Edition
5

D0074185

Teaching Students Who Are Exceptional, Diverse, and At Risk in the General Education Classroom

SHARON VAUGHN
University of Texas, Austin

CANDACE S. BOS
Late of University of Texas, Austin

JEANNE SHAY SCHUMM
University of Miami

PEARSON

Boston   Columbus   Indianapolis   New York   San Francisco   Upper Saddle River
Amsterdam   Cape Town   Dubai   London   Madrid   Milan   Munich   Paris   Montreal   Toronto
Delhi   Mexico City   São Paulo   Sydney   Hong Kong   Seoul   Singapore   Taipei   Tokyo

Vice President and Editor in Chief: Jeffery W. Johnston
Executive Editor: Ann Castel Davis
Editorial Assistant: Penny Burleson
Development Editor: Maxine Effenson Chuck
Vice President, Director of Marketing: Quinn Perkson
Marketing Manager: Erica DeLuca
Senior Managing Editor: Pamela D. Bennett
Project Manager: Sheryl Glicker Langner
Senior Operations Supervisor: Matthew Ottenweller
Senior Art Director: Diane C. Lorenzo
Text Designer: Pre-PressPMG|GGS Higher Education
Resources

Cover Designer: Candace Rowley
Photo Coordinator: Lori Whitley
Cover Image: Super Stock
Media Producer: Autumn Benson
Media Project Manager: Rebecca Norsic
Full-Service Project Management: Kelly Keeler
Composition: GGS|PMG Higher Education Resources
Printer/Binder: Quebecor/Dubuque
Cover Printer: Lehigh Phoenix
Text Font: Garamond Pro

Credits and acknowledgments borrowed from other sources and reproduced, with permission, in this textbook appear on the appropriate page within text.

Every effort has been made to provide accurate and current Internet information in this book. However, the Internet and information posted on it are constantly changing, so it is inevitable that some of the Internet addresses listed in this textbook will change.

Photo Credits: Frank Siteman, pp. 1, 62, 120, 144, 370, 404; David Mager/Pearson Learning Photo Studio, pp. 2, 298, 319; David Young-Wolff/PhotoEdit Inc., pp. 20, 30; Jupiter Unlimited, pp. 38, 92; Pearson Scott Foresman, p. 47; Laura Bolesta/Merrill, pp. 51, 200, 230; Shutterstock, pp. 71, 109; Laura Dwight/PhotoEdit Inc., p. 83; Bob Daemmrich Photography, Inc., pp. 96, 127, 375, 381, 415; Scott Cunningham/Merrill, pp. 100, 336, 409; Sean Cayton/The Image Works, p. 124; Bill Aron/PhotoEdit Inc., pp. 130, 220; Katelyn Metzger/Merrill, pp. 132, 272, 279, 301, 351; David Buffington/Getty Image, Inc.–Photodisc, p. 143; Will Hart/PhotoEdit Inc., pp. 148, 157; Richard Hutchings/PhotoEdit Inc., p. 162; Patrick White/Merrill, p. 174; Anthony Magnacca/Merrill, pp. 176, 211, 257; T. Lindfors/Lindfors Photography, pp. 183, 363; Robin Sachs/PhotoEdit Inc., pp. 191, 235, 240; © Ellen B. Senisi, pp. 204, 254, 287; Bob Daemmrich/PhotoEdit Inc., p. 238; Getty Images/Photodisc, p. 243; Lori Whitley/Merrill, p. 250; Gregory Bull/AP Wide World Photos, p. 262; Michael Newman/PhotoEdit Inc., pp. 285, 423; Comstock Royalty Free Division, p. 297; Corbis RF, p. 304; Courtesy of Julia Weaver, p. 343; Silver Burdett Ginn, p. 386; iStockphoto.com, p. 391; Mark Adams/Getty Images, p. 397; Jupiter Images–FoodPix–Creatas, p. 403; Photos to Go, pp. 438, 449; Jeff Greenberg/PhotoEdit Inc., p. 452.

Library of Congress Cataloging-in-Publication Data
Vaughn, Sharon
  Teaching students who are exceptional, diverse, and at risk in the general education classroom / Sharon Vaughn, Candace S. Bos, Jeanne Shay Schumm.—5th ed.
    p. cm.
  Includes bibliographical references and index.
  ISBN 978-0-13-715179-0 (pbk.)
  1. Mainstreaming in education—United States. 2. Special education—United States. 3. Children with disabilities—Education—United States. 4. Children with social disabilities—Education—United States. 5. Learning disabled children—Education—United States. 6. Inclusive education—United States. I. Bos, Candace S., 1950- II. Schumm, Jeanne Shay, 1947- III. Title.
  LC3981.V28 2011
  371.9'0460973—dc22
                                                                                                    2009032696

10 9 8 7 6 5 4 3 2 1

www.pearsonhighered.com

ISBN 10:   0-13-715179-9
ISBN 13: 978-0-13-715179-0

Today's teaching professionals are assuming considerably more responsibility for meeting the educational needs of students from diverse backgrounds and with diverse learning needs. Teachers identify students with special needs as their greatest challenges and often their greatest rewards. Unfortunately, many general education teachers feel at a loss finding strategies to use in educating their exceptional students. They are eager to provide appropriate instruction, yet often feel inadequately prepared to do so. Furthermore, teachers tell us that what they most want to learn are specific instructional practices that will make a difference for diverse learners, and that they want these practices to enhance the learning of all the students in their classrooms.

The central theme of this book is that general education teachers can make a difference in the lives of all students, particularly students with special needs, by using the tools and strategies described in this text. Our confidence in the effectiveness of these practices comes from our ongoing work in classrooms where these practices are successfully implemented. Many teachers whose stories appear throughout this book implement and extend the recommended practices.

Students in our university classes, as well as practicing teachers, urged us to do more than describe curriculum adaptations; they encouraged us to provide the step-by-step procedures for how to implement curriculum adaptations in the classroom. After reading this book, prospective teachers will have more than increased knowledge about students with special needs—they will have the tools and confidence to adequately meet all of their students' academic and social needs.

This fifth edition includes updated references to the latest research and legislation, allowing readers to look up the most recent studies on topics of interest. Throughout the text we have added new information and described techniques brought to light since the fourth edition was published, and reexamined the ongoing issues surrounding the teaching of diverse learners in general education classrooms.

New to This Edition

We have listened to our users and created a text that will be easier to use in the classroom and more engaging for students. The strength of the book continues to be its numerous learning activities and sample lessons addressing both elementary and secondary classrooms. Changes and enhancements include:

- A thorough reorganization of the content, which is now divided into parts to help the reader and instructor focus on the most important issues and applications teachers experience in the classroom.
- An entirely new chapter on *Response to Intervention and Progress Monitoring,* which reflects the most current research and strategies. In addition, this text integrates and highlights information regarding understanding and using research-based practices within a Response to Intervention (RTI) framework.
- A revised Chapter 5, *Managing Student Behavior and Promoting Social Acceptance,* with an increased emphasis on school-wide behavior management and positive behavioral support, focusing more on "problem kids."
- Evidence-based research practices throughout the text that are based on the most current research and instructional strategies.
- Enhanced classroom-based practices for teaching students with autism and Asperger's syndrome.
- Repurposing of the Research Briefs feature from the fourth edition: Instead of calling out the research, it has been fully integrated within the context in which the research is most relevant.
- Streamlined content that offers more strategies and more examples that bring reader into the classroom.
- Expanded coverage of secondary education via chapter-opening interviews, new photos, and new examples throughout the text.

This edition continues its very popular multi-chapter unit on curriculum adaptations with specific strategies and activities for teaching reading, writing, mathematics, content areas, and study skills. The strong emphasis on teaching secondary learners, professional planning, and collaboration make it an excellent resource for all teachers.

Special Features of This Text

The fifth edition of *Teaching Students Who Are Exceptional, Diverse, and At Risk in the General Education Classroom* retains the most popular features of the prior edition—particularly the emphasis on instructional practices that can be implemented by classroom teachers—with many new additions and enhancements.

The organizational structure of each chapter allows readers to readily locate critical information. Each chapter opens with **Focus Questions** that provide an invitation to the key ideas presented in the chapter, as well as an **Interview** that presents a teacher's, student's, or parent's story that directly relates to the central ideas of the chapter. Each of these stories also identifies issues and personal responses that set the tone for the material that follows.

Each chapter closes with a **Summary** that highlights the key points contained in the chapter. **Think and Apply** questions, activities, and dilemmas challenge the reader to integrate and apply the materials presented. In addition to the organizational features that open and close each chapter, the following features are include within chapters.

The 60-Second Lesson features throughout all chapters present brief mini-lessons that provide specific, concrete examples of how a teacher can make a difference for students with disabilities or diverse needs in only one minute of time.

60 Second LESSON
Homework Buddies: Think–Pair–Share

School days can be long for both teachers and students. With so much activity going on, it can be easy for students to forget assignments or forget books or materials they might need to complete homework assignments. This is true for students who are in a self-contained class or in departmentalized classes when students move from room to room.

At the beginning of the school year, assign each student a homework buddy—two students who sit close to each other. Then, at the end of each school day (in self-contained settings) or at the end of the class period (in departmentalized setting), do a think–pair–share (McTighe & Lyman, 1988).

1. Ask students to take out their homework assignment sheet.

2. Have each student think quietly about what the assignment is and what materials they will need to take home to complete the assignment.

3. Encourage the homework buddies to speak to each other to discuss both the assignment and what they will need to take home.

4. After buddies have conferred, ask the whole class if they have questions they were unable to resolve as a pair.

At first this routine may take more than 60 seconds, but eventually, it will occur smoothly. Taking just a minute or two to get organized for homework will go a long way in helping students get started.

Tips for Teachers in every chapter offer specific advice, guidelines for teaching practice, and step-by-step procedures.

Tips FOR TEACHERS 2.9
USING INTENSIVE INTERVENTIONS

Marla is teaching a 30-minute lesson to a group of second- and third-grade students who are all reading at an upper-first- or a second-grade level. Progress monitoring data indicate that all four students need to build their word study skills. During their first activity, the teacher asks students to review a previously taught word study component—words that end in "ide" or "ike." She asks students to take 1 minute to write all of the words they can think of that have the -ide or -ike rime, or, in other words, are in the same word families. Marla lets them know when time is up, and they count up all of the words they have listed. The student with the most words reads them aloud, while other students check their lists to see if they have written down any words not stated by the first student, and read these aloud. This is a quick warm-up activity that also serves as a review of previously learned material.

Next Marla introduces two-syllable words that have an open, vowel-silent e pattern: be-side, a-like, lo-cate, fe-male, e-rase, do-nate, re-tire, ro-tate, pro-vide, and mi-grate. The last two are "challenge" words because they include blends. Before the lesson began, Marla had written the words on the whiteboard at the front of the classroom, each with a hyphen between syllables. Each student also has a list of the words at his or her desk, one row with the

hyphens in each word and another without them. Marla directs students to count how many syllables are in each word. Next she has them mark vowels and consonants. She asks the students what they notice about the first syllable in each word, and then what they notice about the second syllable in each word (i.e., that all have the vowel-silent e pattern). She points out that they have learned the syllables before, and probably recognize most of them. She asks them to look for syllables they know. Then together the students read the words.

Marla explains and demonstrates what the words mean. For example, for the word *erase*, she erases a word on the board, and for *retire*, she reminds the students that one of their previous teachers has retired. Students practice reading the words, first with the entire group, and then taking turns with a partner. Marla then asks students to look at the story they are reading today. She reminds them of key words previously introduced that they will see in the story. She also asks them to look at the title and the key words and pictures and to make predictions about what they will read or learn. She continues with the lesson, providing students opportunities to read silently and aloud and to ask and answer questions about what they are reading.

Activities for All Learners features present sample lessons that include objectives, procedures, and application suggestions for classroom implementation.

Activities FOR ALL Learners
PROVIDING SCHOOL SUPPORT THROUGH CIRCLE OF FRIENDS

Purpose: To integrate students with disabilities into the general education classroom

Materials: Paper and writing/drawing implements

Procedures: In this activity, each student in the classroom completes a picture of his or her circles of friends, using the following steps:

1. Have students draw four circles.
   - In the first circle, students list the people closest to them, the people they love.
   - In the second circle, students list the people they really like (but not enough to put in the first circle).

- In the third circle, students list groups of people they like or people they do things with (e.g., scouts, soccer team).
- In the fourth circle, students list people who are paid to be in their lives (e.g., doctor, dentist).

2. After students have completed their own circles of friends, describe the circles for a fantasy person who is similar to the student who will be joining the class. For example, a student might have only Mom listed in the first circle, with the second and third circles empty. In the fourth circle are a number of doctors and therapists. Through discussion, talk with the students about how the student must

feel and how this fantasy person is similar to the student with disabilities who is going to join the class.

3. Finally, the teacher and students plan how they can become part of the circles of friends for the student with disabilities through such activities as classroom ambassadors, telephone buddies, lunch buddies, and reading buddies.

Source: Based on Forest, M., & Lusthaus, E. (1989). Promoting educational equality for all students: Circles and maps. In S. Stainback, W. Stainback, and M. Forest (Eds.), Educating all students in the mainstream of regular education (pp. 45–57). Baltimore: Brookes.

NEW: Marginal URLs direct students to websites where they can enhance their knowledge about relevant topics and access tools for teaching and learning.

Go to **www.whatworks.ed.gov**, the What Works Clearing House website provided by the U.S. Department of Education, to find out the research base for the programs, materials, and practices you use.

All new **Tech Tips** features in every chapter describe technological applications that can be used in the classroom to enhance success for all learners, particularly students with special needs.

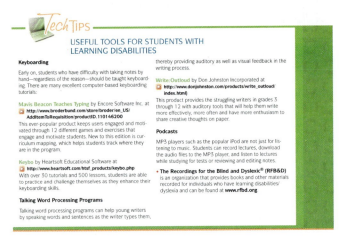

Tech TIPS
USEFUL TOOLS FOR STUDENTS WITH LEARNING DISABILITIES

Keyboarding

Early on, students who have difficulty with taking notes by hand—regardless of the reason—should be taught keyboarding. There are many excellent computer-based keyboarding tutorials:

Mavis Beacon Teaches Typing by Encore Software Inc. at http://www.broderbund.com/store/broder/en_US/AddItemToRequisition/productID.110146200
This ever-popular product keeps users engaged and motivated through 12 different games and exercises that engage and motivate students. New to this edition is curriculum mapping, which helps students track where they are in the program.

Keybo by Heartsoft Educational Software at http://www.heartsoft.com/htsf_products/keybo.php
With over 30 tutorials and 500 lessons, students are able to practice and challenge themselves as they enhance their keyboarding skills.

Talking Word Processing Programs

Talking word processing programs can help young writers by speaking words and sentences as the writer types them,

thereby providing auditory as well as visual feedback in the writing process.

Write:Outloud by Don Johnston Incorporated at http://www.donjohnston.com/products/write_outloud/index.html)
This product provides the struggling writers in grades 3 through 12 with auditory tools that will help them write more effectively, more often and have more enthusiasm to share creative thoughts on paper.

Podcasts

MP3 players such as the popular iPod are not just for listening to music. Students can record lectures, download the audio files to the MP3 player, and listen to lectures while studying for tests or reviewing and editing notes.

- **The Recordings for the Blind and Dyslexic®** (RFB&D) is an organization that provides books and other materials recorded for individuals who have learning disabilities/dyslexia and can be found at **www.rfbd.org**.

Fully integrated **MyEducationLab** online course.

myeducationlab

To enhance your understanding of adapting the classroom with students with disabilities in the general classroom, go to the IRIS Center Resources section of Topic 5: Prereferrals and IEP Process in the MyEducationLab for your course and complete the Module 22: RTI (Part 1): An Overview.

MyEducationLab myeducationlab
The Power of Classroom Practice

"Teacher educators who are developing pedagogies for the analysis of teaching and learning contend that analyzing teaching artifacts has three advantages: it enables new teachers time for reflection while still using the real materials of practice; it provides new teachers with experience thinking about and approaching the complexity of the classroom; and in some cases, it can help new teachers and teacher educators develop a shared understanding and common language about teaching. . . ."[1]

As Linda Darling-Hammond and her colleagues point out, grounding teacher education in real classrooms—among real teachers and students and among actual examples of students' and teachers' work—is an important, and perhaps even an essential, part of training teachers for the complexities of teaching in today's classrooms. For this reason we have created a valuable, time-saving website—MyEducationLab—that provides the context of real classrooms and artifacts that research on teacher education tells us is so important. The authentic in-class video

---

[1] Darling-Hammond, L. & Bransford, J., Eds. (2005). *Preparing Teachers for a Changing World.* San Francisco: John Wiley and Sons.

footage, interactive skill-building exercises, and other resources available on MyEducationLab offers a uniquely valuable teacher education tool.

MyEducationLab is easy to use and integrate into assignments and courses. Whenever the MyEducationLab logo appears in the text, follow the simple instructions to access the interactive assignments, activities, and learning units on MyEducationLab. For each topic covered in the course you will find most or all of the following resources:

Connection to National Standards

Now it is easier than ever to see how coursework is connected to national standards. Each topic on MyEducationLab lists intended learning outcomes connected to the appropriate national standards. All of the Assignments and Activities and all of the Building Teaching Skills and Dispositions in MyEducationLab are mapped to the appropriate national standards and learning outcomes as well.

Assignments and Activities

Designed to save instructors preparation time and enhance student understanding, these assignable exercises show concepts in action (through video, cases, and/or student and teacher artifacts). They help students synthesize and apply concepts and strategies they read about in the book.

Building Teaching Skills and Dispositions

These learning units help students practice and strengthen skills that are essential to quality teaching. They are presented with the core skill or concept and then given an opportunity to practice their understanding of this concept multiple times by watching video footage (or interacting with other media) and then critically analyzing the strategy or skill presented.

IRIS Center Resources

The IRIS Center at Vanderbilt University (http://iris.peabody .vanderbilt.edu – funded by the U.S. Department of Education's Office of Special Education Programs (OSEP) develops training enhancement materials for pre-service and in-service teachers. The Center works with experts from across the country to create challenge-based interactive modules, case study units, and podcasts that provide research-validated information about working with students in inclusive settings. In your MyEducationLab course we have integrated this content where appropriate.

General Resources on Your MyEducationLab Course

The Resources section on MyEducationLab is designed to help students pass their licensure exams, put together effective portfolios and lesson plans, prepare for and navigate the first year of their teaching careers, and understand key educational standards, policies, and laws. This section includes:

- *Licensure Exams*: Contains guidelines for passing the Praxis exam. The *Practice Test Exam* includes practice multiple-choice

questions, case study questions, and video case studies with sample questions.
- *Lesson Plan Builder*: Helps students create and share lesson plans.
- *Licensure and Standards*: Provides links to state licensure standards and national standards.
- *Beginning Your Career*: Educate Offers tips, advice, and valuable information on:
  - *Resume Writing and Interviewing:* Expert advice on how to write impressive resumes and prepare for job interviews.
  - *Your First Year of Teaching:* Practical tips on setting up a classroom, managing student behavior, and planning for instruction and assessment.
  - *Law and Public Policies:* Includes specific directives and requirements educators need to understand under the No Child Left Behind Act and the Individuals with Disabilities Education Improvement Act of 2004.

Visit www.myeducationlab.com for a demonstration of this exciting new online teaching resource.

A Complete Teaching and Learning Package

Online Instructor's Manual with Test Items

The Instructor's Manual and Test Bank is a comprehensive resource available to adopting instructors. For each chapter, the Instructor's Manual also provides a chapter overview, discussion starters, assignments and activities, and a project based on the Building Teaching Skills activities in MyEducationLab. The Test Bank contains multiple-choice items with answer feedback, and essay or case-based applications with answer guidelines.

The electronic Instructor's Manual is available on the Instructor Resource Center at www.pearsonhighered.com. To access the manual with test items, as well as the online PowerPoint lecture slides, go to www.pearsonhighered.com and click on the Instructor Resource Center button. Here you'll be able to log in or complete a one-time registration for a user name and password.

Online PowerPoint Lecture Slides

The PowerPoint lecture slides are available on the Instructor Resource Center at www.pearsonhighered.com. These lecture slides highlight key concepts and summarize key content from each chapter of the text.

Test Bank and MyTest Software

A completely revised test bank of hundreds of questions, available in the computerized MyTest format, also accompanies the text. These multiple-choice, short answer, and essay questions can be used to assess students' recognition, recall, and synthesis of factual content and conceptual issues from each chapter. The MyTest is available in Windows and Macintosh formats, along with assessment software allowing instructors to create and customize exams and track student progress.

Acknowledgments

We have many people to thank for their generous contributions of time, knowledge, experience, and sound advice. We are deeply grateful to the many teachers who have shared their classrooms, students, and experiences with us. In particular, we would like to extend our heartfelt thanks to the teachers and principals of Flamingo Elementary School. We would also like to thank the many students in the teacher preparation programs at the University of Arizona, the University of Miami, and the University of Texas who have helped us better understand the important attitudes, knowledge, and skills for new teachers preparing to teach diverse learners.

Just a few of the many people whose names should be in lights for their generous contribution to this book are:

- Mary Hinson, for sharing her valuable knowledge as a job developer and university instructor for the mainstreaming course for secondary teachers
- Sharon Kutok, for sharing her valuable knowledge as a speech/language pathologist
- Elba Reyes and Manuel Bello, for reviewing and providing insights on teaching students with cultural and linguistic diversity
- Paulette Jackson, for providing expert assistance with manuscript preparation and permissions
- Jean G. Ulman, whose knowledge about technology and special education benefited the Tech Tips

A special thanks to Sandra Bowen, Penny Rosenblum, and Andrea Morrison. Their expertise in educating students with hearing impairments, visual impairments, and mental retardation/severe disabilities, respectively, was a valuable resource. Sandra played an important role in writing the section on hearing impairments. Penny took on a similar role in writing the section on visual impairments in the same chapter. Andrea not only worked on the physical disabilities and health impairments section of the text, but also played a significant role in writing the chapter on developmental disabilities.

We would also like to thank Mark F. O'Reilly, Jeff Sigafoos, and Giulio Lancioni for their contribution of the updated chapter on autism.

Ae-Hwa Kim, Alison Gould Boardman, and Jane Sinagub assisted with all aspects of manuscript preparation, including expert editorial work and good judgment. Their contribution to the book is extensive. I would particularly like to recognize the careful and thoughtful work of Ae-Hwa Kim who made a significant contribution to the third edition and Alison Gould Boardman for her significant contribution to the fourth edition. Alison Gould Boardman provided valuable assistance with the Tips for Teachers, the Appendix, and text reflecting policy changes.

We also benefited from the suggestions and revisions of outstanding reviewers. Thank you for your generous assistance: Helen Dainty, Tennessee Tech University; Marilyn Goodwin, Texas State University; Judy Napier, DePaul University; and Susan Schur, Kent State University.

There are also a handful of individuals who each put their respective areas of research expertise to work for us in a close reading of just a single chapter in their specialty area. Susan Johnston of the University of Utah gave us assistance with the chapter on communication disorders. Kathleen Robins, Janice Day, and Cheryl Winston of the University of Utah provided commentary on the text about vision/hearing/physical challenges. Missy Olive of the University of Texas gave feedback regarding pervasive developmental disorders. Jeff Sigafoos of the University of Texas provided insights on the chapter on developmental disabilities. Alliete Alfano of the University of Miami provided an expert review of the chapter on visual impairments, hearing loss, physical disabilities, health impairments, and traumatic brain injury. Michel Miller, also of the University of Miami, provided valuable comments on the chapter on students with developmental disabilities. Like all authors, we were not always anxious to rewrite but soon realized the benefits from their helpful suggestions and resources.

The personnel at Merrill/Pearson Education provided ongoing support for this book. Initially, Ray Short, Senior Editor, contacted us about writing the book and provided encouragement and continuous positive feedback. He was a wonderful resource when the going got tough, assuring us we were making fine progress. The third and fourth editions of the book have benefited enormously from the caring and careful work of Virginia Lanigan. Upon the sudden death of our co-author Candace Bos, Virginia was a source of social and professional support. She truly guided these editions through completion. We are very grateful to her.

The fifth edition of the book benefited from the insights and suggestions of Ann Davis, editor, and Max Effenson Chuck, development editor. Max was our guide throughout the significant revisions we undertook for this edition. We can not imagine how to adequately thank her or acknowledge the significance of her insights, support, and very fine editorial suggestions. We think you'll agree that this edition is by far our best edition yet.

We also would like to give a very special thank you to our husbands for their steadfast support and personal sacrifices: Jim Dammann and Jerry Schumm.

—SRV
JSS

BRIEF CONTENTS

PART 1

FOUNDATIONS

Chapter 1 Special Education and Inclusive Schooling 2

Chapter 2 Response to Intervention: Developing Success for All Learners 38

Chapter 3 Communicating and Collaborating with Other Professionals and Families 62

Chapter 4 Teaching Culturally and Linguistically Diverse Students 92

Chapter 5 Promoting Social Acceptance and Managing Student Behavior 120

PART 2

CATEGORICAL DIFFERENCES

Chapter 6 Teaching Students with Learning Disabilities and Attention Deficit Hyperactivity Disorder 144

Chapter 7 Teaching Students with Communication Disorders 174

Chapter 8 Teaching Students with Emotional and Behavioral Disorders 200

Chapter 9 Teaching Students with Autism Spectrum Disorders/Pervasive Developmental Disorders 230

Chapter 10 Teaching Students with Developmental Disabilities 250

Chapter 11 Teaching Students with Lower-Incidence Disabilities 272

PART 3

TEACHING PRACTICES

Chapter 12 Facilitating Reading 298

Chapter 13 Facilitating Writing 336

Chapter 14 Helping All Students Succeed in Mathematics 370

PART SECONDARY INSTRUCTION

Chapter 15 Differentiating Instruction and Assessment for Middle and High School Students **404**

Chapter 16 Fostering Strategies for Student Independence **438**

APPENDIX   461

GLOSSARY   473

REFERENCES   483

NAME INDEX   505

SUBJECT INDEX   513

CONTENTS

PART 1 FOUNDATIONS

Chapter 1
Special Education and Inclusive Schooling   2

Introduction   3

Early Foundations of Special Education   4

Early Influences   4
Recent Influences   4

IDEIA and the Vocational Rehabilitation Act   5

Provisions and Guidelines for Implementing IDEA   7
Provisions of the Vocational Rehabilitation Act   8
The Concept of Least Restrictive Environment   9
The Individualized Education Program (IEP)   11

Responsibilities of Classroom Teachers   19

Participating in the Referral and Planning Process   22
Adapting Instruction   25
No Child Left Behind Act   27
Expanding the Impact of IDEA   28

Inclusion   31

Accessing Information About Students   32
Placing Students in the General Education Classroom   34

Chapter 2
Response to Intervention: Developing Success for All Learners   38

Introduction   39

Past and Present Challenges   40

Previous Identification Procedures   40
Initiatives Influencing RTI   41

Components of Response to Intervention   43

Progress Monitoring   44
The Three Tiers of Intervention   46
Implementing Interventions   47
RTI for Students Who Are Culturally and Linguistically Diverse   51
Working with Families   53

Universal Screening   53

Using Screening to Make Educational Decisions   54
Using Progress Monitoring to Assess Students' Response to Interventions   54

Role of Teachers in an RTI Model   56

Collaborating and Consulting   56
Using RTI Data to Identify Students with Disabilities   57
Providing Interventions   57
Using RTI Models in Middle Schools and High Schools   58

Chapter 3
Communicating and Collaborating with Other Professionals and Families   62

Introduction   63

Critical Communication Skills   64

Acceptance   64
Listening   64
Questioning   65
Staying Focused   66

Collaborating with Other Professionals   67

Consultation   68
Collaboration   70
Co-Teaching   71
Collaboration Issues and Dilemmas   77

Working with Parents   78

Family Collaboration   79
Family Adjustment   80
Homework   82
Planned and Unplanned Parent Conferences   84
School-to-Home Communication   86

Chapter 4
Teaching Culturally and Linguistically Diverse Students 92

Introduction 93

Diversity in Classrooms 94

Understanding Diverse Cultures 95
Understanding Cultural Characteristics 97

Multicultural Education 99

Dimensions of Multicultural Education 99
Desired Student Outcomes 101
Multicultural Curricula 101

Linguistic Diversity and Second Language Acquisition 104

Programs for Promoting Second Language Acquisition 104
Framework for Second Language Acquisition 106
Language Variation and Dialect 110
Historical Perspective on ESL Instruction and Bilingual Education 110

Assessment of Students with Cultural and Linguistic Differences 112

Instructional Guidelines and Accommodations for Diverse Students 114

Culturally Responsive Teaching 114
Best Practices in English Language Learning 114

Chapter 5
Promoting Social Acceptance and Managing Student Behavior 120

Introduction 121

Establishing a Positive Classroom Climate 122

Arranging the Physical Space 123
Creating a Learning Community 123
Engaging Students Through Class Meetings 123
Attending to the Safety of Your Students 124

Enhancing Students' Self-Concepts 126

Increasing Social Acceptance of Students with Disabilities and Exceptional Learners 127

Understanding Behavior Management in Culturally Diverse Classrooms 129

Universal Strategies for Managing Student Behavior 130

Focusing on Positive Behaviors 131
Using Reinforcers to Encourage Positive Behavior 132
Establishing Clear Rules with Known Consequences 135
Helping Students to Change Inappropriate Behavior 135
Recognizing Students' Mistaken Goals 138

Practices for Providing Positive Behavior Support 139

Positive Behavior Support as Prevention 139
Schoolwide Positive Behavior Support 140
Positive Behavior Support and Response to Intervention 141

PART 2
CATEGORICAL DIFFERENCES

Chapter 6
Teaching Students with Learning Disabilities and Attention Deficit Hyperactivity Disorder 144

Introduction 145

Learning Disabilities 145

Definitions and Types of Learning Disabilities 146
Diagnosing Students with Learning Disabilities 146
Characteristics of Students with Learning Disabilities 147
Prevalence of Learning Disabilities 150
Identification and Assessment of Students with Learning Disabilities 151
Instructional Techniques and Accommodations for Students with Learning Disabilities 152

Attention Deficit Hyperactivity Disorder 160

Definitions and Types of Attention Deficit Hyperactivity Disorder 161
Characteristics of Students with Attention Deficit Hyperactivity Disorder 163
Prevalence of Attention Deficit Hyperactivity Disorder 165

Identification and Assessment of Students with
Attention Deficit Hyperactivity Disorder   166
Eligibility for ADHD Services and Special Education
Law   166
Instructional Guidelines and Accommodations for
Students with Attention Deficit Hyperactivity
Disorder   167

Chapter 7
Teaching Students with Communication Disorders   174

Introduction   175

Communication Disorders   176

Speech Disorders   176
School-Age Language Disorders   179
Language Content   179
Language Form   183
Language Use   185
Metalinguistics   187

Prevalence of Communication Disorders   188

Identifying and Assessing Students with Communication Disorders   188

Instructional Guidelines and Accommodations for Students with Communication Disorders   190

Facilitating Speech Development   191
Facilitating Language Development   192
Spotlight on Cultural and Linguistic Diversity   197

Working with Parents to Extend Language Concepts   198

Chapter 8
Teaching Students with Emotional and Behavioral Disorders   200

Introduction   201

Definitions of Emotional and Behavioral Disorders   202

Prevalence of Students with Emotional or Behavioral Disorders   203

Types and Characteristics of Emotional or Behavioral Disorders   204

The Diagnostic and Statistical Manual of Mental Disorders   205
Conduct and Aggression   207
Socialized Aggression   207
Immaturity   208
Schizophrenia   209

Causes of Emotional and Behavioral Disorders   209

Biological Causes   209
Environmental Causes   209

Identification and Assessment of Students with Emotional and Behavioral Disorders   210

Initial Identification   210
Response to Intervention for Students with Emotional and Behavioral Disorders   214
Universal Screening and Progress Monitoring   214
Developing a Functional Behavioral Assessment   214

Teaching Guidelines and Accommodations for Students with Emotional or Behavioral Disorders   215

Changing Behavior   217
Resolving Conflicts and Promoting Self-Control   218
Teaching Self-Monitoring Skills   220
Teaching Self-Management Skills   221
Teaching Social Skills   222
Using Social Learning Strategies   224
Implementing School-Based Wraparound   224
Adapting Instruction   226

Chapter 9
Teaching Students with Autism Spectrum Disorders/Pervasive Developmental Disorders   230

Introduction   231

Definitions of Autism Spectrum Disorders/Asperger Syndrome and Pervasive Developmental Disorders   232

Autism   232
Asperger Syndrome   233
Rett Syndrome   235
Childhood Disintegrative Disorder   235
Pervasive Developmental Disorder—Not Otherwise
    Specified   235

Characteristics of Students with Autism Spectrum Disorders/Asperger Syndrome   236

Social Skills   236
Communication Skills   236
Repetitive Behaviors and Routines   237

Identification and Assessment of Students with Autism Spectrum Disorders   237

Curricular and Instructional Guidelines for Students with Autism Spectrum Disorders   237

Assess Preferences   238
Establish a Classroom Routine   238
Teach Communication Skills   239
Teach Social Skills   241

Addressing Challenging Behaviors   245

Using Functional Behavioral Assessment
    (FBA)   245
Using Positive Behavioral Support   247

Chapter 10
Teaching Students with Developmental Disabilities   250

Introduction   251

Types of Developmental Disabilities   251

Intellectual Disabilities   252
Physical Causes of Intellectual Disabilities   253
Severe Disabilities   254

Prevalence and Identification of Students with Developmental Disabilities   257

Identification of Students with Developmental
    Disabilities   258
Teacher's Role in Identifying Students with
    Developmental Disabilities   258
Communicating and Collaborating with
    Families   258

Guidelines for Teaching Students with Developmental Disabilities   259

Role of the General Education Teacher   259
Planning Systems   260
Functional Assessment, Discrepancy Analysis, and Task
    Analysis   262
Authentic and Alternate Assessment   263
Partial Participation   264
Curriculum Adaptations   264
Peer Support and Peer Tutoring   265
Strategies to Support Students in the General
    Education Classroom   265
Providing Opportunities for Functional
    Practice   269
Encouraging Family Involvement   269

Chapter 11
Teaching Students with Lower-Incidence Disabilities   272

Introduction   273

Students with Visual Impairments   274

Definitions and Types of Visual Impairments   274
Characteristics of Students with Visual
    Impairments   275
Prevalence of Visual Impairments   276
Identification and Assessment of Students with Visual
    Impairments   276
Instructional Guidelines and Accommodations for
    Students with Visual Impairments   277

Students with Hearing Loss   280

Definitions and Types of Hearing Loss   281
Characteristics of Students with Hearing Loss   281
Prevalence of Hearing Loss   282
Identification and Assessment of Students with
    Hearing Loss   283
Instructional Guidelines and Accommodations for
    Students with Hearing Loss   284

Students with Physical Disabilities, Health Impairments, and Traumatic Brain Injury   286

Definitions and Types of Physical Disabilities, Health
    Impairments, and Traumatic Brain Injury   286
Characteristics of Students with Physical Disabilities,
    Health Impairments, and Traumatic Brain
    Injury   288

Prevalence of Physical Disabilities Health Impairments, and Traumatic Brain Injury   290

Identification and Assessment of Students with Physical Disabilities, Health Impairments, and Traumatic Brain Injury   291

Instructional Guidelines and Accommodations for Students with Physical Disabilities, Health Impairments, and Traumatic Brain Injury   291

PART 3 TEACHING PRACTICES

Chapter 12
Facilitating Reading   298

Introduction   299

Current Trends in Reading and Reading Instruction   300

Three Key Concepts for Effective Reading Instruction   300

Learning Difficulties in the Process of Reading   301

Components of Reading Instruction   302

Effective Reading Instruction for Struggling Readers   303

Establishing an Environment to Promote Reading   303

Using Response to Intervention to Screen Struggling Readers   304

Using Screening, Assessment, and Progress Monitoring   305

Providing Intensive Instruction   307

Obtaining Early Intervention: Response to Intervention   308

Strategies for Teaching Phonological Awareness and Phonics   308

Teaching Phonological Awareness   309

Teaching Phonics   310

Strategies for Teaching Word Identification   314

Teaching Sight Words   314

Teaching Decoding Strategies   315

Techniques for Teaching Decoding and Sight Words   318

Strategies for Helping Students Develop Fluency   320

Using Response to Intervention (RTI) to Promote Fluency   320

Reading Aloud   321

Repeated Reading   321

Peer Tutoring   323

Strategies for Improving Reading Comprehension   323

K-W-L Strategy   324

Question-Answer Relationships Strategy   325

Questioning the Author   327

Collaborative Strategic Reading   327

Teaching English Language Learners with Reading Difficulties   329

Strategies for Teaching Older Readers with Reading Difficulties   331

Putting It All Together   332

Chapter 13
Facilitating Writing   336

Introduction   337

Current Trends in Writing Curriculum and Instruction   337

Standards-Based Writing Instruction and Research-Based Practices   338

Emphasis on Assessment and Progress Monitoring   339

Progress Monitoring and Writing   339

Response to Intervention and Writing   340

Writing Rubrics and Portfolios   341

Teaching Writing as a Process   342

Writing as an Interactive Process   342

Writing as a Strategic Process   343

Writing as a Process of Constructing Meaning   344

Writing as a Student-Centered Process   345

Writing as a Socially Mediated Language–Learning Activity   345

Strategies for Establishing an Environment That Promotes Writing   345

Physical Environment   345

Social Environment   345

Strategies for Conducting a Writing Workshop   347

Making Adaptations for Struggling Writers: Teachers' Practices 349

Prewriting: Getting Started 350
Composing 351
Revising and Editing 351
Publishing 352
Sharing 352

Strategies for Teaching Narrative Writing 354

Using Story Webs to Plan 354
Instruction in Story Development 354

Strategies for Teaching Expository Writing 354

Paragraph Writing 356
Essay Writing 356
Research Paper Writing 356

Strategies for Teaching Persuasive Writing 357

Strategies for Helping All Students Acquire Spelling Skills 358

Traditional Spelling Instruction 358
Spelling Instruction for Students with Learning Difficulties and Disabilities 359
Principles of Effective Spelling Instruction 362

Strategies for Helping All Students Develop Handwriting and Keyboarding Skills 363

Traditional Handwriting Instruction 363
Students with Difficulty in Handwriting 364
Principles of Effective Handwriting Instruction 364
Principles of Effective Keyboarding Instruction 366

Chapter 14
Helping All Students Succeed in Mathematics 370

Introduction 371

Current Trends in Mathematics Curriculum and Instruction 371

Influences on Math Instruction 372
Math Proficiency 373

Difficulties in Learning Mathematics 375

Developmental Arithmetic Disorder 375
Nonverbal Math Difficulties 375

Effective Math Instruction for All Learners 376

Evaluating Mathematics Curricula 377
Adapting Instruction for Secondary Students with Math Difficulties 378
Adapting Basal Materials for Students with Special Needs 379
Adapting Tests for Students with Special Needs 379
Using Curricular Programs for Students with Math Difficulties 380
Establishing Appropriate Goals 380
Using Peers to Support Instructional Practice 381
Using Response to Intervention: Identifying Students Who Need Help in Math 382
Assessment and Progress Monitoring 382
Assessing Students' Number Sense 384
Helping Students Improve in Math 385
Providing Practice 388

Strategies for Helping All Students Acquire Basic Math Skills 389

Prenumber Skills 389
Working with Numeration 390
Understanding Place Value 392
Learning Fractions 392

Strategies for Helping All Learners Acquire and Use Computation Skills 393

Patterns of Common Computation Errors 394
Computation and Calculators 396

Strategies for Helping All Students Develop Problem-Solving Skills 397

Teaching Problem-Solving Strategies to Secondary Students 397
Integrating Math Problem Solving into the Curriculum 400

PART 4

SECONDARY INSTRUCTION

Chapter 15
Differentiating Instruction and Assessment for Middle and High School Students 404

Introduction 405

Standards-Based Instruction 407

Differentiating Instruction for Secondary Learners   407

What Is Differentiated Instruction?   407

How Can I Differentiate Assignments and Homework?   409

How Can I Plan for Differentiated Instruction?   409

How Can I Accommodate Students Who Are Gifted and Talented?   411

How Can Differenting Instruction Accommodate Multiple Intelligences?   415

How Does Differentiated Instruction Relate to Response to Intervention?   415

Preparing Engaging Lessons for Middle and High School Students   416

Using Prelearning Activities   416

Using Graphic Organizers   416

Creating Listener-Friendly Lectures   419

Giving Demonstrations   420

Facilitating Student Participation   421

Effective Content-Area Reading Instruction for Middle and High School Learners   424

Familiarizing Yourself with the Textbook   424

Understanding How Students Interact with and Respond to Text   424

Making Textbook Adaptations   425

Differentiating Assessment   429

Preparing Students for High-Stakes Tests   431

Helping Students Develop Test-Taking Strategies   432

Grading   435

Chapter 16
Fostering Strategies for Student Independence   438

Introduction   439

Effective Strategy Instruction: The Teaching–Learning Connection   439

The Goals of Strategy Instruction   440

Strategy Instruction Guidelines   440

Difficulties in Developing Independent Learners   443

Developing Independence: Personal Responsibility   443

Self-Monitoring   446

Organizational Systems   448

Time Management   449

Self-Advocacy   450

Developing Independence: Active Learning in the Classroom   451

Participating in Class   451

Listening and Taking Notes in Class   452

Developing Independence: Making Home–School Connections   455

Completing Assignments   456

Organizing and Planning for Long-Term Assignments   456

Remembering Information   457

Appendix   461

Glossary   473

References   483

Name Index   505

Subject Index   513

Part

1

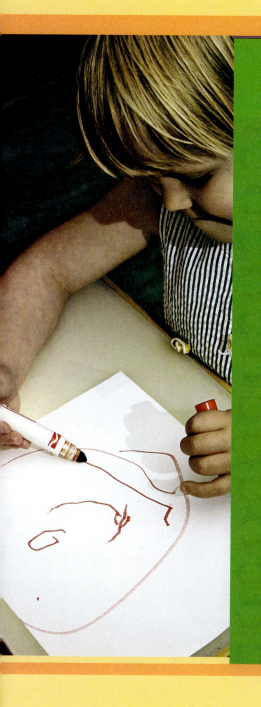

FOUNDATIONS

Chapter 1
Special Education and Inclusive Schooling

Chapter 2
Response to Intervention: Developing Success for All Learners

Chapter 3
Communicating and Collaborating with Other Professionals and Families

Chapter 4
Teaching Culturally and Linguistically Diverse Students

Chapter 5
Promoting Social Acceptance and Managing Student Behavior

Special Education and Inclusive Schooling

CHAPTER 1

FOCUS QUESTIONS

1. What basic laws and procedures govern special education and inclusion?

2. What are the key provisions and guidelines of IDEIA and how do they help shape today's classrooms?

3. As a classroom teacher, what are your responsibilities for your students with special needs? What systems and resources are in place in your school to help you teach students with special needs in your classroom?

4. What concerns do teachers, parents, and schools have about inclusion, and how can these issues be addressed? What are some opportunities and challenges you can expect to find in your inclusive classroom?

INTERVIEW
ELIZABETH DILLER

Elizabeth Diller is a fifth-grade teacher at Cory Elementary School in an urban city in Texas. Elizabeth is an unusual teacher in that she has worked as both a special education teacher and a general education teacher. For the past 2 years, she has served as the lead teacher in a fifth-grade team. What she likes about her job is that she blends her expertise in special education with her new knowledge as a general education curriculum specialist. She assists the other fifth-grade teachers in developing instructional practices and progress monitoring supports for all of the fifth-grade students with disabilities. She also works with the response to intervention (RTI) team to screen and progress monitor students who are at risk for reading and math problems.

Elizabeth has been very successful at keeping students with disabilities in general education classrooms. She also has been a cheerleader for the RTI model of preventing academic difficulties and identifying students for special education in their school. Here is some of her advice for general education teachers working in RTI schools:

- Don't worry if you do not know everything about students with disabilities. Be willing to ask questions and to allow others to help. Many instructional practices that are effective with most students are also effective with students with disabilities.

- Remember that a couple of minutes of focused instructional support that provides additional opportunities for students with disabilities to practice can be very helpful.

- Use ongoing progress monitoring measures in reading and math to inform your instructional decision making.

- Ask the special education teacher, an experienced general education teacher, or the school psychologist to observe students with disabilities in your class. Ask them for advice to improve your instruction.

- Communicate frequently with parents. My class publishes a newsletter every other week that is posted on our class website. If parents like, we print the newsletter and send it home. I also send home weekly notes to parents of students with disabilities to inform them of their child's progress.

Ever since I was little I wanted to be a teacher. When I imagined myself as a teacher, I thought about helping students who needed me the most. I really feel most like a teacher when students who had difficulty learning are now making progress. I like that my classroom includes students with a range of disabilities. We all learn what we can do well and what we need help with, and we always know that there are classmates there to support us.

Introduction

Elizabeth's account reflects the philosophy of this book. Our philosophy rests on the belief that teachers make a difference; that we must teach purposefully to empower all of our students to learn; that even small steps matter; and that if we set ambitious goals, provide research-based instruction, and monitor students' progress, we can ensure their success. The aim of this book is to offer you the basic knowledge, tools, and strategies that will empower you as a classroom teacher to skillfully, confidently, and successfully promote learning for all your students. This book takes a cross-categorical approach—that is, accommodations for exceptional learners are discussed in terms of their shared needs rather than in terms of their identification as members of a disability category.

The basic knowledge you need includes an understanding of the laws and procedures that govern special education and inclusion. This is where we begin.

Early Foundations of Special Education

Before the 1950s, many students with disabilities were excluded from attending public schools. Although children with more severe disabilities were forced either to stay home or to be institutionalized, students with mild or moderate learning problems often dropped out of school long before graduating (Pardini, 2002). It may be difficult for you to imagine, but as recently as 1958, court cases ruled in favor of excluding students with disabilities from a public school education. In *Department of Public Welfare v. Haas* in 1958, the Supreme Court of Illinois maintained that the state's compulsory education laws did not require a "free public education for the 'feebleminded' or to children who were 'mentally deficient' and who, because of their limited intelligence were unable to reap the benefits of a good education" (Yell, 1998, p. 55). Eventually, however, the tide turned in favor of advocating for the education of all students.

Early Influences

Exclusion of students with disabilities would not last forever. A landmark education case paved the way for future legislation that would protect the rights of individuals with disabilities. In *Brown v. Board of Education* in 1954, the Supreme Court ruled that school segregation by race was not constitutional, even if resources were allotted equally. This was the first time the federal government had advocated for students who experienced inequality and prejudice at school, and it set the path for future legislation for individuals with disabilities. See Figure 1.1 for more examples of court cases that have influenced the education of individuals with disabilities.

The Elementary and Secondary Education Act (ESEA) passed in 1965 initiated the role of the federal government in protecting and providing for students from disadvantaged backgrounds so that they would have equal access to the public education system. For example, one of the ESEA provisions established the free and reduced lunch system because children whose basic needs are not met (i.e., being hungry) are not able to benefit fully from instructional programs that are provided. A critical component of ESEA for individuals with disabilities was the grant program that encouraged states to create and improve on programs for students with disabilities. This program was later revised in 1970 as the Education of the Handicapped Act (P.L. 91–230) and continued support for state-run programs for individuals with disabilities although it did not provide any specific guidelines for how to develop these programs or what they should look like.

For many students with disabilities, the initial goal of special education was to ensure that they were provided an opportunity to attend school and profit from education. Not until the passage of P.L. 94–142 in 1975 were schools required to ensure that all children, regardless of

---

FIGURE 1.1 — Influential Court Cases

- *1971—Pennsylvania Association for Retarded Children (PARC) v. Commonwealth of Pennsylvania.* Challenged the constitutionality of excluding individuals with mental retardation from public education and training. The state was not allowed to "deny to any mentally retarded child access to a free public program of education and training."

- *1972—Mills v. Board of Education of the District of Columbia.* Another case in which handicapped children had been excluded from public schools. Similar to the PARC case, this suit required the state to provide "adequate alternative education services" as well as "prior hearing and periodic review of the child's status, progress, and the adequacy of any educational alternative" (348 F. Supp., at 878). In both the PARC and Mills cases, the courts required schools to describe the curricula, objectives, teacher qualifications, and supplemental services that were needed, areas that would later be influential during the drafting of P.L. 94–142.

- *1982—Board of Education of Hendrick Hudson Central School District v. Rowley.* Clarified the definition of a free and appropriate public education (FAPE). Amy Rowley was a deaf fifth-grader who used an FM hearing aid that amplified words spoken by her teacher. She was achieving better than the average student in her class and communicated well with her peers. Although she may not have been achieving maximally and might have benefited from an interpreter, the court ruled that P.L. 94–142 requires states to provide sufficient, but not the best possible, support for students to benefit from a public education at a level typical of nondisabled peers.

- *1988—Honig v. Doe.* Benefited individuals with emotional and/or behavior disorders who have academic and social problems. Ruled that schools could not expel children for behaviors related to their disability.

- *1999—Cedar Rapids v. Garret F.* Garret was paralyzed from the neck down in an accident when he was age 4, but his mental capacities were unaffected. He required nursing services to attend his regular classes, and the court ruled that under IDEA students must be provided with the supplemental services they need to attend school at no extra cost to the parents.

---

their disability, receive a free and appropriate public education. For students with learning disabilities, most of whom were already provided education within the general education system, their special needs would now be identified and they would be provided with a special education.

Initially, defining and providing a special education for students with disabilities were challenges for educators. Little was known about what an effective educational program for students with disabilities should look like.

Recent Influences

President Obama has stated that there will be a change in the name and several guidelines that are currently part of the **No Child Left Behind Act (NCLB) of 2001**. NCLB was enacted to provide a framework "on how to improve the performance of America's elementary and secondary schools while at the same time ensuring that no child is trapped in a failing school" (U.S. Department of Education, 2002b, p. 1). NCLB covers a wide range of areas, from improving teacher quality and supporting instruction for English language learners (ELLs) to efforts to keep schools safe and drug free. Following are the three areas of education that have been affected by NCLB:

■ *Increased accountability*. In perhaps the cornerstone of NCLB legislation, students are required to take statewide assessments (i.e., tests) that are aligned with curriculum **accountability standards** (i.e., state identified grade level learning expectations in key curriculum areas such as reading and math). Furthermore, school districts are expected to make **adequate yearly progress (AYP)** in the areas that are tested. Adequate yearly progress is the amount of gain the school district negotiates with the state that it will make for students who are behind. It is the way the school district can determine whether it is closing the gap between students' current performance and their expected performance at that grade level. Unique to this legislation is the distinction that all students should be included *and* make adequate yearly progress in these high-stakes assessments, regardless of disability, socioeconomic status, language background, race, or ethnicity. Schools that fail to make adequate progress toward proficiency goals are subject to improvement and restructuring efforts as needed to assist them in meeting state standards. Students with disabilities and special education teachers are influenced by this increased accountability, as most students with disabilities will conform to these increased high expectations for performance on outcome assessments.

■ *School choice*. Parents whose children attend schools that do not meet state accountability standards are given the opportunity to send their children to schools with higher performance records. Furthermore, there is more flexibility in how **Title I funds** (special funds allotted to schools with a large proportion of low-income families) are used, as well as support for **charter schools** (schools that develop proposals to use state funds but have independence from the local school district) that provide parents with additional educational options for their children. Critics of school choice raise the concern that charter schools might exclude students with special needs or allow all students to attend without providing the necessary services and resources that would help them succeed (Howe & Welner, 2002).

■ *Greater flexibility for states, school districts, and schools*. A goal of NCLB is to provide states with greater flexibility in how they choose to use federal education funds (including providing a variety of state grant options in areas such as teacher quality, educational technology, and reading) as long as they demonstrate high standards of accountability.

IDEIA and the Vocational Rehabilitation Act

Legislation for individuals with disabilities has provided them with education, employment, housing, and other rights that they previously were denied because of their disabilities. You can imagine how important the following two landmark pieces of legislation have been. The Individuals with Disabilities Education Act (IDEA), P.L. (Public Law) 94–142, and the Vocational Rehabilitation Act, P.L. 93–112, have significantly improved the opportunities for individuals with disabilities.

P.L. 94–142, originally referred to as the Education for All Handicapped Children Act, was enacted in 1975, later reauthorized and expanded as the **Individuals with Disabilities Education Act (IDEA)** in 1990, and most recently amended to the Individuals with

Go to the Assignments and Activities section of Topic 1: Inclusive Practices in the MyEducationLab for your class and complete the activity entitled *Legal Basis for Inclusion*.

Go to **www.wrightslaw.com** for up-to-date information about special education law and advocacy for children with disabilities.

Disabilities Education Improvement Act (IDEIA) in 2004. We do not expect significant changes in the law before 2016. This legislation was designed to ensure that all children with disabilities receive an appropriate education through special education and related services. Figure 1.2 provides a summary of the history of laws governing special education.

FIGURE 1.2

History of the Federal Laws for the Education of Learners Who Are Exceptional

1965 Elementary and Secondary Education Act (ESEA) (Public Law 89–10)
- Supports many initiatives that help low-income families access high-quality education programs
- Includes provisions for free and reduced lunches and additional teachers in disadvantaged communities
- Applies to children who need additional support to benefit from public school education programs

1973 Vocational Rehabilitation Act (VRA) (Public Law 93–112, Section 504)
- Defines *handicapped person*
- Defines *appropriate education*
- Prohibits discrimination against students with disabilities in federally funded programs

1974 Educational Amendments Act (Public Law 93–380)
- Grants federal funds to states for programming for exceptional learners
- Provides the first federal funding of state programs for students who are gifted and talented
- Grants students and families the right of due process in special education placement

1975 Education for All Handicapped Children Act (EAHCA) (Public Law 94–142, Part B)
- Known as the Mainstreaming Law
- Requires states to provide a free and appropriate public education for children with disabilities (ages 5 to 18)
- Requires individualized education programs (IEP)
- First defined *least restrictive environment*

1986 Education of the Handicapped Act Amendments (Public Law 99–457)
- Requires states to extend free and appropriate education to children with disabilities (ages 3 to 5)
- Establishes early intervention programs for infants and toddlers with disabilities (ages birth to 2 years)

1990 Americans with Disabilities Act (ADA) (Public Law 101–336)
- Prohibits discrimination against people with disabilities in the private sector
- Protects equal opportunity to employment and public services, accommodations, transportation, and telecommunications
- Defines *disability* to include people with AIDS

1990 Individuals with Disabilities Education Act (IDEA) (Public Law 101–476)
- Renames and replaces P.L. 94–142 (EAHCA)
- Establishes "people first" language for referring to people with disabilities
- Extends special education services to include social work, assistive technology, and rehabilitation services
- Extends provisions for due process and confidentiality for students and parents
- Adds two new categories of disability: autism and traumatic brain injury
- Requires states to provide bilingual education programs for students with disabilities

- Requires states to educate students with disabilities for transition to employment, and to provide transition services
- Requires the development of individualized transition programs for students with disabilities by the time they reach the age of 16

1997 Individuals with Disabilities Education Act (IDEA) (Public Law 105–17)
- Requires that all students with disabilities continue to receive services, even if they have been expelled from school
- Allows states to extend their use of the developmental delay category for students through age 9
- Requires schools to assume greater responsibility for ensuring that students with disabilities have access to the general education curriculum
- Allows special education staff who are working in the mainstream to assist general education students when needed
- Requires a general education teacher to be a member of the IEP team
- Requires students with disabilities to take part in statewide and districtwide assessments
- Requires states to offer mediation as a voluntary option to parents and educators to resolve differences
- Requires a proactive behavior management plan to be included in the student's IEP if a student with disabilities has behavior problems
- Limits the conditions under which attorneys can collect fees under IDEA

2001 No Child Left Behind Act (NCLB)
- Improves performance of elementary and secondary schools by increasing school, district, and state accountability for all students, including those from minority populations and those with special needs
- Provides more flexibility in how states use federal funds as long as standards of accountability are met
- Offers school choice for students enrolled in failing schools
- Implements early reading interventions

2004 Individuals with Disabilities Education Improvement Act (IDEIA) (Public Law 108–446)
- Allows districts to use a response to intervention (RTI) model for determining whether a child has a specific learning disability, and no longer requires that a child have a severe discrepancy between achievement and intellectual ability to qualify (RTI is described in more detail later in this chapter)
- Increases federal funds to provide early intervention services to students who do not need special education or related services
- Eliminates use of short-term objectives in an IEP except for students who do not take statewide achievement assessments
- Raises standards for special education licensure
- Adopts policies designed to prevent the disproportionate representation of students in special education by race and ethnicity

Provisions and Guidelines for Implementing IDEIA

To ensure that the provisions of this legislation are adhered to, teachers must understand the basic premises that are at its foundation. The following primary provisions and guidelines characterize what schools and teachers must know and do (Turnbull, Stowe, & Huerta, 2008):

- *Zero reject/free appropriate public education.* No child with disabilities can be excluded from education. This is commonly referred to as **zero reject**. Mandatory legislation provides that all children with disabilities be given a **free appropriate public education**. Before IDEIA, school officials who felt that they were not equipped to address the special needs of particular students would not accept such students into their schools.
- *Child find.* States are required to identify and track the number of students with disabilities and to plan for their educational needs. This is commonly called **child find**.
- *Age.* The ages between which children with disabilities must be educated are defined by the law, and these ages exceed those provided for nondisabled students. IDEIA provides for special programs and services for all students with disabilities between the ages of 3 and 21. Infants and toddlers with developmental delays (birth to 2 years of age) are also eligible to receive early intervention services.
- *Nondiscriminatory evaluation.* A **nondiscriminatory evaluation**—an evaluation that does not discriminate on the basis of language, culture, and student background—must be provided for each individual identified for special education.
- *Individualized education program.* An **individualized education program (IEP)**—a plan developed to meet the special learning needs of each student with disabilities—must be written, implemented, and reviewed.
- *Least restrictive environment.* IDEIA defines the educational settings in which students are placed. The **least restrictive environment** is the setting most like that of students without disabilities that also meets each child's educational needs. Inherent in the least restrictive environment is the notion of continuum of services. **Continuum of services** means that a full range of service options for students with disabilities will be provided by the school system. These service options include self-contained classrooms, resource rooms, and homebound and general education programs.
- *Due process.* **Due process** not only ensures that everyone with a stake in the student's educational success has a voice, but also addresses written notification to parents for referral and testing for special education, parental consent, and guidelines for appeals and record keeping. IDEIA guarantees the right to an impartial hearing if appropriate procedures outlined by IDEIA are not followed and parents or schools believe that programs do not meet the student's educational needs.
- *Confidentiality of records.* IDEIA requires **confidentiality of records**. All records and documents regarding students with disabilities must remain both confidential and accessible to parents.
- *Advocacy.* IDEIA requires **advocacy** for students without guardians. Advocates are assigned for individuals with disabilities who lack known parents or guardians.
- *Noncompliance.* IDEIA requires that states mandate consequences for **noncompliance** with the law.
- *Parent participation.* **Parent participation** and shared decision making must be included in all aspects of identification and evaluation of students with disabilities.

Teachers may wonder what some of the guidelines are that pertain to all educational settings. The following guidelines were developed by the U.S. Department of Education after the Individuals with Disabilities Education Improvement Act (2004) was passed to provide this information to school personnel. Critical guidelines include

- Using the **person-first language**. In other words, do not define a child by his or her disability. For example, say "students with learning disabilities" rather than "learning disabled students" or "students with autism" rather than "autistic students."
- Requiring that **transition services** be included in the individualized education programs of all students by at least age 16. Transition services refers to providing activities on behalf of the student with the disability that promote an outcome-oriented process of

supports from school to postsecondary activities that include further schooling, vocational training, and integrated employment.
- Providing for states, as well as school districts, to be sued if they violate IDEIA.
- Including two new special education categories: traumatic brain injury and autism.
- Adding assistive technology as a support service.
- Promoting the involvement of students with disabilities in the general education curriculum.
- Requiring greater accountability for results so that students with disabilities are part of the accountability system.
- Requiring that the IEP not only describe the extent to which a student will be integrated, but also detail the aids and accommodations the student will receive within the general education classroom.
- Allowing states and local districts to use "developmental delay" eligibility criteria through age 9 instead of one of the specific disability categories so that students will not be classified too early.
- Providing further flexibility by allowing IDEIA-funded staff who work with students with disabilities in general education classrooms to work with others who need their help as well.
- Requiring states to include students with disabilities in assessments with appropriate modifications and to develop alternative assessments for the small number of students who cannot participate in regular assessments.

In addition to the above provisions and guidelines, the U.S. Department of Education (n.d.) maps out key features of IDEIA that will help shape how the provisions and guidelines are implemented.

- **Evidence-Based Practice:** One of the significant requirements when Congress reauthorized IDEA in 2004 was the stipulation that students with disabilities receive services based on research—to the extent possible. Students with disabilities are vulnerable for receiving risky practices. Establishing research as the baseline for decision making for individuals with disabilities is a valuable guide.
- **Discipline:** IDEIA allows schools to remove students with disabilities for serious bodily injury and adds new authority to consider discipline on a case-by-case basis.
- **Response to Intervention:** Schools must permit the use of alternative research-based procedures for determining whether a student has a severe learning disability and must not require use of a severe discrepancy.
- **Early Intervention Services:** Schools may provide academic and behavioral support for students not currently identified as special education. They may use not more than 15% of the amount of special education money the LEA (local education agency) receives.
- **Evaluations and Individualized Education Programs:** Not all personnel need to be present if the parents and school agree in writing. However, parents and key educators not present must be informed of any changes to the IEP.
- **Monitoring:** Emphasis is on improving educational results and functional outcomes for each student.
- **Highly Qualified Teachers:** Special education teachers must obtain state certification or pass the state special-education teacher licensing exam.
- **Private Schools:** Students have no individual rights to services and a service plan is developed for individuals with disabilities, not an IEP.

Provisions of the Vocational Rehabilitation Act

The **Vocational Rehabilitation Act** (P.L. 93–112) prevents any private organization that uses federal funds, or any local or state organization, from discriminating against persons with disabilities solely on the basis of the disability. This law made a significant difference in the provision of equal opportunities and services for individuals with disabilities because agencies that accept state or federal monies must comply with the law. It prohibits discrimination not only in public education, but also in the employment of persons with disabilities and in social and health services. Because of this law, many individuals with disabilities now have greater access to opportunities in the workplace, community services, colleges, and universities.

Take, for example, the case of Kathy Carter. "Access to facilities has opened up the world for me and Kathy," said Amy Carter, Kathy's mother.

Since Kathy's mobility is limited to scooting around or the use of a wheelchair, there were many places we could not go. The movie theater closest to our house has a show upstairs where they often show children's movies. I either have to go with another adult who can help me get Kathy up the stairs or we can't go at all. I must say, I've noticed a big difference recently. The new shopping mall near our house is completely wheelchair accessible.

The Concept of Least Restrictive Environment

According to IDEIA (P.L. 108-446), a continuum of educational services must be available for students with disabilities. This **continuum of services** ranges from the full-time general education classroom to a special day school or residential facility. Figure 1.3 shows the continuum of services in terms of the major placement alternatives.

Consideration for **educational placement** is dynamic and ongoing. Students' placements are continually reevaluated for opportunities to move to less restrictive environments. Fundamental to the law is the notion that students cannot be educated in more segregated settings simply because it is easier to do so (Osborne & DiMattia, 1994). The principle behind the least restrictive environment is that students are best served in the settings (most like those of their nondisabled peers) in which they can learn, ideally moving to less and less restrictive settings. A checklist for determining the least restrictive environment is provided in Figure 1.4.

Most students will receive services in the general education classroom, with support services provided as necessary. At times, however, students' needs are best met in other settings. The decision must be made on a student-by-student basis, with any level on the continuum potentially serving as the least restrictive environment for a target student. For example, many parents of children who are deaf prefer that they be educated in settings with other children who are deaf so that their children have opportunities to learn the culture and language of deafness.

Part-Time Placement in Special Education.   Some students whose educational and social needs cannot be met solely within the general education classroom receive special education and related services (that is, counseling, speech, language, occupational or physical therapy, instruction, and so on) outside the classroom. Related services may be provided individually or in small or large groups.

FIGURE 1.3

Continuum of Educational Services for Students with Disabilities

Least restrictive ↓ **Most restrictive**

Level I   General education classroom with consultation from specialists:
Student functions academically and socially in general education classroom full-time. Specialists provide consultation.

Level II   General education classroom; cooperative teaching or co-teaching:
Special education teacher and classroom teacher co-plan and co-teach for part of school day. For entire school day, student is included in general classroom, where support services are provided.

Level III   Part-time placement in special education classroom:
Student is placed in the general education classroom for part of the school day and in the special education classroom, usually the resource room, for a certain number of hours daily.

Level IV   Full-time special education classroom in a general education school:
Student is educated in a special education classroom housed in a general education school. This arrangement—of being educated in the special education room so students have contact with general education peers only during nonacademic periods—may include part-time involvement with general education students for activities such as physical education and lunch.

Level V   Special school:
Student is provided special education services in a special education school.

Level VI   Residential school, treatment center, or homebound instruction:
Student is provided special education services at home, or resides in a school or treatment center in which education is provided.

FIGURE 1.4

Checklist for Determining the Least Restrictive Environment (LRE)

School district decisions are based on formative data collected throughout the LRE process.

✓ Has the school taken steps to maintain the child in the general education classroom?
- What supplementary aids and services were used?
- What interventions were attempted?
- How many interventions were attempted?

✓ Benefits of placement in general education with supplementary aids and services versus special education
- Academic benefits
- Nonacademic benefits (e.g., social and communication)

✓ Effects on the education of other students
- If the student is disruptive, is the education of other students adversely affected?

- Does the student require an inordinate amount of attention from the teacher, thereby adversely affecting the education of others?

✓ If the student is being educated in a setting other than the general education classroom, is he or she interacting with nondisabled peers to the maximum extent appropriate?
- In what academic settings is the student integrated with nondisabled peers?
- In what nonacademic settings is the student integrated with nondisabled peers?

✓ Is the entire continuum of alternative services available from which to choose an appropriate placement?

Source: Yell, M. L. (1995). Least restrictive environment, inclusion, and students with disabilities: A legal analysis. *Journal of Special Education* 28(4), 389–404. Copyright © 1995 by PRO-ED, Inc. Reprinted by permission.

A common educational placement, designed to meet the educational needs of students with disabilities outside the general education classroom, is the **special education resource room**. The resource-room model provides specialized, individualized, and intensive instruction to meet students' needs. Reading, writing, and math are the three academic areas most frequently addressed by the special education teacher in the resource room. Students can work here for as little as a few hours a week in an elementary school or one period a day in a secondary setting. Depending on their needs, students may work nearly full time in a resource setting.

Some resource rooms are designed to meet the needs of students identified as having a particular kind of disability—learning disabilities, for example. Other resource rooms are designed to meet the needs of students with varying exceptionalities. The term *varying exceptionalities* refers to the placement of students who represent a range of disability categories (e.g., students with emotional disorders, learning disabilities, and/or physical impairments, and students who are gifted).

Full-Time Placement in Special Education. The educational and social needs of some students cannot be met through part-time placement in the general education classroom. These students may be placed in a special education classroom located in a general education school. Students placed in full-time special education classrooms often attend elective classes (such as physical education, music, art, and vocational education) with their peers without disabilities. If there are no full-time special education classrooms in the home school, students may be transported to schools outside their neighborhood. Many educators and parents, believing that the relocation of students to another school interferes with the students' social and personal adjustment, discourage such placements. Students who are placed full time in special education classes should be closely monitored so that they can be placed as quickly as possible in the general education classroom.

Special School or Residential Settings. When the problems of students with disabilities are so severe and complex that adequate education cannot be provided in general education classrooms, students may be placed in special schools. These schools may be part of the school system, or the system may contract with private schools that specialize in programs for students with special needs. One advantage of special schools is that total enrollment is usually small, with technical services and individual attention more easily provided. One disadvantage to the school system is cost: Special schools are expensive, and transportation also can be expensive. Disadvantages for students are that travel to and from the school can be time consuming and that they have limited opportunities to interact during the school day with children who do not have disabilities.

Homebound Instruction. Students with health or physical problems that prevent them from attending school regularly and students who have been expelled from school may receive homebound instruction. The primary role of a **homebound teacher** is to provide direct instruction and to coordinate instructional programs between the school and the home. Although students with disabilities sometimes receive long-term homebound instruction, it usually is a short-term remedy until the student is able to return to school. Mariel Simpson explains:

> Over the past eight years my son Jalena, who has spina bifida, has been operated on six times. After each of these operations, he needed to stay at home for eight to twelve weeks to recover. I felt very fortunate to have the homebound teacher come to my home to work with Jalena so that he would not get too far behind in his schoolwork.

In addition to defining the continuum of services, special education laws also identify the types of services to which students with disabilities are entitled. These **related services** include speech therapy, audiology, interpreting services, psychological services, physical therapy, occupational therapy, early identification and assessment, counseling (including rehabilitation counseling), medical services for diagnostic or evaluation purposes, school health services, transportation, social work services, and recreation, including therapeutic recreation. Orientation (including aid in traveling to, from, and around school) and mobility services are also included.

The Individualized Education Program (IEP)

Teachers are required by law to develop an **individualized education program (IEP)** for each student with special educational needs. The purpose of an IEP is to provide an appropriate education that meets the specialized needs of each student with disabilities. IEPs are developed and implemented by the **multidisciplinary team (MDT)**. The MDT serves two purposes. First, the team determines whether the student has a disability and is eligible for special education services. If this is the case, the team then develops the IEP, which provides the foundation for establishing the educational program for the student. The MDT includes a representative of the local education agency, the classroom teacher, the special education teacher, parents or guardians, a person who can interpret the instructional implications of evaluation results, and, when appropriate, the student. Depending on the student's needs, the team also includes professionals from the related services (such as social workers, speech and language pathologists, psychologists, and occupational therapists) and may include other professionals, such as doctors.

Each IEP must include the following information:

- The student's present levels of educational performance, including how the disability affects the student's involvement in the general curriculum.
- Measurable annual goals, including short-term objectives for students who take alternate assessments, that enable the child to participate in the general education curricula and meet other education needs resulting from the disability.
- Special education and related services to be provided to the student and a statement of the program modifications or supports for school personnel that will be provided for the student not only to attain annual goals and be involved in the general education curriculum, but also to participate in extracurricular and other nonacademic activities.
- An explanation of the extent, if any, to which the student will not participate with students without disabilities in the general education class and in the extracurricular and other nonacademic activities.
- Individual modifications in the administration of statewide or districtwide assessments or an explanation of why those assessments are inappropriate for the student and what alternative method will be used to assess the student. Figure 1.5 provides a sample of test accommodations that are relatively easy to implement.
- Projected date for the beginning of services and modifications and their anticipated frequency, location, and duration.
- How the student's progress toward annual goals will be measured.
- What method will be used to inform parents (as often as the parents of nondisabled students) of their child's progress toward annual goals and whether that progress is sufficient to enable their child to achieve the goals by the end of the school year.

PEARSON myeducationlab

Go to Building Teaching Skills and Dispositions section of Topic 5: Prereferrals, Placement, and IEP Process and complete the activity entitled *Conducting or Participating in an IEP Meeting.*

Go to **www.ncset.org** for information and resources for older students with disabilities in the areas of secondary education, transition, and more.

FIGURE 1.5

Test Accommodations

- Extended testing time
- Additional rest breaks
- Writer/recorder of answers
- Reader
- Sign language interpreter (for spoken directions only)
- Braille

- Large print
- Large-print answer sheet
- Audio recording
- Audio recording with large-print figure supplement
- Audio recording with raised-line (tactile) figure supplement

Source: Educational Testing Services. (n.d.). Testing Accommodations for Test Takers with Disabilities. Retrieved March 4, 2009, from http://www.ets.org/portal/site/ets/menuitem.

■ Transition services described under the applicable components of the student's IEP that focus on the appropriate course of study. At age 16, the needed transition services, including, when appropriate, a statement of the interagency responsibilities or any needed linkages, must be specified.

The IEP is a method for planning and assessment that reflects the judgment and input of the school system, specialists, teachers, parents, and students themselves. The IEP is a safeguard not only for students but also for families and school systems. An example of an IEP is presented in Figure 1.6.

IEPs are intended to serve as planning guides for the student with special needs, not as mere paperwork. IEPs provide guidelines for educators for the daily education of the individual. Because the writing and updating of the IEP can be time consuming and tedious, there are a number of commercial software programs available to help simplify the task, enabling the IEP to be discussed, agreed on, and printed all in one meeting. See Tech Tip, for a list of some of these programs.

Unfortunately, classroom teachers at the middle and secondary levels often do not participate in the IEP process and do not know which students in their classrooms have been identified as having special needs (Schumm & Vaughn, 1992a). Carl Turner, a middle-school teacher, put it this way:

> I know that Mike has an IEP and I read it at the beginning of the year, but I haven't really used it in my planning. There may be other students who have learning disabilities in my class, but I won't know until the special education teacher tells me.

*Tech*Tips

IEP SOFTWARE PROGRAMS

The most useful IEP software programs allow teachers to select from skill sequences and author long-term and short-term objectives, freely customizing skills and objectives to meet individual needs. Often school systems or special education units adopt one particular system. You may find that to be the case in your school district. Some programs are installed in individual computers whereas others are web-based. Web-based systems are especially useful because you can access the data from any online computer while maintaining security by the use of a password. It is also easier to move students' records along as they move from teacher to teacher and school to school.

Following is a list of IEP management software names along with their primary web addresses:

- **IEPMaker Pro**, by Chalkware Education Solutions at **www.iepware.com**

- **Class/Bridge IEP Program**, by Class/Bridge at **www.classplus.com**

- **IEP Writer Supreme II**, by Super School Software at **www.superschoolsoftware.com**

Individual Education Program (IEP)

I. DEMOGRAPHIC INFORMATION

DATE (MM/DD/YY)

PRINT STUDENT'S NAME (LAST) (FIRST) (M.I.)

STUDENT I.D. NO.

_____

_____

_____

ADDRESS

PHONE

D.O.B.

_____

_____

_____

HOME SCHOOL NAME

ASSIGNED SCHOOL NAME (Complete after Section X)

_____

_____

II. CONFERENCE INFORMATION

CONFERENCE DATE: _____
        (MM/DD/YY)

☐ Interim Review Date: _____
                (MM/DD/YY)

CONFERENCE TYPE: ☐ Initial ☐ Annual Review ☐ Temporary Assignment ☐ Reevaluation
(Check all that apply.)

☐ Consideration to/from Alternative Education Program ☐ Region Staffing ☐ District Placement Committee

PARENT NOTIFICATION:	TYPE	DATE (MM/DD/YY)	RESPONSE
*Required	*(1) Written (Attach to IEP)		
	*(2)		

Mode/Language of Communication of Parent/Guardian _____

III. SIGNATURES AND POSITIONS OF PERSONS ATTENDING CONFERENCE

☐ PROCEDURAL SAFEGUARDS AVAILABLE TO PARENTS OF EXCEPTIONAL STUDENTS has been received by and was explained to the parent(s) or guardian(s) of the student.

☐ Parent was not in attendance.

Position   Name   Signature

LEA Representative: _____

Parent: _____

General Education Teacher: _____

Special Education Teacher: _____

Evaluation Specialist: _____

Student: _____

Others: _____

(continued)

Figure1.6 Continued

IV. PROGRAM ELIGIBILITY

Meets eligibility requirements as indicated:

☐ Language and Speech Impaired   ☐ Autistic

☐ Specific Learning Disability   ☐ Mentally Retarded

☐ Emotionally Disturbed   ☐ Traumatic Brain Injury

☐ Hearing Impaired   ☐ Deaf/Blind

☐ Visually Impaired   ☐ Multiple Disabilities

☐ Orthopedically Impaired   ☐ Other Health Impaired (specific impairment)_____

V. PRESENT PERFORMANCE LEVELS

Area assessed   Date   Instrument   Findings (Level/Ability)

_____

_____

_____

_____

_____

Include description of the child's academic and behavioral levels and education performance indicators (e.g., statewide assessment results).

_____

_____

_____

_____

VI. TRANSITION PLANNING

☐ Under 16: Transition planning not needed.

☐ 16 years and older: Describe plan and goals for the student's post-high-school years with input from the student, parent, and team members. Include transition assessments, courses of study, and transition services needed to assist student in meeting goals.

VII. PROGRAMS FOR LIMITED ENGLISH PROFICIENT (LEP) EXCEPTIONAL STUDENTS
(Complete this section only if student is LEP.)

Student's home language _____

Student's language proficiency

☐ English only   ☐ Fluent English proficient

☐ Limited English proficient   ☐ Non-English proficient

Determined by _____ Date _____ Primary language level _____

Name of test _____

VIII. MEASURABLE ANNUAL GOAL/BENCHMARKS OF SHORT-TERM OBJECTIVES

Annual Goal:

Benchmarks of Short-Term Objectives (if applicable):

Evaluation Method:

Review Dates and Results:

Method of Reporting Progress to Parents:

IX. SPECIAL EDUCATION AND RELATED SERVICES

Special Education Services	Location	Hours/Week

Related Services/ Supplementary Aids and Services	Location	Hours/Week

X. GENERAL EDUCATION PARTICIPATION
(Regular/vocational education teacher(s) should be included in, or informed of, results of IEP development.)

Description of participation (e.g., specific subjects, art, assemblies, yearbook, lunch, field trips, fund-raising, recess, etc.):

Modifications required:
(select as appropriate)

☐ Increase/decrease instructional time
☐ Vary instructional methodology
☐ Consultation

☐ Use of special communication system
☐ Modification of tests
☐ Other(s): Specify below

SECTION XI. LEAST RESTRICTIVE ENVIRONMENT PLACEMENT

Describe the extent to which the student will not participate in general education settings.

(continued)

Figure 1.6 Continued

Rationale for excluding the student from participation in general education:

☐ Student frustration and stress

☐ Student self-esteem and worth

☐ Disruption of students in general classes

☐ Disruption of students in special classes

☐ Distractibility

☐ Need for lower pupil-to-teacher ratio

☐ Time required to master educational objectives

☐ Need for instructional technology

☐ Mobility problems in a large school setting

☐ Safety concerns due to physical conditions

☐ Health and safety concerns requiring adaptive equipment

☐ Emotional control causing harm to self and others

☐ Social skills causing increased isolation

☐ Difficulty completing tasks

☐ Other(s): _____

XII. PARTICIPATION IN STATEWIDE OR DISTRICTWIDE ASSESSMENT

Will the student participate in state and district assessments? ☐ yes ☐ no

If yes, what accomodations or modifications will be provided?

☐ None ☐ Flexible setting ☐ Flexible presentation ☐ Flexible scheduling ☐ Flexible responding

If no, indicate why state and district assessments are inappropriate.

_____

_____

XIII. OTHER INFORMATION

____ Medications(s): _____

____ Other (e.g., allergies, restrictions): _____

XIV. IEP IMPLEMENTATION

Persons responsible for the implementation of this IEP include:

☐ ESE Teacher   ☐ Occupational Therapist   ☐ Physical Therapist   ☐ Orientation and Mobility Specialist   ☐ Speech/Language Pathologist

☐ Other(s): _____

XV. INITIATION/DURATION DATES

Services delineated on the IEP, unless otherwise indicated:

• will initiate _____,
  (MM/YY)

• and have an anticipated duration through _____.
  (MM/YY)

XVI. PARENT(S)/GUARDIAN(S) COMMENTS

Parent(s)/Guardian(s), if present, please indicate: ☐ agreement or ☐ disagreement

Comments: _____

_____

_____

_____

Persons who are *required by law* to attend the IEP meeting include:

- A representative of the local education agency who is knowledgeable about the special education, the general curriculum, and the availability of resources of the local educational agency.
- A school representative other than the teacher, such as a person designated by the school system.
- Parents or guardians, to ensure that they are informed and involved in the student's placement and progress.
- The student, when appropriate (involving students in the planning of their educational goals is often appropriate, particularly at upper elementary grades and secondary grades).
- The student's general and/or special education teacher (the teacher is involved in identifying realistic and appropriate educational goals for the student).
- An individual who can interpret the instructional implications of evaluation results.
- Others whom the parents or school believe can help develop the IEP (as was mentioned earlier, this may include representatives from a range of related services and professions such as medicine, physical therapy, and psychology).

IDEIA 2004 allows one of the required individuals to be excused from attending an IEP meeting or to provide input in writing with the written consent of the parent. The school should ensure that parents attend IEP meetings by making every reasonable attempt to contact parents and accommodate their schedules. This includes scheduling meetings at times that are convenient for parents, giving ample advance notice of the meeting, securing mutual agreement for the time and place of the meeting, meeting through phone calls or home visits if parents cannot attend, and providing a copy of the IEP to parents on request. If parent involvement cannot be obtained, the school should document all attempts to involve parents, including correspondence and a log of phone calls and visits. Some school districts have a placement specialist who takes responsibility for managing the placement and program development of students with IEPs. In other schools, the special education teacher takes this responsibility.

The role of the general education teacher in the IEP process varies because each school district handles IEP meetings a little differently. As the classroom teacher, however, you will be an important resource, as you will be implementing many of the academic and behavioral suggestions.

Each person is at the meeting because he or she has knowledge and experience that can assist in designing the best educational program for the student. Not everyone knows the same things, so each person's contribution is unique and necessary. For example, the school psychologist often provides expertise on diagnostic test results and interpretation. You, however, are the expert on the curriculum for your content areas and grade levels. Your responsibility is to ensure that the goals that are designed to be implemented in your classroom reflect appropriate content and skills for your classroom. At the same time, everyone's knowledge of the student is useful to establish high, realistic behavioral and academic goals.

Determining Appropriate Accommodations and Modifications. During the IEP conference, parents and professionals work together to identify appropriate accommodations and modifications that will assist the student in learning skills in class. It is important that general education teachers are included in the decisions regarding accommodations and modifications because they will take part in implementing them when students with disabilities are in the general education classroom. For example, if the IEP team decides that a student needs a highlighted textbook in science, someone must be available to do the highlighting or the accommodation cannot be carried out. Furthermore, effective communication systems must be in place so that all teachers and support personnel who will work with the student are aware of the accommodations and modifications that will be implemented.

Student Involvement. By law, students need to attend the IEP meetings only if appropriate. In practice, too often students with disabilities do not attend these meetings, even when the students are in secondary-level settings. However, involving students in this decision-making process helps them develop a commitment to learning and a sense of responsibility and control over the decisions made regarding their learning and may improve their likelihood of being employed after high school (Wehmeyer, 2007; Wehmeyer & Schwartz, 1997).

Why do many students not attend the conference? When junior-high students with learning disabilities and their parents were interviewed, two major reasons were evident (Van Reusen & Bos, 1990). First, parents often are not aware that students can attend. Second, even when students are invited to attend, they choose not to because they feel that they do not know what to say or do, and they are afraid that the major topic of discussion will be "how bad they are doing."

A variety of methods can be used to increase the engagement of individuals with disabilities and their families in IEP planning. This is often called *person-centered planning* or PCP. As the name suggests, PCP involves more than completing an IEP document that addresses a set of issues established by the school or district. The focus in PCP is on developing a more complete understanding of the individual with a disability and his or her family so that his or her specific needs and issues can be addressed (Keyes & Owens-Johnson, 2003). Even with thoughtful and inclusive planning, communication challenges may require facilitation. When this occurs, consider the following practices aimed at facilitating highly effective problem solving at IEP meetings (Mueller, 2009):

- Use a *neutral facilitator* who can listen and interpret fairly the messages from all participants.
- Establish the *agenda* allowing everyone to contribute.
- Allow everyone *adequate time* to discuss their issues.
- Summarize *goals* and *solutions*.
- Provide a comfortable and *relaxed setting*.
- Agree that issues that are brought up but are not on the agenda will be "*parked*" on the side and revisited at the end of the meeting.
- Promote participation and *equity* among all voices at the meeting.

Student participation in IEP meetings can be increased by teaching students how to participate in a meaningful way (Mason, Field, & Sawilowsky, 2004; Myers & Eisenman, 2005). Thus, a component that often accompanies PCP is teaching students ways to become more actively engaged in their own educational planning. Van Reusen and his colleagues developed a self-advocacy strategy (I PLAN) designed to inform students and prepare them to participate in educational planning or transition planning conferences (Deshler & Schumaker, 2006; Van Reusen, Bos, Schumaker, & Deshler, 1994). Teachers can teach students this strategy in about 5 to 6 hours over a 1- to 2-week period. Findings show that junior-high and high-school students with learning disabilities who learn this strategy provide more information during IEP conferences than do students who are only told about the IEP conference but not taught the strategy (Van Reusen & Bos, 1990, 1994). Figure 1.7 describes this strategy and how to teach it.

Focus on Self-Determination.   Another strategy that helps students become part of the decision-making process is focusing on helping students develop self-determination skills.

FIGURE 1.7

I PLAN—An Educational Planning Strategy

Purpose: The I PLAN strategy gives students the knowledge and skills to actively participate in their IEP or transition planning conferences.

Students: The strategy is most effective with upper elementary, secondary, or postsecondary students who will be participating in an IEP or other educational planning meeting.

Group size: Small-group or large-group instruction.

Duration: Five to six hours of instruction.

Description of strategy: The I PLAN strategy is taught in five steps. The first step is completed before the target conference (e.g., IEP meeting), and the remaining steps are practiced first and then implemented during the meeting.

The acronym I PLAN represents the first letter of each phase of the planning strategy (Inventory, Provide, Listen, Ask, and Name):

1. *I*nventory your learning strengths, weaknesses, goals, interests, and choices for learning.
2. *P*rovide your inventory information.
3. *L*isten and respond.
4. *A*sk questions.
5. *N*ame your goals.

Instruction: Teachers focus on gaining commitment from students and encouraging them to actively participate both in learning the I PLAN strategy and in using their new knowledge and skills during the target meeting.

Source: Adapted from Bos, C. S., & Vaughn, S. (2008). *Strategies for teaching students with learning and behavior problems* (7th ed.). Boston: Allyn & Bacon.

Someone who is self-determined is actively involved in making decisions, knows what he or she wants out of life, and is able to influence decisions about his or her life. Although most parents recognize the value of decision making with even very young children, it is difficult for some educators to conceptualize the importance of students with cognitive impairments having a causal role in their life (Marks, 2008). Marks argues that the reason it is important for students with disabilities is the same as for other minorities—to prevent oppression.

In a review of two decades of research, Test and his colleagues (2004) established that instruction in the following self-determination skills leads to positive outcomes for students with a wide range of disabilities:

- Decision making
- Self-advocacy
- Goal setting/attainment
- Problem solving
- Self-regulation
- Participation in IEP meetings
- Self-awareness

The IEP Process. Most school districts have developed their own format and procedures for writing IEPs. All members of the team contribute to the IEP, which should include everyone's ideas about the students' educational goals and objectives. The person who most frequently incorporates what the team agrees on and who writes the IEP is the special education teacher.

Responsibilities of Classroom Teachers

General education teachers often express concerns about the extent to which they need to know and understand the law as it pertains to individuals with disabilities. Leila MacArthur put it this way:

> As a classroom teacher, I'm concerned about all of the children in my classroom. I want to do as good a job as I can, but I also realize that I cannot know everything about every difficulty, learning and behavioral, that the children in my classroom will manifest. I know that I need to know who to contact when I have questions. But I suppose what is of the most interest to me is exactly what I'm responsible for and what I need to know so that I can successfully implement education programs for the students with special needs. Probably my biggest questions center on the law and what I need to do.

When asked what questions she had, Leila provided the following list:

- *Who is responsible for the IEP?*
  The multidisciplinary team is responsible for developing the IEP; the person who is principally responsible for the IEP, however, is the special education teacher. The general education teacher and the parent might be responsible for particular goals described in the IEP.
- *Can I be held responsible if a student in my class does not accomplish all of the objectives in the IEP?*
  The IEP is not a contract but rather an agreement by which the teacher undertakes the optimum educational procedures to help ensure that the student meets the IEP objectives. Teachers cannot be held responsible for students' lack of progress on IEP goals unless it can be proved that teachers have not made efforts to fulfill their responsibilities.
- *What if I was unable to attend the meeting at which the child's IEP was developed?*
  Obtain a copy of the student's IEP from the special education teacher or meet with the special education teacher to identify the IEP goals for which you are responsible.
- *What should I do if I feel a student is not making adequate progress on his or her IEP?*
  Communicate your observations to other members of the multidisciplinary team. Regular meetings with the special education teacher and other professionals who are providing services to the student will ensure that the student's progress is monitored. Also, meetings that involve parents or guardians will help you explain a student's progress and find ways to enhance his or her performance.

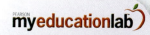

PEARSON
myeducationlab

Go to the Assignments and Activities section of Topic 11: Transition Planning in the MyEducationLab for your class and complete the activity entitled *Impact of Teachers' Attitudes on Students in the Inclusion Classroom.*

Tips FOR TEACHERS 1.1

HOW CAN YOU MEET YOUR SPECIAL EDUCATION RESPONSIBILITIES?

- Ask the special education teacher what reports are relevant to successful instruction of students with disabilities in your class; then read these reports.

- Ask the special education teacher for suggestions for enhancing the learning of students with disabilities in your classroom.

- Ask the special education teacher to co-teach your class or demonstrate lessons that show how his or her suggestions can be implemented.

- Attend relevant meetings (about your students with disabilities) that involve parents and other school personnel.

- Reexamine IEPs quarterly and check that you monitor the progress of students with disabilities in your classroom.

- For each student with disabilities in your classroom, keep a folder of relevant work samples to document progress.

- Maintain parent contact through occasional phone calls and written notes.

- Meet regularly with the special education teacher. If he or she does not already work in your classroom, extend an invitation to come in and help you instruct students with special needs.

- If you are concerned about a student's progress, don't hesitate to inform the special education teacher.

IDEIA is a law aimed at enhancing the quality and equity of education for all students. The law requires reasonable expectations of teachers. Your role is to help students fulfill the goals in the IEP and to provide an appropriate education for all students (see Tips for Teachers 1.1). Although knowledge of the law is important, you should also be aware of the resources available to you when you have questions and need further information. Many people in your school and district can help you. Experienced teachers report that their best resources are the special education teachers in their building, other teachers, the school psychologist, and the principal (Schumm & Vaughn, 1992a).

Octavio Gonzalez, a ninth-grade English teacher, has three students with disabilities in two of his five sections of English. These students receive support services during the school day from the special education teacher, and Octavio meets occasionally with the special education teacher to plan and get suggestions for accommodating their needs in his English class. Octavio comments:

How do classroom teachers participate in the IEP process? What are three ways the teachers participate in the referral and planning process for students with special needs?

At first I was nervous about having students with disabilities in my class. One of the students has a learning disability, one student has serious motor problems and is in a wheelchair, and the third student has vision problems. Now I have to say that the adaptations I make to meet their special learning needs actually help all of the students in my class. I think that I am a better teacher because I think about accommodations now.

An eighth-grade teacher, Lin Chang, put it this way:

At first I was worried that it would be all my responsibility. But after meeting with the special education teacher, I realized that we would work together and I would have additional resources if I needed them. Furthermore, I think more about keeping in touch with the parents so that they are always informed of progress. Doing all of this communication on the telephone is not always possible, so I send a lot of notes home.

Monitoring the progress of students included in general education sometimes becomes the sole responsibility of the special education teacher, but this is not an effective procedure. Students with disabilities are more likely to benefit from collaboration between the special and general education teachers. Our studies with middle- and high-school teachers reveal that obtaining access to students' IEPs and psychological reports (to be used to guide teacher planning for students with disabilities) may be difficult (Vaughn & Schumm,

1994). Teachers believe that their best sources of information are parents, former teachers, or the students themselves (Schumm & Vaughn, 1992a). Thus, middle- and high-school teachers need to consider adaptations that provide for the special learning needs of students with disabilities and also enhance instruction for all their students. It is also important to consider ways to transition older students with disabilities to work settings. The IEP can be an excellent tool for facilitating instructional decision-making (Brooke & McDonough, 2008). Remember, a few minutes of one-on-one purposeful teaching is an effective way to assess progress and provide directed instruction. We have found several accommodations general education teachers can make that not only assist students with disabilities in the general education classroom, but also enhance instruction for all students. These approaches, described in detail later in this book, are summarized in Tips for Teachers 1.2.

PEARSON
myeducationlab

To enhance your understanding of adapting the classroom for students with disabilities in the general classroom, go to the IRIS Center Resources section of Topic 1: Inclusive Practices in the MyEducationLab for your course and complete Module 1: Accessing the General Education Curriculum: Inclusion Considerations for Students with Disabilities.

Tips FOR Teachers 1.2

ADAPTATIONS FOR STUDENTS WITH DISABILITIES IN THE GENERAL CLASSROOM

- Respect all students as individuals with differences and encourage all students to respect included students.

- Coordinate your schedule with specialists who work with students in or out of your classroom (e.g., students don't leave or enter class in the middle of a lesson; specialists are in your classroom at times when they can be the most effective).

- Adapt effective classroom management strategies for students with special needs (e.g., time out, point systems).

- Provide reinforcement and encouragement (e.g., encourage effort; provide support when students get discouraged).

- Establish personal relationships with students (e.g., get to know students as individuals; determine student interests and strengths).

- Communicate frequently with included students (e.g., plan frequent short, one-on-one conferences and discuss potential modifications with students).

- Communicate with professionals and parents of included students (e.g., exchange notes and talk informally with parents; encourage parents to provide support for students' education).

- Establish expectations for all students (e.g., expect the best from every student).

- Make adaptations for students when developing instructional plans (e.g., be alert to problems that could pose special difficulties for students).

- Plan assignments and activities that allow included students to be successful (e.g., try to structure assignments to reduce frustration).

- Allot time for teaching learning strategies as well as content (e.g., test-taking skills, note-taking skills, and so on).

- Adjust physical arrangement of room (e.g., modify seating arrangements).

- Adapt general education classroom materials (e.g., different textbooks, supplemental workbooks).

- Use computers to enhance learning (e.g., as a tool for writing, as a tool for practicing skills).

- Monitor students' understanding of directions and assigned tasks (e.g., ask students to repeat or demonstrate what you have asked them to do; check with students to be sure they are performing assignments correctly).

- Monitor students' understanding of concepts presented in class (e.g., attend to, comment on, and reinforce understanding of vocabulary, abstract ideas, key words, time sequences, and content organization).

- Provide individual instruction (e.g., plan for one-on-one sessions after school; allocate time for individual instruction during class).

- Pair students with a classmate (e.g., to provide assistance with assignments, to provide models for behavior and academics, and for social support).

- Involve students in small-group activities (e.g., allow students from different levels to work in small groups).

- Involve students in whole-class activities (e.g., encourage class participation of included students).

- Provide extra time (e.g., schedule extra time for skill reinforcement and extra practice).

- Adapt pacing of instruction (e.g., break down materials into smaller segments; use step-by-step approaches).

- Keep records to monitor students' progress (e.g., keep a folder of students' papers; keep a progress chart).

- Provide students with ongoing feedback about performance (e.g., meet periodically with students to discuss academic and behavioral performance).

- Adapt evaluations (e.g., use oral testing; give more time for tests; modify administration procedures).

- Adapt scoring/grading criteria (e.g., alter criteria for grades).

Source: Adapted from Heward, W. L. (2009). *Exceptional children.* Upper Saddle River, NJ: Pearson; and Schumm, J. S., & Vaughn, S. (1991). *Making adaptations for mainstreamed students: General classroom teachers' perspectives.* Remedial and Special Education 12(4), 18–27. Copyright © 1991 by PRO-ED, Inc. Adapted and reprinted by permission.

Participating in the Referral and Planning Process

In its 27th annual report, the U.S. Department of Education reported a 26.5% increase in special education enrollment in just the past 10 to 15 years (U.S. Department of Education, 2007). Approximately 14% of the school-age population receives special education services (U.S. Department of Education, 2007). These are students whose educational and social–emotional needs are not expected to be met through traditional instructional procedures alone.

The term **disabilities** refers to conditions that include mental retardation, hearing impairments, vision impairments, speech and language impairments, learning disabilities, serious emotional disturbance, orthopedic impairments, other health impairments, autism, traumatic brain injury, deafness and blindness, and multiple disabilities. The classification of students into categories of disability is controversial. Many people believe that labels are necessary because they provide a common understanding of the student's needs and help to identify appropriate special education services. Others believe that the labels conjure up negative stereotypes, harm students' self-concepts, and cause confusion because each category subsumes many different defining characteristics. Regardless, labels and categories can be used in ways that are helpful as well as harmful. You need to consider how to think of the person first rather than the type of disability. Figure 1.8 shows the system of federal categories and the percentage (by category) of students who are provided with special education.

Students are identified as having special needs through a system of referrals. Students who have obvious disabilities (such as significant hearing, visual, or physical impairments or significant mental retardation) are usually referred and identified before age 5. For these children, the disabilities are often apparent to parents and pediatricians, and intervention begins early in the child's life. Students with mild to moderate disabilities are often identified by classroom teachers or parents after they begin school.

The Prereferral Process.   **Response to intervention (RTI)** has influenced the prereferral process. RTI refers to providing a validated (based on research) intervention to students in the instructional area of need before determining whether a student qualifies for special education services. A student's progress is monitored, and based on this progress additional intervention is provided before the student might be referred for special education. Prior to RTI, classroom teachers initiated referrals for assessment and appropriate intervention services.

Many schools have established school-based **prereferral assistance teams (PATs)** to facilitate assessment and identification of students with special needs. The PAT is a group of teachers and other key educators such as a school psychologist or reading specialist from the same school who meet regularly to discuss the specific progress of students whom other teachers in the school have

FIGURE 1.8

System of Federal Categories and Percentage of Students Served (ages 3–21)

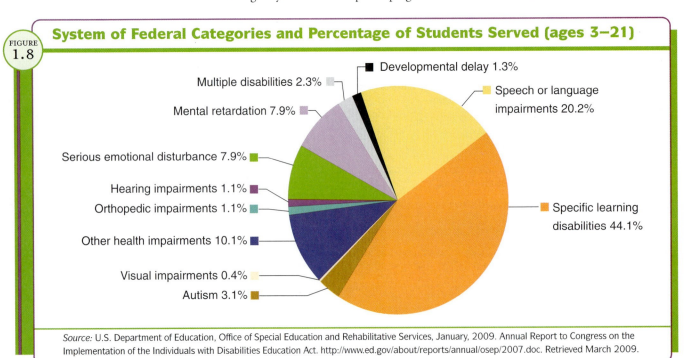

Source: U.S. Department of Education, Office of Special Education and Rehabilitative Services, January, 2009. Annual Report to Congress on the Implementation of the Individuals with Disabilities Education Act. http://www.ed.gov/about/reports/annual/osep/2007.doc. Retrieved March 2009.

brought to their attention. This school-based, problem-solving team is designed to help teachers by making classroom accommodations that maximize opportunities for students to succeed in the general education classroom or by identifying a treatment intervention to determine how the student responds. The idea is to determine whether this student needs additional instruction or has a special need. The model provides a forum in which classroom teachers can be part of the problem-solving process to ensure that each student in their class receives appropriate services and adequate information is available to determine whether they have a special need. Increasingly, students' responses to traditionally successful interventions are used as a data source to determine whether students have a special need.

Currently, individuals who may need special education come to the school's attention because (a) a teacher or parent expresses concerns about the child, (b) a schoolwide screening test suggests possible learning or behavior problems, or (c) students at risk for problems have been provided interventions and the student hasn't responded adequately to the intervention (Elliot, Huai, & Roche, 2007). Whether your school is using a more traditional approach to referral for special education identification or RTI, recommended practice is that students are provided research-based instructional intervention prior to referral for special education. Sometimes instructional and behavioral supports are provided by the classroom teacher and sometimes they are provided by a treatment specialist.

Prereferral teams work toward the following goals:

- Provide suggestions to the classroom teacher.
- Identify a secondary intervention that is associated with improved outcomes for most students.
- Accommodate students' academic and behavioral needs.
- Reduce the need for referral to special education.
- Assist the teacher with the referral process if necessary.

Although prereferral strategies take different forms in different school districts (Jimerson, Burns, & Van Der Heyden, 2007), most school districts use one of the following models:

- Response to intervention model
- Special education teacher as consultant model
- Problem-solving model

Response to Intervention Model. Individuals with learning disabilities have typically been identified based on practices that involve referral by the classroom teacher or parent followed by a complete battery of assessments designed to identify whether the student qualifies as learning disabled. There has been considerable concern about the appropriate use of IQ tests for all students, particularly for minority students, and the extent to which the traditionally used IQ–achievement discrepancy is an appropriate practice for identification of learning disabilities (Bradley, Danielson, & Hallahan, 2002; Jimmerson, Burns, & VanDerHeyden, 2007. Donovan & Cross, 2002). In reaction to these concerns, a significant change in special education law about how students with specific learning disabilities are identified was made in IDEIA 2004. The law stipulates that a student with a learning disability may qualify for special education services if he or she has participated in but does not respond adequately to a scientific, research-based intervention (for example, in reading or math).

What is IQ–achievement discrepancy and what concerns are there about using it? IQ–achievement discrepancy has been the common practice by which the IQ and standardized achievement scores of students referred for learning disabilities are used to establish whether a learning disability exists. A significant discrepancy (higher IQ scores than achievement scores on one or more relevant outcomes) occurs when an individual performs lower than would be expected based on his or her IQ, in one or more areas. Although the presence of an IQ discrepancy was considered a strong indicator of learning disabilities in the past, today there are several concerns about this practice:

- The discrepancy is difficult to determine with young children and may unnecessarily postpone identification until second grade or later.
- Many young children (ages 5–7) benefit greatly from prevention programs, particularly in reading.
- Formal IQ and achievement tests are expensive to administer and interpret, and the money may be better used to provide instruction.
- IQ tests provide little information to improve or alter instruction.

The most frequently suggested alternative to the IQ discrepancy approach to identifying students with learning disabilities is the use of RTI. Using this approach:

- Students who respond adequately to the intervention and are able to make appropriate progress in the classroom are considered high responders to the intervention and are unlikely to require special education.
- Students whose response to the intervention is adequate but who continue to make less than adequate instructional gains in the general education classroom may qualify for special education.
- Students who make little progress when they are provided with research-based instructional methods are very likely to require special education.

The implementation of the RTI approach is relatively new, and therefore questions regarding who will provide the interventions and the extent to which validated instructional practices exist in fields other than reading still need to be addressed. Nevertheless, this approach appears to be a path for identification of learning disabilities that will soon be used by more and more school districts (Vaughn & Fuchs, 2003). See Figure 1.9.

FIGURE 1.9

Response to Intervention

What does RTI look like in schools? Following is an example of RTI in practice. The 3-Tier Reading Model is designed to provide a safety net for struggling readers. The 3-Tier model is currently being used in more than 10 states with promising outcomes for readers at all proficiency levels.

- *It is January of Patrick's kindergarten year, and although most of his classmates have learned all the letter names and most of the letter sounds, Patrick is having difficulty. He identifies a few letter names and letter sounds but does not always remember them.*

- *It is April of second grade, and Mara, who has struggled since first grade with most reading-related tasks, seems to be falling further and further behind. She has difficulty decoding new words, and winter benchmark assessments show she is reading about 35 words a minute, whereas average readers are reading about 90 to 95 words a minute.*

The 3-Tier Reading Model meets the instructional needs of young readers, including those who are slow starters in kindergarten, like Patrick, and those who continue to struggle in the early elementary grades, like Mara. It is a prevention model designed to catch students early, *before* they fall behind, by providing the supports they need throughout the first four years of school. The model consists of three tiers, or levels of intervention.

Tier 1: Core Reading Instruction in the Regular Classroom

Tier 1 consists of three components: (1) core classroom reading instruction provided to all students that is based on scientific reading research, (2) benchmark testing at three times during a year (fall, winter, spring) to determine instructional needs, and (3) ongoing professional development so that teachers are equipped to provide quality reading instruction to their students. In Tier 1 the classroom teacher provides the instruction. Students are at various levels of development in critical early reading skills. Some students are able to acquire the necessary skills through the standard instruction given by the teacher, whereas others require more intensive instruction in specific skill areas. Using flexible grouping and targeting specific skills, classroom teachers are often able to meet the needs of most of the students they teach.

Tier 2: Supplemental Instruction

For some students, focused instruction in the regular classroom setting is not enough. To get back on track, these students require supplemental instruction in addition to the time allotted for core instruction. Tier 2 meets the needs of these students by giving them an additional 30 minutes of intensive small-group reading instruction daily. The goal is to support and reinforce skills being taught by the classroom teacher. At this level of intervention, progress monitoring is used (twice a month) to ensure adequate progress is being made on target skills. Tier 2 instruction may be provided by the classroom teacher, a specialized reading teacher, or another teacher trained in Tier 2 reading methods.

Tier 3: Instruction for Intensive Intervention

A small percentage of students who receive supplemental reading instruction (Tier 2) continue to have difficulty acquiring necessary reading skills. These students require instruction that is more explicit, more intensive, and specifically designed to meet their individual needs. For these students, two additional 30-minute sessions of specialized small-group reading instruction are provided with bimonthly progress monitoring of specific skills. Instruction at this level may be provided by the classroom teacher or another specialist trained in Tier 3 intervention methods.

Movement through the tiers is a dynamic process, with students entering and exiting each level of instruction as needed. Once a student acquires the target skills, he or she may no longer require supplemental instruction. The key components of the 3-Tier model are (1) the use of effective instruction, designed to meet the needs of students at each level, and (2) assessment procedures that measure current skills and growth over time and that are used to provide new instruction to individual students. In contrast to previous interventions for reading, the 3-Tier model provides a system that is responsive to students' changing needs.

Source: Adapted from University of Texas Center for Reading and Language Arts. (2008). *3-Tier reading model: Reducing reading difficulties for kindergarten through third grade students.* Austin: Texas Education Agency.

Consultant Model. The special education teacher as a consultant is a traditional prereferral intervention model. Classroom teachers who have students with learning and behavioral difficulties and other disabilities in their classrooms frequently look to the special education teacher for advice and support. Teachers might ask the special education teacher to observe students in the classroom and in other settings to provide initial suggestions for assistance.

In a second consultant model, the special education teacher works part time in general education classrooms to assist teachers with students who have been identified as requiring special education but whose needs generally can be met in the general education classroom. The special education teacher also assists teachers in implementing practices to enhance academic and social outcomes for students at risk for referral to special education.

Problem-Solving Model. This model provides initial strategies and support for classroom teachers before referring a student for assessment for special education services. Schools may benefit in several ways by using a problem-solving team:

- Classroom teachers have considerable knowledge and talent and can help one another meet the needs of targeted students.
- Classroom teachers can and do help many students with disabilities. Every effort should be made to meet students' needs in the classroom before referral for special education.
- Teachers who work together can solve more problems more effectively than teachers who work alone.
- Teachers can increase their skills and knowledge through solving the academic and social problems of students.

Members of the problem-solving team can include school psychologists, reading specialists, speech and language specialists, and other teachers with experience in effectively teaching students with academic or behavior problems.

Figure 1.10 provides an example of a form that might be used to assist with prereferral. During a problem-solving meeting, team members (using the guidelines in Tips for Teachers 1.3) participate in a problem-solving process that lasts approximately 30 minutes.

Adapting Instruction

In addition to participating in planning, prereferral, and referral procedures, classroom teachers must adapt curriculum and instruction to accommodate students' special needs (see Figure 1.11 for models for adapting instruction). "What does it mean to adapt instruction for students with disabilities?" asked Anna Schmidt, a 10th-grade social studies teacher. "I have certain objectives I need to meet for all of my students. Does this mean I alter these objectives?" Anna's questions are relevant to issues related to effective interventions. Classroom teachers can greatly help their

---

FIGURE 1.10

Prereferral for Special Education Services

Directions: Please complete all sections of this form. The form should be sent to the Teacher Assistance Team. Complete and provide specific information that will assist the team in providing as much assistance as possible. Use behavioral descriptions whenever possible.

Teacher _____

Grade/Class _____

Date _____

Student _____

Age _____

1. Describe what you would like the student to be able to do that he or she does not presently do.
2. Describe what the student does (strengths) and what he or she does not do (difficulties).
3. Describe what you have done to help the student cope with his or her problem.
4. Provide background information and/or previous assessment data relevant to the problem.

Tips FOR TEACHERS 1.3

PROBLEM-SOLVING GUIDELINES FOR TEAM MEETINGS

- Present and review summary information about students from your prereferral form or notes.

- Identify the primary concern and describe interventions you and other teachers have tried.

- Brainstorm and evaluate ideas for potentially solving the problem.

- Select a goal to address the problem and identify objectives and procedures for solving it.

- Discuss suggestions with the classroom teacher and further refine your classroom intervention plan.

- Develop a means of measuring the success of the intervention plan.

- Establish a date and time for a 15-minute follow-up meeting to evaluate the effectiveness of the plan.

students with special needs by making adaptations that positively affect learning for all students in the classroom.

Many of the adaptations you make for students with disabilities will enhance learning for all students in your classroom. For example, Maria Arguelles, an eighth-grade teacher, develops an outline of her lectures. She projects this outline on a screen, pointing out her location in the outline as she presents key information. This procedure not only helps students with disabilities who have difficulty organizing information, taking notes, and identifying key ideas, but also enhances learning for all the students in her classroom.

FIGURE 1.11

Models for Adapting Instruction

A three-year project involving nine elementary and middle schools in integrating students with moderate or severe disabilities into general education classrooms yielded guidelines for change at three phases: planning, implementation, and sustainability (Burstein et al., 2004).

Planning

Participants reported that the most essential features of planning for change are:

- *Change process.* Implement a plan for the change process that includes (a) building a commitment to change with teachers, administrators, and parents; (b) planning for change; and (c) providing support for change.
- *Staff development.* Opportunities to learn about inclusive practices provided motivation and preparation for change and gave participants the tools to meet the needs of students in inclusive settings.
- *Collaborative activities.* Collaborative planning and teaching allowed special education and general education teachers to benefit from the unique expertise that was brought by each group and to create a collaborative environment where meeting the special needs of students became a priority for all teachers.
- *Commitment to change.* Changing practices involved active participation of both administrators and teachers in activities such as making available (administrators) and using (teachers) funds for planning time, staff development, and site visits.

Implementation

Inclusion looked different from school to school and was determined by a variety of factors, including the following:

- *Range of program options.* There was great variation in the types of inclusive practices that occurred in schools. Some served all students with disabilities in general education classrooms and others offered a range of service options. The teachers, administrators, and parents at specific school sites determined how changes were implemented.
- *School site decision making.* Although participants were satisfied with the changes that occurred, the inclusion models implemented looked very different from school to school. This reflects the site-level decision making that was made to address the specific needs of each school.
- *Support services.* Teachers, administrators, and parents required training in effective teaching practices and collaboration and resources such as materials and extra staff to effectively implement inclusive practices.

Long-Term Change

Suggestions for sustaining change were as follows:

- *Leadership at the district level.* Administrators must be committed to supporting long-term change and establishing systems to continue implementation.
- *Teacher satisfaction.* Teachers who see the benefits of the inclusion models for students and faculty in general and special education are likely to sustain the new practices.
- *Ongoing support.* The school district must maintain sufficient resources for ongoing staff development, collaborative planning, and classroom support.
- *Monitor workload.* Teachers were more likely to continue inclusive practices when they were not overloaded with too many students or too many responsibilities in the inclusion model.

Looking for students' strengths and ways to say "good job" also promotes learning for all students. Jane Gordon, a fourth-grade teacher, was a pro at this. She realized that motivation is the key to success, particularly for the students with disabilities in her classroom, and she put considerable effort into knowing the strengths and interests of each student and recognizing those strengths and interests whenever possible.

No Child Left Behind Act

The No Child Left Behind Act requires that at least 95% of students with disabilities participate in the statewide assessments that are used as standard measures of yearly progress for school-age children. According to the National Joint Committee on Learning Disabilities (NJCLD, 2004), the inclusion of students with disabilities in statewide assessments should "lead to informed teaching, improved learning, and the acquisition of needed literacy skills, learning strategies, and social skills that allow students with learning disabilities to access the general education curriculum" (pp. 67–68). The hope is that by including students in all parts of the statewide assessment process (e.g., curriculum alignment, test preparation, assessments, and public reporting of scores), teachers and schools will raise expectations and the quality of instruction for low-achieving students will increase performance in essential knowledge and skills (Ysseldyke et al., 2004).

In a review of the few studies that exist on high-stakes assessments and students with disabilities, Ysseldyke and colleagues (2004) determined that raising expectations for low-achieving students and increasing their participation in statewide assessments can yield positive results when students are given (a) appropriate and individualized accommodations and (b) improved instruction in the content that will be covered on the test. In these situations, students with disabilities gain greater access to the general curriculum and can do well on assessments (see Tips for Teachers 1.4). Test results can also be used to make data-based decisions regarding students' current levels of functioning, goals, and accommodations.

Remember that each test has accommodations that are allowed and those that invalidate results. For example, it is not usually acceptable to read out loud a passage that measures reading comprehension, but it may be okay to read out loud math questions. Recommendations for considering accommodations on high-stakes assessments include the following (NJCLD, 2004; Erickson, Ysseldyke, & Thurlow, 1997):

- *Setting.* Is the student distracted by or distracting to other students? Is the student able to focus in a quiet classroom with 25 to 30 other children? Will alternative delivery or response forms be embarrassing to the student or disruptive to other students?
- *Administration.* Does the child need an alternate form of test (e.g., large print for a student with a vision impairment)? Does the student need the directions or questions read out loud?
- *Timing.* Does the student require extra time? Does the student need frequent breaks to maintain attention? Does the student perform better at certain times of the day than at others? Should the order of the test sections be alternated to improve motivation or decrease anxiety (e.g., allowing the student to choose the order of the test sections)?

Tips for Teachers 1.4

TYPES OF ACCOMMODATIONS USED TO FACILITATE STUDENT PARTICIPATION

What types of accommodations can be used to facilitate participation and success of students with disabilities? According to Salend (2008), accommodations can be organized into five categories:

1. Presentation mode, e.g., clarifying and simplifying language, fewer items on a page

2. Response mode, e.g., extra space on the page, lined or graph paper

3. Timing and scheduling, e.g., shorter segments, more time

4. Setting accommodations, e.g., individual administration, familiar setting

5. Linguistic accommodations, e.g., respond in best language, provide context clues

Source: Salend, S. J. (2008). Determining appropriate testing accommodations. *Teaching Exceptional Children* 40(4), 4–22.

■ *Response.* Should the student respond orally rather than in writing? Does the student need assistance in recording answers (e.g., tracking answers from a test booklet to correctly bubbling responses on the answer sheet)?

Classroom teachers should be aware of the test accommodations that are in place for each student and, as much as possible, should implement similar accommodations during test preparation activities (see also Figure 1.5 on test accommodations). For example, a student who will be given breaks during the statewide assessment should also be allowed to take breaks during practice sessions.

Expanding the Impact of IDEIA

With the amendments, the impact of IDEIA has expanded to include (a) services for infants, toddlers, and young children from birth to age 5 and (b) transition planning and services for adolescents as they move from high school to postsecondary education, adult life, and the world of work.

Early Intervention and Transition from Early Childhood to School.   Part C of IDEIA, or early intervention services, is a state-operated program established in 1986 to serve infants and toddlers (under age 3) and their families. Children who exhibit at least one of the following criteria and who need assistance are served:

■ Diagnosed conditions (e.g., deafness)
■ Development delays (e.g., not reaching developmental milestones for talking or walking)
■ Children who are at risk but who do not currently exhibit a disability or delay (e.g., physical abuse, homelessness)

Early intervention services are comprehensive services that incorporate goals in education, health care, and social services. The emphasis for early intervention services is on supporting family members so they can access resources and manage the care and environment of the infant or toddler with special needs. The important role the IEP plays in program planning for school-age students with disabilities is taken on, for children from birth to 3 years of age, by the **individualized family service plan (IFSP)**. As the name suggests, however, the IFSP broadens the focus to include not only the child but also the family and their needs in supporting a young child with disabilities.

An IFSP must be designed to meet the needs of the child *and* the family. This plan should provide a coordinated array of services that may be provided directly to the child (e.g., speech therapy or occupational therapy) or may be provided to the family to assist the child (e.g., parent training, counseling, or case management). The following services are included:

■ Screening and assessment
■ Psychological assessment and intervention
■ Occupational and physical therapy
■ Speech, language, and audiology services
■ Family involvement, training, and home visits
■ Specialized instruction for parents and the target youngster
■ Case management
■ Health services that may be needed to allow the child to benefit from the intervention service

The IFSP is a family-oriented approach to designing an effective management plan for the youngster with disabilities. The IFSP must be developed by a multidisciplinary team and should include

■ A description of the child's level of functioning across the developmental areas: physical, cognitive, communicative, social or emotional, and adaptive.
■ An assessment of the family, including a description of the family's strengths and needs as they relate to enhancing the development of the child with disabilities.
■ A description of the major goals or outcomes expected for the child with disabilities and the family (as they relate to providing opportunities for the child).

- Procedures for measuring progress, including timelines, objectives, and evaluation procedures.
- A description of natural environments in which the early intervention services will be provided.
- A description of the early intervention services needed to provide appropriate help for the child and family.
- Specifically when the specialized intervention will begin and how long it will last.
- An appointed case manager.
- A specific transition plan from the birth-to-3 program into the preschool program.

If you are a kindergarten teacher, you probably will have the opportunity to teach young children who, having received early intervention services, are making the transition from preschool to your classroom. It is important to remember that for families and children with disabilities, these transitions are among the most significant times in their lives, filled with uncertainty and concern.

As a teacher, you can help parents of children with special needs by recognizing that their fears and concerns are expected and realistic and by providing information about your classroom and the school to help alleviate their concerns (Fowler, Schwartz, & Atwater, 1991; Wolery, 1989). You can also help to facilitate this transition by doing the following:

- Attending the IEP or IFSP meeting before transition so that you are aware of the child's strengths, the goals planned, and the techniques and strategies that have been successful. You can meet the child's parents and current teachers, ask questions, and determine how this child's goals fit with goals for your other students.
- Meeting with the child's parents before the transition to learn about their goals for their child, the child's strengths and needs, and strategies they have found that help their child succeed in preschool.
- Setting up a regular means of communication with the child's parents and former teachers, particularly for the first several months. Invariably, questions will arise that can be answered easily by the parents and those who have been working with the child. Do not hesitate to use these resources.

Section B of IDEIA provides special education or related services to children in the 3-to-5 or 6 age range. At this stage, there is no longer any provision for children who are at risk, and children must exhibit a disability to receive services. However, the term *preschool child with disability* is often used to avoid labeling very young children.

(B) The term "child with a disability" for a child age 3 through 9 may, at the discretion of the State and the local education agency, include a child
  (i) experiencing developmental delays, as defined by the State and as measured by appropriate diagnostic instruments and procedures, in one or more of the following areas: physical development, cognitive development, communication development, social or emotional development, or adaptive development; and
  (ii) who, by reason thereof, needs special education and related services. (Sec. 602[3]; 34CFR 300.7)

Preschool children who qualify are provided with a free and appropriate education that is outlined in an individualized education program. Note that the IEP focuses on educational needs, whereas the IFSP does not. The 2004 revisions to IDEA provide some flexibility for families; for example, children may continue to be served in an infant/toddler program with an IFSP (with educational goals added) after age 3 or move on to a designated preschool program.

Transition from School to Work and Other Postschool Activities. The 2004 amendments to IDEA mandate transition planning and transition services for students from 16 years of age to age 21. In IDEIA, transition services are defined as

a coordinated set of activities for a child with a disability, designed within a results-oriented process, that is focused on improving the academic and functional achievement of the child with a disability to facilitate the child's movement from school to post-school activities, including postsecondary education, vocational education, integrated employment (including supported employment),

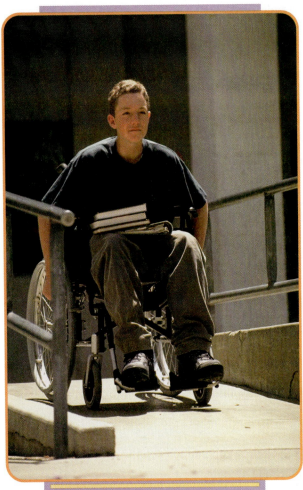

continuing and adult education, adult services, independent living, or community participation. (H.R. 1350, 602[34])

The law also notes that these activities should be based on the student's strengths, preferences, and interests. The activities include instruction, community experiences, the development of employment and other adult-living objectives and, when appropriate, vocational evaluation, rehabilitation counseling, and the acquisition of daily living skills.

This emphasis on transition planning and services came in response to the growing concern about the number of students with disabilities who were unemployed or underemployed as adults and the limited emphasis on vocational education and adult living in many secondary programs for students with disabilities. A consistent finding is that workers with disabilities are twice as likely as workers without disabilities to be in contingent and part-time jobs. A study conducted by Schur (2003) reports that the primary explanation is health problems of individuals with disabilities that make traditional full-time jobs difficult or impossible for them to hold. Even though part-time jobs pay less, individuals with disabilities would not be able to work if it were not for these positions.

A key component of these transition services is the **individualized transition plan** incorporated into the IEP. This transition plan includes the designation of "appropriate measurable postsecondary goals based upon age appropriate transition assessments related to training, education, employment, and, where appropriate, independent living skills" and should also state the transition services (including courses of study) needed to assist the child in reaching his or her goals, as indicated by H.R. 1350 and IDEIA 2004. Specific goals for transition, followed by a list of classes and activities that would provide opportunities for students to meet these goals, are written into the IEP. Sample goals follow:

Why was IDEA expanded to include eligibility for transition planning for individuals with disabilities from birth to age 21? In what transition activities might this student be involved when he is in high school?

- By the end of the semester, Jason will develop the skills to complete job applications successfully (taught in career exploration class and by completing job applications with job developer).
- By the end of the school year, Nancy will develop positive work habits (e.g., arriving on time, interacting with co-workers) (taught in career exploration class and during work experiences supported by the job developer).
- Within the next 3 years, Maria will develop computer skills in word processing, databases, and spreadsheets to the degree that she can effectively use them on a job (taught in computer classes and during work experiences supported by the job developer).

Whereas students with disabilities are underrepresented in postsecondary education settings, students who continue on in school have greater access to employment opportunities and are more likely to get a job and earn a higher salary than those without a postsecondary education (Johnson, Thurlow, Cosio, & Bremer, 2005). High-school teachers, specialists, counselors, and families can prepare students who plan to go on to college in the following ways (National Center on Secondary Education and Transition [NCSET], 2004; Togerson, Miner, & Shen, 2004; Wood, Karvonen, Test, Browder, & Algozzine, 2004):

- Encourage students to actively participate in IEP meetings.
- Help students understand the nature of their disability and how it influences learning.
- Teach strategies for developing self-determination and advocacy.
- Support students in transition activities such as education planning and work-study to prepare for college.
- Help students and families find postsecondary settings that are supportive to students with special needs.
- Ensure that students take courses and have skills required for enrollment in college.

With the increased emphasis on transition, vocational education, and work experience opportunities during high school for students with disabilities, many districts have special education personnel who work in this area. Mary Hinson, a job developer at Catalina High School, is one such person. She comments on her job and the difference it makes in helping students:

> I believe that the work I do as a job developer makes the difference for many students with disabilities and lets them leave high school already employed and adjusted to the world of work. What I do is work with the students, their teachers, and parents to plan a program that allows them to develop job and independent living skills, take relevant course work both at the high school and at the community college, and have relevant work experiences. A big part of my job is developing partnerships with businesses that will provide initial training and "the first job" for students with disabilities.

Clearly, Mary has a different role from that of a typical special education teacher. If you teach in high school, you will want to take the time to find out about transition services and the job developers or persons in charge of transition planning and services. Knowing about a student's transition goals will help you tailor your accommodations so that they are relevant for the student's long-term career goals. For example, if a student with a learning disability is planning to enter the field of drafting, then emphasizing measuring skills in basic math classes and computer-assisted design in computer classes may be particularly beneficial for this student.

The philosophy of this book is that classroom teachers can help their students with disabilities by teaching "on purpose," that is, by being mindful and proactive in using opportunities to make a difference in these students' classroom experiences. See The 60-Second Lesson to learn more about how to incorporate this philosophy into your teaching.

Inclusion

How does inclusion relate to the continuum of services? **Inclusion**, the placement (from part time to full time) of students with disabilities in the general education classroom, is not required by law but is one way to achieve placement in the least restrictive environment. The essential element of inclusion is shared responsibility on the part of all educators in the school for the student with disabilities.

The effectiveness of inclusion has been the subject of extensive discussion in the field of special education (Fuchs & Fuchs, 1994; Kauffman & Hallahan, 1995; Kavale & Forness, 2000; Zigmond, 2003). Research revealed mixed results regarding the effectiveness of inclusion for students with disabilities (Burstein, Sears, Wilcoxen, Cabello, & Spagna, 2004; Carlberg & Kavale, 1980; Klingner et al., 1998; Waldron & McLeskey, 1998; Zigmond et al., 1995). On the basis of available evidence, many factors may influence the effectiveness of inclusion (e.g., the type and severity of disability, and services provided in inclusive settings). Thus, it is important to decide the placement of each student individually on the continuum of services based on his or her unique needs.

In practice, the terms *mainstreaming* and *inclusion* can be used interchangeably. They can have very different meanings, however. **Mainstreaming** refers to the participation of students with disabilities in general education classrooms to the extent that is appropriate to meet their needs. Inclusion refers to the education of students with disabilities with their nondisabled peers, with special education supports and services being provided as necessary. Advocates of

60 *Second* LESSON

TEACHING ON PURPOSE

Contrary to common belief, purposively teaching students with special needs does not need to take a great deal of time. You can make a difference in only a minute. For example, think about having one or two 60-second lessons with each of your students with special needs every day. How is Darnell progressing on a given IEP objective? What directed feedback can you provide to Marlene to help her achieve her goals? To reflect the value of short, targeted lessons in classroom practice, a feature called "The 60-Second Lesson" provides an example in most chapters of this book.

full inclusion believe that all students with disabilities should be educated in the general education classroom all the time (Stainback & Stainback, 1992). **Pull-out services** (e.g., special education resource room models) are not options for full-inclusion advocates because students with disabilities are not educated entirely in the same setting (i.e., the general education classroom) as students without disabilities. A meta-analysis examining research studies on inclusion models indicates that inclusive settings can be effective for some, although not all, students with disabilities (Zigmond, 2003). Similarly, Marston (1996) found that schools offering combined services, rather than inclusion only or pull-out only, had students with significantly greater progress in reading and higher levels of teacher satisfaction.

At issue is the extent to which a continuum of services is maintained. Earlier in this chapter, the range of educational options for students with disabilities (e.g., the self-contained special education classroom, homebound instruction, and resource room) was presented. This is the continuum of services that advocates of inclusion want to maintain. Advocates of full inclusion are concerned, however, that maintaining a continuum of services will prevent real integration of students with disabilities. The concern is that if the option for separation or pull-out from the regular classroom is available, educators will too easily choose it. Debate continues over the extent to which full inclusion should be required for all students with disabilities. We believe that the central issue is the extent to which the academic and social progress of students with disabilities is monitored and adjustments provided if progress is not adequate (Vaughn & Schumm, 1995). Figure 1.12 summarizes guidelines for responsible inclusion.

Accessing Information About Students

How do you learn everything you need to know about your students with disabilities? One of the most difficult aspects of working with students with disabilities is figuring out just what they need and what you need to do to help them be successful while they are in your classroom. The first step is accessing information about your students. At a minimum, teachers should have information about the student's educational and social–emotional needs and about the modifications and accommodations that are required for this student. Although it is

---

FIGURE 1.12

Guidelines for Responsible Inclusion

Responsible Inclusion	Irresponsible Inclusion
The student comes first. The priority is the extent to which the student makes academic and/or social progress.	**The place comes first.** The priority is the place in which the student's education occurs.
Adequate resources are considered and provided for in inclusive classrooms. Both personnel and materials are required to develop and maintain effective inclusive classrooms.	**Resources are not considered before the establishment of inclusion.** Inclusion is established with little consideration for the personnel and physical resources.
A continuum of services is maintained. A range of education programs is available to meet the unique needs of students with disabilities.	**Full inclusion is the only service-delivery model.** All students are placed in general education classrooms, regardless of their needs.
The service-delivery model is evaluated on an ongoing basis. The success of the service-delivery model is evaluated with consideration for the extent to which it meets the student's academic and social needs.	**The service-delivery model is not evaluated on an ongoing basis.** When problems occur, personnel are blamed rather than the model being evaluated.
There is ongoing professional development.	**Professional development is not part of the model.**
The curricula and instruction meet the needs of all students.	**Curricula and instruction that meet the needs of all students are not considered.**

Source: Information from Vaughn, S., & Schumm, J. S. (1995). Responsible inclusion for students with learning disabilities. *Journal of Learning Disabilities* 28(5), 267.

---

important to participate in the IEP process and to read each student's IEP, it is also useful to have information that is easily accessible to you in your classroom.

One way to keep track of the needs of your students is to have a *program outline* for each student with disabilities that provides a quick overview of your student (Thousand, Rosenberg, Bishop, & Villa, 1997). Sometimes a special education teacher will make a program outline for each student, or you can create one yourself by looking at the IEP and other relevant information (see Figure 1.13). This outline does not provide all of the information you will need, but it is a reference sheet you can use to guide the planning and instruction for this student. Items contained in the program outline are information on the disability, strengths and needs, IEP objectives, medical or other needs, grading accommodations, instructional modifications, and contact information. A second piece of useful information is an accommodation checklist. Usually part of the IEP, the checklist should be referenced during planning to ensure that you are providing the student with necessary support and access to the curriculum during your lessons. A sample accommodation checklist is contained in Figure 1.14.

FIGURE 1.13

Program Outline

Student's Name: _____   Grade: _____

Disability: _____   School Year: _____

Daily Schedule

Teacher   Course   Room

_____   _____   _____

_____   _____   _____

_____   _____   _____

_____   _____   _____

Special Education Services

Strengths

IEP Objectives

Academic/Behavioral Modifications

Additional Needs (medical or other)

Grading (If modified grades are used, describe how grades are determined.)

Standardized Assessments (Indicate if the student takes standardized assessments. If yes, list test-taking accommodations.)

Contact Information

Parent/guardian _____   Home phone _____   Work phone _____

Email _____

Special education coordinator _____   Phone _____

Other specialists _____

Source: Adapted from Thousand, J., Rosenburg, R.L., Bishop, K., Villa, R. (1997). The Evolution of Secondary Inclusion. *Remedial and Special Education*, 18, 270–285.

Accommodation Checklist

FIGURE 1.14

Accommodation	Subject Area/Course	Accommodation	Subject Area/Course
1. Highlighted texts		14. Repeat directions	
2. Taped texts		15. Increased verbal response	
3. Simplified texts		16. Check for understanding	
4. Manipulatives		17. Frequent breaks	
5. Note-taking assistance		18. Preferential seating	
6. Access to study aid (e.g., number chart, map, dictionary)		19. Assistive technology (list technology)	
7. Peer buddy		20. Calculator	
8. Peer tutor		21. Study guides	
9. Assignment notebook		22. Extended time on tests	
10. Extended time on assignments		23. Tests in special education classroom	
11. Shortened assignments		24. Oral tests	
12. Alternate presentation format		25. Alternative tests	
13. Small-group instruction		26. Other _____	

Placing Students in the General Education Classroom

The **Regular Education Initiative (REI)** is a concept that promotes the placement of students with disabilities in the general education classroom for all or most of the school day. One primary reason behind the REI is that students with disabilities benefit from placement in general education classrooms. The idea is that general and special education teachers, working cooperatively to meet the individual learning needs of all students in the general education classroom, can better educate the increasing number of students who demonstrate learning problems but do not qualify for special education. The REI has not been without criticism, however, and many educators (e.g., Fuchs & Fuchs, 1994) express concern about the wholesale return of students with disabilities to general education classrooms on a full-time basis.

Recently, the movement within the REI has been expanded to include not only individuals with disabilities but also other support services, such as Chapter 1 reading and migrant education. Individuals who support the REI believe, fundamentally, that the separation of services between special and general education creates an unnecessary burden, restricting the use of funds and limiting the educational opportunities available to all children. Many advocates believe that too many students are identified for special programs and that these students' needs can best be served in general education classrooms.

As previously mentioned, not everyone agrees on every aspect of the education of students with disabilities. One such aspect is that students with disabilities need to be educated in the most normalized environment available and that extensive experience with persons without disabilities is essential to the social and academic growth of students with disabilities. The extent to which these experiences can be provided, while not abolishing required special education support services, should serve as the guiding principle.

The arguments presented in Figure 1.15 are really not for or against inclusion. All advocates believe that students with disabilities should be educated in general education settings to the extent possible. Actually, an examination of data from reports to Congress regarding placement practices for students with learning disabilities over the last 6 years revealed that such students are educated in increasingly less restrictive settings (U.S. Department of Education, 2007). However, the data do not provide insight into how schools have provided appropriate accommodations and support services to these students placed in less restrictive settings. Of concern is the extent to which specialized support services aimed at meeting the learning and behavior needs of students with disabilities should be available.

FIGURE 1.15 — Arguments for Full Inclusion and Maintenance of the Continuum of Services

Arguments for Full Inclusion	Arguments for Maintaining Continuum of Services
• Students with disabilities should be educated in general education classes all the time.	• Students with disabilities should be educated in general education classes to the extent that this meets their educational and behavioral needs.
• Students with disabilities should not be pulled out of the general education classroom to receive specialized education.	• Some students with disabilities need to have their educational needs met outside the general education classroom for part or all of the school day. A continuum of services to meet the needs of students with disabilities is required.
• Benefits of placing students with disabilities in specialized classes, for either their academic or social growth, have not been demonstrated.	• Benefits and pitfalls of full-inclusion models for all students with disabilities have not been empirically documented.
• Comprehensive, professional development that prepares teachers to meet the educational and social needs of all students is required.	• General education teachers are inadequately prepared to meet the specialized needs of all students with disabilities.
• All students with disabilities have the right to education in the most normalized setting—the general education classroom.	• Inclusion is a philosophy, not a place. Students have the right to receive the appropriate educational services to fulfill their learning needs in the most suitable site.

Cortina Fernandez, a fourth-grade teacher, describes the strategy she uses successfully to incorporate students with disabilities into her general education classroom:

First, I work very closely with the special education teacher. Before a student is placed into my classroom, I find out as much as I can about what the student likes, what they can do, what their academic strengths are, what they enjoy doing outside of school, and what they can teach me and other students in the classroom.

Second, I find out what they need to know, where they are in terms of their academic progress, and what skills they need to learn, both academically and socially. I get this information from the student's IEP, from the previous teacher, usually the special education teacher, and, if possible, by interviewing the student and the parent before the student is placed into my classroom.

Third, I work with all of the students in my classroom to assure that every child is a member of our community. Our learning community provides support and assistance for every other member and provides social support as well. This ongoing philosophy maintains a classroom environment in which all children are accepted, an essential ingredient to the success for mainstreaming of students with disabilities. I also make the success of every student in the class the responsibility of every other student. While I'm the teacher in the classroom and take that responsibility seriously, our learning community is one in which each child teaches each other. Thus, it's important to find out what everyone knows and what everyone needs to know so we can all work together. I also closely monitor the progress of every student in my classroom, particularly students with disabilities. I frequently check in with them, make sure they know what they're doing, and assure that they are making expected progress.

Fourth, communication is essential to the successful mainstreaming of students with disabilities. This communication occurs between myself and all the specialists, myself and the parent, as well as myself and other students in my class. However, I do not feel the communication is solely a one-way street. I hold the special education teacher and other specialists responsible for communicating with me, as well as encourage the parents to talk to me as frequently as they feel necessary. In addition, communication is part of the responsibility of students. They need to inform me about what they are doing well and where they need help. I encourage this communication by being open and receptive when they want to talk to me. Successful mainstreaming is more than just what I do as a classroom teacher. It's how I think and how I convey this to all the students and teachers in my school.

Summary

■ The Individuals with Disabilities Education Improvement Act (which incorporates and extends P.L. 94–142) and the Vocational Rehabilitation Act (P.L. 93–112) are the two primary laws that have increased the opportunities and services available to individuals with disabilities.

- IDEIA and the Vocational Rehabilitation Act changed the way students with special needs are educated. Among the provisions of the act is the concept of least restrictive environment, meaning that students are best served in settings most similar to those of their peers without disabilities in which they can learn (ideally, moving to less and less restrictive settings). The individualized education program (IEP) is developed and implemented by the multidisciplinary team, the goal being the appropriate education of all students.

- Among the responsibilities of the classroom teacher are participating in the referral and planning process for students with special needs in their classes as well as working with other professionals such as those who participate in the teacher assistance team.

  IDEIA has been expanded to include services for young children (birth to age 5) and to incorporate transition planning and services for students in secondary schools.

- Inclusion models include mainstreaming and full inclusion. REI promotes proper placement of students with disabilities in the general education classroom.

Think and Apply

1. Now that you have read Chapter 1, review Elizabeth's account of her experience at the beginning of this chapter. If you could talk with Elizabeth directly, what questions would you ask her? List any questions or concerns you currently have about teaching students with disabilities. Then, after you read each chapter, consult your list again and check off any questions that you can answer satisfactorily. File your personal inquiries in your teaching portfolio and record your answers as you progress through the book.

2. Sit in on an IEP meeting. Who were the participants? What roles did each participant play? Based on the roles of the participants, what role do you see yourself playing? The general education teacher? The special education teacher? Why?

3. Interview one or more teachers who have students with disabilities in their classrooms. Ask these teachers to identify any key practices they implement that they believe make a difference. Ask also what they wish they knew more about and what they will do to learn more. What resources do they find most helpful?

PEARSON
myeducationlab

Now go to Topic 1, Inclusive Practices in the MyEducationLab (www.myeducationlab.com) for your course where you can:

- Find learning outcomes for Inclusive Practices along with the national standards that connect to these outcomes.

- Complete Assignments and Activities that can help you more deeply understand the chapter content.

- Examine challenging situations and cases presented in the IRIS Center Resources.

- Apply and practice your understanding of the core teaching skills identified in the chapter with Building Teaching Skills and Dispositions learning units.

Response to Intervention: Developing Success for All Learners

FOCUS QUESTIONS

1. What important issues in special education are addressed by response to intervention (RTI)?

2. Describe an RTI model including the components and implementation practices.

3. How do screening and progress monitoring of students facilitate RTI?

4. What is the role of the teacher in an RTI model?

INTERVIEW
JANE JARRELL

Jane Jarrell has been a second-grade teacher at Horizon Elementary School for 6 years. She previously taught in two other states and as a veteran teacher has taught almost every grade from second through seventh. Because of her experience and training with students with special needs, she often has several students with disabilities in her class.

Jane makes the following comments:

What I like about teaching at Horizon is the student population. I enjoy working with culturally and linguistically diverse students, and this school attracts a range of students from different socioeconomic groups as well as racial backgrounds. I also like that many of the teachers I work with have been here for more than 5 years. Additionally the principal (Mr. Johnston) serves as the curriculum leader and provides new instructional directions. That's why when Mr. Johnston asked me to work with him and several other teachers to design the RTI model for their school, I was eager to participate.

After reading the recommendations from the State Department of Education and checking online with several key resources (http://www.rtinetwork.org and www.nasdese .org), we established the following as our primary goals: To (a) improve the overall instruction for all students in reading and math, (b) establish a schoolwide behavior support plan that would promote positive behavior throughout the school, (c) screen all students at least twice a year for learning difficulties in reading and math, and (d) provide ongoing intervention for students with difficulties.

Jane worked with the principal and a few other teachers to establish an overall training program for the school. They also established guidelines for implementation. Jane summarizes where they are this way: "I'm excited about having a schoolwide model that provides early and ongoing support to all students. I think we can really make a difference and I have renewed commitment to making sure the reading and math instruction for all students is as successful as it can be."

Introduction

In this chapter, you will learn about the issues and challenges of implementing response to intervention (RTI) and how practices implemented within RTI models might help you address the special needs of students with learning and behavior problems in your classroom.

As you think about your role as a classroom teacher, what are some of the challenges that you encounter? One concern that many teachers have is whether they are able to adequately meet the instructional needs of all the students in their class. Also, if you teach students in fifth grade or older, many of their instructional needs may have been unmet for quite a while, thus inhibiting their self-perception and motivation to learn. Many educators perceive that although special education may be available to serve students with disabilities, there are many other students with learning needs who do not qualify for special education. What are some possible solutions to this dilemma? One solution that is recommended in the reauthorization of IDEA (IDEIA 2004) is to provide a **response to intervention (RTI)** as a means of preventing learning and behavior difficulties. RTI is the most current model for screening students and using their response to intervention as a data source to facilitate identifying students who need special education services (Burns, Griffiths, Parson, Tilly, & VanDerHayden, 2007).

As discussed in Chapter 1, students with learning disabilities have most often been identified by determining their potential or ability, usually with an intelligence test, and comparing that with their achievement, as measured by reading or math tests. Students who were assessed as being low in both ability and achievement could not qualify for special education services unless they were so low they were determined to have mental retardation. This process had many difficulties, including (a) overreliance on IQ measures and (b) the requirement to wait for a discrepancy between IQ and achievement (e.g., math or reading performance), which might have meant that students would not be provided services until too late.

RTI is a potential solution to these problems. Most professional organizations and experts in the field are recommending that educators use early screening and intervention as a means of determining students' success and thus subsequent needs. Students who respond well to interventions do not require subsequent support, whereas students whose response to interventions (e.g., supplemental reading instruction for 30 minutes a day) is low may be provided additional supplemental instruction. In addition, the data gathered as a result of monitoring student progress, or **progress monitoring**, might be used to assist in the referral and identification for special education.

As a result of the recommended use of RTI, eligibility and identification criteria for learning disability are described as follows (IDEIA 2004; reauthorization [614(b)(6)(A)-(B)]:

When determining whether a child has a specific learning disability:

- The LEA [local education agency] is not required to consider a severe discrepancy between achievement and intellectual ability.
- The LEA may use a process that determines if a student responds to scientific, research-based intervention as part of the evaluation.

Therefore, RTI may help identify students with learning disabilities by replacing discrepancy criteria and using students' responses to intervention as data to facilitate decision making and provide instruction and learning as critical elements in the assessment process.

Past and Present Challenges

In the past, when students first showed signs of struggling, the prevailing approach was to wait and hope that their progress would improve over time. The idea was that students might simply be slow to achieve academically because of normal developmental or experiential differences and that it would be a disservice to assess them prematurely and place them in special education. Yet students who struggled were provided with few avenues for extra support. Also, young students who were evaluated for possible special education placement sometimes had not yet exhibited enough of a discrepancy between their ability and their achievement to qualify for special education services. For these reasons, this approach was often referred to as the "wait to fail" model.

RTI is different. All students are screened early, often as early as kindergarten, and their progress is assessed frequently so that those students who do not seem to be making adequate progress are provided with timely interventions, before they have a chance to fall further behind. Thus, RTI is a *prevention and intervention model*. As you read this chapter, think about what these changes mean for special educators—and for students.

Previous Identification Procedures

Over the past 30 years, the field of learning disabilities has struggled with numerous challenges related to its definition and identification procedures. Vaughn and Klingner (2007) note that these challenges include

- An increase of more than 200 percent since the category was established.
- Questionable procedures for determining learning disabilities through emphasis on an IQ–achievement discrepancy and processing disorders.
- Students identified using a "wait to fail" model rather than a prevention–early intervention model.
- Subjectivity in student referral for services with teachers' and others' perceptions sometimes weighing too heavily in the process.
- Students' opportunities to learn not adequately considered during the referral and identification process.
- Considerable variation from state to state concerning identification procedures and prevalence rates for learning disabilities.
- An identification process that provides little information to guide instructional decision making.
- Problematic assessment practices, particularly for culturally and linguistically diverse students.
- Disproportionate numbers of culturally and linguistically diverse students inappropriately identified for and served in special education.

These challenges to the traditional model for identifying students with learning disabilities illustrate the importance of adopting the RTI model. RTI provides early and ongoing

PEARSON
myeducationlab

To enhance your understanding of adapting the classroom with students with disabilities in the general classroom, go to the IRIS Center Resources section of Topic 5: Prereferrals and IEP Process in the MyEducationLab for your course and complete Module 22: RTI (Part 1): An Overview.

TABLE 2.1

Identifying Students with Learning Disabilities Prior to IDEIA 2004 and with RTI

PRIOR to IDEIA 2004	RTI
No universal academic screening.	All students are screened.
Little progress monitoring.	Progress monitoring assesses whether students are reaching goals—multiple data points are collected over an extended period of time across different tiers of intervention.
"Wait to fail" model—students frequently not provided with interventions until they have qualified for special education.	Students are provided with interventions at the first sign they are struggling; there is an increased focus on proactive responses to students' difficulties.
Focus on within-child problems or deficits.	Ecological focus. Systems approach to problem solving, focused on instruction and interventions varied in time, intensity, and focus.
Clear eligibility criteria (i.e., a child either did or did not qualify for special education services). Categorical approach—targeted, intensive interventions typically not provided unless a student was found eligible for special education.	Tiered model of service delivery with interventions provided to all students who demonstrate a need for support, regardless of whether they have a disability label.
Multidisciplinary team mostly made up of special education professionals; individual students typically referred by classroom teachers with academic and/or behavioral concerns.	Problem-solving (or interventions) teams include general and special educators; teams consider progress monitoring data and all students who are not reaching benchmarks.
Reliance on assessments, particularly standardized tests.	Collaborative educational decisions based on ongoing school, classroom, and individual student data; adjustments to instruction/intervention based on data.
Assessment data collected during a limited number of sessions.	Multiple data points collected over time and in direct relationship to the intervention provided.
"Comprehensive evaluation" consisting mainly of formal assessments conducted by individual members of the multidisciplinary team, often the same battery of tests administered to all referred children.	"Full and individualized evaluation" relies heavily on existing data collected throughout the RTI process; evaluation includes a student's response to specific validated interventions and other data gathered through observations, teacher and parent checklists, and diagnostic assessments.
LD construct of "unexpected underachievement" indicated by low achievement as compared to a measure of the child's ability (i.e., IQ–achievement discrepancy).	LD construct of "unexpected underachievement" indicated by low achievement and insufficient response to validated interventions that work with most students ("true peers"), even struggling ones.

Source: From Klingner, J. K. (2009). Response to intervention. In Vaughn, S., & Bos, C. S. (2009). *Strategies for teaching students with learning and behavior problems.* Reprinted with permission.

screening of students with early intervention and uses data to facilitate decision making for identification.

The overview in Table 2.1 compares identification of students with learning disabilities before IDEIA 2004 to the identification process with RTI.

Initiatives Influencing RTI

Over the past decade, three contemporary major initiatives set the stage for changes in how we think about students with disabilities and RTI. First, in August 2001, the Office of Special Education Programs brought together leading researchers to discuss numerous issues related to identifying learning disabilities (Bradley, Danielson, & Hallahan, 2002). The team reached consensus on principles related to learning disabilities and the eventual use of RTI to facilitate more appropriate identification of students with learning disabilities (Vaughn & Klingner, 2007):

- Learning disabilities is a valid construct that represents a life span disorder.
- Individuals with learning disabilities require a special education.
- The exact prevalence of learning disabilities is unknown; however, the rate is likely between 2% and 5%.
- The use of IQ–achievement discrepancy is not adequate for identifying students with learning disabilities.

- Linking processing disabilities to learning disabilities has not been adequately established; also, most processing disabilities are difficult to measure and link to treatment.
- The use of reliable and valid data from progress monitoring is a promising addition to identifying individuals with learning disabilities.
- Much is known about effective interventions for students with learning disabilities and yet ineffective interventions continue to be used.

Second, the President's Commission on Excellence in Special Education held public hearings throughout the United States and received hundreds of written comments (*A New Era: Revitalizing Special Education for Children and their Families, 2002*) about the state of special education in the nation's education system. The commission concluded that special educators were spending too much time on paperwork and not enough time teaching. The commission also noted that general education and special education seemed to be operating as two separate systems rather than as a coherent whole. In the report, the commission recommended shifting to a prevention model that takes into account the fact that students with disabilities are also part of general education and that requires special and general educators to work together more closely.

Third, the National Research Council report on the disproportionate representation of culturally and linguistically diverse students in special education provided similar recommendations to those proposed by the Office of Special Education (Donovan & Cross, 2002). The council promoted widespread use of early screening and intervention practices and RTI models. The council's premise was that if schoolwide behavior and early reading programs help culturally and linguistically diverse students receive the support they need and improve their opportunities to learn, then the number of students who exhibit ongoing problems will decrease and the students who continue to struggle will more likely be those who require a special education.

Based on these initiatives, Congress passed the Individuals with Disabilities Education Improvement Act (IDEIA 2004). The new law promoted RTI as a means for preventing learning difficulties and furthering accurate identification of students with learning disabilities. Furthermore, Congress urges the use of *early intervening services* (EIS) to provide students with support as soon as they show signs of struggling. The IDEIA 2004

- Recommends using alternative approaches to identifying students with learning disabilities, but does not require abandoning use of the IQ–achievement discrepancy criterion.
- Urges early screening and early intervention so that students who show signs of struggling do not fall further behind.
- Recommends a **multitiered intervention strategy**. A multitiered intervention strategy is a set of layers of instruction that increase in intensity (e.g., amount of instruction, group size) based on how well students are succeeding in a less intensive instructional format. The first tier in a multitiered intervention approach is typically the classroom instruction; the second tier is often additional instruction that is provided by the classroom teacher; and a third tier of instruction is even more instruction, often provided by a trained person or a specialist such as the special education teacher.
- Asks districts to review practices to accelerate learning so that students make adequate progress in special education.
- Recommends ongoing systematic progress monitoring of students' responses to high-quality, research-based interventions. Progress monitoring provides frequent assessments of how students are learning target knowledge or skills to determine if their response to instruction is adequate.
- Requires better integration of services between general and special education.
- Emphasizes the role of context when referring, identifying, and serving students in special education.

Figure 2.1 provides an overview of the practices related to RTI that are used by states.

There was a strong rationale in support of RTI practices for several reasons, not the least of which was the attempt to better integrate support and services for individuals with disabilities. For example, a student with a learning disability who is included in the general education classroom may also have a speech and language specialist, be taught in reading and math by the special education teacher, have opportunities during the day to work with the Title I reading teacher, and also meet with the school psychologist once or twice a month. One of the goals of RTI is to integrate services and to eliminate settings in which

FIGURE 2.1

Response to Intervention (RTI) Model Recommended by State

GUIDANCE ON RTI	STATE MODEL DEVELOPED	DEVELOPING MODEL	NO MODEL SPECIFIED
	Arizona		
California	Delaware	Alabama	Alaska
Illinois	Florida	Arkansas	New Jersey
Maine	Georgia	Colorado	South Carolina
Maryland	Iowa	Connecticut	
Massachusetts	Kansas	Hawaii	
Missouri	Louisiana	Idaho	
North Dakota	Nebraska	Indiana	
Tennessee	North Carolina	Kentucky	
Texas	Ohio	Michigan	
Virginia	Oregon	Minnesota	
	Pennsylvania	Mississippi	
	Utah	Montana	
	Washington	Nevada	
	West Virginia	New Hampshire	
		New Mexico	
		New York	
		Oklahoma	
		Rhode Island	
		South Dakota	
		Vermont	
		Wisconsin	
		Wyoming	

Source: Berkeley, S., Bender, W. N., Peaster, L. G., & Saunders, L. (2009). Implementation of response to intervention: A snapshot of progress. *Journal of Learning Disabilities, 42*(1), 85–95.

general education teachers do "their thing" and special education teachers are quite separate and disconnected.

Components of Response to Intervention

Because RTI is considered an instructional model for preventing learning difficulties and provides a framework for monitoring the progress of all students, particularly those with difficulties, what are the critical elements that are part of RTI? Fundamentally, there are many frameworks for implementing RTI, not just one. However, within these multiple frameworks, there are critical components that everyone agrees are essential. These are

- Screening and progress monitoring.
- Implementation of effective classroom instructional practices so that all students have an opportunity to learn (Tier 1).
- Provision of secondary intervention (Tier 2) when students fall behind.
- Provision of a more intensive individualized intervention for students for whom secondary intervention is inadequate (Tier 3). Students who are considered special education may be provided services within Tier 3 or within a fourth tier of intervention depending on the instructional framework used by the school or district.

RTI is a schoolwide model that typically starts with students in kindergarten and may continue throughout the elementary grades or even into middle school in some districts. Although no one single model is accepted as the "gold standard," RTI models commonly include four key components (Fuchs, Fuchs, & Vaughn, 2008; Haager, Klingner, & Vaughn, 2007; Vaughn & Fuchs, 2003):

1. **They implement high-quality, research-based instruction matched to the needs of students.** Only instructional practices that generally produce high learning rates for students are used, as demonstrated by scientific research. The implementation of high-quality instructional practices as interventions is intended to increase the probability of positive student responses. Whether you are teaching reading or math at the elementary level or secondary content, the instructional programs, materials, and practices you use should be selected based on the best research available rather than your own ideology or perspective.

2. **They monitor students' learning over time to determine their level and rate of performance (for ongoing decision making).** Educators assess all students' learning to determine if they are making progress toward meeting expected benchmarks at a rate commensurate with that of similar peers. Students who do not seem to be progressing are provided with extra assistance in the form of interventions targeted to their needs. What does this mean for you as an educator? Consider your expectations and goals for learning each week. Create a brief assessment that will help you determine what students know about what you are teaching that week. At the end of the week (or two), use the assessment again to determine how much students have learned. Use this information for reteaching and/or making decisions about additional intervention.

3. **They provide interventions of increasing intensity when students continue to struggle.** The intensity of instruction can be enhanced by reducing group size, increasing time, and/or making sure that interventions are even more carefully tailored to the students' instructional needs. Determine what options for providing intervention are available. Typically, schools provide additional interventions for elementary students in math and reading. It may also be possible to provide additional supports in spelling and writing. For older students, additional reading classes or after-school tutoring may be available. As another option, consider how you might restructure and regroup students so that you can provide additional instruction to those students with the highest needs.

4. **They make important educational decisions based on data.** Decisions about selecting instructional interventions, the intensity of the interventions (e.g., how much time each day and in what group size the intervention is provided), and the duration of the interventions (e.g., 2 weeks, 8 weeks) are based on students' responses to the interventions. As you examine students' performance based on data (e.g., weekly or biweekly assessments), consider instructional adjustments that you could make to ensure that all students have improved outcomes. Also consider whether selected students would benefit from additional instruction.

To learn about useful software and online assessment tools, see Tech Tips. These tools will help you better understand and implement an RTI model.

Progress Monitoring

Progress monitoring involves frequent and ongoing measurement of student knowledge and skills *and* the examination of student data to evaluate instruction. Used with a few students or the entire class, progress monitoring is essential to effective implementation of RTI because it allows key stakeholders, such as the classroom teacher as well as specialists, to determine the rate of growth students are making and to determine whether additional intervention is needed. To better understand why and how to use progress monitoring, see Tips for Teachers 2.1.

The Three Tiers of Intervention

Response to intervention models often discuss instruction or intervention in terms of "tiers." Typically, **tiers** represent the level of intensity of instruction provided to a student or group of students.

As students move through the tiers, the intensity of the interventions they receive increases. Some models include three tiers, and others include a fourth tier. In reading, for example, approximately 80% of all learners make adequate progress in Tier 1, 15% to 20% may require some supplemental instruction in Tier 2, and about 5% to 6% need the intensive intervention implemented in Tier 3.

Go to **www.whatworks.ed.gov**, the What Works Clearing House website provided by the U.S. Department of Education, to find out the research base for the programs, materials, and practices you use.

myeducationlab

Go to the Assignments and Activities section of Pre-referrals, Placement, and IEP in the MyEducationLab for your course and complete the activity entitled *Prereferral Interventions*.

Tech Tips

USING TECHNOLOGY TO IMPLEMENT RTI

A key objective of RTI is to select an instructional strategy to match a student's specific needs. Universal design, authoring software, and assessment software are aspects of technology that can facilitate RTI. Universal design is a growing movement toward designing products and environments to accommodate the diverse needs and abilities of all people.

The concept of universal design can be applied to instructional materials to meet the varied needs of all learners. We need materials that increase the usability for everyone, appealing to different learning styles, methods of input, learner backgrounds, and abilities and disabilities. Such classroom materials may have varying levels of difficulty, multiple means of input, various modes of presentation, and features to customize pace and feedback. Following are some programs that use the concept of universal design:

- **The Early Learning Series** from Marblesoft Simtech at **www.marblesoft.com**. The programs feature multiple difficulty levels, include a built-in recordkeeping system, and allow teachers to customize the learning environment to meet the specific needs of each individual child.

- **IntelliTools, Inc.** at **www.intellitools.com**. This company has marketed three of its most effective classroom programs with a single interface, Classroom Suite 4. The new suite includes a talking word processor and authoring program, an arithmetic authoring program, and a multimedia authoring program. Recommended for Grades PreK–8, these programs offer tremendous possibilities for customizing the curriculum for all learners.

- **The Language Arts Objective Sequence (LOSR)** by Research Press at **www.researchpress.com**. Beyond the traditional assessment software, several assessment packages may be beneficial to teachers practicing RTI. LOSR helps teachers evaluate current language arts performance levels and identify specific goals and objectives.

- **Measures of Academic Progress (MAPS)** by Northwest Evaluation Association (NWEA) at **www.nwea.org/assessments/map.asp**. This research-based, state-aligned assessment tool helps teachers monitor students' growth and progress by having students take adaptive tests in mathematics, reading, science, and language use. Teachers can then use this information to guide their instruction.

Tips for Teachers 2.1

USING PROGRESS MONITORING IN THE CLASSROOM

Why use progress monitoring?

- To keep track of student learning

- To identify students who need additional help

- To assist in arranging small-group instruction

- To design instruction that meets individual student needs

- To refer and identify students for special education based on data gathered during progress monitoring

How do I monitor student progress?

- Assess all students at the beginning of the year in the critical areas for their grade level.

- Use assessments to identify students who need extra help and to create goals for learning. Once you determine which students require extra help, you can plan small-group instruction.

- Monitor the progress of students in small groups more frequently (weekly or monthly) in the specific skill or area being worked on.

- Assess progress by comparing learning goals with actual student progress. Students who are making adequate progress should still be assessed approximately three times a year to ensure that they are learning and continue to achieve at grade level.

What Are the Benefits of Progress Monitoring?

According to the National Center on Monitoring Student Progress, the following are benefits of progress monitoring:

- Increased learning because instructional decisions are based on student data

- Improved accountability

- Better communication about student progress with family and other professionals

- Higher expectations for low-achieving students

- Fewer special education referrals

Primary Instruction, Tier 1. What distinguishes Tier 1 from all of the other tiers of instruction? The primary distinction is that Tier 1 involves all students. For example, in a fourth-grade reading class, the reading instruction provided to all of the students in the class is referred to as Tier 1 instruction, or the math instruction provided to all seventh graders would be considered Tier 1 math instruction.

In Tier 1, general education teachers provide evidence-based instruction to all students in the class. The instruction must be evidenced-based so that when students are not making adequate progress and secondary intervention or Tier 2 instruction is provided, we know that the students have had an adequate opportunity to learn.

What do classroom teachers do during Tier 1 instruction? Classroom teachers or support personnel screen students using easy-to-administer screening measures that are selected for the grade level they are teaching. Typically, screening takes less than 10 minutes per student and can be done at the beginning and middle of the year. Students who are having difficulty in reading or math are administered progress monitoring measures regularly to determine their progress. Teachers differentiate instruction as needed and strive to provide appropriate, effective instruction for their students.

Secondary Intervention, Tier 2. Secondary intervention is provided for those students who are not making adequate progress in Tier 1—in other words, those who are not responding to instruction. Tier 2 interventions are typically provided in small groups with the intention of providing additional instruction that will allow the student to make adequate progress in Tier 1 instruction without further intervention. Tier 2 interventions *supplement* rather than supplant the core curriculum taught in Tier 1 general education classrooms and are intended to reinforce the concepts and skills taught there. Yet the support that students receive in Tier 2 is still under the domain of general education. It is *not* special education. All children who appear to be struggling, as evidenced by their slow rate of progress and low assessment scores, are entitled to this support. Researchers refer to this consideration of both the rate of progress and absolute levels of learning as a *dual discrepancy* (Fuchs, Fuchs, & Speece, 2002).

Teachers continue to monitor the progress of students while they are receiving Tier 2 support. Tier 2 interventions are provided for a fixed duration (e.g., 10 weeks). After this time, educators examine progress monitoring and other data to answer the following questions:

- Is the student making good progress and should he or she return to Tier 1–only instruction?
- Is the student making some but not sufficient progress to move to Tier 1, thereby necessitating that he or she receive another dose of Tier 2 intervention?
- Is the student making very little progress, thereby requiring him or her to be moved to Tier 3?

Tertiary Intervention, Tier 3. Tertiary intervention is provided to those students who continue to experience difficulties and show minimal progress during secondary or Tier 2 interventions. Typically, the majority of students who require intervention benefit from secondary intervention and do not require tertiary intervention. Tertiary intervention is typically provided for a longer time period and more frequently than secondary intervention. Usually students who are provided tertiary intervention are not provided secondary intervention but remain within their primary intervention. Depending on the number of tiers in the RTI model, this tier may or may not be special education. Tier 3 students receive explicit instruction individually or in small groups of two or three students. (See Figure 2.2 for a description of how Tiers 2 and 3 might compare.)

Implementing Interventions

Not everyone agrees on who should decide which interventions to implement in an RTI model, or how these decisions should be made. Some researchers recommend a standard treatment protocol model (Fuchs & Fuchs, 2008). Others prefer a problem-solving model (Marston, Muyskens, Lau, & Canter, 2003). Still others favor a hybrid model that is a combination of these two approaches (Vaughn, Linan-Thompson, & Hickman, 2003). As the National Association of State Directors of Special Education noted, "Some . . . have suggested that multitier systems might use *either* a problem-solving method . . . *or* a standard treatment

PEARSON
myeducationlab

To enhance your understanding of adapting the classroom with students with disabilities in the general classroom, go to the IRIS Center Resources section of Topic 5: Prereferrals, Placement and IEP Process in the MyEducationLab for your course and complete Module 26 (PART 5): A Closer Look at Tier 3.

FIGURE
2.2

How Do Tier 2 and Tier 3 Differ?

	TIER 2 INSTRUCTION	TIER 3 INSTRUCTION
Daily instruction	20 to 30 minutes per day **(plus Tier 1)**	50 minutes per day
Duration	10 to 12 weeks **(1 or 2 rounds)**	10 to 12 weeks **(possibly several rounds)**
Group size	small group/individual	Smallest group possible/individual
Ongoing progress monitoring	Weekly	Weekly

protocol approach. This is an artificial distinction. All RTI systems must consider implementing the best features of both approaches" (Batsche et al., 2005).

Standard Treatment Protocol.   Ms. Tackett was a fourth-grade teacher working in a school that used an RTI framework. During her first year in the school, the principal provided training for all of the kindergarten through fifth-grade teachers on a secondary reading intervention that had been selected by the school district to be used with students who demonstrated reading difficulties. Ms. Tackett was informed that because all students who were at risk for reading problems were using the same intervention (variation within grade level), the school was using a standard protocol model.

Go to **www.texasreading.org** for specific research-based interventions and strategies for instruction.

With the **standard treatment protocol model**, the same empirically validated treatments are used for all children with similar problems (Batsche et al., 2005). The standard treatment protocol does not differ from child to child. The interventions are chosen from those that have an evidence base, and instructional decisions follow a standard protocol. Possible approaches might include explicit instruction in phonological awareness or in phonics skills, fluency or comprehension interventions, or computer programs. Specific research-based interventions for students with similar difficulties are provided in a standardized format to ensure conformity of implementation. Proponents argue that this is the most research-based of the approaches to RTI and leaves less room for error in professional judgment (Fuchs & Fuchs, 2008).

Problem-Solving Model.   Mrs. Denton was a second-grade teacher who was working at a school that was implementing an RTI model throughout the elementary grades. She was asked to attend professional development on how to implement the problem-solving approach to providing secondary intervention (Tier 2) for students in her class with reading and math difficulties.

The problem-solving model is a more individualized or personalized approach. For each child who is not progressing, a problem-solving team—comprised of the classroom teacher, school psychologist, special education teacher, and any other key educational stakeholders (e.g., parent, speech and language therapist)—meets to consider all of the data available so that they can come up with an intervention plan for the child. Interventions are planned specifically for

How is this teacher following a standard protocol to identify students who might be struggling with the lesson?

the targeted student and are provided over a reasonable period of time. The process typically follows these steps:

1. **Define the problem.** Ms. Chung, a fourth-grade teacher, indicated that Thomas was not making progress in math. He seemed easily distracted, did not complete his math work during class, did not participate in team problem solving during math, and had incomplete math homework consistently. She was confident that Thomas was going to fail fourth-grade math. The problem-solving team suggested that the school psychologist observe Thomas during class and meet with him afterwards.

2. **Analyze the problem.** After viewing Thomas in the class, the school psychologist asked Ms. Chung to provide samples of Thomas's work over the past month. Both agreed that Thomas would benefit from small-group instruction in math for about 30 minutes every day. They thought that Thomas was making some progress but it was too slow, and they identified that when he was working in a small group he paid more attention.

3. **Develop a plan.** Several other fourth-grade students lacked progress in math, so they were assembled in a group that met every day with one of the fourth-grade teachers.

4. **Implement the plan.** Thomas started the additional math instruction the following week and received supplemental math instruction daily. His progress in math was monitored every week and this data was retained in a file.

5. **Evaluate the plan.** After 10 weeks, the problem-solving team determined that Thomas was making very good progress, and they attributed it to the additional instruction he was receiving. They projected that after about 10 more weeks of supplemental intervention he would be caught up with his classmates.

This approach maximizes problem-solving opportunities by allowing teams to be flexible. Mrs. Denton appreciated that her professional expertise was valued but realized that it took considerable time to attend meetings with other professionals and design effective interventions for the students in her class who were behind in reading and math. Ms. Chung appreciated the contributions of the problem-solving team and their recommendation to involve the school psychologist. Together, she felt that they had come up with a successful strategy for Thomas.

Differences Between the Standard Protocol and Problem-Solving Models. Ms. Tackett, Mrs. Denton, and Ms. Chung all taught at schools that were implementing RTI frameworks, yet Ms. Tackett was implementing a standard protocol intervention and Mrs. Denton and Ms. Chung were implementing a problem-solving intervention for the students in their classes requiring secondary (Tier 2) interventions. Research suggests that both of the models can be effective, and in fact, most sites implement a hybrid in which aspects of each model are used (Tackett, 2009).

Go to the Assignments and Activities section of Pre-referrals, Placement, and IEP in the MyEducationLab for your course and complete the activity entitled *Prereferral Team Meeting*.

Christ, Burns, and Ysseldyke (2005) note that the fundamental difference between the standard treatment protocol and the problem-solving model is the extent to which decision-making teams engage in analyzing individual student data before selecting and implementing interventions. With a standard treatment protocol, there is little examination of the reasons for a child's struggles. The rationale is that for secondary interventions, there is considerable evidence about what interventions are effective, and the best strategy is to implement an effective intervention. In contrast, the problem-solving model is more flexible. The emphasis is on individualized, targeted interventions based on an analysis of the learning context, environmental conditions, and instructional variables as well as on a student's progress monitoring and other assessment data (Tilly, Reschly, & Grimes, 1999).

Decision-Making Teams. How is the RTI model implemented within schools? Who takes the leadership role for directing RTI? The answers to these questions vary by school and district. It is common to have a team of professionals who work together to guide the RTI process at the school level. Schools might have one or more decision-making teams, and membership might be flexible, depending on the expertise needed for a given situation. You may be asked to be a member of the team to provide insights into curriculum expectations and suggestions for what interventions might be effective with students or you may be asked only to attend team meetings that are relevant to students you teach.

Decision-making teams should include members with relevant expertise. One team member must have expertise in learning disabilities. Another should be an expert in the targeted area of concern (e.g., reading, mathematics, behavior). If the student is an English language

learner, it is critical that someone on the team have expertise in language acquisition, and if relevant, bilingual education.

The overall purpose of the team is to ensure that the RTI model in the school is implemented effectively and that all students who need additional support are identified early, provided appropriate interventions, and monitored over time. See Tips for Teachers 2.2 for more about how team members facilitate the RTI process.

Mr. Chan works in an elementary school in California. He describes how his decision-making team works:

> When the majority of a class is progressing and about 20% or fewer of the students differ from their peers in rate of progress, then the role of the team is to determine which Tier 2 interventions to implement with students who are slower to respond. When students who are receiving Tier 2 interventions continue to experience difficulty, the decision-making team convenes to determine which steps to take next. The team might decide to try different Tier 2 interventions, or perhaps more intensive Tier 3 interventions. The team might decide to initiate a more comprehensive evaluation for possible special education identification.

Mr. Chan's experience is similar to other teachers who are in schools using an RTI framework. Even within the RTI model, however, due process safeguards apply. Families must provide permission for an evaluation to take place. As before the passage of IDEIA 2004, families may request an evaluation for their child.

Responders and Nonresponders to Intervention. One of the important contributions of using a multitiered system in which students are provided primary (Tier 1), secondary (Tier 2), and tertiary (Tier 3) interventions is that it is possible to quickly identify when students are falling behind and provide additional intervention that is targeted to meet their needs. Fortunately, the majority of students respond well when provided additional intervention (Tier 2). We refer to students who respond well to intervention as **responders** or **high responders**. These students may need additional intervention in the future but are generally able to maintain grade-level performance or near grade-level performance with occasional Tier 2 intervention. An example of a good response is when the gap narrows between a student's rate and level of progress and that of her or his peers. In other words, the student seems to be catching up.

On the other hand, students who make minimal or no gains after being taught with high-quality, validated interventions are considered to be inadequately responding to intervention; in other words, they are **nonresponders**. For these students, the gap keeps growing between them and their peers. According to researchers (e.g., Fuchs, Mock, Morgan, & Young, 2003), these students may need more intensive long-term interventions, most likely through special education services. See Tips for Teachers 2.3 for some guidelines regarding what RTI can and cannot do.

Nonresponders do not seem to progress even when instructed with a research-based approach. However, teachers must realize that not all students learn in the same way. They need to understand that although one student may respond well to a given research-based intervention, another student may not. Research can only help us make educated guesses about which instructional practices are most likely to benefit the greatest number of children. But even in the best research studies, some students might actually respond better to an alternative approach. Therefore, when a child does not

PEARSON
myeducationlab

To enhance your understanding of RTI go to the IRIS Center Resources section of Topic 5: Prereferrals and IEP Process in the MyEducationLab for your course and complete Module 23: RTI (Part 2): Assessment.

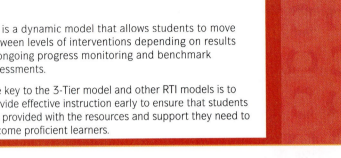

Tips FOR TEACHERS 2.3

WHAT RTI CAN AND CANNOT DO

- RTI neither creates nor fixes learning disabilities. However, models such as 3-Tier Reading provide a safety net for students who might end up in special education simply because they have not been provided adequate instruction or appropriate interventions prior to being referred for special education services.

- RTI is a dynamic model that allows students to move between levels of interventions depending on results of ongoing progress monitoring and benchmark assessments.

- The key to the 3-Tier model and other RTI models is to provide effective instruction early to ensure that students are provided with the resources and support they need to become proficient learners.

seem to be responding to an instructional method, it is important to try a different approach. RTI researcher Amanda VanDerHayden defines nonresponders as "students for whom we have not yet found the right intervention" (personal communication, February 2006). (See Tips for Teachers 2.4 for help in identifying why children may not respond to instruction.)

Teachers vary a great deal in how they apply different instructional approaches. How well a teacher implements a practice affects how well students learn (Al Otaiba & Fuchs, 2006). This common-sense finding has important implications for anyone implementing RTI. Determining whether a program is well implemented and appropriate for students requires observing in classrooms. The program being implemented by the classroom teacher may be appropriate, but the teacher may not be using it effectively. Maybe the teacher is struggling with classroom management and needs assistance in this area before being able to focus more on instruction. In any case, it is important to explore what can be done to improve instruction and to provide group interventions before providing individual interventions (see Tips for Teachers 2.5).

Classroom observations must be part of every RTI model (Vaughn & Fuchs, 2003; Vellutino, Scanlon, Small, Fanuele, & Sweeney, 2007). Vellutino and colleagues (2007) note that, "Intervention at this level is based on the assumption that many if not most struggling readers will be able to profit from relevant modifications in classroom literacy instruction, despite the fact that they were (apparently) less well equipped than their normally achieving

Tips FOR TEACHERS 2.4

IDENTIFYING WHY CHILDREN DO NOT RESPOND TO INSTRUCTION

Before concluding that a child is a nonresponder who needs more intensive services, consider that there are many reasons the child may not be responding to instruction, such as

- The method is not an effective one with this child, and a different approach would yield better results.

- The level of instruction might not be a good match for the child.

- The environment might not be conducive to learning.

Tips FOR TEACHERS 2.5

DETERMINING WHETHER INDIVIDUAL INTERVENTIONS ARE NEEDED

To determine whether teachers should provide individual interventions:

- Examine the program to determine whether it has been validated with students like those in the class.

- Determine whether instruction is at an appropriate level for students and the program is well-implemented.

- Establish whether teachers are sufficiently differentiating instruction to meet diverse student needs.

classmates to compensate for inadequacies in reading instruction" (p. 186). This recognition that many students struggle when their instruction is inadequate is an important one, with significant implications for culturally and linguistically diverse students who often are educated in high-poverty, high-needs schools in which teachers are sometimes not as qualified as in more affluent schools (Harry & Klingner, 2006).

RTI for Students Who Are Culturally and Linguistically Diverse

RTI has the potential to improve outcomes for students who are culturally and linguistically diverse and to more accurately determine which students need special education services (Klingner & Edwards, 2006). RTI practices that are responsive to the cultural and linguistic needs of students can assist teachers in determining whether students' progress is related to what they are being taught, their background experiences, or how they are being taught. The quality of RTI depends on the quality of RTI team involved. Without sufficient knowledge about cultural and linguistic diversity, for example, educators implementing RTI may presume that a child who does not make progress at a certain pace must have a disability rather than recognize that the child may need additional time and support while learning English. Educators may also equate cultural differences with cultural deficits, which may influence their interpretations of their diverse students' behaviors (Klingner & Solano-Flores, 2007).

Although the process of learning to read in a child's second language is similar to learning to read in his or her first language, there also are important differences of which teachers may not be aware (August & Shanahan, 2006). Second language acquisition, best practices for English language learners (ELLs), and cultural variations should be considered when assessing student progress, designing interventions, and interpreting English language learners' responses to interventions.

RTI approaches that respond to the cultural and linguistic diversity of students focus on understanding external or environmental factors that affect their opportunity to learn in addition to personal factors. For RTI to work, team members must have expertise in cultural and linguistic diversity and be knowledgeable about interventions that have been effective with culturally and linguistically diverse students with different needs.

In implementing RTI approaches with ELLs, a significant challenge is determining students' knowledge and skills in their first language and then understanding their performance in their second language (English). For example, there are subgroups of students whose literacy knowledge and skills in their first language (e.g., Spanish) are adequate, but whose literacy skills in their second language (e.g., English) are low. These students have demonstrated the capacity to acquire reading skills and now require instruction so they can apply those skills to the acquisition of English literacy. Other students may have low literacy in both their first language and English because they have not received adequate instruction in either language. Still another group of students, the smallest group, demonstrates low literacy skills in both their first language and English even after receiving adequate instruction. For more on using RTI approaches with ELLs, see Tips for Teachers 2.6.

When students demonstrate reading difficulties, providing small-group intensive interventions that target their instructional needs and then monitoring their progress ensures that instruction is modified to meet the needs of students. To meet their needs, those working with ELLs should consider the following:

- ELLs benefit from teachers who are highly interested in ensuring that their students make adequate progress in reading and that they themselves have the knowledge and skills to provide appropriate instruction.
- ELLs will be better served if teachers and school personnel do not expect or accept low performance and if they do not view students as underserving of effective interventions.
- ELLs who exhibit learning disabilities may be underidentified and undertreated because school personnel may not have the knowledge and skills needed to identify and treat these students.

What can this teacher do to determine whether this child is one of the underidentified children with a learning disability or whether the language barrier is hindering this child's learning?

Tips for Teachers 2.6

USING RTI APPROACHES WITH ENGLISH LANGUAGE LEARNERS

To help determine how you can best provide instruction to your ELLs, consider the following questions:

- *What skills must educators have to effectively implement RTI for ELLs?* Having professional development provided to enhance your knowledge and skills is essential; in addition, a problem-solving team with knowledge and experience working with ELLs can be a valuable resource to facilitate decision making and to design instructional supports. The more you know about the development of oral language, early literacy, students' home language, contextual considerations, and the cultural backgrounds of students, the better informed you will be in making appropriate decisions about interpreting screening and assessment results and in designing appropriate interventions.

- *How is screening implemented with ELLs?* ELLs can be screened on the same early reading indicators as native English language speakers, including phonological awareness, letter knowledge, and word and text reading. Universal screenings must be conducted using native language and/or English measures that have demonstrated high validity and reliability. Provide instructional support to ELLs with low performance in reading areas even when oral language skills in English are low. Interventions should simultaneously address development of language and literacy skills in English.

- *How is progress monitoring effectively implemented with ELLs?* Monitor the progress of ELLs as frequently as you monitor the progress of all other students—a minimum of three times per year for students at grade level or above and three to six times per year for students at risk for reading problems. Consider students' accents and pronunciations when scoring English measures and provide appropriate interpretations when words are mispronounced. Do not penalize students for dialect features. Consider that students may be acquiring word meaning

while acquiring word reading and, thus, oral reading fluency may proceed at an expected rate early (while students are focusing on word reading) and then proceed at a lower than expected rate later when students are focusing more on word meaning.

- *How is primary instruction (Tier 1) provided to ELLs?* Set high but reasonable instructional expectations that provide ongoing instructional support to ensure that these expectations are met. The core reading program for ELLs should include consideration of the foundational skills such as phonemic awareness and phonics early in the reading process, with continued emphasis on vocabulary and concept building throughout the instructional process. Reading words accurately and with prosody, as well as reading for meaning and learning, are emphasized through listening comprehension early and then later through reading comprehension. Scaffold language and opportunities to respond. Scaffolding language includes paraphrasing key words, providing opportunities to extend answers, supporting language by using familiar synonyms (e.g., "that is also like . . .") and familiar antonyms (e.g., "that is also different from . . ."), reframing students' responses, confirming aspects of the answer that are correct, and providing language supports to further explain aspects that require refinement.

- *How are secondary (Tier 2) and tertiary (Tier 3) interventions effectively implemented for ELLs?* Provide intensive reading interventions to ELLs demonstrating low reading skills immediately when needed. These interventions can be effectively implemented as early as first grade, as well as for more mature readers with reading difficulties. You do not need to wait for English oral language to improve before providing reading interventions. Use appropriate practices for building oracy skills and vocabulary development as well as reading skills.

Source: Adapted from *Response to Intervention in Reading for English Language Learners* by Sharon Vaughn and Alba Ortiz. The complete document is available on NCLD website at www.ncld.org; and Gersten, R., Baker, S. K., Shanahan, T., Linan-Thompson, S., Collins, P., & Scarcella, R. (2007). *Effective literacy and English language instruction for English learners in the elementary grades: A practice guide (NCEE 2007-4011)*. Washington, DC: National Center for Education Evaluation and Regional Assistance, Institute of Education Sciences, U.S. Department of Education. Retrieved from http://ies.ed.gov/ncee.

■ Students benefit when school personnel are focused on meeting students' educational needs rather than on finding an external source to explain the educational needs.

Working with Families

Family involvement has been a required part of identifying and monitoring students with disabilities since the earliest version of the IDEA. Family involvement is required with all aspects of identifying students with disabilities—regardless of the model used. If schools are using RTI models, families must be informed and involved in the process. Just as before, families can request a formal evaluation for a disability at any time. A family should also be notified early in the RTI process that a child seems to be struggling and that the school plans to try specific interventions to help. The Council for Exceptional Children (2006–2007) suggests that schools let families know about their child's participation in the RTI process at least by Tier 2. Schools should

■ Describe the RTI process.
■ Provide families with written intervention plans that are clearly explained.

Go to the Assignments and Activities section of Parents and Families in the MyEducationLab for your course and complete the activity entitled *Including Parents on the Collaborative Educational Team.*

- Obtain families' consent.
- Provide families with regular updates about their child's progress.

The National Center for Learning Disabilities (Cortiella, 2006) advises including the following information in written intervention plans:

- A description of the specific intervention
- The length of time (such as the number of weeks) that will be allowed for the intervention to have a positive effect
- The number of minutes per day the intervention will be implemented (such as 30 to 45 minutes)
- The persons responsible for providing the intervention
- The location where the intervention will be provided
- The factors for judging whether the student is experiencing success
- A description of the progress monitoring strategy or approach, such as CBM, that will be used
- A progress monitoring schedule
- How frequently (the parents) will receive reports about (their) child's response to the intervention (p. 5)

Several states have developed documents for parents to assist them in understanding RTI.

Universal Screening

Universal screening in reading, and sometimes in math, is an essential component of RTI models at the Tier 1 level. This process involves administering the same test to all students to determine who is likely to be at risk for academic difficulties, in the same way that schools have checked children's vision for years to screen students for potential problems. In many schools, screening is carried out three times a year: in the fall, winter, and spring. Screening instruments usually have few items and are short in duration. Screening is used to determine whether additional testing is needed. Schoolwide academic screening was rarely implemented with previous models. Instead, it was typically the classroom teacher who first noticed that students were struggling and referred them for an evaluation. Invariably some students were overlooked. With universal screening, however, everyone is tested.

What is an example of universal screening? Texas provides universal screening in reading for all students in kindergarten through second grade. The classroom teacher conducts the screening, and the most frequently used screening measure is the Texas Primary Reading Inventory (TPRI). The TPRI was developed and used to screen Texas students; this diagnostic instrument provides information on a student's reading/language arts development (from kindergarten through third grade). There is a quick screening that takes just a few minutes and is individually administered by the classroom teacher. Students' performance on the quick screen assists teachers in deciding whether a more diagnostic assessment would provide the necessary information to help teachers design instruction. The screening and assessment tool helps teachers decide which of the critical elements in reading (e.g., phonics, fluency, and comprehension) the student needs additional instruction and even provides lessons to facilitate decision making about what instruction should be provided.

Universal screening is also a quick way to identify general performance levels and determine whether students are on track to developing proficiency in the fundamental skills of reading and math. We know much more than we used to about how to predict future reading levels, for example, using phonological awareness and rapid naming tasks. Thus, we can determine with some accuracy which students are at risk and require additional intervention (Vellutino et al., 2007). Foorman and Ciancio (2005) point out that "the purpose of early screening could be identifying students *not* at risk so that instructional objectives can be established for students potentially at risk" (p. 494). Screening also provides valuable information about class performance and identifies teachers who might need further professional development. Once students have been identified as needing additional assistance using a screening measure, interventions are provided.

Numerous assessments can be used as screening instruments (see Table 2.2 for a list of possible reading measures). Some tests assess only one or two elements of reading (such as the C-TOPP, which only tests phonological processing), whereas others tap into several reading components. Some are quite quick to administer, such as the TOWRE, and others take much longer, such as the QRI-4 (Rathvon, 2004).

Go to www.TPRI.org to learn more about TPRI.

TABLE
2.2

Possible Screening Measures for Reading

ASSESSMENT	PUBLISHER AND WEBSITE	GRADES OR AGES	ORAL LANG.	PA	PHON.	WORD ID	FLU.	VOC.	COMP.	COMMENTS
AIMSweb Curriculum-Based Measurement (CBM)	Edformation www.aimsweb.com	K–12	No	Yes	Yes	No	Yes	No	Yes	Offers Web-based data management
Basic Early Assessment of Reading (BEAR)	Riverside www.riverpub.com	K–3	No	Yes	Yes	Yes	Yes	Yes	Yes	Pencil-paper and computerized versions
Comprehensive Test of Phonological Processing (CTOPP)	PRO-ED www.proedinc.com	K–3	No	Yes	No	No	No	No	No	Phonological processing only
Dynamic Indicators of Basic Early Literacy Skills (DIBELS)	Sopris West/Cambium www.dibelsassessment .com	K–3, 4–6	No	Yes	Yes	No	Yes	No	Yes (4–6 only)	Grade 4–6 students assessed only in fluency and comprehension
Fox in a Box-2	CTB McGraw-Hill www.ctb.com	PreK–3	Yes	Yes	Yes	Yes	Yes	Yes	Yes	Includes Prek
Qualitative Reading Inventory-4 (QRI-4)	Allyn & Bacon/ Longman www.ablongman.com	K–12	No	Yes	No	Yes	Yes	No	Yes	Informal Assessment Instrument
Slosson Oral Reading Test (SORT-R3)	Slosson www.slosson.com	K–12	No	No	No	Yes	No	No	No	Word ID only
Scholastic Reading Inventory (SRI)	Scholastic teacher scholastic.com	K–12	No	No	No	No	No	No	Yes	Computer Adaptive; Includes Data Management System
Test of Early Reading Ability (TERA-3)	Pearson http://ags. pearsonassessments .com PRO-ED www .proedinc.com	Ages 3.6–8.6	No	No	No	Yes	No	Yes	Yes	Assesses letter knowledge and environmental print
Texas Primary Reading Inventory (TPRI)	Texas Education Agency www.tpri.org	K–2	Yes	Yes	Yes	Yes	Yes	Yes	Yes	Includes screening section and inventory section
Test of Word Reading Efficiency (TOWRE)	Pearson http://ags.pearson .assessments.com	Ages 6.0–24. 11	No	No	Yes	Yes	No	No	No	Pseudo-word reading and Word ID only

Using Screening to Make Educational Decisions

Screening is useful for providing quick information at the classroom or group level as well as at the student level (Fletcher, Lyon, Fuchs, & Barnes, 1997). When all of the students in a school are screened, school administrators can examine assessment results for patterns across as well as within classrooms. Problems that are widespread across classrooms call for schoolwide interventions. Or it could be that most of the students in the majority of classrooms do well, whereas in one or two classrooms a lot of students seem to be struggling. When this is the case, data indicate a classwide problem in which it may be most appropriate to provide interventions at the class level. When only a few students are struggling relative to their peers, then problems seem to be at an individual level, and individual interventions are warranted.

Using Progress Monitoring to Assess Students' Response to Interventions

Whereas screening is used to assess *all* students to determine who might need additional support, progress monitoring is applied with individual students to assess their response to interventions. Like screening measures, progress monitoring instruments are quick to administer and focus on targeted skills in the core curriculum. The purposes of progress

STEPS IN CONDUCTING PROGRESS MONITORING

When screening students and conducting progress monitoring:

- Screen all students in the fall.

- Rank students by grade level and by classroom. In other words, compile assessment results so that patterns of achievement within classrooms and across classrooms at every grade level can be examined.

- Identify lower-achieving students in each grade or classroom.

- Set goals for individual students.

- Use frequent progress monitoring with students identified as low achievers. Progress monitoring might occur monthly or as often as every week, particularly with the lowest students, on targeted skills (e.g., oral reading fluency).

- Students who score at adequate levels or higher on the screening instrument can be assessed less frequently, for example, three times a year (i.e., in the fall, winter, and spring).

- Create graphs that provide visual displays of students' progress.

- Evaluate progress monitoring data regularly using a systematic set of decision rules to determine whether interventions seem to be effective for individual students.

- Revise interventions as necessary in response to the data.

monitoring are to closely monitor students' progress, to develop profiles of students' learning, and to assess the effectiveness of interventions so that changes can be made if necessary. These data can be quite useful if children continue to struggle and the decision is made to conduct a comprehensive evaluation of their strengths and needs. Progress monitoring measures are administered frequently, perhaps once a month, or as often as once a week in some cases. For more information on progress monitoring measures and procedures specific to reading and mathematics, see Chapters 12 and 14. For a list of steps to follow in completing progress monitoring, see Tips for Teachers 2.7.

Role of Teachers in an RTI Model

At a professional development session designed to improve teachers' knowledge of the RTI model at Sunset Elementary School, Mrs. Jacobs, a 20-year veteran teacher who had taught all grades from second through fifth grade, said, "I think I understand the basic principles of the RTI model, but I just don't understand what I'm supposed to do to facilitate implementation. What is my role?" Amanda VanDerHeyden (2009) indicates that teachers and other school personnel need to establish procedures to accomplish the following:

- Identify students who need intervention. This is typically done using a schoolwide screening in which students who fail the screening at their grade level are considered at risk and provided secondary or tertiary intervention.
- Provide evidence-based interventions that effectively improve learning for the vast majority of students receiving the intervention. Typically the secondary intervention (Tier 2) is provided by the classroom teacher. This may occur in small groups or individually. Sometimes teachers coordinate their Tier 2 instruction by working cooperatively with teachers in their same grade to provide intervention to a small group of students while the other teacher provides a large-class activity.
- Monitor the effects of the intervention to ensure that it positively influences learning. If the classroom teacher is providing the intervention, and if students in Tier 2 intervention are not making adequate progress, the teacher should consult with the special education teacher or school psychologist.
- Make decisions, in consultation with other key professionals, about the need for more or less intensive intervention so that monitoring students' progress through the tiers is possible.
- Meet regularly with interested stakeholders including parents, other teachers, and school psychologists to facilitate successful interventions and identification of students who need special services.

The teacher plays the most important roles in implementing an RTI model. Because the primary focus of the RTI model is early identification of students who need additional assistance, the teacher is a critical link in ensuring that this happens.

Once a student has been identified as needing additional assistance, the special education teacher may be consulted. The special education teacher plays several important roles in a multi-tiered RTI model. These include

- Collaborating with general education teachers and providing consultation services.
- Helping to identify children with disabilities.
- Offering intensive interventions to Tier 3 students.
- Helping Tier 3 students access the general education curriculum.

Special educators may work with struggling students who have not been labeled as having disabilities. In some ways these are similar to the roles special education teachers assumed in the past, and in other ways they are quite different. These shifting roles will require some fundamental changes in the way general education and special education personnel do their work (Burns, Griffiths, Parson, Tilly, & VanDerHeyden, 2007).

Go to the National Center for Learning Disabilities website at **www.ncld.org** to expand your understanding of RTI.

Collaborating and Consulting

As with previous models, particularly co-teaching and inclusion, teachers in an RTI model collaborate with other teachers (e.g., English language development teacher, reading specialist) to provide students who have instructional or special needs with a seamless set of services. Special education teachers may still spend part of their day co-teaching or meeting with general education teachers as part of a collaborative consultation model (see Chapter 3 for an explanation of collaborative models). The purpose of these efforts is to make sure students with disabilities receive accommodations and adaptations so that they have access to the general education curriculum and can participate in the general education program to the extent they are able.

Another way that teachers collaborate is by serving on RTI problem-solving (or intervention) teams that consider progress monitoring and other data and make decisions about teacher and student needs. Teachers provide their expertise when planning interventions or assessments. They are most likely the team member with the greatest expertise about learning difficulties and can offer insights about individual cases.

Using RTI Data to Identify Students with Disabilities

As you recall from the beginning of the chapter, one of the reasons Congress recommended using an RTI approach is that there was considerable concern about the validity of traditional practices for identifying students with learning disabilities (e.g., IQ–achievement discrepancy practice). For this reason, you are likely to work in a school or district that uses data from screening, progress monitoring, and other records related to students' progress in primary and secondary interventions to influence decision making about identifying students with learning disabilities.

How might this work? There is no uniform procedure used in all states; however, many states are using data they accrue during progress monitoring of students in interventions to facilitate referral and decision making about whether students do or do not have a learning disability. When students have participated in targeted interventions at the Tier 2 level and still do not seem to progress, the decision-making team may conclude that a comprehensive evaluation is needed to determine whether the students have learning disabilities. Not all researchers agree about how much and what kind of additional data are needed to make this determination. The National Association of School Psychologists emphasizes that RTI requires a "shift from a within-child deficit paradigm to an eco-behavioral perspective" (Canter, 2006). In other words, the data collected should include information about the instructional environment as well as **within-child factors**. For example, within-child factors that have traditionally been the focus of determining whether a student had special needs include cognitive functioning, which can be measured by an IQ test; academic functioning, often assessed by individually administered tests in reading, math, writing, and spelling; or functioning on such processing measures as auditory and visual tasks. The change in perspective provides less emphasis on these within-child factors and more emphasis on how students are performing in the classroom, whether students are meeting the academic and social demands of their grade level, and whether the classroom environment is conducive to learning.

Most experts agree that RTI data may not be sufficient to identify learning disabilities, but that RTI data should serve as the core of a comprehensive evaluation. It is likely that formal and informal measures of the child's academic skills will be administered in addition to the screening measures, progress monitoring, and other assessment data already collected. The focus should be to develop a profile that includes information about the student's strengths as well as areas of need. The special education teacher and/or other members of the team would observe the child in different contexts to better understand the instructional environment and how appropriate it seems, as well as under what conditions the student seems to thrive or struggle. Observations should include a focus on how well the child is doing in comparison with similar peers.

A psychologist may or may not conduct an evaluation of the student's intellectual ability and cognitive functioning. Just how this is done depends on the state's and district's policies and what the problem-solving team decides is useful data. If the team has concerns about the child's mental and emotional health, the psychologist also conducts assessments in this area. A social worker interviews the parents about the child's background and developmental milestones. The team collects additional information, such as about the child's attendance patterns. The family members are involved in the process as valued team members.

The teacher then works with the team to review and analyze all relevant data to make decisions about the best course of action for the child. They develop an intervention plan and set learning and, if appropriate, behavioral goals. If the team determines that the student has a disability, then they develop an individualized educational plan (see Chapter 1 to review the IEP process).

Providing Interventions

Using a research-based approach to instruction means that the vast majority of students (typically 80%) will be meeting grade-level expectations. These students will not need additional interventions. However, in some schools 20% to 40% of students will require secondary (Tier 2) or tertiary (Tier 3) interventions. What does this mean for the classroom teacher?

Depending on how your school is organized, you can expect to be involved in the delivery of the secondary interventions. This means that a subgroup of students will require additional instruction three to five times per week for 20 minutes or more. Typically this instruction is provided in small groups by the classroom teacher, a paraprofessional, a reading teacher, or other educators trained to provide interventions. Because these students may need instruction that is closely aligned with their instructional needs, the teacher providing the additional instruction uses the data from progress monitoring to guide instruction. Teachers will adjust the pacing of the lesson, provide adequate differentiation, select appropriate materials, provide students with ongoing feedback, and allow students adequate opportunities to respond with guided feedback. Providing students with appropriate feedback is essential to effective interventions. Tips for Teachers 2.8 provides some examples of how to provide this feedback.

Tips FOR Teachers 2.8

THE ROLE OF APPROPRIATE FEEDBACK

Following are examples of how to provide feedback to students that will result in an effective intervention:

- Nod, make eye contact with students, smile, and indicate approval.
- Use verbal praise providing specific feedback about what the student did well.
- Pat the student on the arm to indicate that he or she answered a question correctly.
- Repeat the students' response, adjusting it to indicate the needed change, then ask the student to repeat the answer correctly.
- Write the student's response and then elaborate to extend or expand.
- Ask students to write a response and then give specific feedback on what aspects are correct.
- Describe why the answer or work was correct.

- Describe what the student could say or do to make the answer more correct.
- Summarize what the key ideas were.
- Summarize what students should have learned.
- Ask students to identify what they learned.
- Advise students to start the task again.
- Ask another student to build on what a different student has said.
- Show students how to make specific corrections.
- Ask students to explain how their work is correct or incorrect.
- Ask students to show you where in the text their answer was drawn.

There are several helpful resources to help you with interventions. Figure 2.3 identifies considerations for effectively implementing interventions.

In addition to the instruction provided by the general education teacher, the special education teacher works one-on-one or with small groups of students in reading, math, or other content areas (Vaughn & Linan-Thompson, 2003). Instruction is intense, frequent, and of longer duration than at previous tiers in the RTI model. The special education teacher controls task difficulty and provides ongoing systematic and corrective feedback; progress monitoring continues. See Tips for Teachers 2.9 for an example of how Marla conducts intensive interventions with her reading class.

Using RTI Models in Middle Schools and High Schools

Because RTI was designed as a prevention approach, it is typically provided at the elementary grades. However, there are districts and school sites that are using RTI models with older students, particularly in grades 6 to 8.

FIGURE 2.3

Guidelines for Implementing Effective Tier 2 Interventions

- **Implement universal screening to identify students at risk for reading problems.** Develop procedures for screening all students at least twice a year (beginning of year and middle of year) to determine students at risk for reading or math problems. Provide students at risk with appropriate interventions.

- **Determine students' instructional needs.** Determine students' knowledge and skills related to relevant reading or math skills/knowledge expected at their grade level. For example, for reading it may be several of the following elements: phonemic awareness, alphabet knowledge, phonics, word reading, word or text fluency, vocabulary, spelling, and comprehension.

- **Form same-ability, small groups.** For secondary intervention, form groups of students with similar learning needs. Group sizes should be as small as local resources will allow.

- **Provide daily, targeted instruction that is explicit, is systematic, and provides ample practice opportunities with immediate feedback.** Identify the instructional content in small instructional units (e.g., 3 to 5 minutes per unit) for each lesson.

- **Focus on the reading or math skills that have the highest impact on learning based on students' current performance.** Provide modeled examples before student practice. Scaffold instruction and make adaptations to instruction in response to students' needs and to how quickly or slowly students are learning.

- **Follow a systematic routine.** Use clear, explicit, easy-to-follow procedures and sequence instruction so that easier skills are introduced before more complex ones.

- **Pace instruction quickly so students are engaged and content is covered.** Maximize student engagement, including many opportunities for students to respond.

- **Provide ample opportunities for guided initial practice and independent practice.** Monitor student understanding and mastery of instruction frequently. Adapt instruction so that items are more difficult for some students and easier for other students.

- **Include frequent and cumulative reviews of previously learned material.** Reteach, when necessary.

- **Ensure that students are reading texts at the appropriate level of difficulty.** When students are reading text independently without teacher (or peer) guidance and support, levels of accuracy need to be very high. When students are reading text with teacher guidance and support, lower levels of accuracy may be appropriate. Reading accuracy levels vary from source to source. To calculate reading accuracy, divide the number of words read correctly by the total number of words read. Take into consideration:

  - Independent level: Texts in which no more than approximately 1 in 20 words is read incorrectly (accuracy level: 95%–100%).

  - Instructional level: Texts in which no more than approximately 1 in 10 words is read incorrectly. Students need instructional support from the teacher (accuracy level: 90%–94%).

  - Frustration level: Texts in which more than 1 in 10 words is read incorrectly (accuracy level: less than 90%).

- **Provide many opportunities for struggling readers to apply phonics and word study learning to reading words, word lists, and connected texts.**

  - Have students practice reading words and texts at the appropriate level of difficulty (usually instructional level under the direction of the teacher).

  - Include the reading of word cards or words in phrases or sentences to increase word recognition fluency (often used with high-frequency and irregular words and words that contain previously taught letter–sound correspondences or spelling patterns).

  - Include comprehension instruction that introduces new vocabulary words, incorporates graphic organizers, and teaches comprehension strategies explicitly.

- **Include writing to support reading and spelling.** Have students apply what they are learning about letters and sounds as they write letters, sound units, words, and sentences. Involve parents so they support students' efforts by listening to them read and practicing reading skills.

- **Conduct frequent progress monitoring (e.g., every one to two weeks) to track student progress and inform instruction and grouping.**

Tips for Teachers 2.9

USING INTENSIVE INTERVENTIONS

Marla is teaching a 30-minute lesson to a group of second- and third-grade students who are all reading at an upper-first- or a second-grade level. Progress monitoring data indicate that all four students need to build their word study skills. During their first activity, the teacher asks students to review a previously taught word study component—words that end in "ide" or "ike." She asks students to take 1 minute to write all of the words they can think of that have the -ide or -ike rime, or, in other words, are in the same word families. Marla lets them know when time is up, and they count up all of the words they have listed. The student with the most words reads them aloud, while other students check their lists to see if they have written down any words not stated by the first student, and read these aloud. This is a quick warm-up activity that also serves as a review of previously learned material.

Next Marla introduces two-syllable words that have an open, vowel-silent e pattern: be-side, a-like, lo-cate, fe-male, e-rase, do-nate, re-tire, ro-tate, pro-vide, and mi-grate. The last two are "challenge" words because they include blends. Before the lesson began, Marla had written the words on the whiteboard at the front of the classroom, each with a hyphen between syllables. Each student also has a list of the words at his or her desk, one row with the hyphens in each word and another without them. Marla directs students to count how many syllables they see in each word. Next she has them mark vowels and consonants. She asks the students what they notice about the first syllable in each word, and then what they notice about the second syllable in each word (i.e., that all have the vowel-silent e pattern). She points out that they have learned the syllables before, and probably recognize most of them. She asks them to look for syllables they know. Then together the students read the words.

Marla explains and demonstrates what the words mean. For example, for the word *erase*, she erases a word on the board, and for *retire*, she reminds the students that one of their previous teachers has retired. Students practice reading the words, first with the entire group, and then taking turns with a partner. Marla then asks students to look at the story they are reading today. She reminds them of key words previously introduced that they will see in the story. She also asks them to look at the title and the key words and pictures and to make predictions about what they will read or learn. She continues with the lesson, providing students opportunities to read silently and aloud and to ask and answer questions about what they are reading.

Mr. Morris is one such teacher who worked at a middle school that is implementing an RTI model. As the science teacher, he was unsure what his role would be. He learned that all of the content teachers would be participating in professional development to enhance their knowledge and skills at providing vocabulary and comprehension learning to their students. This was part of the school's Tier 1 instruction and all content area teachers (e.g., math, science, social studies, language arts) were participating.

His class consists of study groups supplemented with in-class modeling and coaching. Reading coaches, who are part of the research team, facilitate monthly study groups with content area teachers, focus on effective practices for teaching students to read and comprehend academic (content area) text, including research-validated instructional practices targeting vocabulary (e.g., providing examples and nonexamples of words, semantic feature analysis) and comprehension (e.g., question generation, summarization strategy instruction, strategic use of graphic organizers). Mr. Morris said, "At first I was skeptical but then I learned some very practical strategies that were actually helpful to me in teaching all of the students. The emphasis is not on preparing content area teachers to teach reading, but on giving them evidence-based instructional approaches to teach students vocabulary and comprehension in their specific content domain."

Mr. Morris went on to explain how their school uses RTI to provide secondary interventions for students identified as at risk for reading problems based on their low scores on the state assessment of reading. Selected teachers provide a standardized reading intervention to students who were at risk for reading problems but scored very close to grade-level expectations. Other teachers provided a more individualized approach to students who had more significant difficulties. Figure 2.4 compares the differences between the standardized and individualized approaches used.

Comparison Between Standardized and Individualized Interventions

FIGURE 2.4

STANDARDIZED	INDIVIDUALIZED
Reduced instructional decision making	Increased instructional decision making based on student assessment results
High control of materials used for instruction	Lower control of materials used for instruction
Highly specified curriculum	Low to moderate specification of curricula
Use of time specified	Flexibility in use of time to address specific student needs
High levels of fidelity to a single approach	Responsive to needs of students
Motivation results from success	Motivation considered in text selection
Systematic and explicit instruction	Systematic and explicit instruction
Fast-paced instruction	Fast-paced instruction
Ongoing progress monitoring	Ongoing progress monitoring

Source: Vaughn, S., Fletcher, J. M., Francis. D. J., Denton, C. A., Wanzek, J., Wexler, J., et al. (2008). Response to intervention with older students with reading difficulties. *Learning and Individual Differences,* 18(3), 338–345.

Summary

- RTI addresses numerous challenges associated with past procedures for supporting student learning and identifying students with learning disabilities. Previous identification criteria focused on establishing a discrepancy between achievement and potential as measured with an IQ test. Yet this way of determining who qualified for special education turned out to be problematic for multiple reasons. Not all students who struggle and need special education demonstrate an IQ–achievement discrepancy. RTI provides an opportunity for schools to integrate a schoolwide approach to prevention and remediation of reading and math difficulties. As a schoolwide approach, RTI integrates school improvement. This entails coordinating screening, instruction, intervention, assessment, and progress monitoring as well as providing ongoing professional development.

- RTI includes several key components. The first is high-quality, research-based instruction that is well matched to students' needs and implemented with fidelity by skilled, caring teachers. Additional components include schoolwide screening to assess the learning levels of all students and progress monitoring designed to assess individual students' learning over time. Thus, an important aspect of RTI is data-based decision making. Data are used to make decisions about which interventions to use, the intensity of interventions, and the duration of the interventions.

- Universal screening and progress monitoring are essential components of RTI. It is through these assessment procedures that data-based decisions can be made about which research-based instructional practices should be used to teach students. Screening is done as part of the first tier of an RTI model. All students are screened. Progress monitoring can also be part of the first tier, but it is an essential component of Tiers 2 and 3. The progress of all students who receive interventions targeted to their instructional needs is monitored frequently. The purposes of progress monitoring are to assess the effectiveness of the interventions so that changes can be made if necessary and also to develop a profile of the student's learning. These data can be quite useful when determining whether a student has a learning disability.

- Teachers play several important roles in an RTI model. The most important role they play is to provide high-quality, research-based instruction so that when students demonstrate low reading or math skills it is because they need additional instruction and not that their current instruction is adequate. They may also assist with screening, progress monitoring, and providing interventions. They collaborate with other educators (e.g., special education teacher, Title I teacher, school psychologist) and other service providers, offering consultation services and helping to identify children with disabilities. They also provide intensive interventions to special education students to help them reach learning objectives in targeted areas, such as in reading and/or math. In addition, they help special education students access the general education curriculum.

Think and Apply

1. Some teachers are confused about different aspects of RTI and uncertain how to deal with some of the challenges they are facing. For example, according to progress monitoring data, more than half of the students in some classes are not reaching benchmarks. What should they do?

2. RTI problem-solving meetings look very much like the Child Study Team Meetings of previous years, focused on possible reasons for a child's struggles from a deficit perspective. The teachers and other school personnel are not clear how the RTI process is similar to and different from the prereferral process. How would you explain these differences?

3. School personnel are unclear about what it means to provide "evidence-based" or "research-based" instruction and the extent to which instruction should be differentiated to meet students' needs in the first tier. How would you explain this? Can you give an example of research-based instruction to illustrate how it is used?

4. School personnel are confused about Tier 2 interventions. They wonder what should "count" as a secondary intervention and whether the special education teacher can provide Tier 2 interventions. They also are not sure what to do about those students who seem to need secondary interventions for an indefinite period of time. How would you respond?

PEARSON
myeducationlab

Now go to Topic 5, PreReferrals, Placement and IEP and Topic 3: Parents and Families in the MyEducationLab (www.myeducationlab.com) for your course where you can:

- Find learning outcomes for these topics along with the national standards that connect to these outcomes.

- Complete Assignments and Activities that can help you more deeply understand the chapter content.

- Examine challenging situations and cases presented in the IRIS Center Resources.

- Apply and practice your understanding of the core teaching skills identified in the chapter with Building Teaching Skills and Dispositions learning units.

students who are gifted, requires collaboration with other professionals and parents. This chapter begins with general suggestions for effective communication. The chapter continues with pointers for working with other professionals and then with guidelines and practices for working with the families of your students.

Critical Communication Skills

Whether you are an elementary or a secondary school teacher, you can expect to work with many adults in the educational community of your school and school district. You will regularly work with the special education teacher, the counselor, and other teachers at your school (Dettmer, Thurston, & Dyck, 2005; Idol, 2002). You might also work with the school psychologist or nurse, the Title I teacher, the English as a second language (ESL) teacher, the teacher of gifted students, and a paraprofessional. You might have students in your class who need specialized services from the speech and language teacher or the occupational or physical therapist. In addition, you will also work with family members of the students in your class.

The school improvement goals of No Child Left Behind (NCLB) continue to challenge many states, school districts, individual schools, parents, and students. In particular, requirements for adequate yearly progress (AYP) have put pressure on educational units to work collaboratively to meet standards for accountability. Collaboration among professionals and the family members of children has been increasingly emphasized and encouraged since IDEIA 2004 and the advent of RTI. As Friend and Cook (2007) point out, collaboration among professionals and with families is mandated or implied in legislation pertaining to assessment, IEP participation, placement, transition, development of behavior support plans, and mediation. Friend (2005a) put it this way:

> Working together is not just rhetoric—it is essential in order to address the increasingly diverse and sometimes daunting needs of students. No single educator can possibly hope to know all that is necessary to effectively reach today's students, and only by pooling expertise—sharing it without losing its focus—respecting and drawing up the differences in perspectives to create new options, can those professionals succeed at their task. (p. 2)

Successful collaboration among adults in the school community requires regular, ongoing communication, and as a classroom teacher, you will often take the lead in initiating such communication. Occasionally communication will take place face-to-face, other times by phone, through written communication, or, increasingly, through electronic means (Merkley, Schmidt, Dirksen, & Fuhler, 2006). Regardless of the mechanism, some teachers communicate effectively with other professionals and families with seemingly little effort. They have acquired the skills to listen effectively and express their point of view. Jacob Levitz, an eighth-grade English teacher, conveys an accepting attitude and is able to make parents feel at ease and willing to disclose information. He is also able to express his views in ways that make parents *want* to listen.

The following sections and Tips for Teachers 3.1 describe basic principles for communicating with parents, teachers, and other professionals.

Acceptance

Acceptance by the teacher is critical to parental and professional participation in the student's program. As the educational workforce and student demographics of our schools become more diverse, understanding and accepting personal perspectives becomes even more pertinent (Harry, 2008; Jairrels, 1999). Lucia Corzo, a third-grade teacher, has been working with parents and professionals for 12 years. Despite expected frustrations and disappointments, she communicates her care and concern to the parents and professionals with whom she interacts and always manages to find the few minutes necessary to meet with them. She says, "Parents have a great deal to teach me about their child. They have spent a lot of time with their child and have seen patterns of behavior that can help me as a teacher. Also, if I can get the parent on my team, we can work together to solve problems."

Listening

Your willingness to genuinely listen to parents and professionals is important to your ability to learn and to work effectively with others. **Effective listening** is more than waiting politely for someone to finish before you speak. You must hear the message the other person is sending students who are gifted, requires collaboration with other professionals and parents. This chapter begins with general suggestions for effective communication. The chapter continues with pointers for working with other professionals and then with guidelines and practices for working with the families of your students.

Critical Communication Skills

Whether you are an elementary or a secondary school teacher, you can expect to work with many adults in the educational community of your school and school district. You will regularly work with the special education teacher, the counselor, and other teachers at your school (Dettmer, Thurston, & Dyck, 2005; Idol, 2002). You might also work with the school psychologist or nurse, the Title I teacher, the English as a second language (ESL) teacher, the teacher of gifted students, and a paraprofessional. You might have students in your class who need specialized services from the speech and language teacher or the occupational or physical therapist. In addition, you will also work with family members of the students in your class.

The school improvement goals of No Child Left Behind (NCLB) continue to challenge many states, school districts, individual schools, parents, and students. In particular, requirements for adequate yearly progress (AYP) have put pressure on educational units to work collaboratively to meet standards for accountability. Collaboration among professionals and the family members of children has been increasingly emphasized and encouraged since IDEIA 2004 and the advent of RTI. As Friend and Cook (2007) point out, collaboration among professionals and with families is mandated or implied in legislation pertaining to assessment, IEP participation, placement, transition, development of behavior support plans, and mediation. Friend (2005a) put it this way:

> Working together is not just rhetoric—it is essential in order to address the increasingly diverse and sometimes daunting needs of students. No single educator can possibly hope to know all that is necessary to effectively reach today's students, and only by pooling expertise—sharing it without losing its focus—respecting and drawing up the differences in perspectives to create new options, can those professionals succeed at their task. (p. 2)

Successful collaboration among adults in the school community requires regular, ongoing communication, and as a classroom teacher, you will often take the lead in initiating such communication. Occasionally communication will take place face-to-face, other times by phone, through written communication, or, increasingly, through electronic means (Merkley, Schmidt, Dirksen, & Fuhler, 2006). Regardless of the mechanism, some teachers communicate effectively with other professionals and families with seemingly little effort. They have acquired the skills to listen effectively and express their point of view. Jacob Levitz, an eighth-grade English teacher, conveys an accepting attitude and is able to make parents feel at ease and willing to disclose information. He is also able to express his views in ways that make parents *want* to listen.

The following sections and Tips for Teachers 3.1 describe basic principles for communicating with parents, teachers, and other professionals.

Acceptance

Acceptance by the teacher is critical to parental and professional participation in the student's program. As the educational workforce and student demographics of our schools become more diverse, understanding and accepting personal perspectives becomes even more pertinent (Harry, 2008; Jairrels, 1999). Lucia Corzo, a third-grade teacher, has been working with parents and professionals for 12 years. Despite expected frustrations and disappointments, she communicates her care and concern to the parents and professionals with whom she interacts and always manages to find the few minutes necessary to meet with them. She says, "Parents have a great deal to teach me about their child. They have spent a lot of time with their child and have seen patterns of behavior that can help me as a teacher. Also, if I can get the parent on my team, we can work together to solve problems."

Listening

Your willingness to genuinely listen to parents and professionals is important to your ability to learn and to work effectively with others. Effective listening is more than waiting politely for someone to finish before you speak. You must hear the message the other person is sending

Margaret Cox is one of two special education teachers at Henry S. West Laboratory School in Miami, Florida. "West Lab" is a professional development school in partnership with the University of Miami. A 37-year veteran teacher, Margaret has taught at West Lab for 11 years.

In that time the nature of her work has changed considerably. Eleven years ago, Margaret pulled out students identified for special education from the general education classroom to bring them to a resource room where she taught math and reading to her assigned students. Although Margaret coordinated curriculum with the general education teachers, she did have a great deal of autonomy in how she managed the resource room and in her dealings with parents of students with disabilities.

However, the movement toward inclusion of students with disabilities in the general education classroom has shifted the bulk of Margaret's work to the general education setting. Rather than teaching in her own resource room, Margaret is engaged in consultation, collaboration, and co-teaching models with several general education teachers in her school, depending of the needs of individual students. She is much more directly involved with teachers and their classrooms and has had to develop the flexibility to work with individuals with very different teaching styles.

In the past 2 years, Margaret's roles and responsibilities have been further altered due to the school's adoption of a response to intervention (RTI) model. Students who do not master weekly learning "benchmarks" attend remediation sessions with her. Margaret uses research-based interventions to help students master key concepts. This includes students who have not been identified for special education services. Thus, Margaret is now working directly with more students (and parents) than ever before.

Margaret has earned the reputation as the school's "learning specialist." In that capacity, she serves as a resource for her general education colleagues, providing research-based strategies, technology applications, and support in making adaptations to help all students learn. In her work with students, she provides strategies for learning or as they would put it, "tips and tricks." She also provides parents with valuable suggestions for supporting learning in the home.

Margaret is very involved in supervising the University of Miami's students enrolled in general education teacher education programs. When students do their field experience rotation at West Lab, Margaret helps them understand her role as a collaborative professional in the school. She also provides suggestions for how they might work with a special educator assigned to their classroom:

> The special education teacher should not be a "wallflower in the classroom." He or she is another teacher who, in a sense, has been displaced from his or her classroom. What is great about inclusion is that students are not "stigmatized" by being sent to a special room. Learning support is right there—on the spot. What is challenging is that there is not always enough time for co-planning. Nonetheless, inclusion works best when the general education teacher views me as another teacher in the classroom, is prepared with specific instructional tasks for me to accomplish, is open to my suggestions for making adaptations, and is willing to make the effort to communicate.

Introduction

As a classroom teacher, your primary responsibility is to instruct your students. However, planning and instruction are only part of your job. As the interview with Margaret Cox exemplifies, increasingly teachers are required to work with other professionals and families and therefore need skills to communicate and collaborate effectively. The need for close collaboration is likely to increase as states and school districts implement RTI models. The increasing diversity in our classrooms, including second language learners, students with disabilities, and

Communicating and Collaborating with Other Professionals and Families

FOCUS QUESTIONS

1. What skills does a teacher need to communicate effectively with professionals and families? Can you identify some good and bad examples of communication with professionals and families?

2. How can you use consultation, collaboration, and co-teaching models to work with other professionals? What conditions are necessary for any type of collaboration to succeed?

3. Working effectively with families requires several skills. What are they? What techniques presented in this chapter might you use to more effectively to collaborate with families?

Think and Apply

1. Some teachers are confused about different aspects of RTI and uncertain how to deal with some of the challenges they are facing. For example, according to progress monitoring data, more than half of the students in some classes are not reaching benchmarks. What should they do?

2. RTI problem-solving meetings look very much like the Child Study Team Meetings of previous years, focused on possible reasons for a child's struggles from a deficit perspective. The teachers and other school personnel are not clear how the RTI process is similar to and different from the prereferral process. How would you explain these differences?

3. School personnel are unclear about what it means to provide "evidence-based" or "research-based" instruction and the extent to which instruction should be differentiated to meet students' needs in the first tier. How would you explain this? Can you give an example of research-based instruction to illustrate how it is used?

4. School personnel are confused about Tier 2 interventions. They wonder what should "count" as a secondary intervention and whether the special education teacher can provide Tier 2 interventions. They also are not sure what to do about those students who seem to need secondary interventions for an indefinite period of time. How would you respond?

PEARSON
myeducationlab

Now go to Topic 5, PreReferrals, Placement and IEP and Topic 3: Parents and Families in the MyEducationLab (www.myeducationlab.com) for your course where you can:

- Find learning outcomes for these topics along with the national standards that connect to these outcomes.
- Complete Assignments and Activities that can help you more deeply understand the chapter content.
- Examine challenging situations and cases presented in the IRIS Center Resources.
- Apply and practice your understanding of the core teaching skills identified in the chapter with Building Teaching Skills and Dispositions learning units.

Tips for Teachers 3.1

FACILITATING EFFECTIVE COMMUNICATION WITH PARENTS AND PROFESSIONALS

- Indicate respect for parents' knowledge and understanding of their child.

- Demonstrate respect for the diverse languages and cultures parents and their children represent.

- Introduce parents to other members of the education team in a way that sets the tone for acceptance.

- Give parents an opportunity to speak and be heard.

- Represent the parents to other professionals and ensure that a language of acceptance is used by all professionals and parents.

- Even when you are busy, take the time to let parents and professionals know that you value them and that you are simply unable to meet with them at *this* time.

- Avoid giving advice unless it is requested. This does not mean that you can never give suggestions; however, suggestions should be given with the expectation that the person may or may not choose to implement them.

- Avoid providing false reassurances to colleagues or parents. Reassurances may make them and you feel better in the short run but are harmful in the long run. When things do not work out as you predicted, everyone can become disappointed and potentially lose trust.

- Ask specific questions. Unfocused questions make a consistent, purposeful conversation difficult to conduct.

- Avoid changing topics too often; you must monitor the topic and direct others to return to it.

- Avoid interrupting others or being interrupted. Interruptions disturb conversation and make effective collaboration difficult.

- Avoid using clichés. A cliché as a response to a problem situation makes the other person feel as though you are trivializing the problem.

- Respond to colleagues and parents in ways that attend to both the content of their message and their feelings.

- Avoid jumping too quickly to a solution. Listening carefully and fully to the message will help you get at the root of the problem.

and ask questions to clarify that you truly understand what others are saying. Effective listening involves the following elements:

- *Listening for the real content in the message.* The **real content** in the message is the main idea or the key information the person wants to convey.
- *Listening for the feelings in the message.* As you listen, consider what the message conveys about the person's feelings about the issue.
- *Restating content and reflecting feelings.* After the person has talked for a while, consider all that he or she has said. Then either ask a question to clarify what you know or restate the main idea to verify that what you heard is correct.
- *Allowing the speaker to confirm or correct your perception.* Give the speaker a chance to correct any misunderstanding you may have or to say more.

Figure 3.1 provides an example of a special education teacher listening effectively to a parent.

Questioning

Questions are an important part of the communication process and have multiple purposes. Questions can be used not only to teach, to establish relationships, to inquire, and to investigate, but also to bully or intimidate. As teachers work with parents and professionals, they need to consider the questions they ask to ensure that they set a tone of acceptance.

Knowing which types of questions to ask helps you obtain the information you need. Questions can be open or closed. An **open question** allows a full range of responses (often beginning with "How," "What," or "Tell me about," for example) and discourages short "yes" or "no" answers. Following are several examples of open-ended questions:

- How do you explain the change in your son's behavior?
- What suggestions do you have about how I might help Mark get a better grade in social studies?
- Tell me your opinion about ways I might adjust my math instruction for Juan.
- How does what I've said about Tanika relate to her behavior at home?

FIGURE
3.1

Effective Listening: An Example

Anna Martinez is the mother of Michael, a student with spina bifida and learning problems who has been placed full time in a fifth-grade classroom. Michael's special education teacher, Joyce, works with him in the general education classroom for part of the school day. Anna made an appointment to meet with Joyce about her son's progress. Their conversation models effective listening.

Anna: (parent) I'm worried about Michael in this new program. I liked it better last year when I knew he was being pulled out of class and getting the help he needed. He seems to have a lot more work, and he complains about homework.

Joyce: (teacher) Let me see if I understand the problem. First, you are concerned about his progress in this new program, and second, Michael seems to have too much work. Is this right? Is there anything else you are concerned about?

Anna: Well, I can't help him with the work because I don't read English that well. He needs help when he comes home, and it can't be from me.

Joyce: The homework he is getting is too hard for him, and there isn't someone to help him at home.

Anna: That's right. He's going to flunk if he does not do his work, yet I can't help him with it, and we are both very worried about it.

Joyce: What if I met with Michael at the end of every day to ensure that he knows how to do his homework by himself. I could also meet with him in the morning before school to make sure he completes it and to help with what he doesn't know. How does that sound?

Anna: I would like to try that. That sounds good.

Joyce: Now let's get back to his placement this year. You indicated some concern about his being in the fifth-grade class all day.

Anna: No, it was really the homework in the class. If we solve that, it will be okay.

Joyce: Well, let's give this plan a try.

- What do you suggest?
- How would you describe Gilbert's behavior?

Antoinette Spinelli, a seventh-grade science teacher, was concerned about Naomi, who was not paying attention in class, seemed sleepy and uninterested, and was not completing assignments. She called Naomi's mother, explained the behavior, and let Naomi's mother give her point of view.

Antoinette (teacher): Naomi has not been paying attention in class and has generally seemed tired and disinterested. What do you think might be happening?

Tracey (parent): Well, I don't know. Maybe she just isn't that interested in science. I don't know why.

Antoinette: Well, the reason I'm concerned is that in the last few weeks Naomi has had more trouble focusing on her work and does not complete assignments as quickly as she has in the past. I wonder if you might be able to help me understand.

Tracey: Maybe it's because there have been so many people in the house the last few weeks. My family is visiting, and they were supposed to stay only one week and now they are starting on their third week. We really don't have room for all of them, so Naomi's had to give up her room. Maybe I need to make sure she is sleeping well enough.

The teacher's questions gave the parent a chance to consider the relationship between her child's behavior and what was occurring at home. This parent was able to identify a change in the household that might be related to her child's poor performance. The parent and teacher were able to identify a possible solution and felt better about their working relationship.

Staying Focused

Finding time to communicate with families and colleagues is often difficult. Therefore, it is important to use the time efficiently and effectively. Staying focused in your communication and keeping others focused is an important skill that contributes to successful collaboration. One thing you can do when someone has difficulty keeping to the topic is redirecting the individual, saying, for example, "Go back to talking about Katelyn. You were providing some suggestions for note-taking skills that might be helpful to her." Another thing you can do is remind him or her of the purpose of the meeting (for instance, "Jackie, let's stick to talking about content-area reading instruction").

Sometimes parents have so many problems of their own that they want to spend their time with you discussing their issues (including such personal problems as financial or marital difficulties) rather than the student's. When this occurs, a good strategy is to have ready a referral list for specialized assistance. It is your responsibility to remind parents that you cannot assist them with *these* problems and to suggest others who can.

Collaborating with Other Professionals

Collaboration between general and special education teachers is occurring in schools across the nation (Dettmer et al., 2005). Greater collaboration among education professionals has grown out of increased awareness that students with disabilities are more likely to succeed in general education classrooms if they receive targeted support services in the classroom. The goal of collaboration models is to ensure that included students remain in the classroom while continuing to receive the accommodations they need to succeed. The goal of collaboration is to achieve ongoing dialogue between all persons who can provide support for the education and social needs of the students.

With increased interest in including students with disabilities in general education classrooms full time, there has been increased movement toward working in cooperative ways using a variety of models. Despite this increased interest, there is limited research data documenting the effectiveness of this approach for meeting the academic needs of students with disabilities (Friend & Hurley-Chamberlain, 2008; Murawski & Swanson, 2001; Scruggs, Mastropieri, & McDuffie, 2007; Zigmond, 2003). Figure 3.2 outlines some perceived benefits and challenges of collaboration models. However, research on the effectiveness of various collaboration and consultation models is still emerging (Murawski & Dieker, 2008; Murawski & Swanson, 2001; Zigmond, 2001). Research is particularly sparse at the secondary level (Magiera, Smith, Zigmond, & Gebauer, 2005; Mastropieri & Scruggs, 2004). We have a great deal to learn not only about administrators', teachers', parents', and students' perceptions of these collaborative models, but also about the impact of these models on student achievement and social adjustment. Therefore, the models implemented at the district and school levels must be evaluated on an ongoing basis (Murawski & Dieker, 2008).

Your interaction with some professionals may be limited to an occasional phone call, a brief meeting, or an IEP staffing. In other cases, your working relationship may be more involved, particularly in working with other professionals. Collaborating with other professionals can be rewarding and can provide the opportunity to learn from others who have different training and experiences. It can also be demanding. In identifying myths and misunderstandings about professional collaboration, Friend (2005b) pointed out that collaboration does not come naturally to everyone. The professional preparation of teachers focuses primarily on working with students. Working with adults can be new territory—and can take skill, practice, and patience. The qualities of collaborative professionals described in Figure 3.3 should be applied regardless of the intensity or duration of the working relationship.

Go to **www.near.org/parents** where you will find a wealth of resources for parents and for teachers in their collaborative work with parents.

PEARSON
myeducationlab

To enhance your understanding of collaboration in the general education classroom go to the IRIS Center Resources section of Topic 2: Collaboration, Consultation, and Co-Teaching in the MyEducationLab for your course and complete the Module 13: Effective School Practices: Promoting Collaboration and Monitoring Students' Academic Achievement.

FIGURE 3.2

Benefits and Challenges of Consultation and Collaboration Models

BENEFITS	CHALLENGES
• Students with special needs are served in the classroom.	• Teachers need greater communication and problem-solving skills.
• Learning for all students is enhanced through spillover effects.	• Special educators' caseloads need to remain realistic.
• Social stigma of exceptionality is reduced.	• Expectations of results need to remain realistic.
• Teachers gain new knowledge and skills.	• Results need to be evaluated for effectiveness.
• Teachers develop more integrated curriculum and instructional variety.	• Students need continued access to the continuum of services.
• Teachers share both burdens and rewards of working with students with disabilities.	• Adequate funding, administrative support, and flexible scheduling need to be maintained.
• Importance of labels and categories of disability decreases.	
• Models work at all grade levels.	

FIGURE 3.3

Qualities of Collaborative Professionals

- Realize that goals are often complex and that the success of achieving these goals requires joint effort. Everyone's effort is needed to solve problems and make schools more effective in meeting the needs of all students.

- Recognize the creativity that occurs when people work together to solve common problems. Collaborative professionals realize that working together makes the problem more manageable and often yields more effective and creative solutions.

- Enjoy the social aspect of problem solving with others. Collaborative professionals respect the other members of the group even when they do not always agree with them. They are able to express their point of view without hostility or put-downs toward others in the group.

- Recognize and value the benefits from working collaboratively. Collaborative professionals realize that many ideas and experiences could not be developed independently; therefore, they value the work of the group.

- Be interested in reflecting on and changing their own practices. Collaborative professionals are willing to consider alternative instructional practices and to think about suggestions and comments that arise during collaboration.

Source: Adapted from Pugach, M. C., & Johnson, L. J. (1995). *Collaborative practitioners, collaborative schools.* Denver, CO: Love.

Different ways in which general education teachers might work with other professionals include consultation, collaboration, and co-teaching.

- *Consultation.* Friend and Cook (2007) define **consultation** as "a voluntary process in which one professional assists another to address a problem concerning a third party" (p. 89). For example, a special education teacher might consult with you about how to develop a behavior management plan for a child with a behavior disorder who is included in your classroom.

- *Collaboration.* According to Friend and Cook (2007), "Interpersonal collaboration is a style for direct interaction between at least two coequal parties voluntarily engaged in shared decision making as they work toward a common goal" (p. 7). **Collaboration** describes the interaction that is occurring: People are working together as equal partners in shared problem solving. For example, you might collaborate with a special education teacher to develop a long-range plan for teaching mathematics to a child with learning disabilities in your class.

- *Co-teaching.* Friend and Cook (2007) define **co-teaching** as "two or more professionals jointly deliver[ing] substantive instruction to a diverse, or blended, group of students in a single physical space" (p. 113). For example, if you are teaching a mathematics lesson in your classroom, you might work with a special education teacher to divide students into two teacher-led groups for guided practice sessions.

The following sections describe various ways in which you can work with other professionals to provide the best learning opportunities for all students. In addition, Tips for Teachers 3.2 provides specific suggestions for working with paraprofessionals.

Consultation

For any professional, understanding the limits of personal expertise is vital, and knowing when and how to solicit advice from colleagues with specialized training is important. From time to time you may feel the need to get input from a school counselor, psychologist, social worker, or other specialist as you try to best serve the needs of students in your classroom. For example, in planning culturally responsive interventions in an RTI model, you may need to consult with a bilingual or ESL specialist (Klingner & Edwards, 2006).

Consultation may be provided for an individual teacher, special education/general education teams, or other groups of teachers. Whatever the configuration of participants, the overall goal of consultation is to tap a consultant's professional expertise to assist a consultee or group of consultees in their efforts to resolve a particular problem or situation. Figure 3.4 is a worksheet that can be used to guide the problem-solving process.

Friend and Cook (2007) identify the following characteristics of consultation:

- *Triadic and indirect relationship.* Typically, consultation involves an expert (the consultant) and parents, teachers, and/or administrators (the consultee) in resolving a problem related to a particular student, group of students, or parent (the client). This triadic

myeducationlab

Go to the Building Teaching Skills and Dispositions section of Topic 2. Collaboration, Consultation, and Co-Teaching in the MyEducaitonLab for your course and complete the activity entitled *Working with Paraprofessionals.*

WORKING WITH PARAPROFESSIONALS

Jamie DeFraites is a first-grade teacher in New Orleans with 22 children in her class. Her multicultural classroom includes 11 Vietnamese children and 2 Hispanic students who are English language learners. Jamie explains, "I love my class and was actually asked to loop to second grade—so I'll have the same students next year!"

Jamie is fortunate enough to work with two paraprofessionals, who join her classroom at different times during the day. Here are Jamie's tips for working with paraprofessionals:

• It's important to have mutual respect and trust. I let the paraprofessionals know how fortunate I feel to have additional adults in the classroom and how important their job is in helping all students learn. I also thank them every chance I get—in the presence of the principal, parents, and students.

• At the beginning of the year, I talk with the paraprofessionals individually about their interests and skills and try to match their duties with their strengths. Both paraprofessionals are bilingual (one in Vietnamese and one in Spanish), so assisting me with parent communication is very important. One of the paraprofessionals is creative and helps me design learning centers. The other is interested in math and helps me with review and extra practice for students with challenges in that area.

• Each of the paraprofessionals is anxious to learn new skills and strategies. It is worth my time to explain instructional strategies to them so that they can do more than grade papers—they can actually interact with children in small groups or individually. It took me a long time to learn to teach—I'm still learning. I don't assume that the paraprofessionals automatically know how to teach. If I can share some of my training, the payoff is big for my students.

• At the beginning of the year, we also clarify roles, responsibilities, classroom routines, and expectations for student learning and behavior. Spending that time in planning and communicating is time well spent. We're on the same page.

• The paraprofessionals both work with several other teachers, so their time in my class is limited. We have to make each minute count. Their tasks have to be well defined. I also plan a backup—what to do when there is nothing to do.

• Finally, I encourage the paraprofessionals to get additional professional training. I let them know about workshops and other opportunities to learn. The more they learn, the more my students benefit!

Jamie admits that she would like to have a regular planning time with the paraprofessionals. As she says, "Often, we have to plan on the run." Also, her school district does not require periodic feedback or performance review sessions. This is something Jamie definitely recommends. "Fortunately, I have not run into problems with either paraprofessional, but if I did, it would be a good idea to have a system for giving feedback in a systematic way."

FIGURE 3.4

Consultation Problem-Solving Worksheet

Collaborative Team Member Name and Position: _____

Team Member's Responsibilities Include: _____

_____

Target Student's Name: _____

Problem Behavior Student Is Exhibiting: _____

_____

Potential Interventions and Consequences Include: _____

_____

Implemented Intervention: _____

Procedures Include: _____

_____

Team Members Involved and Their Responsibilities: _____

_____

Summary Evaluation of the Intervention: _____

_____

Future Interventions/Objectives: _____

arrangement is indirect in that the client is not directly involved in consultation conversations and interactions.

■ *Voluntariness.* Consultation should involve the voluntary participation of both the consultant and the consultee. Typically, consultation is initiated with a request from the consultee (Friend & Bursuck, 2002).

■ *Expert and directional relationship.* The role of the consultant is to provide expertise and guidance in solving a classroom-based or student-based problem.

■ *Problem-solving process with steps or stages.* There are a number of models of consultation, mainly stemming from school psychology literature. Usually, models have steps or stages, although the stages are not always followed in a rigid manner.

■ *Shared but differentiated responsibilities and accountability.* The responsibility of the consultant is to work with the consultee through the problem-solving process. Although a consultant may be available to provide support during implementation of an intervention, this is not always the case. The consultee has implementation responsibility if the consultee chooses to implement the intervention totally, partially, or at all.

Given the range of individual student needs in the classroom, an advantage of consultation is that it provides you with an efficient and effective way to meet those student needs. For example, if you have a student with a hearing impairment, a consultant might help you learn to implement appropriate assistive technology. A special education teacher might consult with you to implement prereferral interventions for a student who has difficulty with phonemic awareness. In short, consultation can provide you with professional development to help students succeed. One disadvantage of consultation is that the "directional relationship" can cause rifts. This is particularly true if a teacher feels that the "expert" is there to "fix" a problem or if the consultee is uncomfortable with the unevenness of expertise. However, if teachers develop a mind-set for learning and a positive attitude about seeking help to bring the best resources to the student, such disadvantages can be overcome.

Collaboration

Collaboration involves more engagement of professionals in both planning and implementing an intervention than does the consultation model. The **peer collaboration model** (Pugach & Johnson, 2002) was developed to help classroom teachers solve problems by providing time and structure to do so. This model is designed for teachers to work with one or two other teachers. By engaging in a structured conversation about a specific problem, teachers increase their awareness of the problem and develop potential solutions.

How might you participate in peer collaboration? Collaboration can occur at varying levels of teacher and school involvement. For example, Michelle Canner is a high-school English teacher who has several students with learning disabilities in her classes. These same students are also in Jonathan Wood's social studies classes and Maria Rodriguez's science classes. The special education teacher and these three teachers established a collaborative team to meet the needs of the target students more effectively. At a middle school, the special education teacher and the speech and language teacher work cooperatively with the general education teachers to develop strategies for facilitating the vocabulary and concept learning of target students.

Procedures for Collaboration. Procedures for peer collaboration include the following five steps (Friend & Cook, 2007; Hudson & Glomb, 1997):

1. *Initiation or facilitation.* Each participant takes a role as either an **initiator**, the teacher with the problem to be addressed, or a **facilitator**, the teacher who guides his or her peer through the process and helps to generate solutions.

2. *Clarifying questions.* The initiator states the problem, and the facilitator asks questions that clarify the problem.

3. *Summarization.* The team takes time to examine and summarize the problem. The format for summarizing the problem includes (a) establishing the pattern of behavior, (b) acknowledging the teacher's feelings about the problem, and (c) identifying aspects of the classroom and school environments that the teacher can modify (Pugach & Johnson, 1995).

PEARSON
myeducationlab

Go to the Assignments and Activities section of Topic 2: Collaboration, Consultation, and Co-Teaching in the MyEducationLab for your course and complete the activity entitled *Understanding Collaboration.*

4. *Interventions and predictions.* The team tries to develop at least three interventions for the problem and to predict the likely outcomes of each one.
5. *Evaluation.* The team develops an evaluation plan that includes strategies for keeping track of the intervention, recording the student's progress, and meeting on an ongoing basis.

Resources Needed for Collaboration.   Time is the most precious and necessary resource for effective collaboration. Unless time is built into teachers' and other professionals' schedules and workloads, collaboration simply cannot occur regularly. Also, if the special education teacher is going to work collaboratively with the social studies teacher, for example, both need to have a planning period at the same time. Although teachers can be resourceful in finding time to collaborate, administrative support is vital. Here are ways some schools have resolved the challenge:

What are the hallmarks of the peer collaboration model? What steps should these teachers follow in planning and problem solving to achieve a successful peer collaboration?

- Administrators designate a common time for collaborating professionals (e.g., all fourth-grade teachers who are members of the same team).
- School boards pay professionals for one extra time period each week that is used for collaboration or for meeting parents.
- School districts provide early dismissal for students one day a week so that team members have a common planning time.
- Teachers schedule brief but focused planning periods with one another as necessary.

Space for meeting is another necessary resource, typically allocated by school administrators. In some schools, overcrowding is such a problem that classroom space is never available for meetings with colleagues. Designated meeting rooms or other conference space may be needed for collaboration to occur.

Administrators can also facilitate successful collaboration by providing an orientation that sets expectations for implementation of the collaborative model in the school and answers basic questions about roles and responsibilities. For example, at the secondary level, when contact is to be made with parents for a meeting with the collaboration team, who contacts the parents and sets the agenda for the meeting? The orientation can also cover what paperwork is required and how it should be completed and submitted.

Co-Teaching

Co-teaching occurs when general and special education teachers work together to coordinate curriculum and instruction and to teach heterogeneous groups of students in the general education classroom setting (Dettmer et al., 2005; Murawski & Dieker, 2008). Key aspects of co-teaching include long-range co-planning, lesson co-planning, lesson co-teaching, and grading. Furthermore, the responsibilities and rewards of meeting the needs of students with disabilities are shared.

How might co-teaching actually work in the classroom? While one of the teachers delivers some instruction to the group as a whole, for example, the other teacher works with small groups or individual students. The special education teacher is not limited to working only with students who have disabilities but can include in the group other students who benefit from the accommodations provided.

Patty Cohen is a special education teacher who works in a cooperative teaching arrangement with Karen Feller, a fifth-grade teacher. Karen has six students with disabilities in her classroom, and Patty spends 2 hours each day in her room. Additionally, Karen has a teaching assistant for 4 hours a day. During a 90-minute language arts period, three teachers are in the classroom. Patty and Karen take turns as lead teacher and small-group teacher. Patty has time to work with students individually or in pairs to teach specific skills. Patty and Karen make cooperative teaching look simple. As you observe them in the classroom, you are aware of how easily the class grouping arrangements flow from one configuration to the next and how comfortably the teachers move from lead teacher to small-group instructor. "It's very easy for us," they say almost in unison. "Both of us have very high expectations for the students, and we strive never to waste a minute of instructional time. This requires planning on our part, but it's worth it."

In some cases, a special educator may work with a single general education teacher; in other cases, the special educator may work with two or more general education teachers (Villa, Thousand, & Nevin, 2008; Walsh & Jones, 2004). For example, Martin Fields is a special educator assigned to a high-school social studies department. Martin works with five different teachers to co-plan and co-teach.

Long-Range Co-Planning. In long-range co-planning, the general education and special education teachers broadly plan their overall goals and desired outcomes for the class and for specific students with disabilities in the class. This co-planning of broad goals occurs quarterly (or more frequently if necessary). This planning fits in with the IEP of each student with disabilities.

In lesson co-planning, the general education and special education teachers plan specific lessons and desired outcomes for the week (Schumm, Vaughn, & Harris, 1997; Schumm, 2006). The teachers decide who will take the lead in the lesson, who will ensure that target students' needs are met, and who will provide individual or small-group instruction. Figure 3.5 illustrates a form for daily co-planning.

The planning pyramid is another excellent tool for co-planning in the general education classroom. The planning pyramid is a framework for or a way of thinking about planning instruction to enhance learning for all students. The pyramid is designed as a flexible tool that teachers can adjust to identify what needs to be taught and, based on student needs, how to teach it. Tips for Teachers 3.3 provides procedures for using the planning pyramid.

Schumm, Vaughn, and Harris (1997) reported that when teachers use the planning pyramid together, they develop a common mind-set about what all students will learn. They also can identify potential trouble spots as well as accommodations for students who may need them. Ruth Rogge, a special education teacher, adapted the planning pyramid lesson plan sheet for her weekly meetings with general education teachers (see Figure 3.6).

Joyce Duryea, a special education teacher, has a set day and time for co-planning with each teacher. Meetings take place during the school day while students are in other classes, such as Spanish, art, or music. "We discuss the planning for the following week and how we can best work together," explains Joyce. Once a month, she and the other teachers go over the goals and objectives from the students' IEPs and discuss whether they are meeting goals or

PEARSON
myeducationlab

Go to the Assignments and Activities section of Topic 2: Collaboration, Consultation, and Co-Teaching in the MyEducationLab for your course and complete the activity entitled *Teacher Collaboration*.

FIGURE 3.5

Lesson Plan Form for Co-Teaching

Date	Instructional Objectives (s)	Co-teaching Model	Tasks for General Ed. Teacher	Tasks for Special Ed. Teacher	Student Assessment	Plan for Reteaching

Information from: Vaughn, S., Schumm, J. S., & Arguelles, M. E. (1997). The ABCDEs of co-teaching. *Teaching Exceptional Children, 30*(2), 7.

PROCEDURES FOR THE PLANNING PYRAMID

The primary component of the planning pyramid, degrees of learning, makes up the body of the pyramid and will help you and your co-teacher examine the content to be taught and decide how you will differentiate instruction for all learners.

Step 1: Examine your state or district curriculum guides or textbooks to identify key standards or objectives to be taught.

Step 2: Decide what will go in the base of the pyramid: the information that is essential for all students to learn. This section is guided by the question, "What do we want *all* students to learn?"

Step 3: Decide what will go in the middle part of the pyramid: the information that is next in importance. This section is guided by the question, "What do we want *most* students to learn?"

Step 4: Decide what you will put at the top of the pyramid: the information that will enhance basic concepts and facts about the topic or subject. This type of information will be acquired only by a few students who have an added interest in and a desire to learn more about the subject.

Step 5: Identify what grouping patterns would facilitate learning and what accommodations are necessary for individual learners.

Step 6: Discuss the roles and responsibilities of you and your co-teacher before, during, and after the lesson.

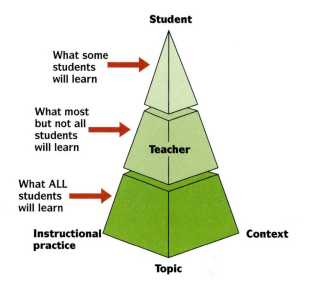

Source: Schumn et al (1994), in *The Reading Teacher* 47(8), 608–615, International Reading Association.

whether they need to switch over to another goal if the students have accomplished the one previously established. As Joyce puts it, "We discuss each student's progress in depth."

Pam Stover works with three general education teachers in the mathematics department at a high school. Finding time each day—or sometimes each week—to meet with each teacher is difficult. Pam and her colleagues have decided to use technology to foster ongoing communication with her colleagues.

> On teacher work days, I have 2-hour planning meetings with each math teacher. Fortunately, each teacher has a web page for students and parents. The webpage outlines curriculum standards and related assignments for each month of the school year. In essence it is a planning calendar for everyone in the loop—students, parents, and the two of us. Before each teacher "releases" the webpage, we discuss curricular goals and think through adaptations necessary for students with disabilities included in the classes. The web page has forced us to do joint planning. In the meantime, we email each other almost daily and focus primarily on any adjustments we need to make to our advance planning based on student progress and interruptions to the schedule that were beyond our control. We use an online grading system. The general education teachers input grades but consult with me about grading adaptations for the students with IEPs.

Lesson Co-Teaching.   For **lesson co-teaching**, the special education and general education teachers are both in the classroom during the same lesson, and both participate in the instruction (Hourcade & Bauwens, 2002; Murawski & Dieker, 2008). Because lessons are co-planned, the specific roles and responsibilities of each teacher are mutually determined ahead of time. Sometimes the general education teacher works with the class as a whole, and the special education teacher adapts assignments for special-needs students, accommodating their learning needs or working with small groups of students. At other times, the class is divided into groups, and each teacher works with a different group. Sometimes the special education teacher takes the lead in providing instruction to the class while the general education teacher moves from student to student, conducting individual lessons or conferences. The roles of both teachers vary according to the goals of the lessons and the needs of the students. Table 3.1 provides an overview of different models of co-teaching.

FIGURE
3.6

Planning Pyramid

Week of: _____

General Educator: _____   Special Educator: _____

	General Educator	Special Educator
Monday		
Tuesday		
Wednesday		
Thursday		
Friday		

Week of: _____   Grade Teacher: _____   Subject: _____

Objectives: _____
_____

Materials/In-Class Assignments

Monday _____

_____

Tuesday _____

_____

Wednesday _____

_____

Thursday _____

_____

Friday _____

_____

Homework Assignments

Monday _____

_____

Tuesday _____

_____

Wednesday _____

_____

Thursday _____

_____

Friday _____

_____

Evaluation: _____
_____

Pyramid	Agenda
	1. _____ 2. _____ 3. _____ 4. _____ 5. _____ 6. _____ 7. _____ Monday _____ Tuesday _____ Wednesday _____ Thursday _____ Friday _____

Source: Ruth Rogge, Silver Ridge Elementary, Broward County, Florida. Used with permission.

Co-Teaching Models

TABLE 3.1

MODEL	GROUPING ARRANGEMENT	TEACHER ROLES	DESCRIPTION
A	Individual students, pairs, or small groups	1 lead teacher 1 teacher "teaching on purpose"	One teacher takes primary responsibility for the overall lesson. The second teacher provides one- to five-minute minilessons for students who need additional help.
B	2 heterogeneous groups	2 teachers— same content	In this model, both teachers teach the same content to small groups. This format works well when complex new information is presented or when students need smaller groups to promote clarifying questions or discussion.
C	2 homogeneous groups	2 teachers— different content	Students are placed in groups based on instructional needs. One group might focus on review and additional practice; a second group might engage in extension activities.
D	Multiple groups	2 teachers— content may vary	This model includes multiple groups—some teacher-led, some student-led. This model includes reading groups and learning centers in which learners are engaged in a variety of activities.
E	Whole class	2 teachers— teaching together	Teachers divide up the agenda for teaching a lesson. Teachers share responsibility for lecturing, demonstrating, modeling note taking, and providing strategies for learning content.

Source: Adapted from Vaughn, S., Schumm, J. S., & Arguelles, M. E. (1997). The ABCDEs of co-teaching. *Teaching Exceptional Children,* 30(2), 4–10.

Joyce, a special education teacher in an inclusive setting, explains her role this way:

I work in three general education classrooms, and in each classroom I do something different. Teachers differ in the extent to which they are willing to share control of their classrooms. Ruby, a second-grade teacher, prefers that I take the lead role when I'm in her class, and she likes to provide me support. Tiffany, the fifth-grade teacher, likes to share control through either co-teaching or alternating the role of lead teacher. Lupita, on the other hand, prefers to maintain the lead role in her class.

Co-teaching requires that both teachers work with all students. When general education and special education teachers co-teach in the same classroom, the goals of the instruction and the needs of all students are the responsibility of both teachers. It is not unusual in co-teaching classrooms for one teacher to assume more of the teaching role than his or her partner (Austin, 2001). Ongoing communication about how best to use the talents and expertise of each partner and how to maximize class time is vital. It is important to have knowledge of the particular school setting and the students within the school to develop co-teaching models that are flexible and efficient (Walsh & Jones, 2004). For example, with careful planning special education teachers might be present only during instructional support. During whole-group lecture time, the special education teacher might not be present. However, the special education teacher is present for follow-up activities, completion of assignments, or reteaching.

Grading.   In thinking about co-teaching, grading is an important consideration when students with disabilities are in general education classrooms. Often the special education co-teacher makes adaptations to homework, assignments, and tests. How do these modifications affect the way students are graded? How can teachers align student grades with state standards and student performance on high-stakes tests? To what extent should students' motivation affect their grades? What about their persistence and their ability? How can these qualities be measured? These issues need to be openly discussed by teachers who have students with disabilities in their classrooms.

The questions about grading are often easier for elementary teachers to answer than for middle- and high-school teachers (Keefe, Moore, & Duff, 2004). At the elementary level, teachers often consider a student's ability and then assign a grade based on the extent to which the student's progress matches his or her ability. At the middle- and high-school levels, however, student performance is often assessed on the basis of established standards. Nonetheless, policies for student grading are not always made clear, so it is important for teachers working together to communicate with one another and with administrators to ensure fair assessment and reporting of student performance (Salend & Duhaney, 2002; McLoughlin & Lewis, 2005).

Standards-based grading and reporting have been offered as an alternative model for reporting students' strengths and areas in need of improvement (Jung & Guskey, 2007). Recognizing the challenge of how best to evaluate and report the performance of students with disabilities in general education, school districts have begun to provide some clarity through the use of standards-based grading (Guskey, 2001). Standards-based grading involves an examination of individual curriculum standards; the process, product, and progress learning goals of the individual student; as well as the appropriate accommodations for the student as determined by the IEP. Depending on the situation, grading could occur on grade-level standards with accommodations and/or grading on modified standards. Although a great deal of work remains in the implementation of this practice in terms of logistics and equity, the promise of standards-based grading is that teachers, parents, and students are provided specific information about progress and instructional goals.

Grading procedures for students with disabilities are often an IEP item, and grading guidelines are written and agreed on during the development of the IEP. This means that students with special needs who are included in general education classrooms often do poorly in these classes. Even when students do their best, their grades are often in the failure range. Students with disabilities need grades that reflect more than the extent to which their performance compares with that of other students in the class. They need encouragement and reinforcement for their work and effort and reasonable accommodations in assessment and grading. Sample criteria for grading a special education student are provided in Figure 3.7.

FIGURE 3.7

Sample of Criteria for Grading a Student with Disabilities

The following procedures could be jointly developed by the school, student, and parent when specifying grading options.

Tests

- Administer tests orally, with questions and answers.

- A teacher, other student, or resource teacher reads the regular test to the student. (Please give the resource teacher at least one day's notice.)

- Administer the regular test using open book, class notes, or both.

- Modify the modality of tests, written or oral, such as multiple-choice instead of essay questions.

- Redo the test if the student does not pass.

- Lower the criterion for passing.

In-Class Assignments

- Give regular assignments with lower criteria for passing.

- Shorten the regular assignment (e.g., half the questions).

- Grade assignments as "complete" rather than with a letter grade.

- Modify the set of questions students will answer.

- Pair the student with another student for help.

- Require the student to give oral answers to a teacher.

- Redo assignments if incorrect.

- Give credit for appropriate behaviors not normally graded, such as taking notes.

Homework

- Same options as "In-Class Assignments."

Class Participation, Behavior, and Effort

- Same expectations as for other class members, but special education students may need extra encouragement and frequent feedback from teacher.

- Focus on a specific study skill or behavior deficit by giving a Pass/No Pass each day for that behavior (examples: coming prepared to class with correct materials or volunteering answers during class discussions).

Other Considerations

- Give extra credit for projects that the student or teacher suggests.

- Have a student aide tape the reading assignments or read aloud to the student.

- Set expectations for attendance.

Source: Gersten, R., Vaughn, S., & Brengelman, S. U. (1996). Grading and academic feedback for special education students with learning disabilities. In *Communicating student learning* (pp. 47–57), T. R. Guskey (ed.), p. 52. Alexandria, VA: Association for Supervision and Curriculum Development.

Collaboration Issues and Dilemmas

At some time, most general education teachers will work with special education personnel in consultation, collaboration, or co-teaching roles. Research has yielded overall support from key stakeholders for collaborative teaching practices (Magiera et al., 2005; Murawski, 2006; Rea, McLaughlin, & Walther-Thomas, 2002; Scruggs et al., 2007). However, research has also identified potential pitfalls and areas for improvement (Murawski & Dieker, 2008; Rea, 2005). Following is a description of issues and dilemmas that frequently occur. Perhaps by considering these issues now, you will be able to work more effectively in future collaborative situations.

Concerns About Co-teaching. For many teachers, co-teaching was not part of their professional preparation. Therefore, when asked to co-teach, teachers often need to adjust from working solo to working collaboratively on an ongoing, sometimes daily basis. Some teachers feel out of place in another teacher's classroom and find it difficult to determine how much control to take. Surveys of teachers in co-teaching settings indicated that general education teachers often take on more responsibility because special educators are seen as the visitors (Austin, 2001). Other teachers find it difficult to adjust to co-teaching and fall into a pattern of one teacher "teaching" and one teacher "roaming" (Magiera & Zigmond, 2005; Scruggs et al., 2007; Weiss & Lloyd, 2003). Some teachers cite lack of administrative support for co-teaching (Rea, 2005). To resolve these concerns, explicit delineation of roles and responsibilities and ongoing monitoring of them are imperative (Schumm, Hughes, & Arguelles, 2001; Villa, Thousand, & Nevin, 2008; Wilson, 2008). Finding the time for co-planning is often difficult, but it is critical for success (Dieker, 2001; Kamens, Loprete, & Slostad, 2003). Informal rating scales can be used as a framework for teachers to discuss their cooperative teaching.

Student Ownership. When students with special needs are placed in general education classrooms for all or part of the day, both general education and special education teachers are responsible for their education. It is not uncommon, however, for teachers to claim "ownership" of or responsibility for some students and not others. Effective programs for all students require teacher attitudes that say, "All students are members of the learning community in my classroom, and I welcome them all."

Individual Versus Class Focus. Traditionally, general education teachers at all grade levels plan instruction for the class as a whole rather than for individual learning needs (McIntosh, Vaughn, Schumm, Haager, & Lee, 1993; Mora-Harder, 2009; Schumm et al., 1995a; Schumm, Moody, & Vaughn, 2000). This approach to planning reflects the need to cover the content for a subject area. Special education teachers, on the other hand, focus on meeting students' individual needs. This difference can lead to conflict. It is important for general–special education partners to discuss these differences and to consider together how to maximize differentiated professional training and skills for the benefit of all students in the classroom (Schumm, Hughes, & Arguelles, 2001). Sallie Gotch, an elementary special education teacher, puts it this way:

> I am a special education teacher, and so the direction of my interest is always with the individual student and how the educational setting can be altered to meet his or her needs. During the last few years, I have been working in a cooperative teaching situation with general education teachers, and I realize that I've needed to adjust my perspective if I am to work effectively with them. When they think about planning, they think about the class as a whole. I have to work cooperatively to think about meeting the needs of individual students without slowing the progress of the class as a whole.

Content Versus Accommodation. When classroom teachers discuss planning and instruction, one of the most consistent themes is content coverage (Keefe et al., 2004; Schumm et al., 1995a; Vaughn & Schumm, 1994). Classroom teachers feel they must cover more content to meet local and state standards and to ensure that students are prepared for the next grade level and for standardized tests. Teachers acknowledge that this need often conflicts with some students' knowledge acquisition but feel obligated to continue teaching new material (Schumm et al., 1995a). Judy Schloss, a seventh-grade science teacher, admits, "I know that when I complete a science

PEARSON
myeducationlab

Go to the Assignments and Activities section of Topic 2: Collaboration, Consultation, and Co-Teaching in the MyEducationLab for your course and complete the activity entitled *Benefits and Challenges of Co-teaching.*

unit, some of the students understand the main concepts and others do not, but I do not have time to reteach. We just move on to new material." As a result of such moving on, many students, particularly students with learning problems, are introduced to a lot of material but learn little about any of it. As Ed Glover, a ninth-grade social studies teacher, says, "If I waited until the students got it, we would never be able to cover all the material."

The issue of content coverage directly influences the instruction of students with special learning needs in general education classrooms. You can imagine the difficulty you might have if you felt pressured to cover extensive amounts of content and at the same time felt pulled to meet the needs of individual students who failed to learn the material. To alleviate this situation, Margaret Cox (the special educator you read about at the beginning of this chapter) works with her general education colleagues to identify students—both with and without IEPs—who are in need of additional accommodations and/or reteaching to master standards in the critical areas of reading and mathematics.

Real World Versus Student's World. Some general education teachers think that treating all students fairly means treating them "the same." Making adaptations in homework or tests is perceived as providing undue advantage for some students. Furthermore, some general education teachers define their mission as preparing all students for the real world, where, they believe, accommodations and adaptations will not be made. Other general education teachers know that the best way to prepare students for the real world is to give them opportunities to be successful in their present world. Maria Pino, a secondary social studies teacher, explains, "My first responsibility is to help students feel successful in their present world—the world of the classroom. Making accommodations helps them feel that success. I also explain to them that employers are required by law to make reasonable adaptations for individuals with disabilities."

Successful collaborative teams emphasize the importance of establishing a community of teachers and learners who share and learn together (Hunt, Hirose-Hatae, Doering, Karasoff, & Goetz, 2000). The ability to collaborate successfully requires flexibility, respect for roles and responsibilities, and the ability to maintain a sense of humor (Schumm, Hughes, & Arguelles, 2001). Based on their experiences in collaborative classrooms and on their understanding of the literature on collaboration, Keefe, Moore, and Duff (2004) have offered the four "knows" of collaborative teaching: (a) know yourself, (b) know your partner, (c) know your students, and (d) know yourself.

In other words, think about your beliefs, goals, and teaching style in the context of working with a colleague to teach students in your class. This type of communication and cooperation requires time, effort, and commitment. However, the potential outcome of working together has benefits for teachers (e.g., developing mutual support, learning from one another's expertise) and students (e.g., enriched curriculum, ongoing scaffolding, reduced student–teacher ratio) (Austin, 2001; Walsh & Jones, 2004).

This section covered several of the issues involved in collaboration and cooperative teaching, such as concerns about cooperative teaching, student ownership, focus on individuals versus the class, content versus accommodation, and the real world versus the student's world. The next section addresses ways to communicate effectively with other professionals and parents.

Working with Parents

Parents are the most influential persons in a child's life. This is particularly true for exceptional students, whose parents serve multiple roles, including those of advocate and information source. Fundamental to the implementation of IDEIA is parent involvement and collaboration (Turnbull, 2005). Parent rights in the educational decision-making process include the following (Yell, 2005):

- Parents should be notified and their permission should be obtained before identification, evaluation, or educational placement of the child.
- Parents may request an evaluation when they think their child needs potential special education and related services.
- Parents may request an independent evaluation at public expense when they disagree with the educational evaluation of the school.

- Parents may request a reevaluation when they think their child's educational placement is no longer appropriate.
- Parents may request that their child be tested in his or her primary language.
- Parents may participate in the development of an IEP or IFSP, including placement.
- Parents may request a due process hearing to resolve differences with the school.
- Parents should be informed about their child's progress at least as often as are parents of children without disabilities.

Family Collaboration

During the middle- and high-school years, students are encouraged to participate in decisions about their education with their parents (Arndt, Konrad, & Test, 2006; Van Reusen & Bos, 1994; Wood, Karvonen, Test, Browder, & Algozzine, 2004). Due to increased accountability demands, IDEIA also outlines the responsibilities of parents and students in education (Turnbull, 2005).

In addition to legal mandates for family involvement in the education of students with disabilities, two other forces have contributed to increased engagement on the part of parents and other family members (Heward, 2009). One is increased parent advocacy for children with disabilities both individually and through involvement in parent support groups and organizations (Turnbull, Turnbull, Erwin, & Soodak, 2007). Another factor is a growing body of research indicating that family involvement has a positive impact on student academic and social outcomes (Epstein & Sanders, 2008). Taken together, these forces have created a climate for positive possibilities with home–school partnerships (Murray & Curran, 2008).

Although progress has been made in family involvement due to legal mandates and parent advocacy, the ideal and reality of collaboration are far from being aligned, particularly when the needs of culturally and linguistically diverse families are concerned (Harry, 2008). The over representation of minorities in special education programs is an issue of national concern and challenges educators to consider how to interact with parents and their children in just and equitable ways (Donovan & Cross, 2002; Harry & Klingner, 2006). Parents of all children bring a rich set of cultural and familial experiences to the educational process that can and should be heard (Moll, Amanti, Neff, & Gonzalez, 1992). Developing patterns of behavior that tap these funds through commitment to the student, equality of power, and mutual trust and respect are key to successful collaborations (Blue-Banning, Summers, Frankland, Nelson, & Beegle, 2004). You as a classroom teacher play a key role in this process.

What can you do so that parents serve as active, collaborative resources? Perhaps it is most important to recognize that home–school communication is a two-way street. As Hallahan, Kauffman, and Pullen (2009) put it, "It's critical to receive information *from* parents as well as to provide information *to* them" (p. 134). Tips for Teachers 3.4 presents some additional ideas.

PEARSON myeducationlab

Go to the Building Teaching Skills and Dispositions section of Topic 2. Collaboration, Consultation, and Co-Teaching in the MyEducaitonLab for your course and complete the activity entitled *Working with Paraprofessionals*

PEARSON myeducationlab

Go to the Assignments and Activities section of Topic 3: Parents and Families in the MyEducationLab for your course and complete the activity entitled *Including Parents on the Collaborative Educational Team*

Tips for TEACHERS 3.4

PARENTS AS ACTIVE COLLABORATORS: WHAT YOU CAN DO

- Remember that a teacher's place is on the parents' side as a team member working for a common goal: the student's success.

- Become aware of your own feelings of defensiveness. Taking a deep breath and putting feelings aside will help teachers to continue building positive relationships. If that is not possible, teachers should postpone interactions until the defensiveness can be handled.

- Remember that the focus must be on the needs and interests of parents and their children, not on their values. It is important to attack the problem, not the person.

- Accept people as they are and stop wishing they were different. This applies to parents as well as to their children.

- Remember that most parents are doing the best they can. Parents do not wake up in the morning and decide, "I think today I will be a poor parent."

- Respect parents' right to have their own values and opinions. Different values are not better or poorer values.

Sources: Dettmer, P., Thurston, L. P., & Dyck, N. J. (2005). *Consultation, collaboration, and teamwork for students with special needs* (5th ed.). Boston: Pearson Education; and Dabkowski, D. M. (2004). Encouraging active parent participation in IEP meetings. *Teaching Exceptional Children, 36*(3), 34–39.

FIGURE 3.8

Epstein's Framework of Six Types of Involvement for Comprehensive Programs of Partnership and Sample Practices

TYPE 1

Parenting

Help all families establish home environments to support children as students.

TYPE 2

Communicating

Design effective forms of school-to-home and home-to-school communications about school programs and their children's progress.

TYPE 3

Volunteering

Recruit and organize parent help and support.

TYPE 4

Learning at Home

Provide information and ideas to families about how to help students at home with homework and other curriculum-related activities, decisions, and planning.

TYPE 5

Decision Making

Include parents in school decisions, developing parent leaders and representatives.

TYPE 6

Collaborating with the Community

Identify and integrate resources and services from the community to strengthen school programs, family practices, and student learning and development.

Source: Adapted from Epstein, J. L., Sanders, M. G., Simon, B. S., Salinas, K. C., Jansorn, N. R., & Van Voorhis, F. L. (2002). *School, family, and community partnerships: Your handbook for action* (2nd ed., p. 14). Thousand Oaks, CA: Corwin Press. Reprinted with permission.

School systems have expended considerable effort to involve parents in their child's educational program. The rationale is that parent involvement is related to their child's adjustment in the educational setting, as well as to academic achievement (O'Shea & O'Shea, 2001). Epstein's (1996) model of parent involvement (see Figure 3.8) indicates the range of ways that parents can become involved in their child's schooling. Parents will vary considerably in terms of their motivation and capacity to become involved. Nonetheless, teachers should be aware of school-based and classroom-based ways to foster parent involvement and to provide leadership in promoting parent partnerships. Teachers also need to understand what parents are expecting from their relationship with their child's school.

To learn more about what parents think about essential components of successful partnerships, Blue-Banning, Summers, Frankland, Nelson, and Beegle (2004) conducted individual and focus group interviews with 137 family members. Participants included parents representing a wide range of cultural and socioeconomic backgrounds and parents of children with and without disabilities. An analysis of the transcripts of interviews resulted in six indicators of successful partnerships: (a) communication, (b) commitment, (c) equality, (d) skills, (e) trust, and (f) respect. The authors concluded that parents viewed "common sense and ordinary human decency" to be the core of what parents want and expect (p. 183). Parents seemed less interested in elaborate, expensive programs and more interested in access to information and the quality of interactions with school personnel. The following section discusses family adjustment and the roles parents can play in supporting their children's education.

Family Adjustment

Family adjustment to having a family member with disabilities can vary considerably. In addition to concerns about health, safety, and academic achievement, family members can also have issues with denial, guilt, dealing with the public, hurt feelings, and stress (Hallahan, Kauffmann, & Pullen, 2009). Parents of children with disabilities have many roles: caregiver, provider, teacher, counselor, behavior support specialist, parent of siblings without disabilities, marriage partner, information specialist, and advocate (Heward, 2009). These issues and roles can affect the parents, siblings, and extended family as well. Some families experience turmoil and suffering as a result of having a family member with disabilities, whereas others learn to cope (Seltzer, Greenberg, Floyd, Pettee, & Hong, 2001). Hallahan, Kauffmann, and Pullen (2009) point out that still other families embrace the opportunity to learn about adjustment and equity through the experience of living with an individual with disabilities.

The needs of parents of children with disabilities are not static, but evolve and change over time (Alper, Schloss, & Schloss, 1994; Turnbull, Turnbull, Erwin, & Soodak, 2007). Moreover, the needs of your students and their families are likely to be highly diverse. Therefore, systematic, ongoing communication is imperative. In general, the needs of families with disabilities fall into five broad categories (Simpson, 1988):

1. *Information exchange.* Parents need conferences, program and classroom information, progress reports, interpretations of their child's academic and social needs, and informal feedback about their child. Teachers can rarely provide too much information to parents (particularly parents of children with special needs, who are already aware of their child's differences).

2. *Consumer and advocacy information.* Parents of students with disabilities sign endless numbers of forms and permissions. Summarize for parents not only the purpose of the forms, but also what the parents are agreeing to by providing their signature. Advocacy for students with disabilities and their families is a lifelong process that includes self-advocacy, social support advocacy, interpersonal advocacy, and legal advocacy (Alper, Schloss, & Schloss, 1994).

3. *Home/community program implementation.* Parents want to assist their children at home and also to involve them in appropriate community activities. How can you help? Provide helpful information. If possible, ask other professionals or community resource people to offer a program to all parents on these topics. Work with other teachers to develop an informational handout or brochure, and provide it in the languages parents read.

4. *Counseling, therapy, and consultation.* When parents request information about support groups, counseling, therapy, and other consultation services, what should you do? First, identify the information sources available from your school or school district, and keep them handy in a folder. Second, ask the school counselor or principal what procedures you should follow.

5. *Parent-coordinated service programs.* Parents need to be able to provide services to and receive services from other parents through advisory councils, parent-to-parent participation, advocacy, and other options.

Family is an important force in a student's learning and development. As a classroom teacher, fostering ongoing collaboration and communication with families is extremely important (Hallahan, Kauffmann, & Pullen, 2009). The primary ways that you can facilitate this connection are homework, parent conferences, and multiple forms of home–school communication. For online resources you can provide to parents, see Tech Tips.

Tech Tips

HELPFUL RESOURCES FOR PARENTS OF CHILDREN WITH SPECIAL NEEDS

There are a number of online resources that you can provide to parents to alert them to suggestions for how they can best advocate for their children. These sites also provide helpful tools and recommendations to parents of children with special needs.

The Parent Teacher Association
▶ www.pta.org/parentinvolvement
This organization provides parents a voice in advocating for the safety and success of other children as well.

National Education Association
▶ www.nea.org/parents
This website provides valuable resources for parents and for teachers in their collaborative efforts with parents.

Exceptional Parent Magazine
▶ www.eparent.com
This website offers vast online resources for parents of students with disabilities.

Homework

Homework (or *home learning*, as some school systems refer to it) gives parents a daily idea of your curriculum and instruction. Researcher Harris Cooper (2006) has conducted in-depth examinations of the research on homework. In reviewing the literature, Cooper recommends the "ten minute rule," or "ten minutes per grade level per night" (2001, p. 36). Thus, a first grader would have 10 minutes of homework per night; a sixth grader 60 minutes of homework per night. This rule of thumb may need to be amended for students with disabilities, depending on the needs of the individual student. Careful attention to crafting assignments that are appropriate in length and complexity for the student to complete independently is important. In addition, ongoing communication with parents about the time and effort it takes students to complete assignments at home can be helpful (Bryan & Burstein, 2004; Margolis, 2005). A "Homework Buddy" 60-second lesson can help students get organized for homework.

60 Second LESSON

Homework Buddies: Think–Pair–Share

School days can be long for both teachers and students. With so much activity going on, it can be easy for students to forget assignments or forget books or materials they might need to complete homework assignments. This is true for students who are in a self-contained class or in departmentalized classes when students move from room to room.

At the beginning of the school year, assign each student a homework buddy—two students who sit close to each other. Then, at the end of each school day (in self-contained settings) or at the end of the class period (in departmentalized settings), do a think–pair–share (McTighe & Lyman, 1988).

1. Ask students to take out their homework assignment sheet.

2. Have each student think quietly about what the assignment is and what materials they will need to take home to complete the assignment.

3. Encourage the homework buddies to speak to each other to discuss both the assignment and what they will need to take home.

4. After buddies have conferred, ask the whole class if they have questions they were unable to resolve as a pair.

At first this routine may take more than 60 seconds, but eventually, it will occur smoothly. Taking just a minute or two to get organized for homework will go a long way in helping students get started.

The goal of helping students with homework and providing an academic support system at home is to enable students to develop independent study skills (see also Chapter 16). For this to happen, parents and teachers need to work cooperatively. One way you can help is to hold evening parent workshops in which parents learn skills for helping with home learning. Often parents want to help but are not certain how to do so (Hughes, Schumm, & Vaughn, 1999). Providing parents with specific strategies that are aligned with what you are doing in the classroom can promote consistency and support for students. Following are some suggestions for providing that guidance.

Start the school year with a written policy statement that begins with a rationale for assigning homework (Cooper, 2001). According to Epstein and Van Voorhis (2001), teachers assign homework for a number of reasons:

- Practice (to help students strengthen skills learned in class)
- Preparation (to prepare for tests)
- Participation (to increase involvement with learning activities)
- Personal development (to build a sense of responsibility and time-management skills)
- Parent–child relations (to increase involvement in home-learning activities)
- Parent–teacher communications (to inform parents about curriculum and student progress)
- Peer interactions (to promote student-to-student support and to prepare for collaborative learning activities)
- Policy (to conform to school and district mandates)
- Public relations (to communicate to parents what students are learning in school)
- Punishment (to correct misbehavior in school)

Using homework for punishment is not particularly effective and can be counterproductive (Feldman, 2004). Homework should not be assigned simply out of routine or homework for homework's sake. It should be purposeful and directly tied to desired student outcomes (Marzano & Pickering, 2007). It is important to communicate why you think homework is important and what positive outcomes it will have for students. Your policy statement should also include a set of expectations: what you expect of the student, what you expect of the parent, and what both the parent and the student can expect of you. Whenever possible, involve parents in developing the policy statement. Tips for Teachers 3.5 provides an outline of issues to address in your policy statement.

One suggestion is to send home regular progress reports. By taking 30 minutes every other week to complete a progress form, you can eliminate problems that arise when parents are uninformed about the student's progress. Some school districts have implemented electronic grade books with online access for parents. Immediate access to grades can help parents stay on top of their child's progress and communicate with the school before it's too late (Lerman, 2006).

Parents are often unsure about how much or how little they should help with special projects such as term papers, book reports, and science fair projects. Parents' resources for providing assistance vary widely. Your policy statement should clarify expectations, such as arranging transportation to the public library and access to a computer and the Internet for researching and writing term papers. When a major project is assigned, let parents know the purpose of the assignment, its components, the due dates, and precisely when and how their assistance may be needed. A special project checklist and contract (see Figure 3.9) will help to clarify the responsibilities of the teacher, parents, and students for the completion of long-term assignments.

What happens when students with special needs fall behind their same-age peers and parents want to help? Particularly for students with disabilities, it is best for the student to work with a trained tutor rather than an untrained parent. This does not mean that parents should not help with homework, coach the child for a spelling test, or assist with a school project. Providing assistance and serving as a tutor are two different roles, however. Our use of the term **tutoring** refers to a systematic plan for supplementing the

What guidance can teachers provide to parents so they can help with their child's homework assignments?

Tips for Teachers 3.5

COMMUNICATING HOMEWORK POLICY

What the Parent and Student Can Expect of You

- Create homework assignments that are meaningful and provide for independent practice of skills taught in class or enrichment of content covered in class.
- Write homework assignments on board daily.
- Provide parents with a general homework schedule (e.g., Monday night, math and spelling; Tuesday night, math and composition).
- Inform parents about long-range projects in advance.
- Provide a system for reporting missing or late homework to parents and students.
- Grade homework in a timely fashion and provide feedback to students.

What You Expect of the Student

- Record homework assignments on an assignment sheet or in an assignment notebook.
- Complete homework assignments in a neat and timely manner.

What You Expect of the Parent

- Help the student set up a homework center.
- Help the student determine a regular homework schedule.
- Monitor and assist as necessary in the completion of homework.
- Write a note if confused about the assignment.

FIGURE
3.9

Special Project Checklist

Step   **Date Done**

☐   1. Decide on a project theme.   _____

☐   2. Have theme approved by a teacher.   _____

      Theme: _____

☐   3. Make a list of what needs to be done and the order in which the tasks should be completed. (List, then number each task.)

☐   4. Decide who is going to do what. (Initial each task.)

☐   5. Set deadlines for completion of each task. (Write in the dates.)

Task	**Date Due**	**Date Done**	**Person Responsible**

☐   6. Make a list of materials needed to do the project.

☐   7. Make a projected budget. (Write the estimated cost of each item.)

Item	**Cost**

☐   8. Send away for resource materials needed.

Resource Material	**Date Requested**	**Date Received**

☐   9. Contact community resources.

Community Resource	**Date Contacted**

☐   10. Visit the library.

Purpose of Visit _____ **Date of Visit** _____

☐   11. Complete the project ON TIME.

Date Handed In: _____ **Year:** _____

Source: This Special Project report is an excerpt from *How to help your child with homework* by Jeanne Shay Schumm, Ph.D. Copyright © 2005. Reprinted courtesy of the author.

student's educational program. Ask parents who are providing their own home tutoring to consider the suggestions provided in Figure 3.10.

Planned and Unplanned Parent Conferences

You will have many opportunities for planned parent conferences. Conferences could be part of the multidisciplinary team meeting, part of an annual parent–student meeting, or a specific meeting scheduled because of an academic or behavioral problem. At the middle- or high-school level, a conference might be with a group of teachers who all teach the same student. Figure 3.11 is a sample letter teachers can send to parents to confirm a planned meeting.

With a planned conference, you will be able to prepare materials and provide background knowledge (Dardig, 2008). At times you may want to include the student in the conference; this is particularly true with middle- and high-school students. If you think including the student is appropriate, talk with the parent first so that there are no surprises.

To prepare for a planned conference:

■ Review the student's materials, grades, and work progress.
■ Meet with and learn the perspectives of other professionals who also work with the student.
■ Review the student's folder, portfolio, and previous assessment information.

FIGURE 3.10

Suggestions for Home Tutors

- Have specific, realistic goals developed with the classroom teacher or the special education teacher.

- Begin and end each tutoring session with an activity that is fun and with which the child is successful.

- Keep the tutoring session brief—not more than 15 minutes for students up to grade 6, and not more than 30 minutes for older students.

- Work on small segments of material at a time.

- Use creative, novel ways of reviewing and teaching new material.

- Prevent the student from making mistakes. If the student does not know the answer, give it.

- Keep a tutoring log in which you record a couple of sentences about what you did and how the student performed.

- Provide encouragement and support. No one learns more by being "corrected" more.

- Practice the activities in fun ways that prevent boredom.

- Work should be challenging but not so difficult that there is not considerable opportunity for success.

- Tutor at the same time and in the same place, so that the student develops an expectation set for what will happen. Do not extend the designated time.

- If you are frustrated or your interactions with your child are strained or stressful during the tutoring, stop. Your relationship with your child is much more important than what you can teach him or her during the tutoring session.

FIGURE 3.11

Sample Note for Parent Conference

It's a Date

Dear Parent of _____,

    Thank you for your response to my request for a meeting about your child. Your appointment has been set for _____ (time) on _____ (day), _____ (date).

    I have set aside _____ minutes for our visit. If you will be bringing any guests, please let me know in advance. If this time is no longer convenient, please let me know.

Looking forward to seeing you,

_____
Teacher's Name

- Obtain samples of the student's most recent work.
- Make an outline of topics to discuss.

Welcome the parent with warmth and try to make the parent as comfortable as possible. Review your outline and ask the parent if he or she has other items to discuss. Begin and end the discussion by saying something positive about the child (Rose, 2005). During the conference, try not to use technical education language that may intimidate or insult the parent (Allen, Harry, & McLaughlin, 1993). Make certain that you have communicated any concerns in a straightforward and sensitive manner, and solicit parent reactions and recommendations to address those concerns (Rose, 2005; Shalaway, 2005). If you are giving the parent feedback about student assessment and academic progress, consider the five pointers in Tips for Teachers 3.6. At the end of the conference, summarize any decisions that were made and review any action plans. If necessary, set up a target date for follow-up by phone, email, or in person.

What happens when conferences are unplanned? Sometimes, at the end of the day, as students line up to go home, you notice a parent waiting by the door to speak with you. This kind of unplanned conference with parents will occur (Turnbull & Turnbull, 2001). Often, parents who come to school to talk with the teacher do so because they are concerned about something they have seen or heard. Their source of information might be their own child, who might not have told the story accurately. Avoid the temptation to resolve complex issues in an

Tips FOR TEACHERS 3.6

WORKING TOWARD EFFECTIVE PARENT CONFERENCES

- *Listen until they are finished.* As difficult as it may be to hear parents out, particularly when the statements they are making are inaccurate, the best way to begin the meeting is to allow them to say everything that is on their minds. Chances are they have thought for a long time about what to say and have even rehearsed it. Listening does not mean that you agree. Let them finish.

- *Take notes.* Write down key phrases the parents say, summarize key points, and jot down notes of things you want to remember to tell them. While you are doing this, be sure to maintain eye contact and composure. Your getting upset increases the likelihood of the parents growing more upset.

- *Summarize their major concerns.* As was stated previously, good communication includes effective summarization of the speaker's words and his or her meaning. Your summary shows parents not only that you have been listening, but also that you care about what they say.

- *State your position calmly.* After you have listened thoroughly and let parents know that you understand their key points, state your position calmly and succinctly. If parents have inaccurate information, now is the time to provide accurate information. Be sure that they understand your point of view. Speak calmly while stating your position and addressing their concerns.

- *Come to closure.* Getting to closure differs according to the situation. Sometimes, for example, you hear a parent's concern and quickly find a solution. "Oh, Mrs. Garcia, Lucy can stay in during lunch while she is sick. That is no problem. Just be sure she remembers to bring her own lunch." At other times, an issue needs to be negotiated. "Well, Mrs. Garcia, I do not think that Lucy has too much homework. The main reason it takes her so long is that she does not work on her math homework during the time allotted at school. Let's first set up a plan to increase her working on math at school."

You can find additional suggestions for planning and implementing parent conferences at www.teacherscholastic.com/professional/parentconf.

Tips FOR TEACHERS 3.7

PROVIDING FEEDBACK ABOUT ASSESSMENT RESULTS

To alleviate this anxiety, Thomas, Correa, and Morsink (2001, p. 281) offer the following tips:

- Provide feedback in a private, safe, comfortable environment.

- Keep the number of professionals to a minimum.

- Begin by asking parents their feelings about the child's strengths and weaknesses.

- Provide evaluation results in a jargon-free manner, using examples of test items and behavioral observations throughout.

- Provide the parents with results from a variety of assessment activities, including standardized tests, criterion-referenced tests, direct behavioral observations, play-based or community-based assessment, and judgment-based approaches.

- Be sensitive to viewing the child as an individual and a "whole" child when reporting various evaluation results.

- Allow the parent time to digest the results before educational planning begins.

- Be sensitive to linguistically different families and the use of interpreters.

- Prepare for the session with other team members, clarifying any possible conflicts before the meeting.

- Use conflict-resolution strategies to clarify any possible conflicts with families.

impromptu meeting. Recognize the importance of the issue and arrange a time to discuss the parent's concerns in a more appropriate setting: either by phone or in person. Parents can be anxious about getting feedback on their child's performance on assessments, whether the assessments are diagnostic, ongoing teacher-made tests, progress monitoring, or high-stakes tests. See Tips for Teachers 3.7 for suggestions that will help you alleviate parents' anxiety.

School-to-Home Communication

Communicating with parents must be an ongoing part of your routine as a teacher. Communication with all parents is important, but it is particularly important with parents of students with special needs. What are some ways to communicate? Letters, notes, calendars, newsletters, phone calls, email, web sites, and surveys are described in this section. Fortunately, many templates for parent notices, calendars, and so forth are now available online.

Teachers have a variety of ways to communicate with parents. In the beginning of the year, it is a good idea to send home a note with students that introduces you and provides a means for parents to contact you (see Figure 3.12 and 3.13). You might also want to send home a **letter** or **bulletin** before any long break (one week or more) to alert parents to activities they can do with their children to reinforce learning while they are out of school or to introduce a new unit of study. Remember, parents want to receive notification about their child: things that are going well, progress reports, your expectations of their child, materials the child needs, problems (early on), and general ideas of how to help their child learn.

Another letter that many parents appreciate is a **progress report** for the year. Joyce (a special education teacher) and the classroom teachers with whom she works sent the letter shown in Figure 3.14 to parents of children with disabilities who are included full time in general education classes.

You can communicate with parents in many ways. Consider some of the following:

- **"Good news" notes** can be used to communicate effectively regarding the positive academic and behavioral progress of students.
- **Student-written learning logs** can document key concepts presented and discussed in class.
- **Weekly and monthly calendars** can be used to communicate key information and to record homework assignments. You can fill in events on a calendar and then copy and distribute it to students to take home. A fourth-grade teacher who regularly sends home a weekly calendar reports that it takes her about 10 minutes to do. Alternatively, you and the special education teachers you work with might decide to provide parents with a weekly list of accomplishments.
- **Newsletters** can be written by the teacher or by students. The purpose of a newsletter is to keep parents informed about what is happening in the classroom. You can use the newsletters to describe your classroom policies or coming events, elicit parent support for projects, or provide ideas for enrichment activities and home learning. Newsletters should not target the poor performance or behavior of a particular student. If your newsletter recognizes student accomplishments, be careful not to name certain students repeatedly while never mentioning others.
- **Phone calls** are an important and often effective means of communicating with parents. Make a list each week of several parents you want to contact with positive reports. Allow 3 to 5 minutes for each call, and make one call at the end of each day. Be sure to keep a phone log of parents contacted by phone during the year.

FIGURE 3.12

Beginning-of-the-Year Letter: Elementary

Dear Parents:

The purpose of this letter is to welcome you and your child to our classroom. We will be co-teaching this year in the fourth-grade classroom. Ms. Anderson has taught at Blake Elementary School for four years; Mr. Westerfield has taught at Blake for six years. We have been working hard this summer to plan for a school year that will be an interesting and productive one for your child and for us.

At the open house on September 15, we will talk with you more about our roles and responsibilities in the classroom. In the meantime, we are sending you our classroom home-learning calendar for August and September. We are also sending you our homework policy and some suggestions for home reading and writing activities.

We hope you will take some time to complete the "Getting to Know You" form also attached to this letter. We are anxious to get to know you and your child. We are also anxious to partner with you in home-learning activities and in the many classroom events we are planning for the school year.

You are welcome to visit the classroom; however, we would appreciate receiving notice ahead of time to be sure your visit will not be interrupted. Feel free to call us at 777–1357 and leave a message. We will return your call as quickly as possible. We look forward to meeting you in person in the near future.

Sincerely,

Julia Anderson
Ben Westerfield

FIGURE
3.13

Beginning-of-the-Year Letter: Secondary

Welcome to U.S. history!

I'm excited to be a faculty member at Ponce de Leon Middle School, and I look forward to being your history teacher this year. As we prepare our journey for the school year, I'd like to share two things with you. First, I'd like to share something personal. Second, I'd like to explain what my expectations are for the coming year as we learn more about our great country and ourselves.

First, let me tell you something about myself by sharing an article printed in *The Miami Herald*, January 20, 2001 (see attached). In 2000, I began my 113-day, 2,225-mile "dream" canoe trip down the Mississippi River. Yes, I dreamed about making this trip for over 40 years. But it was also 40+ years ago that I began dreaming of one day being a social studies/history teacher. Just as my trip down the Mississippi River was a fantastic experience, I know my fifth year at Ponce is going to be another GREAT trip.

Now, let me share some of my hopes for school this coming year. Eighth-grade U.S. history is the climax of the social studies curriculum in middle school. This is where you will use all of the skills and knowledge learned in geography and civics to analyze why certain historical events happened and the effect of these events as a whole. You will learn U.S. history not completely chronologically, but more thematically. For example, we may look at the effects of war in general rather than studying each war separately. Hopefully, by the end of the school year, you will be able to understand the world around you a little bit better because you will know your history! History is fun when you can begin to connect the dots.

In addition to the content we will cover in class, you will have the opportunity to work in small- and large-group settings, participate in simulations, write interesting and thought-provoking essays, and be involved in critical thinking exercises, computer presentations and simulations, research projects, and even some selected and appropriate viewing of historical videotapes.

To begin our study of U.S. history for the first quarter, we will be learning the following topics:

• New World exploration—Your family's roots

• Native American societies—Colonial America

• Separation from England and the American Revolution

• Beginnings of U.S. government

I hope you'll have a better understanding of your country when the year is over. . . . I know I plan to learn something new. It's a great country with a rich heritage.

Attached please find a page titled "Preplanning Prevents Pitiful Pitfalls." The page outlines what I expect of you, what I expect of your family or guardians, and what you both can expect of me. The page also includes information on how your family or guardians can contact me. The goal is to make your school and home-learning experiences positive and productive. We will discuss the details outlined on the handout so that we all have a successful journey this year!

Best of luck to you, and peace,

Dr. Jerry Schumm

More and more teachers are beginning to communicate with parents by electronic communication. Working parents often cannot come to school for meetings during the day, so email communication is a necessary alternative. Using email is great for providing parents with updates and clarifying questions about homework and other activities. Of course, major concerns and dilemmas should be resolved in face-to-face meetings or by phone. It is also important to communicate to parents your availability and guidelines for using email. Spending your evenings or afternoons answering 30 emails might not be the best use of your time.

In addition to email, many schools now have **websites** that provide information about the calendar, major events, and homework tips (Barron & Wells, 2008). Individual **classroom web pages** are also becoming increasingly popular. Johnson (2000) describes four purposes of teacher web pages (see Table 3.2). Moreover, many schools now have electronic grade books that parents can access from home. Electronic grade books can help parents monitor student progress on an ongoing basis.

FIGURE 3.14

Year-End Progress Report

Dear Parents and Guardians:

We thank you all for your cooperation and support this school year. As the school year ends, we always ask parents how they feel the special education program met the needs of their children. We hope you have been satisfied with the results.

Following are your child's scores from the beginning of the year and from the end of the year. Please feel free to call one of us at 555-0000 and leave a message. We will return your call as soon as we can.

	Beginning Scores	**End-of-Year Scores**
Reading Comprehension	_____	_____
Word Recognition	_____	_____
Math Computation	_____	_____
Math Application	_____	_____

Thank you,

Joyce Duryea, Special Education Teacher; Maggie Lowe, Classroom Teacher

Suggestions or Comments:

Salend, Duhaney, Anderson, and Gottschalk (2004) recommend that teachers start slowly with basic homework policies and general guidelines. Homework assignments and models can be added later. Eventually, links to home-learning resources and other procedures for submitting homework online can be incorporated. If you plan to use a web page, it is important to tell parents the purpose of the web page and how often you will update it.

In using electronic communication, keep in mind that not all parents will have access to computers, so other modes of communication need to be made available too.

Still another way to foster communication is through **parent interviews** and **surveys**. Asking family members about their level of satisfaction with programs, curriculum, and services can give family members a voice, put key issues on the table, and lead to program improvement. Inclusion teams can conduct brief interviews or surveys to tap the concerns of family members and to use data to generate possible solutions and to identify necessary resources for program improvement (Salend & Garrick Duhaney, 2002).

TABLE 3.2 — Purposes of Teacher Web Pages

PURPOSES OF WEB PAGES	CONTENT
1. General Class Description	• Teacher name and contact information • Class rules and expectations • Link to school calendar • Supply list • Field trip information • Class news with photos and descriptions of current class activities • Requests and guidelines for parent volunteering • Drop folder for turning in student work electronically • Class electronic mailing list • A counter that records the number of visits to the page
2. Unit Outlines and Timetables	• Lists of units taught in each subject area (elementary) or in each class (secondary) • State requirements met by class or units • Projected dates of units beginning and ending • Major goals for each unit • Samples of final projects from previous years
3. Information about Specific Units and Projects	• Learner outcomes for each unit • Major activities • Homework assignments and due dates • Vocabulary words, spelling lists, number facts, formulas, etc. • Assessment/evaluations for unit and projects • Online practice tests • Active links to on-line resources and web pages • Suggested enrichment activities with which parents can help
4. Student Progress Reporting	• Online gradebook • Final grades for quarter, semester, and year (or equivalent marking period) • GPA and class ranking • Standardized test results • Attendance records

Source: Adapted from Johnson, D. (2000). *Teacher web pages that build parent partnerships.* www.infotoday.com/MMSchools/sep00/johnson.htm. Reprinted by permission of Information Today, Inc., 143 Old Marlton Pike, Medford, NJ 08055. (609) 654-6266. www.infotoday.com.

Summary

■ Effective collaboration with professionals and families requires particular communication skills, such as (a) acceptance, (b) effective listening, (c) appropriate questioning, and (d) focus. Procedures for communicating with other school personnel and parents are delineated in this chapter.

■ Consultation, collaboration, and co-teaching models have grown out of increased awareness that students with disabilities are more likely to succeed in general education classrooms if they get targeted support services in the classroom. For any collaboration model to be effective, several criteria must be in place, including (a) time to co-plan, (b) knowledge of the procedures involved in the particular model, and (c) a location where participants can meet.

■ Ongoing communication with families is vital for student success in school. Teachers need to implement clear and consistent lines of communication, particularly with respect to homework policies.

Think and Apply

1. Have you ever had a conversation during which you did not feel connected? Think about what the other person(s) did and what you did. Using the principles of effective listening identified in this chapter, make a checklist of things you should consider during a conversation (a) with parents and (b) with other professionals.

2. This chapter's Collaboration Issues and Dilemmas section lists four issues you might need to consider if you are involved in a consultation, collaboration, or co-teaching arrangement with another professional. Write your current feelings about each issue (student ownership, individual versus class focus, content versus accommodation, and real world versus student's world). What knowledge and experiences might support your perspectives? What knowledge and experiences might cause you to change your views?

3. Write a homework policy statement for an elementary or secondary classroom. Include in your statement the roles and responsibilities of the teacher, students, and parents.

PEARSON
myeducationlab

Now go to Topic 2: Collaboration, Consultation, and Co-Teaching and Topic 3: Parents and Families in the MyEducationLab (www.myeducationlab.com) for your course where you can:

- Find learning outcomes for these topics along with the national standards that connect to these outcomes.
- Complete Assignments and Activities that can help you more deeply understand the chapter content.
- Examine challenging situations and cases presented in the IRIS Center Resources.
- Apply and practice your understanding of the core teaching skills identified in the chapter with Building Teaching Skills and Dispositions learning units.

*T*eaching Culturally and Linguistically Diverse Students

CHAPTER

4

FOCUS QUESTIONS

1. As a classroom teacher, how can you learn about your culture and your students' cultures and communities? What is the relationship between the macroculture and the microcultures of culturally and linguistically diverse learners?

2. What is multicultural education? As a classroom teacher, how can you incorporate multicultural education into your curriculum?

3. What are common misconceptions about how to teach children who are learning English as a second language? What can you do to support second language acquisition in your classroom?

4. How can assessment of culturally and linguistically diverse students be fair and accurate?

5. As a classroom teacher, how can you practice culturally responsive teaching and promote best practices for culturally diverse and linguistically diverse students in your classroom?

INTERVIEW
KRISTINA ZAYAS-BAZAN

Kristina Zayas-Bazan is assigned to Kensington Park Elementary in South Florida for her 15-week associate teaching experience. On her first day of associate teaching, Kristina steps into a second-grade self-contained classroom full of 27 smiling faces. All of her students are English language learners but they represent a full range of English language proficiency.

Overwhelmed with thoughts of how she can productively divide her instructional time amongst the various learning needs of her diverse students, Kristina implements an interactive pedagogy style aimed to address all possible obstacles. First, through song, kinesthetics, and hands-on experiences, students will actively experiment with the English language in a nonthreatening social arena to further promote the acquisition process. Therefore, Kristina develops a morning routine when students sing, dance, and update the calendar on a daily basis, continually acquiring greater English vocabulary words and phrases through rhythm and rhyme.

Second, thinking about principles of culturally responsive teaching, Kristina creates a learning environment in which students trust her as a teacher, guide, and friend. Kristina encourages her students to take risks with the English language. Kristina's approach allows her to use the students' rich cultures as a stepping-stone on the path toward state and local curriculum goals. Even while Kristina respects the students' native language and traditions, students are simultaneously learning English.

Third, the emphasis on hands-on learning heightens students' educational motivation and interests. Through the continuous incorporation of manipulatives, visuals, and experiments, Kristina is able to relate abstract concepts to pertinent real-world situations that are compatible with the students' life experiences. As Kristina comments,

> My goal is to create a learning environment that complements the uniqueness of each student. Using strategies like that of rhyme, kinesthetics, hands-on experiences, visuals, and bilingual teaching, I am able to reach each and every one of my students regardless of their level of proficiency in English. For us, the English language is not a barrier because we did not let it become one. Via this setup, students smoothly venture down the language acquisition path without ever forgetting who they are or where they come from.

Introduction

Kristina not only teaches children who are new immigrants to the United States, but also, as a kindergartener, was a new immigrant. With this background, her focus is to bring her students the best of both worlds: the riches and value of their native cultures as well as the beauty and excitement of our increasingly diverse country. This chapter focuses on the growing diversity of schools and students in the United States. It also presents the key concepts associated with multicultural education, linguistic diversity, second language learning, and bilingual education. The chapter continues with a presentation of issues regarding the fair and accurate assessment of diverse students. Finally, it discusses instructional strategies for educating students who are culturally and linguistically diverse. As you read this chapter, think about how the ideas presented by Kristina help create a classroom that facilitates the successful education of culturally and linguistically diverse students.

Diversity in Classrooms

The United States is one of the most culturally diverse nations in the world. This diversity continues to increase as new immigrants relocate in the United States. Although the percentage of non-Hispanic Whites is currently roughly two thirds of the U.S. population, it is projected that by the year 2050 that number will be less than half of the total population (U.S. Census Bureau, 2008). The Pew Research Center reports that one of every five students enrolled in public schools is of Hispanic origin (Fry & Gonzales, 2008). Although the majority of these students are born in the United States, many of them are new immigrants or the children of immigrants and are emerging in their use of English. In a policy note issued by the Educational Testing Service (2008), it was reported that over 10% of the nation's students are **English language learners (ELLs)**, students for whom English is a second language. Seven out of 10 of these students do not use English when in the home (Fry & Gonzales, 2008).

Minorities constitute the majority of public school students in more than 20 of the country's largest school systems, including those of Miami, Philadelphia, Baltimore, and Los Angeles. Although many of these students do well in school, a substantial number of students come from homes in which families live in poverty and parents are unemployed or underemployed, have little education and few technical skills, and are not fluent in English (Al-Hassan & Gardner, 2002; KewalRamani, Gilbertson, Fox, & Provasnik, 2007). Furthermore, traditional education practice often does not provide a good match between the students' cultures and the curriculum and instructional practices (Cartledge, Gardner, & Ford, 2009; Ovando, Collier, & Combs, 2006).

The average achievement of African Americans, Native Americans, and Latino Americans is consistently lower than that of middle- and upper-class European Americans at every grade level (KewalRamani et al., 2007). The dropout rates and the grade retention rates are also higher for these groups of students (American Federation of Teachers, 2006; Laird, Cataldi, KewelRamani, & Chapman, 2008; Pinkus, 2006). The dropout rate for students from low-income families is 4.5 times the rate of their peers from high-income families (Laird et al., 2008).

A disproportionately high percentage of African Americans, Latino Americans, and Native Americans have been identified as having learning disabilities, mild mental retardation, and emotional or behavioral disorders (Donovan & Cross, 2002; Harry & Klingner, 2006). In contrast, a disproportionately lower percentage of students from these cultural groups have been identified for more advanced academic programs (Castellano, 2003; Elhoweris, Mutua, Alsheikh, & Holloway, 2005).

Common explanations for the achievement gap are that parents just don't care or value education. These are misconceptions that do not even begin to address the issue (Ladson-Billings, 2007). "It is time to challenge these inherent fallacies and place students' academic struggles in the larger context of social failure, including health, wealth, and funding gaps that harm their school success" (Ladson-Billings, 2007, p. 316). Indeed, the reasons for the limited success of many students are complex and interrelated, but several factors should be considered (Salend, Duhaney, & Montgomery, 2002):

- Role models from minority groups are often limited in school, in that many teachers are European Americans and limited mentor programs are available for these students to connect with leaders in their communities.
- Discrimination against students from minority groups continues in assessment for and placement in advanced and gifted programs (Elhoweris, Mutua, Alsheikh, & Holloway, 2005).
- Curriculum and educational practice are often not culturally responsive, with limited integration of information about different cultural groups into the curriculum (Gay & Kirkland, 2003; Montgomery, 2001).
- Teaching styles might not match the learning styles of students from diverse cultures (Chamberlain, 2005; Ladson-Billings, 1995).
- A greater proportion of students from minority groups live in poverty and their poverty levels are lower than those of European Americans (Hosp & Reschly, 2004; National Center for Children in Poverty, 2008).

The overrepresentation of minorities in special education has long been a dilemma for students, parents, and educators. Although the explanations mentioned above for this persistent problem may or may not hold merit, the fact that students have been subject to misdiagnosis and inadequate instruction cannot be denied (Harry & Klingner, 2006). Response to intervention (RTI) holds great promise for minority students (Haager, 2007; Rinaldi & Samson, 2008). "We are encouraged by the potential of RTI models to improve educational opportunities for culturally and linguistically diverse students and to reduce their disproportionate representation in special education" (Klingner & Edwards, 2006, p. 115). As noted in Chapter 2, the key components of RTI (i.e., early screening, high-quality core instruction, progress monitoring, and intervention with research-based instruction) are designed to promote early success in the acquisition of basic skills rather than the traditional "wait-to-fail" model (Brown & Doolittle, 2008; Haager, 2007). However, research in RTI—particularly as it pertains to culturally and linguistically diverse students—is in its early stages and much is yet to be learned about optimum assessment and instructional practices (Haager, 2007; Klingner & Edwards, 2006).

What can the classroom teacher do? Like Kristina, classroom teachers can strive to develop a **culturally responsive teaching (CRT)** style. "Many ethnically diverse students do not find schooling exciting or inviting; they often feel unwelcome, insignificant, and alienated . . . learning is more interesting and easier to accomplish when it has personal meaning for students" (Gay, 2004, p. 33). Noted scholar Geneva Gay (2000) defines CRT as "using the cultural knowledge, prior experiences, and performance styles of diverse students to make learning more appropriate and effective for them; it teaches to and through the strengths of these students" (p. 29).

CRT is particularly important in thinking about implementation of RTI models (Klingner, Barletta, & Hoover, 2008; Taylor, 2008). However, teachers involved in all tiers of instruction must be prepared to teach in ways that will promote student engagement and address individual needs. Teachers and administrators should also use multiple assessment tools (including student observation) to ensure fair and accurate assessment. Developing an understanding of diverse cultures and cultural characteristics are two of the best steps in becoming a culturally responsive teacher.

Understanding Diverse Cultures

The United States is composed of a shared core culture and many subcultures (Banks, 2008). Students in our schools are influenced by this core culture, sometimes referred to as the **macroculture**. The United States is such a complex and diverse nation that its macroculture is somewhat difficult to describe, but Banks (2008) suggests the following key components:

- Equality, justice, and human dignity
- Individual versus group orientation
- Orientation toward materialism

At the same time, students are influenced by their home and/or regional cultures, or **microcultures** (Banks, 2008). Microcultures are often based on such factors as national origin, ethnicity, socioeconomic class, religion, gender, age, and disability. Sometimes the core values of the macroculture and microcultures are relatively similar, but in other cases the microculture values are quite different from those of the macroculture (Banks, 2008). For example, the emphasis on individuality is generally not as important in African American, Latino American, and Native American ethnic communities as it is in the European American macroculture. Instead, these communities place more importance on group and family values (Hale-Benson, 1986; Irvine & York, 2001; Swisher & Deyhle, 1992). Hence, teaching students to work together to complete assignments rather than compete with each other may be more culturally appropriate for students from these ethnic backgrounds (Cohen & Lotan, 2004). In fact, cooperative learning activities that support equal status contact between majority and minority groups in pursuit of common goals have been shown to increase cross-ethnic friendships in classrooms (e.g., Kagan, Zahn, Widaman, Schwarzwald, & Tyrell, 1985; Oishi, Slavin, & Madden, 1983).

Another example of differences between the macroculture and various microcultures in the United States is the value given to **personalized knowledge** (i.e., knowledge that results

PEARSON
myeducationlab

To enhance your understanding of adapting the classroom with students with cultural and linguistic differences in the general classroom, go to the IRIS Center Resources section of Topic 4: Cultural and Linguistic Diversity in the MyEducationLab for your course and complete Module 12: Cultural and Linguistic Differences: What Teachers Should Know.

from firsthand observation). Although the macroculture values knowledge based on objectivity, and educational institutions emphasize abstract out-of-context knowledge, research on women's ways of knowing suggests that women value personalized knowledge (Belenky, Clinchy, Goldberger, & Tarule, 1986; Gilligan, 1982). Concerns have been raised about the potential bias in educational testing against certain microcultures within our society. Students who have been raised in a microcultures that has not been aligned with the macroculture may have different sets of knowledge and skills than represented on intelligence or achievement tests. This results in the misidentification of minority students in special education placements such as those with learning disabilities, mental retardation, and emotional or behavioral disorders (Donovan & Cross, 2002; Harry, Klingner, & Hart, 2005; Samuels, 2007).

What environmental and instructional measures can teachers take to help diverse students mediate between the microcultures of their homes and communities and the macroculture of their nation and school?

When the core values in the macroculture and microculture are different, teachers can help students understand and mediate differences between the cultures. To act as mediators, teachers need to learn about and incorporate the various microcultures and home communities into school life and the curriculum. For example, Luis Moll and his colleagues (e.g., Gonzalez et al., 1995; Moll & Greenberg, 1990) conducted research in Tucson's barrio schools for a number of years. Moll's research and ethnographic methods of study provide strategies for teachers to integrate the home and school communities by building on the **funds of knowledge** found in the home community. Learning about the funds of knowledge in the students' home community can help teachers to not overgeneralize characteristics that are often attributed to different cultural groups (Harry, Klingner, & Hart, 2005).

If you begin your teaching career in a school in which the students' home communities are neither your home community nor similar to your home communities, you'll need to spend some time learning about your students' cultural backgrounds. One way is to locate at least one person in the community who can serve as your cultural guide. This can often be a fellow staff member who is willing to teach you about the culture and community.

If it is appropriate and within school policy, visits to students' homes can allow you to talk with parents and other family members. This is an ideal opportunity to learn more about the students, the households, and the culture, including interests of the family, the role of the extended family, the way in which jobs are shared, and the ways in which literacy is used in the home.

Also, you'll need to be a learner in the classroom. Discuss with students your interest in learning about their cultures, including community activities. Information that can help guide your learning includes jobs of parents, their special skills and knowledge, special interests of students (at home and in the community), community activities, special occasions and holidays, family structure, and family responsibilities and relationships. Tips for Teachers 4.1 provides additional guidelines for working with culturally and linguistically diverse students.

Understanding Cultural Characteristics

In learning about cultural influences, there is a tendency to make generalizations based on common beliefs about a culture.

> Culture is only one of the characteristics that determine individuals' and families' attitudes, values, beliefs, and ways of behaving. Assuming that culture-specific information applies to all individuals from the cultural group is not only inaccurate but also dangerous—it can lead to stereotyping that diminishes rather than enhances cross-cultural competence. (Lynch & Hanson, 1992, p. 44)

Cultural Characteristics.   Having some knowledge of students' **cultural characteristics** serves as a starting point for understanding individual students' behaviors and learning styles.

Tips FOR TEACHERS 4.1

GUIDELINES FOR WORKING WITH CULTURALLY AND LINGUISTICALLY DIVERSE STUDENTS

- Develop cultural consciousness.

- Become aware of your own cultural background.

- Become aware of culture clashes.

- Develop knowledge of cultural variability and become knowledgeable about how culture influences the teaching/learning process.

- Hold high expectations for all students.

- Resist the blame game.

- Spend time reflecting about teaching practices.

- Gather information about your students.

- Develop an understanding of first and second language acquisition and the challenges students are likely to face in acquiring a second language.

- Develop an understanding of the interaction among language, culture, and disability.

- Teach the rules of the game, and at the same time respect students' cultural background.

- Adopt an integrated approach to instruction.

- Build trusting relationships with students and parents.

- Use a variety of strategies in educating culturally and linguistically diverse students (Chamberlain, 2005).

This knowledge can keep teachers from misinterpreting students' actions. Culturally responsive teachers "recognize the differences between their students and themselves and strive to become nonjudgmental" (Cartledge, Gardner, & Ford, 2009, p. 18). Creating culturally responsive classrooms requires teachers to get to know students, their families, and their cultures. Díaz-Rico (2004) recommends that teachers use multiple resources to learn about the cultures of students in their classroom, including interviews with parents, students, and community members; printed materials; and websites.

Following are general areas and questions you can use to guide inquiry about the cultural characteristics of students in your classroom:

- **Time.** How do students perceive time? How is timeliness regarded in their cultures?
- **Space.** What personal distance do students use in interactions with other students and with adults? How does the culture determine the space allotted to boys and to girls?
- **Dress and food.** How does dress differ for age, gender, and social class? What clothing and accessories are considered acceptable? What foods are typical?
- **Rituals and ceremonies.** What rituals do students use to show respect? What celebrations do students observe, and for what reasons? How and where do parents expect to be greeted when visiting the class?
- **Work.** What types of work are students expected to perform in the home and community, and at what age? To what extent are students expected to work together?
- **Leisure.** What are the purposes for play? What typical activities are done for enjoyment in the home and community?
- **Gender roles.** What tasks are performed by boys? By girls? What expectations do parents and students hold for boys' and girls' achievements, and how do these differ by subject areas?
- **Status.** What resources (e.g., study area and materials, study assistance from parents and siblings) are available at home and in the community? What power do parents have to obtain information about the school and to influence educational choices?
- **Goals.** What kinds of work are considered prestigious or desirable? What role does education play in achieving occupational goals? What education level do the family and student desire for the student?
- **Education.** What methods for teaching and learning are used in the home (e.g., modeling and imitation, didactic stories and proverbs, direct verbal instruction)?
- **Communication.** What roles do verbal and nonverbal language play in learning and teaching? What roles do conventions such as silence, questions, rhetorical questions, and discourse style play in communication? What types of literature (e.g., newspapers, books) are used in

PEARSON
myeducationlab

Go to the Assignments and Activities section of Topic 4: Cultural and Linguistic Diversity in the MyEducationLab for your course and complete the activity entitled *Cultural Bias*.

the home, and in what language(s) are they written? How is writing used in the home (e.g., letters, lists, notes), and in what language(s)?

■ *Interaction.* What roles do cooperation and competition play in learning? How are children expected to interact with teachers?

■ *Behavior.* What are cultural expectations for appropriate behavior in school settings?

Laurel Hopkins's first teaching assignment was in New Orleans. Much to her surprise, her students were primarily new immigrants who had recently come to the United States from Vietnam. As Laurel put it, "I had no idea there was such a large population of Vietnamese in New Orleans." Laurel was pleased to learn that her school had hired a Vietnamese woman, Ms. Nguyen, to work as a paraprofessional to assist with parent communication. Laurel had lunch once a week with Ms. Nguyen to learn more about how to respond to her students' needs. Ms. Nguyen helped Laurel with parent interviews so that she could gather important information about her students and their culture. "Ms. Nguyen was a treasure," explained Laurel. "Not only did I learn about customs and traditions, I also learned about some difficulties parents faced. For example, parents in the Vietnamese culture are honored and have authority. For some parents, having their own children know more English than they did posed a real problem."

The insights that Laurel Hopkins gained from Ms. Nguyen were important. For example, in some instances, there were differences among children and their families. Some were more Americanized than others who resisted Americanization. Laurel learned not to assume that cultural characteristics are common to all members of a cultural group. Rather, understanding characteristics served as a starting point in her education about the cultural diversity of the students she taught.

Go to **www.splcenter.org**, the Southern Poverty Law Center, to find resources that will help you teach students how to combat hate, intolerance, and discrimination.

Cultural Boundaries. Erickson (2005) defines a cultural boundary as "the presence of some kind of cultural difference" (p. 41). Cultural boundaries can occur at many levels, including when there are differences between the student and the teacher or between the student and the culture of schooling. For example, in the Haitian American culture, it is the custom to respect the work of the teacher and to put the responsibility of formal education in the hands of the teacher. Parental involvement in schooling is not typical for some families. When a teacher urges parental involvement, it would mean the crossing of a cultural boundary for parents. Teachers often ask why some cultural groups seem to cross cultural boundaries and succeed in school more easily than others do. The classic work of anthropologist John Ogbu has shed light on cultural boundaries. Ogbu (1978, 1992) has suggested that some cultural groups seem to cross cultural boundaries more easily than other groups. On the basis of his comparative research, Ogbu (1978, 1992) has put forth one explanation. In his work, he classified cultural groups as autonomous minorities, immigrant or voluntary minorities, and castelike or involuntary minorities.

■ *Autonomous minorities* are considered minorities in a numerical sense; they include Jews, Mormons, and the Amish. In the United States, there are no non-White autonomous minorities.

■ *Immigrant or voluntary minorities* are people who have moved to the new society or culture more or less voluntarily because they desire greater economic opportunities and political freedom. The Chinese and Punjabi Indians are representative examples in the United States.

■ *Castelike or involuntary minorities* are people who were brought to the United States or conquered against their will. Examples in the United States are African Americans, Native Americans, early Mexican Americans in the Southwest, and Native Hawaiians.

Ogbu (1992) suggests that voluntary groups experience initial (but not lingering) problems in school because of language and cultural differences. The involuntary minorities, on the other hand, usually experience greater, more persistent difficulties learning in school. This difficulty for involuntary minorities appears related to several factors:

■ **Cultural inversion**, or the tendency to regard certain forms of behavior, events, symbols, and meanings as inappropriate because they are characteristic of European American culture.

■ A **collective identity**, in opposition to the social identity of the dominant group, develops as the involuntary minorities are treated as subordinates by European Americans in economic, political, social, psychological, cultural, and language domains.

Hence, in an effort to retain their own identity and roots, students from involuntary minorities may be more oppositional and less motivated to learn in school. Ogbu (1992) explains, "They fear that by learning the White cultural frame of reference, they will cease to act like minorities and lose their identity as minorities and their sense of community and self-worth" (p. 10). In contrast, because voluntary minorities do not feel the need to protect their cultural identity, they do not perceive learning the attitudes and behaviors required for school success as threatening to their own culture, language, and identities. Instead they interpret such learning as *additive,* that is, adding to what they already have (Chung, 1992).

It is important to note that these are generalized types that include groups who may more appropriately "fit" a different type. For example, Cubans who fled Cuba during the 1960s were an involuntary minority, yet many acculturated and became quite successful in the Miami community.

James Cummins (1992), a leading scholar in bilingual education, suggests that academic success of students from involuntary minority groups is related to the extent that schools reflect the following:

- Minority students' language and culture are incorporated into the school program.
- Minority community participation is encouraged as an integral component of children's education.
- Instruction (pedagogy) is used to motivate students to use language actively to generate their own knowledge.
- Professionals involved in student testing (assessment) become advocates for minority students by focusing primarily on ways in which students' academic difficulties are a function of interactions with and within the school context, instead of locating the problem within the students. (p. 5)

PEARSON
myeducationlab

To hear an expert discuss her work with students with cultural and linguistic differences go to the IRIS Center Resource section of Topic 4: Cultural and Linguistic differences in the MyEducationLab for your course and listen to the Podcast entitled *Donna Ford on cultural and linguistic differences.*

Multicultural Education

Multicultural education is "an educational reform movement whose major goal is to restructure curricula and educational institutions so that students from diverse social-class, racial, and ethnic groups—as well as both gender groups—will experience equal educational opportunities" (Banks, 2008, p. 135). Multicultural education is closely linked to cultural diversity (Ariza, Morales-Jones, Yahya, & Zainuddin, 2006) and fosters pride in minority cultures, assists students in developing new insights into their cultures, reduces prejudice and stereotyping, and promotes intercultural understanding (Rubalcava, 1991). In the fullest sense, multicultural education is a total rethinking of the way we conduct schooling in a diverse society within a democratic, civic framework (Lessow-Hurley, 2008).

Dimensions of Multicultural Education

Multicultural education is much more than a curriculum focused on learning about diverse cultures based on such parameters as gender, ethnicity, and race. It is a thread running through the total curriculum, not a subject to be taught (Gay, 2004; Tiedt & Tiedt, 2006). Banks (2008) suggests that multicultural education has four dimensions: content integration, knowledge construction, prejudice reduction, and an equity pedagogy, as well as an empowering school culture and social structure.

1. **Content integration** focuses on using examples and content from a variety of cultures and groups to illustrate concepts, principles, generalizations, and theories. Ethnic and cultural content is infused into the subject areas in a natural, logical way (Banks, 2008). For example, you can teach students about traditional dress and celebrations in many different cultures by discussing different holidays, the dress worn, and the reasons for the holidays and traditional dress. As a follow-up activity, students can interview their parents and other family members to learn about traditional dress and holidays celebrated by their families.

2. **Knowledge construction** refers to students learning about how implicit cultural assumptions, frames of reference, perspectives, and biases influence the ways in which knowledge is constructed. For example, the discovery of America by Europeans has two very different frames of reference when presented from the perspectives of the Native Americans and the Europeans. Similarly, the power of the mind over the body is viewed differently by Asian and European cultures.

3. **Prejudice reduction** is the idea that when misconceptions and stereotypes about diverse cultural and ethnic groups are dispelled, students can learn to develop an appreciation for individuals from backgrounds other than their own. Teachers can promote prejudice reduction through well-planned units and lessons that help students develop knowledge and positive images of a wide range of groups.

4. With an **equity pedagogy**, the teacher attends to different teaching and learning styles and modifies teaching to facilitate the academic achievement of students from diverse cultures.

An **empowering school culture and social structure** promotes gender, racial, and social class equity. Establishing such a culture entails examining the school culture for biases and prejudices, developing strategies to alleviate them, and replacing them with opportunities that promote positive self-esteem for all students. An initial step in creating an empowering school culture is to have the staff share, learn about, and respect their own diversity.

A school's staff can learn about their school community through many of the activities used to help students learn about one another, such as sharing information about heritage, birthplace, family, traditional foods, and hobbies. For example, Stan Williams, the principal at an urban elementary school, takes time each year at the initial full-staff meeting for the staff to interview each other about their families, cultural backgrounds, areas of educational expertise, traditional foods, and hobbies. Then each interviewer uses the information garnered to introduce the interviewee to at least two other staff members. In the past, Stan has also displayed staff photos and profiles in the staff lounge. Stan comments, "When we take time [for] this activity, the staff immediately begins to learn about each other and find common interests that are fostered throughout the school year. It helps to create a sense of equality across all staff jobs (e.g., teachers, paraprofessionals, office staff, building maintenance staff)."

How can school culture empower all students to succeed? What student outcomes lead to the goal of creating a learning community in which students understand and respect diversity and have equal opportunity to academic success?

To implement multicultural education and integrate these dimensions successfully, teachers should conceptualize multicultural education as much more than a curriculum or a subject to teach. Several leaders in the field have suggested that viewing the school as a social system and studying and reforming the major variables is necessary to create a learning environment in which students have an equal chance for school success (e.g., Banks, 2008; Grant & Sleeter, 1993; Ladson-Billings, 2006; Nieto, 1994; Ogbu, 1992). Banks (2008) suggests that the following aspects of the school as a social system need to be considered:

- School staff: attitudes, perceptions, and actions
- Formalized curriculum and course of study
- School's preferred learning, teaching, and cultural characteristics
- Language and dialects of the school
- Instructional materials
- Assessment and testing procedures
- School culture and hidden curriculum
- The counseling program

As you study the schools in which you teach as social systems and as teaching and learning communities, consider these variables and determine the degree to which they foster the overarching goals of multicultural education. In other words, think about how you can create a learning community in which students have not only equal opportunities for academic success, but also an understanding of and respect for diversity.

Desired Student Outcomes

Given these dimensions of multicultural education and the overall goals, what are some desired student outcomes that lead to these goals? Multicultural teacher educators Tiedt and Tiedt (2006) suggest that students should be able to do the following:

- Identify a strong sense of self-esteem and express the needs and rights of others to similar feelings of self-esteem
- Describe their own cultures, recognizing the influences that have shaped their thinking and behavior
- Identify racial, ethnic, and religious groups represented in our pluralistic society
- Identify needs and concerns universal to people of all cultures and compare cultural variations
- Recognize, understand, and critique examples of stereotypic thinking and social inequities in real life and literature and develop solutions for altering their status
- Discuss special gender-, ethnic-, age-, and disability-related concerns
- Inquire multiculturally as they engage in broad thematic studies related to any field of study

To achieve these outcomes curricula must highlight cultural diversity. The next section discusses curricula for multicultural education.

Multicultural Curricula

Banks (2008) suggests that since multicultural education was introduced in the 1960s, curricular approaches to multicultural education have evolved, based on the degree to which diversity plays a central role in the curriculum. Banks identifies four approaches: contributions, additive, transformation, and social action (see Table 4.1).

Contributions Approach.   The **contributions approach** is characterized by the insertion of ethnic heroes and discrete cultural artifacts into the curriculum—adding culturally diverse inventors and their inventions to a thematic unit on inventions, for example.

This approach is the easiest to use but has several serious limitations. First, because the heroes are usually presented in isolation, students do not gain an overall understanding of the role of ethnic and cultural groups in the United States. Second, this approach does not address issues such as oppression and discrimination. Instead, it reinforces the Horatio Alger myth in that ethnic heroes are presented with little attention paid to how they became heroes despite the barriers they encountered.

Additive Approach.   The **additive approach** is characterized by the addition of content, concepts, themes, and perspectives without changing the basic structure of the curriculum. Typical examples are adding books about different groups to the literature sets (e.g., Mildred Taylor's *Roll of Thunder, Hear My Cry*), adding a unit on Native Americans to an American history course, and adding a course on ethnic or gender studies to a high-school curriculum. This approach offers better integration of multicultural perspectives than the contributions approach but does not result in a restructured curriculum. For example, including a unit on the Plains Indians in a U.S. history class will increase students' understanding of Native Americans but not as clearly as will transforming the curriculum so that the movement to the West is viewed as both an expansion (from a European perspective) and an invasion (from a Native American perspective).

Transformation Approach.   In the **transformation approach**, the basic core of the curriculum is changed and the focus is on viewing events, concepts, and themes from multiple perspectives based on diversity. Banks (2008) suggests that

> When teaching a unit such as "The Westward Movement" using a transformation approach, the teacher would assign appropriate readings and then ask the students such questions as: What do you think the Westward movement means? Who was moving west—the Whites or the Native Americans? . . .The aim of these questions is to help students to understand that the Westward movement is a Eurocentric term . . . The Sioux did not consider their Homeland "the West" but the center of the universe. (p. 49)

Banks's Approaches to Multicultural Curriculum Reform

TABLE 4.1

APPROACH	DESCRIPTION	EXAMPLES	STRENGTHS	PROBLEMS
Contributions	Heroes, cultural components, holidays, and other discrete elements related to ethnic groups are added to the curriculum on special days, occasions, and celebrations.	■ Famous Mexican Americans are studied only during the week of Cinco de Mayo (May 5). African Americans are studied during Black History Month in February but rarely during the rest of the year. ■ Ethnic foods are studied in the first grade with little attention devoted to the cultures in which the foods are embedded.	■ Provides a quick and relatively easy way to put ethnic content into the curriculum. ■ Gives ethnic heroes visibility in the curriculum alongside mainstream heroes. ■ Is a popular approach among teachers and educators.	■ Results in a superficial understanding of ethnic cultures. ■ Focuses on the lifestyles and artifacts of ethnic groups and reinforces stereotypes and misconceptions. ■ Mainstream criteria are used to select heroes and cultural elements for inclusion in the curriculum.
Additive	This approach consists of the addition of content, concepts, themes, and perspectives to the curriculum without changing its structure.	■ Adding the book *The Color Purple* to a literature unit without reconceptualizing the unit or giving the students the background knowledge to understand the book. ■ Adding a unit on the Japanese American internment to a U.S. history course without treating the Japanese in any other unit. ■ Leaving the core curriculum intact but adding an ethnic studies course, as an elective, that focuses on a specific ethnic group.	■ Makes it possible to add ethnic content to the curriculum without changing its structure, which requires substantial curriculum changes and staff development. ■ Can be implemented within the existing curriculum structure.	■ Reinforces the idea that ethnic history and culture are not integral parts of U.S. mainstream culture. ■ Students view ethnic groups from Anglocentric and Eurocentric perspectives. ■ Fails to help students understand how the dominant culture and ethnic cultures are interconnected and interrelated.

Source: Reprinted with the permission of James A. Banks from pp. 262–263 of James A. Banks, "Approaches to Multicultural Curriculum Reform," in James A. Banks & Cherry A. McGee Banks (Editors), *Multicultural Education: Issues and Perspectives* (6th edition, 2007, pp. 247–269). Hoboken, NJ: Wiley.

In developing multicultural units, teachers need to identify the key concept and generalizations associated with that concept. Specific activities can then be planned so that students have the evidence to draw the generalizations and understand the key concept.

Social Action Approach.　The **social action approach** incorporates all the elements of the transformation approach and also includes a cultural critique. Teaching units that use this approach incorporate a problem-solving process in which students make decisions and take actions related to the concept, issue, or problem being studied, following these steps:

1. Identify the problem or question (e.g., discrimination in our school).
2. Collect data related to the problem or question (e.g., what discrimination is, what causes discrimination, what examples are evident in our school).

APPROACH	DESCRIPTION	EXAMPLES	STRENGTHS	PROBLEMS
Transformation	The basic goals, structure, and nature of the curriculum are changed to enable students to view concepts, events, issues, problems, and themes from the perspectives of diverse cultural, ethnic, and racial groups.	■ A unit on the American Revolution describes the meaning of the revolution to Anglo revolutionaries, Anglo loyalists, African Americans, Indians, and the British. ■ A unit on 20th-century	■ Enables students to understand the complex ways in which diverse racial and cultural groups participated in the formation of U.S. society and culture. ■ Helps to reduce racial and ethnic encapsulation. ■ Enables diverse ethnic, racial, and religious groups to see their cultures, ethos, and perspectives in the school curriculum. ■ Gives students a balanced view of the nature and development of U.S. culture and society. ■ Helps to empower victimized racial, ethnic, and cultural groups.	■ The implementation of this approach requires substantial curriculum revision, in-service training, and the identification and development of materials written from the perspectives of various racial and cultural groups. ■ Staff development for the institutionalization of this approach must be continual and ongoing.
Social Action			■ Enables students to improve their thinking, value analysis, decision-making, and social-action skills. ■ Enables students to improve their data-gathering skills. ■ Helps students to develop a sense of political efficacy. ■ Helps students to improve their skills at working in groups.	■ Requires a considerable amount of curriculum planning and materials identification. ■ May be longer in duration than more traditional teaching units. ■ May focus on problems and issues considered controversial by some members of the school staff and citizens of the community. ■ Students may be able to take few meaningful actions that contribute to the resolution of the social issue or problem.

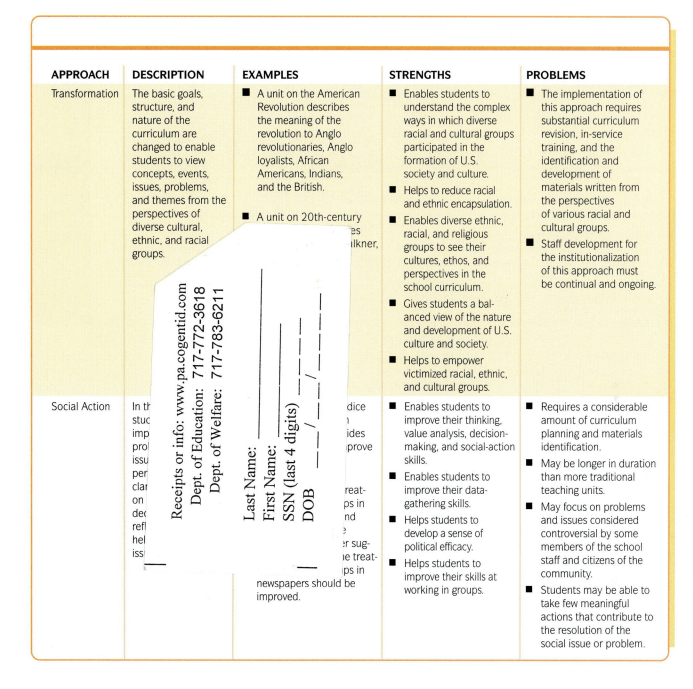

3. Conduct a value inquiry and analysis (i.e., students examine and reflect on their values, attitudes, and beliefs related to discrimination).

4. Make decisions and establish a plan of social action based on a synthesis of the knowledge obtained in step 2 and the values identified in step 3.

As a teacher, you will undoubtedly use all four approaches to multicultural education, with the goal of primarily employing the transformational and social action approaches. Tips for Teachers 4.2 presents general strategies for integrating content about cultural groups into the school curriculum. The curriculum should incorporate opportunities to foster student achievement and cultural competence as well as help students recognize, understand, and critique current social inequities (Ladson-Billings, 1995).

Tips FOR TEACHERS 4.2

GUIDELINES FOR TEACHING MULTICULTURAL CONTENT

- To teach cultural content, you need knowledge of cultural groups. Read books that survey the histories of cultural groups in the United States.

- Make sure that your room conveys positive images of various cultural groups (through bulletin boards, posters, literature, software, and so on).

- Plan time in which you and your students can learn about one another's cultural backgrounds.

- Be culturally conscious in selecting teaching materials. If the materials you use include stereotypes or present only one perspective, point out the limitations to the students.

- Use trade books, films, videotapes, websites, and recordings to supplement the textbook and to present more varied perspectives.

- Use literature to enrich students' understanding of cultural pluralism.

- Be sensitive to the development levels of your students when you select concepts, content, and activities. Use concrete, specific concepts and activities for students in early elementary grades. As students develop, focus on more abstract concepts and problem solving.

- Use group work to promote opportunities for student interaction and conversation.

- Make sure that not only classroom activities but also schoolwide activities (such as plays, sports, and clubs) are culturally integrated.

Linguistic Diversity and Second Language Acquisition

Linguistic diversity is not new in the United States, with its rich history of immigration. Today, as in the past, many students live in homes in which the primary language spoken is not English. This trend is increasing rather than decreasing. José is a good example of such a student. At the age of 4, he emigrated with his parents and three siblings from a rural community in Mexico to an urban Spanish-speaking community in Texas. His parents spoke only Spanish when they arrived. Although he has some exposure to English and his father is taking a night course to learn English, José entered school at age 5 with Spanish as his first language and only a limited knowledge of his second language, English. This same scenario is true of children who emigrate from Central and South American countries, Asian and Pacific Island countries, and eastern European countries.

The implications of this demography are that a growing number of students who enter school in the United States learn English as a second language in school. The teacher's knowledge of second language acquisition and general instructional guidelines can help make school a success for students like José. However, many teachers hold misconceptions about how to teach ELLs (Harper & de Jong, 2004). The four commonly held misconceptions outlined in Figure 4.1 can affect instruction in negative ways. As Harper and de Jong argue, "unless teachers address these misconceptions, their curriculum, instruction, and assessment practices will only partially meet the needs of ELLs in their classrooms and will only superficially include ELLs in mainstream classes" (p. 160).

Programs for Promoting Second Language Acquisition

The programs for ELLs vary tremendously from state to state and even from school to school within a district. Two broad categories of programs have been used in schools in the United States to promote second language acquisition (Ovando, Collier, & Combs, 2006): **English as a second language (ESL)** instruction and **bilingual education**. ESL generally has as its goal the acquisition of English, whereas the goal of bilingual education is to promote bilingualism or proficiency in both the first and second languages. "The most prominent characteristic that defines differences among programs in bilingual/ESL education is how much the primary language of the students is used for instruction" (Ovando et al., 2006, p. 35).

You will need to learn about programs that are available in your school and what your role is in the teaching of ELLs. In addition, you should know some other differences among programs, such as:

- Location—some instruction will take place in the general education classroom, whereas other instruction will be in a resource room

Go to **www.everythingesl.net** to find lesson plans and general teaching suggestions as well as a wealth of resources that will help ESL students feel welcome.

Misconceptions and Realities About the Teaching of English Language Learners

FIGURE 4.1

Misconception 1: Exposure and interaction will result in English language learning.

Reality: Although there are similarities in learning a first and a second language, there are differences as well. In addition to exposure and interaction, ELLs need guided practice and frequent opportunities to learn a second language in both oral and written modes.

Misconception 2: All ELLs learn English in the same way and at the same rate.

Reality: Individual differences in English acquisition occur even though there are some predictable stages of second language development. Many factors can influence different patterns and rates, including cultural differences, prior education in the first language, and whether the student was exposed to English orally first or in written form.

Misconception 3: Good teaching for native speakers is good teaching for ELLs.

Reality: Good teaching for native speakers is necessary but not sufficient for ELLs. Particularly at the secondary level, ELLs are often expected to have the prior knowledge, vocabulary, and reading and writing skills of their classmates in order to complete assignments and tests. Without adaptations and support, learning is difficult if not impossible.

Misconception 4: Effective instruction means nonverbal support.

Reality: Effective instruction means both verbal and nonverbal support. Providing students with visuals and physical prompts may be helpful, but students also need ample opportunity for formal and informal interactions with teachers, other school personnel, and their peers.

Source: Adapted from Harper, C., & de Jong, E. (2004). Misconceptions about teaching English-language learners. *Journal of Adolescent & Adult Literacy,* 48, 152–153. Copyright © 2004 by the International Reading Association.

- Staffing—some instruction is taught by the general education teacher, and other instruction is taught by an ESL specialist
- Duration—placement may be either full-time or part-time

You will also need to be familiar with the programs available in your school district so that you can articulate program possibilities with parents.

Instruction in English as a Second Language.   English as a second language (ESL) instruction uses English to teach students, with limited emphasis on maintaining or developing proficiency in the student's first language. Instruction may be given during a specified instructional time (with students receiving the rest of their instruction in general education classrooms), or it may be integrated into content-area instruction (as is the case of sheltered English).

Sheltered English is a type of ESL instruction in which the goal is to teach English language skills at the same time that students are learning content-area knowledge (Ovando et al., 2006). Typically reserved for students who have some working knowledge of English, sheltered English employs direct experiences, hands-on learning, and meaningful context for instruction. As you will read later in this chapter, many sheltered English techniques can be helpful to you in daily instruction of ELLs.

Schools often use an ESL model when the non-English-speaking students are from several language groups or there are too few students from a common language group to support a bilingual education model. The ESL teacher is usually considered a resource teacher in that he or she works daily, or at least several times a week, with groups of students or whole classes of students for a specified instructional time. An ESL teacher may work in a pull-out program or, more commonly, in an inclusion model. In addition to instructional duties, the ESL teacher is usually responsible for assessing the students' language proficiency in English and, depending on the language, in their first language.

Bilingual Education.   Bilingual education students may spend the entire day in classrooms designated as *bilingual classrooms.* These students are learning English and may be receiving content instruction in their first language, in English, or in both, according to their level of development in English. Frequently, bilingual education approaches are described as *transitional* or *maintenance,* depending on the degree to which the first language is developed and maintained.

The focus of **transitional bilingual education** is to help students shift from the home language to the dominant language. These programs initially provide content-area instruction in students' native language along with ESL instruction. Students transfer from these programs as soon as they are deemed sufficiently proficient in English to receive all academic instruction in English (Baca & Cervantes, 2004). The time taken for this transition from the students' first language to English varies, depending on the program (Ramirez & Merino, 1990). In programs in which literacy is taught in the first language, with other content taught in English, students may make the transition in 2 to 3 years. In other transition programs, at least 40% of the instruction is in the first language—including reading, language arts, math, and sometimes social studies or science—and students usually remain in the programs through fifth or sixth grade (Ramirez, 1992). These programs are sometimes referred to as **early-exit programs**, and concerns have been registered about limited time for learning English (usually 2 years) (Ovando, Collier, & Combs, 2003) and the remedial, segregated structure of some programs (Díaz-Rico, 2004).

When Gloria and Lidia, bilingual education teachers team teaching at Mission Way in southwest Arizona, were asked about their model of bilingual education, they described it as best fitting the transition model, with a relatively late transition to English (fourth to fifth grade). One of the reasons Gloria and Lidia chose to team teach was to better meet the needs of their students as they made the transition from skill and content instruction in Spanish to English. Gloria said,

> During grades 4 and 5, we transition the language of instruction to almost exclusively English. For us, the exception is reading and writing. In our literature-based reading program and writer's workshop, we continue to encourage the students to read some literature written in Spanish and to write some compositions in Spanish, although most instruction is in English. We also discuss the literature in Spanish. In this way, students do not lose those Spanish literacy skills that they have developed in the bilingual programs. We feel that this is important not only for them to stay connected to their home community, but also because being bilingual and biliterate are highly desired job skills.

Maintenance bilingual education, or **late-exit programs**, foster the students' first language and strengthen their sense of cultural identity while teaching the second language and culture (Ovando, Collier, & Combs, 2006). Maintenance programs typically provide native language content-area instruction throughout the elementary grades, with the amount of native language instruction decreasing as students progress through the program. This model values bilingualism and sees the learning of a second language as a positive addition for the students' cognitive development and life success. This model also places a strong emphasis on incorporating the students' culture and heritage into the instruction. A particularly compelling use of the maintenance bilingual model is in the education of Native Americans (Díaz-Rico & Weed, 2002) in which the goal is to increase the number of speakers of Native American languages and preserve their cultural and linguistic heritage (Reyhner, 1992).

Two-way bilingual programs have become an option for students learning English as a second language (Díaz-Rico, 2004). In two-way programs, half the students are native speakers of English and the other half speak another language, usually Spanish. Instruction is in English half the time and in Spanish the other half. The goal is for all students to become fully bilingual and biliterate.

Although much is to be learned about the efficacy of ESL and bilingual programs of all kinds, some recent summaries of research have underscored the importance of maintaining students' first language (Rolstad, Mahoney, & Glass, 2005; Slavin & Cheung, 2005). As a classroom teacher, you can help students bridge the gap from first to second language learning by first understanding how a second language is acquired.

Framework for Second Language Acquisition

Ellis (R. Ellis, 1985, 1994) provides a framework for second language acquisition that can guide you in making accommodations for students whose first language is not English. Ellis suggests that five interrelated factors govern the acquisition of a second language. Figure 4.2 depicts the relationships between these factors.

Situational Factors. The first factors in the framework are **situational factors**, which are related to the context or the situation (i.e., the learning environments) in which the second language learning occurs. Students learn the second language in multiple learning environments—from relatives, friends, and neighbors who speak English; through ESL or bilingual education programs at school; and from peers in the classroom and on the playground.

Environments such as these can provide both formal teaching and more natural opportunities to acquire language. When José's uncle explains the concept "scientist" in Spanish

Go to **www.thegateway.org** where you can find free detailed lesson plans for biligual lessons and other resources.

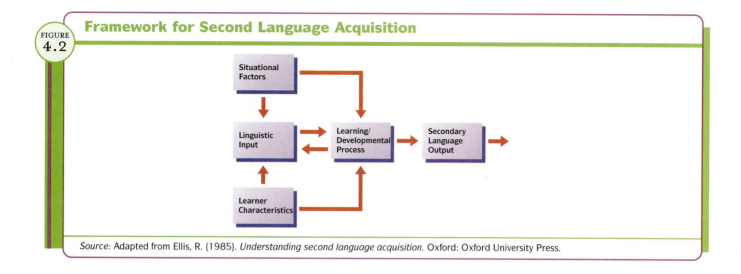

FIGURE 4.2 **Framework for Second Language Acquisition**

Source: Adapted from Ellis, R. (1985). *Understanding second language acquisition.* Oxford: Oxford University Press.

and then pairs it with English, he is providing formal instruction. On the other hand, the instruction is much more natural when José and his uncle converse about what happened in school and his uncle provides José with words in English when José is searching for the English word. One goal of both bilingual education and English as a second language (ESL) instruction is to create environments that are nonthreatening and in which students are willing to take risks and play with the language (Ovando, Collier, & Combs, 2006; Vaughn & Gersten, 1998). Kristina, the associate teacher interviewed at the beginning of this chapter, encourages students to play with the language by experimenting with sounds, words, and syntactic construction. She makes these opportunities for discovery by encouraging experimentation.

Another situational factor that promotes second language acquisition is an environment in which the students' first language and culture are respected and valued. The research consistently demonstrates that valuing students' first language is an important factor for student success (Carter & Chatfield, 1986; Lucas, Henze, & Donato, 1990; Thomas & Collier, 1997). One important aspect of valuing the students' language is learning about their community's funds of knowledge and language.

Linguistic Input.   The second factor in the framework, linguistic input, refers to input received when reading or listening to a second language. Comprehensible input is a key factor for success (Krashen, 1985). Input is made more comprehensible by a number of strategies, including the following:

- Selecting a topic of conversation that is familiar to students
- Creating a context for what is being discussed
- Using simpler sentence construction
- Repeating important phrases
- Incorporating the students' first language into the instruction
- Emphasizing key words to promote comprehensible input

When teaching linguistically diverse students, it is important to consider the linguistic input. Tips for Teachers 4.3 presents guidelines and ideas for making input more understandable.

Learner Characteristics.   The third factor affecting second language acquisition or output is learner characteristics. Relevant learner characteristics include the age at which students learn a second language, their aptitude for learning language, their purposes and degree of motivation for learning the second language, their self-confidence in language learning, and their learning strategies.

Another important variable is the degree of acquisition of proficiency in the first language. Cummins (1991), in a review of research, concluded that the better developed the students' proficiency and conceptual foundation in the first language, the more likely they were to develop similarly high levels of proficiency and conceptual ability in the second language.

Tips FOR TEACHERS 4.3

GUIDELINES FOR MAKING INPUT UNDERSTANDABLE FOR SECOND LANGUAGE LEARNERS

- Begin teaching new concepts by working from the students' current knowledge and incorporating the funds of knowledge from the students' community.

- Use demonstrations and gestures to augment oral communication.

- To the degree possible, create the context in which the concepts occur. For example, when teaching about shellfish, visit an aquarium, watch a film, or display shells in the classroom.

- Discuss connections between the concepts being taught and the students' home cultures.

- Encourage students to share the new vocabulary in their first language and incorporate the first language into instruction.

- If students share a common first language, pair more proficient second language learners with less proficient peers, and encourage students to discuss what they are learning.

- Highlight key words and phrases by repeating them and writing them.

- Use simple sentence constructions, particularly to present a new or difficult concept.

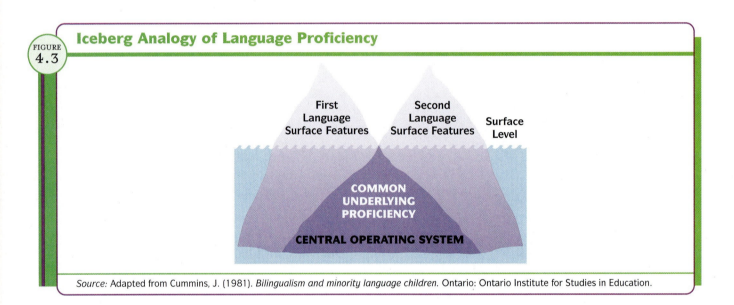

FIGURE 4.3

Iceberg Analogy of Language Proficiency

Source: Adapted from Cummins, J. (1981). *Bilingualism and minority language children.* Ontario: Ontario Institute for Studies in Education.

He has referred to this as the **common underlying proficiency**, using the analogy of an iceberg to explain this hypothesis and relationship between first and second language acquisition (see Figure 4.3) and why proficiency in the first language complements proficiency in the second language (Cummins, 1981). As shown in Figure 4.3, both languages have separate surface features, represented by separate icebergs. Below the surface and less visible, however, is the underlying proficiency common to both languages.

No matter which language the person is using, the thoughts that accompany the talking, reading, writing, and listening come from the same language core. One implication of this analogy is that individuals who are fluent in two languages have an advantage over monolingual individuals in that they have greater cognitive flexibility and a greater understanding of language.

The Learning and Developmental Process. The fourth factor addresses the learning and developmental process of second language acquisition and learning. Cummins (1984) suggested that students generally acquire competency in the **basic interpersonal communication skills (BICS)** before becoming competent in **cognitive academic language proficiency (CALP)**. The BICS, or **social language**, are the conversational competencies we develop with a second language—the greetings and small talk between peers that generally do not require much cognitive effort or social problem solving. The CALP, or **academic language**, by contrast, refers to the more cognitively demanding language skills required for the new learning that occurs in school. In general, BICS develop in a second language before CALP. Cummins (1981) suggested that it takes 1 to 2 years to develop BICS but 5 to 7 years to develop competence in CALP.

Although these guidelines have been shown to vary widely depending on situational factors, linguistic input, and learner characteristics, they do have implications for teachers in general education classrooms. You might assume that because students can converse easily with you in their second language, they are ready to learn new concepts, strategies, and skills in the second language. This is not necessarily the case. For example, when Hoang Hy Vinh entered Sarah Miles's third-grade class, Sarah immediately noticed that he conversed easily with other students and with her. Vinh had emigrated from Vietnam two years before and had begun learning English through the school's ESL program. His parents, who took English in a night course, felt that learning English was important for their economic and personal success in the United States. Still, Vietnamese was the primary language spoken in the home.

As Sarah got to know Vinh, she realized that although his conversational skills were strong enough for him to be comfortable in the classroom community, he was not yet proficient in academic tasks such as reading and writing in English. She also found that for him to learn new concepts in social studies and science she needed to provide a lot of context. Sarah incorporated an extended segment on farming communities into a thematic unit on California, for example, because Vinh and several other students came from other Asian and Mexican farming communities. From the school and public libraries, she checked out books and magazines about farming and rural life in Mexico, Vietnam, and other Asian countries. The students also visited a California market, as well as Asian and Mexican food markets. They compared the foods from the markets and learned how those foods were grown in the three communities. For Vinh and other students from other cultures who were in the process of acquiring English as a second language, providing the link to their cultures helped to give them a context in which to build both their language and their cognitive skills.

This is an example of the **context-embedded communication and instruction** that Cummins (1981) and others (Chamot & O'Malley, 1994; Gersten & Jiménez, 1998; Reyes & Bos, 1998; Ruiz, Garcia, & Figueroa, 1996) recommend as facilitating second language learning. "A good teacher incorporates both social (BICS) and academic (CALP) language into every lesson" (Ovando, Collier, & Combs, 2006, p. 129).

Secondary Language Output.   The fifth factor in the framework is **secondary language output**. Students may understand a language (listening and reading) but not be proficient in producing the language (speaking and writing). An important part of developing speaking proficiency is having the opportunity to engage in meaningful oral exchanges (in the classroom and the community) and to experiment with oral and written language in nonthreatening environments. Swain (1986) emphasized that not only comprehensible input but also opportunities for students to develop **comprehensible output** by oral practice with the language are important for acquiring a second language. Feedback from listeners and from self-monitoring enables second language speakers to develop and fine-tune their oral language.

An important and noteworthy aspect of secondary language output is that receptive language skills typically develop before expressive language skills. It has been well documented that second language learners experience a **silent or nonverbal period** (Ervin-Tripp, 1974; Hakuta, 1974), during which they absorb information and language that they cannot demonstrate or do not yet feel comfortable demonstrating (Coelho, 1994).

According to Ellis's framework for second language acquisition, what five factors will influence this student's acquisition of English? What kinds of instructional activities for second language acquisition might you recommend for this student based on effectiveness research?

Language Variation and Dialect

Language variation, which refers to the fact that language varies from place to place and from group to group, usually relates to the characteristics of groups of people (such as geographical region, social class, ethnic and cultural backgrounds, age, and gender). **Dialect** generally refers to language variations associated with a regional or social group of people. All English speakers use a dialect or variation of the English language. Think for a moment. Do you use the term *pop, soda, soda pop, tonic,* or some other term to label this popular type of drink? The answer depends on your dialect, which most likely relates to where you live and your cultural background. Dialect is also affected by age; for example, use of the term *icebox* rather than *refrigerator* is more evident in older people who grew up in times when iceboxes were used.

A wide range of dialects exists in the United States (Diaz-Rico, 2004). However, in general, there are four dialects that most people recognize: "(1) New York City, (2) New England, (3) the South, and (4) everyone else" (p. 326). Some other dialects include Louisiana French Creole and Hawaiian Creole, to name a few.

Language variation or dialects vary in several ways. Regional dialects tend to be distinguished by pronunciation and vocabulary features, whereas social and cultural dialects show variation not only in these areas but also in grammatical usage. Dialects also reflect conversation patterns. In a good, satisfying conversation in some speech communities, for example, speakers overlap one another's talk. In other communities, the listener waits for a break to enter a conversation, and the speaker is likely to stop talking when someone else starts speaking.

African American Vernacular English (AAVE) is a dialect used by some African Americans. It is the most prevalent native English vernacular dialect in the United States. As with any other language or dialect, there is great language variation among speakers of AAVE. Because of African Americans' historical status as an oppressed and involuntary minority, there has been a tendency to consider AAVE not as a valid language system but rather as random errors (Billings, 2005; Labov, Cohen, Robins, & Lewis, 1968). Like any other language, however, AAVE has an internally consistent linguistic infrastructure and set of grammar rules (Center for Applied Linguistics, 2008; Sealey-Ruiz, 2005).

To be effective in teaching students with dialects other than your own, you need to expand your knowledge about dialects and how they affect learning (Adger, Wolfram, & Christian, 2007). In teaching Standard American English to students who speak a dialect other than Standard English, you should help them understand the systematic differences between the standard and their own. Recognize that **Standard English Language Learners (SELLs)** approach learning through differences in language, not deficits (LeMoine, 2001). See Tips for Teachers 4.4 for recommendations for working with students with dialects.

Historical Perspective on ESL Instruction and Bilingual Education

From the early 19th century to approximately the 1960s, a dominant belief was that bilingualism was detrimental to cognitive development and academic learning. Diaz (1983) summarized the research from before 1962, which built the case for bilingualism as a "language handicap." Researchers found that bilingual children had more limited vocabularies, more deficient articulation, and more grammatical errors than monolingual students. One interpretation was that bilingualism caused "linguistic confusion," which affected students' cognitive ability and

Tips FOR TEACHERS 4.4

STRATEGIES FOR WORKING WITH STUDENTS WITH DIALECTS

1. Teach students pride in their community's dialect.

2. Emphasize that the ability to communicate is more important than the sound of one's accent.

3. Tell students that learning to switch from formal English to informal, and from Standard English to colloquial usages, is part of learning English.

Source: Díaz-Rico, L. (2004). *Teaching English learners: Strategies and methods.* Boston: Allyn & Bacon, p. 336.

academic performance. This research, overall, had many flaws. Bilingual and monolingual groups were not matched for other important variables such as socioeconomic status, for example, and tests for intellectual functioning and learning of bilingual students generally were conducted in English, not in the first or more dominant language.

In 1962, a classic study was published that is now considered the turning point in the history of the relationship between bilingualism and cognition (Peal & Lambert, 1962). This research broke new territory in two respects: it overcame many methodological deficiencies, and it found that bilingualism has cognitive advantages over monolingualism. Researchers Peal and Lambert concluded that bilingualism provides greater cognitive flexibility, greater ability to think more abstractly, and greater ability to form concepts.

Subsequent research has shown that higher degrees of bilingualism are correlated with increased cognitive abilities in such areas as creativity, knowledge of how language works (*metalinguistics*), concept formation, and cognitive flexibility (Galambos & Goldin-Meadow, 1990; Nieto, 1992; Ovando & Collier, 1998; Skutnabb-Kangas, 1981). Bilingual education and teaching **English as a second language (ESL)** for culturally and linguistically diverse students have evolved through the years. Figure 4.4 shows the chronology of this evolution in the United States.

FIGURE 4.4

Developments in Second Language and Bilingual Education in the United States

Before 1914	Many community schools existed to teach a specific language, such as German. Saturday classes were common.
1918	World War I brought about reactions against Germany and a resurgence of patriotic feeling; use of "English only" in schools was legislated in many states.
1945	World War II led to realization of need for knowledge of foreign languages; teaching of foreign languages in schools was encouraged.
1958	Soviet launching of *Sputnik* shocked U.S. leaders, who then funded schools' efforts to promote key subject areas, including foreign languages.
1963	Dade County, Florida, initiated bilingual programs for Spanish-speaking Cuban children coming to Miami.
1964	Civil Rights Act forbade language-based discrimination.
1968	Bilingual Education Act: Title VII of the Elementary and Secondary Education Act promoted bilingual programs in the schools.
1971	Massachusetts Bilingual Education Act: A law mandating bilingual education for non-English-speaking children; Massachusetts was the first state; other states followed.
1974	Bilingual Education Reform Act: Updated the 1968 law; mandated language instruction; added study of history and culture in bilingual programs.
1974	U.S. Supreme Court decision in *Lau v. Nichols* gave non-English-speaking students the legal right to instruction that enables them to participate in education process, and to bilingual instruction, as part of "equal educational opportunity."
1975	The U.S. Department of Education developed guidelines that specified approaches, methods, and procedures for educating students with limited proficiency in English. These Lau Remedies were not enacted.
1981	Senator S. I. Hayakawa first introduced a constitutional amendment to declare English the official language of the United States. (It was defeated.)
1981	*Castenada v. Pickard* established a framework for determining whether school districts are in compliance with *Lau v. Nichols* decision. The framework for compliance included: Theory—Is the program based on sound theory? Implementation—Does the district have an implementation plan? Results—What kinds of results does the district have for implementing the program?
1984	California voters passed a bill to publish ballots and other election material in English only.
1985	U.S. Secretary of Education William Bennett spoke out against federal bilingual education programs.
1994	Reauthorization of the Bilingual Education Act (Title VII of the Improving American Schools Act, formerly Elementary and Secondary Education Act). In this reauthorization, bilingualism was reconceptualized as a valuable national resource. Bilingual programs are no longer defined by types: maintenance, transitional, and immersion.
1994	Reauthorization of Improving American Schools Act resulted in language-minority students being eligible to receive Title I services, even if the source of disadvantage is determined to be language.
1998	The California state legislature passed the English for the Children Initiative that restricts the programs in which ELL students can participate, including the number of years to several years only and the types of programs to ESL programs.
1999	Proposition 227 passed in California eliminating bilingual education programs.
2001	The Elementary and Secondary Education Act (ESEA) was reauthorized as the No Child Left Behind Act.
2006	The National Literacy Panel Report reviewing quantitative and qualitative research on literacy development of language-minority students.

Sources: Adapted from Tiedt, P. L. & Tiedt, I. M. (2005). *Multicultural teaching: A handbook of activities, information, and resources* (7th ed., pp. 16–20). Boston: Allyn & Bacon; August, D., & Shanahan, T. (2006). Developing literacy in second-language learners: Report of the National Literacy Panel on Language-Minority Children and Youth. Mahwah, NJ: Erlbaum; also see http://ourworld.compuserve.com for links to state laws regarding English-only policies.

What is interesting about this chronology is the way bilingualism has been tied to assimilation into American culture and therefore linked to political policy. Bilingualism in our schools and communities dates back to the early colonies. It was common among both the working and the educated classes for many official documents to be published in German and French as well as English. By the late 1800s, however, language restrictions were being placed on schools. Under strong political pressures to assimilate immigrants, bilingual education was virtually eradicated by the 1930s. After World War II, students from minority cultures were described as "culturally deprived" and "linguistically disabled."

In the early 1960s, however, bilingual education was reborn in Dade County, Florida, as Cuban immigrants requested bilingual schooling for their children. Programs were developed throughout the United States, under the authority of the Bilingual Education Act passed (as Title VII of the Elementary and Secondary Education Act) in 1968. Based on the law, suits were brought to ensure better services for students with cultural and linguistic diversities. The most noted case is *Lau v. Nichols,* in which the U.S. Supreme Court ruled that equal treatment is not merely providing students with the same facilities, textbooks, teachers, and curriculum when students do not understand English.

Although the Bilingual Education Act and the Civil Rights Act and their rules and regulations promoted equal access and bilingual education, political developments have moved the country back toward an assimilation philosophy. In 1981, Senator S. I. Hayakawa introduced a constitutional amendment to declare English the official language of the United States. This amendment was defeated, but a growing number of states have passed what has been referred to as "English only" legislation. In 2002, Congress repealed the Bilingual Education Act and subsumed the teaching of ELLs under the umbrella of No Child Left Behind (NCLB). The new law, Title II, the English Language Acquisition, Language Enhancement, and Academic Achievement Act places less emphasis on bilingual education, bilingualism, and biliteracy and greater emphasis on English language learning. Moreover, NCLB mandates the inclusion of ELLs in reporting of adequate yearly progress (AYP) as determined largely on performance on standardized tests.

These changes have resulted in continued controversy about the role of bilingual education in schools in the United States (Crawford, 2004). Those who promote bilingual education offer the following justifications:

- It is the best way to attain the maximum cognitive development of ELL students.
- It is a means of achieving equal educational opportunity.
- It offers a means of easing the transition into the dominant language and culture.
- It is an approach to educational reform.
- It is a means of promoting positive interethnic relations.
- It is a wise economic investment to help ELL students become maximally productive in adult life for the benefit of themselves and society (Baca & Cervantes, 2004).

The forthcoming reauthorization of No Child Left Behind will no doubt have an impact on the immediate future of bilingual education in the United States.

Assessment of Students with Cultural and Linguistic Differences

Although progress has been made in many areas of teaching students with cultural and linguistic differences, the one area still in need of development is assessment (Hurley & Tinajero, 2001; Klingner, 2003; Wagner, Francis, & Morris, 2005). As the Report of the National Literacy Panel on Language-Minority Children and Youth points out, assessment of diverse learners is complex and difficult (Garcia, McKoon, & August, 2006). The IDEIA 2004 demonstrates a growing awareness of the needs of students from different language backgrounds by mandating that assessments for special education services be conducted in the language and form that is most familiar to the student. Nonetheless, the issue of assessment is still a matter of discussion.

Assessment is particularly controversial with respect to mandated standardized tests required by No Child Left Behind (NCLB) and placement into special education (Abedi, 2002; Coltrane, 2002). Such tests may be culturally incompatible for some students and may be linguistically impossible for students who have not reached a level of English academic language development consistent with the examination (Hoover & Barletta, 2008). The controversy about how best to

Go to the National Association for Bilingual Education (NABE) website at **www.nabe.org** to find a set of principles for consideration in the reauthorization of NCLB.

include students with such differences in large-scale, standardized tests has escalated in recent years due to the standards-based instruction and assessment requirements of the NCLB.

Abedi and Dietel (2004) of the National Center for Research on Evaluation, Standards, and Student Testing (CRESST) identify four reasons why standardized tests pose challenges for ELLs:

1. *Historically low ELL performance and slow improvements.* State tests show that ELL students' school performance is far below that of other students, oftentimes 20 to 30 percentage points, and usually shows little improvement over the years.
2. *Measurement accuracy.* CRESST research shows that the language demands of tests negatively influence accurate measurement of ELL performance. For the ELL student, tests measure both achievement *and* language ability.
3. *Instability of the ELL student subgroup.* The goal of redesignating high-performing ELL students as language-proficient students causes ELL high achievers to exit the ELL subgroup. The consequence is downward pressure on ELL test scores, worsened by the addition of new ELL students, who are typically low achieving.
4. *Factors outside of a school's control.* CRESST research shows substantial nonschool (e.g., home, community, and other contextual) effects on student learning even within ELL subgroups. Schools are therefore unable to control all factors related to student achievement. (p. 1)

Chamberlain (2005) points out that culture can also affect student performance on standardized tests. In particular, the content of the tests may include items that assume cultural knowledge and values that are unfamiliar to students. Moreover, the format and procedures for taking standardized tests may be new for students who have not been taught test-taking skills. As mentioned earlier in this chapter, the disproportionate representation of minority students in special education is a concern. Although many factors may affect inappropriate student placement in special education, assessment does play a key role (Demmert, 2005; Salend & Duhaney, 2004). It is often difficult for teachers, and in some cases experts in assessment, to discriminate between learning problems and language or cultural differences (Chamberlain, 2005; Hoover & Barletta, 2008). However, becoming aware of the potential influence of language and culture on formal and informal assessment is a necessary first step. Ongoing professional development and consultation with colleagues with expertise in assessing diverse students are also important.

The role of the classroom teacher in preparing students for standardized tests is pivotal. It is important for you to learn the testing requirements for the diverse students in your state and possible accommodations that are allowable. Whether considering your role in administering standardized tests, interpreting test scores, or selecting and administering classroom assessment tools, principles of **culturally responsive assessment (CRA)** are vitally important. CRA is actually a collection of approaches that promote nondiscriminatory assessment practices (Cartledge et al., 2009). CRA is especially important in the monitoring of student progress that is recommended in RTI models (Fuchs, Stecker, & Fuchs, 2008) and in the research on effective instruction for ELLs (Chamot & O'Malley, 1994). Tips for Teachers 4.5 provides suggestions for CRA.

Tips FOR Teachers 4.5

IMPLEMENTING CULTURALLY RESPONSIVE ASSESSMENT

- Consider the testing environment and how it relates to students' prior experiences.

- Keep students' level of language proficiency in mind.

- Determine students' prior opportunities to learn the skill or concept.

- Implement appropriate accommodations (e.g., dictionary use, administration in first language, extended time).

- Use a variety of authentic assessments (e.g., checklists, performance tasks, group assessment).

- Align assessment with regular instruction and intensive interventions.

- Provide specific and frequent feedback.

- Involve students and families as active participants in the assessment process.

Sources: Based on Barone, D. M. & Xu, S. H. (2008). *Literacy instruction for English language learners pre-k–12.* New York: Guilford; and Cartledge, G., Gardner, R., & Ford, D. Y. (2009). *Diverse learners with exceptionalities: Culturally responsive teaching in the inclusive classroom.* Upper Saddle River, NJ: Merrill/Pearson Education.

Instructional Guidelines and Accommodations for Diverse Students

As a teacher, you will have students from many cultures and students who are in the process of acquiring English as a second language or second dialect. You may or may not be familiar with the culture and language of these students. Moreover, their parents' views about schooling and the roles and responsibilities of parents and teachers (Meyer, Bevan-Brown, Harry, & Sapon-Shevin, 2005), as well as their own experience in schools in the United States and elsewhere, may be very different from your own. It will be your responsibility to help all students feel comfortable in your class and to learn and to reach out to parents in culturally sensitive ways. To accomplish this you can use culturally responsive teaching and best practices in teaching ELLs.

Culturally Responsive Teaching

To promote learning, you should incorporate students' language and culture into the curriculum, demonstrate that you value their culture and language, have high expectations for all of your students, and make accommodations so that they can learn successfully. **Culturally responsive teaching (CRT)** involves teachers who, "recognize the differences between their students and themselves and strive to become nonjudgmental" (Cartledge, Gardner, & Ford, 2009, p. 18).

Research into the characteristics of effective teachers of students with cultural and linguistic diversities (Chamot, 1998; Garcia, 1991; Gersten, Marks, Keating, & Baker, 1998; Graves, Gersten, & Haager, 2004; Ladson-Billings, 1995; Tikunoff, 1983) indicates that such teachers

- Have high expectations of their students and believe that all students are capable of academic success.
- See themselves as members of the community and see teaching as a way to give back to the community.
- Display confidence in their ability to be successful with students who are culturally and linguistically diverse.
- Provide explicit instruction to monitor students' progress, and provide immediate feedback.
- Integrate the students' native language and dialect, culture, and community into classroom activities to make input more relevant and comprehensible, to build trust and self-esteem, and to promote cultural diversity and cultural pluralism.
- Use curriculum and teaching strategies that promote coherence, relevance, progression, and continuity.
- Structure opportunities for students to use English.
- Challenge their students and teach higher-order thinking.

Throughout this chapter we have emphasized the importance of understanding the language and culture of your students. Involving the parents of culturally and linguistically diverse students in their children's education is the key to CRT (Edwards, 2004; Hiatt-Michael, 2007). Most parents want the very best for their children. However, some teachers may think that parents are not interested in their child's education because they do not get involved in school functions, parent conferences, or helping their child with homework. There are many reasons parents do not get involved in traditional ways:

- Some parents do not feel comfortable in schools and are fearful of discrimination and disrespect.
- Others are not comfortable with the English language in either speaking or writing.
- Others may come from cultures in which the teacher has the responsibility of formal schooling and parents customarily do not get involved.
- Still others may have been educated in another system or might not have had the opportunity for schooling at all.

Tips for Teachers 4.6 offers general suggestions for teachers in working with parents from diverse cultural and linguistic backgrounds.

PEARSON
myeducationlab

Go to the Building Teaching Skills and Dispositions section of Topic 4: Cultural and Linguistic Diversity in the MyEducationLab for your course and complete the activity entitled *Culturally Responsive Instruction*.

Tips FOR TEACHERS 4.6

WORKING WITH PARENTS FROM DIVERSE BACKGROUNDS

- Be inviting and welcoming.

- Learn the correct pronunciation of the child's first name and of the family name, and learn a few words of the child's native language.

- When preparing your classroom and curriculum, make certain that the heritage of your students is reflected.

- Explore the best ways to communicate with parents.

- Do not talk down to parents; provide them with the respect you would expect as a parent.

- Enlist the support of a translator or encourage parents to bring a translator or person who can provide support to parent conferences.

- Do your best to provide written communication in the parents' native language.

- Interview parents to determine how they can be a resource at home or at school. All parents have time, treasure, or talent (funds of knowledge) to share in large or small ways.

Best Practices in English Language Learning

A growing body of research is beginning to yield information about best practices in teaching ELLs (Linan-Thompson & Vaughn, 2007). In recent years several summaries and syntheses of research have provided educators with important guidelines for instruction. Across these summaries several consistent themes are echoed: encourage strategic use of first language (Gersten & Baker, 2000; August, Carlo, Dressler, & Snow, 2005; August & Shanahan, 2006), build vocabulary with first language as a foundation (Fitzgerald, 1995; Gersten & Baker, 2000; August et al., 2005; August & Shanahan, 2006), focus on meaning (Fitzgerald, 1995; Gersten & Baker, 2000; August et al., 2005; August & Shanahan, 2006), and provide explicit skill instruction (August & Hakuta, 1997).

Encourage Strategic Use of First Language. Many educators suggest that students should be encouraged to continue to develop proficiency in their first language even if it is not formally supported through bilingual education (e.g., Baker, 1993; Cummins, 1989; Ovando, Collier, & Combs, 2006). To promote this, teachers can do the following:

- Encourage students to use their first language around school.
- Provide opportunities for students from the same language group to communicate with one another in their first language (e.g., in cooperative learning groups, during informal discussions).
- Recruit people who can tutor students in their first language.
- Provide, in classrooms and the school library, books written in various languages.
- Incorporate greetings and information in various languages in newsletters and other official school communications (Cummins, 1989).

For online programs that promote proficiency for culturally and linguistically diverse learners, see TechTips.

Build Vocabulary with First Language as a Foundation. One way to teach vocabulary to ELLs is through cognates. Cognates are words in different languages that sound alike (homophones) or that look alike (homographs) and have roughly or exactly the same meaning. Cognates are very helpful when learning a new language because they make the process a little friendlier. We can say that cognates are "good friends." For example, words that end in *-ción* in Spanish tend to have cognates that end in *-tion* in English; *nación* means "nation," and *constitución* means "constitution." With all of these words looking and sounding alike, you wonder why you don't speak four or five languages. This seems like a breeze, right? Wrong! Beware of *false cognates,* or "false friends." The term was first used by Koessler and Derocquigny in their 1928 book *Les faux amis ou les trahisons du vocabulaire anglais.* The title itself contains a false cognate and a true cognate: *trahisons* is not "treason" but "betrayal," and *vocabulaire* is "vocabulary" (Bello, 2007). Figure 4.5 provides samples of homographs, cognates, and false

TechTIPS

SOFTWARE PROGRAMS AND WEB RESOURCES FOR CULTURALLY AND LINGUISTICALLY DIVERSE LEARNERS

The array of software programs and resources for culturally and linguistically diverse learners keeps growing as the ELL population continues to grow. To help students and teachers with teaching and learning, try the following:

ZipZoom Into English by Scholastic
▶ (http://teacher.scholastic.com/products/zipzoom/overview.htm)
provides teachers and children, K–3, research-based programs that will help children achieve success in mastering English as their second language using a combination of teacher instruction, independent practice, and an interactive software component.

A + RISE: Research-based Instructional Strategies by A-Rise
▶ (http://www.arisek12.com/index.php/site/)
is designed for teachers of K–12 ELLs and provides teachers with more than 70 strategy cards that will show them how to work with ELLs of all ages and at all levels.

Little Explorers Picture Dictionary by Enchanted Learning Software
▶ (www.enchantedlearning.com/Home.html)
has more than 2,400 items in many different collections from English to Portuguese, French, Dutch, German, Italian, Japanese, and more. Many of the pictures link to explanatory text, diagrams, and activities.

In addition to these programs, you might check out the following web resources for dictionaries and translations in various languages:

• www.word2word.com/dictionary.html

• www.babelfish.altavista.com

• http://translation.langenberg.com

• www.freetranslation.com

When using online translators, just be aware that word-to-word translations of English may not be accurate because different languages have different grammatical structures.

FIGURE 4.5

Homographs, Cognates, and False Cognates

Here are some exact Spanish–English homographs:

atlas	atlas
popular	popular
hospital	hospital
metal	metal
fatal	fatal
hotel	hotel
actor	actor

There are many more words that, although not spelled exactly the same, are still understandable:

ácido	acid
alfabeto	alphabet
igual	equal
familia	family
plástico	plastic

Here are some common Spanish–English false cognates:

• *Introducir* means to introduce into, to bring in, to place; to introduce friends, you will need to use *presentar.*

• You will be very embarrassed if you use *embarazada* in the wrong context; it means pregnant, as in "with child." Try *avergonzada/o* for embarrassed instead.

• *Delito* is not delightful; it is a crime. Use *delicia* or *encanto.*

Here are some tips on using cognates in a multicultural or foreign language classroom:

• Take advantage of the students' prior knowledge of language.

• Ask questions like "Does that sound/look like a word in Spanish/English?"

• Use the cognates in different contexts to facilitate understanding.

• Point out the homographic cognates to LEP students.

• Allow the students to repeat and get used to the homophonic cognates (*peace—paz, pleasure—placer*).

• Use words with the same roots to aid in learning others (*appear, disappear—aparecer, desaparecer*).

• Make generalizations about grammatical differences and similarities between the languages.

• Get the students to talk about words and language so that they are more aware of what they know.

• Create a wall of cognates and/or false cognates.

• Use cognates to introduce science lessons (e.g., biology prefixes and roots such as *epi, dermis, itis, geo,* and *lympho*).

• Use cognates to introduce lessons about (language) history, such as words that came into English during the Norman period (French and Latin terms) or Germanic (Anglo-Saxon terms) and the differences between synonyms: *insane/crazy, autumn/fall.*

Source: Bello, M. (2007). Using cognates. In S. Vaughn, C. S. Bos, & J. S. Schumm, *Teaching students who are exceptional, diverse, and at risk in the general education classroom* (4th ed., p. 286). Boston: Allyn & Bacon.

cognates. In addition to cognates, another effective strategy for teaching vocabulary is to focus on meaning.

Focus on Meaning. Students who are acquiring English as a second language are focusing their attention not only on learning content and vocabulary but also on learning English. Depending on their level of language development, meaning is accessed in different ways. Following are stages of second language development related to learning in content classes:

- *Low-beginning.* Students depend on gestures, facial expressions, objects, pictures, a phrase dictionary, and often a translator to understand or be understood. Occasionally, students comprehend words or phrases.
- *Mid-beginning.* Students begin to comprehend more, but only when the speaker provides gestural clues, speaks slowly, and uses concrete referents and repetitions. Students speak seldom and haltingly, show some recognition of written segments, and may be able to write short utterances.
- *High-beginning to low-intermediate.* Students comprehend more, but with difficulty. Students speak in an attempt to meet basic needs but remain hesitant and make frequent errors in grammar, vocabulary, and pronunciation. Students can read very simple text and can write a little (but writing is restricted in grammatical structure and vocabulary).
- *Mid-intermediate.* Students may experience a dramatic increase in vocabulary recognition, but idioms and more advanced vocabulary remain difficult. Students often know what they want to say but grope for acceptable words and phrases. Errors in grammar, vocabulary, and pronunciation are frequent. Students can read text that is more difficult but still concrete and can write with greater ease than before.
- *High-intermediate to low-advanced.* Students begin to comprehend substantial parts of normal conversation but often require repetitions, particularly with academic discourse. Students are gaining confidence in speaking ability; errors are common but less frequent. Students can read and write text that contains more complex vocabulary and structures than before but experience difficulty with abstract language.
- *Mid-advanced.* Students comprehend much conversational and academic discourse spoken at normal rates but sometimes require repetition. Speech is more fluent and meaning is generally clear, but occasional errors occur. Students read and write with less difficulty materials commensurate with their cognitive development but demonstrate some problems in grasping intended meaning.
- *High-advanced.* Students comprehend normal conversation and academic discourse with little difficulty. Most idioms are understood. Students speak fluently in most situations with few errors. Students read and write both concrete and abstract materials and are able to manipulate the language with relative ease (Richard-Amato & Snow, 1992).

Although planning for culturally and linguistically diverse students takes some creative thinking and modifications of the curriculum, these students will broaden both your horizons and those of the class. In your planning, be sure to provide ample time for students to engage in meaningful conversations about topics related to language and culture. Tips for Teachers 4.7 will assist you in your planning.

See the 60-Second Lesson for a quick overview of how to teach a concept to second language learners.

60 Second LESSON

TEACHING A CONCEPT TO SECOND LANGUAGE LEARNERS

When students do not understand a concept, use one or more of the following strategies:

- Draw a picture.
- Have students with the same first language explain it in that language.

- Reexplain, but simplify the language.
- Demonstrate it.
- Provide examples and, if necessary, nonexamples (i.e., use of nonexamples is typical language used in teaching concepts).

Tips FOR TEACHERS 4.7

STRATEGIES FOR PROMOTING CONTENT AND SECOND LANGUAGE LEARNING IN GENERAL EDUCATION CLASSES

Beginning to Mid-Intermediate Proficiency Level

- Provide a supportive environment in which help is readily available to second language learners.

- Establish consistent patterns and routines in the classroom.

- Use gestures, visuals, and demonstrations to present concepts.

- Connect content to students' home cultures.

- Simplify grammar and vocabulary.

- Slow the pace of presentation, enunciate clearly, and emphasize key concepts through gesture, facial expression, intonation, and repetition.

- Record your lectures or talks on tape, and make them available for students.

- Make copies of your notes, or have another student take notes, so that second language learners can concentrate on listening.

- Build in redundancy by restating the concept in a simpler form, providing examples, and giving direct definitions.

- Extend wait time so that second language learners have time to volunteer.

- Avoid forcing second language learners to speak.

- Arrange cooperative learning so that students with the same first language work together.

- Encourage students to use their second language in informal conversations.

- Whenever possible, use tutors who speak the native language of the second language learners.

- Alter criteria for grading.

High-Intermediate to Advanced Proficiency Level

- Add contextual support to your lesson (e.g., advance organizer, study guides, glossaries, videos/films).

- Take into account the linguistic demands of the content.

- Provide opportunities for students to write in the content area.

- Provide opportunities for second language learners to practice critical thinking skills.

- Coach second language learners in appropriate learning strategies for mastering content.

PEARSON
myeducationlab

Go to the Assignments and Activities section of Topic 4: Cultural and Linguistic Diversity in the MyEducationLab for your course and complete the activity entitled *Cultural, Linguistic, and Other Factors That Influence Participation.*

Provide Explict Skill Instruction.   At the beginning of this chapter you read about Kristina and her class of 27 English language learners. Kristina quickly learned that her students not only had a range of English language proficiency, but also a range of prior schooling experiences. She also learned that what she learned in her teacher preparation program about **explicit instruction** was highly relevant to her classroom situation. Linan-Thompson and Vaughn (2007) define explicit instruction as "task-specific, teacher-led instruction that overtly demonstrates a task and can be used to teach students both basic and higher-order reading skills" (p. 6). Kristina realized that the principles of explicit instruction are also applicable when teaching skills in other content areas such as map reading in social studies, computation in mathematics, and experiments in science.

Think about the last time you were trying to learn a new skill. What helped you to learn the skill? Chances are you had a clear idea of what you needed to learn, why you needed to learn it, and steps in how to master the skill. That's explicit instruction. Explicit instruction of a skill begins with a description of what skill is to be learned and why. If necessary, specific instruction in relevant vocabulary helps teacher and student on the same page and to foster understanding of the skill to be learned. The teacher then demonstrates or models the skill, breaking it down into steps if needed. A demonstration is followed by guided practice where the teacher provides support and re-explanations as needed. Finally, the student tries the new skill through independent practice. As Kristina put it, "When I use explicit instruction, my students catch on. Sure, some students need more practice than others. It's so exciting when they 'get it'!" As you read about the instruction activities, strategies, and methods included in this book, think about how you can apply principles of explicit instruction in your planning.

Summary

- The demographics of our nation and schools are changing, and the number of students with cultural and linguistic diversities is increasing. The macroculture represents the dominant culture of the United States; the microcultures represent the students' home cultures. Learning about your students' home cultures and communities and integrating those cultures and communities into the curriculum is important to help them succeed in school and beyond.

- The goal of multicultural education is to change the structure of schools so that students from different cultural groups have an equal chance to achieve in school. Dimensions of multicultural education include content integration, knowledge construction, prejudice reduction, equity pedagogy, and an empowering school culture.

- When teaching students who are second language learners, it is important to keep in mind individual differences including prior educational experiences in the first language, needs for adaptation, and needs for verbal and nonverbal support.

- Assessment of diverse learners is complex and difficult. Culturally responsive assessment can facilitate fair and accurate assessment of students as they progress in learning skills and concepts.

- Culturally responsive teaching and use of best instructional practices can facilitate learning for students who are second language learners. Best instructional practices include strategic use of a first language, building vocabulary with first language as a foundation, focus on meaning, and providing explicit skills instruction.

Think and Apply

1. Now that you have read Chapter 4, think about the interview with Kristina Zayas-Bazan. What questions do you have for her about strategies for working with students who are culturally and linguistically diverse? Make a list of the questions and then ask them of an ESL or bilingual education teacher.

2. Visit a school known for its positive emphasis on multicultural education. Watch for evidence of cultural integration and an empowering school culture. Observe a lesson to see how the teacher builds on the students' cultural diversity.

3. Select a unit you have taught or plan to teach. Review it for its focus on multicultural perspectives. Then, using one of the four approaches to multicultural education (contributions, additive, transformation, social action), modify the unit to include a stronger multicultural emphasis.

PEARSON myeducationlab

Now go to Topic 4: Cultural and Linguistic Diversity in the MyEducationLab (www.myeducationlab.com) for your course where you can:

- Find learning outcomes for this topic along with the national standards that connect to these outcomes.

- Complete Assignments and Activities that can help you more deeply understand the chapter content.

- Examine challenging situations and cases presented in the IRIS Center Resources.

- Apply and practice your understanding of the core teaching skills identified in the chapter with Building Teaching Skills and Dispositions learning units.

Promoting Social Acceptance and Managing Student Behavior

CHAPTER 5

FOCUS QUESTIONS

1. How can you establish a classroom climate that promotes appropriate behaviors and acceptance of all students?

2. What are procedures you can take to nurture your students in developing positive self-concepts?

3. How can you promote acceptance of students with disabilities in your classroom?

4. What factors should you consider in teaching students from diverse cultural and linguistic backgrounds?

5. What are some universal strategies for managing student behavior?

6. What is positive behavior support (PBS) and how does it relate to response to intervention (RTI)?

For the past 7 years, Samantha Dietz has worked with the University of Miami Support Network for novice teachers. This program is designed to provide mentoring and resources for the university's alumni during the first 3 years of teaching. As a licensed clinical social worker and an expert in emotional and behavioral disorders, Samantha's job is to provide advice regarding general classroom management techniques as well as working with students with special conduct issues.

The Support Network begins with a 3-day summer institute with follow-up sessions during the academic year. Participants are also assigned an experienced teacher as a mentor who provides one-to-one support throughout the first year of teaching. On the third day of the summer institute, Samantha uses a sociometric technique as a vehicle for a discussion of stressors about what participants are about to face during the upcoming school year. She asks the participants to move to one of four quadrants in a large assembly room. The quadrants represent four potential areas of stress for novice teachers: knowing their own subject, establishing positive school relationships (e.g., administrators, parents), managing the general classroom, and dealing with problem behavior. From year to year the results are consistent. As Samantha describes it:

> For the most part, the participants place themselves in one of two quadrants—managing the general classroom

or dealing with problem behavior. As a result of their undergraduate classes and student teaching experience, they feel they have a basic background for what they are about to encounter. They are excited and even thrilled about having their own classroom. However, there is still high anxiety about whether or not they will be able to handle the complexities of the classroom and how they are going to put the theory they know into practice. There is a fear of the unknown coupled with a fear of exactly how to put all the pieces together.

This sociometric activity has proven to be a powerful tool to trigger discussions in small groups and with participants' individual mentors about their fears of failure, adequacy, and needs. As the school year progresses, students are taught in follow-up sessions specific ways to identify problem areas, garner resources (both human and otherwise) to address those problems, and generate solutions. Samantha explains:

> Our goal is to help participants understand that their feelings are normal and natural. Eventually they learn from veteran teachers and from each other how to muster up their self-confidence and to take the risk to ask for help and advice. I've been labeled the "feel good" woman. Indeed our participants do feel good when they take the responsibility for their own professional growth and learn how to gather resources to do so.

Introduction

How can I set up my classroom so that I spend more time teaching and less time managing student behavior? How can I establish a classroom community where students work together and all students feel accepted and valued? How can I manage my classroom so that I can help students in my classroom recognize their strengths and learn to cope with personal challenges in behavior and learning? How can I help students with disabilities feel welcome and accepted in my classroom? In her work with novice teachers, Samantha is frequently asked these questions. The purpose of this chapter is to provide the principles of promoting student acceptance, managing student behavior, and providing positive behavior supports so that you will be prepared to create a classroom that enhances student learning.

This chapter begins with three sections that focus on ways to foster acceptance of all children in your classroom by establishing a harmonious classroom climate, considering the needs of students based on ethnic and socioeconomic factors, and increasing the acceptance of students with disabilities by peers and professionals. The chapter continues with an overview of the basic principles of managing student behavior followed by a discussion of positive behavior supports and schoolwide programs. The principles and practices you'll learn in this chapter will enable you to prevent and address most of the student behavior challenges elementary and secondary teachers encounter on a day-to-day basis.

Establishing a Positive Classroom Climate

One of the first things Samantha Dietz recommends to novice teachers is starting the year off right by establishing a positive classroom climate that will be conducive to learning. Classroom climate includes both physical and social elements.

Arranging the Physical Space

You cannot control certain aspects of the physical classroom climate. The condition of the building, the size of your classroom, the type of furniture, and the nature of the ventilation are examples of important elements in your environment that affect you and your students but over which you are likely to have little or no control.

Working with what you have, however, you can create an environment using classroom space and seating arrangements that communicate, "Learning happens here!" Look around your classroom or that of another teacher and evaluate whether the physical environment supports or detracts from the student's ability to behave appropriately. The physical arrangement may have a significant effect on the classroom climate as well as on student behavior.

Interior designers often use paper scale models to plan room arrangements. You can use such a model to plan student seating (e.g., small-group pods, individual seats, pairs), computer work areas, and centers (Downing, 2007). Your seating arrangement should communicate that all students are part of the classroom and none are being "singled out." Nonetheless, some special considerations may be necessary for students who are easily distracted, have vision or hearing problems, or need to be in close contact with you or a paraprofessional. In addition, as you work on your model, create an organizational plan that will ensure smooth traffic flow from one activity to the next, easy access to instructional materials, and limitations to distractions.

Most students work best in organized, structured environments in which materials, equipment, and personal items are well maintained, neatly arranged, and presented in a predictable way. You can establish a classroom committee composed of elected students or students you appoint on a rotating basis that allows all students to participate over the school year. This committee might meet weekly to assess the classroom environment and address issues raised by students (perhaps in a student suggestion box). See Tips for Teachers 5.1 for other strategies for creating a structured environment.

CREATING A STRUCTURED PHYSICAL ENVIRONMENT

- Keep the classroom uncluttered, clean, attractive, and uncrowded, especially in high-traffic areas (e.g., group work areas, space around the pencil sharpener, doorways, supply areas).

- Make sure necessary materials are accessible, organized, and stored appropriately.

- Ensure that the classroom is well ventilated with appropriate lighting.

- Maintain an appropriate noise level. Consider which objects might be removed or changed to make the room less noisy.

- Establish personal physical space, desk, and materials for each student.

- Be sure all students are easily seen and accessible to the teacher and that all students can easily see instructional presentations and displays.

- Post a schedule that provides a predictable routine.

- Post classroom rules and consequences so that students can see them.

Source: Emmer, E., Everston, C., & Worsham, M. E. (2006). *Classroom management for elementary teachers* (7th ed.). Boston: Allyn & Bacon.

Perhaps an even more important factor than the physical arrangement of the room are the procedures that you, the teacher, implement to create a classroom climate that is respectful and accepting of all students.

Creating a Learning Community

Classrooms are for learning. Your role as a teacher is to establish a classroom that is conducive for learning to occur. To create a positive and productive learning community, consider the following guiding principles:

- **Recognize that students are children or adolescents first.** Teachers who remember this look beyond the visible and less obvious ways in which students differ and respect their common needs and goals—to be accepted, recognized, and valued members of the community. The classroom community is one of the most important places this needs to occur. An attitude that places children or adolescents first recognizes that students are more alike than different.

- **Focus on abilities.** To foster an accepting classroom climate, you must establish an environment in which teachers and students seek and use knowledge about the abilities and expertise of *all* class members. In Laureen Rankin's third-grade class, a picture of each student was framed in a decorated star and hung in the classroom. Attached to each star were lists of self- and teacher-identified strengths or abilities. In addition, all students were encouraged to recognize their fellow students' abilities (which, when identified, were added to the appropriate star).

- **Celebrate diversity.** Celebrating diversity means conveying to students the value of students who learn or behave differently, are physically challenged, speak other languages, or represent other cultural backgrounds. Sharon Andreaci, a sixth-grade teacher, was delighted that many of the students in her classroom spoke Spanish and represented the cultural backgrounds of several Hispanic groups (e.g., Cuban, Nicaraguan, Colombian, and Mexican). She often asked students about their backgrounds and encouraged them to share their knowledge and practices with others in the classroom. For example, she routinely asked such questions as "Juan, how would you say that in Spanish? Ana, would you say it the same way? Is there another way to say it in Spanish?"

- **Demonstrate high regard for all students.** Students know when teachers prefer particular students, even when teachers go out of their way to disguise their preference. Demonstrating high regard for all students means treating each of them as the most important student in the class. Carlos Rivera, a ninth-grade science teacher, recommends the following:

  Listen carefully and attentively to each student's responses, not just those of the brighter students. Look for ways to connect each student's response to what you are talking about now or in a previous lesson. Make eye contact with each student; do not always look at the brighter students. Be sure to call on each student at least every day. Get to know a few personal things about each student and check on them periodically.

- **Provide opportunities for students to work in mixed-ability groups.** Students prefer, and benefit from, opportunities to work with their peers in groups that represent a range of abilities. Be sure that each group member plays a genuine role in which he or she contributes to the group process. Particularly for students with disabilities, work to ensure that each student's role is active and linked to the group's success.

Engaging Students Through Class Meetings

Another way to improve the classroom climate is to engage students in taking responsibility for their classroom through **class meetings**. Class meetings are formal or informal meetings to set mutual goals, solve problems, or plan activities (Schaps, 2003). Joan McGinnis is a fifth-grade teacher who uses class meetings to involve students in the management of their class. Joan has a regularly scheduled Friday afternoon meeting. She uses class meetings to solve crises and to deal with immediate problems. She also uses class meetings to prevent problems, identify potential or occurring problems, teach problem solving, and foster class responsibility for the cohesion and functioning of the classroom.

The format of the class meeting is much the same at both the elementary and secondary levels. You can start the class meeting by forming a circle so that everyone can see everyone else.

The change in the seating structure of the classroom reminds students that this is a special time (Nelson, Epstein, Bursuck, Jayanthi, & Sawyer, 1998). Here's how Joan structures class meetings:

1. The first 10 minutes of the meeting are used for compliments and appreciations, which can be handled in several ways. Joan uses a *recognition box,* a decorated shoe box into which students and teachers place written recognitions of classmates or teachers who have done helpful or special things, such as helping a classmate, doing well on a paper, or ignoring someone who is bothering them. Recognitions also include personal information, such as winning a swim meet. When the class meeting starts, Joan passes the recognition box around the circle. Each student selects one slip until all the slips have been removed from the box. Students take turns reading the recognitions. Joan often allows several minutes during which students can contribute recognitions they did not submit to the recognition box.

2. The second part of the class meeting—follow-up on prior solutions—takes approximately 15 minutes. During this time, problems that had been brought up at previous meetings are discussed and evaluated. Students and teachers share their perceptions in answer to the following questions:
   - How frequently does the problem occur? More or less than before?
   - How well are people implementing the selected solution? Is this still a problem? Is the solution effective?

3. The third part of the meeting—new problems—takes approximately 15 minutes and gives students and teachers an opportunity to identify problems and work with the group to identify potential solutions to the problems. Joan cautions that it is important not to let this part of the meeting turn into a gripe session and to be sure not to allow students to complain about a specific student. Joan teaches all her students how to solve problems and encourages them to use those skills.

4. The fourth part of the meeting—future plans—takes approximately 10 minutes. Joan describes this section of the meeting:

   I try to keep this part of the meeting very upbeat with an emphasis on future projects, school events, or field trips. I use this time to engage the students not just in the social plans of the class and school but also in my academic plans for the future weeks. If I have a special project planned, I use this time to introduce the new project to the students.

Even though Joan is an elementary school teacher, she recognizes that the same format can be used for middle- and high-school students as well. She comments on these meetings:

I feel that it is an essential aspect of a successful classroom. The students in my room are not only better behaved, [but] they work more as a team. They take more responsibility for their own behavior as well as that of other students in the class. I think the benefits go way beyond classroom management and include academic gains as well. I guess you can tell I'm pretty enthusiastic about their function.

What instructional and management goals can be met throughout a class meeting format? How might class meetings increase students' stake in the day-to-day cohesion and operation of their classroom?

Attending to the Safety of Your Students

Every day, we hear and read about risks to the health and safety of young people at home and at school. Millions of young people face risks that not only inhibit learning, but also can be life threatening or can compromise normal growth and development. Poor nutrition, lack of adequate rest, lack of access to health care, exposure to harmful substances, and exposure to sexually transmitted diseases contribute to students' health problems. Stories about safety issues are equally sobering. We hear about child abuse and neglect, school shootings, and domestic and neighborhood violence. Consider these U.S. statistics from the Children's Defense Fund (2008):

- 1 out of 9 children come from families with no health insurance.
- 1 out of 13 live in extreme poverty (less than half of poverty line income or $10,600 or less).
- Between 1979 and 2005 more than 104,000 children were killed by firearms.

Children who experience threats to their health, safety, and basic well-being are at risk of having academic and socioemotional problems at school. It is imperative that you, as a classroom teacher, become familiar with your school district's procedures for student health and safety as well as signs and symptoms of student substance abuse or a child who is physically or emotionally abused (see Figure 5.1). School districts have policies and procedures for reporting

---

FIGURE 5.1

Signs and Symptoms of Child Abuse and Neglect

Signs and Symptoms of Student Substance Abuse

- Abrupt changes in work or school attendance, quality of work, work output, grades, discipline
- Unusual flare-ups or outbreaks of temper
- Withdrawal from responsibility
- General changes in overall attitude
- Deterioration of physical appearance and grooming
- Wearing of sunglasses at inappropriate times
- Continual wearing of long-sleeved garments, particularly in hot weather, or reluctance to wear short-sleeved attire when appropriate
- Association with known substance abusers
- Unusual borrowing of money from friends, co-workers, or parents
- Stealing small items from employer, home, or school
- Secretive behavior regarding actions and possessions; poorly concealed attempts to avoid attention and suspicion, such as frequent trips to storage rooms, restroom, basement, etc.

Signs and Symptoms of Child Abuse and Neglect

Physical Abuse

Physical Symptoms

- Unexplained bruises or burns in various stages of healing
- Welts, human bite marks, bald spots
- Unexplained fractures, abrasions, or other injuries

Behavioral Warning Signs

- Self-destructive behavior
- Nervous, hyperactive, aggressive, disruptive, and destructive behavior
- Unusual apprehensiveness of physical contact
- Demonstrating fear of parents or caretaker
- Expressing little or no emotion when hurt
- Unusual shyness, passiveness, or withdrawn behavior

Sexual Abuse

Physical Symptoms

- Sleep disturbances or nightmares
- Difficulty walking or sitting
- Pain, itching, bruising, or bleeding in the genitalia
- Frequent urinary tract or yeast infections
- Pregnancy

Behavioral Warning Signs

- Engaging in sexual activity that is not age appropriate
- Detailed and sophisticated understanding of sexual behavior
- Going back to a behavior such as bedwetting, or speech loss (regression)
- Unwillingness to change into gym clothes or participate in physical education
- Poor interpersonal relationships with peers

Emotional Abuse

Physical Symptoms

- Speech disorders
- Delayed physical or emotional development
- Ulcers, asthma, and severe allergies

Behavioral Warning Signs

- Habits such as sucking, rocking, and biting
- Extreme passivity and undemanding demeanor
- Low self-esteem
- Exceedingly demanding, aggressive, and angry behavior
- Conduct disorder, including antisocial and destructive behavior
- Depression and/or suicidal ideation
- Attention-seeking behavior

Neglect

Physical Symptoms

- Constant lack of supervision
- Unattended medical needs; pale and listless appearance
- Abandonment by parents or caretaker
- Constant hunger, inappropriate dress, poor hygiene, lice, and distended stomach
- Falling asleep in class and regularly displaying fatigue

Behavioral Warning Signs

- Poor social skills
- Craving attention and indiscriminate demonstration of affection
- Self-destructive behavior
- Begging for or stealing food
- Frequent school absence or tardiness

Source: Smith, T. W., & Lambie, G. W. (2005). Teachers' responsibilities when adolescent abuse and neglect are suspected. *Middle School Journal,* 33–40.

cases of child abuse or neglect, and you must be responsible for knowing them (Smith & Lambie, 2005). Certainly, you would not want to accuse a parent or guardian unfairly; nonetheless, failure to report cases of suspected or confirmed abuse or neglect is a crime in some states. Similarly, you need to become familiar with your school's procedures for school safety in the case of an emergency and to create a classroom climate that puts safety first.

Enhancing Students' Self-Concepts

Ask parents what they most want for their children, and a frequent response is that they want their children to be happy. They want their children to like themselves and be proud of what they do and who they are. This section identifies procedures that teachers can implement to enhance students' self-concepts.

How do you feel about yourself? Do you think you are a valuable person, worthy of love and appreciation from others? Do you think you have friends and are liked by others? Do you think you do well in school and are likely to succeed? How do you feel about the way you look? What about your ability to play sports? Your answers to these questions provide insight into your self-concept. Individuals with positive self-concepts generally feel as though they are worthwhile and deserve the respect, recognition, and appreciation of others. They have positive feelings about themselves in multiple settings, including at school, with friends, and with family. They generally like the way they look and who they are.

Students who have disabilities, are at risk, or are exceptional face greater challenges to their self-concept as their situation sets them apart from their mainstream peers. In addition, because individuals who are at risk or disabled often receive more negative feedback than other students do, their self-concepts may be lower, on the average, than those of other students (Haager & Vaughn, 1995; Vaughn, Elbaum, & Boardman, 2001; Sze & Valentin, 2007).

To help enhance the self-concepts of students with disabilities, teachers can

- Hold all students to high standards, and then provide the encouragement and support students need to meet those standards (Marzano & Marzano, 2003). Teachers often have lower expectations for students who demonstrate learning and behavior problems than for other students. These lowered expectations, however unintentional, limit the opportunities available to these students as compared with those for whom we have high standards.
- Discover students' talents, abilities, or interests, and recognize them personally. Every student in the classroom can be an expert on something. Be sure to find out what expertise every student in your classroom possesses. It is important to understand that students with disabilities who excel in an extracurricular activity such as sports or music demonstrate levels of self-concept similar to those of academically average students when their strengths are acknowledged (Kleinert, Miracle, & Sheppard-Jones, 2007).
- Provide opportunities for students who struggle academically to succeed in other ways. One parent described it this way: "The best thing that happened to my son is swimming. He joined a swim team when he was 6, and all his friends know he has won many swimming awards. No matter how discouraged he is about school, he has one area in which he is successful."
- Recognize students' difficulties with learning, and explain their problems to them in a way they can understand. Sometimes, teachers and parents try to protect students and do not explain to them why they are having problems in school. An honest explanation (that they have attention problems, learning problems, physical problems, etc.) often helps students understand why some things are more difficult for them than for other students. Group counseling can be an effective process for improving the self-concept of middle-school students with disabilities (Elbaum & Vaughn, 2001).

Go to the Council for Children with Behavior Disorders at **www.ccbd.net** for access to helpful information and resources.

Remember the important role that teachers play in influencing students' self-concepts (both negatively and positively). They exert an enormous influence over the self-perceptions of students, even students who they feel pay too little attention to them. Students know (much better than you might imagine) what teachers think and how they feel about them. Tips for Teachers 5.2 gives suggestions for providing opportunities for student success.

PROVIDING OPPORTUNITIES FOR STUDENT SUCCESS

- When you correct papers, point out correct responses rather than mistakes.

- Before students submit papers, ask them to look carefully to see whether they can find an error. Call on students to describe mistakes they find, and praise them for finding and correcting the mistakes. Point out that everyone makes mistakes and that with practice they can reduce the number and types of mistakes they make.

- Find opportunities for a student to "shine" in front of classmates. Even small recognitions are valuable.

- When a student with emotional or behavioral disorders asks for help, start by asking the student to find something correct on his or her paper.

- Notice improvement. If the student usually gets three right on the weekly spelling test and this week gets five right, let the student know that you notice the change. Recognition of progress toward a goal motivates students more than recognition that comes only after the goal has been attained.

Increasing Social Acceptance of Students with Disabilities and Exceptional Learners

Judith Warner, a veteran 10th-grade teacher, is well respected by her students, their parents, and her fellow teachers for the effective way she manages students' behavior. She has experienced a great deal of success with teaching students with disabilities who are placed in her classroom. Judith indicates that the secret to her success is establishing a personal relationship with each student in her class:

> I spend the first month of class getting to know each of my students, what they are like, what they do outside of school, who is special to them at home and in their community, what their strengths are, and what makes them tick. I use this information to facilitate their adjustment to the classroom community and to establishing a relationship with me that will influence our year together. Yes, you can say that each student learns very early in the year that I genuinely respect and care about each of them. When students are not behaving, I always assume initially that it is because they do not know that they are bothering me or another student. I pull them aside and tell them what they are doing and how it is affecting me or others. With older students, giving them feedback privately is important. It usually works.

Go to the Educators section of **http://www.ldonline.org/** for useful links to material on fostering social competence and engaging in effective interactions with students with disabilities.

As she just described, Judith does a number of things to ensure that all of the students in her classroom are accepted.

1. **She treats all students with respect.** Her classroom is not segmented into those who know and those who do not. She genuinely communicates respect for each student and expects students to communicate respect to one another.

2. **She teaches students concern for one another.** The students in Judith's classes learn quickly that they are responsible for themselves and for one another.

3. **She and her class point out students abilities.** Judith insists that when a negative statement is made about a student, something positive about that student must be said: "Yes, Myla [a student who uses a wheelchair] does slow us down going to lunch, but Myla is the class artist. She provides artistic guidance and gifts to all of us."

Conveying acceptance of all students in the classroom is an important responsibility of the classroom teacher. It is particularly important for you to demonstrate acceptance of students with disabilities. Remember that your students may have limited experience in meeting and interacting with students with

As a teacher, what is your role in promoting the social acceptance of students with disabilities? How will you model social acceptance for your students, and what other strategies will you use?

Tips for Teachers 5.3

PREVENTING BULLYING AND TEASING OF INDIVIDUALS WITH DISABILITIES

As a classroom teacher, you have the responsibility to stop bullying in your classroom. Failure to recognize bullying or stop it can have dire consequences for your students. The acronym STOP IT summarizes key steps you can take.

Stop bullying the moment you see it—intervene immediately.

Teach your students school rules regarding bullying, how to recognize bullying, and how to react when another student bullies you.

Observe your students in the playground, lunchroom, hallways, and bus lines. Be vigilant for signs for bullying and work with colleagues to do the same.

Provide support for students who have been bullied and let them know that you are there to help.

Inform yourself about procedures for referring bullying to administrators and parents. Also, inform yourself about best practices in dealing with bullying.

Take necessary steps to deal with the bully and to provide him or her with positive support to overcome this pattern of behavior.

Source: Based on Limber, S. P. (2004). What works and doesn't work in bullying prevention and intervention. Student Assistance Journal, 16–19; and Olweus, D. (2003). A profile of bullying at school. *Educational Leadership,* 60, 12–17.

---

disabilities. Their natural curiosity might take unfortunate turns, resulting in pity, ridicule (Salend, 2004), or even bullying and teasing.

Schools and educators have reported that bullying and excessive teasing are a serious school problem. Bullying often involves picking on or harming someone because he or she is "different." Therefore, students with learning and behavior problems and those with physical or health impairments may be particularly susceptible to harassment and bullying (Hoover & Stenhjem, 2005).

Bullying is the most common form of aggression in youths. It is an intentional act and can result in mental and physical danger for the victim. Unfortunately, 25% of teachers do not perceive bullying as wrong and therefore rarely intervene, and most students perceive that schools do little to respond to bullying (Hoover & Stenhjem, 2005). When evidence of nonacceptance arises, teachers must serve as advocates to promote social acceptance. Tips for Teachers 5.3 presents ideas related to the prevention of bullying of students with disabilities.

Likewise, serving as an advocate for all of your students with other professionals is another critical role that teachers should play. Students with special needs may be more likely than other students in your class to receive criticism from other professionals. Another way to help students experience social acceptance is to be aware of technological options open to them, such as those listed in Tech Tips.

PEARSON
myeducationlab

Go to the Assignments and Activities section of Topic 6: Classroom/Behavior Management in the MyEducationLab for your course and complete the activity entitled *Classroom Strategies for Bullying.*

Tech Tips

USING COMPUTERS TO PROMOTE SOCIAL ACCEPTANCE

Teachers can use computers to enhance socialization skills by encouraging learners to work cooperatively at the computer. Activities that encourage students to make decisions and cooperate with other students can foster appropriate interaction whether they are playing games or doing a research project together.

Simulations, programs that require students to make real-life decisions, are popular options:

Zoo Tycoon and Zoo Tycoon 2 by Microsoft at
▶ www.microsoft.com/games/zootycoon
This program allows children to create an animal adventure together and to be part of an online community where they can ask the zookeeper questions or play mini games.

Sims 2 by Electronic Arts Inc. at
▶ http://thesims2.ea.com/
This is a current version of one of the original simulation programs. Children can create and be part of communities that they and others create. These programs continue to be creative, engaging, and highly entertaining.

Community Success by Tom Caine Associates at
▶ http://caineassociates.com/products/
community-success-p-76.html
This program is for students K–12. It allows children to practice social skills and learn about appropriate and inappropriate behaviors in different situations with the help of realistic illustrations and auditory cues. There are 45 activities that take place in a variety of settings.

Understanding Behavior Management in Culturally Diverse Classrooms

Teachers often misinterpret the behavior of minority students and thus respond inappropriately to their behavior (Chamberlain, 2005; Harry & Klingner, 2006). The miscommunications between minority students and their teachers may cause misunderstandings that lead to discipline problems. For example, educators tend to have low expectations of poor, African American, Native American, and Hispanic students (e.g., Donovan & Cross, 2002; Harry & Klingner, 2006; Ogbu, 1990). It is likely that teachers also hold low expectations for individuals with disabilities, and these low expectations influence the extent to which the teachers interact with these students.

How might these low expectations influence how teachers manage these students' behavior? This question is particularly relevant because disproportionate numbers of students from minority groups are identified as needing special education, although many of them remain in the general education classroom for all or part of the school day (Donovan & Cross, 2002; Harry & Klingner, 2006). Although little information is available about how teachers' attitudes might influence their treatment of students' behavior problems in their classrooms, there is little doubt that when teachers have lowered expectations for students, student motivation and learning are hampered. Because teachers are likely to expect students from traditionally underrepresented groups to be problematic, in an attempt to stop problems before they get out of control they provide overcorrection for problems they might be willing to overlook in nonminority students. African American males are particularly vulnerable to disproportionate discipline by educators (Harry, Klingner, & Cramer, 2007; Townsend, 2000). The primary solution to the problem is awareness of prejudices and the subtle and not so subtle ways in which these prejudices might influence the way you manage the behavior of students in your classroom. (See Tips for Teachers 5.4.)

Following are cautions and considerations that should help you better manage and understand your culturally diverse classroom (Grossman, 1995; Chamberlain, 2005; Townsend, 2000):

- Behaviors that are acceptable and encouraged in the home and the community may be incompatible with behaviors at school. Students may not only receive conflicting messages about their behavior, but also be forced to choose between loyalty to home and community or to school. For example, in some immigrant homes, homework time is a group activity with lots of talking and interaction between parents and children. At school, students may be required to work quietly and independently—a direct contrast to what is encouraged at home. Teachers should avoid placing any student in this position by learning as much as they can about the expectations of all students' homes and communities and communicating acceptance of these practices. So informed, teachers can help students determine which behaviors are acceptable in which settings.

Tips for Teachers 5.4

QUESTIONS TO ASK YOURSELF WHEN TEACHING CULTURALLY DIVERSE STUDENTS

Keep the following questions in your desk, and read and reflect on them frequently:

- What behaviors bother me as a teacher? Who is exhibiting these behaviors? Am I sure that *all* students who behave in these ways are treated in the same way?

- Who are the students I have the most difficulty managing? What socioeconomic, cultural, and linguistic background(s) do they represent? How does this affect my attitude?

- To what extent have I reached out and demonstrated genuine caring and concern to *all* students in my class?

- If students were asked to identify which students in the class I like best and least, what would they say? What does this say about me?

- How are students from traditionally underrepresented groups performing in my class? What behaviors do I demonstrate to promote their success?

- What steps am I taking to better engage all students in instruction and learning?

How does the miscommunication between students with cultural and linguistic diversity and their teachers influence the way the teachers manage the behaviors of the students? What considerations will help the teachers cope more effectively with the behaviors of students with cultural and linguistic diversity?

■ Behaviors that are indicative of problems in one group of students might not be so in another. For example, teachers may overlook signs of internalizing behaviors in African American students, who may express such behaviors differently. Also, teachers who know that Hispanic students might not ask for help may check frequently with these students to determine how they are proceeding. Finally, behaviors of some students may be viewed as aggressive and acting out when their intention is merely to fit in and be recognized.

■ Some behaviors that students exhibit may be wrongly attributed and interpreted by teachers who do not understand the students' culture or background. For example, some students who are English language learners may fail to respond, make limited eye contact with the teacher, or appear defiant because they lack confidence. Some students from other cultures (e.g., Asian groups) are accustomed to clearly defined rules and regulations and may have difficulty interpreting more implicit rules.

Universal Strategies for Managing Student Behavior

Creating a climate of acceptance and understanding serves as a firm foundation for a successful school year for your students and for you. You can build on that foundation by implementing some basic principles of managing student behavior, including looking for the positive, using reinforcers to encourage positive behavior, establishing clear rules with known consequences, helping students to change inappropriate behavior, and recognizing students' mistaken goals. These basic principles are sometimes referred to as **universal strategies** (Anderson & Spaulding, 2007) in that they are used for all students in a classroom. Following these principles can avoid situations such as the following.

Glen Nichols, a seventh-grade science teacher, felt frustrated. One of his science classes included several students with disabilities, and he was interested in modifying his usual routine to ensure that they had an adequate opportunity to learn. He had spent considerable time preparing a science experiment for the laboratory, one he thought students would learn from and enjoy. He arranged the materials ahead of time, identified the key concepts he wanted to teach, and was optimistic that the lesson would go well. What happened? Glen described it this way:

> First of all, the students came to the lab and were more interested in who their lab partner would be than the topic. They seemed to have a more difficult time settling down than usual, and talking seemed to occur during the entire session. There were a few students who seemed to follow the procedures and get something out of it, but for the most part I think it was a waste of my time.

Glen understood well the content he was teaching, but was less able to manage student behaviors so that he could teach effectively. Glen is not alone. Many teachers identify classroom management not only as a cause of stress, but also as their reason for leaving the profession (Cangelosi, 2004; Emmer & Stough, 2001).

Glen was becoming increasingly frustrated and said so during lunch in the faculty lounge. Frank, a special education teacher, suggested that Glen needed to look for positive behaviors. Glen threw up his hands and said, "There weren't any! The poor behavior far outweighed the good." In response, Frank volunteered to videotape Glen's class and to view and discuss the lesson with Glen. When Glen examined the videotape of his lesson and Frank asked him to make a written list of student behaviors that he found acceptable, he noticed quite a few.

Glen, like many teachers, got into the habit of noticing and calling attention to *misbehavior* instead of noticing appropriate behavior and providing positive reinforcement. Frank asked him to list the behaviors he most wanted to see in his students. Glen was then asked to look for and say something positive to students who were performing those behaviors.

Focusing on Positive Behaviors

Teachers tend to think they speak positively to students more often than they actually do. When someone counts the positive comments in the classroom, teachers are surprised at how few they actually made. McIntosh and colleagues (1993) found that even general education teachers who were identified as effective and accepting of students with special needs made very few positive statements during a lesson. As third-grade teacher Nina Zaragoza explains: "At the end of the day, I think I have been so positive, calling out specific behaviors I like and describing the behaviors of students I want to see more of, yet I realize that with what I view as a nonstop positive onslaught, many students are still not getting enough positive feedback."

Positive feedback to students must be specific and must be presented immediately after you witness the target behaviors you want the students to continue (and other students to model). At the elementary level, teachers can comment on which students are displaying the desired behavior: "Mark, Jacob, and Cynthia are looking at me with their books open. I can tell they are ready. Who else knows what to do to show me they are ready?"

Elementary students find public recognition in front of the entire class more rewarding than do older students, who prefer to receive individual feedback that is more private. This does *not* mean that you should not have a positive attitude and look for appropriate behavior in older students. All students like to be told when they are doing something right. They all like a classroom in which the atmosphere is positive and upbeat and the teacher looks for good things, rather than only for bad behaviors. Table 5.1 provides a list of positive teacher comments to use in response to students' behaviors.

TABLE 5.1

Positive Responses to Students' Classroom Behaviors

STUDENT BEHAVIORS		TEACHER RESPONSES
Appropriate/Desired	*Inappropriate/Undesired*	
Sitting with bottoms flat on carpet	Kneeling up	"I'm glad so many people remember how to sit in Magic Five."
Raising hand to speak	Calling out a response	"It really helps me to know if you have something to say when you raise your hand."
Sitting inside the tape	Sitting outside the tape/leaning on the wall	"It's important to sit inside the tape because it helps you remember what you're supposed to be looking at and thinking about."
Looking in the direction of whoever is speaking	Talking to another person or playing with something	"It's so polite to look at someone when it's their turn to speak."
Walking quickly and quietly to desk	Running to desk or stepping on and over a chair; Yelling to friends while going to desks	"I like how _____ went to her desk so quickly and got started. _____ did a great job walking quietly to his desk."
Working on the right assignment	Drawing instead of working on assignment	"People are working so hard on this assignment."
Using quiet voices	Yelling or talking too loudly	"It's so important to use quiet voices at our desks so we don't disturb our friends who are working."
Finding something appropriate to do when work is done	Wandering around the room when work is done or drawing or playing an inappropriate game	"_____ is a great thing to do when all your work is done. Good idea."

Source: Carpenter, S. L., & McKee-Higgins, E. (1996). Behavior management in inclusive classrooms. *Remedial and Special Education* 17(4), 200. Reprinted with permission.

What reinforcer is being used? What other types of reinforcers could be used to enhance positive behavior? If this were your classroom, what reinforcers might you consider using?

Several authors distinguish between positive feedback and encouragement (Dreikurs, Cassel, & Ferguson, 2004; Dreikurs, Grunwalk, & Pepper, 1982). The primary difference is that **positive feedback** often provides some judgment from the teacher about the appropriateness of the behavior, whereas **encouragement** recognizes the behavior but does not provide teacher judgment. An example of positive feedback is a teacher saying, "Shana is waiting in line quietly. Good job, Shana." An example of encouragement is to say, "I'm sure that you know how to stand in line when we get ready for lunch." Encouragement focuses on the process (Dweck, Kamins, & Person, 1999), as in the following: "The ending of this paper is quite strong. Can you reread the ending and consider how to improve the introduction?" Both encouragement and positive feedback are effective procedures for noticing what is positive about your students' behavior.

Using Reinforcers to Encourage Positive Behavior

Positive reinforcement is the presentation, following the target behavior, of a **stimulus** (a verbal response; a physical response, such as touching; or a tangible response, such as a reward) to maintain or increase the target behavior. **Negative reinforcement** is the removal of a stimulus to increase engagement in desirable behaviors. If a teacher rings a bell until the students are quiet, then the removal of the bell sound is a negative reinforcer for quieting student behavior. Because "negative" is often misinterpreted to mean "harmful," the implication is that positive reinforcement is good and negative reinforcement is bad, but this is not necessarily the case. However, although negative reinforcement can be effective, positive reinforcement is the best way to increase desirable student behaviors.

Larrivee (2005) describes a hierarchy of reinforcers ranging from tangible or extrinsic rewards (raisins, stickers, school supplies) to internal or intrinsic rewards (student satisfaction). The hierarchy of reinforcers includes the following types:

- Consumable (raisins, crackers, jelly beans)
- Tangible (school supplies, toys)
- Token (stickers, checks, coupons)
- Activity (computer time, free time)
- Privilege (errands, line leader)
- Peer recognition (peer acceptance, approval)
- Teacher approval (recognition, praise)
- Self-satisfaction (motivation, seeing one's accomplishments)

Figure 5.2 provides a list of reinforcers that teachers can use to increase appropriate behavior.

In addition to thinking about the type of reward, you will also want to consider group versus individual rewards (Anderson & Spaulding, 2007). Lauren Angelo, a third-grade teacher, uses whole-class, small-group, and individual rewards. If all students bring in their homework, Lauren rewards her students by letting them dance to a favorite CD. Since starting this practice homework has improved to 100% completion. Lauren's students are seated in clusters of six seats, which she refers to as teams. Teams can earn points that lead to earning the right to work in independent centers. They earn points by following directions for independent or cooperative learning activities. Finally, Lauren uses individual rewards such as stickers, certificates, and stamps to acknowledge individual accomplishments on both academic and social goals.

For some additional suggestions for positive reinforcement, see Tips for Teachers 5.5.

Some teachers, particularly those who have students with exceptional behavioral problems in their classrooms, may need to establish a **token system** (or token economy). In a token system students earn tokens (e.g., chips, points) for following classroom rules and meeting target

FIGURE 5.2

Reinforcers That Can Increase Appropriate Behavior

Activities

- Students can perform an activity they like (e.g., drawing) after they complete the desired activity (e.g., the activity during that class period).
- Students can perform their tasks on a computer.
- Students can perform their tasks with a partner they select.

Adult Approval

- Teacher provides verbal recognition that student is behaving appropriately. ("John, you are following directions on this assignment.")
- Teacher provides physical recognition of appropriate student behavior. Teacher moves around classroom, touching the shoulder of students who are behaving appropriately.
- Teacher informs parents or other professionals of students' appropriate behavior. This can be accomplished orally or with "good news" notes.

Peer Recognition

- Teacher informs other students of a student's appropriate behavior. ("The award for Student of the Day goes to the outstanding improvement in behavior demonstrated by [student's name].")
- Students can place in a special box the names of students who have demonstrated appropriate behavior. These names can be read at the end of the week.
- A designated period of time is allocated at the end of the class period (high school) or day (elementary school) to ask students to recognize their fellow classmates who have demonstrated outstanding behavior.

Privileges

- Students are awarded free time after displaying appropriate behavior.
- Students are allowed to serve in key classroom roles after demonstrating outstanding behavior.
- Students are awarded passes that they can trade for a night without homework.

Students Provide Self-Reinforcers

- Students give themselves points for behaving well.
- Students say positive things to themselves. ("I'm working hard and doing well.")
- Students monitor their own behavior.

Tokens

- Tokens are items (e.g., chips, play money, points) that can be exchanged for something of value.
- Use tokens to reward groups or teams who are behaving appropriately.
- Allow groups or individuals to accumulate tokens they can "spend" on privileges, such as no homework or free time.

Tangibles and Consumables

- Tangibles are rewards, objects that students want, but usually not objects they can consume (e.g., toys, pencils, erasers, paper, crayons).
- Consumables are rewards that students can eat (e.g., raisins, pieces of cereal, candy).
- Tokens can be exchanged for tangible reinforcers or for consumable reinforcers.
- Tangible reinforcers or consumables can be used to reward the class for meeting a class goal.
- Tangible reinforcers or consumables may be needed to maintain the behavior of a student with severe behavior problems.

Tips FOR Teachers 5.5

SUGGESTIONS FOR POSITIVE REINFORCEMENT

By using a menu of positive rewards, students can select and work toward specific activities or privileges that are particularly interesting to them. The following list gives examples of rewards that can be used to motivate students in the classroom:

- Read story to teacher or independently.

- Visit or help another class.

- Assist the teacher.

- Care for class pets, plants, etc.

- Pass out or collect materials.

- Write on or erase boards, clean desks, organize books.

- Help the custodian, in school office, in lunchroom.

- Participate in after-school activity.

- Decorate classroom.

- Go to the library.

- Eat lunch with teacher, principal, or favorite adult.

- Choose friend for a game or an activity.

- Have free time to use specific supplies (e.g., computer, books on tape, music, art supplies).

- Sit in special place (teacher's desk, next to friend) for specified period of time.

- Tutor in class or with younger students.

- Take a short break.

- Get time to work on a special project.

- Omit specific assignments.

- Choose a free homework night.

- Have extra or longer recess.

- Display student's work.

- Selected as "Student of the Week."

- Remove lowest grade.

- Take turn as hall monitor or line leader.

- Use teacher's materials (hole punch, paper cutter, dry erase pens).

- Keep score for class game.

behavioral objectives. Students can exchange the tokens for tangible and/or consumable rewards. Juanita Cowell is a middle-school teacher who has five students with special needs in her classroom. One of her students has difficulty staying on task, not disrupting others, and raising his hand when he has something to say. Unfortunately, several students seemed to be learning his "bad" behavior instead of his learning the good behavior of other students. Juanita had tried many of the reinforcers mentioned in Figure 5.2 (such as adult, peer, and activity reinforcers, as well as privileges), and although the class had more good days than bad, she was still concerned about the behavior of several students. She decided to establish a token system whereby she would place a token in a glass bank to indicate that the student was behaving appropriately. The tokens were deposited

- At the end of every period (usually about 50 minutes) if the student followed rules during the period.
- At the beginning of each new period if the student made a quiet transition to the new task.
- For exceptional student behavior, such as ignoring another student's interfering behavior or helping a student who was distracted get back to work.
- For successfully completing activities.

 Go to **http://cases.coedu.usf .edu** for a variety of teaching cases on topics such as behavior management and social skills training.

Juanita removed a token from the jar when rules were broken. The target student added up the tokens at the end of each day. If the student earned 10 tokens or more, a note was sent home. The number of tokens each day was recorded, and when the student reached 200 (approximately 10 days of good behavior), the student could exchange the tokens for a pizza party at lunch with two students of his or her choice. Juanita soon found that she could shake the jar as a signal to quiet down or as a warning that the student was about to lose a token.

Ayllon (1999) provides several points to consider when implementing a token system:

- Clearly identify the behavior(s) you want to change.
- Make the tokens readily available and easy to administer.

- Identify items, activities, or reinforcers that are highly rewarding for the student and that can be obtained by exchanging the tokens.
- Give regular opportunities to exchange the tokens.

When students have a clear incentive that is within reach, the token system is most effective. Another strategy for guiding students' behavior is by establishing rules for behavior and consequences for unwelcome behaviors.

Establishing Clear Rules with Known Consequences

Effective management of student behavior requires clearly specified guidelines and consequences when students do not follow those guidelines. *Guidelines* in the classroom consist of procedures and rules (Brophy, 2003). *Procedures* are classroom routines that occur at specified times and allow the classroom to run effectively. These procedures need to be taught to students and used consistently so that the classroom will run smoothly. Each teacher needs to establish procedures for record keeping (taking attendance, for example), passing out papers and materials, storing materials and books, collecting papers and materials, entering and leaving the room (alone and with the class), and making the transition between tasks.

Rules provide the structure for acceptable and unacceptable classroom behaviors. Like procedures, rules need to be taught explicitly (Anderson & Spaulding, 2007). Instead of trying to develop a rule to govern every possible misbehavior, teachers should develop a few general rules that guide students in determining whether behavior is acceptable. These rules should be based on the teacher's criteria for what constitutes a behavior problem (Emmer, Evertson, Sanford, Clements, & Worsham, 1989; Marzano & Marzano, 2003) as well as on schoolwide policies for rules and discipline.

Some teachers involve students in determining class rules and consequences. **Consequences** are the repercussions associated with appropriate behavior (e.g., gaining a token) and inappropriate behavior (e.g., losing a token). When students are involved in the development of the consequences, the teacher needs to play an active role. Students often want to establish consequences far harsher than those established by the teacher. Following are examples of general rules:

- Raise your hand if you have something to contribute.
- Do not interfere with your fellow students' learning.
- Do not interfere with the teacher's instruction.
- Complete tasks and homework on time.
- Do not bring to school materials (e.g., toys, action figures) that interfere with your learning.

Some teachers show each new class the rules from the previous year and allow the current students to make changes.

Students need to know what the consequences are of not following a procedure or rule and teachers need to be consistent in implementing consequences. Like many first-year teachers, Allison Frost had a hard time establishing and implementing consequences. She had difficulty anticipating the kinds of problems she would face and had limited experience in providing consequences for student behavior. She implemented a strategy in which consequences for breaking class rules were as closely related to the problem as possible. For example, students who interfered with the their classmates' learning suffered the consequences of being removed from the group for a designated period of time.

Allison also established a system for classroom procedures. Every Friday, two students were selected to distribute and collect papers and materials during the following week. She identified these students by using a lottery system, with eligibility based on meeting weekly behavior goals. Also, so that students would understand what was expected of them, all students practiced procedures for transitions between centers, going to and from their classroom, and other routines. Rules were handled through the new token system she established. On Friday, she counted the number of tokens for the week, and students solved math problems about the number of tokens needed to win the prize.

Helping Students to Change Inappropriate Behavior

What should a teacher do when focusing on positive behaviors does not change the negative behaviors? Three alternative techniques are ignoring on purpose, time out, and punishment. Effective procedures for implementing these techniques follow.

PEARSON myeducationlab

Go to the Building Teaching Skills and Dispositions section of Topic 6: Classroom/Behavior Management n the MyEducationLab for your course and complete the activity entitled *Establishing Classroom Rules and Routines*.

Go to **http://www.thinkkids.org/** for helpful resources that can help teachers who work with children with challenging behaviors.

Ignoring on Purpose.   The goal of **ignoring on purpose** or **planned ignoring** is to eliminate (extinguish) a student's undesirable behavior, which is being reinforced through attention (Lewis, Lewis-Palmer, Newcomer, & Stichter, 2004). Many teachers and students unknowingly maintain the unwanted behaviors of students by attending to these behaviors. When teachers recognize that an undesirable behavior is being maintained by either their attention or the attention of fellow students and then plan to eliminate the attention, the strategy for elimination is called **extinction**. For example, a teacher might want to extinguish a student's behavior of shouting out. Having determined that telling the student to raise his hand provides the attention the student wants, the teacher decides to ignore the student (with the intention of reducing the behavior through ignoring on purpose).

Ignoring can be a very effective strategy to reduce undesirable behaviors but is harder to implement than most people think. Let's return to the example of the student who continually shouted out in class. If this student's behavior was reinforced not only by the attention of the teacher, but also by that of his classmates, then both teacher and classmates need to ignore the undesirable behavior. It is important for the teacher to understand that during extinction, the target behavior will increase in rate or intensity before decreasing. To be effective, this strategy requires patience and the ability to control reinforcement.

Time Out.   **Time out** occurs when the student is removed from the classroom situation. This eliminates the opportunity to receive reinforcement. In the classroom, the student receives reinforcement from classmates, the teacher, and ideally, the environment. When a student is removed from this setting, he or she is no longer able to receive these reinforcers. The underlying principle behind the successful use of time out is that the environment the student leaves must be reinforcing and the time-out environment must not. In general, the amount of time spent out is gauged by a student's age—1 minute per year (i.e., a 6 year old would have 6 minutes of time out) (Downing, 2007). Guidelines for implementing time out in the classroom are provided in Tips for Teachers 5.6.

Punishment.   **Punishment** is "the presentation or removal of a stimulus or event after a response, which decreases the likelihood or probability of that response" (Kazdin, 2001, p. 56). Punishment can take multiple forms, including the following (Downing, 2007).

- **Verbal reprimands** are short, targeted comments designed to address a specific misbehavior (e.g., "Isaiah, turn around in your seat and look at me.").
- **Overcorrection** refers to the act of having the student perform a duty or task to compensate for what happened (e.g., "Frank, you threw paper on the floor. During recess

GUIDELINES FOR IMPLEMENTING TIME OUT

- Time out should be used as a last resort.

- Time-out procedures should be discussed with school administrators and parents before implementation.

- Students should be provided in advance with information about behaviors that will result in time out.

- The amount of time the student is in time out should be brief (between 15 and 20 minutes).

- The amount of time the student is in time out should be specified ahead of time.

- The student should be told to go to time out. If the student does not comply, the teacher should unemotionally place the student in time out.

- Time out should be implemented *immediately* following the inappropriate behavior.

- Contingencies should be established in advance for the student who fails to comply with time-out rules.

- Do not leave the time-out area unmonitored.

- When time out is over, the student should join his or her classmates.

- The teacher should look for ways to provide reinforcement for appropriate behavior after time out.

you can pick up paper in the school yard for 15 minutes."). It can also involve redoing an action in the correct manner for the purposes of practicing appropriate behavior (e.g., "Sarah, you ran into the room, did not pick up your writing journal, and started talking with Megan. Please walk into the room again and show me how we get ready for journal writing in the morning.").

- **Response cost** involves the loss of something tangible or intangible (e.g., "Samantha, because you were talking during independent work time, you will not be allowed to go to the computer center today.").

Although punishment often reduces the undesired behavior, it does not ensure that the desired behavior will occur (Lee & Axelrod, 2005). For example, a student who is punished for talking in class might stop talking in that class, yet he or she might not attend to his or her studies for the remainder of the day.

Many educators argue against the use of punishment for these reasons:

- Punishment is often ineffective in the long run.
- Punishment often causes undesirable emotional side effects such as fear, aggression, and resentment.
- Punishment provides little information about what to do, teaching the individual only what *not* to do.
- The person who administers punishment is often associated with it and subsequently viewed as harsh or negative.
- Punishment frequently does not generalize across settings; therefore, it needs to be readministered.
- Fear of punishment often leads to escape behavior (e.g., running away, skipping class, reluctance to attend school).

Despite the many arguments against the use of punishment, parents and teachers frequently use it for the following reasons:

- They may be unfamiliar with the consequences of punishment.
- They are unable to effectively implement a more positive approach.
- It is often reinforcing to the person who administers it. When punishment rapidly changes the undesirable behavior, the person who implements the punishment is highly rewarded.

Punishment should be used as a last resort and when behaviors are harmful to a student or others. For example, Tracy Takamura, a second-grade teacher, felt she had no choice but to punish Monique Jackson, whose fighting on the playground was harmful to others. Despite Tracy's positive attempts to change her behavior, Monique continued to attack others when they did not do what she wanted. To address Monique's bullying, Tracy implemented the following procedures, which are necessary to make punishment effective:

- Tell the student ahead of time what the consequences will be the next time the student engages in the undesirable behavior.
- Deliver punishment immediately after the undesirable behavior (e.g., fighting) each time it occurs.
- Unless a sharp decrease in the frequency and intensity of the behavior occurs, the punishment is ineffective and should be altered.
- Identify and reinforce the appropriate behaviors of the target student.

Be aware that discipline procedures (e.g., school suspension) are different for a student whose infraction is related to his or her disability. For example, IDEIA 2004 includes limits on the number of days a student can be moved to an alternative placement. Check with your school counselor or special education teacher regarding the specific discipline procedures outlined in IDEIA 2004 that apply to students with disabilities. Table 5.2 provides a summary of behavioral techniques for increasing students' desirable behavior and decreasing undesirable behavior.

TABLE
5.2

Summary of Behavioral Techniques to Moderate Students' Behaviors

PROCEDURES FOR INCREASING DESIRABLE BEHAVIORS	METHODS FOR DECREASING UNDESIRABLE BEHAVIORS
• *Positive reinforcement*: The application of a pleasurable consequence following the display of a desirable behavior. Positive reinforcement increases the target behavior that it follows. Positive reinforcement can be social (e.g., a smile, a pat on the back) or tangible (e.g., a sticker or food).	• *Extinction*: The removal of positive reinforcement. For example, when a student shouts in class and other students laugh at this behavior, that laughter can be a positive reinforcer for the shouting behavior. In such cases, the teacher may want to have a class meeting when the target student is not present and elicit the cooperation of classmates, asking them to help reduce or extinguish the shouting behavior by not laughing when the student shouts.
• *Negative reinforcement*: The removal, following a behavior, of an unpleasant consequence that increases the likelihood of that behavior being maintained or increased.	• *Punishment*: The application of an unpleasant or aversive consequence immediately following an undesirable behavior. In many cases, teachers think only of physical punishment. Other forms of punishment include any behavior that is extremely unpleasant or undesirable to the student and that reduces the occurrence of the student's target behavior. Sometimes staying after school or staying in the classroom during lunch is used as punishment. It is important for teachers to remember that a consequence is punishing only if it reduces the occurrence of the target behavior.
• *Contract*: An oral or written agreement between student and teacher that identifies the expected behavior and the consequences for exhibiting or not exhibiting that behavior. For example, the teacher and student write up the specific behavior to be demonstrated, how often it should occur, and the positive consequences of fulfilling the contract.	
• *Premack principle*: The **Premack principle** provides the opportunity for behaviors (acceptable to both teachers and students) to serve as reinforcers for behaviors that teachers want, as well as other behaviors that are acceptable to teachers but less acceptable to students.	• *Time out*: The removal of a student from a positively reinforcing situation. Many teachers use time out ineffectively, removing students from classroom situations that are not positively reinforcing. Also, time out should be for a very specific period of time, not more than 15–20 minutes, and students should be told ahead of time when they will be allowed to return to the reinforcing situation.

Recognizing Students' Mistaken Goals

Rudolf Dreikurs, who was a follower of Alfred Adler and director of the Adler Institute, is well known for his contribution to understanding the classroom behavior of students (Dreikurs & Cassel, 1972; Dreikurs et al., 1982; Dreikurs et al., 2004). He believed that all behavior is purposeful and that student behavior and misbehavior can be better dealt with by teachers if they better understand the purpose behind the behavior.

The following principles form the foundation of Dreikurs's approach to discipline:

■ Students (like the rest of us) are social beings, and their behaviors are attempts to be liked and accepted.
■ Students can control their own behavior.
■ When students display inappropriate behavior, they do so because they have the **mistaken goal** that it will get them the recognition and acceptance they want.

Many students learn that they can garner the acceptance and recognition they need by behaving appropriately and completing school tasks. Other students do not feel capable or worthy of obtaining recognition in these ways; they attempt to obtain the acceptance and recognition they need by displaying inappropriate behavior and not completing their school tasks. Over time, they begin to feel that the only way to get recognition is through inappropriate behavior.

Dreikurs identified four mistaken goals that categorize the behavior of most students:

1. Attention
2. Power or control
3. Revenge or getting even
4. Display of inadequacy

According to Dreikurs, the best way to determine a student's mistaken goal is to identify what the student is doing and how you feel about or react to the behavior. Table 5.3 provides a description of a student's mistaken goal, the student's behavior, and the teacher's reaction. Dreikurs indicates that the teacher's job is to identify the student's mistaken goal and to discuss it with him or her. Teachers also need to identify their own reaction to the student's behavior and how that might contribute to the student's mistaken goal. See Charles and Senter (2005) for further information on the application of Dreikurs's approach to classroom management.

PEARSON
myeducationlab

To enhance your understanding behavior management strategies in the classroom, go to the IRIS Center Resources section of Topic 6: Classroom/Behavior Management in the MyEducationLab for your course and complete Module 37 entitled *Who's in Charge? Developing a Comprehensive Behavior Management System.*

TABLE
5.3

Students' Mistaken Goals

STUDENT'S GOAL	STUDENT'S BEHAVIOR	TEACHER'S FEELING
Attention	Repeats aversive behavior	Annoyed
Power	Refuses to stop behavior	Threatened, loss of control
Revenge	Becomes hostile, tries to hurt others	Hurt
Exhibition of inadequacy	Refuses to participate or cooperate	Helpless, gives up

Practices for Providing Positive Behavior Support

As part of her work with novice teachers, Samantha Dietz emphasizes a problem-solving model to prevent inappropriate behavior in the classroom and to both teach and reinforce appropriate behavior. In the previous section, you were introduced to principles of behavior management that classroom teachers can use to improve students' behavior and to reduce behavior problems. In recent years, the principles of more traditional behavior management have been applied to schoolwide models for the prevention of problem behavior, a system for monitoring student behavior, and a coordinated plan for dealing with problem behavior when it occurs. In place of individual and often disjointed classroom and school discipline procedures, a continuum of policies and procedures for all students is implemented throughout the school. This modification of behavior management principles is called **positive behavior support (PBS)** (OSEP Technical Assistance Center on Positive Behavioral Interventions and Supports, 2009). It is described as being problem-solving oriented, data-based, evidence-based, and systemic (Klotz & Canter, 2007). PBS for students with disabilities is not just good practice; it's part of the law under IDEIA 2004. Moreover, PBS works hand-in-hand with the RTI approach you read about in Chapter 2 and facilitates a problem-solving model with collaboration and communication with all key stakeholders (administrators, teachers, students and their families). Thus, individual teachers are not working alone in dealing with students with challenging behavioral issues.

Positive Behavior Support as Prevention

Many schools today are coping with increasing numbers of behavior problems such as fighting and bullying, discontent among students, and general lack of discipline within a positive climate of support in the schools. This problem does not exist because teachers or administrators lack concern or caring for the issue. It occurs because a schoolwide adoption of a consistent and fluent model has not taken place. The focus of PBS is on developing individualized interventions that occur within a coordinated schoolwide system. The interventions emphasize preventing problem behaviors through effective educational programming to improve the individual's quality of life (Janney & Snell, 2008; Sandomierski, Kincaid, & Algozzine, 2009; Simonsen, Sugai, & Negron, 2008).

PBS involves careful observation of circumstances and the purpose of the problem behavior. A significant number of negative behaviors can be dealt with by modifying the environment (e.g., who sits near a student, how a student is responded to). PBS also emphasizes teaching appropriate behaviors to replace the inappropriate behavior in the target setting (Epstein, Atkins, Cullinan, Kutash, & Weaver, 2008; Janney & Snell, 2008).

Juan was a fifth-grade student who had a physical and cognitive disability, poor social skills, and difficulty interacting with peers. He hit other children and got into fights for no apparent reason. When Juan's teacher and the school counselor observed Juan's interactions with peers and his behaviors, they learned that hitting was Juan's way of saying, "Get off my back." He was sensitive to teasing, and students learned that they could get him very mad very easily by teasing him. Through PBS, Juan was taught to say, "Get off my back" and walk away instead of hitting. He was also taught to recognize teasing and to not let the other students control his behavior. Furthermore, the students primarily associated with teasing Juan were

PEARSON
myeducationlab

Go to the Assignments and Activities section of Topic 6: Classroom/Behavior Management in the MyEducationLab for your course and complete the activity entitled *Positive Behavior Support in the Classroom.*

taught to have fun in other ways. All the teachers in the school reminded Juan to use his words instead of his hands to communicate. He was also taught other specific skills necessary for successful social interactions, such as joining a group and initiating and maintaining a conversation. All students were rewarded with tokens when Juan did not get into a fight or hit someone; thus, everyone was interested in seeing Juan's behavior improve. Teachers tried to pair Juan with other students during classroom activities to provide him with opportunities to practice his new skills.

In this case, Juan's behavior and the environment in which target behaviors occurred were observed. Once the causes, circumstances, and purposes of the behaviors were identified, the classroom teacher met with other teachers to discuss and enlist their help in providing Juan with the support he would need. The teachers also developed a list of specific social skills to teach him. Over time, Juan's problem behaviors decreased, his social skills improved, and he made friends with a few students.

Schoolwide Positive Behavior Support

Go to the Assignments and Activities section of Topic 6: Classroom/Behavior Management in the MyEducationLab for your course and complete the activity entitled *Schoolwide Positive Behavior Support*.

Go to **www.pbis.org** for research-based information on the implementation of positive behavior supports and interventions.

Schoolwide positive behavior support (SWPBS) models begin with a **primary prevention model** in which the focus is on preventing behavior problems schoolwide (Sugai, Horner, & Gresham, 2002). All school personnel know the rules and expectations that are established and that a concerted effort is made to ensure that all students and their parents are aware of positive school behavior and rules.

Typically, a SWPBS leadership team of administrators, teachers, and staff is established. This team coordinates efforts including working with faculty to develop rules and expectations, providing professional development for teachers in evidence-based practices, examining student data (e.g., discipline referrals, suspensions, teacher ratings of behavior), monitoring progress of students identified for interventions, communicating rules and expectations to students and families, and evaluating the SWPBS plan on a regular basis. Though initially time-consuming to establish, SWPBS yields high results over time, reduces behavior problems, and improves the school climate (Fairbanks, Simonsen, & Sugai, 2008). Tips for Teachers 5.7 highlights the essential elements of a schoolwide PBS approach.

Many schools are in the early stages of implementing SWPBS plans. To change from a more traditional system of behavior management to one that is preventive and positive, the OSEP Center on Positive Behavioral Interventions and Supports (2009) suggests that schools must

- Develop programs that consider behavioral issues for all students.
- Consider whether the behavioral practices recommended are empirically valid.
- Consider the connections between academic and behavioral success.
- Approach behavior management from a prevention perspective.
- Involve all key stakeholders in the school, home, and community in developing team-building and behavioral problem-solving skills.

Tips FOR TEACHERS 5.7

ESSENTIAL ELEMENTS OF A SCHOOLWIDE PBS APPROACH

To change from a more traditional system of behavior management to one that is preventive and positive, the OSEP Center on Positive Behavioral Interventions and Supports (2009) suggests that schools must

- Consider the needs of all children because every child needs some type of behavior support.

- Use research-based methods that have been validated and are relevant to the population.

- Work toward both academic and behavioral success for all students.

- Emphasize prevention first to create and maintain a safe and supportive school environment.

- Think beyond the school site to expand the use of effective PBS models to district, county, regional, and state levels.

- Collaborate with community agencies (e.g., education, juvenile justice, community mental health, family, and medical).

- Develop the schoolwide (including students, staff, and administration) use of team-building and problem-solving skills through instruction, high expectations, and reinforcement.

How will you know if your school is ready for PBS? The Center on Positive Behavioral Interventions and Supports (2009) provides the following guidelines for ensuring that a school is prepared to implement an effective schoolwide PBS model:

- Establish a leadership team consisting of administrators, teachers, support staff, specialists, and parents.
- Establish a commitment of support and active participation from the school administration and at least 80% of the staff.
- Conduct a self-assessment of the current schoolwide discipline system. Use the data to create an implementation action.
- Set up a system to collect discipline referrals and other relevant data on a regular basis to track progress and evaluate the effectiveness of schoolwide PBS efforts.

It is not just up to the schools to implement PBS; parents and other family members can get involved as well. Considerable evidence shows that PBS can be taught to and used by parents very effectively (Lucyshyn, Dunlap, & Albin, 2002). Parents and other family members have successfully engaged children with severe problem behaviors in alternative behaviors and modified contexts that no longer support the behavior problems. Much like general and special education teachers who have students with extreme behavior problems, parents can identify the behavior problems through assessment and then alter their feedback so that their child's behavior problems are no longer supported and thus become ineffective (Lucyshyn, Horner, Dunlap, Albin, & Ben, 2002). This yields more positive and constructive parent–child interactions.

Positive Behavior Support and Response to Intervention

How does PBS link to RTI? In Chapter 2 you read about tiers of intervention. In that chapter tiers were discussed in terms of level of intensity of instruction. In the case of PBS, the focus is less on academics and more on instruction of appropriate behavior.

Tier 1 instruction involves many of the universal strategies for creating a positive classroom climate and managing student behavior that you have already read about in this chapter. However, PBS advocates also recommend that universal strategies are lodged within a well-articulated schoolwide plan (Sandomierski et al., 2009; Simonson et al., 2008). Key to the success of Tier 1 is setting expectations for positive behaviors, teaching those expectations to all students, and recognizing when students exhibit those behaviors (Fairbanks et al., 2008). When behavior challenges arise with individual students, teachers work with other professionals in the school to implement high-quality behavioral interventions. If those interventions are not successful, students may be in need of additional help.

Tier 2 supports are provided for students who need additional support, individually or in small groups; these supports may take place inside or outside of the general education classroom (Fairbanks et al., 2008). Interventions can focus on social skills, counseling, or mentoring depending on individual needs. Like academic interventions, it is recommended that evidence-based interventions for behavior are used to provide such support (Sandomierski et al., 2009). With Tier 2, students spend limited time away from the classroom and progress monitoring is used to gauge students' growth and to determine whether Tier 3 intervention is necessary.

Tier 3 instruction is at the individual level and is meant for students who have not made satisfactory progress with Tier 2 supports, have persistent or severe disciplinary infractions, or might endanger themselves or others. It involves more detailed assessment of student behavior and the development of an individual behavior improvement plan that may involve individual or group interventions and possibly alternative placements. In Chapter 8, you'll learn more about PBS/RTI and Tier 2 and 3 interventions and your role as a general education teacher.

In the introduction to this chapter, Samantha Dietz emphasized the need for teachers to be proactive in gathering resources to address challenges in the classroom. The promise of PBS and RTI is that teachers will have expanded access to such resources and that as a result all students can become successful learners and productive citizens.

Summary

- Your role as a teacher is to establish a classroom that is conducive for learning to occur. Both physical and social aspects of classroom climate need to be planned and implemented.

- Students who have disabilities, are at risk, or are exceptional face greater challenges to their self-concept as their situation sets them apart from their mainstream peers. As a classroom teacher you can take steps to nurture positive self-concepts among all students in your classroom.

- Conveying acceptance of students with disabilities is an important part of your role as a teacher. You will serve as a model for your students and will help them learn to recognize the strengths and talents of their peers.

- Classroom behavior needs to be considered within a cultural context. Learn as much as you can about your students' background before making decisions about behavioral issues.

- Universal strategies for behavior management include looking for the positive, using reinforcers to encourage positive behavior, establishing clear rules with known consequences, helping students to change inappropriate behavior, and recognizing students' mistaken goals.

- IDEIA 2004 mandates the implementation of schoolwide positive behavior support and response to intervention models to prevent misbehavior and to provide evidence-based interventions to teach appropriate behavior.

Think and Apply

1. As the interview with Samantha Dietz revealed, many preservice teachers identify classroom management as the issue they are most concerned about before teaching, and practicing teachers identify it as the issue with which they have the most difficulty. Interview five practicing teachers and ask the following questions: What classroom management strategies do you find most useful? What aspects of classroom management do you wish you knew more about? What advice about classroom management would you offer?

2. Establishing a climate for acceptance is key to creating a productive learning environment. What are some specific things you plan to do to create an accepting environment for culturally and linguistically diverse students in your classroom? Describe some ways you can promote acceptance of students with disabilities in your classroom; in other words, how would you manage this inclusive classroom?

3. This chapter identified universal strategies for effective classroom management. On a sheet of paper, list the strategies for effective classroom management. Now add several others to the list, based on information provided in this chapter and from your own experience. Rank these strategies according to their importance to you. As you continue reading, return to your list of classroom management strategies and see whether there are any you would rewrite or reorder.

PEARSON myeducationlab

Now go to Topic 6: Classroom/Behavior Management in the MyEducationLab (www.myeducationlab.com) for your course where you can:

- Find learning outcomes for this topic along with the national standards that connect to these outcomes.

- Complete Assignments and Activities that can help you more deeply understand the chapter content.

- Examine challenging situations and cases presented in the IRIS Center Resources.

- Listen to Teacher Talk to hear how one teacher creates a community of learners.

- Apply and practice your understanding of the core teaching skills identified in the chapter with Building Teaching Skills and Dispositions learning units.

CATEGORICAL DIFFERENCES

Chapter 6

Teaching Students with Learning Disabilities
and Attention Deficit Hyperactivity Disorder

Chapter 7

Teaching Students with Communication Disorders

Chapter 8

Teaching Students with Emotional and Behavioral Disorders

Chapter 9

Teaching Students with Autism Spectrum
Disorders/Pervasive Developmental Disorders

Chapter 10

Teaching Students with Developmental Disabilities

Chapter 11

Teaching Students with Lower-Incidence Disabilities

Teaching Students with Learning Disabilities and Attention Deficit Hyperactivity Disorder

CHAPTER 6

FOCUS QUESTIONS

1. According to IDEIA, what are the major components of the definition and criteria for determining a specific learning disability?

2. What are the characteristics of students who have learning disabilities?

3. What information should you collect about a student with a possible learning disability to share at a multidisciplinary conference?

4. What techniques could you incorporate into your teaching to benefit students with learning disabilities?

5. What is attention deficit hyperactivity disorder (ADHD)? How does it affect a student in school?

6. What are the characteristics of students with hyperactive–impulsive-type ADHD and of students with inattentive-type ADHD, and why is it difficult to determine the prevalence of ADHD?

7. What are some strategies you can use to help students with ADHD be successful in school?

INTERVIEW
TAMMY GREGORY

Tammy Gregory is a third-year teacher who has one student with learning disabilities, Adrian, and one student with attention deficit hyperactivity disorder, Lenny, in her class with 26 other second graders. Tammy is strongly committed to providing the most effective instruction and a supportive learning environment for all of her students. Adrian has a learning disability that is represented in the speed at which he processes information. He responds slower than other students, it takes him a while to process what the teacher and other students are saying, and he reads and performs math problems very slowly. When he writes, it takes him longer and he is often the last student to complete assignments.

Tammy regularly makes accommodations for Adrian so that he is a successful learner in her classroom. She may reduce the length of the assignment so that he can complete it in the time allowed. Tammy says, "The key is that Adrian understands and has mastered the skill. If he can demonstrate mastery answering 5 problems instead of 10 problems in math, then he has learned and reached his goal."

Although speed of processing can make Adrian appear slow and not very adept at many skills, his teacher has taken the time to learn about his interests and his strengths and to share these with the other students. It is not unusual to hear Tammy say to the class, "Check with Adrian on that. He's a real expert."

Tammy had more difficulties finding appropriate accommodations for Lenny, a student with attention deficit hyperactivity disorder. He moved constantly (even when sitting) and was always out of his seat, sharpening his pencil and talking to and bothering the other students. He rarely completed assignments. Tammy felt that Lenny could do much of the work but that his attention problems got in the way of his being a successful learner. To help Lenny, Tammy thought about and modified the structure of her classroom and schedule. Tammy reviewed the schedule each day with the entire class ensuring that Lenny knew what was planned and expected of him. She provided a list of daily activities that Lenny checked off and asked him to rate himself on three criteria: paying attention, effort, and work completed.

Introduction

Think about Tammy's philosophy and practice of teaching students with learning disabilities (LD) and attention problems. To what extent do the practices she implements with Adrian and Lenny reflect the type of teacher you are or want to be? The first section of this chapter provides an overview of students with learning disabilities (LD), and the second section focuses on students with attention deficit hyperactivity disorder (ADHD). As you read, think about ways the strategies suggested for these students can also be used for other students in elementary and secondary classrooms.

Learning Disabilities

The disabilities of students who have visual impairments, are deaf or hard of hearing, or have overall cognitive delays are usually apparent. In contrast, you probably will not recognize students with LD in your classroom until you have the opportunity to see how they learn. Only in the last 35 years have learning disabilities, sometimes referred to as the "invisible disability," been recognized in our schools. This section provides definitions and characteristics of learning disabilities, as well as suggestions for meeting the needs of students with LD in your classroom.

Definitions and Types of Learning Disabilities

The issue of how to define learning disabilities has received considerable attention in the field since 1963, when Samuel Kirk suggested the term *specific learning disabilities* at the organizational meeting of the Learning Disabilities Association of America (LDA) (formerly called the Association for Children with Learning Disabilities [ACLD]). The LDA is a parent and professional organization that provides many resources related to learning disabilities. In the early 1960s, children with LD were referred to by such terms as *perceptually handicapped, brain-injured,* and *neurologically impaired* and were served in classrooms for students with mental retardation or, in most cases, were not receiving any specialized services in the public schools.

The term **specific learning disabilities** represents a heterogeneous group of students who, despite adequate cognitive functioning and the ability to learn some skills and strategies relatively quickly and easily, have great difficulty learning other skills and strategies. For example, students with specific reading disabilities may participate quite well in class discussions but have difficulty reading the text and taking tests. Other students may have great difficulty with math but have little difficulty with tasks that incorporate reading and writing.

The operational guidelines for the definition of specific learning disabilities are identified in the rules and regulations for IDEIA 2004 and indicate that a multidisciplinary team may determine that a child has a specific learning disability if

- The student does not achieve commensurate with his or her age and ability level in one or more of several specific areas when provided with appropriate learning experiences.
- The student has participated in but does not respond adequately to a scientific, research-based intervention (for example, in reading or math). In the updated definition, a child no longer needs to have a severe discrepancy between achievement and intellectual ability to qualify for a specific learning disability (Individuals with Disabilities Education Improvement Act of 2004, sec. 614[b][2], [3]).
- The student needs special education services.

A student is not regarded as having a specific learning disability if the deficit is primarily the result of any of the following:

- Visual, hearing, or motor disability
- Mental retardation
- Emotional disturbance
- Environmental, cultural, or economic disadvantage
- Lack of appropriate instruction in reading

The term **children with specific learning disabilities** means those children who have a disorder in one or more of the basic psychological processes involved in understanding or in using language, spoken or written, that may manifest itself in an imperfect ability to listen, think, speak, read, write, spell, or do mathematical calculations. These disorders include such conditions as perceptual handicaps, brain injury, minimal brain dysfunction, dyslexia, and developmental aphasia. Such terms do not include children who have learning problems that are primarily the result of visual, hearing, or motor handicap; of mental retardation; of emotional disturbance; or of environmental, cultural, or economic disadvantage. The major components of this definition include the following:

- Difficulty with academic and learning tasks
- Discrepancy between expected and actual achievement that can be documented through low response to intervention
- Disorder in basic psychological processing
- Exclusion of other causes

Diagnosing Students with Learning Disabilities

Determining that students have a learning disability has always been a difficult and somewhat controversial task. This is largely because it is difficult to distinguish between a learning problem and a learning disability. Furthermore, until relatively recently, most professionals believed that a discrepancy between IQ and achievement defined discrepancy. Discrepancy is no longer required when diagnosing a student as having a learning disability and instead many professionals are using response to intervention.

In 2002, Stuebing and colleagues evaluated 46 different studies conducted between 1973 and 1998 that addressed IQ–achievement discrepancy. These studies included measures of behavior, academic achievement, and cognitive abilities. These studies found little relationship between IQ and word reading.

Recently, concern has been raised about the federal criteria for determining a specific learning disability. The discrepancy is difficult to determine with young children and may unnecessarily postpone identification until second grade or later. At the same time, longitudinal research has demonstrated that 75% of students who do not learn to read by the third grade will continue to have reading disabilities throughout their schooling career (Lyon, Fletcher, & Barnes, 2003).

IDEIA 2004 includes the use of response to intervention (RTI) as an alternative to the traditional aptitude–achievement discrepancy approaches to identifying students with learning disabilities. Recall from Chapters 1 and 2 that RTI is a model for providing support to struggling readers in the primary grades at the intensity and level that is required to meet the needs of individual students. RTI provides a validated intervention to students in the instructional area of need before determining their qualifications for special education. Students who respond adequately to the intervention and are able to make appropriate progress in the classroom are unlikely to require special education. Students whose response to the intervention is low are very likely to require special education. Possible difficulties of the RTI approach include questions of who will provide the interventions and the extent to which validated instructional practices exist in fields other than reading, but this approach appears to be a path for identification of learning disabilities that will be taken by more and more school districts (Fuchs, Fuchs, & Vaughn, 2008; Vaughn & Fuchs, 2003).

Although many definitions of learning disabilities have been developed, secondary science teacher Joseph Blankenship's ideas about learning disabilities are similar to those of many other general education teachers. He comments that initially these students may not seem different from other students. They participate in classroom discussions and may appear to understand the content covered. But as assignments are submitted and tests given, he quickly realizes that students with LD have difficulties with reading, writing, math, studying, and organizing their time.

RTI neither creates nor fixes learning disabilities. However, models such as 3-Tier Reading provide a safety net for students who might end up in special education simply because they have not been provided adequate instruction or appropriate interventions prior to being referred for special education services. RTI is a dynamic model that allows students to move between levels of interventions depending on results of ongoing progress monitoring and benchmark assessments. The key to the 3-Tier Reading Model and other RTI models is to provide effective instruction early to ensure that students are provided with the resources and support they need to become proficient readers.

Characteristics of Students with Learning Disabilities

Because learning disabilities are heterogeneous, it is difficult to list a set of characteristics that adequately describes all students with LD. You will find that students with LD seem more different from one another than alike in relation to how they learn, but certain overriding characteristics will help you identify these students:

- *Unexpected* difficulty or low performance in one or more academic areas (unexpected in that your general impressions of the student would not lead you to predict that he or she would have difficulty)
- Ineffective or inefficient information-processing or learning strategies in the area(s) of difficulty

Furthermore, the reasons for this low performance vary according to the strengths and weaknesses of the learner and the learning strategies he or she employs.

For example, Tamara and Manuel, two students in Carla Huerra's third-grade classroom, were identified as having specific learning disabilities and were reading and spelling at an early first-grade (primer) level. Both students have difficulty learning to recognize and spell words automatically when reading and writing, but the strategies they use are very different, as are

What are some learner characteristics that might help you identify a student with possible learning disabilities? How might you work with an inclusion specialist or special education teacher to plan and design an education program to support such a student?

PEARSON myeducationlab

Go to the Assignments and Activities section of Topic 12: Learning Disabilities in the MyEducationLab for your course and complete the activity entitled *Differentiated Instruction for Students with Learning Disabilities.*

the individualized education programs that Carla and the special education teacher, David Ross, use with each student.

Carla's observations reveal that Tamara has strong oral language skills. She capitalizes on these skills when she reads and uses the meaning and the syntax (word order or grammar) of the language as her primary strategies for figuring out unknown words. When she does not know a word, she skips it or substitutes a word that more or less makes sense. She shows little evidence of using phonics beyond using the initial sound to figure out unknown words. Carla notes that even though Tamara sees a word many times, either in context or written by itself, it is not easy for her to recognize it automatically so that it becomes part of her sight vocabulary. When Carla observes Tamara's writing, she notes that Tamara has wonderful ideas but spends much of her time asking other students how to spell words or changing what she was originally going to write so that she can use words she knows how to spell.

Like Tamara, Manuel has difficulty with reading and writing automatically. Manuel's reading is very slow and he sounds out the words (uses his phonic analysis skills). He is able to get a number of the individual sounds but has trouble blending them together to make a word. Although the words that result may not make sense, he does not seem to monitor this by going back and rereading. Manuel's writing also reflects his use of somewhat successful phonic analysis, in that even high-frequency, irregular words are spelled phonetically (e.g., "cum" for *come,* "wuz" for *was*).

In talking with David Ross, Tamara and Manuel's special education teacher, Carla learned that both students have visual-memory and auditory-processing difficulties that make it hard for them to learn to automatically recognize words. Each student, however, uses different strategies and strengths to compensate (i.e., Tamara relies on her strong oral language skills, and Manuel relies on "somewhat successful" phonic analysis).

Together, Carla and David have planned and designed educational programs to support these students. For studying content areas such as science and social studies, Carla relies on using books written at different reading levels. She also allows students to demonstrate their knowledge through oral reports, posters, and pictures rather than only through traditional written reports and tests. During writers' workshops, Carla helps each student develop a spelling dictionary. For reading, Carla and David work together to help Tamara and Manuel expand the strategies they use to decode unknown words. For Tamara, this includes learning to use phonic analysis along with meaning to help her identify the unknown word. They are also helping Tamara to see similar spelling patterns in words (e.g., word families: *-ake, make, take, lake*). For Manuel, their help includes using repeated reading to get him to build fluency and take more risks when decoding words. Manuel is also learning to ask himself the question "Does this make sense?" to monitor his decoding and comprehension.

Figure 6.1 presents some characteristics that, although they might not apply to all students with LD, have helped signal to general education teachers which students might have specific learning disabilities. Several of these characteristics refer to difficulties in attention. Students with LD often have difficulties with attention and, in some cases, hyperactivity. More than 40% of students with learning disabilities or behavior disorders also exhibit difficulties with attention problems (Zentall, 2006), and boys are four times more likely to be diagnosed with attention deficit disorder than are girls (Barkley, 2005).

Learning disabilities represent a group of disorders that cause students to have learning and academic difficulties. Currently, although no generally accepted classification systems exist for students with LD (Fletcher et al., 2007; Keogh, 1993; Speece, 1994), types of learning disabilities have been discussed in the literature and used in medical and psychological reports for many years. Some of the most frequently used terms are *dyslexia, dysgraphia,* and *dyscalculia.*

FIGURE
6.1

Signals for Possible Learning Disabilities

Signals for learning disabilities are characteristics of students with learning disabilities. Because these students are a heterogeneous group, only certain signals will apply to any one student.

- Has trouble understanding and following directions

- Has a short attention span; is easily distracted

- Is overactive and impulsive

- Has difficulty with handwriting and fine motor activities

- Has difficulty with visual or auditory sequential memory

- Has difficulty memorizing words or basic math facts

- Has difficulty allocating time and organizing work

- Is unmotivated toward tasks that are difficult

- Has difficulty segmenting words into sounds and blending sounds

- Confuses similar letters and words, such as *b* and *d*, and *was* and *saw*

- Listens and speaks well but decodes poorly when reading

- Has difficulty with tasks that require rapid naming of pictures, words, and numbers

- Is not efficient or effective in using learning strategies

- **Dyslexia** refers to severe difficulty in learning to read, particularly as it relates to decoding and spelling.
- **Dysgraphia** refers to severe difficulty in learning to write, including handwriting.
- **Dyscalculia** refers to severe difficulty in learning mathematical concepts and computation.

Reading difficulties are the most frequent characteristic of students with LD. For students who are learning to read, evidence suggests that this problem is related to difficulties in phonemic awareness, developing the alphabetic principle, and rapid naming tasks (see for reviews Ehri, 2004; Klingner, Vaughn, & Boardman, 2007; Lovett, Barron, & Benson, 2003). **Phonemic awareness** is the ability to blend, segment, and manipulate speech sounds (for example, *trash* has four speech sounds or phonemes: *t-r-a-sh*). The **alphabetic principle** is learning how speech maps to print or learning letter–sound relationships. Understanding letter–sound relationships allows students to decode unknown words by making the speech sounds associated with letters and then blending them together to make the word (e.g., *c-a-t* is *cat*). **Rapid naming** entails having children quickly name familiar objects, letters, or numbers. This skill is important in building reading fluency. Students with LD may also have difficulty with reading comprehension, and many students who have difficulty learning to read continue to have difficulty with decoding, which affects their reading comprehension. Examples of the types of reading disabilities frequently exhibited and the activities that teachers can use to instruct students are provided in Tips for Teachers 6.1.

Students with LD, even those who read fairly well, may have problems with written language (Harris, Graham, Mason, & Fiedlander, 2008). These difficulties can occur in handwriting, spelling, productivity, writing mechanics, organization, and composition (Gersten & Baker, 2003).

Although not as prevalent as reading disabilities, a substantial number of students with LD in elementary and secondary grades experience difficulties with mathematics (Fuchs, Fuchs, & Prentice, 2004). Difficulty may be in basic math calculations or more complex mathematical problem solving. Students with LD often require instruction in both basic math skills and math problem solving.

What are the lifelong outcomes for students with LD? There is no single answer for all students, but we do have evidence that some individuals with LD are quite successful in adult life and that they learn to adjust and make accommodations for their disabilities (e.g., Albert Einstein, Nelson Rockefeller, and Thomas Edison all had significant learning disabilities). Overall, however, students with LD have higher rates of unemployment and underemployment, fewer live independently, and fewer succeed in postsecondary programs than students in general.

What are the social and education factors that predict success for individuals with LD? Research indicates that successful adults with LD make realistic adaptations for their LD, take control of their lives, are goal oriented, and persist at these goals. Successful adults with LD have indicated that one or more significant people have supported their adjustments during school, postsecondary training, and young adult life (e.g., Raskind, Goldberg, Higgins, & Herman, 1999; Speckman, Goldberg, & Herman, 1993), including engaging them in planning for the transition from middle and high school to other work or learning experiences (Neubert, 2003). Increased access to vocational training programs and support programs in

Go to **www.interdys.org** to learn more about how you can help students with dyslexia and their families.

Go to **www.ld.org** for information on awareness, advocacy, education, and treatment of LD.

READING DIFFICULTIES AND SUGGESTIONS FOR INSTRUCTION

Phonological Awareness

- Blending phonemes (e.g., blending sounds to make words such as /m/, /a/, /n/)

- Segmenting phonemes (e.g., this is the opposite of blending and requires identifying the sounds separately in a word; teacher says "not" and student says, /n/, /o/, /t/)

- Integrating phonemic awareness with letters and print (e.g., as students are blending phonemes and segmenting phonemes, point to the letter, move the letters as tiles or blocks, or ask students to write, point to, or move the letters)

Phonics

- Letter–sound correspondence, letter combinations, affixes, and roots (e.g., examine a core reading program with a strong phonics strand and identify the key phonics elements taught at each grade level, determining which ones the student knows and doesn't know)

- Blending regular words (e.g., fin, trump, sunshine, sailor)

- Structural analysis to decode words (e.g., use prefixes such as "pre" and "un," suffixes such as "ly" and "ed," and key words to detect compound words)

- Strategies for decoding multisyllabic words (e.g., recognize the letter combinations that trigger multiple syllable words such as the "double letter" in simmer and endings such as "ly" and "ing")

- Reading irregular words with extensive review (e.g., high frequency irregular words such as "said," "the," "from," "was")

- Integrating phonics instruction with text reading and spelling (e.g., asking students to read words in context for which they know the phonics rules and asking students to use spelling to reinforce phonics rules)

Fluency

- Models of fluent reading (e.g., tapes of adult readers, older students, or better readers serving as models for reading the passages)

- Strategies for chunking text (e.g., phrasing and organizing text to read fluently)

- Rereading text with feedback (e.g., listening to students read and providing feedback about phrasing, prosody, and accuracy)

Vocabulary

- Oral discussions of new words and meanings (e.g., ask students to build word meanings through discussion)

- Instruction in specific word meanings for words used frequently in print (e.g., identify key words in text and preteach meanings using student-friendly descriptions)

- Practice making connections between related words (e.g., gallop describes how someone or something moves, what other words describe movement?)

- Repeated exposure to new vocabulary in a variety of contexts (e.g., words read in reading and language arts are encountered in other contexts)

- Strategies for determining word meanings independently (e.g., using context to understand word meaning)

Comprehension

- Generating questions (e.g., teach students to develop questions about what they read)

- Understanding features of text formats (e.g., story structure)

- Summarizing and generating main ideas (e.g., model and then practice main idea and summarize of different text types)

---

colleges has also increased success (Barkley, Murphy, & Fischer, 2008; Gerber, Ginsberg, & Reiff, 1992; Vogel, Hruby, & Adelman, 1993), with many students with LD and ADHD performing on par with nondisabled students in college (Sparks, Javorsky, & Philips, 2004). Success after high school also means success in living independently, having positive relationships with co-workers, having friends, and enjoying family and community life (Ferguson & Ferguson, 2006).

Prevalence of Learning Disabilities

Today, more students are identified as having specific learning disabilities than any other type of disability. According to the *Twenty-Seventh Annual Report to Congress on the Implementation of the Individuals with Disabilities Education Act* (U.S. Department of Education, 2007), approximately 9% of school-age children were identified as having disabilities, and just over 47% of this group, or approximately 4% of the school-age population, were identified as having specific learning disabilities. During the last three decades, the number of students identified as having LD has increased substantially—more than doubling. The percentage of school-age children identified as having a learning disability varies considerably by state, ranging from 1.5% to 5.2%.

Why does the percentage of students with LD continue to increase? Several factors are considered, including the following (Hallahan, 1992; Kavale, Holdnack, & Mostert, 2005):

- *Growing public awareness of LD.* As more parents and general education teachers learn about the characteristics of students with LD, they become more attuned to watching for signs and seeking assistance within the school system.
- *Greater social acceptance.* Learning disabilities are viewed as more socially accepted and have fewer negative connotations than others.
- *Limited alternatives for other students at risk.* Owing to limited alternative programs, the tendency is to identify any students who are failing as having learning disabilities so that they can receive services.
- *Social and cultural influences on central nervous system integrity.* Demographics suggest that more children are being born to parents whose income falls below the poverty level, who may be addicted to drugs and alcohol, and who are teenagers (all factors that increase chances of these children being at risk for LD).
- *Increasing needs for literacy at work and in daily life.* As we move into an information age that requires better-educated individuals, schools are demanding more of students, and higher literacy levels are necessary for jobs and the tasks of daily life.

Also of interest is the number of boys versus girls identified as having learning disabilities, boys being identified from twice to as many as eight times more often than girls. Data from the U.S. Department of Education (2008) indicate a ratio of approximately four boys to every girl. Recent research on the genetic bases of dyslexia would suggest that the ratio of boys to girls should be more equal (Fletcher, Lyon, Fuchs, & Barnes, 2007; Shaywitz, 2003) even though males do have more of a biological vulnerability than females. Males may also be more vulnerable to referral and identification because boys generally exhibit more disruptive behaviors, including attention deficit disorder (Liederman, Kantrowit, & Flannery, 2005).

Identification and Assessment of Students with Learning Disabilities

Most students with LD are identified because of difficulties with academic achievement. Teachers—usually the first professionals to notice the students' learning strengths and weaknesses and academic skills—play an important role in identifying students with LD. Louise Parra, a first-grade teacher, comments on the importance she places on being alert for students who may have LD:

> As a first-grade teacher, it is very important that I understand LD and keep alert for children who are not learning at the same rate or with the same ease that I would expect of them. If I notice these children in the first grade and begin collaborating with the special education teacher, other specialists, and the children's families, then I can assist in preventing these children from developing the poor self-esteem that frequently develops if they continue to fail and are not supported.

Of all the members of a prereferral or multidisciplinary team, classroom teachers and parents have the most experience with a student. Referral from the classroom teacher is one of the most important predictors of whether a student will be identified as learning disabled. One of the most important things you can do to ensure that you are appropriately referring students for learning disabilities is to ask yourself the following questions:

- Have you provided effective instruction?
- Have you given the student additional support and modifications?
- Is this student a distinctly different learner than others you have taught?
- Are there other explanations for this student's learning problems other than a possible learning disability?

Tips for Teachers 6.2 provides suggestions for what classroom teachers should consider before referring a student who seems to have LD.

Jackie Darnell, a fifth-grade teacher, shared observations and information about a student, Cassandra, at a multidisciplinary conference, during which it was decided that, because of math disabilities, Cassandra was eligible for special education services (see Figure 6.2). Jackie used a

Tips FOR TEACHERS 6.2

WHAT TO CONSIDER IN REFERRING STUDENTS SUSPECTED OF HAVING LEARNING DISABILITIES

- In which academic areas of learning (e.g., listening comprehension, oral expression, basic reading skills, reading comprehension, basic writing skills, written expression, math computation, math reasoning and problem solving) is the student successful, and in which areas is the student having difficulties?

- What are the academic achievement levels in these areas and what are representative examples of the student's work?

- How does the student compare with other students in the classroom in areas of success and difficulty?

- What factors (other than specific learning disabilities) might be contributing to the learning problems experienced by the student (e.g., frequent moves, absences, recent traumatic life events, vision or hearing impairments, emotional disorders)?

- Are the student's first language and language of instruction the same, or is the student learning academics while also acquiring a second language or dialect?

- What learning or compensatory strategies does the student currently use to aid in learning?

- How does the student perceive him- or herself as a learner, and what is the student's attitude toward school and learning?

- What strategies and accommodations have been tried, and how did they work?

variety of assessments to collect information about Cassandra, including observations and analysis of work samples, curriculum-based assessments taken from the math curriculum and textbook, and informal math assessments designed by Jackie to pinpoint skills on which students need to work to gain mastery. The information Jackie provided clearly identified her concerns in the area of math computation. She also provided information about strategies she had already tried with Cassandra. Documenting what has been tried and its success is key to justifying that a student needs special education services.

Because Cassandra enjoyed working on the computer, she and the special education teacher worked together to identify additional computer programs for Cassandra. In addition, the special education teacher planned to work with Cassandra on how to use a calculator and build skills in computation of multiplication problems. Both teachers also planned to use manipulatives (e.g., tokens, fraction cards, pegs) to build Cassandra's understanding of division and fractions.

Instructional Techniques and Accommodations for Students with Learning Disabilities

No one approach or technique is appropriate for all students with LD because students with LD are so diverse. In fact, many special education teachers describe having to be eclectic in their philosophy and approaches to teaching to match the different learning patterns these students exhibit. Effective classroom teachers report that they must use their "best teaching practices" to teach students with LD. Len Hays, a seventh-grade English teacher, elaborates on best teaching practices:

> When I work with students who have been identified as having LD or who are at risk, it requires my best teaching. By this I mean that I must be very organized in the manner in which I present a literature unit or an English lesson. First, I give an overview of the lesson and explain the activities and what is expected of the students. I also make sure that when I lecture, I display the important information so that all students can see it. If I want the students to understand a process, such as how to revise an essay to add "color," then using a projector lets me demonstrate the process and my thinking as I edit. This allows me to model the questions I ask myself as a writer and to show the changes I make. It is also important that I organize the learning activities and working groups so that students have the opportunity to practice the skills that are the focus of the lesson. Whether we are working on editing skills or doing a critical analysis of a book, I always work to relate the learning to the students' daily lives. Finally, I try to be creative and humorous. That is just part of being a middle-school teacher and dealing with adolescence.

Several instructional practices are associated with improved outcomes for students with learning disabilities. These instructional practices have emerged from more than 100 studies

FIGURE 6.2

Information Shared by Jackie Darnell, the Classroom Teacher, at a Multidisciplinary Conference

Name: Cassandra   **Age:** 10   **Grade:** 5th

Literacy:

• 4th- to 5th-grade level.

• Participates in literature discussion groups and can answer a variety of questions about the literature, including underlying theme and application questions.

• Can write a report with introduction and two supporting paragraphs.

• Spells at fourth-grade level, using phonic and structural analysis for unknown words.

• Can use a word processor to write and revise written work.

Progress monitoring data used to determine performance levels: Fall and winter benchmark testing.

RTI: No specialized intervention needed. Progress steady.

Math:

• Second-grade achievement level.

• Adds and subtracts with regrouping but makes computation errors in the process and with basic facts.

• Understands basic concept of multiplication but does not know basic facts or how to use for simple word problems.

• Has difficulty understanding simple one- and two-step word problems.

• Understands concept of multiplication as repeated addition. Does not compute multiplication problems.

• Demonstrates concept of simple fractions 1/2, 1/3, 1/4.

• Solves word problems. Errors are generally in computation and basic facts rather than problem representation.

• Describes math as least favorite subject.

• Struggles to learn basic math facts despite incentive program, coordination with parents, and use of computer programs at school.

Progress monitoring data used to determine performance levels: Weekly tests in +, −, *, / (number correct out of 10).

RTI: 15 minutes minimum daily small-group instruction. Progress minimal.

Social–Emotional:

• Well liked by peers, both boys and girls.

• Quiet, does not ask for help when needed.

• Works well in cooperative groups but usually does not take leadership roles.

• Good sense of humor.

(e.g., Fletcher, Lyon, Fuchs, & Barnes, 2007; Gersten & Baker, 2003; Kim, Vaughn, Wanzek, & Wei, 2004; Swanson, 1999; Swanson & Deshler, 2003).

On the basis of this work, several common practices were identified as powerful predictors of the academic success of students with LD:

■ Controlling task difficulty (i.e., teaching at the student's instructional level and sequencing examples and problems to maintain high levels of student success)
■ Teaching students with LD in small interactive groups of six or fewer students
■ Using graphic organizers and other visual displays to illustrate key ideas and concepts
■ Using a combination of direct instruction and cognitive strategy instruction
■ Providing modeling and "think alouds" to demonstrate strategies and learning practices
■ Teaching students to self-regulate and self-monitor their learning and to "fix-up" when they have learning problems
■ Providing opportunities for extended practice with feedback

Providing a Framework for Learning.   Students are more successful when they have a good idea of where they are going. Research on the use of **advance organizers** (i.e., activities that orient students to the task and the materials) suggests that this is even more important for students with LD, learning problems, or limited background knowledge for the task being taught (Bulgren, Deshler, & Lenz, 2007; Kim et al., 2004).

Colleagues at the University of Kansas identified steps for using advance organizers and concept maps to improve learning across the content area (Bulgren, 2006; Bulgren, Deshler, & Lenz, 2007; Lenz, Deshler, & Kissam, 2003). Lenz (1983) found that when content-area teachers in middle and high schools used advance organizers for learning, adolescents with LD could experience significant improvements in both the quality and quantity of learning. Three factors seem important to the success of advance organizers. First, students with LD are taught how to listen for and use the advance organizer. Students might complete a worksheet (see Figure 6.3) as they listen to the teacher introduce each part of the advance organizer. Second, after using the advance organizer worksheet, the teacher and students discuss the effectiveness of its use and how and when it might be used in various content classes. Third, before an advance organizer is presented, the teacher cues the students that it is going to be used.

One critical aspect of the advance organizer is that it provides basic information or activates the students' background knowledge (refer to step 5 in Tips for Teachers 6.3). Students with LD often have information about the topics, skills, or strategies being taught but do not automatically think about this information. The chapters on reading and content-area instruction discuss specific techniques for activating students' background knowledge.

Using Thinking Aloud and Instructional Conversations.   One key to success for students with LD is to make the learning visible. Think back to your experiences as a student. How did you learn to find the main idea when you were reading? Many teachers traditionally used the technique of repeatedly asking students questions such as "What is the main idea of this story?" until a student provided the right answer (e.g., Durkin, 1978–1979). Students were expected to infer how to find the main idea. However, intervention research on teaching reading comprehension and other cognitive processes has emphasized that teachers and students should model and discuss the **cognitive strategies** (i.e., thinking processes) they use for tasks such as finding the main idea of the story (e.g., Harris, Graham, Mason, & Friedlander, 2007; Klingner, Vaughn, &

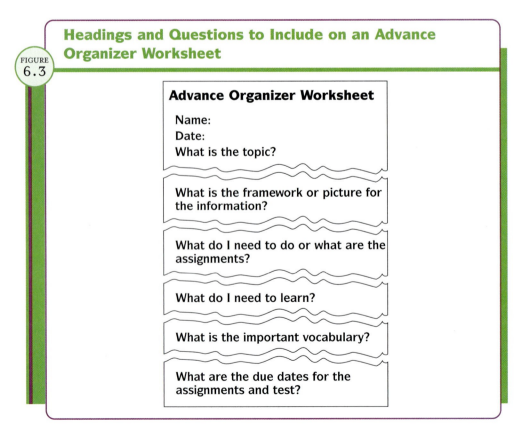

FIGURE 6.3

Headings and Questions to Include on an Advance Organizer Worksheet

Advance Organizer Worksheet

Name:
Date:
What is the topic?

What is the framework or picture for the information?

What do I need to do or what are the assignments?

What do I need to learn?

What is the important vocabulary?

What are the due dates for the assignments and test?

Tips FOR TEACHERS 6.3

STEPS IN USING AN ADVANCE ORGANIZER

1. Inform students of advance organizers.
   - Announce advance organizer.
   - State benefits of advance organizer.
   - Suggest that students take notes on the advance organizer.
2. Identify topics or tasks.
   - Identify major topics or activities.
   - Identify subtopics or component activities.
3. Provide an organizational framework.
   - Present an outline, list, or narrative of the lesson's content.
4. Clarify action to be taken.
   - Explain your actions.
   - State actions expected of students.
5. Provide background information.
   - Relate topic to the course or to a previous lesson.
   - Relate topic to new information.
6. State the concepts to be learned.
   - State specific concepts and ideas from the lesson.
   - State general concepts and ideas broader than the lesson's content.
7. Clarify the concepts to be learned.
   - Clarify by examples or analogies.
   - Clarify by nonexamples.
   - Caution students about possible misunderstandings.
8. Motivate students to learn.
   - Point out relevance to students.
   - Be specific, personal, and believable.
9. Introduce vocabulary.
   - Identify and define new terms.
   - Repeat and define difficult terms.
10. State the general outcome desired.
    - State objectives of instruction and learning.
    - Relate outcomes to test performance.

Source: Adapted from Lenz, B. K. (1983). Promoting active learning through effective instruction. *Pointer* 27(2), 12. Reprinted with permission.

Boardman, 2007; Wong, Harris, & Graham, 2003). Teachers and students can use thinking aloud to comment on or make visible their thought processes as they are doing cognitive tasks such as finding the main idea. Teachers can use discussions (referred to as **instructional conversations**) to make visible the thinking processes needed for understanding.

Mr. Waterhouse, a middle-school science teacher, had numerous students with disabilities in his classroom. He frequently used "think aloud" practices to help students identify key words and concepts and their meaning. For example, he would ask students to turn to a page in the science book and would say, "In paragraph 2, there is a key word, *mitosis*. Turn to page 139, paragraph 2, and find the word *mitosis*. I want you to listen to me read the paragraph aloud. As I read the paragraph I am going to ask myself if there are any clues to help me understand what mitosis means. After I find the clues, I'm going to generate a description of mitosis. As I continue reading the text, I will look for additional information to confirm or modify the meaning I've established."

In the following dialogue, the teacher is helping students to better understand story elements using an instructional conversation to make learning more visible (Englert, Raphael, & Mariage, 1994). In this example, the teacher is working with two third-grade students who have partner-read a narrative story about a bear and are now telling the rest of the students about the story.

T: Tell us about the story.
Ann: [Begins . . . by retelling random incidents from the story]
T: You already said we were going to talk about the characters, setting, and problem. Who are the characters in that story?
Dee: There is Brother Bear, Papa Bear, and . . . [Shows pictures from the book]
T: Who would you say is the main character?
Ann: They were all main characters because they were all together throughout the story.
T: When we try to figure out the main character, what is the question we ask ourselves?
Ann: What the author wants us to know.
T: Remember when we try to figure out the main character, we ask ourselves, "Who is ..."
Ann: [Ann fills in] ". . . the story mostly about?"
T: Could you answer that question by saying it's mostly about everybody there? (p. 21)

Rather than providing the answer, the teacher is modeling what question to ask to determine who the main character is. Research on students with LD has consistently demonstrated that whether the teacher is teaching reading, math, or written expression, making the learning strategies visible improves learning significantly.

Teaching Self-Regulation and Self-Monitoring.　By having students keep track of how well they are understanding or performing, students can gain incentives for learning and change their learning patterns to more effective ones. Research suggests that students with LD are not as adept as their peers at monitoring their own performance (e.g., Klingner, Vaughn, & Boardman, 2007; Wong et al., 2003), and effective teachers promote self-monitoring (Pressley, in press; Pressley et al., 2001). One way to help students with LD is to teach them to ask themselves questions about their learning and performance. General questions that students can ask themselves include the following:

- What is my purpose for learning or doing this?
- What is my plan for doing this task?
- Does what I am learning, reading, or doing make sense?
- What do I already know about this topic?
- How am I doing with my work?
- What are the main points I am learning?
- How can I use this elsewhere?

The use of **self-monitoring** and graphing has been shown to be effective for students with learning and attention problems (e.g., Fletcher, Lyon, Fuchs, & Barnes, 2007; Hitchcock, Dowrick, & Prater, 2003; Klingner, Vaughn, & Boardman, 2007). For example, teaching students to self-monitor reading fluency can provide a means for them to set goals and see their progress. Students should read material written at their instructional to independent reading levels (e.g., word recognition 90% or greater). To calculate fluency, have the students use the following formula:

$$\frac{\text{Total words read} - \text{Errors}}{\text{Number of minutes of reading}} = \text{Words correct per minute}$$

Fluency information can be plotted onto graphs like the one shown in Figure 6.4. Having students record their own progress serves as a motivation for reading, provides immediate feedback, and allows the students to set goals and see concrete evidence of their progress. Generally, for students with fluency problems, the goal should be an increase of one to two words correct per minute per week. However, use past performance to help students set goals.

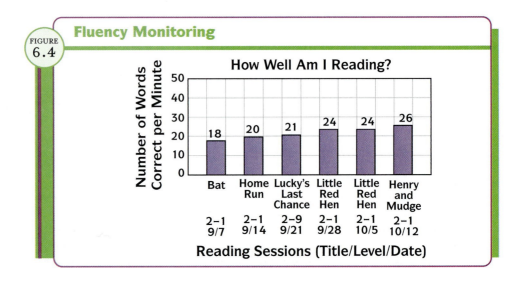

FIGURE 6.4

Fluency Monitoring

Providing Extended Practice and Application.
Students with LD need extended practice and additional opportunities to apply their learning to ensure continued mastery (Kameenui & Simmons, 1990; Lovett et al., 2003; Swanson & Hoskyn, 1998). When teachers present complex materials and skills to adolescents with LD, extended practice with feedback is particularly important and helps to minimize difficulties with complex cognitive activities (Scammacca et al., 2007; Swanson & Hoskyn, 1998; Vaughn, Gersten, & Chard, 2000). To create these opportunities when other students in the class may not benefit from them, teachers must be adept at instructional management.

Sonya Rieden, a sixth-grade teacher, comments on the way she organizes her classroom to promote opportunities for extended practice and maintenance of skills and strategies:

> One of the most difficult aspects of teaching is juggling the grouping of students and scheduling of activities to ensure that students who need more time to learn have that opportunity available. Here is the way I do it. I select the skills/strategies based on students' needs, and we usually work on those skills/strategies for one to three weeks. I usually teach nine 10- to 15-minute lessons a week so that I focus on three skills/strategies at the same time. The students who are most academically at risk usually work on two of the three skills/strategies. This allows the students who need the most guidance to receive regular small-group instruction and to work consistently on a specific skill or strategy. In their learning folders students keep a list of these skills/strategies and space to record progress and to provide work samples. When I meet with students (either individually or in small groups), we review the skill/strategy list, update the records, monitor progress, and set goals. We prioritize activities and expected learning for the future.

Several other instructional principles that are important for students with LD and are helpful for many students include the following:

- Using learning tools and aids
- Adjusting workload and time
- Presenting and having students demonstrate their learning in multiple ways
- Teaching students to use memory strategies

What are eight general teaching strategies that are helpful for all students but are especially effective for students with learning disabilities?

Using Learning Tools and Aids. With new technology and its increasing availability, more students with reading, writing, and math disabilities are able to overcome their academic problems through the use of technologically based learning tools (Quinlan, 2004; Rose & Meyer, 2002).

Also, teachers are better able to organize their classrooms and use technology to facilitate effective cooperative learning activities (see Tech Tips to learn about some useful technologies). Computers, with their peripherals and programs, offer a number of effective tools for students, with new programs being created and older programs being updated. Some examples include:

- Students with handwriting and spelling disabilities have been helped by word processing programs with built-in spell checkers.
- Through speech synthesizers and software, students with reading and writing difficulties have had the opportunity to hear what they write and then to read along with the computer. Drill-and-practice programs for math facts, such as *Math Blasters Plus,* have provided students with the opportunity to review and practice their math facts in an interactive game format.
- Other learning tools that are recommended for students with LD include calculators, spell checkers, tape recorders, and handheld organizers.

Adjusting Workload and Time. Adjustments of workload and time allocations can be useful accommodations for students with LD. Workload adjustments can include both the amount of work given and the manner in which it is given. Reducing the amount of work may be a reasonable

PEARSON
myeducationlab

Go to the Assignments and Activities section of Topic 12: Learning Disabilities in the MyEducationLab for your course and complete the activity entitled *Accommodations: Additional Time.*

accommodation when the goal of an assignment or test is for the student to demonstrate mastery (and it can be demonstrated with less work). For example, if the purpose of a math assignment is to demonstrate mastery in using addition and subtraction with regrouping to solve verbal math problems, then completing the odd-numbered problems rather than all the problems may provide adequate evidence of mastery. This type of accommodation is reasonable for students who are slow in math computation because their knowledge of math facts is not at an automatic level. The accommodation of providing time extensions for tests or completion of large projects has also been helpful for students with LD.

Another way to adjust work is to divide it into smaller sections or tasks. Having students work on groups of 5 problems at a time rather than the complete set of 20 can make a task more manageable for the student and give the teacher additional opportunities to provide feedback and encouragement as each five-problem set is completed. Helping students to break a complex task, such as reading a book and writing a report, into smaller tasks and to develop a timeline for completing each task can also encourage successful task completion.

Presenting Information in Multiple Ways. Students with LD may have difficulty processing information when it is presented in only one way. To assist these students, it is important to present the information in multiple ways. Bruce Ford, a ninth-grade science teacher, incorporates a number of activities, materials, and ways of presenting information as he plans a unit on cells:

When I think about planning for biology class, I think about what are the key knowledge and skills that I want the students to understand and use. I know that if I just present the information using a lecture and have the students read the textbook, a good number of the students will not be able to access the information. So I find myself being creative and constantly on the lookout for additional resources that I can integrate into the unit. Right now, when we do the unit on cells, I have a great video from *Nova* that I use. I have also developed a study guide that I have students complete as we go through the unit. It incorporates pictures of cells and allows students to label the parts of the cell and their functions. It also includes Internet sites that provide accurate information on cells.

The study guide provides the outline for my lecture notes. The study guide is critical because many of the students in my class cannot take adequate notes, and the study guide serves as a structure for their note taking. One activity that I use is an experiment where students have to view cells during the reproduction cycle with a microscope. This activity allows the students to work in teams and develop a group report of their findings. I ask the students to be sure to include drawings. I have found that some of my students with LD excel at this activity.

By presenting information in multiple ways, teachers allow students to demonstrate their learning in multiple ways. This benefits many students, particularly because the majority of students with LD have writing problems that persist over time (Gersten & Baker, 2001; Graham & Harris, 2003). A high-school teacher who teaches students with LD explains: "The adolescents in my program do not want to write. They do not even want to answer questions in writing. Writing a theme for a class is torture." Yet writing and tests are the major vehicles used to demonstrate learning. Modifying the manner in which students demonstrate learning enables students with LD to be more successful in the classroom. Tips for Teachers 6.4 suggests ideas for presenting information and demonstrating learning in multiple ways.

Teaching Students to Use Memory Strategies. Research has consistently demonstrated that students with LD are less effective at employing memory strategies than their peers (McNamara & Wong, 2003; Swanson & Saez, 2003; Swanson & Siegel, 2001). This is particularly important when students with disabilities are included in general education classrooms where they are exposed to large amounts of information during content-area instruction. For the classroom teacher, this means that students with LD will not automatically use **memory strategies** such as rehearsing information they are learning, categorizing the information to make it easier to learn, using visual imagery to "see" the information mentally, and using

Tips FOR TEACHERS 6.4

IDEAS FOR PRESENTING INFORMATION AND DEMONSTRATING LEARNING IN MULTIPLE WAYS

Ideas for Presenting Information

- Demonstrate the process or strategy.

- Lecture, writing key points so that they are visible to students as you talk.

- Lecture, stopping at natural breaks so that students, working in pairs, can discuss what they see as the major ideas.

- Use a graphic organizer or map to show the relationships among the ideas you are presenting.

- Use a video or movie that presents the key points.

- Have students listen to audio-recorded books.

- Have students conduct experiments to test hypotheses or discover relationships.

- Use pantomimes and skits to explain concepts.

- Have students role-play.

- Use computer simulations.

- Use manipulatives to demonstrate and then have the students use manipulatives.

- Use analogies, metaphors, and examples to further explain concepts.

- Have students use visualization and imagery to see ideas and their relationships.

Ideas for Demonstrating Learning in Math

- For students who have difficulties aligning numbers, use graph paper.

- Have students draw a visual representation of the story problem and then complete the math computation. Give partial credit for correct visual representation, even if math computation is incorrect.

- Allow students who do not know their math facts to use math fact matrixes or calculators.

- Allow for time extensions.

Ideas for Demonstrating Learning in Content Areas

- Give tests orally and have students respond orally (students can tape record their responses). (The special education teacher or paraprofessional can often assist in this activity.)

- Allow time extensions on tests and projects.

- For projects, help students divide the project into steps and develop a timeline for completing each step.

- Have students use a picture or sequence of pictures to demonstrate understanding of a concept or process.

- Have students develop a skit or pantomime and present it to the class.

- Use word processing programs and spell checkers.

TEACHING STUDENTS TO DEVELOP ACRONYMS

One activity that students of all ages seem to enjoy and profit from is learning to develop and memorize acronyms for lists of information that must be learned. When you teach a list to students, have them form cooperative groups, with each group working on developing an acronym to help them remember the list. Then each group can report on its acronym.

acronyms to remember lists. By teaching students with LD how to organize and associate information, how to use mnemonic devices and key words, and how to use rehearsal strategies, you can help them remember information, whether they are beginning readers developing an automatic sight vocabulary or high-school students studying for a science test. Take, for example, the use of acronyms to remember lists of information. The sentence "**K**ings **p**lay **c**ards **o**n **f**ine **g**reen **s**ofas" can help students remember the biological classification system:

Kingdom   **P**hylum   **C**lass   **O**rder   **F**amily   **G**enus   **S**pecies

It is important not only to teach students memory strategies, but also to cue students to use their memory strategies when they work on a task. The 60-Second Lesson describes a fun way to have students develop acronyms.

Overall, key strategies for teaching students with LD include the following:

- Controlling task difficulty
- Teaching students with LD in small interactive groups of six or fewer students
- Using a combination of direct instruction and cognitive strategy instruction
- Providing a framework for learning
- Modeling process and strategies using thinking aloud and instructional conversations
- Teaching self-regulation and self-monitoring
- Providing opportunities for extended practice and application
- Using learning tools and aids
- Adjusting workload and time requirements
- Presenting information and having students demonstrate learning in multiple ways
- Teaching memory strategies

As a teacher, you will find that many of the strategies and accommodations suggested in this section will also assist students with attention deficit hyperactivity disorder as well as other learners.

Attention Deficit Hyperactivity Disorder

Many students with LD also demonstrate attention problems. Danny Moreira, a tenth-grade student, found out during the ninth grade that he has an attention deficit hyperactivity disorder (ADHD):

Go to **www.ldonline.org** for information about resources that cater to educators, students, and their parents about LD and ADD/ADHD.

It has been an enormous relief to me, because all of my life I have been called names like "spaced out," "lazy," "hyper," and "daydreamer," yet I always knew that I was doing the best I could and that it was difficult for me to behave any other way. Ever since I was very young I was very intense and had extra energy to work on areas of interest, but I also became easily bored and distracted. I've been reading and talking to my counselor about ADHD, and what they say is that people with ADHD have a hard time making friends. That has sure been true for me. I get bored with what people are saying. I interrupt. I am also somewhat impulsive so that if I am thinking something I just blurt it out and sometimes I say the wrong thing. I've gotten much better and the friends I have now understand me. I must say, though, that finding out I had an attention deficit really took the weight off of me. I feel like I've had a boulder removed from my shoulders.

School was a disaster for me, largely because I was so bored and the work all seemed so repetitive and tedious. I've only had one teacher who I felt understood me, Mrs. Golding, my third-grade teacher. I'll never forget her. For math, she would tell me I only had to do the problems until I got five in a row right, then I could stop. At recess she would help me get involved in games with other children and insist that I be included.

Students with attention deficit hyperactivity disorder have been identified for well over a century (e.g., Still, 1902), but only recently have we begun to address the educational implications of their disorder in schools. The terms *attention deficit disorder (ADD)* and **attention deficit hyperactivity disorder (ADHD)** have been used to describe students with this disability. Parent groups such as Children and Adults with Attention Deficit Disorders (CHADD) have applied pressure at the local, state, and national levels so that appropriate educational services would be developed for their children. Additionally, teachers and other school personnel, recognizing that students with ADHD come to school with behaviors that interfere with their successful learning, are increasingly requesting information that provides instructional guidelines that will help them meet the needs of students with ADHD. Linda Wellens, a veteran kindergarten teacher, explains her experiences with ADHD this way:

Go to **www.add.org** for information pertaining to individuals with ADHD.

> I know that every year at least one of the students in my class will have serious attention problems. I don't mean the usual behaviors that a 5-year-old and 6-year-old display—I mean serious problems focusing on what we are doing, controlling themselves, and following directions even after everyone else in the room has caught on to the routines. I can usually tell after the first two weeks of school, but I try everything I can think of to structure the classroom for the child before I mention it to the parents or school counselor. I find that parents are relieved to discover that another adult has confirmed what they know about their child. Most of these parents are totally stressed out having to deal with the problems day and night and are looking for help.

Definitions and Types of Attention Deficit Hyperactivity Disorder

Research studies provide compelling evidence that ADHD is a true disorder (American Psychiatric Association, 2000; Barkley, 2008; CHADD, 2005). For example, magnetic resonance imaging research has demonstrated decreases in blood flow in areas of the brain associated with attention (e.g., Roth & Saykin, 2004).

Despite compelling information scientifically documenting that ADHD is a true disorder, there are considerable myths and misunderstandings about ADHD. Ellison (2003) summarizes these myths:

- ADHD is not a real disorder and was "drummed up" by the pharmaceutical or psychiatric communities. Overwhelming evidence reports that ADHD is a real disorder with detrimental consequences for children, adolescents, and adults.
- ADHD is a disorder that only affects young children. ADHD affects individuals across the lifespan.
- ADHD is overdiagnosed and many individuals who are labeled ADHD are not. Though occasional misdiagnosis is possible with all disabilities, prevalence rates for ADHD vary from 3% to 5% (National Institute of Mental Health [NIMH], 2008).
- ADHD is likely to result in overmedicating children. The increase in medication is likely a result of better diagnosis and treatment across the lifespan.
- ADHD is a result of poor parenting. ADHD is attributable to genetics in the vast majority of cases.

The American Psychiatric Association (2002) publishes the *Diagnostic and Statistical Manual of Mental Disorders* (referred to as DSM-IV), which addresses mental health disorders for children and adults. The description in the DSM-IV of ADHD is as a general term and subdivides individuals into:

1. ADHD, Predominantly Inattentive Type
2. ADHD, Predominantly Hyperactive–Impulsive Type
3. ADHD, Combined Type

Students who display either or both of these characteristics can be identified as having ADHD. Furthermore, there is evidence to suggest that ADHD often coexists with other conditions such as depression, anxiety, and learning disabilities (CHADD, 2005). There is increasing support for the notion that youngsters with ADD without hyperactivity display different achievement patterns from those with both attention deficit disorder and hyper-

PEARSON
myeducationlab

Go to the Assignments and Activities section of Topic 13: Attention Deficit Hyperactivity Disorders in the MyEducationLab for your course and complete the activity entitled *Common Characteristics of Attention Deficit Hyperactivity Disorder.*

activity (Barkley, 2005). **Inattention** refers to consistent (over 6 months) and highly inappropriate levels of at least six of the following behaviors:

- Failing to pay close attention to details and making careless mistakes that are inconsistent with the child's developmental level
- Failing to sustain attention to tasks and/or play activities
- Failing to listen, even when spoken to directly
- Failing to complete tasks
- Having difficulty with organization
- Resisting working on tasks that require sustained attention
- Losing materials and objects
- Becoming easily distracted
- Being forgetful

Hyperactivity–impulsivity refers to consistent (over 6 months) and highly inappropriate levels of at least six of the following behaviors:

HYPERACTIVITY

- Fidgeting or squirming
- Having a difficult time remaining seated during class, even when other students are able to do so
- Running or climbing excessively when it is not appropriate
- Having difficulty playing quietly
- Acting as though he or she is "driven by a motor"
- Talking too much

IMPULSIVITY

- Blurting out answers
- Having difficulty waiting for his or her turn
- Interrupting others or butting into activities

These characteristics of inattention and/or hyperactivity–impulsivity should be present before the age of 7 and in two or more separate settings (e.g., at school and at home). There should also be clear evidence that these characteristics significantly impair social, academic, or occupational functioning.

What are some signs of hyperactivity and impulsivity in students identified as having attention deficit hyperactivity disorder? What can you do to help students with ADHD in your classroom?

1. The first type of ADHD is the predominantly inattentive type. Teachers recognize these students as daydreamers who are often forgetful and easily distracted. Hallowell and Ratey (1995) describe these students as daydreamers,

    the kids—often girls—who sit in the back of the class and twirl their hair through their fingers while staring out the window and thinking long, long thoughts. These are the adults who drift off during conversations or in the midst of reading a page. These are the people, often highly imaginative, who are building stairways to heaven in the midst of conversations, or writing plays in their minds while not finishing the day's work, or nodding agreeably and politely while not hearing what is being said at all. (p. 153)

2. The second type of ADHD is predominantly hyperactive–impulsive. These students have difficulty sitting still, talk out of turn, are the most challenging to parents and teachers, and are more likely to develop oppositional and defiant disorder or conduct disorder in adolescence.

3. The third type of ADHD is the combined type and describes students who have features of both inattention and hyperactivity–impulsivity. It is estimated that 85% of students

TABLE 6.1

Differences Between Inattentive and Hyperactive–Impulsive Types of ADHD

TRAIT	HYPERACTIVE–IMPULSIVE TYPE	INATTENTIVE TYPE
Decision making	Impulsive	Sluggish
Boundaries	Intrusive, rebellious	Honors boundaries, polite, obedient
Assertion	Bossy, irritating	Underassertive, overly polite, docile
Attention seeking	Shows off, egotistical, best at worst	Modest, shy, socially withdrawn
Popularity	Attracts new friends but doesn't bond	Bonds but doesn't attract
Most common diagnosis	Oppositional defiant, conduct disorder	Depression, energy focused in

Source: Taylor, J. F. (2001). *Helping your ADD child* (3rd ed.). New York: Three Rivers Press. Copyright © 1994, 1999 by John Taylor. Used by permission of Random House, Inc.

with ADHD are the combined type (Barkley, 2006). Table 6.1 lists some characteristics that highlight the differences between the students with the inattentive and the hyperactive–impulsive types of ADHD. Those with the combined type may exhibit features of both but are generally more like students with hyperactivity–impulsiveness.

Although many teachers and parents think that inattention is the key characteristic of ADHD, there is growing evidence and consensus that inattention, as well as hyperactivity and impulsivity, is the result of problems in behavioral inhibition and self-control (Barkley, 2006, 2008), as discussed in the next section.

Characteristics of Students with Attention Deficit Hyperactivity Disorder

There is general agreement that ADHD manifests early in a youngster's life. In fact, the precursors to ADHD have been identified in infancy (Barkley, 2006). Some early indicators of ADHD include poor sleeping and eating habits, a difficult temperament, and high levels of activity. By the time youngsters are 3 years old, approximately 50% of those who will later be identified as having ADHD demonstrate such behaviors as high levels of activity, behavior problems, and short attention spans (Barkley, 2006). Therefore, it is not uncommon for children to demonstrate many of the behaviors associated with ADHD as early as kindergarten and first grade. The core characteristics of ADHD include the following:

- Feeling fidgety and restless
- Blurting out answers
- Having poor sustained attention and vigilance and being easily distracted
- Skipping from one incomplete task to the next, thus rarely completing work
- Being impulsive or having poor delay of gratification
- Being hyperactive or having difficulty regulating activity
- Exhibiting diminished rule-governed behavior
- Having increased variability of task performance

Even though preschool children may be diagnosed as having ADHD at age 4, some will not have the same diagnosis by later childhood or early adolescence (Barkley, 2006). These children may no longer be diagnosed with a disability or may develop LD as the academic tasks become more challenging. However, in the majority of those children in whom this early pattern of ADHD lasts for at least a year, ADHD is likely to continue into the school-age years, including adolescence. Parents describe these young children as restless, always on the go, acting as if driven by a motor, persistent in their wants, demanding of parental attention, and insatiable in their curiosity about their environment.

The common developmental features that distinguish ADHD from mild attention or hyperactive problems are the following:

- Onset in early childhood
- Chronic over time

Tips FOR TEACHERS 6.5

EIGHT TIPS PARENTS AND TEACHERS CAN USE TO EXPLAIN ADHD TO OTHERS

1. *Tell the truth.* This is the central, guiding principle. First, educate yourself about ADHD, and then put what you have learned into your own words, words the child can understand. Don't just hand the child a book or send the child off to some professional for an explanation. Explain it to yourself, after you have learned about it, and then explain it to the child. Be straightforward, and honest and clear.

2. *Use an accurate vocabulary.* Use accurate words even if they are technical. The child will carry the explanation you give him or her wherever he or she goes.

3. *Answer questions.* Solicit questions from students. Remember, children often have questions you cannot answer. Don't be afraid to say you don't know the answer. Then go find the answer.

4. *Be sure to tell the child what ADHD is not.* ADHD is not stupidity, retardation, defectiveness, badness, and so on.

5. *Give examples of positive role models.* Use role models either from history, such as Thomas Edison, or from personal experience, such as a family member (mom or dad).

6. *If possible, let others know the child has ADHD.* Let others in the classroom know (after discussing this with the child and parents), and let others in the extended family know. Again, the message should be that there is nothing to hide, nothing to be ashamed of.

7. *Caution the child not to use ADHD as an excuse.* Most kids, once they catch on to what ADHD is, go through a phase of trying to use it as an excuse. ADHD is an explanation, not an excuse. They still have to take responsibility for what they do.

8. *Educate others.* Educate the other parents and children in the classroom, as well as members of the extended family. The single strongest weapon we have to ensure that children get proper treatment is knowledge. Spread the knowledge as far as you can; there is still a great deal of ignorance and misinformation out there about ADHD.

- Generally pervasive behaviors across situations
- Deviant from age-based standards
- Increased likelihood of having another difficulty such as a learning or psychiatric disorder

Typically, teachers notice that these students are restless, are inattentive, and have a difficult time with routines. Parents often confirm these observations. Tips for Teachers 6.5 describes what teachers and parents can do to understand ADHD and to help others such as family members and community personnel understand as well.

In the early elementary years, teachers often view these children as having "immature" behaviors and making slow academic progress. About 20% to 25% are likely to have difficulty learning how to read. The students struggle not only with phonological processing tasks, but also with overall regulation of their behavior and control over their learning related to both reading and behavior (Barkley, 2008; Pennington, Groisser, & Welsh, 1993; Pisecco, Baker, Silva, & Brooke, 2001).

Research suggests that the key characteristic of ADHD lies in difficulty with behavioral inhibition or self-control (Barkley, 2006, 2008; Caspi, Henry, McGee, Moffitt, & Silva, 1995). **Behavioral inhibition** refers to the ability to withhold a planned response, halt a response that has been started, protect an ongoing activity from interfering activities, and delay a response (Rubia, Oosterlaan, Sergeant, Brandeis, & van Leeuwen, 1998). Teachers note that children with ADHD have difficulty waiting their turn, refraining from interrupting conversations, delaying immediate gratification, working for long-term rewards, and resisting potential distractions when working (Barkley & Murphy, 1998). The ability to delay one's response to external stimuli permits the development of the executive functions involved in self-control. **Executive functioning** is the ability to regulate one's thinking and behavior through the use of working memory, inner speech, control of emotions and arousal levels, and analysis of problems and communication of problem solutions to others. For example, students can use **inner speech** to "talk to themselves" about various solutions when in the midst of solving a problem. Students with ADHD have problems in guiding their behavior in situations that demand the ability to follow rules or instructions. These students also have more limited persistent goal-directed behavior and can find it exceedingly difficult to stay focused on tasks that require effort or concentration but that are not inherently exciting (Barkley, 2006).

As with learning disabilities, in the 1970s there was a common belief that children would outgrow ADHD as they reached adolescence and adulthood. Although there is evidence that

Go to **http://www.chadd.org** to learn how to provide instructional accommodations for students with ADHD.

outward signs of hyperactivity may be reduced, many individuals with ADHD continue to experience attentional problems in adolescence and adulthood. Approximately 40% of children diagnosed with ADHD are likely to continue to have the characteristics of ADHD as adults and about 36% would be considered to have recovered from ADHD (Barkley, Murphy, & Fischer, 2008).

Individuals with ADHD do get better as they get older, but more than half of them continue to complain of impulsivity, inattention, low self-esteem, and restlessness as adults (Barkley, Murphy, & Fischer, 2008). As in high school, at work, adults with ADHD may have significant problems with their ability to work independently of supervision, meet deadlines and work schedules, be persistent and productive in getting assigned work done, and interact cordially with fellow workers (Barkley, 2000).

Perhaps one of the most distinctive characteristics of ADHD is the likelihood that it will co-occur with another disability and be associated with difficulties such as occupational and social functioning (Adler, 2006; Shaywitz & Shaywitz, 1988). Approximately 65% display oppositional and defiant behaviors, and as many as 45% may progress to the more severe diagnosis of conduct disorders (Barkley, 1998, 2009; Fowler, 1992). Thus, students with ADHD frequently have other behavioral or academic difficulties. Tips for Teachers 6.6 lists 10 things that adolescent students with ADHD would like their teachers to know about them.

Prevalence of Attention Deficit Hyperactivity Disorder

Current best estimates of the prevalence rate of ADHD are from 3% to 5% (American Psychological Association, 2000; Barkley, 2006; Mayo Clinic, 2002; NIMH, 2008). The number of individuals with ADHD is difficult to determine because many children with ADHD have not been identified. Furthermore, recording the number of students with ADHD is difficult because there is no specific category for ADHD under the Individuals with Disabilities Education Improvement Act. Students with ADHD may be identified as having a health impairment or a secondary condition when ADHD and another disability (e.g., learning or emotional disabilities) coexist. Other students, who do not qualify under IDEIA as students with ADHD, do qualify under Section 504 of the Vocational Rehabilitation Act (discussed in Chapter 1). Again, however, as in the case of IDEIA, the number of students with ADHD is not recorded.

Prevalence estimates of students with ADHD consistently report higher rates for males than for females. Some reports indicate that the ratio of males to females is 3 to 1, with other

---

Tips for TEACHERS 6.6

TEN THINGS TEENS WITH ADHD WANT THEIR TEACHERS TO KNOW

1. I am not stupid. I may be frustrated after struggling for so long, but I want and need your help to succeed in school—even if I don't always ask for it.

2. I may need help to organize my schoolwork. I really do complete my homework. I often lose papers, leave them at home, or can't find them when I need them.

3. ADHD is not an excuse. It is hard for me to do well in school.

4. I really do forget things. I'm not trying to be difficult. Sometimes I just don't remember.

5. I don't like to be singled out. Please talk to me in private about my behavior. Do not embarrass or humiliate me in front of the class. Don't advertise to everyone the modifications I need.

6. Sometimes I act without thinking. Help me navigate social and academic situations so that I can control my impulsive behavior.

7. It can be very hard for me to make friends. Cooperative learning and other organized activities that allow me to interact with my peers will help me make and maintain friendships.

8. I do better when I have a clearly organized plan and a routine to follow. If the routine changes, I may need more help than other students to adapt.

9. I am a person with feelings, needs, and goals. Include me in planning and decision making whenever possible.

10. Learn more about ADHD so you can understand the challenges I face every day at home and at school.

Source: Information from Bailey, E. (2005). 12 things high school students with ADD/ADHD would like their teachers to know. Retrieved from http://add.about.com.

studies reporting ratios as high as 6 to 1 (e.g., Barkley, 1998, 2009; Willcutt & Pennington, 2000). The ratio is highest for children referred to clinics. It is difficult to determine why the rate is so much higher for boys, but there is some reason to believe that ADHD may manifest differently in girls than in boys and that the identification instruments are based on the behavioral manifestations of ADHD in boys. Oftentimes, girls with ADHD are more likely to be withdrawn and diagnosed as ADHD without hyperactivity (and thus less likely to be identified) than boys with ADHD, who are likely to be hyperactive and more aggressive. For example, Roisen and colleagues (1994) found that of girls identified with ADHD, 29.3% had the inattentive subtype, compared with 2.3% of boys.

Identification and Assessment of Students with Attention Deficit Hyperactivity Disorder

Go to the Assignments and Activities section of Topic 13: Attention Deficit Hyperactivity Disorder in the MyEducationLab for your course and complete the activity entitled *Personal and Educational Implications of ADHD.*

Unlike learning disabilities, initial identification of ADHD often involves a medical evaluation from a pediatrician, psychologist, or psychiatrist outside the school system. This evaluation should rule out other reasons for the student's behavior problems and evaluate the student's difficulty with attention and behavioral inhibition. This is usually accomplished through the use of interviews and/or the completion of behavioral rating scales by parents, teachers, and, when appropriate, the student. The information that you provide as a teacher can be helpful in determining whether attentional problems are severe enough to be identified as ADHD and how the attentional and behavioral problems are affecting the student in school both socially and academically. For example, keeping a record of the characteristics from the DSM-IV criteria that you observe in the child can be helpful in making initial identification and planning for accommodations.

A number of rating scales have been developed specifically for the identification of ADHD. A frequently used scale is a teacher-rating scale in which teachers consider the behavior of a specific student and then rate items based on their knowledge of this student's behavior (Conner, 2008). Teachers and parents are asked to rate descriptive statements about the child's behavior based on presence of the behavior (not at all present, just a little present, pretty much present, very much present) or frequency of occurrence (never or rarely, sometimes, often, very often). Examples of behaviors include distractible, restless, always up, excitable, impulsive, excessive demands, unaccepted by peers, no sense of fair game, and fails to finish tasks. The assessment is normed for students ages 6 to 18.

Because the identification of ADHD is based on the perceptions of those rating the student, it is important to take into consideration cultural and ethnic factors that may result in the overdiagnosis or underdiagnosis of ADHD. Some students may have activity levels and behavioral patterns that are culturally and ethnically appropriate but differ significantly from majority-culture, same-age peers (Harry & Klingner, 2007). For example, Hispanic students, especially those from Puerto Rico, and African American students, particularly males, may manifest more body movements, gestures, and expressions that may be interpreted as hyperactive than European American students (Neal, McCray, & Webb-Johnson, 2001). Teachers must be cautious in using and interpreting these behavioral assessments. Furthermore, although certain behaviors may occur more frequently owing to cultural influences, individuals vary widely within cultural groups. Instruments such as the Child Behavior Checklist–Direct Observation Form (Achenbach, 2000) allow for direct observation and comparison to peers from the same cultural group. The Committee on Minority Representation in Special Education (Donovan & Cross, 2002) recommended that states adopt a universal screening and intervention approach within general education for early identification of students with learning, attention, and behavior problems. This approach to universal screening provides opportunities for students' problems to be detected based on performance criteria and educational and behavioral needs.

Eligibility for ADHD Services and Special Education Law

Two federal laws guarantee children with ADHD a **free and appropriate public education (FAPE)**. These two laws are the Individuals with Disabilities Education Improvement Act (IDEIA) and Section 504 of the Rehabilitation Act of 1973 (Section 504). The two laws have different provisions for eligibility and services for students with ADHD, and it is important for parents and professionals to understand these differences. Whereas IDEIA mandates procedures for identifying students with disabilities and how services should be provided and monitored, Section 504 focuses on equity and access in all areas of life but does *not* detail how services will be provided. Following are brief descriptions of how the two laws influence services for students with ADHD.

IDEIA. IDEIA provides a special education for those students who meet the eligibility criteria for one or more disability *and* whose disability adversely affects their educational performance. ADHD is listed under the category "Other Health Impairment."

Evaluation and diagnosis of ADHD in the "Other Health Impairment" category is subject to the same referral and assessment procedures as other disabilities as specified in IDEIA. Examples of additional IDEIA provisions for a student with a disability are the development and regular evaluation of the IEP, parent participation and consent, procedures for handling suspensions and expulsions, and guidelines for determining how and where students are to receive special education services.

Section 504. Section 504 is a civil rights statute. It requires that schools do not discriminate against children with disabilities and that they provide children with reasonable accommodations (Sands, Kozleski, & French, 2000). Eligibility for Section 504 is based on "the existence of an identified physical condition that substantially limits a major life activity" (CHADD, 2005, p. 3). If it is determined that the ADHD substantially limits a child's ability to learn, he or she meets the 504 eligibility criteria. Unlike IDEIA, fewer regulations are placed on procedures for eligibility and services in Section 504. This makes 504 a more flexible and faster way to receive accommodations and services. Furthermore, students who may not meet eligibility criteria for a disability under IDEIA may still be eligible for 504. However, because IDEIA contains more specific guidelines for all aspects of referral, placement, and services, it may be more appropriate for students who require greater assistance and safeguards in order to succeed at school. It is important for parents and professionals to understand the advantages and disadvantages of both laws and their influence on services for students with ADHD.

Instructional Guidelines and Accommodations for Students with Attention Deficit Hyperactivity Disorder

What are the characteristics of teachers who are effective with students with ADHD? According to Lerner and colleagues, "in many respects, they are simply good teachers" (1995, p. 96). Lerner and colleagues indicate that the following characteristics help teachers work successfully with students who have ADHD:

- *Positive attitudes toward inclusion of students with ADHD.* These attitudes are reflected in the way teachers accept students and promote students' acceptance by the classroom community.
- *Ability to collaborate as a member of an interdisciplinary team.* Teachers who have students with ADHD in their classrooms have an opportunity to work with other professionals and family members who will be monitoring the students' academic and behavioral progress, response to medication, and self-esteem.
- *Knowledge of behavior-management procedures.* Most students with ADHD will demonstrate difficulty following directions, remembering routines, staying on task, and organizing themselves and their work. Behavior-management skills are essential to adequately meet the needs of students with ADHD.
- *Personal characteristics.* Teaching students with ADHD requires understanding, compassion, patience, concern, respect, responsiveness, and a sense of humor.

Educational Interventions. Although teachers often focus on providing interventions to students with ADHD that reduce inappropriate behaviors, these students benefit the most when behavioral interventions are accompanied by effective instruction designed to meet their individual learning needs (Salend, Elhoweris, & Van Garderen, 2003). Teachers should begin any educational intervention by planning. Maria Nahmias has served as a consultant to parents and teachers on how to effectively meet the needs of students with ADHD in the classroom, and Susan Stevens is a teacher and consultant with many years of experience working with students with ADHD. On the basis of their experiences, they recommend that teachers consider the following key points when planning **educational interventions** for students with ADHD (DuPaul & Stoner, 2003; Nahmias, 1995; Stevens, 2001):

- *Use novelty in instruction and directions.* Highlight important instructions and key points with colored pens, highlight markers, or felt-tip pens. Put key information in boldface or underline it. For example, have students highlight the operation signs on a math page before completing the page. Use oral cueing to identify key words or ideas in the directions.

- *Maintain a schedule.* As indicated earlier, students with ADHD have a difficult time learning rules and routines; therefore, it is critical that these be changed as infrequently as possible. Change is difficult for students to adjust to and often promotes behavior problems. Post rules and schedules in the room and on index cards on the students' desks.

- *Prepare students for transitions and provide support in completing transitions.* Alert students to upcoming transitions (e.g., "We'll be going to recess in 3 minutes. Finish what you are doing and put your materials away."). Provide guidance and encouragement as students complete transitions (e.g., "You have all your materials put away. All you need to do is line up when I call your table.").

- *Emphasize time limits.* Individuals with ADHD (adults even more so than children) have a poor concept of the time needed to complete tasks. Teach students to plan ahead and use the rule that to be considered "satisfactory," assignments are to be completed according to directions, with a passing grade, and turned in on time. Any adjustments in time should be arranged well before the deadline, not at the last minute.

- *Provide organizational assistance.* Provide guidelines for how the students should maintain their desks, materials, and schedules. Provide opportunities at the beginning of each week for students to organize, and then reward them for doing so. Ask students to keep a planner and a notebook for each of their classes and to write their assignments and due dates in the notebook.

- *Provide rewards consistently and often.* All students like to receive positive feedback about their performance and behavior; however, the frequency, intensity, and consistency of rewards need to be increased for students with ADHD. Whenever possible, involve the student in selecting the rewards.

- *Be brief and clear.* Think about instructions before stating them, and provide them as briefly and in as well organized a way as possible. Present the critical information in chunks so that it is more easily understood and remembered. Keep instructional lessons brief to maintain students' attention.

- *Arrange the environment to facilitate attention.* Consider where the student is sitting. Are other students who might promote good behavior and organizational skills sitting nearby? Are you able to quickly and easily maintain eye contact as well as physical contact with the student? Be sure to consider how to minimize distractions.

- *Provide optimal stimulation.* There is some support for the notion that optimal stimulation facilitates learning for students with ADHD. For example, students with ADHD who were provided with background music while doing arithmetic problems performed better than non-ADHD students under the same conditions (Abikoff, Courtney, Szeibel, & Koplewicz, 1996).

- *Allow for movement and postures other than sitting.* Arrange activities so that they include movement as part of the activity, such as writing, typing, drawing, or using manipulatives. Have students demonstrate their learning by using the board or overhead projector.

- *Promote active participation through effective questioning techniques.* Ask questions that promote student participation and provide feedback to the teacher about student learning. Effective questioning techniques include varying the types of questions to include high-level questions that require students to think critically about the material, adjusting question content for individual skill levels, using language that is understandable to students, pausing so that students have time to organize a response, valuing all responses so that not only the "correct" answer is acceptable, and rephrasing or summarizing student responses for the rest of the class.

Planning lessons for students with ADHD within the context of planning for the class as a whole is a challenge. The primary focus of planning should be on what accommodations are needed to make the lesson effective for all students, including students with ADHD. Table 6.2 lists types of problems frequently manifested by students with ADHD and provides potential solutions.

Educational Interventions

TABLE 6.2

PROBLEM	SOLUTION
Listening	Provide visual displays (flowcharts, pictorials, wheels); preread questions/terms at end of chapter; assigned reading; keyword note-taking system to expand memory jogs during daily review; advance note-taking organizers from subtitles in textbook.
Distractibility	Minimize visual distractors in the environment; don't have interesting activities going on in one corner of the room while expecting the student to do his or her seatwork.
Attention Span	Have student work in short units of time with controlled activity breaks (i.e., reading break or magazine break); activities need to be interspersed throughout instruction.
Short-Term Memory	Offer review systems in a flashcard style so frequent practice can be done independently; material may need to be reviewed frequently.
Task Completion	Present work in short units (i.e., five problems on paper cut into quarters rather than on one sheet); timeframes should be short, with clear deadlines and checkpoints to measure progress; have a model available so product can be examined if directions can't be retained.
Distractibility	Have as few distractions as possible; provide a "quiet corner" for anyone who wishes a distraction-free place to work.
Impulsivity	Show the student how to do the work; have a checklist for what he or she needs to do, and have a reward system tied to the completion of all the steps.
Inattention to Detail	Emphasize detail through color coding or isolation.
Test Taking	Have the student review critical details and main ideas in a flashcard system to support attention and practice specific retrieval.

Source: Rooney, K. J. (1995). Teaching students with attention disorders. *Intervention in School and Clinic* 30(4), 221–225. Copyright © 1995 by PRO-ED, Inc. Reprinted by permission.

A problem frequently noted by parents and teachers of students with ADHD is homework (Salend et al., 2003; Weyandt, 2001). These students have a difficult time recording assignments, knowing when they are due, and establishing an organizational sequence that enables them to complete the task on time. For this reason, homework record sheets are often developed and implemented by teachers and then monitored by parents. Figure 6.5 provides an example of a daily assignment and homework log.

Tips for Teachers 6.7 provides guidelines that will help reduce the trauma often associated with homework for students with ADHD. Tips for Teachers 6.8 lists some of the ways teachers can help children they suspect may have ADHD.

Although no one educational treatment package has been demonstrated to yield successful outcomes for students with ADHD (Barkley, 1998; Guyer, 2001), the best treatment procedures to date are those that involve a range of instructional and behavioral supports and accommodations and may be implemented in conjunction with medication (NIMH, 2008).

Medication as One Aspect of Treatment for ADHD. The identification of ADHD in children frequently involves a pediatrician, psychologist, and/or psychiatrist. These professionals may recommend that the student be given medication as one aspect of treatment for ADHD. The most typical type of medication is **stimulant medication**, which includes Ritalin (methylphenidate). Other drugs that have been approved for youngsters (meaning that the drug has been tested and decided to be safe) include amphetamine, methylphenidate, pemoline, dextroamphetamine, and dexmethylphenidate. About 70% to 80% of children with ADHD respond positively to stimulant medications, but they are only one aspect of a treatment plan and should be paired with behavioral and/or academic interventions (Barkley, 2006; NIMH, 2008).

Many adults and parents are concerned about providing medications to children. It is important that a highly qualified physician as well as other well-trained personnel (e.g., psychologist or psychiatrist) be involved in decision making. However, youngsters who are provided either medication-management alone or medication-management with a behavior therapist have been associated with superior results compared to than youngsters who were provided routine community treatment or only behavioral intervention (NIMH, 2008).

Daily Assignment and Homework Log

FIGURE
6.5

Student: _____   Week of: _____

Day/ Subject	Class Assignment	Finished Y N	Homework Assignment	Materials Needed	Finished Y N

Special Projects	Materials/ Clothes Needed
Tests	Teacher/Parent Notes

Tips FOR TEACHERS 6.7

GUIDELINES THAT HELP REDUCE TRAUMA ASSOCIATED WITH HOMEWORK FOR STUDENTS WITH ADHD

- *Keep homework assignments separate from unfinished classwork.* Unfinished classwork should remain in class. This helps students to differentiate between classwork and homework. If unfinished classwork becomes homework (as an add-on to the already assigned homework), students can easily become overwhelmed.

- *Establish routines for assigning, collecting, and evaluating homework so that students know what to expect.* Students are more likely to buy in to homework if they understand how it fits into the classroom routine.

- *Use homework as practice for material that has already been taught.* Don't use homework as a means for teaching new information. Homework should be on the student's independent reading level and provide for review and practice.

- *Identify the minimum amount necessary to demonstrate learning.* Understanding and mastering the task are more important than completing an extensive amount of work. Consider shortening the task for these students. It is better that they do a small amount well than a lot of work poorly.

- *Provide timelines for tasks associated with long-term assignments.* Rather than telling students the date a long-term assignment is due, help them problem solve a timeline for completing the key components of the assignment. Pair them with a buddy or work cooperatively with parents to ensure that each component in the timeline is completed.

- *Involve families.* Communication with families (e.g., homework notebooks, recorded messages that state assignments, homework hot lines, email, websites) about both the value of homework as well as specific assignments and timelines helps families support students in completing work outside of school.

Tips FOR TEACHERS 6.8

TEN WAYS TEACHERS CAN HELP STUDENTS THEY SUSPECT MIGHT HAVE ADHD

1. Discuss with other professionals such as the school psychologist or counselor to confirm the behaviors you are observing.

2. Discuss with the parents to determine whether they observe the same behaviors at home and other settings.

3. Ask other professionals to observe you and the students in your class to provide suggestions for how you might improve behavior and learning for the target students.

4. Get a formal diagnosis. Work with the school or choose a specialist who has knowledge and experience with ADHD. An evaluation should be able to determine other learning, psychological, or physical problems that may look like or coexist with ADHD.

5. If a diagnosis is made, gather information about medication and behavioral treatments. Write notes about how these interventions are working outside of school.

6. Play an active role in IEP or Section 504 plan development. Parents are valuable resources to professionals and can help design a program that works for the family and the school. Keep records of all documentation. This is especially important if parents and the school disagree at any point in planning or implementing services.

7. Work with the parents and school to identify problems and possible solutions. Parents and children with ADHD are protected by federal laws. If parents and the school cannot agree on services, try mediation; as a last result, consider a due process hearing to ensure that the child with ADHD is getting the services and support he or she needs to be successful at school.

8. Consider seeking behavioral therapy or social skills training to support the students' behavior.

9. Organize the classroom schedule so that predictable routines are provided and made clear to the student.

10. When students break rules, respond to them in a calm and matter-of-fact way, reminding them of the rules and applying reasonable consequences.

The decision to use medication as one part of a treatment program can be a tumultuous one for parents who, unsure about the outcomes associated with medical treatment, fear negative side effects. As a teacher, you will want to monitor the positive and negative effects of medication and work with the parents so that the physician can be informed. It is not unusual for teachers to be asked to complete behavior rating forms as the physician works to adjust the medication dosage. Linda Wellens, a kindergarten teacher, comments:

> This year I had a student, Alex, who was identified as ADHD with hyperactivity–impulsivity. His mother called me frequently to check on how he was doing in school. He had been kicked out of three preschools before he even started kindergarten, and she was worried about how he would perform. Alex just couldn't sit still. He would try to stay in his seat and then would jump up and start playing with toys or building with blocks. He just seemed to need a frequent release. He was a handful, but I managed to set up a behavior modification program that was highly effective. One of the things that helped the most is that his parents and his behavioral pediatrician agreed that he would benefit from medication. Then we worked as a team to monitor his reaction and progress.

Stimulant medication works like a pair of eyeglasses, helping the individual to focus. It can also reduce the sense of inner turmoil and anxiety that is so common with ADHD. Stimulant medication works by adjusting a chemical imbalance that affects the neurotransmitters in the parts of the brain that regulate attention, impulse control, and mood (Barkley, 2006). See Table 6.3 for a list of common medications to treat ADHD.

As a classroom teacher, your role in monitoring the medication is important. Work with the parents and doctor to observe the following:

- Changes in impulsivity, attentiveness, activity level, frustration level, organizational skills, behavioral inhibition, and interest in schoolwork
- Changes in academic performance
- Changes related to changes in dosage of the medication
- Possible side effects (loss of appetite, stomachaches, sleepiness, headaches, mood changes, irritability)
- Duration of the medication dosage

TABLE
6.3

Common Medications Used to Treat ADHD

MEDICATION	EFFECTS
Methylphenidate (better known by its brand name, Ritalin)	Methylphenidate drugs help many youngsters and teenagers with ADHD concentrate and focus better.
Dopamine	This is a neurotransmitter that is increased with methylphenidate, and it sends messages between nerve cells in the brain.
Concerta, Focalin, Metadate, and Methylin	These are all types of methylphenidate.
Atomoxetine (and other related drugs)	These medications are antidepressants.

The one thing all professionals agree on about treatment of ADHD with medication is that it should always be considered one component of an overall treatment plan (Barkley, 2006; NIMH, 2008). Medical treatment is one part of a complete management and intervention program. School districts are prohibited from requiring a child to get a prescription for medications as a condition of school attendance or receiving services under IDEIA 2004. Schools, parents, the physician, and the counselor or psychologist all need to work as a team to develop a coordinated effort to meet the needs of students with ADHD.

Summary

- The term *learning disabilities* is used to describe a heterogeneous group of students who, despite adequate cognitive functioning, have difficulty learning, particularly academics. Dyslexia, dysgraphia, and dyscalculia are three types of learning disabilities that refer to extreme difficulty learning to read, write, and do mathematics, respectively.

- Students with learning disabilities represent a range of characteristics that include low performance in one or more academic areas, unexpected low performance considering their overall ability, and ineffective or inefficient information processing.

- Because the characteristics of students with learning disabilities are heterogeneous, the types of learning accommodations vary. Accommodations that generally assist students with learning disabilities include teaching the students at their instructional level, using interactive groups of six or fewer, and using a combination of direct instruction and cognitive strategy instruction. Other strategies that facilitate their learning include providing a framework for learning, modeling the processes and strategies, teaching self-regulation, providing opportunities for extended practice and application, using learning tools and aids, adjusting workloads and time requirements, presenting information and allowing students to demonstrate learning in multiple ways, and teaching students to use memory strategies.

- Attention deficit hyperactivity disorder (ADHD) refers to difficulty in attention and has two factors: inattention and hyperactivity–impulsivity. Students can display one or both of these factors.

- The core characteristics of ADHD are lack of behavior inhibition and difficulty with executive functioning, or the ability to regulate one's thinking and behavior. Other characteristics include poor sustained attention and vigilance, impulsivity with poor delay of gratification, hyperactivity and poorly regulated activity, diminished rule-governed behavior, and increased variability of task performance.

- Classroom interventions to assist students with ADHD include using novelty in instruction and directions, maintaining a schedule, providing organizational assistance, providing rewards consistently and often, communicating briefly and clearly, and arranging the environment to facilitate attention.

Think and Apply

1. Now that you have read Chapter 6, review Tammy's experiences in working with Adrian and Lenny. If you could talk to Tammy and the parents of Adrian and Lenny, what questions would you ask them and what advice would you provide?

2. Select a lesson in which you are going to teach a new skill or strategy. Think about how you can modify the lesson to provide more opportunities for you and the students to model or demonstrate the skill or strategy, and more opportunities for the students to practice the skill or strategy. Consider how you might make adjustments for students with learning disabilities and also students with ADHD.

3. Prepare for an interview as a teacher with a principal in which you know the question will be, "How do you plan to support the students with learning disabilities in your class"?

PEARSON
myeducationlab

Now go to Topic 12: Learning Disabilities and Topic 13: Attention Deficit Hyperactivity Disorders in the MyEducationLab (www.myeducationlab.com) for your course where you can:

- Find learning outcomes for these topics along with the national standards that connect to these outcomes.
- Complete Assignments and Activities that can help you more deeply understand the chapter content.
- Examine challenging situations and cases presented in the IRIS Center Resources.
- Apply and practice your understanding of the core teaching skills identified in the chapter with Building Teaching Skills and Dispositions learning units.

Communication Disorders

Communication is the process of exchanging ideas, information, needs, and desires (Owens, 2005). Both in school and in society, oral and written communication are powerful resources. We use communication to do the following:

- Develop and maintain contact and relationships with others
- Gain and give information
- Control and persuade
- Create and imagine
- Communicate feelings
- Monitor our own behavior when we talk to ourselves

Even though written communication plays a key role in school, speaking and listening are the most frequently used means of learning. Consequently, students with communication disorders may experience difficulties in many aspects of school, including both academically and socially.

The term **communication disorders** refers to students who demonstrate difficulties with exchanging knowledge, ideas, opinions, desires, and feelings (Owens, 2008). Communication is thought to be problematic when it deviates enough to interfere with the transmission of messages, stands out as being unusual or different, or produces negative feelings or responses (National Dissemination Center for Children with Disabilities [NICHCY], 2000; Payne & Taylor, 1998). Communication disorders range in severity from mild to profound. They may be developmental or acquired through injuries or diseases that affect the brain. A communication disorder may be the primary disability, or it may be secondary to other disabilities (American Speech-Language-Hearing Association [ASHA], 2008). For example, students with learning disabilities and mental retardation often have secondary language disabilities and receive services from a speech and language pathologist. A **speech and language pathologist** is trained to provide screening, assessment, and treatment for students who have difficulties with speech (including pronunciation) as well as with language (including stuttering, inadequate language development, and poor use of syntax).

When students enter school, they are expected to communicate by listening and speaking. Some students may have difficulty transmitting the message or information. Although many children "outgrow" early language difficulties, 20% to 25% of children with delayed language development at age 2 continue to have communication problems throughout their preschool and school years, and two-thirds of kindergarteners who have difficulties with language will continue to have language problems in middle and high school (Owens, 2008).

Consider the following two examples. When Sarah entered kindergarten, her speech was so difficult to understand that both the teacher and the other students had to listen to her for several days before they began to figure out what she was trying to communicate. Sarah has difficulty with speech, or the vocal production of language. Jeffrey, by contrast, has difficulty understanding the messages of others and communicating messages to others. His speech (vocal production) is adequate, but the message is unclear. Jeffrey's difficulties have to do with communicating through using language. The American Speech-Language-Hearing Association (2005) has divided communication disorders into these three broad categories: speech disorders, language disorders, and hearing disorders. This chapter deals with speech and language disorders; Chapter 11 discusses students with hearing disorders.

In what ways might developmental delays in language be manifested? What aspects of communication are important in identifying students with possible language-learning disabilities?

Speech Disorders

Individuals with **speech disorders** have difficulty with the verbal means of communication. The major components of speech are articulation, fluency, and voice. *Articulation* has to do with the production of speech sounds, *fluency* refers to the flow and rhythm of language, and *voice* focuses on the quality of speech, including resonance, pitch, and intensity.

Communication Disorders

Communication is the process of exchanging ideas, information, needs, and desires (Owens, 2005). Both in school and in society, oral and written communication are powerful resources. We use communication to do the following:

- Develop and maintain contact and relationships with others
- Gain and give information
- Control and persuade
- Create and imagine
- Communicate feelings
- Monitor our own behavior when we talk to ourselves

Even though written communication plays a key role in school, speaking and listening are the most frequently used means of learning. Consequently, students with communication disorders may experience difficulties in many aspects of school, including both academically and socially.

The term **communication disorders** refers to students who demonstrate difficulties with exchanging knowledge, ideas, opinions, desires, and feelings (Owens, 2008). Communication is thought to be problematic when it deviates enough to interfere with the transmission of messages, stands out as being unusual or different, or produces negative feelings or responses (National Dissemination Center for Children with Disabilities [NICHCY], 2000; Payne & Taylor, 1998). Communication disorders range in severity from mild to profound. They may be developmental or acquired through injuries or diseases that affect the brain. A communication disorder may be the primary disability, or it may be secondary to other disabilities (American Speech-Language-Hearing Association [ASHA], 2008). For example, students with learning disabilities and mental retardation often have secondary language disabilities and receive services from a speech and language pathologist. A **speech and language pathologist** is trained to provide screening, assessment, and treatment for students who have difficulties with speech (including pronunciation) as well as with language (including stuttering, inadequate language development, and poor use of syntax).

When students enter school, they are expected to communicate by listening and speaking. Some students may have difficulty transmitting the message or information. Although many children "outgrow" early language difficulties, 20% to 25% of children with delayed language development at age 2 continue to have communication problems throughout their preschool and school years, and two-thirds of kindergarteners who have difficulties with language will continue to have language problems in middle and high school (Owens, 2008).

Consider the following two examples. When Sarah entered kindergarten, her speech was so difficult to understand that both the teacher and the other students had to listen to her for several days before they began to figure out what she was trying to communicate. Sarah has difficulty with speech, or the vocal production of language. Jeffrey, by contrast, has difficulty understanding the messages of others and communicating messages to others. His speech (vocal production) is adequate, but the message is unclear. Jeffrey's difficulties have to do with communicating through using language. The American Speech-Language-Hearing Association (2005) has divided communication disorders into these three broad categories: speech disorders, language disorders, and hearing disorders. This chapter deals with speech and language disorders; Chapter 11 discusses students with hearing disorders.

In what ways might developmental delays in language be manifested? What aspects of communication are important in identifying students with possible language-learning disabilities?

Speech Disorders

Individuals with **speech disorders** have difficulty with the verbal means of communication. The major components of speech are articulation, fluency, and voice. *Articulation* has to do with the production of speech sounds, *fluency* refers to the flow and rhythm of language, and *voice* focuses on the quality of speech, including resonance, pitch, and intensity.

INTERVIEW
LORRI JOHNSON

Lorri Johnson is one of five third-grade teachers at Drexel Elementary School. In her class of 27 students, one student (Samantha) has a communication disorder. Lorri also has two students with learning disabilities, one of whom receives support from both the speech and language pathologist and the special education teacher. Lorri believes that all children can learn and that her job is to create a learning community that supports this belief.

Samantha is a student with a communication disorder who works with the speech and language pathologist, Nancy Meyers, for 30 minutes twice a week. Nancy and Lorri check with each other informally about once a week regarding Samantha's progress. Lorri's description of Samantha clearly shows that she understands Samantha's needs and makes accommodations to help her communicate successfully in the classroom. Lorri notes,

> The way I would describe Samantha is as a late bloomer when it comes to language. Early in the year, Nancy and I sat down with Samantha's file, and we discussed her history and needs. Samantha did not start talking until she was almost 3 years old. At age 4, Samantha began attending Head Start and was identified as a child with a speech and language disorder. She started working with a speech and language pathologist at that time. She has continued to receive services since then. Her sentences are short, and she continues to have difficulty producing complex sentence structures, does not use adjectives and adverbs to elaborate, and has significant difficulty

with verb tenses and irregular verbs. Samantha also has a limited vocabulary when she speaks, and I am unsure if she is getting the concepts that I am teaching.

I feel that I work to make my class successful for Samantha in several ways. First, I usually don't call on Samantha in large-class discussions unless she raises her hand. We have a deal that she can't use this rule to escape listening and learning and that I expect her to contribute to large-group discussions at least several times a day. But this way she gets to pick the opportunities. Second, I frequently "check for understanding" by asking students questions that allow me to determine whether they really are learning the key ideas of my instruction. To keep the class active, I have them use thumbs up, stand up, clap hands, and so on to indicate whether they understand. I think Samantha and the other students feel comfortable telling me they don't understand, for I encourage and praise them for the questions they ask. Third, I ask Samantha to take leadership roles that require her to talk when we work in small groups, and I encourage her to help other students when doing independent seatwork. Finally, through reading and writing, I can focus on the areas that are difficult for her in oral language. For example, we have been working on using adjectives to make our writing more interesting. Samantha has really improved in this area of writing, and now I am asking the students to take their new descriptive written language and use it more when they talk.

I guess, overall, I feel that Samantha is a successful learner in my class, but I would like to know more about communication disorders so I can provide more encouragement and assistance.

Introduction

Many other teachers (both elementary and secondary) share Lorri's feelings. They learn a lot about teaching reading and writing but much less about the development of oral communication, the characteristics of students with communication disorders, strategies for identifying these students, and techniques for promoting oral communication and language development in general education classrooms. This chapter focuses on those areas and should provide you with a number of techniques and strategies for working with students who have communication disorders or other disabilities that result in delayed communication development.

Teaching Students with Communication Disorders

FOCUS QUESTIONS

1. Communication is a powerful tool. What are communication disorders and in what areas of communication might students have difficulty?

2. What percentage of students have communication disorders, and how does this percentage change from preschool to elementary school?

3. Language is sometimes described in terms of content, form, and use. What signs would you look for at school if students are having difficulty in each of these areas and with whom would you work to determine whether a student needs further assistance in the area of communication? What practice would be helpful in working with parents of students who have communication difficulties?

4. Why is it important to take into consideration the student's culture and dialect and whether the student is learning English as a second language when making decisions about a student who might have a communication disorder?

5. What practices might you suggest to parents of a child with language disorders to support the child's communication?

Think and Apply

1. Now that you have read Chapter 6, review Tammy's experiences in working with Adrian and Lenny. If you could talk to Tammy and the parents of Adrian and Lenny, what questions would you ask them and what advice would you provide?

2. Select a lesson in which you are going to teach a new skill or strategy. Think about how you can modify the lesson to provide more opportunities for you and the students to model or demonstrate the skill or strategy, and more opportunities for the students to practice the skill or strategy. Consider how you might make adjustments for students with learning disabilities and also students with ADHD.

3. Prepare for an interview as a teacher with a principal in which you know the question will be, "How do you plan to support the students with learning disabilities in your class"?

PEARSON
myeducationlab

Now go to Topic 12: Learning Disabilities and Topic 13: Attention Deficit Hyperactivity Disorders in the MyEducationLab (www.myeducationlab.com) for your course where you can:

- Find learning outcomes for these topics along with the national standards that connect to these outcomes.
- Complete Assignments and Activities that can help you more deeply understand the chapter content.
- Examine challenging situations and cases presented in the IRIS Center Resources.
- Apply and practice your understanding of the core teaching skills identified in the chapter with Building Teaching Skills and Dispositions learning units.

Articulation Disorders.   By far the most common speech disorders, articulation disorders occur when students are unable to produce the various sounds and sound combinations of language (Hulit & Howard, 2006). It is not unusual for speech and language pathologists to work with elementary-age children who have a delay in the development of articulation, because the ability to produce the speech sounds continues to develop through age 8 (Smit, 1993). Learning to produce the speech sounds, no matter what the language, usually proceeds in a fairly consistent sequence, but there may be as much as a 3-year variance between the time early learners start producing a particular sound and the time late learners start producing the sound (Bernthal & Bankson, 1998; Yavas, 1998). Figure 7.1 demonstrates the developmental progression of speech sounds and clarifies why many children enter school still in the process of learning to produce such sounds as /r/, /l/, /s/, /ch/, /sh/, /z/, /j/, /v/, /zh/, and voiced and voiceless /th/.

The production of speech sounds generally develops earlier in girls than in boys. Table 7.1 compares the development of girls and boys, noting the age at which 90% of girls and boys can articulate the sounds. If you teach kindergarten through second grade, you will have the opportunity to hear these sounds developing in some of your students. Even if these sounds are not fully developed, children's speech, by the time they enter kindergarten, should be at least 90% intelligible.

Types of articulation errors include sound substitutions, omissions, additions, and distortions. The errors can occur at the beginning, middle, and/or end of words. Substitutions and omissions are the most common errors. In *substitutions,* one sound is substituted for another. Common substitutions at the beginning of words include /w/ for /r/ (*wabbit* for *rabbit*), /t/ for /c/ (*tat* for *cat*), /b/ for /v/ (*balentine* for *valentine*), and /f/ for /th/ (*free* for *three*). *Omissions* occur when a sound is not included in a word. Because blends (two consonant that go together and make two separate sounds such as /br/, /pl/, /cr/, and /gl/) are later in developing, many omission errors occur when young children or students with communication difficulties leave off the second sound in the blend (e.g., *boo* for *blue, pity* for *pretty*). Final sounds also are commonly omitted, particularly the later-developing sounds such as /s/, /sh/, /z/, and voiced and voiceless /th/. For example, youngsters might say *mi* instead of *miss* or *mat* instead of *math*. As a classroom teacher, you must listen for children whose articulation might be developmentally delayed or whose articulation errors are so frequent that they significantly affect intelligibility. You will want to talk with the speech and language pathologist and the parents of these children to learn more.

Articulation is affected not only by development but also by regional dialects and cultural uses. Variations or dialects of a language are products of historical, cultural, geographic, social, economic, ethnic, and political factors (Hedge, 1998; Owens, 2008). For example, Bostonians often use /er/ for /a/ (as in *idea/ider* and *data/dater*), and Southerners draw out vowels. We all speak a dialect of English—it is interesting to learn and appreciate the dialects of other English speakers.

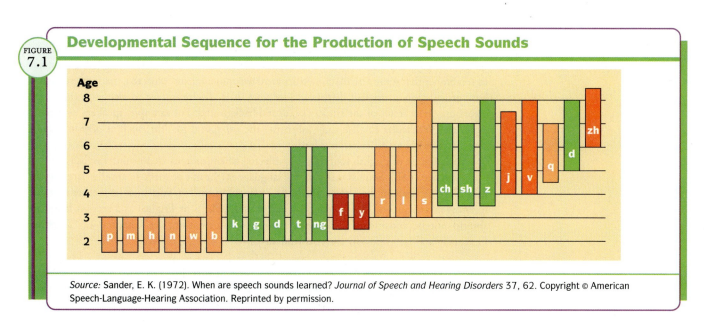

FIGURE 7.1

Developmental Sequence for the Production of Speech Sounds

Source: Sander, E. K. (1972). When are speech sounds learned? *Journal of Speech and Hearing Disorders* 37, 62. Copyright © American Speech-Language-Hearing Association. Reprinted by permission.

TABLE 7.1 Comparison of the Development for Speech Sound Production in Boys and Girls*

BOYS

Age	3	4	5	6	7
	p	ng	y	zh	f
	b			wh	l
	m			j	r
	h				ch
	w				sh
	d				s
	n				z
	k				th (voiceless)
	t				v
	g				th (voiced)

GIRLS

Age	3	4	5	6	7
	p	l	j	sh	s
	b	t	y	ch	z
	m			r	th (voiceless)
	w			zh	v
	d		f	f	th (voiced)
	n			wh	
	k				
	g				
	h				
	ng				

*The age at which 90 percent of boys and girls can articulate sounds. *Note:* Vowel sounds are produced correctly by 90 percent of all children by age 3. Consonant blends—*tr, bl, pr,* and so on—develop between ages 7 and 9.

Source: Work, R. S. (1994). Articulation disorders. In S. Adler & D. A. King (Eds.), *Oral communication problems in children and adolescents* (p. 3). Copyright © 1994 by Pearson Education. Reprinted by permission of the publisher.

How can a teacher determine whether students have an articulation disorder? When a student in your class has difficulty saying sounds that are said correctly by other students, the student may have an articulation problem. This is particularly true if the student's first language is English and the errors make it difficult for others to understand them. It is important to remember that some articulation errors are developmental and expected; many preschoolers have articulation errors that disappear over time. It is also important to recognize that some errors may be a result of the student's cultural background. For example, speakers of African American Vernacular English may substitute the /d/ sound for /th/, such as *dem* instead of *them*. This is not an articulation error.

Articulation of English sounds is also affected when students are learning English as a second language (ESL). Sounds made in one language might not be made in another language or might not be made in the same manner. As a classroom teacher, you must remember that differences in articulation due to regional or cultural dialects or English as a second language should not be considered disorders. (For more information, see Chapter 4, "Teaching Culturally and Linguistically Diverse Students.")

Fluency Disorders.   Whereas articulation disorders involve difficulty with the production of sounds, fluency disorders involve difficulty with the rate and flow of speech. All of us are non-fluent to some degree when we communicate. We hesitate in the middle of sentences, break the flow of language with meaningless sounds and fillers (e.g., *ah, um, you know, like*), repeat parts of words, and speak quickly. We are more nonfluent in stressful, novel, or exciting situations. When we have difficulty thinking of a word, we may become **dysfluent**. However, when a child's dysfluencies become more intense and are more problematic than the dysfluencies of normal speakers, the child might have a problem of fluency referred to as stuttering. One of the most common types of fluency disorders, **stuttering** is characterized by an interruption of the forward flow of speech (Palmer & Yantis, 1990).

Most young children, at different times during the preschool years, are nonfluent in a manner that resembles stuttering. Stuttering usually first appears between the ages of 2 and 4 and then for the vast majority of youngsters (approximately 75%), stuttering disappears by age 10. Boys are three to four times more likely to stutter than are girls (ASHA, 2008).

Go to **www.stuttersfa.org** for information on books, videos, and websites on stuttering and related disorders.

Voice Disorders.   **Voice disorders** relate to the quality of the voice itself. Usually, three dimensions are considered:

- Quality (hoarse, breathy, hypernasal/hyponasal)
- Pitch (high or low, monotone)
- Intensity (loud or soft)

One common type of voice disorder found in school-age children is caused by the presence of **vocal nodules**. These nodules are the result of yelling and other forms of vocal abuse that affect voice quality. Vocal nodules, which develop because the vocal mechanism is used incorrectly or overused, are somewhat like calluses on the vocal folds. If the nodules become too large, students can lose their voices and require surgery. Generally, it takes consistent and prolonged abuse for nodules to develop, but it is important to provide students with information about good vocal hygiene, including

- Keeping yelling to a minimum
- Breathing from the stomach
- Limiting time spent talking in noisy places
- Avoiding vigorous coughing (Lue, 2001)

Few school-age children have the other types of voice disorders, such as those related to pitch and intensity. Should you notice students whose speech quality, pitch, and/or intensity seems to be affected, talk with your school's speech and language pathologist.

School-Age Language Disorders

Language functions as an integral part of the communication process because it allows us to represent ideas using a conventional code. A person's ability to understand what is being communicated is referred to as **comprehension** or **receptive language**, whereas a person's ability to convey the intended message is referred to as **production** or **expressive language**.

Students with **language disorders** may have developmental delays in comprehension or receptive language. These students frequently ask for information to be repeated or clarified. In school, these students may have difficulties with following directions, understanding abstract concepts, and comprehending multiple meanings. Students with production or expressive language difficulties generally communicate less frequently than their peers. These students may have difficulty using correct grammar, thinking of the right word to convey meaning, and repairing communication when the listener doesn't understand.

To help us think about language and language disorders, language has been divided into **content** (semantics), **form** (phonology, morphology, and syntax), and use (pragmatics) (Bloom & Lahey, 1978). It is the interaction of content, form, and use that creates language.

Language Content

Semantics refers to the meaning or content of words and word combinations. When you teach a lesson (as in social studies or science), you are teaching concepts and the labels for those concepts (vocabulary). For example, students often ask for the label for an idea (e.g., "What is that?" or "What are you doing?"), and they ask about what a word means (e.g., "What is a penguin?" or "What does freedom mean?").

Teaching content focuses on teaching vocabulary, word categories and relationships, multiple meanings, and figurative language. Gloria Huerra, a high-school social studies teacher, comments:

> Grouping words by categories and using relationship words (like *if . . . then* and *because*) are often difficult for students with language impairments or for English language learners. It is also the multiple meanings of words and the figurative language that holds up their learning. I consistently highlight these in our discussions of social studies. One way that I highlight them is by writing them so that they can be projected and visible to all students and then discussing them prior to reading. Then I cue the students to look for them when they read. We discuss them after reading by finding them in the text and reviewing their use.

Go to the Assignments and Activities section of Topic 16: Communication Disorders in the MyEducationLab for your course and complete the activity entitled *1-1 Speech and Language Intervention*.

Vocabulary. As students develop language, their vocabulary, or stock of words, and their ability to understand and talk about abstract concepts increase quickly. For example, children's speaking vocabulary, vocabulary that is used as part of their oral language, is estimated to be about 2,600 words at age 6, and their receptive vocabulary, words that they understand the meaning of but may not use in their oral language, consists of about 20,000 to 24,000 words. By the age of 12, students' receptive vocabulary has increased to 50,000 words (Owens, 2008). In comparison, when technical words are discounted, average adult speakers use about 10,000 words in everyday conversation, and an estimated 60,000 to 80,000 words are known and used by the average high-school graduate (Carroll, 1964).

As Mary Armanti got to know Krista, a student with communication disorders in her third-grade class, she discovered that Krista's vocabulary was very limited. During sharing or small-group discussion, Krista used simple words and did not expand on her ideas (compared to the other students). Concerned about Krista's limited vocabulary, Mary worked with the speech and language pathologist to develop some classroom strategies to increase Krista's vocabulary. These strategies included Mary elaborating on what Krista said—that is, to model for Krista how to use a more complex, richer vocabulary. For example, when Krista volunteered, "The egg hatched," as she watched a bird nest outside the classroom window, Mary elaborated on her statement: "Yes, the bird's egg just hatched. The new bird is so tiny and fuzzy."

The oral language of the students in your classes is influenced significantly by the oral language they are exposed to at home. Of the words in a child's vocabulary, 86% to 98% are words contained in their parents' vocabularies (Hart & Risley, 2003). Betty Hart and Todd Risley (2003) conducted more than 1,300 observations of 42 families over a two-and-a-half year period. Families all had children who were learning to talk and were observed talking and interacting casually at home. By the age of 3, children had very different home language experiences. For example, the average child in a welfare family was exposed to 616 words an hour, the working-class child was exposed to 1,251 words an hour, and the average child in a professional family was exposed to 2,153 words an hour. Early language experience also predicted later language ability and school performance. What can teachers do when students come to school with low language and vocabulary development? As we discuss in more detail in Chapter 12, teachers can provide daily and ongoing development of word meanings as part of their everyday instruction. Furthermore, teachers can advocate for intensive early intervention services for children and families to close the language gap between children from different types of families.

Word Categories and Word Relationships. From kindergarten through 12th grade, students' ability to learn to understand and organize words and concepts improves significantly (Owens, 2008). Students learn to group concepts by abstract features (such as animate and inanimate), spatial features, temporal relationships, or function. For example, in learning about fossils, students learn to simultaneously classify different types of fossils (e.g., trilobites, crinoids, brachiopods) according to plant/animal, extinct/not extinct, and location (e.g., sea, lakes, or land). By using semantic feature analysis, in which the categories or critical features are placed along one axis of a matrix and the specific vocabulary along the other axis, teachers can guide student discussion about the relationships among concepts and then visually represent those relationships (see Figure 7.2). Relationships can be noted as positive, negative, or no relationship or can be rated as to the degree of relationship along a scale.

FIGURE 7.2

Semantic Feature Analysis for a Chapter on Fossils

RELATIONSHIP CHART

Important Words	Type of Life		Location			Extinct?	
	Plant	Animal	Sea	Lakes	Land	Extinct	Not Extinct
Trilobites							
Crinoids							
Giant cats							
Coral							
Bryozoans							
Guide fossils							
Dinosaurs							
Fresh water fish							
Brachiopods							
Small horses							
Ferns							
Enormous winged bugs							
Trees							

Key:
+ = positive relationship
− = opposite or negative relationship
o = no relationship
? = uncertain

Understanding the relationships among concepts is important to successful learning. Types of relationships include the following categories:

- Comparative (*taller than*)
- Spatial (*above, under*)
- Temporal–sequential (*before, first*)
- Causal (*because, therefore*)
- Conditional (*if . . . then*)
- Conjunctive (*and*)
- Disjunctive (*either . . . or*)
- Contrastive (*but, although*)
- Enabling (*so that, in order that*)

Teaching relationship vocabulary is important for students' understanding of content subjects such as science, social studies, and math.

Multiple Meanings. Children also learn about the **multiple meanings** of words during the school-age years (Menyuk, 1971; Nippold, 1998). For example, the word *bank* has several meanings and can function as both a noun and a verb:

- "Lou sat on the bank fishing."
- "You can bank on him to be there."
- "Put your money in the bank for now."

Many students with communication disorders have more limited vocabularies, and their word meanings are generally more concrete and less specific than those of other students.

These students also have greater difficulty understanding multiple meanings and when to apply which meaning.

Figurative Language. Another area of language content, **figurative language**, represents abstract concepts and usually requires an inferential rather than a literal interpretation. Figurative language allows students to use language in truly creative ways (McLaughlin, 1998; Nippold, 1998; Owens, 2008). The primary types of figurative language include the following:

- Idioms ("It's raining cats and dogs.")
- Metaphors ("She watched him with an eagle eye.")
- Similes ("He ran like a frightened rabbit.")
- Proverbs ("The early bird catches the worm.")

Figure 7.3 presents some common American English idioms.

Students with language disorders, students from other cultures or regions, and students for whom English is a second language may have difficulty with figurative language. Yet figurative

---

FIGURE 7.3

Common American English Idioms

Animals

a bull in a china shop

as stubborn as a mule

going to the dogs

playing possum

a fly in the ointment

clinging like a leech

grinning like a Cheshire cat

thrown to the wolves

Body Parts

on the tip of my tongue

raised eyebrows

turn the other cheek

put your best foot forward

turn heads

put their heads together

Clothing

dressed to kill

hot under the collar

wear the pants in the family

fit like a glove

strait-laced

Colors

gray area

once in a blue moon

tickled pink

has a yellow streak

red-letter day

true blue

Games and Sports

ace up my sleeve

cards are stacked against me

got lost in the shuffle

keep your head above water

paddle your own canoe

ballpark figure

get to first base

keep the ball rolling

on the rebound

Foods

eat crow

humble pie

that takes the cake

a finger in every pie

in a jam

Plants

heard it through the grapevine

resting on his laurels

shrinking violet

no bed of roses

shaking like a leaf

withered on the vine

Tools and Work

bury the hatchet

has an axe to grind

hit the nail on the head

jockey for position

throw a monkey wrench into it

doctor the books

has a screw loose

hit the roof

nursing his wounds

sober as a judge

Vehicles

fix your wagon

like ships passing in the night

on the wagon

don't rock the boat

missed the boat

take a back seat

Weather

calm before the storm

haven't the foggiest

steal her thunder

come rain or shine

right as rain

throw caution to the wind

Source: Owens, Jr., R. E. (2010). *Language disorders: A functional approach to assessment and intervention* (5th ed., pp. 320–21). Boston: Allyn & Bacon. Copyright © 2010 by Allyn & Bacon. Reprinted by permission. Compiled from Clark (1990); Gibbs (1987); Gulland & Hinds-Howell (1986); Nippold & Rudzinski (1993).

---

language, particularly idioms, prevails in the classroom. Classroom research shows that teachers use idioms in approximately 11% of what they say and that approximately 7% of the sentences in third- to eighth-grade reading programs contain idioms (Lazar, Warr-Leeper, Nicholson, & Johnson, 1989). Understanding and using figurative language is associated with higher performance among adolescents on literacy (Dean Qualls, O'Brien, Blood, & Scheffner Hammer, 2003).

Language Form

Difficulties with the form of language are usually quite noticeable to classroom teachers. Students not only have difficulty pronouncing certain sounds and using prefixes, suffixes, and endings on words, but also use sentences that have poor word order and grammar. As was mentioned earlier, form refers to the structure of the language and includes phonology, morphology, and syntax.

Phonology. **Phonology** focuses on the sounds of language and the rules that determine how those sounds fit together. **Phonemes** are the smallest linguistic units of sound that can signal a meaning difference. In English there are approximately 45 phonemes or speech sounds, classified as either consonants or vowels. (The section on articulation disorders also includes information relevant to the development of phonemes.) The ability to listen to and produce sounds is important not only for oral language but also for reading and writing (written language). As students learn to decode unknown words while reading and to spell words as they write, one strategy they use is to "sound out the word" or "sound spell." Students who have difficulty generating rhyming words, segmenting words into their individual sounds, or producing individual sounds and then blending them together to make words often have difficulty using the "sound out" or "sound spell" strategies. These skills develop in the preschool and early elementary years as students experiment with sounds and sound patterns while they play with words and learn to read and write. These skills, referred to as **phonological awareness**, pertain to students' ability to understand that words contain sounds and that sounds can be used as linguistic building blocks to construct words (Mann, 1984). This difficulty with phonological awareness has been identified as a strong predictor of later reading and spelling problems (Catts, Fey, Zhang, & Tomblin, 2001; Passenger, Stuart, & Terrell, 2000; Van Kleek, 1995). Consequently, the ability to listen to and produce sounds plays an important role in the development not only of oral language but also of written language.

PEARSON
myeducationlab

Go to the Assignments and Activities section of Topic 19: Reading Instruction in the MyEducationLab for your course and complete the activity entitled *Phonemic Awareness*.

Morphology. Whereas phonology focuses on sounds, **morphology** focuses on the rule system that governs the structure of words and word forms. And as phonemes are the smallest sound units, **morphemes** are the smallest units of language that convey meaning. There are two different kinds of morphemes: *free morphemes,* which can stand alone (e.g., *cat, run, pretty, small, inside*), and *bound morphemes* (prefixes, suffixes, and inflectional endings), which cannot stand alone but, when added to words, change their meaning. For example, *s* is a common morpheme in English that when used at the end of a noun changes it to plural. Students who understand both orally and in print that *cat* is singular and *cats* is plural have better understanding

What competencies in the pragmatics of language do these students probably possess? How does the way children typically use language change as they mature into adolescence?

of what they hear and read. Another example is the prefix *re*, which is often used to mean *do again*. Students who understand that rewrite means to write again will be able to generalize *re* to other words and their meaning.

Learning the different bound morphemes and their meanings can help elementary and secondary students to decode words, spell words, and determine the meaning of words. For example, students who do not recognize or know the meaning of the word *predetermination* can break it into the free morpheme *determine* (to decide) and the bound morphemes *pre* (before) and *tion* (denoting action in a noun). Then the students can decode the word and decide that the meaning of *predetermination* is "a decision made in advance."

Developmentally, inflectional endings are the easiest to learn, followed by suffixes and then prefixes (Owens, 2008; Rubin, 1988). Although inflectional endings may be acquired through conversation, suffixes and prefixes usually require more direct instruction in both oral and written form. What does this mean for the teacher? Most students will learn how *ing* and *s* adjust the meaning of a word through listening and reading. However, they will require instruction in prefixes (e.g., *un*, *re*, *pre*) to understand their meaning and use. This is also true for suffixes such as *ful* and *ment*. You can use the common prefixes, suffixes, and inflectional endings presented in Table 7.2 as a guide for teaching morphology.

TABLE 7.2

Common Prefixes, Suffixes, and Inflectional Endings

DERIVATIONAL		INFLECTIONAL
PREFIXES	*SUFFIXES*	
a- (in, on, into, in a manner)	-able (ability, tendency, likelihood)	-ed (past)
bi- (twice, two)	-al (pertaining to, like, action, process)	-ing (at present)
de- (negative, descent, reversal)	-ance (action, state)	-s (plural)
ex- (out of, from, thoroughly)	-ation (denoting action in a noun)	-s (third person marker)
inter- (reciprocal, between, together)	-en (used to form verbs from adjectives)	-'s (possession)
mis- (ill, negative, wrong)	-ence (action, state)	
out- (extra, beyond, not)	-er (used as an agentive ending)	
over- (over)	-est (superlative)	
post- (behind, after)	-ful (full, tending)	
pre- (to, before)	-ible (ability, tendency, likelihood)	
pro- (in favor of)	-ish (belonging to)	
re- (again, backward motion)	-ism (doctrine, state, practice)	
semi- (half)	-ist (one who does something)	
super- (superior)	-ity (used for abstract nouns)	
trans- (across, beyond)	-ive (tendency or connection)	
tri- (three)	-ize (action, policy)	
un- (not, reversal)	-less (without)	
under- (under)	-ly (used to form adverbs)	
	-ment (action, product, means, state)	
	-ness (quality, state)	
	-or (used as an agentive ending)	
	-ous (full of, having, like)	
	-y (inclined to)	

Source: Owens, Jr., R. E. (2010). *Language disorders: A functional approach to assessment and intervention* (5th ed., p. 444). Boston: Allyn & Bacon. Copyright © 2010 by Allyn & Bacon. Reprinted by permission.

Syntax. Syntax focuses on the rules that govern the order of words in sentences. During the school-age years, students continue to grow in their ability to use more complex sentence structures (Owens, 2008). Even though most students understand and generate basic sentences by age 5 (McNeill, 1970; Nippold, 1998), first-graders produce sentences that are neither completely grammatical (*He'll might go to jail*) nor reflect the syntactical complexities of the English language.

Students with language impairments and English language learners may experience difficulties in the area of syntax. Students who are learning English as a second language may understand complex syntax, particularly if similar syntax is found in their first language, but may be uncomfortable producing it.

Regardless of the reason for the delay, one helpful strategy for identifying children's needs relative to syntax is to listen to the students' language and determine where they are in the developmental sequence. For example, Rebecca Blair, a third-grade teacher, noticed that several of her students with language-learning disabilities were not using the past participle (*has/have* + verb) during class discussions, on the playground, or during small-group discussions. She talked with Jean Gleason, the speech and language pathologist, who agreed that this would be a good skill to work on, because all three students were able to use the simple past tense. To teach the skill directly, Rebecca interacted with the three students as they worked together to create and write a story in which she controlled the use of verb tense by requiring them to use the past participle. The story follows:

> Once upon a time, there was a very hungry boy named Jason. Jason decided that he would eat everything he could find in the refrigerator. All day long, he has gone to the refrigerator and eaten whatever food he could find. By the end of the day,
>
> Jason has eaten 3 pickles.
> Jason has eaten 5 olives.
> Jason has eaten 8 slices of cheese.
> Jason has eaten 25 grapes.
>
> Now Jason has a stomachache.

In discussing the story, Rebecca compared the simple past tense with the past participle and had the students think of other instances in which they could use the past participle. Rebecca had the students tell and write other stories with similar formats, and Jean, at the same time, worked on the same skill with the students. Rebecca also gave each student a quick "thumbs up" whenever she heard them use the past participle. Within 3 months, the past participle became part of their everyday language.

As sentence complexity increases, so does the average length of the sentences. During the early elementary grades, students also continue to increase in their ability to use irregular noun plurals (e.g., *mice, sheep, men*) and irregular verbs (see Table 7.3). In students with communication disorders and other disabilities, development of these irregular forms is often delayed by several years (Koziol, 1973; Nelson, 1998; Owens, 2008).

Language Use

The area of most important linguistic growth during the school-age years is language use, or pragmatics (Owens, 2008). **Pragmatics** refers to the purposes or functions of communication, or how we use language in a social context (Lue, 2001). During the school years, students become quite adept at using communication for a variety of functions. Students can use language to give and receive compliments, engage in role-playing, deal with conflicts, and ask for help (Lue, 2001). Students also learn to vary their communication style, or **register**, according to the listener's characteristics and knowledge of the topic. By the age of 13, students can switch from peer register to adult register (depending on the person with whom they are talking) and from formal register to informal register, depending on the setting and circumstances (McKinley & Larson, 1991; Owens, 2008).

Young children use language for such functions as gaining and holding attention, obtaining and giving information, directing and following others, expressing feelings, and role-playing (White, 1975). By adolescence, students demonstrate communication competence (Mobbs, Reed, & McAllister, 1993; Nippold, 1998; Owens, 2008; Wiig & Semel, 1984) in that they are able to do the following:

- Express positive and negative feelings and reactions to others
- Present, understand, and respond to information in spoken messages about people, objects, events, or processes that are not immediately visible

TABLE
7.3

Development of Irregular Verbs

AGE IN YEARS	IRREGULAR VERBS
3–0 to 3–5	Hit, hurt
3–6 to 3–11	Went
4–0 to 4–5	Saw
4–6 to 4–11	Ate, gave
5–0 to 5–5	Broke, fell, found, took
5–6 to 5–11	Came, made, sat, threw
6–0 to 6–5	Bit, cut, drove, fed, flew, ran, wore, wrote
6–6 to 6–11	Blew, read, rode, shot
7–0 to 7–5	Drank
7–6 to 7–11	Drew, dug, hid, rang, slept, swam
8–0 to 8–5	Caught, hung, left, slid
8–6 to 8–11	Built, sent, shook

Source: Information from Shipley, K., Maddox, M., & Driver, J. (1991). Children's development of irregular past tense verb forms. *Language, Speech, and Hearing Services in Schools* 22, 115–122.

- Take the conversational partner's perspective
- Comprehend the speaker's mood
- Comprehend nonverbal communication
- Understand and present complex messages
- Adapt messages to the needs of others
- Use clarification and repair in conversation
- On the basis of prior experience, approach verbal interaction with expectations of what to say and how to say it
- Relate a narrative cohesively and sequentially
- Communicate a point of view logically
- Select different forms of messages according to the age, status, and reactions of listeners
- Use sarcasm, humor, and multiple meanings
- Make deliberate use of figurative language

Language is used for many different communication activities. One activity that occurs frequently in school and in other settings is conversation. To determine whether students are having difficulty with the use of language, you can assess their conversational skills. See Tips for Teachers 7.1 for ideas on how to assess conversational skills.

 **Tips FOR TEACHERS 7.1**

ASSESSING YOUR STUDENTS' CONVERSATIONAL SKILLS

Take a few minutes to think about several students you know or with whom you are currently working. Think about how they use language to communicate in social contexts.

- Do they vary their communication style depending on the listener?

- Do they present enough information for the listener to understand the message?

- If the listener is not understanding, do they take action to clarify what they said?

For students who do have difficulty with these areas, working on language use may be an appropriate goal.

Metalinguistics

Students who use **metalinguistics** can think about, analyze, and reflect on language as an object in much the same way they can describe what a picture or figure looks like to someone who cannot see it or vividly describe their friends to others (Hulit & Howard, 2006; Wallach & Miller, 1988). Metalinguistics also involves understanding that language is a code for representing sounds, words, and ideas.

Young children learn to use language without really understanding how it operates and functions. They use the linguistic rules that govern language, but if you asked them to tell you about or explain the rules, they would have great difficulty. As children mature, however, they become more sophisticated language learners. They develop metalinguistic skills, or the ability to talk about and reflect on language as if it were an object. Berko Gleason (2001) notes that metalinguistics involves talking about words and language, seeing language as an entity separate from its function. Metalinguistics is the ability to judge the correctness of language and to correct it.

Teachers can use information about the development of metalinguistic skills to consider instruction in prereading and reading. For example, Wallach and Miller (1988) organized the development of metalinguistic skills to correspond to Piaget's stages of cognitive development (see Figure 7.4). It is evident from this figure that during Stage Two (ages 2 to 6) children develop the metalinguistic skills critical for decoding words (when reading) and for learning to spell (when writing). These skills include ascertaining word boundaries in spoken and printed sentences, rhyming, making sound substitutions, segmenting words into syllables and sounds, and blending syllables and sounds into words. Research consistently demonstrates the reciprocal relationship between early reading and writing and the development of these metalinguistic skills (e.g., Fletcher, Lyon, Fuchs, & Barnes, 2007; Speece, Roth, & Cooper, 1999).

FIGURE 7.4

Stages of Children's Metalinguistic Development

Stage One (Ages $1\frac{1}{2}$ to 2)

- Distinguishes print from nonprint
- Knows how to interact with books: right side up, page turning from right to left
- Recognizes some printed symbols, e.g., TV character's name, brand names, signs

Stage Two (Ages 2 to $5\frac{1}{2}$ or 6)

- Ascertains word boundaries in spoken sentences
- Ascertains word boundaries in printed sentences
- Engages in word substitution play
- Plays with the sounds of language
- Begins to talk about language parts and about talking (speech acts)
- Corrects own speech/language to help the listener understand the message (spontaneously or in response to listener request)
- Self-monitors own speech and makes changes to more closely approximate the adult model; phonological first; lexical and semantic speech style last
- Believes that a word is an integral part of the object to which it refers (word realism)
- Able to separate words into syllables
- Inability to consider that one word could have two different meanings

Stage Three (Ages 6 to 10)

- Begins to take listener perspective and use language form to match
- Understands verbal humor involving linguistic ambiguity, e.g., riddles
- Able to resolve ambiguity: lexical first, as in homophones; deep structures next, as in ambiguous phrases ("Will you join me in a bowl of soup?"); phonological or morphemic next (Q: "What do you have if you put three ducks in a box?" A: "A box of quackers.")
- Able to understand that words can have two meanings, one literal and the other nonconventional or idiomatic, e.g., adjectives used to describe personality characteristics such as *hard, sweet, bitter*
- Able to resequence language elements, as in pig Latin
- Able to segment syllables into phonemes
- Finds it difficult to appreciate figurative forms other than idioms

Stage Four (Ages 10 +)

- Able to extend language meaning into hypothetical realms, e.g., to understand figurative language such as metaphors, similes, parodies, analogies, etc.
- Able to manipulate various speech styles to fit a variety of contexts and listeners

Source: Wallach, G. P. & Miller, L. (1988). *Language intervention and academic success* (p. 33). San Diego: College Hill. Reprinted with permission.

60 Second LESSON

PROMOTING LANGUAGE THROUGH WORD GAMES

Often, teachers find themselves before or just after a transition with several minutes that need to be filled. Playing word games is a great way to fill the time and to promote language and metalinguistic skills. Listed here are several word games you and your students can play. You might want to make lists based on the words you generate from these games and post them for student reference.

FOR YOUNGER STUDENTS

Rhyming Words.   Select a word. Use a word from a word family (e.g., *-at, -ight, -an, -end*) to provide lots of opportunities for rhyming. Or have a student select a word. Then have the other students give rhyming words. You might want to write the words so that students can see the similarities between words. If you want students to select the words, put each word on a slip of paper and place them in a container such as a hat or jar, and then have students draw words from the container.

Sound Substitutions.   Select a word (e.g., *hat*). (Again, use of word-family words helps.) Say the word and write it on the board. Then ask students what word will be made if the first sound (e.g., /h/) is changed to another sound (e.g., /b/).

Syllables.   Have a student select a word and say it. Then repeat the word slowly and have the students clap once for each syllable in the word.

Opposites.   Select pairs of simple word opposites (e.g., *hot*/cold, *easy/hard, big/little, happy/sad*). Say one word from each pair and have students say the opposite.

FOR OLDER STUDENTS

Antonyms.   Select pairs of word opposites (e.g., *cool/warm, hard/soft, cruel/gentle, empty/full, tame/wild*). Write one word from the pair on a card and put it in a container. Have a student draw a card, say the word, and have other students say or write the opposite word.

Synonyms.   Select a word with several synonyms (e.g., *eat, pretty, pants, laugh*). Say one word and have students name as many synonyms as they can.

Homonyms.   Select a word with at least one homonym (e.g., *fare, sale, male*). Say and spell one word and have students give the homonyms.

Multiple Meanings.   Select a word that has several meanings, write it on the board, and have students give examples of sentences that use the different meanings of the word (e.g., I have a *run* in my stocking. Let's go for a *run*. In the long *run* it isn't very important. I have to *run* and pick up a sandwich).

Suffixes.   Select a suffix (e.g., *-tion*). Discuss its meaning and then have students provide examples of words that use this suffix (e.g., *determination, nomination, participation*). Have students also tell what the root word is. (You can play the same game with prefixes.)

As a teacher, you will want to talk about language, how it works, and the rules that govern language. Playing word games such as the ones suggested in the 60-Second Lesson is one way to build this type of language learning into those free moments during the day.

Prevalence of Communication Disorders

The prevalence of youngsters in the elementary grades with communication disorders ranges from 7% to 9% (Ziegler, Pech-Georgel, Alario, & Lorenzi, 2005) with the number of students actually receiving services for speech or language disorders reported at 18.7% (U.S Department of Education, 2005). Why such a range from communication disorders and speech and language? This is because many students receive speech services in the early grades that are then readily corrected and they no longer receive services in the upper elementary grades. The vast majority of students, 88%, are included in the general education classroom and thus you, as a teacher, will likely be coordinating services for these students with the speech and language specialist (U.S. Department of Education, 2005). Of school-age children with communication disorders, most have difficulties in the areas of language and articulation. Within this population, communication disorders occur more often in boys than in girls (ASHA, 2008).

Identifying and Assessing Students with Communication Disorders

Most students with communication disorders are identified in preschool or during the early elementary grades. As a teacher, consider the following steps if you suspect a student has a communication disorder.

- Talk with the speech and language specialist in your school district and ask her or him to schedule some time to observe the student in class and to interact with the student. The speech and language specialist is likely to recommend a hearing screening to determine whether there is interference in language development based on any hearing loss.
- Call the student's parents and ask them about the student's communication at home.
- Determine whether the student needs an evaluation. The evaluation for possible language delays or disorders often includes collecting a language sample. Sampling involves tape-recording students as they interact, and then analyzing the students' utterances for characteristics such as mean length of utterance, types of utterances, vocabulary, topic maintenance, and turn taking.

One role that general education teachers play is that of observer and listener for students who have significant difficulty communicating. Particularly in the elementary grades, the classroom teacher spends more time with the students than any other individual in school. When Sharon Kutok, a speech and language pathologist, spoke about what teachers should watch for, she commented, "Classroom teachers are good at identifying students with language disabilities. When identifying students with receptive language problems, typical teacher comments are 'When these students are listening to a presentation they look away and don't focus. When I ask a question, they don't seem to know what is going on. I don't know if the students don't understand me or if they can't answer my question.'"

For expressive language difficulties, Sharon noted that "classroom teachers indicate that these students give answers that have no relationship to the question. They use short sentences or just words, and sometimes the words are out of order. Those are the kinds of symptoms that teachers notice when identifying students with language difficulties."

As a classroom teacher, you have the opportunity to observe students using language in the classroom (during both academic and social activities) as well as on the playground and during other activities such as art, music, and physical education. What should you look for in the area of language? Tips for Teachers 7.2 presents questions you can ask about your students

PEARSON
myeducationlab

Go to the Assignments and Activities section of Topic 16: Communication Disorders in the MyEducationLab for your course and complete the activity entitled *Informal Expressive Language Assessment.*

Tips for Teachers 7.2

IDENTIFYING A STUDENT WITH POSSIBLE LANGUAGE DISORDERS

Language Form

- Does the student mispronounce sounds or words and omit endings more than other students in the classroom do?

- Does the student comprehend and produce types of sentences similar to those of other students in the classroom?

- Is the student's language as elaborate and descriptive as that of other students in the classroom?

- Are the student's comprehension and production of grammatical rules similar to those of other students in the classroom?

Language Content

- Does the student comprehend and produce vocabulary as rich and varied as that of other students in the classroom?

- Does the student comprehend others' ideas and express his or her ideas as effectively as other students in the classroom?

- When talking, does the student have significant difficulty finding the word he or she wants to use (i.e., word-finding difficulties)?

- Does the student comprehend and use figurative language and multiple meanings of words similar to that of other students in the classroom?

Language Use

- Does the student use language for different purposes, including to gain attention, ask for and tell about information, express and respond to feelings, use imagination to understand and tell stories and jokes, express opinions and persuade, and for greetings, introductions, and farewells?

- Does the student take turns appropriately in conversations?

- Does the student initiate conversations?

- Does the student stay on topic during a conversation?

- Does the student have more than one style of interacting, depending on the listener, situation, and topic?

- Does the student recognize when the listener is not understanding and act to clarify communication for the listener?

to determine the possibility of difficulties with language. The questions are grouped according to the three areas of language: form, content, and use. If a language delay is evident, you should consider making a referral to the speech and language pathologist.

If students are English language learners (ELL) or if their first dialects are other than Standard English, consult with a speech and language pathologist and a bilingual education or ELL teacher when observing students for language differences associated with second language or dialect acquisition or possible language difficulties. (See Chapter 4 for additional information.)

The role of the school-based speech and language pathologist (SLP) has changed significantly within the past few decades due to legislative changes in special education. Traditionally, the speech and language pathologist has used a clinical/medical model of assessment and intervention, treating students individually or in small groups in a separate therapy or resource room. Educational reform statutes such as the Education for All Handicapped Children Act of 1986 and the later Individuals with Disabilities Education Act (IDEA) and its 1997 and 2004 amendments have mandated increased participation of students with disabilities in the general education classroom.

Speech and language pathologists now work closely with other school professionals and parents in a team model, using a combination of direct and indirect service methods to assist students with communication disorders. In addition to providing individual or group therapy, they may also collaborate with classroom teachers to develop modifications and strategies for students within the classroom. The role of the speech and language pathologist may vary due to differences in caseload, state or district regulations, and staffing needs (ASHA, 2006). The changing role is largely a function of the large caseloads most speech and language pathologists are asked to serve, which averages about 50 students per specialist (ASHA, 2006). The following are some ways that the speech and language pathologist can help the child with language difficulties within the school setting (ASHA, 2000):

LITERACY AND LANGUAGE

- Collaborate with the teacher to implement developmentally appropriate language arts and literacy programs.
- Assist in modifying and selecting language and instructional strategies that integrate oral and written communication skills.
- Provide information and training to school personnel regarding the linguistic bases of reading and writing.
- Provide information and support for parents of at-risk children regarding language and literacy activities in the home environment.
- Collaborate with reading professionals and classroom teachers to augment the success of children with language and reading impairments.

SOCIAL–EMOTIONAL COMMUNICATION SKILLS

- Provide information regarding the link between social–emotional problems and social communication skills (pragmatics).
- Assist in training school staff to use effective verbal and nonverbal communication strategies in conflict resolution.
- Demonstrate lessons to enhance pragmatic communication skills (problem solving, social communication).

Go to **www.asha.org** for membership information for the American Speech-Language-Hearing Association. Find articles and the latest related research.

Instructional Guidelines and Accommodations for Students with Communication Disorders

Most students with communication disorders are educated in general education classrooms. Although these students may work (individually or in small groups) with a speech and language pathologist several times a week for 30 minutes or so, they spend the rest of their school days with the classroom teacher and students. Consequently, students with communication disorders have many more opportunities to develop effective communication in the classroom than in the limited time spent with the SLP. As a classroom teacher, you will play a major role in facilitating the development of effective communication for these students.

Speech and language pathologists are one of your best resources for ideas about facilitating speech and language development. As more schools adopt inclusion policies, speech and language pathologists are more frequently teaming with classroom teachers. Two major benefits of these teams are that you and the SLP have more opportunities to learn from each other and that students other than those identified as having communication disorders profit from the communication activities.

Facilitating Speech Development

Generally, specific remediation of articulation errors, voice disorders, and stuttering is provided by the SLP. The major goal of the general education teacher is to provide opportunities for the student to communicate in the classroom using the most natural, supportive situations possible. If students are to generalize what they are learning in therapy, you will also need to work with the SLP to get specific information on the skills students are targeting and to discuss strategies you can use to help them generalize those skills. One such strategy is to develop a personal cueing system for students who have difficulty responding in a large group. Robert Encino, a seventh-grade science teacher, explains how he developed such a system with Kim:

These students are working in a cooperative learning group. Which instructional accommodations described in this chapter might the teacher use for her students who have communication difficulties?

> Kim was a student in my fifth period who stutters. I was aware that she often knew an answer and wanted to share her knowledge, but I was unsure of when she felt confident enough to do so. I met with Kim one day during planning period, and we agreed on a system where she would open her hand, palm-side up on her desk, if she wanted to respond. What I found was that this reduced her anxiety, and during the semester her hand was open more and more frequently. Eventually, we discontinued the system because she felt that she didn't need it any longer.

It is also important for students with speech disorders that the classroom be a safe environment in which to practice oral communication. Tips for Teachers 7.3 provides some strategies for helping to promote a classroom community that accepts and encourages meaningful student communication.

PEARSON myeducationlab

Go to the Building Teaching Skills and Dispositions section of Topic 16: Communication Disorders in the MyEducationLab for your course and complete the activity entitled *Collaborating with the Speech Language Pathologist.*

Tips FOR TEACHERS 7.3

CREATING AN ACCEPTING CLASSROOM COMMUNITY FOR STUDENTS WITH SPEECH DISORDERS

- Create an atmosphere of ease and comfortable pacing. Avoid an atmosphere that creates time pressures and tensions.

- Listen in a calm and thoughtful manner to what students have to say. Allow time for students to finish their thoughts. Don't disregard ideas just because students have difficulty expressing them.

- Do not criticize or point out speech errors. You may, however, demonstrate correct speech by correctly repeating what the students said.

- Establish classroom rules that do not allow for ridicule of students or their speech errors.

- Take care not to place students with speech problems in situations in which their communication difficulties might interfere or are highlighted.

- Use flexible grouping so that students have opportunities to talk in small groups and with a partner.

- Allow time for students to respond. Students often need time to get their ideas organized and to plan their communication. Speech may be labored and slow.

- Develop cueing systems that allow students to let you know when they are comfortable responding.

- Read aloud in a slow, easy manner to give students an opportunity to practice fluency strategies or new sounds they are learning. Students become more fluent with multiple readings, so the use of repeated reading may be beneficial.

- Avoid competition among students, particularly when it highlights oral communication.

Go to **www.isaac-online.org** for information about membership information and the latest research, resources, and discussion groups.

Some students with physical disabilities and other severe disabilities cannot communicate effectively through speech and therefore rely on **augmentative and alternative communication (AAC) systems**. AAC refers to ways (other than speech) that are used to send and receive messages. We all use AAC strategies such as facial expressions, gestures, and writing in our daily interactions. Individuals with severe physical and/or cognitive disabilities use these strategies as well as individualized AAC systems. Augmentative communication systems attempt to compensate for, temporarily or permanently, the impairment and disability patterns of individuals with severe expressive and receptive language disorders (ASHA, 1993). Augmentative communication is a means for students with limited or no speech to interact with peers and teachers in the classroom environment. Tech Tips describes different issues related to augmentative and alternative communication.

Facilitating Language Development

Opportunities for teaching oral language abound during general education classroom activities—whether they occur in the classroom itself or on the playground, during field trips, or in the lunchroom. Language also becomes more natural and purposeful in these settings than is the case in the therapy setting. As a classroom teacher, you are constantly teaching oral language. When you teach students new concepts and vocabulary in content-area subjects, you are teaching oral language. When students learn how to give oral reports or retell a story, how to introduce themselves, or how to use irregular verbs, they are developing language skills. What are some general guidelines you can use to facilitate language development in your classroom? Vaughn and Bos (2009) suggest the following guidelines to help shape your instruction.

Go to **www.aacproducts.org**, the website of the Communication Aid Manufacturers Association, which contains information related to workshops, catalogs, and related links.

Teaching Language in Purposive Contexts. Whether you are teaching students causal relationships such as the effect of heat on water or how to request information by telephone, it is important to teach language in the context of meaningful activities. It is difficult to imagine teaching someone how to use a screwdriver or a needle and thread without having the tools at

---

Tech TIPS

AUGMENTATIVE COMMUNICATION TOOLS FOR STUDENTS WITH COMMUNICATION DISORDERS AND PERVASIVE DEVELOPMENTAL DISORDERS

There are a number of different augmentative technologies that can assist students with communication disorders and pervasive developmental disorders.

Communication Boards

One relatively simple communication solution for learners who cannot speak is the communication board. Typically, with a board, the user points to the desired symbol, word, or picture. The communication board could be a laminated page with pictures, words, or symbols to which the learner points, or a small book of pages the learner flips through to express needs or feelings.

Boardmaker Software Family? by Mayer-Johnson **www.mayerjohnson.com** is a widely used computer program that simplifies the creation of communication boards by providing many useful templates and an extensive collection of picture communication symbols.

Interactive Software Programs

For learners with poor communication skills, there are computer programs that can help improve oral language skills.

TalkTime with Tucker and Tiger's Tale by Laureate **www.laureatelearning.com** are voice-activated software programs that require the learner to speak to the computer, thereby encouraging expressive language and stimulating speech. In TalkTime with Tucker, Tucker, an animated character, talks and moves with the speaker's vocalizations. Clear articulation is not required. In Tiger's Tale, an animated tiger has lost his voice, calling on the learner to speak for this unfortunate big cat. The learner can then play back the completed movie, listening to his or her own voice recorded with the software speaking for the tiger.

ReadPlease® by ReadPlease Corporation **www.readplease.com/** is an easy-to-use, reasonably priced software that is an effective text-to-speech product for students, allowing almost any text to be read out loud by the computer. An effective technology for students with developmental and/or communication disorders.

Using Barrier Games to Promote Language

Objectives: Helping students build their comprehension and production of descriptive language

Grades: Pre-K through grade 3

Materials: Blocks for building or paper and crayons for making a picture

It is not always possible to create authentic learning environments when you teach language, but we know that the best and quickest way to learn language is when it is purposeful and taught in context. One way to promote purposeful language and to help students build their comprehension and production of descriptive language, particularly locative prepositions, is to use barrier games. These games (frequently used by speech and language pathologists to teach prepositions) can be a great activity for the entire class or used as a filler activity after students complete their work.

Teaching procedure: Students work in pairs, with a barrier placed between them so that they cannot see each other's work.

- The lead student builds a simple structure or draws a simple design or picture. Then the lead student describes to the second student how to make what he or she has built or drawn.

- The second student is encouraged to ask questions when the directions are unclear.

- After the second student has finished his or her project, the barrier is removed, the two projects are compared, and differences are discussed. Then the roles are reversed.

Students can keep track of the number of projects that resemble the one that was presented to them orally. Another way to facilitate clearer communications is to provide a picture to one student and not to the second student. The student with the picture is given an allocated amount of time, e.g., 60 seconds, to talk about the picture without stating what it is. The second student guesses what it is based on the description.

hand, demonstrating how to use them, and then letting students practice. The same is true for language. Hence, when you cannot create a "real" situation, use such techniques as simulations and role-playing to create authentic learning experiences. Activities for All Learners explains how to use barrier games to teach language.

Teaching Comprehension and Production. Give students opportunities to develop both their understanding of (comprehension) and their ability to express (production) the new structures (form), vocabulary (content), and ways of using language (use) they are learning. When teaching the vocabulary associated with a new unit, for example, provide students with opportunities not only to listen to explanations but also to discuss their knowledge of the vocabulary and to use the new terms in their discussion and writing. The pause procedure provides these opportunities (Di Vesta & Smith, 1979; Ruhl, Hughes, & Gajar, 1990). Using this procedure, the teacher pauses at logical breaks in the lecture or discussion, and the students discuss what they are learning (with a partner or in a small group) and review their notes.

Presenting New Concepts. Critical to students' learning of new content or concepts is the use of effective teaching strategies. As you may recall from the earlier discussion of vocabulary development, students' knowledge of concepts grows exponentially during the school-age years. By using effective teaching strategies (see Tips for Teachers 7.4), you help students with language impairments and English language learners to gain the concepts and content necessary for success in content-area classes.

Demonstrating Connections Between Concepts. One important way we learn about concepts is by understanding the relationships or connections between concepts. If you listen to a conversation in which a new idea is being explained, you'll undoubtedly hear statements such as "It's like," or "You can compare it to," or "It's like … except that," or "It's almost the opposite of." These phrases all help students understand and see the connections between concepts. Because students with language problems have difficulty making those connections, it is important that you highlight them as you and the students discuss new concepts. For example, when Peggy, a first-grade teacher, was introducing the concept of "squirm" because it was

Tips FOR TEACHERS 7.4

PRESENTING NEW LANGUAGE CONCEPTS OR CONTENT

When teaching new language concepts or patterns, keep the following strategies in mind:

- Gear the activities to the students' interests and cognitive level.

- Get the students' attention before engaging in communication activities.

- Bombard the students with the concept or skill frequently throughout the day in a functional manner.

- When speaking, place stress on the target concept or language pattern.

- Pause between phrases or sentences so that the students have time to process the new concept or language pattern.

- Decrease the rate of presentation when first introducing the concept or language pattern.

- When introducing a new concept or language pattern, use familiar vocabulary that can be readily visualized.

- If possible, present the new concept or language pattern by using more than one input mode (e.g., auditory, visual, kinesthetic). Gestures and facial expressions that are paired with a specific language pattern often assist students in understanding the form. For example, giving a look of puzzlement or wonder when asking a question can serve as a cue to the students.

- Pair written symbols with oral language. For instance, demonstrating morphological endings such as -s (plurals) and -ed (past tense) can be done in writing. The students can then be cued to listen for what they see.

---

important for understanding the book her students were to discuss and read, she asked the students, "What does *squirm* mean?" "Show me with your body how you can squirm." "What other things can squirm?" "Now that we know what *squirm* is, what other words mean something similar to squirm?" "Is *squirm* similar to *wiggle*?" "What would be the opposite of *squirm*? If you weren't squirming, you would be _____."

At more advanced levels, when students make comparisons between books written by the same author, when they compare the relationships between addition and multiplication versus subtraction and division, and when they compare the similarities between the Korean and Vietnam Wars, the emphasis is on making connections. These kinds of discussions help students see the relationships between concepts and better understand semantic relationships (such as contrastives, comparatives, causals, and conditionals). The use of semantic feature analysis and other graphic organizers such as semantic maps and concept diagrams (see Chapter 14) can help students see the relationships.

PEARSON
myeducationlab

Go to the Assignments and Activities section of Topic 16: Communication Disorders in the MyEducationLab for your course and complete the activity entitled *Encouraging Participation*.

Using Conversation. As students with language impairments work, think, and play in your classroom, you need to create opportunities for them to engage in conversations with you and with other students. One way to do this is to use discussion groups rather than a question-and-answer format for reviews of books and current events. Nancy Meyers, the speech and language pathologist who works with Lorri Johnson, chose to work in Lorri's classroom while the literature groups meet. Once a week, she joins Samantha's literature group. As she listens and joins in the conversation about the book being discussed, Nancy has the opportunity to model language patterns on which Samantha is working.

At least several times a week, engage students in conversation. This may take some forethought and effort on your part, for observational research has shown that classroom teachers, in general, are not as responsive to students with language impairments as they are to average and high-achieving students (Pecyna-Rhyner, Lehr, & Pudlas, 1990). Let the students direct the topics of these conversations, which need not be long and, in secondary settings, can be accomplished as students enter the room. Do not fire away questions but give the student time to think, talk, and engage. Children like when adults "play with language" and are a little silly. Most importantly, be interested in the children and what they have to say.

Using Wait Time.   When speech and language pathologist Sharon Kutok talks about the most important principles in teaching students with language impairments, the first one she mentions is **wait time**. "For some students, waiting is important. Wait time gives students the opportunity to understand what has been said and to construct a response. These students may have particular difficulty with form (e.g., syntax) and need the extra time to think about the form they should use in constructing their response."

Students who have difficulty with content may also have difficulty with **word retrieval** or word finding (German, 1992). A word retrieval problem is like having the word on the tip of your tongue but not being able to think of it. Two examples demonstrate how difficulty with word retrieval can affect the flow of communication. The first conversation (about making an Easter basket) is a dialog between two third-graders, one with typical language and the other with word retrieval problems (Vaughn & Bos, 2009).

> **Susan:** Are you going to make, uh, make, uh, one of these things (pointing to the Easter basket on the bookshelf)?
> **Cori:** Oh, you mean an Easter basket?
> **Susan:** Yeah, an Easter basket.
> **Cori:** Sure, I'd like to, but I'm not sure how to do it. Can you help me?
> **Susan:** Yeah, first you need some, uh, some, uh, the things you cut with, you know.
> **Cori:** Scissors.
> **Susan:** Yeah, and some paper and the thing you use to stick things together with.
> **Cori:** Tape?
> **Susan:** No, uh, uh, sticky stuff.
> **Cori:** Oh, well, let's get the stuff we need.
> **Susan:** Let's go, to, uh, uh, the shelf, uh, where you get, you know, the stuff to cut up.
> **Cori:** Yeah, the paper, and let's also get the glue. (p. 76)

In the second example, an adolescent explains how to fix a tire:

> Well . . . to fix a tire . . . or your wheel . . . you gotta take the tire off . . . you gotta lift up . . . you jack up the car and use this thing . . . it's square metal wrench . . . to loosen the bolts . . . you know the nuts . . . then you take the wheel off the axel. First you ask the guy at the garage if he will fix the tire. You lock up the car so it won't . . . you put the car in gear so it stays put. (Chappell, 1985, p. 226)

It is clear from these two examples that wait time is important for students with word retrieval problems. In addition to increasing wait time, strategies that teachers can use during classroom discussions include the following:

- Using multiple-choice formats so that students need recognize only one word in a group, rather than having to generate the word
- Providing a cue, such as the initial sound or syllable, the category name or function, a synonym or description, or a gesture demonstrating the word
- Restating a question so that it requires a yes-or-no response rather than an open-ended answer

By teaching students with word-finding problems to categorize words, make visual images of words, learn synonyms, and make word associations (e.g., *bread/butter, plane/fly*), you can help them recall words, thereby increasing the accuracy and fluency of their expressive language (Gerber, 1993; German, 1993; McGregor & Leonard, 1995; Owens, 2008).

Adjusting the Pace.   Students with language delays and other disabilities and English language learners often have difficulty comprehending what is being said during class, particularly in content-area classes. Teachers need to adjust the pace so that these students have time to process information. The flow of instruction does not have to suffer, but when you discuss new or difficult concepts or ideas, slow the pace and highlight key ideas by writing them on the board or using technology to project them. Reducing the amount of information in each segment is helpful. For example, Bob Stern, a high-school science teacher, used to introduce the terms for a new science chapter by writing them on the board and discussing them as a group when he introduced the chapter. After Bob noticed that his students with language problems listened to the first five words and recorded three of them in their science notebooks, he decided to chunk the words into groups of three to five, introducing them when they were needed.

Using Self-Talk and Parallel Talk.   Students, particularly young students with language delays, need to hear language that is connected to activities. When teachers use **self-talk**, they describe what they are doing or thinking; in **parallel talk**, teachers describe what students are doing or thinking. As you and your students work or play, describe what everyone is doing. Maria Ferraro, a first-grade teacher who works in an inner-city school, regularly uses parallel talk and self-talk when she joins students at the different centers in her classroom:

> When I join a center, I try to sit down and join in the activities rather than asking students questions. My goal is to become part of the group. As I join in the activity, I describe what I am doing and what other students in the group are doing. For example, I might say, "José is making a clay animal. It's blue and right now he is putting a ferocious snarl on the animal's face. I wonder what kind of animal it is? I think I'll ask José." In this way, the students get to hear how words can describe what someone is doing, and it focuses the attention on José and the ongoing activities.

Using Modeling.   Modeling, using the oral language you want students to use, plays an important role in the process of learning language. Whether students are learning a new sentence structure, a new vocabulary, or a new function or use for language, modeling is a powerful tool. For example, Sharon Kutok and Armando Rivera, the speech and language pathologist and the eighth-grade English teacher at Vail Middle School, respectively, decided to improve their students' conversational skills during literature groups. Both Armando and Sharon were concerned about the number of students who did not clarify what they were saying when other students obviously did not understand (but did not request clarification).

To teach clarification skills, Armando and Sharon began discussing clarifying conversations. During their discussion, they role-played, first as students who could not effectively clarify what they were saying, and then as students who clarified effectively. They exaggerated the examples, and the students seemed to really enjoy their modeling. Next, Armando and Sharon joined the literature groups and continued to model as they participated in discussions. At the end of the period, they asked students to summarize what they had learned and whether they thought they could become more effective at clarifying what they said and asking others to clarify if they did not understand. During the next 2 weeks, Armando had the students in each literature group rate the group's effectiveness in clarification. When Sharon returned in 2 weeks, both teachers observed a difference in the students' discussions, particularly in their ability to clarify ideas and ask for clarification. The students also thought that their skills had improved. In discussing the change, both teachers and students agreed that the modeling Armando and Sharon had done on the first day was an important key to their learning.

Promoting Language Through Expansion and Elaboration.   Language **expansion** is a technique used to facilitate the development of complex language form and content. By repeating what students say but in a slightly more complex manner, the teacher demonstrates how their thoughts can be more fully expressed. For example, Susie Lee, a first-grade teacher, is working to get Rob to use adverbs to describe his actions. As he finished several math problems, Rob reported, "I got the first one easy. The second one was hard." Susie replied, "Oh, you got the first one easily. That's good." Note that you do not want to imply that you are correcting the student; you are simply showing him or her a more complex way of expressing the thought. Note also that you should expand only one element at a time. Otherwise, the expansion will be too complex for the student to profit from it.

You can use language **elaboration** to build on the content of the student's language and provide additional information on the topic. For example, Chris, a fourth-grade student with language disabilities, was explaining that snakes have rough skin. Teacher Peggy Anderson elaborated on Chris's idea by commenting, "Yes, and snakes have smooth skin on their bellies and so do lizards. Are there other animals in the desert that have smooth skin on their bellies?"

Using Language as an Intrinsic Motivator.   Language is a powerful enabling tool and carries a great deal of intrinsic motivation for students. Rather than using praise (e.g., "I like the

Go to the Assignments and Activities section of Topic 16: Communication Disorders in the MyEducationLab for your course and complete the activity entitled *Collaboration to Support Communication*.

way you said that" or "Good talking"), you can capitalize on the naturally reinforcing nature of language. During a cooking activity, for example, teacher Jon Warner asked students, "How can we figure out how much two thirds of a cup plus three fourths of a cup of flour is?" After Lydia explained, Jon said, "Now we know how to figure that out. Shall we give it a try?" Later, Jon asked how to sift flour. After Randa explained, Jon said, "I've got it. How about the rest of you? Do you think you can sift the flour just the way Randa explained to us?" Instead of commenting on how "good" their language was and disrupting the flow of communication, Jon complimented Lydia and Randa by letting them know how useful the information was.

When students' purposes and intents are fulfilled because of their language, their language is naturally reinforcing, and students learn that language is a powerful tool for controlling their environment (Owens, 2008; Vaughn & Bos, 2009). Tips for Teachers 7.5 provides strategies for promoting effective communication in your classroom.

Spotlight on Cultural and Linguistic Diversity

Language knowledge, vocabulary development, and understanding of word use all influence the writing of English language learners. Knowledge of the conventions of writing such as noun–verb agreement and other grammatical features may interfere with the writing production of English language learners. For this reason teachers must know what the learner knows about the language and expect that the development of the student's writing will reflect this knowledge. Thus, we would not expect the same level of grammatical accuracy from English language learners as we might from most native English speakers. However, it is important to provide English language learners with many opportunities to use written expression and to promote and support their acquisition of writing skills. Many of the approaches to writing that are discussed in this chapter are highly appropriate for English language learners. Haley and Austin (2004) provide the following guidelines for assisting English language learners with writing:

- Do they have an idea of what they want to write about?
- Are they comfortable using their personal, family, and relevant experiences in their writing?
- Do they use what they know to support their writing?
- What strategies are helpful in getting them to start thinking about their composition?
- Do they try to use new words in their writing?
- Do they get suggestions for their writing from family and friends?
- Do they use procedures for deciding what is important and not important in their writing?
- Do they choose different ways to express their ideas and feelings in their writing?
- Do they increasingly use more appropriate and effective language in their writing?

PEARSON
myeducationlab

Go to the Assignments and Activities section of Topic 16: Communication Disorders in the MyEducationLab for your course and complete the activity entitled *Promoting Communication in the Classroom*.

Tips FOR TEACHERS 7.5

PROMOTING EFFECTIVE COMMUNICATION IN YOUR CLASSROOM

- Use consistent verbal, visual, or physical cues to get attention (e.g., "1-2-3, eyes on me").

- Give instructions and important information only when students are paying attention.

- Be brief and specific when giving directions.

- Use students' names when speaking with them.

- Use gestures and facial expressions to help convey meaning when speaking.

- Use consistent routines to maximize engagement and discussion during peer group and partner work.

- Provide time for conversations during class so that students can share ideas and demonstrate understanding.

- Allow students to speak for themselves (e.g., avoid completing students' thoughts or having a peer speak for the student).

Source: Information from Smith, T. E. C., Polloway, E. A., Patton, J. R., & Dowdy, C. A. (2004). *Teaching students with special needs in inclusive settings* (4th ed.). Boston: Pearson.

Working with Parents to Extend Language Concepts

Children are more likely to learn new vocabulary and language structures when they are active participants in their learning and can practice new concepts in different contexts (home and school). The following are some suggestions for using newly learned language concepts in a variety of environments. Keep all language activities short and fun so that parents do not view communication as "homework." When planning language activities, be aware of cultural and linguistic differences in the home. If the family does not speak English, encourage the child to complete these activities in the language of the home:

FOR YOUNGER STUDENTS

- Send home a short description or picture of a recent classroom activity or field trip. Encourage the parents to ask open-ended rather than closed questions about the activity. For example, parents might ask: "I understand that you made a papier-mâché vase today. How did you do that?"
- Inform the parents of new vocabulary the child is learning. Have the child write a note to his or her family about what he or she learned. The child might say, "I learned the word *notorious* today."
- Have the child bring new words to class that he or she has heard at home. Create a word "treasure chest" and encourage the children to be vocabulary "hunters."
- Inform parents of new social language concepts that the child has practiced in class. Have the child describe the concept to his or her parent. For instance, the child might say, "I learned what to say if someone is bullying me." Encourage the parents to practice similar role-plays with the child at home.
- When possible, have students ask their parents questions about topics the students are learning in class. For example, if you are discussing the food pyramid, have the children ask their families about favorite foods and set aside a time for them to report back to the class on their findings.
- To practice figurative language, have children tell jokes or word puns to their families at home.
- To practice asking questions and listening skills, have the students ask their families about hypothetical situations discussed in class. Themes may come from journal topics such as "What would you do if you had a million dollars?"
- Encourage parents to discuss books that they read to or with their children. Send home some tips to encourage discussion of a book (e.g., talk about the pictures; relate the story to the child's own experiences).

FOR OLDER STUDENTS

- Encourage families to let students take responsibility for communicating in the community by asking for help from a store clerk, ordering for themselves in a restaurant, or calling a business to ask for directions or store hours.
- Encourage parents to ask students to explain school assignments and homework and jointly come up with a plan for accomplishing tasks.
- Model and encourage following conversation rules such as turn taking, active listening, and topic maintenance.
- Listen to students' stories, goals, and needs and help them problem solve solutions. Effective listening can open the door to conversations with adolescents who may be reluctant to share with their families.

Because some adolescents with language disorders may misunderstand what has been said or have difficulty understanding nonverbal cues, it is important that parents are clear with their messages, check for understanding, and are patient if the student becomes frustrated during a conversation. If something is very important, parents should communicate the information in words and with a written note and encourage students to do the same.

Summary

- Communication is one of the most essential tools in school and society. We communicate to develop and maintain relationships, to gain and give information, to express feelings, and to control others and the environment.

- Communication disorders include speech, language, and hearing disorders. Speech disorders involve difficulties with articulation, fluency, and voice. Language disorders involve difficulties with content (semantics), form (phonology, morphology, and syntax), and use (pragmatics).

- Although most basic language skills develop before children enter school, language continues to evolve through the school-age years, a process that includes a large growth in vocabulary, more complex sentence structures, use of prefixes and suffixes, multiple meanings, figurative language, complex semantic relationships (e.g., causal, conditional, enabling), and more sophisticated uses of language (e.g., adjustments to the register of communication, the use of sarcasm and humor).

- An important role classroom teachers play is to identify students who might have speech and language impairments.

- For students with speech disorders, the classroom teacher's role is to create a nonthreatening environment in which the students can communicate.

- Classroom teachers play an important role in facilitating the development of language. The classroom is an ideal setting to use such language techniques as self-talk and parallel talk, expansion and elaboration, modeling, and conversations. It is also important to adjust the pace and wait time and to communicate effectively with parents about the communication development of their child.

Think and Apply

1. Assume that you are a new teacher at Drexel Elementary School and Lorri Johnson is your teaching mentor. Make a list of one or two instructional practices you have learned about teaching content, form, and use with respect to supporting students with language difficulties. Provide these suggestions to your mentor teacher for feedback.

2. Determine the questions or concerns you have about teaching students with communication disorders. Discuss your questions with your fellow students, your instructor, and a speech and language pathologist. Record your answers and file your personal inquiry in your teaching portfolio.

3. When teaching or observing a teacher, consciously use the techniques of parallel talk, expansion, and elaboration. How does this affect the expressive language of the students whose language is typically less elaborated and complex?

PEARSON
myeducationlab

Now go to Topic 16: Communication Disorders in the MyEducationLab (www.myeducationlab.com) for your course where you can:

- Find learning outcomes for this topic along with the national standards that connect to these outcomes.

- Complete Assignments and Activities that can help you more deeply understand the chapter content.

- Examine challenging situations and cases presented in the IRIS Center Resources.

- Apply and practice your understanding of the core teaching skills identified in the chapter with Building Teaching Skills and Dispositions learning units.

Teaching Students with Emotional and Behavioral Disorders

FOCUS QUESTIONS

1. Who are students with emotional or behavioral disorders?

2. What percentage of the students in your class would you expect to have prevailing emotional and behavioral disorders?

3. What characteristics would you expect of students with emotional or behavioral disorders?

4. What are some causes of emotional and behavioral disorders and how might these disorders be treated both medicinally as well as behaviorally?

5. What is the general education teacher's role in the identification and assessment of students with emotional or behavioral challenges?

6. What characteristics of the teacher–student relationship enhance positive outcomes for students with emotional and behavioral problems? What types of positive behavior supports are likely to facilitate the social and academic development of students with emotional and behavioral problems?

Adalyn Saladrigas has been a middle-school teacher for over 10 years. Adalyn holds certification in special education and has elected to focus on teaching students who are identified as emotionally and behaviorally disordered. She explains, "I love these kids—and have learned when to be tough, when to be strong, and when to be compassionate."

She has taught in self-contained classes of students with emotional and behavior disorders as well as in inclusion settings where she has co-taught with general education colleagues. After recently earning a graduate degree in educational leadership, her role at her current school, Ponce de Leon Middle Community School, has changed. Part of her role is as an administrative assistant. As such, she serves as a resource for teachers, parents, and students in terms of social and behavioral issues. Someone is always knocking at her door for advice on specific incidents as well as more chronic problems with an individual child or group of students. Her second role is as a consultant for individual students who are mainstreamed in general education classrooms. Adalyn describes services for students with emotional and behavior disorders at her school as follows:

> We have three possible placements for students who have been identified for special services because of emotional or behavioral difficulties. Some students are placed in self-contained classes where we have one teacher for every eight students. Other students are placed in general education classrooms with a co-teaching arrangement. Still others are fully independent and mainstreamed for all classes with minimal support from me. I monitor these students carefully and consult with parents and teachers about their progress and needs.

Adalyn relies on positive behavior supports when making recommendations to parents and teachers. She realizes that some students need specific instruction in how to behave in a variety of settings and how to get along with others. Often that is the curriculum they need to succeed at school and beyond.

Introduction

The relationships established between classroom teachers and their students with emotional and behavioral disorders (EBD) are often among the more meaningful relationships experienced by both. Sharon Andreaci, a sixth-grade teacher, describes a student with emotional problems who was included in her classroom part time and spent the rest of the day in the special education resource room:

> Diana was her name, and you could just tell by looking into her eyes that something was wrong. She had been raped by a member of her family, and she never seemed to recover. She would see spirits and think evil things were coming to get her. She would say very strange things to me and to other students in the class. I felt that the support she got that year from me and the [other] students . . . really helped her feel better accepted. I have followed her in school and checked to see how she is doing. Now she is in a regular ninth-grade class and is participating in counseling.

General education teachers indicate that the students they feel are the most difficult to have in their classrooms are students who demonstrate serious emotional and behavioral disorders (Landers, Alter, & Servilio, 2008; Scott, Park, Swain-Bradway, & Landers, 2007). As Juana Lopez, a third-grade teacher, says, "Overall, my students are terrific and respond well to the lessons I plan and teach. But when my two students with behavioral problems are present, I really earn my paycheck." Even special education teachers like Adalyn Saladrigas find students with serious emotional and behavioral problems to be a challenge; yet, for teachers who understand and implement the types of instructional adaptations necessary to meet these students' educational needs, the results can be very satisfying. As many experienced teachers have reported, the positive impact their efforts have on their students' lives can greatly reward teachers and stay with them forever.

Although some students with EBD receive at least part of their educational program in self-contained special education classrooms or in specialized settings (e.g., alternative schools for students with specific problems, hospital settings), approximately 50% of students who are identified as having emotional or behavioral disorders spend more than 21% of their school day in general education classrooms (National Center for Educational Statistics, 2009). Therefore, general education teachers must be knowledgeable in the techniques and skills necessary to work with students with EBD.

Definitions of Emotional and Behavioral Disorders

What does it mean have an emotional or behavioral disorder? What types of behaviors would you expect to see? As with many other disabilities, there is no clear line between those who have emotional and behavioral disorders and those who do not. Often the question is decided by the severity and persistence of the problem. As a teacher, you will come in contact with students who display a range of emotional and behavioral problems.

Like other areas of special education, the field of emotional and behavioral disorders has grappled with definitional issues. How a disability is defined can have implications for public policy, assessment, and placement in special education services (Cullinan, 2004). Although definitions among professional groups may differ, they do have some commonalities. In general, describing someone as having **emotional disorders** or **behavioral disorders** commonly refers to students whose behavior falls considerably outside the norm, is chronic in nature, and is socially or culturally unacceptable (Hallahan, Kauffman, & Pullen, 2009). A number of definitions exist, but the two most prevalent are the U.S. federal government definition and that of the Council for Exceptional Children's division, Council for Children with Behavioral Disorders (CCBD).

The federal government uses the term *emotional disturbance* in its criteria for placement of students in special education. The federal definition of emotional disturbance is provided in Figure 8.1. Critics of this definition point out that it is vague and ambiguous. Terms such as *satisfactory* or *inappropriate* can be interpreted in different ways in different contexts (Walker, Ramsey, & Gresham, 2004; Walker & Severson, 1992). A larger concern is that the exclusion of students who are socially maladjusted, but not emotionally disturbed, is potentially dangerous for students who are in dire need of special services.

The CCBD definition was proposed as an alternative to the federal definition (see Figure 8.2). Advocates of this alternative point out that it couches emotional and behavior disorders in school, age, and ethnic/cultural contexts and focuses on early identification and intervention (Cullinan, 2004). Moreover, it incorporates the idea that students can have

Go to **www.ccbd.net**, The Council for Children with Behavioral Disorders website, for information and resources related to working with students with EBD.

FIGURE 8.1

The Federal Definition of Emotional Disturbance

The federal government defines "emotionally disturbed" as follows:

(i) The term means a condition exhibiting one or more of the following characteristics over a long period of time and to a marked degree, which adversely affects educational performance including:

  (A) An inability to learn that cannot be explained by intellectual, sensory, or health factors;

  (B) An inability to build or maintain satisfactory interpersonal relationships with peers and teachers;

  (C) Inappropriate types of behavior or feelings under normal circumstances;

  (D) A general pervasive mood of unhappiness or depression; or

  (E) A tendency to develop physical symptoms or fears associated with personal or school problems.

(ii) The term includes children who are schizophrenic. The term does not include children who are socially maladjusted, unless it is determined that they are emotionally disturbed.

Source: U.S. Department of Education. (2004). *Building the legacy: IDEA 2004.* Retrieved June 2, 2009, from http://idea.ed.gov/

FIGURE
8.2

Council for Children with Behavioral Disorders Definition of Emotional and Behavioral Disorders

1. The term "emotional" or "behavioral disorder" means a disability that is characterized by emotional or behavioral responses in school programs so different from appropriate age, cultural, or ethnic norms that the responses adversely affect educational performance, including academic, social, vocational, or personal skills; more than a temporary, expected response to stressful events in the environment; consistently exhibited in two different settings, at least one of which is school-related; and unresponsive to direct intervention in general education, or the condition of the child is such that general education interventions would be insufficient.

2. The term includes such a disability that co-exists with other disabilities.

3. The term includes a schizophrenic disorder, affective disorder, anxiety disorder, or other sustained disorder of conduct or adjustment, affecting a child if the disorder affects educational performance as described in paragraph (1). (*Federal Register*, February 10, 1993, p. 7938).

Source: Federal Register, February 10, 1993, P.7938.

more than one disability, referred to as **co-morbidity**. For example, Sam is a fourth-grade student who qualifies for services in two areas: learning disability and emotional disorder.

Although it is not the responsibility of general education teachers to determine whether a student has an emotional or behavioral disorder, because teachers are on the front line, they may be involved in the initial identification of students for referral for possible special education placement. Indeed, general education teachers serve as the primary source for referrals for students with emotional or behavioral challenges (Gresham & Kern, 2004). General education teachers may also be responsible for teaching students with EBD while they are in general education classroom, full or part time. Therefore, teachers must become familiar with local and state policies and procedures for such students.

Prevalence of Students with Emotional or Behavioral Disorders

Prevalence of students with emotional and behavioral disorders varies, depending on the criteria used to classify students. Higher prevalence rates are reported for mild emotional or behavioral disorders, and lower prevalence rates for more severe disorders. Current reports of the prevalence of emotional and behavioral disorders in the general population range from 6% to 10% of the school-age population (Kauffman & Landrum, 2009). Although 50% of referrals for special services occur in the elementary grades, referrals peak with students in their early teens (Kauffman, Brigham, & Mock, 2004). These numbers are especially worrisome given the preponderance of evidence documenting the importance of early (at or before entrance to school) identification and intervention. Thus, students with emotional or behavioral disorders are regarded as underserved.

Kauffman, Brigham, and Mock (2004) summarized the following issues as reasons for the underidentification of students with emotional and behavioral disorders:

- Social stigma is associated with the label "seriously emotionally disturbed."
- Eligibility for categorization as emotionally disordered is not clearly defined.
- The identification process lacks uniformity.
- Co-morbidity can make identification difficult.
- A lack of funding may limit school districts' willingness to identify and provide services for these students.
- There is often a lack of appropriate services when students are identified, and identification limits a school's ability to take disciplinary action against misbehavior.
- Adequate assessment measures to facilitate identification are few.

Although most professionals agree that students with emotional and behavioral disorders are underidentified, there is less certainty as to why so many of the students who are identified are males. For decades males have consistently outnumbered females in all prevalence reports for emotional disturbance (Quay & Werry, 1986; Rosenberg, Wilson, Maheady, & Sindelar, 1997; Wagner, Kutash, Duchnowski, Epstein, & Sumi, 2005). Students from minority populations are also disproportionately represented in the emotional and behavioral disorders category (Skiba et al., 2008). The issue of overrepresentation of minority students is complex and is viewed in terms of a combination of factors, including cultural bias, poverty, and the historical practice of segregation and discrimination in schools (Donovan & Cross, 2002; Harry & Klingner, 2006; Skiba et al., 2008).

What is the prevalence rate of students with disabilities in juvenile correction services? A survey conducted by Quinn, Rutherford, Leone, Osher, and Poirier (2005) reveals that 33.4% of all youth in juvenile justice were identified and receiving services for special education. This is more than four times as many as are provided services in the public schools. Of the individuals in juvenile justice receiving special education services, the majority were identified as having emotional disturbances (47.8%), with the next largest group identified as having specific learning disabilities (38.6%). Most of these students exhibit significant difficulties with reading and writing as well as social and emotional difficulties.

Types and Characteristics of Emotional or Behavioral Disorders

As Adalyn Saladrigas has learned over the years, students with behavior disorders display a wide range of characteristics. Perhaps the most consistent characteristic of these students is their inability to maintain satisfying relationships with others (e.g., Kauffman, 2004). Nonetheless, there is a spectrum of emotional and behavioral characteristics that elementary and secondary educators may experience among their students.

Think about classrooms where you have observed or taught. Which students got your attention first: those who were quiet and withdrawn or those who were acting out and disturbing others? Not surprisingly, students who demonstrate such externalizing behaviors as aggression, hitting, lack of attention, and impulsivity are much more likely to come to the teacher's attention and therefore to be identified as behavior-disordered (Furlong, Morrison, & Jimerson, 2004). On the other hand, there are students who exhibit more internalizing behaviors, such as shyness, withdrawal, depression, fears/phobias, or anxiety (Gresham & Kern, 2004).

Emotional and behavioral disorders can be classified broadly as externalizing or internalizing (Cooper & Bilton, 2002). Students who exhibit **externalizing behaviors** (e.g., conduct disorders, acting out, aggression, tantrums, and bizarre behaviors) tend to interfere with others. Students who exhibit **internalizing behaviors** (e.g., fear, immaturity, tenseness, withdrawal, worry) tend to be less disturbing to others but still very distressing to themselves and their families.

For example, two students identified for special education services were placed in Maribel Sterling's sixth-grade class. A special educator in the school, Greg Hauser, oriented Maribel to their IEPs and provided support for setting expectations and for positive behavioral supports. Their behavior patterns were strikingly different. Steven was excessively shy and reluctant to make friends or speak in class. In addition, completing tests and assignments caused Steven a great deal of fear and anxiety. Tara, on the other hand, had a long history of exhibiting aggressive behavior toward peers and defiance of teachers and administrators. When aggravated, Tara would throw tantrums and use language inappropriate at school. Tara was placed in a self-contained special education setting to learn strategies for self-control, and her parents and teachers agreed that she was ready again for the general education classroom. Maribel and Greg worked together to address ways to help Steven with his internalizing behaviors and Tara with her externalizing behaviors. Greg met with Maribel weekly to check on their progress and to make changes as needed.

What internalizing behaviors might signal the possible presence of emotional or behavioral disorders? How would you identify signals for externalizing problems?

Classifying students' behaviors as either externalizing or internalizing can be useful for classroom teachers. First, it helps teachers become aware that students with internalizing problems also need help, even though they do not call attention to themselves in the same way as those with externalizing problems. It is important for classroom teachers to recognize the special needs of these students even though they might not interfere with instruction or the learning of others. Second, being able to identify the type of behavior problem provides a framework for establishing a plan to help. However, research has revealed that there is often overlap of both externalizing and internalizing behaviors among some students; thus, it is important to realize that the categories are not discrete (Kauffman, 2004). During your career as a teacher, you will have students who display a range of these behaviors, some mild and some severe. Understanding these categories will help you not only to more accurately describe your students' behavior to professionals, but also to respond appropriately to your students. One classification system frequently used by counselors, psychologists, and physicians is described next.

The *Diagnostic and Statistical Manual of Mental Disorders*

The *Diagnostic and Statistical Manual of Mental Disorders* classification system is based on the reference book of the same name, published by the American Psychiatric Association (APA). Currently in its fourth edition, the book is commonly referred to as the DSM-IV-TR (APA, 2000). Its purpose is to provide a uniform nomenclature that clinicians and researchers can use to discuss, research, diagnose, and treat mental disorders. The book describes specific criteria necessary for the diagnosis of each disorder as well as symptoms, indicators of severity, and any variations of the disorder.

Counselors, psychologists, psychiatrists, and medical doctors who have had extensive training in diagnostic procedures generally use the DSM-IV-TR. Although teachers need not be fluent in its content, having it as a reference allows teachers to facilitate communication with school counselors, psychologists, and doctors who may use DSM-IV-TR disorder classification titles, symptoms, and codes.

Students with emotional and behavioral disorders frequently experience co-morbidity or the co-occurrence of more that one disability. Learning disabilities, ADHD, and developmental disabilities can co-occur with emotional and behavioral disorders. The DSM-IV-TR can assist trained professionals in the detection of co-morbidity. It can also be helpful in identifying particular types of emotional and behavioral disorders based on characteristics such as anxiety, mood, defiance, conduct and aggression, socialized aggression, and immaturity. DSM-IV also is used by mental health specialists to identify rare conditions such as schizophrenia.

Anxiety. The term **anxiety** involves extreme worry, fearfulness, and concern (even when little reason for those feelings exists). Simple reassurance is rarely effective. After nearly choking on a piece of candy, Trent developed a fear of eating. Neither his parents nor teacher could convince him to eat solid food. His internalizing behaviors persisted over an extended period of time and began to take a toll on his family life as well as his work in school. Trent was eventually diagnosed as having an **anxiety disorder**.

The National Institute of Mental Health (2009a) lists five primary types of anxiety disorder:

1. *Generalized Anxiety Disorder*—reoccurring fears about everyday situations
2. *Obsessive-Compulsive Disorder*—persistent thoughts about worrisome subjects (e.g., germs, objects out of order, safety) that result in ritual routines to alleviate those thoughts (e.g., hand washing, reorganizing objects, taking safety precautions)
3. *Panic Disorder*—sudden onset of intense fear resulting in extreme mental and physical reactions
4. *Posttraumatic Stress Disorder*—persistent anxiety resulting from a traumatic experience such as a death of a family member, natural disaster, or life-threatening experience
5. *Social Phobia (or Social Anxiety Disorder)*—exaggerated fear of social situations and anticipations of nonacceptance and ridicule from others

Some students with anxiety disorder frequently withdraw from others and appear reclusive, preferring solitary activities. Withdrawn students are often timid or bashful around others—even

PEARSON
myeducationlab

Go to the Assignments and Activities section of Topic 15: Emotional and Behavioral Disorders in the MyEducationLab for your course and complete the activity entitled *Students with Emotional and Behavioral Disorders in the Inclusive Classroom*.

Go to **www.air.org/cecp** where you can find out more about eligibility, characteristics, identification, and services for individuals with emotional disturbances.

people they know. In class they may avoid participating in group work, volunteering, or answering questions. Some exhibit tendencies toward perfectionism and are afraid of making mistakes. Excessive fear and anxiety can have an impact on socialization and academic performance (Anxiety Disorders Association of America, 2009; Schoenfeld & Janney, 2008).

Mood. When asked what they want for their children, most parents say, "I want them to be healthy and happy." When children and adolescents are constantly irritable, sad, or fatigued, adults are naturally concerned about their well-being. Such was the case with Miriam Schatz, a tenth grader. Miriam was normally a well-adjusted, high-achieving student with a small but close circle of friends. Late in the fall semester, Miriam became increasingly sullen, withdrawn, and distracted. Her school attendance became irregular and her grades plummeted. Several of Miriam's teachers noticed these changes in her disposition and referred her to the school counselor. As secondary-school teachers, they were accustomed to temporary mood changes among their students, but in Miriam's case the changes in her behavior were drastic and prolonged.

Many students with emotional and behavioral disorders are also prone to **mood disorders**. Mood disorders include various types of **depression** including **bi-polar disorder**. Depression involves prolonged and persistent feelings of dejection that interfere with life functioning (American Academy of Child and Adolescent Psychiatry [AACAP], 2009). Bi-polar disorder (formerly referred to as manic depression) is characterized by extreme mood swings (Cash & Cowan, 2006; Senokossoff & Stoddard, 2009; U.S. Department of Health and Human Services, 2009). All forms of mood disorders can vary in terms of frequency and degree. Some are caused by genetic factors; others by environment; still others by a combination of genetic and environmental factors (Cancro, 2008).

Mental health workers and educators have long realized that depression is a widespread, serious problem among children and adolescents (Forness, 1988), but it has only been in recent years that intensive attention has been focused on the disorder (National Institute of Mental Health, 2009b). Whereas depression is more prevalent in adult women than men, young boys are as likely as girls to exhibit depression (e.g., Kovacs, Obrosky, & Sherrill, 2003). However, after the onset of puberty, depression in girls increases dramatically (Galambos, Leadbeater, & Barker, 2004). As girls with depression get older, they have an increased risk for acquiring eating disorders, whereas boys with depression often go on to exhibit aggressive behaviors and substance abuse (Kovacs et al., 2003). Teachers often have difficulty identifying students who are depressed (AACAP, 2009). This is particularly true at the middle and high school when students have multiple teachers. To recognize signs of depression in students, see Tips for Teachers 8.1, Recognizing Signs of Depression.

Of particular concern is the fact that students who experience depression may grapple with thoughts of suicide. Indeed suicide ranks third in leading causes of death among children ages 5 to 14 (AACAP, 2009). A number of situations can trigger suicidal thoughts. Family conflict, changes in family situations, drug/alcohol abuse, and preexisting suicidal thoughts are the among the conditions that may cause suicide among children and adolescents (AACAP, 2009;

RECOGNIZING SIGNS OF DEPRESSION

The following behaviors may indicate depression:

- Acting sad, lonely, and apathetic

- Exhibiting low self-esteem or hopelessness

- Decreased interest in activities (particularly avoiding social experiences)

- Having chronic complaints about physical ailments, such as stomachaches or aching arms or legs, with no apparent cause

- Frequently being absent from school

- Talking of suicide or self-destructive behavior (e.g., cutting)

- Persistent boredom or low energy

- Poor school performance

- Increased irritability, anger, or hostility

Brent, Melhem, Bertille Donohoe, & Walker, 2009). The American Foundation for Suicide Prevention (2009) explains that suicide is preventable and that the emotional states that trigger suicide are often treatable. In the unlikely event that a student reveals suicidal thoughts to a classroom teacher, that teacher must discuss the matter with the school counselor immediately. Also, if a student seems deeply depressed over a sustained period of time (over 2 weeks), seek advice from the school counselor as well.

Defiance.   It is not unusual for elementary and particularly secondary students to be defiant or disobedient from time to time. However, when students habitually question authority, intentionally misbehave and ignore rules, are temperamental and negative, and blame others for their actions, or when social and/or academic progress is inhibited as a result, it may indicate signs of an **oppositional defiant disorder (ODD)** (Hommersen, Murray, Ohan, & Johnston, 2006; Skoulos & Shicktryon, 2007). ODD is a disorder that often occurs with other disorders such as mood disorders and conduct disorders.

Go to **www.mentalhealth.com** for resources related to a variety of mental health disorders.

The onset of ODD often occurs before age 8 and frequently exacerbates with age (Hommersen et al., 2006). In the case of Marcus Wagner, it all began in kindergarten. Each day after the pledge to the flag and a moment of silence, students recited their school's mission statement, which included language about being a good citizen and following rules. It didn't register with Marcus. Marcus spent most of the school day ignoring rules; talking back to his teacher, Megan O'Conner, and refusing to take blame for his actions. Given that defiant behavior is likely to persist, early diagnosis, intervention, and collaboration with parents is important (Downing, 2007).

Conduct and Aggression

Behaviors associated with misconduct and aggression can be covert (stealing, lying, burglary, use of drugs and alcohol) or overt (coercion, bullying, manipulation of others, escalated interactions with teachers, parents, and peers) (AACAP, 2009; Loeber et al., 1993). When students are consistent in ignoring the rights of others and are cruel, destructive, deceitful, or truant, they may be diagnosed as having a **conduct disorder**. Some students with conduct disorders, like eighth-grader Derek Curtis, provoke peers into hitting them or others. When his teacher, Patrick Anthony, called Derek's home to describe his conduct, he discovered frustrated parents who feel that Derek is not as responsive to them as they would like.

The chance that aggression and problem behaviors will continue throughout a student's lifetime is compounded by the number and duration of risk factors he or she is exposed to (Mack, 2004). As a result of the multidimensional nature of conduct disorder, remediation, especially in older children and teens, is difficult and complex (AACAP, 2004). Although their intelligence is often well within the normal range (Sattler, 1988), students with conduct disorder often display low academic achievement (Gold & Mann, 1972; Kazdin & Crowley, 1997; Mack, 2004).

Behavior-management strategies and cooperation among the school counselor, psychologist, and parents are often effective for students with mild to moderate conduct disorder. For students with more extreme conduct disorder, however, such strategies may not be as effective and more dramatic measures may be required such as removing the student from the classroom for all or part of the school day and moving the student into a special education setting where small class sizes and low student–teacher ratio are provided.

Socialized Aggression

Antisocial behavior involves acts that can cause mental or physical harm to others or to their property. Although many people have intentionally or unintentionally engaged in some type of antisocial behavior at some point in their lives, the term **socialized aggression** is used to refer to students who routinely engage in antisocial behavior. Adults may describe them as hanging around with the wrong kinds of kids, displaying behaviors that are not typical of others in their age group, and engaging in behaviors such as harassing others and stealing and damaging property. These students may also cut classes or skip school.

Socialized aggression is also associated with **group behavior**; that is, these behaviors are displayed in the presence of other group members. Students with socialized aggression often belong to gangs. Students' attraction to gang life is apparent in many inner cities as well as in suburban and rural areas and, since 2000, has been on the rise (Egley & O'Donnell, 2009). Law enforcement agencies categorize **gangs** into the following four groups:

1. *Delinquent* youth gangs, which are loosely structured and recognize one another by the way they dress and look
2. *Turf-based* gangs, which are also loosely structured but committed to defending a reputation or neighborhood
3. *Crime-oriented* gangs or drug gangs, which engage in robbery, burglary, or sale of controlled substances for monetary gain
4. *Violent* hate gangs, whose members commit assaults or hate crimes against specific types of people

Students may be attracted to gangs due to a desire for companionship, acceptance, and success or for the perception of safety they believe may be afforded to them with gang membership (Thornberry, Huizinga, & Loeber, 2004). Many such students feel that they have not been accepted by traditional society.

A high rate of overlap exists between conduct disorder, attention problems, and socialized aggression. For example, many students who have attention problems might also display behaviors associated with conduct disorder, such as aggression and acting out. There may be as many as five types of aggression (Lancelotta & Vaughn, 1989):

1. In *provoked physical aggression,* one student hits or taunts another, who retaliates.
2. In *unprovoked physical aggression,* a student acts aggressively with no apparent prompting.
3. In *verbal aggression,* one student screams, yells, or uses other verbal expressions to attack another.
4. In *outburst aggression,* a student "blows up."
5. In *indirect aggression,* a student does something sneaky or tricky to get back at another student. Neither boys nor girls like students who use indirect aggression.

Both sexes are the most tolerant of provoked aggression, but girls are less tolerant of all types of aggression than are boys. All subtypes of aggression except provoked physical aggression are related to low social acceptance by classmates. See Tips for Teachers 8.2 to better understand how to respond to students' violent behaviors.

Immaturity

Behaviors associated with **immaturity** include lack of perseverance, failure to finish tasks, a short attention span, poor concentration, and frequent daydreaming or preoccupation. Students might stare into space excessively; appear absentminded, inattentive, or drowsy; or seem clumsy or poorly coordinated. Immaturity alone would not necessarily qualify a student

Go to the Building Teaching Skills and Dispositions section of Topic 15: Emotional and Behavioral Disorders in the MyEducationLab for your course and complete the activity entitled *Discouraging Bullying at School.*

UNDERSTANDING VIOLENT BEHAVIOR

- Do not dismiss violent behavior, even in very young children, as a passing phase. Violent behavior at any age should be taken seriously.

- Act immediately if you are concerned about a child's violent behavior. Contact the school or district mental health professional. He or she will arrange a comprehensive evaluation and/or conduct a functional behavior assessment to identify and address the needs of the child.

- Be aware of the risk factors for violent behavior. They include previous aggressive or violent behavior, being the victim of physical or sexual abuse, exposure to violence, genetic factors, exposure to violence in the media, use of drugs/alcohol, presence of firearms in the home, family stress (e.g., poverty, unemployment, marital problems), and brain damage from head injury.

- Watch for warning signs that may precede violent behavior, such as intense anger, frequent loss of temper, extreme irritability or impulsivity, and very low thresholds of frustration.

Source: American Academy of Child and Adolescent Psychiatry. (2001). Understanding violent behavior in children and adolescents. Retrieved September 25, 2009, from http://www.aacap.org/cs/root/facts_for_families/

for special education services, but many students with emotional and behavioral disorders may exhibit signs of immaturity.

Immature students often come to the attention of teachers because they show little interest in schoolwork and need prodding to participate. Teachers might feel frustrated at the amount of effort necessary to keep these students interested and involved.

These students often seem overly dependent on parents or caretakers and have difficulty being responsible members of a group (whether the classroom or the family). Students with severe immaturity often have difficulty interacting with other people, using social skills, and playing with children their own age. These students may frequently retreat into fantasy and develop fears that are out of proportion to the circumstances.

Schizophrenia

The National Institute of Mental Health defines schizophrenia as "a chronic, severe, and disabling brain disorder that has been recognized throughout recorded history" (National Institute of Mental Health, 2009c). It is one of a family of psychotic disorders. Schizophrenia is rare among children and typically emerges in the late teens or early 20s (Konopasek & Forness, 2004). Individuals with schizophrenia experience hallucinations and delusions, and have disorders of both thought and movement (National Institute of Mental Health, 2009c). Fortunately, treatment procedures (both with medication and social therapy) for schizophrenia have improved over the years and have allowed individuals with the disorder to live productive lives (Lehman, Kreyenbuhl, Buchanan, Dickerson, Dixon, & Goldberg, 2004).

Causes of Emotional and Behavioral Disorders

Our best understanding is that emotional and behavioral disorders result from both biological and environmental factors. In many cases, causes of a disorder are complex and multiple. Because of the social nature of emotional and behavioral disorders, biological causes usually do not work independently of environmental causes. Typically, no one cause precipitates emotional and behavioral disorders (Hallahan et al., 2009).

Biological Causes

Three primary biological causes are potential contributors to emotional and behavioral disorders: brain disorders, genetics, and temperament (Hallahan et al., 2009; Heward, 2009; Pierangelo & Giuliani, 2007). Biological causes can work independently or in conjunction with each other.

1. Brain disorders can result from injuries (see the discussion in Chapter 11 on traumatic brain disorder), prenatal damage, infection, or other brain defects. Chemical imbalances can also affect the brain and nervous system.
2. Mental illness can have genetic roots. For example, depression is a disorder that has a tendency to run in families and maternal depression is a strong predictor of problem behavior in young children (Nelson, Stage, Duppong-Hurley, Synhorst, & Epstein, 2007).
3. Temperament is considered to be a biologically determined or inborn condition (Hallahan et al., 2009; Kagan & Snidman, 2004).

Environmental Causes

Environmental causes of emotional and behavioral disorders stem from unsettling circumstances in the home or community. What happens in the environment can affect students' quality of life, emotional well-being, and ultimately success or failure at school (Sacks & Kern, 2008). Sometimes these circumstances are temporary; at other times, they are an ongoing part of the student's life. Although the educational impact (both short-term and long-term) of environmental causes varies from student to student, it is important that you, as a teacher, create a classroom atmosphere that is a safe haven from the unpredictable circumstances that affect your students' lives.

Home Conditions.   Home conditions that can potentially affect student academic performance include family poverty, family instability, and family violence. According to the Children's

Defense Fund (2009), one out of five children come from families living below the poverty level. Students whose families live in poverty often come to school without their basic needs of food, clothing, shelter, and health care being met. The limitations poverty places on families are likely to affect students' quality of life, level of stress, and performance in school (Donovan & Cross, 2002; Park, Turnbull, & Turnbull, 2002). Families with financial burdens often cannot afford educational materials, home computers, and extended vacations or day trips that broaden horizons and reduce stress. Older students may also have extended work responsibilities, such as caring for siblings or contributing to the family income.

One of the most common jolts to family stability is divorce. Divorce can cause students to become depressed and angry and can affect their desire to achieve in school (Wallerstein, Lewis, & Blakeslee, 2000). Although the emotional impact of divorce on individual children may vary, a divorce does cause inevitable changes in the home routine (Kelly & Emery, 2003). For example, after a divorce, children may have two homes instead of one, which can disrupt homework and study patterns, as well as such basic routines as getting dressed and ready for school.

Family stress and violence can create a volatile home situation that can result in child neglect and mental or physical abuse (Mattison, 2004). As you read in Chapter 5, it is imperative that you follow local guidelines in reporting neglect and abuse. As a teacher, you have little control about what happens in the home; however, you can work with school counselors, social workers, and psychologists to provide parents and children with the support they need.

Community Conditions.   Every day we hear and read about risks to the safety of children in our communities. Millions of young people face life-threatening circumstances through neighborhood violence. Children who experience threats to their safety and well-being in their communities are at risk for having academic and socioemotional problems at school. Some safety risks are chronic and ongoing; others are the product of particular crises.

National tragedies continue to challenge our community and our teachers in how best to help students cope with safety issues that are beyond most of our experience. Well-publicized shootings at schools have undermined students' feelings of safety. We can only begin to imagine the impact of our national tragedy of September 11, 2001. Traumatic natural disasters such as Hurricane Katrina resulted in high numbers of children in need of counseling and support. Organizations such as the Council for Exceptional Children (CEC) and the Association for Supervision and Curriculum Development (ASCD) provide updated resources to general and special education teachers for helping students through crises and trying times. Many schools are implementing violence-prevention and conflict-resolution programs to address these issues. It is imperative that you, as a classroom teacher, become familiar with your school district's procedures for student safety.

PEARSON
myeducationlab

Go to the Teacher Talk section of Topic 15: Emotional and Behavioral Disorder in the MyEducationLab for your course and listen to high school teacher, Susanne Frensley discuss how important it is to treat student who are in pain with respect and love; in return they become giving human beings.

Identification and Assessment of Students with Emotional and Behavioral Disorders

Students with severe emotional and behavioral disorders are often recognized by parents and other adults before they start attending school. These students may receive early treatment through a combination of educational interventions, medications, play therapy, and family counseling. Other students have emotional and behavioral disorders that remain latent until students are older. In some of these cases, the disorders become apparent once the students are in structured settings such as the school.

Formal identification and assessment requires involvement of professionals who are specifically trained to do so (e.g., psychologists, physicians). As a classroom teacher, you may be involved in the initial identification process and, as a part of the response to intervention, universal screening, progress monitoring, and functional behavior assessment to determine appropriate levels of support.

Initial Identification

Part of your responsibility as a classroom teacher is to handle the everyday situations when students do not meet established behavioral expectations. Realistically, you will encounter students with emotional or behavioral patterns that cause you concern and that warrant more intensive intervention and professional input (Downing, 2007). How should classroom teachers decide whether a student's behavior is problematic enough to warrant referral for more intensive interventions? The following criteria provide indications of disturbance that may trigger referral (e.g., Clarizio & McCoy, 1983; Morgan & Reinhart, 1991):

■ **Behavior–age discrepancy.** The social and behavioral problems exhibited must be unusual or deviant for the student's age. For example, clinging to adults is common in very young children but is deemed inappropriate for school-age children.

■ **Frequency of occurrence of the behavior.** Under stress, all people exhibit characteristics of emotional or behavioral disorders, such as whining, withdrawal, mood swings, or depression. These behaviors and feeling states are not considered problems if they occur only occasionally.

■ **Number of symptoms.** The display of one or more behavior problems at some time does not indicate that a person has an emotional or behavioral disorder, but students who frequently display several related symptoms should be considered for referral. The greater the number of symptoms, the greater the likelihood of a serious emotional disturbance.

■ **Inner suffering.** Signs of inner suffering include low self-esteem, less interaction with others, appearance of sadness or loneliness, and general malaise. Inner suffering interferes with learning, social relationships, and achievement.

■ **Harm to others.** The student consistently harms others or animals intentionally and shows little remorse for hurting others.

■ **Persistence of the behavior.** Persistence refers to the continuation of the emotional or behavioral problems over time, despite substantive efforts on the part of adults and the student to change the behaviors. A behavior problem is persistent when several types of interventions have not resulted in long-term change.

What criteria would you use to determine whether this student's behavior warrants referral for evaluation for the presence of an emotional or behavioral disorder?

■ **Self-satisfaction.** Students who appear to be generally happy with themselves reflect a measure of self-satisfaction. They show positive affect and the willingness to give and receive affection and pleasure. A lack of self-satisfaction contributes to problems that interfere with personal growth and development as well as academic and social success, but that might not signal the presence of an emotional or behavioral disorder.

■ **Severity and duration of the behavior.** All dimensions of a student's behavior can be classified in terms of two important criteria: severity and duration. *Severity* refers to how extreme the problem is and the extent to which it varies from expected behavior. *Duration* (or persistence) refers to the length of time the problem has existed. A problem that persists over a long period is said to be *chronic*. Most students who are identified as having emotional or behavioral disorders must deal with their problems throughout their lifetimes.

When identifying a student with possible emotional or behavioral disorders, teachers need to be prepared to answer the following questions:

■ How often does the behavior occur? How long has the problem persisted?
■ Under what conditions does the behavior occur? To what extent does this behavior occur in different settings, such as the classroom, playground, or home?
■ What are the *antecedents* of the behavior; that is, what events occur before the behavior is exhibited, triggering the behavior? What are the *consequences;* that is, what occurs as an outcome of the behavior after the student exhibits the behavior?
■ Does the problem not arise in certain situations?
■ To what extent does the student develop and maintain positive relationships with other people? Does the student seem happy or display satisfaction at any time?
■ How severe is the problem? To what extent is the behavior deviant from that of other students of the same age?
■ To what extent is this a problem in the relationship between you and the student or a problem within the student?
■ What have you and/or the family done to reduce or eliminate the problem?

Go to the Assignments and Activities section of Topic 15: Emotional and Behavioral Disorders for the MyEducationalLab for your course and complete the activity entitled *Individual Behavior Interventions: Problem Solving Model.*

Tips for Teachers 8.3 offers suggestions for gathering information before referring a student with possible emotional or behavioral disorders.

Tips FOR TEACHERS 8.3

MAKING REFERRALS FOR STUDENTS WITH EMOTIONAL OR BEHAVIORAL DISORDERS

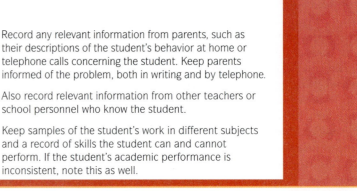

- Keep a journal that includes the dates, times, and contexts of student behaviors that you regard as deviant or bizarre.

- Be specific, using behavioral terms to describe what occurs. As much as possible, avoid including value judgments. For example, a journal entry might read "Mark got up from his seat, pushed John out of his chair, and then ran out of the room."

- Record any relevant information from parents, such as their descriptions of the student's behavior at home or telephone calls concerning the student. Keep parents informed of the problem, both in writing and by telephone.

- Also record relevant information from other teachers or school personnel who know the student.

- Keep samples of the student's work in different subjects and a record of skills the student can and cannot perform. If the student's academic performance is inconsistent, note this as well.

Response to Intervention for Students with Emotional and Behavioral Disorders

Katie Newberg, a fifth-grade teacher, has the reputation among parents, fellow teachers, and her administrator as being highly organized. Year in and year out she creates a welcoming classroom that makes students want to learn, and they do. From the outset of this school year, Katie knew that she was working with a special group of children and that all of her attention to classroom organization, consistent following of rules, and predictable routines was not going to be enough to meet the needs of three students in particular: Mike, who exhibits disruptive behaviors; Carlton, who is often defiant and ignores rules; and Phoebe, who is extremely withdrawn and often is absent due to a great deal of anxiety about school. Katie kept careful anecdotal records on each child in preparation for meeting with parents and other school-based colleagues. Discussions with the school counselor, special education teacher, and parents led to the initial screening of the children and attempts to implement appropriate interventions. Nothing seemed to work. It was clear that each of her students needed additional support to make progress.

In Katie's case, Tier 1 of RTI involved implementation of the following as part of a school-wide positive behavior supports model: explicit teaching of rules and consequences, use of research-based universal strategies for general classroom management, and universal screening to identify students with special needs (Fairbanks, Simonsen, & Sugai, 2008). Katie worked with parents and other professionals in the classroom to target problem behaviors and decide what additional positive behavioral supports might be appropriate for her to implement in the classroom.

Tips for Teachers 8.4 provides general research-based recommendations for interventions for children with emotional and behavioral disorders.

Ongoing monitoring of Mike, Carlton, and Phoebe indicated that more support was necessary. Thus, Tier 2 (or secondary) behavior interventions were launched. Tier 2 interventions are typically small-group interventions that can provide students with the self-control, self-monitoring, social, and self-management skills they need to benefit from universal strategies (Lembke & Stichter, 2006). The special educator, school counselor, and Katie met with each of the children's parents to identify concrete interventions for implementation. Katie's school uses a **check-in, check-out (CICO) procedure** where students earn points for appropriate behaviors in small-group instructional or mentoring sessions and in the classroom (Campbell & Anderson, 2008; Hawken & Horner, 2003). (See Tips for Teachers 8.5 for more details on CICO.) All three students were monitored weekly for a period of 6 weeks. In that time, Mike's disruptive behavior began to subside as the result of the small-group interventions. Phoebe, although still somewhat withdrawn, demonstrated decreases absenteeism and increased participation in peer tutoring and small-group activities. However, Carlton's defiance and tendency to ignore rules continued to escalate. His aggressive behaviors (hitting, bullying) were endangering other students in the classroom. Moreover, his academic performance, particularly in reading, was an area that needed intervention as well.

Tips for Teachers 8.4

RECOMMENDATIONS FOR EFFECTIVE INTERVENTIONS

- Link assessment data of student's behavior with interventions.

- Implement interventions across settings and placements. For example, a behavior contract used in the special education classroom can also be used in a general class setting.

- Provide a range of interventions for improving behavior. The effect of a single intervention is likely to be short-lived.

- Use interventions that address not only the behavior related to a single disciplinary action, but also the related behaviors and contributing factors.

- Implement interventions that are proactive, corrective, and instructive. In this way, interventions can support

prosocial behaviors and the self-management strategies that students need to mediate their own behavior.

- Ensure that interventions are developmentally appropriate and address the unique strengths and weaknesses of the individual.

- Accompany student supports with parent education and family therapy.

- Devote resources to early interventions to reduce the need for more extensive and expensive treatment later. Interventions are the most effective when provided early in life.

- Recognize that the intensity and the duration of the intervention will vary depending on individual student needs.

Source: National Dissemination Center for Children with Disabilities. (2003). Interventions for chronic behavior problems. Retrieved September 25, 2009, from http://www.nichcy.org/InformationResources/Documents/NICHCY%20PUBS/rb.1.pdf

Tips for Teachers 8.5

STEPS FOR IMPLEMENTING CHECK-IN/CHECK-OUT (CICO)

Check-in/check-out serves as a way to conduct progress monitoring with students with emotional and behavioral disorders. It is a point system that serves as an ongoing report card of student behavior. The follow steps can be used to implement CICO.

Step 1: Understand how CICO fits into the overall positive behavior support program in your school and who serves as the CICO coordinator.

Step 2: Understand specifically what behaviors are being targeted for each student involved.

Step 3: Learn what school personnel will be involved with CICO for each student and if and how parents are to be involved.

Step 4: Review procedures for when points are to be recorded, and reviewed, and when rewards are to be given.

Step 5: Evaluate the CICO plan with the CICO coordinator to decide if intervals for recording and reviewing need to be adjusted and whether rewards are appropriate.

At Katie's school, Tier 3 (or tertiary) interventions for students with emotional and behavioral issues begin with a comprehensive functional behavior assessment (see following section). After a careful analysis of the externalizing behaviors Carlton displayed, a more intensive individual intervention program was deemed necessary. Specific replacement behaviors and academic objectives were targeted and taught to Carlton in one-on-one sessions (Lembke & Stichter, 2006). In Carlton's case, the school decided to employ multiple supports (family, teacher, school counselor, social worker, and school psychologist) to ensure consistency of intervention implementation at home, in school, and in community settings.

RTI is new to many schools and school districts. State and local guidelines coupled with the wide range of individual differences in student needs and local resources mean that the procedures at Katie's school might be very different than your own. A great deal of research is needed to validate RTI practices at each tier for students with emotional and behavioral disorders. Consequently, schools may differ considerably at each tier in terms of

- Assessments, screening, and monitoring used
- Implementation of functional behavior assessment

- Interventions employed
- School personnel involved
- Venue for interventions (e.g., general education classroom, resource room)
- Decision points for placement in special education and IEP development

As part of your role as a general education teacher in the implementation of RTI, you will likely be involved in universal screening and progress monitoring as well as in functional behavioral assessment.

Universal Screening and Progress Monitoring

Key to RTI are the goals of early identification of emotional and behavioral disorders, appropriate intervention, and ongoing monitoring of student progress. As you read in Chapter 2, universal screening can provide quick information about what students may need additional academic supports. Screening of all students early in the school year can also be used to identify students who need emotional or behavioral supports as well.

Initial screening might involve basic student data: number of absences, discipline referrals, and teacher requests for additional support with a child. Information from previous years and schools may also be reviewed to provide archival data. Beyond that, you may be asked to complete a screening checklist or scale to provide additional information (Downing, 2007). Longitudinal research of students at risk for emotional and behavioral disorders indicates that teacher ratings are stable predictors of later identification (Montague, Enders, & Castro, 2005). Some commonly used rating scales are Social Skills Rating System for Children (Gresham & Elliott, 1990), Childhood Behavior Checklist (Achenbach & McConaughy, 2003), and Systematic Screening for Behavior Disorders (Walker, Ramsey, & Gresham, 2004). Interpretation of findings from such screening measures is best from individuals who are trained to do so based on specific decision rules (Gresham, 2007). Universal screening should occur early in the school year to ward off escalation of potential problem behaviors.

When individual students have been identified as being in need of additional positive behavior supports, frequent progress monitoring is vital (Griffiths, VanDerHeyden, Parson, & Burns, 2006). Monitoring can determine whether interventions can be discontinued, continued under similar or adapted conditions, or intensified. Monitoring of student progress should be coupled with an evaluation of intervention implementation **fidelity**, or the degree to which the intervention has been administered with consistency and according to prescribed guidelines (Gresham, 2007). The format used for progress monitoring should be aligned with the targeted objective and can involve observation, checklists, point systems, interviews, or logs and journals. If appropriate, parents can serve as partners in progress monitoring and students can become engaged in self-assessment. Data from progress monitoring should be reviewed systematically to make necessary adjustments in intervention. One process that works hand-in-hand with progress monitoring is functional behavioral assessment.

Developing a Functional Behavioral Assessment

New advances in assessment and intervention provide a wealth of information for teachers of students with emotional or behavioral disorders. In fact, much of the distress associated with these disorders can be minimized with the implementation of timely and appropriate interventions and supports (National Health Information Center, 2004). At school, an important component of identifying *and* addressing the needs of students with emotional or behavioral disorders is to develop a **functional behavioral assessment (FBA)**. Functional behavioral assessments are a method of gathering data to design the most effective positive support plans and to monitor students' progress. Mandated by IDEIA, all students with disabilities who have significant behavior problems that interfere with either their own learning or the learning of other students must have an FBA.

An FBA and a **behavioral improvement plan (BIP)** are designed to identify behavior problems of students and to develop an intervention plan to treat these behavior problems. The procedures and practices for developing an FBA are not nearly as well defined as those for an IEP, and many school personnel still are unclear about how and when to design and use FBAs and BIPs. If students' behavior is interfering with their learning, the design and use of an FBA is required. Because it is much more likely that the FBA will assist students rather than interfere

PEARSON
myeducationlab

To enhance your understanding using RTI to support students with behavior management and academic concerns, go to the IRIS Center Resources section of Topic 5: Prereferrals, Placement and IEP Process in the MyEducationLab for your course and complete Module 34 entitled *The Prereferral Process: Procedures for Supporting Students with Academic and Behavioral Concerns.*

with their learning, it is always a good idea to develop an FBA and a BIP. As a general education teacher, you'll work with a special education colleague and possibly other professionals in the school to develop both.

According to Shippen, Simpson, and Crites (2003), there are several critical steps in designing an effective FBA. These include:

- Defining the target behavior in behavioral terms. Clearly specify the behavior(s) you would like to see the student perform in observational terms that can be recorded and monitored.
- Collecting and monitoring the target behaviors through ongoing data collection that considers frequency, intensity, and rate.
- Recording the events and behaviors that precede and follow the target behavior. In this way, the antecedent, behavior, and consequences are noted.
- Developing a hypothesis of the conditions under which the target behavior occurs. This hypothesis guides the intervention plan.
- Developing an intervention plan that considers the antecedents and reinforcers and is built to test the hypothesis.

Although the FBA is often used in reaction to problem behaviors (as mandated in IDEIA), it is perhaps most effective when used to determine the educational needs of students before behavior has gotten out of control. It may also be used as part of an RTI model, to collect data and to track progress and the effectiveness of interventions before referral to special education (Ryan, Halsey, & Matthews, 2003). Figure 8.3 provides an example of a functional behavioral assessment.

The FBA is not a static procedure (Fairbanks et al., 2008) and can be implemented during any tier of RTI depending on individual needs. Through FBA, it is possible to identify specific events that predict and maintain behavior and to design a support plan that effectively addresses those variables. FBA methods can, and should, vary across circumstances but typically include *record reviews, interviews,* and *direct observation.*

Teaching Guidelines and Accommodations for Students with Emotional or Behavioral Disorders

Think about the teachers that you remember most from your elementary and secondary school days. What made these teachers special to you? Chances are that you felt they really cared about you, what you learned, and how well you liked school, your teacher, and your classmates. Establishing good relationships with all students is important, but especially so for students with emotional and behavioral disorders. These students probably have had few positive relationships with adults and may act as if they dare you to care about them.

Trust is the foundation for success with students with emotional and behavioral disorders. Students learn to trust you when you act in predictable ways and do what you say you are going to do. They also learn to trust you when they believe you will do what is best for them rather than what is best for you.

Remember that disliking the student's behavior is not the same as disliking the student, who needs your respect and caring. "Respect the student, dislike the behavior" is an important motto when you work with students with emotional and behavioral disorders. Think about the language you use when you reprimand students or enforce consequences for inappropriate behavior. Be sure you convince students that it is their behavior that is unacceptable, not they. Jason Landis, a high-school English teacher, says it this way:

When I correct students, I always talk about the behavior, and I always let the student know that anyone who behaves like this will be treated the same way. For example, the other day in class, I needed to remind a student that no one swears in the class and those who swear will get a detention and therefore, here is your detention. Later on in the period, I encouraged the same student to respond to a question and provided positive feedback for the part of the answer he answered correctly.

Many teachers realize that understanding and recognizing the behaviors of students with emotional and behavioral disorders is the first step in providing appropriate interventions. Tips for Teachers 8.6 offers further suggestions for creating an appropriate emotional environment.

Methods of Functional Behavioral Assessment (FBA)

FIGURE 8.3

Functional behavioral assessment (FBA) is a systematic process for gathering information to determine the relationships between a person's problem behavior and aspects of his or her environment. Through FBA, it is possible to identify specific events that predict and maintain behavior and to design a support plan that effectively addresses those variables. FBA methods can, and should, vary across circumstances but typically include *record reviews, interviews,* and *direct observation.*

Method	Sample Sources/Tools	Examples/Products
Record reviews	Diagnostic/medical records, psychological reports, assessments from therapies, developmental profiles, social histories, previous behavior management plans, IEPs, ISPs, anecdotal records, incident reports, discipline referrals	Sammy's records contained: History of allergies and asthma Some effective educational strategies used in the past Patterns of discipline referrals
Structured interviews	People who know the individual well and represent a range of environments (the person, family members, teachers, friends, direct service providers, etc.) may be interviewed. Some interview tools: *Functional Assessment Interview, Student-Directed Functional Assessment Interview* (O'Neill et al., 1997) *Motivational Assessment Scale* (Durand & Crimmins, 1988)	Interviews of Delores's family, friends, and job coach addressed her preferences for "low-key" settings, difficulty with dramatic changes in routine, and beliefs that she is motivated to avoid demanding social circumstances
Direct observation	Observations should be conducted across a variety of times and circumstances. Some observation tools: *ABC (Antecedent-Behavior-Consequence) Recording Scatterplot* (Touchette, MacDonald, & Langer, 1985) *Frequency Measures across Conditions*	Scatterplot data indicate that Ben's biting is most likely to occur when he is getting ready to leave in the morning and immediately after lunch

FBA methods range from highly precise and systematic to relatively informal. Particular tools and strategies should be selected based on the circumstances, individuals involved, and goals of intervention. The goal of FBA, regardless of which methods are used, is to answer certain questions:

1. Under what circumstances is the behavior most/least likely to occur (e.g., when, where, with whom)?
2. What outcomes does the behavior produce (i.e., what does the person get or avoid through his or her behavior)?

To answer these questions, the information gathered must be analyzed and summarized. Hypothesis (or summary) statements describe the specific patterns identified through the FBA and, if supported by the data, provide a foundation for intervention. A hypothesis statement must describe the behavior and surrounding conditions and be clear, comprehensive, and unbiased to be useful. Example: "When Steven finishes his work early, he makes noises and destroys his materials. His behavior prompts his supervisor to initiate an alternative activity."

Frequently Asked Questions

1. *When and why should a functional behavioral assessment be completed?* An FBA may be initiated when a person's behavior interferes with performance, progress, and/or participation within typical daily routines and environments. It is completed for the purpose of designing an effective intervention that will allow the person with challenging behavior to be successful across all circumstances.
2. *Who should do a functional behavioral assessment (e.g., what qualifications are needed)?* It is important to have individuals who are experienced and skilled in FBA, competent in promoting collaboration, and proficient in designing effective positive behavioral support strategies involved in the process. Such individuals may come from varying backgrounds (e.g., applied behavioral analysis, school psychology).

3. *Are there shortcuts (e.g., one-page forms) for conducting FBAs?* Yes and no. A variety of tools are available for data collection and synthesis. In many cases, an informal or abbreviated approach can lead to reasonable interventions. However, in other circumstances, a more comprehensive and systematic process is required. An appropriate FBA is one that is matched to the circumstances and leads to an effective behavioral support plan.
4. *What is the difference between functional behavioral assessment and functional analysis? Functional behavioral assessment* is a broad term referring to the information-gathering and hypothesis-development process. It can involve a variety of methods, including functional analysis. Functional analysis is a rigorous experimental procedure in which hypotheses are tested by manipulating antecedents and consequences to see what impact they have on behavior. Whereas functional analysis may be useful in some circumstances, it is not always necessary or appropriate.

Other Resources

Crone, D. A. & Horner, R. (2003). *Building positive behavior support systems in schools: Functional behavioral assessment.* New York: Guilford Press.

Crone, D. A., Horner, R. H., & Hawken, L. S. (2004). *Responding to problem behavior in schools: The behavior education program.* New York: Guilford Press.

OSEP Center on Positive Behavioral Interventions and Supports. (2004). *School-wide positive behavior support: Implementers' blueprint and self-assessment.* Eugene: Center on Positive Behavioral Interventions and Supports, University of Oregon. Available at www.pbis.org.

Scott, T. M., Liaupsin, C. J., Nelson, C. M., & Jolivette, K. (2003). Ensuring student success through team-based functional behavioral assessment. *Teaching Exceptional Children 35*(5), 16–21.

Source: Based on *Methods of Functional Behavior Assessment.* Positive Behavioral Interventions and Support Technical Assistance Center; Behavioral Research and Training; 5262 University of Oregon; Eugene, OR 97403-5262; PBIS@oregon.uoregon.edu.

CREATING AN APPROPRIATE EMOTIONAL ENVIRONMENT

- *Respond to students' feelings and intentions* rather than to overt behavior. When students with emotional and behavioral disorders act out or become aggressive, your first reaction might be to respond with anger or hostility, but the student is really saying, "I'm hurting. Pay attention to me."

- *Listen.* Before responding, no matter how certain you are that the student is in the wrong, give the student an opportunity to explain and give his or her version of what occurred. You may not always agree with the interpretation, but by taking the time to listen you demonstrate caring and concern to the student. Listening is a sign of acceptance, an important first step in helping students.

- *Develop a positive relationship* with the student about one topic. All students are interested in and can succeed at something that you can recognize. Discover what this area is and what the student knows about it, and then make him or her the class expert.

- *Establish rules and consequences* to help provide the structure that students with emotional and behavioral disorders need.

- *Consider changes you can make.* Evaluate the classroom routines, instructional procedures, and discipline practices you use that may be contributing to the student's behavioral problems.

- *Catch the student being good.* You have many opportunities to recognize the student's inappropriate behavior. A greater challenge is to catch the student being good and to recognize that appropriate behavior several times a day.

- *Use humor* to build relationships and to decrease tension. Look for the fun in the way students relate to one another and to you.

- *Create an emotionally safe classroom* environment in which students accept one another's strengths and weaknesses and treat one another with respect and consideration.

Although this first step is necessary, it is not sufficient. In Chapter 5 you read about positive behavior supports as part of a schoolwide plan to prevent student discipline referrals and to use a problem-solving approach to managing student behavior. Positive behavior support is important for all of your students, but particularly for those who experience challenges emotionally, behaviorally, and socially (Hendley & Lock, 2007; Rafferty, 2007; Scott, Park, Swain-Bradway, & Landers, 2007).

This section provides an overview of interventions and accommodations you can implement to provide positive behavior supports and to facilitate the social and academic growth of students with emotional and behavioral disorders. No single approach to intervention works for all students with severe emotional and behavioral problems. However, a systematic, well-organized plan and documentation of changes in behavior will help you determine whether an intervention is working. Keep in mind that some students with emotional and behavioral disorders may have co-morbidity with learning disabilities or may otherwise have difficulty with making academic progress. Thus, we conclude with suggestions for academic adaptations.

PEARSON
myeducationlab

To enhance your understanding of how to promote positive behavior support for students who experience behavioral challenges, go to the IRIS Center Resources section of Topic 15: Emotional and Behavioral Disorders in the MyEducationLab for your course and complete Case 7 entitled *Encouraging Appropriate Behavior.*

Changing Behavior

The student behaviors that teachers most want to change are those they regard as undesirable, such as those that interfere with instruction, other students, or the student's learning. *Desirable behaviors*—those that enhance instruction, relations with others, and the student's success— are the behaviors teachers most want to see increased. Tips for Teachers 8.7 provides guiding principles that will help you promote desirable behaviors and decrease undesirable ones.

Changing student behavior is a daunting task and it does not happen overnight. Give yourself positive feedback for what you do to enhance student learning and social functioning. Do not be too hard on yourself, especially when you make mistakes. At the end of the day, focus on the positive. Although there are limitations to what any effective teacher can do, there are always opportunities to be successful in teaching students with emotional and behavioral disorders. See Tips for Teachers 8.8 to learn about how to target key behaviors that you want to change.

Other techniques exist as well. Figure 8.4 provides an example of a behavior contract between a student and a teacher. The Activities for All Learners shows how even simple devices can work.

PROMOTING DESIRABLE BEHAVIORS AND DECREASING UNDESIRABLE ONES

- Do not use threats; instead, issue consequences that you are prepared to execute if students do not behave appropriately. When you make remarks such as "You're going to do this math paper if you have to sit here all day," students soon learn that consequences are not real and that your words cannot be trusted.

- Establish consequences that do not punish you as well as your student. If you are stressed or inconvenienced by the consequence, you might resent the student (a circumstance that would surely interfere with the quality of the relationship you need to establish). For example, staying in at lunch, giving up your planning period, or driving the student home can punish you as much as the student.

- Listen and talk to your student but avoid arguing. If you are tempted to argue, recognize that you need a break and set another time to finish the discussion.

- Use logic, principles, and effective guidelines to make decisions. Do not flaunt your authority as a teacher to make students do something; always provide a clear sense of what is the right or best thing to do.

- Focus on the problems that interfere most; that is, ignore minor misbehaviors.

- Build into your instruction a strategy that shows students that the work they complete is necessary and meaningful.

- Avoid comparing a student with emotional or behavioral problems to other students. Comparisons do not help students understand and accept themselves or be understood and accepted by others.

- Resist the temptation to solve students' problems for them. Students need to learn how to resolve conflicts for themselves. The long-term goal of any behavior-management strategy is to motivate students to behave appropriately and to shift the responsibility of "controlling behavior" from teacher to student.

- Recognize your feelings and do not let them control your behavior. When you are upset by a student's behavior in class, it is important not to respond by further upsetting the student. Never "strike back" by humiliating, embarrassing, or berating a student.

- Let your student know how many chances he or she has before a consequence will be applied (and do not add chances later). When you tell a student, "This is the last chance," and he or she continues to behave inappropriately, you need to follow through on whatever consequence was designated.

FOSTERING CHANGE BY TARGETING KEY BEHAVIORS

- Whenever possible, involve students and parents in identifying the target behavior. In this way, you work at changing the behavior both at school and at home.

- As when making referrals, describe the behavior in as much detail as possible, including when and with whom it typically occurs.

- Get the student's input on the behavior, as well as his or her suggestions for what might help to reduce it.

- Describe the target behavior in writing, using the terms expressed by the student, the parent, and yourself so that everyone involved understands the problem.

- Establish a procedure for eliminating the behavior and providing positive consequences when the behavior does not occur. Involve parents in distributing positive consequences as well.

Resolving Conflicts and Promoting Self-Control

Dealing with conflict between students and between a student and a teacher is an ongoing issue for teachers at all grade levels. Conflicts are inevitable in a classroom community; they occur among all students, not just those who have emotional and behavioral disorders (Albrecht, 2008). Adalyn Saladrigas says, "With some of our students with emotional and behavioral disorders I can often see it coming on with their body language. In particular, when they clench their fists, something's going to happen."

What about extreme cases? School districts have guidelines for procedures regarding restraining students. In general, the rule of thumb is—don't restrain unless you are specifically trained to do so. If a student seems violent, get other students out of harm's way and

FIGURE
8.4

Sample Student–Teacher Contract

Date: _____

Ms. Gonzalez will draw a star next to Paul's name on the bulletin board and give Paul one point when he does any of the following in her classroom:

1) He raises his hand and waits for the teacher to call on him before talking.

2) He stays seated in his chair while working on class assignments.

3) When other kids in the class are bothering him, he tells the teacher about their behavior instead of yelling at and/or hitting the other kids.

After Paul has earned 12 points from his teacher, Ms. Gonzalez, he may select one of the following rewards:

1) He may have extra time to work on the computer.

2) He may serve as the teacher's helper for a day.

3) He may be in charge of caring for the class pet for a day.

4) He may serve as a peer tutor for a day (for a subject decided upon by the teacher).

After Paul has received 12 points, he begins earning the points again. Another reward will be given when 12 points have been earned.

I, Paul B. O'Brien, agree to the conditions stated above, and understand that I will not be allowed any of the rewards until I have earned 12 points by doing the activities stated above.

_____

(student's signature)

I, Ms. Gonzalez, agree to the conditions stated above. I will give Paul one of the aforementioned reinforcers only after he has received 12 points.

_____

(teacher's signature)

Activities FOR **ALL** Learners

USING A TIMER TO CHANGE BEHAVIOR

Purpose: To increase appropriate behavior, such as on-task behavior, and to reduce inappropriate behavior, such as being out of seat

Materials: Kitchen timer

Procedures:

1. Show students the kitchen timer and indicate that you will be using it to cue students to look for on-task behavior in the class. Discuss with students what behaviors will be included (e.g., working, performing an assignment, asking a question, reading a text).

2. Indicate that the timer will ring at different intervals and that all groups or individuals who are on task when the timer rings will be awarded a point.

3. Set the timer initially for a range of times (from 5 to 10 minutes), and then for longer periods of time.

Source: Adapted from Wolf, M. M., Hanley, E. L., King, L. A., Lachowicz, J., & Giles, D. K. (1970). The timer-game: A variable interval contingency for the management of out-of-seat behavior. *Exceptional Children, 37* 113–117.

give the student time to decompress. Call security or an administrator according to policy in your building.

To assist students in resolving conflicts, Larrivee (2005) established a model for conflict resolution that teachers can use in class and that is applicable to most situations you will encounter (see Figure 8.5). The idea is that students have a large number of strategies to apply individually or in combination in order to solve problems. Although all students can benefit from conflict-resolution strategies, this model is particularly effective for students

FIGURE
8.5

Larrivee's Model for Conflict Resolution

GROUP WORK SOLUTIONS

- **Compromising.** Requires cooperation and also negotiation in order to find a workable solution. In a compromise, everyone gives up a little while still getting some of what he or she originally wanted.

- **Sharing.** Individuals decide to share for mutual benefit (e.g., working together to complete the assignment). This is a difficult concept for children to understand because it requires waiting for the benefit to occur in the future.

- **Taking turns.** A simple strategy; it is important to teach that the student who goes second has not "lost." It is often effective to let students decide the order in turn taking.

- **Chance.** Another strategy to alleviate a dispute around turn taking; flip a coin, draw straws, or use another method that leaves the resolution to chance.

COMMUNICATION STRATEGIES

- **Apologizing.** Admitting responsibility if you recognize that your behavior was wrong. It can also be a way to recognize the other person's feelings without having to take responsibility for causing the problem.

- **Sending an I-message.** Express how you feel without blaming the other person. For example, "I was angry when you used my book without asking."

- **Active listening.** This is the most difficult of the communication strategies. Active listening involves trying to understand how another person is feeling by listening carefully to what he or she says. This is particularly difficult because conflicts often arise when people do not listen or misinterpret what another person is trying to say.

- **Self-talk.** This strategy is a self-control method used to reduce stress or remain calm by engaging in rehearsed positive self-talk (e.g., "You are in control; don't lose it.").

DIFFUSING A POTENTIALLY VOLATILE CONFLICT

- **Distracting/postponing.** Attention on the conflict is diverted or postponed to diffuse a conflict. It allows students to cool off before addressing the conflict (e.g., "You know what, let's try this game again tomorrow.").

- **Humor/exaggerating.** Another strategy to diffuse a volatile situation is to poke fun at the situation or to engage in an exaggerated recounting in order to help students put their issues in perspective. These strategies should be taught with caution as they can result in hurt feelings if all parties are not able to share in the "joke."

- **Abandoning.** If a person realizes he or she can't handle a situation, walking away may be the best way to exercise self-control.

- **Seeking assistance.** An individual or group should seek assistance if other conflict resolution strategies are not working, if the situation is volatile, or if the problem is too complex to solve without help.

Source: Information from Larrivee, B. (2005). *Authentic classroom management: Creating a learning community and building reflective practice* (2nd ed.). Boston: Allyn & Bacon.

What steps should this teacher take to help students resolve their conflict? What specific skills can students be taught to use in preventing future interpersonal conflicts?

who are easily frustrated or who become volatile when conflicts arise between or among peers. Teaching these techniques requires modeling, practice, feedback, and patience as students learn to recognize and support one another when they or their peers use strategies to solve problems.

Teaching Self-Monitoring Skills

By teaching students to identify their problem behaviors, to set personal goals, and to monitor their academic and social behavior, you also help them to develop self-control (Menzies, Lane, & Lee, 2009; Polsgrove & Smith, 2004; Vanderbilt, 2005). Setting and monitoring positive personal goals contribute to students' positive self-concept and higher self-esteem. What are the benefits of teaching self-monitoring strategies? Daly and Ranalli (2003) summarize several of the advantages of self-monitoring:

- It is practical and takes little extra time on the part of the teacher; consequently, it can free up time for the teacher to work with other students.
- It can be used to improve a variety of academic or social skills.
- It uses monitoring systems, such as charting progress using graphs, charts, and checklists that provide the student with concrete evidence of improved behavior.

- It provides more immediate feedback than a teacher is able to provide.
- It increases students' independence and helps them become responsible for their own behavior.
- It facilitates communication with parents by providing data that can be easily shared during meetings.
- It encourages individual improvement rather than competition across students, so each student can work toward his or her own goals.

Self-monitoring has helped students with disabilities make positive behavior changes in a variety of areas, including improving on-task behavior (Hutchinson, Murdock, Williamson, & Cronin, 2000; Rock, 2005), decreasing aggressive behavior (Gumpel & Shlomit, 2000), improving other social behaviors such as peer interactions and cooperative behavior (McDougall, 1998), and improving academic performance (Levendoski & Cartledge, 2000; Rock, 2005). For example, Marcia Rock (2005) studied the use of a self-monitoring intervention in which elementary school students with EBD in inclusion math and reading classes were taught to self-monitor their attention to an academic task and their performance on the task. The strategy involved students in setting an individual performance goal for the lesson, creating a plan to achieve the goal, using self-talk to reflect during the lesson, and evaluating progress. To make the monitoring of appropriate behaviors concrete, teachers took pictures of students demonstrating on-task behavior. Students looked at the pictures of themselves periodically during class as a way to monitor and correct their behavior. The intervention helped students take control of their learning by supporting self-management skills that resulted in improved academic performance. The Activities for All Learners below describes a simple activity for helping students establish personal goals.

Teaching Self-Management Skills

Self-monitoring helps students to become more aware of their own behaviors. Self-management enables students to govern the reinforcers for their behaviors (Cooper, Heron, & Heward, 2007). Furthermore, teaching students self-management skills enables them to depend less on the teacher. Recall from the basic principles of managing student behavior introduced in Chapter 5 that much of the responsibility for targeting behavior, identifying reinforcers, and implementing a behavior change plan rested with the teachers. Self-management skills require that students learn some principles of behavior management and then implement the selected reinforcers. Self-management requires a more active role from the student and a more collaborative role from the teacher.

Margarite Rabinsky is a fourth-grade teacher whose student, Eduardo Cora, was not completing assignments. Although Margarite worked closely with Eduardo to ensure that the assignments were not too difficult and that Eduardo understood how to complete them, he was still unsuccessful at turning in completed assignments on time. Deciding to

HELPING STUDENTS ESTABLISH PERSONAL GOALS

Purpose: To establish personal goals

Materials: Index card or small piece of paper, pencil or pen

Procedures:
1. Ask students to think about people they most admire. For younger students, discuss the meaning of "admire."

2. Ask students to identify the qualities of people they admire and examples of their behavior that demonstrate these qualities.
3. Now ask each student to write on the index card one quality for which they would like to be admired.
4. Ask students to keep the card in a prominent place (taped on their assignment folder or inside their desk, for example).

5. Throughout the year, ask students to look at the card and assess the extent to which they express the quality or trait for which they most want to be admired.

Self-Management Plan

Name: Eduardo Cora

Target Behavior: Submit completed assignments to teacher on time or meet with teacher before assignment is due to agree on alternative date and time.

When Behavior Occurs: Mostly on Thursdays and Fridays.

Where Behavior Occurs: Social Studies and Science.

Goals:

1. Eduardo will write down assignments and due dates in a separate assignment book for each subject.

2. Eduardo will look at each assignment and be sure that he knows how to complete it. Eduardo will ask questions, as necessary.

3. Eduardo will tell the teacher ahead of time if an assignment is going to be late.

Timeline: Meet each Friday to review the progress on the plan, and then revise the plan in three weeks.

Reinforcer: Eduardo will receive 15 minutes of extra time to work on the computer each day his assignments are completed.

Evaluation: Eduardo will write a brief description of the program's success.

Go to the Assignments and Activities section of Topic 15: Emotional and Behavioral Disorders for the MyEducationaLab for your course and complete the activity entitled *Conflict Resolution*.

involve Eduardo in a self-management plan, Margarite implemented the following steps for developing a self-management plan:

1. ***Teacher and student identify and agree on the behavior to be changed.*** Margarite and Eduardo agreed on the behavior to change and put it in writing (see Figure 8.6).

2. ***Identify when and where the behavior most frequently occurs.*** Margarite stated, "First, let's think about what classes it occurs in most, and then let's think about whether there are certain days when it occurs." Eduardo volunteered that he started the week off pretty well and then felt he got worse on Thursday and Friday. Margarite indicated that she did not think he had difficulty with math, as he most frequently turned in his math work, but that he seemed to have trouble with social studies and science. Eduardo agreed, and they summarized this on the form.

3. ***Establish realistic goals for changing the behavior.*** Margarite and Eduardo discussed his behavior and then established the goals listed in Figure 8.6.

4. ***Identify a timeline showing how long the behavior change plan will be in effect.*** Because neither Margarite nor Eduardo had done this before, they decided to meet for 5 minutes every Friday to review the progress for the week and to have a longer meeting in 3 weeks to determine how effective the program had been.

5. ***Identify reinforcers and consequences.*** Margarite and Eduardo reexamined their goals and discussed what reinforcers should be provided if Eduardo met the goals. They also discussed consequences if the goals were not met. These reinforcers and consequences were written into the plan in Figure 8.6.

6. ***Self-evaluate the success of the program each day.*** Margarite explained to Eduardo that he would be responsible, at the end of each day, for writing a brief evaluation of how effective the plan was for that day. Margarite observed a noticeable change in Eduardo's behavior after 1 week. After 2 weeks, Eduardo's behavior was more like the behavior of other students in the class. Though Eduardo would still have bad days, they were far less frequent.

Teaching Social Skills

Go to **www.ldonline.org** where the Teachers section provides several useful links to material on social skills training and fostering social competence.

Have you ever met someone who seems to know the right thing to say and do no matter what the situation might be? We often watch these people with envy as they move from person to person, always seemingly at ease. We refer to them as demonstrating good social skills or social competence. **Social skills** or **competence** are defined as "those responses, which within a given situation, prove effective, or in other words, maximize the probability of producing, maintaining, or enhancing positive effects for the interactor" (Foster & Ritchey, 1979, p. 26) and, it should be added, while causing no harm to others. Social skills allow individuals to

Examples of Social Skills Deficits

FIGURE 8.7

- Deficits in social perception and social cognition that inhibit students' abilities to interact with others
- Lack of consequential thinking
- Difficulty expressing feelings
- Difficulty in feeling empathy for others
- Difficulty delaying gratification (impulsive)
- Inappropriate grooming and hygiene
- Failure to understand and fulfill the role of listener
- Inability to take the perspective of another
- Less time spent looking and smiling at a conversational partner
- Unwilling to act in a social situation to influence the outcome
- Less likely to request clarification when given ambiguous or incomplete information
- Lack of self-confidence and tendency to portray learned helplessness behaviors
- Aggressive or antisocial behaviors
- Tendency to talk more or less than non-LD peers
- More likely to approach teacher and ask inappropriate questions
- Less proficient in interpersonal problem solving
- Less proficient in planning for the future

adapt and respond to the expectations of society. Social competence is a process that begins at birth and continues throughout life.

Many students with disabilities have difficulties with social skills (see Figure 8.7). This is particularly true for students with emotional and behavioral disorders (Kavale, Mathur, & Mostert, 2004; Maag, 2006). Children with deficits in social skills may have difficulty with *acquisition* (they are simply unaware of the social skill), *performance* (they are aware of the skill, but don't know how to implement it), or *fluency* (knows how to implement the skill, but is awkward in doing so) (Gresham, Sugai, & Horner, 2001; Patterson, Jolivette, & Crosby, 2006). Consequences of having social skills deficits include alienation from peers, isolation, unsatisfying social relationships, academic failure, and difficulties in living independently as an adult (Maag, 2006).

Social skills training (SST) provides students with specific instruction in acquisition, performance, and fluency of social skills. SST is "a positive, proactive intervention, designed to teach specific social behavior by replacing negative behaviors with more desirable ones" (Patterson et al., 2006, p. 23). Although results of research on SST have been mixed (Cook, Gresham, Kern, Barreras, & Crews, 2008; Forness & Kavale, 1999; Gresham, Cook, Crews, & Kern, 2004; Gresham, Sugai, & Horner, 2001; Maag, 2006), there is still optimism about the potential for its success and recommendations for its continued research and development (Kavale et al., 2004; Patterson et al., 2006).

A number of SST programs have emerged in recent decades (McIntosh & MacKay, 2008), including a host of commercial SST curriculum products. Although there are differences among programs, there are several principles of SST that generalize across most programs (see Figure 8.8). For such programs to be successful, they should (1) teach necessary social skills; (2) have an extended duration; and (3) provide sufficient opportunities for practice in classroom settings (Gresham, Van, & Cook, 2006; McIntosh & MacKay, 2008).

As a classroom teacher, how might you be involved with SST? Because it is recommended that SST occur in natural settings with peers and adults involved (McIntosh & MacKay, 2008), you may be involved in teaching and reinforcing target social skills. Your school may have adopted a commercial program or you can work with the special education teacher and/or school counselor to plan, implement, and evaluate social skills interventions. Activities for All Learners, page 225, presents an example of an SST program for adolescents, ASSET.

Go to **www.whatworks.ed.gov** to visit the What Works Clearinghouse, which includes reviews of SST programs.

FIGURE
8.8

Principles for Conducting Social Skills Training

1. *Develop cooperative learning.* Classrooms can be structured so there is a win–lose atmosphere in which children compete with one another for grades and teacher attention, or classrooms can be structured so children work on their own with little interaction between classmates, or classrooms can be structured for cooperative learning so children work alone, in pairs, and in groups, helping one another master the assigned material.

2. *Involve peers in the training program for low social status students.* An important function of social skills training is to alter the way peers perceive students identified as low in social status. Including popular peers in the social skills training program increases the likelihood that they will have opportunities to observe the changes in target students and to cue and reinforce appropriate behavior in the classroom.

3. *Use principles of effective instruction.* Teaching social skills requires implementing principles of effective instruction. These have been used and explained throughout this text and include obtaining student commitment, identifying target behavior, pretesting, teaching, modeling, rehearsing, role-playing, providing feedback, practicing in controlled settings, practicing in other settings, posttesting, and following up.

4. *Teach needed skills.* Many social skills training programs fail because youngsters are trained to do things they already know how to do. Social skills that learning- and behavior-disordered students frequently need to be taught include reading body language (e.g., what his or her body "says," gestures, eye contact, facial reactions), using greetings, initiating and maintaining a conversation, giving and accepting positive feedback, identifying feelings in self and others, and using problem solving/conflict resolution.

5. *Teach for transfer of learning.* For social skills to generalize to other settings, the program must require the rehearsal and implementation of target skills across settings. Social skills training programs need to ensure that learned skills are systematically demonstrated in the classroom, on the playground, and at home.

6. *Empower students.* Many students with learning difficulties feel discouraged and unable to influence their learning. They turn the responsibility for learning over to the teacher and become "passive" learners. You can empower students by offering choices, teaching about consequences, documenting progress, and helping students to exercise control of what happens to them.

7. *Identify strengths.* Knowing something about the students' areas of strength might be helpful in identifying social contexts that may be promising for promoting positive peer interactions. Students with social skills deficits may benefit from acquiring strengths in appearance and athletic activities so they have areas of strength from which to build their social skills. Other areas such as hobbies or special interests can be presented in the classroom so that the student with difficulties with social relationships has an opportunity to be perceived as one who is knowledgeable.

8. *Encourage reciprocal friendships.* Reciprocal friendship is the mutual identification as "best friend" by two students. Thus, a student who identifies a person as his or her best friend is also identified by that same person as a best friend. Because it is unlikely that all youngsters in the classroom are going to like all the other students equally, the notion of developing a reciprocal friendship is a more realistic goal.

When developing social skills interventions, it may be important to consider the nature of children's friendships or social support outside of the school setting (LaGreca & Vaughn, 1992; Lane, Wehby, Menzies, Doukas, Munton, & Gregg, 2003). Students with learning and behavior disorders who are not well accepted by their classmates may have friends in the neighborhood or within their families (e.g., cousins). Perhaps the most important point to remember is that because a child is not well accepted by peers at school does not necessarily mean that the child does not have effective social relationships outside of the school setting. Thus, getting input from key family members is important in planning SST.

Using Social Learning Strategies

Social learning also contributes to the success of students with emotional and behavioral disorders. **Social learning** involves observing and modeling or imitating the behavior of others (e.g., Bandura, 1971, 1973). To what extent can you expect students to imitate the appropriate behaviors of classmates, and what can you do to accelerate this process? Research suggests that students with emotional and behavioral disorders are unlikely to imitate "better" behaviors in the classroom unless teachers provide directed experiences to promote this behavior (Kauffman & Landrum, 2009). Tips for Teachers 8.9 offers a strategy for guiding students to learn appropriate behaviors from classmates.

Implementing School-Based Wraparound

Students with behavior disorders and emotional disturbances are among the most highly segregated students with disabilities. Furthermore, systems operating independently of one another (e.g., schools, mental health agencies, juvenile justice) have repeatedly failed to adequately support individuals with EBD and their families (e.g., Eber & Keenan, 2004). In response, schools are starting to implement **wraparound** processes that provide coordinated services to families and students with emotional or behavior disorders (Bruns, Walrath, &

THE ASSET METHOD FOR TEACHING SOCIAL SKILLS TO SECONDARY STUDENTS

Purpose: To develop the social skills of adolescents with special needs who demonstrate difficulties in social functioning

Materials: The leader's guide (Hazel, Schumaker, Sherman, & Sheldon-Wildgen, 1982) from the ASSET program provides instructions for running the groups and teaching the skills. Eight teaching sessions are provided on videotapes that demonstrate the skills. Program materials include skill sheets, home notes, and criterion checklists. Each lesson is taught to a small group of adolescents.

Procedure: Each social skill is taught by implementing the following nine-step procedure:

Step 1 *Review.* Previously learned skills are reviewed and homework is evaluated and integrated.

Step 2 *Explain.* The skill that is the focus of the lesson is explained and discussed.

Step 3 *Rationale.* A rationale for why the skill is important and why the students need to learn it is provided.

Step 4 *Example.* Examples of situations in which the skill can be used are provided. These examples relate directly to the experiences and interests of the students.

Step 5 *Examine.* A skills sheet that lists the component skills (refer to text for list of skills for following directions) is provided to each student.

Step 6 *Model.* Through videotapes that can be purchased with the curriculum, or as implemented by the teacher, the skills are demonstrated and modeled.

Step 7 *Verbal Rehearsal.* The procedure of verbally stating the components of each skill so that they can be learned by the student is

implemented. The students practice saying the skill components and play games and engage in activities that teach them the skills.

Step 8 *Behavioral Rehearsal.* Students practice performing each subskill and overall skill, and demonstrate proficiency.

Step 9 *Homework.* Designed to enhance generalization, homework provides students with directed activities that allow them to practice the subskills and skills outside the classroom.

Source: Information from Hazel, J. S., Schumaker, J. B., Sherman, J. A., & Sheldon-Wildgen, J. (1982). Group training for social skills: A program for court-adjudicated, probationary youths. *Criminal Justice and Behavior* 9, 35–53.

Tips FOR TEACHERS 8.9

GUIDING STUDENTS TO LEARN APPROPRIATE BEHAVIORS FROM CLASSMATES

- Identify student "models" and the behaviors that you want other students to emulate. For example, "Joaquin has his math book open to page 38 and is looking at me to indicate that he is ready. Show me that you are ready by doing the same thing."

- Monitor whether the student with emotional or behavioral disorders follows the model. Look for approximations and provide positive reinforcement. For example, "Sheilah [student with emotional or behavioral problems] is getting her math book out. What are the next two things you need to do, Sheilah, to indicate that you are ready?"

- Provide frequent feedback when the student performs the desired behaviors. Look for as many chances as possible to recognize desirable behaviors.

- Students who view themselves as "like" a model are more likely than not to imitate desirable behaviors. You can facilitate this process by identifying ways in which students' behaviors are similar. For example, "Sheilah [student with emotional or behavioral disorder] and Joaquin are not talking while they are getting ready for the homework assignment. Good for them!"

Sheehan, 2007; Eber, Breen, Rose, Unizycki, & London, 2008; Eber & Keenan, 2004; Nordness, 2005). Wraparound planning involves focusing on the actual needs of the students within their home–school community. It has been recommended as a process for Tier 3 interventions for the 1% to 2% of high-needs students with emotional and behavioral disorders (Eber et al., 2008).

Wraparound services can be used to provide supports that are coordinated through school, home, and community settings. Because wraparound planning considers the entire family, some supports may be included in the IEP (e.g., coordinating professionals who will implement interventions for the student), whereas others may not (e.g., parent training or support for siblings). Typically a social worker, school counselor, or school psychologist will serve as the wraparound facilitator. As a classroom teacher, you may be a member of a wraparound team. Keep the following elements of successful wraparound systems of care in mind as you participate as a team member (Eber & Keenan, 2004):

- Use services that are based in the community.
- Individualize supports and services and base them on student strengths.
- Use culturally appropriate practices.
- Involve families as active participants.
- Collaborate with family, child, agencies, and community services to create a plan and provide services as a team (e.g., coordinate IEP planning with wraparound planning).
- Investigate flexible use of resources and funding.
- Involve a collaborative team in establishing goals and evaluating outcomes.
- Maintain a strong commitment to the wraparound system.

A **wraparound facilitator** or case manager will most likely be responsible for coordinating services. As a classroom teacher you may be asked to be part of the wraparound team to ensure a systematic approach to address the needs of the student.

Adapting Instruction

Students with emotional and behavioral problems often have academic difficulties, may be underachievers in school, and are often missing basic academic skills (Gonzales, Vannest, & Reid, 2008); McEvoy & Welker, 2000). In addition, because many are eligible for services due to a diagnosed learning disability, academic challenges are compounded (Ryan, Pierce, & Money, 2008). The relationship between EBD and academic failure has resulted in dropout rates for EBD students that are much higher than those of students with other disabilities (Cohen & Smerdon, 2009; Pierce, Reid, & Epstein, 2004). Moreover, requirements for schools to demonstrate adequate yearly progress via standardized testing place greater emphasis on the academic progress of all students with disabilities, including those with emotional and behavioral disorders (Vannest, Temple-Harvey, & Mason, 2009).

An important factor that positively affects students with emotional and behavioral disorders is the extent to which they are busy in purposeful activities. Students need to view the activities as personally relevant and related to skills they need to learn. To engage their students, effective teachers need to explain to students *why* they are studying a topic, *why* they are given a particular assignment, and *how* their learning will contribute to their success as students and in the future.

Academic failure or frustration can exacerbate a student's emotional or behavioral disorder (Conroy, Sutherland, Snyder, Al-Hendawi, & Vo, 2009). Without creating a parallel program or watering down the curriculum, teachers can adapt and modify assignments and expectations so that students can succeed. One simple strategy is to look for opportunities to reinforce and reward students for what they know or have done correctly. Tips for Teachers 8.10 offers additional suggestions for giving students opportunities for success. Also see Tech Tips for online tools for students with EBD.

Adalyn Saladrigas loves her work, because she knows she is making a difference in the lives of the middle-school students she teaches. Some students feel helpless and that their emotional reactions and behavioral patterns are beyond their control. Through positive behavior supports and through interactions with teachers and parents, she helps her students get in control of their lives. The stakes are high: academic failure, dropping out of school, decreased chances for professional success, and increased chances of substance abuse and incarceration (Crews et al., 2007). Success with her students is, in Adalyn's words, "priceless."

Go to **www.pacer.org/ebd**, which introduces the project for parents of children with EBD.

Tips FOR TEACHERS 8.10

ADAPTING INSTRUCTION FOR STUDENT SUCCESS

- *Use different groupings—individual, small groups, pairs, and large groups—to give students opportunities to acquire academic and social skills.* Students with emotional and behavioral disorders may have difficulty learning in whole-class instruction but do well in small-group or paired learning situations. Also provide opportunities for students to be tutored and to serve as tutors themselves. Learning to work with others is an important skill for students with emotional and behavioral disorders. In a review of research, peer-mediated learning methods (cross-age, same-age, or classwide peer tutoring, and cooperative learning) were successful for students with emotional or behavior disorders in a range of academic subject areas and grade levels.

- *Use materials that will generate high interest.* When teachers design assignments to increase the likelihood of student success, it helps reduce incidences of inappropriate behaviors. Teachers can do this by using high-interest materials; for example, some students may enjoy working on computers while others might like to write or use artistic means for approaching. Consequently, having students compose essays, practice skills on a computer, or illustrate responses may provide better motivation than more traditional activities.

- *Provide alternative ways for students to complete tasks and demonstrate learning.* For example, students might give oral recitations to describe what they know to other students who have already mastered the material. Allow students to express their individual learning-style preferences. For instance, some students work better standing up, others while sitting on the floor, still others while sitting in beanbag chairs. As long as students are working, learning, and not interfering with the progress of others, providing appropriate alternatives for completing tasks makes sense.

Sources: Ryan, J. B., Pierce, C. D., & Mooney, P. (2008). Evidence-based teaching strategies for students with EBD. *Beyond Behavior* 22–29; Ryan, J. B., Reid, R., & Epstein, M. H. (2004). Peer-mediated intervention studies on academic achievement for students with EBD: A review. *Remedial and Special Education* 25(6), 330–341; and Stevens, K. B., & Lingo, A. S. (2005). Constant time delay: One way to provide positive behavioral support for students with emotional and behavioral disorders. *Beyond Behavior* 10–15.

Tech TIPS

TOOLS FOR TEACHING STUDENTS WITH EBD

A number of resources are available for teachers who have students with EBD in their classrooms. Some provide classroom activities and others provide teachers with resources and strategies.

PEGS, by STEPS Professional Development at
▶ www.pegsforteachers.com
Practice in Effective Guidance Strategies (PEGS) is an interactive classroom simulation program that has versions for preschool, elementary, and secondary classrooms. This program provides a variety of simulated classroom activities to help teachers promote appropriate participation with each learner. Teachers can learn how to apply specific behavioral strategies to match individual needs and observe the results of interventions.

Intervention Central created by school psychologist and administrator in Central New York, Jim Wright at
▶ www.interventioncentral.org/
This site offers scientifically based online tools to help teachers promote positive classroom behaviors that enhance learning.

OSEP Center for Positive Behavioral Interventions and Supports at
▶ www.pbis.org
This website provides current information related to research-based practices and schoolwide strategies for creating positive learning environments for all children.

Summary

- Students with emotional and behavioral disorders exhibit behaviors that are significantly different from the norm and that persist over a long period.

- In general, higher prevalence rates are reported for students with mild emotional or behavioral disorders, and lower rates for more severe disorders. Current estimates range from 6% to 10% of the school-age population.

- Students with emotional and behavioral disorders may exhibit problems in one or more of the following areas: anxiety, mood, defiance, conduct and aggression, socialized aggression, and immaturity.

- Emotional and behavioral disorders result from both biological and environmental factors. In many cases, causes of a disorder are complex and multiple.

- Students with severe emotional and behavioral disorders are often recognized by parents and other adults. Other students have disorders that are latent or become apparent after school entry. As a classroom teacher, you may be involved with initial referrals for some students and with ongoing functional behavioral assessment and monitoring of progress for most students with emotional and behavioral disorders assigned to your classroom.

- Positive behavior supports for students with emotional and behavioral disorders can include direct instruction focused on behavior change and include the teaching of (a) ways to change behavior, (b) conflict resolution and self-control, (c) self-monitoring skills, (d) self-management skills, (e) social skills, and (f) social learning strategies. For students with greater needs, you may be involved on a school wraparound team to provide more support. Students may also need academic adaptations to ensure success in meeting curricular objectives.

Think and Apply

1. Adalyn Saladrigas has vast experiences in meeting the behavioral, social, and academic needs of students with emotional and behavioral disorders. If you could meet Adalyn, what would be some key questions you would ask about what she has learned from her experience?

2. Michelle is a student in your sixth-grade class. Michelle is aggressive and defiant to you and verbally abusive to her classmates. Several of the parents of children in your class have explained that Michelle is a bully and that their children are afraid to come to school because of her. Michelle is aware that school is a no bullying zone, but despite your best attempts her behavior persists. Learn about the process for referring students like Michelle for special services for an emotional or behavioral disorder in your state and school district. What online resources are available for learning about your roles and responsibilities in this process? What are Tier 1 and 2 interventions that may help change Michelle's behavior?

PEARSON myeducationlab

Now go to Topic 15: Emotional and Behavioral Disorders in the MyEducationLab (www.myeducationlab.com) for your course where you can:

- Find learning outcomes for this topic along with the national standards that connect to these outcomes.

- Complete Assignments and Activities that can help you more deeply understand the chapter content.

- Examine challenging situations and cases presented in the IRIS Center Resources.

- Listen to Teacher Talk to hear how one teacher treats her students who are in pain with love and respect.

- Apply and practice your understanding of the core teaching skills identified in the chapter with Building Teaching Skills and Dispositions learning units.

Teaching Students with Autism Spectrum Disorders/Pervasive Developmental Disorders

FOCUS QUESTIONS

1. What are autism spectrum disorders (ASD) and what disabilities are included in this category?

2. What are the most prevalent characteristics of children with autism spectrum disorders?

3. What types of assessments are done to identify students with autism spectrum disorders?

4. What general instructional accommodations would you consider for students with an autism spectrum disorder?

5. What might you do to assess a student with an autism spectrum disorder who engages in severe challenging behavior such as self-injury or aggression?

CONTRIBUTORS TO THIS CHAPTER:

Mark F. O'Reilly, The University of Texas at Austin

Jeff Sigafoos, Victoria University, New Zealand

Giulio Lancioni, The University of Bari, Italy

Russell Lang, The University of California at Santa Barbara

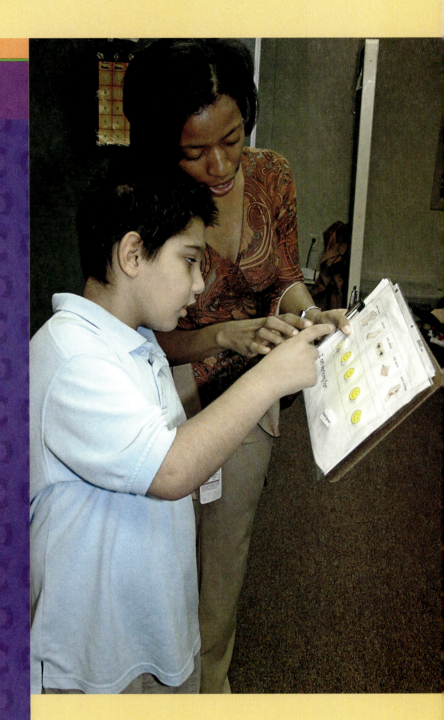

Kelly Page is a public elementary school special education teacher in the Southwest. Her job involves supporting teachers and students within inclusive general education settings. She is responsible for 10 students with a variety of disabilities. Several of these students are diagnosed with an autism spectrum disorder (ASD).

One of my students is Carl. Carl is 11 years old and is diagnosed with Asperger syndrome. He has excellent language skills and can carry on a conversation. In fact, Carl has the ability to engage in conversations using words and constructs far above his age level. However, he only wants to talk about insects and spiders. He seems to know everything there is to know about bugs. For hundreds of different insects and spiders, he can tell you their Latin names, what they eat, and where they live. No matter what else you try to talk to him about he always seems to find a way to tie it back to this topic. When I started to work with him initially he had no classroom friends, struggled completing his schoolwork, and often got very upset. When plans changed at the last minute or when he did not want to complete his schoolwork, he would cry, scream, and occasionally try to leave the classroom without permission. On the playground he would catch bugs and take them to show to people. The other children made fun of him and would not include him in their games. Carl attended general education classes and did excellent in Science, but he struggled in English. One of the more common tasks in English class was creative writing and Carl absolutely refused to participate. His English teacher saw no reason why such an intelligent student would not complete his work and would throw such a fit. She often wanted to punish Carl with bad grades and send him out of the classroom to go to the office. My initial goals for Carl included improving social skills, eliminating his tantrums, and improving his performance in English. The first priority was explaining Asperger syndrome to his English teacher and modifying the creative writing assignment to be on Carl's level. Just because Carl excels in some areas does not mean he excels everywhere. In fact the abstract thinking and imagination required in the creative writing assignments is exactly the type of thing individuals with Asperger's may struggle with.

Another of my students is Erin. Erin also has an ASD, but she and Carl are very different. Erin is a 5-year-old kindergartener with a diagnosis of severe mental retardation and autism. Erin currently spends half of her day in a typical kindergarten class and the other half of her day working one-on-one with me. Erin does not have any functional language and often intentionally hits her head on solid objects when she gets upset. We try and block her from doing this, but she frequently gets in a hard hit. She has had a red bruise on her face and forehead for most of the year. I spend a lot of time worrying about her safety. Erin also waves her hands in front of her face pretty constantly and seems unaware or disinterested in other people. Eye contact with Erin is rare and she will almost always turn her head or close her eyes if I try to make her look at me. Goals for Erin include simple self-help skills (toileting), requesting items with sign language, and reducing her self-injury. I noticed that head hitting seems to increase after she has worked on something for a few minutes. Specifically, if we work on sign language for too long she gets really upset. I think head hitting may be Erin's way of asking for a break from work. I have decided to plan Erin's instruction so that she only works for brief periods of time and practices requesting only items she really likes, and when she starts to look like she may be about to get upset, I prompt her to sign for a break from work.

Introduction

Both Carl and Erin have been diagnosed with autism spectrum disorders (ASD). Students with ASD have difficulty communicating or interacting socially with other people. Some of these students may have mental retardation. A lot of these students also engage in challenging behavior such as aggression, tantrums, and self-injury. They also tend to be rigid in terms of what they want to talk about and things they like to do. These students can get very upset when anyone interferes with their interests and activities, as seen in the examples of Kelly's students. In this chapter, we first describe the characteristics of ASD and then outline the best ways to organize the curriculum to teach students with ASD.

Definitions of Autism Spectrum Disorders/Asperger Syndrome and Pervasive Developmental Disorders

You will note that the chapter title mentions two conditions: autism spectrum disorders (ASD) and pervasive developmental disorders (PDD). The term **pervasive developmental disorder (PDD)** is a diagnostic category used by the American Psychiatric Association to describe five related disabilities, namely, autistic disorder or autism, Rett syndrome, childhood disintegrative disorder, Asperger syndrome, and pervasive developmental disorder–not otherwise specified (PDD–NOS) (American Psychiatric Association, 2000; National Research Council, 2001). **Autism spectrum disorders (ASD)** has recently become a popular term to describe a subgroup of PDD, namely, autism and Asperger syndrome.

The number of individuals diagnosed with ASD has risen dramatically in the last 10 years (Centers for Disease Control and Prevention, 2009). In 2006, approximately 211,610 students who were classified with autism received special education services in our schools. This is nine times more than the number of students receiving school services in 1994. Data from several studies using the current diagnostic criteria place the numbers of students with this disorder somewhere between 2 and 6 per 1,000 individuals. The most commonly cited statistic at the time of writing this chapter was 1 in 150 children age 8 have an ASD (Centers for Disease Control and Prevention, 2009. It is unclear why there is such a rise in students diagnosed with ASD. The rise may be due to changes in diagnostic practices (Rutter, 2005) and the inclusion of autism as a special education category in the early 1990s. Nevertheless, some true rise in the rate of ASD cannot be firmly discounted. However, research findings on the influence of environmental factors, such as the measles-mumps-rubella vaccine, have not shown a relationship between these vaccines and the increases in ASD (Honda, Shimizu, & Rutter, 2005).

One of the main reasons for using the term *ASD* to describe autism and Asperger syndrome is that these disabilities incorporate many of the same symptoms and differ primarily in the severity of expression of those symptoms. The other categories of PDD are extremely rare (i.e., Rett syndrome, childhood disintegrative disorder) or may not be very clear (PDD–NOS). In this section, each of the five PDD categories is described. However, the remainder of the chapter focuses on teaching students with ASD. There are quantitative and qualitative differences in the learning and behavioral characteristics exhibited by individuals who have each disability. Table 9.1 displays each disorder as well as the characteristics that set the disorders apart. Delays are usually noted in early childhood and may co-occur with mental retardation. At this time, there is no identified cause for many of these disabilities. Given the lack of knowledge about cause, there are no empirically validated strategies for prevention or cure at this time.

Autism

Autism is a developmental disability that typically appears during the first 3 years of life. Although people diagnosed with autism are considered to have a severe disability, the range in ability level within this group is varied (National Research Council, 2001). Some individuals with autism may function independently or almost independently.

To be diagnosed with autism, a child must have documented features in three areas:

1. *Six or more of any combination of the following*:
   - Impairments in social interactions (e.g., poor eye contact, lack of responsiveness, inability to establish relationships)
   - Impairments in communication (e.g., no formal spoken language, robotic sounding speech with little tone inflection, use of made-up gibberish words, and repeating exactly what has been heard)
2. *Stereotypical behavior* (e.g., body rocking, hand flapping, or fascination with objects or specific parts of objects)

TABLE
9.1

Comparison of Disabilities Across Developmental Areas

	SOCIAL INTERACTION	COMMUNICATION	STEREOTYPES	COGNITION
Autism	Little or no eye contact Autistic leading Unawareness of social situations	Little to no verbal communication Repetitive, echolalic, or robotic speech	Inflexible routines Motor repetitions (finger flapping, body rocking)	May have mental retardation May have savant characteristics
Rett Syndrome	Loss of social skills within the first few years Loss of interest in social environment	Severely impaired expressive and receptive language	Develops hand movements such as hand-wringing or hand-washing between ages 5 and 30 months	Often associated with severe or profound mental retardation
Childhood Disintegrative Disorder	Loss of interest in environment but not until 2–10 years of age Lack of social or emotional reciprocity	Loss of language skills around 2–10 years of age Repetitive use of language Lack of make-believe play	Develops repetitive motor movements such as hand-flapping and finger waving Restricted interests and activities	Usually associated with mental retardation as the loss of skills in all areas is progressive
Asperger Syndrome	Lack of ability to read social cues Awkward eye contact Interest in social environment	No clinically significant delay in language Use of language (pragmatics) may be delayed (e.g., loudness or socially appropriate use)	Restricted areas of interest (e.g., preoccupation with a topic) Inflexible adherence to certain routines Repetitive motor movements	No clinically significant delay in cognition

3. *Onset before age 3* (note, this is not necessarily as a loss of skills but rather as an emergence of delay in skill development). The child must not meet criteria for Rett syndrome or childhood disintegrative disorder, in which loss of skills is reported before age 5.

The physical features of people with autism might not suggest a disability. Rather, the disability is generally manifested in their language and their personal and social behavior. The Individuals with Disabilities Education Improvement Act (2004) defines *autism* as follows:

> A developmental disability significantly affecting verbal and nonverbal communication and social interaction, generally evident before age 3, that adversely affects a child's performance. Other characteristics often associated with autism are engagement in repetitive activities and stereotyped movements, resistance to environmental change or change in daily routines, and unusual responses to sensory experiences. The term does not apply if a child's educational performance is adversely affected primarily because the child has a serious emotional disturbance.

After having Terry, a student with autism, in his seventh-grade language block for several months, Thomas Salome expressed these thoughts:

> I was worried about how it would work with the other students; if it would take away time and attention from them. I was concerned that Terry would be a distraction to the students. But now that Terry has been part of our class for several months, I feel that the more he is in the classroom, the less the children even notice the noise or occasional outbursts. The students have learned that Terry does things that are not okay for them to do.

Tips for Teachers 9.1 presents Thomas's advice for working with students like Terry in the classroom.

Asperger Syndrome

Asperger syndrome is the next most common PDD. Despite serious impairments in social skills, abstract thinking, and the ability to relate to and identify emotions, these students are often in the normal IQ range and may have extensive verbal abilities. As a result many people

Go to **www.autism-society.org**, the website of The Autism Society of America, to learn more about autism. This site serves the needs of students with autism and their families.

WORKING WITH STUDENTS WITH AUTISM

- *Don't let the behavior overwhelm you.* Develop a behavior-management plan and implement small steps. Decide what you will put up with and what behaviors must stop, and target those.

- *Talk to the student's parents and other teachers.* Find out what works and what does not work with this student. For example, does the child like to be offered choices during the day (e.g., what to do next) or would the child prefer a more set schedule with a routine?

- *Systematically expect more and more of the student.* At first, it might be enough that the student sits with the class during circle time. However, over time you may require increased participation (e.g., answering questions).

- *Develop a picture and word schedule for daily activities.* Picture schedules may have photographs or drawings that represent activities that will occur during the day. Referencing this schedule may help the child understand what is coming next and transition between activities and environments more smoothly. This type of schedule will help you introduce changes in routine slowly, and let the student know in advance that these changes are going to occur.

- *Use peers to help redirect the student's behavior.* Classmates can be a source of support for a student with ASD. They can help prompt appropriate behavior and even praise a student for his or her accomplishments.

- *Take ownership of the student.* Every child in your class is your responsibility and you have been entrusted with their education and well-being. Children with ASD can be challenging, but you will feel a deep sense of accomplishment when they make progress.

do not immediately recognize the child with Asperger syndrome in the classroom. Asperger syndrome is diagnosed by documenting behaviors in six different areas:

1. Qualitative impairment in social interaction (e.g., eye contact, failure to develop peer relationships) and lack of social or emotional reciprocity

2. Stereotypical behavior such as abnormal preoccupation with one or more areas of interest in either intensity or focus (e.g., Carl's interest in insects from the beginning of the chapter), inflexible adherence to routines or rituals, and stereotyped motor mannerisms (e.g., finger flapping)

3. Presence of an impairment in a social, occupational, or vocational area (e.g., inability to get a job or make friends)

4. No clinically significant delay in language; in other words, in terms of vocabulary and semantics, language ability is comparable to a same-age peer without a disability, but speech may sound robotic or monotone

5. No clinically significant delays in cognition, self-help, adaptive skills, (e.g. eating, dressing, toileting), or curiosity about the environment

6. Must not meet the criteria for schizophrenia, because schizophrenia would likely better explain the majority of the symptoms shared with Asperger syndrome

Because Asperger syndrome is not immediately obvious, this disability can create unique challenges for school systems and teachers (Portway & Johnson, 2005). If students with Asperger syndrome are overlooked and considered just to be quirky or immature, they are not likely to receive the supports and services they need. Without support, many of these students will experience social isolation, anxiety, and depression (Rayner, 2005). Parents of children with Asperger syndrome state that once school personnel understand the characteristics of Asperger syndrome they do a better job of making accommodations and providing support (e.g., teaching social skills and modifying class assignments). In turn, these supports have a positive effect on these students' quality of life (Brewin, Renwick, & Schormans, 2008).

Consider the example of Rusty. Rusty is a 15-year-old boy who just started high school. In middle school his teacher (Mrs. Page) was well aware of his Asperger diagnosis and made the minor accommodations necessary for him to make progress and feel successful at school. Among other things, Mrs. Page would reexplain complex directions for some assignments in very concrete terms, which Rusty was better able to understand. She would also offer Rusty slightly modified assignments to scaffold his learning experiences to better meet his current

Go to **www.udel.edu/bkirby/ asperger** for information and support for individuals with Asperger syndrome.

abilities and educational goals. However, now in high school, Rusty changes classes and has many teachers. Many of his new teachers are unaware of his diagnosis and think of Rusty as just a peculiar kid who fails to complete work or participate in class because of laziness. In his history class Rusty is asked to work in a team of three students to prepare a presentation for the class. The topic of the presentation is how different people in different countries interpreted certain events during World War II. Rusty struggles to understand the topic and to recognize the frustration of the other members in his group. Ultimately, he is embarrassed and earns a poor grade. With slight modifications (e.g., allowing independent work and better explanation of the assignment), Rusty may have succeeded. However, because the teacher did not recognize the disability or understand its implications, Rusty experienced unnecessary failure.

Rett Syndrome

To be diagnosed with **Rett syndrome**, a child must have normal prenatal and perinatal development, normal psychomotor development for the first 5 months, and normal head circumference at birth. The child also exhibits normal development in the following areas until a loss of skills occurs between 5 and 48 months. These deficits include the following:

- Deceleration of head growth
- Loss of hand skills with subsequent development of stereotyped hand movements (e.g., hand washing or hand wringing)
- Loss of social engagement
- Poor gait or trunk movements
- Severely impaired receptive and expressive communication (Sigafoos et al., 2009)

This syndrome is extremely rare, occurring in approximately 1 in 15,000 live births, and occurs only in females (National Institutes of Health, 2001). A genetic cause for Rett syndrome has been isolated. As these girls begin to regress developmentally, they exhibit symptoms that are superficially similar to autism (e.g., loss of communication skills). These children eventually suffer from multiple disabilities. For guidelines on working with children with multiple disabilities, see Chapter 10, "Teaching Students With Developmental Disabilities."

What physical behaviors do children with autism exhibit? What other impairments may occur in people diagnosed with autism?

Childhood Disintegrative Disorder

To be diagnosed with **childhood disintegrative disorder**, a child must have a normal pattern of development through age 2. Between the ages of 2 and 10, the child must demonstrate a regression of skills in two of the following: language, social skills, adaptive skills, bowel or bladder control, play skills, and motor skills. The child must also exhibit delays in social interaction, communication, and stereotypical behaviors. Last, the child must not meet the criteria for any other PDD or schizophrenia. This is an extremely rare condition, occurring in approximately 1 in 50,000 live births (Frombonne, 2002).

Pervasive Developmental Disorder–Not Otherwise Specified

A child is diagnosed with **pervasive developmental disorder–not otherwise specified (PDD–NOS)** when delays are exhibited in social interaction or communication or if stereotypical behaviors develop and the child does not meet the criteria for another PDD. Essentially, the diagnosis is used when no other diagnosis seems appropriate but there are obvious delays for no apparent reason, such as traumatic birth or neurological development.

Go to **www.autism.org** where you can find a variety of links on several autism-related issues and interventions for individuals with autism.

Characteristics of Students with Autism Spectrum Disorders/Asperger Syndrome

Autism spectrum disorders cover a wide range of abilities and difficulties as described earlier in the chapter. Three core deficits are common to ASD: in social skills, in communication skills, and in repetitive behaviors and routines. Each student with ASD will possess these deficits to some degree. Being aware of these core areas of functioning can help you tailor your curriculum and instruction to the needs of a specific student.

Social Skills

Students with ASD do not interact with other people in a typical fashion (National Research Council, 2001). In fact, they may not wish to interact with people at all. They can have difficulty interpreting the social cues of other people. For example, they may be unable to discriminate the different intentions of a wink versus a frown. They may appear not to notice other people at all and can give the impression that they are deaf. Other students with ASD may be interested in people but lack core social skills to initiate, respond to, and maintain social interactions.

Additionally, students with ASD have difficulty seeing the world from the perspective of another person. They are unable to "get in the head" of another person and recognize that other people have goals and feelings. This means that they are unable to comprehend the behavior of other people. The social world may therefore be an unpredictable place for students with ASD.

A related problem is that many students with ASD have difficulty regulating their emotions. They may engage in what appears to be spontaneous outbursts of aggression (hitting other students), self-injury (banging their heads), or sadness (weeping). This pattern can also impede social integration.

Communication Skills

Many children with autism do not talk at all and others only develop extremely limited verbal language, which they use to make one-word requests (Charman, Drew, Baird, & Baird, 2003). Some of these children seem to pass the early milestones of language acquisition (e.g., babbling), but then they stop. Others may develop some language later, at age 9 or 10, for example.

Those who develop language use it in unusual ways. Many use single words or phrases but do not combine these words and phrases into meaningful sentences. They may repeat what they hear verbatim, a condition called **echolalia**. For example, when you ask, "Would you like a cookie?" they might repeat, "Would you like a cookie?" instead of answering the question. Other students may have mild delays in language development or may, in fact, possess large or even precocious vocabularies, yet they have difficulty sustaining conversations with others. This last difficulty is typical of students with high-functioning autism and Asperger syndrome. A student with Asperger syndrome may be more than able to carry on a detailed monologue about a favorite topic (e.g., Carl and his insects described before) but will not give any other students an opportunity to engage in a conversation about the topic. They appear to talk *at* people and seem oblivious to any attempts at initiation by others. These students may also have difficulty interpreting the body language, tone of voice, and turn of phrase of other students.

Body language, including facial expressions, posture, orientation, and gestures, rarely matches what these students are saying. Tone of voice is often monotone, high-pitched, or robotic. Students with Asperger syndrome will often speak like adults and will not use the vocal nuances of their peer group. A child with Asperger syndrome may be expressing genuine interest in a topic or an individual but fail to accurately communicate this interest. For example, after hearing a joke they enjoyed instead of saying, "That was cool joke, can you tell another?" they may instead say "I require a second amusing anecdote now." When making this sincere, yet peculiar and precocious request they might also fail to make eye contact and their voice and expression may make them appear bored or disinterested.

With such deficits in communication skills, these students can have difficulty expressing their wants and needs. They may therefore communicate their intent by other means such as grabbing, pulling, screaming, hitting, and self-injury. Young adults with high-functioning autism (i.e., those students with autism who may not have a diagnosis of mental retardation or who may have mild levels of mental retardation) or Asperger syndrome may become aware of these difficulties. This awareness that they are different can in some instances cause frustration, embarrassment, and social isolation, which may ultimately result in secondary psychiatric issues such as anxiety and depression.

Repetitive Behaviors and Routines

Many students with ASD engage in **repetitive motor behaviors** (National Research Council, 2001). These can be subtle (repeated head turning when they appear to be alone) or blatant (continuous and vigorous body rocking). Other typical types of repetitive motor behaviors include hand flapping, finger flicking, and toe walking.

Children with ASD tend to insist on sameness or consistency in the environment. For example, they will engage with certain toys but not play with them in a typical fashion. Instead of pretend play with toy cars, they may endlessly line them up in rows. Any change in daily routines such as time, venue, and menu for meals; route to school; personal hygiene; and bedtime routines can result in challenging behavior. These children may also be intensely preoccupied with very specific interests such as train schedules, dinosaurs, or specific TV shows.

It appears that such behaviors and routines may underpin consistency and predictability in the child's world. As a result, any attempt to interfere with the repetitive behaviors and routines can result in extreme upset and challenging behavior.

Identification and Assessment of Students with Autism Spectrum Disorders

Children with severe ASD will most likely have a diagnosis before arriving in your classroom. However, it is also possible you may be involved in initial evaluations or screenings for ASD. If this is needed, you may be asked to document student performance in the areas of language, social, academic, or adaptive behaviors. You may even be asked to complete rating scales describing student behavior in your class. These rating scales are often simple and require little, if any, specialized knowledge to complete.

If you are not involved in the identification evaluation, you will certainly be involved in ongoing assessment and reevaluation. As a classroom teacher, you may be expected to monitor progress in areas in which delays are commonly reported. For example, you might have to monitor how a child with Asperger syndrome uses language in conversations and interacts with his or her peers. Keeping some sort of record or data concerning progress is paramount. For example, consider Carl's case described in the beginning of this chapter. Carl struggles with peer relationships. You might want to keep track of how often Carl interacts with his classmates without discussing insects. By simply making a note in a special folder at the end of the day detailing any interaction you witnessed, over time you may be able to gauge some progress. If his appropriate interactions increase, then you have some evidence that he may be making improvements in both controlling his perseverations and social skills.

The assessment of contextual variables is also important for this population of students. A contextual variable is something that is unique to a particular situation, for example, the environmental differences between the classroom and the lunchroom and even the differences between one teacher and another. Students with ASD may learn something in one context but then fail to generalize the ability to another context. For example, during lunch, your student with autism may be able to demonstrate appropriate use of a napkin, but he may not be able to demonstrate this in home economics when his class is working on table manners. Additionally, a student's behavior may be substantially different in different environments (Lang et al., 2008, 2009). It is not uncommon for parents to say, "but my child never behaves that way at home." A well-prepared and organized teacher will keep a log documenting where students perform certain skills as well as under what conditions the skills are missing. This type of assessment can help you better understand exactly where, by whom, and the other contextual variables that may be important when teaching a particular student.

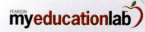

Go to the Assignments and Activities section of Topic 6: Assessment in the MyEducationLab for your course and complete the activity entitled *Using Assessment to Drive Instruction*.

Curricular and Instructional Guidelines for Students with Autism Spectrum Disorders

In this section, we outline some suggestions for organizing the curriculum and designing instruction for students with ASD. These guidelines are not exhaustive. In fact, we recommend that you also read Chapter 10, "Teaching Students With Developmental Disabilities," because the curricular and instructional guidelines for students with developmental disabilities are equally applicable to students with ASD. To develop an effective instructional program for students with ASD, you should consider the key processes discussed in the following sections.

Assess Preferences

At the beginning of the school year, try to get a comprehensive picture of the students' likes and dislikes in terms of activities by conducting a **preference assessment**. A preference assessment form can be as simple as a piece of paper listing the items the student likes. Assess what contexts students find challenging. For example, some students might find that structured classroom tasks they complete individually are not a challenge, whereas cooperative learning might be. As part of this process, generate a list of items such as toys, foods, and activities that the students like. You can generate this list by interviewing parents and previous teachers and then tailor the emphasis to each student.

Preference assessments should be conducted at least two times during the academic year, because children's preferences change over time. Also, as you work with students, you may see changes in their preferred activities and items. This information will be invaluable when designing the classroom routine and selecting instructional strategies.

Establish a Classroom Routine

When we discussed some of the difficulties experienced by students with ASD, we noted that they may be particularly challenged when a routine is absent or unpredictable. These students may be prone to challenging behavior when placed in a new classroom situation. It is important to establish a classroom routine quickly and to communicate this routine to the student.

When first establishing the **classroom routine**, consider the demands of the regular classroom routine, such as what the students are supposed to do when they first enter the classroom, when they go to lunch, and when they finish their work. The routine for the

Why is it important to establish a classroom routine? How do daily routines benefit students with autism spectrum disorders?

student with an ASD should fit within this larger routine as much as possible. When designing the routine, teachers should consider information regarding the student's high- and low-preference activities and then design the student's routine judiciously. For example, intersperse high- and low-preference activities. Do not expect the student to spend extended periods of time engaged in low-preference activities. Low- and high-preference activities should be evenly balanced. For example, consider Erin's case presented at the beginning of the chapter. Erin did not enjoy working on sign language, and if she is required to do this task for too long, she engages in challenging behavior. However, Erin does enjoy coloring and scribbling on paper. An appropriate routine for Erin that could minimize challenging behavior might alternate brief periods of sign language work with periods of coloring.

Some students may experience difficulties transitioning from high-preference to low-preference activities. In these cases it may be helpful to incorporate a neutral activity (i.e., something the child does not dislike, but is also not highly preferred) following a high-preference activity (e.g., coloring for Erin) and before a low-preference activity (e.g., sign language drills for Erin). When this is done, the child is not being asked to give up something they enjoy to do something they hate, but instead this eases the transition and may also reduce the likelihood of challenging behavior.

It is important to establish a routine as early as possible in the school year. The daily routine should be communicated to students through a daily schedule. This schedule can be presented to students in different formats. For the student with Asperger syndrome, the schedule can be written into a personal diary that the student carries with him or her. For the student with autism, the schedule could be posted on the wall with pictures attached identifying the daily activities and the times they will occur. At the beginning of each school day, you should review the activities on the schedule for that day with each individual student.

It is important to involve the student, as much as possible, in preparing this schedule. So, within the constraints of mandated classroom activities, the student could choose the sequence of activities for the day. Certain time periods may be left blank during the day. When a blank period arises, you might offer the student a choice between different activities. For example, consider Carl's case again. After English class Carl could be scheduled for a preferred activity as a reward. Carl's teacher, Mrs. Page, could offer Carl two choices of how to spend his free time, perhaps playing on the computer or looking at an insect picture book. For higher functioning students, it may be sufficient to simply offer the choices verbally. However, for some students pictorial representations of the activities may more clearly explain the choices. In these instances Carl could select the picture of the insect book to indicate his preference.

This form of active scheduling is an important antecedent intervention to enhance self-control and communication skills. It also reduces the probability of challenging behavior from students with ASD (Flannery & Horner, 1994; O'Reilly, Sigafoos, Lancioni, Edrishina, & Andrews, 2005). See Tips for Teachers 9.2 for more suggestions for working with students with ASD.

PEARSON
myeducationlab

Go to the Assignments and Activities section of Topic 17, Autism Spectrum Disorders in the MyEducationLab for your course and complete the activity entitled *Picture Schedules.*

Teach Communication Skills

Communication skills are typically very difficult for students with ASD; consequently, it is essential that you develop a comprehensive plan that maps out the skills you plan to teach and how you are going to teach them. Once you have established your daily schedule for the student, it is helpful to target communication skills to teach during each activity, such as requesting preferred items or naming objects. For example, during snack time, Erin's teacher is going to teach the sign for popcorn (a preferred food) and have Erin use the sign to get her snack. Teaching in this way makes the skill relevant to the situation. A creative teacher will find a way to target at least one communication skill during every schedule activity.

Portions of the daily schedule might involve intensive instruction in communication skills using a **massed trials strategy**. A massed trials strategy means that the same instructional trial is repeated again and again to a predefined criterion of correct performance. For example, you might ask the child to name certain items that are presented individually on a table or to point to an item from an array of items presented simultaneously. Each trial begins with the teacher asking a question: "What is this?" or "Point to the ___." Initially, the teacher will immediately give the answer: "A doll." The student is expected to repeat the answer. As training progresses, the teacher systematically delays the answer to the question (e.g., by 2 seconds) in order to give the student the opportunity to respond independently. All of the student's correct responses receive **reinforcement** (reward) from the teacher. This reinforcement should be selected from the information obtained in the preference assessment described earlier. For example, if it was determined that Erin liked popcorn, using a small piece of popcorn as reinforcement during massed trials might be appropriate. Alternatively, for some children

Tips FOR TEACHERS 9.2

WORKING WITH STUDENTS WITH ASD

- *Use picture and word schedules for daily activities.* Picture schedules may have photographs or drawings that represent activities that will occur during the day. Referencing this schedule may help the child understand what is coming next and transition between activities and environments more smoothly. This type of schedule will help you introduce changes in routine slowly, and let the student know in advance that these changes are going to occur.

- *Establish routines early in the school year.* Students with ASD often rely heavily on routines. Communicate clearly about any changes in the routine, and post them in your picture schedule.

- *Learn about augmentative and alternative communication.* Students with delays in social communication often use a

different mode of communication. You may have students who use picture wallets, communication boards, or even voice output communication aids to communicate. Learn to feel comfortable using these devices.

- *Establish collaborative relationships with families.* Parents know their child best, and they can assist you when you have questions or concerns. Communicate regularly with parents so that they are aware of any changes in your class. Ask them to communicate to you about changes at home.

- *Be aware of your classroom environment.* Students with ASD may be hypersensitive to environmental conditions such as noise, lighting, and temperature. Become familiar with your individual students' needs and make adjustments to your classroom environment as needed.

What forms of augmentative and alternative communication are available for students with autism?

physical contact (e.g., high-five or a hug) and praise may be sufficient reinforcement.

Communication skills should also be taught as part of the ongoing natural context. This type of communication instruction is often called **milieu** or **naturalistic instruction**. These instructional strategies are similar to massed trials strategies. The main difference with milieu training is that the communication training occurs when there is a natural opportunity for the child to communicate. For example, at lunchtime the child could be presented with an empty glass. You hold the container of milk. The child motions toward the glass. You then present the container of milk with the request, "I want milk please." The student repeats the phrase and is then given the milk. The consequence of the request (receiving the milk) acts as a natural positive consequence of engaging in the request. No arbitrary consequences selected from the preference assessment are necessary using this strategy. Over time, you can delay using the phrase until the natural conditions (e.g., empty glass and container of milk) elicit the request spontaneously from the student.

Children with autism often have profound language delays (Charman et al., 2003). Addressing communication difficulties is a common and often high-priority education goal. Communication can occur through gestures, facial expressions, eye blinks, and behavior, and through augmentative and alternative communication (AAC) (such as the high- and low-technology communication devices introduced in Chapter 7). Low-technology devices can involve pictures or drawings at which the student points to convey a message. High-technology devices can provide voice output (speech synthesizers) and can be programmed with many messages.

A **communication board** is one example of augmentative communication. The essential elements are the board itself and the symbols or pictures. The board can be made of sturdy paper or an actual board, or it can be a regular or simplified computer keyboard or a computer screen. The symbols or symbol systems that are selected depend on the learner and the environment in which he or she lives. Symbols should be selected according to what students need and want to communicate. In constructing communication boards, Lewis (1993) suggests that the following questions need to be addressed:

- What choices will the student be able to make?
- How will the choices be represented on the board?
- How will the student make his or her selections?
- How many choices will be available and how will they be arranged on the board?
- How will the communication board be constructed?

Figure 9.1 presents examples of common symbol systems, which include Core Picture Vocabulary (Johnson, 1985), Talking Pictures (Leff & Leff, 1978), Pic Syms (Carlson, 1984), Oakland Schools Picture Dictionary (Kirstein & Bernstein, 1981), Picture Communication Symbols (Johnson, 1985), and Blissymbols (Bliss, 1965).

The goals and strategies of communication instruction should be identical for students who do not speak and those who do speak. You will need to work closely with your speech and language pathologist to find the best AAC solution for your student. To find the best solution for your student, you need to identify your communication goals for your student and present this information to the speech pathologist as you discuss the optimal AAC device for the student in question.

The communication skills chosen for instruction will depend on such factors as the level of the student's disability and family priorities. The communication skills of many students with autism will be at what is described as a **prelinguistic level**. For example, the child may lead you to an area (e.g., locked cupboard) where a desired item is present (e.g., favorite toy). This leading behavior is common in autism and is often referred to as **autistic leading**. It is important to identify these prelinguistic behaviors and replace them with more appropriate communication skills, such as orally requesting an item, using the instructional strategies previously described. Other children may not even present with prelinguistic behaviors, appearing almost

FIGURE
9.1

Picture Symbol Systems for Communication Boards

	Core Picture Vocabulary	Talking Pictures	Pic Syms	Oakland	Picture Communication Symbols	Blissymbols
Man						
Wash						
Want		No symbol				
Hello		No symbol		No symbol		
Happy		No symbol				
House						
Car						

Source: Glennen, S. (1992). Augmentative and alternative communication. In G. Church and S. Glennen (Eds.), *The handbook of assistive technology* (p. 100). San Diego, CA: Singular Publishing Group. Reprinted with permission.

comatose. For these students, rudimentary skills such as making and maintaining eye contact may need to be encouraged.

Because students with ASD tend not to efficiently generalize skills they have been taught, you will need to encourage generalization of the targeted communication skills in as many different environments as possible. One way to facilitate this is to involve parents as trainers. Parents spend more time with their children than you do and will have many opportunities to implement milieu or naturalistic strategies. Therefore, involving the parents in the process of teaching communication skills can be very beneficial. Parents can be effective teachers, and involving them in their child's instruction can have a positive effect on reducing the stress involved in interacting with their child.

See the Tech Tips for information on computer programs that are helpful in instructing students with ASD.

Teach Social Skills

The distinction between communication skills and social skills is a somewhat arbitrary one. In a sense, one must possess adequate communication skills in order to engage socially with others. For the purposes of this chapter, social skills include the ability to initiate appropriate social interactions, respond to social initiations from others, and terminate social interactions appropriately.

COMPUTER PROGRAMS FOR STUDENTS WITH AUTISM SPECTRUM DISORDERS

In selecting computer programs to use with students, we must look beyond the content of the program to determine whether the material is presented in a way most suited to each individual student's learning style and ability—a critical issue for learners with autism. You should consider the suggestions here in general terms rather than as specific solutions for any single individual.

Typically, because many learners with autism can process visual material better than auditory, carefully selected computer programs may help them to improve basic skills more easily on the computer than in a classroom setting. Look for educational software that is self-paced, offers clear guidelines for expectations, and requires minimal teacher assistance. Consider the following:

Boardmaker
▶ **www.mayerjohnson.com**

Many teachers have had success in using this program to help learners with autism with organization, structure, and expectations. A visual calendar can be useful, as can visual images of sequential steps for specific activities—such as

washing hands, checking out a book, or dressing to go outside in the winter. Also useful are visual signals to help the learner with transitions throughout the day—when to stop playing a game or when to put away materials. For example, prepare green (go), yellow (warning), and red (stop) signs. As the student begins an activity, give her the green sign. When the time for that activity is almost over, exchange the green sign for the yellow one, announcing that time is almost up.

Pyramid Educational Consultants
▶ **www.pecs.com**

Picture Exchange Communication System (PECS) has designed this site for use by persons with autism and related developmental disabilities. PECS has received worldwide recognition for focusing on the initiation component of communication. The PECS system employs applied behavior analysis in conjunction with the development of functional communication skills that focus on the initiation of communication and the design of effective educational environments.

Go to the Assignments and Activities section of Topic 17: Autism Spectrum Disorders in the MyEducationLab for your course and complete the activity entitled *Social Skills*.

Go to **www.teacch.com**, the Division of TEACCH (Treatment and Education of Autistic and related Communication-handicapped Children) where you can find information and resources about various educational approaches to working with children with autism.

A person is perceived to be socially competent by others if he or she is able to interact socially in an effective manner, generalize these interaction styles across multiple social situations, and maintain such interactions over time. Social skills targeted for instruction include the following:

- Initiating conversations with others
- Responding to initiations
- Maintaining conversations
- Responding to criticism

These skills have been taught within a multitude of social contexts such as play and leisure situations (e.g., initiating interactions with peers on the playground), the home environment (e.g., responding appropriately to parent initiations), and work settings (e.g., expanding interactions with co-workers). Strategies for teaching social skills are varied and can include verbal, gesture, and physical prompts; role-play; and a variety of self-management strategies (self-monitoring, self-instruction, and self-reinforcement).

You should focus your efforts on teaching social skills to students with ASD when they possess communication skills but fail to discriminate how to use these skills effectively with peers and others. In other words, social skills interventions should be a major focus for students with autism who are higher functioning and students with Asperger syndrome. As mentioned earlier, a variety of social skills intervention strategies are available; you need to select an intervention that will be maximally effective for these students. Remember that social skills deficits occur for a number of reasons, including the inability to understand the social context, such as the intentions, feelings, and perceptions of others. Therefore, many of the popular instructional strategies that focus primarily on teaching overt social skills without teaching the person to understand the perceptions of others may not be effective.

Two social skills teaching strategies that may prove helpful with these students are **social problem solving** and **Social Story™ interventions**. Both of these intervention strategies teach the student with ASD to understand the social context in addition to responding to or behaving appropriately in that social context.

Social Problem Solving.   Social problem solving involves teaching the social skills you want your students to perform (e.g., maintaining appropriate distance from a person when initiating an interaction) as part of a generic process of engaging in social interactions. In other words, you will teach students a set of strategies to monitor or manage their own social skills in addition to the very specific social skills you want them to perform.

A number of empirical studies have examined the effectiveness of teaching social problem solving to people with disabilities (e.g., O'Reilly & Glynn, 1995; O'Reilly, Lancioni, & Kierans, 2000; O'Reilly, Lancioni, Sigafoos, O'Donoghue, Lacey, & Edrisinha, 2004; Park & Gaylord-Ross, 1989). Replicating previous research from supported employment studies, O'Reilly and Glynn (1995) taught social problem-solving skills in school settings to students with disabilities who were socially withdrawn. Students learned to initiate appropriately with teachers following training. They also generalized the skills trained to the schoolyard setting with peers. The results of this and similar studies indicate that social problem solving is a powerful strategy for teaching social skills that generalize to real-world settings and are maintained over time.

In school settings, teachers often teach these skills in an environment removed from the regular classroom context, because the training involves one-to-one rehearsal and feedback with the teacher or paraprofessional. This problem-solving strategy is taught using a combination of role-play, feedback, modeling, and verbal instruction with you or a paraprofessional. See Tips for Teachers 9.3 for guidance on how to design this instruction.

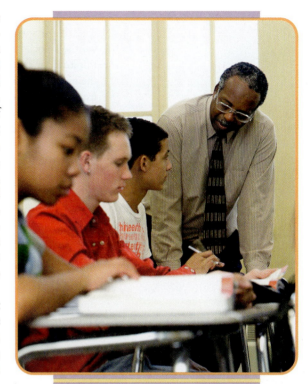

What strategies will you use to teach social skills in your classroom? What social skills are needed in a situation similar to the one pictured here?

Social Story Interventions.   Social Story interventions have very similar goals to those of the social problem-solving approach. Unlike social problem solving, however, Social Stories are a relatively recent social skills intervention technique. Although some positive research on this technique has been published, more research is needed to clarify best practices in using Social Stories.

Social Story interventions are based on the premise that children with ASD are unable to interpret the social context or imagine the perspectives of others during social interactions. Additionally, social interactions may evoke challenging behavior because they are unpredictable and hence possibly aversive to students with ASD. Effective social interventions must involve teaching students to understand the social context and to perform appropriately within that specific context.

Tips FOR TEACHERS 9.3

USING SOCIAL PROBLEM-SOLVING STRATEGIES

- Schedule two to three 30-minute periods during the first week of training to give the student ample exposure to the skill. Thereafter, you can provide brief feedback to the student during the regular classroom routine as he or she performs the social skill targeted during training.

- Teach the student to ask and answer a series of questions in relation to the social context in which the targeted social skill occurs.

- Teach the student to discriminate the salient social stimuli by asking himself or herself, "What's happening here?" The student must then accurately describe the social situation.

- Help the student make decisions about how to behave by asking himself or herself: "What should I do?" These prompts help the student generate a series of alternative

action plans and select the most appropriate social interaction for the current context. At this point, the student performs the overt social skill (e.g., initiating the conversation, responding to an initiation from another).

- The teacher or paraprofessional should role-play the social partner at this point of the training and give immediate feedback regarding the student's performance of the targeted social skill.

- Have the student evaluate the social interaction by asking, "What happened when I [description of how he or she behaved]?" The student is prompted to generate a description of the responses of other people in the social interaction and to evaluate whether these responses were positive or negative.

A **Social Story** is an individualized short story designed to clarify a particular social context, the perspectives of others in that context, and the social skills to be performed. In other words, a Social Story provides "information on what people in a given situation are doing, thinking, or feeling, the sequence of events, the identification of significant social cues and their meaning, and the script of what to do and say" (Attwood, 2000, p. 90). Social Stories are usually developed based on a series of guidelines (Gray, 2000):

- Stries should be tailored to a student's comprehension level.
- A story may consist of a series of simple sentences and/or picture cues that describe the context and provide examples of desired responses, explain the perspectives of others, and explain the rules of social engagement.
- A Social Story should provide a description of a social context and social exchange and be directive in telling the student how to behave.

Social Stories usually use role-play, modeling, and feedback immediately before the target social situation in order to facilitate acquisition and generalization of the social skills. An example of a Social Story used to reduce screaming, crying, hitting, and falling during homework for a 7-year-old student with ASD is included in Figure 9.2. This student's parents read the story aloud to him before homework (Adams, Gouvouis, VanLue, & Waldron, 2004).

Selecting Social Skills for Intervention.   Take some time at the beginning of the school year to observe how your students with ASD interact with peers and others during the school day. Cue in to such skills as their ability to initiate social interactions, to respond to others' interactions, and to terminate interactions appropriately. Carefully examine their body language. Does body language match the intent of the verbal interactions? How is their social performance during structured versus unstructured parts of the school day? By making these careful observations, you may be able to develop a list of key social deficits and the social situations in which they occur. This information will form the basis of your social skills curriculum. When designing this curriculum, you should only target individual or small numbers of social skills at a time. Intervene using a problem-solving intervention strategy and then (unobtrusively) prompt performance of the target social skills throughout the school day. Once these skills begin to improve, target another set of social skills. Remember to involve paraprofessionals (see Tips for Teachers 9.4 for additional information on working with paraprofessionals) and the students' families in training these social skills across settings, because these students do not generalize new skills without specific training.

FIGURE 9.2

Example of a Social Story Used to Decrease Challenging Behavior During Homework for Peter, a 7-Year-Old Boy with ASD

Almost every day I do my homework.

Mom and Dad help me with my homework.

Sometimes I have to do reading.

Sometimes I have to do spelling.

Sometimes I have to do math.

When homework is hard, sometimes I get upset.

When I get upset, sometimes I want to cry and scream.

Sometimes I want to fall off my chair.

Sometimes I hit the table or other things.

Sometimes I say that I don't want to do my homework.

Mom and Dad are sad when I get upset.

They are sad when I cry, scream, fall off my chair, and hit.

They are sad when I say I don't want to do my homework.

When I do my homework and it gets hard Mom and Dad will help me.

I can ask Mom and Dad for help.

I don't have to cry, scream, fall off my chair, or hit.

In a quiet voice I can tell Mom or Dad that I don't understand.

In a quiet voice I can tell Mom or Dad that I don't remember.

In a quiet voice I can tell Mom or Dad that I need help.

When I use my quiet voice Mom and Dad are happy.

Mom and Dad are happy when I use my quiet voice.

I will use my quiet voice to tell Mom and Dad that I don't understand.

I will use my quiet voice to tell Mom and Dad that I don't remember.

I will use my quiet voice to tell Mom and Dad that I need help.

Source: Adams, L., Gouvousis, A., VanLue, M., & Waldron, C. (2004). Social story intervention. Improving communication skills in a child with an autism spectrum disorder. *Focus on Austism and Other Developmental Disabilities* 19, 87–94.

WORKING WITH PARAPROFESSIONALS

- *Keep your paraprofessional informed.* Students may have quirks such as having tantrums when they are touched. Inform paraprofessionals about these and other unique characteristics of your students.

- *Educate your paraprofessional.* Paraprofessionals may have limited formal education. They may benefit from some tips on working with students with ASD.

- *Create a schedule.* Use a schedule to help your paraprofessional understand your classroom. If you are out of the class, the schedule can still be followed.

- *Communicate clearly.* Just as it is important to communicate clearly with parents, you should communicate regularly with your paraprofessional so that he or she is aware of minor changes in your classroom or with your students and their families.

- *Vary responsibilities.* Paraprofessionals may become frustrated when they are expected to supervise a student in the restroom day after day. Rotate staff responsibilities so that no person gets stuck with the "dirty work" on a regular basis.

Addressing Challenging Behaviors

Many students who are diagnosed with ASD engage in challenging behaviors. **Challenging behavior** is defined as behavior by a child that results in self-injury or injury to others, causes damage to the physical environment, interferes with the acquisition of new skills, and/or socially isolates the child (Sigafoos, Arthur, & O'Reilly, 2003). Challenging behavior can include disruption, aggression, and self-injury. Disruptive behaviors that students most often exhibit include noncompliance, throwing materials, talking out of turn, and disturbing other students. **Aggression** can include any behavior that involves one student striking another (hitting, kicking, and biting). **Self-injury** includes behaviors in which a student injures himself or herself (e.g., head banging or eye poking).

Challenging behaviors are often a form of communication for students with disabilities. Specifically, students with disabilities engage in challenging behavior because it results in desired outcomes. Given their delays in language, communicating their wants and needs becomes more difficult, and thus challenging behavior becomes an effective form of communication. For example, consider Erin's case from the beginning of the chapter. Erin does not want to work on her sign language; however, she lacks the verbal ability to request a break from work. What Erin has learned is that if she engages in self-injury (head hitting), the teacher will give her a break. In this way head hitting is seen as a form of communication between Erin and her teacher in which Erin is in effect saying, "I do not want to do this." There are many possible messages that children with ASD communicate via challenging behavior. They may use challenging behavior to access a preferred item (Carl's insect book), gain adult attention, or escape from work. These consequences or outcomes of challenging behaviors are known as functions of behavior (Sigafoos et al., 2003).

Using Functional Behavioral Assessment (FBA)

You can determine the function of a student's challenging behavior by completing a functional behavioral assessment (FBA). There are three steps to an FBA (see also Chapter 8 and Tips for Teachers 9.5 for more information on how to handle challenging behavior):

1. Indirect assessments
2. Direct assessments
3. Functional analysis

Indirect Assessments.   These assessments should be completed before direct assessments. **Indirect assessments** include interviews with parents and previous teachers, as well as the completion of rating scales. These interviews and rating scales allow you to clearly describe the challenging behavior, along with some of the possible reasons for why it occurs.

Direct Assessments.   This type of assessment involves observing your student and documenting the sequence of behaviors around the challenging behavior. One example of a **direct assessment** is an ABC sequence chart. Observational assessment should be conducted

PEARSON
myeducationlab

Go to the Building Teaching Skills and Dispositions section of Topic 17: Autism Spectrum Disorders in the MyEducationLab for your course and complete the activity entitled *Using Social Supports and Social Skills Instruction.*

MANAGING CHALLENGING BEHAVIORS

• *Understand why behaviors are occurring.* Students engage in challenging behavior for reasons, usually as a form of communication. A functional behavioral assessment will help you understand why the behaviors are occurring.

• *Be consistent.* All interventions should be implemented consistently so that the student understands what is expected on a daily basis.

• *Make sure that everyone is aware of the student's behavior intervention plan (BIP).* Challenging behaviors usually

occur in all settings. Therefore, everyone, including bus drivers, secretaries, and parents, should implement intervention components.

• *Monitor challenging behavior closely.* It may be difficult to notice when a behavior decreases from 50 times a day to 25 times a day. Use systematic data collection and analysis to monitor your student's progress.

FIGURE 9.3

An ABC Analysis

Child: Manuel
Date and Time of Observation: April 4, 9:40–11:20 AM

What happened before the behavior	Target behavior	What happened after the behavior
Teacher says, "What word is this, Manuel?"	✔	Teacher moves away and asks another student.
Teacher points to a letter and asks, "What letter is this Manuel?"	✔	Teacher moves on to a different topic with the class.
Teacher asks Manuel to open his book.	✔	Teacher does not persist but moves on to another student.

---

during those times of the day when challenging behavior is most likely to occur; it should also be conducted for approximately five school days. Because of the intensity of this observational process, it may be best for a consultant, such as a behavior or autism specialist, to conduct these observations.

An example of an ABC analysis for Manuel, a student with ASD and challenging behavior, is presented in Figure 9.3. The ABC assessment presents data on Manuel's target behavior (head hitting) between 9:40 A.M. and 11:20 A.M. (the time of day when Manuel is most likely to engage in challenging behavior) during a given school day. Each time the target behavior occurs, the teacher places a check mark in the target behavior box (center column). The teacher then describes what happened immediately before the behavior. In the final column, the teacher describes what people did in response to the student's behavior. Three incidents of the target behavior are included in Figure 9.3. You can see from this brief assessment that head hitting occurred when a task demand was placed on Manuel. When he engaged in head hitting, the task was removed. This brief assessment from this particular school day would seem to indicate that Manuel hit his head in order to communicate his desire to escape from demanding tasks.

Functional Analysis. If steps 1 and 2 do not clearly identify the function of your student's challenging behavior, you might need to seek the assistance of a behavioral specialist who can help you design and implement a functional analysis, step 3 of the FBA. A **functional analysis** consists of an experiment in which you manipulate one variable in your classroom to determine its effects on challenging behavior. All possible variables must be manipulated, and rates of challenging behavior must be compared across each condition. For example, if you think your student is trying to escape independent math or is trying to obtain peer attention, you have four manipulations to implement: getting out of math, not getting out of math, getting peer attention, and not getting peer attention. Because this third step of the FBA is time consuming and sometimes provokes more challenging behavior, it is often reserved for research purposes or for times when the function of behavior is not clear after steps 1 and 2 have been completed.

Using Positive Behavioral Support

In the past, teachers and parents addressed challenging behavior by attending to the form of the behavior (e.g., hitting) rather than the function (e.g., obtaining teacher attention). The intervention was implemented after challenging behavior occurred. For example, when a student hit a peer, the teacher told the child to stop hitting. Hypothetically, this reprimand was intended to teach the student that hitting was not tolerated and thus help the student learn not to hit anymore.

Research has shown that these reactive procedures are not as effective at addressing challenging behaviors as the strategy of **positive behavioral supports** (Sigafoos et al., 2003). Positive behavioral supports comprise several key features. First, the approach is based on the sound behavioral science of human behavior. Second, interventions must be practical and based on FBA results. Interventions are implemented in a proactive manner rather than in a traditional reactive manner and focus on teaching new skills that foster independence, improve adaptive skills, or increase effective communication. These interventions also allow individuals with disabilities to access natural communities of reinforcement. Candy and other treats are not provided following the demonstration of a new skill such as talking. Rather, an individual is taught to request pizza in the lunchroom where pizza occurs naturally. Interventions are monitored through systematic data collection and analysis to determine intervention effectiveness.

Another feature of positive behavioral supports is the consideration of social values during the assessment and intervention processes. Behavior change should be observed across all environments of the child's day; it should be durable, lasting through the school and postschool years. Behavior change should be relevant and result in concomitant improvements in social behavior.

Over the years, Horner and his colleagues have conducted a series of studies on the use of positive behavioral supports with students who engaged in challenging behavior. In these studies:

- Teachers conducted functional behavioral assessments.
- A team approach to problem solving and intervention design was used.
- Teachers implemented practical and effective interventions.
- The students were taught new skills.
- Ongoing data collection and monitoring were used.

For example, Todd, Horner, and Sugai (2000) examined a fourth-grade student who was taught to self-monitor, self-evaluate, and self-recruit teacher attention. Teaching him these skills resulted in a decrease in frequency of challenging behavior, an increase in on-task behavior, and an increase in task completion. Vaughn and Horner (1997) compared levels of challenging behavior when students received instruction during preferred and nonpreferred tasks and when teachers rather than students selected tasks. They reported that for two students, rates of challenging behavior were lower when students were able to select tasks, regardless of task preference. Last, Day, Horner, and O'Neill (1994) described an intervention in which students were taught alternative communication in place of challenging behavior. In this study, three participants engaged in challenging behavior to escape difficult tasks or to obtain preferred items. Once they were trained in an alternative communication, challenging behavior decreased and new communication increased.

You will note from this description of research on positive behavioral supports that many of the goals and strategies of positive behavioral support (e.g., to enhance self-control, choice making, communication training) were discussed earlier in this chapter. In fact, you may be able to prevent challenging behavior with many of these students if you use the strategies outlined earlier.

PEARSON
myeducationlab

Go to the Assignments and Activities section of Topic 7: Classroom/Behavior Management in the MyEducationLab for your course and complete the activity *Positive Behavior Support in the Classroom.*

Summary

- PDD includes a number of disabilities, including autism, Asperger syndrome, Rett syndrome, childhood disintegrative disorder, and PDD–NOS. Both Rett and childhood disintegrative disorder are extremely rare. ASD is a subgroup of the PDD categories and includes autism and Asperger syndrome. Both of these diagnostic categories have similar symptoms but differ in terms of the severity of expression of these symptoms.

- The core difficulties experienced by students with ASD include communication and social skills deficits or excesses and rigidity of behavior patterns. These students may also engage in challenging behavior, including self-injury, aggression, and property destruction.

- Although teachers often know who those students are that have been identified with ASD, there may be others who they suspect may need additional supports. In both cases, teachers should document student performance in the areas of language, social, academic, or adaptive behaviors. In some cases, teachers are asked to complete rating scales describing student behavior. Documenting behaviors and monitoring progress helps teachers assess students' progress.

- Key processes for effective instruction for students with ASD include assessing preferences, establishing a classroom routine at the beginning of the year, teaching communication skills, and teaching social skills.

- Many students with ASD engage in challenging behavior. You must understand when, where, and why they engage in such behaviors. This can be accomplished using the FBA process. The results of the FBA can then be incorporated into a behavioral support plan that involves teaching communication skills and modifying the curriculum to make challenging behavior less necessary for the student.

Think and Apply

1. Interview the parents and teachers of a student with ASD to identify preferences for that student. Make a list of five activities/contexts and items that the student likes and dislikes. Then identify ways in which you can incorporate student preferences into the student's instructional routine.

2. Teach a targeted communication skill to a student with ASD using the massed trials format. Then find at least five opportunities to implement the milieu intervention strategy with that same student for the same communication skill.

3. Identify two students with ASD who engage in severe challenging behavior. With their teachers, review the results of their FBA and observe the implementation of the positive behavioral support plan.

PEARSON
myeducationlab

Now go to Topic 17: Autism Spectrum Disorders; Topic 7: Classroom/Behavior Management; and Topic 6: Asssessment in the MyEducationLab (www.myeducationlab.com) for your course where you can:

- Find learning outcomes for these topics along with the national standards that connect to these outcomes.

- Complete Assignments and Activities that can help you more deeply understand the chapter content.

- Examine challenging situations and cases presented in the IRIS Center Resources.

- Apply and practice your understanding of the core teaching skills identified in the chapter with Building Teaching Skills and Dispositions learning units.

Teaching Students with Developmental Disabilities

FOCUS QUESTIONS

1. Who are students with developmental disabilities? How do students with developmental disabilities differ in terms of the nature and degree of their physical, intellectual, and social challenges?

2. What is the prevalence of developmental disabilities? What is your role in the identification process?

3. What are some general guidelines that you, as a classroom teacher, can follow to plan for the needs of students with developmental disabilities in your classroom?

Three years ago, Chris Johnson's experience as a middle-school teacher changed tremendously. For the first time, Chris was assigned a student with intellectual disabilities. Chris remembers his reaction on hearing that he would have Darrell, a student with mild intellectual disabilities, in his eighth-grade applied math class: "One of my main concerns was what am I going to do for Darrell? How am I possibly going to teach him anything? I don't have a special education degree. I feel as if I need one in order to teach him. How is Darrell going to fit in as a member of the class?"

To alleviate these feelings, Chris met with Darrell's special education teacher, Martha Anderson. They reviewed the applied math curriculum in relation to Darrell's IEP goals and objectives. What they quickly realized was that many of Darrell's goals (including skills in measurement, making change, and using fractions and percentages) could be met within the general curriculum.

Each week, Chris discussed the activities and assignments with Martha, and she gave him ideas for modifications. Once a week, Martha worked in the room with Chris so that she could keep up with the curriculum and Darrell's progress. Martha uses math manipulatives and computer programs to provide additional support in learning and applying new concepts. At the end of the first month, Chris said,

> Darrell is a member of our class, just like any of the [other] students. He works on math assignments, although I usually modify them by giving him less to complete, by allowing him to use manipulatives and a calculator, and in some cases giving him different assignments from the other students. Darrell has a great sense of humor and makes a contribution to a positive classroom environment.

By the end of the school year, Chris learned more about Darrell's strengths and challenges as a learner. He also developed genuine ways for Darrell to share his talents with his classmates and to build friendships. Chris also learned a great deal from Darrell's parents and how they worked to build a positive quality of life for their son. As a result of this experience, Chris not only volunteered to partner with Martha in teaching other students with disabilities, but also became involved as a volunteer with his local Best Buddies organization.

Introduction

Chris's initial concerns are those expressed by many general education teachers. Teachers want to give each student their best, but feel that they may not have sufficient knowledge and experience to provide students with developmental disabilities with the support they need. Because IDEIA 2004 mandates access to the general education curriculum, you may have a student like Darrell in your classroom. This chapter provides information about students with developmental disabilities, including intellectual, severe, and multiple disabilities. It also presents guidelines you can use to support students with developmental disabilities in your classroom in their academic and social development. As Chris Johnson learned, working with students with developmental disabilities can be both challenging and rewarding.

Types of Developmental Disabilities

The population of individuals who are considered to have developmental disabilities is quite heterogeneous. **Developmental disabilities** are mental or physical disabilities that impair the person's functioning in language, learning, mobility, self-care, or other important areas of living. These disabilities may range from mild to severe. Students with developmental disabilities present a wide range of characteristics, strengths, and challenges. This section discusses the definitions and types of developmental disabilities.

The U.S. Centers for Disease Control and Prevention (2009) defines developmental disabilities as

> a diverse group of severe chronic conditions that are due to mental and/or physical impairments. People with developmental disabilities have problems with major life activities such as language, mobility, learning, self-help, and independent living. Developmental disabilities begin anytime during development up to 22 years of age and usually last throughout a person's lifetime. (p. 1)

When you consider these major life activities, remember that not every student will experience difficulties in all areas. Moreover, the degree to which limitations manifest themselves in any given area can range from mild to severe. In general, *developmental disabilities* is an umbrella term that can refer to a wide spectrum of intellectual disabilities and severe disabilities including multiple or dual sensory disabilities.

Intellectual Disabilities

Students with **intellectual disabilities** have limited cognitive functioning, which affects their learning. These students have slower rates of learning and are particularly challenged by complex and abstract tasks. Quite often students with intellectual disabilities may have challenges with **adaptive behavior** or the age-appropriate social and practical skills necessarily for daily living (Luckasson et al., 2002; Wehmeyer, Buntinx, Lachapelle, Luckasson, Schalock, & Verdugo, 2008). Students with intellectual disabilities are just like other students in your class in that they are members of families, have friends and neighbors, have personalities shaped by both their innate characteristics and their life experiences, and have aspirations to become adults, get jobs, and fall in love (Orelove, Sobsey, & Silberman, 2004). Yet to be successful in general education classrooms, they also need additional support and accommodations. In planning for this support, it is helpful to have some knowledge about intellectual disabilities and how they affects learning.

The federal definition of **mental retardation** as included in IDEIA 2004 is as follows: "significantly subaverage general intellectual functioning, existing concurrently with deficits in adaptive behavior and manifested during the developmental period, that adversely affects a child's educational performance" (IDEA 34 CFR 300.7[c][6]). However, the term *intellectual disability* is increasingly being used to refer to individuals with mental retardation (Schalock, Luckasson, & Shogren, 2007; Smith, 2008). Indeed, in 2007 the American Association on Mental Retardation (AAMR) officially changed its name to the American Association on Intellectual and Developmental Disabilities (AAIDD). Historically, the view of mental retardation focused primarily on limitations in intellectual functioning (as measured by intelligence tests). Recently, a more optimistic perspective about the quality of life for individuals with mental retardation has evolved. The term *intellectual disabilities* reflects this optimism. The AAIDD has adopted this terminology to reflect evolving views of mental retardation. Similarly, the American Psychological Association's Division of Mental Retardation and Developmental Disabilities changed its name to Division of Intellectual and Developmental Disabilities in 2007.

This current shift reflects a long history of issues and opinions related to mental retardation (Thompson & Wehmeyer, 2008). Indeed, the AAMR, founded in 1876, has issued 10 definitions since 1908. AAMR defined *mental retardation* as follows in 2002: "Mental retardation is a disability characterized by significant limitations both in intellectual functioning and in adaptive behavior as expressed in conceptual, social, and practical adaptive skills" (Luckasson et al., 2002, p. 1).

The following five assumptions are essential to the application of this definition:

1. Limitations in present functioning must be considered within the context of community environments typical of the individual's peers and culture.
2. Valid assessment considers cultural and linguistic diversity, as well as differences in communication, sensory, motor, and behavioral factors.
3. Within an individual, limitations often coexist with strengths.
4. An important purpose of describing limitations is to develop a profile of needed supports.
5. With appropriate personalized supports over a sustained period, the life functioning of the person with mental retardation generally will improve. (Luckasson et al., 2002, p. 1)

In comparison to definitions before 1992, the 2002 definition stressed the interactions among (a) the environment in which the person functions, (b) the person's capabilities, and

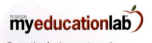

Go to the Assignments and Activities section of Topic 14: Intellectual Disabilities in the MyEducationLab for your course and complete the activity entitled *Students with Mental Retardation in the Integrated Inclusion Classroom*.

(c) the need for varying levels of support (Luckasson et al., 2002). **Systems of support** are the coordinated set of services and accommodations matched to a student's needs and can include teachers and specialists, specialized programs and methodologies, and assistive technology. When appropriate supports are provided over a sustained period, the life functioning of students with mental retardation will generally improve (Luckasson et al., 2002).

In 2007, the AAIDD adapted the 2002 definition as follows: "Intellectual disability is characterized by significant limitations both in intellectual functioning and adaptive behavior as expressed in conceptual, social, and practical skills" (Schalock et al., 2007, p. 118). In essence, the definition refers to the same group of individuals, but reflects language that is less offensive and more consistent with international terminology. Moreover, it retains the importance of appropriate systems of support based on individual needs. The most recent (2007) definition is based on a theoretical framework including five dimensions where individuals with intellectual disabilities may need support: (a) intellectual functioning in school and in daily living; (b) adaptive behavior; (c) health; (d) participation in a variety of social, educational, and professional arenas; and (e) environmental and personal contextual factors (Wehmeyer, Buntinx, Lachapelle, Luckasson, Schalock, & Verdugo, 2008). Systems of support across all five dimensions should be considered in planning for optimal human functioning for individuals with intellectual disabilities.

Before the adoption of the 1992 definition of mental retardation, a traditional classification system was used. The traditional system emphasized the individual's degree of retardation (i.e., mild retardation: IQ scores of 50–55 to 70–75; moderate retardation: IQ scores of 35–40 to 50–55; severe retardation: IQ scores of 20–25 to 35–40; profound retardation: IQ scores below 20–25) (American Psychiatric Association, 2000). These categories are published in the *Diagnostic and Statistical Manual of Mental Disorders* (DSM-IV-TR). The fifth edition of this manual is currently underway with a projected publication date of 2012. The upcoming edition is projected to use the term *intellectual disability* rather than *mental retardation*.

The AAIDD publishes an assessment scale based on levels of support. The Supports Intensity Scale (Thompson et al., 2004) identifies the level of support individuals may need in home living, community living, lifelong learning, employment, health and safety, social interaction, and protection and advocacy. Case managers, psychologists, or social workers complete the scale by interviewing the individual with disabilities and key family members or caretakers to determine the needs for each of the support areas. The intent of this measure is to focus more on the supports needed to function as independently as possible.

Go to **www.aamr.org/**, the website of the American Association on Intellectual and Developmental Disabilities, where you will find a variety of resources including journal articles, newsletters, and more.

Physical Causes of Intellectual Disabilities

There are multiple causes for intellectual disabilities including genetic, other physical causes, and nonphysical causes. *The Educator's Diagnostic Manual of Disabilities and Disorders* (Pierangelo & Giuliani, 2007) lists 50 potential causes of intellectual disabilities using the following superordinate categories: chromosomal abnormalities, disorders of brain formation, metabolic disorders, maternal infections, fetal intoxicant exposure, gestational disorders, postnatal environmental problems, and other causes (e.g., postnatal conditions, intoxicants, or brain diseases). As many as 40% to 50% of individuals with intellectual disabilities may not have the cause of the disability identified (Luckasson et al., 2002). Although it is beyond the scope of this chapter to describe *each* of the potential causes, we will focus on some that you are most likely to encounter: chromosomal disorders, fragile X syndrome, and fetal alcohol syndrome.

Chromosomal Disorders. Chromosomal disorders are probably the best-known cause of intellectual disabilities. **Down syndrome** is one of the most common chromosomal disorders and is often what people think of when mental retardation is mentioned. Down syndrome occurs in about 1 in 733 to 1,000 live births (National Down Syndrome Society, 2009). Individuals with Down syndrome experience mild to moderate intellectual disability and have strong promise for success in school and in the world of work with proper supports. Although they are prone to health problems such as congenital heart defects and thyroid conditions, with improved health care life expectancy of individuals with Down syndrome has steadily increased.

Fragile X Syndrome.   **Fragile X syndrome** is the most common form of intellectual disability that is passed from parent to child (National Institutes of Health and Human Development, 2009). Individuals with fragile X syndrome can manifest a range of intellectual disabilities from mild to severe. Their challenges can also include social and emotional difficulties, speech and language problems, and sensitivity to sensory input such as bright light or loud sounds. Some, but not all, males with fragile X syndrome have physical symptoms including an elongated face and large ears. The symptoms associated with fragile X syndrome are typically more severe with boys than with girls. Similarly, the prevalence of fragile X syndrome is higher with males (1 in 3,600 live births) than with females (1 in 4,000 to 6,000 live births) (National Fragile X Foundation, 2009).

Fetal Alcohol Syndrome.   **Fetal alcohol syndrome (FAS)**, one of the top three known causes of birth defects, refers to a spectrum of birth defects caused by the mother's drinking during pregnancy and is fast becoming the leading cause of mental retardation. Estimates are as high as 1 in 100 live births resulting in FAS according to the National Organization on Fetal Alcohol Syndrome (NOFAS) (2009). Children with FAS may experience some degree of intellectual disabilities, poor coordination, psychosocial behavior problems, physical abnormalities, and speech and language problems (NOFAS, 2009). In addition to alcohol, maternal use of drugs or tobacco can also cause birth defects and potential intellectual disabilities (March of Dimes, 2006).

Other Physical Causes of Intellectual Disabilities.   Other physical causes include infections, low birth weight, diseases (e.g., measles, meningitis), malnutrition, and exposure to toxins (Pierangelo & Giuliani, 2007). Nonphysical causes include various forms of child abuse (e.g., shaken baby syndrome) and neglect (e.g., inadequate health care), poverty (e.g., unsafe neighborhoods), lack of stimulation, and lack of opportunity to develop communication, social, and adaptive skills (AAIDD, 2009b; Pierangelo & Giuliani, 2007).

Numerous nonprofit organizations have been organized and broadened to address the needs of individuals with intellectual disabilities (e.g., American Association on Intellectual and Developmental Disabilities, www.aamr.org; The ARC of the United States, www.thearc.org; National Down Syndrome Society, ww.ndss.org). Although their foci and missions vary, most organizations do provide resources for research in addition to providing information for individuals with disabilities and their families as well as for teachers and the community at large. Most nonprofit organizations serve as advocacy groups for the individuals they represent and emphasize the supports needed to ensure a high quality of life.

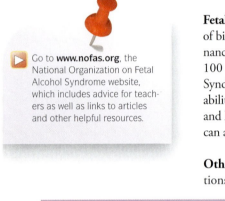

Go to **www.nofas.org**, the National Organization on Fetal Alcohol Syndrome website, which includes advice for teachers as well as links to articles and other helpful resources.

What types of resources are available to teachers to help them help their students with physical and intellectual disabilities participate in classroom activities?

Severe Disabilities

Severe disabilities are often described as conditions in which typical life activities are significantly affected. Among those who are considered to have severe disabilities are

- Students whose intellectual disability is severe or profound
- Students who have multiple disabilities (e.g., significant intellectual disability and physical disabilities or intellectual disability and a sensory disability)
- Students who have dual sensory impairments (i.e., deaf–blind)

The Association for Persons with Severe Handicaps (TASH) defines persons with severe disabilities as

Individuals with disabilities of all ages, races, creeds, national origins, genders and sexual orientations who require ongoing support in one or more major life activities in order to participate in an integrated community and enjoy a quality of life similar to that available to all citizens. Support may be required for life activities such as mobility, communication, self-care, and learning as necessary for community living, employment and self-sufficiency. (TASH, 2000, p. 1)

In general, students with severe disabilities may experience difficulties in intellectual, motor, communication, and/or social skills. The combination of needs is unique to each student, thus you will want to know as much as possible about a student enrolled in your class from parents, caregivers, and other professionals.

PEARSON
myeducationlab

Go to the Teacher Talk section of Topic 14: Intellectual Disabilities in the MyEducationLab for your course and listen to teacher Conney Dahn talk about her high expectations for her students with severe disabilities.

Intellectual Skills.   Although students with severe disabilities have many diverse learning characteristics, they generally learn slowly and often fail to notice relevant features of what is being taught, do not demonstrate learned skills spontaneously, and have difficulty generalizing learned skills to new situations (Heward, 2009). These students also have difficulty learning complex skills and abstract concepts, have difficulty making generalizations, and learn less overall than other students do. Many students with developmental disabilities experience memory deficits, either remembering incorrectly or not remembering automatically.

Motor Skills.   The physical disabilities commonly found among individuals with severe disabilities include cerebral palsy, spina bifida, seizure disorders, hydrocephalus, and cardiovascular disorders. (Chapter 11 discusses physical disabilities in more detail.) Many students with severe disabilities cannot move independently and need assistance from wheelchairs, walkers, and braces. Other students may have limited voluntary movement of any type and may experience difficulty grasping items, holding up their heads, and rolling over.

Communication Skills.   Communication is important for students with severe disabilities because it gives them some control over their environment and a way to fulfill their wants and needs (see Chapter 7 for more about communication disorders). It is also an important key to being socially accepted. Students with severe disabilities might not acquire speech, or their speech might be difficult to understand for people who do not interact with them often (Arthur-Kelly, Foreman, Bennett, & Pascoe, 2008). Yet it is important to realize that a lack of speech does not preclude communication.

Communication can occur through gestures, facial expressions, eye blinks, and behavior and through augmentative and alternative communication. Low-technology devices can involve pictures or drawings at which the student points to convey a message. High-technology devices can provide voice output (speech synthesizers) and can be programmed with many messages. Ideas to help students with developmental disabilities develop communication skills are discussed in Tips for Teachers 10.1.

Tips FOR TEACHERS 10.1

HELPING STUDENTS DEVELOP COMMUNICATION SKILLS

- *Give students a reason to communicate.* By anticipating the needs of students with mental retardation and severe disabilities, we often deprive them of reasons to communicate. Create situations that motivate students to communicate. For example, you might "accidentally" forget to give them their lunch tickets when the rest of the class receives their tickets, or have every student tell you about the drawing they just did before they can go out to recess. Working on communication skills during everyday activities is known to significantly increase students' desire to communicate.

- *Determine the best mode of communication.* Make sure that students have a way, as well as a reason, to communicate. If your students do not use speech, they should have an augmentative communication device. If your students do not have a mode of communication, talk with the school's speech and language pathologist or inclusion specialist about developing or purchasing one.

- *Give students a way to make choices.* Self-stick notes provide a quick and easy way to give students with disabilities on-the-spot choices (choosing a word to fill in the blank, choosing a color) to facilitate their participation in class. Just write the choices on the notes and stick them on the students' desks so that they can make the choices. To help students choose a partner, take pictures of all the students in the class (or use individual class photos) and paste them in a little book or on a board so that the student with a disability can choose the person with whom he or she wants to work on a class assignment.

PROVIDING SCHOOL SUPPORT THROUGH CIRCLES OF FRIENDS

Purpose: To integrate students with disabilities into the general education classroom

Materials: Paper and writing/drawing implements

Procedures: In this activity, each student in the classroom completes a picture of his or her circles of friends, using the following steps:

1. Have students draw four circles.
   - In the first circle, students list the people closest to them, the people they love.
   - In the second circle, students list the people they really like (but not enough to put in the first circle).
   - In the third circle, students list groups of people they like or people they do things with (e.g., scouts, soccer team).
   - In the fourth circle, students list people who are paid to be in their lives (e.g., doctor, dentist).

2. After students have completed their own circles of friends, describe the circles for a fantasy person who is similar to the student who will be joining the class. For example, a student might have only Mom listed in the first circle, with the second and third circles empty. In the fourth circle are a number of doctors and therapists. Through discussion, talk with the students about how the student must feel and how this fantasy person is similar to the student with disabilities who is going to join the class.

3. Finally, the teacher and students plan how they can become part of the circles of friends for the student with disabilities through such activities as classroom ambassadors, telephone buddies, lunch buddies, and reading buddies.

Source: Based on Forest, M., & Lusthaus, E. (1989). Promoting educational equality for all students: Circles and maps. In S. Stainback, W. Stainback, and M. Forest (Eds.), *Educating all students in the mainstream of regular education* (pp. 45–57). Baltimore: Brookes.

Because students are unable to express their desires or dislikes verbally, they express them through their behavior. Students with severe disabilities often engage in isolated inappropriate behaviors such as stereotypic or self-injurious behaviors. **Stereotypic behaviors** include rocking, flapping fingers, twirling or spinning objects, and grinding teeth. **Self-injurious behavior** may consist of head banging, scratching, or self-biting and is difficult to understand. One of several theories about why children exhibit these behaviors is that they are a means of communicating or regulating the child's own level of awareness (Helmstetter & Durand, 1991; Johnson, Baumgart, Helmstetter, & Curry, 1996).

Social Skills.   Students with developmental disabilities have friends and participate in social activities but often have difficulties developing friendships. Such difficulties may be due to behaviors that deter interactions or to lack of opportunity (Westling & Fox, 2009). With the move toward inclusion of students with developmental disabilities in the general education classroom, they have more opportunities to develop friendships and build solid social relationships (Hunt & McDonnell, 2007).

Circles of Friends (Forest & Lusthaus, 1989; Fredrickson & Turner, 2003; Miller, Cooke, Test, & White, 2003) is one example of an activity that can promote social support for students with disabilities as they are integrated into general education classrooms. In this activity, each student in the classroom completes a picture of his or her circles of friends, following the steps in Activities for All Learners.

Multiple Disabilities.   Individuals with **multiple disabilities** have mental retardation that is severe or profound, as well as one or more significant motor or sensory impairments or special health needs. For example, a person with severe mental retardation might also have cerebral palsy or epilepsy (Orelove et al., 2004; Westling & Fox, 2009). Types of multiple disabilities include mental retardation with physical disabilities (e.g., cerebral palsy, spina bifida, seizure disorders), mental retardation with severe behavior disorders, and mental retardation with a visual or hearing impairment. It is reasonable to expect that two of every five students with severe and multiple disabilities will have a sensory impairment (Sobsey & Wolf-Schein, 1996). IDEIA 2004 defines *multiple disabilities* as

concomitant impairments (such as mental retardation–blindness, mental retardation–orthopedic impairments, etc.), the combination of which causes such severe educational needs that cannot be accommodated in special education programs solely for one of the impairments. The term does not include deaf–blindness. (IDEA 34 CFR 300.7 [c][7])

Like all students, students with multiple disabilities have learning needs that require a *holistic* approach to education (an approach in which the student is viewed as a whole person). In determining educational goals and teaching strategies, professionals consider factors such as the student's emotions, cognitive processes, and other factors that interact with the environment to produce behavior (Downing, 2002).

Dual Sensory Impairments. Students with **dual sensory impairments** (also referred to as **deaf–blind**) present unique challenges in that the two main channels (auditory and visual) of receptive communication and learning are impaired. Although difficult to determine, the cognitive abilities of students with dual sensory impairments can vary from severe retardation to giftedness. Individuals who are deaf–blind may have diverse combinations of vision and hearing impairments with normal or gifted intelligence, or they may have additional mental, physical, and behavioral disabilities (Downing & Eichinger, 2003; Orelove et al., 2004). The IDEIA 2004 defines deaf–blindness as follows:

What factors must be taken into account when planning instruction for students with severe or multiple disabilities?

> Deaf–blindness means concomitant hearing and visual impairments, the combination of which causes such severe communication and other developmental and education needs that they cannot be accommodated in special education programs solely for children with deafness or children with blindness. (IDEA 34 CFR 300.7 [c][2])

Because these individuals do not receive clear and consistent information from either sensory modality, a tendency exists to turn inward. These individuals may appear passive, not responding to or initiating interactions with others.

Go to **www.unl.edu/spedsev/resource.html** for links to resources on students with severe disabilities.

Prevalence and Identification of Students with Developmental Disabilities

The prevalence of persons with developmental disabilities is difficult to determine because different definitions and methodologies are used to determine various conditions under this large umbrella (Stoneman, 2009). Generally, however, prevalence is estimated to be about 1% of the school population (National Center for Educational Statistics, 2009). According to the federal government, 487,854 students were eligible for IDEIA services and were identified as individuals with mental retardation (National Center for Educational Statistics, 2009). Prevalence of multiple disabilities is also difficult to determine, as different states use different classification systems (e.g., some states include students with multiple disabilities under the category of physical disabilities). In 2008, the same federal report indicated 13,347 receiving services under the category of multiple disabilities. In the category of deaf–blind, the federal government reported in 2008 that 1,310 students were served under IDEIA.

Before the passage of the Individuals with Disabilities Education Act (IDEA) in 1975, many students with developmental disabilities were not allowed to attend public schools. This federal legislation required that educational services be provided for all students, including students with severe and profound retardation and severe disabilities. One result was the need for better methods of identification and assessment for educational purposes. With the passage of IDEA amendments in 1986 (P.L. 99–457), these children became eligible to receive special education services as infants and toddlers and in preschool (see Chapter 1). More recent amendments to IDEA in 2004 have ensured access to the general education curriculum.

Identification of Students with Developmental Disabilities

For students with all but mild mental retardation, initial identification is usually a medical diagnosis made at birth or shortly thereafter. For students with mild mental retardation, initial identification often occurs during preschool when the child's rate of development in cognitive, language, and motor skills is not typical. For these students, the emphasis is on developmental and educational assessment, which usually includes measures of general intelligence and measures of adaptive behavior.

Standardized assessments such as the Wechsler Intelligence Scale–IV (Kaplan, Fein, Kramer, Delis, & Morris, 2004) are widely used to gauge eligibility for special education services. Although intelligence tests are commonly used to determine whether students have developmental disabilities, a number of concerns have been raised. First, it can be difficult to know whether the tests accurately reflect the students' capacity to learn, particularly given their difficulty with communication and their delayed responses. Second, there is continuing concern regarding cultural influences and biases in tests of intellectual functioning (Klingner, Blanchett, & Harry, 2007). Factors influencing student performance on intelligence tests include family history and home life, duration of study in the United States, language proficiency, socioeconomic status, prior educational experiences, test-wiseness, and cultural background. Given the disproportionate representation of minorities (particularly African American) students receiving special education services for developmental disabilities, issues related to equity and intelligence tests need continued exploration (Klingner et al., 2007).

Another area used to determine evidence of developmental disability is the student's adaptive behavior. One frequently used adaptive behavior scale is the second edition of the AAMR Adaptive Behavior Scale—School (Dixon, 2007; Lambert, Nihira, & Leland, 1993), which includes domains for both adaptive and social behaviors. The AAIDD is currently in the process of developing a new standardized assessment tool, the Diagnostic Adaptive Behavior Scale (DABS), which is scheduled for availability in 2010 (AAIDD, 2009a). DABS is being designed to assess conceptual, social, and practical skills domains. Unlike previous assessments normed only on individuals with impaired adaptive behaviors, DABS is being normed on individuals with and without such challenges to compare performance on the assessment with the general population. Klingner and colleagues (2007) caution that assessment of adaptive behavior must be evaluated within a cultural context and that assessment should occur before placement in special education.

Teacher's Role in Identifying Students with Developmental Disabilities

As a classroom teacher, what is your role in the identification of students with developmental disabilities or in their identification for special education services? If you observe a student in your classroom with persistent difficulties in learning tasks or adaptive behavior, begin documenting your observations quickly. Follow procedures in your school district about whom to contact first (e.g., the school principal, counselor) and when and how to approach parents about your concerns. You may be asked to participate in prereferral interventions to determine whether, with available supports, the student can function successfully. Once the referral process begins, administration and interpretation of findings from intelligence tests and adaptive behavior assessments will be the responsibility of a school psychologist or an independently contracted professional. You may be asked (along with parents) to provide input on the adaptive behavior assessments. You may also be asked to provide anecdotal records, student test scores, and work samples.

Communicating and Collaborating with Families

Along the way, your role in communicating and collaborating with families in positive and supportive ways is vital. For all students, but particularly for students with developmental disabilities, families play an important role in assessment. This is evident in the IDEIA emphasis on the role of families in identifying and assessing students with disabilities and in planning for the students' individual education programs. Classroom teachers can also benefit from family input when students with developmental disabilities are included in their classrooms. No one knows the student better than his or her family.

PEARSON myeducationlab

Go to the Assignments and Activities section of Topic 5: Prereferrals, Placement and IEP Process in the MyEducationLab for your course and complete the activity entitled *Prereferral Interventions*.

Guidelines for Teaching Students with Developmental Disabilities

Teachers who have students with developmental disabilities in their classrooms are asked to participate in their students' educational plans, work with the students, and communicate and work with the paraprofessionals and specialists who provide support. Douglas Akers, a fifth-grade teacher, has been working for several months with Amy, a student with Down syndrome and moderate retardation, who is being included in general education classes for the first time. Reflecting on Amy entering his class, Doug comments:

> I wanted to establish a good rapport with Amy. I wanted her to take directions from me, not just to rely on her aide or the special education teacher. I wanted Amy to develop a relationship with me and feel comfortable coming to me or the other students for assistance. I knew this would take time because she has always been in a self-contained special education class. But now she does come to me with her work and with questions.

The instructional guidelines and accommodations discussed here will help you to include students with developmental disabilities in your class and to develop a social support network that will facilitate these students' success. Tech Tips will provide you with tools that can help students with a variety of developmental disabilities.

PEARSON
myeducationlab

Go to the Assignments and Activities section of Topic 14: Intellectual Disabilities in the MyEducationLab for your course and compete the activity entitled *Assistive Technology*.

Role of the General Education Teacher

With the move toward inclusive schools, the roles of special education and general education teachers have changed considerably in the past two decades. The role of the general education teacher is to be involved in and problem solve adaptations and curriculum modifications for all students.

At the beginning of this chapter, you read about the changes Chris Johnson experienced when Darrell was enrolled in his middle school class. With the help of his special education colleague, Chris learned there are three key roles that he could assume to guide students with disabilities.

1. Take ownership of students with disabilities by demonstrating that these students are members of the class and that they are valued (Downing & Peckham-Hardin, 2007). When this happens, students with disabilities develop a sense of belonging and being accepted. For Chris and his class, Darrell was just another member of the applied math class.

TechTips

ASSISTIVE TECHNOLOGIES FOR STUDENTS WITH DEVELOPMENTAL DISABILITIES

Once teachers become familiar with students' limitations due to their developmental disabilities, whether they are physical or intellectual, there are many sources for assistive devices. Finding the right tool for students can help them both reach their potential and become part of the classroom community. Sources include the following:

Enabling Devices at
▶ http://enablingdevices.com/catalog/useful-devices provides a wide array of products for individuals with disabilities such as a Perceptual Motor Trainer, which helps teach hand–eye coordination and a Slant Board, which helps with handwriting training.

Enable Mart at
▶ www.enablemart.com offers assistive technologies, both hardware and software, that accommodate individuals with disabilities and communication disorders.

Ablenet Inc. at
▶ www.ablenetinc.com provides tools and resources for children and teachers to accommodate students with intellectual and physical disabilities.

RJ Cooper & Associates at
▶ www.rjcooper.com provides assistive technologies to schools or individuals to help students with special needs.

2. Become familiar with the full range of goals and objectives on the student's IEP. Appropriate planning and adaptation for students with developmental disabilities requires careful analysis of tasks to be accomplished and some creativity (Downing & Peckham-Hardin, 2007). Having a strong command of the IEPs makes planning more fluent and systematic.

3. A paraprofessional or aide may be assigned to a student with disabilities for all or part of the school day. Your role is to plan curriculum and adaptations for all students in the classroom, frequently in collaboration with a special educator. Although paraprofessionals can be involved in the planning process, they should not take on that responsibility in isolation. Because most paraprofessionals do not have preparation in curriculum and instruction, their role is to supplement your planning and instruction (Giangreco, 2009; Pickett, 2008). With appropriate preparation and supervision, paraprofessionals can provide vital instructional roles (Keller, Bucholz, & Brady, 2007). When a student is assigned a paraprofessional on a one-to-one basis, in-class isolation of the student with disabilities can result (Causton-Theoharis & Malmgren, 2005; Giangreco, 2009). Thus, you should also discuss specific strategies for using peer support and for developing meaningful interactions with peers to promote inclusion and formation of friendships (Hebdon, 2008).

Planning Systems

Planning is critical for all students, but it is particularly so for students with developmental disabilities, whose learning goals may differ from those of other students in the class. The standards-based reform movement has strong implications for academic outcomes of students with developmental disabilities (Browder, Trela, Gibbs, Wakeman, & Harris, 2009; Lee, Soukup, Little, & Wehmeyer, 2009). The No Child Left Behind Act (NCLB, 2001) and the 2004 reauthorization of IDEA have mandated increased access to the general education curriculum for students with disabilities (Hardman & Dawson, 2008). This includes requirements for students with disabilities to meet academic standards and, to the degree outlined in the student's IEP, to participate in high-stakes testing (Downing & Peckham-Hardin, 2007; Parrish & Stodden, 2009).

In the past, students with developmental disabilities have often been assigned low academic expectations and alternative instructional activities emphasizing life skills and adaptive behaviors (Friend, 2005a; Wehmeyer, Lattin, Lapp-Rincker, & Agran, 2003; Weiner, 2005). Although some educators maintain that alternative instructional activities are appropriate, others argue that with careful planning and adaptations, there is hope that the level of expectations and student academic outcomes can be raised. Indeed, some states are rewriting curricular standards with specific considerations for students with cognitive disabilities. For example, in the State of Florida, specific requirements for students with disabilities have been identified for state standards to facilitate appropriate instruction for students with cognitive disabilities (State of Florida, 2009).

The movement toward increased access to the general education curriculum for students with disabilities makes joint planning by the special education and classroom teachers imperative (Parrish & Stodden, 2009). When Jeannette Robinson heard that she was going to have a student with developmental disabilities in her third-grade classroom (Steven), she was concerned that she would be responsible for writing lesson plans and making all the adaptations. She felt overwhelmed until she realized that it was a team process and that the special education teacher would help her plan. She said, "I'm so relieved. I feel much more positive now. I didn't know how I was going to do it." Realizing that it is a team process and that everyone has knowledge to contribute is important. In the following sections several planning systems that can support joint planning are presented.

Planning Pyramid. One planning system is the planning pyramid (Schumm, Vaughn, & Leavell, 1994; Schumm & Avalos, 2009). As you read in Chapter 3, the planning pyramid is a framework for planning for differentiated instruction in the general education classroom.

Jeannette Robinson was planning for a unit on weathering and erosion. She wrote in the base of the pyramid what she wanted *all* students to learn based on state curricular standards. The first year she used the planning pyramid, this goal was appropriate for all the students in

FIGURE
10.1

Planning Pyramid with Modifications for a Student with Significant Disabilities

What some students will learn.
- How earth looked during Ice Age
- Disasters caused by sudden changes
- Geographic examples of slow and fast changes

What most students will learn.
- Compare and contrast weathering and erosion
- How humans cause physical and chemical weathering
- Basic types of rocks

What ALL* students should learn.
- Basic components of Earth's surface
- Forces that change crust are weathering and erosion

Steven—identify 3 types of weather and the appropriate clothing.

her class, but when Jeannette taught the unit the next year, Steven, a student with autism and limited language and cognitive skills, was assigned to her class. During weekly planning time, Jeannette talked about the unit with the inclusion specialist and paraprofessional who supported Steven. They decided that Steven's content goals would be to identify three types of weather (e.g., sunny, rainy, and snowy) and the type of clothing worn in each type of weather. Jeannette noted these specific goals on the unit planning sheet. Refer to Figure 10.1 to see how Jeannette planned her unit on weathering and erosion to accommodate all of her students.

Although Steven would participate in a number of the activities planned for the unit and continue to work on his general language and social goals (e.g., working with others and sharing, communicating wants and feelings), the paraprofessional would work with him on these content goals. The paraprofessional also prepared materials for Steven to take home for home learning assignments.

McGill Action Planning System (MAPS).   When working with a student with severe disabilities, you should participate in planning for the student's long-range goals, which are incorporated into the IEP. The **McGill Action Planning System (MAPS)** (Circle of Inclusion Project, 2002; Klein-Ezell, LaRusso, & Ezell, 2008; Lusthaus & Forest, 1987) is one example of such a planning system. The purpose of this planning activity is to foster relationships to improve the quality of life for people with severe disabilities and to facilitate participation in inclusive settings such as a general education classroom.

In the MAPS process, the student, his or her family and friends, and special and general educators establish a team. Because peers are important to the process, students from the classroom generally participate in the team (Hamill & Everington, 2002; Vandercook, York, & Forest, 1989). This team answers seven questions, using them to brainstorm methods to plan the student's future in an inclusive environment. Answers to the seven questions help to determine the goals and objectives. Figure 10.2 provides an example of the MAPS questions and ideas for Tyrone, a high-school student with severe mental retardation.

Choosing Outcomes and Accommodations for Children (COACH).   This planning system is designed for developing an appropriate educational program for students with severe disabilities in the general education setting (Giangreco, Cloninger, & Iverson, 1998). COACH focuses on individualization, family participation, and the active involvement of related service providers.

Person-Centered Planning.   For students with developmental disabilities, it is important to plan beyond the students' school experiences, particularly as these students reach middle and high school. **Person-centered planning** for their transition into adult life in terms of vocation and adult living is critical to their success (Wehmeyer, Sands, Knowlton, & Kozleski, 2002). Person-centered planning (Dunlap & Carr, 2007: Holburn & Cea, 2007; Schwartz, Jacobson, & Holburn, 2000) builds from such techniques as MAPS and Circles of Friends to

myeducationlab

Go to the Building Teaching Skills and Dispositions section of Topic 11: Transition Planning in the MyEducationLab for your course and complete the activity entitled *Participating in the Creation of an Effective Transition Plan*.

FIGURE 10.2

MAPS Questions and Ideas Generated for Tyrone

1. What is the individual's history?
Tyrone developed meningitis shortly after birth, which resulted in brain damage. He learned to walk and talk much later than normal.

2. What is your dream for the individual?
Tyrone will find a job in the community, where he can interact with many people, and a place to live with friends.

3. What is your nightmare?
Tyrone will be alone after we (parents) pass away.

4. Who is the individual?
Tyrone is a young man who loves music and talking to people. He is an only child. He is a sophomore in high school. He loves sports. He gets lonely and bored when alone for long periods of time.

5. What are the individual's strengths, gifts, and abilities?
He loves to laugh and smiles a lot. He works hard. He has a great sense of humor. He's energetic. He is sensitive to others' moods.

6. What are the individual's needs?
He needs friends his own age with whom to do things. He needs to be more assertive and ask for help when necessary. He needs to be more independent in food preparation and in getting around the community.

7. What would the individual's ideal day at school look like and what must be done to make it happen?
A Circles of Friends should be done with Tyrone so that he has friends to meet when he gets off the bus and to hang out with during lunch and breaks. Tyrone should participate in some community-based instruction. Tyrone should take a Foods class.

---

provide long-range planning and transition. As part of the process, the student's circle of support map is developed by the student, family, educators, and other key support persons. As a classroom teacher, you may be involved in this process and in the process of aligning school-based curriculum with the transition goals.

Functional Assessment, Discrepancy Analysis, and Task Analysis

Functional assessment, discrepancy analysis, and task analysis are important planning tools for determining the skills the students with developmental disabilities need to reach established goals. In a **functional assessment**, each goal or activity is broken into steps or subskills, and the student's present performance level is determined for each subskill or step in the activity. A **discrepancy analysis** reviews each specific step or skill and determines how the student does the step or skill compared to nondisabled peers. Next, a **task analysis** (a further breakdown of each individual step or skill, with the necessary adaptations) is used as a guide to teach the step or skill to the student. For example, the 60-Second Lesson describes how to develop a picture task analysis.

In Figure 10.3, a functional analysis and discrepancy analysis is done for Marta, an eighth-grade student with moderate mental retardation and cerebral palsy. Notice how when Marta is unable to perform a step or skill, such as going to her locker, it is indicated in the third column (i.e., a discrepancy exists). From there, the teacher determines whether the student should be taught that particular step or skill or whether an adaptation should be made to help the student perform the skill. The fourth column shows the adaptations and instruction that will occur as a result of the functional assessment and discrepancy analysis.

The same goals can be assessed across the different environments in which the activities occur. Mary Hinson, Marta's high-school job developer, assessed "arriving and getting started" as part of placing Marta in her first job in an

How would you identify the skills the student needs to succeed? What opportunities does this learning situation provide for the functional practice of these skills?

60 Second LESSON

DEVELOPING A PICTURE TASK ANALYSIS

Picture task analyses, by providing visual cues of the steps of a task, enable students with mental disabilities to gain meaningful skills and independence. A picture is taken of each step in a task. Then the pictures are glued (in sequential order) in a manila folder, with a number under each picture. Laminating the whole folder helps to preserve the photographs. An erasable pen enables students to cross off pictures as the steps are completed. How might you develop a picture schedule for Marta (see Figure 10.3)?

For more information, see "Using a Picture Task Analysis to Teach Students With Multiple Disabilities," by W. Roberson, J. Gravel, G. Valcante, and R. Maurer (1992), in *Teaching Exceptional Children, 24*(4), 12–16.

office: putting on labels and doing simple packaging. For a number of steps, the adaptations made at school could easily be made at work.

Authentic and Alternate Assessment

Authentic assessment makes a link between goals and objectives for your students and the documentation of progress toward meeting those goals and objectives (Layton & Lock, 2007). Many of the types of authentic assessment you read about in this book can be adapted for students with developmental disabilities. Curriculum-based assessment and portfolio assessment are two approaches appropriate for students with developmental disabilities (Hamill & Everington, 2002; Klein-Ezell et al., 2008). **Curriculum-based assessment (CBA)** is a way to monitor ongoing progress in acquisition of basic skills. Hammill and Everington note that some adaptations (e.g., extended time, alternative response modes) may need to be made for students with developmental disabilities. **Portfolio assessment** involves compilation of multiple artifacts or student work samples.

FIGURE 10.3

Functional Assessment and Discrepancy Analysis

Student: Marta is an eighth-grade student with moderate mental retardation and cerebral palsy.
Activity: Arriving at school

Steps of the Activity	Student Performance	Discrepancy Analysis	Teach or Adapt
1. Arrives at school by bus	+		
2. Goes to locker	−	Cannot propel herself	Peers will wait by bus
3. Opens locker	−	Doesn't remember combination	Use key lock
4. Gets notebooks, etc., out	−	Can't reach items	Put items in backpack on hook
5. Hangs out/does hair until class	−	Doesn't initiate conversations	Develop "Circles of Friends"
6. Goes to class when bell rings	−	Can't self-propel that far	Ask classmates to help
7. Listens to announcements in homeroom	+		
8. Raises hand to indicate will eat lunch	+		
9. Goes to first hour when bell rings	−	Doesn't know which class is at this time	Teach to review a picture schedule and ask for help

Code: + = can do step − = cannot do step

Although somewhat cumbersome and time consuming, portfolios provide tangible evidence of student progress.

In addition to the authentic assessment tools you use in your class, you should also become familiar with **alternate assessment** policies in your state and school district for students with disabilities in meeting requirements for high-stakes tests. IDEIA 2004 and No Child Left Behind (2001) require that students with disabilities participate in high-stakes testing. In many cases, accommodations such as extended time will be sufficient for participation. For some students, alternate means are necessary to provide fair and equitable assessment (Towles-Reeves, Kleinert, & Muhomba, 2009). Alternate assessments are based on alternate achievement standards (AA-AAS) for students with disabilities. AA-AAS is "the primary method through which students with the most significant cognitive disabilities participate in measures of educational assessment and school accountability" (Towles-Reeves et al., 2009). Portfolios, checklists, and one-to-one performance assessment are the most commonly used methods for alternate assessment that states might use (Roeber, 2002).

Partial Participation

An opportunity to participate should not be denied because a person cannot independently perform the needed skills; instead, individualized adaptations should be developed to allow participation and learning, even if of only part of the skill. The concept of **partial or parallel participation** assumes that an individual has the right to participate in all activities to the extent possible (Hamill & Everington, 2002). Active participation not only helps to maintain students' physical health, but also enhances their image, as peers see them partaking in a meaningful activity. Say, for example, that a class is working on writing sentences using correct punctuation. A classmate randomly selects three small pictures and places them on Heather's desk. Heather, a student with a severe disability, has to reach out and point to one of the pictures. Her goals are to reach and point, to look at her peer, and to make decisions in a timely fashion. The peer then holds up the picture for the class to see. The class writes a sentence about it, and Heather must answer a question about it.

Curriculum Adaptations

In looking at the variables that contribute to successful access to the general education curriculum, researchers Lee, Soukup, Little, and Wehmeyer (2008) concluded that curriculum adaptations were extremely important for students with intellectual and developmental disabilities. Wolfe and Hall (2003) recommend that special education–general education teams use a **cascade of integration options**. As they put it, "This cascade of services highlights the need to individualize and base decisions for placement on the student's unique needs" (p. 56). The cascade of integration options can be used to guide teams in making decisions about the appropriate activities (same, similar, different), objectives (same, related, or unrelated), and settings (inside or outside the general education classroom) for instruction. Table 10.1 presents examples of curriculum for students with developmental disabilities.

TABLE 10.1	Adapted Curriculum Outcomes for Students with Developmental Disabilities		
	GRADE LEVEL	**TYPICAL OUTCOMES**	**ADAPTED OUTCOMES**
	Grade 2: Reading	Learn 10 words per week, and be able to spell them correctly.	Learn 5 grocery words (e.g., *apple, shampoo*), and be able to recognize them.
	Grade 4: Writing	Read a story and write a report, using correct grammar, punctuation, and spelling.	Listen to taped story, and record a personal reaction to the story.
	Grade 6: Social Studies	Locate all continents on a map, and name 3 countries per continent.	Locate own continent on a map, and name 3 countries on own continent.

Source: Adapted from Wehman, P. (1997). *Exceptional individuals in school, community, and work* (p. 131). Austin, TX: PRO-ED.

Peer Support and Peer Tutoring

Peers may be the most underrated and underused human resource available in general education classrooms. Nondisabled peers are often creative problem solvers and staunch supporters of students with developmental disabilities (Carter, Cushing, Clark, & Kennedy, 2005; Stenhoff & Lignugaris/Kraft, 2007). Peers can provide both academic and social support (Munk & Van Laarhoven, 2008).

It is important, however, that students not always take the role of "helping" a student with disabilities, which can get in the way of their developing a friendship. Initially, peer support and tutoring require adult facilitation as needs and strategies are identified, but adult participation should be reduced as friendships and tutoring routines develop. Tips for Teachers 10.2 provides general suggestions for making the most of working in pairs. Tips for Teachers 10.3 presents steps for peers to provide survival skills support for students with developmental disabilities.

Go to **www.bestbuddies.org** to learn more about this international volunteer organization that pairs students with cognitive disabilities with a partner.

Strategies to Support Students in the General Education Classroom

A number of general strategies can be used to support students with developmental disabilities in the general education classroom.

Increasing a Student's Sense of Belonging.   The first key to success is creating a community to which the student with disabilities has a sense of belonging. Developing and implementing routines is one way to ensure a sense of belonging. When students can predict what is going to happen, they are more likely to feel a part of the classroom. Project PLAI (Promoting Learning through Active Interaction) (Chen, Alsop, & Minor, 2000) developed a set of routines for students who are deaf–blind. Learning routines such as lining up, distributing materials, taking turns, and taking time for communication are important aspects of helping students feel at home in the classroom. Tips for Teachers 10.4 lists strategies to increase this sense of belonging.

Using Routines to Ensure Safety.   Teaching students with developmental disabilities safety routines is vitally important (Mechling, 2008). Review emergency procedures with key personnel and with students. Students with developmental disabilities may need direct, explicit instruction not only in emergency procedures, but also in day-to-day routines such as getting on the bus, crossing the street, and using telephones. Practice fire drills before an actual fire drill occurs to avoid confusion and emotional distress. If a student has a condition that may impede evacuation, a plan for emergencies should be documented in the IEP.

Tips for Teachers 10.2

MAKING THE MOST OF WORKING WITH PAIRS

Set Procedures for Peer Tutoring

1. Give everyone a chance to be a tutor—every student has something to share with a peer.

2. Give the tutor very specific suggestions about what to teach and how to teach it.

3. Keep tutoring sessions short for students with short attention spans.

Set Procedures for Collaborative Pairs

1. Give specific guidelines about the responsibilities of each partner.

2. Hold each partner accountable for fulfilling responsibilities.

3. Give students the opportunity to work with a variety of partners.

Set Rules

1. Talk only to your partner.

2. Talk only about the assignment (project).

3. Use a low voice.

4. Cooperate with your partner.

5. Try to do your best.

Source: Used by permission of Douglas and Lynn Fuchs, Vanderbilt University.

TIPS FOR TEACHERS 10.3

PEER-SUPPORTED STRATEGY TO PROMOTE CLASSROOM SURVIVAL SKILLS

Step	Description
Step 1	Peer tutors explain why the classroom survival skills are important to learn.
	Example: *"In class when the bell rings, in seat when the bell rings, bring appropriate materials to class, greet the teacher, greet other students, ask questions, answer questions, sit up straight, pay attention to the teacher, acknowledge comments from other students."*
Step 2	Peer tutors give one example for each survival skill.
	Example: *"I am going to show you how you can teach yourself to be in class when the bell rings. You need to stop what you are doing outside of the classroom during recess and come to the class when the bell rings."*
Step 3	Peer tutors give one counterexample for each survival skill.
	Example: *"Staying in the cafeteria when the bell rings is not being in class when the bell rings."*
Step 4	Peer tutors explain how to count and self-record survival skills.
	Example: *"Were you in class when the bell rang? If you were in the class when the bell rang, mark Yes. If not, mark No."*
Step 5	Peer tutors prompt for appropriate survival skills when necessary.
Step 6	Peer tutors provide feedback and praise for appropriate survival skills.

Source: Information from Gilberts, G. H., Agran, M., Huges, C., & Wehmeyer M. (2001). The effects of peer delivered self-monitoring strategies on the participation of students with severe disabilities in general education classrooms. *Journal of the Association for Persons with Severe Handicaps*, 26(1), 25-36.

Accepting Varied Learning Goals. The most frequently asked question about inclusion is "How are students going to benefit from my class? What will they get out of it?" Students with developmental disabilities may be working on their own goals during class activities; it is important that these goals, however different, be regarded as meeting valued educational needs. Sean Miller, a high-school biology teacher, says his biggest concern was how to grade the student with mild retardation in his class. He comments, "I didn't know what to do. The student was trying and doing her work, but it wasn't high-school level. I wondered if I gave her a passing grade, was it fair to the other students? We (the special education staff and I) ended

TIPS FOR TEACHERS 10.4

STRATEGIES TO INCREASE SENSE OF BELONGING

- Give the student the same things as the other students (e.g., desk, typical seating, locker, name on classroom charts).

- Demonstrate respect for the student by using age-appropriate language and being a good role model.

- Involve the student in the typical classroom routine.

- Work with your educational team and students to find ways for the student to participate actively in classroom activities.

- Consult with specialists for ideas, and express your concerns.

- Encourage students to find ways to increase learning opportunities for classmates who are challenged.

- Promote equality and interactions with other classmates (e.g., remember to use the word *friend* instead of *peer tutor*, and say "go together" rather than "take _____ with you."

- Make connections among students who have common interests (e.g., sports, animals) with students with disabilities to generate interaction.

Sources: Causton-Theoharis, J., & Malmgren, K. (2005). Strategies to help paraprofessionals promote peer interaction. *Teaching Exceptional Children*, 37, 18–24; Frisbee, K., & Libby, J. (1992). *All together now.* Concord, NH: Cubb Life America.

FIGURE 10.4 — IEP Goal–Activity Matrix

Student **Manny** Semester **Fall 2010**

Grade **2nd grade** Teachers **Ms. Nichols, Mr. O'Brian**

IEP Goal Areas	Opening	Reading/ Language Arts	Recess	Math Their Way	Lunch	Science/ Social Studies
Writes name and functional words		X		X		X
One-to-one correspondence				X		X
Decision making	X	X	X	X	X	X
Initiating communication	X	X	X	X	X	X
Functional reading	X	X				X

up sitting down and reviewing her goals and determining a grade based on that. I was comfortable with that idea."

When encountering a situation like Sean's, it can help to create something like the IEP Goal–Activity Matrix shown in Figure 10.4. The matrix was created for Manny, a second-grade student with a moderate mental disability. The Xs indicate the logical subject or activity in which Manny will work on his IEP goals during his school day.

Making Environmental Accommodations. Environmental accommodations are changes made to the physical learning environment so that each student can participate successfully. These changes are often as simple as having a beanbag chair in the classroom so that a student with cerebral palsy can be on the floor with peers during story time, or lifting the legs of a desk a few inches so that a wheelchair fits comfortably underneath it. Tips for Teachers 10.5 provides suggestions for environmental accommodations.

Cooperative Learning. Cooperative learning is an effective instructional method for including students with developmental disabilities (Demchak, 2005; Hunt & McDonnell, 2007; Lee, Soukup, Little, & Wehmeyer, 2008). In cooperative learning situations, the class is divided for learning activities into groups that have cooperative goals. Each student has a role, and it is important that each role is valued. Cooperative learning fosters interdependence and is a strong vehicle for bringing access to the general education curriculum to students with developmental disabilities (Soukup, Wehmeyer, Bashinski, & Bovaird, 2007).

Barbara Mykel uses cooperative learning groups to support her fifth graders in reading social studies textbooks. She assigns students to mixed-ability groups and gives each student a role within that group. Two students take turns as readers, one leads the group in generating possible test questions, and one serves as a notetaker. Kevin, a student with moderate intellectual disabilities, participates in these cooperative groups. Kevin serves as the announcer and makes sure that everyone in the group contributes possible test questions. The paraprofessional, Gilbert Gomez, makes flash cards for later review with Kevin and for home learning.

Providing Hands-On Instruction. Hands-on, or experientially based, instruction relates learning to what students already know and uses real-life activities as teaching tools. This type of instruction provides greater opportunity for students with developmental disabilities to be

Tips for Teachers 10.5

ENVIRONMENTAL ACCOMMODATIONS

- Develop a tactile schedule for your student. Each activity of the day has an object that represents it. For example: math—calculator; lunch—spoon; reading—a small book.

- Along with the schedule, objects can be used to make choices, get information from the environment, or convey a message (e.g., handing the teacher a small pillow might mean the student wants his or her position changed, choosing a small ball would communicate what the student wants to do during recess).

- Tactually or visually identify your student's belongings with a consistent, meaningful symbol. This will help facilitate independence (e.g., a pencil taped on the desk, a safety pin on the tag of his or her coat).

- Have clear pathways marked with objects that serve as cues. Consistent furniture or tactile or visual runners on

the wall help to promote orientation and the student's independent mobility. Important places should be distinguished by special cues.

- To encourage your student to use his or her remaining hearing or vision, add light, color, sound, vibration, interesting textures, and colors to objects.

- Firmly touch the student's shoulder to signal that an interaction is going to occur.

- Introduce yourself by using a consistent symbol for your name. This could be a ring, watch, or other piece of jewelry you always wear that the student could easily touch, or it could be a distinguishing feature, such as your hair or glasses. Name signs or the finger spelling of the first letter of your name could also be signed in the palm of the student's hand as a consistent symbol for your name.

Source: Adapted from Rikhye, C. H., Gotheif, C. R., & Appell, M. W. (1989). A classroom environment checklist for students with dual sensory impairments. *Teaching Exceptional Children,* 22(1), 44–46; California Deaf–Blind Services. (1992). *How to interact with individuals with dual sensory impairments* (Fact Sheet). California: Author.

actively involved (Scruggs, Mastropieri, & Okolo, 2008). Learning centers, math manipulatives, science projects, art projects, and computers are examples of hands-on activities that give students with developmental disabilities the opportunity to participate. Downing and Eichinger (2003) explain that working with materials helps students with developmental disabilities learn how to follow directions and handle items in appropriate ways. Tips for Teachers 10.6 lists additional ways you can teach skills and strategies to students with developmental disabilities.

Self-Determination. One aspect of teaching students with developmental disabilities is development of self-determination (Wehmeyer, Martin, & Sands, 2008). **Self-determination** is the ability to make informed decisions that will lead to positive outcomes. Self-determination is important for transition to life beyond the school and ultimately for quality of life

Tips for Teachers 10.6

PROMOTING SKILLS AND STRATEGY ACQUISITION

- Engage students actively in learning.

- Teach the strategy or skill in small steps or segments.

- Teach students how to use the specific strategies.

- Check frequently for understanding and provide feedback.

- Use actual materials and real-life experiences or simulations.

- Provide concrete examples in instruction.

- Have students perform the skill or strategy repeatedly.

- Provide many examples and multiple contexts to promote generalization.

- Reinforce generalization.

- Use the skill or strategy in several different learning situations to promote generalization.

- Create learning environments that provide students with successful experiences.

- Limit the number of concepts presented in any one period.

(Carter, Lane, Pierson, & Stang, 2008). There are seven components of self-determination: (a) problem solving, (b) self-management, (c) decision making, (d) goal setting, (e) choice making, (f) self-awareness, and (g) self-advocacy (Bremer, Kachgal, & Schoeller, 2003; Council for Exceptional Children, 2003). These domains may be represented on your student's IEP, and you'll need to work with your special education colleagues to implement systematic and intensive ways for your students to develop these skills, particularly with students in middle and high school.

Providing Opportunities for Functional Practice

Students with developmental disabilities may not independently make connections between what they are learning in school and their daily lives. Functional practice can help make those links. **Functional practice** is relevant practice to help students easily see the connection between what they are practicing and its use in real life. For example, you can incorporate into reading instruction activities that stress reading for fun or to obtain information needed for daily life. Tips for Teachers 10.7 provides information on how to incorporate functional tools and activities into the classroom. Functional activities can often predict the degree to which they will function successfully as adults.

Encouraging Family Involvement

Every teacher realizes the importance of family involvement in a student's education. In recent decades research on families that include children with developmental and intellectual disabilities has expanded tremendously (Odom, Horner, Snell, & Blacher, 2007). Their parents, guardians, caretakers, and extended family members play key roles in determining the students' educational program, and their preparation for adult life.

Knowing the family's goals for their child can help everyone work together as a team. Regular communication is the key to success.

Tips FOR Teachers 10.7

BRINGING FUNCTIONAL TOOLS AND ACTIVITIES INTO THE CLASSROOM

Following are some tools you can use to help make learning activities relevant:

- Directions (e.g., for cooking, building a model, repairing an appliance)
- Directional orientation and maps
- Menus
- Labels on foods, medicines, and clothing
- Telephone book
- Catalogs and advertisements (for selecting something to order)
- Schedules (e.g., bus, train, television)
- Signs
- Newspapers and magazines

Writing activities also can be centered on daily activities, such as:

- Sending an e-mail to a friend
- Writing a letter to request something or to complain
- Writing a postcard or letter to a relative
- Making a shopping list
- Completing a job application or an application for a library card
- Ordering something by filling out a form
- Writing down a telephone message

Functional math activities include the following:

- Making change
- Counting money
- Making a purchase
- Using a checking account
- Using a credit card
- Budgeting money
- Telling and estimating time
- Reading a calendar
- Reading a thermometer
- Measuring
- Determining weight and height

Turnbull and Turnbull (2001) talk about successful home–school partnerships as **reliable alliances**. Reliable alliances occur when there is mutual trust; ongoing communication; sensitivity to family culture, basic needs, and choices; and high yet realistic expectations. Keep in mind the influence of family culture on expectations (Harry, Rueda, & Kalyanpur, 1999; Harry & Klingner, 2006; Sparks, 2008).

As students with developmental disabilities are increasingly included in general education classrooms, it is important that you learn strategies for accommodating these students in your class. You might need to adapt the curriculum or have the students work on goals that are not specified in the curriculum. As Chris Johnson discovered, a key to successful integration is collaboration with and support from the student's family as well as specialists who work with students such as Darrell. If you make time for co-planning and ongoing communication, you can help to ensure that students are successful and that you feel positive about the learning experiences of all the students in your class.

Summary

- Students with developmental disabilities represent a diverse group of individuals with varied learning needs and abilities who, with proper supports, can improve their quality of life both in school and beyond. Students with developmental disabilities include individuals with intellectual disabilities, severe disabilities, multiple disabilities, and the deaf–blind. The challenges students with developmental disabilities face can be physical, intellectual, and social and can vary from mild to severe.

- The prevalence of persons with developmental disabilities is difficult to determine because different definitions and methodologies are used to determine various conditions under this large umbrella. Generally, however, prevalence is estimated to be about 1% of the school population. IDEIA 2004 mandates access to the general education curriculum. Many students with developmental disabilities will be identified for special services before entering your class. However, if you observe a student with persistent difficulties in learning tasks or adaptive behavior, follow your school district guidelines for providing support and, if necessary, determining what your role is in the referral process.

- As a general education teacher, you will be involved in the planning and implementation of adaptations and curriculum modifications for all students. A variety of planning systems and functional assessment and discrepancy analysis techniques are available to facilitate appropriate assessment and instruction. Using these systems and techniques as well as curricular adaptations, peer support, functional practice, and input from families can help you provide high-quality instruction for students with developmental disabilities.

Think and Apply

1. Think about Chris Johnson's special education colleague Martha Anderson's role as an inclusion specialist in relation to your role as a classroom teacher. If one of Martha's students were to join your class, how would you plan, communicate, and work with Martha so that she could support both you and the student? List the questions you would want to ask Darrell before the student joined your class.

2. Check your state and school district websites for information about access to the general education curriculum for students with developmental disabilities. Has your state or school district adapted curricular standards for students with developmental disabilities? What requirements and accommodations are available for students with developmental disabilities in your state's high-stakes testing?

3. Check your state and school district websites for information about how students with developmental disabilities are identified for special education. Investigate the general education teacher's role in identification, in particular with RTI.

4. Plan a lesson for one of your state's academic standards in your curriculum area. Include in your plan activities for partial or parallel participation for students with intellectual disabilities.

Peggy Kirkland teaches fourth grade and has a group of 25 students. The school year got off to a great start and Peggy felt wonderful about the attitude and enthusiasm of all of her students. She knew it was going to be a terrific year. Shortly after the beginning of school, Peggy was told that one of her students, Kerri Albride, was hospitalized due to an accident at a playground near her home. Kerri sustained broken bones and injuries to the head. Doctors later confirmed that she had a traumatic brain injury.

Kerri was one of the most popular students in Peggy's class. She was a fluent reader, participated in class discussions, and had a large circle of friends. Her classmates were very upset when the accident occurred. Peggy asked the school counselor, Mark Romano, to meet with her students to help them cope with their concerns about Kerri.

After a long hospital stay and recuperation at home, Kerri finally returned to school. Physically, there was little change; the broken bones were healed. But a very different Kerri came back to fourth grade. Here are Peggy's observations:

> Other than slightly slurred speech, you really couldn't tell that Kerri might have some difficulties in making the adjustment back to school. But slowly other symptoms started to pop up. Kerri had trouble following directions, responding to questions, and reading. She got frustrated when she couldn't find the right words. Her problems weren't just academic; they were social as well.

Kerri didn't see herself as being very different than she was before—at least socially. But we all noticed that her temperament was very different. Kerri would lash out at her classmates and they were bewildered by her actions. It soon became clear that we were going to have to continue to learn about what Kerri could and couldn't do and that it was going to take a team effort to help her adjust. It soon became clear to me that Kerri, her parents, her classmates, and I were all dealing with a loss for which we were not prepared.

Peggy was aware that she could not help Kerri or the other students she taught without support. The school counselor, Mark Romano, brought together a team that included Kerri's parents, the special education teacher, an occupational therapist, and a speech therapist. Kerri's physicians shared information that was useful for their planning. Together the team was able to develop an IEP that addressed Kerri's academic and social needs. Peggy also talked with the team about how she could help her other students adjust to Kerri's changed behavior and how to set a positive classroom climate. Toward the end of the school year, Peggy observed:

> Kerri and her parents have many challenges ahead of them. What we all learned this year is the importance of teamwork. We're not sure if or when Kerri will recover fully. Her parents do have a strong support team that will help them along each step of the way.

Introduction

Peggy Kirkland is an experienced teacher who, from time to time, has had students with sensory (hearing and vision), physical, and health impairments in her classroom. Peggy recognizes that students have individual needs (based on the extent of their disabilities) and may need support from other professionals. When you work with students with sensory, physical, or health impairments or disabilities, like Peggy you will likely be part of a team that includes you, the parents, the student, and other teachers and specialists. This chapter is divided into three sections: visual impairments; hearing loss or deafness/hardness of hearing; and physical disabilities, health impairments, and traumatic brain injury. You will learn about your role in the possible identification of special needs as well as strategies to promote student academic and social success.

Students with Visual Impairments

Think about classrooms you have visited and how many activities involve vision. According to the American Optometric Association (2009) as much as 80% of what children learn comes through visual input. This section's discussion of students with visual impairments focuses on appropriate instructional strategies you can use to support their learning. So that you can better understand their needs, the section begins with definitions of types of visual impairments, along with information about the characteristics, prevalence, and identification of students with visual impairments.

Definitions and Types of Visual Impairments

The visual system is a complex system that includes (a) the surrounding structures such as the skeletal structure of the face, the eyelid, and the tear system; (b) the eye globe itself, including each of the parts such as the iris, lens, and retina; and (c) the neurological system, including the optic pathways and vision centers of the brain such as the occipital lobes. In defining this system, Hallahan, Kauffmann, and Pullan (2009) note that visual impairments are typically defined within legal or educational frameworks.

Legal Definitions.   Have you ever stood in line in a school nurse's office to read a chart of letters of increasingly smaller size on a chart? Such a chart is a Snellen chart, a tool to gauge **visual acuity** or the ability to see detail clearly. **Legal blindness** is defined as a visual acuity of 20/200 with best correction in the best eye or a visual field loss resulting in a visual field of 20 degrees or less. An individual with good vision can stand 200 feet away to read the largest line on the Snellen chart, whereas an individual who has a visual impairment of 20/200 must stand only 20 feet away to read the same line. Such an individual would be classified as legally blind and may be eligible for special services. Additionally, how well an individual can see using peripheral or side vision is called **visual field**. When someone experiences a significant visual field loss that leaves the person with a field of 20 degrees or less, he or she is then classified as legally blind (Corn & Koenig, 2002) and can be eligible for tax benefits or special materials and resources.

Some people who are classified as legally blind may be able to read standard print, see and identify the faces of friends and family, view objects at a distance, and discriminate details in objects or pictures. Others may have difficulty with these same tasks and may even have difficulty detecting objects, colors, and the location of light sources. Therefore, each individual's visual impairment is unique. **Total blindness** refers to a very small minority of individuals who have visual impairments and who are unable to see anything, including objects or light sources (Huebner, 2000). **Partial sight** is a phrase that was previously used to specify individuals who had a visual acuity in the range of 20/70 to 20/200. This terminology is no longer used as widely as it once was (Corn & Koenig, 1996b). **Low vision** is the term more typically used for individuals with visual acuity in that range who continue to have difficulty with vision even with corrective lenses (glasses) (Hallahan et al., 2009). Corn and Koenig define *low vision* as the preferred terminology for individuals who have an impairment and who with standard corrective lenses (glasses) continue to have "difficulty accomplishing visual tasks but can enhance [their] ability to accomplish these tasks with the use of compensatory visual strategies, low-vision and other devices, and environmental modifications" (Corn & Koenig, 2002, p. 4).

Educational Definition.   An educational definition of visual impairment emphasizes academic tasks, particularly reading more and visual acuity less (Hallahan et al., 2009):

> *Visual impairment including blindness* means an impairment in vision that even with correction, adversely affects a child's educational performance. This term includes both partial sight and blindness. (IDEA 300.8 [c][13])

Causes of Visual Impairment.   The many causes of visual impairment are usually grouped in the following three areas:

- Structural impairments (i.e., damage or impairment to one or more parts of the visual system)
- Refractive errors (i.e., an inability of the eye to focus the light rays onto the retina correctly)

- Cortical visual impairments (i.e., a problem with the neurological pathways, including reception and interpretation of the visual information) (Heward, 2009)

While vision impairment can occur any time during life, the Centers for Disease Control and Prevention (CDC) (2009b) reports that most children with vision impairment in the 3- to 10-year age range had causes that occurred in infancy. Abnormal blood vessel growth or scarring of the retina of the eye were typical causes and more common among children with low birth weights (CDC, 2009b). While it is helpful to know the cause of a student's visual impairment, it is more important to know how the student uses his or her vision to accomplish desired tasks.

Characteristics of Students with Visual Impairments

Even though a student with a visual impairment is more like sighted peers than different from them, a visual impairment has an impact on all aspects of development. Its effect on each student varies considerably (Ferrell, 2000). Children with visual impairments are thought to have a more difficult time developing basic concepts owing to their vision loss. Although the other senses help young children gain information about their world, a visual impairment will limit the range and scope of information available to the child. In its position statement on the educational needs of students with visual impairments, the American Foundation for the Blind (2009) states: "No other sense can stimulate curiosity, combine information, or invite exploration in the same way, or as efficiently and fully as vision. Students with visual impairments can and do succeed, but at different rates and often in different sequences" (p. 3).

Additionally, a young child will have difficulty learning from the activities of others (incidental learning) because the child might not be able to determine visually what someone, such as a parent, is doing and what the results of the activity are (Ferrell, 1996). Preparing a simple snack is an example of such an activity. A child who has sight can watch a parent retrieve the food from the cupboard or refrigerator, prepare it, and then bring it to the child. A child who is visually impaired might not have access to any of this information because the child cannot see the location of the cupboard or refrigerator and might not even know what items are stored there. The child will not know how to prepare the food (e.g., spread peanut butter on bread) and will not know what utensils are needed. Finally, the child might not know how to open and close containers and will need repeated experiences to learn this skill.

Children with visual impairments do typically reach the developmental milestones in each of the five developmental domains of cognition including concept development, communication, motor skills (fine and gross) and mobility, self-help, and social and emotional development. However, students may be delayed in these areas in the following ways:

- *Concept development.* Areas in which the child has not had a direct experience may be underdeveloped. In addition, children with visual impairments may not have access to clues such as color that can aid in conceptual development and vocabulary.
- *Communication.* There is general agreement that a visual impairment does not have a direct impact on oral language development (Rosel, Caballer, Jara, & Oliver, 2005). However, lack of access to appropriate adaptive materials may limit development in communication through the written word (Steinman, LeJeune, & Kimbrough, 2006).
- *Motor skills and mobility.* Children may be delayed in large (gross) motor skill development and may engage in fewer activities that use visual-motor skills (e.g., running, jumping, and kicking) (Bouchard & Tetreault, 2000). They may also have delays in fine motor skills (e.g., writing, cutting, and grasping small items). Moreover, issues related to safety may inhibit mobility and access to the physical environment.
- *Self-help.* If children have not been given responsibilities and guidance, they might not be able to fix a simple snack, independently select clothing, or dress themselves.
- *Social skills.* Children might not know when individuals are speaking to them. Additionally, children might be unable to see how others initiate interactions, how they give nonverbal indications of their feelings and desires, and how peers are responding to interactions and common situations (Campbell, 2007; Sacks & Wolffe, 2006; Wagner, 2004). As a result, children with visual impairments may also be more isolated than their sighted peers (Kelly & Smith, 2008) and less involved in after-school clubs, activities, and work opportunities.

PEARSON
myeducationlab

Go to the Assignments and Activities section of Topic 19: Visual Impairment in the MyEducationLab for your course and complete the activity entitled *Effect of Visual Impairment on Daily Life*.

Go to **www.aph.org,** the American Printing House for the Blind website, where you can find information about special media, tools, and materials for students with visual impairments.

It is important to remember that children with visual impairments need opportunities to directly interact with the environment. These children need to touch, listen, and explore new objects. They need to participate actively in all activities, have opportunities to talk about their experiences, and have opportunities to travel to and explore new environments. Teachers should provide additional time for these students to explore and ask questions about their environment and objects within the environment (Cox & Dykes, 2001).

Prevalence of Visual Impairments

Visual impairments are considered a low-incidence disability, which means that comparatively fewer students have visual impairments than have high-incidence disabilities such as learning disabilities. Most of the students with visual impairments placed in your class are likely to have some usable vision (Griffin, Williams, Davis, & Engleman, 2002). The U.S. Department of Education (2007) reports that during the 2005-2006 school year, 25,855 school-age students (ages 6–21) with vision impairments were served under IDEIA. An additional 1,310 deaf–blind students also received services. Because students with visual impairments may also be classified under the umbrella of another disability, these numbers are not necessarily representative of children with visual impairments you might have in your classroom. According to the American Foundation for the Blind (2007), approximately 93,000 visually impaired or blind students are served in special education. This total includes 10,800 who are deaf–blind. Of these students with visual impairments, approximately two thirds have some other disability (often mental retardation).

Approximately 25% of students with visual impairments are *visual* readers (use large print or some means of enlarging the print), 10% are *braille* readers (use braille for reading), and 7% are *auditory* readers (listen to tapes or others reading) (American Printing House for the Blind, 2007). The remaining students are either *prereaders* (young children) or *nonreaders* who, in addition to their visual impairment, have other disabilities (usually mental retardation) that interfere with their ability to read. The American Printing House for the Blind (2007) reports that 48,080 children with visual impairments attend public schools and 5,085 children attend residential schools for children with visual impairments. Note that the American Printing House for the Blind counts only children who are legally blind, so there are children with significant vision impairments (acuity better than 20/200) who are not reported in the preceding figures.

Identification and Assessment of Students with Visual Impairments

Certain indicators may help you identify students who need to be referred for evaluation. Following are common physical characteristics that might indicate visual impairments:

- Red-rimmed, swollen, or encrusted eyes
- Excessive blinking
- Itchy eyes
- Eyes that are tearing
- One or both eyes turn inward, outward, upward, or downward
- Extreme sensitivity to light
- Tilting or turning the head to one side to see an object
- Squinting
- Covering one eye to view an object
- Thrusting the head forward to view an object
- Headaches, fatigue, or dizziness after doing close work
- Tripping, bumping into objects, or appearing disoriented
- Recurring sties (i.e., inflamed swelling of the gland at the margin of the eyelid)

You may also observe some performance characteristics while students are reading, such as loss of place, omitting or inserting words or letters, or avoiding reading and writing tasks.

If you suspect that a student has a visual impairment, you should refer the student to the school nurse and the school or district's teacher who works with students who have visual impairments. To receive educational services from a special education teacher specializing in visual impairments, students must have a documented visual impairment. Written documentation in the form of an eye report is obtained from an ophthalmologist or optometrist.

After a student's visual impairment is identified, the special education teacher who specializes in visual impairments assesses the student's functional vision in multiple environments, including the academic setting. The **functional vision assessment** will include the student's ability to view at both near and distant points and the student's ability to sustain visual function throughout daily academic settings. Environmental conditions such as lighting, contrasts, optimal print size, seating preference, and visual features of the environment are part of a functional vision assessment. A **learning media assessment** to determine the student's dominant learning modality should also be included as part of the assessment battery. Compensatory skills assessments may also be appropriate to determine the services needed for the student. **Compensatory skills** include listening skills, orientation and mobility skills, social skills, and daily living skills. These important skills must be taught in the environments in which they will be used.

Instructional Guidelines and Accommodations for Students with Visual Impairments

Although most districts already provide adapted materials to students with visual impairments, the 2004 update of IDEA mandates that states adopt the National Instructional Materials Accessibility Standard (NIMAS) to provide appropriate instructional materials to individuals who are blind and to those with visual impairments. Fortunately, thanks to developments in technology, avenues for access to the general education curriculum are on the rise. The National Federation of the Blind (2009) maintains a webpage presenting a Technology Resource List. This list is updated regularly and provides information about resources available for students and adults with visual impairments.

Some general education teachers feel apprehensive when they see the materials and equipment that a student with visual impairments needs in the classroom (Corn & Wall, 2002). Ron Cross, an eighth-grade science teacher, was concerned when Diane, a special educator, and Brandy, his student, first indicated the materials and adaptations that Brandy would require. Brandy's equipment included the science textbook in braille (12 volumes) and an electronic brailler and braille paper (i.e., the machine and special paper used to write braille). During the year, Diane also provided tactile diagrams of cells and insects (i.e., diagrams that are raised and textured so that the features can be felt). Diane explained that the specialized equipment and materials would enable Brandy to succeed in science class.

General Accommodations.   In planning for students with visual impairments, teachers should think about auditory, tactile, and visual accommodations (Cox & Dykes, 2001). Students may not have a wide range of visual images to draw from. Therefore, when giving directions or lecturing, you may need to activate the students' prior knowledge and vocabulary. You may also need to provide some auditory signs or cues to key students into vital information. Tactile accommodations include opportunities for students to touch and feel objects related to a learning activity. Children should be encouraged to touch with both hands and to have repeated opportunities to touch before, during, and after a lesson (Castellano, 2003). Visual accommodations include making certain that the student is seated in a way so as to get an unobstructed view, creating printed materials with appropriate font size, and writing in large letters on the board and overheads. Tips for Teachers 11.1 includes additional suggestions for students who have some usable vision.

Using Braille and Braille Devices.   Some students may have some usable vision but rely on tactile and auditory information gained by using these learning channels. These students use **braille**, a system of embossed or raised dots that can be read with the tips of the fingers. The basic unit of braille is a cell that contains six dots in two vertical rows of three dots each. Combining the dots forms letters of the alphabet, numbers, punctuation marks, and contractions. Contractions are used to save space (for example, the entire word *understand* is written as ⠠⠥⠝⠙⠻⠌⠯, whereas the contraction for *understand* takes up only four cells: ⠨⠥⠯⠙). When students learn braille, they learn to spell both the full and the contracted forms. Figure 11.1 gives examples of braille forms. There are several ways to write braille: by using a *brailler* (also called a *braillewriter*), by using a noiseless portable note taker such as Braille 'n Speak or a mobile manager such as Braille+, and by using a slate and stylus. Young children who are

Go to the Assignments and Activities section of Topic 19: Visual Impairments in the MyEducationLab for your course and complete the activity entitled *Using Large Print, Braille, and Braille Notes.*

Tips FOR TEACHERS 11.1

MODIFYING THE ENVIRONMENT FOR STUDENTS WITH VISUAL IMPAIRMENTS

Physical Environment

- Announce your presence and identify yourself (e.g., "Hi, girls, it's Mr. Johnson. May I join your science group to see how you are working together?"). Also announce your departure (e.g., "Thank you, girls, for letting me join you. I'm going to check in with Ryan's group now.").

- Leave doors fully opened or closed and drawers closed so that the student does not run into them.

- Describe the locations of things, especially after rearranging the classroom. Start with the door and travel around the room systematically, noting locations.

- Provide an extra desk or shelf space for the student to store materials.

- Provide access to an outlet for audio equipment, braillers, lamp, or other electrical equipment.

- Allow early dismissal from class so that the student has time to travel to other classes.

Learning Environment

- Familiarize students with classroom materials (e.g., give them time to visually or tactually explore a globe before asking them to locate the longitude and latitude of a city).

- Have concrete examples students can touch (e.g., in science, have fossils, not just pictures of fossils).

- Provide lessons with tactual and auditory components, and adapt assignments so that students can participate.

- Consider lighting conditions. Some students do best with natural lighting, others do better with lamps. Backlighting reduces visibility, so avoid standing in front of a window when you present material to the class. Low contrast in materials and between backgrounds and foregrounds reduces visibility, so make sure the contrast is as high as possible (for example, black background with brown letters).

- Provide written copies of any materials you use on an overhead projector or board. When you use an overhead projector or board, say what you are writing as you do it.

- Allow a peer to take notes for the student, but check that the student is still paying attention and participating.

- Provide opportunities for students to work in groups, especially when the assignment has a visual component (e.g., conducting experiments in science class).

- Modify writing activities as necessary by allowing students to dictate into a tape recorder.

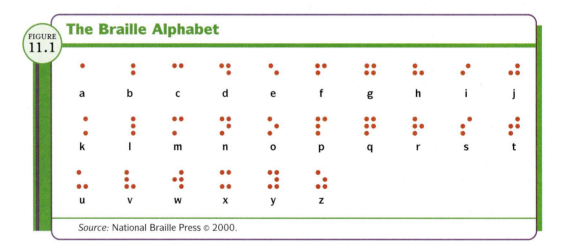

FIGURE 11.1

The Braille Alphabet

a b c d e f g h i j

k l m n o p q r s t

u v w x y z

Source: National Braille Press © 2000.

exposed to braille before they start school are as ready to learn to read and write as their normally sighted peers (Durando, 2008; Steinman et al., 2006).

Go to **www.nfb.org**, the website of the National Federation of the Blind, for access to information about blindness with a particular emphasis on braille technology.

Using Orientation and Mobility Skills. Orientation and mobility specialists teach students with visual impairments to travel independently in their environments. "The goal is to enable the student to enter any environment, familiar or unfamiliar, and to function safely, efficiently, gracefully, and independently" (Hill & Ponder, 1976, p. 1). Consequently, it is not unusual for the student and specialist to work not only in school but also in the community.

The student needs to develop both **orientation skills** (which include understanding one's own body, one's position in space, and abstract concepts such as the layout of a city block) and **mobility skills** (which include going up and down stairs, crossing streets, and using public transportation). The orientation and mobility specialist or the special education teacher who specializes in visual impairments can help you arrange your classroom to facilitate the student's mobility within the classroom and other key places in the school (e.g., cafeteria, library, bus loading zone, playground). In addition, students with visual impairments need to know procedures related to safety and emergencies (Cox & Dykes, 2001; Emerson & Corn, 2006).

The long cane is the mobility device most frequently used by individuals with visual impairments, including children. The cane has a handle (generally black or red); a shaft, which is white; and a red reflective material at the bottom of the shaft. The tip of the cane varies considerably, some being small and others quite large. The type of tip used on the cane will be determined by the orientation and mobility specialist. When students have canes at school, they are responsible for their cane. Mobility specialists have shown them how to store their cane when it is not in use (sometimes by hanging it on a hook, other times by folding it and placing it in their bag). The cane is not a toy and is used solely for the purpose of providing the visually impaired traveler with information about the terrain as he or she walks. Instruction from the orientation and mobility specialist is essential for the child with a visual impairment to develop the skills to be a safe and efficient cane user (Emerson & Corn, 2006; Griffin-Shirley, Trusty, & Rickard, 2000).

Using Optical, Nonoptical, and Instructional Aids.   Students who have difficulty seeing street signs, building numbers, and bus signs might use a *monocular,* an optical aid that magnifies a distant object. Other optical aids include many types of magnifiers—handheld, lighted, or with a stand—as well as prescription lenses (glasses or contacts). The special education teacher trained to work with students with visual impairments has learned techniques to employ in teaching students to use both distance optical devices such as the monocular and near optical devices such as magnifiers (Corn, Wall, Jose, Bell, Wilcox, & Perez, 2002; D'Andrea & Farrenkopf, 2000; Presley & D'Andrea, 2009).

Large print is another option for students with visual impairments (Kitchel, 2004). Large-print books are costly and difficult to store, however, and sometimes embarrass the students. Reading large print may also be tiring, in that it requires exaggerated head movements and adaptive seating positions. The American Printing House for the Blind has designated guidelines for the use of large print (Kitchel, 2004).

Optical aids, by contrast, are more compact, less costly, and give students access to all materials (Corn, Wall, & Bell, 2000; Corn et al., 2002; Farmer & Morse, 2007). The key is to have the teacher who specializes in visual impairments assess the student's needs and abilities in multiple environments and provide appropriate training on all necessary equipment and devices.

General educators, parents, and special educators must not assume that all children with visual impairments need large print and will benefit from it. Many children with low vision are candidates for optical aids and should be evaluated by a doctor trained in low vision. Once optical aids are prescribed, teachers who are certified teachers of children with visual impairments need to provide students with instruction in how to use these devices. When selecting and preparing a text, teachers must make sure that it is clearly written, has adequate spacing between letters and words, and is on good-quality paper. Reducing the amount of background patterns on the page or providing good contrast between the color of the print and the color of the page is important (Barraga & Erin, 2001). Nonoptical aids also can help students to maximize visual potential. **Nonoptical aids** are devices that, although not prescribed by a doctor, promote efficient use of vision. Following are some examples of nonoptical aids:

- *Lamp* (provides additional light). Lamps with adjustable necks help to minimize glare.
- *Reading stand* (used to bring printed material closer to the eyes). Also reduces poor posture and fatigue.
- *Bold-line paper* (makes writing easier for students with visual impairments). The American Printing House for the Blind manufactures writing paper, graph paper, and large-print paper with music staffs.

PEARSON
myeducationlab

To enhance your understanding of adapting the classroom to accommodate students with disabilities in the general education classroom, go to the IRIS Center Resources section of Topic 6: Classroom/Behavior Management in the MyEducationLab for your course and complete the Module 2: *Accommodations to the Physical Environment: Setting up a Classroom for Students with Visual Disabilities.*

What low-tech and high-tech solutions available for students with vision impairments can students use in your classroom?

Tips FOR Teachers 11.2

ACCOMMODATIONS FOR TESTS IN THE GENERAL EDUCATION CLASSROOM

- Provide test materials in the student's primary learning medium (e.g., braille, large print, audiotape).

- Allow extra time to complete test items.

- As a general rule, give students who read braille twice as much time as other students to complete a test.

- As a general rule, give students who read regular or large print time and a half to complete a test (e.g., if the time limit is 30 minutes, give them 45 minutes).

- Read written instructions to students with visual impairment to minimize the amount of reading they need to do (so as to reduce eye fatigue).

- Present test items orally if doing so will not compromise the integrity of the test.

- Allow students to write answers on the test material instead of a bubble sheet, or provide a large-print bubble sheet.

- *Hats and visors* (can help to reduce the amount of light). Helpful for students who are sensitive to light (photophobic).
- *Color acetate* (a plastic overlay that darkens print or increases contrast). Yellow is the color favored by many students with visual impairments.

Several nonoptical aids, available mainly from the American Printing House for the Blind, include the following:

- *Cranmer abacus*—an adapted device for the rapid computation of basic math functions, decimals, and fractions
- *Raised-line paper*—writing and graph paper with raised lines that can be followed tactually
- *Writing guides*—rectangular templates designed to enable the writer to accurately place a signature, address an envelope, or write a check
- *Measurement tools*—items such as braille clocks, rulers, and measuring kits with raised marks

Testing Accommodations.   Classroom tests should be modified to make them accessible to students with visual impairments. Modifications may include assigning alternative items, orally reading sections of the test to the student, using large-print or braille answer sheets, providing real objects for items shown in pictures, or coloring pictures to make them easier to see. Tip for Teachers 11.2 provides some additional ideas for making accommodations for tests. The special education teacher who works with the student with visual impairments is also an excellent resource for suggesting several simple testing accommodations.

Students with Hearing Loss

You may have the opportunity to teach a student who is deaf or hard of hearing. Nancy Shipka, a fifth-grade math and science teacher who had that opportunity, worked with a special education teacher specializing in hearing loss and a sign language interpreter. Nancy had no idea what to expect when two students who were deaf joined her math and science class. She was concerned not only that the students' academic performance would not measure up to that of the normally hearing students in her class, but also about working with a special education team. With the help of the special education team, however, Nancy worked with the students to determine where they should sit so that they could clearly see her, the interpreter, the whiteboard, and the computer monitor. She also learned to face the students directly when speaking and to vary her teaching methods, emphasizing hands-on activities and demonstrations. As part of her own education, Nancy came to understand that the role of the interpreter is one of facilitating communication. In this capacity, Nancy told the interpreter about difficult concepts ahead of time and also provided written summaries and class notes so that the interpreter would be prepared to sign difficult or technical concepts.

Like Nancy, you could also find yourself in a classroom with a student with hearing loss. If this is the case, you will have questions about how to best meet your student's needs. This section explains deafness, hearing loss, and how to best accommodate students with hearing loss.

Definitions and Types of Hearing Loss

Hearing loss, although often associated with aging, can occur at any time, including from birth. Hearing loss can occur as the result of several factors, including heredity, illness or disease, and excessive prolonged exposure to loud noises. Many of the causes of hearing loss in infants are unknown. Young children who are identified as having hearing loss before they learn language (2 to 3 years of age) are identified as prelingually deaf. This early loss of hearing significantly affects language development. The U.S. federal government identifies hearing loss as one form of sensory impairment with the following definition:

> Hearing—the capacity to hear, with amplification, is limited, impaired, or absent and results in one or more of the following: reduced performance in hearing acuity tasks; difficulty with oral communication; and/or difficulty in understanding auditorally-presented information in the education environment. The term includes students who are deaf and students who are hard-of-hearing. (IDEA 300.7[c][5])

Hearing loss can occur in one ear (unilateral) or both ears (bilateral). It can be described by type and degree. The type of hearing loss depends on where it occurs in the ear. A hearing loss is referred to as conductive when the outer and middle ears do not transfer enough acoustic energy to the inner ear fluids. Blockage of the ear canal by congenital malformation, abnormalities of the middle ear structures, or otitis media (infection of the middle ear) are some of the causes of conductive hearing loss. Medicine or surgery may sometimes help with this type of hearing loss. A hearing loss is sensorineural when there is damage to the cochlea (inner ear) or to the auditory nerve. This type of hearing loss is usually permanent. Hearing loss is called **mixed hearing loss** when the loss is both conductive and sensorineural.

The degree of hearing loss is assessed by observing a person's responses to sounds. The intensity of a sound (loud versus quiet) is measured in decibels (dB); the frequency of the sound (high versus low) is measured in hertz. An audiologist tests and plots an individual's responses to sounds on a graph called an **audiogram**, a visual representation of an individual's ability to hear sound. Figure 11.2 shows a comparison of the frequency and intensity of various environmental and speech sounds, plotted on an audiogram (Stach, 1998). As you can see from the diagram, the rustling sound of a palm tree is quiet (5 dB), whereas rock music is quite loud (100–110 dB). Speech sounds are somewhere in between in a configuration called the "Speech Banana."

Characteristics of Students with Hearing Loss

Normal hearing falls within the range of 0–15 dB. Hearing losses are described by degree in terms such as *minimal, mild, moderate, severe,* and *profound:*

- 16–25 dB = minimal loss
- 25–40 dB = mild hearing loss
- 40–65 dB = moderate hearing loss
- 65–90 dB = severe hearing loss
- Greater than 90 dB = profound hearing loss

A person with a mild to moderate loss is usually referred to as being **hard of hearing**. Someone with a severe or profound loss is usually described as **deaf**.

Hearing loss affects normal speech and language development, which in turn affects reading development. Students who are deaf or hard of hearing may be significantly delayed in vocabulary development and reading skills. Some students who are deaf use vision as their primary mode of communication and learning. Other students who are deaf or hard of hearing develop communication and learning skills through the use of **residual hearing**, or the amount of hearing remaining after a hearing loss. Students with hearing losses to different degrees have difficulty accessing their environment and language system. Even though their vocal apparatuses function normally, they experience difficulty learning to produce the speech sounds, because they might not get accurate or complete feedback from hearing the sounds

Go to **www.commtechlab.msu .edu/sites/aslweb** where you will find thousands of ASL signs and video clips of signing.

FIGURE
11.2

Comparison of the Frequency and Intensity of Various Environmental and Speech Sounds

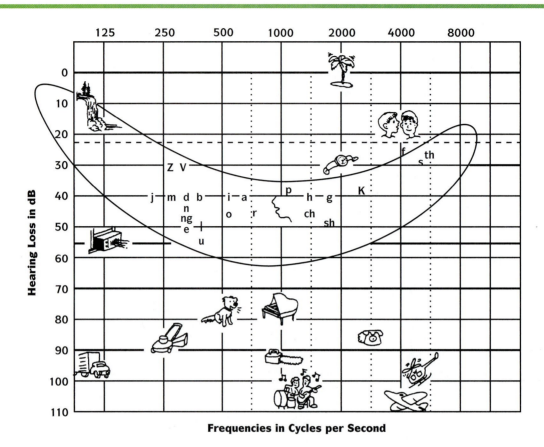

Source: Watkins, S. (Ed.). (1993). *SKI-HI resource manual* (p. G9). Logan, UT: H.O.P.E. Reprinted with permission.

they are producing. Many students who are deaf use **American Sign Language (ASL)** as their primary mode of communication. Other deaf or hard-of-hearing students use spoken English or a signed English system as their primary mode of communication. ASL is a visual, gestural language: It is not a visual representation of English, it is not a simplified language or communication system, nor is it a universal language. ASL has its own unique grammar and usage. **Finger spelling** is a system for representing the English alphabet manually. Finger spelling is used to "spell" names and proper nouns, as well as English words for which no sign exists. Figure 11.3 shows the American finger-spelling alphabet.

Because many students and adults who are deaf speak a common language, ASL, and share similar backgrounds (in that they are deaf), they regard themselves as members of the Deaf culture. Members of the Deaf culture view hearing loss not as a disability but as a common characteristic among their members (Padden & Humphries, 2006).

Prevalence of Hearing Loss

Since the implementation of the Individuals with Disabilities Education Act (IDEA), public schools have served more students with hearing loss than have state residential schools. On the basis of an annual survey of children and youth who are deaf or hard of hearing by the Gallaudet Research Institute (2008), which included 37,352 students, 42.4% received instruction in the general education classroom and 12.1% received instruction in a resource setting. The remainder were in special schools, home-schooled, or in self-contained classrooms. In the 2005–2006 school year, 71,332 students with hearing impairments received

FIGURE
11.3

American Finger-Spelling Alphabet

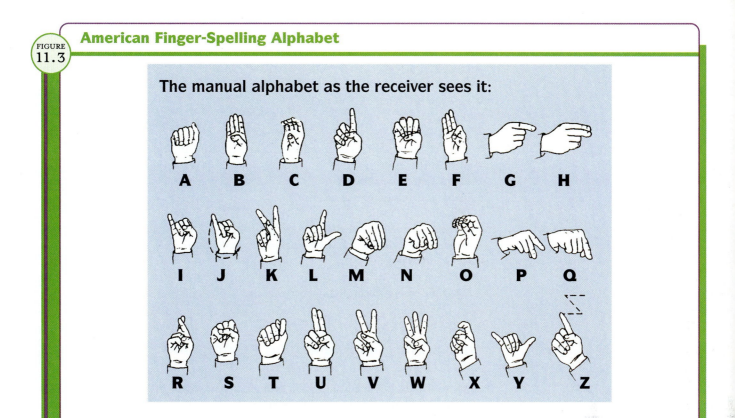

The manual alphabet as the receiver sees it:

A B C D E F G H

I J K L M N O P Q

R S T U V W X Y Z

special education services (U.S. Department of Education, 2007). However, like students with vision impairments, the number of students with hearing impairments in your classroom may be larger if the student has multiple disabilities.

Identification and Assessment of Students with Hearing Loss

Melanie Brooks, a kindergarten teacher, recalls her first experience of identifying a student with hearing loss. Chelsea had difficulty following directions, often asked that information be repeated, and had difficulty locating the speaker in group discussions. Melanie was also concerned about Chelsea's persistent colds, and she contacted the school nurse.

Together, the school nurse, Chelsea's parents, and Melanie began to identify ways to help Chelsea. They discovered that Chelsea had failed her kindergarten hearing screening and by talking with her parents, the nurse, and Melanie learned that Chelsea had incurred numerous ear infections as an infant and toddler. The district audiologist conducted further testing with Chelsea, discovering a mild to moderate hearing loss in both ears. To address the hearing loss, Chelsea was fitted with hearing aids. Melanie and the special education teacher specializing in hearing loss worked with Chelsea to provide resources and adaptations to help her learn better.

Some losses, particularly if they are mild to moderate ones, may first be detected during kindergarten screening and by classroom teachers. Most moderate, severe, and profound hearing losses have already been detected and identified by the time they reach your class. Early identification and intervention are key to the development of language and learning for children with hearing loss (Moeller, 2000). In 1993, the National Institutes of Health's Consensus Development Conference on Early Identification of Hearing Loss concluded that all infants should be screened for hearing loss, preferably before hospital discharge. Currently 37 states have passed legislation requiring newborn hearing screening for all babies born in their state (National Center for Hearing Assessment & Management, 2009). However, not all hearing loss occurs at birth, not all hearing losses are detected by a newborn hearing screening, and not all states have a systematic early detection system in place.

You may be able to assist in identifying children in your classroom with hearing loss by being aware of the following warning signs:

- Daydreaming
- Inattention
- Behavior problems and frustration
- Lethargy
- Failure to follow simple verbal commands
- Using verbal expressions of misunderstanding (e.g., "Huh?" and "I don't know")
- Articulation errors
- Limited speech or vocabulary
- Inappropriate responses to questions
- Difficulties with verbal tasks
- Difficulty decoding phonetically
- Unusual voice quality (soft, nasal, high pitch, monotonal)
- Mouth breathing
- Persistent colds
- Watching other students for instructional cues

Instructional Guidelines and Accommodations for Students with Hearing Loss

If you have a student with hearing loss in your classroom, you become an important member of a team that will make educational decisions that will affect that child. In addition to you, the team can include a special education teacher specializing in hearing loss, a sign language interpreter, the student, the parents, a speech and language pathologist, an audiologist, and other resource personnel.

Using Amplification.   Depending on the nature and extent of the hearing loss, students may use a **hearing aid** or an **implant**, which is a device inserted into the ear through surgery. Such devices do not regenerate hearing but amplify or give the sensation of hearing.

Even a mild hearing loss can have significant educational effects if it is not recognized. Lauren Resnick, a first-grade teacher, commented that she was surprised at the difference hearing aids made for Rider, a student in her class who had a mild hearing loss. When Rider was not wearing his hearing aids, he was often off task or seemed uninterested in class activities. With his hearing aids, however, he functioned like the other students in the class.

Technological advances provide many options in hearing aid selection. In classroom situations, however, hearing aids have limitations. They may amplify all sounds in the environment, and the student may hear other noises (background and reverberation) in addition to the desired signal such as the teacher's voice. Although some hearing aids can greatly reduce these problems, many considerations must be taken into account in selecting and fitting amplification for children. To help create an environment that provides an optimum listening environment for children with hearing loss, teachers should try to reduce background noise and decrease the listening distance of the student to the speaker.

Implants are increasingly being used for individuals who cannot benefit from the use of hearing aids. As with hearing aids, the success of implantation is very individual. Different types of implants serve different individual needs and functions (Hear-it Org, 2009):

- *Cochlear implants* are for individuals who are profoundly deaf; the devices provide a sensation of hearing.
- *Middle ear implants* are for individuals with conductive or mixed hearing loss; they are microphones that transmit sound from the middle to the inner ear.
- *Bone-anchored implants* are for a variety of hearing losses; they conduct sound from an implant in the skull behind the ear to the inner ear.
- *Auditory brain implants* are for individuals who do not have adequate auditory nerves; they are electrodes applied to the brain stem that provide electric signals leading to a sense of hearing and resulting in support for lipreading.

PEARSON
myeducationlab

Go to the Building Teaching Skills and Dispositions section of Topic 20: Hearing Loss and Deafness in the MyEducationLab for your course and complete the activity entitled *Using Visual Teaching Techniques*.

Go to **www.asha.org**, the American Speech-Language-Hearing Association website, for more information about technologies and resources that you can use to accommodate students with hearing loss.

Making Classroom Accommodations. Accommodations for students must be individualized. The Tips for Teachers 11.3 provides you with some general guidelines to help you meet the needs of your students with hearing loss.

As you plan your lessons, think of visual teaching for students with hearing loss not only in terms of instruction but also with respect to classroom management (Luckner, Bowen, & Carter, 2001). Rule charts, daily schedules, and task organizers can help students become full participants in ongoing activities.

Using Assistive Technology. In classroom situations, students often use **assistive listening devices (ALDs)** such as personal FM (frequency modulation) units (Plumley, 2008). With a *personal FM unit*, the teacher wears a wireless microphone, and the student wears a wireless receiver incorporated with a hearing aid. The microphone amplifies the teacher's voice 12 to 15 dB above the classroom noise and is not affected by distance. A *sound field FM system* may be another option for a student with hearing loss in the classroom. The teacher wears a small wireless microphone, and speakers are placed in strategic locations within the classroom. This system creates a favorable signal-to-noise ratio and accessibility to teacher instruction (Flexer, 2000). The American Speech-Language-Hearing Association points out that the number and variety of ALDs is vast and growing due to advances in technology (American Speech-Language-Hearing Association, 2009). Amplified answering machines and telephones, paging systems, and wake-up alarms are examples of ALDs that your student's audiologist may recommend for use.

What are some advantages and disadvantages of amplification systems for students with hearing loss? What communication alternatives are available for students who are deaf?

Tips FOR TEACHERS 11.3

ACCOMMODATING STUDENTS WITH HEARING LOSS

Provide Preferential Seating

- Minimize listening distance by having the student sit near you. Seat students away from loud noises (e.g., high-traffic areas, doors, air conditioning and heating units).

- Make sure the student can see you, the interpreter, and visual aids clearly.

- Eliminate glare from windows or lights.

Minimize Environmental Noise

- Use carpets, rugs, cork, and curtains to help absorb noise.

- Avoid unnecessary background noise (e.g., music, hallway noise).

Use Visual Clues and Demonstrations

- Face the student directly when you talk.

- Use an overhead projector rather than the board so that you can face the student while you write.

- Use natural gestures.

- Use modeling to demonstrate how to do different procedures and tasks.

- Use pictures, diagrams, and graphic organizers.

- Provide opportunities for experiential learning.

Maximize the Use of Visual Media

- Provide closed-captioned television (see Tips for Teachers 11.4).

- Provide access to computers.

Monitor the Student's Understanding

- Ask the student to repeat or rephrase important information or directions.

- Reword statements for clarification.

- Provide written instructions and summaries.

Promote Cooperation and Collaboration

- Use peer and classroom tutors and note takers.

- Identify speakers in a group discussion.

- Inform interpreters of topics before class, and provide study guides or teaching notes.

USING CLOSED CAPTIONING

Closed captioning is the process of encoding dialogue and sound effects from a program into readable text at the bottom of the television screen (similar to the subtitles in foreign films). *Decoders* are devices that enable you to view the words in a closed-captioning program.

In 1993 the federal Television Circuitry Decoder Act (passed in 1990) took effect. Thanks to this act, all televisions marketed in the United States must be capable of decoding closed-captioned signals. With this

development, one does not need a special captioning machine to view closed-captioned text. How does this apply to the classroom?

Today, many films, DVDs, and educational resources are captioned and available for use in the classroom. When you order a film or video, find out whether you can order it captioned. For more information, contact the Described and Captioned Media Program (www.dcmp.org).

In addition to ALDs, visual systems can be used in classrooms to promote learning for students with hearing impairments. Emails can be used for teacher-to-student or student-to-student communication (Lynne, 2007). Computerized speech recognition where computers transform human speech to print can be used to assist with composition and communication. Closed captioning with a television and CDs can also be used to improve access to the curriculum (see Tips for Teachers 11.4).

Using Interpreters and Note Takers. Sign language interpreters and note takers are valuable resources in the classroom. It is important that students who use a sign language system have an interpreter in the educational setting. Although an interpreter facilitates communication between the teacher and the student, the interpreter is not a substitute for you (the classroom teacher). Students may at first rely on the interpreter for answers and guidance but will learn to shift their confidence to you.

Go to **www.agbell.org** for information about programs, advocacy, and resources, including a site for teens who are deaf and hard of hearing.

To understand the information being presented, students need to be visually attentive. By permitting these students to photocopy your lecture notes or a classmate's notes or by providing duplicating paper to a peer note taker, you allow them to focus all their attention on what is taking place in the classroom. Peer or adult note takers and tutors can also help to clarify and explain topics, preteach vocabulary, or review technical terms. Keep in mind that careful attention to teaching techniques that support language and concept development will be beneficial for all your students.

Students with Physical Disabilities, Health Impairments, and Traumatic Brain Injury

Students with physical disabilities, health impairments, and traumatic brain injury are a small but diverse group. Disabilities can range from asthma, a comparatively mild condition, to cerebral palsy, which may involve neurological impairment that affects mobility and other functional skills, to traumatic brain injury, which can vary greatly in its effect on learning and daily functioning.

One of Lanetta Bridgewater's second-grade students, Emma, has cerebral palsy and is unable to speak but understands what others are saying and is developing academic skills at a rate similar to her classmates. In planning and working with Emma, Lanetta worked closely with Susie Speelman, an inclusion support teacher. Among the strategies Lanetta and Susie used to facilitate Emma's successful inclusion in Lanetta's classes were taking time to plan together, making the classroom more accessible for Emma and her wheelchair, using technology (particularly assistive devices to enable Emma to make choices and demonstrate her understanding), and reducing the amount of work (so that Emma has enough time to respond).

Definitions and Types of Physical Disabilities, Health Impairments, and Traumatic Brain Injury

Students with significant physical disabilities, health impairments, and traumatic brain injury generally qualify for special education services under three IDEIA categories: orthopedic impairment, other health impairment, and traumatic brain injury. Under IDEIA 2004 **orthopedic impairment** is defined as

> a severe orthopedic impairment that adversely affects a child's educational performance. The term includes impairments caused by congenital anomaly (e.g., clubfoot, absence of some member, etc.), impairments caused by disease (e.g., poliomyelitis, bone tuberculosis, etc.), and impairments from other causes (e.g., cerebral palsy, amputations, and fractures or burns that cause contractures). (IDEA 300.7[8])

Orthopedic impairments represent a wide range of conditions. They may not only interfere with the students' coordination and mobility, but also affect their ability to communicate, learn, and adjust. Orthopedic impairments are frequently referred to in education circles as **physical disabilities** (Turnbull, Turnbull, & Wehmeyer, 2010). The two general categories of physical disabilities are orthopedic impairments and neuromotor impairments (Heward, 2009). Orthopedic impairments are directly related to the skeletal system (e.g., bones, joints). **Neuromotor impairment** is an abnormal performance caused by a dysfunction of the brain, spinal cord, and nerves, thereby creating transmission of improper instructions, uncontrolled bursts of instructions from the brain, or incorrect interpretation of feedback to the brain (Pierangelo & Giuliani, 2007). Some types of neurological impairmentd are seizure disorders, cerebral palsy, and spina bifida. Neuromotor impairments can also involve both the nerves and the muscles. Muscular dystrophy, polio, and multiple sclerosis are examples of this type of physical disability. Although the cause of the physical impairment may vary from student to student, many of the challenges they face in movement are similar (Pierangelo & Giuliani, 2007).

IDEIA also provides special education services for students with other health impairments. **Other health impairment** is defined as

> having limited strength, vitality, or alertness, including a heightened alertness to environmental stimuli, that results in limited alertness with respect to the educational environment, that is due to chronic or acute health problems such as asthma, attention deficit disorder or attention deficit hyperactivity disorder, diabetes, epilepsy, a heart condition, hemophilia, lead poisoning, leukemia, nephritis, rheumatic fever, sickle cell anemia, and Tourette syndrome; and adversely affects academic performance. (IDEA 300.8 [c][9])

Students with health impairments are characterized by their chronic or acute health problems that result in limited strength, vitality, or alertness. Two subgroups of students with health impairments are medically fragile and/or technologically dependent individuals (Heward, 2009). **Medically fragile** children are at risk for medical emergencies on a regular basis and may also have progressive diseases such as cancer or AIDS. **Technologically dependent** students often require life support or specialized support systems such as ventilators.

With the 1990 amendments to IDEA, **traumatic brain injury** was identified as a category of disability and defined as

> an acquired injury to the brain caused by an external physical force, resulting in total or partial functional disability or psychosocial impairment, or both, that adversely affects a child's education performance. The term applies to open or closed head injuries resulting in impairments in one or more areas, such as cognition; language; memory; attention; reasoning; abstract thinking; judgment; problem-solving; sensory, perceptual, and motor abilities; psychosocial behavior; physical functions; information processing; and speech. The term does not apply to brain injuries that are congenital or degenerative, or brain injuries induced by birth trauma. (IDEA 300.8[c][12])

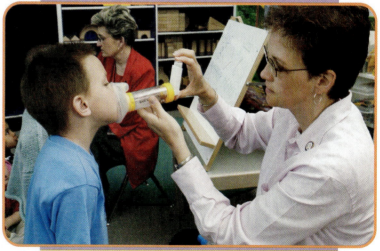

As classroom teacher, how will you assess and address the needs of a student with a serious health impairment?

Common causes of traumatic brain injuries are motorcycle, automobile, and off-road vehicle accidents; sports injuries; and accidents from violence, such as gunshot wounds and child abuse (Langlois, Rutland-Brown, & Thomas, 2006).

Characteristics of Students with Physical Disabilities, Health Impairments, and Traumatic Brain Injury

During your teaching career, you undoubtedly will have students with physical disabilities, health impairments, and traumatic brain injury. This section describes some of the more prevalent of these disabilities.

Asthma. The chronic health condition that your students are most likely to experience in your classroom is asthma. Asthma is a persistent inflammation of the air passages that causes episodes of difficulty in breathing (American Lung Association, 2009). Asthma is the most common chronic condition among children. The American Lung Association (2009) reports that 6.8 million children 18 years and younger have asthma and that 12.8 million school days a year are lost due to the condition. Asthma can be caused by allergies, but can also be caused by nonallergic factors such as stress, viruses, and smoke (Asthma Allergy Foundation of America, 2009). As a classroom teacher, you will want to learn what triggers an asthma attack (e.g., exercise, chalk dust, carpets, odors or fumes), any dietary restrictions, and procedures to follow if an episode occurs.

Cerebral Palsy. Students with **cerebral palsy** constitute one of the largest groups of children with physical disabilities (Heward, 2009). Cerebral palsy is caused by damage to the brain before or during birth. Conditions are classified according to the areas affected and the types of symptoms. The degree of severity varies and is often evidenced by lack of coordination, speech disorders, motor problems, and extreme weakness. Cerebral palsy generally has accompanying problems in such areas as learning, vision, hearing, cognitive functioning, skin disorders (because of pressure sores), and social and emotional growth (United Cerebral Palsy, 2009). The condition can interfere with head control, arm use, sitting positions, balance, posture, and mobility, and these problems can be exacerbated by fatigue and stress.

As a classroom teacher of a student with cerebral palsy, you will want to be aware of the student's level of fatigue and stress. Paul Nichols, a high-school math teacher, mentioned that his student, Allison, appeared stressed during tests, particularly if they were long or timed.

> I noticed that whenever we had a timed test with essays, Allison would have difficulty sitting up and holding up her head. At first I thought it was just a way for her to try to get out of the test, so I tried to be firm with her. When I spoke to the physical therapist, he mentioned that she may be tired or stressed and then he taught her some relaxation techniques. She is doing better but it is still a difficult time for her. I did explain to her that the timed part was not as important as doing the work, so now I give her extended time by allowing her to finish the test with the special education teacher during her resource period.

Spina Bifida. **Spina bifida**, a birth defect that occurs when the spinal cord fails to close properly, often causes paralysis of parts of the body but seldom affects intellectual functioning (Bigge, Best, & Heller, 2001; Spina Bifida Foundation, 2009). Most students with spina bifida walk with difficulty and lack complete bladder and bowel control. Some students need to use a catheter, which necessitates training in hygiene and extra time during the day to take care of the catheter. Generally, the school nurse or a special education teacher provides this training if it has not already been provided. This type of support is often provided by a paraprofessional.

Epilepsy. The most common neurological impairment in school-age children is convulsive disorders, or **epilepsy**. Epilepsy is characterized by a tendency to have recurrent seizures—sudden, excessive, spontaneous, and abnormal discharges of neurons accompanied by alteration in motor function, sensory function, or consciousness (Epilepsy Foundation, 2009).

There are two major types of seizures. **Absence seizures (petit mal)** are characterized by short lapses in consciousness. Students may appear inattentive and often do not realize that they are having seizures. **Tonic–clonic seizures (grand mal)** are characterized by convulsions followed by loss of consciousness. Usually, a tonic phase, in which the muscles are rigid, is followed by a clonic phase, in which the arms and legs jerk. Often the student loses consciousness and awakens disoriented and tired. Hallahan and colleagues (2009) note that seizures differ in the following dimensions: duration, frequency, onset, movements, causes, associated disabilities, and control (e.g., through medication). Talk with your student's family

Go to **www.aafa.org,** the Asthma and Allergy Foundation of America website, for facts, resources, and expert information about asthma and related conditions.

PEARSON myeducationlab

Go to the Assignments and Activities section of Topic 18: Physical Disabilities and Health Impairments in the MyEducationLab for your course and complete the activity entitled *Paraprofessionals and Children with Physical Disabilities*.

Go to **www.epilepsyfoundation .org,** the Epilepsy Foundation website, where you can find information about how to help individuals with epilepsy and how to help students make academic and social adjustments.

Tips FOR Teachers 11.5

HOW TO RESPOND TO A STUDENT HAVING A TONIC–CLONIC (GRAND MAL) SEIZURE

- Ease the student to the floor and clear the area around him or her.

- Put something soft under the student's head to keep it from banging on the floor.

- Do not interfere with the seizure. Turn the student gently on his or her side, but do not put anything in the student's mouth, and do not try to hold his or her tongue.

- Have someone stay with the student until he or she is fully awake.

- Allow the student to rest afterward.

- Seek emergency assistance if the seizure lasts longer than 5 minutes or if the student requests it.

to learn more about what you might expect in terms of the nature and type of seizures your student experiences.

Although these seizures usually last less than 5 minutes, they can be a frightening event for you and your students. Tips for Teachers 11.5 provides some pointers for handling this type of seizure. If a student in your class has this type of seizure disorder, be sure to help the other students in the classroom understand the condition and respond appropriately to the student.

Muscular Dystrophy. **Muscular dystrophy** is a chronic disorder characterized by the weakening and wasting of the body's muscles. People with muscular dystrophy progressively lose their ability to walk and effectively use their arms and hands (Muscular Dystrophy Association, 2009). There is no cure for muscular dystrophy at this time, and the only prevention is genetic counseling (the condition appears to run in families). Helping the student maintain independence through regular physical therapy, exercise, and necessary physical aids is important. School personnel need to be careful not to lift or pull a student with muscular dystrophy by his or her arms, because doing so may cause dislocation of limbs. Most students with muscular dystrophy have a diminished ability to walk by the age of 10 to 14, and teachers should be alert for signs of fatigue (Heward, 2009).

Go to **www.mda.org**, the Muscular Dystrophy Association website, where you can find a wide range of resources to help students with academic and social adjustments.

HIV and AIDS. **Human immunodeficiency virus (HIV)** is a condition that infects and eventually destroys cells in the immune system that protect the body from disease. A viral infection transmitted through bodily fluids, HIV is responsible for **acquired immunodeficiency syndrome (AIDS)** (CDC, 2009a). Most children with HIV/AIDS contracted the disease through their mother: either before or during birth or through breastfeeding (CDC, 2007). Adolescents may contract HIV/AIDS through sexual activity (CDC, 2008).

Students infected with HIV may eventually experience loss of stamina, developmental delays, motor problems, progressive neurological defects, repeated bacterial infections, psychological stresses, and death (Foulk, Gessner, & Koorland, 2001). HIV progresses through stages. In the latency stage, which generally lasts from 2 to 10 years in children, there are no outward symptoms. As the disease progresses through the middle stages, individuals experience a general weakening of the immune system, which results in persistent fevers and infections. In the final stages, opportunistic infections increase in frequency and severity.

In its position statement on Education of Children with HIV, the American Academy of Pediatrics (2001, 2007) recommends that students with the infection should receive the same opportunities for education as other children with chronic illnesses. Most school districts have established policies regarding the inclusion of students with HIV in general education classrooms. This includes policies on confidentiality and disclosure (DePaepe, Garrison-Kane, & Doelling, 2002). If students in your classroom are identified as having HIV, consult with individuals knowledgeable about these policies and work with the special education teacher and school nurse in planning for these students. One important question to ask is how the condition currently affects the student's physical and mental health. Students whose frequent absences are due to recurrent infections might need a homebound teacher. Students may also exhibit anxiety about their condition, about visits to the doctor, or about facing death (DePaepe et al., 2002).

PEARSON
myeducationlab

To enhance your understanding of the role of the school nurse when working with students who have health impairments, go to the IRIS Center Resources section of Topic 18: Physical Disabilities and Health Impairments in the MyEducationLab for your course and complete Module 29: School Nurses: Roles and Responsibilities in the School Setting.

By knowing and adjusting to the student's capabilities, you enable the student to participate more fully and successfully in classroom activities. For example, Shirley Meeder, an eighth-grade social studies teacher, found that she could adapt assignments for Joey, a student in the middle stages of HIV, by reducing the amount of work required, giving him the option of listening to the textbook on tape, having a note taker, and letting Joey take tests orally. These modifications helped Joey deal with his limited stamina. The special education teacher helped Shirley provide many of these accommodations. When Joey suffered from a prolonged infection, he received homebound instruction so that he could keep up with his classmates.

You may not be informed that a student in your class has HIV. Therefore, taking precautions when coming in contact with blood or other bodily fluids of any student is wise (DePaepe et al., 2002). Keep latex gloves available in case a student in your class has a cut or other injury.

Traumatic Brain Injury. Because traumatic brain injury may occur at different developmental stages, with a wide variety of severity and complexities and various responses to recovery, the characteristics and educational needs of these students are unique (Lash, 2000). Key points to consider about the characteristics of individuals with traumatic brain injury are the following:

- The degree of initial recovery from the injury will vary widely and require frequent review of the student's individual educational program.
- Memory, attention, and executive function difficulties are common.
- Slowed processing of information and faulty reasoning are common.
- Preinjury skills may be preserved but are not predictive of new learning abilities.
- Lowered social inhibition and judgment, lowered impulse control, depression, and overestimation of abilities are typical.
- Less initiative and motivation are typical, as is general fatigue.
- Services and supports are often needed in at least four areas: cognition, speech and language, social and behavioral skills, and physical functioning.

Go to **www.biausa.org**, the Brain Injury Association website, where you can find information to help meet students' educational needs.

For example, when Justin returned to high school 3 weeks after being in a car accident in which he sustained a head injury, Ms. Claudia Ruiz, his math teacher, immediately recognized the changes in his cognitive functioning. His response time was slower, and concepts that had been easy for him to grasp were fuzzy and required reteaching. Claudia worked with the special education teacher to identify key concepts for Justin to relearn and new concepts to be reinforced. Over the next 3 months, Claudia recognized a significant change in Justin's learning patterns. His response time quickened, and he was able to learn new concepts at a faster rate. During these first 3 months, Claudia stayed in especially close contact with the special education teacher and Justin's parents so that she could facilitate the recovery of his cognitive functioning.

The following are typical behaviors associated with traumatic brain injuries:

- Lowered social inhibition, judgment, and impulse control
- Faulty reasoning
- Numerous cognitive processing difficulties
- Lowered initiative and motivation
- Overestimation of abilities
- Depression
- Flat affect with sudden outbursts
- Agitation and irritability
- Fatigue (Keyser-Marcus, Briel et al., 2002; National Dissemination Center for Children with Disabilities, 2006)

Prevalence of Physical Disabilities, Health Impairments, and Traumatic Brain Injury

Despite advances in medical research and treatment, in some areas of chronic health conditions (such as asthma) prevalence figures are actually on the rise (van der Lee, Mokkink, Grootenhuis, Heymans, & Offringa, 2007). Depending on how chronic health conditions are defined, prevalence figures vary from .22% to 44% of children in the United States (van der Lee et al., 2007). To further complicate prevalence figures, students with physical disabilities or health impairments may be identified in the system under another disability category including multiple disabilities. U.S. Department of Education (2007) figures indicate that in the 2005–2006 school year 60,100 students with orthopedic impairments and 625,187 students with other health impairments received special education services under IDEIA.

The most common cause of disability is traumatic brain injury (Keyser-Marcus, Briel, Sherron-Targett, Yasuda, Johnson, & Wehman, 2002). Although approximately 450,000 children and adolescents sustain a brain injury each year and are treated in emergency rooms (Langlois et al., 2006), the number of students who receive services under IDEIA is substantially less, approximately 23,805 (U.S. Department of Education, 2007). The occurrence of traumatic brain injury increases dramatically during adolescence (15 to 24 years of age) owing to increased participation in contact sports, greater access to and use of automobiles and motorcycles, more frequent use of racing and mountain bikes, and injuries from firearms. Boys are two to three times more likely to receive head injuries than girls (Langlois et al., 2006).

Identification and Assessment of Students with Physical Disabilities, Health Impairments, and Traumatic Brain Injury

Medical diagnosis usually provides the initial identification of physical disabilities, health impairments, and traumatic brain injury. Assessments are carefully designed to take into account these students' potential for delayed motor skills or problems staying on task for long periods of time. Remember that, as a classroom teacher and a member of the education team, you are a valuable resource of information.

Depending on the student, assessments in the following areas are often appropriate:

- Activities of daily living (personal hygiene, eating, dressing, using public transportation)
- Attention, concentration, initiation, or sustained effort
- Adaptations for learning (academic and physical adaptations to help students achieve academic success and independence)
- Communication (students' ability to express and understand language)
- Mobility (students' current and potential range and mode of mobility)
- Physical abilities and limitations (positioning and necessary adaptive equipment and techniques that facilitate students' independence)
- Psychosocial development (effects of impairment on students' social and emotional functioning)
- Transition skills (skills needed for a successful transition into and from school and between grade levels)

Instructional Guidelines and Accommodations for Students with Physical Disabilities, Health Impairments, and Traumatic Brain Injury

Three basic principles can help you accommodate students with physical disabilities, health impairments, and traumatic brain injury in your classroom:

1. *Use others as resources.* Call on the expertise of the student, parents, other school personnel, and others in health-related professions, as well as the student's classmates.
2. *Be flexible in your planning.* Be willing to make last-minute changes in response to day-to-day changes in the student's condition and readiness to learn.
3. *Be ingenious and creative.* One of the greatest rewards from working with students is helping them discover their strengths and ways to demonstrate them.

Transdisciplinary Teaming and Support Providers. Because many students with physical disabilities or health impairments receive services from special education teachers, an occupational or physical therapist, an adaptive physical education teacher, and possibly a speech and language pathologist, effective teaming and communication are crucial. In transdisciplinary teaming, all members of the team work together and view the student as a whole instead of working only on their area of specialty (Orelove, Sobsey, & Silberman, 2004). All team members are aware of the student's goals and observe one another as they work with the student so that they can share and generalize successful techniques and strategies. Tips for Teachers 11.6

Tips FOR TEACHERS 11.6

SUGGESTIONS FOR WORKING WITH SERVICE PROVIDERS

- Become aware of what support service providers have to offer.

- Approach support service staff as collaborators rather than experts.

- Make sure team members agree on expectations and goals for students.

- Clarify your role as a team member and your relationship with other team members.

- Be clear about the types of supports you need and want.

- Distinguish between needing an "extra pair of hands" and more specialized help.

- Make sure support service providers understand your classroom routines.

- Participate in scheduling support services.

- Have the team evaluate the effectiveness of support services for the student.

- Make sure support services are helping you do a better job.

Source: Adapted from Giangreco, M. F. (1997). *Quick-guides to inclusion: Ideas for educating students with disabilities.* Baltimore: Brookes.

provides further suggestions for working with these and other service providers. You will find these individuals to be an important support team for you and one key to the student's success.

Using Assistive Technology   The 2004 reauthorization of IDEA defines **assistive technology** as "any item, piece of equipment, or product system whether acquired commercially off the shelf, modified, or customized, that is used to increase, maintain, or improve functional capabilities of individuals with disabilities" (Pub. L. No. 108-466, Part A, Sec. 602, pp. 11–12). Assistive technology devices are particularly useful for increasing mobility, improving communication, gaining access to computers, performing daily living skills, enhancing learning, and manipulating and controlling the environment (Bryant & Bryant, 2003; Dell, Newton, & Petroff, 2008; Johnston, Beard, & Carpenter, 2007). By using such assistive technology as eye-gaze pointing, communication boards, and writing implements encased in plastic tubing or bicycle handle grips, for example, Lanetta's student, Emma, described earlier, is able to participate more fully in classroom life. The implementation of any assistive technology should be based on student needs as identified on the IEP. In thinking about the use of technology and assistive technology, consider these points (Marino, Marino, & Shaw, 2006):

- Determine the people who are responsible for assistive technology at your school, district, or region and use them as resources.
- Check your school district policy on using equipment at home and on maintaining and repairing equipment.
- Ask for training on the equipment that your student will be using.
- Collaborate with others to share your knowledge and learn from them.

See TechTips for more information on using assistive technologies.

Making Environmental Modifications.   In addition to the necessary accessibility modifications (e.g., wide aisles for wheelchairs, low drinking fountains, appropriate handles), other environmental modifications facilitate independence for students with physical disabilities, health impairments, and traumatic brain injury. Wright and Bigge (1991) discuss four types of environmental modifications:

- Changes in location of materials and equipment (e.g., so that students in wheelchairs can reach items independently)
- Work surface modifications (e.g., raising a desk so that a wheelchair fits under it)
- Object modifications (e.g., attaching clips to a student's desk to secure papers)
- Manipulation aids (e.g., using a page turner to reduce dependency on others)

Tech Tips

ASSISTIVE TECHNOLOGIES FOR STUDENTS WITH VISUAL AND HEARING IMPAIRMENTS AND TRAUMATIC BRAIN INJURIES

When you are teaching children with special needs, you will make accommodations, based on individual needs, to enable those learners to accomplish the same work as their classmates who do not have disabilities. The computer empowers these children, more than any other population, to accomplish the same work in general education classes as their peers without disabilities. With appropriate accommodations, barriers to the general education curriculum imposed by a disability can be minimized or even eliminated.

IntelliTools by Cadmium Learning at
▶ **www.intellitools.com** offers alternative keyboards, some that are programmable, for students with physical disabilities. IntelliKeys USB keyboard has Overlay Maker software that you can use to easily design overlays to meet individual needs.

Mountbatten Brailler by Quantum Technology at
▶ **www.quantech.com.au/** offers four models of braille instruction from introductory through the high-school years. These research-based products connect to PCs and allow teachers to prepare braille materials for students and allow students to communicate with teachers.

Alliance for Technology Access at
▶ **www.ataccess.org/** is a nonprofit community of vendors and service providers who offer information and services for children and adults with disabilities and give them access to a technology.

Providing Instruction for Motor Skills. For students with physical disabilities, health impairments, and traumatic brain injury, working on motor skills is an important component of their education program. Many activities that support motor skills can be incorporated easily into daily classroom activities, such as increasing control by looking at a classmate during cooperative learning activities or improving fine motor skills by drawing or writing. The special education teacher, occupational therapist, physical therapist, and adaptive physical education teacher can be valuable resources in integrating instruction in motor skills into the curriculum.

Promoting Literacy Development. Promoting literacy development (reading, writing, listening, and speaking) is very important for individuals with physical disabilities (Downing, 2005; Johnston, McDonnell, & Hawken, 2008). It provides students access to language, a means to communicate their ideas, and a way to increase their experiences and knowledge. It also provides a lifelong pleasurable activity. Facilitating literacy development includes such suggestions as the following:

■ *Positioning.* Adaptive wheelchairs or other seating devices may act as barriers to the students' ability to see print and pictures. Position students so that they can see the print and pictures while listening. This helps them begin to make the connection between print and speech. Ideally, students should be situated in a way that allows them to help turn the pages so that they begin to recognize the left-to-right orientation of text. Following the text with a finger or a bookmark also helps a person develop this concept.

■ *Siblings and peers.* Because children with physical disabilities might not have the ability to question and retell a story, the inclusion of peers or siblings during storytime could help make the storytime livelier. Parents have reported that children related text to real-life activities and asked and answered a greater variety of questions when peers or siblings were present. The other children also act as models for the child with disabilities.

■ *Print in the environment.* Having print everywhere in the students' environment is important. Remember that for students with physical disabilities the print needs to be at their eye level based on their adaptive equipment.

■ *Accessing literacy.* Students with disabilities need a method by which to independently access storybooks, writing instruments, and other literacy-related items. These could be books on tape, podcasts, or switches to access computer programs for reading, writing, and drawing. Drawing and writing can be made easier with adaptive holders for the writing utensil. Taping the paper down or stabilizing items with Velcro also helps the student draw or write. Tips for Teachers 11.7 provides more quick and easy ideas for helping students become more independent and successful.

PROMOTING INDEPENDENCE FOR STUDENTS WITH PHYSICAL DISABILITIES

- Retrace or enlarge print with a dark marker to help students see material more clearly.

- Schedule study buddies to help a student with disabilities gather learning materials.

- Assign a classmate or ask for a volunteer to take or copy notes for a student with disabilities.

- Ask students for whom writing is difficult whether they would prefer an oral assignment or test.

- Ask the special education teacher to provide (or advise you on acquiring) materials for securing small objects.

Velcro and a Dycem mat on a student's desk prevent books, calculators, pencil boxes, and the like from slipping off.

- Ask parents to provide a bandanna or sweatband, worn on the wrist, to help a student with limited control of facial muscles wipe off excess saliva.

- Arrange with the special education teacher for the assistance of a paraprofessional in moving a student from a wheelchair to a beanbag chair during floor activities so that the student can be both supported physically and seated on the same level as peers.

Educating Classmates.   For students with health impairments and physical disabilities, some of the most important modifications relate to informing other students in the class. Classmates, particularly of younger students with rare diseases or severe disabilities, will most likely have limited knowledge and many questions. For example, Sexson and Madan-Swain (1993) found that students most often asked the following questions about a classmate with a health problem:

- What's wrong with the student?
- Is the disease contagious?
- Will (the student) die from it?
- Will the student lose anything (such as limbs, hair)?
- Should we talk about the student's illness or ignore it?
- What will other students think if I'm still friends with this student?

It may also be helpful to talk about how a student might be different when he or she returns from a prolonged absence or a traumatic brain injury. Using children's and juvenile literature and DVDs are other ways in which students and you can learn about different disabilities and support a student with a specific physical or health-related impairment (Conner & Bejoian, 2006; Prater & Dyches, 2008).

Go to **http://www.hospicenet .org/** for books and support group information that you can pass on to families to help them through these difficult times.

Dealing with Chronic Illness and Death.   During your teaching career, you may have a student in your class who is dying. Children in your class may also experience a death of someone close to them: a friend, family member, teacher, classmate, or pet. Open communication with the student, parents, counselor, and other members of the education team becomes very important so that you can deal with the student's feelings and fears in a consistent and open manner. You may work directly with the school counselor, but you need written permission from parents before you can contact a student's private counselor or psychologist. You will also want to work with the school counselor as you develop a plan for communicating with and supporting classmates as they deal with the illness and/or death of a friend. There are abundant resources including websites to turn to so you can learn more about how to support children, their classmates, and their families (e.g., The Dougy Center, National Center for Grieving Children and Families, and hospice care).

Interviews with children who are cancer survivors shed light on the needs of children who have a chronic illness (Bessell, 2001). Students emphasized how important attending school was to their sense of normalcy. A caring and understanding teacher and the acceptance of their peers were seen as particularly important. Teachers who made accommodations for their special needs were viewed positively. Homebound instruction can be necessary when students are in treatment or otherwise unable to attend school. If this is the case, Bessell recommends that teachers make every effort to "keep students in the loop." Using technologies such as email and Skype can assist in keeping the communication flowing.

For decades it has been recognized that individuals can go through stages as they move toward accepting death (Berner, 1977; Cassini & Rogers, 1990; Kübler-Ross, 1969). Although not all children go through all stages and some stages may be experienced simultaneously, knowledge of these stages can help you understand the behaviors and emotions that may be exhibited by a student who is dying. Moreover, for children stages may not occur in a predictable order (Wolfelt, 2002; Worden, 1996). The stages include the following:

- Shock and disbelief
- Crying (sometimes hysterical)
- Feelings of isolation and loneliness
- Psychosomatic symptoms, which may distract the student from the fatal condition
- Panic
- Guilty feelings that he or she is to blame
- Hostility or resentment toward others
- Resistance to usual routines and continuing to live
- Reconciliation and beginning acceptance of the inevitability of death
- Acceptance

Although the suggestions in Table 11.1 are from parents of children with cancer (Candlelighters Childhood Cancer Foundation, 1993), many apply also to children with other life-threatening illnesses, such as HIV/AIDS and cystic fibrosis.

Finally, the loss of the child will be a loss for you as well. Make certain that you have identified a support network that can assist you as you cope with your own grieving process (Hunt & Munson, 2005).

As you work with students who have visual, hearing, physical, or health impairments, your repertoire of teaching strategies and knowledge of classroom accommodations and assistive technology will grow. With the help of a number of specialists, who can assist both you and the student, you should feel confident of success in educating your students.

TABLE 11.1

Parents' View: What Teachers Should and Should Not Do for a Student with Cancer

HELPFUL TEACHERS	LESS HELPFUL TEACHERS
✓ Take time to learn about the treatments and their effects on school performance.	✓ Fail to learn about the disease and its effects and treatments.
✓ Demonstrate support for parents as well as student.	✓ Show fear about having the student in class.
✓ Listen to parents' concerns and fears.	✓ Allow other students to pity the student.
✓ Call or visit during absences.	✓ Fail to keep ongoing communication with parents and student during absences.
✓ Encourage classmates to call or write during extended absences.	✓ Ignore problems classmates have in adjusting to friend's disease.
✓ Before reentry, talk with the student about any fears or concerns.	✓ Before reentry, fail to share information about the student and the disease with classmates.
✓ Adjust lessons and assignments based on the student's endurance.	✓ Do not give the student the benefit of the doubt on assignments and homework.
✓ Follow parental and medical instructions regarding snacks, wearing a hat, bathroom visits.	✓ Make an issue of the student's differences in front of others.
✓ Treat the student as normally as possible and include the student in as many class activities as possible.	✓ Do not give the student an opportunity to attempt what others are doing.

Source: Information from Candlelighters Childhood Cancer Foundation (1993). Advice to educators (adapted from a survey by A Wish with Wings). In *Educating the child with cancer (pp. 21–22).* Bethesda, MD: Author.

Summary

- Legal definitions of visual impairments are based on visual acuity and visual fields. Educational definitions are based on student's ability to perform academic tasks. It is important when planning for a student with a visual impairment to consider the student's functional vision and to consider auditory, tactile, and visual accommodations.

- Definitions of hearing impairment include individuals who are deaf and those who are hard of hearing. Although most children with significant hearing loss are identified before beginning school, it is important to watch for signs of mild hearing loss. Arranging the classroom to reduce background noise and using interpreters and note takers provide means for students with hearing loss to better access the general education curriculum.

- Students who have physical disabilities, health impairments, and traumatic brain injury may need environmental modifications such as changes in location of materials, work surface modifications, object modifications, and manipulation aids. When working with students who have physical disabilities, health impairments, and traumatic brain injury, you will want to collaborate with specialists such as physical and occupational therapists, speech and language pathologists, assistive technology specialists, and school nurses and other medical professionals.

Think and Apply

1. In the opening interview, Peggy Kirkland was afraid that she lacked the knowledge and experience to work with students like Kerri. What systems are in place to help Peggy? Make a list of your questions, the people you would ask, and the meetings or activities you would plan before a student with disabilities joins your class.

2. Try to find a classroom that includes students who have visual impairments in your school district. Arrange to spend some time in a classroom and observe the strategies teachers use to communicate with and instruct their students.

3. Interview and observe a speech and hearing specialist. Find out about the students with whom they work, their roles and responsibilities, and how they team with general classroom teachers.

4. Interview several adolescents or young adults with a physical disability, health impairment, or traumatic brain injury. Ask the following questions:

   - What impact does (the disability) have on your daily life?
   - How do your routines differ because of (the disability)?
   - How do others react to your disability?
   - What advice would you give classroom teachers about helping other students with (the disability)?

PEARSON
myeducationlab

Now go to Topic 18: Physical Disabilities and Health Impairments; Topic 19: Visual Impairments; and Topic 20: Hearing Loss and Deafness in the MyEducationLab (www.myeducationlab.com) for your course where you can:

- Find learning outcomes for these topics along with the national standards that connect to these outcomes.

- Complete Assignments and Activities that can help you more deeply understand the chapter content.

- Examine challenging situations and cases presented in the IRIS Center Resources.

- Apply and practice your understanding of the core teaching skills identified in the chapter with Building Teaching Skills and Dispositions learning units.

Part

3

TEACHING PRACTICES

Chapter 12

Facilitating Reading

Chapter 13

Facilitating Writing

Chapter 14

Helping All Students Succeed in Mathematics

Facilitating Reading

CHAPTER

12

FOCUS QUESTIONS

1. What are current trends and issues in reading instruction, particularly for struggling readers, and how might they affect your planning for reading instruction in your classroom? What are the components of reading instruction and how would you vary instruction for a beginning and an advanced reader?

2. What are principles of effective reading instruction for struggling readers?

3. What guidelines and teaching strategies can you implement for students who have difficulty with phonological awareness, letter–sound correspondence, and the alphabetic principle?

4. What guidelines and teaching strategies can you use to help your students identify words when they are reading?

5. What are some activities you can use to help your students become more fluent readers?

6. What strategies can you teach to help improve students' comprehension before, during, and after they read?

7. What are some key similarities and differences between teaching older struggling readers and younger struggling readers?

INTERVIEW
INES LEZCANO

Ines Lezcano is a third-grade teacher at Flamingo Elementary School in Miami, Florida. Of the 29 students in her classroom, eight are originally speakers of languages other than English who have transitioned into speaking, reading, and writing in English. Four are children with learning disabilities (LD) who are in her class full time. Ines works with the special education teacher, Joyce Duryea, to plan for the reading and writing instruction of these four students. However, Joyce is a great support for all students because she co-teaches lessons and makes instructional adaptations for students with LD.

For the last 2 years, I have also [had] a classroom in which most of the students with disabilities are placed. Even though I received a lot of support from Joyce, I was still concerned about whether or not I could adequately meet the academic needs of the students with LD in my classroom. What I've learned is that it can be done, but I've had to rethink my instructional practices—especially for reading. For my students who have reading skills that are substantially below those of the other students in my class, I keep on having to think, "How can I meet their needs and still keep things going for everyone else in the classroom?" I've figured out how to do this through multilevel activities, adaptations during whole-group activities, and small-group instruction.

My favorite multilevel activity is classwide peer tutoring. During classwide peer tutoring, everyone is reading to a partner. I like it because the students really get involved and learn how to give each other help with their reading. This practice gives me an opportunity to work closely with students with reading disabilities. I also teach comprehension strategies such as finding the main idea or making a story map as multilevel activities. I teach the whole class the strategy and then have the students work in groups and practice using text that is appropriate for their reading levels.

When I do give whole-class assignments in reading that I think are going to be hard for the students with reading problems, particularly with recognizing the words, I have to plan for adaptations. For example, sometimes we read a story from the basal reader. I have a listening station set up in my room so that my lowest readers can listen to an audiotape of the story. Volunteer readers from the fifth-grade class make the audiotapes of the stories. It's important to keep in mind how to give kids the support they need to do well.

A few of my students need intensive instruction in reading sight words, and I have found that phonics instruction for about 15 minutes a day really supports their reading. Joyce has helped me establish instructional goals and activities for the students with disabilities. We're monitoring their progress and really starting to see some growth.

The reading [and] language arts block is my favorite time of the day. It's fun to see my students get excited about reading. It is also rewarding to watch their progress and to see how much more fluent and competent they're becoming as readers. It's a challenge to think about what each one needs, but I'm getting better at observing them and thinking of ways to help them become independent learners. I feel that during reading [and] language arts time I'm giving them the tools they need to be successful learners in all of their subjects.

Introduction

Ines values the interactive role that the special education teacher, Joyce, provides in designing and implementing instructional routines for all of her students but especially those with disabilities. Both Ines and Joyce are on the lookout for strategies, instructional materials, and computer-assisted instruction that can make all students successful learners. Students with moderate to severe disabilities are frequently denied opportunities to learn to read and become participating members of our literate society, even though many of them are able to successfully learn to read or to make meaning from messages in our environment (Copeland & Keefe, 2007). This chapter focuses on what general education teachers can do to provide effective instruction for students who struggle with learning to read.

Current Trends in Reading and Reading Instruction

The goal of reading instruction is to provide students with the skills, strategies, and knowledge to read fluently and to understand and construct meaning from text for purposes of enjoyment and learning, whether reading a book, magazine, sign, pamphlet, email message, or information on the Internet. Reading is considered by many to be the most important area of education, and proficiency in reading is becoming even more critical in our technological society. Can you even imagine how difficult it would be to succeed not just in school but in life if you have difficulty reading? For example, consider a middle-school boy with significant reading problems who explained that after he learned to read, what he really appreciated was being able to read the menu for lunch and not have to wait to look at the food. Skill in reading is a prerequisite for many of the learning activities in content-area classes such as social studies, science, and vocational education and for successful employment and daily living.

We have been concerned for decades about improving reading instruction. Fundamentally, there is nothing more important than learning to read and reading to learn. Although there is much agreement that learning to read is important, there have always been rather contentious discussions on how best to accomplish this goal. National panels of experts have reviewed the research and written summaries of research-based practices for reading instruction. These committees represented national experts on reading research and a few selected practitioners and assembled two reports:

■ The Committee on Prevention of Reading Difficulties in Young Children published the report *Preventing Reading Difficulties in Young Children* (Snow, Burns, & Griffin, 1998).
■ The National Reading Panel (a panel charged by Congress to assess the research-based knowledge in teaching reading) published *Teaching Children to Read: An Evidence-Based Assessment of the Scientific Research Literature on Reading and Its Implications for Reading Instruction* (National Reading Panel, 2000).

Both reports stressed the importance of a balanced approach to teaching early reading, including the important role of phonological awareness and phonics instruction as well as the critical role that repeated reading plays in the development of reading fluency and the importance of teaching reading comprehension strategies, vocabulary, and text structure. Even though these reports did not focus on individuals with disabilities, many of the practices recommended are also effective for these students (Boyle, 2008).

Go to **www.NationalReading Panel.org** for a current review of the research on teaching reading.

Three Key Concepts for Effective Reading Instruction

Whether you become an elementary teacher, a language arts teacher in middle or high school, or teach a content area such as social studies, science, or vocational education, three overarching concepts will be important to employ when you support students in reading.

1. *Reading is a skilled and strategic process in which learning to decode and read words accurately and rapidly is an essential feature.* Reading requires a variety of thinking skills and strategies, including those for recognizing words, sometimes called **decoding** or **word identification**. Reading entails using attention, perception, memory, and retrieval processes so that the reader can automatically identify or decode words. Readers use selective attention and perception coupled with their knowledge of the letter–sound relationships and context to help them automatically recognize the words. As students become proficient readers, they recognize most words with little effort. But as students are learning to read or when readers encounter unknown words, they use their knowledge of the **alphabetic principle** (how speech relates to print), **phonological awareness skills** (distinguishing the sounds in a word and being able to segment and blend them) (e.g., *-at, -ight,* prefixes, suffixes, syllables), and their decoding strategies (e.g., phonic analysis, structural analysis, context) to assist in decoding. When students have difficulty identifying words, they also have difficulty with **fluency** (reading quickly and smoothly) because so much effort is spent just on figuring out the words. When decoding is fluent, effort can be focused on comprehension. Therefore, one goal of reading instruction is to teach phonological awareness, the alphabetic principle, decoding, and fluency so that students decode quickly and effortlessly and attention can focus on comprehension (Moats, 2009).

2. *Reading entails understanding and constructing meaning from text and is dependent on the reader's active engagement and interpretation.* Reading also entails developing skills and strategies for understanding or constructing meaning from text (**reading comprehension**) and for monitoring understanding (**comprehension monitoring**). Understanding is influenced both by the text and by the readers' prior knowledge (Klingner, Vaughn, & Boardman, 2007). When readers read, the text does not simply convey ideas to the readers but stimulates readers to actively engage in the following comprehension strategies:

- *Predicting* to make hypotheses about the meaning
- *Summarizing* to put the major points in the text into their own words
- *Questioning* to promote and check for understanding
- *Clarifying* when concepts are not clear

What happens as these students read? What processes are involved that students with disabilities might find difficult?

Effective readers regularly monitor their comprehension to determine whether they understand what they are reading. When they are not sure, they might decide to employ "fix-up" strategies such as rereading or reading on for further clarification, or they might decide not to worry about the confusion, depending on the purpose for reading. Hence, a second goal of reading instruction is to teach comprehension and comprehension-monitoring strategies.

3. *Reading is a socially mediated language-learning activity.* Because reading is a mode of communication, learning to read, like learning to listen, speak, and write, is socially mediated (Vygotsky, 1978). When students and teachers ask questions and discuss what they are reading, they share what they already know about the topic and integrate their knowledge with that of the text. When students and teachers talk about the reading process, they share the strategies they use to decode words and construct meaning, sometimes referred to as *instructional conversations* (Tharp, Estrada, Dalton, & Yamaguchi, 1999). Therefore, a goal of reading instruction is to use a social context in which to engage students in discussions about what they are reading and the reading process (Snow, Porche, Tabors, & Harris, 2007).

PEARSON
myeducationlab

Go to the Assignments and Activities section of Topic 9: Reading Instruction in the MyEducationLab for your course and complete the activity entitled *Effective Reading Instruction*.

Learning Difficulties in the Process of Reading

Because reading is a complex process, it involves many areas of potential difficulties. As Figure 12.1 indicates, a variety of interrelated factors influence whether students experience success in learning how to read. A leading reading researcher, Dr. Keith Stanovich (1986), refers to this combination of factors as **reciprocal causation**—essentially a domino effect, in which an initial factor leads to a second factor, which leads to a third, and so on. For example, children who are not read to during their preschool years might not have the opportunity to become familiar with books and how print and sounds relate to each other, which may lead to greater challenges in learning how to read, which may lead to limited motivation to read, which may then result in the child not choosing to read and thus having less opportunity to practice reading skills and less opportunity to develop new concepts and vocabulary through reading.

As a classroom teacher, you must be sensitive to the factors that influence reading and to the individual needs of your students in their attempts to tackle this complex process. For example, some of the students in your classes will have overall low reading skills and will need instructional support in all of the critical elements of reading including learning to read words, reading connected text, knowing what words mean, and understanding how to grapple with text to improve understanding. Other students may only need support in learning the meanings of words and improving their comprehension. Still others will have inadequate word reading interfering with their understanding of text. Identifying students' specific needs and then developing instructional programs that prioritize instruction in these areas leads to effective outcomes.

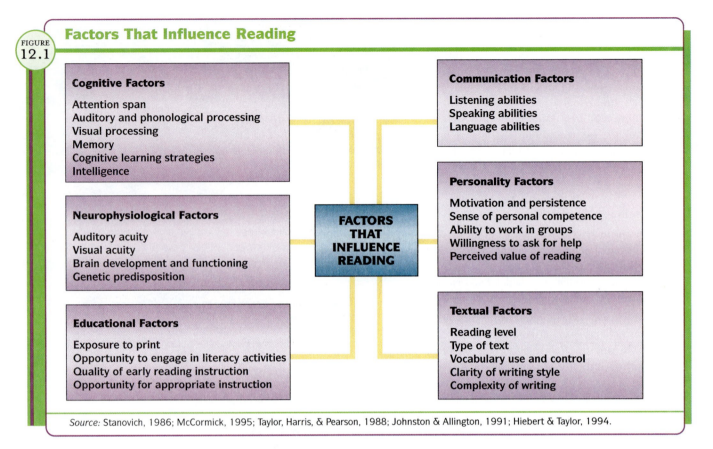

Factors That Influence Reading

FIGURE 12.1

Cognitive Factors

Attention span
Auditory and phonological processing
Visual processing
Memory
Cognitive learning strategies
Intelligence

Neurophysiological Factors

Auditory acuity
Visual acuity
Brain development and functioning
Genetic predisposition

Educational Factors

Exposure to print
Opportunity to engage in literacy activities
Quality of early reading instruction
Opportunity for appropriate instruction

FACTORS THAT INFLUENCE READING

Communication Factors

Listening abilities
Speaking abilities
Language abilities

Personality Factors

Motivation and persistence
Sense of personal competence
Ability to work in groups
Willingness to ask for help
Perceived value of reading

Textual Factors

Reading level
Type of text
Vocabulary use and control
Clarity of writing style
Complexity of writing

Source: Stanovich, 1986; McCormick, 1995; Taylor, Harris, & Pearson, 1988; Johnston & Allington, 1991; Hiebert & Taylor, 1994.

Components of Reading Instruction

Components of an effective and efficient reading program are depicted in Figure 12.2. Depending on the student's level of development and needs, you will want to emphasize certain components. Yet at the same time you will need to integrate these components to obtain a balanced approach to teaching reading. Consider the following examples.

FIGURE 12.2

Components of Reading and Reading Instruction

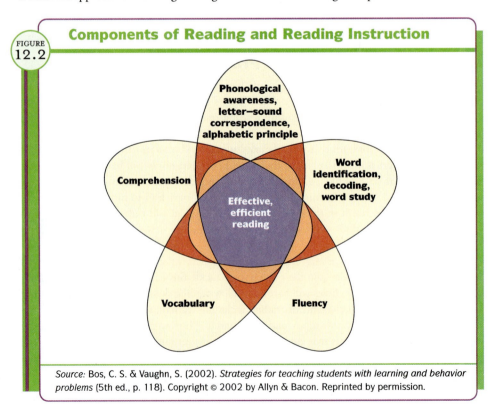

Source: Bos, C. S. & Vaughn, S. (2002). *Strategies for teaching students with learning and behavior problems* (5th ed., p. 118). Copyright © 2002 by Allyn & Bacon. Reprinted by permission.

Stephanie is a third grader with a specific reading disability who receives reading instruction in her classroom and also works with the special education teacher on reading. She reads at a beginning level and is able to recognize only about 30 words. When she comes to a word she does not recognize, she sometimes attempts to sound out the word. However, she has difficulty remembering common letter–sound relationships. She also struggles to blend the sounds so she can generate a word that is close enough to the correct word that she can figure it out. Her reading instruction focuses primarily on building phonological awareness, letter–sound relationships, decoding strategies, and fluent word identification. However, her instructional program also includes repeated and partner reading of instructional-level decodable books (i.e., books that primarily use words that reflect the phonic and word patterns she has already learned) to build fluency. She also listens to and discusses a wide variety of literature and content-area materials with her classmates to support her development of vocabulary and comprehension. It is important that Stephanie pairs readings and writing activities so that, as she builds reading decoding skills, she works simultaneously on spelling (see Chapter 13). Similarly, as she develops an understanding of different types of text and genres (e.g., narratives such as folktales, adventure stories, and mysteries and expositions such as descriptions, comparisons/contrasts, persuasions), it is also important that she explores writing in different genres and different types of texts (see Chapter 13).

Go to **www.pbs.org/wgbh/ mis understoodminds/ reading basics.html** for strategies on how to work with students with reading difficulties.

Manuel is an eighth grader who is reading at approximately the fourth-grade level. He entered school speaking both Spanish and English. He struggled with learning to read in Spanish because of his limited vocabulary knowledge and comprehension skills (e.g., getting the main idea, comprehension monitoring). He began reading in English during third grade and continued to struggle with vocabulary knowledge and comprehension and also had difficulty with decoding in English because its letter–sound relationships are not as regular as those in Spanish. As an eighth grader, he is taking English language arts from Ms. Gonzalez, who works with Manuel and a group of six students on building their vocabulary, comprehension, and advanced decoding skills. To build both decoding of multisyllabic words and vocabulary, they have learned to identify and separate prefixes and suffixes. They also learn the meaning of these affixes and of root words. For example, if the word is *construction,* they make a "struct" web with words such as *destruction, construct, reconstruction,* and *deconstruct.* (You will find more ideas for teaching vocabulary in Chapter 15 in the sections on teaching content-area subjects.) For comprehension enhancement, Manuel and his classmates have been working with Ms. Gonzalez and the special education teacher to learn to use comprehension strategies. These include activities such as previewing the key words, headings, or pictures before reading and practices for identifying the main idea of what they read and then summarizing accurately what they've read or learned. The students work in collaborative learning groups, and they have been using social studies content.

Effective Reading Instruction for Struggling Readers

It is important that you, as a classroom teacher, provide effective reading instruction and support for all your students, including those who struggle with reading. Features of effective reading instruction include the following:

- Establishing an environment to promote reading
- Using appropriate and ongoing screening, assessment, and progress monitoring so that you know the students' reading levels and what skills and strategies your students have mastered and need to develop
- Providing intensive instruction
- Obtaining early intervention when needed

Collaborating with the reading specialist, special education teacher, and grade-level team members will be important in implementing effective instruction (Hall, 2008).

Establishing an Environment to Promote Reading

Research has documented the importance of engaging in reading and reading with others for building vocabulary and reading skills (Guthrie, 2007). Jane Saunders, a second-grade teacher in a culturally and linguistically diverse school, has a room that provides an environment filled

Go to **www.reading.org**, the website for the International Reading Association, where you will find a variety of resources for teaching reading.

with print that interests students and is readily available to them. When her second graders walk into the classroom on the first day of school, they feel right at home. There are curtains on the windows, a basket for writing supplies at the center of each cluster of four student desks, and a reading center with a couch and carpet for informal reading. The writing center has materials for making books. The library center is well stocked with reading materials (e.g., newspapers, magazines, catalogs, brochures) and organized with books color-coded according to genre and reading levels. The word study center has lots of activities and games for making words using different phonics elements, spelling patterns, and common prefixes and suffixes. The listening station has books on tape that can be used for reading along or for repeated reading to build fluency.

The social environment for reading is also critical. Jane plans times when students can engage in recreational reading. She also models reading by reading aloud to students daily and talking about the books with the students. She uses echo and choral reading so that students have more opportunities to practice their newly learned reading skills. Parents, grandparents, school personnel, and community leaders frequently visit Jane's class to read to students and to listen to students read. Reading is valued, reading is emphasized—reading happens!

These students are using newspapers to find words with prefixes and suffixes. How might you use newspapers to teach skills in your classroom?

Using Response to Intervention to Screen Struggling Readers

Preventing reading difficulties and appropriately serving students with reading disabilities requires an understanding of how to implement elements of response to intervention (RTI). As discussed in Chapter 2, the critical elements of RTI include

- Ongoing screening
- Progress monitoring
- Early intervention in reading for students at risk for reading problems and ongoing assessment and treatment as needed

Ongoing screening, assessment, and progress monitoring are discussed in the next section, with instructional practices for teaching students with reading difficulties presented in the subsequent section.

How do you know if students are responding to instruction? The answers to several questions can provide valuable information for determining students' response to intervention:

- Have students received scientifically-based reading instruction in the appropriate elements of reading (e.g., phonemic awareness and phonics for beginning readers, and fluency, vocabulary, and comprehension for all readers)?
- Have students received adequate opportunities to respond, obtain feedback, and see modeling and scaffolding to support their learning?
- How does the performance of students who are low responders compare with the performance of other students in the class?
- Have students received instructional opportunities in small groups to acquire reading proficiency?
- Have students been adequately engaged and had opportunities to select text of interest to read?
- Is progress monitoring data available to show the slope of the student's progress?

Answering these questions can help you determine whether students have received adequate instruction and thus whether their low response to reading instruction is a function of exceptional needs of the student. Knowing the opportunities students have to learn and being able to examine their progress using data assists in determining the severity of the problem and designing interventions.

How do we know if students are responding adequately to reading instruction? If students are receiving scientifically based reading instruction, we can then determine (a) how they are responding relative to others in their class and in the same grade in other classes in the school, and (b) what the slope of their progress is based on progress monitoring measures acquired at least every 2 weeks. If a student's progress is significantly below other students in the class and/or the slope for their progress based on progress monitoring is lower than expected, the student may not be responding adequately to instruction.

PEARSON
myeducationlab

Go to the Assignments and Activities section of Topic 9: Reading Instruction in the MyEducationLab for your course and complete the activity entitled *Reading Instruction that Reaches All Students*.

Using Screening, Assessment, and Progress Monitoring

Screening is a mechanism for determining how students perform relative to their grade level peers in order to determine whether further assessment or instruction would be beneficial. Most schools provide some measure to all students at each grade level at the beginning of the year to determine their relative standing in reading. These screening measures allow teachers to determine whether they have students who are reading considerably above grade level and also to determine whether students are below level. Often these screening measures assist teachers in grouping students for instruction, selecting texts at appropriate reading levels, and planning instruction.

Types of Assessments.   Several critical aspects of assessments should be considered in choosing a test:

- The purpose of the testing (screening, progress monitoring, diagnostic, outcome)
- The specific information needed about the student's reading (specific skills assessment, reading level)
- The number of students being tested (whether you can test individually, in small groups, or in the whole class)
- The examiner's qualifications (whether the tester can acquire the skills to give highly specific tests)

Selecting a test to match the specific assessment needs is key. Assessments that tell us specifically how a student is performing and what else he or she needs to know are referred to as **diagnostic assessments**. Some assessments help us to determine how the student's performance compares with other students of the same age or in the same grade. This gives us some idea of what students need to know to achieve grade-level performance. These assessments are referred to as **norm-based assessments**. Appropriate assessments can also allow us to monitor the progress of students and determine whether their progress is on track and appropriate or whether we need to alter instruction to improve their performance. These assessments are referred to as *progress monitoring assessments* or *curriculum-based measures*. There are a number of assessments available to meet specific needs. Tips for Teachers 12.1 describes some of these assessments.

Progress Monitoring.   Progress monitoring, or **curriculum-based measurement (CBM)**, is a means of measuring students' progress and highlights the close tie between curriculum and student performance. It uses frequent samplings from the curriculum materials to assess the students' academic performance (e.g., Deno, 1985). CBM has been used successfully in general education classrooms to increase word recognition, reading fluency, and reading comprehension (e.g., Fuchs, Fuchs, & Burish, 2000; Fuchs, Fuchs, Hamlett, Phillips, & Bentz, 1994; Mathes, Fuchs, Roberts, & Fuchs, 1998). For example, to assess reading comprehension, students read passages at their instructional level and complete a maze task. For this task, the first sentence is left intact, but thereafter, every seventh word is deleted. Students select from three choices the one semantically correct word that fills in the blank. CBM provides ongoing data for making instructional decisions by considering

- How performance is affected by changing the instructional level
- The rate of learning (as reflected by changes in the slope of the trend line) compared to the goal
- The variability in the consistency of the performance

The 60-Second Lesson provides procedures for monitoring student progress in fluency and comprehension.

TYPES OF ASSESSMENT RESOURCES

- *Yopp-Singer Test of Phoneme Segmentation* (Yopp, 1995). This test assesses students' ability to orally segment phonemes separately in words. Students receive credit if they say all of the sounds in the word correctly. Like most phonemic-awareness measures, this one is administered individually to children.

- *Comprehensive Test of Phonological Processing* (CTOPP; Wagner, Torgesen, & Rashotte, 1999). The CTOPP is administered individually to students to determine their skill in phonological awareness and to guide the teacher in designing appropriate instruction. The test is designed for individuals between the ages of 5 and 24 and assesses three areas: phonological awareness, phonological memory, and rapid naming ability. If teachers are interested in assessing more specific areas of phonological awareness, additional subtests are available.

- *Test of Oral Reading Fluency* (TORF; Children's Educational Services, 1987). The TORF is an individually administered reading fluency assessment for grades K–6. It takes about 2 to 3 minutes per student to administer. There are 18 different passages at each level to give plenty of text for monitoring students' progress.

- *Dynamic Indicators of Basic Early Literacy Skills* (DIBELS; Good & Kaminski, 2004). The DIBELS consists of timed measures for grades K–6: Letter Naming Fluency (automatic letter recognition); Initial Sound Fluency and Phoneme Segmentation Fluency (phonological awareness); Nonsense Word Fluency (alphabetic principle); Oral Reading Fluency (fluency); Retell Fluency (comprehension); and Word Use Fluency (vocabulary). There are 20 forms of each measure. The measures are individually administered and require 1 to 3 minutes each. The fluency assessment passages are also available for grades K–3 in Spanish (Indicadores Dinámicos del éxito en la lectura; Good, Bank, & Watson, 2004).

- *Comprehensive Reading Assessment Battery* (CRAB; Fuchs, Fuchs, & Hamlett, 1989). The CRAB provides assessment in fluency and comprehension for students in grades K–6. It takes 30 to 40 minutes to administer all sections of the test to an individual student.

- *Gates-MacGinitie Reading Tests* (MacGinitie et al., 2000). This comprehension assessment is designed for group administration. There are levels of the test available for grades K–12 as well as for adults. The assessment requires 55 to 75 minutes to complete.

When working with struggling readers, progress monitoring provides the teacher with necessary data to inform decision making about grouping and instruction. Progress monitoring assists teachers in identifying students who are at risk for failing to acquire necessary skills and allows the teacher to monitor the progress students make in response to instruction. Two important aspects of progress monitoring measures are that (a) they should be predictive of later reading ability, and (b) they need to guide instruction.

60 *Second* LESSON

MONITORING STUDENT PROGRESS IN FLUENCY AND COMPREHENSION

1. Select two to three passages that are unfamiliar to the student and that are at the student's instructional or independent word recognition levels. Make two copies of each passage of text you are using with the targeted student: one for recording errors and one for the student to read.

2. Tell the student: "When I say 'begin,' start reading aloud at the top of the page. Do your best reading. If you come to a word that you don't know, I'll tell it to you."

3. Have the student read for one minute. If the student does not read a word within 3 seconds, pronounce the word.

4. Follow along as the student reads and mark your copy by putting a slash (/) through words read incorrectly. This includes mispronunciations, substitutions, omissions, words pronounced after hesitations of more than 3 seconds, and reversals. Do not count insertions, self-corrections, or

repetitions. Also note if the student is having difficulty with phrasing; ignoring punctuation; reading slowly, word-by-word, or laboriously; and/or has frequent extended pauses, false starts, sound-outs, and repetitions.

5. Note the last word read by the student when the one minute is up. If the student is in the middle of a sentence when the time has finished, have him or her finish the sentence but count only those words read up to the stop point.

6. Calculate fluency using the following formula:

# of words read in one minute − # of errors = words correct per minute (WCPM)

For example, if a student reads 83 words during a one-minute sample and makes 6 errors, then the WCPM would be 83 minus 6 equals 77.

Criteria for Determining Reading Level

FIGURE 12.3

	WORD RECOGNITION	WORD COMPREHENSION
Independent	95–100%	90% and above
Instructional	90–95%	75–90%
Frustration	Below 90%	Below 75%

Informal reading inventories and curriculum-based measurement are means for monitoring ongoing student progress. Using **informal reading inventories**, students read lists of words and passages that are leveled by grade, and retell or answer comprehension questions about the passages they have read. As a teacher, you not only can determine the independent, instructional, and frustrational reading levels of the students, but also can gain insight into the decoding and comprehension strategies the students use when reading. Typical criteria used for determining reading level are illustrated in Figure 12.3.

The following three guidelines provide a means for increasing the likelihood that students are reading appropriate materials.

1. The **independent reading level** is characterized by the students reading on their own without support from others.
2. The **instructional reading level** is the level at which instruction should occur. At this level, students are challenged by the reading and still need some support (e.g., preteaching words the students do not recognize automatically, teaching new vocabulary, making predictions about the story).
3. At the **frustration reading level**, the material is too difficult for the students to read with understanding even with assistance.

Assessment includes measures used by state departments of education or school districts to determine accountability (e.g., the California Reading Initiative, Texas Reading Initiative, No Child Left Behind). When matched to state standards or benchmarks in reading, these assessments can provide helpful information in determining what reading skills the students have developed. Although they are one source of information it is important to remember that for struggling readers these assessments can be particularly difficult and might not provide a good picture of their reading skills. Furthermore, standardized tests tend to focus on the "product" of reading and ignore salient factors that influence success or failure in literacy development.

Providing Intensive Instruction

For students with special learning needs in reading, whole-class instruction can be treacherous. Therefore, it is important to find ways to provide instruction that is both appropriate for meeting individual students' needs and intensive enough for progress to occur. Research has demonstrated that a substantial number of students who are identified as initially having difficulty learning to read can profit from intensive small-group instruction or working as pairs in structured peer tutoring formats (Elbaum, Vaughn, Hughes, & Moody, 2000; O'Connor, 2000; Wanzek & Vaughn, 2007).

Reading instruction is appropriate and intensive when

- Students have a clear understanding of teacher expectations and the goals of instruction.
- Instruction provided matches the reader's instructional reading level and needs.
- Adequate texts are used that are engaging to the students and at their reading levels.
- Instruction is explicit and direct in the skills and strategies the reader needs in order to become proficient and more independent.
- Students are grouped appropriately, which includes ability-level grouping.
- Instruction includes frequent opportunities for responding with feedback.
- Student progress is monitored frequently and used to make instructional decisions.
- Teachers and peers support the students when necessary.

Teachers frequently ask, "What skills do I teach?" and "How do I decide what students to put in a particular skill group?" Tips for Teachers 12.2 provides some suggestions.

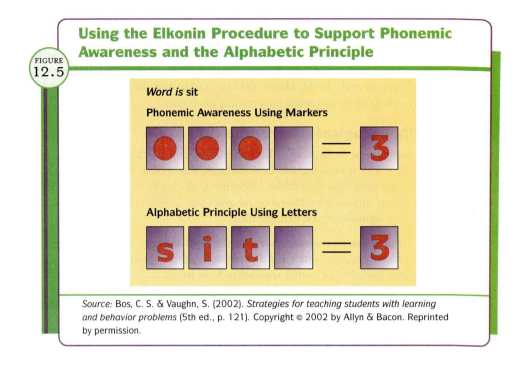

FIGURE 12.5

Using the Elkonin Procedure to Support Phonemic Awareness and the Alphabetic Principle

Word is sit

Phonemic Awareness Using Markers

● ● ●   = 3

Alphabetic Principle Using Letters

s i t   = 3

Source: Bos, C. S. & Vaughn, S. (2002). *Strategies for teaching students with learning and behavior problems* (5th ed., p. 121). Copyright © 2002 by Allyn & Bacon. Reprinted by permission.

To teach rhyming and alliteration, use books that are based on rhyme and alliteration, such as *There's a Wocket in My Pocket* (Seuss, 1974) and *Each Peach Pear Plum* (Ahlberg & Ahlberg, 1979). You can have students create, say, and listen/look for rhymes, alliterations, and "silly sayings." To build blending and segmenting skills, you might want to use the Elkonin procedure (Elkonin, 1973). As a phonological task, students listen to a word and push a marker, block, or other small object into a printed square for each sound they hear (see the first row in Figure 12.5). As students gain knowledge about the letter–sound relationships, they can push or write letters in the boxes (see the second row in Figure 12.5). This is one way to make an oral language activity more visible and kinesthetic. Other ways are tapping one finger to the thumb for each sound and watching your mouth in a mirror, feeling the facial movements by placing your fingers on your cheeks, and concentrating on how your mouth changes when different sounds are made.

General guidelines for teaching phonological awareness activities include the following (Bos & Vaughn, 2008):

- Consider the students' levels of development and tasks that need to be mastered.
- Model each activity.
- Use manipulatives and movement to make auditory/oral tasks more visible.
- Move from less to more difficult tasks, considering level of development (syllables, onset-rimes, phonemes), phoneme position (initial, final, medial), number of sounds in a word (*cat* is easier than *split*), and phonological features of the words (e.g., continuing consonants such as /m/, /n/, and /s/ are easier than stops or clipped sounds such as /t/, /b/, and /d/).
- Provide feedback and opportunities for practice and review.
- Make learning fun!

A number of programs and resources are available for teaching phonological awareness and the alphabetic principle (see Tips for Teachers 12.3 for a selected list).

Teaching Phonics

Students who are able to distinguish the sounds in words and to segment and blend them orally (phonological awareness) are more likely to be successful in applying their knowledge to making connections between sounds and print. As students learn letter–sound correspondences and how to blend, segment, and manipulate sounds, it is important that they associate speech with print (Chard & Dickson, 1999; Smith, 1998; Torgesen, 1999), thereby teaching

Tips FOR TEACHERS 12.3

SELECTED PROGRAMS AND RESOURCES FOR TEACHING PHONOLOGICAL AWARENESS

- *Ladders to Literacy: A Kindergarten Activity Book* by O'Connor, R., Notari-Syverson, A., and Vadasy, P. F., 2005, Baltimore, MD: Paul H. Brookes.

- *Phonemic Awareness in Young Children: A Classroom Curriculum* by Adams, M. J., Foorman, B. G., Lundberg, I., and Beeler, T., 1998, Baltimore, MD: Paul H. Brookes.

- *Phonological Awareness and Primary Phonics* by Gunning, T. G., 2000, Boston: Allyn & Bacon.

- *Road to the Code: A Program of Early Literacy Activities to Develop Phonological Awareness* by Blachman, B. A., Ball, E. W., Black, R., and Tangel, D. M., 2000, Baltimore, MD: Paul H. Brookes.

- *Interventions for Reading Success* by Haager, D., Domino, J. A., and Windmueller, M. P., 2006, Baltimore, MD: Paul H. Brookes.

- *Speech to Print* by Moats, L. C., 2000, Baltimore, MD: Paul H. Brookes.

- *The Lindamood Phoneme Sequencing Program for Reading, Spelling, and Speech* by Lindamood, P. A., and Lindamood, P., Austin, TX: PRO-ED.

- *Phonological Awareness Assessment and Instruction: A Sound Beginning* by Lane, H. B., and Pullen, P. C., 2004, Boston: Allyn & Bacon.

- *A Basic Guide to Understanding, Assessing, and Teaching Phonological Awareness* by Torgesen, J. K., and Mathes, P. G., 2000, Austin, TX: PRO-ED.

Websites with Instructional Activities and Lessons
www.nationalreadingpanel.org
www.texasreading.org
www.fcrr.org
www.readingrockets.org

---

the **alphabetic principle** (understanding that the sequence of letters in written words represents the sequence of sounds in spoken words). Almost all early reading programs are developed to teach letter–sound correspondence and phonics to students. There are also programs designed specifically for students with reading difficulties or disabilities:

- *Corrective Reading* (Engelmann, Meyer, Carnine, Becker, Eisele, & Johnson, 1999)
- *Lindamood Phoneme Sequencing Program for Reading, Spelling, and Speech* (Lindamood & Lindamood, 1998)
- *Wilson Reading System* (Wilson, 1996)
- *Word Detectives: Benchmark Word Identification Program for Beginning Readers* (Gaskins, 1996)

Most programs that are designed to teach phonics to students with reading difficulties have these instructional features:

- Teach a core set of frequently used consonants and short vowel sounds that represent clear sounds and nonreversible letter forms (e.g., /a/, /i/, /d/, /f/, /g/, /h/, /l/, /n/, /p/, /s/, /t/).
- Begin immediately to blend and segment the sounds in order to read and spell the words and read the words in **decodable text** (i.e., text in which most of the words are composed of letter–sound correspondences that have been taught).
- Separate the introduction of letter sounds with similar auditory or visual features (e.g., /e/ and /i/, /m/ and /n/, /b/ and /d/).
- Use a consistent key word to assist students in hearing and remembering the sound (e.g., *b, ball,* /b/).
- Teach that some letters can represent more than one sound. For each letter, first teach the most frequent sound and then teach other sounds (e.g., /c/ in *cat,* then /s/ in *city;* /g/ in *gate,* then /j/ in *gem*).
- Teach that different letters can make the same sound, such as the /s/ in *sit* and *city.*
- Teach that sounds can be represented by a single letter or a combination of letters (e.g., /a/ in *make* and *rain,* /sh/ in *fish*) and may be represented in boxes with a dotted line.

f	I	S	H

- Color-code consonants and vowels so that the two categories of sounds are highlighted.

Go to the Assignments and Activities section of Topic 9: Reading Instruction in the MyEducationLab for your course and complete the activity entitled *Phonics.*

GUIDELINES FOR USING PHONICS INSTRUCTION

- Build on a child's foundation of phonological awareness and rich concept of how print functions.

- Use direct and systematic instruction, as follows:

  - Begin with simple VC (*in*) and CVC (*pet*) words, and then move to more complex sound patterns, such as CCVC (*slim*), CVCC (*duck*), CVCe (*make*).

  - Demonstrate and have the students point to each letter sound as they say the sound, and then have them sweep their fingers under the word when they say it fast.

- Provide practice with feedback.

- Integrate phonics instruction into a balanced reading program.

- Teach only the most salient and needed patterns (e.g., silent *e*).

- Develop automatic word recognition so that students can devote their attention to comprehension rather than identifying words.

■ Add a kinesthetic component by having students trace or write the letter as they say the sound.

■ Have students use mirrors and feel their mouths to see and feel how sounds are different.

With respect to phonics instruction, research reviews (e.g. Ehri, 2004; National Reading Panel, 2000) make the following recommendations (also see Tips for Teachers 12.4):

■ Systematic phonics instruction results in significant benefits in decoding and spelling for students in kindergarten through sixth grade.

■ Synthetic phonics instruction (i.e., teaching students explicitly to convert letters into sounds and then blend the sounds to form recognizable words) was particularly effective for students with reading/learning disabilities and students from low socioeconomic backgrounds.

■ Although conventional wisdom has suggested that kindergarten children might not be ready for phonics instruction, this assumption was not supported by the research.

■ Invented spellings should be encouraged, in that they help students develop the necessary phonological awareness skills for reading and spelling. Students should also be taught to transition to conventional spellings.

■ Teaching of some phonics rules and generalizations can be helpful if they bring attention to spelling patterns. But learning rules is no substitute for practicing with spelling patterns.

■ Teaching of onset-rimes and the blending and segmenting of sounds is particularly important for building decoding and spelling skills.

■ Teachers need to be flexible in their phonics instruction to adapt to the strengths and needs of individual students.

■ Systematic phonics is only one component, but a necessary one, of a total reading program.

■ Students should be taught how to use their phonics rules in multisyllabic words.

■ Teachers should spend enough time teaching and applying phonics rules to help students read new words but not too much time to detract from opportunities to read.

Teaching phonics is a key element in understanding the alphabetic principle and learning to read and spell words. However, programs that focus too much on teaching phonics and not enough on putting the rules of phonics to work by reading words automatically and understanding text are likely to be ineffective. Through modeling and discussion, students need to understand that the purpose for learning these relationships is to apply them to their reading and writing activities. For example, when students in Ms. Wanzek's class have trouble reading a word, she asks them to use the phonics rules they know to decode the word. When her student Michael was stuck on the word *happen*, she reminded him about the phonics rule he knew about dividing the word into syllables when two consonants were doubled in the middle of a word. He then was able to read "hap" and "pen" and put it together to read the word *happen*. See Activities for All Learners for additional activities to use to encourage successful reading for all students.

READING ACTIVITIES FOR ALL LEARNERS

Phonological Awareness Songs 1

Objective: To teach sound matching, isolation, blending, and segmentation

Grades: Kindergarten to third grade

Materials: Song sheets or poster with words to songs

Teaching Procedures:

1. For younger students, the singing and rhyming may occur only as a listening activity.

2. For older students, words and letters could be added using song sheets or posters with words to the songs.

Sound Matching Activity 2

(To the tune of "Jimmy Crack Corn and I Don't Care")
Teacher: Who has an /m/ word to share with us?
Who has an /m/ word to share with us?
Who has an /m/ word to share with us?
It must start with the /m/ sound.

Child: Man is a word that starts with /m/.
Man is a word that starts with /m/.
Man is a word that starts with /m/.
Man starts with the /m/ sound.

Sound Isolation Activity 3

(To the tune of "Old MacDonald Had a Farm")
What's the sound that starts these words:
Turtle, time, and teeth? (wait for a response)
T is the sound that starts these words:
Turtle, time, and teeth.
with a /t/, /t/ here, and a /t/, /t/ there,
Here a /t/, there a /t/, everywhere a /t/, /t/.
T is the sound that starts these words:
Turtle, time, and teeth.
(This can be used with medial and final sounds as well.)

Blending Activity 4

(To the tune of "If You're Happy and You Know It, Clap Your Hands")
If you think you know this word, shout it out!
If you think you know this word, shout it out!
If you think you know this word,
Then tell me what you've heard,
If you think you know this word, shout it out!
(Sound out a word slowly such as /m/-/a/-/n/ and have students blend the sounds to make a word.)

Segmentation Activity 5

(To the tune of "Twinkle, Twinkle, Little Star")
Listen, listen
To my word
Then tell me all the sounds you heard: cape (slowly)
/k/ is one sound
/a/ is two
/p/ is last in cape
It's true.
Thanks for listening
To my words
And telling all the sounds you heard!

Source: Yopp, H. (1992). Developing phonemic awareness in young children. *The Reading Teacher, 45,* 696–703. Copyright by the International Reading Association.

Sound Magic Game 6

Objective: To improve phonological awareness of beginning, medial, and ending sounds

Grades: Primary

Materials: List of one-syllable words

Teaching Procedures:

1. Decide whether you want to play Sound Magic with the whole class or with small groups of students.

2. Place all participating students in a circle.

3. Begin by introducing a one-syllable word.

4. Explain that you play the game by moving the word around the circle from person to person. To move the word, you make a new word by changing the beginning, middle, or end sound and say the new word out loud. For example, you might start out with the word *sit.* The first child might form the new word *hit,* the next child *hat,* the next child *mat,* and so on.

5. If a child can't think of a word in a reasonable period of time, the child can pass.

6. Keep going until there are three passes in a row.

7. Start again with a new word and with the next child.

8. The object of the game is to make new words out of one word and to break the group's record.

Compound Concentration 7

Objective: To give the students practice in identifying compound words and to illustrate

how words may be combined to form compound words

Grades: Intermediate and secondary

Materials: 36 index cards (3" × 5") on which the two parts of 18 compound words have been written; make sure each part can only be joined with one other part

Teaching Procedures: Explain the game. Have the students shuffle the cards and place them face down in six rows with six cards each. Each player takes a turn at turning over two cards. The student then decides whether the two words make a compound word. If they do not, the cards are again turned face down and the next player takes a turn. If the words make a compound word, the player gets the two cards and turns over two more cards. The student continues playing until two cards are turned over that do not make a compound word. The game is over when all the cards are matched. The player with the most cards wins.

Adaptations: Students can match synonyms, antonyms, prefixes, suffixes, initial or final consonants, categories, and sight words.

Source: Vaughn, S. & Bos, C. S. (2008). *Strategies for teaching students with learning and behavior problems* (7th ed.). Boston: Allyn & Bacon.

How Short Can You Make It? 8

Objective: To improve summarizing skills

Grades: Intermediate grades and above

Materials: Any reading material

Teaching Procedures:

1. Decide whether to play this game as a whole-class or small-group activity.

2. Have students read a sentence or paragraph aloud or silently.

3. Give students time to think how to reduce the sentence or paragraph to its most important ideas, write down their reduction, and make edits as needed.

4. Have students "bid" on how short they can make it. For example, one student might say, "I can reduce it to six words"; another might say, "I can reduce it to four words."

5. The lowest bidder then reads his or her reduction. If the group agrees that it maintains all key ideas, then the lowest bidder gets to conduct the next round of bidding. If not, then necessary revisions are made and the teacher runs the next round of bidding.

(continued)

(continued)

WH-Game

⑨

Objective: To provide students practice in answering who, what, when, where, why, and how questions

Grades: All grades

Materials: (1) Generic game board, spinner or die, and markers. (2) WH cards: cards with "WH-Game" written on one side and one of these written on the other: Who, What, When, Where, Why, How. (3) Sets of story and article cards: copies of short stories and articles mounted on cards. There should be one set for each player. Select topics of interest for the students' age level.

Teaching Procedures: Explain the game to students or have them read the directions. First, the players set up the game. Next, they select a set of story or article cards. All players read the card and place it face down. Each player then takes a turn by throwing the die or spinning and selecting a WH card. The player must make up a question using the WH word and answer it correctly to move his or her marker the indicated number of spaces. If another player questions the validity of a player's question or answer, the players may look at the story or article card. Otherwise, these cards should remain face down during play. After 10 questions have been asked using one story or article card, another set is selected. The students read this card, and the game continues. The first player to arrive at the finish wins.

Adaptations: Students may also work in pairs, with one person on the team making up the question and the other person answering it.

Source: Vaughn, S. & Bos, C. S. (2008). *Strategies for teaching students with learning and behavior problems* (7th ed.). Boston: Allyn & Bacon.

Comp Checks

⑩

Objective: To help students learn to monitor their own comprehension

Grades: All grades

Materials: Paper strips (2″ × 8″); assigned reading

Teaching Procedures:

1. As you prepare a reading assignment, think about the characteristics of the text, your purpose for having students read the assignment, and your goals for learning about students' response to the text.

2. Identify key comprehension-monitoring goals. For example, you might want to know during a social studies reading assignment when a student is bored or confused, when a student thinks an idea is important, and when a student encounters a surprising new fact.

3. Brainstorm with students to create a code. For example, Bored = ^, Confused = ?, Important idea = *, Suprising fact = !

4. While students read, have them record page numbers and codes on paper strips.

5. After reading, focus the discussion on what students found to be boring, confusing, important, and surprising.

Strategies for Teaching Word Identification

Reading words quickly and easily is one key to successful reading (Beck, 2005; Ehri, 2003). Successful readers identify words fluently and, if a word is unknown, have effective decoding strategies to decipher the word. Therefore, it is important that students develop a sight word vocabulary (i.e., the words that students recognize without conscious effort) and decoding strategies to support them when they encounter an unknown word.

Teaching Sight Words

A **sight word** is a word for which the student can recognize the pronunciation and meaning automatically. In reading words by sight, the words are processed quickly and accessed from information in memory. LaBerge and Samuels (1974) are two early researchers who developed the theoretical basis underlying the importance of fluency in reading instruction. They argue that it is important for students to develop **automaticity** (quick word recognition) so that they can focus on comprehension. Some students have difficulty with automatic recognition of words in print, particularly with **high-frequency words**—words such as *the, you, and,* and *was*—that serve as the basic glue of our language. According to Fry, Kress, and Fountoukidis (2003), about 50% of written language contains 100 high-frequency words, such as those presented in Table 12.1.

You can select words to teach on the basis of the materials the students are reading, words the students are having difficulty learning, key vocabulary from content-area textbooks, or high-frequency words from graded word lists. Consider two factors: usefulness (words that occur most frequently) and ease of learning (Gunning, 2006). The words *the, of, and, a, to, in, is, you, that,* and *it* account for more than 20% of the words that students will encounter. Nouns and words with distinctive shapes are generally easier to learn. See Tips for Teachers 12.5 for guidelines for teaching sight words, particularly those that are less predictable on the basis of phonics and spelling patterns (e.g., *was, want, come*).

TABLE 12.1

The Instant (Sight) Words

THE FIRST 100 WORDS (APPROXIMATELY FIRST GRADE)				THE SECOND 100 WORDS (APPROXIMATELY SECOND GRADE)			
GROUP 1A	GROUP 1B	GROUP 1C	GROUP 1D	GROUP 2A	GROUP 2B	GROUP 2C	GROUP 2D
the	he	go	who	saw	big	may	ran
a	I	see	an	home	where	let	five
is	they	then	there	soon	am	use	read
you	one	us	she	stand	ball	these	over
to	good	no	new	box	morning	right	such
and	me	him	said	upon	live	present	way
we	about	by	did	first	four	tell	too
that	had	was	boy	came	last	next	shall
in	if	come	three	girl	color	please	own
not	some	get	down	house	away	leave	most
for	up	or	work	find	red	hand	sure
at	her	two	put	because	friend	more	thing
with	do	man	were	made	pretty	why	only
it	when	little	before	could	eat	better	near
on	so	has	just	book	want	under	than
can	my	them	long	look	year	while	open
will	very	how	here	mother	white	should	kind
are	all	like	other	run	got	never	must
of	would	our	old	school	play	each	high
this	any	what	take	people	found	best	far
your	been	know	cat	night	left	another	both
as	out	make	again	into	men	seem	end
but	there	which	give	say	bring	tree	also
be	from	much	after	think	wish	name	until
have	day	his	many	back	black	dear	call

Source: Reprinted by permission of Edward Fry, author.

Teaching Decoding Strategies

What decoding or word identification strategies do readers employ to decode words they do not know automatically? Research on teaching struggling readers, including those with specific reading disabilities, would suggest that five strategies are helpful in teaching these students to decode words. Figure 12.6 defines these five strategies and each one of them is described in detail in the next sections.

Phonic Analysis. *Identify and blend letter–sound correspondences into words.* This is referred to as **phonic analysis**, which is the use of phonics to decode words. This strategy builds on the alphabetic principle and assumes that the students have basic levels of phonological awareness and knowledge of some letter–sound correspondences. Students with reading difficulties need systematic word identification instruction, including phonics instruction.

Onset-Rime. *Use common spelling patterns to decode words by blending.* One salient feature of the English language is the use of spelling patterns, also referred to as **onset-rimes**,

PEARSON
myeducationlab

Go to the Assignments and Activities section of Topic 9: Reading Instruction in the MyEducationLab for your course and complete the activity entitled *Sight Words*.

Tips FOR TEACHERS 12.5

GUIDELINES FOR TEACHING SIGHT WORDS

- Teach the most frequently occurring words.

- Check to see that students understand the meaning, particularly if they have limited language, have a specific language disability, or are English language learners.

- Introduce these new words before students encounter them in text.

- Limit the number of words introduced in a single lesson.

- Reinforce the association by adding a kinesthetic component such as tracing, copying, and writing from memory.

- Introduce visually similar words (e.g., *where* and *were, was* and *saw*) in separate lessons to avoid confusion.

- When students confuse visually similar words (e.g., *what* for *when*), highlight the differences.

- Provide multiple opportunities, including games and computer-assisted instruction, for the students to read the words in text and as single words until they automatically recognize the words.

- Review words that have been previously taught, particularly if the students miscall them when reading text.

Sources: Bos & Vaughn, 2008; Cunningham, P. M. (2000). *Phonics they use: Words for reading and writing* (3rd ed.). New York: Longman; Gunning, 2006.

phonograms, or *word families.* When using spelling patterns to decode an unknown word, the students segment the word between the onset (/bl/ in the word *blend*) and the rime (*-end*) and then blend the onset and rime to make the word (*blend*). Figure 12.7 presents a list of 37 common rimes that make almost 500 words (Wylie & Durrell, 1970). Guidelines for teaching onset-rimes follow the same guidelines as those suggested for teaching phonic analysis except that the word is segmented at the level of onset-rime rather than at the phoneme level.

Structural Analysis and Syllabication.   *Use knowledge of word structures such as compound words, root words, suffixes, prefixes, and inflectional endings and syllabication to decode multisyllabic words.* Between third and seventh grades, children learn from 3,000 to 26,000 words, most of them multisyllabic words encountered through reading; only a limited number are taught directly (Wysocki & Jenkins, 1987). Teach students **structural analysis** for examining smaller words they know within a larger word (e.g., Manhattan has "man" and "hat" in it). Structural analysis can also be used to identify root words, prefixes, suffixes, and inflectional endings, because (a) such analysis provides students with ways to segment longer, multisyllabic words into decodable (and meaningful) parts, and (b) it assists students in determining the meanings of words (Henry, 1997). For example, the word *unbelievable* can be segmented into three parts: *un–believe–able.* Chunking not only makes this word easier to decode, but also tells us about the meaning. In the case of *unbelievable, un-* means "not," and *-able* means "is or can be." Hence, *unbelievable* means something that is not to be believed. When teaching students to divide words into meaning parts, begin with analyzing compound words. Teach high-frequency prefixes (e.g., *re-, pre-, un-*), suffixes (e.g., *-er/-or, -ly, -tion/-ion,-ness, -ful*), and inflection endings (e.g., *-s, -es, -ing, -ed*). See Tips for Teachers 12.6 for ideas and guidelines for teaching and reinforcing structural analysis.

Strategies for Decoding Unknown Words

FIGURE 12.6

- *Phonic Analysis*: Identify and blend letter–sound correspondences into words.

- *Onset-Rime:* Use common spelling patterns (onset-rimes) to decode words by blending the initial sound(s) with the spelling pattern or by using analogy.

- *Structural Analysis and Syllabication:* Use knowledge of word structures such as compound words, root words, suffixes, prefixes, and inflectional endings and syllable types to decode multisyllabic words and assist with meaning.

- *Syntax and Semantics:* Use knowledge of word order (syntax) and context (semantics) to support the pronunciation and confirm word meaning.

- *Use Other Resources:* Use other resources such as asking someone or using a dictionary.

FIGURE
12.7

Common Spelling Onset-Rimes from Primary-Grade Texts

-ack	-ail	-ain	-ake	-ale
-ame	-an	-ank	-ap	-ash
-at	-ate	-aw	-ay	
	-ell	-est		
-eat				
-ice	-ick	-ide	-ight	-ill
-in	-ine	-ing	-ink	-ip
-ir				
-ock	-oke	-op	-ore	-or
-uck	-ug	-ump	-unk	

FIGURE
12.8

Root Word Map of *Friend*

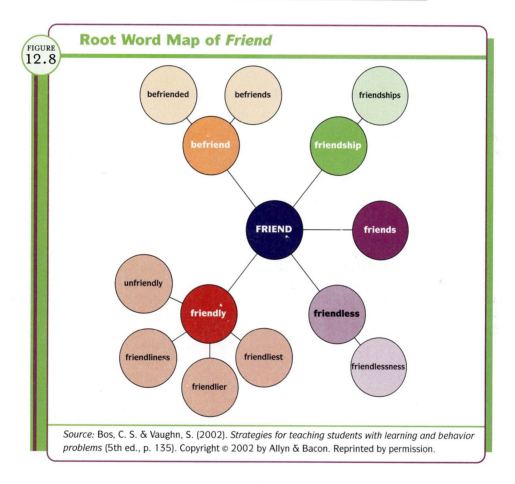

Source: Bos, C. S. & Vaughn, S. (2002). *Strategies for teaching students with learning and behavior problems* (5th ed., p. 135). Copyright © 2002 by Allyn & Bacon. Reprinted by permission.

Dividing words by common syllable types, or **syllabication**, can also provide struggling readers with clues for decoding multisyllabic words. A high percentage of more than 600,000 English words can be categorized as one of six syllable types or a combination of different syllable types (Carreker, 1999; Knight-McKenna, 2008). English language learners also benefit from instruction in these syllable types (Vaughn, Mathes, Linan-Thompson, & Francis, 2005). By providing examples (listed in Table 12.2), you can lead students to discover the six types and how to apply them when decoding unknown words.

Syntax and Semantics. *Use knowledge of word order (syntax) and context (semantics) to support the pronunciation and confirm word meaning.* Whereas students with reading difficulties often overrely on syntax and context to decode an unknown word, good readers use syntax and context for cross-checking their pronunciation and monitoring comprehension

GUIDELINES FOR TEACHING AND REINFORCING STRUCTURAL ANALYSIS

- Teach the meanings along with recognition of the meaning parts.

- Explain and demonstrate how many "big words" are just "smaller words" with prefixes, suffixes, and endings.

- Ask students to decode words they do not know by covering all but one part of the word and having them

identify it, then uncovering the next part and identifying it, and so on.

- Create a class or student dictionary that has each word part, its meaning, and several example words.

- Use a word map to demonstrate how one root word can make a cadre of related words (see Figure 12.8 on page 317).

(Schumm, 2006). This is evident when students reread a word, phrase, or sentence because "it doesn't make sense." Key questions that students can ask are the following:

- Does that sound right here?
- Does that make sense?

Techniques for Teaching Decoding and Sight Words

A number of programs and strategies have been developed for teaching decoding strategies and sight words. The techniques of making words, word sorting, and using word walls have been used by many teachers. Even secondary teachers who are instructing older students with reading disabilities are using word analysis practices to bolster students' success at decoding and accurately reading words.

Making Words, Word Sorting, and Using Word Walls. A number of activities can be developed around making words, word sorts, and word walls. *Making Words* and *Words Their Way* were initially developed for students in the primary grades to develop sensitivity to manipulating sounds and building decoding strategies (Bear, Invernizzi, Templeton, & Johnston, 2008; Cunningham, 2000b), but can also be used with upper-elementary or middle-school students who need to work on common spelling patterns, prefixes, and suffixes (Deshler, Palincsar, Biancarosa, & Nair, 2007; Scammacca et al., 2007) and with English language learners who can learn more about word meaning and word reading (Bear, Helman, Invernizzi, & Templeton, 2007). *Making Words* provides opportunities to construct words using magnetic letters, letter tiles, or laminated letters to see how

TABLE 12.2

Six Types of Syllables

TYPE	DESCRIPTION/EXAMPLES
Closed (CVC)	Ends in at least one consonant; vowel is short. *bed, lost, and, magnet, dap-* in *dapple, hos-* in *hostel*
Open (CV)	Ends in one vowel; vowel is long. *me, mo-* in *moment, ti-* in *tiger, ta-* in *table*
Vowel-consonant-e (CVCe)	Ends in one long vowel, one consonant, and a final *e* that is silent. *name, slope, five, -pite* in *despite, -pete* in *compete*
Vowel team (CVVC)	Uses two adjacent vowels. Sounds of vowel teams vary. *rain, sweet, -geal* in *congeal, train-* in *trainer, bea-* in *beagle*
R-controlled (CV + r)	Vowel is followed by /r/, and vowel pronunciation is affected by /r/. *fern, burn, car, forge, charter*
Consonant-le (-C + le)	Unaccented final syllable with a consonant plus /l/ and silent *e*. *-dle* in *candle, -tle* in *little, -zle* in *puzzle*

words are affected. For example, the teacher might start with the sounds /s/, /t/, /r/, /n/, and /a/ and ask the students to do the following:

> **Teacher:** What two sounds make the word at?
> Now add a letter sound to the beginning to make the word *sat*.
> Remove the /s/. What one sound would you add to the beginning to make the word *rat*?
> Now listen. We're going to make a three-letter word. Take off the /t/ sound at the end of the word. Now add the one sound that will make the word *ran*.

Using a specific set of letters (e.g., *a, c, h, r, s, t*), students make approximately 15 words beginning with two-letter words (e.g., *at*) and progressing to three-, four-, and five-letter words (e.g., *tar, cart, star, cash*) until the final "mystery word" is made (e.g., *scratch*). Students complete a three-step process that includes making words, word sorting, and making words quickly to build fluency (see Activities for All Learners). The whole sequence (including distribution of materials) takes about 30 minutes.

Using a **word wall** can reinforce students' learning to recognize and spell words. The word wall is a large space dedicated to displaying word types that are the focus of the week's instruction. These word types can represent the phonics rules being learned, review previously learned phonics rules, and/or represent sight words that are the focus of instruction that week. Words can be displayed based on the sound units they represent (e.g., all words that end in "ay" are organized together), or they can be displayed in alphabetical order, or in whatever order makes sense based on the goals of instruction. When new words are added, the teacher and students talk about the word pattern and its meaning, use the word in a sentence, and determine whether its spelling follows a regular or irregular pattern. Students can use

How can a teacher reinforce the use of the words students recommend for the word wall?

Activities FOR **ALL** Learners

STEPS IN MAKING WORDS

Objective: To improve students' ability to make words

Grades: Using simple words, such as *mat, him, it* (Grades 1–3); using more complex words, such as *weather, marriage, champion* (Grades 3–6)

Materials: Laminated letters, sentence strip board, word cards

Teaching Procedures:

Step 1. Making Words Slowly (about 15 minutes)

- Students make 12 to 15 words, using a set of individual laminated letters.
- The last word includes all the letters a student has been given that day. For example, a student might be given the letters "eudhnrt."

- Direct students to spell words such as *red, Ted, Ned, her, hut, rut,* and *under.* The final word would be *thunder.*
- After the students spell the words with their own letters, show or have a student show the correct spelling, using large letters and a sentence strip chart in the front of the room. Students correct their own work.

Step 2. Word Sorting (about 10 minutes)

- Put up on the sentence strip board word cards with all the words spelled that day.
- Ask students how some of the words are alike.
- Have a volunteer sort the words on the sentence strip board by putting all like words together (e.g., *fat, rat, sat*).

- Have the other students in the class then guess why those words are grouped together, which helps students focus on word patterns.

Step 3. Making Words Quickly (about 2 minutes)

- Have students write as many words as they can using the day's letters, writing the words in a "making words" log.
- Have students take 1 minute to write the date and the day's letters at the top of the page.
- When you say, "Go," they write words for 2 minutes.

This activity helps build fluency. Because each lesson starts with easy words and ends with more difficult words, all students in the class can participate.

these words to help them spell words they are writing and eventually learn to read and spell the words through repeated practice. Some teachers provide folders or word boxes in which students can retain the words they are working on in reading, vocabulary, or spelling.

Using the DISSECT Strategy.   As students become more advanced in their reading, they begin to use structural analysis (e.g., compound words, prefixes, and suffixes) and syllabication to identify multisyllabic words. Lenz, Schumaker, Deshler, and Beals (1984) developed a strategy for secondary students with learning disabilities to approach multisyllabic words in a strategic way that has been validated through several research studies (e.g., Woodruff, Schumaker, & Deshler, 2002). This strategy, known by the acronym **DISSECT**, includes the following steps:

1. *D*iscover the word's context.
2. *I*solate the prefix. Students look at the beginning of the word to see whether the initial letters of the word match a prefix they know. If they do recognize a prefix, they isolate it (e.g., *pre*/*heat*). If students do not recognize a prefix, they proceed to step 3.
3. *S*eparate the suffix. Students look at the end of the word to see whether the letters match a suffix they know. If they do recognize a suffix, they separate it; if not, they go on to the next step.
4. *S*ay the stem.
5. *E*xamine the stem. Students dissect the stem into easy-to-pronounce parts, two or three letters at a time. When they can pronounce the whole word, students reread the whole sentence to check their understanding. If students still cannot figure out the word, they go on to the last steps.
6. *C*heck with someone.
7. *T*ry the dictionary.

DISSECT can be taught to your whole class. Students can then practice using the strategy in small groups or pairs. You may also want to put the steps for DISSECT on a poster in front of your room and remind students regularly about the steps.

Strategies for Helping Students Develop Fluency

Fluency is the ability to read a text quickly, accurately, and with expression (Chard, Vaughn, & Tyler, 2002; Stahl, 2003). Students are fluent in reading when they can recognize printed words quickly and effortlessly and are therefore able to focus more of their attention on comprehension. Because struggling readers often take longer and require more exposure to words in order to automatically recognize and rapidly recall words than do typical readers, it is important that fluency instruction provides multiple opportunities for practice (Wexler et al., 2008). Use the suggestions in this section to help students become more fluent readers.

Using Response to Intervention (RTI) to Promote Fluency

Oral reading fluency is the number of words a student reads correctly in one minute. Typically, students are provided with grade-level passages and asked to read for one minute. The teacher then counts the number of words read correctly.

Monitoring the number of words students read correctly in a minute is frequently used in the lower grades (first through third grade) to monitor students' progress in reading. For this reason, it is also used as means for determining how students with reading difficulties may be responding to interventions. For example, many schools screen students in first, second, and third grades using oral reading fluency to identify students who are at risk for reading problems. They then provide a standardized intervention to these students (four to five times per week) for 20 to 40 minutes per day over an 8- to 12-week period. During this intervention, students typically receive an oral reading fluency test every week or two so that the slope of their progress can be determined. Thus, based on students' overall progress and the extent to which they are closing the gap between their oral reading fluency prior to intervention and during intervention, a decision is made about participation in subsequent interventions.

To illustrate, Jeanine, a second grader, was making adequate progress in reading after she was placed in an intervention (more than two words correct per week gain on average) and

PEARSON
myeducationlab

Go to the Assignments and Activities section of Topic 9: Reading Instruction in the MyEducationLab for your course and complete the activity entitled *Building Reading Fluency*.

Go to **http://reading.uoregon.edu/** where you will find useful links to information on both fluency and comprehension.

appeared to be very close to meeting expected reading performance. Her teachers decided that it would be in her best interest to continue the intervention for another 10 weeks.

Max displayed a different pattern of learning. His overall progress was very low (less than one word correct per week on average) and teachers were concerned that he needed even more intensive intervention. They adjusted his instruction both in the classroom and in the intervention and provided one-on-one support to determine his RTI over time. Thus, oral reading fluency provided an important data source for decision making related to response to intervention. We know considerably less about the role of oral reading fluency and its application within RTI models with older readers.

Reading Aloud

Reading aloud is typically used at the elementary level to preview a book or model fluent reading (Hickman, Pollard-Durodola, & Vaughn, 2004; Reutzel & Hollingsworth, 1993; Trelease, 1995). Reading aloud and previewing a book promote reading fluency in a number of ways:

- **Reading aloud models fluent reading.** For younger children, **big books** (books with large pictures and words that can be seen by the whole class) are ideal because they allow you to point to the text while reading and use the pictures to create more interest in the story.
- **Students can become familiar with the story.** Reading aloud gives you the opportunity to preview the book (e.g., to discuss with the students the content of the story and to introduce difficult vocabulary).
- *Students can listen to and discuss books that may be too difficult for them to read.* Struggling readers may have listening comprehension that is several years more advanced than their reading comprehension due to difficulties with word recognition. This will allow them access to more advanced books and literature.
- *English language learners can improve their word knowledge and concept development.*
- *Less adept older readers can read books to young children and serve as cross-age tutors.*
- *Older readers can listen to books on tape and then read those same texts as a way to improve reading fluency.*

Repeated Reading

Repeated reading consists of reading short, meaningful passages several times until a satisfactory level of fluency is reached. The general format for this reading procedure is to have the students repeatedly read short passages (50–200 words long) that are at the students' instructional to independent reading levels (90%–100% word recognition) until they reach a fluent reading rate.

The reading rate is most frequently measured by the words read correctly per minute (WCPM) and through observations of phrasing, smoothness, and pace. Having students read for one minute and then counting the total number of words read minus the incorrect words (e.g., mispronunciations, substitutions, omissions, and words pronounced after a hesitation of more than 3 seconds) provide the WCPM. Guidelines (words correct per minute) for reading fluency for grades 1 through 8 (Behavioral Research and Reading, 2005) are presented in Table 12.3.

For example, Jeff, a fourth-grade student with an instructional level at second grade, read the second-grade passage on whales at the rate of 25 words per minute. He and his teacher set

TABLE 12.3	Guidelines for Repeated Reading		
GRADE	**FALL**	**WINTER**	**SPRING**
1	—	23–47	53–82
2	51–79	72–100	89–117
3	71–99	92–120	107–137
4	94–119	112–139	123–152
5	110–139	127–156	139–168
6	127–153	140–167	150–177
7	128–156	136–165	150–177
8	133–161	146–173	151–177

a goal of Jeff reading the passage at 55 words per minute. It took him five repeated readings to reach this goal, and he graphed his progress. If you are measuring fluency across passages such as those depicted in the graph in Figure 6.4 on page 156, increases of one to two WCPM per week are realistic goals (e.g., from 25 WCPM to 27 WCPM) (Fuchs, Fuchs, Hamlett, Walz, & Germann, 1993).

Younger students reading below grade level who have used repeated reading have consistently demonstrated gains in both fluency and reading comprehension (Chard, Vaughn, & Tyler, 2002; Mastropieri, Leinart, & Scruggs, 1999; Meyer & Felton, 1999). However, older students with reading difficulties do not consistently benefit from repeated reading activities (Wexler, Edmonds, & Vaughn, 2008; Wexler, Vaughn, Edmonds, & Reutebuch, 2008). Although many older students with reading disabilities demonstrate reading fluency challenges, we are still struggling to identify the most effective practices for these youngsters.

From these reviews of research, several instructional guidelines for using repeated reading are apparent (see Tips for Teachers 12.7). You can incorporate repeated reading into whole-class or small-group routines. You can also pair students to read to each other. Tech Tips provides ideas for using technology to support fluent reading.

 **Tips FOR TEACHERS 12.7**

GUIDELINES FOR USING REPEATED READING TO IMPROVE FLUENCY

- Use repeated reading with younger readers with reading difficulties to increase reading speed, accuracy, expression, and comprehension.

- Select text materials at the students' independent to instruction reading levels (90–100% word recognition).

- Provide a good model reading the passage before asking the student to read.

- Ask students to reread passages three to five times.

- Demonstrate how to use phrases so that students can also do multiple readings of phrases.

- Provide adult guidance and feedback during reading.

- Preteach words and phrases from the text.

- Model reading with expression.

- Use short, frequent sessions of fluency practice (10–15 minutes).

- Have students set goals and record progress.

 **Tech TIPS**

USING TECHNOLOGY TO HELP STRUGGLING READERS

The computer is an ideal tool for helping students learn phonological awareness and phonics, build fluency, increase their vocabulary and word recognition, and enhance comprehension. The following programs are designed to help struggling readers achieve these goals.

Lexia by Lexia Learning Systems, Inc.,
▶ http://www.lexialearning.com/research/3tier.html
This program is used with K–8 students and is used in conjunction with the three-tiered RTI model to support struggling readers. Students practice phonological awareness and phonics to help them improve their reading skills.

Reading Assistant by Scientific Learning,
▶ http://www.scilearn.com/products/reading-assistant/index.php
Reading Assistant is a scientifically based intervention that helps struggling readers of all ages. Using speech recognition technology, this program allows students to practice their reading with the benefit of instant feedback and progress monitoring as the student moves through the program.

Read Naturally by Read Naturally, Inc.,
▶ http://www.readnaturally.com/
This program uses reaching strategies such as modeling, repeat reading, and assessment strategies to help students develop phonological awareness, phonics, fluency, word recognition, and reading comprehension.

Peer Tutoring

Several related practices, **peer-assisted learning (PAL)** (What Works Clearing House: Intervention Peer-Assisted Learning Strategies, July 16, 2007: ies.ed.gov/ncee/wwc/pdf/wwc.pals) and **classwide peer tutoring (CWPT)** (What Works Clearing House: Intervention Classwide Peer Tutoring, July 9, 2007: ies.ed.gov/ncee/wwc/pdf/wwc_cwpt), promote the use of students working together to provide practice and feedback on improving reading fluency. In both approaches, students of different reading levels are paired, one average or high reader with one low reader. The reading material for the tutoring sessions can be a basal reader, trade book, or magazine; what is important is that the less able reader in the pair can read it easily. During peer tutoring sessions, which last approximately 30 minutes, the pairs work through a sequence of structured activities in which partners read orally, share story retelling, and summarize what was read. Students earn points as they work through the series of activities. When reading, first the stronger reader reads aloud to serve as a model, and then the other reader reads.

There are many responsibilities for the teacher to ensure that peer tutoring is effective. It is important, for example, to teach students how to be both tutors/listeners and tutees/readers and provide role-play practice and feedback. For the tutors, give guidelines for how they should correct errors during oral reading (e.g., point out the word, pronounce the word, and have the tutee say the word) and the questions they should ask when the students have finished reading (e.g., What is the story about? What is happening in the story now? What do you think will happen next?). Many students are not experienced in providing effective feedback to their partners. Teachers can assist students by modeling the type of feedback that is helpful. For example, Mr. Zayer provides a list of phrases for students to use with each other to help shape positive and effective feedback (e.g., "you read that paragraph with no mistakes," "look at that word, read it again.").

Peer tutoring has been researched extensively in various school settings (e.g., McMaster, Shu-Hsuan, Insoon, & Cao, 2008). Results indicate that when the procedure is implemented consistently (three times a week over a period of 16 weeks), the amount of reading practice time increases substantially, and students of all ability levels improve in fluency and comprehension.

Strategies for Improving Reading Comprehension

Understanding, appreciating, and learning from what we read is the ultimate goal. For many students, however, reading the words is not enough to make understanding happen. Ms. Lockerson teaches a sixth-grade reading class for students who have reading problems and/or reading disabilities. She claims that the biggest problem she encounters are students who can read the words, albeit slowly, but do not understand what they read. "Even after they read a passage silently and then we reread the passage aloud, if I ask students what the passage is mostly about, there will be either few answers or incomplete answers." In this section of the chapter, we will discuss practices that Ms. Lockerson can do to enhance the understanding of the students in her class.

Students with reading difficulties need to learn specific ways to get ready for reading, to understand what they are reading while they read it, and to summarize and reflect on what they have read. In other words, many struggling readers need **comprehension strategies** to use before, during, and after reading. Students also need to learn strategies for dealing with both *narrative* and *expository* text (stories and informational writing, respectively) and to monitor their comprehension (comprehension monitoring).

Effective comprehension instruction includes many of the following features (e.g., Carlisle & Rice, 2002; Gersten & Baker, 2003; Klingner, Vaughn, & Boardman, 2007):

- *Activating background knowledge.* Thinking about what you already know about the topic and how your knowledge relates to what you are reading
- *Predicting.* Making predictions about what is going to happen or what will be learned from reading the text
- *Generating and answering questions.* Asking and answering relevant questions that promote understanding, such as who, what, when, where, why, and how questions
- *Clarifying.* Clarifying unclear concepts or vocabulary

- *Summarizing.* Determining the main ideas and important concepts related to the main idea
- *Using text structure.* Using knowledge of different text structures (e.g., narrative, expositions) as a framework for comprehension
- *Monitoring comprehension.* Checking for understanding and using fix-up strategies (e.g., rereading, clarifying a concept) to facilitate comprehension
- *Engaging text and conversations about reading.* Texts that are engaging and interesting and comprehension practices that involve students in conversations about what they read readily support understanding text

Go to the Assignments and Activities section of Topic 9: Reading Instruction in the MyEducationLab for your course and complete the activity entitled *Vocabulary and Fluency.*

Vocabulary knowledge is also pertinent to student comprehension of text (Beck, McKeown, & Kucan, 2002). *Vocabulary* refers to the words a person understands and uses in listening, speaking, reading, and writing. Students can learn word meanings through direct and indirect experiences with oral and printed language. *Indirect experiences* that serve to increase student vocabularies include opportunities to engage in oral discussions of new experiences and new words that build on previous knowledge. For example, MaryAnn Radkin, a second-grade teacher, uses teacher read-alouds of narrative text in the morning and information text in the afternoon as a means of teaching new vocabulary words and concepts and encouraging students to use these new words as they talk about what they are hearing. She realizes that specifically teaching word meanings is necessary to increase student exposure to novel words (Brett, Rothlein, & Hurley, 1996; Seals, Pollard-Durodola, Foorman, & Bradley, 2007) and is most effective when words are selected and incorporated in text based on their usefulness in language and importance to comprehension (Beck, McKeown, & Stahl, 2002). Juan Gonzalez, an eighth-grade science teacher, also preteaches key vocabulary and concepts before discussing new ideas or asking students to read text. He recognizes that students learn more about science when they know the meaning of the key words.

Following the initial introduction of words, students need repeated exposure to the new vocabulary in a variety of contexts to ensure significant reading gains (Willis, 2008). Students will encounter novel words in print throughout their reading careers. Therefore, instruction in independent strategies for learning new word meanings is also necessary, such as using context (Hiebert, 2005; Stahl, 1983). Teachers should provide student-friendly definitions consisting of words that students know:

- Introduce a vocabulary word (e.g., *immigrant*), and ask students to repeat the word so that they know how to pronounce the word.
- Discuss the meaning of the word using synonyms, examples, and/or definitions (e.g., *Immigrant* means "someone who comes from abroad to live permanently in another country").
- Test students on their understanding of the word by asking students to figure out positive or incorrect examples and to explain why. (Positive example of the word *immigrant*: "Tom's grandparents came to the United States from England in 1912. They lived in the United States until they passed away." Ask the students, "Are Tom's grandparents immigrants? Why or why not?" An example of an incorrect use of the word *immigrant*: "Recently, many international students came to the United States to study." Ask the students, "Are the international students immigrants? Why or why not?")

Each of the teaching techniques in this section focuses on teaching comprehension strategies and comprehension monitoring and can be used with a variety of texts. Tips for Teachers 12.8 provides instructions for using story retelling to enhance fluency.

K-W-L Strategy

K-W-L is a strategy used to help students become actively engaged in comprehension before, during, and after reading (Carr & Thompson, 1996; Ogle, 1986). The **K-W-L strategy** is based on research that underscores the importance of activating prior knowledge as a means of connecting what we know with what we are reading and also in promoting engagement and comprehension monitoring during reading. When using K-W-L, consider the following components:

1. Accessing what I **K**now
2. Determining what I **W**ant to learn
3. Recalling what I **L**earned

Tips FOR TEACHERS 12.8

USING STORY RETELLING TO ENHANCE FLUENCY

Fluency is an excellent predictor of reading comprehension for classroom teachers because it provides a reasonable and feasible means for determining whether students understand what they read and whether they are likely to pass high-stakes reading comprehension tests. In addition, comprehension can be monitored by asking students to retell the most important parts of the text they have just read. One advantage to story retelling is that the teacher is able to learn a great deal about what the students understand and is able to determine what additional comprehension skills need to be taught.

1. Ask young students to read a brief passage (1–2 minutes) aloud. Ask older students to read a brief passage (1–2 minutes) silently. Select passages that are at the students' instructional or independent reading level.

2. Tell the students, "Start at the beginning and you tell me the story" (Lipson, Mosentha, & Mekkelson, 1999).

3. Score the story retelling based on the depth of information provided. Teachers may want to consider whether students mentioned characters, the story problem, events, problem resolutions, and/or story quality.

During the Know step, teachers and students engage in a discussion about what they already know about a topic. This can be done very quickly and requires teachers to make linkages, align with the text they are reading, and build background knowledge. During the Want-to-learn step, teachers and students describe what they hope to learn from reading about the topic. Finally, during the Learned stage, teachers and students discuss what they learned after reading the passage and what information the passage did not provide. As with many reading comprehension strategies, K-W-L can also be used as a listening comprehension strategy before and after lectures. Ogle (1989) added a fourth column, "what we still want to know." Schmidt (1999) referred to it as K-W-L-Q with the "Q" representing more questions. Figure 12.9 shows a K-W-L-Q worksheet you can use to help students learn this strategy.

Question–Answer Relationships Strategy

Is asking students questions after they read text the same as reading comprehension instruction? Probably not. Though teacher's manuals and student workbooks, readers, and textbooks contain many comprehension questions for students to answer, these questions more often provide an index for the teacher of whether the student understood some element of the text. They may not help the student better understand the text. What is a more effective practice is to instruct students in how to develop good questions about what they read and to ask and answer these questions. Moving students into the role of developing the questions also teaches them to monitor their comprehension while they are reading and to think about what they read.

FIGURE 12.9

K-W-L-Q Chart for Pond and Pond Life

All about Ponds (K-W-L-Q)

What We Know	What We Want to Know	What We Learned	More Questions We Have
Contains water	How does the pond get its water?	Underground springs and rain	Why do ponds die?
Smaller than a lake			What happens to a pond in winter?
Fish	Why are ponds green and muddy?	Algae and other plants make it green	How do algae help or hurt a pond?
Ducks	What fish live in the pond?	Blue gill, trout, bass, catfish	
Frogs	What insects live on the pond?	Dragonflies, mosquitoes, water fleas	
Muddy			
Algae			
Insects on top			

Source: Information from Schmidt, P.R. (1999). KWLQ: Inquiry and literacy learning in science, *The Reading Teacher, 52,* 789–792.

For example, Simmons, Vaughn, and colleagues (2008) developed question cards that they used to assist students in designing different types of questions during and after reading. Students learned to ask questions in which the answer was one word. For example, "Who was this story mostly about?" or "What country did the characters live in?" After students learned to ask questions that had one-word answers, they were taught to ask questions in which the answer was in text but required more than one word to answer it. For example, "What happened after the dolphins were released in the gulf?" Students were then taught to ask questions that involved "why" and "how," requiring even more complex answers. Overall, students learned to think more about their text and their overall comprehension improved.

Pearson and Johnson (1978) developed a way to classify questions on the basis of the relationship between the question and the location of its answer. From this classification system, a strategy for teaching students how to answer different types of questions was also developed. This strategy, called the **question–answer relationships (QAR) strategy** (Raphael, 1982, 1984, 1986), helps students realize that when answering questions, they need to not only consider the text and their prior knowledge, but also use strategic behavior to adjust the use of each of these sources. As a result, student comprehension is enhanced (Simmonds, 1992).

The four question–answer relationships are based on the source of information and the types of reasoning involved:

1. *Right there.* Words used to create the question and words used for the answer are in the same sentence.
2. *Think and search.* The answer is in the text, but words used to create the question and those used for an appropriate answer are not in the same sentence.
3. *Author and you.* The answer is implied in the author's language, style, and tone.
4. *On my own.* The answer is found not in the text but in one's head on the basis of personal experience.

Teaching QAR involves having students learn to differentiate first between the two sources of information and then between the four question–answer relationships. Students also learn how to identify the types of questions they are trying to answer. Figure 12.10 presents a cue card students can use during instruction.

Adapted from Raphael (1986), the following are procedures for introducing the QAR strategy to students from elementary to middle school:

1. On the first day you are introducing QAR, inform students that you are going to show them how questions and answers relate in text and how they can be developed to be increasingly difficult. Either read several short passages aloud or ask students to read them

---

FIGURE 12.10

Question–Answer Relationships (QARs)

IN THE BOOK QAR

Right There

The answer is in the text, usually easy to find. The words used to make up the question and words used to answer the question are **Right There** in the same sentence.

Think and Search (Putting It Together)

The answer is in the story, but you need to put together different story parts to find it. Words for the question and words for the answer are not found in the same sentence. They come from different parts of the text.

IN MY HEAD QAR

Author and You

The answer is not in the story. You need to think about what you already know, what the author tells you in the text, and how it fits together.

On My Own

The answer is not in the story. You can even answer the question without reading the story. You need to use your own experience.

Source: Adapted from Raphael, T. E. (1986). Teaching question–answer relationships, revisited, *The Reading Teacher, 39*(6), 519. Copyright by the International Reading Association.

silently. Ask students to identify the type of QAR, the answer to the question, and the strategy they used for finding the answer. The progression for teaching should be from highly supportive to independent. In highly *supportive* teaching, the educator provides text, questions, answers, the QAR label for each question, and reasons the label is appropriate. In highly *independent* teaching, students generate their own questions, QAR labels, and reasons for their choices.

2. When students have a clear picture of the difference between "in my head" and "in the book," teach the next level of differentiation for each of the major categories. First, work on "in the book," then go to "in my head." The key distinction between the two "in my head" subcategories is "whether or not the reader needs to read the text for the questions to make sense" (Raphael, 1986, p. 519).

3. When students can use the QAR strategy effectively in short passages, gradually increase the length of the passages and the variety of reading materials. Review the strategy, model its use on the first question, and then have students use the strategy on the rest of the questions.

4. When students are proficient, use expanded or alternative QAR activities:
   - Have students work in pairs or cooperative learning groups, using QAR to answer comprehension questions.
   - Ask students to write stories with questions. Have other students determine the answer to each question and what kind of question it is.
   - Play a detective game in which students answer questions in their search for clues to solve the case and cite the source for their evidence.
   - Divide students into teams and have the teacher read a short passage, followed by questions. The teams earn points by answering questions and determining the QAR labels.

Questioning the Author

Questioning the Author (QtA) (2006) is an instructional conversation designed to provide engaging discussions about texts as though the author were present and contributing. QtA provides students with well-scaffolded instruction that supports students' thinking about text. It allows students to interact with each other as though the "author" were available for comment and conversation and also gives the students the opportunity to give the author feedback. Using QtA as a teaching strategy, the teacher has distinct goals and uses questions to assist students in reaching those goals. To use QtA, teachers should use the following steps:

1. Select text for students to read that is engaging and at an appropriate level. The text can be from traditional textbooks (e.g., social studies or science) or from other sources. Text that provides opportunities for students to engage in discussion is essential.

2. Make sure that students have some background knowledge of the topic they are reading about. The teacher can provide this information or have students do some prior reading. Background knowledge allows students to have an informed discussion about what they are reading.

3. Develop interesting questions that promote discussion and understanding of text. One of the primary goals is to promote students' thinking and to have them grapple with ideas and constructs while they read and then again after they read. Teachers can help guide these discussions by asking such questions such as "What is the author trying to tell us?" and "Why do you think the author is saying this?"

When effectively implemented, QtA can take students to a higher level of understanding.

Collaborative Strategic Reading

Collaborative strategic reading (CSR) is a multicomponent learning strategy that is typically used with students in grades 4 through 12 and combines essential reading comprehension strategies that have been demonstrated as effective in improving students' understanding of text (Lederer, 2000; Palincsar, 1986; Rosenshine & Meister, 1994) with cooperative learning groups or paired learning. CSR takes advantage of the growing understanding that youngsters need to be taught and provides specific strategies to enhance their understanding of text; however, students should not be overwhelmed with so many strategies that they are unable to decide which ones to use. CSR is based on reciprocal teaching (Palincsar & Brown, 1984) and teaches four strategies using the following steps: *preview* (i.e., predicting), *click and clunk* (i.e., questioning and clarifying), *get the gist* (i.e., summarization), and *wrap-up* (i.e., summarization). Preview is used only before reading the text and wrap-up only after reading the entire

PEARSON
myeducationlab

To enhance your understanding of how to use CSR for struggling readers, go to the IRIS Center Resources section of Topic 9: Reading Instruction in the MyEducationLab for your course and complete Module 11: CSR: A Reading Comprehension Strategy.

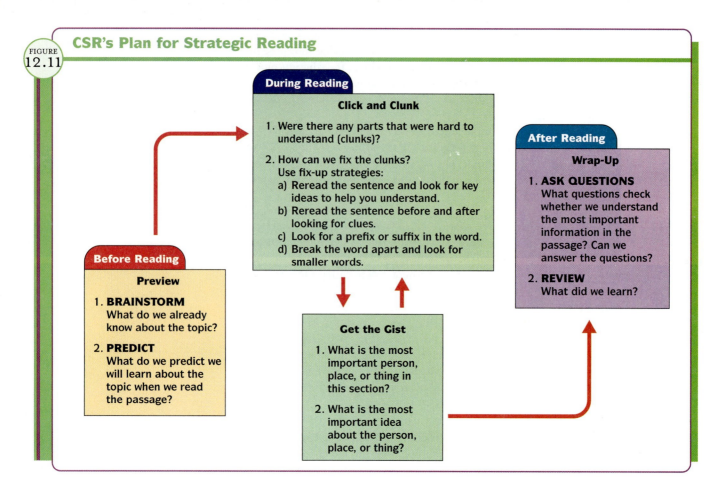

FIGURE 12.11 CSR's Plan for Strategic Reading

During Reading

Click and Clunk

1. Were there any parts that were hard to understand (clunks)?

2. How can we fix the clunks? Use fix-up strategies:
   a) Reread the sentence and look for key ideas to help you understand.
   b) Reread the sentence before and after looking for clues.
   c) Look for a prefix or suffix in the word.
   d) Break the word apart and look for smaller words.

Before Reading

Preview

1. **BRAINSTORM** What do we already know about the topic?

2. **PREDICT** What do we predict we will learn about the topic when we read the passage?

Get the Gist

1. What is the most important person, place, or thing in this section?

2. What is the most important idea about the person, place, or thing?

After Reading

Wrap-Up

1. **ASK QUESTIONS** What questions check whether we understand the most important information in the passage? Can we answer the questions?

2. **REVIEW** What did we learn?

Go to **www.readingrockets.org/** and read about research findings on effective reading instruction. You will also find links that provide an overview of reading comprehension and reading fluency.

text. Figure 12.11 presents the four CSR steps with key questions students can ask as they complete the process.

1. *Previewing.* The goals of previewing are for students to (a) learn as much about the passage as they can in 2 to 3 minutes, (b) activate their background knowledge about the topic, (c) make predictions about what they will read, and (d) pique their interest in the topic and engage them in active reading. In previewing, teach the students to check out the headings, key words, pictures, tables, graphs, and other key information. Jane Gordon, a sixth-grade teacher, uses previewing with her students by teaching them proper nouns and key words before they read. She then asks them to quickly examine the text and make sensible predictions about what they will read. If students make guesses that are not linked to the content of the text, she gives them feedback or asks them to justify their prediction.

2. *Click and Clunk.* Students "click and clunk" while reading each section of the text. "Clicks" refer to the portions of the text that make sense, and "clunks" are the portions about which comprehension isn't clear (e.g., students do not know the meaning of a word). Clicking and clunking is designed to help students monitor their comprehension and employ fix-up strategies to clarify their understanding. Clunk cards read as follows:

- Reread the sentence and look for ideas that help you understand the word.
- Reread the sentence leaving out the "clunk." What word makes sense?
- Reread the sentences before and after the sentence with the "clunk."
- Look for prefixes or suffixes in the word.
- Break the word apart and look for smaller words you know.

Jane Gordon encourages her students to be "clunk experts" by identifying key words and ideas they don't know and working with their partners to uncover their meaning. Students learn to select clunks carefully, which helps them monitor their comprehension while they read.

3. *Getting the Gist.* Students learn to get the gist (get the main idea) by reading each section and then asking and answering in their own words and in 10 words or less:

- Who or what is it about?
- What is most important about the who or what?

Teaching students to restate the most important point in 10 words or less is a way of making sure they understood what they read. Students repeat the second and third steps for each paragraph or section of the passage. The students in Jane Gordon's class, for example, appreciate that they not only have to read the material, but also have to write a brief sentence about the main idea. Initially they had a difficult time figuring out what a paragraph was about, but Jane helped them by asking students

- To read or display their gists from commonly read material
- To provide support for aspects of the gist that were valuable
- To rewrite it

Over time, students improved in their gist writing.

4. *Wrap-Up.*   During wrap-up, students formulate questions and answers about the key ideas from the entire passage and discuss what they have learned. The goal is to improve students' knowledge, understanding, and memory of what they read. For students with learning and language disabilities, it may be necessary to explicitly teach them to ask questions using the WH + How questions (*What?, When?, Where?, Why?,* and *How?*). Students can use the gists they have generated for the different sections to think about the most important information in the whole passage.

Cooperative Learning Groups.   Once students have developed proficiency in applying the comprehension strategies through teacher-led activities, the students learn to use CSR in peer-led cooperative learning groups of about four or five students (Johnson & Johnson, 1989). Typical roles used during CSR include the following:

- *Leader.* Leads the group by saying what to read and what strategy to use next
- *Clunk expert.* Reminds students to use clunk strategies to figure out a difficult word or concept
- *Announcer.* Calls on different members to read and share ideas
- *Encourager.* Watches the group and gives encouragement and feedback
- *Reporter.* During the whole-class wrap-up, reports to the class the important ideas learned and favorite questions
- *Timekeeper.* Keeps time and lets the group know when it is time to move on

Roles should change on a regular basis. After students wrap up in their cooperative groups, a whole-class wrap-up is completed to give the teacher and groups the opportunity to report and discuss the content.

CSR has been used in diverse classrooms, including students with reading problems and English language learners, to help students in upper-elementary, middle, and high school read content-area materials more efficiently and effectively (Klingner & Vaughn, 1998, 2000; Klingner, Vaughn, & Boardman, 2007; Klingner, Vaughn, & Schumm, 1998; Vaughn & Klingner, 1999, 2004; Vaughn, Klingner, & Bryant, 2001). Tiffany Royal, a fifth-grade inclusion teacher, notes, "What I like best is that my students learn how to understand what they read while they improve their vocabulary. Also, it helps on our standardized achievement tests."

Teaching English Language Learners with Reading Difficulties

Many of the critical content components that are essential for monolingual English speakers are effective for English language learners (ELLs). English language learners typically speak a language other than English in the home and are more comfortable listening and speaking in their home language. However, whether you are teaching them to read in their home language or English, the essential components of learning to read are also effective for these students.

ELLs benefit from having phonological awareness and, with guidance, can readily transfer their phonological awareness knowledge in their home language to English. They benefit from instruction in phonics, fluency, and comprehension. If they are not yet successful readers in English, learning to use listening comprehension strategies similar to reading comprehension strategies will help them be more effective at understanding what they hear and then transferring this knowledge later to what they read. Perhaps the most important component is to adequately build vocabulary, concept, and comprehension knowledge.

Unfortunately, there is substantially more knowledge about teaching students with reading difficulties who are monolingual English students than there is about teaching students who are ELLs. However, there is a growing knowledge base to inform our instruction in early reading with ELLs (Denton, Anthony, Parker, & Hasbrouck, 2004; Linan-Thompson & Vaughn, 2006; Vaughn, Cirino et al., 2006). A summary of findings reveals that

- English language learners who were given direct instruction in early reading in English benefited in the number of words read correctly per minute (Gunn et al., 2000).
- Bilingual students with significant reading problems who participated in 22 tutoring sessions in a systematic and explicit approach to phonics and word and sentence reading significantly improved on word identification when compared with control groups who did not receive this type of instruction (Denton et al., 2004).
- ELLs who were second graders at risk for reading disabilities participated in 58 sessions (35 minutes each) of supplemental intervention in group sizes of one to three students (Linan-Thompson et al., 2003). Students in the treatment made gains on reading outcomes such as word attack, passage comprehension, phoneme segmentation, and oral reading fluency. Only three students made less than 6 months' growth during the 3-month intervention.
- In a study with young children with problems learning to read in English but who spoke Sylheti (a dialect from Bangladesh), students who participated in a phonics program rather than story reading made significant gains on phonics recognition and recall and writing sounds, as well as on reading words and reading nonwords (Stuart, 1999). Findings indicate that a more structured, systematic approach that includes phonics resulted in better outcomes for ELLs than interventions without these elements.
- Young bilingual students (Spanish/English) with low literacy and oralcy skills taught to read in English made considerable gains over their first-grade year and maintained these advantages into second grade (Vaughn, Cirino et al., 2006; Vaughn, Mathes et al., 2006). Similarly, young bilingual students (Spanish/English) with low literacy and oralcy skills taught to read in Spanish also made considerable gains, outperformed comparison students, and maintained these gains into second grade (Vaughn, Cirino et al., 2006; Vaughn, Linan-Thompson et al., 2006).

In summary, good readers—whether they are monolingual English or English language learners—rely primarily on decoding words (understanding the sound-to-print correspondence or alphabetic principle). They do not rely primarily on context or pictures to identify words. When they use context, it is to confirm word reading or to better understand text meaning. Well-developed phonics instruction provides ELLs with the knowledge they need to develop the skills and strategies needed to effectively and efficiently establish a map for making sense of how English language works in print. As with monolingual students, phonics instruction is a piece of the reading instruction and not the entire program. Good phonics instruction is well integrated into language activities, story time, and small-group support to create a balanced reading program. Learning to read in languages in which the print is less consistently connected to sounds (like English) takes longer than learning to read in languages that have more consistent orthographies (e.g., Spanish) (Seymour, 2006).

Teachers who implement effective instructional practices with ELLs (Linan-Thompson & Vaughn, 2007; Vaughn & Bos, 2008)

- Consider the commonalities between reading instruction in English and the reading instruction that is provided in the student's native language (assuming native language instruction has occurred).
- Identify procedures for instructing students in all of the critical elements of reading, including phonemic awareness, spelling, phonics, vocabulary, language development, fluency, and comprehension.
- Recognize that English is the most difficult language of all alphabetic languages to learn to read and therefore many of the foundation skills such as spelling and phonics require more explicit and systematic instruction than they might in other alphabetic languages such as Spanish or Italian.
- Make connections between the home language and the language of instruction at school.
- Capitalize on every opportunity to use and promote language development during instruction and give opportunities for students to engage in higher order questions.

- Promote all opportunities to teach and engage in vocabulary and concept building.
- Use peer pairing and cooperative groups to enhance learning.

Strategies for Teaching Older Readers with Reading Difficulties

In the upper-elementary grades, middle school, and high school, reading instruction focuses more on comprehension and reading for learning in the content areas. Even so, it is not unusual for students who decode at a third-grade level or below to be members of heterogeneous classes. What can you do when only a few students are nonreaders? Tips for Teachers 12.9 presents some strategies for teaching older students to read.

Teaching older students with significant reading difficulties to read is not substantively different from teaching younger students. Many of the practices we've discussed apply to older readers with a few important exceptions. First, few older readers require instruction in phonological awareness. Second, phonics and other word-study practices are taught with more complex multisyllable words as opposed to the single syllable words used with younger children. This way, students learn to read "big" words at a level that is not demeaning.

The REWARDS program (Reading Excellence: Word Attack & Rate Development Strategies) (Archer, Gleason, & Vachon, 2005) is a flexible teaching strategy used with older students for reading longer, multisyllabic words instead of a more stringent set of syllabication rules. The strategy is based on the fact that many words in the English language (80%) contain at least one prefix and one suffix and all decodable parts of words contain at least one vowel. Therefore, students are taught to identify affixes and vowel sounds to break a word into manageable parts. The students are then taught to say the word part by part and then say the whole word. The goal is to achieve a close enough approximation of the word that students can then correct the pronunciation if necessary using context. Students are taught to circle prefixes and suffixes, underline vowels, say the parts of the word, say the whole word, and then make it into a real word.

Many teachers of older students with reading difficulties or disabilities are eager to learn more about instructional programs that have been developed and tested specifically with older students. Deshler, Palincsar, Biancarosa, and Nair (2007) provide an overview of more than 50 programs that have been developed and evaluated with older students with reading difficulties/disabilities. These programs are rated based on content and research. If you are thinking about using a program, you might want to check to see whether they have reviewed it.

PEARSON
myeducationlab

Go to the Building Teaching Skills and Dispositions section of Topic 9: Reading Instruction in the MyEducationLab for your course and complete the activity entitled *Fostering Reading Development in Students of Different Ages.*

Tips for TEACHERS 12.9

STRATEGIES IN READING INSTRUCTION FOR OLDER STUDENTS

- *Be an advocate for nonreaders.* As a content-area teacher, you might not be able to teach these students to decode, but you can be an advocate for them as individuals and for nonreaders collectively.

- *Work collaboratively with other professionals in the school.* What resources are available to help you teach and for students to receive additional help?

- *Work out a plan for what you can reasonably do in your classroom.* Communicate the plan to administrators, other professionals, parents, and students, and follow it regularly.

- *Continue to make knowledge available to students who cannot adequately access knowledge through reading.* Students who cannot read the text for content-area

instruction can be left out of learning without teachers who provide alternative ways for them to access the content. Teach key words, concepts, and principles orally and provide opportunities to review this knowledge. Allow for engaging and interactive activities to promote access to knowledge for students who read poorly.

- *Include in your plan ways to provide support for students to complete reading assignments and tests by using audiotaping, parent support, or peer support.* Work out a way to have assignments and tests read aloud to students if they cannot read them on their own.

- *Find out about and build on the strengths of nonreaders.* Make certain that in your class they have an opportunity to share their gifts and talents with classmates.

Putting It All Together

Perhaps one of the most challenging but also exciting and important aspects of teaching reading to students with reading difficulties and disabilities is determining students' instructional needs and then meeting them. The feedback from students who say, "I didn't really think I could ever learn to read—but now I can," are the magic words that make students with real learning challenges the most exciting of all our students. Tables 12.4, 12.5, and 12.6 provide an overview of the critical elements that teachers may want to consider when students are not meeting grade-level expectations in reading. This flow of reading instruction will help you "put it all together" so that the satisfaction of teaching all students to read is possible to achieve.

TABLE 12.4

Supplemental Reading Instruction for Kindergarten

INSTRUCTIONAL COMPONENT	OBJECTIVES	ACTIVITIES	LESSON COMPONENTS
Phonological Awareness	• To accurately and automatically manipulate onset and rimes (first semester) and phonemes (second semester)	• Identifying, blending, segmenting, and substituting words in sentences, and syllables in words, onset/rime, and phonemes with or without support	• Focus on one or two types of manipulation (e.g., blending and segmenting) • Conduct all activities orally initially, and then link to print • Allow students to respond individually and as a group • Use manipulatives if desired
Phonics and Word Study	• To understand that sounds are represented by letters • To apply sound–letter correspondences to reading words accurately and fluently	• Identifying letter names and sounds, consonants in initial and final positions, and short vowels • Blending sounds to read words • Dictating letters and words	• Introduce letters and sounds systematically • Have students combine sounds to form words • Allow students to practice writing the letters and words they are learning
Listening Comprehension	• To construct meaning from stories using comprehension strategies	• Reading narrative and expository text out loud • Predicting and activating background knowledge before reading • Summarizing periodically during reading • Questioning and retelling activities after reading	• Introduce strategies systematically • Model strategies • Focus on the most important idea • Use different types of questions

Source: Vaughn, S. & Linan-Thompson, S. (2004). *Research-based methods of reading instruction, grades K–3.* Alexandria, VA: Association for Supervision and Curriculum Development.

TABLE 12.5 — Supplemental Reading Instruction for First Grade

INSTRUCTIONAL COMPONENT	OBJECTIVES	ACTIVITIES	LESSON COMPONENTS
Fluency	• To automatically recognize words, both in isolation and in connected text	• Partner reading (student–adult or student–student) • Choral reading • Tape-assisted reading	• Provide a good and explicit model • Provide opportunities to reread text • Have students reread text at least three times • Establish performance criteria
Phonological Awareness	• To be able to manipulate phonemes	• Blending and segmenting words at the phoneme level with or without support	• Focus on one or two types of manipulation (e.g., blending and segmenting) • Use print • Provide opportunities for students to respond individually and as a group • Use manipulatives if desired
Phonics and Word Study	• To apply sound–letter correspondences to read words accurately and fluently • To use decoding strategies to read unknown words	• Blending sounds to read words • Reading decodable text • Dictating words and sentences	• Read books that contain words students have learned • Let students use decoding strategies • Introduce patterns and rules systematically • Combine sounds to form words
Comprehension	• To use comprehension strategies before, during, and after reading text to construct meaning	• Engaging in comprehension strategies before, during, and after listening to or reading a text • Predicting and activating background knowledge • Self-questioning, self-monitoring, and generating and answering questions	• Model use of self-monitoring and comprehension strategies • Provide opportunities for students to use self-monitoring and comprehension strategies

Source: Vaughn, S. & Linan-Thompson, S. (2004). *Research-based methods of reading instruction, grades K–3.* Alexandria, VA: Association for Supervision and Curriculum Development.

TABLE 12.6 — Supplemental Reading Instruction for Second and Third Grade

INSTRUCTIONAL COMPONENT	OBJECTIVES	ACTIVITIES	LESSON COMPONENTS
Fluency	To automatically recognize words in connected text	• Partner reading (student–adult or student–student) • Choral reading • Tape-assisted reading • Fluency building at the word and phrase level	• Provide a good and explicit model • Provide opportunities for student to reread text at least three times • Establish performance criteria
Vocabulary	To use advanced word recognition strategies with unknown words	• Teaching words and their extended meanings systematically	• Model and teach the use of both explicit and implicit vocabulary instruction activities • Provide multiple opportunities to practice and use key vocabulary
Comprehension	• To use comprehension strategies before, during, and after reading text to construct meaning • To use self-monitoring strategies	• Predicting and activating background knowledge before reading • Providing decoding support and monitoring comprehension during reading • Answering and generating questions and summarizing after reading	• Make sure books are at instructional level • Preview vocabulary when introducing books • Model the use of self-monitoring and comprehension strategies • Provide opportunities for students to use self-monitoring and comprehension strategies

Source: Vaughn, S. & Linan-Thompson, S. (2004). *Research-based methods of reading instruction, grades K–3.* Alexandria, VA: Association for Supervision and Curriculum Development.

Summary

■ In the last decade, national, state, and local initiatives have emphasized balanced approaches to teaching reading and the use of research-based strategies for teaching students how to read. Balanced means that students are provided with appropriate instruction in all critical elements of reading, including phonemic awareness, phonics, fluency, comprehension, and vocabulary. Effective reading instruction for struggling readers encompasses several areas (phonological awareness, letter–sound correspondence, alphabetic principle, word identification, fluency, vocabulary, and comprehension) that teachers balance on the basis of the students' current reading levels and needs and the purposes of instruction.

■ In planning and using effective reading instruction for struggling readers, teachers should establish an environment that promotes reading, use appropriate and ongoing assessment, use RTI strategies, provide intensive instruction, and obtain early intervention.

■ Students, especially struggling readers, need systematic instruction in phonological awareness, letter–sound correspondence, and decoding strategies, including phonics instruction. This instruction includes modeling and guided practice with feedback in context and with words in isolation.

- Some students have difficulty automatically recognizing words in print and need specific instruction with sight words.
- Students are fluent in reading when they can recognize printed words quickly and effortlessly. Repeated reading, reading aloud to students, and classwide peer tutoring promote reading fluency. Fluency instruction should be integrated with instruction in word identification and comprehension.
- Asking students to predict and make connections with prior knowledge before reading, monitor their understanding during reading, and summarize key ideas after reading assists them in improving their comprehension.
- There are some key similarities and differences between teaching young struggling readers and older struggling readers. REWARDS is an effective strategy for teaching older readers.

Think and Apply

1. Now that you have read Chapter 12, what strategies can you use to teach phonological awareness, phonics, word identification, fluency, and comprehension to students with reading difficulties?

2. Think about several students you have taught or are currently teaching who are struggling with reading. Which factors are influencing their learning? What components of the reading process pose the most problems for each student? How have you integrated the components to meet their needs?

3. Plan a lesson to teach phonological awareness or reading comprehension. Describe the follow-up activities, including the instructional grouping formats, you plan to use to reinforce learning and meet individual student needs. Describe how you will monitor progress.

PEARSON
myeducationlab

Now go to Topic 9: Reading Comprehension in the MyEducationLab (www.myeducationlab .com) for your course where you can:

- Find learning outcomes for this topic along with the national standards that connect to these outcomes.
- Complete Assignments and Activities that can help you more deeply understand the chapter content.
- Examine challenging situations and cases presented in the IRIS Center Resources.
- Apply and practice your understanding of the core teaching skills identified in the chapter with Building Teaching Skills and Dispositions learning units.

Facilitating Writing

FOCUS QUESTIONS

1. What are the current trends in writing curriculum and instruction and how do they align with your beliefs about writing instruction? How do your beliefs compare with belief statements published by the National Council of Teachers of English?

2. What are advantages of teaching writing as a process and how does this process promote effective writing instruction for all learners?

3. What strategies can you implement to establish an environment that promotes writing?

4. What strategies can you implement for conducting effective writing workshops?

5. What strategies can you implement for students who have difficulties writing stories?

6. What strategies can you implement for students who have difficulties with narrative writing?

7. What strategies can you implement for students who have difficulties with informational writing?

8. What strategies can you implement to help students who have difficulties with persuasive writing?

9. What strategies can you implement to help all students develop spelling skills?

10. What strategies can you implement to help all students develop handwriting skills?

INTERVIEW
MICHELLE LANGLOIS

Michelle Langlois is a special education teacher who has worked for 5 years at the elementary level as an "inclusion" teacher providing instructional support to teachers and specialized instruction to students with disabilities in kindergarten through third grade. During the past year she decided to tackle a new challenge and accepted a transfer to a middle school where she worked as a resource teacher with 18 students with disabilities. Michelle was very confident about her successes in teaching writing at the elementary school but was less confident after her first year teaching middle school.

Well I'm not sure who learned more this year, the students or me. I'm just kidding—I think—but it was a big learning experience for me. You see, when I taught elementary inclusion classes I worked cooperatively with a team of the kindergarten through third-grade teachers to establish writing centers that would give students experience in all of the elements of writing including composing, editing, rewriting, and publishing. We all agreed that students needed time to practice the craft of writing and to learn that good writers read and rewrite their work and then receive feedback from others including their classmates before revising and publishing. We didn't just let students develop writing independently but provided explicit instruction in those critical skills associated with effective writing including spelling, punctuation, and elements of grammar. However, we all seemed to agree on the procedures and shared a common language for how we talked about writing and instruction to students.

I found that when I came to the middle school, many of the teachers were not accustomed to having the special education teacher be an active member of the team. I was hoping that I could extend many of the practices I used at the elementary level to establish and promote writing instruction across the content area using research-based instructional practices that would promote writing for all learners but especially for students with disabilities. For example, we know that when students identify the topic they are writing about and use a graphic organizer to help them include critical ideas, key words, and important parts of the writing piece (e.g., introduction, summary), students produce better writing. I was encouraging all of the middle-school teachers to work with me to identify common writing strategies we would all use—that way students could learn the new strategies and practice them across content areas. I was optimistic that I could then reinforce these instructional strategies by teaching and applying them in the resource room. I was not as successful at instituting these practices as I would like to have been though I am optimistic that many of the teachers I worked with last year had a positive experience and that we will start off this next year with these teachers eager to continue our work together.

Introduction

Like many teachers who have acquired knowledge about effective instructional practices and are eager to share them with other teachers, Michelle found that the process works best when the professional development includes open communication and careful planning. In this chapter, you will first read about current trends in writing curricula. The chapter continues with suggestions for helping all students succeed in composition of various genres, spelling, and handwriting.

Current Trends in Writing Curriculum and Instruction

Michelle realized that research-based writing practices can be applied at both the elementary and the secondary level and are especially helpful to students with disabilities who are included in general education classrooms. However, there are competing issues such as high-stakes assessment that influence writing curriculum. Current trends in writing curriculum and instruction include

- Movement toward standards-based writing instruction and research-based practices.
- Increased emphasis on assessment.
- Emphasis on balanced and effective writing instruction for all students.
- Implementation of writing practices that are based on research and represent standardized writing and spelling outcomes.

Standards-Based Writing Instruction and Research-Based Practices

Teachers such as Michelle realize that they need to consider the writing standards of the state in which they teach. Most frequently, state standards are based on standards recommended by professional organizations such as the International Reading Association and the National Council of Teachers of English (see Figure 13.1).

One way to ensure high-quality writing instruction is through the use of research-based practices. No Child Left Behind mandates "an emphasis on implementing education programs and practices that have been clearly demonstrated to be effective through rigorous scientific

---

FIGURE 13.1 **International Reading Association/National Council of Teachers of English Standards**

IRA/NCTE Standards for the English Language Arts

The 12 Standards

The vision guiding these standards is that all students must have the opportunities and resources to develop the language skills they need to pursue life's goals and to participate fully as informed, productive members of society. These standards assume that literacy growth begins before children enter school as they experience and experiment with literacy activities—reading and writing, and associating spoken words with their graphic representations. Recognizing this fact, these standards encourage the development of curriculum and instruction that make productive use of the emerging literacy abilities that children bring to school. Furthermore, the standards provide ample room for the innovation and creativity essential to teaching and learning. They are not prescriptions for particular curriculum or instruction.

1. Students read a wide range of print and nonprint texts to build an understanding of texts, of themselves, and of the cultures of the United States and the world; to acquire new information; to respond to the needs and demands of society and the workplace; and for personal fulfillment. Among these texts are fiction and nonfiction, classic and contemporary works.

2. Students read a wide range of literature from many periods in many genres to build an understanding of the many dimensions (e.g., philosophical, ethical, aesthetic) of human experience.

3. Students apply a wide range of strategies to comprehend, interpret, evaluate, and appreciate texts. They draw on their prior experience, their interactions with other readers and writers, their knowledge of word meaning and of other texts, their word identification strategies, and their understanding of textual features (e.g., sound–letter correspondence, sentence structure, context, graphics).

4. Students adjust their use of spoken, written, and visual language (e.g., conventions, style, vocabulary) to communicate effectively with a variety of audiences and for different purposes.

5. Students employ a wide range of strategies as they write and use different writing process elements appropriately to communicate with different audiences for a variety of purposes.

6. Students apply knowledge of language structure, language conventions (e.g., spelling and punctuation), media techniques, figurative language, and genre to create, critique, and discuss print and nonprint texts.

7. Students conduct research on issues and interests by generating ideas and questions, and by posing problems. They gather, evaluate, and synthesize data from a variety of sources (e.g., print and nonprint texts, artifacts, people) to communicate their discoveries in ways that suit their purpose and audience.

8. Students use a variety of technological and information resources (e.g., libraries, databases, computer networks, video) to gather and synthesize information and to create and communicate knowledge.

9. Students develop an understanding of and respect for diversity in language use, patterns, and dialects across cultures, ethnic groups, geographic regions, and social roles.

10. Students whose first language is not English make use of their first language to develop competency in the English language arts and to develop understanding of content across the curriculum.

11. Students participate as knowledgeable, reflective, creative, and critical members of a variety of literacy communities.

12. Students use spoken, written, and visual language to accomplish their own purposes (e.g., for learning, enjoyment, persuasion, and the exchange of information).

Source: National Council of Teachers of English and International Reading Association. (1998–2008). *Standards for the English language arts* (p. 3). Urbana, IL: Authors. Reprinted with permission.

Tips for Teachers 13.1

RESEARCH-BASED WRITING PRACTICES

- Teaching students writing strategies that include planning, revising, and editing their compositions. Many of the writing strategies discussed previously were developed to meet this recommendation.

- Helping students to combine sentences to achieve more complex sentence types and to summarize texts.

- Providing opportunities for students to work together in pairs and groups toward cooperative written products to facilitate quality of composition.

- Establishing goals for students' writing to improve outcomes.

- Giving students access to and instruction in word processing to facilitate writing.

- Assisting students in developing prewriting practices that help generate or organize ideas for writing.

- Using inquiry activities to analyze data related to writing reports.

- Using writing process approaches that provide extended time for writing and revision.

- Providing students with good models of writing to study and to compare with their own writing.

- Integrating writing as a tool to enhance content knowledge.

Source: Information from Graham, S. & Perrin, D. (2007). A meta-analysis of writing instruction for adolescent students. *Journal of Educational Psychology, 99,*445–476.

research" (U.S. Department of Education, 2004, p. 5). A growing body of knowledge exists that can ensure success in learning to write—even among students for whom learning to write is difficult, including students with learning disabilities (Graham & Perin, 2007) and English language learners (Graves, Valles, & Rueda, 2000). However, Baker, Gersten, and Graham (2003) emphasize the importance of teaching students strategies for composing text and for giving students specific feedback to help them improve their writing. Some of the research-based instructional practices for improving writing are provided in Tips for Teachers 13.1.

Emphasis on Assessment and Progress Monitoring

Many states now require high-stakes writing tests that potentially affect student promotion and graduation from high school. The emphasis on student outcomes has spawned greater emphasis on ongoing student progress monitoring and providing students with specific feedback about their performance. Although the debate about high-stakes tests will continue, the importance of learning to communicate in the written word using a variety of media and technologies remains. Students need feedback and monitoring to help them achieve success in written communication. Moreover, students with difficulties in writing need intensive and sustained interventions to improve their writing (e.g., Ferretti, Andrews-Weckerly, & Lewis, 2007). Figure 13.2 provides features of exemplary writing instruction.

Progress Monitoring and Writing

Why is it a good idea to monitor the progress of students with writing difficulties? When teachers monitor students' progress on critical elements regularly (at least every 2 weeks), students may make notable progress. Teachers record students' progress so that they, the students, and parents can see progress, such as the number of words written for younger children and developing a checklist of story elements and their quality for older students.

Teachers monitor students' progress by noting

- Whether students can complete the written project
- How proficient they are at each element of the writing process (e.g., planning, spelling, handwriting, composing)
- Whether they can apply the skills and knowledge to other contexts (e.g., at other times during the day)
- How they explain the process they are using

myeducationlab

Go to the Building Teaching Skills and Dispositions section of Topic 6: Assessment in the MyEducationLab for your course and complete the activity entitled *Assessing Students' Written Work.*

Go to **www.nwrel.org/edservices**, where you can read about writing assessment and instruction called 6 + 1 Trait Writing as well as other programs.

Features of Exemplary Writing Instruction

FIGURE 13.2

- A literate classroom environment where students' written work is prominently displayed, the room is packed with writing and reading material, and word lists adorn the walls.

- Daily writing with students working on a wide range of writing tasks for multiple audiences, including writing at home.

- Extensive efforts to make writing motivating by setting an exciting mood, creating a risk-free environment, allowing students to select their own writing topics or modify teacher assignments, developing assigned topics compatible with students' interests, reinforcing children's accomplishments, specifying the goal for each lesson, and promoting an "I can" attitude.

- Regular teacher–student conferences concerning the writing topic the student is currently working on, including the establishment of goals or criteria to guide the child's writing and revising efforts.

- A predictable writing routine where students are encouraged to think, reflect, and revise.

- Overt teacher modeling of the process of writing as well as positive attitudes toward writing.

- Cooperative arrangements where students help each other plan, draft, revise, edit, or publish their written work.

- Group or individual sharing where students present work in progress or completed papers to their peers for feedback.

- Instruction covering a broad range of skills, knowledge, [and] strategies, including phonological awareness, handwriting and spelling, writing conventions, sentence-level skills, text structure, functions of writing, and planning and revising.

- Follow-up instruction to ensure mastery of targeted writing skills, knowledge, and strategies.

- Integration of writing activities across the curriculum and the use of reading to support writing development.

- Frequent opportunities for students to self-regulate their behavior during writing, including working independently, arranging their own space, and seeking help from others.

- Teacher and student assessments of writing progress, strengths, and needs.

- Periodic conferences with parents and frequent communications with home about the writing program and students' progress as writers.

Source: Information from Graham, S., Harris, K.R. & Larsen, L. (2001). Prevention and intervention of writing difficulties for students with learning disabilities. *Learning disabilities research and practice, 16,* 74–84.

For example, as students write, teachers notice what strategies they use to compose text (e.g., outline, notes, keywords), reflect on the appropriateness of the task and teaching presentation, and keep written records to document student progress, such as notes, checklists, and samples of students' work. Monitoring students' progress in writing involves evaluating written products and observing the writing process. Teachers can observe students as they write and use conference times to assess and record their progress. By observing and examining writing processes and products, teachers can plan instruction to meet individual needs.

Many teachers keep anecdotal records by creating a record sheet to quickly document students' progress on writing projects. They include a summary of what they observe, the date, and context, and they list skills and writing strategies that need to be taught. Collections of students' written work help teachers, parents, and students to document growth and development as it occurs during the school year. Journals and writing folders also provide insight into writing growth. Teachers may periodically review and select representative pieces to show writing development and use progress monitoring as a means to establish writing goals for students.

Perhaps the most important activity is to determine how the teacher will measure writing progress for each student. For example, for young students, the teacher may monitor the number of words written, number of words spelled correctly, and use of capital letters and punctuation. As students mature in their writing, the teacher may decide to monitor the use of adjectives and vivid verbs, facility in editing and revising, and overall quality of the writing. It is important to focus on only one or two things at a time. After students demonstrate progress in the target areas, the teacher can add other elements of writing. This way, progress is recorded, and students are not overwhelmed by the number of writing conventions that they need to monitor.

Response to Intervention and Writing

Documenting students' response to writing instruction is a useful way of providing valuable information that would assist in determining whether they require special education or, for those students already receiving special education, whether they are making adequate progress in writing. How might response to intervention be used for students with writing difficulties? Students with extreme writing challenges should be provided extra time each day (20 minutes) and extra instruction to determine whether their writing improved. Teachers can maintain copies of students' writing to determine whether adequate progress in writing has occurred.

Writing Rubrics and Portfolios

Writing rubrics and portfolios can be used to structure assessment. These tools are helpful for both teachers and students in that they serve as a gauge of student progress.

Writing Rubrics.   A **writing rubric** is a scoring guide that outlines expected performance on a written product. There are many variations of formats for rubrics (Arter & McTighe, 2000; Flynn & Flynn, 2004), but most include levels of performance from unacceptable to proficient. Rubrics can be developed by schools, district, or states based on required standards for writing. Textbook publishers are including more rubrics as supplemental material. A number of rubrics and "rubric generators" are available online. Teachers and students can construct rubrics as well (see examples in Figure 13.3). Often rubrics are accompanied by writing samples or exemplars that demonstrate different levels of performance.

Whatever the source, rubrics are best used to clarify what students are being expected to do and to provide a framework for self-, peer, and teacher evaluation. Rubrics can also be used to give guided feedback that will direct students in reaching higher levels of performance. It is useful for parents to be informed about the number of levels in your rubric (the more levels the better) and the meaning of the categories in the rubric (e.g., what do you mean by "mechanical errors"), so that they can provide support to their youngster at home.

Writing Portfolios.   You can use several types of writing portfolios in your classroom. Strickland, Galda, and Cullinan (2004) mention four types:

1. Showcase portfolios (featuring best work)
2. Documentation portfolios (includes artifacts over a period of time)
3. Process portfolios (evidence of development of a single piece from beginning to end)
4. Evaluation portfolios (used to determine grades based on a predetermined set of standards)

The type of portfolio you use will depend on your state and district requirements and on your own decision about how you want to track student progress and report to parents and administrators. Tips for Teachers 13.2 provides suggestions for implementing writing portfolios in your classroom.

FIGURE 13.3

Sample Rubric for Writing

	TIP TOP	PRETTY GOOD	GETTING THERE	KEEP WORKING
MEANING	Message clear, easy to follow	Message mostly clear and easy to follow	Message somewhat clear or easy to follow	Message not clear, hard to follow
PARAGRAPHS	Indented, has a main idea, and connects with paragraphs before and after	Mostly indented, has a main idea, and connects with paragraphs before and after	Mostly indented, has a main idea, or connects with paragraphs before and after	Not indented, has no main idea, and does not connect with paragraphs before and after
SENTENCES	Expresses complete thoughts and uses correct punctuation	Mostly expresses complete thoughts and uses correct punctuation	Mostly expresses complete thoughts or uses correct punctuation	Does not express complete thoughts nor use correct punctuation
WORDS	Spelling correct, capitalization correct, and uses a variety of words	Spelling mostly correct, capitalization mostly correct, and/or some use of a variety of words	Spelling needs correction, capitalization needs correction, or needs more use of a variety of words	Spelling needs correction, capitalization needs correction, and needs more use of a variety of words
NEATNESS	Easy to read and follows directions for format	Mostly easy to read and follows directions for format	Mostly easy to read or follows directions for format	Hard to read and does not follow directions for format

Source: Schumm, J.S. (2005). *How to help your child with homework* (p. 71). Copyright © 2005. Used with permission of Free Spirit Publishing, Inc., Minneapolis, MN; 1-866-703-7322; www.freespirit.com. All rights reserved.

IMPLEMENTING WRITING PORTFOLIOS

- Introduce the portfolio. Describe the purpose for the portfolio, intended use and audience, type of artifacts to include, and examples.

- Introduce the rubric or scoring guide. Explain how the portfolio will be evaluated and by whom (e.g., teacher, parent, peer, self).

- Explain guidelines for inclusion of artifacts, including electronic artifacts.

- Outline logistical and ethical issues: how materials will be housed and maintained, appropriate times and procedures for working on the portfolio, and who has access to materials.

- Assist student in setting personal goals and planning artifacts/projects to meet those goals.

- Provide guided experiences for students to reflect on their work and to document those reflections.

Source: Adapted from Gredler, M. E. & Johnson, R. L. (2004). *Assessment in the literacy classroom.* Boston: Allyn & Bacon. Copyright © 2005 by Pearson Education. Adapted by permission of the publisher.

Teaching Writing as a Process

Think about some of your recent experiences as a writer. Perhaps you were writing a research paper for school. You might have been writing a letter or an email message to a friend. Maybe you were carefully crafting a letter of application for a job. Think about the process. To compose, you needed to do the following:

- Formulate your message in your head.
- Organize your ideas in a logical fashion.
- Think about the reader and how he or she might understand and react to the message.
- Choose words carefully to make the flow of language, or syntax, smooth.
- Select individual words to convey your meaning succinctly.
- Attend to your spelling, capitalization, and punctuation.
- Consider the appearance of the final product (the legibility of your handwriting, typing, or word processing).

As a teacher, you need to help your students write using this same process.

Go to **www.literacyconnections .com** for more ideas for teaching language arts, including sections on writing, to all students.

Writing as an Interactive Process

Writers use the sounds, grammar, and meaning of our language system to **encode** (or to put language into print) and to communicate a message to the reader. In writing, as in reading, students may have problems with any aspect of the language system—with using language interactively and with using it fluently. In addition, students may have problems with the physical act of writing. For example, Grant Ellsworth, a fifth grader with learning disabilities, loves to tell stories, especially about fishing with his father, but he is reluctant when asked to write them. Grant is a poor speller and for some reason cannot get the hang of capitalization and punctuation rules. In addition, his handwriting is illegible, and he hasn't learned to use a keyboard. Writing a single sentence takes Grant so long that he soon loses his story and its intended meaning. Even though Grant can tell stories in an entertaining way, he cannot get them on paper.

Effective teachers understand what research has demonstrated: Students need to know the mechanics of writing if they are going to communicate effectively with others. Earlier instruction in writing often focused too much on the mechanics and too little on conveying meaning. Today, some teachers may overemphasize a process approach to writing focusing too much on the meaning and too little on the mechanics. Successful teachers know that both are essential elements to successful writing and are best taught in an integrated fashion (National Council of Teachers of English [NCTE], 2004). For example, Mrs. Zakibe, Grant's teacher, knows that she must ensure that Grant and all her students understand the rules of language, including capitalization, punctuation, and spelling as well as the value of a well-organized story structure.

When teachers implement effective intervention approaches that use both the conventions of writing, such as capitalization, punctuation, and sentence structure, and strategies for improving written expression, such as planning and composing, the results are positive (Gersten & Baker, 2001). Effective writing instruction requires the following critical points (Fearn & Farnan, 2001):

- Attention to conventions does not disrupt the flow of writing but is part of the discipline of writing.
- Focus on the conventions of writing does not inhibit growth in writing but facilitates it.
- Even very young children can learn and perform simple conventions automatically.
- Students with disabilities need to spend about 20% of their instructional time in writing addressing the use and application of the conventions of writing.

Writing as a Strategic Process

Because writing is such a complex task, successful writers need a strategy or plan for communicating ideas clearly. It is important to have systematic procedures for being successful and productive at each stage of the authoring process. Students, especially those with learning and behavior problems, often have difficulty not only planning their writing but also monitoring and regulating themselves while they write. Since the 1980s, researchers have worked to develop ways to teach students to become strategic writers (Englert, Berry, & Dunsmore, 2001; Graham & Harris, 2006; Mason & Graham, 2008). Fortunately, research-based practices that can help students become more strategic writers are emerging in several areas, including learning the stages of the writing process, learning narrative and expository text structures, and getting systematic and specific feedback (Baker, Gersten, & Graham, 2003). Students may find a checklist like the one in Tips for Teachers 13.3 helpful for monitoring their own writing.

Should children be encouraged to write before they can read or spell? Why or why not?

Tips for Teachers 13.3

CHECKLIST THAT HELPS STUDENTS MONITOR THEIR WRITING

_____ I found a quiet place to work.
_____ I set up a schedule for when I would work on this paper.
_____ I read or listened to the teacher's directions carefully.
_____ I thought about who would read my paper.
_____ I thought about what I wanted my paper to accomplish.
_____ I started planning my paper before I actually started writing it.
_____ I tried to remember everything I already knew about the topic before I started to write.
_____ I got all the information I needed before starting to write.
_____ I organized my information before starting to write.
_____ I thought about the reader as I wrote.
_____ I thought about what I wanted to accomplish as I wrote.
_____ I continued to develop my plans as I wrote.
_____ I revised the first draft of my paper.
_____ I checked what I wrote to make sure that the reader would understand it.
_____ I checked to make sure that I accomplished my goals.
_____ I reread my paper before turning it in.
_____ I asked other students, the teacher, or my parents when I needed help.
_____ I rewarded myself when I finished my paper.

Source: Harris, K. R. & Graham, S. (1992). *Helping young writers master the craft: Strategy instruction and self-regulation in the writing process.* Boston: Brookline Books. Reprinted by permission.

Writing as a Process of Constructing Meaning

When writers compose, they need to keep potential readers in mind. Readers need to have background information and specific links (such as examples and definitions of new terms) to help them connect the new information with what they already know. In short, writers need to take responsibility for helping readers to construct meaning.

Students with writing difficulties might not understand the role of audience or potential readers or how to help readers construct meaning by providing background knowledge and using predictable story or informational writing structures. For example, Terry Macinello, a fifth grader, wrote a story about a recent trip but did not indicate where or why he went on his trip and gave only sketchy details of one event. In his narrative, which had no distinguishable beginning, middle, or end, he referred to family members without letting the reader know who they were. Terry doesn't realize that when he writes a story, it is for someone to read and that he needs to fill in some gaps so that readers can understand and enjoy his story.

The majority of students with disabilities benefit from effective instruction that assists them in progressing as writers. For example, in three year-long case studies, Zaragoza and Vaughn (1992) followed the progress of gifted, low-achieving, and learning disabled students over the course of the academic year. All three of the students benefited from participating in the writing process and from teacher's scaffolding of instruction. One student with learning disabilities was very hesitant about writing. He asked for constant teacher assistance and would not write unless a teacher worked closely with him. He wrote slowly and neatly, even on first drafts. His first piece of writing was untitled and incomplete. He was insecure about working with other students and never volunteered to share his writing. His piece, titled "Disneyworld," demonstrated an understanding that you can write down what you really think. He included his own dog in a Disneyworld theme ("Goofy is a dog I like to play with but Goofy is not better than my dog."). The other students loved this story, and asked him to read it again and again. Subsequently, he frequently volunteered to share his writing with the class. He had a flair for good endings and became the class expert on developing endings. For example, in "The Spooky Halloween," he ended with "Halloween is nothing to play with." "Freddy Is in My Room" ended with "Give it up."

Other students, like third grader Maya Bradley, get so wrapped up in basic writing skills (e.g., spelling, grammar, handwriting) that they lose track of the purpose of writing. When asked about good writing, Maya defines it as "when I am neat and get the words spelled right." Teachers often spend more time teaching basic skills to students who struggle (Graham, Harris, Fink-Chorzempa, & MacArthur, 2003). However, all students need to be taught the purpose of writing as a way to communicate a message. As the Tech Tips suggests, technology can provide support for students in communicating their message.

Tech TIPS

WRITTEN EXPRESSION

Computer programs can help learners with written expression in many ways. The following software programs are
particularly useful in helping students to master the writing
process by giving them tools that help them compose with
confidence.

Write:Outloud by Don Johnston Incorporated
▶ **www.donjohnston.com/products/write_outloud/
index.html**
This program, for students in grades 3 through 12, is a
talking word processor that allows students to hear letters,
words, sentences, and paragraphs spoken as they type.
Other speech features include speaking any selected text
and changing voice and speed. Learners who can benefit
from hearing what they have typed should have access to a
talking word processor.

The Secret Writer's Society from SmartKids Software
▶ **www.smartkidssoftware.com/99v.htm**
This program is designed for students in grades 8 and up
has levels (missions) of teaching topics such as
capitalization, end punctuation, sentence writing, paragraph
writing, planning and ordering sentences, and revision and
editing. A final level guides the learner through the five-step
writing process.

Draft: Builder by Don Johnston Incorporated
▶ **www.donjohnston.com/products/draft_builder/**
This word processing and writing program, designed for
students in grades 3 though 8, helps students map and
organize their written products. It also helps them to edit
and revise their work.

Writing as a Student-Centered Process

The emphasis of a **student-centered model** of writing is on giving students ample opportunities to find personal meaning in what they write. Rather than being taught in isolation, as they are in more traditional models, skills are part of connected, meaningful experiences in communication. The work of Donald Graves (2003) has provided a major contribution to the understanding of writing as a student-centered activity. His observations of children as they write reveal that even young children go through an interactive **authoring process** of prewriting, composing (drafting), and postwriting (revising, editing, and publishing), providing educators with procedures for implementing this authoring process in the classroom and for helping students and teachers realize the importance of authorship and audience.

Charles Schwartz teaches eighth-grade language arts using a student-centered model. Charles integrates reading, writing, speaking, and listening activities in his language arts program. To document students' progress in writing, Charles uses writing samples, self- and peer evaluations, and teacher observation checklists. His classroom looks like a writers' workshop. Charles says that his role is to serve as a writing coach, providing not only encouragement but also direct skills instruction.

Although the student-centered model promotes creativity and student productivity, critics claim that teaching of skills is incidental, inconsistent, and not intensive enough for students who have problems learning to write. This chapter provides specific suggestions for making a student-centered model work for all students in your classroom by ensuring that the mechanics of writing are an essential feature of instruction.

Writing as a Socially Mediated Language-Learning Activity

To become more proficient writers, students must have social interactions with others to move forward (Vygotsky, 1978). Students who have experienced failure in learning to write may be reluctant to share their writing with teachers and peers because they are embarrassed about their lack of skill in writing mechanics. It is important, however, that students have the opportunity not only to share their writing but also to have that sharing focus on the intended meaning rather than on how many words are misspelled. It is also important for young writers to have time to talk with the teacher about composing strategies (Bereiter & Scardamalia, 1982; Mason & Graham, 2008). For students who are English language learners, interacting with teachers and peers during the process of writing builds language fluency (Peregoy & Boyle, 2005).

Strategies for Establishing an Environment That Promotes Writing

From what you have already read about current trends and effective writing instruction, you can imagine the importance of planning the environment in which writing is taught. Gina Terry, a general education teacher, and her teaching partner, Galia Pennecamp, a special education teacher, have created a classroom environment that encourages their fourth-grade students to write. Gina and Galia have learned that the classroom's physical and social environment both need to be considered when teachers establish a writing community.

Go to **http://www.read writethink.org/**, where you will find a wealth of resources for teaching writing.

Physical Environment

As they planned the physical arrangement of their classroom at the beginning of the year, Gina and Galia decided to create a writer's studio in their co-taught classroom. According to Graves (2003), the classroom setting should create a work atmosphere similar to that of a studio, which promotes independence and in which students can easily interact. Gina and Galia felt that structuring their classroom as a studio was especially important for students who had already experienced failure in writing. The message they wanted to convey from day one was "This is a place for writers, and all of us are writers. Enjoy!"

A publishing center is set up for making books. Writing materials and supplies are plentiful and readily available to students. At the beginning of the year, Gina and Galia explain guidelines for using materials in responsible ways. In addition to individual writing folders for ongoing writing projects, each student has an assessment portfolio that serves as a record of his or her progress in writing. Individual folders and portfolios are located in a permanent place in the classroom, ready for student or parent conferences. Gina and Galia wanted the room arranged so that students could work together or individually. They planned spaces for writing conferences of small groups of students, teacher and student, and student and student.

Gina and Galia also realized that many students with disabilities would benefit from having technology and tools readily available to facilitate their writing. For this reason, the following tools and technologies were available in their classroom:

- Computer
- Charts and markers
- Paper with raised lines, highlighted lines, etc.
- Adaptive grip for pencil or pen
- Word cards/word book/key words in a file
- Pocket dictionary
- Pocket thesaurus
- Electronic talking dictionary/thesaurus
- Voice recognition software
- Keyboard with easy access
- Adaptive devices for students with disabilities such as mouth stick/head pointer with alternate or standard keyboard
- Head mouse/head master with onscreen keyboard

Although not every classroom can be equipped with all of the tools that Gina and Galia were able to provide, there are still ways to establish an environment that is literature-rich and encourages writing.

Social Environment

Realizing that for students to write well, an environment of mutual trust and respect is essential, Gina and Galia posted the writing workshop's student guidelines (see Figure 13.4) in their classroom. The guidelines these teachers follow to establish a social environment for a productive writing community are presented in Tips for Teachers 13.4.

Tips for Teachers 13.4

ESTABLISHING A SOCIAL ENVIRONMENT FOR PRODUCTIVE WRITING

- *Have students write every day for at least 30 minutes.* Students need time to think, write, discuss, rewrite, confer, revise, talk, read, and write some more. Good writing takes time.

- *Encourage students to develop areas of expertise.* At first, students will write broadly about what they know. With encouragement, however, they can become class experts in a particular area, subject, or writing form. Take the time to help students discover their own writing "turf."

- *Model the writing process.* Write with students in the classroom. Using an overhead or easel, teachers may share how they compose.

- *Share writing.* Include in the writing time an opportunity for the whole class to meet to read their writing to others and to exchange comments and questions.

- *Read to the students.* Share and discuss books, poems, and other readings. Young authors can learn from the writing of others.

- *Expand the writing community outside the classroom.* Place books published by your students in the library so that other students can use them and so that students can share their writing with other classes. Encourage authors from other classrooms to visit and read their writing.

- *Develop students' capacity to evaluate their own work.* Students need to develop their own goals and document their progress toward them. By conferring with the teacher, they will learn methods for evaluating their own work.

- *Slow the pace.* Graves (1985) says, "Teachers need to slow down so kids can hurry up." When teachers ask questions, they need to be patient, giving students time to answer.

FIGURE 13.4

Writing Workshop

Writing Workshop

1. Write three first drafts.
2. Pick one draft to publish.
3. Self-edit your draft.
4. Have a friend edit your draft.
5. Take your draft to an adult to edit.
6. Publish your draft.
7. Read over your final copy and make corrections.
8. Give a friend your final copy to make corrections.
9. Give an adult your final copy to make corrections.
10. Put your final copy in a cover.
11. Share, help others, go back to step 1.

Our Rights

- ☺ We have the right to use the things in our classroom.
- ☺ We have the right to receive caring from our teachers.
- ☺ We have the right to be listened to by our teachers and friends.
- ☺ We have the right to call our families in cases of emergency.
- ☺ We have the right to be decision makers in our classroom.

Our Responsibilities

- ☺ We have the responsibility to encourage and be caring toward our friends and teachers.
- ☺ We have the responsibility to treat all things in our classroom carefully.
- ☺ We have the responsibility to participate in all activities and help our community to become strong and positive.
- ☺ We have the responsibility to help others to meet their responsibilities successfully.

Classroom Rules

- ☺ We try our best.
- ☺ We listen and look when others talk.
- ☺ We are kind and helpful to others.
- ☺ We help others remember the rules.

Rewards

- ☺ We feel proud.
- ☺ We have parties and free time.
- ☺ We call, tell, write our family.

Consequences

- ☹ We feel sad and disappointed.
- ☹ We lose parties and free time.
- ☹ We call, tell, write our family.

Source: Zaragoza, N. & Vaughn, S. (1995). *Writing workshop manual.* Unpublished manuscript.

Strategies for Conducting a Writing Workshop

If you were to visit Gina and Galia's classroom during their writing workshop, the first thing you would notice is the variety of activities. Some students would be working individually on a writing project; others would be working in small groups or pairs, generating ideas for a book or putting the final touches on a story. You would also observe that the teachers are busy. You might see Gina **conferencing** with a student. During conferencing Gina's goals are related to the individual student and would include asking the student to read part of his or her writing aloud, commenting on what particular aspects of the writing are successful, and asking questions that "teach" the student to revise and adjust for improved writing. These conferences typically end with joint decisions about what the student will do next to improve the writing.

In addition to conferencing, you might see Gina or Galia teaching a mini lesson on punctuation to a small group. You would discover that students often choose their own topics but also are expected to provide writing products that reflect a broad range of writing formats (e.g., letter to a pen pal, story biography, persuasive argument). Also, students often have two or three writing projects in progress at a time. Some students have even elected to co-author with a classmate. You would also note that amid all this activity, there is routine. Students seem to know exactly what to do and how to get help if they need it. See Activities for All Learners for writing activities that can include all learners.

Writing Activities for All Learners

① INTERVIEW A CLASSMATE

Objective: To give students practice in developing and using questions as a means for obtaining more information for the piece they are writing

Grades: Adapted for all levels

Materials: Writing materials and a writing topic, a list of possible questions, a tape recorder (optional)

Teaching Procedures: Using the format of a radio or television interview, demonstrate and role-play "mock" interviews with sports, movie, music, and political celebrities. Give the students opportunities to play both roles.

1. Discuss what types of questions allow the interviewee to give elaborate responses (e.g., open questions), and what types of questions do not allow the interviewee to give a very expanded answer (e.g., closed questions). Practice asking open questions.

2. Use a piece that you are writing as an example, and discuss whom you might interview to obtain more information. For example, "In writing a piece about what it might be like to go to the New York World's Fair in 1964, I might interview my grandfather, who was there, to obtain more information."

3. Ask the students to select an appropriate person to interview for their writing piece and to write possible questions. In pairs, the students refine their questions for the actual interview. The students then conduct the interviews and later discuss how information from the interview assisted them in writing their piece.

② FLASHWRITING

Objective: To improve writing fluency

Grades: Intermediate and above

Materials: Paper and pencil; timer

Teaching Procedures:

1. Give students 1 or 2 minutes to think of a topic.

2. Start the timer and give students 5 to 10 minutes to flashwrite about the topic.

3. The goal is to keep writing about the topic. If ideas don't come, just write, "I can't think of what to write," until an idea pops up.

4. At the end of the designated time, have pairs of students share their writing.

5. Have the pairs circle key ideas that might be worth developing during extended writing periods.

③ SENTENCE STRETCHING

Objective: To help students learn to elaborate simple sentences

Grades: Intermediate, middle school

Materials: Paper and pencil

Teaching Procedures:

1. On the board, write a simple sentence of two to four words—for example, "The king fell."

2. Have students expand the sentence by adding words and phrases.

3. If you choose, have students illustrate their expanded sentences and share with the class.

④ UP IN THE AIR FOR A TOPIC

Objective: To provide support to students with problems with topic selection

Grades: Primary and intermediate

Materials: Poster with suggestions for topic selection; paper and pencil

Teaching Procedures:

1. During writing workshop, discuss topic selection and ask students what they do when they are "stuck" for a topic.

2. Present the following suggestions on a poster:
   Check your folder and reread your idea list.
   Ask a friend to help you brainstorm ideas.
   Listen to others' ideas.
   Write about what you know: your experiences.
   Write a make-believe story.
   Write about a special interest or hobby.
   Write about how to do something.
   Think about how you got your last idea.

3. Model or solicit examples for each suggestion, add students' other suggestions, and post the chart in the room for students to consult whenever they are "stuck" for a topic.

What is involved in the writing process?

- In **prewriting**, a writer collects information about a topic by observing, remembering, interviewing, and reading.
- In **composing** (or **drafting**), the author attempts to get ideas on paper in the form of a draft. The drafting process tells the author what he or she knows or does not know.
- In **postwriting**, the author revises, edits, and publishes the work.
  - During **revising**, the focus is on meaning; points are explored further, ideas are elaborated, and further connections are made.
  - When the author is satisfied with the content, **editing** takes place as the author reviews the piece line by line to determine whether each word is necessary. Punctuation, spelling, and other mechanical processes are checked.
  - The final element is **publishing.** If the author considers the piece a good one, it is published.

FINDING THE TOPIC BY USING THE GOLDILOCKS RULE ⑤

Objective: To help students brainstorm for expository writing topics

Grades: Intermediate and above

Materials: Timer, paper, and pencil

Teaching Procedures:

1. Describe the "Goldilocks procedure."
   Brainstorm as many ideas as possible in 5 minutes.
   Write down all ideas. Don't stop to read or judge them.
   Stop when timer goes off.
   Organize ideas into categories with the Goldilocks Rule:
   Too broad
   Too narrow
   Just right
   Choose a topic from the Just Right category.

2. Model the use of the Goldilocks procedure.

3. Try out the procedure as a whole-class activity.

4. Have students try out the procedure independently and then share their topics in small groups.

Source: Schumm, J. S., & Radencich, M. (1992). School power. Minneapolis: Free Spirit Publishing.

TELL IT AGAIN ⑥

Objective: To help students learn story elements

Grades: Primary, intermediate

Materials: Paper, pencil, crayons, markers

Teaching Procedures: Story retellings are a good way to determine which elements of a story are familiar (and unfamiliar) to your students. To help students "Tell It Again," follow these steps:

1. Provide a story for your students. It might be a story you read, a story they read independently or with a partner, or a story they hear on TV or on a video.

2. Decide on a retelling format. Students can retell the story by drawing pictures of major events (making a wordless picture book), rewriting and illustrating the story, dramatizing the story, or orally retelling the story to you or to a friend.

3. Keep tabs on the story elements your students include in their retellings. If a story element (such as setting, character or plot) is missing, provide instruction (either individually, in small groups, or with the class as a whole) about one element at a time. Monitor that element in subsequent retelling assignments.

THE RAFT TECHNIQUE ⑦

Objective: To help students learn to vary their writing with respect to writer's role, audience, format, and topic

Grades: Intermediate and above

Materials: Paper and pencil

Teaching Procedures: The RAFT technique was developed by Santa (1988) to help secondary students write in the content areas. RAFT provides a framework for thinking about how to write for different purposes by varying the writer's role, audience, format, and topic. Here's how to teach it:

1. Explain the components of RAFT:
   Role of the writer. Who are you? A professor? A volcano? An ancient Egyptian?
   Audience. Who will be your reader? A friend? A famous athlete? A lawyer?
   Format. What form will your writing take? A brochure? A letter? A newspaper article?
   Topic. What topic have you chosen? Hazards of smoking? Need for gun control? How cheese is made?

2. Write R–A–F–T on the board or on a transparency. Brainstorm with students about possible roles, audiences, formats, and topics. Following is an example:
   R—Role = a liver
   A—Audience = alcoholic
   F—Format = script for TV commercial
   T—Topic = the ill effects of drinking

3. Have students work in cooperative groups to generate other RAFT ideas.

4. Have students work independently to complete a RAFT assignment.

Making Adaptations for Struggling Writers: Teachers' Practices

How do teachers adapt writing instruction for struggling writers? Graham, Harris, Fink-Chorzempa, and MacArthur (2003) surveyed 153 primary-grade teachers to learn more about the adaptations they make. Twenty percent of the teachers reported that they made no adaptations at all; 24% made only one or two adaptations. The majority of adaptations involved additional instruction in basic writing skills. With respect to the writing process, additional instruction in the planning and revising stages was most common. In general, teachers reported that they spent more time reteaching, conferencing, and encouraging struggling writers. Graham and colleagues emphasized the importance of getting young writers off to a good start and the complexities they face in achieving a command of writing.

Students with writing problems differ in the degree to which components of the writing process are difficult for them (Scott & Vitale, 2003). Many students with writing problems experience significant difficulty in editing and writing final copy because they have difficulty with mechanics. These students often produce well-developed stories that are hard to read because of the mechanical errors. Other students with writing problems have difficulty organizing during the composing stage and need to rethink the sequencing during revision. There is considerable agreement that students use the writing process best when they are taught explicitly how to use each of the elements (e.g., prewriting, revising, conferencing) (Baker, Gersten, & Graham, 2003; Thompkins, 2008).

Prewriting: Getting Started

"What should I write about?" As a teacher, it's easy to say, "Write about what you did during your summer vacation," but the key to engaging students as writers is to have them select topics. Saying to students "Just write about anything" isn't enough. The following section shows how to help students approach topic selection.

Selecting Topics.   Deciding what you say to students to help them generate a list of topics they either know about or want to learn about varies somewhat by grade level. It is critical to each grade level that teachers provide students with some time to generate their own topics of interest in addition to writing about topics generated by the teacher.

For example, with elementary students, you might say, "You know lots of things about yourself, about your family, and about your friends. You have hobbies and activities that you like to do. You have stories about things that have happened to you and to people you know. You have lots of things to share with others. I want you to make a list of things you would like to share with others through writing. Do not put them in any specific order—just write them down as you think of them. You will not have to write on all of these topics. The purpose of this exercise is to think of as many topics as you can. I will give you about 10 minutes. Begin."

For older students, teachers might want to talk about the different genres of writing, including personal biography, persuasion, sarcasm, humor, narrative story, and reporting, as a means to facilitate topic generation. You might say, "Identify two to four of the genres you might like to use for your writing. Then under each genre, identify two to four topics you would like to write about."

One way to model brainstorming for a topic is to use an LCD or overhead projector. Write a list of things you do very well—in which you're an expert. Then select one item from the list to write about. Have your students develop their own "expert list" and add it to their writing folder (Thompkins, 2008). Model the process by writing as many topics as you can think of during the assigned time. When time is up, tell the students to pick a partner and share their topics. They may add any new topics they think of at this time. Then share your list with the entire group and comment on topics you are looking forward to writing about. Ask for volunteers to read their topic lists to the entire group. Have students select the three topics they are most interested in writing about and place their topic lists in their writing folders as a resource for future writing. Finally, ask students to select one of their top three topics and begin writing.

Teachers may want to hold students accountable for writing in multiple genres. For example, you might say, "During this 6-week period, I need you to submit a completed composition in each of the following areas: story, opinion, and expository factual report on a topic of interest."

Problems in Topic Selection.   Maintaining a supply of writing topics is difficult for some students. When students tell you stories, ask them whether the story generates a topic they might want to write about. When students read or you read to them, ask whether the reading has given them ideas for their own writing. If they were going to write the end of the story, how would they do it? If they were going to continue this story, what would happen? If they were going to add characters to the story, what types of characters would they add? Would they change the setting?

Some students want to repeat the same topic or theme, especially students with writing problems, who may find security in such repetition. Before suggesting that students change topics, check whether their stories are changing in other ways (through development of vocabulary, concept, story, or character). Students may be learning a great deal about writing, even though the topic is the same.

Planning. Prewriting entails developing a plan for writing. Planning for writing includes the following three steps:

1. *Identify the intended audience.* To make a writing project meaningful, the writer must identify the audience. Who will be the reader? The audience might be family, friends, business people, politicians, teachers, potential employers—or oneself.
2. *State a purpose for writing.* The purpose for writing may be to inform, entertain, or persuade. An example of a purpose statement might be: "I am writing this story about my imaginary pet shark, Gums, to entertain my friends."
3. *Decide on a format.* Before writing begins, it's good to have a general idea of how the piece will be structured. Although the structure may change during drafting and revision, writers should have an initial road map at the prewriting stage.

Some students are limited in text-organization skills because they have difficulty categorizing ideas related to a specific topic, providing advance organizers for the topic, and relating and extending ideas about the topic (Mason & Graham, 2008; Tomlinson, 2008). As you teach the thinking process that goes into a piece of writing, you can model your own thinking as you move from topic selection to planning for audience, purpose, and format to drafting. During whole-class sharing time, you can also encourage students to describe how they generated topics and planned for their own writing.

What are the stages of the writing process? What are some effective strategies for teaching each stage to students?

Composing

The purpose of the composing stage is to develop an initial draft that will be refined later. Some teachers call this a *sloppy copy.* Many students with learning and behavior problems think of a topic and, without much planning, begin writing. Composing is also difficult for students who lack fluency in the mechanics of writing or in the physical act of writing (Scott & Vitale, 2003). During composing, you should assume the role of coach and encourage students to concentrate on getting their ideas on paper.

Revising and Editing

The purpose of revision is to make certain that the meaning is clear and that the message can be understood by others. *Editing* focuses mainly on mechanics, such as proofreading. After the students and teacher are happy with the content, it is time to finalize the correction of spelling, capitalization, punctuation, and language.

During editing, students circle words whose spelling they are not sure of, put boxes where they are unsure of punctuation, and underline sentences in which they feel the language may not be correct. Students are not expected to correct all errors, but are expected to correct known errors. Revising and editing are difficult tasks for all writers, especially beginning writers and students for whom writing is difficult. Getting the entire message down on paper the first time is difficult enough; making changes so that the piece is at its best and can be understood by others is a most formidable task.

Revising, which means attending to meaning and making adjustments to a written document, is an ongoing process. Through modeling and feedback, students will learn that they may need to revise once, twice, or more until their intended meaning is expressed clearly and completely. Most students with learning and behavior problems have difficulty revising their work (Scott & Vitale, 2003). Teachers often find it best initially to let students move to publication without much revision and then gradually show them the benefits of revision and editing. Explicit teaching of the differences between revising and editing and structured formats for this aspect of composition is necessary (Bradley, 2001; Saddler, 2004).

Adolescents with disabilities can learn procedures such as *compare, diagnose,* and *operate* to assist them during the revision process (De La Paz, Swanson, & Graham, 1998; Wong, Butler,

Tips for Teachers 13.5

TEACHING STUDENTS TO COMPARE, DIAGNOSE, AND OPERATE

1. Compare and diagnose. Read your writing and consider the following:

   - Does it ignore the obvious point against my idea?
   - Does it have too few ideas?
   - Part of the essay doesn't belong with the rest.
   - Part of the essay is not in the right order.

2. Tactic operations.

   - Rewrite.
   - Delete.
   - Add.
   - Move.

3. Compare. Reread the paper and highlight problems.

4. Diagnose and operate.

   - This doesn't sound right.
   - This isn't what I intended to say.
   - This is an incomplete idea.
   - This part is not clear_____.
   - The problem is.

   The following suggestions to help students remove the mechanical barriers from their writing:

   - Have students dictate their story to improve the flow of their writing.
   - Provide students with a list of key words and difficult-to-spell words to assist with writing and editing.
   - Promote peer collaboration in editing.

Source: Information from Isaacson, S. & Gleason, M. M. (1997). Mechanical obstacles to writing: What can teachers do to help students with learning problems? *Learning Disabilities Research and Practice, 12*(3), 188–194.

Ficzere, & Kuperis, 1997). When teachers model, demonstrate, and provide feedback using the procedure described in Tips for Teachers 13.5, students' revisions and writing improve.

In addition to revising and editing their own work, students can serve as editors for the work of their peers. **Peer editing** can work several ways. One way is to have students edit their own work first and then ask a friend to edit it. Another way is to establish a class editor who is responsible for reading the material and finding mechanical errors. The role of class editor can rotate so that every student has an opportunity to serve in that capacity.

It is important that students not be too critical while revising and editing one another's work. You can communicate that the purpose of revising and editing is to support the author in developing a finished piece. You can also model acceptable ways to give feedback.

Publishing

Not all student writing is published; often only one in five or six pieces is published. **Publishing** means preparing a piece so that others can read it. Publication is often in the form of books with cardboard bindings decorated with contact paper or scraps of wallpaper. Books can include a picture of the author, a description of the author, and a list of books published by the author. Young children writing short pieces may publish every 2 weeks; older students who spend more time composing and revising publish less frequently.

Publishing is a way to confirm a student's hard work and share the piece with others. Publishing is also a way to involve others in school and at home with the students' writing. It is important for all students to publish, not just the best authors.

Sharing

Sharing work with others is important during all stages of the writing process. The author's chair (Graves & Hansen, 1983) is a formal opportunity to share writing. When Romain, a student who recently moved from Haiti to the United States, signed up for author's chair early in the school year, Galia and Gina were surprised. Romain, the most reluctant writer in their class, was also extremely self-conscious about not being able to spell. During author's chair, Romain sat on a special stool in a circle of peers and read his letter to an imaginary pen pal in Haiti. He described life in Miami and ended with a wish: "I hope that you are happy and have enough food to eat." It turned out that most of Romain's story wasn't written at all—he held a paper in front of him and made up the letter as he spoke. But because Romain got a positive response from his audience about how well he communicated his ideas, he was encouraged to become a writer. The author's chair experience was his launching point. Using author's chair can be facilitated by having the student present the writing on a computer and then projecting it on an LCD so that all of the students can view the work at the same time (Labbo, 2004).

Teachers often need to set rules for students' behavior when a classmate is sharing work in the author's chair. Such rules might include raising one's hand, asking a question, making a positive comment, and giving feedback when asked. A simple but powerful framework within which students can give one another feedback about their writing is called **TAG** (Zaragoza, 1987):

Tell what you like.
Ask questions.
Give suggestions.

After an author has read his or her writing, the author leads the class in a TAG session, asking class members the three questions "What did you like?," "Do you have any questions?," and "Do you have any suggestions?" Three or four responses are usually allowed for each question. TAG sessions give authors valuable feedback about their writing as well as a chance to lead a class discussion.

Conferencing.   The heart of the writing workshop—the student–teacher writing conference—is ongoing. The student comes to the writing conference prepared to read his or her piece, to describe problem areas, and to respond to questions. Students know that the teacher will listen and respond and that they will be asked challenging questions about their work. Questions should be carefully selected, with enough time allotted for the student to respond. Even though you may see many problems with the piece of writing, try to focus on only one or two specific areas. Some key points about conferencing with students are presented in Tips for Teachers 13.6.

Tips for Teachers 13.6

GUIDELINES FOR CONDUCTING A WRITING CONFERENCE

Big Principles of a Writing Conference

- *Follow the student's lead during the conference.* Avoid imposing your ideas about the topic or the way you would write the story.

- *Listen to and accept what the student says.* When you talk more than the writer does during conferences, you are being too directive.

- *Ask questions that teach.* Ask students questions that help them understand what needs to be revised and what steps to take next with their writing.

- *Make conferences frequent and brief.* Although conferences can range from 30 seconds to 10 minutes, most last 2 to 3 minutes.

- *Listen to what students have written and tell them what you hear.* Learning to listen to what they are communicating from the perspective of a reader is essential for students to learn to make effective revisions.

Suggestions to Compliment Writing

- I like the way your paper began in this way . . .

- I like the part where . . .

- I like the way you explained . . .

- I like the order you used in your paper because . . .

- I like the details you used to describe . . .

- I like the way you used dialogue to make your story sound real. In particular, this section . . .

- I like the action and the descriptive words you used in your writing, such as . . .

- I like the facts you used, such as . . .

- I like the way the paper ended because . . .

- I like the mood of your writing because it made me feel . . .

Questions and Suggestions to Improve Writing

- I got confused in the part about . . .

- Could you add an example to the _____ part about . . .

- Could you add more to this part because . . .

- Do you think your order would make more sense if you . . .

- Do you think you could leave this part out because . . .

- Could you use a different word for _____ because . . .

- Is this _____ paragraph on one topic?

- Could you write a beginning sentence to "grab" your readers?

- What happens in the end?

- Can you think of another word for "said"?

Teaching Writing Skills.   A frequently asked question is, "When do I teach skills?" This question is especially important for teachers whose students have poor writing skills to begin with. Prolific writing without help from a teacher will not lead to improvement (Graham & Perin, 2007).

Skills lessons can be taught to the class as a whole and then in small groups composed of students who need additional knowledge and practice with a specified skill. Skills lessons, or mini lessons, should be brief (15–20 minutes), and the topics for these lessons should be based on the students' needs. Ideas for topics can come from your observations of student writing, requests for help, and data from writing conferences.

After teaching a skill and providing ample opportunities to practice it, help students to generalize and apply the skill in their daily writing. As Graham (1992) recommended for students with writing problems, skills are best taught in the context of "real" writing and have the most impact when they bring the greatest rewards in writing improvement.

Strategies for Teaching Narrative Writing

In the elementary grades and in middle school, students typically practice **narrative writing** (writing stories). For many students, story writing is not a problem. Through hearing and reading stories, they have learned the basic elements of a story and can incorporate them into their own storytelling and writing. Students with writing problems may be aware of story elements but may not incorporate them into their writing in a systematic way unless they are provided instructional support (Graham & Harris, 2006; Montague & Graves, 1993). Students with writing problems may also exhibit the following problems when they compose stories:

- Lack of organization
- Lack of unity and coherence
- Lack of character development
- Incomplete use of story elements

Story webbing and direct instruction on the development of story elements are effective ways to address these difficulties.

Using Story Webs to Plan

Story webs, or *maps,* were originally developed as visual displays to help students understand the structure of the stories they read. Stories are composed of predictable elements and have a characteristic narrative structure or story grammar. Elements of stories include the setting, characters, a problem statement, the goal, the event sequence or episodes, and the resolution or ending. Using story webs such as the one shown in Figure 13.5, students can trace these elements when they read, plan, or write a story.

You can conduct mini lessons on webbing with your whole class or just with students who need help with story planning. To introduce the story web, first talk about its components and model its use in planning a story. You might want to have students work together in small, mixed-ability groups to plan a group story.

Instruction in Story Development

As previously stated, some students might include a story element, such as a main character, in their stories but fail to develop the element fully. Graves and Hauge (1993) developed the cue sheet shown in Figure 13.6 to help students improve their story writing.

Strategies for Teaching Expository Writing

Expository writing, or informational writing, once reserved for middle and upper grades, is now being included in the curriculum for even very young students. Expository writing poses particular problems for students with writing problems who may be unaware of the purpose of informational writing (Englert et al., 1988; Mason & Graham, 2008). Graham and Harris (1989b) reported that the informational writing of students with learning disabilities often contains irrelevant information and inappropriate conclusions.

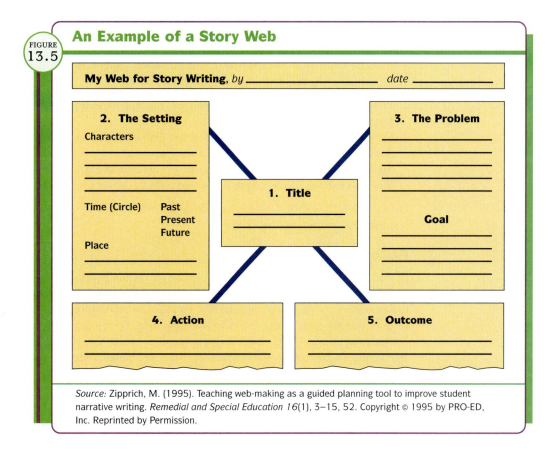

FIGURE 13.5

An Example of a Story Web

My Web for Story Writing, *by* _____ *date* _____

2. The Setting

Characters

_____
_____
_____

Time (Circle)   Past
                Present
                Future

Place

_____

1. Title

_____

3. The Problem

_____
_____
_____

Goal

_____
_____

4. Action

_____
_____

5. Outcome

_____
_____

Source: Zipprich, M. (1995). Teaching web-making as a guided planning tool to improve student narrative writing. *Remedial and Special Education 16*(1), 3–15, 52. Copyright © 1995 by PRO-ED, Inc. Reprinted by Permission.

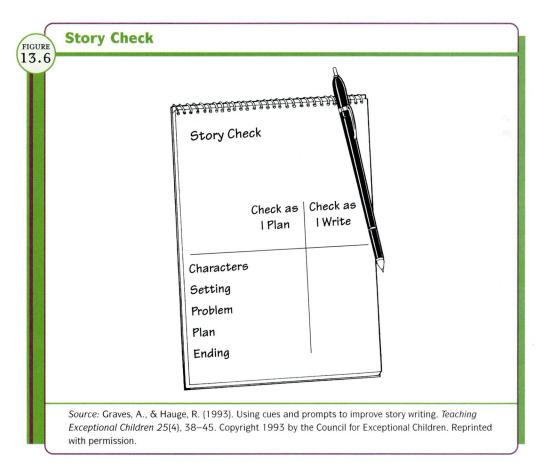

FIGURE 13.6

Story Check

Story Check

	Check as I Plan	Check as I Write
Characters		
Setting		
Problem		
Plan		
Ending		

Source: Graves, A., & Hauge, R. (1993). Using cues and prompts to improve story writing. *Teaching Exceptional Children 25*(4), 38–45. Copyright 1993 by the Council for Exceptional Children. Reprinted with permission.

Paragraph Writing

Students with writing problems often have difficulty developing coherent, logical paragraphs. The **PLEASE strategy** (Welch, 1992; Welch & Link, 1989) was developed to provide students with a step-by-step procedure for paragraph writing:

Pick the topic, audience, and paragraph type (cause/effect, compare/contrast, etc.).
List information about the topic.
Evaluate whether the list is complete and also determine how to order items in the list.
Activate your writing by starting with a topic sentence.
Supply supporting or detail sentences, using items from the list.
End with a strong concluding sentence, and evaluate the paragraph by revising and editing.

Developing coherent paragraphs is a challenge for many students. Consequently, this strategy is an effective tool to use with all writers.

Essay Writing

As students mature and move through the grades, they must progress from writing paragraphs to writing well-developed essays. Some parents and educators resist what is referred to as "formulaic writing" or the five-paragraph essay. Formulas for developing a five-paragraph essay are variations on the same theme. For example, bing, bang, bongo: paragraph 1—list bing, bang, bongo; paragraph 2—write about bing; paragraph 3—write about bang; paragraph 4—write about bongo; paragraph 5—summarize bing, bang, and bongo. Despite resistance, many teachers find such formulas helpful in preparing students for standardized writing tests, particularly for students who need scaffolding and structure.

Graham and Harris (1989a, 1989b) developed a three-step strategy for helping students learn to write essays:

1. Think about the audience and purpose for writing the essay.
2. Plan the essay, using the **TREE method**:
   - Write a **T**opic sentence.
   - Think of **R**easons to support the topic sentence.
   - **E**xamine your reasons.
   - Think of an **E**nding or conclusion.
3. Write the essay.

Standardized writing tests frequently require students to write an essay to a **prompt**. A writing prompt includes a situation and directions for writing. An example from the Florida Department of Education (2005) follows:

Situation: Everyone has jobs or chores.
Directions: Before you begin writing, think about why you do one of your jobs or chores. Now explain why you do one of your jobs or chores.

Student writing products are often graded using a holistic scoring rubric that evaluates the essay based on focus, organization, conventions (e.g., spelling, punctuation), understanding of topic, and support for ideas presented.

Research Paper Writing

As students progress through the grade levels, summarizing information in the form of a research paper is a common assignment. Korinek and Bulls (1996) offer a strategy to help students get organized for what can be a cumbersome task—not just for students with disabilities, but for any student with organizational problems or who has difficulty with long-range, multiphase assignments. The mnemonic tool, referred to as **SCORE A** (the goal for a grade) is used to identify the steps:

Select a topic.
Create categories.
Obtain reference tools.
Read and take notes.
Evenly organize the information using note cards.
Apply writing process steps (i.e., prewriting, drafting, etc.).

Once students are able to master this process, they are more likely to succeed in producing a well-thought-out paper. This success will then contribute to future successes.

Strategies for Teaching Persuasive Writing

Many state assessments include persuasive writing components. Writing persuasive essays can be incorporated into content areas such as science and social studies. **Persuasive writing** is a format in which the writer provides evidence in order to convince or persuade the reader of his or her position or opinion. Writing persuasive essays involves planning and critical thinking. Whereas most students have difficulty with persuasive writing, many students with LD have even more problems (De La Paz, 2001). To help all students compose well-developed and supported persuasive pieces, De La Paz and Graham (1997) developed and researched the **STOP and DARE strategy**. Here are the steps:

1. *Suspend judgment.* First, ask students to suspend their own judgment about the topic, keep an open mind, and write a list of pros and cons about the topic.
2. *Take a side.* Next, ask students to decide which side they believe in and can build the best argument.
3. *Organize ideas.* Tell students to reflect on their pro/con sheet and identify the strongest points they can make to support their point of view. Have students identify points from the opposite side that they want to refute.
4. *Plan more as you write.* As students refine and reorganize their essays, ask them to keep the components of DARE in mind (see the STOP and DARE cue card in Figure 13.7).

PEARSON
myeducationlab

Go to the Assignments and Activities section of Topic 10: Content Area Teaching in the Building Teaching Skills and Dispositions for your course and complete the activity entitled *Scaffolding Writing.*

FIGURE 13.7

STOP and DARE Cue Cards

Step 1

> **S**uspend judgment
> Did I list ideas for both sides? If not, do this now.

> **S**uspend judgment
> Can I think of anything else?
> Try to write more.

> **S**uspend judgment
> Another point I haven't considered is . . .
> Think of possible arguments.

Step 2

> **T**ake a side
> Place a "+" at the top of one box to show the side you will take in your essay.

Step 3

> **O**rganize ideas
> Put a star next to ideas you want to use.
> Choose at least _____ ideas to use.

> **O**rganize ideas
> Did I star ideas on both sides?
> Choose at least _____ arguments that you can dispute.

> **O**rganize ideas
> Number your ideas in the order you will use.

Step 4

> **P**lan more as you write
> Remember to use all four essay parts:
> **D**evelop your topic sentence.
> **A**dd supporting ideas.
> **R**eject possible arguments.
> **E**nd with a conclusion.

Source: Information from De La Paz, S. (2001). STOP and DARE: A persuasive writing strategy, *Intervention in school and clinic, 36.* 237. Copyright 2001 by PRO-ED, Inc.

For additional strategies that will help students understand and practice persuasive writing, find examples of persuasive writing for them to consider. There are examples all around in our everyday lives, including advertisements, commercials, letters to the editor, campaign speeches, and movie or book reviews (Medina, 2006).

Strategies for Helping All Students Acquire Spelling Skills

Even in the age of computers with spell-check programs, learning how to spell is important. If a writer is bogged down with the spelling of even commonly used words, progress in writing is stymied. Many students with reading and other disabilities are poor spellers. Spelling, like reading, involves phonological awareness (see Figure 13.8).

Spelling instruction is important for all students, but the students in your class are likely to differ in terms of their stages of development, the types of errors they make, and what they need to learn in spelling to become more fluent writers. What instructional methods can you use to teach all your students to spell?

PEARSON
myeducationlab

Go to the Assignments and Activities section of Topic 10: Content Area Teaching in the MyEducationLab for your course and complete the activity entitled *Direct Instruction: Spelling Lessons.*

Traditional Spelling Instruction

Mary Jacobs uses a traditional spelling instruction model in her third-grade class. All students in the class have the same third-grade spelling book. Each lesson in the speller focuses on a particular pattern (e.g., long vowels, short vowels, vowel plus *r*, prefixes). On Monday, Mary gives a spelling pretest on the 15 new words, and for homework students write (five times) each word they missed. On Tuesday and Wednesday nights, students are assigned exercises in the spelling book. On Thursday night, they write one sentence for each word on the list.

FIGURE 13.8

Characteristics of Learners in Five Stages of Development

Stage 1: Precommunicative Spelling

- Uses scribbles, letter-like forms, letters, and sometimes numbers to represent a message.

- May write from left to right, right to left, top to bottom, or randomly on the page.

- Shows no understanding of phoneme–grapheme correspondences.

- May repeat a few letters again and again or use most of the letters of the alphabet.

- Frequently mixes upper- and lowercase letters but shows a preference for uppercase letters.

Stage 2: Semiphonetic Spelling

- Becomes aware of the alphabetic principle that letters are used to represent sounds.

- Uses abbreviated one-, two-, or three-letter spelling to represent an entire word.

- Uses letter–name strategy to spell words (e.g., U for you).

Stage 3: Phonetic Spelling

- Represents all essential sound features of a word in spelling.

- Develops particular spellings for long and short vowels, plural and past tense markers, and other aspects of spelling.

- Chooses letters on the basis of sound, without regard for English letter sequences or other conventions.

Stage 4: Transitional Spelling

- Adheres to basic conventions of English orthography.

- Begins to use morphological and visual information in addition to phonetic information.

- May include all appropriate letters in a word but reverse some of them.

- Uses alternate spellings for the same sound in different words, but only partially understands the conditions governing their use.

- Uses a high percentage of correctly spelled words.

Stage 5: Correct Spelling

- Applies the basic rules of the English orthographic system.

- Extends knowledge of word structure, including the spelling of affixes, contractions, compound words, and homonyms.

- Demonstrates growing accuracy in using silent consonants and doubling consonants before adding suffixes.

- Recognizes when a word doesn't "look right" and can consider alternate spellings for the same sound.

- Learns irregular spelling patterns.

- Learns consonant and vowel alternations, and other morphological structures.

- Knows how to spell a large number of words.

Source: Gentry, J. R. (1982). An analysis for developmental spelling in GYNS at WRK. *The Reading Teacher, 36,* 192–200. Copyright by the International Reading Association.

On Friday during class, Mary gives students a spelling test on the 15 words. Some teachers vary this traditional pattern by selecting words from the basal reader or from the current science or social studies unit.

Spelling Instruction for Students with Learning Difficulties and Disabilities

How appropriate is the traditional approach for classrooms that include students of different academic levels? Many students who are good spellers know all the words at the beginning of the week and so have no real challenge. For students with learning difficulties, 15 words may be too many to learn, feedback about their errors may be ineffective, and the amount of practice may be insufficient. In addition, traditional spelling instruction does not teach for transfer to new situations. Students often learn words from their spelling list and get 100% on the test, but misspell those same words in their compositions.

Go to **www.edbydesign.com**, then under the section on Learning Resource, you will find practical resources for spelling and writing.

A review of spelling interventions (Gordon, Vaughn, & Schumm, 1993; Wanzek, Vaughn, Wexler, Swanson, Edmonds & Kim 2006) indicated that spelling practices that provide students with spelling strategies or systematic study and word practice methods yield the highest rates of spelling improvement. Findings from the studies can be grouped into seven areas of instructional practice:

1. *A weekly list of words.* Students perform better in spelling when they have a list of words each week that are related (e.g., same spelling patterns or thematically related), when they are required to demonstrate proficiency, and when they realize that spelling these words correctly in their writing is expected.
2. *Error imitation and modeling.* Students with learning disabilities need to compare each incorrectly spelled word with the correct spelling. The teacher copies the incorrect spelling and then writes the word correctly, calling attention to features in the word that will help students remember the correct spelling.
3. *Unit size.* Students with learning disabilities tend to become overloaded and have difficulty when they have to study several words at once. These students can learn to spell if the unit size of their assigned list is reduced to three words a day and if effective instruction is offered for those three words.
4. *Modality.* When studying words, students with learning disabilities learned equally by (a) writing the words, (b) arranging and tracing letter shapes or tiles, and (c) typing the words at a computer. Most students preferred to practice their spelling words at a computer.
5. *Computer-assisted instruction.* Computer-assisted instruction (CAI) has been shown to be effective in improving the spelling skills of students with learning disabilities. CAI software programs for spelling improvement often emphasize awareness of word structure and spelling strategies and make use of time delay, voice simulation, and sound effects.
6. *Peer tutoring.* A teacher's individual help is preferable, but structured peer tutoring can be a viable alternative. Burks (2004) and Keller (2002) have adapted classwide peer tutoring to structure peer support for learning to spell.
7. *Study techniques.* Study techniques provide a format and a standard procedure that help students with learning disabilities organize their study of spelling. Wheatley (2005) advocates strategic spelling rather than rote memorization of words. Figure 13.9 is a flow chart that can be used with intermediate grade and secondary students to help them become more strategic spellers.

Meredith Millan is a third-grade teacher whose three students with learning disabilities require that they receive specialized instruction. Meredith and the special education teacher have agreed that Meredith will assign students their weekly spelling words. Meredith has worked hard to integrate spelling instruction into her ongoing writing program. She likes the idea of having weekly spelling tests but knows that the range of student spelling levels in her class is too broad for all students to benefit from having the same words and the same number of words to learn. The following sections describe the way Meredith has structured her spelling program.

Selecting Words.   Meredith teaches spelling words that correspond with the phonics rules she is teaching in reading. For example, if she is teaching students the **VCe rule** (vowel, consonant, long e as in "time") by which the first vowel says its name, as part of word study she

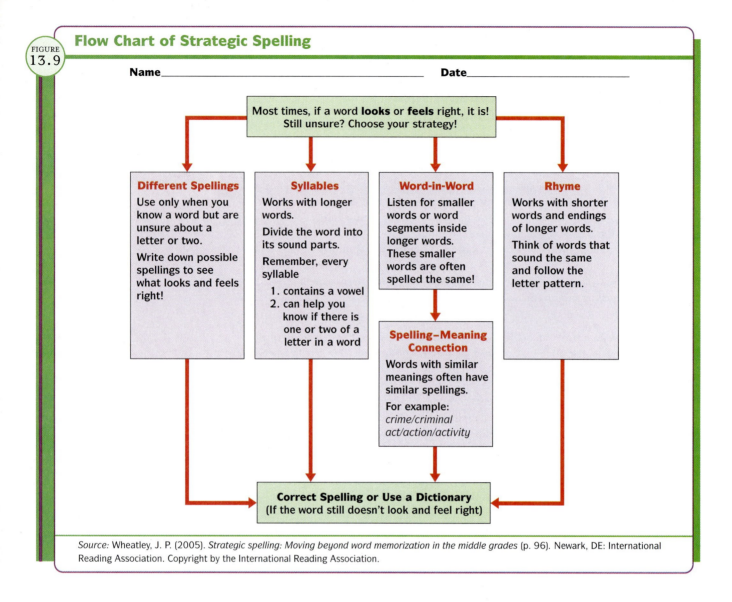

Flow Chart of Strategic Spelling

FIGURE 13.9

Name_____ Date_____

Most times, if a word **looks** or **feels** right, it is!
Still unsure? Choose your strategy!

Different Spellings

Use only when you know a word but are unsure about a letter or two.

Write down possible spellings to see what looks and feels right!

Syllables

Works with longer words.

Divide the word into its sound parts.

Remember, every syllable

1. contains a vowel
2. can help you know if there is one or two of a letter in a word

Word-in-Word

Listen for smaller words or word segments inside longer words. These smaller words are often spelled the same!

Spelling–Meaning Connection

Words with similar meanings often have similar spellings.

For example:
crime/criminal
act/action/activity

Rhyme

Works with shorter words and endings of longer words.

Think of words that sound the same and follow the letter pattern.

Correct Spelling or Use a Dictionary
(If the word still doesn't look and feel right)

Source: Wheatley, J. P. (2005). *Strategic spelling: Moving beyond word memorization in the middle grades* (p. 96). Newark, DE: International Reading Association. Copyright by the International Reading Association.

also uses VCe word types for her spelling list. This allows her to connect reading and spelling rules and capitalize on the patterns of language (Carreker, 1999; Moats, 2000). This procedure can be used for older students as well. If students are progressing beyond rule-based instruction in reading, then spelling words can be selected from their writing errors or from key words needed in their social studies and science instruction.

Each student in Meredith's class keeps a spelling log, which is a running list of words. At the beginning of the week, students select words from the log for the Friday spelling test and write the words on their homework sheet. Meredith and each student agree in advance on the number of words. Some students have 5 or 6 words, others as many as 20. Meredith also assigns all students 2 to 3 words from the thematic unit they are studying at the time. Words that students misspell are taken from the edited drafts of their compositions. During a writing conference, Meredith not only discusses the words a student should add to his or her spelling log, but also asks, "Are there other words you really would like to learn to spell?" and adds them to the log.

Providing Instruction and Practice. Meredith provides spelling instruction and practice in four ways: through mini lessons, student pairs, parental involvement, and collaboration with the special education teacher. Each week Meredith provides mini lessons on spelling patterns. For example, she noticed that about 20 students were using *-ing* words in their writing and spelling them incorrectly. Meredith met with this group for 2 weeks, gave them mini lessons on adding *-ing,* and included *-ing* words on their spelling tests.

Early in the school year, Meredith figured out that 10 of her students needed more practice preparing for spelling tests. She decided to have these students work in pairs. The pairs meet for 15 minutes three times a week, usually while other students are composing during writing workshop. Meredith involves parents in the spelling program in two ways. First, at the beginning of the year, she writes parents a letter about the spelling program and ways in which parents can help their child study for spelling tests. Second, she invites parents to add one or two words to the spelling list each week. Parents observe their children's writing at home and can pick up on important misspellings.

Two of the students with learning disabilities, Kara and Mitchell, need additional help learning their words. In collaboration with Meredith, the special education teacher helps Kara and Mitchell learn and maintain new words by using individualized approaches to word study including ensuring that students know the phonics patterns in the words and use practices for writing, checking, correcting, and rewriting spelling words until they are written correctly and automatically.

Monitoring Student Progress. There are basically three ways to assess student spelling: dictation, error detection or proofreading tasks, and examination of student spelling in their composition products (Hallahan, Lloyd, Kauffman, Weiss, & Martinez, 2005). Meredith includes a spelling rubric she uses in writing workshop (see Figure 13.10). She includes both dictation and error detection formats as part of her weekly spelling tests.

All students take their Friday spelling test during the same class period. Because it is not possible to give 36 students individual spelling dictation tests based on the words in their spelling logs, Meredith pairs the students so they can test each other. Students follow these strict guidelines during the test period:

- You can talk only to your partner and only about the test.
- You cannot give or receive information about how to spell words.
- You must take your test in ink—no erasing allowed.

FIGURE 13.10

Spelling Rubric

Name: _____   Date: _____

Spelling Rubric

Title of Writing Assignment: _____   Spelling Strategy Used: _____

CRITERIA	5	4	3	2	1
Circles all misspelled words	Student found and circled all misspelled words.	Student circled 75%–99% of misspelled words.	Student circled 50%–74% of misspelled words.	Student circled 25%–49% of misspelled words.	Student circled 1%–24% of misspelled words.
Accurately corrects all circled misspelled words	Student accurately corrected all circled misspelled words.	Student accurately corrected 75%–99% of circled misspelled words.	Student accurately corrected 50%–74% of circled misspelled words.	Student accurately corrected 25%–49% of circled misspelled words.	Student accurately corrected 1%–24% of circled misspelled words.
Always uses sounding-out, spell checker, dictionary, or similar words to spell words without help	Student always used one of the taught spelling strategies to spell words correctly on his or her own.	Student almost always used one of the taught spelling strategies to spell words correctly on his or her own.	Student sometimes used one of the taught spelling strategies to spell words correctly on his or her own.	Student always used one of the taught spelling strategies to spell words correctly with some help from an adult.	Student sometimes used one of the taught spelling strategies to spell words correctly with some help from an adult.
Spells all words correctly in writing	Student correctly spelled all the words in his or her writing.	Student correctly spelled 75%–99% of the words in his or her writing.	Student correctly spelled 50%–74% of the words in his or her writing.	Student correctly spelled 25%–49% of the words in his or her writing.	Student correctly spelled 1%–24% of the words in his or her writing.
Grade	/20 points	% =	Letter grade =		

Source: Loeffler, K.A. (2005). No more Friday spelling tests? An alternative spelling assessment for students with learning disabilities. *Teaching Exceptional Children, 37,* 24. Copyright 2005 by the Council for Exceptional Children. Reprinted with permission.

Meredith monitors the test process, collects and grades papers, and adds words missed to next week's spelling list.

Each week Meredith also gives an error detection test with words representing phonics patterns she taught that week as well as review patterns. The test consists of 20 word pairs. Each word pair consists of a correctly and incorrectly spelled word. Students are directed to circle the correct spelling.

Principles of Effective Spelling Instruction

The following sections describe principles of effective spelling instruction that Meredith observes. Any approach that is used with students who have spelling problems should include these principles.

Teaching Spelling Patterns. Learning to spell can be facilitated by understanding the patterns of our language. That is why early phonics instruction and later instruction in multisyllable words helps students become better spellers. Thus, students benefit when they are taught common word patterns such as base words, prefixes, suffixes, consonants, consonant blends, digraphs, and vowel sound–symbol associations.

Teaching in Small Units. Teach students with spelling problems three words a day rather than four or five. In one study, students with learning disabilities who were assigned three words a day performed better than a control group of students with learning disabilities who were assigned four or five words (Bryant, Drabin, & Gettinger, 1981).

Providing Sufficient Practice and Feedback. Give students opportunities to practice words each day, with feedback. Many teachers do this by having students work with spelling partners who ask them words and provide immediate feedback. Another procedure for self-correction and practice is presented in the 60-Second Lesson.

Selecting Appropriate Words. The most important strategy for teaching spelling is to make sure that students know how to read the word and already know its meaning. Selection of spelling words should be based on students' existing vocabularies.

Maintaining Previously Learned Words. For students to be able to remember how to spell words, you must frequently assign (for review) words they have already learned, along with new words. Previously learned words must be reviewed frequently to be maintained.

Teaching for Transfer of Learning. After spelling words have been mastered, provide opportunities for students to see and use the words in different contexts.

Motivating Students to Spell Correctly. Using games and activities, selecting meaningful words, and providing examples of the use and need for correct spelling are strategies that help motivate students and give them a positive attitude about spelling (Graham & Miller, 1979).

60 Second LESSON

PROCEDURE OF SELF-CORRECTION AND PRACTICE

To help students learn how to correct misspellings, try the following procedure:

1. Fold a paper into five columns, and write the correctly spelled words in the first column.

2. The student studies one word, folds the column back, and writes the word in the second column. The student then checks his or her spelling against the correctly spelled word in column 1.

3. After folding columns 1 and 2 back, the student writes the word in the third column. When the word is spelled correctly three times, the student moves on to the next word. The student continues until each word is spelled correctly from memory three times in a row.

Including Dictionary Training. Dictionary training (which includes alphabetizing, identifying target words, and locating the correct definition when several are provided) should be developed as part of the spelling program. Some teachers may decide to use computers to assist with this instruction.

Strategies for Helping All Students Develop Handwriting and Keyboarding Skills

Before computers, legible handwriting was a must. Even though children grow up using computers, learning how to write legibly is still important for students who are physically able. For most students, learning how to write legibly and fluently is a key to success in school. Indeed, many states have writing examinations that require students to write manually rather than using a computer.

Traditional Handwriting Instruction

In traditional handwriting instruction in the United States, students learn **manuscript writing** (printing) in the early grades and move to **cursive writing** (script) in the later grades (second or third, depending on the district). Clare Whiting, a third-grade teacher, teaches handwriting as a whole-class activity. To plan her lessons, she uses a commercial handwriting program that includes individual student booklets and extra worksheets to serve as models. Clare begins the school year by reviewing manuscript writing and then introduces the cursive alphabet after the first grading period. Clare assigns grades on the basis of her judgment of the legibility of students' handwriting.

What strategies work with students who have difficulty learning to spell? How can you help students who have difficulty with handwriting?

Critics of traditional handwriting instruction say that spending valuable class time on developing legible handwriting is not time well spent, and that time could be better spent teaching students to keyboard. Some educators maintain that handwriting should be taught during composition rather than whole-class instruction. Others argue against teaching two handwriting systems, some arguing for manuscript and others for cursive (see Figure 13.11). Frose (1981) proposed that both systems be maintained and that students be allowed to decide individually which form is most comfortable for them. The controversy over manuscript and cursive handwriting adds to the problems of students who have difficulties learning to write.

There are some advantages to learning early and well to print since it corresponds more obviously with the print students read (Spear-Swerling, 2006). In general, manuscript should be taught early on and maintained. Students who can make the transition to cursive should have the opportunity to do so.

FIGURE 13.11

Manuscript versus Cursive

Manuscript

1. It more closely resembles print and facilitates learning to read.

2. It is easier for young children to learn.

3. It is more legible than cursive.

4. Many students write manuscript at the same rate as cursive and this rate can be significantly influenced through direct instruction.

5. It is better for students with learning disabilities to learn one writing process well than to attempt to learn two.

Cursive

1. Many students want to learn to write cursive.

2. Many students write cursive faster.

3. Many adults object to students using manuscript beyond the primary grades.

Students with Difficulty in Handwriting

Students with dysgraphia have severe problems learning to write. Hamstra-Bletz and Blote (1993) define **dysgraphia** as follows:

> *Dysgraphia* is a written-language disorder that concerns the mechanical writing skill. It manifests itself in poor writing performance in children of at least average intelligence who do not have a distinct neurological disability and/or an overt perceptual–motor handicap. Furthermore, dysgraphia is regarded as a disability that can or cannot occur in the presence of other disabilities, like dyslexia or dyscalculia. (p. 690)

Poor handwriting, whether of students with dysgraphia or others, can include any of the following characteristics (Weintraub & Graham, 1998):

- Poor letter formation
- Letters that are too large, too small, or inconsistent in size
- Incorrect use of capital and lowercase letters
- Letters that are crowded and cramped
- Inconsistent spacing between letters
- Incorrect alignment (letters do not rest on a base line)
- Incorrect or inconsistent slant of cursive letters
- Lack of fluency in writing

With direct instruction and regular practice, most of these problems can be handled and corrected. There are six letters that account for 48% of the errors students make when forming letters: *q, j, z, u, n,* and *k* (Graham, Berninger, & Weintraub, 1998). It may be useful to spend more time teaching these letters and ensuring that students know how to connect them to other letters without changing their formation.

Principles of Effective Handwriting Instruction

It is important to address handwriting problems for several reasons. For one thing, they are associated with reduced interest in writing and thus influence written expression. Also, students with handwriting difficulties spell worse than those without handwriting problems even when spelling interventions are provided (Berninger et al., 1998). See Tips for Teachers 13.7 for some helpful strategies for teaching effective handwriting.

To teach handwriting, you must focus on two major components—legibility and fluency—both of which can be improved when students have correct posture, pencil grip, and paper position.

- *Posture.* Lower back touches the back of the chair and feet rest on the floor. The torso leans forward slightly in a straight line. Both forearms rest on the desk, with elbows slightly extended.

TIPS FOR TEACHERS 13.7

INSTRUCTIONAL PRINCIPLES FOR EFFECTIVE HANDWRITING

- Use direct instruction.
- Use individualized instruction.
- Use a variety of techniques and methods, matching the students' individual needs.
- Teach handwriting frequently (several times a week).
- Teach brief handwriting lessons within the context of students' writing.

- Teach handwriting skills separately and then encourage students to use them.
- Have students evaluate their own handwriting and, when appropriate, the handwriting of others.
- Present your handwriting as a model for the students to follow.
- Teach handwriting not as only a visual task or only a motor task, but as both.

Source: Information from Hagins, R. A. (1983). Write right or left: A practical approach to handwriting. *Journal of Learning Disabilities, 16,* 266–271.

- *Pencil grip.* The pencil is held lightly between the thumb and first two fingers, about one inch above the point. The first finger rests on top of the pencil. The end of the pencil points toward the shoulder.
- *Paper position.* For manuscript writing, the paper is held straight in front of the writer, and the nonwriting hand holds the paper in place. For cursive writing, the paper is slanted counterclockwise for a right-hander and clockwise for a left-hander.

Monitoring Student Progress. At the beginning and end of the school year, have students copy a short poem to get a sample of their handwriting and to indicate progress—you will be amazed at what you see. Hallahan and colleagues (2005) recommend using student writing samples on a variety of tasks to assess their legibility and fluency: freewriting, dictation, near-point copying, and far-point copying (see Table 13.1).

Legibility. Legibility is the most important goal of handwriting, and incorrect letter formation is the most frequent obstacle to reaching that goal. A survey of primary teachers indicated that their students displayed the following handwriting problems: overall neatness (76%), spacing between words (66%), letter size (59%), letter formation (57%), alignment of letters (54%), and reversals (52%) (Graham et al., 2008).

Teaching letter formation includes

- Identifying the critical features of the shapes of letters by comparing and contrasting them.
- Using physical prompts such as guiding the student's hand.
- Providing paper and materials that have the letters faded or with dots so that students have a model for tracing the letters.

TABLE 13.1

Guidelines for Assessing Handwriting

	PURPOSE	DIRECTIONS	ACCURACY STANDARD	SPEED STANDARD
FREEWRITING	To provide a baseline for evaluating other tasks and for assessing programs	Identify the letters (i.e., alphabet) or words (e.g., names and familiar words) that the student can write readily. Direct the student to write the identified materials repeatedly, as quickly as possible.	95–100%	60 characters per minute (cpm); 100 cpm, better
DICTATION	To evaluate a student's production of writing when she or he does not know what will come next	Decide whether to test individual letters, words, or phrases. Identify items you are sure the student can write without requiring much thinking (i.e., "known" items); you can use the same item several times in a test. Direct the student to write items as you say them. Watch closely, and, as the student finishes an item, say the next one.	90–100%	70% of standard for freewriting
NEAR-POINT COPYING	To evaluate a student's production of writing when she or he copies from materials on the desk	1. Familiar: Select highly familiar material for the student to copy. 2. Unfamiliar: Select material the student has not previously seen but that is at about the same difficulty level as in the familiar condition. Compare the performances to estimate the contribution of familiarity.	95–100%	75–80% of standard for freewriting
FAR-POINT COPYING	To evaluate a student's production of writing when she or he copies from a distant source (e.g., the chalkboard)	1. Familiar: Select highly familiar material for the student to copy. 2. Unfamiliar: Select material the student has not previously seen but that is at about the same difficulty level as in the familiar condition. Compare the performances to estimate the contribution of familiarity.	90–100%	75–80% of standard for freewriting

Source: Adapted from Hallahan, D. P., Lloyd, J. W., Kauffman, J. M., Weiss, M. P., & Martinez, E. A. (2005). *Learning disabilities: Foundations, characteristics, and effective teaching* (p. 412). Boston: Allyn & Bacon. Copyright © 2005 by Pearson Education. Reprinted by permission of the publisher.

- Giving students specific reinforcement for letters or parts of letters that are formed correctly and then giving specific feedback and correction for letters or parts of letters that need to be rewritten.

Hanover (1983) provided a system for teaching cursive writing based on the similarities of letters or letter families. Because students learn letters in groups with similar strokes, learning to write letters is easier. The position of the pencil when you start the letter and some of the significant "loops" or "shapes" used to form the letter allows you to teach letters with common shapes together. It makes sense that some letters can be taught in more than one family. Letter families in the **Hanover method** (Hanover, 1983) are shown here in the order recommended for teaching them:

e family:	*e, l, h, f, k*
hump-shaped family:	*n, m, s, y*
c family:	*c, a, d, o, q, g*
hump family:	*n, m, v, y, x*
back-tail family:	*f, q*
front-tail family:	*g, p, y, z*

One of the most effective ways to develop legibility is to provide a **moving model**. Modeling how to form letters and words is more helpful to students than simply having them copy letters and words (Wright & Wright, 1980). To provide a moving model, sit next to the student. As you form a letter or word, talk the student through the motions you are making. If the child writes with a different hand from you, have another child, a volunteer, or another teacher who writes with that hand provide the model. If you decide to have whole-class handwriting lessons, first provide a model by using the chalkboard or overhead projector; then circulate around the room, providing an individual moving model for students who seem to need the extra support.

Fluency.   After students begin to master basic letter forms and their writing becomes more legible, the next goal is to learn to write quickly and with ease. Tom Reynolds helps students in his class improve their fluency through timed writings and journal writing.

Tom has three students in his fifth-grade class who have improved the legibility of their writing considerably during the school year but who still need to learn to write more quickly. He decided to group the three students together for timed writings. (In a timed writing, students copy a 50-word passage and record the number of minutes the process takes.) When the group met for the first time, Tom showed them how to conduct a timed writing and keep records. For each student, he set up a folder with a collection of passages and a chart for recording progress. During this first meeting, Tom also explained that the idea is to work toward personal improvement, not to compete, and he talked about ways in which they could encourage one another. In time, the students could see that each was becoming a more fluent writer.

The daily 15-minute journal-writing activity Tom plans for all his students is a good way to enhance fluency. Because students know that their journals will not be graded for spelling or handwriting, they take risks and write more. Tom encourages students to evaluate their own journal writing and makes certain that students with fluency problems evaluate how much they write.

At the beginning of the year, Tom talked with the first-grade teacher, Helen Byers, and they decided to initiate a dialog journal activity (Atwell, 1984; Bode, 1989; Gambrell, 1985). A **dialog journal** is an ongoing written conversation between two students (or, in some cases, between a student and an adult). Each of Tom's fifth graders was paired with one of Helen's first graders. Once a week, the fifth graders visit the first-grade class and tell or read aloud a story to their first-grade partners. Then the pairs spend some time writing in a dialog journal.

Principles of Effective Keyboarding Instruction

Using the computer is frequently recommended as an adaptation for students who have difficulty with handwriting and spelling (Lerner, 2006). Learning to keyboard or type is essential for school success. Grade 4 is typically recommended for formal keyboarding instruction (see Table 13.2). Many software programs are available for teaching keyboarding skills. Such programs can monitor

Keyboarding Curriculum

TABLE 13.2

	TOPIC	TIME FRAME	SKILL LEVEL ALPHABETIC COPY
Grade 1 or 2	Home keys	3–4 hours	Don't measure
Grade 2 or 3	1. Alphabetic keys and commonly used punctuation marks 2. Spelling words and other short activities	30–35 hours	20 wam*
Grade 4 or 5	1. Review alphabetic keys and introduce numbers and commonly used symbols. 2. Incorporate in language arts.	25 hours	30 wam
Grade 6 or 7 or 8	Review skills. Use skills in all language arts. Use for personal use, reports, essays, letters, etc.	min. of 1 semester— 190 hrs 1 yr if preparing for vocational skill	40 wam
Grades 9–10	Introduction to business skills (word processing, database, spreadsheets, etc.)	1 semester	40–50 wam
Grades 11–12	Advanced business skills (word processing, database, spreadsheets, etc.)	1–2 semesters	50+

Note: Students can use word processing programs and microcomputers at any grade level where equipment is available.
*Words a minute—a standard word is five strokes, spaces, etc.

Source: Bartholome, L. W. (2003). Typewriting/keyboarding instruction in elementary schools. Retrieved June 10, 2005, from www.usoe.k12.ut.us/ate/keyboarding/Articles/Bartholome.

student progress and give feedback about accuracy. However, they may be lacking in that students' fingering cannot be monitored directly. Direct instruction with feedback and sufficient time for practice are necessary. Although students may exhibit some frustration using word processing to compose, when keyboarding fluency develops the frustration often fades (Cotton, 2001).

Summary

- Current trends in writing curriculum and instruction include (a) movement toward standards-based writing instruction and research-based practices, (b) increased emphasis on assessment, and (c) emphasis on balanced and effective writing instruction for all students.

- Writing is a complex process with many areas of potential difficulty for students. In addition to needing extra time for writing, students who have difficulty need direct instruction in composing, spelling, and handwriting. As a process, writing (like reading) is (a) interactive, (b) strategic, (c) constructed by meaning, (d) student centered, and (e) socially mediated.

- The elements of the authoring process include prewriting, composing, revising, editing, and publishing.

- Skills lessons can be taught in conjunction with students' ongoing writing using flexible grouping practices. The topics of skills lessons can be based on observations of student writing, requests for help, and data collected from writing conferences.

- Writing portfolios and writing rubrics can be used to assess student compositions and as guides for self-, peer, and teacher assessment.

- Although students with writing problems may be aware of the elements of a story, they do not necessarily incorporate these elements into their writing. Students need direct instruction in narrative writing.

- Students need instruction in expository writing, including typical informational writing patterns and strategic planning for composing informational text.

- Spelling is an important tool for writers. Effective instruction for students with spelling problems includes teaching spelling patterns, teaching in small units, providing feedback and practice, selecting appropriate words, and maintaining previously learned words.

- Because handwriting is still necessary for success in school, students need specific instruction in how to write legibly and fluently. Handwriting assessment should include assessment of freewriting, dictation, near-point copying, and far-point copying.

Think and Apply

1. Now that you have read Chapter 13, reread the interview with Michelle Langlois. What strategies does she use to plan a writing program that meets state standards and encourages student appreciation for the writing process?

2. Think about your own experience in developing your writing skills. What instructional methods and procedures were most helpful? Least helpful? Develop a personal writing portfolio to share with your students. In your portfolio include samples of your own writing from different phases of the authoring process. If possible, include some samples of your writing (and perhaps pictures of yourself) as a child. The portfolio will demonstrate to your students that you are a writer and will illustrate your own progress as a writer.

3. Plan the following activities: story writing, informational writing, spelling, and handwriting mini lessons. Then, make a list of all the tools and technologies you might use to make accommodations and adaptations for students with disabilities who have difficulties writing.

PEARSON
myeducationlab

Now go to Topic 6: Assessment; Topic 8: Instructional Practices and Learning Strategies; and Topic 10: Content Area Teaching   in the MyEducationLab (www.myeducationlab.com) for your course where you can:

- Find learning outcomes for these topics along with the national standards that connect to these outcomes.

- Complete Assignments and Activities that can help you more deeply understand the chapter content.

- Examine challenging situations and cases presented in the IRIS Center Resources.

- Apply and practice your understanding of the core teaching skills identified in the chapter with Building Teaching Skills and Dispositions learning units.

Helping All Students Succeed in Mathematics

FOCUS QUESTIONS

1. What are some of the current trends in math curriculum and instruction?

2. What are some of the reasons students with learning problems have difficulty with traditional mathematics curricula?

3. What are the recommended changes to traditional mathematics curricula and the implications of such changes for students with learning problems?

4. What teaching strategies are most important in helping all students acquire basic math skills?

5. How can teachers ensure that students understand the meaning of a mathematical operation and not just the answer to the problem?

6. How can teachers help students develop and use problem-solving strategies both in math as well as in other content areas?

INTERVIEW
ONE STUDENT'S EXPERIENCE

Shawn is an undergraduate at a small university. But unlike most first-year students, he is 21 years old, not 18. Since Shawn was very little, his parents have known he was not like the other children in the family or other children they knew. He was extraordinary in many ways and had problems in other ways. These problems were apparent when Shawn started school. Although few subjects were easy for him, all subjects were easier than math.

Through elementary and high school, Shawn received poor grades in mathematics, but not because of a lack of effort on his part. Shawn says, "No matter how much I studied, I just did not get it. When I say I can't do math, I mean it's not that I'm not trying, it's that it just really doesn't make any sense to me." Shawn recalls that in fourth grade he had a teacher who seemed to really understand his challenges with math and who worked hard to help him visualize what he was doing when he was solving math problems. She used objects such as colored chips to represent ones, tens, and hundreds and tried to make math real to him. He said that these accommodations helped and improved his attitude about learning math. Overall, though, he felt that the type of intensive support for math he needed was just not available. He explains: "I was mainstreamed into classrooms where there were at least 25 other students. I think the attitude toward students, especially students with learning disabilities, is 'Why should I change my teaching style just for you?'" Shawn describes his years in school this way: "It's like somebody saying we are going to make you do this even though you don't know how to. It was so hard and frustrating all of the time."

In high school, Shawn began to advocate for himself and seek out assistance with his courses, but again he describes his math experiences as unsuccessful. Shawn's experiences with mathematics have been so negative that he currently goes to great strides to exclude math from his life. "I don't take math. I switched my major so I won't have to take math. Math is just not a part of my life."

As a student with learning disabilities, what advice would Shawn give teachers? "The reason a student is coming to you with a problem and saying that they're LD is not because they want to give you more problems in your life, it's because they want you to help them."

Introduction

The purpose of this chapter is to introduce procedures for effectively instructing students like Shawn who have extraordinary problems learning mathematics. Think about how you felt about mathematics instruction. What do you think were some of the factors that influenced how you felt about mathematics instruction? Surely the teachers you had and the way mathematics was taught had a great deal of influence on how you feel about the subject today. Unfortunately, far too few students consider mathematics an exciting subject, and many students with disabilities perform poorly in mathematics because of low expectations for success and poor instruction (Baker, Gersten, & Lee, 2002; Bryant, Hartman, & Kim, 2003; U.S. Department of Education, 2008).

Current Trends in Mathematics Curriculum and Instruction

A central topic in education is mathematics instruction. This issue has been paramount for students with learning difficulties. There is growing national concern that students across all achievement groups are not faring well in mathematics compared with students in countries such as Belgium, Canada, England, Finland, Hungary, Japan, New Zealand, Scotland, and Sweden. Some think that the mathematics performance of students in the United States is related to the way in which mathematics is taught. In fact, the National Mathematics Advisory Panel (U.S. Department of Education, 2008) indicated that mathematics instruction is broken and needs to be fixed. The most important message they provide is to put "first things first"—meaning that students need to master important skills and knowledge sequentially.

Influences on Math Instruction

Mathematics instruction has been in a state of change over the past 30 years, with considerable emphasis on developing mathematical literacy through helping students construct knowledge (U.S. Department of Education, 2008). The Mathematics Advisory Panel included the outstanding research scientists in mathematics education in the United States who met and reviewed research on effective mathematics instruction. In their lengthy report (U.S. Department of Education, 2008) the Mathematics Advisory Panel offered six recommendations including:

1. Streamline the mathematics curriculum so that only the most essential elements of mathematics instruction are taught. These essential elements include whole numbers, computational proficiency, measurement, geometry, proficiency with fractions including decimals, percentage, and negative fractions.
2. Use findings from rigorous mathematics research to (a) give students an early start in mathematics, (b) teach in ways that recognize the importance of both conceptual understanding of mathematics and fluency and automaticity in mathematical facts, and (c) recognize that persistence in teaching and learning mathematics (i.e., effort) is important, not just inherent talent.
3. Provide preservice and professional development for teachers of mathematics so that they are knowledgeable about math content as well as effective instructional practices.
4. Use both student-centered and teacher-directed instruction. Students with learning difficulties and disabilities respond positively to explicit instruction in mathematics.
5. Emphasize mathematics instruction that leads to success in algebra.
6. Read and implement findings from rigorous research on math instruction.

The professional mathematics instruction group, the National Council of Teachers of Mathematics (NCTM), has been significantly influential in defining instructional core content in mathematics. In 1989, this group set curriculum standards for the development and implementation of mathematics curricula (NCTM, 1989). Since that time, NCTM has created professional standards (in 1991), assessment standards (in 1995), and most recently, a set of standards that builds on the three previous standards documents (published in 2000) and are summarized in Figure 14.1. Since the NCTM standards were published, NCTM went one step further and created "Curriculum Focal Points," which are the topics in mathematics that are most important at each grade level. These related ideas, concepts, and skills define the key instructional practices for teachers for each grade (NCTM, 2006) and are available for each grade level from prekindergarten through grade 8. As a prospective or practicing teacher, these focal points may be useful to you as you select curriculum and design instruction for students with special needs.

You can see from reviewing the Math Standards that mathematical problem solving is a major focus of the NCTM standards. When students with disabilities or math difficulties demonstrate challenges in mathematics problems solving, it is of particular concern because it interferes with students' access to higher-level math content and with applying math skills to everyday problems.

In an effort to determine how effective mathematical textbooks are in teaching math problem-solving standards to all students, Jitendra and colleagues (2005) reviewed five mathematical textbooks to determine the extent to which they addressed NCTM's problem-solving standards. These researchers also looked at the extent to which the texts provided design features associated with improved instructional outcomes for students with disabilities (e.g., prerequisite skills, teaching examples, practice problems, review, and feedback). Most textbooks provided an adequate number of problem-solving opportunities for students. However, with respect to instructional design criteria that would enhance instruction and support learning for students with disabilities, the textbooks were rated quite low, with few textbooks meeting even three instructional design features. To best accommodate students with disabilities, these

FIGURE 14.1

NCTM Standards 2000

Instructional programs for prekindergarten through grade 12 in the following areas should enable all students to use the following concepts:

1. Number and operations
   - Understand numbers, ways of representing numbers, relationships among numbers, and number systems
   - Understand meanings of operations and how they relate to one another
   - Compute fluently and make reasonable estimates

2. Algebra
   - Understand patterns, relations, and functions
   - Represent and analyze mathematical solutions and structures using algebraic symbols
   - Use mathematical models to represent and understand quantitative relationships
   - Analyze change in various contexts

3. Geometry
   - Analyze characteristics and properties of two- and three-dimensional geometric shapes, and develop mathematical arguments about geometric relationships
   - Specify locations and describe spatial relationships using coordinate geometry and other representational systems
   - Apply transformations and use symmetry to analyze mathematical situations
   - Use visualization, spatial reasoning, and geometric modeling to solve problems

4. Measurement
   - Understand measurable attributes of objects and the units, systems, and processes of measurement
   - Apply appropriate techniques, tools, and formulas to determine measurements

5. Data analysis and probability
   - Formulate questions that can be addressed with data and collect, organize, and display relevant data to answer them
   - Select and use appropriate statistical methods to analyze data
   - Develop and evaluate inferences and predictions that are based on data
   - Understand and apply basic concepts of probability

6. Problem solving
   - Build new mathematical knowledge through problem solving
   - Solve problems that arise in mathematics and in other contexts
   - Apply and adapt a variety of appropriate strategies to solve problems
   - Monitor and reflect on the process of mathematical problem solving

7. Reasoning and proof
   - Recognize reasoning and proof as fundamental aspects of mathematics
   - Make and investigate mathematical conjectures
   - Develop and evaluate mathematical arguments and proofs
   - Select and use various types of reasoning and methods of proof

8. Communication
   - Organize and consolidate their mathematical thinking through communication
   - Communicate their mathematical thinking coherently and clearly to peers, teachers, and others
   - Analyze and evaluate the mathematical thinking and strategies of others
   - Use the language of mathematics to express mathematical ideas precisely

9. Connections
   - Recognize and use connections among mathematical ideas
   - Understand how mathematical ideas interconnect and build on one another to produce a coherent whole
   - Recognize and apply mathematics in contexts outside of mathematics

10. Representation
    - Create and use representations to organize, record, and communicate mathematical ideas
    - Select, apply, and translate among mathematical representations to solve problems
    - Use representations to model and interpret physical, social, and mathematical phenomena

authors suggest that teachers will need to provide more specific and explicit instruction with additional examples as well as specific feedback.

Think about your own mathematics instruction when you were in school. Was the emphasis on worksheets and learning computation, or was it on problem solving and activities? Math educators suggest that students need to learn both and that an early emphasis on critical skills such as mathematical computational fluency is important, especially with opportunities to understand the computations conceptually and to apply them (U.S. Department of Education, 2008). In other words, it is not important to pick either mathematical computation or problem solving and application—students need to learn both.

Math Proficiency

The National Research Council (NRC) has conducted an examination of U.S. mathematics education from kindergarten through graduate study. This joint activity was conducted by the Mathematical Sciences Education Board, the Board on Mathematical Sciences, the Committee

FIGURE
14.2

The National Council of Teachers of Mathematics Recommendations

- Do not alter curricular goals to differentiate students; change the type and speed of instruction.

- Make mathematics education student oriented, not an authoritarian model that is teacher focused.

- Encourage students to explore, verbalize ideas, and understand that mathematics is part of their lives.

- Provide opportunities on a daily basis for students to apply mathematics and to work problems that are related to their daily lives. Relate what they are learning to real-life experiences.

- Teach mathematics so that students understand when they can estimate an answer and when they need to compute an exact answer.

- Teach problem solving, computer application, and use of calculators to all students.

- Teach students to understand probability, data analysis, and statistics as they relate to daily decision making, model building, operations, research, and application to computers.

- Shift from relying primarily on paper-and-pencil activities to use of calculators, computers, and other applied materials.

on the Mathematical Sciences, and the National Research Council. The extensive report resulting from the work of these committees not only outlines problems in mathematics education but also charts a course for remedying them. The suggestions that relate to students with learning and behavior problems are presented in Figure 14.2.

In addition to the guidelines in Figure 14.2, the National Research Council (2001) indicates that "mathematical proficiency" is the essential goal of instruction. What is mathematical proficiency? The aspects of mathematical proficiency are described here. As you read them, consider how you might integrate these ideas into your instruction for students with disabilities. Think about how you might document whether students are making progress.

- *Conceptual understanding* refers to understanding mathematic concepts and operations.
- *Procedural fluency* refers to being able to accurately and efficiently conduct operations and mathematics practices.
- *Strategic competence* refers to the ability to formulate and conduct mathematical problems.
- *Adaptive reasoning* refers to the thinking about, explaining, and justifying mathematical work.
- *Productive disposition* refers to the ability to appreciate the useful and positive influences of understanding mathematics and how one's disposition toward mathematics influences success.

Despite this plea for additional emphasis on problem solving, computation is still an essential component of the mathematics curriculum. Some feel that students with learning problems potentially have the most to lose as the curriculum shifts away from computation and toward an emphasis on problem solving and teaching students to think mathematically, thus the recent focal points for mathematics instruction (NCTM, 2006) provide an opportunity for teachers to identify the critical elements of instruction for their grade level and to determine whether students have mastered the previous focal points. This emphasis on the high-priority skills and practices at each grade level will ensure that the National Mathematics Advisory Panel's recommendation (U.S. Department of Education, 2008) to do first things first and to do the most important things at each grade level—not everything—can be accomplished.

For example, in fourth grade, the focal points (NCTM, 2006) emphasize that students demonstrate quick recall of multiplication and division facts and are very fluent with whole number multiplication. Fourth graders are also supposed to demonstrate understanding of decimals and the connection between decimals and fractions as well as an understanding of area and how to determine the area of two-dimensional shapes. How can James Frist, a fourth-grade teacher with two students with disabilities, consider these math focal points for all of the students in his class including his students with disabilities? Following are some guidelines to help James:

- Students with disabilities may be slower and require more practice, but they are not necessarily less accurate. Consider that the students with disabilities may need more time to complete the problem.
- Students with disabilities may need more support (e.g., additional instruction), to have the problem read to them, guidance about the key ideas to focus on, and reminders about which operation to use. At the same time, however, they should have access to learning the same focal points in mathematics.

- When students work in pairs or groups, it is not uncommon that the students with disabilities are assigned passive and unimportant roles where they have little opportunity for learning and participating. Consider ways to alter this practice and to include them more actively in partner or group work.
- Students with disabilities may not have adequate fluency with basic math facts and may need additional practice and opportunities to acquire this proficiency.

Understanding why your students are having difficulty learning math will help you to better meet their needs. The following sections offer specific information about why students struggle.

Difficulties in Learning Mathematics

Students with behavior disorders, mental retardation, learning disabilities, and attention problems typically score below their same-age peers on measures of math achievement (Zentall & Smith, 1993). Some of their difficulties in mathematics relate to understanding the problem. In other instances, they lack the computation skills to adequately complete the problem. Typically, students with disabilities have difficulties with both math facts and procedures (Barnes et al., 2006). Interestingly, not all of their difficulties in mathematics relate to their knowledge of math; some reflect other problems such as memory, difficulty in considering math problems from a "reasonable" perspective, poor calculation skills, number reversals, and difficulty understanding operation signs (Bryant, Hartman, & Kim, 2003).

What kinds of difficulties in mathematics do students with disabilities have? How can teachers help students with these kinds of difficulties?

Despite the significant difficulties many individuals with disabilities have with mathematics, they do not report lower self-perceptions of their math skills than average-achieving students (Montague & van Garderen, 2003).

Students who have both math and reading disabilities are more at risk than students with math disabilities alone (Jordan & Hanich, 2003). This is because students with both reading and math disabilities have additional problems associated with processing symbols and text (Bryant, Bryant, & Hammill, 2000; Bryant, Hartman, & Kim, 2003).

Developmental Arithmetic Disorder

Students with **developmental arithmetic disorder** have significant difficulties learning arithmetic—difficulties that are unexpected given the students' overall cognitive functioning and academic performance in other subject areas. For example, Shawn, the student introduced at the beginning of this chapter, demonstrated a significant arithmetic disorder. His performance in arithmetic was unexpectedly low given his overall cognitive performance. His difficulty in mathematics was also long lasting, not related to an area of mathematics or a particular teacher. Good teaching is likely to help students with developmental arithmetic disorder but probably not enough to ensure grade-level performance.

Nonverbal Math Difficulties

Johnson and Myklebust (1967) were the first to introduce the notion of **nonverbal math disabilities**. They were referring to a small group of students who displayed good reading and verbal expression but extreme difficulty with mathematics. Other problems associated with students who display nonverbal mathematics problems include the following:

- Social immaturity
- Disorientation
- Deficits in visual, motor, and self-help skills
- Problems estimating distance and time

Go to **www.ldonline.org/ ld_indepth/math_skills/ adapt_cld.html**, where you will find information on instructional adaptations of mathematics for students with learning disabilities.

Saje, a third-grade student with disabilities, was a successful reader but demonstrated significant difficulties in mathematics and was really a puzzle to his teacher, Theresa Ramirez. She could not figure out why, despite Saje's high verbal expression and good vocabulary, he continually mixed up old and new rules. He not only had problems in math but also was frequently inattentive and disorganized and avoided responsibility. No matter how often she reminded Saje to keep his math paper neat, the papers he turned in had frayed edges, had numbers all over the place (instead of problems written in neat columns), and were covered with eraser marks and holes. Theresa asked the special education teacher how to help Saje. The special education teacher worked with Saje, administered some tests, and explained to Saje's classroom teacher that he had a nonverbal math difficulty.

Although math would always be challenging for Saje, the special education teacher suggested some things that the classroom teacher could do to help Saje:

1. First, she taught only one mathematical principle at a time until Saje became masterful and fluent with that principle.
2. She used word games, songs, and other verbal activities to enhance instruction.
3. She devised organizational aids such as graph paper with large boxes that Saje could use to write numbers.
4. She provided Saje with devices such as computers and tape recorders as alternatives to pencil and paper.

Students who demonstrate nonverbal math difficulties are capable of acquiring meaningful understanding of mathematics and solving mathematical problems. Providing effective instructional accommodations such as the ones provided for Saje can improve their mathematical performance not only in your class, but in the future as well.

Effective Math Instruction for All Learners

Go to the Assignments and Activities section of Topic 10: Content Area Teaching in the MyEducationLab for your course and complete the activity entitled *Mathematical Concepts*.

Students can display poor math performance for several reasons. The one that can be most readily corrected is the inappropriate or inadequate instruction in mathematics that many students receive. Many professionals believe that the math difficulties among students with learning problems are compounded by ineffective instruction. Most teachers know how they learned to compute math problems but are not aware of alternative ways to compute them (e.g., they memorized successfully multiplication tables but are unfamiliar with adding numbers to resolve multiplication). Few teachers have procedures for using concrete approaches and how to successfully use manipulatives to teach computation. Tips for Teachers 14.1 provides a summary of guidelines for instructional practices for students with disabilities in a general education classroom.

As a general education teacher, you will also need to be prepared to meet the instructional needs of students who are mathematically gifted. There is a debate about whether to accelerate the pacing of instruction for gifted students or to provide differentiated instruction. Johnson (2000) indicated that most experts recommend a combined approach. Tips for Teachers 14.2 provides some suggestions for meeting the needs of mathematically gifted students.

Tips for Teachers 14.1

INSTRUCTIONAL PRACTICES FOR STUDENTS WITH DISABILITIES

- Select appropriate, comprehensive math content.
- Select goals that establish high expectations.
- Provide systematic and explicit instruction.
- Teach students to understand math concepts.

- Monitor the progress of students.
- Teach to mastery.
- Promote a positive attitude toward math.
- Teach students to generalize the math skills they learn.

Additional tips for teachers can be located at these websites: www.ldonline.org/ld_indepth/math_skills and www.superkids.com/aweb/tools/math

Tips FOR TEACHERS 14.2

INSTRUCTIONAL PRACTICES FOR GIFTED STUDENTS

- Give preassessments so that students who already know the material do not have to repeat it, keeping instruction and activities meaningful. In the elementary grades, gifted learners still need to know their basic facts. If they do not, don't hold them back from other, more complex tasks, but continue to work concurrently on the basics.

- Create assessments that allow for differences in understanding, creativity, and accomplishment; give students a chance to show what they have learned. Ask students to explain their reasoning both orally and in writing.

- Choose textbooks that provide more enriched opportunities. Because most textbooks are written for the general population, they are not always appropriate for gifted students. Use multiple resources. No single text will adequately meet the needs of these learners.

- Be flexible in your expectations about pacing for different students. While some may be mastering basic skills, others may work on more advanced problems.

- Use inquiry-based, discovery learning approaches that emphasize open-ended problems with multiple solutions or multiple paths to solutions. Allow students to design their own ways to find the answers to complex questions. Gifted students may discover more than you thought was possible.

- Use a lot of higher-level questions. Ask "why" and "what if" questions.

- Provide units, activities, or problems that extend beyond the normal curriculum. Offer challenging mathematical recreations such as puzzles and games.

- Provide AP level courses in calculus, statistics, and computer science, or encourage prepared students to take classes at local colleges if the supply of courses at the high school has been exhausted.

- Differentiate assignments. It is not appropriate to give more problems of the same type to gifted students. You might give students a choice of a regular assignment; a different, more challenging one; or a task that is tailored to interests.

- Expect high-level products (e.g., writing, proofs, projects, solutions to challenging problems).

- Provide opportunities to participate in contests such as Mathematical Olympiads for the Elementary School (grades 4–6), Math Counts (grades 7–8), the American Junior High School Mathematics Exam (grades 7–8), or the American High School Mathematics Exam (grades 9–12). Give feedback to students on their solutions. After the contests, use some of the problems as the basis for classroom discussions.

- Provide access to male and female mentors who represent diverse linguistic and cultural groups. They may be individuals within the school system, volunteers from the community, or experts who agree to respond to questions by email. Bring speakers into the classroom to explain how math has opened doors in their professions and careers.

- Provide some activities that can be done independently or in groups based on student choice. Be aware that if gifted students always work independently, they are gaining no more than they could do at home. They also need appropriate instruction, interaction with other gifted students, and regular feedback from the teacher.

- Provide useful, concrete experiences. Even though gifted learners may be capable of abstraction and may move from concrete to abstract more rapidly, they still benefit from the use of manipulatives and hands-on activities.

Source: Adapted from Johnson, D. T. (2000, April). Teaching mathematics to gifted students in a mixed-ability classroom. *ERIC Digest E594* (ERIC Document Reproduction Service No. ED441302). Reprinted by permission of the author.

Evaluating Mathematics Curricula

Considering the mathematical focal points by NCTM (2006) and the guidance provided by the National Mathematics Advisory Panel (U.S. Department of Education, 2008), it is likely that math curricula will be influenced and aligned with the math panel guidelines described in the section "Influences on Math Instruction." Students with disabilities and math difficulties will benefit from teachers who consider the following:

- ■ *Students have difficulty reading the information provided.* Because the reading vocabulary is too difficult and the reading level is too high, students with math difficulties are able to learn very little by reading their math books. Consequently, teachers must provide supports that make the information accessible. For example, Max Diamond, a tenth-grade math teacher, assigned several pages of reading in the math textbook as homework. Realizing that several of his students would not be able to read and understand the text adequately, Max had these pages read into a tape recorder and made the tapes and recorders available to all students in his class.

- ■ *Math concepts are often presented poorly.* Multiple concepts are introduced at one time, and information is often presented in a scattered fashion. For this reason, Dawn McQueen reorganizes the information in the math text so that she can teach computation skills to mastery rather than skipping around teaching many new ideas in 2 weeks. Dawn introduces only one concept at a time, teaching that concept until *all* students in her class (not just those with learning problems) learn it. Then she moves on to the next concept. Although Dawn follows a sequence of pages different from that presented in the book, she believes that her efforts are worthwhile because her students seem to understand better.

- ***There are insufficient problems covering any one concept or operation and too few opportunities for application of knowledge learned.*** The problems are not presented in enough different situations for students to learn and transfer what they know. Janice Kauffman, a sixth-grade teacher, addresses this problem by developing her own supportive materials to supplement the book. She also provides practice with problem solving, reasoning, and real-life applications that helps students transfer their knowledge to real-life settings.
- ***Students often do not have the necessary prerequisite skills assumed by the text (and so the next level is too difficult).*** As Margaret Gardner plans each math unit she teaches, she spends considerable time considering the prerequisite skills students need to master the concept or operation she is teaching. After identifying these prerequisite skills, she tells students directly that she is looking to see whether they know them. She prepares activities and exercises so that she knows which students do and which do not possess the skills they need to move on to the next math concept or operation.
- ***The pages and organizational format of the text vary considerably and make learning from the text difficult.*** Linda Saumell, having recognized this problem, walks students through the text section by section, explaining the format to them.
- ***Students have difficulty transferring knowledge to real problems.*** Many of the steps necessary to help students transfer what they know mathematically to selected problems are not taught explicitly and so students fail to perform correctly. With problem solving, for example, students often know how to do pieces of the problem but do not know how to assemble these pieces to correctly generalize what they know to the new problem.

To shape the mathematics curricula so that it accommodates the learning needs of all students, particularly students with learning problems, teachers need to adapt traditional math curricula to best meet the learning needs of students in their classrooms. The teachers cited above are successful in addressing inherent limitations, improving their students' potential for a positive outcome.

Adapting Instruction for Secondary Students with Math Difficulties

Older students with mathematical problems require instructional considerations to access and learn mathematics. Though the research base is better developed for teaching mathematics to younger students with learning difficulties, there are instructional practices with older students that are associated with improved outcomes. See Tips for Teachers 14.3 for some suggestions for teachers working with older students who have experienced years of challenge and frustration in learning math.

Many older students benefit from real-world problem solving that includes a gamelike experience. Shaftel, Pass, and Schnabel (2005) provide an example of a game that gives adolescent students with learning disabilities an opportunity to use a checkbook and keep track of their expenses. Teachers can create a game board on which each "space" has a real-life experience. Examples of these experiences include

- Pay rent for your apartment: $300.
- Receive your monthly paycheck of $800.
- Unexpected dental expense; pay $180.

Each student is provided with a checkbook and checks. Students can all be given a designated amount of money at the beginning of the game. Based on where they land on the game board, they add or subtract money. After a specified period of time, the student with the most money in his or her checkbook is the winner.

Using real-world examples such as paying bills and keeping a checkbook heightens students' interest in doing math. It also shows them that there are important reasons to master math skills, as they really do need to use these skills in their every day lives.

Go to **www.ldonline.org/ indepth/math** for additional information on teaching students who struggle with math.

Tips for Teachers 14.3

WORKING WITH OLDER STUDENTS WHO HAVE EXPERIENCED FRUSTRATIONS LEARNING MATH

- *Provide explicit instruction.* For many students, this means clearly identifying the steps in solving the problem, facilitating background knowledge and skills, and demonstrating clearly all aspects of problem resolution. One way teachers can improve explicit instruction is to determine whether they have made transparent to the learner all critical parts of solving the mathematical problem.

- *Provide clear and a sufficient number of examples; most commercial materials fall short in this area.* Students with learning difficulties benefit from more examples and nonexamples. This means showing them the application several ways. It is also useful to demonstrate a counterexample that illustrates a faulty application.

- *Give real-life applications for students.* Students with mathematical difficulties find math abstract and conceptually difficult to understand. For this reason, teachers who link the problems to real-life situations are more successful.

- *Provide ample opportunities to be successful.* Students with mathematical difficulties need not only lots of examples from the teacher, but also lots of opportunities to practice the problem-types until they master them. One of the critical difficulties experienced by students with math problems is that they never really master a problem-type before they are introduced to something new.

- *Use cooperative learning activities, but include individual accountability as a key component.* Although cooperative learning (asking students to work in small groups with three to five other students in which they all attempt to solve the same problem) may be useful for students with mathematical difficulties because it provides them ready access to able students as models and guides, it also can have the negative consequence of leaving the target student out of the learning. Unless there is a focus on individual accountability, where every student is responsible for demonstrating learning, it is possible that cooperative groups can give students with mathematical difficulties a free ride.

Adapting Basal Materials for Students with Special Needs

Teachers need to do several things to adapt basal materials. One is to select appropriate math content. There is considerable concern among educators that poor math content is a result of the **spiral curriculum**, which occurs when the same skills (e.g., mathematics skills) are woven into every year of school and students continually "relearn" the same skills in the same area. Jason, an eighth-grade student, said it this way: "It seems every year we start with multiplication and then go to division and then we learn something about fractions and then we stop. Then the next year, we do it all over again." One approach to teaching mathematics, the Corrective Mathematics Program (Engelmann & Carnine, 1992), is designed to avoid the problems of the spiral curriculum and provide satisfactory pacing of instruction.

Teachers can also use instructional design principles to assist students with learning problems in acquiring proficiency in mathematics. These design principles include (a) teaching big ideas, (b) making strategies conspicuous, (c) using instructional time efficiently, (d) making instruction on strategies clear and explicit, and (e) providing appropriate practice and review (Pressley & Harris, 2006).

A key aspect of selecting the appropriate curriculum is that it be comprehensive. A fifth-grade teacher, Mr. Lanca, reflected, "I know my curriculum should be more comprehensive than just the facts and computation, but I'm not sure what else I should teach. Also, the students seem to really need the time to learn computation." Working on other skills in mathematics does not mean that computation is left behind; in fact, computation can often be enhanced while other components of math are taught. Students need to be taught and involved in a full range of mathematics skills that include basic facts, computation, word problems, operations, problem solving, mathematical reasoning, time, measurement, fractions, and math application.

Adapting Tests for Students with Special Needs

How effective are test accommodations in mathematics for students with disabilities? The idea behind test accommodations is that individuals with disabilities profit more from them than individuals without disabilities—thus the test accommodations are more responsive to their individual needs. Elbaum (2007) reports that when mathematics tests are read aloud to students with disabilities and their performance on these tests are compared with students without disabilities, the read-aloud condition is more helpful to elementary students with disabilities than elementary students without disabilities. However, the reverse is true for secondary students with disabilities whose improved performance with accommodations is overall lower than for students without disabilities.

Using Curricular Programs for Students With Math Difficulties

Other than the basal curriculum books, math workbooks, and the curriculum guidebooks published by many state departments of education, what curriculum resources are available to teachers? The following list provides brief descriptions of some resources that are helpful for students who have difficulty learning math.

Go to www.greatschools.net/LD/assistive-technology/math-tools.gs?content = 949 where you will find technology to help students learn mathematics.

- **Vmath** (Voyager Expanded Learning, 2008) was developed for students in grades 3 through 8 who may need extra instruction to meet mathematics learning goals. Vmath is designed at each grade level to assess and monitor the progress of students so that through a systematic approach to instruction they can develop into independent learners in math and help students meet grade-level goals in math.
- The **Corrective Mathematics Program** stresses direct instruction through a highly sequenced format that provides immediate feedback to students (Engelmann & Carnine, 1992). The arithmetic kits come with a detailed teacher's guide, workbooks, teaching book, and take-home sheets for homework and parent involvement. The entire program is based on behavioral principles of learning and provides explicit instructions for the teacher. The materials are designed to be fast paced with a lot of oral drill.
- The **Computational Arithmetic Program** provides 314 worksheets for teaching basic math skills to students in grades 1 through 6 (Smith & Lovitt, 1982).
- **NCTM Navigation Series** is a series of graded and topical books with CD-ROMs published by NCTM. The books focus on activities for teaching algebra, geometry, numbers and operations, and the like, based on the NCTM principles and standards.
- **Math Exploration and Applications** provides instruction, games, and manipulatives for building fluency in math skills in English and Spanish (Bereiter, Hilton, Rubinstein, & Willoughby, 1998).
- **Key Math Teach and Practice** is designed to provide remedial practice in and diagnosis of math difficulties (Connolly, 1988). Materials include a teacher's guide, a student progress chart, and a sequence chart, as well as activities and worksheets.
- **ETA/Cuisenaire** provides a variety of supplemental mathematics materials. This company specializes in math manipulatives that emphasize learning principles through hands-on learning. One of their earliest products was the Cuisenaire rods. Cuisenaire rods come in various lengths and colors and can be used to represent numbers. Students with disabilities can be taught to use Cuisenaire rods as manipulatives to facilitate their successful understanding of word problems. Over time, they are able to generalize to similar problems when the rods are not used (Marsh & Cooke, 1996).
- **Saxon Math** was designed for kindergarten through fourth grade (Larson, 2004) and eighth through twelfth grades (Saxon, 2003), addressing math concepts with an emphasis on solving math problems. Strategies for solving math problems are scaffolded through step-by-step problem solving.

Being aware of these options equips teachers with alternatives for helping all students achieve some success in math. When necessary, working with the special education teacher can help teachers identify the best programs for struggling students.

Establishing Appropriate Goals

Students and teachers who establish feasible goals in mathematics and monitor the progress of these goals are more likely to demonstrate improved success (Fuchs et al., 1992). How can teachers do this? One way is to establish goals for all students, including those with disabilities, and discuss or establish these goals with their students. Why is this important? Often the goals and expectations teachers set for students with learning problems are too low. Students benefit when they are challenged to meet realistic but rigorous academic goals.

Marie Fernandez, a middle-school teacher, realized that she often responded to students' low self-image and low motivation by setting low goals for them. She did not expect that students would be interested and work hard, and they met her low expectations. Several of the students with learning problems in her class would indicate that the work was too difficult or that there was too much work, and she would respond by lessening their load instead of thinking of alternatives. With the help of the special education teacher at her school, Marie Fernandez instituted some of the following changes:

- **Students use goal setting and self-monitoring with teacher support.** In the goal-setting process, students were asked to set realistic goals for how much work they could complete and how many problems they could solve. For example, students would determine that they would be able to complete six mathematical problems that involved multiplication of two-digit numbers with no errors in 5 minutes.

- **Teacher models and thinks aloud how to solve the problem.** Rather than giving up when students thought the problems were too difficult, Marie Fernandez began showing students how to do the problems by conducting them step by step and thinking aloud the procedures. For example, "First I read the numbers out loud and estimate how much it will be. Let's see—86 plus 22 is going to be more than 100, but not much more. Now I start on the right and add the column. Now I add the column on the left. The total is 108."

- **Teacher guides the student to solve the problem.** Thanks to the teacher's prompts and guidance, the student does not have to work through the verbalization alone. When the student has difficulty, the teacher fills in. The teacher does not do the work but guides the student through it so that he or she has accomplished the problem successfully.

- **Students have opportunities to work in small groups or alone to successfully complete the problems.** After students have succeeded in completing the problems with support from the teacher, the next step may be to have them work in small groups or pairs to complete problems before they work independently to do them. This phasing from teacher instruction to guided practice to practice with peers and then independent practice provides a scaffold so that all students can succeed.

Using Peers to Support Instructional Practice

Effective ways to facilitate learning of mathematics for students with difficulties is to engage peers in the process. One way is through peer pairing in which two students work together (usually a stronger student in math is paired with a less able student). Students are provided instruction by the teacher and then through pairs complete designated problems. The idea is that by working together they can learn to solve and practice the problems effectively (Dion, Fuchs, & Fuchs, 2007; Gardner, Nobel, Hessler, Yawn & Heron, 2007) as well as practice these skills (Fuchs et al., 1997).

Peer tutoring is effective not only for the student who is tutored, but also for the student who does the tutoring. Teaching not only helps enhance students' self-concept, but also helps them learn a great deal. Cooperative learning occurs when the teacher divides the class into small groups (ordinarily three or four students per group), usually not based on ability, and asks these groups to work together to solve problems. Maheady, Harper, and Sacca (1988) conducted a cooperative learning math instruction program for ninth- and tenth-grade students with mild disabilities. The study showed that students who participated in the cooperative teams performed better in mathematics and received higher grades than those who did not.

Slavin, Madden, and Leavey (1984; Slavin, 1995) designed **team-assisted individualization**, in which individualized instruction is provided in a cooperative learning model. Each of the four or five students in the heterogeneous learning team is assigned individualized

How can teachers guide peer tutors to help the students with whom they are paired? What makes this dynamic effective?

mathematics material at his or her own level. Students on the same team help one another with problems and also manage checking and record keeping for the individualized math materials. Students work independently, but teachers teach skills to groups of students who are at the same level by pulling them from various teams.

Using Response to Intervention: Identifying Students Who Need Help in Math

Math, like reading and writing, is an academic area where response to intervention (RTI) can be implemented. One of the best ways to use RTI in mathematics is to screen students for math difficulties and then to provide them with early and intensive intervention to ensure their progress. There are several measures that can be used to determine students' early math knowledge (Clarke & Shinn, 2004; Fuchs et al., 2007):

1. *Number identification.* Students are asked to identify orally numbers between 0 and 20 when these are presented randomly on a piece of paper.
2. *Number writing.* Students are asked to write a number between 1 and 20 when the number is provided to them orally.
3. *Quantity discrimination.* Students are asked to identify which of two numbers is the larger (or smaller).
4. *Missing number.* Students are provided with a string of numbers and are asked to identify the number that is missing.
5. *Computation.* Students are asked to complete computations that are representative of their grade level. Students are provided 2 minutes to complete as many problems as possible.

Many of the same principles that apply to the use of RTI in reading also apply to math, including

- *Screening*—students can be screened to determine whether they have math problems in numeracy, math calculations, and/or problem solving.
- *Evidence-based math*—schools and districts can ensure that the math instruction for all students is based on the best research available.
- *Interventions*—when students have difficulties that are not adequately addressed through the evidence-based math program in the classroom, additional instruction through short-term interventions (10–20 weeks) can be implemented.
- *Progress monitoring*—students' progress in the classroom and in interventions can be documented to ensure that they are staying on track and meeting curriculum benchmarks.

Assessment and Progress Monitoring

Effective math instruction involves checking students' work frequently and providing feedback. When students demonstrate math difficulties, their progress needs to be assessed by their classroom math teacher approximately every 2 weeks, and if students are not progressing adequately, accommodations including reteaching and guided practice need to be provided to ensure success. The math assessments used should align with the instructional curriculum.

Students in teacher Alex Chinn's fifth-grade class were asked to complete a worksheet to practice a new skill he had taught them for using dollar signs and decimal points in subtraction problems. Alex told the students to complete only the first problem. After they completed the problem, they were to consider whether the answer made sense and whether dollar signs and decimal points were used correctly. If so, they were to place a *C* next to the problem. If they were not sure whether the problem was correct, they were to mark it with a question mark (?); and if they thought the problem was wrong, they were to use a star (*). Alex moved quickly from student to student, checking the first problem and providing them with feedback and reinforcement: "Jacob, you were right, you did have the problem correct. Maxine, what are you unsure about? Now, look at it again. What do you think? Yes, that's right, it's correct. Beth, let's do this problem together." The teacher then guides the student by facilitating problem completion and then provides additional opportunities for the student to do similar problems independently.

Being a Model in Math.   Most of the time, a positive attitude toward math comes from effective instruction and the interest the teacher shows in mathematics. Tips for Teachers 14.4 offers suggestions for promoting positive attitudes toward math.

PROMOTING POSITIVE ATTITUDES TOWARD MATH

- Provide multiple opportunities for success.

- Select real-world problems that address issues of importance to the students.

- Be certain that students have the prerequisite skills to adequately solve the problem.

- Teach students to chart their progress—success is the best motivator.

- Provide calculators and other tools to support success.

- For complex problems, ask students to solve the problem in steps so that they get feedback as they proceed.

- When appropriate, encourage students to work with partners.

Diagnosing Students' Learning Needs in Mathematics. When students have persistent difficulties in math that continue after teachers have made adequate instructional accommodations, teachers may need to provide further diagnosis to pinpoint the students' math learning needs. Jana is a first-year special education teacher. She is fortunate to work in a middle school with three other special education teachers who have been working at the school for several years and are used to team teaching. Jana's school administrator asked her whether she would be comfortable teaching mathematics to all of the special education students. Because she is pretty good at mathematics herself, Jana thought this arrangement would give her an opportunity to learn to teach one content area very well. She quickly realized that her first task would be to determine the performance levels in mathematics of all her students. She also realized that she needed to select a measure that would tell her what students knew and did not know and also how they compared with other students in their grade. Although there is general information on the IEP about the student's math performance, she wanted more precise, diagnostic information.

There are a number of ways in which Jana can obtain the information she needs to develop instructional programs for her students. One of the first questions Jana needs to address is whether she has the time to give an *individually administered assessment* or whether she needs to use a group administered measure. For students with special needs, individually administered measures yield the most information for teachers. Second, Jana needs to decide whether the measure is designed for students in the age range of the students she is teaching. Table 14.1 provides a list of mathematics measures, states whether they are group or individually administered, and lists the age range for which they are appropriate.

How can teachers best make decisions about whether students are learning mathematics effectively? Also, how can teachers monitor the progress of their students so that they can document the rate and progress students are making in mathematics? Perhaps the best way to determine student progress is to implement curriculum-based measurement (CBM), which is a method of determining whether the student is learning the curriculum that is taught. Teachers prioritize the most important skills students need to learn each week and then assess students prior to and following instruction. These tests can be group administered, teacher developed, and take as little as a few minutes to administer. Based on the findings from the pretest, teachers can identify what they need to teach all students and what they need to teach some of the students. Posttesting at the end of the week tells the teacher who needs additional instruction. There is considerable and growing evidence that when teachers use CBM to monitor their students' progress and to adjust their instruction accordingly, students make gains at much more rapid rates than when CBM is not used (Stecker & Fuchs, 2000).

What is CBM for math? Simply stated, it is a way of documenting the extent to which the student is learning the critical elements you have targeted in the curriculum. To illustrate, consider the case of Ricky, a fifth-grade boy with learning and attention problems, who is struggling with math. His goals for the next 10 weeks are (a) to know all subtraction facts up to 100 automatically, (b) to quickly be able to do addition with regrouping word problems, and (c) to be able to use basic measurement terms such as *inches, feet,* and *yards* appropriately. Ricky's teacher, Mr. Rojas, pretested Ricky on all 100 subtraction facts in random order, timing him while he completed the worksheet. He then showed Ricky how to graph his

TABLE
14.1

Measures to Assess Mathematics Performance

TEST NAME	HOW ADMINISTERED	AGE/GRADE APPROPRIATE	OTHER INFORMATION
Comprehensive Math Assessment	Group	Grades 2–8	Based largely on the National Council of Teachers of Mathematics' critical elements in mathematics instruction
Diagnostic Achievement Battery	Individual	Most grade levels	Provides normative data on student performance but not specific information for identifying strengths and weaknesses
Wide Range Achievement Test	Individual or Group	Most grade levels	Provides normative data on student performance but difficult to identify students' needs for instruction
Woodcock Johnson III Tests of Achievement	Individual	Most grade levels	Provides normative data on student performance but may not provide adequate information for designing instruction
Test of Early Mathematics Ability	Individual	Ages 3–9	Provides information to assist with designing and monitoring instruction
BRIGANCE Diagnostic Comprehensive Inventory of Basic Skills—Revised	Individual	Prekindergarten–grade 9	Provides information to assist with designing and monitoring instruction
Comprehensive Mathematical Ability Test	Individual	Grades 1–12	Provides information to assist with designing instruction
Key Math—Revised	Individual	Grades 1–12	Provides information to assist with designing instruction
Test of Mathematical Abilities	Individual	Grades 3–12	Provides information to assist with designing instruction
Math—Level Indicator: A Quick Group Math Placement Test	Group	Grades 4–12	Takes approximately 30 minutes, and because it is group administered, it quickly determines the performance levels of a large group of students. The problems are based on the NCTM standards.

Source: Bos, C. S. & Vaughn, S. (2006). *Strategies for teaching students with learning and behavior problems* (6th ed.). Boston: Allyn & Bacon.

performance in two ways: first, by graphing how long it took him to complete the worksheet, and second, by graphing the number of problems correct. Together they agreed that he would take a version of this test once every week to determine whether he could decrease the amount of time he needed to complete the test and increase the number of problems he got correct. Next, they established a schedule of work assignments and practice sessions. His teacher followed a similar procedure with measurement and problem solving to determine what Ricky knew and what he needed to know, and then he established a simple graph that Ricky could complete to monitor his progress. Ricky and his teacher frequently discussed Ricky's progress and modified assignments and instruction to facilitate his learning.

As a teacher, you may want to consider using a computerized application of CBM procedures, which is available for mathematics as well as for spelling and reading (Fuchs, Fuchs, & Hamlett, 1990). Remember, CBMs should be easy to administer, cost efficient, and sensitive to small changes in learning (Kamee'enui et al., 2005).

Assessing Students' Number Sense

One promising practice for monitoring the progress of young children in mathematics and identifying children who have mathematics difficulties or disabilities is by assessing their "number sense." **Number sense** refers to whether a student's understanding of a number and its use and meaning is flexible and fully developed. In terms of assessment, number sense is particularly important because it assists teachers in determining which students currently have mathematical difficulty; it also serves as a predictor for students who may have learning difficulties in the future.

Several counting measures for students' beginning math skills (ages 4–8) can be used as effective screening tools for students with mathematic difficulties or used to monitor students' progress in this area.

- Count to 20. This is a beginning-level skill requiring students to count to 20, recording which numbers were known in the correct sequence and which ones were not.
- Count by 3 and 6. This skill requires students to count from a predetermined number, say 5, in increments of 3 or 6. Teachers record the accuracy and speed with which students perform this task.
- Count by 2, 5, and 10. This skill requires that students count by the designated number— 2, 5, or 10—in increments up to a specified number, such as 20 for 2s, 30 for 5s, or 100 for 10s.

Teachers are interested in assessment to help them determine what students know and what they need to know. Assessing students' number sense can also tell teachers how students compare with others at their same age or grade level. Finally, appropriate assessments allow teachers to monitor students' progress and regularly make effective instructional decisions that influence students' performance.

Helping Students Improve in Math

The most important thing to remember as a teacher is to begin with the concrete and then move to the abstract when you are teaching new math concepts or when a student is having difficulty learning a math concept. Because all students have had opportunities to interact with objects, the process makes sense to them. By using examples from the manipulation to develop problems and to write them numerically, you bridge the gap between the abstractness of mathematics and students' need to learn the information concretely. You might start instruction using elements that contribute to systematic and explicit instruction, which include (Christenson, Ysseldyke, & Thurlow, 1989; Fuchs & Fuchs, 2003; Fuchs et al., 2008)

- The teaching strategy of demonstration–prompt–practice (see Tips for Teachers 14.5).
- Explicit instruction that not only involves highly organized step-by-step presentations related to the specific target skill, but also provides information about why learning this skill facilitates student learning.
- Assurance that students understand the directions and the task demands. Periodic checks are necessary to determine whether students understand the directions, and the teacher must monitor students' progress.
- The systematic use of learning principles. This refers to maintaining and using positive reinforcement, providing varied practice, and ensuring motivation.
- The use of everyday examples that are understandable and make sense to a wide range of youngsters based on their own experiences.
- Clearly articulated models with scripted examples of how these models can be used to promote instruction.

Go to **www.aplusmath.com/ Worksheets** where you can create worksheets for various math concepts.

Tips for Teachers 14.5

PROVIDING FEEDBACK THAT ENHANCES STUDENT LEARNING

Teachers are often reluctant to give feedback to students with disabilities, wondering whether they will do more damage than good. Specific feedback helps students learn when it is provided with teaching the student as the goal. Consider the following:

- Provide feedback informing students that their response is not accurate and cue them as to what is wrong. Give students an opportunity to try again. Recognize positively if students are successful in the next try. If not successful, provide even more instruction with another opportunity to demonstrate success.

- Remind students of what they know and have done successfully in the past that is related to the problem. Encourage them to use previous knowledge to solve the new problem.

- Ask students to monitor their problem resolution and reinforce them for checking and monitoring their learning.

- Provide readily available answers and feedback so that students wait a minimal amount of time after completing problems to know what they did right and what needs to be redone.

What can teachers do to ensure that students will improve their math performance? Baker, Gersten, and Lee's (2002) synthesis of the research suggests the following:

- Collect ongoing progress monitoring data to identify what students are learning and how quickly they are learning.
- Have peers assist one another in learning, applying, and reviewing math problems.
- Use explicit and systematic instruction in all elements of mathematics, including computation and problem solving. This type of instruction guides students through problems and calculations rather than relying on students to "figure it out" independently.
- Provide parents with information on how their children are performing and engage them as supporters and motivators for their children's progress in mathematics.

Math Manipulatives. Learning the language of mathematics is an important skill for all students. Peterson, Mercer, and O'Shea (1988) examined the effectiveness of a three-stage teaching sequence on students' abilities to learn place value. The sequence included going from concrete to semiconcrete and then to abstract teaching strategies. In the *concrete* stage, the mathematical concept was taught by using manipulative objects such as pegs. In the *semiconcrete* stage, pictorial representations were used for instruction. In the *abstract* stage, only numbers were used. Students who used this three-step process for learning place values significantly outperformed a control group. Tips for Teachers 14.6 shows another way to help students move from the concrete to the abstract.

What procedures can teachers develop for using concrete approaches and manipulatives in mathematics instruction? What instructional strategies work for helping students move from the concrete to the abstract?

Teaching for Comprehension. Teach students to understand math concepts. Most instruction is provided to ensure that the answer is correct, the math computation has been accurately completed, or the math fact is memorized. Additional emphasis on ensuring that students understand the math process needs to be included in the math curriculum. Jan Hughes, a third-grade teacher, continually asks students to say in their own words what she has just said. During math problem solving, she often asks students to work in groups of three to write story problems that go along with an operation she has just taught. She continually thinks about ways to make the mathematics she teaches "real" to students. The following section describes ways to check for comprehension in math instruction.

Tips for Teachers 14.6

HELPING STUDENTS MOVE FROM CONCRETE TO ABSTRACT LEARNING

- *Concrete.* Provide manipulative and interactive opportunities to integrate the new mathematical concept. For example, use pictures, blocks, rods, or other representations to demonstrate understanding of the answer. Encourage students to use both oral and written language to relate to the new mathematical vocabulary and concept.

- *Pictorial.* Represent the mathematics problem with pictures. Provide the problem and have students interpret it and draw pictures to represent it.

- *Linking.* Encourage students to talk about what they have learned and to explain it to others. By recording or

demonstrating what they have learned in meaningful ways, they can link their language to the mathematical algorithm.

- *Symbolic.* Have students demonstrate knowledge about the symbols by talking about them and demonstrating through drawing, pointing, or replicating the meaning of the symbol or algorithm.

- *Abstract.* Have students teach the steps for computing or problem solving with alternative solutions, and then solve problems in new and creative ways without using concrete or pictorial representations.

Checking for Comprehension: The Case of Trinette. Be certain that students understand the *meaning* of an operation, not just the answer. Students who have memorized the facts by rote often operate with little understanding of what they are doing. For example, Trinette was asked to write the answer to the following math problem:

$$3 \times 2 =$$

Answering correctly, she wrote 6. But when Trinette's teacher asked her to illustrate the problem with pictures of flowers, this is what Trinette drew:

Trinette demonstrated that she did not understand the problem, although she had successfully memorized the answer and her facts.

The following drawing illustrates how rows of chips can be used to illustrate multiplication. For example, ask, "How many fours make twenty?" "Fours are placed on the board _____ times."

$$4 \times \rule{3cm}{0.4pt} = 20$$

Other ways to check for comprehension include having students "talk aloud" about what is involved in solving a problem. Instead of letting them merely *read* the problem, ask them to *explain* what it means. For example, 63 − 27 could mean that someone had 63 pieces of gum and gave 27 pieces to a friend. Another strategy is to have one student explain the process to another student by using block manipulatives. For example, 24 + 31 is the same as adding 4 one-block pieces to 1 one-block piece and 2 ten-block pieces to 3 ten-block pieces. Some teachers use vocalization or have students close their eyes and use noises to illustrate operations. To illustrate multiplication, for example, the teacher and student might tap to indicate groups of six.

Using Constant Time Delay Procedure. Constant time delay is a procedure for teaching math facts that provides for the systematic introduction of teacher assistance. This nearly errorless technique employs a controlling prompt to ensure the successful performance of the student (Gast, Ault, Wolery, Doyle, & Belanger, 1988; Stevens & Schuster, 1988). In general, the procedure involves presentation of a stimulus (e.g., a word or math fact), after which the student is allowed a specific amount of time (e.g., 3 seconds) to provide the correct answer (e.g., read the word or answer the fact). If the student does not respond within the time allowed, a controlling prompt (typically a teacher modeling the correct response) is provided. The controlling prompt is a cue that ensures that the student will respond correctly (i.e., the word name or the answer to the problem is modeled). The student then repeats the teacher's model. Although correct responses before and after the prompt are reinforced, only correct responses given before the prompt count. The effectiveness of the constant time delay procedure has been demonstrated with a variety of academic skills, students, and instructional arrangements as demonstrated in the 60-Second Lesson (Mattingly & Bott, 1990; Schuster, Stevens, & Doak, 1990; Stevens & Schuster, 1987; Wolery, Cjybriwsky, Gast, & Boyle-Gast, 1991).

Providing Correction and Feedback. Immediate correction and feedback are essential to the success of students with math difficulties. Saying, "Orlando, the first six problems are correct, and then the third row is all wrong. Please redo them." is an example of insufficient feedback. Teachers often tell students which problems are correct and which are wrong and hope that this feedback is adequate. For students with learning problems, it is not. They need more sustained interaction to help them acquire not only the skills for identifying what they did wrong, but also the procedures for how to do it differently. The teacher must analyze the problem and also obtain sufficient information from the student to determine why the problem was not done correctly. A better model for correction and feedback follows: "Orlando, point to the problems you think are correct. Think about each problem before you point." (The teacher positively reinforces Orlando as he points to problems that are right.) "Yes, those are all correct. You did an excellent job with those. You started on the right, added them correctly, carried numbers when you needed to."

When students are first learning a math concept or operation, teachers need to provide a great deal of assistance to ensure that students perform correctly. Over time, teachers need to systematically reduce the amount of help they give students.

Providing Practice

Practice is important if students are to exhibit high levels of accuracy consistently and across multiple problem types. **Mastery** occurs when students meet expectations for accuracy and speed in different types of problems. In operations, mastery refers to the ability to use multiple algorithms to solve an operation so that students truly learn (rather than memorize). Denise, a ninth-grade student, expresses her frustration this way: "I never seem to be able to really learn anything. Just when I feel like I'm starting to get it, we move on to a different thing. I wish I could just stay with something until I really get it." As a teacher, you need to know when there are students like Denise who need additional support.

Counting by Numbers. Students are taught to "count by" numbers, beginning with 2, 10, and 5, and then 3, 4, 6, 7, 8, and 9. This is done by group counting, singing the numbers in sequence, writing the numbers, erasing some numbers in the sequence and having students fill them in, and having students work on worksheets with the count-by sequences.

After students have learned to count by numbers, they can apply the strategy to multiplication by using the following steps:

1. Ask students to point to the number they can count by.
2. Make hash marks to represent the number on the other side of the multiplication sign.
3. When you count by the number, point to each of the hash marks. The last number said when you reach the end of the hash marks is the answer to the problem.

Games. Games can be an important way for students to learn mathematics skills. Larson and Slaughter (1984) provide the following suggestions for using games in mathematics instruction:

■ *Choose games that reinforce present instruction.* Be sure that the selected game reinforces much of what students already know.

- *Consider the complexity of the game* so that students do not spend more time learning the game's procedures and rules than they spend learning the math-related material.
- *Foresee potential problems associated with games,* such as disruptive behavior and shouting out.
- *Provide an answer key if an adult is not available.*
- *Play at least one round of the game with students* to ensure that they understand the rules and procedures and are acquiring the mathematics skills desired.
- *Use aides or parent helpers to monitor the games.*

Strategies for Helping All Students Acquire Basic Math Skills

Mathematics instruction once focused on the acquisition of the basic math skills, saving problem solving for later in the math curriculum. We now realize that teaching basic skills and problem solving must be coordinated from the beginning of math instruction. Key components of basic math skills include the following:

- Prenumber
- Numeration
- Place value
- Fractions

Prenumber Skills

Many young students with learning problems come to school without certain basic prenumber skills necessary for initial success in mathematics. Sonya Perez, a first-grade teacher, described Malcolm in this way: "When he came to my class, he knew how to count to 10, but he didn't know what he was doing. He didn't know what the numbers meant. As far as he knew, he could have been saying his ABCs." She realized that he first needed to learn one-to-one correspondence.

One-to-One Correspondence.   Students demonstrate understanding of one-to-one correspondence when they are able to determine that each object corresponds to another object. For example, when a student puts out cereal bowls for himself, his sister, and his mother, he learns that each bowl represents one person. Early humans used one-to-one correspondence to keep track of their accounts. For example, a man might put a rock in a bucket to represent each bag of grain he gave to a neighbor. The following activities can be used to teach one-to-one correspondence:

- *Use everyday events to teach one-to-one correspondence.* Allow students with difficulties in this area to pass out materials. "Allison, please get one pair of scissors for each student in your group. Naja, you need to have a chair for each member of your group. How many chairs are there? How many more do you need?"
- *Use objects when you work with small groups of students who need help with one-to-one correspondence.* Give each student 10 small blocks. Place 3 blocks in the center. Say, "I want you to place a block next to each one in the center. As you place a block, I want you to say the number. I will do the first one, and then you do what I did."
- *Give students a set of cards with pictures on each card.* Ask students to put the correct number of objects (e.g., pegs) on top of each number card. Reverse the task by giving objects to students and asking them to put the correct picture card next to the objects.

Classification.   Classification, the ability to group or sort objects based on one or more common properties, is an important prenumber skill because it focuses students, making them attend to the common properties of objects and reduce large numbers of objects to smaller groups. Classification can be by size, color, shape, texture, or design. Most students are naturally interested in sorting and think that activities related to this prenumber skill are fun. Examples of such activities follow:

- Provide students with a bag of miscellaneous articles that vary in size, shape, and color. Ask students to sort the articles any way they like into an empty egg carton or empty plastic containers. After they finish, ask them to tell you the rules for sorting their articles.

After they have had a chance to listen to others, give them a chance to sort the articles again and to explain their rules for sorting.

■ Provide students with an empty egg carton and a box of small articles. Ask students to sort the articles by a single property, such as color. Now ask them whether there is another way in which they might be able to sort the articles. For example, ask them to consider size, texture, and so on.

■ Ask students to work in small groups, and provide them with a bag of articles. Ask one student to sort several of the articles by a property. Then ask other students in the group to guess the property that qualifies the articles for the group.

■ Use pictures for sorting tasks. Good pictures include ones that represent animals, foods, plants, and toys.

■ Board games and bingo games can be played by sorting or classifying shapes, colors, and pictures.

Seriation.   Seriation, the ability to rank objects according to the degree to which they possess a certain common characteristic, is similar to classification in that it depends on the recognition of common attributes of objects but differs from classification in that the order in which objects are placed depends on the extent to which each object possesses the attribute. For example, seriation can occur by length, height, color, or weight. Sample activities for teaching seriation follow:

■ Give students a long piece of string. Ask them to cut the string into pieces of various lengths. Then ask them to put the lengths in order from shortest to longest. Now ask students to work in groups of three. Have them use those same piles of string to create one long seriation, from shortest to longest. Continue to ask students to work in different groups to sort the string sizes.

■ Ask students to work in groups of eight. In these groups, ask them to put themselves in order from shortest to tallest. Now ask them to put themselves in order from longest to shortest hair. Continue asking students to put themselves in seriation based on different attributes.

■ Using a peg with various sizes of rings, ask students to put the rings on the peg from largest to smallest.

■ Fill jars of the same size with different amounts of sand or water and ask students to put them in order.

See Activities for All Learners later in the chapter for more activities.

Working with Numeration

Numeration is the understanding of numbers and their manipulations. Do not assume that because students can count or identify numbers that they understand the value and the meaning of the numbers. This is a mistake that many teachers and parents make.

Understanding numerals is an extremely important basic concept, one that throws many children into mathematical confusion early. A good example is Michelle, whose early experiences with math were positive. She learned to say, read, and write numbers with little or no difficulty. In first and second grade, she mastered addition and subtraction facts and did these problems easily. When Michelle was asked to do problems that involved addition with regrouping (adding numerals and then converting them to tens, hundreds, thousands etc.), her lack of knowledge of numerals and their meaning quickly became evident. Following are examples of the way Michelle did some problems:

$$27 + 15 = 312$$
$$49 + 36 = 715$$

As you can see from Michelle's answers, she remembered her math facts, such as 7 + 5 and 2 + 1, or 9 + 6 and 4 + 3, but did not understand what the numbers meant. Michelle added 7 plus 5 to get 12 and then 2 plus 1 to get 3 resulting in the answer 312; however, Michelle did not understand the importance of place value nor did she "check" her answer by estimating a reasonable answer and determining if she was even close.

Understanding numeration and place value is necessary for progress in computation. Like Michelle, many students fail to make adequate progress in math because they do not understand the meaning of the numerals and the place value with which they are working. For example, students who understand the meaning of the numerals 25 and 17 would be less likely to make the following conceptual error:

$$25 - 17 = 12$$

Estimating. Many students with learning difficulties in math do not have a sense of how much a certain amount really is—what it means to have five dollars, for example, or how many eggs are in a dozen, or about what 15 and 15, added together, should equal. These students cannot check their answers to determine how far off they are because they do not have a good idea of what an answer that makes sense would be.

Estimating is something that can be done throughout the day and throughout the curriculum. For example, start the day by asking students to estimate how many children are absent. Estimation can be included in subject matters as well. You can use estimation in science, social studies, and even with art projects.

Why is extra practice in estimation and other basic math skills important for students with math difficulties? How can instruction in those skills be modified for students with learning problems?

Students who do not understand the real meaning of numerals have difficulty applying computation to everyday problems. For example, when Michelle's teacher posed the following problem, Michelle did not understand how to begin to find the answer: "Let's pretend that you had three one-dollar bills and you were going to McDonald's to buy lunch. Let's pretend that your hamburger costs 89 cents, your French fries cost 74 cents, and your medium-sized Coke costs 69 cents. How much money would you have left to spend?"

Mistakes occur when students attempt problems that are entirely too difficult for them or when they do not understand the idea behind the problem. In such cases, the solutions students provide are totally unreasonable given the problem. One of the best ways to help students who demonstrate this problem is to continually ask them to think about the problem and estimate what their answer probably will be. For example, before computing the problem 24 plus 73, ask students what they would estimate the answer would be. If students have difficulty even identifying a reasonable response, help them round up or down the two numbers so they are easier to estimate. In the previous problem, students can round up 24 to 25 and 73 to 75. That way they can guess that the answer will be very close to 100. When students are taught to consider what a reasonable answer should be, they are better able to catch their mistakes. These problems are particularly severe for students with disabilities who demonstrate low understanding of mathematical problems and the meaning of numbers (Lucangeli, Coi, & Bosco, 1997).

Understanding Regrouping. Regrouping refers to converting from tens to ones or hundreds to tens, etc., so that borrowing can occur. Many children have difficulty with regrouping. Regrouping errors are less likely to occur when students understand numeration. Following are examples of regrouping errors:

$$39 + 27 = 516$$
$$56 - 18 = 42$$
$$41 - 24 = 23$$

Examine the errors students make and use the information to provide instruction. For example, some students subtract the smaller number from the larger number regardless of the problem. These students need practicing reading the entire number and determining which number is larger. Practicing reading numbers and stating which one is bigger or smaller may be helpful to them. Furthermore, students who consistently make errors in regrouping can practice subtracting smaller numbers (e.g., single digit numbers) until they can do so automatically and correctly before doing more complex numbers.

Understanding Zero. Students need to understand that zero is a number and means more than "nothing." In the number 30, for example, students need to understand that the number zero is a placeholder. For the number 306, students need to understand that there are 0 tens and that zero is serving as a placeholder.

Understanding Place Value

Before students can understand place value, they must understand numeration. Students who know the meaning of numbers will have far less difficulty understanding place value. For example, if a student knows what 56 actually means, then when someone talks about the tens place equaling 50, the student will not be confused. When someone talks about the ones place equaling 6 ones, the student will understand what is meant.

Grouping by Ones and Tens. To teach grouping, start with manipulatives (buttons, sticks, and blocks are useful), then pictures, and then numbers. Ask students to practice grouping by ones and tens. Students can also develop a table to record their answers, as follows:

HUNDREDS	TENS	ONES	NUMERALS
1	3	1	131
1	2	3	123
1	4	5	145

Use "ten blocks" and "single blocks" to represent numerals. For example, 35 can be represented as follows:

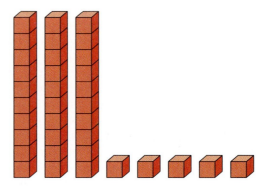

Naming Tens. Teach students to identify numerals by the number of tens. For example, 6 tens is 60, 4 tens is 40, 8 tens is 80, and so on. Give students opportunities to count by tens and then name the number. For example, "Count by tens three times." "10, 20, 30." "Count by tens seven times." "10, 20, 30, 40, 50, 60, 70." Also give students opportunities to draw picture diagrams that represent the place values of tens and ones and to identify the number.

Place Value Beyond Two Digits. When students can accurately group and identify numbers at the two-digit level, introduce them to three- and four-digit numbers. It is a good idea to be certain that students have mastered the concept of two-digit place value before you introduce numerals and place value. Give students plenty of opportunity to group, orally name, and sequence three- and four-digit place values.

Because place value is a skill taught during the primary grades, older students who have not adequately learned the skill will have difficulty with computation and word problems and may have little opportunity to learn place value. Many of the games and activities designed to teach place value are aimed at young children and are less appropriate for older students. Tips for Teachers 14.7 provides sources of numbers that may be useful for teaching place value to older students.

Learning Fractions

Although often thought of as one of the more difficult mathematical skills, fractions are actually introduced early in the mathematics curriculum. Children between the ages of 3 and 5 discover fractions when they begin to cook. "Pour in ½ cup of milk and ⅓ cup of raisins" is often a youngster's introduction to fractions. Sharing—as in "Give half of your cookie to your sister"—is also a good way for children to discover fractions.

SOURCES OF NUMBERS FOR TEACHING PLACE VALUE TO OLDER STUDENTS

- An odometer
- Numbers from students' science or social studies texts
- Numbers from school population (e.g., number of first-year students, sophomores, juniors, seniors, and so on)
- Population data from town, county, state, or country
- Financial data page from the newspaper

The teaching of fractions, mirroring that of other computations, proceeds from concrete to abstract. Many manipulative aids can be used to teach fractions: colored rods, cardboard strips and squares, blocks, fractional circle wheels, cooking utensils such as measuring cups and spoons, and any unit divider (e.g., egg cartons and muffin pans).

Students with learning problems are unlikely to learn fractions, however, unless they are taught directly and systematically (Engelmann, Carnine, & Steely, 2005). Such teaching includes the following:

- ■ *Systematic practice in discriminating among different problem types.* Students with learning disabilities and behavior problems often confuse algorithms when they compute fractions. For example, when adding fractions the denominator stays the same as in ¼ plus ¾ = ⁴⁄₄ or 1. However, when dividing with fractions the denominator changes.
- ■ *Separation of confusing elements and terminology.* Because much of the language of learning fractions is unfamiliar and confusing, students are more likely to learn fractions successfully when the language and concepts are clearly explained and illustrated.
- ■ *Use of a wide range of elements to illustrate each concept.* Students have a difficult time generalizing beyond the number of examples provided by the teacher; therefore, by providing many different examples, you help students understand.

The teaching sequence for fractions, which ensures that each student can do certain work, follows:

1. *Manipulate concrete models.* Students must use fraction blocks and pegs and use instruments that require understanding of fractions (such as measuring cups, spoons, and rulers).
2. *Match fractional models.* Students must match halves, thirds, and fourths. One way to do this is to think about the role of fractions when dividing food such as pizza or pieces of cake.
3. *Point to fractional model when the teacher names a fraction.* When the teacher says "half," the student selects a model of "half" from several answers.
4. *Name fractional units when the teacher selects it.* When the teacher points to a fractional unit such as a "fourth," the student names it.
5. *Draw diagrams or use manipulatives to represent fractional units.* When the teacher says or writes fractional units such as "whole," "half," and "third," the student uses manipulative drawings to represent these units.
6. *Write fraction names when given fractional drawings.* When the teacher shows the student a picture of a fractional unit, the student writes the name of the fraction.
7. *Use fractions to solve problems.* Fractions are very helpful for dividing the cost of a bill when eating out or when dividing food such as a pie.

Strategies for Helping All Learners Acquire and Use Computation Skills

The emphasis on problem solving from NCTM (2000) does not mean that students do not need to learn math computation. In fact, students will be unsuccessful problem solvers if they spend too little time on math computation. You can help students with special needs, who often have difficulty with math computation, by addressing the following issues that present obstacles for these students.

Go to **www.superkids.com/ aweb/tools/math,** where you can create worksheets on addition, subtraction, multiplication, division, fractions, and more. There are also games available on the site.

Patterns of Common Computation Errors

The computation errors that students make fit certain patterns. Rourke (1993) identifies common types of mechanical arithmetic errors, described in the following sections. Tips for Teachers 14.8 has suggestions for helping students learn computational techniques.

Tips for Teachers 14.8

TEACHING STUDENTS COMPUTATIONAL STRATEGIES

1. *Use doubles.* Students know that $2 + 2 = 4$, $3 + 3 = 6$, and $5 + 5 = 10$. With this basic information, they can easily compute related facts. For example, if $3 + 3 = 6$, what is $3 + 4$? Yes, it is one more.

2. *Count on.* Students do not need to resort to counting from 1 to solve math facts. They can learn to count on from the largest numeral in an addition fact. For example, $8 + 3$ means counting on 3 more from 8, for a sum of 11. Students learn to count on 3 more from 8: "9, 10, 11." The answer is the last number they say after they have counted on the correct number. Students can use this same principle for subtraction. For example, when asked to solve the following problem:

$$8 - 3 =$$

   they now count backward from eight, "7, 6, 5." Again, the last number is the answer.

3. *Use the commutative idea.* With addition and multiplication, the order of the numbers does not matter—it always yields the same answer. For example, $3 + 4 = 7$ and $4 + 3 = 7$. With multiplication, this is also true: $4 \times 6 = 24$ and $6 \times 4 = 24$. Give students many opportunities to use this principle to be sure they understand and apply it.

4. *Think one more or one less than a known fact.* When students know a math fact, teach them that they also know related math facts. For example, Guido knew that $6 + 7 = 13$. When he was faced with the problem $6 + 8 = \rule{1cm}{0.4pt}$, he panicked. When his teacher told him that 8 is one more than 7, thus the answer is one more than $6 + 7 = 13$, he was able to solve the problem quickly. Pictures such as the following can help to illustrate the principle:

   $5 + 5 = 10$ ♥♥ ♥♥
   ♥♥♥ + ♥♥♥ =
   $5 + 6 =$ ♥♥ ♥♥
   ♥♥♥ + ♥♥♥ =
   $5 + 4 =$ ♥♥ ♥♥
   ♥♥♥ + ♥ =

5. *Using tens.* Students can learn that $10 +$ any single-digit number merely changes the 0 in the 10 to the number they are adding to it, as in the following examples:

$$10 + 4 = 14$$
$$10 + 8 = 18$$

6. *Using nines.* There are two strategies students can apply to addition facts that involve nines. First, they can think of the 9 as a 10 and then subtract 1 from the answer. In the following example, the student is taught to "think" of the 9 as a 10:

9	think	10
+6		+6
		$16 - 1 = 15$

   Second, students can think that whenever there is a 9 in an addition problem, the answer in the ones column is always one less than the number they are adding to the 9. For example:

9	8	9
+4	+9	+6
13	17	15

7. *Counting by twos, threes, fours, fives, and tens.* Beginning with 10, teach students to count by the number. This can be done with individual students or with a small group. It is sometimes helpful to develop a rhythm to the counting sequence:

$$10-20-30-40-50-60-70-80-90-100$$

   After students can count by tens to 100, ask them to count aloud by 10 from two points other than 10 and 100. For example, "Count aloud from 20 to 80." After students have learned to count by tens, they should be taught to count by fives and then by twos, threes, and fours. Being able to count by multiples helps in addition, multiplication, and division. Multiplication facts can be taught by interpreting 3×4 as counting by threes four times. Division facts, such as 8 divided by 2, can be interpreted as "How many times do you count by twos before you reach 8?"

8. *Relationship between addition and subtraction and between multiplication and division.* After students learn addition facts, they can be shown the relationship between the addition fact and subtraction. For example, students who know $7 + 6 = 13$ can learn the relationships between the known addition fact and the subtraction fact, $13 - 7 = \rule{1cm}{0.4pt}$. Whenever possible, reinforce this principle as students are working: "You know $8 + 4 = 12$, so $12 - 4$ must be $\rule{1cm}{0.4pt}$." Give students known facts and ask them to form subtraction problems. These sample relationships can be used to teach multiplication and division facts.

Sources: Adapted from Bley, N. S., & Thornton, C. A. (2001). *Teaching mathematics to students with learning disabilities;* Thornton, C. A., & Toohey, M. A. (1985). Basic math facts: Guidelines for teaching and learning. *Learning Disabilities Focus, 1,* 44–57; and Thornton, C. A., Tucker, B. F., Dossey, J. A., & Brazik, E. F. (1983). *Teaching mathematics to children with special needs.* Menlo Park, CA: Addison-Wesley.

Spatial Organization. Mistakes in spatial organization are those that occur because students misalign numbers in columns. These mistakes can occur when students copy problems incorrectly or as they solve problems. One way to help students correct misaligned numbers is to tell them to draw vertical lines through their numbers to ensure that ones, tens, and hundreds are all in the right place. Another way to help is to provide graph paper with large squares so that students can write the numbers in boxes and more easily align them.

Visual Detail. Mistakes involving **visual detail** occur when students misread one aspect of the arithmetic problem—misreading a minus sign as a plus sign, for example, or disregarding a dollar sign. Because many of the problems that occur in mathematics can be easily corrected by the student, teach students to stop and reread the problem and their answers before they go to the next problem to be sure that they neither misread nor omitted something.

Procedural Error. **Procedural error** occurs when students misapply a procedure from one arithmetic operation to another. For example, a student learns that $5 \times 5 = 25$, and when asked to complete the problem $5 + 5$ misapplies information from multiplication and writes the answer 25.

Failure to Shift Operations. A **failure to shift operations** occurs when students fail to move to another operation after completing one operation. This occurs in word problems that involve more than one step, such as subtraction and addition. To help students who demonstrate this problem, ask them to reread the problem and tell you whether more than one operation is involved. Ask them to identify the types of operations involved and to provide an example of each one. Ask them to tell you how they will monitor their process and to determine how they will ensure accuracy in switching from one operation to the next.

Motoric Problems. Mistakes resulting from **motoric problems** can occur when the students' writing is so difficult to read that it leads to errors in arithmetic. Many students with learning problems demonstrate such poor writing ability that it interferes with their ability to successfully perform arithmetic computations. These students have difficulty not only writing their numbers but also reading them. They often mistake their fives for threes, their twos for threes, and so on. Therefore, their calculations may be accurate, according to their interpretation of the number, but the answers are wrong because they have mistaken the number.

Memory Problems. Mistakes resulting from **memory problems** occur when students forget or misremember a fact that leads to an error in arithmetic calculation. As a teacher, you can help students with learning problems by providing them with adequate time and frequent opportunities to rehearse and learn arithmetic facts.

Difficulty with Zero. **Difficulty with zero** can lead to mistakes that occur when students do not understand the multiple meanings and uses of zero. Many students with learning problems learn that zero means "nothing," and they never really understand that zero is a number or the role of zero as a placeholder. The best way to help students who have difficulty with zero is to ensure that they understand how zero can be used as a placeholder. To facilitate understanding and adequate use of zero, you can teach a mini lesson to a small group of students who demonstrate difficulty with this concept such as the one described in the 60-Second Lesson.

PEARSON
myeducationlab

Go to the Building Teaching Skills and Dispositions section of Topic 8: Instructional Practices and Learning Strategies in the MyEducationLab for your course and complete the activity entitled *Helping Learners Remember and Retrieve Information.*

60 *Second* LESSON

The Meaning of "Zero"

In a 60-second lesson the teacher might indicate that the term *zero* has several meanings.

- "What is one of the meanings of *zero*?" "Yes, zero means 'nothing'."

- "If you have zero candy, you have no candy."

- "A different meaning of zero is as a placeholder when we are writing numbers. For example, in the number 100, the zeros

tell us that the number is a LOT more than 1." The teacher can then delete the zero at the end of the number 100.

- The teacher then asks, "What number is this? Yes, the new number is 10. The zero at the end tells us that the number is more than 1 but a lot less than the previous number 100."

The teacher can then add additional examples.

Computation and Calculators

There is a preponderance of evidence that calculators assist in the acquisition of mathematics achievement for students with learning problems. Reviews of the calculator research have drawn the following conclusions:

- Calculators for instructional purposes do not impede the acquisition of basic skills. In fact, calculators can increase skill acquisition.
- The advantages of using calculators are more obvious for problems that include computation than for problem solving.
- Students who use calculators on criterion tests produce higher achievement scores than students who do not.
- Studies indicate that students do not develop a negative attitude toward math because of calculator use. In fact, calculators improve students' attitudes toward mathematics.
- It is appropriate to introduce calculators at the same time that the paper-and-pencil methods are taught.
- Students can develop their own complex problems and then solve them with use of the calculator. This also serves to increase their self-concept about math skills.

Students are more likely to be persistent in solving math problems and have a better attitude toward math when they use technology supports (Cawley, Foley, & Doan, 2003). Tech Tips provides examples of some of these supports.

Geary (2003) and Hofmeister (1989) provide a summary of the research on math problem solving:

- Most students with significant learning problems have well-developed number concepts but do have difficulties with even simple arithmetic.
- Some generalization of problem-solving skills should be planned for and systematically taught. This generalization is most likely to occur across problems without a domain. Transfer across domains will depend on the similarity of the problem.
- It may be unreasonable to expect the majority of specific problem-solving strategies in one domain, such as ratio-based word problems, to transfer to another domain, such as geometry proofs.
- The development of practical problem-solving skills will require a considerable investment of time and explicitly taught strategies and practices.
- Teaching of problem-solving strategies should be integrated with the teaching of other content in the domain, such as computational and factual knowledge.

Understanding the research on teaching problem-solving skills to all students will better prepare you to apply effective strategies for teaching students problem-solving skills.

 *Tech* TIPS

TECHNOLOGY THAT HELPS STUDENTS SOLVE MATH PROBLEMS

Many educational software programs, with varying foci. are designed to enhance mathematics instruction. As a tool or utility, programs that offer students and teachers ease of use can be extremely helpful in accommodating all learners in your class.

MathPad and MathPad Plus and Number Concepts by Cabmium LearningTechnologies, Inc. at
▶ http://store.cambiumlearning.com/SearchResultsHP.aspx? searchtype = Subject&sorttype = Subject&Query = Mathematics&site = itc
These programs, designed for students K–8, enable learners to do arithmetic directly on the computer. These programs are ideal for learners who need help organizing or navigating through math problems or who have difficulty using pencil and paper with math.

AAA Math at
▶ www.aaamath.com
This web resource for math activities is loaded with explanations, interactive practice, and games, along with teacher resources.

Ten Tricky Tiles by Sunburst Technologies at
▶ http://store.sunburst.com/Category.aspx?MODE = RESULTS&CATID = 3360
This program is for young children who are developing their arithmetic and number skills. Sunburst Technologies offers numerous math programs for all ages and skill levels.

Strategies for Helping All Students Develop Problem-Solving Skills

Teaching problem-solving skills is an important aspect of effective math instruction. There are several unifying components that include

- A mathematics knowledge base.
- An application of knowledge to new and unfamiliar situations.
- An ability to actively engage in thinking processes and apply this knowledge base to problems.

Each of these components must be present in order to help all students understand how to develop problem-solving skills.

Teaching Problem-Solving Strategies to Secondary Students

Mercer and Miller (1992) have developed a procedure called FAST DRAW to teach the concrete–representational–abstract teaching principle advocated in mathematics instruction. The Strategic Math Series is the name of their program. Following is an explanation of the **FAST DRAW** strategy:

Find what you're solving for.
Ask yourself, "What are the parts of the problem?"
Set up the numbers.
Tie down the sign.
Discover the sign.
Read the problem.
Answer or draw a conceptual representation of the problem, using lines and tallies, and check.
Write the answer.

Since many students with disabilities benefit from cognitive problem-solving instruction (Alter, Wrick, Brown, & Lingo, 2008; Montague, 1992), teachers are finding a multistep process useful:

1. Read the problem aloud. If students have difficulty reading, read the problem to them.
2. Ask students to think about and identify the key words in the problem using their own words.
3. Ask students to visualize the problem or draw it.
4. Guide students in putting the key parts of the problem in their own words.
5. Help students determine a reasonable hypothesis for solving the problem.
6. Ask students to estimate an answer.
7. Provide guided instruction as students calculate the answer.

Solving algebra word problems is a challenging task for many older students with math difficulties. Cognitive strategies such as asking themselves questions (self-question), thinking aloud, providing guided practice, and using graphs to monitor their progress may be helpful. Students displayed increased abilities to solve problems and transferred their skills to other settings. The self-questions Hutchinson (1993) used included the following:

- Have I read and understood the sentence?
- Do I have the whole picture, a representation, for this problem?
- Have I written the representation on the worksheet?

In summary, when teaching story problems to students with learning and behavior difficulties, keep the following guidelines in mind (Bos & Vaughn, 2006):

- Be certain students can perform the arithmetic computation before introducing the computation in story problems.

By acquiring a good mathematics knowledge base, students learn the strategies for developing problem-solving skills.

PEARSON myeducationlab

To enhance your understanding of how to use learning strategies to teach intermediate algebra, go to the IRIS Center Resources section of Topic 10: Content Area Teaching in the MyEducationLab for your course and complete Case 1: Algebra (Part 1): Applying Learning Strategies to Beginning Algebra.

- Develop a range of story problems that contain the type of problem you want students to learn to solve so that they have adequate opportunities to practice and learn the pattern of the story problem.
- Instruct with one type of problem until mastery is attained.
- Teach students to read through the word problem and visualize the situation. Ask them to read the story aloud and tell what it is about.
- Ask students to reread the story, this time to get the facts.
- Identify the key question. In the beginning stages of problem solving, students should write the key question so that it can be referred to when computation is complete.
- Identify extraneous information. Tell students to note that this information will not be used.
- Reread the story problem and attempt to state the situation in a mathematical sentence. The teacher plays an important role in this step by asking the students questions and guiding them in formulating the arithmetic problem.
- Tell students to write the arithmetic problem and compute the answer. Students can compute some problems in their heads without completing this step.
- Tell students to reread the key questions and be sure that they have completed the problem correctly.
- Ask students whether their answer is likely, based on their estimate.

What should teachers consider when they design math problem-solving activities for students with special needs? To what extent will these designs benefit other students? The instructional practices that we recommend for teaching problem solving will benefit all students. Tips for Teachers 14.8 should be helpful as you design and implement problem-solving activities for students with learning problems.

Integrating Math Problem Solving into the Curriculum

Problem solving does not have to occur only during math time; it is an interesting and fun activity to integrate into the rest of the curriculum as well. Math story problems are especially easy to integrate into the reading curriculum. How? Take stories that children are reading or books that you are reading to the entire class and change the stories so that they include numbers and problems the students need to answer.

Joan Lindquist, a third-grade teacher, asked students the following questions about a story they were reading in class: "How many friends has Marcia told us about? How many friends does Linda have? Altogether, how many friends do they have? How many more friends does Linda have than Marcia?" Teachers can also add information to the stories and then ask children to solve word problems based on the additional information provided. They can then have students work in pairs to write their own word problems from the stories they are reading and have them read their word problems to the entire class so that the class can solve them.

Word problems can be easily integrated into the social studies curriculum as well. When dates are discussed, ask students to compute how many years ago the event occurred. Ask students word problems about the age of central figures in the social studies lesson. Add numbers and information to the lesson and construct word problems. Integrating math into other content areas is an important means of promoting generalization of math concepts. See Activities for All Learners for a variety of mathematics activities suitable for all learners.

Return to the interview at the beginning of this chapter, where you met Shawn, a college student with learning disabilities who had extreme difficulty with math. What questions would you want to ask him? If Shawn were in your class, how would you implement the suggestions in this chapter to ensure that his experiences in mathematics would be as positive as possible? Remember, you *can* make a difference in students' lives.

Activities FOR ALL Learners

Mathematics Activities for All Learners

Slap it!!!

Objective: To provide practice in responding quickly to math

Grades: Second through eighth grade

Materials: A set of 4-inch by 6-inch cards on which the answers to math facts are written; cards can be established as answers to addition, subtraction, multiplication, or division facts

Teaching Procedures:

1. Students and teacher stand around a small table (preferably round), and teacher shows students the cards, each with a number (the answer to a math fact). Teacher spreads the cards (approximately 10) on the table with the number side up.

2. Students are told to keep both hands on the table until the teacher says, "Go." Students who lift either hand prior to the "go" signal are eliminated from that round of competition.

3. The teacher says a computation problem, followed by the word go. For example, "6 × 7 = (go)."

4. Students slap the card that has the correct answer. The first hand on the card gets to keep the card. The student with the most cards gets to be the teacher.

Adaptations:

1. Teachers can use the same game with word problems.

2. Teachers can use more than one computation during the game.

MEASUREMENT

Objective: To reinforce understanding of perimeter and area

Grades: Third grade and above

Materials: 1-inch graph paper, scissors, teacher-made table worksheet

Teaching Procedures:

1. Have students cut out squares of graph paper of different sizes: a 1-inch square, a 2-inch square, a 3-inch square, a 4-inch square, and a 5-inch square.

2. Measure the number of small squares in each large cutout square, and complete the following table:

edges	1	2	3	4	5	6
perimeter						
area						

3. Ask, "What happens to the perimeter and area each time the edges are doubled?"

4. Have students experiment with different-size squares and then complete the table.

Source: Reprinted with permission of the publisher, Teaching K–8, Norwalk, CT 06854. From the April 1993 issue of Teaching K–8.

SUBTRACTION WITH MONEY

Objective: To introduce the concept of subtraction of three-digit numbers with regrouping, using play money

Grades: Third grade and above

Materials: Play money (20 one-dollar bills, 20 dimes, and 20 pennies for each student), place-value board for each student

Teaching Procedures:

1. Review 100 pennies = 1 dollar

    10 pennies = 1 dime

    10 dimes = 1 dollar

2. Write example on the board: $5.36
    $$-1.27$$

3. Student makes $5.36 on place-value board.

4. Teacher begins questioning: "You have 6 pennies; you have to give me 7 pennies. Do you have enough pennies?" "Can you trade something?" "That's right. 1 dime = 10 pennies. Take 1 dime from your dimes place and trade it for 10 pennies from your bank. Put the 10 pennies in the pennies place." "Now, how many pennies do you have?" "Can you take 7 pennies

away? How many are left?" (Teacher writes 9 in the ones column.) "Can you take 1 dollar away? How many are left?" (Teacher writes 3 in the hundreds place.)

5. Give students ample guided practice with one trade before giving them independent practice in pairs. Encourage students to self-question while completing each step.

Modifications: When students become proficient in subtracting with one trade, provide examples of problems involving two trades.

"99"

Objective: To generalize and practice adding numbers in one's head or on paper

Grades: Intermediate to high school

Materials: (1) Playing cards; (2) paper and pencils

Teaching Procedures: Explain that the objective of this game is to add cards up to a score of 99. Establish the following rules:

    Jacks and Queens = 10
    Kings = 99
    Nines = "free turn" pass; to be used anytime
    Fours = pass
    Aces = 1
    Other cards = face value

Each player is dealt three cards. The rest of the cards go face down on a draw pile. The players take turns discarding one card from their hand face up on a discard pile and drawing one card from the draw pile to put back in their hand. As a player discards his or her card, he or she must add the number from the card to any previous score acquired up to that point in the game and give the new score out loud. Note the exception: If a player plays a nine, he or she receives a free-turn pass. If a player plays a four, he or she has to pass a turn with no score. The first player to score higher than 99 loses the game.

Source: Adapted from Bos, C. S., & Vaughn, S. (2006). Strategies for teaching students with learning and behavior problems (6th ed.). Boston: Allyn & Bacon.

Differentiating Instruction and Assessment for Middle and High School Students

FOCUS QUESTIONS

1. What is the standards-based movement and what challenges does it bring to secondary teachers?

2. What is differentiated instruction and how can it be implemented in secondary classrooms?

3. What can you do to prepare lessons that can engage all students?

4. What procedures can you use to learn the strengths and weaknesses of your textbook and how can you differentiate reading assignments for students with reading difficulties?

5. How can you differentiate assessment to meet the needs of all learners?

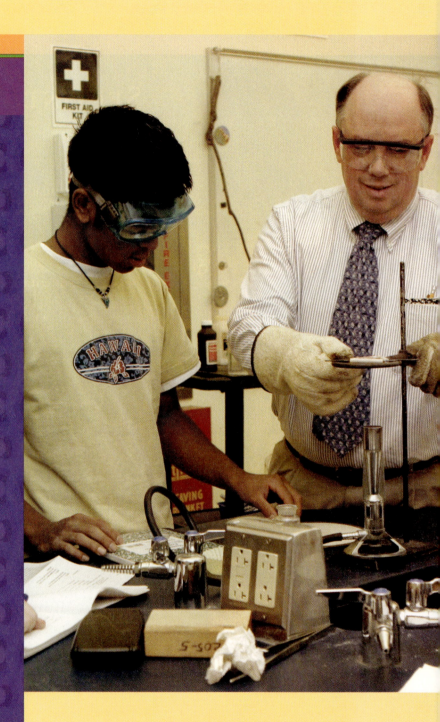

Jerry Schumm is a social studies teacher at Ponce de Leon Middle Community School, an urban school that is among the most ethnically mixed in the city of Miami, Florida. He teaches approximately 175 eighth graders in six different U.S. history classes. Twelve of his students have been school-identified as having learning disabilities. Thus, Jerry's students represent a wide range of cultural, linguistic, and academic diversity. The challenge of meeting the needs of diverse learners is coupled with a challenging, fast-paced curriculum.

Jerry explains, "We are expected to provide an overview of all of U.S. history in eighth grade. Not only do we teach to demanding state standards, we also are expected to take some class time out to have students complete reading passages and questions that are similar to what they will have on their high-stakes tests. We are on block schedule—so I see each class for 100 minutes every other day. Needless to say the time rushes by and it is very tough to keep up, much less teach anything in depth."

Jerry Schumm recognizes that standards help to focus instruction and to make links with teacher-made assessments. Many of the standards in social studies are aligned with reading competencies on the state's high-stakes test. Nonetheless, trying to address all standards is daunting. As Jerry put it, "Since I took U.S. history in middle school, we've added 40 years of U.S. history. Trying to cover it all—even in a survey class—is tough. I work hard to examine the curriculum carefully, select instructional materials that are motivating and directed to the standards, and design tests and assignments that hit key ideas. I also think about what support my struggling students will need to meet standards and what more advanced students might need to stretch."

Introduction

The challenges Jerry experiences are the same that face many secondary teachers, both novice and seasoned. For many middle and high school teachers striking a balance between somewhat conflicting demands can be daunting. This chapter begins with a discussion of the standards-based movement and the challenges it brings to secondary teachers. Next, the chapter provides a definition of differentiated instruction and why it is necessary for secondary learners. It continues with concrete suggestions for preparing lessons and textbook readings that can accommodate a range of student needs. Finally, the chapter provides information about how you can differentiate assessment. In Chapter 15 the focus is on teacher actions and activities. In Chapter 16 you'll learn more about how you can empower students to become independent, successful learners.

Standards-Based Instruction

Like Jerry Schumm, teachers in middle and high school are often required to plan their instruction according to a set of standards determined by state or school district curriculum frameworks. An educational standard "is a statement that depicts what students should know or be able to do as a result of teaching and learning" (Conley, 2005, p. 5). Some states also adopt benchmarks or specific student behaviors that indicate they have mastered a particular standard. Figure 15.1 includes samples of standards that Jerry incorporates in his lessons.

The standards movement was ignited by the 1983 report of the National Commission on Excellence in Education titled *A Nation at Risk,* which brought public attention to the state of education in the United States. Although controversial, the report did spawn school reform and the standards movement (Marzano & Haystead, 2008; Ravitch, 1995; Resnick & Zurawsky, 2005). Standards are intended to bring coherence and comprehensiveness to curricula and serve as curricular frameworks. The National Council of Teachers of Mathematics (NCTM) was the first

FIGURE
15.1

Sample U.S. History Standards

Standard 4. The student understands United States history to 1880.

1. Knows factors involved in the development of cities and industries (e.g., religious needs, the need for military protection, the need for a marketplace, changing spatial patterns, and geographical factors for location such as transportation and food supply).

2. Knows the role of physical and cultural geography in shaping events in the United States (e.g., environmental and climatic influences on settlement of the colonies, the American Revolution, the Civil War).

3. Understands the impact of significant people and ideas on the development of values and traditions in the United States prior to 1880.

4. Understands ways state and federal policy influenced various Native American nations throughout United States history (for example, Cherokee and Choctaw removals, loss of Native American homelands, Black Hawk War, removal policies in the Old Northwest).

Source: Florida Sunshine State Standards, grades 6–8 Social Studies. Retrieved from myflorida.com February 14, 2009.

professional organization to introduce standards for the teaching of mathematics (NCTM, 1989). Since that time, professional organizations representing other content areas have developed sets of standards as well.

Since the authorization of No Child Left Behind (2001), states have adopted curriculum standards for middle and high school subjects. State and local curriculum standards are typically more detailed versions of professional standards (Darling-Hammond, 2007; Vacca & Vacca, 2008). State standards vary widely in terms of content and rigor (Peterson & Hess, 2008), so it is important that you become familiar with the standards for your subject area. Your state department of education website lists standards for the subject areas and grade levels you teach.

Advocates of standards-based on instruction cite potential benefits such as alignment with content on high-stakes tests, focused instruction, and uniformity of curriculum (Resnick & Zurawsky, 2005; Schmoker & Marzano, 1999). Proponents also pose that standards can form the basis for differentiating instruction based individual student performance in relationship to each standard (Cooper & Kiger, 2009). Critics of curriculum standards maintain that student outcomes are not necessarily rising as a result of standards-based education (Amrein & Berliner, 2002) and that authentic learning and student engagement are dwindling (Certo, Cauley, Moxley, & Chafin, 2008; Pedulla et al., 2003). Some educators and students argue that standards are too high for some students and not high enough for others (Glass, 2004; Matus, 2009; Viadero, 2007). Still others observe that because of the sometimes-excessive number of standards, content coverage is gained while in-depth inquiry is lost (Certo, Cauley, Moxley, & Chafin, 2008; Marzano & Haystead, 2008; Mastropieri et al., 2005). Gunning (2003) advises, "Although controversial and undoubtedly incorporating a number of drawbacks, the standards movement is now well established. Perhaps the best plan is to take advantage of its positive aspects . . . and work to ameliorate or eliminate its negative features" (p. 11). Tips for Teachers 15.1 provides suggestions for how to make standards-based instruction work for you.

Tips for Teachers 15.1

MAKING STANDARDS-BASED INSTRUCTION WORK FOR YOU

Select—choose the standard you want to address.

1. Adopt—use the standard as is to serve as the framework for your planning.
OR

2. Adapt—adapt the standard to meet the needs of your students (e.g., teach one part of the standard, plan for adaptations for students with diverse needs).

3. Invent—use multiple resources to create innovative ways to address the standard in terms of lessons, assignments, and student assessment.

4. Assess—evaluate your approach to inform future planning.

Source: Information from Conley, M. (2005). *Connecting standards and assessment through literacy.* Boston: Allyn & Bacon.

Differentiating Instruction for Secondary Learners

Why do students in middle and high school have difficulty learning? You could answer that question by summarizing all you have learned in this textbook about different students' needs. The advent of inclusion of students with disabilities and students identified as gifted and talented in the general education classroom as well as increased cultural and linguistic diversity have initiated increased attention on how best to meet the needs of a wide range of students.

In addition to issues related to individual student differences, at the secondary level typical content-area classes pose particular problems for students. These problems include the following:

- Not all subjects are uniformly interesting to all students.
- Not all subjects are consistent with students' cultural backgrounds and prior knowledge.
- Learning in some content areas requires basic skills in reading, writing, and mathematics that some students do not have.
- The pace of instruction in some content areas is too fast for some students and too slow for others.
- The level of conceptual complexity and density in some content areas is overwhelming for some students.
- Textbooks in content-area classes can be dull and encyclopedic.
- Content-area classes require both regular homework and assignments and long-term projects.
- Taking tests is a required component of many content-area classes.

These individual differences pose challenges for secondary teachers who view themselves primarily as teachers of a specific content area (e.g., mathematics, social studies, science). Professional organizations such as the National Middle School Association and the National Association of Secondary School Principals advocate teacher preparation that includes not only solid grounding in content, but also understanding developmentally appropriate instructional practices for older learners: a balanced approach. In a joint statement, these associations and others argued, "Thomas Edison knew science, but could he have taught a class of seventh graders? Some may have considered him highly qualified, but would his students have passed a proficiency test?" (National Middle School Association, 2006, p.1). Vacca and Vacca (2008) put it this way: "Teachers who are wedded to a discipline walk a tightrope between content and process. It's a balancing act every time the attempt is made to influence what is learned (content) and how it should be learned (process)" (p. 7).

Differentiated instruction (DI) has been identified as one means to plan for individual student needs and for secondary teachers to bridge content and process. This section is organized around questions secondary teachers typically pose about DI:

- What is differentiated instruction?
- How can I differentiate assignments and homework?
- How can I plan for differentiated instruction?
- How can I accommodate students who are gifted and talented?
- How can differentiated instruction accommodate multiples intelligences?
- How does differentiated instruction relate to response to intervention?

What Is Differentiated Instruction?

The call for DI has come from a number of fields, including reading, special education, gifted education, teaching English as a second language, and multiple intelligence (Schumm & Avalos, 2009). Consequently, a number of definitions for DI have evolved and teachers often have misconceptions about what it is and what it entails. Schumm and Avalos (2009) offer the follow basic components of differentiated instruction:

- DI is both a philosophy of instructing students based on individual needs as well as instructional practices aligned with the philosophy.
- DI draws on a wide variety of practices (some research based; some not).
- DI at the secondary level can occur not only in the general education classroom, but also in advanced placement classes, resource rooms, or pull-out settings.

Carol Tomlinson, an expert in DI, offers the following definition:

A differentiated classroom offers a variety of learning options designed to tap into different readiness levels, interests, and learning profiles. In a differentiated class, the teacher uses (1) a variety of ways for students to explore curriculum content, (2) a variety of sense-making activities or processes through which students can come to understand and "own" information and ideas, and (3) a variety of options through which students can demonstrate or exhibit what they have learned. (Tomlinson, 2005, p. 1)

Components of Differentiated Instruction.   DI involves curriculum enhancement and curriculum modification (Koga & Hall, 2004). Curriculum **curriculum enhancement** involves no changes to the curriculum, but involves instructional strategies that promote learning for all students. For example, preteaching vocabulary and using graphic organizers are examples of curriculum enhancers.

Curriculum **curriculum modification** is more complex and is targeted to the individual needs of students. It includes both accommodation and adaptation. **Accommodation** involves no changes in curriculum requirements for students, but may make modifications to how the material is presented and what is required of the student. For example, a student with learning disabilities might listen to an audiotaped version of a science textbook rather than completing the reading assignment. The student would take the same test as his or her peers, but in an oral format. **Adaptations** go one step further in that curriculum requirements might be altered. For instance, if middle school students are working on a three-point essay in language arts class, a student with identified difficulties in writing may be assigned a paragraph writing activity. Accommodations and adaptations are more time consuming for teachers, but are critical for providing students with the support they need to succeed (Koga & Hall, 2004).

A **learning contract** is one strategy that is recommended for organizing differentiated instruction (Tomlinson, 2001). Learning contracts are particularly helpful when planning long-term assignments and research projects. With a learning contract, you identify target standards or objectives and then negotiate with students about the pathway and products they will produce to determine mastery.

Differentiated Instructing Using Flexible Grouping.   As you implement differentiated instruction in your classroom, you will want to plan for a variety of grouping patterns. Group size and membership should be flexible, with formats that change according to the goals of the lesson as well as your students' characteristics. A variety of grouping patterns can be referred to as **multiple grouping formats**.

At the middle and high school levels, your students may be **tracked** or placed in the same class by achievement level. Quite often the decision whether to track students or group them in mixed-ability classes is a school or district decision. Even in "same-ability" classes, however, you will quickly note that students in your class have a range of differences to which you need to attend.

Grouping patterns are determined by two basic variables:

1. They can be categorized by group size: whole class, small group, pairs, and single student.
2. Group composition may be **homogeneous grouping** (students at similar achievement levels) or **heterogeneous grouping** (students at a wide range of achievement levels).

Depending on the purpose of the learning activity, you can branch beyond these two basic variables and group students by interest, skills to be learned, or prior knowledge of a topic. To mix things up a bit, you may give students time to create their own small groups for activities such as discussing with classmates the books they read independently over the weekend.

For multiple grouping structures to be successful, careful planning is essential. The temptation becomes not to group at all, but instead to fall into the pattern of whole-class teaching followed by individual practice. As you think about a lesson, keep grouping in mind by asking yourself the following questions:

- What is the best group for teaching this lesson?
- What is the best group size for follow-up activities?
- What is the best composition of learners for each group with respect to student academic ability and work habits?
- What materials are needed for each group?

- Will the groups be teacher-led, student-led, or cooperative?
- What room arrangement is necessary for the grouping plan?
- When students move from one group to another, how can I ensure a quick and smooth transition?
- What issues related to students' behavior and social needs should I consider?

If you decide to have your students work cooperatively in small groups or in pairs, students may need explicit instruction in how to work together. In **cooperative learning groups**, students work together toward a common goal, usually to help one another learn academic material (Slavin, 1991). Working collaboratively, students must learn such lessons as how to give and receive help, how to listen and respond to the ideas of others, and how to complete a task as a team. Teachers cannot assume that middle and high school students automatically know how to work in groups. Most of the time, these skills need to be taught explicitly and practiced, just like skills in any other academic area.

What might be some advantages of working in cooperative learning groups for students with special needs? What can teachers do to ensure that all group members get the most out of their group activity?

How Can I Differentiate Assignments and Homework?

Students' success or failure in a content-area class is often based on their performance on assignments and homework. But what about students with learning and behavior problems? Should they have the same assignments and tests as everyone else? What if a student cannot read? What if a student cannot work under timed conditions?

Teacher surveys, interviews, and classroom observations indicate that teachers of all grade levels (elementary through high school) do not often make individual adaptations to homework, assignments, and tests (Ness, 2008; Schumm & Vaughn, 1991, 1992a; Schumm et al., 1995a). Constructing individual assignments and tests may not be feasible on a day-to-day basis and may not even be necessary. In this section, you learn about ways to prepare effective assignments and homework for all students.

In Chapter 3 you read about the importance of having a homework policy and communicating that policy to students and their families. But there is more you can do to make assignments clear and comprehensible. After conducting a comprehensive review of the literature, Cooper and Nye (1994) concluded that homework assignments for students with disabilities should be brief, focused on reinforcement of old material rather than new material, monitored carefully, and supported through parental involvement.

The most important aspect of making assignments is to give complete information. You need to let students know why the assignment is important, when it is due, what support they will have for completing the task, and the steps necessary for getting the job done. Having complete information helps to motivate students. The procedure in Tips for Teachers 15.2 can help you provide students with a complete set of directions.

Class assignments and homework can be adapted for special learners so that they can experience success without undue attention being brought to their learning difficulties. The key to success is to make assignments appropriate in content, length, time required to complete, and skill level needed to accomplish the task. It is also important that students know how and where to get help when they get stuck.

How Can I Plan for Differentiated Instruction?

Planning for the success of all students in your class involves careful consideration of the needs of individuals as well as those of the class as a whole. If you ask experienced teachers how they plan to meet a wide range of student needs, you are likely to get a collection of very different answers. In most cases, teachers have a single lesson or unit plan and make adaptations on the spot for individual students. The unfortunate consequence is that adaptations

Tips for Teachers 15.2

STRATEGIES FOR GIVING ASSIGNMENTS

- Explain the purpose of the assignment. Stress what you expect students to learn and why learning the skill or concept is important. Connect the skill or concept to real-life applications.

- Explain in detail the procedures for completing the assignment. Ask one or two students to summarize the procedures to check for understanding.

- Get students started by modeling one or two problems or by providing an example.

- Describe the equipment and materials needed to complete the assignment.

- Anticipate trouble spots, and ask students how they might tackle difficult parts in the assignment.

- Tell students when the assignment is due.

- Explain how the assignment will be graded and how it factors into the overall grade for the class.

- Describe appropriate ways to get help or support in completing the assignment.

- For an in-class assignment, explain your expectations for student behavior while they complete the assignment and what students who finish early should do.

- Address student questions.

become incidental, inconsistent, and (for students with disabilities) not representative of what is mandated on their IEPs.

A number of systems have been recommended for planning for differentiated instruction (see Table 15.1). Recall from Chapter 3 that the planning pyramid is an effective framework to use when planning instruction that will meet the needs of all of your students. To be

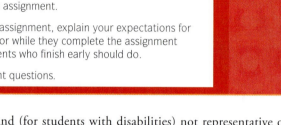

TABLE 15.1	**Ways to Provide Access to Content-Area Instruction for All Learners**		
	SOURCE	DESCRIPTION	BENEFITS FOR STUDENTS WITH SPECIAL NEEDS
Planning Pyramid	Schumm, Vaughn, & Leavell (1994); Schumm, Vaughn, & Harris (1997)	A three-tiered framework for planning instructional units and lessons for diverse learners. Key concepts are identified and appropriate assignments and adaptations are incorporated.	Serves as a tool to integrate learning for all students and as a way for special and general education teachers to coordinate planning and instruction.
Universal Design for Learning	Hitchcock, Meyer, Rose, & Jackson (2002); Voltz, Sims, Nelson, & Bivens (2005)	A system for identifying appropriate goals, materials, methods, and assessments for all students.	Assignments and assessments are at an appropriate level of challenge. Exceptional students are viewed as participants, not outliers.
Curriculum Mapping	Hayes-Jacobs (1997); Koppang (2004)	A calendar-based system used to gather data about content, skill instruction, and assessment within and across grade levels in a school.	Specialists have a clear picture of what is going to be taught and when. Assists in planning of appropriate accommodations.
Concept Anchoring Routine	Bulgren, Schumaker, & Deshler (1994); Deshler et al. (2001)	A series of instructional methods to help students with disabilities master key concepts in the general education curriculum.	Helps students to connect new information with prior knowledge.

Sources: Koppang, A. (2004). Curriculum mapping: Building collaboration and communication. *Intervention in School and Clinic, 39,* 154–161; Schumm, J. S. & Avalos, M. A. (2009). Responsible differentiated instruction for the adolescent learner: Promises, pitfalls, and possibilities. In W. Blanton & K. Wood (Eds.) *Promoting literacy with adolescent learners.* New York: Guilford; Schumm, J. S., Vaughn, S., & Leavell, A. G. (1994). Planning pyramid: A framework for planning for diverse student needs during content area instruction. *The Reading Teacher, 47* (8), 608–615; Lenz, B. K., & Deshler, D. D. (2004). *Teaching content to all: Evidence-based inclusive practices in middle and secondary schools.* Boston: Allyn & Bacon; Rock, M. L., Gregg, M., Ellis, Edwin, & Gable, R. A. (2008). REACH: A framework for differentiated classroom instruction. *Preventing School Failure, 52,* 31–47; Rose, D. H., & Meyer, A. (2002). *Teaching every student in the digital age: Universal design for learning.* Alexandria, VA: Association for Supervision and Curriculum Development; and van Garderen, D., & Whittaker, C. (2006). Planning differentiated, multicultural instruction for secondary inclusive classrooms. *Teaching Exceptional Children, 38,* 12–20.

effective, you will need to take into consideration the degrees of learning—what and how much do you expect all, more, or some of your students to learn? Consider, for example, sixth-grade teacher Sara Hood, who used the planning pyramid to plan a two-and-a-half-week unit on Latin American countries for her middle school students. Sara has two students with learning disabilities in her class. One student, Carlos, has difficulty with decoding; another, Miriam, struggles with reading comprehension. Her state-adopted textbook is very difficult for these students, and her planning needs to include accommodations to help both students learn content.

To prepare for the lesson, Sara examined the whole unit in the textbook and chose the fundamental ideas she wanted students to learn. The bottom of the pyramid (see Figure 15.2) listed topics that all groups would research and on which all students would be tested. The middle and top of the pyramid listed student-selected material.

One major concern Sara had in planning was finding activities that would keep her middle school students involved in learning and provide Carlos and Miriam the support they needed. To address these concerns, she planned to divide the classes into mixed-ability cooperative learning groups, each of which would select a country and present what they learned to the rest of the class. Sara provided the students with a checklist with her expectations for the cooperative learning groups' oral presentations in class. In the cooperative learning groups, material was read aloud to facilitate access to the information for Carlos. Also, groups worked together to identify key information, thus assisting Miriam with comprehension.

In addition to using cooperative learning groups to facilitate differentiated instruction, Sara also planned to include differentiated assessment. In his IEP, Carlos is allowed to have tests administered orally. Thus, Sara's special education colleague administered his unit exam orally to Carlos. Miriam's IEP calls for extended time in taking tests, and the special educator facilitated that as well. Both Carlos and Miriam participated in their groups' oral presentations.

Planning is a critical component for successful differentiated instruction in the general education classroom. The planning pyramid can serve as a framework for such planning—not only for students with learning and behavior problems, but also for students who are identified as gifted and talented.

How Can I Accommodate Students Who Are Gifted and Talented?

Consider the following quotation:

Of all the students you are teaching in a given class, which group do you think will probably learn the least this year? It may surprise you to find that in a class that has a range of abilities (and which

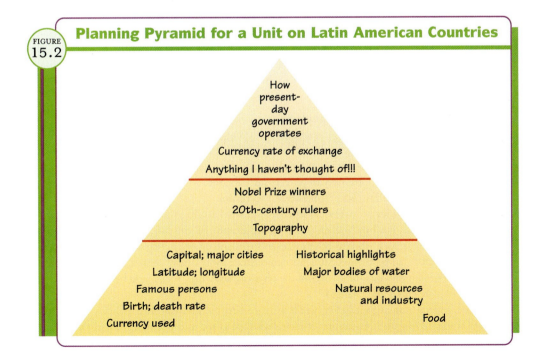

FIGURE 15.2

Planning Pyramid for a Unit on Latin American Countries

How present-day government operates

Currency rate of exchange

Anything I haven't thought of!!!

Nobel Prize winners

20th-century rulers

Topography

Capital; major cities   Historical highlights

Latitude; longitude   Major bodies of water

Famous persons   Natural resources and industry

Birth; death rate

Currency used   Food

class doesn't?), it is the most able, rather than the least able, who will learn less new material than any other group. (Winebrenner & Espeland, 2000, p. 1)

How can this occur?

Think about Rick, a tenth-grade student who knows all the vocabulary for an English test at the beginning of the week. He gets a grade of 100% on the test, but has he learned anything?

Think about Mina, a sixth-grade student who is a voracious reader and is particularly interested in astronomy. She skims the chapter in her general science textbook, quickly gets its gist, and realizes that the content is basic and boring. The class lecture does not go beyond answering the end-of-chapter questions. Mina does not have the opportunity to share what she really knows and "tunes out" during class discussion. She gets a grade of 70% on a chapter test because she simply doesn't care about "proving" what she knows.

Think about Caroline, an eighth-grade student who has known all about the eight parts of speech since third grade. Even if she had forgotten the eight parts of speech in third grade, it wouldn't have mattered because they were also taught in fourth, fifth, sixth, and seventh grades. She gets a grade of 100% on a grammar unit test, but has she learned anything?

Think about Thaddeus. Thaddeus loves to draw and does so constantly at home and at school. Unfortunately, he would rather draw than do anything else, and his teacher frequently reprimands him for "doodling" rather than completing assignments.

You've got the picture. Frequently, students who are gifted or talented and other high-achieving students already know the material being covered in the general curriculum. Can you imagine spending 7 hours a day, 5 days a week, school year after school year, reviewing information you already know? Can you imagine having genuine artistic talent and not having the opportunity to develop that talent or to share it with others? Can you imagine drilling on standards that you have already mastered (Glass, 2004; Viadero, 2007)?

Go to www.hoagiesgifted.org where you will find Hoagies' Gifted Education page, which includes online resources for students, parents, and teachers.

Characteristics of Students Who Are Gifted and Talented.   As a classroom teacher, you'll need to recognize the characteristics of students with extraordinary gifts and talents so that you can help identify students for special services and provide appropriate instruction for gifted students who are members of your class. There is disparity among states in terms of how giftedness is defined, how students are identified for gifted education services, and how services are provided (pull-out programs, full-time programs, inclusion programs) (Hallahan, Kauffman, & Pullen, 2009). There is a clear trend toward increased inclusion of students who are gifted and talented in the general education classroom (Van Tassel-Baska, Quek, & Feng, 2007). Thus, it is important that you investigate local policies and understand your role in identifying students with special gifts and talents and designing instruction that meets their needs.

What you should also be aware of is that the gifted population is very diverse (Soller, 2003). Part of this diversity is due to definitional differences and local criteria for admission to gifted programs (Stephens & Karnes, 2000); part is due to individual differences (Robinson, Zigler, & Gallagher, 2000); and part is due to the degree of giftedness (Ziegler & Heller, 2000).

Underidentified High-Achieving Students.   Another group that is of particular interest to many general education teachers is that of high-achieving students who are not identified for special programs. Frequently, teachers will notice a child with extraordinary talents and abilities who might not meet state or school district criteria to qualify for a special program. It becomes the general education teacher's responsibility to provide such children with the support, encouragement, and stimulation they need to feel productive and successful.

Table 15.2 provides an overview of characteristics of gifted and talented students and instructional suggestions for addressing those characteristics. As you can see, some characteristics relate to academic factors, whereas others refer to social and emotional factors. It is important to note that not all gifted or talented students demonstrate every one of these characteristics; there is a wide range of individual differences in the physical, academic, social, and behavioral traits of students who are gifted and talented.

As a general education teacher, you'll want to become familiar with policies and procedures for identifying and instructing students who are gifted and talented. In addition, you'll want to learn about what resources are available to you and to your students. You'll also want

TABLE
15.2

Classroom Strategies and Adaptations for Gifted Students

CHARACTERISTICS OF GIFTED AND TALENTED STUDENTS	CLASSROOM STRATEGIES AND ADAPTATIONS
Advanced vocabulary for chronological age	• Develop word relationship skills (e.g., analogies, homonyms, etc.).* • Encourage use of wide variety of words. • Suggest keeping a journal of "word of the day" or "word of the week."* • Provide experiences in second language learning.*
Outstanding memory; possesses lots of information	• Teach ways to summarize information. • Work on specific product development.* • Provide exhibition space for student products.* • Allow for oral reports before the class.* • Provide unstructured activities, allowing the student to choose the medium of expression.*
Curious; asks endless questions ("Why?" "And then what?")	• Plan exploratory, interdisciplinary curriculum.**
Operates on higher levels of thinking than same-age peers; is comfortable with abstract thinking	• Emphasize thinking strategies, problem solving, creative solutions, and decision making within the context of specific subject areas.** • Teach debating skills.* • Regularly include open-ended, higher-order thinking questions in classroom discussions.
Has many interests, hobbies, and collections	• Develop interest-group assignments that enable gifted students to work together with others who share similar interests.** • Encourage and provide time to pursue free reading based on student interests.* • Create centers where students select topics and work together on projects that require several types or levels of skills.**
May have a passionate interest that has lasted for many years (example: dinosaurs)	• Encourage reading biographies and autobiographies of individuals who shared interests in common with the student.* • Use outside resources to help students develop their talents.** • Find mentors.
Intense; gets totally absorbed in activities and thoughts	• Allow some time for uninterrupted reading and thinking. • Teach time-management skills. • Teach strategies for transitioning from one task to another. • Give a 5-minute warning when it is time to wind down one task and start another.
Strongly motivated to do things of interest; may be unwilling to work on other activities	• Adapt assignments to focus on in-depth work on most difficult aspect of assignment and to skip easiest components. • Provide interesting things to do if student finishes assignment before others in the class.
Prefers complex and challenging tasks to "basic" work	
Catches on quickly, then resists doing work, or works in a sloppy, careless manner	• Create open-ended, self-paced assignments.** • Help students set their own high, yet realistic, outcomes for assignments that vary in complexity.** • Co-create a "contract" for completion of assignments signed by teacher, parent, and student.
Comes up with "better ways" for doing things; suggests them to peers, teachers, and other adults	• Set expectations for working collaboratively with peers, teachers, and other adults. • Model appropriate ways of offering suggestions for "better ways" of doing things. • Teach leadership skills. • Recognize ideas when appropriate and expand and elaborate on them.
Aware of global issues that are uninteresting to many age-level peers	• Develop a reading list of books, journals, and magazines to foster interest in global issues. • Provide support in conducting informal research using print and nonprint sources.
Sophisticated sense of humor; may be "class clown"	• Set guidelines for appropriate timing of humor in the classroom. • Encourage student to explore the use of humor in a variety of genres.

* Information from *Teaching gifted kids in the regular classroom* by Susan Winebrenner. Copyright 1992. Used with permission from Free Spirit Publishing, Inc., Minneapolis, MN (800) 735-7323. All rights reserved.

** Information from *Excellence in educating gifted and talented learners* by Joyce Van Tassel-Baska. Copyright 1998.

Go to **www.nagc.org**, the National Association for Gifted Children website, where you will find resources for educators, parents, and students who are gifted and talented.

to learn about policies related to acceleration and enrichment. **Acceleration** refers to the procedure of moving them quickly through the grades or through the curriculum. With the idea that some students might not be socially ready for the demands of acceleration to higher grades, **enrichment** evolved as an alternative to acceleration. Gifted education programs in the United States have varied in their emphasis on acceleration or enrichment. In some cases, programs in general education have elected to incorporate elements of both.

There are several approaches to DI for gifted students suggested in the literature. Two commonly recommended approaches for general education classrooms are curriculum compacting and the Parallel Curriculum Model.

Curriculum Compacting. Experts in the field of gifted education suggest that general education teachers work cooperatively with teachers in gifted programs to compact the general education curriculum for gifted students (Reis & Renzulli, 2005). Research indicates that gifted and high-achieving students may already know 40% to 50% of concepts and skills at the outset of a lesson (Reis & Purcell, 1993). **Curriculum compacting** provides students with the opportunity to demonstrate what they already know about a subject. Teachers can then eliminate content that is repetitive or review for students, replacing it with advanced learning experiences. To assess what your students know, see the 60-Second Lesson.

Curriculum compacting is a three-step identification process:

1. What the student already knows about a topic
2. What a student needs to learn
3. What adaptations or activities are appropriate for facilitating student learning

Parallel Curriculum Model. Tomlinson, Kaplan, Renzulli, Purcell, Leppien, and Burns (2001) developed a framework for differentiated instruction called the **Parallel Curriculum Model (PCM)**. PCM takes into consideration four curriculum design components:

1. Core Curriculum—key concepts to be learned
2. Curriculum of Connections—making interdisciplinary linkages
3. Curriculum of Practice—supporting students in learning to think like a practitioner
4. Curriculum of Identity—helping students make personal meaning and clarification of what they are learning

The parallel curriculum components can be used together, separately, or in various combinations depending on the teacher's goals. Like the planning pyramid, PCM forces teachers to think about what is important to learn and how to facilitate instruction for a wide range of student needs.

Although DI is a viable way to accommodate individual differences, the National Association for Gifted Children (2005) also offers some cautions and comments about the

 **LESSON**

ASSESSING PRIOR KNOWLEDGE

When you begin a new unit or topic, you need to find out what your students already know and what they need to learn. Finding out what students know will help you plan differentiated lessons and think about accommodations you might need for students with special needs. Some teachers skip this very important step because they don't want to take the time to construct a pretest. Here are some efficient ways to assess prior knowledge:

1. One quick way to assess prior knowledge (a way that takes little preplanning) is "most difficult first" (Winebrenner, 1992). In a list of tasks organized by relative difficulty, identify the most difficult tasks and have students who are willing to take the challenge do them

first. Allow students who demonstrate mastery to go on to a self-selected task. Students who are gifted or high achieving frequently get bored with undue repetition and practice. "Most difficult first" can help to circumvent this problem.

2. Put three or four structured questions that relate to the core of a lesson on the board or an overhead transparency. Have the students respond in writing to the questions.

3. Free recall is another way to assess prior knowledge. Provide students with the topic of the lesson and have them generate as many ideas as they can about the topic within a brief time limit.

practice. Differentiated instruction should not mean "just more work" for advanced students. It should offer opportunities for both acceleration and enrichment. Thus, differentiated instruction holds great promise, but involves careful planning and ongoing evaluation.

How Can Differentiated Instruction Accommodate Multiple Intelligences?

In his book *Frames of Mind* (1983), Howard Gardner proposes the theory of **multiple intelligences**. Gardner suggests that human beings are capable of exhibiting intelligence in seven domains: linguistic, logical–mathematical, spatial, musical, bodily–kinesthetic, interpersonal (i.e., discerning and responding to the needs of others), and intrapersonal. Later, Gardner identified an eighth intelligence, the naturalistic, which consists of the ability to, "recognize, categorize and draw upon certain features of the environment (Gardner, 1999, p. 48). Gardner (2006) has also suggested a ninth intelligence, the existential, which refers to the ability to identify big issues and fundamental life questions.

What determines the number of individuals in the student population who are identified as academically or creatively exceptional? What groups tend to be underidentified and why?

Traditional intelligence tests tap only linguistic and logical–mathematical intelligence. Gardner advocates a revamping of assessment procedures to evaluate all eight areas in ways that are sensitive to culture, age, gender, and social class (Checkley 1997; Gardner & Hatch 1989). Assessment needs to investigate skills that are needed to survive in society, not skills associated with the ability to succeed in a school setting. Gardner and his colleagues have developed assessment procedures aligned with multiple intelligence theory through their Project Zero and Project Spectrum at Harvard University. The main tenet of Gardner's theory to remember when planning educational programs is the responsibility to help all students realize and enhance their potential and strengths by showing children joy and interest in learning while helping them with the mastery of skills and curriculum (Gardner, 2006).

Gardner explains that the approach does not mean that teachers "need to create nine different lesson plans. Instead, design rich learning experiences that nurture each student's combination of intelligences" (Moran, Kornhaber, & Gardner, 2006, p. 22). Classroom applications of the theory have emerged (e.g., Armstrong, 2003; Christodoulou, 2009; Stanford, 2003), and there is emerging evidence that the approach results in higher engagement and motivation among minority students (Williams, 2009). Key to the implementation of multiple intelligence theory are differentiated assessment and instruction using thematic units as a vehicle. Students can tune into learning through multiple channels.

How Does Differentiated Instruction Relate to Response to Intervention?

Response to intervention (RTI) at the middle and high school levels offers challenges not inherent at the elementary level. First, students at secondary levels are more likely to be placed in departmentalized settings. Second, scheduling problems can inhibit time for Tier 2 and Tier 3 instruction. Third, the pacing of instruction is much more rapid with little time for review or reteaching. Much is to be learned from research and practice about how best to provide tiered instruction for middle and high school students (Mastropieri & Scruggs, 2005). Because students in middle and high schools settings may remain undiagnosed for special services, ongoing research in this area is warranted.

Much of what you read in this chapter about differentiated assessment and instruction can be incorporated into Tier 1 strategies. The steps you take to address individual needs through implementation of evidence-based strategies can form the foundation for RTI.

Because RTI in secondary settings is in its infancy, caution in implementation is warranted. You'll want to familiarize yourself with the legal requirements of RTI, engage in professional development to learn more about tiered instruction and progress monitoring, and develop strong communication with your peers (Canter, Klotz, & Cowan, 2008). You'll also want to know how Tiers 2 and 3 are implemented at your school and how and when student progress monitoring occurs (Burns, 2008). At the middle and high school levels, identifying and addressing student needs may offer students their last chance.

Go to the Teacher Talk section of Topic 6: Assessment in the MyEducationLab for your course and listen to middle school teacher Beth Oswald talk about how she uses a variety of strategies for engaging and assessing her students.

Preparing Engaging Lessons for Middle and High School Students

Jerry Schumm is known for his wardrobe. He has costumes for most periods of history that he teaches. As he tells his students, "I don't want you just to learn history, I want you to feel history. I want you all to plug in!" Jerry knows that keeping adolescents engaged takes a big bag of tricks that he replenishes frequently. This section provides ideas for expanding your bag of tricks by (a) using prelearning activities, (b) using graphic organizers, (c) creating listener-friendly lectures, (d) giving demonstrations, and (e) facilitating student participation.

Using Prelearning Activities

Prelearning activities are strategies that teachers use to activate students' prior knowledge and to preteach vocabulary and concepts—essentially, to prepare students to learn. Lauren Lopez, who teachers ninth-grade science, describes her students as follows:

> Some of my students have traveled all over the world; others have never left their neighborhood. Some of my students have had solid instruction in science in the elementary grades; others have had none. The time I spend with prelearning activities sets the stage for learning and helps build common vocabulary. It saves lots of reteaching time.

Like Lauren, you can use purpose-setting activities and preteaching vocabulary to help students prepare to learn new information.

Purpose Setting.   **Purpose-setting activities** provide students with a reason for completing a reading assignment or for listening to a lecture. Setting a purpose for learning helps to guide the reading and listening process and helps students improve the depth of their comprehension. Purpose-setting activities are important for all learners but particularly for students with motivational and attentional problems. Although teachers often set a purpose for reading or listening, students can engage in purpose setting as well (Gunning, 2010). Tips for Teachers 15.3 provides guidelines for setting a purpose before you give a lecture or a reading assignment.

Tips FOR TEACHERS 15.3

SETTING A PURPOSE FOR A LESSON

- Keep the purpose brief, but make it powerful. Students become more actively involved in listening, reading, or participating in a classroom activity when they have a reason for doing so.

- Set a single purpose. When students are given too many purposes, they can lose their focus.

- Make certain that the purpose statement is not too narrow in scope and that it does not reveal too much content, which can actually inhibit comprehension.

- Have a regular purpose-setting routine. For example, write the purpose for learning on the board or demonstrate how the purpose was set.

- After reading, begin discussion with a reiteration of the purpose for reading.

- Help students learn how to set their own purposes. Talk about the importance of setting a purpose and how to develop purpose statements.

- Keep the written purpose statement in full view of students while they are participating in a class activity. Some students may need to be reminded about the purpose of the lesson.

Source: Blanton, W. E., Wood, K. D., & Moorman, G. B. (1990). The role of purpose in reading instruction. *The Reading Teacher, 43*(7), 486–493.

Preteaching Vocabulary.   In recent years, vocabulary instruction has taken a front seat in research and practice (Pearson, Hiebert, & Kamil, 2007). Before beginning a content-area unit or lesson, you can help students gain a better understanding of what they are about to read or hear through direct preteaching of a few key words. Teaching too many new technical vocabulary words can confuse students. Preteaching is helpful for all students, particularly those with limited prior knowledge of the topic.

In selecting the words you are going to preteach, begin by identifying the key concepts you want students to learn in a unit or lesson (McCoy & Ketterlin-Geller, 2004). Next, identify the key vocabulary related to the concept that would be most helpful for your students to learn up front. If you are experienced with the content of the unit or lesson and if you have spent time getting to know your students and their background, this selection should be relatively easy.

Chiappone (2006) lists seven principles of excellent vocabulary instruction:

1. Develop awareness of the stages of word knowledge.
2. Build experiential background for students.
3. Relate word learning to students' backgrounds.
4. Develop depth of meaning through multiple sources and repeated exposures.
5. Foster appreciation and enthusiasm for word learning.
6. Teach strategies to build independent word learning.
7. Teach words in context.

Keeping these principles in mind, use a wide variety of methods and materials to preteach vocabulary. Some examples include semantic feature analysis, the key word method, and graphic organizers.

Using Graphic Organizers

One set of tools that Rita Menendez uses almost daily is **graphic organizers**. Vacca and Vacca (2005) describe a graphic organizer as "a diagram that uses content vocabulary to help students anticipate concepts and their relationships to one another in the reading material. These concepts are displayed in an arrangement of key technical terms relevant to the important concepts to be learned" (p. 271). Rita explains that she uses not only a variety of graphic organizers but also a variety of materials. "Sometime I just use the white board, sometimes the SmartBoard or PowerPoint, and sometimes overhead transparencies." Rita then adds, "Starting a lesson with a graphic organizer helps, but refining the organizer as we read or listen and using the organizer as a tool for reviewing what we have learned [are] important as well."

For students with learning disabilities and other students with reading comprehension difficulties, graphic organizers provide a visual representation of key ideas in the text and the relationships among those ideas. Using lines, arrows, and flow charts, graphic organizers can help students conceptualize key ideas. Kim, Vaughn, Wanzek, and Wei (2004) conducted a synthesis of the research on the use of graphic organizers for teaching reading comprehension to students with learning disabilities. Twenty-one articles (published between 1963 and 2001) were identified, coded, and analyzed for statistical significance. Most of the studies were conducted with students in intermediate and secondary grades. In general, the researchers found support for the use of graphic organizers in terms of student outcomes on teacher-made or researcher-made tests. Use of graphic organizers appeared to assist in learning material in typical classroom instruction. What remains to be discovered is whether this comprehension tool can be used to improve student outcomes on standardized tests.

Semantic Maps.   Providing students with visual representations of concepts and vocabulary to be learned is a powerful prelearning tool, particularly for special learners. One visual tool that is commonly used in prelearning activities is a **semantic map** (Irwin, 2007; Pearson & Johnson, 1978), a visual aid that helps students see how ideas are related to one another and to what students already know.

Lists of words prepared in advance by the teacher or generated by students through teacher-guided brainstorming are placed on the board. After discussing the meanings of the words, students discuss how to cluster the words and work together to develop a map to represent visually the relationships that exist among the ideas. For example, Figure 15.3 shows a semantic map for the words for a chapter on Egypt. Students can use the map as a listening or

FIGURE
15.3

Example of a Semantic Map

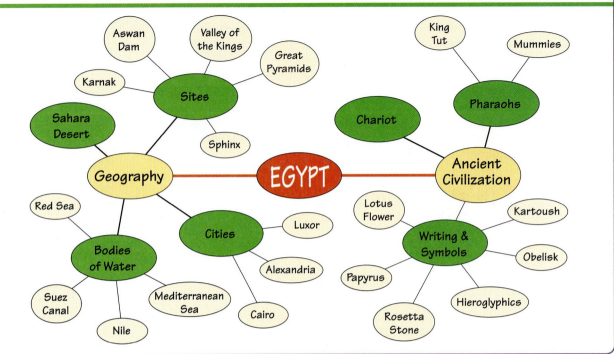

reading guide. The map can also serve as a framework for postlistening and postreading discussions and as an aid for studying for tests or quizzes.

Concept Diagrams. Concept diagrams (Lenz & Deshler, 2004) are another way to introduce a lecture or reading assignment. A **concept diagram** (see Figure 15.4) is similar to a semantic map, but also helps students determine the definitions, characteristics, examples, and nonexamples of a concept.

Concept diagramming is time consuming. Select concepts with care. Choose those that are pivotal to the curriculum and that students need to understand thoroughly. See Tips for Teachers 15.4 for recommendations for creating concept diagrams.

Timelines. Timelines can be used to provide students with a way to visualize and sequence content-area information as they read, listen, and discuss. They can be used in math (e.g., sequences of

CREATING CONCEPT DIAGRAMS

- Identify major concepts to teach.

- List important characteristics of the concepts. Think about whether each characteristic is always present, sometimes present, or never present.

- Locate examples and nonexamples of the concept.

- Construct a definition of the concept by naming the superordinate concept, its characteristics, and the relationships among characteristics.

- Introduce the concept diagram to students using an advance organizer.

- Elicit a list of key words or ideas that relate to the concept.

- Explain or review the parts of the concept diagram and their intended use.

- Name and define the concept with students.

- Discuss characteristics that are always present, sometimes present, and never present in the meaning of the concept.

- Discuss examples and nonexamples of the concept.

- Link the examples and nonexamples to the characteristics.

Concept Diagram

FIGURE 15.4

Concept Name: fossils

Definitions: Fossils are remains or prints of plants or animals who lived thousands of years ago which have been preserved in the earth.

Characteristics Present in the Concept:

Always	Sometimes	Never
remains or prints	frozen in ice	still alive
plants or animals	trapped in tar	still decaying
thousands of years old	crushed by water	
preserved in the earth	in volcanic ash	

Example:

tigers in La Brea tar pits

petrified forest in Arizona

Siberian mammoth

fish skeleton in limestone layers

Nonexample:

your pet cat

tree limbs and leaves in your yard

elephant in Africa today

fish in supermarket

Source: Bos, C. S. & Vaughn, S. (1994). *Strategies for teaching students with learning and behavior problems* (3rd ed.). Copyright © 1994 by Allyn & Bacon. Reprinted by permission.

events in word problems), science (e.g., seasons of the year), reading (e.g., biographies or story plots), and art (e.g., timeline of classic art) and as a study skills tool (e.g., assignments for the month and activities needed to complete each assignment) (Fry & Kress, 2006). Timelines can be more than simple listings of facts on a horizontal black line (Kelly & Clausen-Grace, 2007). They can be illustrated or include photographs as well.

Creating Listener-Friendly Lectures

When using computer software or navigating Internet sites, people talk about them as being "user-friendly." When teachers, like website developers, keep the audience in mind and anticipate points of potential difficulty, the product is user-friendly. Listener-friendly lectures are lectures structured to facilitate listening and learning. Such lectures are not only well organized, but also help students discern what is most important and connect new ideas to what they already know. Well-designed lectures are particularly beneficial for students with learning disabilities, English language learners, and listeners with relatively limited language skills and/or little prior knowledge of the content.

The goal of lectures is to enhance student understanding. One key to enhancing understanding is **instructional clarity**—the clear, direct, explicit presentation of information. McCaleb and White (1980) list the following five components of instructional clarity:

1. *Understanding*—connecting new information with what students already know
2. *Structuring*—providing a clear format for the presentation, one that students can follow easily
3. *Sequencing*—arranging a presentation in a logical order
4. *Explaining*—defining key terms and providing examples as necessary
5. *Presenting*—delivering material in an articulate and lively manner with correct pacing, and using visual aids and multimedia as necessary

In all classroom presentations, clarity should be your goal. Clarity is important for all students but particularly for students who have difficulty with language or organizational skills or who have little prior knowledge of a topic. Instructional clarity is particularly important during lectures. Giving lectures is often necessary to generate interest in a topic, to provide information that is not included in textbooks, or to clarify or embellish textbook information. Although

TIPS FOR CREATING LISTENER-FRIENDLY LECTURES

- Use advance organizers.

- Use cue words or phrases to let students know what information is important (e.g., "It is important that you know," "The key information to remember is," "In summary").

- Repeat important information.

- Write important information on the board, the transparency, and a handout.

- Stress key points by varying the tone and quality of your voice.

- Number ideas or points (e.g., first, second, next, then, finally).

- Write technical words or words that are difficult to spell.

- Use a study guide that lists the major concepts, with space for students to add other information.

- Use pictures, diagrams, and semantic maps to show relationships among ideas.

- Provide examples and nonexamples of the concepts you are discussing.

- Ask questions or encourage discussion that requires students to relate the new information to ideas they already know (from their own background or your previous lectures).

- Stop frequently and have students work with partners to discuss what they have learned.

- Allow time at the end of a lecture for students to look over their notes, summarize, and ask questions.

lectures tend to be overused, used properly they can be an effective way to teach. By improving your lectures, you help students improve their note taking. See Tips for Teachers 15.5 for tips on how to create listener-friendly lectures.

Many teachers are using PowerPoint presentations to organize their lectures. Leigh and Johnson (2004) recommend the following:

- When preparing PowerPoint presentations, give careful attention to font size and color and background color. The goal is for all students to be able to read the print clearly, even if they are sitting at the back of the room.
- Carefully plan the amount of information you provide on each slide—not too much information, not too little.
- When presenting the slides, don't go through them too quickly, particularly if students do not have handouts of the slides.

While giving lectures, use cues to help students become more active listeners and better note takers (see Figure 15.5).

Another way to make your lectures more friendly is to use the pause procedure (Armbruster, 2009; Ruhl, Hughes, & Gajar, 1990). The **pause procedure** is a technique that helps students learn more from lectures. During logical breaks in a lecture (approximately every 10 minutes), the teacher pauses for 2 minutes. During that time, teachers have pairs of students compare their notes to make certain that key concepts have been recorded. Students also ask each other questions to check for understanding. At the end of the 2 minutes, ask students whether they have any questions or concepts that need further discussion or clarification. After this quick monitoring for student understanding, the lecture continues.

Giving Demonstrations

Demonstrations can be used to show students how to perform a skill, complete a task, or solve a problem. Demonstrations can be for the whole class, small groups, or individual students. They can be preplanned or can occur on the spot as part of interactive planning when students need more explanation. The key to demonstrations is that they must engage students, especially passive learners who will watch your demonstration and then forget every step of it. The important thing is to get students involved and thinking about what you are doing.

As with any lesson, before you give a demonstration be sure to set a purpose, define key vocabulary, and provide an overview or advance organizer of the presentation, including key things to observe (Good & Brophy, 2007). Also provide guidelines for student participation during the presentation. Should they take notes? Should they ask questions before, during, or after the demonstration (Good & Brophy, 2007)?

FIGURE
15.5

Using Cues When Giving Lectures

Use the following list of cues to help students learn how to listen and watch for important information. Encourage students to listen and watch for additional cues and add them to the list. When integrating a content unit with a unit on note taking, you can place on a handout or post on a wall chart the information presented in this activity.

Type of Cue	Examples
Organizational cues	"Today, we will be discussing . . ."
	"The topic I want to cover today . . ."
	"There are (number) points I want you to be sure to learn . . ."
	"The important relationship is . . ."
	"The main point of this discussion is . . ."
	Any statement that signals a number or position (e.g., first, last, next, then)
	"To review/summarize/recap, . . ."
Emphasis cues: verbal	"You need to know/understand/remember . . ."
	"This is important/key/basic/critical."
	"Let me repeat this, . . ."
	"Let me check, . . . now do you understand?"
	Any statement repeated.
	Words are emphasized.
	Teacher speaks more slowly, loudly, or with more emphasis.
	Teacher stresses certain words.
	Teacher spells words.
	Teacher asks rhetorical question.
Emphasis cues: nonverbal	Information written on overhead or board.
	Information handed out in study guide.
	Teacher emphasizes point by using gestures.

Note: For more information, see Suritsky, S. K. & Hughes, C. A. (1996). Notetaking strategy instruction. In D. D. Deshler, E. S. Ellis, & B. K. Lenz (Eds.), *Teaching adolescents with learning disabilities* (2nd ed., pp. 267–312). Denver: Love.

After the demonstration, ask students to summarize the steps, or have one or two students repeat the demonstration for the class. Rivera and Deutsch-Smith (1988) offer an additional strategy for giving demonstrations to students with learning problems: the **demonstration plus model strategy**. To use this strategy, after completing your demonstration by following the steps outlined in the preceding paragraph, add these two steps:

1. After the students have viewed the demonstration, have a student perform each step, verbalizing each step as you did.
2. Have all students complete additional practice exercises independently, using the steps.

You can also improve a demonstration by describing your thinking as you move through the demonstration. Teacher **think alouds** are a metacognitive strategy used to model how to think and learn (Block & Israel, 2004; Oczkus, 2009). Think alouds are most frequently used to model reading processes, but they can also be used to model thinking during a demonstration. Davey (1983) listed the following five powerful uses of think alouds:

1. Making predictions or showing students how to develop hypotheses
2. Describing your visual images
3. Sharing an analogy or showing how prior knowledge applies
4. Verbalizing confusing points or showing how you monitor developing understanding
5. Demonstrating fix-up strategies (p. 45)

Facilitating Student Participation

As you have seen, student engagement can be fostered through cooperative learning groups and involvement in hands-on learning activities. In Chapter 16, you will read more about what students can do to develop personal responsibility for their own learning and for participation in class. This section includes additional suggestions for facilitating participation of all students in your class through two common content-area practices: questioning and discussion.

Questioning.   When Grace Demming did her college field experience in urban high schools in the late 1990s, one of the most frequent instructional patterns she observed was questioning routines. Teachers asked questions; students gave answers. Grace remarked, "It was like watching a tennis match—back and forth; back and forth." Searfoss and Readence (1989) refer to the typical exchange that goes on in a classroom as *ping-pong discussion.* The teacher asks questions and students answer, back and forth. When teachers "serve the ball" only to students who are most capable of supplying the answer, other students become mere spectators.

Meichenbaum and Biemiller (1998) talk about the "art of questioning" and compare it to a dance: "each partner needs to be attuned to the other, following the other's lead" (p. 153). Questioning is important for helping you to monitor student understanding of content and also for understanding how students are processing what they learn. Good and Brophy (2007) write about the "diagnostic power" of questioning. Questioning can also be used to scaffold and support student learning.

Asking simple yes/no questions or "guess what I'm thinking" questions has little diagnostic value in the classroom. Effective questioning strategies include the following:

- Distribute questions evenly among all students.
- Make certain that questions are clearly stated.
- Ask a variety of question types—lower and higher order questions.
- Ask all kinds of students all kinds of questions.
- Give students specific feedback about their answers.
- Let students explain why an answer is right.
- Let students explain their thinking when they get an answer wrong.
- Sequence the questions in such a way that they provide structure for learning.
- Ask questions in a nonthreatening, natural way.
- Encourage students to ask questions of you and of one another.
- Make questions relevant to students and to real-world applications.

One of the most important aspects of question asking is wait time (Rowe, 1974). No one likes to be put "on the spot." Giving students 3 to 5 seconds to think about an answer results in more thoughtful answers, more elaborated responses, and greater likelihood of participation from a wide range of students. There are benefits to asking fewer questions and giving students more time to give thoughtful answers (Zwiers, 2008). See the 60-Second Lesson for more suggestions for questioning strategies.

TECHNIQUES FOR TEACHING QUESTION ANSWERING

Scaffolded questioning: When a student answers a question incorrectly, rather than giving the student the correct answer or moving on to another student, provide scaffolded questioning to promote student learning. Scaffolded questioning is not asking questions that lead to the answer you have in your head. Rather, scaffolded questioning is a set of sequenced prompts that begin with general questions and then provide increased guidance. The goal is not just for the student to arrive at the right answer; it is also to help students learn strategies for problem solving and answering questions. Some examples of scaffolded questions are:

• What information do you need to answer this question?

• Do you need me to repeat the question?

• What are some key words in my question? How can the key words help you answer the question?

• Look at the graphic organizer we started at the beginning of the lesson. What information in the graphic organizer can help you answer the question?

Group responding: When reviewing material for a test or when helping students develop fluency in answering the question, group responding can be helpful. Choral or group responding occurs when the teacher asks the whole class a question and the entire class responds simultaneously. Group responding should be used judiciously because it is more difficult to monitor individual student responses.

Sources: Irwin, J. W. (2007). *Teaching comprehension processes* (3rd ed.). Boston: Allyn & Bacon; and Meichenbaum, D., & Biemiller, A. (1998). *Nurturing independent learners: Helping students take charge of their learning.* Newton, MA: Brookline Books.

Discussions. When done well, classroom discussions can be stimulating for students and for teachers as well. However, leading classroom discussions can be challenging for teachers (Ezzedeen, 2008; Wolsey & Lapp, 2009; Zwiers, 2008). Effective classroom discussions involve not only setting a positive classroom environment that encourages participating and risk-taking, but also planning a great deal (Zwiers, 2008). The goal is to engage students in **vibrant discussions** (Bean, 1985), in which student participation is high, students' thinking is stimulated, and students have opportunities to connect what they are learning to their personal knowledge and experience. Vibrant discussions help students learn how to express ideas, justify positions, listen to the ideas of others, and ask for clarification when they don't understand (Kauchak & Eggen, 1993; Zwiers, 2008).

Your role in a discussion is that of moderator and encourager. As a moderator, you help the group to establish a focus and stay on the topic. As an encourager, you engage reluctant participants and make certain that students are free to express their points of view. To encourage vibrant discussions, try the alternatives to traditional questioning in Tips for Teachers 15.6 (Dillon, 1979).

The **discussion web** (Alvermann, 1991) is a graphic aid to help students prepare for classroom discussions in content-area classes. As Figure 15.6 shows, the discussion web is designed to help students examine both sides of an issue. It is appropriate for elementary and secondary students and can be used before and after lectures.

Alvermann suggests the following procedure for implementing the discussion web:

What qualities are present in a vibrant discussion group? How can discussion skills be directly taught?

- Prepare students for reading or listening by introducing key vocabulary, activating prior knowledge, and setting a purpose for reading.
- After students have read a selection or listened to a lecture, introduce the discussion web with a provocative question. For example, after giving a lecture about the First Amendment, you could ask, "Should rap music be censored?" Provide time for students to discuss the pros and cons of the issue in pairs and complete the discussion web as a team. Students should take turns filling in as many "Yes" and "No" statements as the team can generate.
- Regroup pairs of students into teams of four students, who then compare their discussion webs and build consensus on an answer to the question.
- Have the group select and record the strongest argument and the reason for their choice.
- Have a spokesperson from each group take 3 minutes to report the results, and give individual students with dissenting or unrepresented points of view an opportunity to state their positions.
- Assign students an individual activity in which they write a position statement about their point of view on the issue.

TECHNIQUES FOR STIMULATING DISCUSSION

- *Declarative statements.* Provide information to which students can respond or react.

- *Declarative restatements.* Summarize student comments.

- *Indirect questions.* Ask questions that begin "I wonder . . ." or "What would happen if . . ."

- *Imperatives.* Make statements that encourage students to tell more about what they were thinking or to provide examples.

- *Student questions.* Invite students to ask questions of one another.

- *Deliberate silence.* Give everyone time to think and to gather their thoughts.

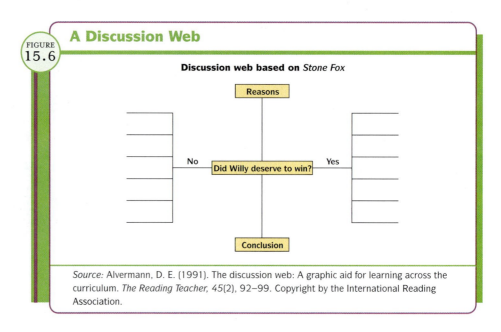

A Discussion Web

Discussion web based on *Stone Fox*

Reasons

No | Did Willy deserve to win? | Yes

Conclusion

Source: Alvermann, D. E. (1991). The discussion web: A graphic aid for learning across the curriculum. *The Reading Teacher, 45*(2), 92–99. Copyright by the International Reading Association.

The discussion web provides a structure for *critical thinking*—examining both sides of an issue carefully before making a judgment.

Effective Content-Area Reading Instruction for Middle and High School Learners

In your academic career you've developed strategies for navigating textbook reading assignments. Lots of practice and, perhaps, some direct instruction on how to read and learn from text have helped you along the way. For many students, textbooks can be labor intensive (Stahl, 2004; Wood, Lapp, Flood, & Taylor, 2008). This is certainly true for students who struggle with reading, but can also be true for some usually high-achieving students who have not learned approaches for efficient and effective textbook reading. This section shows you how to become familiar not only with the strengths and weaknesses of your textbook, but also with the ways in which students interact with and respond to the text. This section also contains effective techniques for making textbook adaptations for special learners.

Familiarizing Yourself with the Textbook

As a classroom teacher, you might not have the opportunity to select the textbook that is used in your content-area classroom. Typically, state selection committees decide on a limited number of state-adopted textbooks from which school districts can choose. At the district level, the list is shortened by a district committee. At the school level, grade- or committee-level teams frequently choose the textbook. Chances are, you will inherit a textbook that someone else has chosen for you. To familiarize yourself with your textbook, you need to consider text-based factors that contribute to the many challenges students encounter with textbook reading: readability level and friendliness level.

Go to **www.lexile.com** to learn more about the Lexile Framework™ for Reading.

Readability Level. Traditionally, a textbook's level of difficulty is gauged by its **readability level**, expressed as a grade level. For example, you might hear a teacher say, "This science book is intended for 10th graders, but the readability level is 11th grade." Readability levels are determined by applying to the text one or more readability formulas (e.g., Dale & Chall, 1948; Fry, 1977; Raygor, 1977). Such formulas are based on sentence complexity (measured by sentence length) and word difficulty (measured by word length and frequency). Keep in mind that readability levels are overall estimates of the textbook level of difficulty and that within each textbook some passages might vary—in some textbooks as much as three or four grade levels.

Another way to estimate the level of difficulty of a text is by **Lexile levels**. The Lexile Framework˚ for Reading estimates the student's reading level and a text's readability level. If a student has the same Lexile level as the Lexile level of a text, the student should be able to read the book with 75% accuracy. Lexile scores range from 200L (beginning readers) to 1700L (advanced readers).

Your teachers' manual will report the readability level and/or Lexile level of your text. Why is this important to know? Fran Hampton teaches 10th-grade biology. Some of her students are students with learning disabilities, some are English language learners, and a few are garden variety poor readers who have not been placed in special services. The reading levels of her students range from about 4th-grade level to 12th-grade level. The textbook has a stated readability level of 10th grade. Thus, Fran needs to make adaptations to the textbook to promote learning for all students in her classroom.

Friendliness Level. In addition to the readability level of your textbook, you should also become familiar with the text features included in your text that can support readers. **Friendly text** or **considerate text** is written and formatted in such a way that information can be extracted easily and support is available when the reader does not understand (Armbruster & Anderson, 1988; Singer, 1986). The degree to which text is considered friendly or considerate to the reader is determined by the number of features included in the text that promote learning (such as headings and subheadings, vocabulary in boldface type, and chapter summaries).

Familiarize yourself with the textbook you plan to use, and learn to recognize friendly text features that support student learning as well as areas in which you will need to intervene. Friendly text has *organization, explication, conceptual density, metadiscourse,* and *instructional devices*.

- *Organization* is sequence in which the author presents information in the text. Organization includes the general structure of the text as well as consistency and connectedness of ideas.
- *Explication* is how the author explains ideas and teaches the reader. Explication includes necessary background information and examples.
- *Conceptual density* is the number of new vocabulary terms or concepts the author introduces.
- *Metadiscourse* is the degree to which the author "talks" to the reader. Metadiscourse includes direct explanations of how to learn from the text and how to connect ideas from one part of the text to another.
- *Instructional devices* are the number of learning tools the author provides. Examples of learning tools are a table of contents, marginal annotations, and a glossary.

At the beginning of the school year, Fran Hampton does a textbook walk-through with her students. She holds a class discussion about the friendly text features in their book and brainstorms about ways students can use those text features to prepare for class discussions, labs, and tests.

Understanding How Students Interact with and Respond to Text

As you examine the textbook you will be using, you should anticipate how you will need to supplement it. The ultimate judge of the readability and friendliness of a textbook is the reader. The **FLIP chart strategy** helps students learn to evaluate text on their own (Schumm & Mangrum, 1991). ("FLIP" stands for **F**riendliness, **L**anguage, **I**nterest, and **P**rior knowledge.) By filling out forms like the one shown in Figure 15.7, students learn what is comfortable for them individually as readers. After students have completed the FLIP chart, you can learn (through class discussions and individual conferences) what is difficult for them in terms of text friendliness, language, interest, and prior knowledge. Students with reading and learning problems especially need to learn how to talk about the textbook and any problems they have with it. Classroom discussions based on the FLIP chart strategy also help students think as a group about effective strategies for coping with text they find difficult.

Making Textbook Adaptations

Suppose you learn that the textbook is too difficult for some of your students. What will you do? Research indicates that most content-area teachers seldom implement many adaptations for a number of reasons (Schumm & Vaughn, 1992a; Schumm, Vaughn, & Saumell, 1992).

FIGURE
15.7

The FLIP Chart

Title of assignment _____

Number of pages _____

General directions: Rate each of the four FLIP categories on a 1–5 scale (5 = high). Then determine your purpose for reading and appropriate reading rate, and budget your reading/study time.

F = Friendliness: How friendly is my reading assignment?
   Directions: Examine your assignment to see if it includes the friendly elements listed below.

Friendly text features

Table of contents	Index	Glossary
Chapter introductions	Headings	Subheadings
Margin notes	Study questions	Chapter summary
Key terms highlighted	Graphs	Charts
Pictures	Signal words	Lists of key facts

1_____2_____3_____4_____5

No friendly text features   Some friendly text features   Many friendly text features

Friendliness rating _____

L = Language: How difficult is the language in my reading assignment?
   Directions: Skim the chapter quickly to determine the number of new terms. Read three random paragraphs to get a feel for the vocabulary level and number of long, complicated sentences.

1_____2_____3_____4_____5

Many new words;   Some new words;   No new words;
complicated sentences   somewhat complicated sentences   clear sentences

Language rating _____

I = Interest: How interesting is my reading assignment?
   Directions: Read the title, introduction, headings/subheadings, and summary. Examine the pictures and graphics included.

1_____2_____3_____4_____5

Boring   Somewhat interesting   Very interesting

Interest rating _____

P = Prior knowledge: What do I already know about the material covered in my reading assignment?
   Directions: Think about the title, introduction, headings/subheadings, and summary.

1_____2_____3_____4_____5

Mostly new information   Some new information   Mostly familiar information

Prior knowledge rating _____

Overall, this reading assignment appears to be at:

☐ a comfortable reading level for me

☐ a somewhat comfortable reading level for me

☐ an uncomfortable reading level for me

Source: Schumm, J. S. & Mangrum, C. T. (1991). FLIP: A framework for textbook thinking. *Journal of Reading, 35,* 120–124. Copyright by the International Reading Association.

First, adapting textbooks takes time, and teachers' time for planning and preparing for instruction is already limited. Second, textbook adaptations often slow down instruction, and teachers cannot cover as much material as they would like. Third, some teachers think that making adaptations for the few students who need them is not fair to the high-achieving students who are ready to work at a faster pace. Fourth, some teachers feel that they do not

Tips for Teachers 15.7

GUIDELINES FOR ADAPTING CONTENT-AREA TEXTBOOKS

Substitute the textbook for students who have severe word-recognition problems:

- Audiotape textbook content.
- Read textbook aloud to students.
- Pair students to master textbook content.
- Use direct experiences, films, videotapes, recorders, and computer programs as substitutes for textbook reading.
- Work with students individually or in small groups to master textbook material.

Simplify the textbook for students whose reading level is far below that of the textbook used in class:

- Construct abridged versions of the textbook content or use the publisher's abridged version.
- Provide students with chapter outlines or summaries.
- Use a multilevel, multimaterial approach.

Highlight key concepts for students who have difficulty comprehending textbook material:

- Preview reading assignments with students to orient them to the topic and provide guidelines for budgeting reading and study time.
- Provide students with a purpose for reading.
- Provide an overview of an assignment before reading.
- Structure opportunities for students to activate prior knowledge before starting a reading assignment.

- Introduce key vocabulary before assigning reading.
- Develop a study guide to direct learning.
- Summarize or reduce textbook information to guide classroom discussions and independent reading.
- Color-code or highlight textbooks.
- Reduce length of assignments.
- Slow down the pace of reading assignments.
- Provide assistance in answering text-based questions.
- Demonstrate or model effective reading strategies.
- Place students in cooperative learning groups to master textbook content.
- Teach comprehension-monitoring techniques to improve ongoing understanding of text material.
- Teach students to use graphic aids to understand textbook information.

Increase idea retention for students who have difficulty with long-term memory:

- Structure postreading activities to increase retention of content.
- Teach reading strategies to improve retention.
- Teach students to record key concepts and terms for study purposes.
- Teach memory strategies to improve retention of text material.

Source: Schumm, J. S. & Strickler, K. (1991). Guidelines for adapting content area textbooks: Keeping teachers and students content. *Intervention in School and Clinic,* 27(2), 79–84. Copyright © 1991 by PRO-ED, Inc. Reprinted by permission.

have the training they need to make adaptations (Hall, 2005; Mallette, Henk, Waggoner, & Delaney, 2005). Fortunately, with professional development and use of a broadening array of instruction resources, teachers can make the adaptations students want and need (Cantrell, Burns, & Callaway, 2009). Tips for Teachers 15.7 lists textbook adaptations you might consider, three of which are discussed here in greater depth: text highlighting, multiliteracies, and listening to learn.

Text Highlighting.   Students with comprehension problems have difficulty sifting out important information. Underlining or highlighting key points in the textbook can help students attend to the most salient information (Santa, Havens, & Valdes, 2004; Wood & Wooley, 1986). As you read the textbook, highlight the information you think is most important. Then student or adult volunteers can use your book as a guide to highlight the same information in books for students with reading and learning disabilities. Keep in mind that this is an intermediate step. Students should also be taught how to highlight and identify key information on their own (Santa et al., 2004). You can use cooperative learning groups to support students in learning how to draw salient information from textbooks. Students can work collaboratively to develop text coding or "text graffiti" systems using colored pens and sticky notes (Buehl, 2009).

Multiliteracies.   After you and your students have taken a careful look at your textbook, you might realize that you will need to go beyond the textbook to provide your students with alternative reading material. Living in a digital age requires students to learn skills for dealing with multiples sources of information or **multiliteracies** (Bean, Readence, & Baldwin, 2008; Burniske, 2008; Wood et al., 2008). "No longer can we refer to traditional books alone as text. Now the term *text* has expanded to include print, graphic novels, art, music, digital and visual media, technical writings, popular culture such as music and television programs and characters, and Internet texts (webpages, blogs, instant messaging for example)" (Wood et al., 2008, p. 6).

Although Fran Hampton uses the textbook for her core curriculum, like more and more content-area teachers, she has begun using trade books (both fiction and nonfiction) and other reading materials (e.g., magazines and journals) to supplement content-area textbooks. Trade books and other alternative reading sources can be used to spark interest and to help students develop lifelong reading habits. In addition to informational books, she also uses historical fiction, biographies, and autobiographies as part of her planning to make the study of biology alive and relevant. Because informational trade books at lower readability levels have been produced in recent years, it's possible to locate books on the same theme at varying levels as a basis for classroom discussion (Fitzpatrick, 2008). Regardless of how you choose to integrate trade books in content-area instruction, try to select (or help your students select) books that are engaging and that will grab their interest, and don't forget to share your own enthusiasm for reading and learning beyond the textbook.

Fran has not limited herself to traditional print media. She encourages students to use the Internet. Fran identifies appropriate websites and creates inquiry-based activities based on web content. Students work in teams in the school's computer lab to complete the activity and then later to engage in class discussion about what they learned. She also encourages her students to use **cybaries**, or cyber libraries, to find links to websites that can be useful in their research (e.g., *Nettrekker*). As Fran puts it, "I'm continuing to keep an open mind about multiliteracies, but do so with caution. On the one hand my students are increasingly more tech savvy and motivated to use digital resources. On the other hand, I want to ensure that we use safe Internet practices." See Tech Tips to learn about some supporting technology.

Go to **www.cast.org**, the website of the Center for Applied Special Technology, where you will learn more about gaining access to the general education curriculum through technology.

Listening to Learn.   For over 60 years the nonprofit organization Recording for the Blind & Dyslexic (RFB&D) has provided audiobook library services for students who have difficulty with traditional texts. The organization offers recorded books in both CD-ROM and downloadable versions to assist students who are blind, have low vision, or have learning disabilities.

Tech TIPS

USING TECHNOLOGY TO SUPPORT LEARNING IN CONTENT AREAS

Learners with difficulties in reading and comprehending written text often experience failure in content-area classes such as social studies and science. Although learners may be receiving support in their reading and writing skills, they also need support in their content-area classes. There are many programs online that you can use in the classroom or that students can use on their own. Consider some of the following:

On-line science museum by the Smithsonian at
▶ www.smithsonian.org/
The Smithsonian Institution home page, with extensive links to art, design, history, culture, science, and technology collections, is a treasure trove of information for students looking to learn about content areas that will enrich their knowledge base.

Cast e-reader by CAST, Inc. at
▶ www.cast.org
This website uses the universal design framework for accommodating all learners. Using a wide array of technologies and media, this site allows educators to assess all students accurately and to provide instruction that will meet students' needs.

Bookshare by Benetech at
▶ http://www.bookshare.org/
For students with visual, learning, or physical disabilities, this site is an online library that provides access to online books, periodicals, newspapers, and textbooks. Once students provide proof of their disability, they may become eligible to become members of Bookshare.

SUGGESTIONS FOR RECORDING READING ASSIGNMENTS

- Instead of recording an entire chapter verbatim, read the key sections and paraphrase the less important sections.

- Code the text so that readers or listeners will know whether the person on the tape is reading or paraphrasing.

- Provide a short advance organizer on the tape to help students get ready to read and listen.

- Insert questions that readers or listeners can stop to think about.

- Remind readers or listeners to stop periodically to think about what they have read.

- Use a natural tone of voice and a comfortable reading rate. Have students experiment with recorded texts to see whether they comprehend better with or without the accompanying printed text.

Their expanded website offers information for how to access recorded materials and suggestions for implementing them in your classroom.

With the advent of portable media players, audiobooks are increasingly popular and acceptable to students. Students can listen to the books in a listening center in classrooms, resource rooms, school libraries, or at home. If the material is not available through RFB&D, Tips for Teachers 15.8 provides suggestions for recording reading assignments.

Boyle and colleagues (2002) recommend pairing the listening of recorded text with other learning strategies to get maximum results. In particular, they recommend the SLiCK sequence to structure learning from recorded text. The steps in the SLiCK strategy are as follows:

- **S**et up the CD-ROM playback machine.
- **L**ook ahead or preview the printed chapter and any organizational aspects of the CD-ROM to identify headings, subheadings, and key words.
- **C**omprehend the recorded text through careful listening and reading along with the text.
- **K**eep notes from text for further review and to prepare for tests and classroom discussions.

Effective content-area reading instruction coupled with listener-friendly lectures can serve as the foundation for students' success in middle and high school. Activities for all Learners includes additional ideas you can use to promote student learning in secondary grades.

Another key element that determines student success or failure is student assessment. But what about students with learning and behavior problems? Should they have the same assessments and tests as everyone else? What if a student cannot read? What if a student cannot work under timed conditions? In the next section, you'll learn about key ideas in thinking about differentiating assessment.

Differentiating Assessment

In classrooms that include highly diverse learners, differentiated assessment should go hand in hand with differentiated instruction. Learners may have different assessment needs. For example, some children with challenges in learning basic skills may need more intensive and frequent progress monitoring than others. For children who are English language learners or students with disabilities, testing accommodations such as extended time may be appropriate. Differentiated assessment involves to use of formal assessments and informal measures (Chapman & King, 2004; Wormeli, 2006b). It also involves accommodations and adaptations to meet individual needs. Tomlinson (2003) identifies four ways that assessment and instruction can be linked:

1. Preassessment is necessary to find out what each student knows and needs to learn.
2. Ongoing assessment is needed to monitor student learning during instructional units and to make adjustments as necessary.
3. Teachers identify multiple ways for students to demonstrate what they have learned.
4. Students become actively engaged in setting instructional goals and in self-assessment in meeting those goals.

CONTENT-AREA INSTRUCTIONAL ACTIVITIES FOR ALL LEARNERS

① CONVERSATIONAL DISCUSSION GROUPS

Objective: To help students become comfortable in classroom discussions

Grades: Middle school and above

Teaching Procedures: The idea behind conversational discussion groups is that discourse about reading assignments and lectures should be more like conversations. Authentic oral language experiences with peers can be particularly helpful for English language learners (Wolsey & Lapp, 2009). Discussion groups can be held after reading a book or other selection, listening to a lecture, hearing a guest speaker, or viewing a video in class. There are three steps to implementing conversational discussion groups:

1. *Introduce/review rules.* Before dividing students into conversation groups, either introduce or review rules. You will need to determine rules in advance or perhaps have the group generate rules related to etiquette for speaking in a group, participation, staying on task, and behavior.

2. *Lines of thought.* During the discussion time, the teacher presents students with three questions—one at a time. When students finish with one question, the teacher goes to the group to hear and respond to their answer and then gives a second question. Questions are related to background knowledge, summarizing the story or lecture, and making personal reactions or reflections.

3. *Debriefing.* Students then spend some time reflecting on and evaluating their experiences in the conversational discussion group. The reflection is guided by three questions: (a) How did we go about getting our answers today? (b) How did we do? and (c) What can we do to improve next time?

Depending on the group of students, they may need more or less teacher direction and modeling in how to discuss what they have read or heard. The real goal of conversational discussion groups is to get beyond a formalized structure and to encourage students to have productive, personally meaningful discussions with their peers.

Sources: O'Flahavan, J. F. & Stein, C. (1992, December). The conversational discussion groups project. In K. Jongsma (Chair), *Understanding and enhancing literature discussion in elementary classrooms*. Symposium conducted at the 42nd Annual Meeting of the National Reading Conference, San Antonio, TX; and Wolsey, T. H. & Lapp, D. (2009). Discussion-based instruction in the middle and secondary school classroom. In K. D. Wood & W. E. Blanton (Eds.), *Literacy instruction for adolescents: Research-based practices* (pp. 368–391). New York: Guilford.

② JIGSAW PUZZLE METHOD

Objective: To help students work cooperatively to learn content-area material

Grades: Middle school and above

Materials: Expert sheets

Teaching Procedures:

1. Select a unit of material for students to learn that can be broken up into four sections. For example, a social studies chapter on Italy might be broken up into imports and exports, natural resources, famous sights, and native foods.

2. Assign students to four different "expert" groups. The members of each group are responsible for learning the material in their assigned section—they must become experts.

3. Allow expert groups enough time to complete "expert sheets." Expert sheets are handouts you have prepared for students to record important information they have learned.

4. Prepare a quiz (two or three questions) that each group member must pass to truly become an expert. Students who do not pass the test can work with you or with group mates to learn the information. You can decide whether students can use their expert sheets to take the quiz.

5. Move the students into their jigsaw groups. A jigsaw group consists of one expert from each of the four different groups.

6. Each expert then teaches the content he or she learned to members of the jigsaw group.

Source: Aronson, E. & Patnoe, S. (1997). *The jigsaw classroom: Building cooperation in the classroom* (2nd ed.). New York: Addison-Wesley/Longman; and Paratore, J. R., & McCormack, R. L. (2009). *Grouping in the middle and secondary grades: Advancing content and literacy knowledge.* In K. D. Wood & W. E. Blanton (Eds.), *Literacy instruction for adolescents: Research-based practices* (pp. 420–441). New York: Guilford.

③ SEND A PROBLEM

Objective: To help students learn content-area material

Grades: Middle school and above

Materials: Index cards

Teaching Procedures:

1. Students work individually to generate questions about a reading assignment or lecture.

2. Students record their questions on the front of an index card; they record answers on the back of the same card.

3. Students are assigned to work in groups of three or four to review the questions and answers for accuracy of the answers. Answers are revised if needed.

4. The stack of question cards is then passed to another group of students. Members of the group take turns asking and answering questions.

5. The process of passing continues until time is up or until all groups have had the opportunity to review the cards of every group.

This section begins with a discussion of formal assessment including high-stakes testing and teacher-made tests. It continues with ideas for informal or alternative assessment including suggestions for engaging secondary students in self-assessment. The chapter concludes with ideas for assigning student grades.

Preparing Students for High-Stakes Tests

The passage of the No Child Left Behind Act mandated large-scale assessment for all students, including students with disabilities and English language learners. High-quality instruction that is direct and focused on concepts to be learned, clarification of student misunderstandings, attention to level of difficulty of assignments, and support to guide problem solving are some of the best ways to promote student achievement (Vaughn, Gersten, & Chard, 2000).

PEARSON
myeducationlab

Go to the Assignments and Activities section for Topic 6: Assessment in the MyEducationLab for your course and complete the activity entitled *High Stakes Testing*.

Implementation of high-stakes tests varies considerably, especially among those students who qualify for accommodations. Other than providing high-quality instruction, how teachers prepare students for taking high-stakes tests depends on the nature of state-identified standards and the format of the examination used (Katsiyannis, Zhang, Ryan, & Jones, 2007). Tips for Teachers 15.9 provides questions that can guide your thinking about how to prepare students for high-stakes tests in content areas such as science and social studies. At the middle and high school levels, some content areas are not included in statewide assessments. Nonetheless, teachers in all subject areas are increasingly being provided with professional development and resources to align their teaching in a way that promotes student achievement on tests in reading, writing, and mathematics. Tips for Teachers 15.9 also provides questions you can ask curriculum leaders in your school.

Your state, school district, and school may have policy statements and procedures for appropriate and ethical ways to prepare your students for high-stakes tests. As a classroom teacher, you should become familiar with those policies and procedures. You will also want to find out what adaptations or exam alternatives are available for which individual students in your class may be eligible (Wasburn-Moses, 2003).

Tips for Teachers 15.9

QUESTIONS THAT WILL GUIDE YOU IN PREPARING STUDENTS FOR HIGH-STAKES TESTING IN CONTENT AREAS

- What state standards are designated for students in my grade level?

- How are state standards aligned with district and school requirements?

- What materials do I have that are aligned with the standards?

- What is the format of the state exam?

- Are there resources available to help me design my teacher-made exams to align with the format of the state test?

- Does my state or district maintain a website with resources that can assist me in planning, assessment, and instruction?

- When students do not seem to be making progress on state standards, what classroom interventions can I implement?

- When classroom interventions do not work, are there resources for my students at the school or district level for more intensive intervention?

- How can I integrate standards into my ongoing teaching to keep students motivated and engaged?

- What accommodations or alternative assessments are available for students with disabilities or those who are English language learners?

Here are some questions you can ask of curriculum leaders in your school:

- What is the format of high-stakes tests in our state?

- What types of questions can I include in my class discussions and tests that support question formats used on state examinations?

- What formats for writing assessment are used on state assessments? What ways can I incorporate those formats into my assignments and tests?

Helping Students Develop Test-Taking Strategies

There is growing evidence that helping students develop test-taking strategies can enhance performance on high-stakes tests (Carter, Hughes, & Wehby, 2005). Keeping local requirements in mind, Thurlow, Elliott, and Ysseldyke (2002) suggest three general ways a teacher can help students prepare for high-stakes tests: test approach skills, test-taking skills, and test preparedness.

1. **Test approach skills** are skills that can help students get physically and mentally ready for exams. Sending flyers home to parents about the importance of sleep and nutrition can help prepare students physically. Miyasaka (2002) emphasizes the importance of reducing test anxiety. Teaching test-taking and test preparedness skills will help alleviate student anxiety. However, the positive attitude you set in your classroom is vital for the reduction of anxiety. Talk with your school counselor about students who seem to have an unusually high level of anxiety about the examination.

2. **Test-taking skills** are skills that students use during the examination (Flippo, Becker, & Wark, 2009). You can help students develop test-taking skills by providing suggestions for taking specific types of tests (multiple-choice, true/false, matching, short-answer, essay) and by teaching testing vocabulary. Table 15.3 presents cue words related to essay examinations that help middle and high school students construct better answers on open-ended items on high-stakes tests.

3. **Test preparedness skills** are skills related to knowing both the general content and the format of the test. Critics of high-stakes tests point out that teachers are reduced to "teaching to the test" and that instruction becomes stilted and narrow. Gulik (2003) warns, "A teacher should not engage in instruction that addresses only those portions of knowledge included on the test" (p. 2). Many teachers find this easier said than

---

TABLE 15.3

Instruction Cue Words for Answering Essay Questions

CUE	MEANING	CUE	MEANING
Analyze	Break into parts and examine each part.	List	Provide a numbered list of items or points.
Apply	Discuss how the principles would apply to a situation.	Outline	Organize your answer into main points and supporting details. If appropriate, use outline format.
Compare	Discuss differences and similarities.	Prove	Provide factual evidence to support your logic or position.
Contrast	Discuss differences and similarities, stressing the differences.	Relate	Show the connections among ideas.
Critique	Analyze and evaluate, using criteria.	Review	Provide a critical summary in which you summarize and present your comments.
Define	Provide a clear, concise statement that explains the concept.	State	Explain precisely.
Describe	Give a detailed account, listing characteristics, qualities, and components as appropriate.	Summarize	Provide a synopsis that does not include your comments.
Diagram	Provide a drawing.	Trace	Describe the development or progress of the idea.
Discuss	Provide an in-depth explanation. Be analytical.	**Add your own instruction cue words and definitions!**	
Explain	Give a logical development that discusses reasons or causes.		
Illustrate	Use examples or, when appropriate, provide a diagram or picture.		
Interpret	Explain and share your own judgment.		
Justify	Provide reasons for your statements or conclusion.		

Source: Adapted from Bos, C. S. & Vaughn, S. *Teaching students with learning and behavior problems* (4th ed., p. 326). Boston: Allyn & Bacon. Copyright © 2006 by Pearson Education. Reprinted by permission of the publisher.

done. Guthrie and Wigfield (2000) offer suggestions for making connections between standards, test content, and student motivation:

- *Learning and knowledge goals.* Set core learning goals that are co-developed by the teacher and the students.
- *Real-world interactions.* Make connections between the academic curriculum and the personal experiences of learners.
- *Interesting subject content.* Students will devote effort, attention, and persistence to topics that are enjoyable and intriguing.
- *Strategy instruction.* Provide direct instruction, scaffolding, and guided practice.
- *Praise and rewards.* Give informative compliments that make learners feel a sense of accomplishment and pride in their work.

Teacher-Made Tests. Tests are the primary means teachers use to determine whether students have learned new concepts and can apply them. Regular classroom tests can be teacher made, department or district made, or come from supplemental textbook materials. If you use department-made, district-made, or textbook-made exams, read the exams thoroughly to make sure the content is representative of what you have covered in class or in reading assignments. It is a good idea to take the tests yourself as a way of reviewing test content. One of the primary steps you can take is to create student-friendly tests.

Tests are also a way to find out what students need to learn and what they have learned. Pretests can be used to identify what students already know about a topic and help you plan for differentiated instruction. Tests can also be used for ongoing monitoring of student progress and for outcomes at the end of a lesson or unit. The best way to discover what students have learned is to construct student-friendly tests, adapt test administration and scoring as necessary, consider alternatives to testing (such as assessment portfolios), and teach test-taking skills.

Student-friendly tests are considerate to the test taker in content and format. The content has been covered in class or assigned readings, and students have been told explicitly that they are responsible for learning it. The format is clear and easy to understand. To construct student-friendly tests, you must first decide what skills and concepts to include. The lesson and unit planning pyramids can be particularly helpful here; to complete them, you decide which concepts are most important and prioritize those concepts for instructional purposes. You know what you want all, most, and some of your students to know, and you have told them your expectations. You can cover those skills and concepts on the test. Avoid asking trivial questions (Conderman & Koroghlanian, 2002).

In a test format, directions should be clear and unambiguous, and items should be legible and properly spaced. Students should have sufficient room to place their answers and specific guidelines if answers are to be written on a separate sheet (Salend, 1994). Attention to format is important for all students but particularly for those who have difficulty reading and taking tests and those who are anxious about test taking. Tips for Teachers 15.10 provides some suggestions for teacher-made tests.

Even with student-friendly tests, students with learning problems may have difficulty reading tests, working within time constraints, or resisting distractions during a test. Other special learners may have physical needs that inhibit performance on a test (they may tire easily, for example). As you decide which, if any, adaptations to use, consider the material to be covered by the test, the test's task requirements (e.g., reading, taking dictation), and the particular needs of special learners. Consult with the special education teacher and other specialists in your school to get advice about the most appropriate adaptations for individual students. Tips for Teachers 15.11 provides suggestions for making adaptations for students with special needs.

Alternative Assessments. In addition to tests, alternative assessments can be used for preassessment, ongoing monitoring, and assessment of student outcomes at the end of a lesson or unit. The idea with alternative assessments is to offer students variety in terms of how they can demonstrate what they have learned and can do. The following are some examples of alternative assessments:

- Audiotapes, videotapes, CD-ROMs, photographs
- Teacher, peer, and self checklists
- Lists of books read
- Lists of accomplishments

Tips for Teachers 15.10

WRITING EFFECTIVE TEST QUESTIONS

True/False Questions

- Test one idea.
- Write items without any qualification.
- Avoid using negatives.
- Avoid items that are obviously true or false.
- Write items of the same length.
- Write an equal number of true and false items.

Multiple-Choice Questions

- Write direct questions.
- Make the stem longer than the choice.
- Avoid using *all* or *none* choices.

- Arrange choices in logical order.
- Avoid clues within the item or test.
- Avoid using negatives.
- Write items of the same length.
- Scatter the correct choices equally.

Matching Questions

- Use homogenous lists.
- Place longer phrases in the left column.
- Include more responses than premises.
- Arrange response in a logical order.
- Restrict the number of matches to 10 or fewer.

Source: Conderman, G., & Koroghlanian, C. (2002). Writing test questions like a pro. *Intervention in School and Clinic, 38,* 83–87. Copyright 2002 by PRO-ED, Inc. Reprinted with permission.

Tips for Teachers 15.11

TESTING ADAPTATIONS

- Teach students test-taking skills.
- Give frequent quizzes rather than only exams.
- Give take-home tests.
- Test on less content than the rest of the class.
- Change types of questions (e.g., essay to multiple choice).
- Use tests with enlarged print.
- Use black-and-white copies (versus dittos).
- Highlight key words in questions.
- Provide extra space on tests for answering.
- Simplify wording of test questions.
- Allow students to answer fewer questions.
- Give extra help preparing for tests.
- Give the actual test as a study guide.

- Give practice questions as a study guide.
- Give open-book and note tests.
- Give tests to small groups.
- Give extended time to finish tests.
- Read test questions to students.
- Allow use of learning aids during tests (e.g., calculators).
- Give individual help with directions during tests.
- Allow oral instead of written answers (e.g., tape recorders).
- Allow answers in outline format.
- Allow word processors.
- Give feedback to individual students during test.

Source: Jayanthi, M., Epstein, M. H., Polloway, E. A., & Bursuck, W. D. (1996). Testing adaptations: A national survey of the testing practices of general education teachers. *Journal of Special Education, 30,* 99–155.

- Samples of home learning
- Goals statements and record of goal attainment
- Journals and self-reflections
- Graphs of individual student progress
- Copies of passages read fluently

Both tests and alternative assessment artifacts can be organized into an assessment portfolio. **Assessment portfolios** are collections of work samples that document a student's progress in a content area (Wormeli, 2006a). You can use portfolios to provide tangible evidence of student performance over a period of time. Portfolios can include writing samples of all stages of the writing process and in all genres. Suggestions for developing assessment portfolios are included in Tips for Teachers 15.12.

Assessment portfolios can be organized according to subject-area standards that students need to master. Students can gather evidence that demonstrates their progress in meeting standards and benchmarks. Thus, students can become actively engaged in self-assessment. For this to happen, students need to be aware of academic goals, criteria for mastery, and what constitutes adequate evidence (Andrade & Valtcheva, 2009; McMillan & Hearn, 2008). Checklist and self-reflection prompts can be used to get students actively engaged in gauging their progress in meeting goals (Wormeli, 2006a). Although secondary students can become actively involved in monitoring their performance, their assessment should only represent a small portion (perhaps 5%) of their grade (Andrade & Valtcheva, 2009).

Grading

Perhaps few other topics related to differentiated assessment and instruction generate more discussion than grading. Teachers, administrators, parents, and students struggle with what is fair in terms of individual student rights, equity among all students in the classroom, and accountability to state and local standards (Nunley, 2006; Wormeli, 2006a). Even though local policies are in place that address grading issues, there are no easy answers as to what is fair and equitable for all students.

In general, when differentiating assessment and grading, keep in mind what you want your students to know and be able to do to demonstrate mastery of a standard. The pathway that students take to mastery may be very different (Nunley, 2006). One way to make your expectations

Tips FOR TEACHERS 15.12

DEVELOPMENT OF ASSESSMENT PORTFOLIOS

- Develop a portfolio plan consistent with your purposes for the assignment.

- Clarify what work will go into portfolios.

- Start with only a couple of different kinds of entries and expand gradually.

- Compare notes with other teachers as you experiment with portfolios.

- Have as a long-term goal the inclusion of a variety of assessments that address content, process, and attitude goals across the curriculum.

- Make portfolios accessible in the classroom. Students and teachers should be able to add to the collection quickly and easily.

- Develop summary sheets or graphs that help to describe a body of information (e.g., "I can do" lists, lists of books read, or pieces of writing completed). Let students record these data when possible.

- Work with the student to choose a few representative samples that demonstrate the student's progress.

- Review portfolios with students periodically (at least four times during the school year). The review should be a time to celebrate progress and to set future goals.

- Encourage students to review portfolios with a classmate before reviewing with the teacher. Students should help make decisions about what to keep.

- In preparation for a parent conference, have students develop a table of contents for the portfolio.

Source: Radencich, M. C., Beers, P. C., & Schumm, J. S. (1993). *A handbook for the K–12 reading resource specialist* (pp. 119–120). Boston: Allyn & Bacon.

Objective: To help students learn to use rubrics effectively

Grades: Grades 6 and above

Teaching Procedures: To complete this activity, you will need a rubric and some student work samples. Give the students examples of high-quality work, average work, and less than satisfactory work, and have them complete the following **RUBRIC** process:

Read the rubric and the material to be graded.

Use the rubric to give an initial score.

Bring a buddy to help you rate again.

Review the material together.

Identify and award the scores together.

Check the scores again.

Source: Jackson, C. W., & Larkin, M. J. (2002). RUBRIC—Teaching students to use grading rubrics. Teaching Exceptional Children, 35, 40–45.

and grading guidelines clear to students is through the use of **rubrics** or **scoring guides**. Such tools are increasingly being used to give students explicit information about expected performance on tests and assignments (Whittaker, Salend, & Duhaney, 2001; Wormeli, 2006a). Rubrics are of two general types: **analytic rubrics** (process-oriented instruments that break an activity into component parts) and **holistic rubrics** (product-oriented instruments used with parts that are interrelated) (Jackson & Larkin, 2002). Although the construction of rubrics does take some time, they typically streamline the grading process. Rubrics also make your expectations more tangible for students and their parents. Activities for All Learners provides a strategy to help secondary students become proficient in the use of rubrics.

Summary

- Since the authorization of No Child Left Behind (2001), states have adopted curriculum standards for middle and high school subjects. It is important that you become familiar with the standards for your subject area in the state where you plan to teach.

- Differentiated instruction (DI) has been identified as one means to plan for individual student needs. DI is both a philosophy of instructing students based on individual needs as well as instructional practices aligned with the philosophy.

- Content-area teachers can use prelearning activities such as purpose setting, preteaching vocabulary, and graphic organizers to improve students' comprehension and depth of learning. Student participation in class can be improved through the planning and implementation of well-structured questions and vibrant discussions.

- Textbook adaptations include study guides, highlighting, and alternative reading materials. You can become familiar with the strengths and weaknesses of your textbook by evaluating its subject matter content, readability level, and friendliness level. One way to learn how your students interact with and respond to the textbook is to use the FLIP chart.

- In classrooms that include highly diverse learners, differentiated assessment should go hand in hand with differentiated instruction. Differentiated assessment involves use of formal assessments and informal measures such as surveys, rubrics, checklists, projects, and home learning activities.

Think and Apply

1. Now that you have read Chapter 15, think about how Jerry Schumm met the challenges he faced in content-area instruction. What practices did he use? What additional strategies would you use in your own class?

2. On your department of education website, locate the instructional standards for your state in a subject area you plan to teach. Identify three standards and think about what

challenges the standards might pose for high-, average-, and low-achieving students; for students with learning and behavior problems; for students who are English language learners; and for students who are gifted.

3. Work in a cooperative learning group to brainstorm the potential pitfalls of differentiated instruction and how you might overcome those pitfalls in your middle or high school classroom.

PEARSON
myeducationlab

Now go to Topic 6: Assessment; Topic 8: Instructional Practices; and Learning Strategies; and Topic 9: Reading Instruction in the MyEducationLab (www.myeducationlab.com) for your course where you can:

■ Find learning outcomes for these topics along with the national standards that connect to these outcomes.

■ Complete Assignments and Activities that can help you more deeply understand the chapter content.

■ Examine challenging situations and cases presented in the IRIS Center Resources.

■ Listen to Teacher Talk to hear how one teacher holds high expectations for her students with severe disabilities.

■ Apply and practice your understanding of the core teaching skills identified in the chapter with Building Teaching Skills and Dispositions learning units.

Fostering Strategies for Student Independence

FOCUS QUESTIONS

1. How can you provide effective strategy instruction to help your students learn how to learn?

2. What are some difficulties students have in taking responsibility for their learning?

3. What are some ways you can teach students to take personal responsibility for their learning?

4. What are some effective ways to help students become active learners in the classroom?

5. What are some strategies you can use to help students navigate the home–school connection?

Andrew Post is in his fifth year of teaching seniors in a large, urban high school. He teaches six periods of American Government (first semester) and Economics (second semester) to honors students. Andrew teaches at the same high school he attended and chose teaching as a profession largely because of the rich experience he had when taking the classes he now teaches. As Andrew puts it, "It's the exact reason I went into teaching."

The companion classes are designed to promote student responsibility and independent learning. The American Government class is taught using a Mock Congress simulation. Each student researches a specific state and then composes a bill, tracks the bill through committee, and eventually to a congressional vote. The Economics class uses a simulated personal finance experience (Budget World) as an instructional foundation. Students work individually and in investment groups to generate income and then develop a budget to manage their resources (Personal Finance Project). Student engagement is high due to the hands-on approach and the "hot-topics" that are naturally generated.

Both courses incorporate assignments that encourage individual and group responsibility. Course requirements include traditional textbook/test requirements, but also debate, presentations, reports on committee work, and participation in classroom discussions. "We use a million ways to assess so that all students can plug in and be successful."

When Andrew first started teaching seniors, he realized that even in honors classes there was a wide range of student preparedness to work independently, pace themselves in completion of assignments, and tackle long-range projects. The type of activities Andrew plans paves the way for his students in their next steps: typically college or in some cases a vocational track. However, Andrew has become an advocate for teaching study strategies early on. He now teaches a one-day-a-week "Freshman Focus" course that teaches "Tools for Success." All freshmen are required to complete this mini-course that focuses on areas such as time management, conflict management, active listening, and note taking.

Introduction

Most teachers would like their students to become independent, successful learners. As high-school seniors, Andrew's students have a short timeline toward independence. Thus, the support he provides in fostering learning and study strategies among his students is vital. This chapter begins with a discussion of effective strategy instruction with an emphasis on the teaching–learning connection. It continues with a discussion of why some students have difficulty becoming independent learners. Finally, the chapter presents ideas for developing independence through personal responsibility and active learning inside and outside of the classroom.

Effective Strategy Instruction: The Teaching–Learning Connection

Andrew has learned that the time he spends teaching his high-school seniors strategies for learning has big payoffs. His students not only master the content, but also learn how to take more responsibility for their own learning. **Strategies** are step-by-step cognitive processes and plans for reading, studying, and problem solving (Holschuh & Aultman, 2009; Montague, 2008). Strategies actively engage students in **metacognition** or "knowledge of one's knowledge, processes, and cognitive and affective states; and the ability to consciously and deliberately monitor and regulate one's knowledge, processes, and cognitive and affective states" (Hacker, 1998, p. 11).

The Goals of Strategy Instruction

What is the difference between strategies and skills? Some authors and classroom teachers use these terms interchangeably or inconsistently (Devine & Kania, 2003; Mulcahy-Ernt & Caverly, 2009). To address this confusion, literacy researchers Afflerbach, Pearson, and Paris (2008) conducted an historical review of the terms in the hope of bringing clarity for teachers and their students. They concluded that skills are automatic processes whereas strategies are deliberately controlled processes. "Reading strategies are deliberate, goal-directed attempts to control and modify the reader's efforts to decode text, understand words, and construct meanings of text. Reading skills are automatic actions. . . . The reader's deliberate control, goal-directedness, and awareness define a strategic action" (Afflerbach et al., 2008, p. 368). Strategies and skills are interconnected. Deliberate strategies are used to complete new or difficult tasks. When the strategies are applied automatically and effortlessly, they become skills.

The goal of strategy instruction is to support students as they develop independence in completing learning tasks and eventually become skilled in their use. Schumm and Post (1997) refer to independent learners as **executive learners**. Executive learners are students who

- Are knowledgeable about personal learning strengths and challenges.
- Have a clear understanding about tasks to be accomplished.
- Have a repertoire of learning strategies that can be applied in independent learning situations.
- Have developed a set of **help-seeking behaviors** to activate when additional assistance is needed.

Strategy Instruction Guidelines

Go to **www.how-to-study.com** to find tips for all areas of study skills and strategies.

How can you help students in your class become executive learners? One way is to incorporate strategy instruction into your instructional repertoire. When you teach strategies, keep in mind the teaching–learning connection. Most students need direct instruction and sufficient practice to learn how to learn. Following are key guidelines to keep in mind when planning for strategy instruction.

Guideline 1: Choose Strategies Carefully.   There is a wide array of strategies from which you can choose. In fact, several books on the market are actually encyclopedias of potential strategies for use with secondary students:

- *Classroom Strategies for Interactive Learning* (Buehl, 2009)
- *Informed Choices for Struggling Adolescent Readers: A Research-Based Guide to Instructional Programs and Practices* (Deshler, Palinscar, Biancarosa, & Nair, 2007)
- *Project CRISS (Creating Independence Through Student-Owned Strategies)* (Santa, Havens, & Valdes, 2004)

So which strategies should you select? See Tips for Teachers 16.1.

Guideline 2: Present Content and Strategies Concurrently.   Strategy instruction is not new. In fact, Frances Robinson (1941) introduced the reading strategy Survey, Question, Read, Recite, Review (SQ3R) in the 1940s! Often strategies are taught in isolation and students are on their own in determining when and how to use the strategy. Most often they don't use the strategy at all. You can increase the odds of your students' strategy use when you teach content and strategies concurrently (Bean, Readence, & Baldwin, 2008). For instance, if Andrew were teaching his high-school seniors about the different types of bills that are introduced in Congress (e.g., enabling bill, amendment), he might also teach summarization strategies at the same time. Students would be assigned a textbook reading that provided an overview of each type of bill. Then students would write brief summaries of the essential components of each variety of bills.

Guideline 3: Teach Strategies in Stages.   Strategy instruction involves a gradual release of responsibility from the teacher to the learner (Buehl, 2009). The goal is to move from teacher-regulated to student-regulated use of strategies through scaffolded instruction (Buehl, 2009). There are different stages of strategy learning that lead to skilled, executive learning. If students learn a strategy only at a superficial level, they are not likely to use it on a regular basis.

To enhance your understanding of strategies that will help support student learning, go to the IRIS Center Resources section of Topic 8: Instructional Practices and Learning Strategies in the MyEducationLab for your course and complete Module 35: Using Learning Strategies: Instruction to Enhance Student Learning.

CHOOSING STRATEGIES TO MEET ALL STUDENTS' NEEDS

- Different strategies are designed for different purposes. Select a strategy that will help your students meet the standards or instructional goals you intend.

- All strategies may not work with all students. Some strategies were researched and developed specifically for students with disabilities; others for more general audiences. In selecting a strategy, think about the needs of the students in your classroom and whether your students are ready for the strategy in terms of their knowledge base and capacity. You might choose a few generic strategies to teach to the whole class in depth. Strategies to meet the needs of individuals or small groups of students can be taught in collaboration with a special education teacher or in small, teacher-led groups at appropriate times.

- For strategies to be useful for students, they must be presented in a memorable form. Strategies that are short and easy to remember are more likely to be internalized and actually used.

- The strategies you select must meet the "reality check" for you. Choose strategies that are consistent with the time, materials, and other resources you have available.

Sources: Bean, T. W., Readence, J. E., & Baldwin, R. S. (2008). *Content area literacy: An integrated approach* (9th ed.). Dubuque, IA: Kendall/Hunt; Lenz, B. K., & Deshler, D. D. (2004). *Teaching content to all: Evidence-based inclusive practices in middle and secondary schools.* Boston: Pearson; and Montague, M. (2008). Self-regulation strategies to improve mathematical problem solving for students with learning disabilities. *Learning Disability Quarterly, 31,* 37–44.

Yet, most students—including high-achieving students—appreciate learning "tricks" that will help them learn more efficiently and effectively.

When introducing a strategy to your students, provide instruction and practice that will lead them to the following higher levels of strategy learning and ultimately to the automatic skill level as presented in the following stages:

1. **Stage 1:** *Awareness*—initially becoming introduced to a new strategy and the rationale for its use
2. **Stage 2:** *Knowledge*—developing insights about how the strategy works, when the strategy is most appropriate, and procedures for using the strategy
3. **Stage 3:** *Simulation*—trying the strategy out with simulated drills or exercises
4. **Stage 4:** *Practice*—trying the strategy out in actual reading and studying
5. **Stage 5:** *Skill*—making the strategy a part of a regular study routine

When Andrew introduces a strategy to his Freshman Focus classes, he builds in opportunities for students to move toward higher stages of strategy learning. For example, if Andrew were introducing the K-W-L strategy (Ogle, 1986) (see Chapter 12), he would do the following:

- Provide an overview of the strategy, describe that its purpose is to activate prior knowledge, and give a pep talk about how the strategy can be helpful in promoting active reading and comprehension.
- Give an in-class lecture and demonstration to introduce the K-W-L strategy to develop general awareness of steps and procedures involved.
- Use a think-aloud strategy to model his own use of the strategy.
- Have his students take notes in their learning log and participate in a class discussion about when and where to use the strategy.
- Have his students write a reflection in their log to demonstrate knowledge.

Students then would work in cooperative learning groups to try out K-W-L. For these simulations, Andrew would choose high-interest, low-vocabulary materials so that the focus in on the strategy itself. See Activities for All Learners to learn about two types of K-W-L approaches. To provide additional practice, Andrew would provide a strategy guide for students to gain independent practice in implementing the strategy in their homework. **Strategy guides** are graphic and questioning materials that provide support to students as they learn to use metacognitive strategies (Wood, Lapp, Flood, & Taylor, 2008). They can be used independently or in small groups, as a class activity, or as a home learning assignment (see Tips for Teachers 16.2). Often strategy guides are teacher-developed; however, publishers are including them in supplementary text material such as workbooks.

K-W-L: TWO VARIATIONS

Objective: To provide students with additional scaffolding as they read content-area material using two variations of K-W-L

Grading: Middle schools and above

Teaching Procedures: While Donna Ogle's K-W-L is a popular teaching method used to activate students' prior knowledge, it lacks a clear description of school district standards and learner outcomes that are required in schools today.

1. To address this issue, Laura Alatorre-Parks devised K-W-E-L to teach her high-school English students what the school district deemed they were expected to learn.
   - K-W-E-L is essentially the same as K-W-L; the critical difference is that K-W-E-L includes an in-depth discussion about district objectives or standards after the brainstorming (what I know and what I want to learn).
   - Alatorre-Parks also engages her students in planning how to merge their interests and wants with what they are expected to learn. She reports that this simple extension helps students to become more aware of what is expected of them and to develop a sense of ownership about their learning.

2. Another variation is K-W-H-H-L and was developed after Susan Szabo, a middle-school reading specialist, conducted a content analysis of her students' K-W-L journals.
   - She learned that her students needed more structure in targeting essential material from text and in making personal responses to what they read.
   - She added two additional headers: H (hard words) to help students identify key vocabulary and H (heart) to have students reflect about content based on personal experience and emotional reactions.

Sources: Alatorre-Parks, L. (2001). Aligning student interests with district mandates. *Journal of Adolescent and Adult Literacy, 44,* 330–332; Ogle, D. (1986). K-W-L: A teaching model that develops active reading of expository text. *The Reading Teacher, 39,* 564–570; and Szabo, S. (2006). KWHHL: A student-driven evolution of the KWL. *American Secondary Education, 34,* 57–67.

Tips for TEACHERS 16.2

DEVELOPING STRATEGY GUIDES

- Analyze the learning task, think about student needs, and identify a strategy that will help students accomplish the task you have identified.

- Design guides that are graphically appealing, promote engagement, and foster higher order thinking.

- Embed adaptations for English language learners and students with disabilities as necessary.

- Embed extension activities for students who want or need a "stretch."

- Introduce the guide with emphasis on (a) the task to be accomplished and (b) how the strategy will assist in accomplishing the task.

- If necessary, model the use of the strategy guide.

- If students need additional support, particularly for new strategies, have them work in cooperative learning groups or pairs to try out the guide.

- After completion of the guide, conduct a metacognitive discussion to discuss what was learned and how the strategy facilitated learning.

Guideline 4: Make Strategy Discussion a Regular Part of Class Routines. Learning how to learn can be empowering to students. You can teach targeted strategies in class, but students also pick up constructive learning tips from other teachers, parents, and each other. Brief classroom discussions about specific learning tasks and how best to accomplish those tasks can be beneficial. Such discussions have been labeled as **metacognitive conversations** (Buehl, 2009). Metacognitive conversations need not be lengthy, but can be time well spent in helping students become executive learners.

You can also use metacognitive conversations as a vehicle for student evaluation of the strategies you present. The Strategy Satisfaction Survey, shown in Figure 16.1, can serve as a springboard for discussion.

FIGURE
16.1

Strategy Satisfaction Survey

Name of Student _____

Name of Strategy _____

How did you learn the strategy?

What was easy about using the strategy?

What was difficult about using the strategy?

How would you change the strategy to meet your learning needs?

Would you use the strategy in the future? If so, how?

Overall, how much did the strategy help you learn?

_____ A lot

_____ A little bit

_____ Not at all

Keep in mind that there are no "lock step" procedures in terms of strategy instruction. Although the guidelines mentioned above are solid, use your own judgment about your students and their needs. The approach you use to teach strategies can vary. You can present the strategy and its steps, or you can have students develop their own steps in cooperative groups, through class discussion, or independently. Students can also get involved in developing study guides for themselves and for fellow students. Keep the focus on helping students learn how to learn—to become executive learners.

Difficulties in Developing Independent Learners

In reflecting on what you have already read in this textbook, you can easily list reasons why students are not independent, successful learners. The reasons can be cognitive, cultural, communicative, educational, motivational, or organizational. For older students, family obligations, part-time jobs, and extracurricular activities can have an impact on study time. There can be a single reason or a complex web of reasons—over many of which you have little control.

Your students can also come up with a host of reasons:

- "There isn't enough time."
- "My teachers didn't prepare me for this level of work."
- "I don't have a quiet place to study at home."
- "I have to work after school."
- "I don't have a computer at home."

Many of the reasons you hear from students are beyond your control as well. Things you can control are (a) your focus on teaching students how to learn in your own classroom and (b) your advocacy for schoolwide strategy learning programs. To make sure that strategy instruction is not superficial or inconsistent within and across classrooms, see Tips for Teachers 16.3 to learn about things you can do to support your students in becoming independent learners.

The study habits checklist (Figure 16.2) and the help-seeking inventory (Figure 16.3) can be used as guides for setting personal goals. The inventories will provide you with valuable information in guiding your students toward independence.

The following section discusses ways in which you can help your students develop personal responsibility.

Developing Independence: Personal Responsibility

Tom Ellis is a high-school sophomore. In fourth grade, he was diagnosed with a learning disability and has received special education services in inclusion and resource settings. When Tom was in middle school, he had a hard time moving from class to class. He was disorganized and frequently forgot assignments and books and did not study for tests. At the annual

PEARSON
myeducationlab

To enhance your understanding of strategies that will help support student learning, go to in the IRIS Center Resources section of Topic 8: Instructional Practices and Learning Strategies in the MyEducationLab for your course and complete Module 31 SOS: Helping Students Become Independent Learners.

Tips FOR TEACHERS 16.3

HELPING STUDENTS TO BECOME INDEPENDENT LEARNERS

- Teach strategies with sufficient depth and breadth.

- Integrate strategy instruction with ongoing content and curriculum.

- Get your students actively involved in assessing their strengths and challenges in learning strategies, setting goals for improvement, and monitoring their progress toward meeting those goals.

- Talk about personal responsibility and setting expectations for your students to meet.

- Teach your students about appropriate help-seeking behaviors.

- Communicate your expectations with parents and solicit their support as partners in learning.

FIGURE 16.2

Study Habits Checklist

Name _____   Date _____

Evaluate each statement by checking the column that describes your study habits.

STATEMENT	RARELY	GENERALLY	ALMOST ALWAYS
1. I set aside a regular time to study.			
2. I do not take calls or allow interruptions during study time.			
3. I take short breaks when I get tired but return to work.			
4. I take a few minutes at the beginning to organize my study time.			
5. I begin with the hardest assignments.			
6. I finish one assignment before going on to the next one.			
7. I break long projects down into short tasks and work on the tasks over time.			
8. I begin studying for a test at least three days before the test.			
9. I have someone I can contact when I get stuck.			
10. I write down questions I need to ask the teacher.			

Source: Adapted from Strichart, S..S. & Mangrum, C. T., II (1993). *Teaching study strategies to students with learning disabilities* (p. 356). Boston: Allyn & Bacon.

---

meeting to discuss Tom's IEP, Tom and his parents, one of his general education teachers, his special education teacher, and his school counselor determined objectives related to organizational strategies. The special education teacher helped Tom set learning goals, monitor those goals, and develop checklists to assist with personal organization. As Tom puts it, "Now that I am in high school, I'm more on my own. Staying organized is always going to be tough for me. But I'm learning that organization takes time and discipline. I'm getting it together."

Like Tom, many students have difficulties with **self-monitoring**. Others have difficulty with **self-determination**—articulating what they want and need in appropriate ways. Teaching students strategies related to self-initiative and personal organization can help with academic achievement. Moreover, teaching students how to assume personal responsibility can help them move beyond passivity and learned helplessness (Hallahan, Kauffman, & Pullen, 2009).

You can support your students' move toward assuming personal responsibility for their own learning by teaching strategies for goal setting and monitoring, organizational systems, time management, and self-advocacy.

Go to **www.focusonlearning. org/handcrafted2.asp** where you will find interactive tools for students and educators.

FIGURE
16.3

Help-Seeking Inventory

Purpose: To help you reflect on your help-seeking style.

Directions: Think of a time when you are studying and you are having some difficulty learning material or completing an assignment. Sometimes you might ask for help; other times you might not. These questions have to do with deciding whether to get some help. In each of the following situations, indicate how likely you are to ask for help. **Use a scale of 1–5, in which 1 is "Not at all likely" and 5 is "Very likely."**

How Likely Are You to Ask for Help When

1. You don't understand how to do a problem or exercise.   1 2 3 4 5
2. You need help with something the teacher already explained how to do.   1 2 3 4 5
3. You are having trouble during class and your teacher seems busy or in the middle of a lecture.   1 2 3 4 5
4. You are having trouble and your teacher seems to have too busy a schedule to meet with you outside of class.   1 2 3 4 5
5. You think you might get a bad grade if you don't get help.   1 2 3 4 5
6. You can't remember something that you need to know in order to do an assignment or problem.   1 2 3 4 5

Benefits of Help Seeking

7. I think that asking questions during class helps me learn.   1 2 3 4 5
8. I feel smart when I ask a question during class.   1 2 3 4 5
9. I think that asking teachers questions helps me learn.   1 2 3 4 5
10. I think that studying with friends helps me learn.   1 2 3 4 5
11. I think that asking friends for help enables me to learn.   1 2 3 4 5

Costs of Help Seeking

12. I think the teacher might think I'm dumb if I ask a question.   1 2 3 4 5
13. I think the teacher might think I'm unprepared if I ask a question.   1 2 3 4 5
14. I feel scared about asking questions during class.   1 2 3 4 5
15. I feel scared about asking questions outside of class.   1 2 3 4 5

16. I think the teacher will get angry with me if I ask a question.   1 2 3 4 5
17. I feel shy about asking questions.   1 2 3 4 5
18. I feel it's too much of a bother to ask questions.   1 2 3 4 5
19. I do not like to waste time seeking out help from teachers.   1 2 3 4 5
20. I think my friends might think I'm dumb if I ask for their help.   1 2 3 4 5
21. I do not like to waste time seeking out help from friends.   1 2 3 4 5

Help-Seeking Practices

22. I usually need a lot of help with my work.   1 2 3 4 5
23. I am aware of my teachers' office hours.   1 2 3 4 5
24. I have a listing of all teachers' office hours.   1 2 3 4 5
25. I have a telephone number of a fellow student from each class.   1 2 3 4 5
26. I have asked a fellow student in each class to take notes for me if I am absent and have agreed to do the same for that student in return.   1 2 3 4 5
27. I am aware of the free or low-cost tutoring services available to me on my campus.   1 2 3 4 5
28. I typically can monitor my learning and ask for help before it is too late.   1 2 3 4 5
29. Overall, how effective do you think your help-seeking behaviors and practices are with your fellow students?
    _____ effective
    _____ somewhat effective
    _____ could be more effective
30. Overall, how effective do you think your help-seeking behaviors and practices are with teachers?
    _____ effective
    _____ somewhat effective
    _____ could be more effective
31. My goals for help seeking this semester are:
    A. _____
    B. _____
    C. _____

Sources: Newman, R. S. (1990), Children's help-seeking in the classroom: The role of motivational factors and attitudes, *Journal of Educational Pyschology, 82*(1), 80; Newman, R. S., & Goldin, L. (1990), Children's reluctance to seek help with schoolwork, *Journal of Educational Psychology, 82,* 100. Copyright © 1990 by the American Psychological Association, Adapted with permission.

Self-Monitoring

Self-monitoring includes both self-evaluation and self-recording (Hallahan et al., 2009). **Self-evaluation** involves self-analysis and goal setting for either academic or behavioral tasks. **Self-recording** is written documentation of incremental progress made in meeting goals. Whether the task is working on finishing a term paper or saving enough money to buy a car, it is important to set goals, make a plan to accomplish the goals, and monitor progress.

Van Reusen and Bos (1992) developed a strategy that students can use for setting goals and monitoring progress. The strategy uses the acronym **MARKER** (it gives students a *mark* to work toward and is a *marker* of their progress) and includes the following steps:

Make a list of goals, set the order, and set the dates.
Arrange a plan for each goal and predict your success.
Run your plan for each goal and adjust if necessary.
Keep records of your progress.
Evaluate your progress toward each goal.
Reward yourself when you reach a goal, and set a new goal.

For each goal, students use a goal-planning sheet (see Figure 16.4) to answer the following questions:

- Can I describe my goal?
- What is the reason or purpose for the goal?
- Where am I going to work on and complete this goal?
- How much time do I have to complete the goal?

FIGURE 16.4

Goal-Planning and Monitoring Sheet

Name:_____ Class:_____ Date:_____

1. Goal: _____

2. Reason(s) for working on goal: _____

_____

3. Goal will be worked on at: _____

4. Date to reach goal (due date): _____

5. Materials needed: _____

_____

6. Steps used to reach the goal: _____

_____

7. Progress toward the goal: Record in each box the date and progress rating.

   3—Goal reached   2—Good progress made   1—Some progress made   0—No progress made

Date / Rating				
Date / Rating				
Date / Rating				

8. Reward for reaching goal: _____

Source: Adapted from Van Reusen, A. K. & Bos, C. S. (1992). *Use of the goal-regulation strategy to improve the goal attainment of students with learning disabilities* (Final Report). Tucson: University of Arizona.

- What materials do I need to complete the goal?
- Can I divide the goal into steps or parts? If so, in what order should I complete each step or part?
- How am I going to keep records of my progress?
- How will I reward myself for reaching my goal?

Students usually work on one to three goals at a time, keeping progress data on each goal.

This strategy can be taught as a unit in almost any class but is particularly appropriate for social studies and life skills classes. When Van Reusen and Bos (1992) used this strategy with middle- and high-school students with learning disabilities and behavior disorders, they found that students accomplished more goals and gained a more informed perspective on their educational and personal goals.

For students in departmentalized settings, adjusting to different teaching styles and class requirements can be difficult. Setting course-specific goals can help students with the adjustment. Figure 16.5 provides a framework for analyzing courses and for setting course-specific goals.

FIGURE 16.5

Setting Course-Specific Goals: Long-Range Task Analysis

Purpose: To provide a structure with which to examine the demands and requirements of each of your courses this semester.

Directions: Make copies of this form and complete one for each of your courses.

Course number _____   Course title _____

Lectures

Does the teacher deliver content through class lectures?

_____ Yes _____ No

Are the lectures generally easy to understand?

_____ Yes _____ No

Is it easy to capture key vocabulary and ideas from the lectures?

_____ Yes _____ No

Is it easy to take notes from the lectures?

_____ Yes _____ No

Are the lectures presented in the same order as the information in the textbook?

_____ Yes _____ No

Are the lectures made up of information not presented in the text at all?

_____ Yes _____ No

Reading Assignments

Does the teacher have required reading assignments?

_____ Yes _____ No

Is the reading material generally easy to understand?

_____ Yes _____ No

Is it easy to capture key vocabulary and ideas from the reading material?

_____ Yes _____ No

Is it absolutely necessary to read the textbook in detail to prepare for class discussions?

_____ Yes _____ No

Is it absolutely necessary to read the textbook in detail to prepare for tests?

_____ Yes _____ No

Other Assignments

List other assignments for this course:

Quizzes and Examinations

Number of quizzes _____

Number of exams _____

Is the final exam cumulative?

_____ Yes _____ No

The format of the quizzes and examinations is typically

_____ multiple-choice

_____ true/false

_____ identification/short answer

_____ essay

_____ other _____

Quizzes and examinations cover content from

_____ lectures

_____ reading assignments

_____ other _____

Course Analysis

Given the level of difficulty and my level of interest in this course, my goal for a grade in this course is _____.

My other goals for this course are:

_____

_____

_____

Source: Schumm, J. S. & Post, S. A. (1997). *Executive learning: Successful strategies for college reading and studying* (pp. 79–81). Upper Saddle River, NJ: Pearson. Adapted by permission of Pearson Education, Inc.

Organizational Systems

In addition to goal setting and self-monitoring, students need to organize their study environment and notebook(s). The "personal organization" business is large and growing in the United States. Newspapers, magazines, websites, and television shows offer suggestions for simplifying personal and professional environments and streamlining daily tasks at home and on the job. Although students are typically receptive to learning organizational tips, some students will need more support and continuity in learning how to get organized.

To help students get organized, at the beginning of the school year, let parents know—through a letter, on your website, or on a class Facebook page, if you have one—that students will be assessing and thinking about modifying their home study environment to promote studying. After students complete a study environment checklist (see Figure 16.6), have them meet in groups to discuss the results and their ideas for modifying their study environments.

Meet with each student individually to summarize the results and to write one to three goals for improving the study environment, if warranted. Individual meetings are appropriate in that students may have personal or family issues they may not be willing to discuss in a group. For example, students whose parents are divorced may have two homes. Going back and forth between two different settings can pose logistical problems. Other students may not have access to a computer or other resources for learning in the home.

Have students report on their progress toward meeting their goals soon after the goals are set and several times each grading period thereafter. Also, alert students that you will be reviewing their notebooks for organization and will provide a list of recommended materials, including the following:

- Three-ring notebook, so that pages can be added easily
- Supply pouch and school supplies such as pens, pencils, erasers, calculator, hole punch, package of file cards, ruler
- Labeled dividers—one for each class, plus others labeled "Schedules and Calendar," "Reference Information," "Notebook Dictionary," "Personal Word List," "Notebook Paper," "Graph Paper," and "Computer Paper"

Work with students to organize their notebooks, using the following suggestions:

- Include a semester calendar, weekly schedules, and to-do lists in the section on schedules and calendar.

FIGURE 16.6

Study Environment Checklist

Name _____   Date_____

Evaluate each statement by checking the column that describes the place where you study.

STATEMENT	RARELY	GENERALLY	ALMOST ALWAYS
1. I study in a consistent place.			
2. The place where I study is quiet.			
3. It has good light.			
4. There are no visual distractions.			
5. There are a comfortable desk/table and a chair.			
6. The materials I need are at my desk.			
7. The study area is available when I need it.			

Source: Adapted from Strichart, S. S. & Mangrum, C. T., II. (1993). *Teaching study strategies to students with learning disabilities* (p. 356). Boston: Allyn & Bacon.

- After the divider for each class, organize materials for that class (starting with class outline or syllabus).
- Date notes and place them in order.
- In the personal word list, alphabetically list frequently misspelled words.

Time Management

Time management is the organization and monitoring of time so that tasks can be scheduled and completed in an efficient and timely manner. Effective time management includes the following:

- Identifying the tasks to be completed
- Estimating the time needed to complete the tasks
- Prioritizing tasks and estimating time
- Scheduling the time
- Working toward meeting deadlines
- Monitoring progress and adjusting deadlines or tasks
- Reviewing deadlines after task completion and adjusting schedules and priorities based on past performance

Go to **www.collegeboard.com/ student/plan/college-success/ 116.html** to help students learn about time-management strategies.

As a classroom teacher, long-range and short-range planning are essential parts of your professional life—for both you and your students. Planning takes time; consequently, you will need to build a rationale that explains to students the importance of planning. Students will want to know why they need to take some time every month to do extended planning and to monitor their plan on a weekly or daily basis. Following are some suggestions for building a rationale:

- Scheduling your time helps you get jobs done so you have more time for fun and for time with your friends.
- Parents will "get off your back" when they see you getting your work done on time.
- If you write down what you have to do, you don't have to try to remember everything.
- If you set a time to begin, it is easier to get started and not procrastinate.
- When you set a time frame for completing an assignment, it helps you focus on working toward your goal.
- When you have a schedule, you're less likely to let a short break become a long break.
- Being in control of time makes you feel like you have more control of your life.
- When you get assignments and you finish them on time, then you can really enjoy your free time. (Bos & Vaughn, 2002, pp. 308–309)

Content Class Integration. A unit on time management is easily integrated into any class. It can be the first unit of the year in a math class, emphasizing time use and computation of time. It can be integrated into an economics class, emphasizing how time relates to productivity, or into a life skills class.

Teaching Time Analysis. You can get your students started on time management through time-analysis exercises. Have student groups identify usual activities and estimate the time it takes to complete them. Distribute a blank schedule form to students, and have them use the form to keep track of their activities for one week. Also have students list each school assignment and note whether they had "too much time" (+), "the right amount of time" (×), or "too little time" (−) to complete it.

At the end of the week, have student groups review their schedules and compare how much time they spent on different activities such as sleeping, eating, studying, attending class, and so on. Also have students compare their estimates with the actual time it took to complete the activities. Usually students underestimate their time by about 50%.

What time-management strategies can you, as a teacher, teach your class?

Planning and Monitoring a Schedule. Many middle schools and high schools provide students with academic calendars or assignment notebooks. If your school does not provide them, require your students to get a calendar and/or assignment notebook small enough to carry but large enough to record assignments and due dates. Some students are beginning to use their cell phones or a portable computer for recording assignments. Regardless of the format students use, planning a schedule requires several steps:

1. Record due dates for assignments, tests, and other important projects.
2. Record regularly scheduled activities, study times, and personal times.
3. Identify complex tasks or projects, break them into smaller tasks, and determine the due dates for each smaller task.
4. Make a to-do list for each day (refer to Figure 16.7) so that you can see how you need to plan your time, particularly study time.
5. Set priorities; if there is a lot to do, make a list of everything and rank each task as high, medium, or low priority.

Monitoring task completion is the key to successful use of schedules and to-do lists. Following are some suggestions for monitoring:

- Have students spend about 5 minutes during the class period to update their schedules and cross off tasks they have completed. This can be done at the beginning of class when you are taking attendance.
- Meet with students, as necessary, to review their schedules and their monitoring.
- Have students adjust their schedules as necessary.

Self-Advocacy

Self-advocacy occurs when individuals effectively communicate and negotiate for their interests, desires, needs, and rights by making informed decisions and taking responsibility for those decisions (Brewer, Fowler, & Test, 2005; Van Reusen, Bos, Schumaker, & Deshler, 1994). Self-advocacy is a subset of the skills, knowledge, and beliefs that constitute self-determination (Algozzine, Browder, Karvonen, Test, & Wood, 2001; Campbell-Whatley, 2008; Carter, Lane, Pierson, & Stang, 2008). Other aspects of self-determination include choice making, decision making, and self-awareness, to name a few. Self-advocacy can be

myeducationlab

Go to the Assignments and Activities section of Topic 12: Learning Disabilities in the MyEducationLab for your course and complete the activity entitled *Teaching Self-Advocacy*.

FIGURE 16.7

To-Do List: Daily Planning Worksheet

Things to do on _____

Priorities	Daily Homework Assignments	Tasks to Be Completed for Long-Range Assignments
Phone Calls, Emails, and Letters	Flyers and Papers for Parents to Read/Sign	Clubs and Activities
Personal Activities	Home Chores/Tasks	Other

Source: Schumm, J. S. (2001). *School power: Study skill strategies for succeeding in school* (p. 102). Copyright © 2001. Used with permission of Free Spirit Publishing, Inc., Minneapolis, MN; 1-866-703-7322; www.freespirit.com. All rights reserved.

taught; there is evidence that direct instruction of these skills is beneficial to students with learning and cognitive disabilities (Algozzine et al., 2001; Brewer et al., 2005; Campbell-Whatley, 2008; Pocock et al., 2002; van Belle, Marks, Martin, & Chun, 2006).

Recall from Chapter 1 the **I PLAN** self-advocacy strategy that helps students develop their advocacy skills (Van Reusen & Bos, 1990). Think about how effective this strategy is for older students who are becoming more independent learners.

In revisiting this strategy, consider the five steps. During the first step, students work in instructional groups to develop their own personal inventories (**I**). The remaining four steps in the strategy focus on the communication skills needed to present the information and advocate with teachers, parents, counselors, and others. These steps are presented, discussed, and then practiced through role-playing.

Inventories are created by each individual in instructional groups; these inventories focus on students' strengths, areas to improve or learn, goals, and choice for learning or accommodations.

Provide your inventory information.

Listen and respond.

Ask questions.

Name your goals.

Students also learn the following **SHARE** behaviors to promote positive communication:

Sit up straight.

Have a pleasant tone of voice.

Activate your thinking.

- Tell yourself to pay attention.
- Tell yourself to participate.
- Tell yourself to compare ideas.

Relax.

- Don't look uptight.
- Tell yourself to stay calm.

Engage in eye communication.

I PLAN and SHARE can be taught using role-playing activities. For example, two students could role-play how to communicate with a teacher when the student feels he or she needs an adaptation to complete a test or assignment. The whole class could then reflect on the role-play and make suggestions for improved communication.

Developing Independence: Active Learning in the Classroom

Tinisha Robinson teaches seventh-grade civics. Students in her class come from a self-contained elementary school setting in sixth grade. So at the beginning of the school year, her students need a lot of support and structure as they adapt to having multiple teachers. Her school has block scheduling, so Tinisha has long stretches of time (1 hour and 45 minutes) to teach both content and process. Tinisha explains,

> I don't want any passive learners in my classroom. I want them engaged and participating. But many of my students don't know how or are reluctant to take a risk to do so. I teach my students how to ask questions, how to be an active member in a group, how to listen, and how to take notes. When they leave my class, they have the tools to succeed.

Listening to lectures, asking questions, and taking notes are skills critical for success in school. Teachers are generally more willing to accommodate students who actively participate in class, and these students tend to be more successful academically (Schumm & Vaughn, 1991).

Participating in Class

In Tinisha's class, nonparticipation is not an option: "I want my reluctant learners to become risk takers. I want my English language learners to practice their new language. I want my kids who always seem to have the right answers [to] learn to listen to their peers." Tinisha talks with her students about her expectations for participating in general class discussions and group work.

FIGURE
16.8

Classroom Discussions

Do . . .

ask legitimate questions based on reading you've done ahead of time.

ask legitimate questions about what others say in class.

listen carefully to what others have to say.

add any information you may have to a point someone else makes.

share personal experiences related to the topic when this will enhance the discussion.

make statements or ask questions showing that you came to class prepared.

give yourself three to five seconds of thinking time before answering a question. Your answers will be more accurate and interesting.

be kind when you disagree with what somebody else says.

Don't . . .

make comments that take up too much class time.

make comments just to hear yourself talk.

make a habit of going off the subject.

interrupt others.

get into arguments.

Source: Schumm, J. S. (2001). *School power: Study skill strategies for succeeding in school* (p. 37). Copyright © 2001. Used with permission of Free Spirit Publishing, Inc., Minneapolis, MN; 1-866-703-7322; www.freespirit.com. All rights reserved.

Classroom discussions go beyond teacher questions and student responses. Genuine discussions provide opportunities for expression of multiple points of view, critical thinking, and information seeking (Strickland, Galda, & Cullinan, 2004). Figure 16.8 provides some guidelines for students as they become active participants in classroom discussions.

Cooperative learning groups and student pairs can be excellent ways to promote class participation. Throughout this book, you have read about various strategies for implementing small-group instruction. But as Vacca and Vacca (2005) explain, "Small-group learning is complex, and cooperative teams don't run by themselves. Students must know how to work together and how to use techniques they have been taught" (p. 255).

What can you do during class time to help students organize their notes? How can you make your lectures more listener friendly?

Listening and Taking Notes in Class

Secondary teachers typically base test material on assigned readings and on material presented in class. To perform well on tests, students need to take notes to make a record of lecture content (Boyle, 2007). There are two purposes for note taking: the **external storage function** and the **encoding function** (DiVesta & Gray, 1972; Igo, Riccoinini, Bruning, & Pope, 2006). The external storage function means that taking notes in class provides the student with a record of what was presented and discussed in class. This record can be used to prepare for tests and class discussions.

The second function, encoding, means that the physical act of taking notes promotes student engagement and learning. There is growing evidence that when students are actively engaged in taking notes, they retain more information than when complete sets of notes are simply handed to them (Austin, Lee, & Carr, 2004; Grabe, Christopherson, & Douglas, 2004-2005; Neef, McCord, & Ferreri, 2006).

Tinisha uses class discussion or cooperative groups to have students generate a rationale for the importance taking notes for school success. If students do not mention the following reasons, Tinisha points out that

- Note taking increases attention.
- Note taking requires a deeper level of thinking because students must make sense of the information as they write down ideas.
- Because students must process information on a deeper level, note taking makes learning and remembering information easier.

Guidelines for Effective Note Taking.   Next, Tinisha teaches guidelines for effective note taking. Effective note taking includes activities that students need to accomplish before, during, and after a lecture (Boyle, 2007). You can brainstorm with your students to generate a list of their ideas about best practice before, during, and after taking notes. Make a poster of their ideas and keep the poster in a highly visible spot in your classroom. Here are some general guidelines.

Before the lecture, students can skim or read a chapter from the textbook to get ready to listen. If the lecture is part of a series, reviewing notes from the previous lecture is helpful. During the lecture, students should both listen and write. For students with auditory, memory, or attention problems or difficulties with writing fluency, taking notes can be quite difficult. Developing good note-taking habits can help students overcome obstacles. Schumm (2001) offers the following suggestions for taking notes:

- Write down the date and title of each lecture.
- Don't worry about punctuation or grammar.
- Use abbreviations for speed and efficiency.
- Don't write down every word the teacher says.
- Record what the teacher puts on the board or includes in PowerPoint presentations or transparencies.
- Underline, circle, or star anything the teacher repeats or emphasizes.
- Don't write more than one idea per line.
- Listen for digressions (times when the teacher gets off the subject). It's okay to take a mental break during these—but don't fall asleep.
- Write down any questions the teacher asks, because these are likely to appear on future tests.
- Don't cram your writing into a small space. Leave room to add more notes later.
- Put question marks by any points you don't understand. Check them later with the teacher. (p. 25)

Two-column note taking is frequently recommended to provide structure for taking notes (Bean et al., 2008; Pauk, 1989; Santa, Havens, & Valdes, 2004). Originally developed by Walter Pauk at Cornell University, two-column notes consist of a cue column, where students record main ideas or prompts, and a recording column, where students record details, examples, illustrations, and other key facts (see Figure 16.9 for an example). Two-column notes can be used for taking notes during lectures but can also be used to take notes when reading textbooks.

After the lecture, students should clean up and review their notes within 24 hours. Because students may have trouble deciphering what they wrote or what they meant when they wrote something down, waiting a week or two to revise their notes or waiting until it is

FIGURE
16.9

Sample Two-Column Note-Taking Format

Date: _____   Page: _____

Topic: _____

KEY CONCEPTS/QUESTIONS	NOTES

FIGURE 16.10

Listening and Note-Taking Inventory

Part A: Listening Inventory

What kind of listener are you? Find out by taking this Listening Habits Inventory.

You'll need a piece of paper and something to write with. Number the paper from 1–12. For each statement, give yourself 2 points if you *always* do it, 1 point if you *sometimes* do it, and 0 points if you *never* do it.

1. I'm in my seat and ready to listen soon after the bell rings.
2. I don't do other things while the teacher is talking.
3. I don't talk with friends while the teacher is talking.
4. I listen carefully to directions.
5. I ask questions when I don't understand directions or other information the teacher presents.
6. I take notes when the teacher presents a lot of information.
7. I know when the teacher is making an important point.
8. If I catch myself daydreaming, I try to get back on track.
9. I look at the teacher when she or he is talking.
10. I concentrate on what the teacher is saying.
11. If someone else is keeping me from listening, I ask that person to stop talking. If this doesn't work, I ask the teacher to help or change my seat.
12. I spend more time listening than talking in class.

Scoring: Add up your points.
16–24 points: You're a good listener!
12–15 points: You need to be a better listener!
11 points or less: Huh?

Part B: Note-Taking Inventory

From time to time, it's smart to check the quality of your notes to see how you're doing. Then you'll know if you need to make any changes or improvements. Use this Note-Taking Inventory whenever you feel the need. Simply check it against that day's class notes.

You'll need a piece of paper and something to write with. Number the paper from 1–10. Give yourself one point for each item you find in your notes.

1. Date of lecture
2. Title of lecture
3. Writing neat enough for you to read (that's all that counts)
4. No more than one idea per line
5. Plenty of blank space to add extra ideas later
6. All main ideas brought up during class
7. All important details mentioned during class
8. All key terms and definitions given during class
9. Abbreviations used where necessary
10. No unnecessary words

Scoring: Add up your points.
9–10 points: You're a great note-taker!
7–8 points: You're a good note-taker.
5–6 points: You need to take better notes.
4 points or less: Make a note of this—practice, practice, practice.

time to study for a test might be too late. Cleaning up notes involves reorganizing, supplementing notes with textbook information, and writing out abbreviations. It can also involve finding the correct spelling of key technical vocabulary words. Reviewing notes involves highlighting key ideas, writing notes to ask the teacher in class, and thinking about ways to remember important information for tests and class discussions. See also Figure 16.10 for listening and note-taking inventories students can use to guide their note-taking practice.

Teaching Note Taking. Teaching note-taking skills to students in your class is a good investment of time and effort. When you teach note-taking skills, keep in mind that students need to master four key areas (Gunning, 2003):

- *Selectivity* —selecting the most important main ideas and details
- *Organization* —showing how key ideas are related
- *Consolidation* —shrinking the key ideas in a telegraphic style
- *Fluency* —rapid and efficient note taking

As you teach a content unit, you can use the procedure in Tips for Teachers 16.4 to evaluate your students' note-taking skills and to introduce and teach alternative ways to take notes.

Students who are new to note taking or who have some difficulties taking notes may need more support (Boyle, 2007). Students with more severe problems may need a note-taking buddy to assist with taking notes. For some students, graphic organizers such as Venn diagrams can help them better conceptualize lessons. For others, note-taking frames that accompany PowerPoint presentations provide a very structured framework for listening and taking notes.

Tips FOR TEACHERS 16.4

EVALUATING STUDENTS' NOTE-TAKING SKILLS

- *Have students evaluate the effectiveness of their current note-taking skills.* Give a lecture from the content unit and have students take notes as usual. The next day give students an open-note quiz. Have them evaluate the completeness, format, and legibility of their notes, as well as their ease of use for review. You can also have students review their listening and note-taking habits as a springboard for discussion.

- *Use videotaped lectures to teach students to listen effectively and take notes.* Use a videotape of your lecture so that students can listen and watch for cues you give to signal important information. When students notice a cue, stop the videotape and replay it so that all the students can hear and see it.

- *Control the difficulty of the lectures.* Select the first unit of the year to teach note taking. This unit usually contains simple information that was presented the previous year.

- *Discuss with students ways to record notes* (e.g., record key ideas, not sentences; use consistent abbreviations; use an outline format; spell a word the way it looks or sounds). As a class, have students develop a set of abbreviations to be posted on a wall chart.

- *Teach students how to review their notes, add missing information, and clarify information that is unclear.* Have students, working as partners or in cooperative groups, use their notes to study for tests. Teach students how to use their notes to create questions, and then check to see that they can answer them.

- *Have students monitor their note taking.* Have them keep track of how often they use their note-taking skills in your class (and others), and record how they are doing on tests and assignments (and the effect of their improved note-taking skills).

Source: Schumm, J. S. (2001). *School power: Study skill strategies for succeeding in school.* Minneapolis, MN: Free Spirit.

Giving students structured support may be necessary for some students, but teachers should keep in mind that too much support may hinder the goal of working toward independence.

Although note taking is frequently cited as an important skill for high-school and college success (Armbruster, 2009), relatively little research exists in this area, particularly for students with disabilities. To add to the knowledge base, Boyle and Weishaar (2001) examined the effects of a strategic note-taking procedure on the note-taking performance of students with learning disabilities and students with mental retardation. Thirteen high-school students with disabilities received a 50-minute training in strategic note taking. Thirteen other students were in a no-treatment control group. Both groups were asked to take notes on two videotaped lectures on topics about which they had no prior knowledge.

Student notes based on the videotapes were examined for number of words recorded. In addition, students completed immediate free recall, delayed free recall, and a comprehension test. Students in the strategic note-taking group outperformed the no-treatment control group on all measures.

With relatively little instructional time, students in this investigation were able to see dramatic improvements in their note taking. Although the investigators recognize that additional research is needed, they anticipate that the strategy has promise not only for students with disabilities, but also for other students who have problems in learning to listen and take notes.

Developing Independence: Making Home–School Connections

Robert Pierre is a tenth-grade mathematics teacher. Robert grew up in the Little Haiti section of Miami and now teaches at the high school where he graduated 5 years ago. Many of Robert's students are new immigrants to the United States. Many are still developing proficiency in English. Some attended school regularly in Haiti; others did not. Robert can identify with his students' struggles to learn, but he also serves as a role model of the merits of hard work and determination. Robert explains:

> My students know that they need to perform well on the state examinations if they are going to earn a college degree. It's a lot of pressure for them. At the beginning of the year I set guidelines (I call them Pierre's Pointers) for completing assignments and preparing for tests. I spend class time teaching them how to study so that we can bridge what's going on in class with what they are doing at home and on their own.

Spending class time teaching strategies for completing assignments, remembering information, and preparing for examinations can set the stage for what students do when they are on their own.

Completing Assignments

Classroom and homework assignments should be structured in such a way that they are purposeful and provide opportunities for students to practice, reinforce, or extend what was taught in school (Cooper, 2001). In addition, there should be definite rules about due dates and consequences for not meeting them (Good & Brophy, 2007). Most importantly, assignments should be checked, feedback provided, and intervention implemented as needed (Good & Brophy, 2007).

When students are habitually handing in assignments that are late or incomplete, you need to do some investigation to figure out whether the problem is with the level of difficulty of the work, clarity of directions, situations in the home, or personal learning or organizational issues. Students within all grade and achievement levels sometimes have problems with short-term assignments, long-term assignments, or both.

Jeremy Johnston was a bright, energetic eighth grader who was failing in school. His performance on tests was no less than a C, but he was failing because he seldom if ever handed in homework and rarely completed in-class assignments. When Jeremy's case was discussed during the middle-school team meeting, the team discovered that Jeremy was having the same problem with short-term assignments across the board.

Students like Jeremy who have difficulty completing assignments may benefit from getting direct instruction in how to do so. The **PROJECT** strategy was developed for middle-school students with learning disabilities to provide structure for assignment completion (Hughes, Ruhl, Schumaker, & Deshler, 2002). PROJECT leads students through steps that occur at school and at home. The strategy steps are as follows:

Prepare your assignment sheet.
Record and ask.
Organize.
   Break the assignment into parts.
   Estimate the number of study sessions.
   Schedule the sessions.
   Take your materials home.
Jump into it.
Engage in the work.
Check your work.
Turn in your work.

You can teach the PROJECT strategy in class. Also, let parents know through a flyer, letter, email, or on your website that you have taught the strategy and are encouraging your students to use the strategy for home learning.

Organizing and Planning for Long-Term Assignments

For many students, developing the skills to organize and plan long-term assignments and projects is new territory. Particularly in middle school, breaking big assignments down into manageable tasks, setting deadlines for those tasks, and seeing an assignment to completion is an essential learning process.

Michelle Miller is an eighth-grade language arts teacher. Each year she assigns a multiphase career project. First, students conduct a literature review on their career of choice and submit a three-page paper. Next, they construct an interview protocol to administer to someone in that career. After Michelle approves and grades the protocol, students interview their contact person and write a three-page summary of the experience. The final product is a 5-minute PowerPoint presentation that students give to the class. By embedding multiple due dates and assignments in the career project, Michelle can provide students support in developing a finished product of which they can be proud. Figure 16.11 is a project planning form you can use to assist students in planning long-term assignments.

Project Planning Sheet

1. Decide on a project theme.   **Date Done** _____

2. Have the theme approved by your teacher.   **Date Done** _____

   Theme: _____

3. Make a list of things you need to do to complete your project. Rank them in the order they should be completed.

   Will Need Help With: **Who Will Help Me:**

4. Set deadlines for finishing each part of your project. Write the deadline dates on your calendar.

   Task   **Date Due**   **Date Done**   **Person Responsible**

5. Make a list of materials you will need. Estimate how much they will cost.

   Item   **Cost**

6. Send away for resource materials.

   Resource Material   **Date Requested**   **Date Received**

7. Contact community resources.

   Community Resource   **Date Contacted**   **Result(s)**

8. Visit the library.

   Purpose of Visit   **Date of Visit**

9. Complete your project on schedule.

   Date Turned In: _____   **Grade:** _____

Remembering Information

Using memory strategies to learn information is critical for success in school. Students, particularly students with disabilities and those who are at risk, often have difficulty memorizing information (Scruggs, Mastropieri, & Okolo, 2008). Sometimes students do not understand the information, but in some cases, students may not perform well because they have difficulties retrieving information or because they do not use deliberate memory strategies.

PEARSON
myeducationlab

Go to the Building Teaching Skills and Dispositions section of Topic 8: Instructional Practices and Learning Strategies in the MyEducationLab for your course and complete the activity entitled *Helping Learners Remember and Retrieve Information*.

As a classroom teacher, there are some general practices you can implement to enhance student memory of what they learn in class:

- Cue students when important information is being presented.
- Activate prior knowledge and help students make connections between old and new knowledge.
- Use visual aids such as semantic maps and diagrams to make the information more memorable.
- Limit the amount of information presented; group related ideas.
- Control the rate at which information is presented.
- Provide time to review, rehearse, and elaborate on the information.
- Teach students how to use and apply memory strategies and devices.
- Provide opportunities for distributed practice and encourage overlearning.

Distributed practice means breaking up the material to be learned into manageable chunks and then holding several short study sessions over a period of time. The opposite of distributed practice would be to try to learn a large amount of material in one sitting. **Overlearning** means learning to mastery. Sometimes students say, "I knew it last night and then forgot it during the test." Typically when this happens, the student did not rehearse or practice the material a sufficient number of times to get to the point of mastery.

Direct teaching of memory strategies can enhance student performance on tests, vocabulary learning, and retention of key concepts (Rummel, Levin, & Woodward, 2003; Uberti, Scruggs, & Mastropieri, 2003). This has been demonstrated with students with learning disabilities (Bryant, Goodwin, Bryant, & Higgins, 2003; Scruggs et al., 2008) and English language learners (Zhang & Schumm, 2000).

Mnemonics. **Mnemonic devices** are memory-triggering techniques that help us remember and retrieve information by forming associations that do not exist naturally in the content. The word *mnemonics* is derived from the name of the Greek goddess of memory, Mnemosyne. There are several types of mnemonic devices recommended to promote student independent learning. Two of the most versatile mnemonic strategies are letter strategies and key word strategies (Fontana, Scruggs, & Mastropieri, 2007). As you read in Chapter 6, memory strategies (also known as mnemonic devices) are particularly helpful for students with learning disabilities, but may be helpful for other students – and for you!

Two types of **letter strategy** mnemonics are acronyms and acrostics. **Acronyms** are words created by joining the first letters of a series of words. Examples are *radar* (radio detecting and ranging), *scuba* (self-contained underwater breathing apparatus), and *laser* (light amplification by stimulated emission of radiation). **Acrostics** are sentences created by words that begin with the first letters of a series of words. A popular example of an acrostic is "Every good boy does fine," which represents the notes on the lines of the treble clef staff: E, G, B, D, F. By teaching students to construct acronyms and acrostics, sharing them in class, and then cueing students to use them when they study and take tests, you help them to learn and retrieve information.

The **FIRST-letter** mnemonic strategy is one strategy you can teach to help students construct lists of information to memorize and develop an acronym or acrostic for learning and remembering the information. The strategy includes an overall strategy (LISTS) and a substrategy for making a mnemonic device (FIRST). The steps in the overall strategy include the following:

Look for clues. In class notes and textbooks, look for lists of information that are important to learn. Name or give a heading to each list.

Investigate the items. Decide which items should be included in the list.

Select a mnemonic device, using FIRST. Use the FIRST substrategy, explained shortly, to construct a mnemonic.

Transfer the information to a card. Write the mnemonic and the list on one side of a card and the name of the list on the other side of the card.

Self-test. Study by looking at the name of the list, using the mnemonic to recall the list.

To complete the selection step, students use the FIRST substrategy to design an acronym or acrostic:

Form a word. Using uppercase letters, write the first letter of each word in the list; see whether an acronym—either a recognizable word or a nonsense word—can be made.

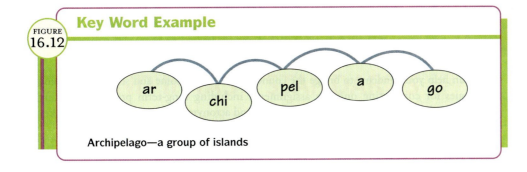

FIGURE
16.12

Key Word Example

ar

chi

pel

a

go

Archipelago—a group of islands

Insert a letter(s). Insert letter(s) to see whether a word can be made. (Be sure to use lowercase letters so that you know they do not represent an item on the list—BACk, for example.)

Rearrange the letters. Rearrange the letters to see whether a word can be made.

Shape a sentence. Using the first letter of each word in the list, try to construct a sentence (an acrostic).

Try combinations. Try combinations of the preceding steps to generate the mnemonic.

This strategy can be taught in any content-area class, but it is particularly effective in science and social studies classes in which lists of information are to be learned. The strategy provides a systematic method for students to review text and class notes, construct lists, and develop acronyms and acrostics that help them remember and retrieve information.

The **key word strategy** is a research-based mnemonic that can be used to remember both vocabulary and concepts (Atkinson, 1975; Uberti et al., 2003). The method uses both verbal and visual cues to create images that prompt recall and retention. The key word method involves three steps:

1. Identify a target word or concept to be learned.
2. Identify a concrete, easily imagined "key word" that is either phonetically or semantically related to the target word.
3. Identify a visual image that links the key word to the meaning of the target word.

For example, in a social studies class the target word to be learned might be *archipelago,* or a group of islands. The target word is *archipelago,* the key word could be *arch,* and the visual image could be a series of islands connected by arches (see Figure 16.12).

Although research has demonstrated the potential usefulness of mnemonic devices (Fontana et al., 2007; Kretlow, Lo, White, & Jordan, 2008), Lenz and Deshler (2004) offer one caution. If students do not make a final link between the memory prompt and the term or concept, the mnemonic can be troublesome. In addition, students may spend more time creating the mnemonics than actually rehearsing the material to be learned. Students need direct instruction in mnemonic strategies, but they also need time to reflect on what worked, what didn't work, and why.

Andrew Post's high-school courses in American Government and Economics had a phenomenal impact on him as a secondary student. He not only learned content, but also learned how to become an independent, executive learner. These are lessons he now conveys to his own freshman and senior students.

Summary

- The goal of strategy instruction is to support students in becoming independent in completing learning tasks. Most students need direct instruction and sufficient practice to become skilled in learning how to learn.

- There are many reasons why students experience difficulties in taking responsibility for their learning. Providing opportunities to examine their study habits and help-seeking styles can guide students in setting academic and personal goals.

- Self-monitoring strategies can help students reach both academic and personal goals. Establishing organizational systems, time management, and planning help students set the stage for efficient studying.

	CEC		INTASC	
Major Chapter Headings	**Knowledge and Skill Core Standard**	**Associated Subcategories**	**Core Principle**	**Associated Special Education Subcategories**
Strategies for Helping All Students Develop Problem-Solving Skills	**4.** Instructional Strategies	**ICC4S2** Teach individuals to use self-assessment, problem solving, and other cognitive strategies to meet their needs.	**4.** Instructional Strategies	**4.03** All teachers use research-based practices to support learning and generalization of concepts and skills.

Part 4: Secondary Instruction

Chapter 15 Differentiating Instruction and Assessment for Middle and High School Students

Standards-Based Instruction	**7.** Instructional Planning	**ICC7K2** National, state or provincial, and local curricula standards.	N/A	
Differentiating Instruction for Secondary Learners	**2.** Development and Characteristics of Learners	**ICC2K5** Similarities and differences of individuals with and without exceptional learning needs.	**3.** Learner Differences	**3.02** All teachers understand and are sensitive to cultural, ethnic, gender, and linguistic differences that may be confused with or misinterpreted as manifestations of a disability.
Preparing Engaging Lessons for Middle and High School Students	**5.** Learning Environments and Social Interactions	**ICC5S4** Design learning environments that encourage active participation in individual and group activities.	**2.** Student Learning	**2.04** All teachers are knowledgeable about multiple theories of learning and research-based teaching practices that support learning.
Effective Content-Area Reading Instruction for Middle- and High-School Learners	**4.** Instructional Strategies	**GC4S11** Use instructional methods to strengthen and compensate for deficits in perception, comprehension, memory, and retrieval.	**4.** Instructional Strategies	**4.03** All teachers use research-based practices to support learning and generalization of concepts and skills.
Differentiating Assessment	**4.** Instructional Strategies	**GC4K2** Strategies to prepare for and take tests.	**8.** Assessment	**8.04** All teachers engage all students, including students with disabilities, in assessing and understanding their own learning and behavior.

Chapter 16 Fostering Strategies for Student Independence

Effective Strategy Instruction: The Teaching–Learning Connection	**4.** Instructional Strategies	**GC4K5** Strategies for integrating student-initiated learning experiences into ongoing instruction.	**4.** Instructional Strategies	**4.01** All teachers share responsibility for the education of students with disabilities, including providing effective instruction to support students' learning.
Difficulties in Developing Independent Learners	**2.** Development and Characteristics of Learners	**ICC2K2** Educational implications of characteristics of various exceptionalities.	**2.** Student Learning	**2.02** All teachers examine their assumptions about the learning and development of students with disabilities and use this information to create challenging and supportive learning opportunities.
Developing Independence: Personal Responsibility	**4.** Instructional Strategies	**ICC4S5** Use procedures to increase the individual's self-awareness, self-management, self-control, self-reliance, and self-esteem.	**4.** Instructional Strategies	**4.07** All teachers use strategies to promote the independence, self-control, and self-advocacy of students with disabilities.

	CEC		INTASC	
Major Chapter Headings	**Knowledge and Skill Core Standard**	**Associated Subcategories**	**Core Principle**	**Associated Special Education Subcategories**
Strategies for Helping All Students Develop Problem-Solving Skills	**4.** Instructional Strategies	**ICC4S2** Teach individuals to use self-assessment, problem solving, and other cognitive strategies to meet their needs.	**4.** Instructional Strategies	**4.03** All teachers use research-based practices to support learning and generalization of concepts and skills.

Part 4: Secondary Instruction

Chapter 15 Differentiating Instruction and Assessment for Middle and High School Students

Standards-Based Instruction	**7.** Instructional Planning	**ICC7K2** National, state or provincial, and local curricula standards.	N/A	
Differentiating Instruction for Secondary Learners	**2.** Development and Characteristics of Learners	**ICC2K5** Similarities and differences of individuals with and without exceptional learning needs.	**3.** Learner Differences	**3.02** All teachers understand and are sensitive to cultural, ethnic, gender, and linguistic differences that may be confused with or misinterpreted as manifestations of a disability.
Preparing Engaging Lessons for Middle and High School Students	**5.** Learning Environments and Social Interactions	**ICC5S4** Design learning environments that encourage active participation in individual and group activities.	**2.** Student Learning	**2.04** All teachers are knowledgeable about multiple theories of learning and research-based teaching practices that support learning.
Effective Content-Area Reading Instruction for Middle- and High-School Learners	**4.** Instructional Strategies	**GC4S11** Use instructional methods to strengthen and compensate for deficits in perception, comprehension, memory, and retrieval.	**4.** Instructional Strategies	**4.03** All teachers use research-based practices to support learning and generalization of concepts and skills.
Differentiating Assessment	**4.** Instructional Strategies	**GC4K2** Strategies to prepare for and take tests.	**8.** Assessment	**8.04** All teachers engage all students, including students with disabilities, in assessing and understanding their own learning and behavior.

Chapter 16 Fostering Strategies for Student Independence

Effective Strategy Instruction: The Teaching–Learning Connection	**4.** Instructional Strategies	**GC4K5** Strategies for integrating student-initiated learning experiences into ongoing instruction.	**4.** Instructional Strategies	**4.01** All teachers share responsibility for the education of students with disabilities, including providing effective instruction to support students' learning.
Difficulties in Developing Independent Learners	**2.** Development and Characteristics of Learners	**ICC2K2** Educational implications of characteristics of various exceptionalities.	**2.** Student Learning	**2.02** All teachers examine their assumptions about the learning and development of students with disabilities and use this information to create challenging and supportive learning opportunities.
Developing Independence: Personal Responsibility	**4.** Instructional Strategies	**ICC4S5** Use procedures to increase the individual's self-awareness, self-management, self-control, self-reliance, and self-esteem.	**4.** Instructional Strategies	**4.07** All teachers use strategies to promote the independence, self-control, and self-advocacy of students with disabilities.

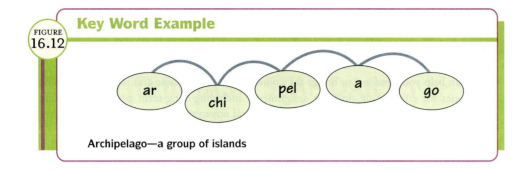

Key Word Example

FIGURE
16.12

ar — chi — pel — a — go

Archipelago—a group of islands

Insert a letter(s). Insert letter(s) to see whether a word can be made. (Be sure to use lowercase letters so that you know they do not represent an item on the list—BACk, for example.)

Rearrange the letters. Rearrange the letters to see whether a word can be made.

Shape a sentence. Using the first letter of each word in the list, try to construct a sentence (an acrostic).

Try combinations. Try combinations of the preceding steps to generate the mnemonic.

This strategy can be taught in any content-area class, but it is particularly effective in science and social studies classes in which lists of information are to be learned. The strategy provides a systematic method for students to review text and class notes, construct lists, and develop acronyms and acrostics that help them remember and retrieve information.

The **key word strategy** is a research-based mnemonic that can be used to remember both vocabulary and concepts (Atkinson, 1975; Uberti et al., 2003). The method uses both verbal and visual cues to create images that prompt recall and retention. The key word method involves three steps:

1. Identify a target word or concept to be learned.
2. Identify a concrete, easily imagined "key word" that is either phonetically or semantically related to the target word.
3. Identify a visual image that links the key word to the meaning of the target word.

For example, in a social studies class the target word to be learned might be *archipelago,* or a group of islands. The target word is *archipelago,* the key word could be *arch,* and the visual image could be a series of islands connected by arches (see Figure 16.12).

Although research has demonstrated the potential usefulness of mnemonic devices (Fontana et al., 2007; Kretlow, Lo, White, & Jordan, 2008), Lenz and Deshler (2004) offer one caution. If students do not make a final link between the memory prompt and the term or concept, the mnemonic can be troublesome. In addition, students may spend more time creating the mnemonics than actually rehearsing the material to be learned. Students need direct instruction in mnemonic strategies, but they also need time to reflect on what worked, what didn't work, and why.

Andrew Post's high-school courses in American Government and Economics had a phenomenal impact on him as a secondary student. He not only learned content, but also learned how to become an independent, executive learner. These are lessons he now conveys to his own freshman and senior students.

Summary

- The goal of strategy instruction is to support students in becoming independent in completing learning tasks. Most students need direct instruction and sufficient practice to become skilled in learning how to learn.

- There are many reasons why students experience difficulties in taking responsibility for their learning. Providing opportunities to examine their study habits and help-seeking styles can guide students in setting academic and personal goals.

- Self-monitoring strategies can help students reach both academic and personal goals. Establishing organizational systems, time management, and planning help students set the stage for efficient studying.

FIGURE
16.12

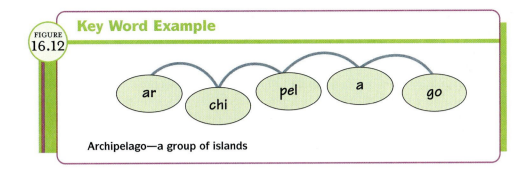

Key Word Example

Archipelago—a group of islands

Insert a letter(s). Insert letter(s) to see whether a word can be made. (Be sure to use lowercase letters so that you know they do not represent an item on the list—BACk, for example.)

Rearrange the letters. Rearrange the letters to see whether a word can be made.

Shape a sentence. Using the first letter of each word in the list, try to construct a sentence (an acrostic).

Try combinations. Try combinations of the preceding steps to generate the mnemonic.

This strategy can be taught in any content-area class, but it is particularly effective in science and social studies classes in which lists of information are to be learned. The strategy provides a systematic method for students to review text and class notes, construct lists, and develop acronyms and acrostics that help them remember and retrieve information.

The **key word strategy** is a research-based mnemonic that can be used to remember both vocabulary and concepts (Atkinson, 1975; Uberti et al., 2003). The method uses both verbal and visual cues to create images that prompt recall and retention. The key word method involves three steps:

1. Identify a target word or concept to be learned.
2. Identify a concrete, easily imagined "key word" that is either phonetically or semantically related to the target word.
3. Identify a visual image that links the key word to the meaning of the target word.

For example, in a social studies class the target word to be learned might be *archipelago,* or a group of islands. The target word is *archipelago,* the key word could be *arch,* and the visual image could be a series of islands connected by arches (see Figure 16.12).

Although research has demonstrated the potential usefulness of mnemonic devices (Fontana et al., 2007; Kretlow, Lo, White, & Jordan, 2008), Lenz and Deshler (2004) offer one caution. If students do not make a final link between the memory prompt and the term or concept, the mnemonic can be troublesome. In addition, students may spend more time creating the mnemonics than actually rehearsing the material to be learned. Students need direct instruction in mnemonic strategies, but they also need time to reflect on what worked, what didn't work, and why.

Andrew Post's high-school courses in American Government and Economics had a phenomenal impact on him as a secondary student. He not only learned content, but also learned how to become an independent, executive learner. These are lessons he now conveys to his own freshman and senior students.

Summary

- The goal of strategy instruction is to support students in becoming independent in completing learning tasks. Most students need direct instruction and sufficient practice to become skilled in learning how to learn.

- There are many reasons why students experience difficulties in taking responsibility for their learning. Providing opportunities to examine their study habits and help-seeking styles can guide students in setting academic and personal goals.

- Self-monitoring strategies can help students reach both academic and personal goals. Establishing organizational systems, time management, and planning help students set the stage for efficient studying.

- Teachers need to plan systematic ways to teach students how to participate in class discussions and small-group learning situations. Note taking in class helps students become active learners and to learn how to record important information for home learning. Skilled note taking involves selectivity, organization, consolidation, and fluency.
- You can help your students to bridge the connection between home and school by teaching strategies for completing ongoing assignments including long-term projects. Teaching mnemonic devices such as the key word method and acronyms can improve retention of key concepts and vocabulary for tests.

Think and Apply

1. Reread the interview with Andrew Post at the beginning of this chapter. Andrew's own life experience informs his teaching in the classroom. Think about your own journey as a student. Write a brief reflection paper about how and when you learned to study. What interested you most? How will your own experience affect what you plan for your own students?

2. Develop a series of lesson plans you would use to introduce a strategy to middle- or high-school students. Include in your plans the stages of strategy learning, a strategy guide, and a metacognitive conversation.

3. Many teachers struggle with motivating students to turn in homework assignments on time. Explain your position on turning in homework and consequences for not turning in homework on time. How would you work with students and parents to improve your students' personal responsibility for homework completion?

PEARSON
myeducationlab)

Now go to Topic 8: Instructional Practices and Learning Strategies and Topic 12: Learning Disabilities in the MyEducationLab (www.myeducationlab.com) for your course where you can:

- Find learning outcomes for these topics along with the national standards that connect to these outcomes.
- Complete Assignments and Activities that can help you more deeply understand the chapter content.
- Examine challenging situations and cases presented in the IRIS Center Resources.
- Apply and practice your understanding of the core teaching skills identified in the chapter with Building Teaching Skills and Dispositions learning units.

APPENDIX

CEC AND INTASC STANDARDS

The Council for Exceptional Children (CEC) Standards and the Interstate New Teacher and Assessment Consortium (INTASC) Principles are guidelines that must be mastered by all beginning inclusive educators. Together, these standards detail the knowledge and skills that all educators should possess in order to be effective teachers of students with disabilities. The following tables connect the basic knowledge and skills described in the CEC Standards and INTASC Principles that can be applied to each major section of each chapter in this text. Other standards may also be applied to the chapters.

	CEC		INTASC	
Major Chapter Headings	**Knowledge and Skill Core Standard**	**Associated Subcategories**	**Core Principle**	**Associated Special Education Subcategories**
Part 1: Foundations				
Chapter 1 Special Education and Inclusive Schooling				
Early Foundations of Special Education	**1.** Foundations	**ICC1K1** Models, theories, philosophies, and research methods that provide the basis for special education practice.	**1.** Subject Matter	**1.04** All teachers have knowledge of the major principles and parameters of federal disabilities legislation.
IDEIA and the Vocational Rehabilitation Act	**1.** Foundations	**ICC1K5** Issues in definition and identification of individuals with exceptional learning needs, including those from culturally and linguistically diverse backgrounds.	**1.** Subject Matter	**1.04** All teachers have knowledge of the major principles and parameters of federal disabilities legislation.
Responsibilities of Classroom Teachers	**1.** Foundations	**ICC1K3** Relationship of special education to the organization and function of educational agencies.	**7.** Instructional Planning	**7.01** All teachers contribute their expertise as members of a collaborative team to develop, monitor, and periodically revise individualized educational plans for students with disabilities.
Inclusion	**1.** Foundations	**ICC1K4** Rights and responsibilities of students, parents, teachers, and other professionals, and schools related to exceptional learning needs.	**10.** Collaboration, Ethics, and Relationships	**10.01** All teachers share instructional responsibility for students with disabilities and work to develop well-functioning collaborative teaching relationships.

	CEC		INTASC	
Major Chapter Headings	**Knowledge and Skill Core Standard**	**Associated Subcategories**	**Core Principle**	**Associated Special Education Subcategories**
Chapter 2 Response to Intervention: Developing Success for All Learners				
Past and Present Challenges	**1.** Foundations	**GC1K3** Historical foundations, classic studies, major contributors, major legislation, and current issues related to knowledge and practice.	**1.** Subject Matter	**1.05** All teachers know about and can access resources to gain information about state, district, and school policies and procedures regarding special education, including those regarding referral, assessment, eligibility, and services for students with disabilities.
Components of Response to Intervention	**7.** Instructional Planning	**GC7K3** Interventions and services for children who may be at risk for learning disabilities.	**8.** Assessment	**8.01** All General and Special Education Teachers understand the purposes, strengths, and limitations of formal and informal assessment approaches for making eligibility, placement, and instructional decisions for students with disabilities.
Universal Screening	**8.** Assessment	**ICC8K3** Screening, prereferral, referral, and classification procedures.	**8.** Assessment	**8.02** All teachers use a variety of assessment procedures to document students' learning, behavior, and growth within multiple environments appropriate to the student's age, interests, and learning.
Role of Teachers in an RTI Model	**8.** Assessment	**ICC8S6** Use assessment information in making eligibility, program, and placement decisions for individuals with exceptional learning needs, including those from culturally and/or linguistically diverse backgrounds.	**8.** Assessment	**8.04** All teachers engage all students, including students with disabilities, in assessing and understanding their own learning behavior.
Chapter 3 Communicating and Collaborating with Other Professionals and Families				
Critical Communication Skills	**10.** Collaboration	**ICC10S3** Foster respectful and beneficial relationships between families and professionals.	**7.** Instructional Planning	**7.02** All teachers plan ways to modify instruction, as needed, to facilitate positive learning results within the general curriculum for students with disabilities.
Collaborating wth Other Professionals	**10.** Collaboration	**ICC10K2** Roles of individuals with exceptional learning needs, families, and school and community personnel in planning of an individualized program.	**10.** Collaboration, Ethics, and Relationships	**10.01** All teachers share instructional responsibility for students with disabilities and work to develop well-functioning collaborative teaching relationships.
Working with Parents	**10.** Collaboration	**ICC10K3** Concerns of families of individuals with exceptional learning needs and strategies to help address these concerns.	**10.** Collaboration, Ethics, and Relationships	**10.04** All teachers accept families as full partners in planning appropriate instruction and services for students with disabilities, and provide meaningful opportunities for them to participate as partners in their children's instructional programs.

	CEC		INTASC	
Major Chapter Headings	**Knowledge and Skill Core Standard**	**Associated Subcategories**	**Core Principle**	**Associated Special Education Subcategories**
Chapter 4 Teaching Culturally and Linguistically Diverse Students				
Diversity in Classrooms	**5.** Learning Environments and Social Interactions	**ICC5K8** Ways to create learning environments that allow individuals to retain and appreciate their own and each others' respective language and cultural heritage.	**3.** Learner Differences	**3.04** All teachers understand and are sensitive to cultural, ethnic, gender, and linguistic differences that may be confused with or misinterpreted as manifestations of disability.
Multicultural Education	**5.** Learning Environments and Social Interactions	**ICC5K7** Strategies for preparing individuals to live harmoniously and productively in a culturally diverse world.	**2.** Student Learning	**2.04** All teachers are knowledgeable about multiple theories of learning and research-based practices that support learning and use this information to inform instruction.
Linguistic Diversity and Second Language Acquisition	**6.** Communication	**ICC6K1** Effects of cultural and linguistic differences on growth and development.	**4.** Instructional Strategies	**4.03** All teachers use research-based practices to support learning and generalization of concepts and skills.
Assessment of Students with Cultural and Linguistic Differences	**8.** Assessment	**ICC8S6** Use assessment information in making eligibility, program, and placement decisions for individuals with exceptional learning needs, including those from culturally and/or linguistically diverse backgrounds.	**9.** Reflective Practitioner	**9.04** All teachers reflect on the potential interaction between a student's cultural experiences and their disability.
Instructional Guidelines and Accommodations for Diverse Students	**6.** Communication	**ICC6S2** Use communication strategies and resources to facilitate understanding of subject matter for students whose primary language is not the dominant language.	**2.** Student Learning	**2.03** All teachers recognize that students with disabilities vary in their approaches to learning depending on factors such as the nature of their disability, their level of knowledge and functioning, and life experiences.
Chapter 5 Promoting Social Acceptance and Managing Student Behavior				
Establishing a Positive Classroom Climate	**5.** Learning Environments and Social Interactions	**ICC5K2** Basic classroom management theories and strategies for individuals with exceptional learning needs.	**5.** Learning Environment	**5.03** All teachers take deliberate action to promote positive social relationships among students with disabilities and their age-appropriate peers in the learning community.
Enhancing Students' Self-Concepts	**4.** Instructional Strategies	**ICC4S5** Use procedures to increase the individual's self-awareness, self-management, self-control, self-reliance, and self-esteem.	**4.** Instructional Strategies	**4.07** All teachers use strategies that promote the independence, self-control, and self-advocacy of students with disabilities.
Understanding Behavior Management in Culturally Diverse Classrooms	**5.** Learning Environments and Social Interactions	**ICC5S1** Create a safe, equitable, positive, and supportive learning environment in which diversities are valued.	**2.** Student Learning	**2.04** All teachers are knowledgeable about multiple theories of learning and research-based practices that support learning and use this information to inform instruction.

	CEC		INTASC	
Major Chapter Headings	**Knowledge and Skill Core Standard**	**Associated Subcategories**	**Core Principle**	**Associated Special Education Subcategories**
Universal Strategies for Managing Student Behavior	**1.** Foundations	**GC1K9** Theory of reinforcement techniques in serving individuals with disabilities.	**5.** Learning Environments	**5.02** All teachers help students with disabilities develop positive strategies for coping with frustrations in the learning situation that may be associated with their disability.
Practices for Providing Positive Behavior Support	**7.** Instructional Planning	**GC7S1** Plan and implement individualized reinforcement systems and environmental modifications at levels equal to the intensity of the behavior.	**5.** Learning Environments	**5.05** All teachers participate in the design and implementation of individual behavioral support plans and are proactive in responding to the needs of individual students within the learning community.

Part 2: Categorical Differences

Chapter 6 Teaching Students with Learning Disabilities and Attention Deficit Hyperactivity Disorder

Learning Disabilities	**3.** Individual Learning Differences	**GC3K1** Impact of disabilities on auditory and information processing skills.	**2.** Student Learning	**2.01** All teachers have a sound understanding of physical, social, emotional, and cognitive development. They are familiar with the general characteristics of the most frequently occurring disabilities and have a basic understanding of the ways that disabilities impact learning.
Identification and Assessment of Students with Learning Disabilities	**3.** Individual Learning Differences	**ICC3K1** Effects an exceptional condition(s) can have on an individual's life.	**8.** Assessment	**8.01** All General and Special Education Teachers understand the purposes, strengths, and limitations of formal and informal assessment approaches for making eligibility, placement, and instructional decisions for students with disabilities.
Attention Deficit Hyperactivity Disorder	**3.** Individual Learning Differences	**ICC3K1** Effects an exceptional condition(s) can have on an individual's life.	**7.** Instructional Planning	**7.02** All teachers plan ways to modify instruction, as needed, to facilitate positive learning results within the general curriculum for students with disabilities.

Chapter 7 Teaching Students with Communication Disorders

Communication Disorders	**2.** Development and Characteristics of Learners	**ICC2K1** Typical and atypical growth and development.	**6.** Communication	**6.04** All teachers provide multiple opportunities to foster effective communication among students with disabilities and other members of the classroom as a means of building communication and language skills.
Prevalence of Communication Disorders	**9.** Professional and Ethical Practice	**ICC9S10** Access information on exceptionalities.	**2.** Student Learning	**2.01** All teachers have a sound understanding of physical, social, emotional, and cognitive development. They are familiar with the general characteristics of the most frequently occurring disabilities and have a basic understanding of the ways that disabilities impact learning.
Identifying and Assessing Students with Communication Disorders	**10.** Collaboration	**ICC10S9** Communicate with school personnel about the characteristics and needs of individuals with exceptional learning needs.	**6.** Communication	**6.02** All teachers collaborate with speech/language pathologists and other language specialists to identify the language and communication skills that need to be developed and work cooperatively to teach those skills across settings.

	CEC		INTASC	
Major Chapter Headings	Knowledge and Skill Core Standard	Associated Subcategories	Core Principle	Associated Special Education Subcategories
Instructional Guidelines and Accommodations for Students with Communication Disorders	**6.** Communication	**ICC6S1** Use strategies to support and enhance communication skills of individuals with exceptional learning needs.	**6.** Communication	**6.01** All teachers have knowledge of the general types of communication strategies and assistive technologies that can be incorporated as a regular part of instruction. They understand that students with disabilities may have communication and language needs that impact their ability to access the general education curriculum.
Working with Parents to Extend Language Concepts	**4.** Instructional Strategies	**ICC4S4** Use strategies to facilitate maintenance and generalization of skills across learning environments.	**10.** Collaboration	**10.04** All teachers accept families as full partners in planning appropriate instruction and services for students with disabilities and provide meaningful opportunities for them to participate in their children's instructional programs and life at school.

Chapter 8 Teaching Students with Emotional and Behavioral Disorders

	CEC		INTASC	
Definitions of Emotional and Behavioral Disorders	**1.** Foundations	**GC1K1** Definitions and issues related to the identification of individuals with disabilities.	**2.** Student Learning	**2.01** All teachers have a sound understanding of physical, social, emotional, and cognitive development. They are familiar with the general characteristics of the most frequently occurring disabilities and have a basic understanding of the ways that disabilities impact learning.
Prevalence of Students with Emotional or Behavioral Disorders	**2.** Development and Characteristics of Learners	**GC2K4** Psychological and social-emotional characteristics of individuals with disabilities.	**3.** Learner Differences	**3.04** All teachers understand and are sensitive to cultural, ethnic, gender, and linguistic differences that may be confused with or misinterpreted as manifestations of disability.
Types and Characteristics of Emotional or Behavioral Disorders	**1.** Foundations	**GC1K2** Models and theories of deviance and behavior problems.	**2.** Student Learning	**2.01** All teachers have a sound understanding of physical, social, emotional, and cognitive development. They are familiar with the general characteristics of the most frequently occurring disabilities and have a basic understanding of the ways that disabilities impact learning.
Causes of Emotional and Behavioral Disorders	**2.** Development and Characteristics of Learners	**GC2K1** Etiology and diagnosis related to various theoretical approaches.	**2.** Student Learning	**2.03** All teachers recognize that students with disabilities vary in their approaches to learning depending on factors such as the nature of their disability, their level of knowledge and functioning, and life experiences.
Identification and Assessment of Students with Emotional and Behavioral Disorders	**8.** Assessment	**GC8S4** Assess reliable method(s) of response of individuals who lack typical communication and performance abilities.	**8.** Assessment	**8.02** All teachers use a variety of assessment procedures to document students' learning, behavior, and growth within multiple environments appropriate to the student's age, interests, and learning.

	CEC		INTASC	
Major Chapter Headings	**Knowledge and Skill Core Standard**	**Associated Subcategories**	**Core Principle**	**Associated Special Education Subcategories**
Teaching Guidelines and Accommodations for Students with Emotional or Behavioral Disorders	**7.** Instructional Planning	**GC7K1** Integrate academic instruction and behavior management for individuals and groups with disabilities.	**5.** Learning Environments	**5.05** All teachers participate in the design and implementation of individual behavioral support plans and are proactive in responding to the needs of individual students within the learning community.

Chapter 9 Teaching Students with Autism Spectrum Disorders/Pervasive Developmental Disorders

Definitions of Autism Spectrum Disorders/Asperger Syndrome and Pervasive Developmental Disorders	**2.** Development and Characteristics of Learners	**ICC2K6** Similarities and differences among individuals with exceptional learning needs.	**1.** Subject Matter	**1.04** All teachers have knowledge of the major principles and parameters of federal disabilities legislation.
Characteristics of Students with Autism Spectrum Disorders/Asperger Syndrome	**2.** Development and Characteristics of Learners	**ICC2K2** Educational implications of characteristics of various exceptionalities.	**2.** Student Learning	**2.01** All teachers have a sound understanding of physical, social, emotional, and cognitive development. They are familiar with the general characteristics of the most frequently occurring disabilities and have a basic understanding of the ways that disabilities impact learning.
Identification and Assessment of Students with Autism Spectrum Disorders	**8.** Assessment	**GC8S3** Select, adapt and modify assessments to accommodate the unique abilities and needs of individuals with disabilities.	**8.** Assessment	**8.02** All teachers use a variety of assessment procedures to document students' learning, behavior, and growth within multiple environments appropriate to the student's age, interests, and learning.
Curricular and Instructional Guidelines for Students with Autism Spectrum Disorders	**6.** Communication	**ICC6S1** Use strategies to support and enhance communication skills of individuals with exceptional learning needs.	**6.** Communication	**6.04** All teachers provide multiple opportunities to foster effective communication among students with disabilities and other members of the classroom as a means of building communication and language skills.
Addressing Challenging Behaviors	**5.** Learning Environments and Social Interactions	**ICC5K6** Strategies for crisis prevention and intervention.	**5.** Learning Environment	**5.05** All teachers participate in the design and implementation of individual behavioral support plans and are proactive in responding to the needs of individual students within the learning community.

Chapter 10 Teaching Students with Developmental Disabilities

Types of Developmental Disabilities	**1.** Foundations	**ICCIKI** Models, theories, philosophies, and research methods that provide the basis for special education practice.	**2.** Student Learning	**2.03** All teachers recognize that students with disabilities vary in their approaches to learning depending on factors such as the nature of their disability, their level of knowledge and functioning, and life experiences.

| Major Chapter Headings | CEC | | INTASC | |
	Knowledge and Skill Core Standard	Associated Subcategories	Core Principle	Associated Special Education Subcategories
Prevalence and Identification of Students with Developmental Disabilities	**1.** Development and Characteristics of Learners	**ICC2K2** Educational implications of characteristics of various exceptionalities.	**2.** Student Learning	**2.01** All teachers have a sound understanding of physical, social, emotional, and cognitive development. They are familiar with the general characteristics of the most frequently occurring disabilities and have a basic understanding of the ways that disabilities impact learning.
Guidelines for Teaching Students with Developmental Disabilities	**7.** Instructional Planning	**ICC7S4** Use functional assessments to develop intervention plans.	**2.** Student Learning	**2.02** All teachers examine their assumptions about the learning and development of students with disabilities and use this information to create challenging and supportive learning opportunities.

Chapter 11 Teaching Students with Impairments, Disabilities, or Traumatic Brain Injury

Major Chapter Headings	Knowledge and Skill Core Standard	Associated Subcategories	Core Principle	Associated Special Education Subcategories
Students with Visual Impairments	**7.** Instructional Planning	**ICC7S9** Incorporate and implement instructional and assistive technology into the educational program.	**3.** Learner Differences	**3.02** All teachers recognize that a specific disability does not dictate how an individual student will learn.
Students with Hearing Loss	**5.** Learning Environments and Social Interactions	**GC5S2** Use and maintain assistive technologies.	**4.** Instructional Strategies	**4.08** All teachers expect and support the use of assistive and instructional technologies to promote learning and independence of students with disabilities.
Students with Physical Disabilities, Health Impairments, and Traumatic Brain Injury	**9.** Professional and Ethical Practice	**ICC9S3** Act ethically in advocating for appropriate services.	**2.** Student Learning	**2.02** All teachers examine their assumptions about the learning and development of students with disabilities and use this information to create challenging and supportive learning opportunities.

Part 3: Teaching Practices

Chapter 12 Facilitating Reading

Major Chapter Headings	Knowledge and Skill Core Standard	Associated Subcategories	Core Principle	Associated Special Education Subcategories
Current Trends in Reading and Reading Instruction	**7.** Instructional Planning	**ICC7K1** Theories and research that form the basis of curriculum development and instructional practice.	**1.** Subject Matter	**1.01** All teachers have a solid base of understanding of the major concepts, assumptions, issues, and processes of inquiry in the subject matter content areas that they teach.
Effective Reading Instruction for Struggling Readers	**8.** Assessment	**ICC8S8** Evaluate instruction and monitor progress of individuals with exceptional learning needs.	**2.** Student Learning	**2.04** All teachers are knowledgeable about multiple theories of learning and research-based practices that support learning and use this information to inform instruction.
Strategies for Teaching Phonological Awareness and Phonics	**4.** Instructional Strategies	**GC4S14** Implement systematic instruction in teaching reading comprehension and monitoring strategies.	**7.** Instructional Planning	**7.02** All teachers plan ways to modify instruction to facilitate positive learning results within the general education curriculum for students with disabilities.

	CEC		INTASC	
Major Chapter Headings	**Knowledge and Skill Core Standard**	**Associated Subcategories**	**Core Principle**	**Associated Special Education Subcategories**
Strategies for Teaching Word Identification	**4.** Instructional Strategies	**GC4S16** Implement systematic instruction to teach accuracy, fluency, and comprehension in content area reading and written language.	**4.** Instructional Strategies	**4.02** All teachers understand how different learning theories and research contribute to effective instruction for students with disabilities.
Strategies for Helping Students Develop Fluency	**4.** Instructional Strategies	**GC4S4** Use reading methods appropriate to the individual with learning disabilities.	**4.** Instructional Strategies	**4.** Instructional Strategies
Strategies for Improving Reading Comprehension	**4.** Instructional Strategies	**GC4S16** Implement systematic instruction to teach accuracy, fluency, and comprehension in content area reading and written language.	**4.** Instructional Strategies	**4.03** All teachers use research-based practices to support learning and generalization of concepts and skills.
Strategies for Teaching Older Readers with Reading Difficulties	**4.** Instructional Strategies	**GC4S4** Use reading methods appropriate to the individual with learning disabilities.	**3.** Learner Differences	**3.02** All teachers recognize that a specific disability does not dictate how an individual student will learn.
Chapter 13 Facilitating Writing				
Current Trends in Writing Curriculum and Instruction	**7.** Instructional Planning	**ICC7K1** Theories and research that form the basis of curriculum development and instructional practice.	**1.** Subject Matter	**1.01** All teachers have a solid base of understanding of the major concepts, assumptions, issues, and processes of inquiry in the subject matter content areas that they teach.
Teaching Writing as a Process	**4.** Instructional Strategies	**GC4S16** Implement systematic instruction to teach accuracy, fluency, and comprehension in content area reading and written language.	**1.** Subject Matter	**1.03** All teachers understand that students with disabilities may need accommodations, modifications, and/or adaptations to the general curriculum.
Strategies for Establishing an Environment That Promotes Writing	**5.** Learning Environments	**ICC5S4** Design learning environments that encourage active participation in individual and group activities.	**5.** Learning Environment	**5.04** All teachers recognize factors and situations that are likely to promote intrinsic motivation, and create learning environments that encourage engagement and self-motivation.
Strategies for Conducting a Writing Workshop	**4.** Instructional Strategies	**GC4S15** Teach strategies for organizing and composing written products.	**4.** Instructional Strategies	**4.03** All teachers use research-based practices to support learning and generalization of concepts and skills.
Making Adaptations for Struggling Writers: Teachers' Practices	**4.** Instructional Strategies	**ICC4S3** Select, adapt, and use instructional strategies and materials according to characteristics of the individual with exceptional learning needs.	**7.** Instructional Planning	**7.02** All teachers plan ways to modify instruction to facilitate positive learning results within the general education curriculum for students with disabilities.
Strategies for Teaching Narrative Writing	**4.** Instructional Strategies	**GC4S15** Teach strategies for organizing and composing written products.	**4.** Instructional Strategies	**4.04** All teachers understand that it is particularly important to provide multiple ways for students with disabilities to participate in learning activities. They modify tasks and accommodate individual needs of students with disabilities.

	CEC		INTASC	
Major Chapter Headings	**Knowledge and Skill Core Standard**	**Associated Subcategories**	**Core Principle**	**Associated Special Education Subcategories**
Strategies for Teaching Expository Writing	**4.** Instructional Strategies	**GC4S10** Identify and teach basic structures and relationships within and across curricula.	**2.** Student Learning	**2.04** All teachers are knowledgeable about multiple theories of learning and research-based practices that support learning and use this information to inform instruction.
Strategies for Teaching Persuasive Writing	**4.** Instructional Strategies	**GC4S12** Use responses and errors to guide instructional decisions and provide feedback to learners.	**8.** Assessment	**8.04** All teachers engage all students, including students with disabilities, in assessing and understanding their own learning and behavior.
Strategies for Helping All Students Acquire Spelling Skills	**6.** Communication	**GC6S2** Teach strategies for spelling accuracy and generalization.	**7.** Instructional Planning	**7.02** All teachers plan ways to modify instruction to facilitate positive learning results within the general education curriculum for students with disabilities.
Strategies for Helping All Students Develop Handwriting and Keyboarding Skills	**6.** Communication	**GC6S4** Teach methods and strategies for producing legible documents.	**4.** Instructional Strategies	**4.08** All teachers expect and support the use of assistive and instructional technologies to promote learning and independence of students with disabilities.
Chapter 14 Helping All Students Succeed in Mathematics				
Current Trends in Mathematics Curriculum and Instruction	**7.** Instructional Planning	**ICC7K1** Theories and research that form the basis of curriculum development and instructional practice.	**7.** Instructional Planning	**7.02** All teachers plan ways to modify instruction to facilitate positive learning results within the general education curriculum for students with disabilities.
Difficulties in Learning Mathematics	**2.** Development and Characteristics of Learners	**ICC2K2** Educational implications of characteristics of various exceptionalities.	**2.** Student Learning	**2.03** All teachers recognize that students with disabilities vary in their approaches to learning depending on factors such as the nature of their disability, their level of knowledge and functioning, and life experiences.
Effective Math Instruction for All Learners	**4.** Instructional Strategies	**GC4S5** Use methods to teach mathematics appropriate to the individuals with disabilities.	**4.** Instructional Strategies	**4.04** All teachers understand that it is particularly important to provide multiple ways for students with disabilities to participate in learning activities. They modify tasks and accommodate individual needs of students with disabilities.
Strategies for Helping All Students Acquire Basic Math Skills	**4.** Instructional Strategies	**GC4K6** Methods for increasing accuracy and proficiency in math calculations and applications.	**1.** Subject Matter	**1.01** All teachers have a solid base of understanding of the major concepts, assumptions, issues, and processes of inquiry in the subject matter content areas that they teach.
Strategies for Helping All Learners Acquire and Use Computation Skills	**4.** Instructional Strategies	**ICC4S3** Select, adapt, and use instructional strategies and materials according to characteristics of the individual with exceptional learning needs.	**1.** Subject Matter	**1.03** All teachers understand that students with disabilities may need accommodations, modifications, and/or adaptations to the general curriculum.

	CEC		INTASC	
Major Chapter Headings	Knowledge and Skill Core Standard	Associated Subcategories	Core Principle	Associated Special Education Subcategories
Strategies for Helping All Students Develop Problem-Solving Skills	**4.** Instructional Strategies	**ICC4S2** Teach individuals to use self-assessment, problem solving, and other cognitive strategies to meet their needs.	**4.** Instructional Strategies	**4.03** All teachers use research-based practices to support learning and generalization of concepts and skills.

Part 4: Secondary Instruction

Chapter 15 Differentiating Instruction and Assessment for Middle and High School Students

Major Chapter Headings	Knowledge and Skill Core Standard	Associated Subcategories	Core Principle	Associated Special Education Subcategories
Standards-Based Instruction	**7.** Instructional Planning	**ICC7K2** National, state or provincial, and local curricula standards.	N/A	
Differentiating Instruction for Secondary Learners	**2.** Development and Characteristics of Learners	**ICC2K5** Similarities and differences of individuals with and without exceptional learning needs.	**3.** Learner Differences	**3.02** All teachers understand and are sensitive to cultural, ethnic, gender, and linguistic differences that may be confused with or misinterpreted as manifestations of a disability.
Preparing Engaging Lessons for Middle and High School Students	**5.** Learning Environments and Social Interactions	**ICC5S4** Design learning environments that encourage active participation in individual and group activities.	**2.** Student Learning	**2.04** All teachers are knowledgeable about multiple theories of learning and research-based teaching practices that support learning.
Effective Content-Area Reading Instruction for Middle- and High-School Learners	**4.** Instructional Strategies	**GC4S11** Use instructional methods to strengthen and compensate for deficits in perception, comprehension, memory, and retrieval.	**4.** Instructional Strategies	**4.03** All teachers use research-based practices to support learning and generalization of concepts and skills.
Differentiating Assessment	**4.** Instructional Strategies	**GC4K2** Strategies to prepare for and take tests.	**8.** Assessment	**8.04** All teachers engage all students, including students with disabilities, in assessing and understanding their own learning and behavior.

Chapter 16 Fostering Strategies for Student Independence

Major Chapter Headings	Knowledge and Skill Core Standard	Associated Subcategories	Core Principle	Associated Special Education Subcategories
Effective Strategy Instruction: The Teaching–Learning Connection	**4.** Instructional Strategies	**GC4K5** Strategies for integrating student-initiated learning experiences into ongoing instruction.	**4.** Instructional Strategies	**4.01** All teachers share responsibility for the education of students with disabilities, including providing effective instruction to support students' learning.
Difficulties in Developing Independent Learners	**2.** Development and Characteristics of Learners	**ICC2K2** Educational implications of characteristics of various exceptionalities.	**2.** Student Learning	**2.02** All teachers examine their assumptions about the learning and development of students with disabilities and use this information to create challenging and supportive learning opportunities.
Developing Independence: Personal Responsibility	**4.** Instructional Strategies	**ICC4S5** Use procedures to increase the individual's self-awareness, self-management, self-control, self-reliance, and self-esteem.	**4.** Instructional Strategies	**4.07** All teachers use strategies to promote the independence, self-control, and self-advocacy of students with disabilities.

	CEC		INTASC	
Major Chapter Headings	**Knowledge and Skill Core Standard**	**Associated Subcategories**	**Core Principle**	**Associated Special Education Subcategories**
Developing Independence: Active Learning in the Classroom	**5.** Learning Environments and Social Interactions	**ICC5S9** Create an environment that encourages self-advocacy and increased independence.	**4.** Instructional Strategies	**4.03** All teachers use research-based practices to support learning and generalization of concepts and skills.
Developing Independence: Making Home–School Connections	**4.** Instructional Strategies	**ICC4S4** Use strategies to facilitate maintenance and generalization of skills across learning environments.	**4.** Instructional Strategies	**4.04** All teachers understand that it is particularly important to provide multiple ways for students with disabilities to participate in learning activities. They modify tasks and accommodate individual needs of students with disabilities.

GLOSSARY

A

Absence seizures (petit mal) A type of seizure characterized by short lapses in consciousness

Academic language Refers to the more cognitively demanding language skills required for the new learning that occurs in school

Acceleration The procedure of moving students quickly through the grades or through the curriculum

Accommodation Involves no changes in curriculum requirements for students, but may make modifications to how the material is presented and what is required of the student

Accountability standards State identified grade level learning expectations in key curriculum areas such as reading and math

Acquired immunodeficiency syndrome (AIDS) A viral infection transmitted through bodily fluids that may eventually cause a loss of stamina, developmental delays, motor problems, progressive neurological defects, repeated bacterial infections, psychological stresses, and death

Acronyms Words created by joining the first letters of a series of words

Acrostics Sentences created by words that begin with the first letters of a series of words

Adaptations Might involve changes in curriculum requirements

Adaptive behavior Refers to the effectiveness or degree with which individuals meet the standards of personal independence and social responsibility expected for the person's age and cultural group

Additive approach A strategy characterized by the addition of content, concepts, themes, and perspectives without changing the basic structure of the curriculum

Adequate yearly progress (AYP) The amount of gain the school district negotiates with the state that it will make for students who are behind

Advance organizer Information presented in advance of and at a higher level of generality, inclusiveness, and abstraction than the learning task itself

Advocacy One of the primary characteristics of the Individuals with Disabilities Education Act, which involves the assignment of representatives (advocates) for individuals with disabilities who lack parents or guardians

African American Vernacular English (AAVE) A dialect used by some African Americans; it is the most prevalent native English vernacular dialect in the United States

Aggression A form of behavior characterized by hostile or destructive actions

Alliteration The repetition of beginning sounds in words; one aspect students can use to identify similarities and differences in words

Alphabetic principle The use of the letters of the alphabet to form words

Alternate assessment State and school district policies for students with disabilities in meeting requirements for high-stakes tests

American Sign Language (ASL) A visual, gestural language

Analytic rubrics Scoring guides for evaluating student work that is made up of component parts of the activity and a scoring method to indicate level of performance on each part

Antisocial behavior Acts that can cause mental or physical harm to others or to their property

Anxiety A type of problem behavior involving extreme worry, anxiousness, or depression

Anxiety disorder A disorder that involves extreme worry, fearfulness, and concern (even when little reason for those feelings exists)

Articulation disorders Occur when students are unable to produce the sounds and sound combinations of language

Asperger syndrome A disorder in which the individual has a normal IQ and language development but also exhibits autisticlike behaviors and marked deficiencies in social and communication skills

Assessment portfolios Collections of work samples that document student progress in one or more subject areas

Assistive listening devices Tools that aid in the process of hearing

Assistive technology Any item, piece of equipment, or product system whether acquired commercially off the shelf, modified, or customized, that is used to increase, maintain, or improve functional capabilities of individuals with disabilities

Attention deficit hyperactivity disorder (ADHD) A disorder consisting of two subtypes of behavior: inattention and hyperactivity–impulsivity

Audiogram A visual representation of an individual's ability to hear sound

Augmentative and alternative communication (AAC) systems Systems that attempt to facilitate and compensate for, temporarily or permanently, the impairment and disability patterns of individuals with severe expressive and/or language comprehension disorders

Authentic assessment Assessment that makes a link between goals and objectives for your students and documentation of progress toward meeting those goals and objectives

Authoring process A cycle of prewriting, composing (drafting), and postwriting (revising, editing, and publishing)

Autism A developmental disability characterized by extreme withdrawal and communication difficulties

Autism spectrum disorders (ASD) A subgroup of pervasive developmental disorders, namely, autism and Asperger syndrome

Autistic leading Leading behavior that is common in autism

Automaticity Automaticity in decoding refers to recognizing the words on sight

B

Basic interpersonal communication skills (BICS) The conversational competencies that develop with a second language

Behavioral disorders Behavior that falls considerably outside the norm

Behavioral improvement plan (BIP) A plan designed to identify behavior problems of students and to develop an intervention plan to treat these behavior problems

Behavioral inhibition The ability to withhold a planned response, halt a response that has been started, protect an ongoing activity from interfering activities, or delay a response

Big books Books with large pictures and words that can be seen by a whole class and used for shared reading activities

Bilingual education An educational program involving instruction in two languages, the goal being to promote bilingualism (proficiency in both languages)

Bipolar disorder A type of depression characterized by extreme mood swings

Blending Putting sounds or phonemes together to form words

Braille A system of embossed or raised dots that can be read with the tips of the fingers

Bulletin A way to communicate with parents

Cascade of integration options The options special education/general education teams use to individualize and make instructional decisions based on a student's specific needs

Cerebral palsy Results from damage to the brain before or during birth; conditions are classified according to the areas affected and the types of symptoms

Challenging behavior A pattern of inappropriate behavior that interferes with learning or social situations.

Charter schools Schools that develop proposals to use state funds but have independence from the local school district

Check-in, check-out (CICO) procedure A procedure where students earn points for appropriate behaviors in small-group instructional or mentoring sessions and in the classroom

Child find A requirement that each state identify and track the number of students with disabilities and plan for their educational needs

Childhood disintegrative disorder A neurologic condition generally classified in the pervasive developmental disorders (PDDs) that is characterized by normal development through age 2 followed by a severe deterioration of mental and social functioning, with regression to a state suggestive of autism

Children with specific learning disabilities Those children who have a disorder in one or more of the basic psychological processes involved in understanding or in using language, spoken or written, that may manifest itself in an imperfect ability to listen, think, speak, read, write, spell, or do mathematical calculations

Class meetings Meetings that include all students in the class, as well as the teacher; used to foster students' involvement in the management of their classes

Classification The ability to group or sort objects by one or more common properties

Classroom routine The organization of classroom activities throughout the school day

Classroom web pages An individual classroom web page that provides information about the calendar, major events, and homework tips

Classwide peer tutoring (CWPT) Students of different reading levels are paired (one average or high and one low) and read materials that can be easily read by the less able reader in the pair

Cognitive academic language performance (CALP) Refers to the more cognitively demanding language skills required for the new learning that is characteristic of school settings

Cognitive strategies Thinking processes used by students to complete their academic work

Collaboration A style for direct interaction between at least two coequal parties voluntarily engaged in shared decision making as they work toward a common goal

Collaborative strategic reading (CSR) A multicomponent learning strategy that combines essential reading comprehension strategies that have been demonstrated as effective in improving students' understanding of text

Collective identity An identity that develops as the involuntary minorities are treated as subordinates by European Americans in economic, political, social, psychological, cultural, and language domains

Common underlying proficiency The phenomenon that the better developed the students' first language proficiency and conceptual foundation, the more likely they are to develop similarly high levels of proficiency and conceptual ability in the second language

Communication board An example of augmentative communication that includes the board itself and symbols or pictures

Communication disorders Difficulties with the transfer of knowledge, ideas, opinions, and feelings

Comorbidity The idea that students can have more than one disability

Compensatory skills Skills needed for independence, which may include the use of Braille, a slate and stylus, or an abacus

Composing Process in which the author attempts to get ideas on paper in the form of a draft

Comprehensible input Refers to input received and made understandable when listening to or reading in a second language

Comprehensible output Output that is transmitted and made understandable when speaking

Comprehension A person's ability to understand what is being communicated

Comprehension monitoring Refers to monitoring understanding

Comprehension strategies Techniques designed to improve students' understanding of text

Computational Arithmetic Program A program that provides 314 worksheets to teach basic math skills in grades 1 through 6

Concept diagram A way to introduce a lecture or reading assignment (similar to a semantic map) that also helps students determine the definitions, characteristics, examples, and nonexamples of a concept

Conduct disorder Includes behaviors such as hitting, fighting, throwing, temper tantrums, and acting defiant or disobedient, and characteristics such as being irritable or overactive, difficult to get along with, uncooperative, inconsiderate, resistive, jealous, quarrelsome, distractible, teasing, irresponsible, and inattentive

Conferencing An ongoing student–teacher meeting prepared to read the student's writing piece, to describe problem areas, and to respond to questions

Confidentiality of records The requirement of the Individuals with Disabilities Education Act that all records and documents regarding students with disabilities remain undisclosed to the public but accessible to parents

Consequences The ramifications of not following classroom guidelines

Considerate text Text that is written and formatted in such a way that information can be extracted easily, with support available when the reader does not understand

Constant time delay A procedure for teaching math facts that provides for the systematic introduction of teacher assistance

Consultation An interactive process that enables people with diverse expertise to generate creative solutions to mutually defined problems

Content The semantics of language

Content integration Focused use of examples and content from different cultures and groups to illustrate concepts, principles, generalizations, and theories

Context-embedded communication and instruction Providing a link between students' culture, the instruction they receive, and the mode in which they receive it

Continuum of services A full range of service options for students with disabilities, provided by the school system

Contributions approach Characterized by the insertion of ethnic heroes and discrete cultural artifacts into the curriculum

Cooperative learning Groups in which students work together toward a common goal, usually to help one another learn academic material

Cooperative learning groups Groups of students working together toward a common goal, usually to help one another learn academic material

Corrective Mathematics Program A math program that requires only minimal reading skills and provides remedial math for students in grades 3 through 12

Co-teaching Occurs when general and special education teachers work together to coordinate curriculum and instruction and to teach heterogeneous groups of students in the general education classroom setting

Cultural characteristics Traits or aspects that characterize a particular culture

Cultural inversion The tendency to regard certain forms of behavior, events, symbols, and meanings as inappropriate because they are uncharacteristic of European-American culture

Culturally responsive assessment (CRA) A collection of approaches that promote nondiscriminatory assessment practices

Culturally responsive teaching (CRT) Using the cultural knowledge, past experiences, and learning styles of diverse students to make learning more appropriate and effective for them

Curriculum compacting Provides students with the opportunity to demonstrate what they already know about a subject by eliminating repetitive or review content and replacing it with advanced learning experiences

Curriculum enhancement Involves no changes to the curriculum, but involves instructional strategies that promote learning for all students

Curriculum modification Modifications targeted to individual needs of students

Curriculum-based assessment (CBA) A way to monitor ongoing progress in acquisition of basic skills

Curriculum-based measurement (CBM) A means of measuring student progress that highlights the close tie between curriculum and student performance

Cursive writing Script writing typically introduced in third grade

Cybaries Cyber libraries

D

Deaf Describes a person with a severe or profound loss of hearing

Deaf–blind Also known as dual sensory impairment; involves impairments in the two main channels (auditory and visual) of receptive communication and learning

Decodable books Books that primarily use words that reflect the phonic and word patterns already learned

Decodable text Text in which most of the words are composed of letter–sound correspondences that have been taught

Decoding A strategy for recognizing words

Demonstration plus model strategy A strategy for giving demonstrations to students with learning problems that includes completion of the demonstration, having a student perform each step, verbalizing each step as the teacher did, and having all students complete additional practice exercises independently, using the steps

Depression A mental illness characterized by prolonged and persistent feelings of sadness, irritability, or anxiety that interfere with life functioning

Developmental arithmetic disorder Refers to students who have significant difficulties learning arithmetic (difficulties that are unexpected, given the students' overall cognitive functioning and/or academic performance in other subject areas)

Developmental disability Refers to a disability that is attributable to mental retardation or related conditions that include cerebral palsy, epilepsy, autism, or other neurological conditions when such conditions result in impairment of general intellectual functioning or adaptive behavior similar to that of a person with mental retardation

Diagnostic and Statistical Manual of Mental Disorders A reference book published by the American Psychiatric Association

Diagnostic assessments Assessments that tell us specifically how a student is performing and what else he or she needs to know

Dialect Refers to language variations associated with a regional or social group of people

Dialog journal An ongoing written conversation between two students (or in some cases between a student and an adult)

Difficulty with zero Refers to students' misunderstanding of the multiple meanings and uses of zero that causes errors in arithmetic

Direct assessment Assessment that involves observing students and documenting the sequence of behaviors around challenging behavior

Disabilities Conditions that include mental retardation, hearing impairments, vision impairments, speech and language impairments, learning disabilities, serious emotional disturbance, orthopedic impairments, other health impairments, autism, traumatic brain injury, deafness and blindness, and multiple disabilities

Discrepancy analysis A review of each specific step or skill and determination of how a student does the step or skill compared to what is expected

Discussion web A graphic aid to help students prepare for classroom discussions in content-area classes

DISSECT A learning strategy for secondary students with learning disabilities to approach a multisyllable word in a strategic way

Distributed practice The practice of breaking up the material to be learned into manageable chunks and then having several short study sessions over a period of time.

Down syndrome One of the most common chromosomal disorders, usually associated with mental retardation

Drafting See **Composing**

Dual sensory impairments Refers to impairments in the two main channels (auditory and visual) of receptive communication and learning

Due process Ensures that everyone with a stake in the student's educational success has a voice; also addresses written notification to parents for referral and testing for special education, parental consent, and guidelines for appeals and record keeping

Dyscalculia Severe disability in learning mathematical concepts and computation

Dysfluent Difficulty with the rate and flow of speech

Dysgraphia Severe difficulty learning to write (including handwriting)

Dyslexia Severe difficulty learning to read, particularly as it relates to decoding

E

Early intervention services Comprehensive services that incorporate goals in education, health care, and social services

Early-exit programs Transition programs in which at least 40% of the instruction is in the first language

Echolalia Repeating what was heard verbatim

Editing The process that takes place as the author reviews the written work line by line to determine whether the overall content is appropriate and the mechanics are correct

Educational interventions Special strategies for meeting the diverse needs of students

Educational placement The type of educational setting in which a particular student is instructed; examples include general education classrooms, resource rooms, special schools, and other types of settings

Effective listening Requires hearing the message being sent and often requires asking questions to clarify the true message being sent

Elaboration Teacher extension of language that builds on the content of the student's language and provides additional information on the topic

Emotional disorders Behavior that falls considerably outside the norm

Empowering school culture and social structure A culture that promotes gender, racial, and social class equity

Encode To change written language to symbols; to write

Encoding function The physical act of taking notes promotes student engagement and learning

Encouragement Teacher recognizes a behavior but does not provide judgment

English as a Second Language (ESL) instruction Teaching English as a second language, with limited emphasis on maintaining or developing proficiency in the student's first language

English language learners (ELLs) Students for whom English is a second language

Enrichment Adding breadth and depth to the traditional curriculum

Environmental accommodations Changes made to the physical learning environment so that each student can participate successfully

Epilepsy A condition characterized by the tendency to have recurrent seizures caused by sudden, excessive, spontaneous, and abnormal discharges of neurons accompanied by alteration in motor function and/or sensory function and/or consciousness

Equity pedagogy Attending to different teaching and learning styles and modifying teaching to facilitate the academic achievement of students from diverse cultures

Executive functioning Refers to the ability to regulate one's thinking and behavior through the use of working memory, inner speech, control of emotions and arousal levels, and analysis of problems and communication of problem solutions to others

Executive learner A student who is aware of personal learning strengths and challenges, understands tasks to be accomplished, has a repertoire of learning strategies, and has developed help-seeking behaviors

Expansion A technique used to facilitate the development of more complex language form and content

Expository writing Informational writing

Expressive language A person's ability to convey the intended message

External storage function One of two purposes of notetaking; students take notes to record what was presented and discussed in class; this record can be used for preparing for tests and class discussions

Externalizing behaviors Behaviors such as aggression, hitting, and shouting that are readily observable and tend to affect others

Extinction The elimination of a student's undesirable behavior by removing reinforcers

F

Facilitator The teacher who guides his or her peer through the process and helps to generate solutions

Failure to shift operations Occurs when the student fails to move to the next operation after completing a previous operation

Family adjustment A family's changes in response to having a child with severe disabilities, mental retardation, or physical disabilities

FAST DRAW A type of mnemonic used to teach the concrete-representational-abstract teaching principle advocated in mathematics instruction (Find what you're solving for; Ask yourself "What are the parts of the problem?"; Set up the numbers; Tie down the sign; Discover the sign; Read the problem; Answer or draw a conceptual representation of the problem, using lines and tallies, and check; Write the answer)

Fetal alcohol syndrome (FAS) Refers to a spectrum of birth defects caused by the mother's drinking during pregnancy

Fidelity The degree to which an intervention has been administered with consistency and according to prescribed guidelines

Figurative language Represents abstract concepts and usually requires an inferential rather than literal interpretation

Finger spelling A system for manually representing the English alphabet

FIRST-letter A mnemonic strategy in which students construct lists of information to memorize and develop an acronym or acrostic for learning and remembering the information

FLIP Chart Strategy Helps students learn to evaluate the difficulty of text on their own by examining text friendliness and language as well as their interest in and prior knowledge of the topic

Fluency The ability to recognize printed words quickly

Form The phonology, morphology, and syntax of language

Fragile X syndrome The most common form of intellectual disabilities that is passed from parent to child

Free appropriate public education (FAPE) The legal mandate that all children with disabilities be given a free and appropriate public education

Friendly text A text that features elements that support student learning

Frustration reading level The reading level at which students have difficulty reading even with assistance, because reading materials are too difficult

Full inclusion A movement that advocates educating all students with disabilities in the general education classroom full time

Functional analysis Involves analysis of the skills needed to complete a particular activity or task

Functional assessment Assessment in which each goal or activity is broken into steps or subskills, and the student's present performance level is determined for each subskill or step in the activity

Functional behavior assessment A method of gathering data to design the most effective positive support plans and to monitor their progress

Functional practice Relevant practice that helps students to easily see the connection between what they are practicing and its use in real life

Functional vision assessment Assessment that includes the student's ability to view at both near and distant points and to sustain visual function throughout daily academic settings

Funds of knowledge The information and resources available in the student's home community

G

Gangs Groups of individuals working to unlawful or antisocial ends

Graphic organizer A visual framework used to assist students in organizing information or making connections between concepts

Group behavior Behaviors displayed in the presence of other group members

H

Hanover method A system for teaching cursive writing based on the similarities of letters or letter families

Hard of hearing Describes a person with a mild to moderate loss of hearing

Hearing aid A device that amplifies hearing

Help-seeking behaviors A set of behaviors that exhibit a student's skill in seeking assistance in appropriate and effective ways

Heterogeneous grouping Groups consisting of students at a wide range of achievement levels

High responders Students who respond well to intervention

High-frequency words Words that occur frequently in spoken language and in written text

Holistic rubrics Scoring guides for evaluating a student product; the scoring method indicates level of performance on the product as a whole

Homebound teacher A teacher who provides direct instruction and coordinates instructional programs between the school and the home

Homogeneous grouping The practice of putting students at approximately the same achievement level together for instruction (also called *same-ability grouping*)

Human immunodeficiency virus (HIV) A virus that infects and eventually destroys cells in the immune system that protect the body from disease

Hyperactivity–impulsivity Refers to a group of behaviors associated with restlessness, excess motor activity, and an inability to control one's own actions

I PLAN A strategy for developing student self-advocacy skills during IEP or transition planning conferences; the plan includes five steps: **I**nventory your learning strengths, weaknesses, goals, interests, and choices for learning; **P**rovide your inventory information; **L**isten and respond; **A**sk questions; **N**ame your goals

Ignoring on purpose A method of eliminating a student's undesirable behavior by purposely removing the teacher's and other students' attention to that behavior

Immaturity Behaviors that include lack of perseverance, failure to finish tasks, short attention span, poor concentration, and frequent daydreaming or preoccupation

Implant A device inserted into the ear through surgery

Inattention Refers to difficulty sustaining attention

Inclusion The situation in which students with disabilities are educated with their nondisabled peers, with special education supports and services provided as needed

Independent reading level The reading level at which students read on their own without support from others

Indirect assessments Assessments providing information about student strengths and needs that do not involve direct observation or direct contact with the student

Individualized education program (IEP) A written plan, developed to meet the special learning needs of each student with disabilities

Individualized family service plan (IFSP) A plan, for children from birth to 3 years of age, developed to meet not only the special needs of each student with disabilities but also those of his or her family

Individualized transition plan A plan, for students from 16 years of age (or 14 years and even younger, if appropriate) to age 21, that states what transition services are necessary and, when appropriate, includes a statement of the interagency responsibilities and linkages

Individuals with Disabilities Education Act (IDEA) Legislation designed to ensure that all children with disabilities receive an appropriate education through special education and related services

Informal reading inventory An individually administered reading assessment designed to help a teacher determine a student's reading instructional needs. The student reads lists of words and passages that are leveled by grade and retells or answers comprehension questions about the passages

Initiator The teacher who addresses the problems to his or her peer

Inner speech Talking to one's self about various solutions when in the midst of solving a problem

Instructional clarity The clear, direct, and explicit presentation of information

Instructional conversations Conversations between students and teachers on the reading process (e.g., sharing the strategies the students use to decode words and construct meaning)

Instructional reading level The reading level at which instruction should occur and at which students are challenged by the reading but still need some support

Intellectual disabilities Limited cognitive functioning, which affects learning

Internalizing behaviors Behaviors such as shyness, withdrawal, or depression that tend to be less readily observable and negatively affect the individual exhibiting the behaviors

Key Math Teach and Practice A program designed to diagnose math difficulties and provide remedial practice

Key word strategy A mnemonic strategy that uses both verbal and visual cues to create images to prompt recall and retention of information

Knowledge construction Refers to students' learning about how implicit cultural assumptions, frames of reference, perspectives, and biases influence the ways that knowledge is constructed

K-W-L strategy A strategy (based on research underscoring the importance of activating prior knowledge before reading) to help students become actively engaged in comprehension before, during, and after reading

Language disorders A major area of communication disorders

Language variation Refers to the fact that language varies from place to place and from group to group

Late-exit programs Programs that foster the students' first language and strengthen their sense of cultural identity while teaching the second language and culture

Learner characteristics The third factor affecting second language acquisition or output; includes the age at which students learn a second language, their aptitude for learning language, their purposes and degree of motivation for learning the second language, their self-confidence in language learning, and the learning strategies they have for learning language

Learning contract A contract that identifies target standards or objectives and allows the teacher to negotiate with students about the pathway and products they will produce to determine mastery

Learning media assessment An assessment to determine a student's dominant learning modality

Least restrictive environment The instructional setting most like that of nondisabled peers that also meets the educational needs of each student with disabilities

Legal blindness The visual impairment of an individual who with the best possible correction in the better eye has a measured visual acuity of 20/200 or worse or a visual field restricted to 20 degrees or less

Lesson co-planning Collaboration of general and special education teachers to plan activities for students

Lesson co-teaching Teaching in which the special education and general education teachers are both in the classroom during the same lesson and both participate in the instruction

Letter A way to communicate with parents

Letter strategy A type of mnemonics

Lexile levels An estimate of a student's reading level and a text's readability; levels can range from 200 for beginning readers to over 1700 for advanced text

Linguistic input Input received when listening or reading in a second language

Long-range co-planning Planning in which the general education and special education teachers broadly plan their overall goals and desired outcomes for the class and for specific students with disabilities in the class

Low vision Describes an individual who is either partially sighted or legally blind

Macroculture The core culture in a school

Mainstreaming The participation of students with disabilities in general education classrooms to the extent appropriate for meeting their needs

Maintenance bilingual education Education that attempts to foster the students' first language and strengthen their sense of cultural identity

Making words A whole-class guided activity that helps students develop phonological awareness and become more sensitive to common spelling patterns

Manipulating A type of phonological awareness skill: deleting, adding, and substituting syllables and sounds

Manuscript writing Print writing

MARKER A strategy for setting goals and monitoring progress: **M**ake a list of goals, set the order, and set the dates; **A**rrange a plan for each goal and predict your success; **R**un your plan for each goal and adjust if necessary; **K**eep records of your progress; **E**valuate your progress toward each goal; **R**eward yourself when you reach a goal, and set a new goal

Massed trials strategy A technique whereby the same instructional trial is repeated again and again to a predefined criterion of correct performance

Mastery Meeting accuracy, speed, and knowledge expectations

McGill Action Planning System (MAPS) A planning activity that fosters relationships in order to improve the quality of life for persons with severe disabilities while facilitating participation in inclusive settings

Medically fragile A subgroup that has emerged within the health disabilities, characterized by an individual being at risk for medical emergencies on a regular basis and often requiring life support or specialized support systems such as ventilators

Memory problems Forgetting or misremembering a fact; lead to errors in arithmetic calculation and other areas

Memory strategies Mental techniques for increasing students' abilities to memorize information and utilize information in memory

Mental retardation Limited intellectual functioning that affects an individual's learning

Metacognition Knowledge of one's knowledge, processes, and cognitive and affective states; and the ability to consciously and deliberately monitor and regulate one's knowledge, processes, and cognitive and affective states

Metacognitive conversations Brief classroom discussions about specific learning tasks and how best to accomplish those tasks

Metalinguistics Involves thinking about, analyzing, and reflecting on language as an object in much the same way one reflects on a table or a friend

Microcultures Home cultures based on such factors as national origin, ethnicity, socioeconomic class, religion, gender, age, and disability

Milieu instruction Communication training occurring during natural opportunities for children or students to communicate

Mistaken goal Evidenced when students display inappropriate behavior because they believe it will get them the recognition and acceptance they desire

Mixed hearing loss Hearing loss that is both conductive and sensorineural

Mnemonic devices Memory-triggering techniques used to help remember or retrieve information by forming associations that do not exist naturally in the content

Mobility skills Skills such as going up and down stairs, crossing streets, and using public transportation

Modeling A technique for teaching language that involves following examples illustrated by others

Mood disorders Disorders that include various types of depression

Morpheme The smallest unit of language that conveys meaning

Morphology Word study that focuses on the rule system that governs the structure of words and word forms

Motoric problems Difficulty of writing and reading numbers

Moving model Modeling for students how to form letters and words in order to develop their legibility

Multicultural education An educational reform movement whose major goal is to change the structure of educational institutions so that female students; exceptional students; and students who are members of diverse racial, ethnic, and cultural groups have an equal chance to achieve in school

Multidisciplinary team (MDT) A group that usually includes a representative of the local education agency, the classroom teacher, the special education teacher, parents or guardians, and, when appropriate, the

student; together they develop and implement the IEP

Multiliteracies Skills for dealing with multiples sources of information

Multiple disabilities The combination of severe or profound mental retardation and one or more significant motor or sensory impairments and/or special health needs

Multiple grouping formats The use of a variety of grouping patterns

Multiple intelligences The theory that human beings are capable of exhibiting intelligence in eight domains: linguistic, logical–mathematical, spatial, musical, bodily–kinesthetic, interpersonal (i.e., discerning and responding to the needs of others), intrapersonal (i.e., having detailed and accurate self-knowledge), and naturalistic (i.e., differentiating between living things and accurate knowledge of the natural world)

Multiple meanings Applies to words that have more than one meaning

Multitiered intervention strategy A set of layers of instruction that increase in intensity (e.g., amount of instruction, group size) based on how well students are succeeding in a less intensive instructional format

Muscular dystrophy A chronic disorder characterized by the weakening and wasting of the body's muscles

Narrative writing The writing of stories

Naturalistic instruction Communication skills taught as part of the ongoing natural context

NCTM Navigation Series Refers to a series of graded and topical books that focus on teaching algebra, geometry, numbers, and operations based on the NCTM principles and standards

Negative reinforcement The removal of a stimulus to increase responding

Neuromotor impairment An abnormal performance caused by a dysfunction of the brain, spinal cord, and nerves, thereby creating transmission of improper instructions, uncontrolled bursts of instructions from the brain, or incorrect interpretation of feedback to the brain

No Child Left Behind Act (NCLB) of 2001 An act that provides a framework on how to improve the performance of America's elementary and secondary schools while at the same time ensuring that no child is trapped in a failing school

Noncompliance Failure to comply with the law; the Individuals with Disabilities Act requires that states mandate consequences for noncompliance

Nondiscriminatory evaluation An evaluation that does not discriminate on the basis of language, culture, and student's background; must be provided for each individual who is assessed for special education

Nonoptical aids Devices that, although not prescribed by a doctor, promote efficient use of vision

Nonresponders Students who make minimal or no gains after being taught with high-quality, validated interventions

Nonverbal math disabilities Students who display good reading and verbal expression but who have extreme difficulty with mathematics

Norm-based assessments Assessments used to determine how a student's performance compares with other students of the same age or in the same grade

Number sense Whether a student's understanding of a number and its use and meaning is flexible and fully developed

Numeration The understanding of numbers and their manipulations

One-to-one correspondence A situation in which each object corresponds to another object

Onset-rime Onset is the word's initial consonant or consonant combination (e.g., /g/), and rime is the rhyming part of the word (e.g., /et/)

Open question A question that allows a full range of responses and discourages short "yes" or "no" answers

Oppositional defiant disorder (ODD) A disorder in which students habitually question authority, intentionally misbehave and ignore rules, are temperamental and negative, and blame others for their actions or when social and/or academic progress is inhibited as a result

Oral reading fluency The number of words a student reads correctly in one minute

Orientation skills Includes understanding one's own body, one's position in space, and physical concepts such as the layout of a city block

Orthopedic impairment Includes deficits caused by congenital anomaly (e.g., clubfoot, absence of some member), impairments caused by disease (e.g., poliomyelitis, bone tuberculosis), and impairments from other causes (e.g., cerebral palsy, amputations, and fractures or burns that cause contractures)

Other health impairments (OHI) Limited strength, vitality, or alertness (caused by chronic or acute health problems such as heart condition, tuberculosis, rheumatic fever,

nephritis, asthma, sickle-cell anemia, hemophilia, epilepsy, lead poisoning, leukemia, or diabetes) that adversely affects a student's educational performance

Overcorrection The act of having a student perform a duty or task to compensate for what happened

Overlearning The continued study or practice of new content after initial proficiency levels are reached in order to reinforce the learned content; learning to mastery

Parallel Curriculum Model (PCM) A framework for differentiated instruction that takes into consideration four curriculum design components

Parallel talk A process in which the teacher describes what students are doing or thinking

Parent interviews A way to foster communication by asking family members about their level of satisfaction with programs, curriculum, and services

Parent participation Involvement of parents in all aspects of identifying and evaluating students with disabilities, including decision making

Partial or parallel participation A concept that assumes that an individual has the right to participate, to the extent possible, in all activities

Partial sight Describes an individual who with best possible correction in the better eye has a measured visual acuity between 20/70 and 20/200

Pause procedure A technique in which, during logical breaks in a lecture (approximately every 10 minutes), the teacher pauses for 2 minutes to allow pairs of students to compare their notes to make certain that key concepts have been recorded

Peer collaboration model A model designed for classroom teachers to work with one or two other teachers.

Peer editing Process in which students revise and edit each other's work

Peer-assisted learning (PAL) An instructional practice promoting the use of students working together to provide practice and feedback on improving reading fluency; higher and lower readers are paired together and work through a series of structured activities. *See* **Classwide peer tutoring (CWPT)**

Personalized knowledge Knowledge that results from firsthand observation

Person-centered planning Planning for students' transition into adult life in terms of vocation and adult living

Person-first language Language that does not define a child by his or her disability

Persuasive writing A writing format in which the writer provides evidence in order to convince or persuade the reader of his or her position or opinion; writing persuasive essays involves planning and critical thinking

Pervasive developmental disorder (PDD) A disorder characterized by impairments in social interaction and verbal and communication skills, a limited number of interests, imaginative activity, and activities that tend to be repetitive

Pervasive developmental disorder–not otherwise specified A disorder in which a child exhibits stereotypical behaviors or delays in social interaction or communication, but does not meet the criteria for another PDD

Phoneme The smallest unit of speech sound

Phonemic awareness The understanding of how to listen to and produce sounds

Phonic analysis Identifying and blending letter–sound correspondences into words

Phonological awareness Possession of skills such as rhyming, alliteration recognition, blending, and segmentation

Phonology Focuses on the sounds of language and the rules that determine how the sounds fit together

Physical disabilities Orthopedic impairments and neuromotor impairments

PL 94–142 This legislation, designed to ensure that all children with disabilities receive an appropriate education through special education and related services, was originally referred to as the *Education for All Handicapped Children Act,* enacted in 1975, and later reauthorized and expanded as the Individuals with Disabilities Education Act (IDEA)

Planned ignoring A strategy to eliminate (extinguish) a student's undesirable behavior, which is being reinforced through attention, by ignoring

PLEASE strategy A strategy developed to provide students with a step-by-step procedure for paragraph writing

Portfolio assessment Assessment that involves compilation of multiple artifacts or student work samples

Positive behavioral support The modification of behavior management principles applied in various community settings with supports to reduce problem behaviors and develop appropriate behaviors that lead to enhanced social relations and lifestyle

Positive feedback Recognizing a student behavior by providing some judgment about the appropriateness of the behavior

Positive reinforcement The presentation of a stimulus (verbal response, physical response such as touching, or tangible response such as a reward) following the target behavior to maintain or increase the target behavior

Postwriting Process in which authors revise, edit, and publish their written work

Pragmatics The purposes or functions of communication or how we use language to communicate

Preference assessment An assessment of students' likes and dislikes

Prejudice reduction The dispelling of misconceptions and stereotypes about diverse cultural and ethnic groups

Prelearning activities Strategies teachers use to activate students' prior knowledge and to preteach vocabulary and concepts—essentially, to prepare students to learn

Prelinguistic level The communication skills of many students with autism, such as autistic leading

Prereferral assistance team (PAT) A group of teachers from the same school who meet regularly to discuss the specific progress of students brought to their attention by other teachers in the school

Prewriting Process in which a writer collects information about a topic through observing, remembering, interviewing, and reading

Primary prevention model A model in which the focus is on preventing behavior problems schoolwide

Procedural error Misapplying a procedure from one arithmetic operation to another

Production A person's ability to convey the intended message

Progress monitoring The frequent assessment of academic performance used to evaluate the effectiveness of instruction for students. *See* **Curriculum-based measurement (CBM)**

Progress report A letter sent to parents

PROJECT A multi-step strategy for completing assignments: **P**repare your assignment sheet; **R**ecord and ask; **O**rganize; **J**ump into it; **E**ngage in the work; **C**heck your work; **T**urn in your work

Prompt A situation and directions for writing an essay

Publishing Preparing a written work in a way that enables others to read it

Pull-out services Programs in which children are pulled out of their general education classroom for supplemental instruction in basic skills

Punishment The opposite of reinforcement, in that it follows a behavior and decreases the strength of the behavior or the likelihood the behavior will continue to occur

Purpose-setting activities Activities that give students a reason to complete a reading assignment or listen to a lecture

Question–answer relationships (QAR) strategy A strategy for teaching students how to answer different types of comprehension questions

Rapid naming Tasks such as naming a series of random numbers or letters

Readability level The level of difficulty of a textbook

Reading comprehension The ability to understand individual words, phrases and clauses, sentences, paragraphs, and larger units of text

Real content The main idea or key information that someone wants to convey

Receptive language A person's ability to understand what is being communicated

Receptive vocabulary Words that children understand the meaning of but may not use in their oral language

Reciprocal causation The combination of factors related to a student's reading problems

Register A language style the speaker uses to communicate to meet the needs or expectations of the speaker; includes such features as choice of words, sentences, intonation, and formality

Regular Education Initiative (REI) A concept that promotes coordination of services between regular and special education

Reinforcement Rewards from the teacher

Related services The types of services to which students with disabilities are entitled, including speech therapy, audiology, psychological services, physical therapy, occupational therapy, recreation, early identification and assessment, counseling, medical services for diagnostic or evaluation purposes, school health services, transportation, and social work services

Reliable alliances Home/school partnerships that occur when there are mutual trust; ongoing communication; sensitivity to family culture, basic needs, and choices; and high yet realistic expectations

Repeated readings Process of reading passages over and over again to develop fluency in reading

Repetitive motor behaviors Physical movements that are continuously repeated; examples are rocking, hand flapping, or rapid blinking

Residual hearing Usable hearing

Responders Students who respond well to intervention

Response cost Punishment that involves the loss of something tangible or intangible

Response to intervention (RTI) The practice of making educational decisions for students based on the student's level of performance and rate of progress after receiving high-quality, validated instruction or intervention

Rett syndrome An extremely rare disorder that primarily affects females, characterized by the following symptoms occurring between 5 and 48 months: deceleration of head growth, loss of hand skills with subsequent development of stereotyped hand movements, loss of social engagement, poor gait or trunk movements, and severely impaired receptive and expressive communication

Revising Stage of writing during which points are explored further, ideas are elaborated on, and further connections are made

Rhyming Identifying similarities and differences in word endings

RUBRIC A strategy for helping students learn to use rubrics effectively: **R**ead the rubric and the material to be graded; **U**se the rubric to give an initial score; **B**ring a buddy to help you rate again; **R**eview the material together; **I**dentify and award the scores together; **C**heck the scores again

Saxon Math A K–12 math program addressing math concepts with a scaffolded approach and an emphasis on solving math problems

Schizophrenia A chronic, severe, and disabling brain disorder

SCORE A A type of mnemonic used to identify the writing steps (Select a topic; Create categories; Obtain reference tools; Read and take notes; Evenly organize the information using notecards; Apply writing process steps)

Scoring guides Guidelines indicating what students should know and be able to do to demonstrate mastery of a standard

Secondary language output The level of proficiency in producing (speaking and writing) a language

Segmenting Process of dividing ideas into words and words into syllables and individual phonemes

Self-advocacy Occurs when individuals effectively communicate and negotiate for their interests, desires, needs, and rights

Self-determination A set of skills related to development of independence in setting and reaching goals including self-advocacy, choice making, decision making, and self-awareness

Self-evaluation Student self-analysis and goal setting for academic or behavioral tasks

Self-injurious behavior Behavior that may consist of head banging, scratching, or self-biting

Self-injury A behavior that may consist of head banging, scratching, or biting oneself

Self-monitoring Keeping track of how well one is understanding or performing by oneself

Self-recording Written documentation of incremental progress in meeting academic or behavioral goals

Self-talk A technique in which the teacher describes what he or she is doing or thinking

Semantic feature analysis A vocabulary-enhancement procedure that involves the placement of categories or critical features along one axis and the specific vocabulary along the other axis

Semantic map A prelearning activity for increasing students' comprehension

Semantics The content of language

Seriation The ability to rank objects according to the degree to which they possess a certain common characteristic

Severe disabilities Conditions that significantly affect typical life activities

SHARE A multi-step strategy for promoting positive communication: **S**it up straight; **H**ave a pleasant tone of voice; **A**ctivate your thinking; **R**elax; **E**ngage in eye communication

Sheltered English A type of ESL instruction in which the goal is to teach English language skills at the same time that students are learning content-area information

Sight word Words that are recognized immediately upon seeing them

Sight word association procedure (SWAP) A learning technique that helps students associate spoken words with their printed forms

Silent or nonverbal period A time during which children are absorbing information and language that they cannot demonstrate or do not yet feel comfortable demonstrating

Situational factors Factors related to the context or situation in which the second language learning occurs

Social action approach An approach that incorporates all the elements of the transformation approach but also includes cultural

critique and problem solving that require students to make decisions and take actions related to the concept, issue, or problem being studied

Social language Part of the conversational competencies we develop with a second language—the greetings and "small talk" between peers, which generally do not require much cognitive effort or social problem solving

Social learning Involves observing and modeling or imitating the behavior of others

Social problem solving Social skill instruction taught within the process of engaging in social interactions and involving a set of strategies students learn to monitor or manage their own social skills

Social skills The ability to initiate appropriate social interactions, respond to social initiations from others, and terminate social interactions appropriately

Social skills training (SST) Training that provides students with specific instruction in acquisition, performance, and fluency of social skills

Social Story An individualized short story designed to clarify a particular social context, the perspectives of others in that context, and the social skills to be performed

Social Story interventions Social skill instruction involving individualized short stories designed to clarify a particular social context, the perspectives of others in that context, and the social skills to be performed

Socialized aggression Routinely engaging in antisocial behavior

Speaking vocabulary Vocabulary that is used as part of children's oral language

Special education resource room A placement outside the general education classroom where students with disabilities receive specialized, individualized, and intensive instruction to meet their needs

Specific learning disabilities Represents a heterogeneous group of students who, despite adequate cognitive functioning and the ability to learn some skills and strategies quickly and easily, have great difficulty learning other skills and strategies

Speech and language pathologist A person trained to provide screening, assessment, and treatment for students who have difficulties with speech (including pronunciation) as well as with language (including stuttering, inadequate language development, and poor use of syntax)

Speech disorders Disorders that involve unintelligible or unpleasant communication

Spina bifida A birth defect that occurs when the spinal cord fails to close properly

Spiral curriculum Occurs when the same skills (e.g., mathematics skills) are woven into every year of school and students continually repeat knowledge acquisition in the same area

Standard English Language Learners (SELLs) Learners who approach learning through differences in language, not deficits

Standard treatment protocol model The same empirically validated treatments are used for all children with similar problems

Stereotypic behavior Behaviors that characterize a disorder or condition such as rocking, flapping fingers, twirling or spinning objects, and grinding teeth

Stimulant medications Medications that are frequently used in the treatment of attention deficit and hyperactivity disorders

Stimulus Something that incites activity or attention

STOP and DARE strategy A multi-step strategy for persuasive writing: **S**uspend judgment; **T**ake a side; **O**rganize ideas; **P**lan more as you write; **D**evelop your topic sentence; **A**dd supporting ideas; **R**eject possible arguments; **E**nd with a conclusion.

Story webs Visual displays developed to help students understand the structure of the stories they read

Strategies Step-by-step cognitive processes and plans for reading, studying, and problem solving

Strategy guides Graphic and questioning materials that provide support to students as they learn to use metacognitive strategies

Structural analysis Analysis involving the use of root words, prefixes, and suffixes to determine the pronunciation and meaning of a word, including multisyllable words and merged words such as compounds (*buttermilk, pancake*) and contractions (*don't, can't*)

Student-centered model An educational model in which students have ample opportunity to create personal meaning from what they are reading and writing

Stuttering The most common fluency disorder, involving an interruption of the forward flow of speech

Surveys A way to foster communication with parents

Syllabication Dividing words by common syllable types

Syntax The rules that govern the order of words in sentences

Systems of support A coordinated set of services and accommodations matched to the student's needs

T

TAG A strategy for students to provide each other with feedback about their writing

Talent pool approach Procedure used to avoid overlooking students with exceptional talents and abilities who might not be identified through IQ tests or teacher nominations alone

Task analysis A breakdown of each individual step or skill, with the necessary adaptations, that will be used as a guide for teaching the step or skill to the student

Team-assisted individualization Provision of individualized instruction within a cooperative learning model

Technologically dependent Requiring life support or specialized support systems such as ventilators

Test approach skills Skills that can help students get physically and mentally ready for exams; sending flyers home to parents about the importance of sleep and nutrition can help prepare students physically

Test preparedness skills Skills related to knowing both the general content and the format of an exam

Test-taking skills Skills that students use to complete an examination in a timely and effective way

Think alouds A way to model how to think and learn

Tiers The level of intensity of instruction provided to a student or group of students

Time out Time during which the student is removed from the opportunity to receive reinforcement

Title I funds A federally funded program that provides financial assistance for schools with high numbers or percentages of students from low-income families; funds must be used to provide services for students who have demonstrated academic difficulties or are at risk of academic difficulties

Token system A system in which students receive tokens in exchange for meeting classroom objectives and can exchange the tokens for rewards

Tonic–clonic seizures A type of seizure that is characterized by convulsions followed by loss of consciousness

Total blindness Refers to a very small minority of individuals who have visual impairments and who are unable to see anything, including objects or light sources

Tracked The practice of placing students with similar needs together for extended periods of the school day

Transdisciplinary teaming The teaming of a group of experts who work together and view the student as a whole instead of working independently in a single specialty area

Transformation approach An approach in which the basic core of the curriculum is changed, and goals focus on viewing events, concepts, and themes from multiple perspectives, based on diversity

Transition services Services that provide activities on behalf of the student with the disability that promote an outcome-oriented process of supports from school to postsecondary activities that include further schooling, vocational training, and integrated employment

Transitional bilingual education A program that helps students shift from the home language to the dominant language

Traumatic brain injury An injury to the brain, caused by an external physical force, that causes total or partial functional disability or psychosocial impairment, or both, which adversely affects a student's educational performance

TREE method A type of mnemonic used to plan an essay (write a **T**opic sentence; think of **R**easons to support the topic sentence; **E**xamine your reasons; think of an **E**nding or conclusion)

Tutoring A systematic plan for supplementing the student's educational program

Two-way bilingual programs A program in which half the students are native speakers of English and the other half speak another language, usually Spanish. Instruction is delivered in English half the time and in the other language the other half

U

Universal screening Screening that administers the same test to all students to determine who is likely to be at risk for academic difficulties

Universal strategies Basic principles of managing student behavior

V

VCe rule Vowel, consonant, silent e as in "time"

Verbal reprimands Short, targeted comments designed to address a specific misbehavior

Vibrant discussions Discussions in which student participation is high, students' thinking is stimulated, and students have opportunities to connect what they are learning to their personal knowledge and experience

Visual acuity The clarity with which an individual can see an object from a distance of 20 feet

Visual detail Ability to perceive details in the visual field; difficulties in this area may lead to academic problems such as misreading an aspect of an arithmetic problem

Visual field How well an individual can see using peripheral or side vision

Vocabulary An individual's working knowledge of words

Vocal nodules Nodules that develop because the vocal mechanism is used incorrectly or overused

Vocational Rehabilitation Act This act (P.L. 93–112) prevents any private organization that uses federal funds, or any local or state organization, from discriminating against persons with disabilities solely on the basis of those disabilities

Voice disorders Disorders that relate to the quality of the voice itself

W

Wait time Time provided to allow students to understand what has been said and to construct a response

Websites School websites that provide information about the calendar, major events, and homework tips

Within-child factors Factors that have traditionally been the focus of determining whether a student has special needs, such as cognitive functioning, academic functioning, or functioning on such processing measures as auditory and visual tasks

Word identification A strategy for recognizing words involved in reading

Word retrieval Finding words from memory

Word wall A large, permanent bulletin board to which words are added each week and grouped in alphabetical order; used for word recognition and spelling

Wraparound Processes that provide coordinated services to families and students with emotional or behavior disorders

Wraparound facilitator A case manager responsible for coordinating services

Writing rubrics Scoring guides that outline expected performance on a written product

Z

Zero reject An element of IDEA that states that no child with disabilities can be excluded from receiving a free and appropriate education

AACAP. (2004). *The depressed child.* Retrieved from http://aacap.org/publications/factsfam/depressed.htm

Abedi, J. (2002). *Assessment and accommodations of English language learners: Issues, concerns, and recommendations.* Retrieved from www.icsac.org/jsi/2002v3il/assessment

Abedi, J., & Dietel, R. (2004). *Challenges in the No Child Left Behind Act for English language learners.* Los Angeles: National Center for Research on Evaluation, Standards, and Student Testing.

Abikoff, H., Courtney, M. E., Szeibel, P. J., & Koplewicz, H. S. (1996). The effects of auditory stimulation on the arithmetic performance of children with ADHD and nondisabled children. *Journal of Learning Disabilities, 29*(3), 238–246.

Achenbach, T. M. (2000). *Achenbach system of empirically based assessment.* Burlington: University of Vermont.

Achenbach, T. M., & McConaughy, S. H. (2003). The Achenbach system of empirically based assessment. In C. R. Reynolds & R. W. Kamphaus (Eds.), *Handbook of psychological and educational assessment of children: Personality, behavior, and context* (2nd ed., pp. 406–432). New York: Guilford Press.

Adams, L., Gouvousis, A., VanLue, M., & Waldron, C. (2004). Social story intervention: Improving communication skills in a child with an autism spectrum disorder. *Focus on Autism and Other Developmental Disabilities, 19,* 87–94.

Adger, C. T., Wolfram, W., & Christian, D. (2007). *Dialects in schools and communities.* Mahwah, NJ: Erlbaum.

Adler, L. (2006). *Scattered minds: Hope and help for adults with attention deficit hyperactivity disorder.* New York: Putnam.

Adler, L., Barkley, R. A., & Newcorn, J. (2008). ADHD and comorbidity in adults. *Journal of Clinical Psychiatry, 69,* 1328–1335.

Afflerbach, P., Pearson, P. D., & Paris, S. G. (2008). Clarifying differences between reading skills and reading strategies. *The Reading Teacher, 61,* 364–373.

Ahlberg, J., & Ahlberg, A. (1979). *Each peach pear plum.* New York: Viking Press.

Al Otaiba, S., & Fuchs, D. (2006). Who are the young children for whom best practices in reading are ineffective? *Journal of Learning Disabilities, 39,* 414–431.

Albrecht, S. F. (2008). Time away: A skill-building alternative to discipline. *Preventing School Failure, 53,* 49–55.

Algozzine, B., Browder, D., Karvonen, M., Test, D. W., & Wood, W. M. (2001). Effects of interventions to promote self-determination for individuals with disabilities. *Review of Educational Research, 71,* 219–277.

Al-Hassan, S., & Gardner, R. (2002). Involving immigrant parents of students with disabilities in the educational process. *Teaching Exceptional Children, 34,* 52–58.

Allen, N., Harry, B., & McLaughlin, M. (1993). *The parent-professional partnership: African-American parents' participation in the special education process.* Final Report, Grant No. H023C901254. College Park, MD: Institute for the Study of Exceptional Children and Youth, Department of Special Education, University of Maryland College.

Alper, S., Schloss, P., & Schloss, C. (1994). *Families of students with disabilities.* Boston: Allyn & Bacon.

Alter, P. J., Wrick, A., Brown, E. T., & Lingo, A. (2008). Improving mathematics problem solving skills for students with challenging behavior. *Beyond Behavior, 17*(3), 2–7.

Alvermann, D. E. (1991). The discussion web: A graphic aid for learning across the curriculum. *The Reading Teacher, 45*(2), 92–99.

American Academy of Child & Adolescent Psychiatry. (2009). *FAQs on child and adolescent depression.* Retrieved from www.aacap.org/cs/child_and_adolescent_depression_resource_center/faqs

American Academy of Pediatrics. (2001, 2007). *Policy statement: American Academy of Pediatrics: Education of children with human immunodeficiency virus infection.* Retrieved from www.aappolicy.aappublications.org/cgi/content/full/pediatrics;105/6/1358

American Association of Intellectual and Developmental Disabilities. (2009a). *Diagnostic Adaptive Behavior Scale.* Retrieved from www.aamr.org/content_106.cfm?navID=23

American Association of Intellectual and Developmental Disabilities. (2009b). *FAQs on intellectual disability.* Retrieved from www.aamr.org/content_104.cfm?navID=22

American Association of Intellectual and Developmental Disabilities. (2009c). *What is the Supports Intensity Scale?* Retrieved from www.siswebsite.org/

American Association on Mental Retardation. (2002). *Mental retardation: Definition, classification, and systems of support* (10th ed.). Washington, DC: Author.

American Foundation for Suicide Prevention. (2009). *Warning signs of suicide.* Retrieved from www.afsp.org/index.cfm?page_id=0519EC1A-D73A-8D90-7D2E9E2456182D66

American Foundation for the Blind. (2007). *Estimates of severely visually impaired children.* Retrieved from www.afb.org/Section.asp?SectionID

American Foundation for the Blind. (2009). *Educating students with visual impairments for inclusion in society.* Retrieved from www.afb.org/Section.asp?SectionID

American Lung Association. (2009). *Asthma & children fact sheet.* Retrieved from www.lungusa.org/site/pp.asp?c=dvLUK9O0E&b=44352

American Optometric Asssociation. (2009). *School-aged vision: 6 to 18 years of age.* Retrieved from www.aoa.org/X9451.sml?prt

American Printing House for the Blind. (2007). *Distribution of eligible students.* Retrieved from www.aph.org/fedquotpgm/dist07.html

American Psychiatric Association. (2000). *Diagnostic and statistical manual of mental disorders: DSM-IV-TR* (4th ed., text rev.). Washington, DC: Author.

American Speech-Language-Hearing Association. (1993). Definitions: Communicative disorders and variations. *ASHA, 35* (Suppl. 10), 40–41.

American Speech-Language-Hearing Association. (2000). Retrieved from www.asha.org/default.htm

American Speech-Language-Hearing Association. (2005). Retrieved from www.asha.org/default.htm

American Speech-Language-Hearing Association. (2006). *2006 schools survey report: Caseload characteristics.* Rockville, MD: Author.

American Speech-Language-Hearing Association. (2008). *Incidence and prevalence of communication disorders and hearing loss in children.* Retrieved from www.asha.org/members/research/reports/children.html

American Speech-Language-Hearing Association. (2009). *Assistive technology.* Retrieved from www.asha.org/public/hearing/treatment/assist_tech.htm

Amrein, A. L., & Berliner, D. C. (2002, March 28). High-stakes testing, uncertainty, and student learning, *Education Policy Analysis Archives, 10*(18). Retrieved from www.epaa.asu.edu/epaa/v10n18/

Anderson, C. M., & Spaulding, S. A. (2007). Using positive behavior support to design effective classrooms. *PBS in the Classroom, 27*–31.

Andrade, H., & Valtcheva, A. (2009). Promoting learning and achievement through self-assessment. *Theory Into Practice, 48,* 12–19.

Anxiety Disorders Association of America. (2009). *Anxiety disorders in children and teens.* Retrieved from www.adaa.org/GettingHelp/FocusOn/Children&Adolescents.asp

Archer, A. L., Gleason, M. M., & Vachon, V. (2005). *REWARDS reading excellence: Word attack & rate development strategies.* Longmont, CO: Sopris West Educational Services.

Armbruster, B. (2009). Notetaking from lectures. In R. F. Flippo & D. C. Caverly (Eds.), *Handbook of college reading and study strategy research* (2nd ed., pp. 220–248). New York: Routledge.

Armbruster, B. B., & Anderson, T. H. (1988). On selecting "considerate" content area textbooks. *Remedial and Special Education, 9,* 47–52.

Armstrong, T. (2003). *Multiple intelligences of reading and writing: Making the words count.* Alexandria, VA: Association for Supervision and Curriculum Development.

Arndt, S. A., Konrad, M., & Test, D. W. (2006). Effects of the self-directed IEP on student participation in planning meetings. *Remedial and Special Education, 27,* 194–207.

Arter, J., & McTighe, J. (2000). *Scoring rubrics in the classroom: Using performance criteria for assessing and improving student performance.* Thousand Oaks, CA: Corwin Press.

Arthur-Kelly, M., Foreman, P., Bennett, D., & Pascoe, S. (2008). Interaction, inclusion and students with profound and multiple disabilities: Towards an agenda for research and practice. *Journal of Research in Special Education Needs, 8,* 161–166.

Asthma Allergy Foundation of America. (2009). *Asthma overview.* Retrieved from www.aafa.org/display.cfm?id=8

Atkinson, R. C. (1975). Mnemotechnics in second-language learning. *American Psychologist, 30,* 821–828.

Attwood, T. (2000). Strategies for improving the social integration of students with Asperger syndrome. *Autism, 4,* 85–100.

Atwell, N. (1984). Writing and reading literature from the inside out. *Language Arts, 61,* 240–252.

August, D., & Hakuta, K. (Eds.). (1997). *Improving schools for language-minority children: A research agenda.* Washington, DC: National Academies Press.

August, D., & Shanahan, T. (2006). *Developing literacy in second-language learners: Report of the National Literacy Panel on Language-Minority Children and Youth.* Mahwah, NJ: Erlbaum.

Austin, J., Lee, M., & Carr, J. (2004). The effects of guided notes on undergraduate student recording of lecture content. *Journal of Instructional Psychology, 31,* 314–320.

Austin, V. L. (2001). Teachers' beliefs about co-teaching. *Remedial and Special Education, 22,* 245–254.

Ayllon, T. (1999). *How to use token economies and point systems.* Austin, TX: PRO-ED.

Baker, C. (1993). *Foundations of bilingual education and bilingualism.* Clevedon, England: Multilingual Matters.

Baker, S., Gersten, R., & Graham, S. (2003). Teaching expressive writing to students with learning disabilities: Research-based applications and examples. *Journal of Learning Disabilities, 36,* 109–123.

Baker, S., Gersten, R., & Lee, D. (2002). A synthesis of empirical research on teaching mathematics to low-achieving students. *The Elementary School Journal, 103*(1), 51–73.

Bambara, L. M., Wilson, B. A., & McKenzie, M. (2007). Transition and quality of life. In S. L. Odom, R. H. Horner, M. E. Snell, & J. Blacher (Eds.), *Handbook of developmental disabilities* (pp. 271–389). New York: Guilford Press.

Bandura, A. (1971). *Psychological modeling.* Chicago: Aldine/Atherton.

Bandura, A. (1973). *Aggression: A social learning analysis.* Englewood Cliffs, NJ: Prentice-Hall.

Banks, J. A. (2008). *An introduction to multicultural education* (4th ed.). Boston: Pearson.

Barkley, R. A. (1998). *Attention-deficit hyperactivity disorder: A handbook for diagnosis and treatment* (2nd ed.). New York: Guilford Press.

Barkley, R. A. (2000). *Taking charge of ADHD: The complete, authoritative guide for parents* (rev. ed.). New York: Guilford Press.

Barkley, R. A. (2005). *Attention-deficit hyperactivity disorder: A handbook for diagnosis and treatment* (3rd ed.). New York: Guilford Press.

Barkley, R. A. (2008). *Attention-deficit hyperactivity disorder: A handbook for diagnosis and treatment* (4th ed.). New York: Guilford Press.

Barkley, R. A., & Murphy, K. R. (1998). *Attention-deficit hyperactivity disorder: A clinical workbook* (2nd ed.). New York: Guilford Press.

Barkley, R. A., & Murphy, K. R. (2006). *Attention-deficit hyperactivity disorder: A clinical workbook.* New York: Guilford Press.

Barkley, R. A., Murphy, K. R., & Fischer, M. (2008). *ADHD in adults: What the science says.* New York: Guilford Press.

Barnes, M. A., Wilkinson, M., Khemar, E., Boudescuie, A., Dennis, M., & Fletcher, J. M. (2006). Mathematics errors in spina-bifida. *Journal of Learning Disabilities, 39*(2), 174–187.

Barraga, N. C., & Erin, J. N. (2001). *Visual handicaps and learning* (3rd ed.). Austin, TX: PRO-ED.

Batsche, G., Elliott J., Graden, J. L., Grimes, J., Kovaleski. J. F., Prasse, D., Reschly, D., Tilly, W. D. (2005). *Response to intervention: Policy considerations and implementation.* Alexandria, VA: National Association of State Directors of Special Education.

Bean, T. W. (1985). Classroom questioning: Directions for applied research. In A. C. Graesser & J. Black (Eds.), *Psychology of questions* (pp. 335–358). Hillsdale, NJ: Erlbaum.

Bean, T. W., Readence, J. E., & Baldwin, R. S. (2008). *Content area literacy: An integrated approach* (9th ed.). Dubuque, IA: Kendall/Hunt.

Bear, D. R., Helman, L., Invernizzi, M., & Templeton, S. R. (2007). *Words their way with English learners: Word study for spelling, phonics, and vocabulary instruction.* Upper Saddle River, NJ: Merrill/Prentice Hall.

Bear, D. R., Invernizzi, M., Templeton, S., & Johnston, F. (2008). *Words their way: Word study for phonics, vocabulary, and spelling instruction* (4th ed.). Upper Saddle River, NJ: Merrill/Prentice Hall.

Beck, I. L. (2006). *Making sense of phonics.* New York: Guilford Press.

Beck, I. L., & McKeown, M. G. (2006). *Improving comprehension with questioning the author.* New York: Scholastic.

Beck, I. L., McKeown, M. G., & Kucan, L. (2002). *Bringing words to life.* New York: Guilford Press.

Belenky, M. F., Clinchy, B. M., Goldberger, N. R., & Tarule, J. M. (1986). *Women's ways of knowing: The development of self, voice, and mind.* New York: Basic Books.

Bello, M. (2007). Using cognates. In S. Vaughn, C. S. Bos, & J. S. Schumm (Eds.), *Teaching students who are exceptional, diverse, and at risk in the general education classroom* (4th ed., p. 286). Boston: Allyn & Bacon.

Bereiter, C., Hilton, P., Rubinstein, J., & Willoughby, S. (1998). *SRA math explorations and applications,* Level 5, teachers edition. Boston: McGraw Hill.

Bereiter, C., & Scardamalia, M. (1982). From conversation to composition. In R. Glaser (Ed.), *Advances in instructional psychology* (Vol. 2). Hillsdale, NJ: Erlbaum.

Berko Gleason, J. (2001). *The development of language* (5th ed.). Boston: Allyn & Bacon.

Berner, R. (1977). What parents and teachers should know about death education. *DOPHHH Journal, 3,* 17–21.

Berninger, V., Abbott, R., Rogan, L., Reed, E., Abbott, S., Brooks, A., Vaughan, K., & Graham, S. (1998). Teaching spelling to children with specific learning disabilities: The mind's ear and eye beat the computer or pencil. *Learning Disability Quarterly, 21*(2), 106–122.

Bernthal, J. E., & Bankson, N. W. (1998). *Articulation and phonological disorders* (4th ed.). Boston: Allyn & Bacon.

Bessell, A. G. (2001). Children surviving cancer: Psychosocial adjustment, quality of life, and school experience. *Exceptional Children, 67*(3), 345–359.

Bigge, J. L., Best, S. J., & Heller, K. W. (2001). *Teaching individuals with physical, health, and multiple disabilities* (4th ed.). Upper Saddle River, NJ: Prentice Hall.

Billings, A. C. (2005). Beyond the Ebonics debate: Attitudes about Black and Standard American English. *Journal of Black Studies, 36,* 68–81.

Blachman, B. A. (2000). Phonological awareness. In M. L. Kamil, P. B. Mosenthal, P. D. Pearson, & R. Barr (Eds.), *Handbook of reading research* (Vol. 3, pp. 251–284). Mahwah, NJ: Erlbaum.

Bley, N. S., & Thornton, C. A. (2001). *Teaching mathematics to students with learning disabilities* (4th ed.). Austin, TX: PRO-ED.

Bliss, C. (1965). *Semantography.* Sydney, Austrialia: Semantography Publications.

Block, C. C., & Israel, S. E. (2004). The ABCs of performing highly effective think alouds. *The Reading Teacher, 58,* 154–167.

Bloom, L., & Lahey, M. (1978). *Language development and language disorders.* New York: Wiley.

Bode, B. A. (1989). Dialogue journal writing. *The Reading Teacher, 42,* 568–571.

Bos, C. S., & Vaughn, S. (2002). *Strategies for teaching students with learning and behavior problems* (7th ed.). Boston: Allyn & Bacon.

Bos, C. S., & Vaughn, S. (2006). *Strategies for teaching students with learning and behaviour problems* (6th ed.). Boston: Allyn & Bacon.

Bouchard, D., & Tetreault, S. (2000). The motor development of sighted children and children with moderate low vision aged 8–13. *Journal of Visual Impairment and Blindness, 94*(9), 564–573.

Boyle, E. A., Washburn, S. G., Rosenberg, M. S., Connelly, V. J., Brinckerhoff, L. C., & Banerjee, M. (2002). Reading's SLICK with new audio texts and strategies. *Teaching Exceptional Children, 35,* 50–55.

Boyle, J. R. (2007). The process of note taking: Implications for students with mild disabilities. *The Clearing House, 80,* 227–230.

Boyle, J. R. (2008). Reading strategies for students with mild disabilities. *Intervention in School and Clinic, 44,* 3–9.

Boyle, J. R., & Weishaar, M. (2001). The effects of notetaking on the recall and comprehension of lecture information for high school students with learning disabilities. *Learning Disabilities Research and Practice, 16,* 133–141.

Bradley, D. H. (2001). 20 ways to help students who struggle with writing become better writers. *Intervention in School and Clinic, 37,* 118–121.

Bradley, R., Danielson, L., & Doolittle, J. (2005). Response to intervention. *Journal of Learning Disabilities, 38,* 485–486.

Bradley, R., Danielson, L., & Hallahan, D. P. (2002). *Identification of learning disabilities: Research to practice.* Mahwah, NJ: Erlbaum.

Bremer, C. D., Kachgal, M., & Schoeller, K. (2003). Self-determination: Supporting successful transition. *Research to Practice Brief, 2,* 1–6.

Brent, D., Melhem, N., Donohoe, B. & Walker, M. (2009). The incidence and course of depression in bereaved youth 21 months after the loss of a parent to suicide, accident, or sudden natural death. *American Journal of Psychiatry, 166,* 786–794.

Brett, A., Rothlein, L., & Hurley, M. (1996). Vocabulary acquisition from listening to stories and explanations of target words. *Elementary School Journal, 96*(4), 415–422.

Brewer, D. M., Fowler, C. H., & Test, D. W. (2005). A content and methodological review of self-advocacy intervention studies. *Exceptional Children, 72,* 101–125.

Brewin, B. J., Renwick, R., & Schormans, A. F. (2008). Parental perspectives of the quality of life in school environments for children with Asperger syndrome. *Focus on Autism and Other Developmental Disabilities, 23,* 242–252.

Brooke, V., & McDonough, J. T. (2008). The facts ma'am, just the facts. *Teaching Exceptional Children, 41*(1), 58–65.

Brophy, J. E. (2003). *Teaching problem students.* New York: Guilford Press.

Browder, D. M., Trela, K., Gibbs, S. L., Wakeman, S., & Harris, A. A. (2007). Academic skills: Reading and mathematics. In S. L. Odom, R. H. Horner, M. E. Snell, & J. Blacher (Eds.), *Handbook of developmental disabilities* (pp. 292–309). New York: Guilford Press.

Brown, J. E., & Doolittle, J. (2008). A cultural, linguistic, and ecological framework for response to intervention with English language learners. *Teaching Exceptional Children, 40,* 66–72.

Bruns, E. J., Walrath, C. M., & Sheehan, A. K. (2007). Who administers wraparound? An examination of the training, beliefs, and implementation supports for wraparound providers. *Journal of Emotional and Behavioral Disorders, 15,* 156–168.

Bryant, D., & Bryant, B. (2003). *Assistive technology for people with disabilities.* Boston: Allyn & Bacon.

Bryant, D. P., Bryant, B., & Hammill, D. (2000). Characteristic behaviors of students with LD who have teacher-identified math weaknesses. *Journal of Learning Disabilities, 33,* 168–177, 199.

Bryant, D. P., Goodwin, M., Bryant, B. R., & Higgins, K. (2003). Vocabulary instruction for students with learning disabilities: A review of the research. *Learning Disabilities Quarterly, 26,* 117–128.

Bryant, D. P., Hartman, P., & Kim, S. A. (2003). Using explicit and systematic instruction to teach division skills to students with learning disabilities. *Exceptionality, 11*(3), 151–164.

Bryant, N. D., Drabin, I. R., & Gettinger, M. (1981). Effects of varying unit size on spelling achievement in learning disabled children. *Journal of Learning Disabilities, 14*(4), 200–203.

Buehl, D. (2009). *Classroom strategies for interactive learning* (3rd ed.). Newark, DE: International Reading Association.

Bulgren, J. A. (2006). Integrated content enhancement routines: Responding to the needs of adolescents with disabilities in rigorous inclusive secondary content classes. *Teaching Exceptional Children, 38*(6), 54–58.

Bulgren, J., Deshler, D. D., & Lenz, B. K. (2007). Engaging adolescents with LD in higher order thinking about history concepts using integrated content enhancement routines. *Journal of Learning Disabilities, 40*(2), 121–133.

Burks, M. (2004). Effects of classwide peer tutoring on the number of words spelled correctly by students with LD. *Intervention in School and Clinic, 39,* 301–304.

Burniske, R. W. (2008). *Literacy in the digital age.* Thousand Oaks, CA: Corwin Press.

Burns, M. K. (2008). Response to intervention at the secondary level. *Principal Leadership, 8,* 12–15.

Burns, M. K., Griffiths, A., Parson, L. B., Tilly, W. D., & VanDerHayden, A. (2007). *Response to intervention: Research for practice.* Alexandria, VA: National Association of State Directors of Special Education.

Burstein, N., Sears, S., Wilcoken, A., Cabello, B., & Spagna, M. (2004). Moving toward inclusive practices. *Remedial and Special Education, 25*(2), 104–116.

Campbell, A., & Anderson, C. M. (2008). Enhancing effects of check-in/check-out with function-based support. *Behavior Disorders, 33,* 233–245.

Campbell, J. (2007). Understanding the emotional needs of children who are blind. *Journal of Visual Impairment and Blindness, 101,* 351–355.

Campbell-Whatley, G. D. (2008). Teaching students about their disabilities: Increasing self-determination skills and self-concept. *International Journal of Special Education, 23,* 137–144.

Cancro, R. (2008). Depression. *The Exceptional Parent, 38,* 67–68.

Candlelighters Childhood Cancer Foundation. (1993). Advice to educators (adapted from a survey by A Wish with Wings). In *Educating the child with cancer* (pp. 21–22). Bethesda, MD: Author.

Cangelosi, J. S. (2004). *Classroom management strategies: Gaining and maintaining students' cooperation.* Hoboken, NJ: Wiley.

Canter, A. (2006). Problem solving and RTI: New roles for school psychologists. *NASP Communiqué, 34*(5). Retrieved from www.nasponline.org/publications/cq/cq345rti.aspx

Canter, A., Klotz, M. B., & Cowan, K. (2008). Response to intervention: The future for secondary students. *Principal Leadership, 8,* 12–15.

Cantrell, S. C., Burns, L. D., & Callaway, P. (2009). Middle- and high-school content area teachers' perceptions about literacy teaching and learning. *Literacy Research and Instruction, 48,* 76–94.

Carlberg, C., & Kavale, K. (1980). The efficacy of special versus regular class placement for exceptional children: A meta-analysis. *The Journal of Special Education, 14,* 295–309.

Carlisle, J., & Rice, M. (2002). *Improving reading comprehension: Research-based principles and practices.* Baltimore, MD: York Press.

Carlson, R. (1984). *Picsyms categorical dictionary.* Lawrence, KS: Baggeboda Press.

Carr, S. C., & Thompson, B. (1996). The effects of prior knowledge and schema activation strategies on the inferential reading comprehension of children with and without learning disabilities. *Learning Disability Quarterly, 19*(1), 48–61.

Carreker, S. (1999). Teaching spelling. In J. R. Birsh (Ed.), *Multisensory teaching of basic language skills* (pp. 217–256). Baltimore, MD: Paul H. Brookes.

Carroll, J. (1964). *Language and thought.* Englewood Cliffs, NJ: Prentice-Hall.

Carter, E. W., Cushing, L. S., Clark, N. M., & Kennedy, C. H. (2005). Effects of peer support interventions on students' access to the general curriculum and social interactions. *Research and Practice for Persons With Severe Disabilities, 30,* 15–25.

Carter, E. W., Hughes, C., & Wehby, J. (2005). Preparing adolescents with high-incidence disabilities for high-stakes testing with strategy instruction. *Prevention School Failure, 49,* 55–62.

Carter, E. W., Lane, K. L., Pierson, M. R., & Stang, K. K. (2008). Promoting self-determination for transition-age youth: Views of high school general and special educators. *Exceptional Children, 75,* 55–70.

Carter, T. P., & Chatfield, M. L. (1986). Effective bilingual schools: Implications for policy and practice. *American Journal of Education, 5*(1), 200–234.

Cartledge, G., Gardner, R., & Ford, D. Y. (2009). *Diverse learners with exceptionalities: Culturally responsive teaching in the inclusive classroom.* Upper Saddle River, NJ: Merrill.

Cash, R. E., & Cowan, K. C. (2006). Mood disorders: What parents and teachers should know. *Communique, 35,* 1–4.

Caspi, A., Henry, B., McGee, R. O., Moffitt, T. E., & Silva, P. A. (1995). Temperamental origins of child and adolescent behavior problems: From age 3 to age 15. *Child Development, 66,* 55–68.

Cassini, K. K., & Rogers, J. L. (1990). *Death in the classroom.* Cincinnati, OH: Griefwork.

Castellano, C. (2003). *Tips for classroom teachers.* Retrieved from www.blindchildren.org/textonly/to_edu_dev/3_5_4.html

Castellano, J. A. (2003). *Special populations in gifted education: Working with diverse gifted learners.* Boston: Allyn & Bacon.

Catts, H., Fey, M., Zhang, X., & Tomblin, B. (2001). Estimating the risk of future reading difficulties in kindergarten children: A research-based model and its clinical implementation. *Language, Speech, and Hearing Services in Schools, 32*(1), 38–50.

Causton-Theoharis, J., & Malmgren, K. (2005). Building bridges: Strategies to help paraprofessionals promote peer interaction. *Teaching Exceptional Children, 37,* 18–24.

Cawley, J. F., Foley, T. F., & Doan, T. (2003). Giving students a voice in selecting arithmetical context. *Teaching Exceptional Children, 36,* 8–17.

Centers for Disease Control and Prevention. (2007). *Mother-to-child (perinatal) HIV transmission and prevention.* Retrieved from www.ced.gov/hiv

Centers for Disease Control and Prevention. (2008). *HIV/AIDS among youth.* Retrieved from www.ced.gov/hiv

Centers for Disease Control and Prevention. (2009). *Autism spectrum disorders, 2009*. Retrieved from www.cdc.gov/ncbddd/autism/index.html

Centers for Disease Control and Prevention. (2009). *Developmental disabilities*. Retrieved from www.cdc.gov/ncbddd/dd/dd1.html

Centers for Disease Control and Prevention. (2009a). *Basic information*. Retrieved from www.cdc.gov/hiv/topics/basic/print/index.htm

Centers for Disease Control and Prevention. (2009b). *Vision impairment*. Retrieved from www.ced.gov/ncbddd/dd/vision3.htm

Certo, J. L., Cauley, K. M., Moxley, K. D., & Chafin, C. (2008). An argument for authenticity: Adolescents' perspectives on standards-based reform. *The High School Journal, 91*, 26–39.

CHADD. (2005). Retrieved from www.chadd.org

Chamberlain, S. P. (2005). Recognizing and responding to cultural differences in the education of culturally and linguistically diverse learners. *Intervention in School and Clinic, 40*, 195–211.

Chamot, A. U. (1998). Effective instruction for high school En-glish language learners. In R. M. Gersten & R. T. Jimenez (Eds.), *Promoting learning for culturally and linguistically diverse students* (pp. 186–209). Belmont, CA: Wadsworth.

Chamot, A., & O'Malley, J. M. (1994). *The CALLA handbook: Implementing the cognitive academic language learning approach*. Reading, MA: Addison-Wesley.

Chapman, C., & King, R. (2004). *Differentiated assessment strategies: One tool doesn't fit all*. Thousand Oaks, CA: Sage.

Chappell, G. (1985). Description and assessment of language disabilities of junior high school students. In C. Simon (Ed.), *Communication skills and classroom success: Assessment of language-learning disabled students*. San Diego, CA: College-Hill.

Chard, D. J., & Dickson, S. V. (1999). Phonological awareness: Instructional and assessment guidelines. *Intervention in Clinic and School, 34*(5), 261–270.

Chard, D. J., Vaughn, S., & Tyler, B. (2002). A synthesis of research on effective interventions for building reading fluency with elementary students with learning disabilities. *Journal of Learning Disabilities, 35*(5), 386–406.

Charles, C., & Senter, G. (2005). *Building classroom discipline* (8th ed.). Boston: Allyn & Bacon.

Charman, T., Drew, A., Baird, C., & Baird, G. (2003). Measuring early language development in pre-school children with autism spectrum disorder using the MacArthur Communicative Development Inventory (Infant Form). *Journal of Child Language, 30*, 213–236.

Checkley, K. (1997). The first seven . . . and the eighth: A conversation with Howard Gardner. *Educational Leadership, 55*, 8–13.

Chen, D., Alsop, L., & Minor, L. (2000). Lessons from Project PLAI in California and Utah: Implications for early intervention service to infants who are deaf-blind and their families. *Deaf-Blind Perspectives, 7*, 1–9.

Chiappone, L. L. (2006). The wonder of words: Learning and expanding vocabulary. In J. S. Schumm (Ed.), *Reading assessment and instruction for all learners* (pp. 297–332). New York: Guilford Press.

Children's Defense Fund. (2008). *State of America's children 2008*. Washington, DC: Author.

Children's Defense Fund. (2009). *About child poverty*. Retrieved from www.childrensdefensefind.org/help-americas-children/ending-child-poverty/about.html

Christ, T. J., Burns, M. K., & Ysseldyke, J. E. (2005). Conceptual confusion within response-to-intervention vernacular: Clarifying meaningful differences. NASP *Communiqué, 34*(3). Retrieved from www.nasponline.org/publications/cq/cq343rti.aspx

Christenson, S. L., Ysseldyke, J. E., & Thurlow, M. L. (1989). Critical instruction factors for students with mild handicaps: An integrative review. *Remedial and Special Education, 10*(5), 21–31.

Christodoulou, J. A. (2009). Applying multiple intelligences. *School Administrator, 66*, 22–26.

Chung, J. P-L. (1992). *The out-of-class language and social experience of a clique of Chinese immigrant students: An ethnography of a process of social identity information* (Unpublished doctoral dissertation). State University of New York, Buffalo.

Circle of Inclusion Project. (2002). *The MAPS process: Seven questions*. Retrieved from www.circleofinclusion.org/english/guidelines/modulesix/a.html

Clarizio, H. F., & McCoy, G. F. (1983). *Behavior disorders in children*. New York: Crowell.

Clarke, B., & Shinn, M. R. (2004). A preliminary investigation into the identification and development of early mathematics curriculum-based measurement. *School Psychology Review, 33*, 234–248.

Coelho, E. (1994). Social integration of immigrant and refugee children. In F. Genesee (Ed.), *Educating second language children: The whole child, the whole curriculum, the whole community* (pp. 301–328). Cambridge, England: Cambridge University Press.

Cohen, E. G., & Lotan, R. (2004). Equity in heterogeneous classrooms. In J. A. Banks & C. A. M. Banks (Eds.), *Handbook of research on multicultural education* (2nd ed., pp. 736–750). San Francisco: Jossey-Bass.

Cohen, J. S., & Smerdon, B. A. (2009). Tightening the dropout tourniquet: Easing the transition from middle to high school. *Preventing School Failure, 53*, 177–184.

Coltrane, B. (2002). *English language learners and high-stakes tests: An overview of the issues*. Retrieved from www.cal.org/resources/digest/0207coltrane.html

Conderman, G., & Koroghlanian, C. (2002). Writing test questions like a pro. *Intervention in School and Clinic, 38*, 83–87.

Conley, M. W. (2005). *Connecting standards and assessment through literacy*. Boston: Allyn & Bacon.

Conner, C. K. (2008). *Attention deficit hyperactivity disorder in children and adolescents: The latest assessment and treatment strategies*. Kansas City, MO: Compact Clinicals.

Conner, D. J., & Bejoian, L. M. (2006). Pigs, pirates, and pills: Using film to teach the social context of disability. *Teaching Exceptional Children, 39*, 52–60.

Connolly, A. J. (1998). *Key math-revised: A diagnostic inventory of essential mathematics*. Circle Pines, MN: American Guidance Service.

Conroy, M. A., Sutherland, K. S., Snyder, A., Al-Hendawi, M., & Vo, A. (2009). Creating a Positive Classroom Atmosphere: Teachers' Use of Effective Praise and Feedback. *Beyond Behavior*, 18–26.

Cook, C. R., Gresham, F. M., Kern, K., Barreras, R. B., & Crews, S. D. (2008). Social skills training for secondary students with emotional and/or behavioral disorders. *Journal of Emotional and Behavioral Disorders, 16*, 131–144.

Cooper, H. (2001). *The battleground over homework: Common ground for administrators, teachers, and parents* (2nd ed.). Thousand Oaks, CA: Corwin Press.

Cooper, H., & Nye, B. (1994). Homework for students with learning disabilities: The implications of research for policy and practice. *Journal of Learning Disabilities, 27*(8), 470–479.

Cooper, J. D., & Kiger, N. D. (2009). *Literacy: Helping students construct meaning* (7th ed.). Boston: Houghton Mifflin.

Cooper, J. O., Heron, T. E., & Heward, W. L. (2007). *Applied behavioral analysis* (2nd ed.). Upper Saddle River, NJ: Merrill/Prentice Hall.

Cooper, P., & Bilton, K. M. (2002). *Attention deficit/hyperactivity disorder: A practical guide for teachers* (2nd ed.). Great Britain: David Fulton Publishers.

Copeland, S. R., & Keefe, E. B. (2007). *Effective literacy instruction for students with moderate or severe disabilities*. Baltimore, MD: Paul H. Brookes.

Corn, A. L., & Koenig, A. J. (Eds.). (1996a). *Foundations of low vision: Clinical and functional perspectives*. New York: American Foundation for the Blind.

Corn, A. L., & Koenig, A. J. (1996b). Perspectives on low vision. In A. L. Corn & A. J. Koenig (Eds.), *Foundations of low vision: Clinical and functional perspectives* (pp. 3–25). New York: American Foundation for the Blind.

Corn, A. L., & Koenig, A. J. (2002). Literacy instruction for students with low vision: A framework for delivery of instruction. *Journal of Vision Impairment and Blindness, 96*, 305–321.

Corn, A. L., & Wall, R. S. (2002). Access to multimedia presentations for students with visual impairments. *Journal of Visual Impairment and Blindness, 96*, 197–211.

Corn, A. L., Wall, R., & Bell, J. (2000). Impact of optical devices on reading rates and expectations for visual functioning of school aged children and youth with low vision. *Visual Impairment Research, 2*, 33–41.

Corn, A. L., Wall, R. S., Jose, R. T., Bell, J. K., Wilcox, K., & Perez, A. (2002). An initial study of reading and comprehension rates for students who received optical devices. *Journal of Visual Impairment and Blindness, 96*, 322–334.

Cortiella, C. (2006). *A parent's guide to response to intervention*. National Center for Learning Disabilities. Retrieved from www.ncld.org/images/stories/downloads/parent_center/rti_final.pdf

Cotton, K. (2001). *Teaching composition: Research on effective practices*. Portland, OR: Northwest Regional Educational Laboratory.

Council for Exceptional Children. (n.d.). *Response-to-intervention: The promise and the peril.* Retrieved from www.cec.sped.org/AM/Template.cfm?Section=Home&CONTENTID=8427&TEMPLATE=/CM/ContentDisplay.cfm

Council for Exceptional Children. (2003). *What every special educator must know. Ethics standards, and guidelines for special educators* (5th ed.). Arlington, VA: Author.

Cox, P., & Dykes, M. (2001). Effective classroom adaptations for students with visual impairments. *Teaching Exceptional Children, 33,* 68–74.

Crews, S. D., Bender, H., Cook, C. R., Gresham, F. M., Kern, L., & Vanderwood, M. (2007). Risk and protective factors of emotional and/or behavioral disorders in children and adolescents: A mega-analytic synthesis. *Behavior Disorders, 32,* 64–77.

Cullinan, D. (2004). Classification and definition of emotional and behavioral disorders. In R. B. Rutherford, M. M. Quinn, & S. R. Mathur (Eds.), *Handbook of research in emotional and behavioral disorders* (pp. 32–53). New York: Guilford Press.

Cummins, J. (1981). *Bilingualism and minority language children.* Toronto, Ontario: Institute for Studies in Education.

Cummins, J. (1984). *Bilingualism and special education: Issues in assessment and pedagogy.* Clevedon, England: Multilingual Matters.

Cummins, J. (1989). A theoretical framework for bilingual special education. *Exceptional Children, 56,* 111–119.

Cummins, J. (1991). Interdependence of first- and second-language proficiency in bilingual children. In E. Bialystok (Ed.), *Language processing in bilingual children.* Cambridge, England: Cambridge University Press.

Cummins, J. (1992). The empowerment of Indian students. In J. Reyhner (Ed.), *Teaching American Indian students* (pp. 1–12). Norman, OK: University of Oklahoma Press.

Cunningham, P. M. (2000a). *Phonics they use: Words for reading and writing* (3rd ed.). New York: Longman.

Cunningham, P. M. (2000b). *Systematic sequential phonics they use: For beginning readers of any age.* Greensboro, NC: Carson-Dellosa.

D'Andrea, F. M., & Farrenkopf, C. (2000). *Looking to learn: Promoting literacy for students with low vision.* New York: AFB Press.

Dabkowski, D. M. (2004). Encouraging active parent participation in IEP meetings. *Teaching Exceptional Children, 36*(3), 34–39.

Dale, E., & Chall, J. (1948). A formula for predicting readability. *Educational Research Bulletin, 27,* 37–54.

Daly, P. M., & Ranalli, P. (2003). Using Countoons to teach self-monitoring skills. *Teaching Exceptional Children, 35*(5), 30–35.

Darling-Hammond, L. (2007). Standards and accountability movement needs to push, not punish. *Journal of Staff Development, 28,* 47–50.

Davey, B. (1983). Think-aloud: Modeling the cognitive processes of reading comprehension. *Journal of Reading, 27,* 44–47.

Day, M. H., Horner, R. H., & O'Neill, R. E. (1994). Multiple functions or problem behaviors: Assessment and intervention. *Journal of Applied Behavior Analysis, 27,* 279–289.

De La Paz, S. (2001). Stop and dare: A persuasive writing strategy. *Intervention in School and Clinic, 36,* 234–243.

De La Paz, S., & Graham, S. (1997). Strategy instruction in planning: Effects on the writing performance and behavior of students with learning difficulties. *Exceptional Children, 63*(2), 167–183.

De La Paz, S., Swanson, P. N., & Graham, S. (1998). The contribution of executive control to the revising by students with writing and learning difficulties. *Journal of Educational Psychology, 90*(3), 448–460.

Dean Qualls, C., O'Brien, R. M., Blood, G. W., & Scheffner Hammer, C. (2003). Contextual variation, familiarity, academic literacy, and rural adolescents' idiom knowledge. *Language, Speech, and Hearing Services in Schools, 34,* 69–79.

Dell, A. G., Newton, D., & Petroff, J. (2008). *Assistive technology in the classroom: Enhancing the school experiences of students with disabilities.* Upper Saddle River, NJ: Merrill.

Demchak, M. A. (2005). Teaching students with severe disabilities in inclusive settings. In M. L. Wehmeyer & M. Agran (Eds.), *Mental retardation and intellectual disabilities: Teaching students using innovative and research-based strategies* (pp. 57–77). Washington, DC: American Association on Mental Retardation.

Demmert, W. G. (2005). The influences of culture on learning and assessment among native American students. *Learning Disabilities Research & Practice, 20,* 16–23.

Deno, S. L. (1985). Curriculum-based measurement: The emerging alternative. *Exceptional Children, 52,* 219–232.

Denton, C., Anthony, J. L., Parker, J., & Hasbrouck, J. (2004). Effects of two tutoring programs on the English reading development of Spanish-English bilingual students. *Elementary School Journal, 104,* 289–305.

DePaepe, P., Garrison-Kane, L., & Doelling, J. (2002). Supporting students with health needs in schools: An overview of selected health conditions. *Focus on Exceptional Children, 35,* 1–24.

Deshler, D. D., & Schumaker, J. B. (2006). *Teaching adolescents with disabilities: Accessing the general education curriculum.* Thousand Oaks, CA: Corwin Press.

Deshler, D., Palinscar, A. S., Biancarosa, G., & Nair, M. (2007). *Informed choices for struggling adolescent readers: A research-based guide to instructional programs and processes.* Newark, DE: International Reading Association.

Dettmer, P., Thurston, L. P., & Dyck, N. J. (2005). *Consultation, collaboration, and teamwork for students with special needs* (5th ed.). Boston: Pearson Education.

Devine, T. G., & Kania, J. S. (2003). Studying: Skills, strategies, and systems. In J. Flood, D. Lapp, & J. R. Squire (Eds.), *Handbook on research on teaching the English language arts* (2nd ed., pp. 942–954). Mahwah, NJ: Erlbaum.

Di Vesta, F. J., & Smith, D. A. (1979). The pausing principle: Increasing the efficiency of memory for ongoing events. *Contemporary Educational Psychology, 4,* 288–296.

Diaz, R. (1983). Thought and two languages: The impact of bilingualism on cognitive development. *Review of Research in Education, 10,* 23–34.

Díaz-Rico, L. (2004). *Teaching English learners: Strategies and methods.* Boston: Allyn & Bacon.

Díaz-Rico, L. (2005). *Teaching English learners: Methods and strategies,* MyLabSchool edition. Boston: Allyn & Bacon.

Díaz-Rico, L., & Weed, K. Z. (2002). *The crosscultural, language, and academic development handbook: A complete K–12 reference guide* (2nd ed.). Boston: Allyn & Bacon.

Dieker, L. A. (2001). What are the characteristics of "effective" middle and high school co-taught teams for students with disabilities? *Preventing School Failure, 46,* 14–23.

Dillon, J. (1979). Alternatives to questioning. *High School Journal, 62,* 217–222.

Dion, E., Fuchs, D., & Fuchs, L. S. (2007). Peer-mediated programs to strengthen classroom instruction: Cooperative learning, reciprocal teaching, classwide peer tutoring, and peer-assisted learning strategies. In L. Flonan (Ed.), *Handbook of special education* (pp. 450–459), London: Sage.

DiVesta, E. J., & Gray, G. S. (1972). Listening and notetaking. *Journal of Educational Psychology, 64,* 321–325.

Dixon, D. R. (2007). Adaptive behavior scales. In J. L. Matson (Eds.), *International review of research in mental retardation: Vol. 34. Handbook of persons with disabilities* (pp. 99–140). San Diego, CA: Elsevier.

Donovan, M. S., & Cross, C. T. (2002). *Minority students in special and gifted education.* Washington, DC: National Academies Press.

Downing, J. (2002). *Including students with severe and multiple disabilities in typical classrooms: Practical strategies for teachers* (2nd ed.). Baltimore, MD: Paul H. Brookes.

Downing, J. A. (2007). *Students with emotional and behavioral problems: Assessment, management, and intervention strategies.* Upper Saddle River, NJ: Merrill.

Downing, J. E. (2005). *Teaching literacy to students with significant disabilities: Strategies for the K–12 inclusive classroom.* Thousand Oaks, CA: Corwin Press.

Downing, J. E., & Peckham-Hardin, K. D. (2007). Inclusive education: What makes it a good education for students with moderate to severe disabilities? *Research and Practice for Persons With Severe Disabilities, 32,* 16–30.

Downing, J., & Eichinger, J. (2003). Creating learning opportunities for students with disabilities in inclusive classrooms. *Teaching Exceptional Children, 36,* 26–31.

Dreikurs, R., & Cassel, P. (1972). *Discipline without tears.* New York: Hawthorn.

Dreikurs, R., Cassel, P., & Ferguson, E. D. (2004). *Discipline without tears: How to reduce conflict and establish cooperation in the classroom.* Hoboken, NJ: Wiley.

Dunlap, G., & Carr, E. G. (2007). Positive behavior support and developmental disabilities: A summary and analysis of research. In S. L. Odom, R. H. Horner, M. E. Snell, & J. Blacher (Eds.), *Handbook of developmental disabilities* (pp. 469–482). New York: Guilford Press.

DuPaul, G. J., & Stoner, G. (2003). *AD/HD in the schools: Assessment and intervention strategies* (2nd ed.). New York: Guilford Press.

Durando, J. (2008). A survey on literacy instruction for students with multiple disabilities. *Journal of Visual Impairment and Blindness, 102,* 40–45.

Durkin, D. D. (1978–1979). What classroom observations reveal about reading comprehension instruction. *Reading Research Quarterly, 14,* 481–533.

Eber, L., Breen, K., Rose, J., Unizycki, R. M., & London, T. H. (2009). Wraparound as a tertiary level intervention for students with emotional/behavioral needs. *Teaching Exceptional Children, 40,* 16–22.

Eber, L., & Keenan, S. (2004). Collaboration with other agencies: Wraparound and systems of care for children and youths with emotional and behavioral disorders. In R. B. Rutherford, M. M. Quinn, & S. R. Mathur (Eds.), *Handbook of research in emotional and behavioral disorders* (pp. 502–516). New York: Guilford Press.

Educational Testing Service. (2008). Addressing achievement gaps: The language acquisition and education achievement of English-language learners. *Policy Notes, 16,* 1.

Edwards, P. A. (2004). *Children's literacy development: Making it happen through school, family, and community involvement.* Boston: Allyn & Bacon.

Egley, A., & O'Donnell, C. E. (2009, April). Highlights of the 2007 national youth gang survey. *OJJDP Fact Sheet.*

Ehri, L. C. (2003). *Systematic phonics instruction: Findings of the National Reading Panel.* Paper presented at the invitational seminar organized by the Standards and Effectiveness Unit, Department for Education and Skills, British Government, London, England.

Ehri, L. (2004). Teaching phonemic awareness and phonics: An explanation of the National Reading Panel Meta-analyses. In P. McCardle & V. Chhabra (Eds.), *The voice of evidence in reading research* (pp. 153–186). Baltimore, MD: Paul H. Brookes.

Elbaum, B. (2007). Effects of an oral testing accommodation on the mathematics performance of secondary students with and without learning disabilities. *Journal of Special Education, 40*(4), 218–229.

Elbaum, B., & Vaughn, S. (2001). School-based interventions to enhance the self-concept of students with learning disabilities: A meta-analysis. *Elementary School Journal, 101*(3), 303–329.

Elbaum, B., Vaughn, S., Hughes, M., & Moody, S. W. (2000). How effective are one-to-one tutoring programs in reading for elementary students at risk for reading failure? A meta-analysis of the intervention research. *Journal of Educational Psychology, 92,* 605–619.

Elbaum, B., Vaughn, S., Hughes, M., Moody, S. W., & Schumm, J. S. (2000). How reading outcomes of students with disabilities are related to instructional grouping formats: A meta-analytic review. In R. Gersten, E. Schiller, & S. Vaughn (Eds.), *Contemporary special education research* (pp. 105–135). Mahwah, NJ: Erlbaum.

Elhoweris, H., Mutua, K., Alsheikh, N., & Holloway, P. (2005). Effect of ethnicity on teachers' referral and recommendation decisions in gifted and talented programs. *Remedial and Special Education, 26,* 25–31.

Elkonin, D. B. (1973). U.S.S.R. In J. Downing (Ed.), *Comparative reading* (pp. 551–579). New York: Macmillan.

Ellis, R. (1985). *Understanding second language acquisition.* Oxford, England: Oxford University Press.

Ellis, R. (1994). *The study of second language acquisition.* Oxford, England: Oxford University Press.

Emerson, R. S. W., & Corn, A. L. (2006). Orientation and mobility content for children and youths: A Delphi approach pilot study. *Journal of Visual Impairment and Blindness, 100,* 331–342.

Emmer, E., Evertson, C., Sanford, J. P., Clements, B. S., & Worsham, M. E. (1989). *Classroom management for secondary teachers* (2nd ed.). Englewood Cliffs, NJ: Prentice-Hall.

Emmer, E., Everston, C., & Worsham, M. E. (2002). *Classroom management for elementary teachers* (6th ed.). Boston: Allyn & Bacon.

Emmer, E., & Stough, L. (2001). Classroom management: A critical part of educational psychology, with implications for teacher education. *Educational Psychologist, 36,* 103–112.

Engelmann, S., & Carnine, D. (1992). *Early corrective mathematics.* Columbus, OH: McGraw Hill.

Engelmann, S., Carnine, D., & Steely, D. (2005). *Corrective mathematics.* Columbus, OH: McGraw Hill.

Engelmann, S., Meyer, L., Carnine, L., Becker, W., Eisele, J., & Johnson, G. (1999). *Corrective reading program.* Columbus, OH: SRA/McGraw-Hill.

Englert, C. S., Raphael, R. E., & Mariage, T. V. (1994). Developing a school-based discourse for literacy learning: A principled search for understanding. *Learning Disability Quarterly, 17,* 2–32.

Englert, C. S., Berry, R., & Dunsmore, K. (2001). A case study of the apprenticeship process: Another perspective on the apprentice and the scaffolding metaphor. *Journal of Learning Disabilities, 34*(2), 152–171.

Englert, C. S., Raphael, T. E., Anderson, L. M., Anthony, H. M., Fear, K. L., & Gregg, D. D. (1988). A case for writing intervention: Strategies for writing informational text. *Learning Disabilities Focus, 3*(2), 98–113.

Epilepsy Foundation. (2009). *About epilepsy.* Retrieved from ww.epilepsyfoundation.org/about/

Epstein, J. L. (1996). *Partnership-2000 schools manual.* Baltimore, MD: Johns Hopkins University.

Epstein, M., Atkins, M., Cullinan, D., Kutash, K., & Weaver, R. (2008). *Reducing behavior problems in the elementary school classroom.* Washington DC: Institute of Education Sciences National Center for Education Evaluation and Regional Assistance.

Erickson, F. (2005). Culture in society and in educational practices. In J. A. Banks & C. M. Banks (Eds.), *Multicultural education: Issues and perspectives* (5th ed., pp. 31–60). Hoboken, NJ: Wiley.

Erickson, R. N., Ysseldyke, J. E., & Thurlow, M. L. (1997). Neglected numerators, drifting denominators and fractured fractions: Determining participation rates for students with disabilities in statewide assessments. *Diagnostique, 23*(2), 105–116.

Ervin-Tripp, S. (1974). Is second language learning like the first? *TESOL Quarterly, 8* (June), 111–127.

Evertson, C., Emmer, E., & Worsham, M. (2006). *Classroom management for elementary teachers* (7th ed.). Boston: Allyn & Bacon.

Ezzedeen, S. R. (2008). Facilitating class discussions around current and controversial issues: Ten recommendations for teachers. *College Teaching, 56,* 230–236.

Fairbanks, S., Simonsen, B., & Sugai, G. (2008). Classwide secondary and tertiary tier practices and systems. *Teaching Exceptional Children, 40,* 44–52.

Farmer, J., & Morse, S. E. (2007). Project Magnify: Increasing reading skills in students with low vision. *Journal of Visual Impairment and Blindness, 101,* 763–768.

Fearn, L., & Farnan, N. (2001). *Writing effectively: Helping children master the conventions of writing.* Boston: Allyn & Bacon.

Ferguson, P. M., & Ferguson, D. L. (2006). The promise of adulthood. In M. E. Snell & E. Brown (Eds.), *Instruction of students with severe disabilities* (6th ed.). Upper Saddle River, NJ: Merrill/Prentice Hall.

Ferrell, K. A. (1996). Your child's development. In M. C. Holbrook (Ed.), *Children with visual impairments* (pp. 73–96). Bethesda, MD: Woodbine House.

Ferrell, K. A. (2000). Growth and development of young children. In M. C. Holbrook & A. J. Koenig (1993), *Foundations of education: Instructional strategies for teaching children and youth with visual impairments* (Vol. I, 2nd ed., pp. 135–160). New York: AFB Press.

Fitzgerald, J. (1995). English-as-a-second-language instruction in the United States: A research review. *Journal of Reading Behavior, 27,* 115–152.

Fitzpatrick, D. (2008). Constructing complexity: Using reading levels to differentiated reading comprehension activities. *English Journal, 98,* 57–65.

Flannery, K. B., & Horner, R. H. (1994). The relationship between predictability and problem behavior for students with severe disabilities. *Journal of Behavioral Education, 4,* 157–176.

Fletcher, J. M., Lyon, G. R., Fuchs, L. S., & Barnes, M. A. (2007). *Learning disabilities: From identification to intervention.* New York: Guilford Press.

Flexer, C. (2000). The startling possibility of sound field. *Advance for Speech-Language Pathologists and Audiologists, 36,* 5, 13.

Flippo, R. F., Becker, M. J., & Wark, D. M. (2009). Test taking. In R. F. Flippo & D. C. Caverly (Eds.), *Handbook of college reading and study strategy research* (2nd ed., pp. 249–286). New York: Routledge.

Florida Department of Education. (2005). *Types of writing prompts.* Retrieved from www.firn.edu/doe/sas/fw/fwapprmp.htm

Flynn, L. A., & Flynn, E. M. (2004). *Teaching writing with rubrics.* Thousand Oaks, CA: Corwin Press.

Fontana, J. L., Scruggs, T., & Mastropieri, M. A. (2007). Mnemonic strategy instruction in inclusive secondary social studies classes. *Remedial and Special Education, 28,* 345–355.

Foorman, B. R., & Ciancio, D. J. (2005). Screening for secondary intervention: Concept and context. *Journal of Learning Disabilities, 38*(6), 494–499.

Forest, M., & Lusthaus, E. (1989). Promoting educational equality for all students: Circles and maps. In S. Stainback, W. Stainback, & M. Forest (Eds.), *Educating all students in the mainstream of regular education* (pp. 45–57). Baltimore, MD: Paul H. Brookes.

Forness, S. R. (1988). School characteristics of children and adolescents with depression. In R. B. Rutherford, C. M. Nelson, & S. R. Forness (Eds.), *Bases of severe behavioral disorders of children and youth.* Boston: Little, Brown.

Forness, S., & Kavale, K. (1999). Teaching social skills in children with learning disabilities: A meta-analysis of the research. *Learning Disability Quarterly, 19,* 2–13.

Foster, S. L., & Ritchey, W. L. (1979). Issues in assessment of social competence in children. *Journal of Applied Behavior Analysis, 12,* 625–638.

Foulk, D., Gessner, L. J., & Koorland, M. A. (2001). Human immunodeficiency virus/acquired immune deficiency syndrome (HIV/AIDS): Content in introduction to exceptionalities textbooks. *Action in Teacher Education, 23,* 47–54.

Fowler, M. (1992). *CH.A.D.D. educator's manual: An in-depth look at attention deficit disorders from an educational perspective.* Plantation, FL: Children and Adults with Attention Deficit Disorders.

Fowler, S. A., Schwartz, I., & Atwater, J. (1991). Perspective on the transition from preschool to kindergarten for children with disabilities and their families. *Exceptional Children, 58,* 136–145.

Fredrickson, N., & Turner, J. (2003). Utilizing the classroom peer group to address children's social needs: An evaluation of the Circle of Friends Intervention Approach. *The Journal of Special Education, 36,* 234–245.

Friend, M. (2005a). *Special education: Contemporary perspectives for school professionals.* Boston: Allyn & Bacon.

Friend, M. (2005b). *Thoughts on collaboration for the 21st century school professionals . . . Moving forward or lost in space?* Retrieved from www.ctserc.org/initiatives/teachandlearn/mfriend.shtml

Friend, M., & Bursuck, W. D. (2002). *Including students with special needs: A practical guide for classroom teachers* (3rd ed.). Boston: Allyn & Bacon.

Frombonne, E. (2002). Prevalence of childhood disintegrative disorder. *Autism, 6,* 149–157.

Frose, V. (1981). Handwriting: Practice, pragmatism, and progress. In V. Frose & S. B. Straw (Eds.), *Research in the language arts: Language and schooling* (pp. 227–243). Baltimore: University Park Press.

Fry, E. B. (1977). Fry's readability graph: Clarifications, validity, and extension to level 17. *Journal of Reading, 21,* 242–252.

Fry, E. B., & Kress, J. E. (2006). *The reading teacher's book of lists.* San Francisco: Josey-Bass.

Fry, E. B., Kress, J. E., & Fountoukidis, D. L. (2003). *The reading teacher's book of lists* (4th ed.). Englewood Cliffs, NJ: Prentice Hall.

Fry, R., & Gonzalez, F. (2008). *One-in-five and growing fast: A profile of Hispanic public school students.* Retrieved from http://pewresearch.org/pubs/937/

Fuchs, D., & Fuchs, L. S. (1994). Inclusive school movement and radicalization of special education reform. *Exceptional Children, 60,* 294–309.

Fuchs, D., Fuchs, L. S., & Burish, P. (2000). Peer-assisted learning strategies: An evidence-based practice to promote reading achievement. *Learning Disabilities Research and Practice, 15*(2), 85–91.

Fuchs, D., Fuchs, L. S., & Vaughn, S. (Eds.). (2008). *Response to intervention: A framework for reading educators.* Newark, DE: International Reading Association.

Fuchs, D., Mock, D., Morgan, P. L., & Young, C. L. (2003). Responsiveness to intervention: Definitions, evidence, and implications for the learning disabilities construct. *Learning Disabilities Research & Practice, 18,* 172–186.

Fuchs, D., Stecker, P. M., & Fuchs, L. S. (2008). The role of assessment within the RTI framework. In D. Fuchs, L. S. Fuchs, & S. Vaughn (Eds.), *Response to intervention: A framework for reading educators* (pp. 27–49). Newark, DE: International Reading Association.

Fuchs, L. S., & Fuchs, D. (1992). Identifying a measure for monitoring student reading program. *School Psychology Review, 21*(1), 45–58.

Fuchs, L. S., & Fuchs, D. (2003). Enhancing the mathematical problem solving of students with mathematics disabilities. In H. L. Swanson, K. R. Harris, & S. Graham (Eds.), *Handbook of learning disabilities* (pp. 306–322). New York: Guilford Press.

Fuchs, L. S., Fuchs, D., Compton, D. L., Bryant, J. D., Hamlett, C. L., & Seethuler, P. M. (2007). Mathematics screening and progress monitoring at first grade: Implications for response to intervention. *Exceptional Children, 73*(3), 311–330.

Fuchs, L. S., Fuchs, D., & Hamlett, C. L. (1990). Curriculum-based measurement: A standardized, long-term goal approach to monitoring student progress. *Academic Therapy, 25*(5), 615–632.

Fuchs, L. S., Fuchs, D., Hamlett, C. L., Phillips, N. B., & Bentz, J. (1994). Classwide curriculum-based assessment: Helping general educators meet the challenge of student diversity. *Exceptional Children, 60,* 518–537.

Fuchs, L. S., Fuchs, D., Hamlett, C. L., Phillips, N. B., Karns, K., & Dutka, S. (1997). Enhancing students' helping behavior during peer-mediated instruction with conceptual mathematical explanations. *Elementary School Journal, 97,* 223–250.

Fuchs, L. S., Fuchs, D., Hamlett, C. L., Walz, L., & Germann, G. (1993). Formative evaluation of academic progress: How much growth can we expect? *School Psychology Review, 22,* 27–48.

Fuchs, L. S., Fuchs, D., & Prentice, K. (2004). Responsiveness to mathematical problem-solving treatment among students with risk for mathematics disability, with and without risk for reading disability. *Journal of Learning Disabilities, 27,* 273–306.

Fuchs, L. S., Fuchs, D., & Speece, D. L. (2002). Treatment validity as a unifying construct for identifying learning disabilities. *Learning Disability Quarterly, 25,* 33–45.

Fuchs, L. S., Seethaler, P. M., Powell, S. A., Fuchs, D., Hamlett, C. L., & Fletcher, J. M. (2008). Effects of preventative tutoring on the mathematical problem solving of third-grade students with math and reading difficulties. *Exceptional Children, 74*(2), 155–173.

Fuchs, L., Compton, D., Fuchs, D., Paulsen, K., Bryant, J. D., & Hamlett, C. L. (2005). The prevention, identification, and cognitive determinants of math difficulty. *Journal of Educational Psychology, 98*(1), 29–43.

Fuchs, L., Fuchs, D., & Hamlett, C. (1989). Monitoring reading growth using student recalls: Effects of two teacher feedback systems. *Journal of Educational Research, 83,* 101–111.

Furlong, J. J., Morrison, G. M., & Jimerson, S. (2004). Externalizing behaviors of aggression and violence and the school context. In R. B. Rutherford, M. M. Quinn, & S. R. Mathur (Eds.), *Handbook of research in emotional and behavioral disorders* (pp. 243–261). New York: Guilford Press.

Galambos, N. L., Leadbeater, B. J., & Barker, E. T. (2004). Gender differences in and risk factors for depression in adolescence: A 4-year longitudinal study. *International Journal of Behavioral Development, 28*(1), 16–25.

Galambos, S., & Goldin-Meadow, S. (1990). The effects of learning two languages on metalinguistic development. *Cognition, 34,* 1–56.

Gallaudet Research Institute. (2008). *Regional and national summary report of data from the 2006–2007 annual survey of deaf and hard of hearing children and youth.* Washington, DC: GRI, Gallaudet University.

Gambrell, L. B. (1985). Dialogue journals: Reading-writing interaction. *The Reading Teacher, 38,* 512–515.

Garcia, E. E. (1991). Effective instruction for language minority students: The teacher. *Journal of Education, 173*(2), 130–141.

Gardner, H. (1983). *Frames of mind.* New York: Basic Books.

Gardner, H. (1999). *Intelligence reframed. Multiple intelligences for the 21st century.* New York: Basic Books.

Gardner, H. (2006). *Multiple intelligences: New horizons.* New York: Basic Books.

Gardner, H., & Hatch, T. (1989). Multiple intelligences go to school: Educational implications of the theory of multiple intelligences. *Educational Researcher, 18*(8), 4–9.

Gardner, R. III, Nobel, M. M., Hessler, T., Yawn, C. D., & Heron, T. E. (2007). Tutoring system innovations: Past practice to future prototypes. *Intervention in School and Clinic, 43*(2), 71–81.

Gaskins, I. W. (1996). *Word detectives: Benchmark extended word identification program for beginning readers.* Media, PA: Benchmark School.

Gast, D., Ault, M., Wolery, M., Doyle, P., & Belanger, S. (1988). Comparison of constant time delay and the system of least prompts in teaching sight word reading to students with moderate retardation. *Education and Training in Mental Retardation, 23,* 117–128.

Gay, G. (2000). *Culturally responsive teaching: Theory, research, & practice.* New York: Teachers College Press.

Gay, G. (2004). The importance of multicultural education. *Educational Leadership, 61,* 30–35.

Gay, G., & Kirkland, K. (2003). Developing cultural critical consciousness and self-reflection in preservice teacher education. *Theory Into Practice, 42,* 181–187.

Geary, D.C. (2003). Learning disabilities in arithmetic: Problem-solving differences and cognitive deficits. In H. L. Swanson, K. R. Harris, & S. Graham (Eds.), *Handbook of learning disabilities* (pp. 199–212). New York: Guilford Press.

Gerber, A. (1993). *Language related learning disabilities: Their nature and treatment.* Baltimore, MD: Paul H. Brookes.

Gerber, P. J., Ginsberg, R., & Reiff, H. B. (1992). Identifying alterable patterns in employment success for highly successful adults with learning disabilities. *Journal of Learning Disabilities, 25,* 475–487.

German, D. J. (1992). Word-finding intervention for children and adolescents. *Topics in Language Disorders, 13*(1), 33–50.

German, D. J. (1993). *Word finding intervention program.* Austin, TX: PRO-ED.

Gersten, R. M., & Jiménez, R. T. (Eds.). (1998). *Promoting learning for culturally and linguistically diverse students.* Belmont, CA: Wadsworth.

Gersten, R., & Baker, S. (2000). What we know about effective instructional practices for English-language learners. *Exceptional Children, 66,* 454–470.

Gersten, R., & Baker, S. (2001). Teaching expressive writing to students with learning disabilities: A meta-analysis. *Elementary School Journal, 101*(3), 251–272.

Gersten, R., & Baker, S. (2003). The contemporary research base in learning disabilities on teaching writing, promoting higher order thinking, and enhancing self-concept: Introduction to the special issue. *Journal of Learning Disabilities, 36*(2), 98–99.

Gersten, R., Marks, S. U., Keating, T., & Baker, S. (1998). Recent research on effective instructional practices for content areas ESOL. In R. M. Gersten & R. T. Jiménez (Eds.), *Promoting learning for culturally and linguistically diverse students* (pp. 57–72). Belmont, CA: Wadsworth.

Giangreco, M. F. (2009). *Critical issues brief: Concerns about the proliferation of one-to-one paraprofessionals.* Arlington, VA: Council for Exceptional Children, Division on Autism and Developmental Disabilities. Retrieved from www.dddcec.org/positionpapers.htm

Giangreco, M. F., Cloninger, C. J., & Iverson, V. (1998). *Choosing outcomes and accommodations for children: A guide to educational planning for students with disabilities (COACH)* (2nd ed.). Baltimore, MD: Paul H. Brookes.

Gilligan, C. (1982). *In a different voice: Psychological theory and women's development.* Cambridge, MA: Harvard University Press.

Gillon, G. T. (2007). *Phonological awareness from research to practice.* New York: Guilford Press.

Glass, T. F. (2004). What gift? The reality of the student who is gifted and talented in public school classrooms. *Gifted Child Today, 27,* 25–29.

Gold, M., & Mann, D. (1972). Delinquency as a defense. *American Journal of Orthopsychiatry, 42,* 463–479.

Gonzales, J. E., Vannest, K. J., & Reid, R. (2008). Early classification of reading performance in children identified or at risk for emotional and behavioral disorders. *The Journal of At-Risk Issues, 14,* 33–40.

Gonzalez, N., Moll, L. C., Floyd-Tenery, M., Rivera, A., Rendón, P., Gonzales, R., & Amati, C. (1995). Teacher research on funds of knowledge: Learning from households. *Urban Education, 29,* 443–470.

Good, R. H., Kaminski, R. A., Smith, S., Laimon, D., & Dill, S. (2003). *Dynamic indicators of basic early literacy skills* (6th ed.). Eugene, OR: University of Oregon.

Good, T. L., & Brophy, J. E. (2007). *Looking in classrooms* (10th ed.). Boston: Allyn & Bacon.

Gordon, J., Vaughn, S., & Schumm, J. S. (1993). Spelling interventions: A review of literature and implications for instruction for students with learning disabilities. *Learning Disabilities Research & Practice, 8*(3), 175–181.

Grabe, M., Christopherson, K., & Douglas, J. (2004–2005). Providing introductory psychology students access to online lecture notes: The relationship of note use to performance and class attendance. *Journal of Educational Technology Systems, 33,* 293–308.

Graham, S. (1992). Helping students with LD progress as writers. *Intervention in School and Clinic, 27,* 134–144.

Graham, S., Berninger, V., & Weintraub, N. (1998). The relationship between handwriting style and speed and legibility. *Journal of Educational Research, 91,* 290–297.

Graham, S., & Harris, K. (1989a). Cognitive training: Implications for written language. In J. Hughes & R. Hall (Eds.), *Cognitive behavioral psychology in the schools: A comprehensive handbook* (pp. 247–279). New York: Guilford Press.

Graham, S., & Harris, K. R. (1989b). Improving learning disabled students' skills at composing essays: Self-instructional strategy training. *Exceptional Children, 56,* 201–214.

Graham, S., & Harris, K. R. (2003). Students with learning disabilities and the process of writing: A meta-analysis of SRSD studies. In H. Swanson, K. R. Harris, & S. Graham (Eds.), *Handbook of learning disabilities* (pp. 323–344). New York: Guilford Press.

Graham, S., & Harris, K. R. (2006). Preventing writing difficulties: Providing additional handwriting and spelling instruction to at-risk children in first grade. *Teaching Exceptional Children, 38,* 64–66.

Graham, S., Harris, K. R., Fink-Chorzempa, B., & MacArthur, C. (2003). Primary grade teachers' instructional adaptations for struggling writers: A national survey. *Journal of Educational Psychology, 95,* 279–292.

Graham, S., Harris, K. R., Mason, L., Fink-Chorzempa, B., Moran, S., & Saddler, B. (2008). How do primary grade teachers teach handwriting: A national survey. *Reading & Writing: An Interdisciplinary Journal, 21,* 49–69.

Graham, S., & Miller, L. (1979). Spelling research and practice: A unified approach. *Focus on Exceptional Children, 13*(2), 1–16.

Graham, S., & Perrin, D. (2007). A meta-analysis of writing instruction for adolescent students. *Journal of Educational Psychology, 99,* 445–476.

Grant, C. A., & Sleeter, C. E. (1993). Race, class, gender, and disability in the classroom. In J. A. Banks & C. A. Banks (Eds.), *Multicultural education: Issues and perspectives* (2nd ed., pp. 48–67). Boston: Allyn & Bacon.

Graves, A., & Hauge, R. (1993). Using cues and prompts to improve story writing. *Teaching Exceptional Children, 25,* 38–45.

Graves, A. W., Valles, E. C., & Rueda, R. (2000). Variations in interactive writing instruction: A study in four bilingual special education settings. *Learning Disabilities Research & Practice, 15*(3), 1–9.

Graves, D. H. (2003). *Writing: Teachers and children at work* (Rev. ed.). Portsmouth, NH: Heinemann.

Graves, D. H. (1985). All children can write. *Learning Disability Focus, 1*(1), 36–43.

Graves, D., & Hansen, J. (1983). The author's chair. *Language Arts, 60*(2), 176–183.

Gray, C. (2000). *The new social story book.* Arlington, TX: Future Horizons.

Gresham, F. M. (2007). Response to intervention and emotional and behavioral disorders: Best practices in assessment for intervention. *Assessment for Effective Intervention, 32,* 214–221.

Gresham, F. M., Cook, C. R., Crews, S. D., & Kern, L. (2004). Social skills training for children and youth with emotional and behavior disorders: Validity considerations and future directions. *Behavioral Disorders, 30,* 32–46.

Gresham, F. M., & Elliott, S. N. (1990). *Social skills rating system.* Circle Pines, MN: American Guidance Service.

Gresham, F. M., & Kern, L. (2004). Internalizing behavior problems in children and adolescents. In R. B. Rutherford, M. M. Quinn, & S. R. Mathur (Eds.), *Handbook of research in emotional and behavioral disorders* (pp. 262–281). New York: Guilford Press.

Gresham, F. M., Sugai, G., & Horner, R. H. (2001). Interpreting outcomes of social skills training for students with high-incidence disabilities. *Exceptional Children, 67*(3), 331–344.

Gresham, F. M., Van, M. B., & Cook, C. R. (2006). Social skills training for teaching replacement behaviors: Remediating acquisition deficits in at-risk students. *Behavioral Disorders 31,* 363–377.

Griffin, H., Williams, S., Davis, M., & Engleman, M. (2002). Using technology to enhance cues for children with low vision. *Teaching Exceptional Children, 35,* 36–42.

Griffin-Shirley, N., Trusty, S., & Rickard, R. (2000). Orientation and mobility. In A. J. Koenig & M. C. Holbrook (Eds.), *Foundations of education: Instructional strategies for teaching children and youth with visual impairments* (Vol. 2, 2nd ed., pp. 529–568). New York: AFB Press.

Griffiths, A., VanDerHeyden, A. M., Parson, L. B., & Burns, M. K. (2006). Practical applications of response-to-intervention research. *Assessment for Effective Intervention, 32,* 50–56.

Grossman, H. (1995). *Special education in a diverse society.* Boston: Allyn & Bacon.

Gulik, C. (2003). Preparing for high-stakes testing. *Theory Into Practice, 42*(1), 42–50.

Gumpel, T. P., & Shlomit, D. (2000). Exploring the efficacy of self-regulatory training as a possible alternative to social skills training. *Behavioral Disorders, 25,* 131–141.

Gunn, B., Biglan, A., Smokowski, K., & Ary, D. (2000). The efficacy of supplemental instruction in decoding skills for Hispanic and non-Hispanic students in early elementary school. *The Journal of Special Education, 34*(2), 90–103.

Gunning, T. G. (2003). *Building literacy in the content areas* (6th ed.). Boston: Allyn & Bacon.

Guthrie, J. T. (2007). *Engaging adolescents in reading*. Thousand Oaks, CA: Corwin Press.

Guthrie, J. T., & Wigfield, A. (2000). Engagement and motivation in reading. In M. T. Kamil, P. T. Mosenthal, P. D. Pearson, & R. Barr (Eds.), *Handbook of reading research* (Vol. III, pp. 403–422). Mahwah, NJ: Erlbaum.

Guyer, B. P. (Ed.). (2001). *ADHD: Achieving success in school and life*. Boston: Allyn & Bacon.

Haager, D. (2007). Promises and cautions regarding response to intervention with English language learners. *Learning Disabilities Quarterly, 30*, 213–218.

Haager, D., Klingner, J. K., & Vaughn, S. (2007). *Evidence-based reading practices for response to intervention*. Baltimore: Paul H. Brookes.

Haager, D., & Vaughn, S. (1995). Parent, teacher, peer, and self-reports of the social competence of students with learning disabilities. *Journal of Learning Disabilities, 28*(4), 205–215.

Hacker, D. J. (1998). Definitions and empirical foundations. In D. J. Hacker, J. Dunlosky, & A. C. Graesser (Eds.), *Metacognition in theory and practice* (pp. 1–23). Mahwah, NJ: Erlbaum.

Hakuta, K. (1974). A report on the development of grammatical morphemes in a Japanese girl learning English as a second language. *Working Papers in Bilingualism* (Vol. 4, pp. 18–44). Toronto: OISE Press.

Hale-Benson, J. E. (1986). *Black children: Their roots, culture, and learning styles* (rev. ed.). Baltimore, MD: Johns Hopkins University Press.

Haley, M. H., & Austin, T.Y. (2004). *Content-based second language teaching and learning: An interactive approach*. Boston: Allyn & Bacon.

Hall, L. A. (2005). Teachers and content area reading: Attitudes, beliefs, and change. *Teaching and Teacher Education, 21*, 403–414.

Hall, S. L. (2008). *A principal's guide: Implementing response to intervention*. Thousand Oaks, CA: Corwin Press.

Hall, T. (2002). *Differentiated instruction*. Wakefield, MA: National Center on Accessing the General Curriculum. Retrieved from www.cast.org/publications/ncac/ncac_diffinstruc.html

Hallanan, D. P. (1992). Some thoughts on why the prevalence of learning disabilities has increased. *Journal of Learning Disabilities, 25*(8), 523–528.

Hallahan, D. P., Kauffman, J. M., & Pullen, P. C. (2009). *Exceptional learners: An introduction to special education*. Boston: Pearson.

Hallanan, D. P., Lloyd, J. W., Kauffman, J. M., Weiss, M P., & Martinez, E. A. (2005). *Learning disabilities: Foundations, characteristics, and effective teaching*. Boston: Allyn & Bacon.

Hallowell, E. M., & Ratey, J. J. (1995). *Driven to distraction: Recognizing and coping with attention deficit disorder from childhood through adulthood*. New York: Touchstone.

Hamill, L., & Everington, C. (2002). *Teaching students with moderate to severe disabilities: An applied approach for inclusive environments*. Upper Saddle River, NJ: Prentice Hall.

Hamstra-Bletz, L., & Blote, A. W. (1993). A longitudinal study on dysgraphic handwriting in primary school. *Journal of Learning Disabilities, 26*, 689–699.

Hanover, S. (1983). Handwriting comes naturally? *Academic Therapy, 18*, 407–412.

Hardman, M. L., & Dawson, S. (2008). The impact of federal public policy on curriculum and instruction for students with disabilities in the general classroom. *Preventing School Failure, 52*, 5–11.

Harper, C., & de Jong, E. (2004). Misconceptions about teaching English-language learners. *The Reading Teacher, 48*, 152–153.

Harris, K. R., Graham, S., Mason, L. H., & Friedlander, M. A. (2008). *Powerful writing strategies for all students*. Baltimore, MD: Paul H. Brookes.

Harry, B., & Klingner, J. (2006). *Why are so many minority students in special education? Understanding race and disability in schools*. New York: Teachers College Press.

Harry, B., & Klingner, J. (2007a). Discarding the deficit model. *Educational Leadership, 64*, 16–21.

Harry, B., & Klingner, J. K. (2007b). *Case studies of minority student placement in special education*. New York: Teachers College Press.

Harry, B., Klingner, J., & Cramer, E. (2007). *Case studies of minority student placement in special education*. New York: Teachers College Press.

Harry, B., Klingner, J. K., & Hart, J. (2005). African American families under fire: Ethnographic views of family strengths. *Remedial and Special Education, 26*, 101–112.

Harry, B., Rueda, R., & Kalyanpur, M. (1999). Cultural reciprocity in sociocultural perspective: Adapting the normalization principle for family collaboration. *Exceptional Children, 66*, 123–136.

Hart, B., & Risley, T. R. (2003). The early catastrophe: The 30 million word gap by age 3. *American Educator, 27*(1), 4–9.

Hawken, L. S., & Horner, R. (2003). Evaluation of a targeted group intervention with a schoolwide system of behavior support. *Journal of Positive Behavior Interventions, 9*, 94–101.

Hazel, J. S., Schumaker, J. B., Sherman, J. A., & Sheldon-Wildgen, J. (1982). Group training for social skills: A program for court-adjudicated, probationary youths. *Criminal Justice and Behavior, 9*, 35–53.

Hear-it Org. (2009). *Implants*. Retrieved from http://hear-it.org/printpage.dsp?printable=yes&page=2021

Heath, M. A., Leavy, D., Hansen, K., Ryan, K., Lawrence, L., & Sonntag, A. G. (2008). Coping with grief: Guidelines and resources for assisting children. *Intervention in School and Clinic, 43*, 259–269.

Hebdon, H. M. (2008). The use of one-on-one paraprofessionals in the classroom: Does this assistance help to build necessary life skills? *The Exceptional Parent, 38*, 88–89.

Hedge, M. N. (1998). *Coursebook on aphasia and other neurogenic language disorders* (2nd ed.). Florence, KY: Thomson Learning.

Helman, L. A., & Burns, M. K. (2008). What does oral language have to do with it? Helping young English-language learners acquire a sight vocabulary. *The Reading Teacher, 62*, 14–19.

Helmstetter, E., & Durand, V. M. (1991). Nonaversive interventions for severe behavior problems. In L. Meyer, C. Peck, & L. Brown (Eds.), *Critical issues in the lives of people with severe disabilities* (pp. 559–600). Baltimore, MD: Paul H. Brookes.

Hendley, S. L., & Lock, R. H. (2007). 20 ways to . . . use positive behavior support for inclusion in the general education classroom. *Intervention in School and Clinic, 42*, 225–228.

Henry, M. (1997). The decoding/spelling curriculum: Integrated decoding and spelling instruction from pre-school to early secondary school. *Dyslexia, 3*, 178–189.

Heward, W. L. (2009). *Exceptional children: An introduction to special education* (9th ed.). Upper Saddle River, NJ: Merrill.

Hiatt-Michael, D. B. (Ed.). (2007). *Promising practices for teachers to engage families of English language learners*. Charlotte, NC: Information Age Publishing.

Hickman, P., Pollard-Durodola, S., & Vaughn, S. (2004). Storybook reading: Improving vocabulary and comprehension for English language learners. *The Reading Teacher, 57*(8), 720–730.

Hiebert, E. H. (2005). *Teaching and learning vocabulary: Bringing research to practice*. Mahwah, NJ: Erlbaum.

Hill, E. W., & Ponder, P. (1976). *Orientation and mobility techniques*. New York: American Foundation for the Blind.

Hitchcock, C. H., Dowrick, P. W., & Prater, M. A. (2003). Video self-modeling intervention in school-based settings: A review. *Remedial & Special Education, 24*(1), 36–46.

Hofmeister, A. M. (1989). Teaching problem-solving skills with technology. *Educational Technology, 29*(9), 26–29.

Holburn, S., & Cea, C. D. (2007). Excessive positivism in person-centered planning. *Research and Practice for Persons With Severe Disabilities, 32*, 167–172.

Holschuh, J. P., & Aultman, L. P. (2009). Comprehension development. In R. F. Flippo & D. C. Caverly (Eds.), *Handbook of college reading and study strategy research* (2nd ed., pp. 121–144). New York: Routledge.

Hommersen, P., Murray, C., Ohan, J. L., & Johnston, C. (2006). Oppositional defiant disorder rating scale: Preliminary evidence of reliability and validity. *Journal of Emotional and Behavioral Disorders, 14*, 118–125.

Honda, H., Shimizu, Y., & Rutter, M. (2005). No effect of MMR withdrawal on the incidence of autism: A total population study. *Journal of Child Psychology and Psychiatry, 46*, 572–579.

Hoover, J., & Stenhjem, P. (2005). Bullying and teasing of youth with disabilities: Creating positive school environments for effective inclusion. *Issue Brief: Examining Current Challenges in Secondary Education and Transition, 2*(3), 1–6.

Hosp, J. L., & Reschly, D. J. (2004). Disproportionate representation of minority students in special education: Academic, demographic, and economic predictors. *Exceptional Children, 70,* 185–199.

Hourcade, J. J., & Bauwens, J. (2002). *Cooperative teaching: Rebuilding and sharing the schoolhouse* (2nd ed.). Austin, TX: PRO-ED.

Howe, K. R., & Welner, K. G. (2002). School choice and pressure to perform déjà vu for children with disabilities? *Remedial and Special Education, 23,* 212–221.

Hudson, P., & Glomb, N. (1997). If it takes two to tango, then why not teach both partners to dance? Collaboration instruction for all educators. *Journal of Learning Disabilities, 30*(4), 442–448.

Huebner, K. M. (2000). Visual impairment. In M. C. Holbrook & A. J. Koenig (Eds.), *Foundations of education. Volume I: History and theory of teaching children and youths with visual impairment* (2nd ed., pp. 55–76). New York: AFB Press.

Hughes, C. A., Ruhl, K. L., Schumaker, J. B., & Deshler, D. D. (2002). Effects of instruction in an assignment completion strategy on the homework performance of students with learning disabilities in general education classes. *Learning Disabilities Research and Practice, 17,* 1–18.

Hughes, M. T., Schumm, J. S., & Vaughn, S. (1999). Home literacy activities: Perceptions and practices of Hispanic parents of children with learning disabilities. *Learning Disability Quarterly, 22,* 209–222.

Hulit, L., & Howard, M. (2006). *Born to talk: An introduction to speech and language development* (4th ed.). Boston: Allyn & Bacon.

Hunt, N., & Munson, L. J. (2005). Teachers grieve: What can we do for our colleagues and ourselves when a student dies? *Teaching Exceptional Children, 37,* 48–51.

Hunt, P., Hirose-Hatae, A., Doering, K., Karasoff, P., & Goetz, L. (2000). "Community" is what I think everyone is talking about. *Remedial and Special Education, 21,* 305–317.

Hunt, P., & McDonnell, J. (2007). Inclusive education. In S. L. Odom, R. H. Horner, M. E. Snell, & J. Blacher (Eds.), *Handbook of developmental disabilities* (pp. 269–291). New York: Guilford Press.

Hurley, S. R., & Tinajero, J. V. (Eds.). (2001). *Literacy assessment of second language learners.* Boston: Allyn & Bacon.

Hutchinson, N. L. (1993). Effects of cognitive strategy instruction on algebra problem solving of adolescents with learning disabilities. *Learning Disability Quarterly, 16,* 34–63.

Hutchinson, S. W., Murdock, J. Y., Williamson, R. D., & Cronin, M. E. (2000). Self-recording plus encouragement equals improved behavior. *Teaching Exceptional Children, 32*(5), 54–58.

Idol, L. (2002). *Creating collaborative and inclusive schools.* Austin, TX: PRO-ED.

Igo, L. B., Riccoinini, P. J., Bruning, R. H., & Pope, G. G. (2006). How should middle-school students with LD approach online note taking? A mixed-methods study. *Learning Disability Quarterly, 29,* 89–100.

Individuals With Disabilities Education Act (IDEA) Data. (2004). *Number of children served under IDEA Part B by disability and age group, 2006.* Retrieved from https://www.ideadata.org/arc_toc8.asp#partbCC

Irvine, J. L., & York, E. D. (2001). Learning styles and culturally diverse students: A literature review. In J. A. Banks & C. A. M. Banks (Eds.), *Handbook of research on multicultural education* (pp. 484–497). San Francisco: Jossey-Bass.

Irwin, J. W. (2007). *Teaching comprehension processes* (3rd ed.). Boston: Allyn & Bacon.

Jackson, C. W., & Larkin, M. J. (2002). RUBRIC—Teaching students to use grading rubrics. *Teaching Exceptional Children, 35,* 40–45.

Janney, R., & Snell, M. E. (2008). *Behavior support: Teachers' guides to inclusive practices* (2nd ed.). Baltimore, MD: Paul H. Brookes.

Jimerson, S. R., Burns, M. K., & Van Der Heyden, A. M. (2007). *Handbook of response to intervention: The science and practice of assessment and intervention.* New York: Springer.

Jitendra, A. K., Griffin, C., Deatline-Buchman, A., Dipipi-Hoy, C., Sczesniak, E., Sokol, N. G., & Xin, Y. P. (2005). Adherence to mathematics professional standards and instructional design criteria for problem-solving in mathematics. *Exceptional Children, 71*(3), 319–337.

Johnson, D. (2000). *Teacher Web pages that build parent partnerships.* Mankato, MN: MultiMedia Schools. Retrieved from www.infotoday.com/MMSchools/sep00/johnson.htm

Johnson, D., & Johnson, R. (1989). Cooperative learning: What special education teachers need to know. *Pointer, 33*(2), 5–10.

Johnson, D. J., & Myklebust, H. R. (1967). *Learning disabilities: Educational principles and practices* (Report No. EC–001–107). New York: Grune & Stratton, Inc. (ERIC Document Reproduction Service No. ED 021 352).

Johnson, D. R., Thurlow, M., Cosio, A., & Bremer, C. D. (2005). High school graduation requirements and students with disabilities. *Information Brief* (NCSET publication), *4*(2).

Johnson, J. M., Baumgart, D., Helmstetter, E., & Curry, C. A. (1996). *Augmenting basic communication in natural contexts.* Baltimore, MD: Paul H. Brookes.

Johnson, R. (1985). *The picture communication symbols: Book II.* Solana Beach, CA: Mayer-Johnson.

Johnston, L., Beard, L., & Carpenter, L. B. (2007). *Assistive technology: Access for all students.* Upper Saddle River, NJ: Merrill.

Johnston, P., & Allington, R. (1991). Remediation. In R. Barr, M. L. Kamil, P. Mosenthal, & P. D. Pearson (Eds.), *Handbook of reading research* (Vol. 2, pp. 984–1012). New York: Longman.

Johnston, S. S., McDonnell, A. P., & Hawken, L. S. (2008). Enhancing outcomes in early literacy for young children with disabilities: Strategies for success. *Intervention in School and Clinic, 43,* 210–217.

Jordan, N. C., & Hanich, L. B. (2003). Characteristics of children with moderate mathematics deficiencies: A longitudinal perspective. *Learning Disabilities Research & Practice, 18*(4), 213–221.

Kagan, S., Zahn, G. L., Widaman, K. F., Schwarzwald, J., & Tyrell, G. (1985). Classroom structural bias: Impact of cooperative and competitive classroom structures on cooperative and competitive individuals and groups. In R. E. Slavin, S. Sharan, S. Kagan, R. Hertz-Lazarowitz, C. Webb, & R. Schmuck (Eds.), *Learning to cooperate, cooperating to learn* (pp. 177–209). New York: Plenum.

Kameenui, E. J., & Simmons, D. C. (1990). *Designing instructional strategies: The prevention of academic learning problems.* Columbus, OH: Merrill.

Kamens, M. W., Loprete, S. J., & Slostad, F. A. (2003). Inclusive classrooms: What practicing teachers want to know. *Action in Teacher Education, 25,* 20–26.

Kaplan, E., Fein, D., Kramer, J., Delis, D., & Morris, R. (2004). *Wechsler Intelligence Scale–Fourth Edition.* San Antonio, TX: Pearson.

Katsiyannis, A., Zhang, D., Ryan, J. B., & Jones, J. (2007). High-stakes testing and students with disabilities. *Journal of Disability Policy Studies, 18,* 160–167.

Kauchak, D., & Eggen, P. (1993). *Learning and teaching: Research-based methods* (2nd ed.). Boston: Allyn & Bacon.

Kauffman, J. M. (2004). *Characteristics of emotional and behavioral disorders of children and youth* (8th ed.). Upper Saddle River, NJ: Prentice Hall.

Kauffman, J. M., Brigham, F. J., & Mock, D. R. (2004). Historical and contemporary perspectives on the field of emotional and behavioral disorders. In R. B. Rutherford, M. M. Quinn, & S. R. Mathur (Eds.), *Handbook of research in emotional and behavioral disorders* (pp. 15–31). New York: Guilford Press.

Kauffman, J. M., & Hallahan, D. P. (1995). *The illusion of full inclusion: A comprehensive critique of a special education bandwagon.* Austin, TX: PRO-ED.

Kauffman, J. M., & Landrum, T. J. (2009). *Characteristics of emotional and behavioral disorders of children and youth* (9th ed.). Upper Saddle River, NJ: Prentice Hall.

Kavale, K. A., & Forness, S. R. (2000). History, rhetoric, and reality: Analysis of the inclusion debate. *Remedial and Special Education, 17,* 217–225.

Kavale, K. A., Holdnack, J. A., & Mostert, M. P. (2005). Responsiveness to intervention and the identification of specific learning disabilities: A critique and alternative proposal. *Learning Disability Quarterly, 28,* 2–16.

Kavale, K. A., Mathur, S. P., & Mostert, M. P. (2004). Social skills training and teaching social behavior to students with emotional and behavioral disorders. In R. B. Rutherford, M. M. Quinn, & S. R. Mathur (Eds.), *Handbook of research in emotional and behavioral disorders* (pp. 446–461). New York: Guilford Press.

Kazdin, A. E. (2001). *Behavior modification in applied settings* (6th ed.). Belmont, CA: Wadsworth.

Kazdin, A. E., & Crowley, M. J. (1997). Moderators of treatment outcome in cognitively based treatment of antisocial children. *Cognitive Therapy and Research, 19*(3), 357–372.

Keefe, E. B., Moore, V., & Duff, F. (2004). The four "knows" of collaborative teaching. *Teaching Exceptional Children, 36,* 36–42.

Keller, C. L., Bucholz, J., & Brady, M. P. (2007). Yes, I can! Empowering paraprofessionals to teach learning strategies. *Teaching Exceptional Children, 39,* 18–23.

Keller, M. (2002). Handwriting club: Using sensory integration strategies to improve handwriting. *Intervention in School and Clinic, 37,* 9–12.

Kelly, J. B., & Emery, R. E. (2003). Children's adjustment following divorce: Risk and resilience perspectives. *Family Relations, 52,* 352–362.

Kelly, M. J., & Clausen-Grace, N. (2007). *Comprehension should be silent: From strategy instruction to student independence.* Newark, DE: International Reading Association.

Kelly, S. M., & Smith, T. J. (2008). The digital social interactions of students with visual impairments: Findings from two national surveys. *Journal of Visual Impairment and Blindness, 102,* 528–539.

Keogh, B. K. (1993). Linking purpose and practice: Social-political and developmental perspectives on classification. In G. R. Lyon, D. B. Gray, J. R. Kavanagh, & N. A. Krasnegor (Eds.), *Better understanding learning disabilities* (pp. 311–323). Baltimore, MD: Paul H. Brookes.

Keyes, M. W., & Owens-Johnson, L. (2003). Developing person-centered IEPs. *Intervention in School and Clinic, 38*(3), 145–152.

Keyser-Marcus, L., Briel, L., Sherron-Targett, P., Yasuda, S., Johnson, S., & Wehman, P. (2002). Enhancing the schooling of students with traumatic brain injury. *Teaching Exceptional Children, 34,* 62–67.

Kim, A., Vaughn, S., Wanzek, J., & Wei, S. (2004). Graphic organizers and their effects on the reading comprehension of students with LD: A synthesis of research. *Journal of Learning Disabilities, 37*(2), 105–118.

Kirstein, I., & Bernstein, C. (1981). *Oakland schools picture dictionary.* Pontiac, MI: Oakland Schools Communication Enhancement Center.

Kitchel, J. E. (2004). *Large print: Guidelines for optimal readability and APHont™, a font for low vision.* Retrieved from www.aph.org/edresearch/lpguide.htm

Kleinert, H. L., Miracle, S. A., & Sheppard-Jones, K. (2007). Including students with moderate and severe disabilities in extracurricular and community activities. *Teaching Exceptional Children, 39,* 33–38.

Klein-Ezell, C. E., LaRusso, R., & Ezell, D. (2008). Alternate assessment for students with developmental disabilities. In H. P. Parette & G. R. Peterson-Karlan (Eds.), *Research-based practices in developmental disabilities* (2nd ed., pp. 415–430). Austin, TX: PRO-ED.

Klingner, J. K. (2003). Introduction to Right #5. In P. A. Mason & J. S. Schumm (Eds.), *Promising practices for urban reading instruction* (pp. 222–228). Newark, DE: International Reading Association.

Klingner, J. K., Barletta, L. M., & Hoover, J. J. (2008). Response to intervention models and English language learners. In J. K. Klingner, J. J. Hoover, & L. M. Baca (Eds.), *Why do English language learners struggle with reading: Distinguishing language acquisition from learning disabilities* (pp. 37–56). Thousand Oaks, CA: Corwin Press.

Klingner, J. K., Blanchett, W. J., & Harry, B. (2007). Race, culture, and developmental disabilities. In S. L. Odom, R. H. Horner, M. E. Snell, & J. Blacher (Eds.), *Handbook of developmental disabilities* (pp. 55–75). New York: Guilford Press.

Klingner, J. K., & Edwards, P. (2006a). Cultural considerations with response-to-intervention models. *Reading Research Quarterly, 41,* 108–117.

Klingner, J. K., & Edwards, P. A. (2006b). RTI (response to intervention): Rethinking special education for students with reading difficulties (yet again). *Reading Research Quarterly, 41,* 108–117.

Klingner, J. K., & Solano-Flores, G. (2007). Cultural responsiveness in response-to-intervention models. In *Accommodating students with disabilities: What works?* Educational Testing Service.

Klingner, J. K., & Vaughn, S. (1998). Using collaborative strategic reading. *Teaching Exceptional Children, 30*(6), 32–37.

Klingner, J. K., & Vaughn, S. (1999). Promoting reading comprehension, content learning, and English acquisition through collaborative strategic reading. *The Reading Teacher, 52*(7), 738–747.

Klingner, J. K., & Vaughn, S. (2000). The helping behaviors of fifth-graders while using collaborative strategic reading during ESL content classes. *TESOL Quarterly, 34*(1), 69–98.

Klingner, J. K., Vaughn, S., Arguelles, M. E., Hughes, M. T., & Leftwich, S. A. (2004). Collaborative strategic reading: Real-world lessons from classroom teachers. *Remedial and Special Education, 25*(5), 291–302.

Klingner, J. K., Vaughn, S., & Boardman, A. (2007). *Teaching reading comprehension to students with learning difficulties.* New York: Guilford Press.

Klingner, J. K., Vaughn, S., Hughes, M. T., Schumm, J. S., & Elbaum, B. (1998). Outcomes for students with and without learning disabilities. *Learning Disabilities Research and Practice, 13*(3), 153–161.

Klingner, J. K., Vaughn, S., & Schumm, J. S. (1998). Collaborative strategic reading during social studies in heterogeneous fourth-grade classrooms. *Elementary School Journal, 99,* 3–22.

Klotz, M. B., & Canter, A. (2007). *Response to intervention (RTI): A primer for parents.* Washington, DC: National Association of School Psychologists.

Knight-McKenna, M. (2008). Syllable types: A strategy for reading multisyllabic words. *Teaching Exceptional Children, 40*(3), 18–24.

Koga, N., & Hall, T. (2004). *Curriculum modification.* Wakefield, MA: National Center on Accessing the General Curriculum. Retrieved from www.cast.org/publications/ncac/ncac_curriculummod.html

Konopasek, D., & Forness, S. R. (2004). Psychopharmacology in the treatment of emotional and behavioral disorders. In R. B. Rutherford, M. M. Quinn, & S. R. Mathur (Eds.), *Handbook of research in emotional and behavioral disorders* (pp. 352–368). New York: Guilford Press.

Korinek, L., & Bulls, J. A. (1996). SCOREA: A student research paper writing strategy. *Teaching Exceptional Children, 28,* 60–63.

Kovacs, M., Obrosky, D. S., & Sherrill, J. (2003). Developmental changes in the phenomenology of depression in girls compared to boys from childhood onward. *Journal of Affective Disorders, 74*(1), 33–48.

Koziol, S. (1973). The development of noun plural rules during the primary grades. *Research in the Teaching of English, 7,* 30–50.

Krashen, S. (1985). *The input hypothesis: Issues and implications.* London: Longman.

Kretlow, A. G., Lo, Y., White, R. B., & Jordan, L. (2008). Teaching test-taking strategies to improve the academic achievement of students with mild mental disabilities. *Education and Training in Developmental Disabilities, 43,* 397–408.

Kubler-Ross, E. (1969). *On death and dying.* New York: Macmillan.

Labbo, L. D. (2004). Author's computer chair. *The Reading Teacher, 57,* 688–691.

LaBerge, D., & Samuels, S. J. (1974). Toward a theory of automatic information processing in reading. *Cognitive Psychology, 6,* 293–323.

Labov, W., Cohen, P., Robins, C., & Lewis, J. (1968). *A study of the non-standard English of Negro and Puerto Rican speakers in New York City* (Report on Cooperative Research Project 3288). New York: Columbia University.

Ladson-Billings, G. (1995). Toward a theory of culturally relevant pedagogy. *American Educational Research Journal, 32,* 465–491.

Ladson-Billings, G. (2006). From the achievement gap to the education debt: Understanding achievement in U.S. Schools. *Educational Researcher, 35,* 3–12.

Ladson-Billings, G. (2007). Pushing past the achievement gap: An essay on the language of deficit. *The Journal of Negro Education, 76,* 316–323.

LaGreca, A. M., & Vaughn, S. (1992). Social functioning of individuals with learning disabilities. *School Psychology Review, 21,* 423–427.

Laird, J., Cataldi, E. F., KewalRamani, A., & Chapman, C. (2008). *Dropout and completion rates in the United States: 2006* (NCES 2008-053). Retrieved from http://nces.ed.gov/pubsearch/pubsinfo.asp?pubid=2008053

Lambert, N., Nihira, K., & Leland, H. (1993). *AAMR Adaptive Behavior Scale—School: Examiner's manual* (2nd ed.). Austin, TX: PRO-ED.

Lancelotta, G. X., & Vaughn, S. (1989). Relation between types of aggression and sociometric status: Peer and teacher perceptions. *Journal of Educational Psychology, 81,* 86–90.

Landers, E., Alter, P., & Servilio, K. (2008). Students challenging behavior and teachers' job satisfaction. *Beyond Behavior, 26–33.*

Lane, K. L., Wehby, J., Menzies, H. M., Doukas, G. L., Munton, S. M., & Gregg, R. M. (2003). Social skills instruction for students at risk for antisocial behavior: The effects of small-group instruction. *Behavioral Disorders, 28,* 229–248.

Lang, R., O'Reilly, M., Lancioni, G., Rispoli, M., Machalicek, W., Chan, J. M., . . . & Franco, J. H. (2009). Discrepancy in functional analysis results across two applied settings: Implications for intervention design. *Journal of Applied Behavior Analysis, 42,* 393–398.

Lang, R., O'Reilly, M., Machalicek, W., Lancioni, G., Rispoli, M., & Chan, J. M. (2008). A preliminary comparison of functional analysis results when conducted in contrived versus naturalistic settings. *Journal of Applied Behavior Analysis, 41,* 135–139.

Langlois, J. A., Rutland-Brown, W., & Thomas, K. E. (2006). *Traumatic brain injury in the United States: Emergency department visits, hospitalizations, and deaths.* Atlanta: Centers for Disease Control and Prevention, National Center for Injury Prevention and Control.

Larrivee, B. (1992). *Strategies for effective classroom management.* Boston: Allyn & Bacon.

Larrivee, B. (2005). *Authentic classroom management: Creating a learning community and building reflective practice* (2nd ed.). Boston: Allyn & Bacon.

Larson, C. N., & Slaughter, H. (1984). The use of manipulatives and games in selected elementary school classrooms, from an ethnographic study. In A. E. Uprichard & J. V. Perez (Eds.), *Focus on learning problems in mathematics* (pp. 31–49). Framingham, MA: Center for Teaching/Learning of Mathematics.

Larson, N. (2004). *Teacher reference materials: Saxon Math 2: Test preparation and practice for ISTEP.* Norman, OK: Saxon.

Lash, M. H. (2000). *Resource guide: Children, adolescents and young adults with brain injuries.* Wake Forest, NC: L & A Publishing/Training.

Layton, C. A., & Lock, R. H. (2007). 20 ways to . . . use authentic assessment techniques to fulfill the promise of No Child Left Behind. *Intervention in School and Clinic, 42,* 169–173.

Lazar, R. T., Warr-Leeper, G. A., Nicholson, C. B., & Johnson, S. (1989). Elementary school teachers' use of multiple meaning expressions. *Language, Speech, and Hearing Services in Schools, 20,* 420–430.

Lederer, J. M. (2000). Reciprocal teaching of social studies in inclusive elementary classrooms. *Journal of Learning Disabilities, 33*(1), 91–106.

Lee, D. L., & Axelrod, S. (2005). *Behavior modification: Basic principles* (3rd ed.). Austin, TX: PRO-ED.

Lee, S.-H., Soukup, J. H., Little, T. D., & Wehmeyer, M. L. (2008). Student and teacher variables contributing to access to the general education curriculum for students with intellectual and developmental disabilities. *Journal of Special Education, 43,* 29–44.

Leff, S., & Leff, R. (1978). *Talking pictures.* Milwaukee, WI: Crestwood Company.

Lehman, A. F., Kreyenbuhl, J., Buchanan, R. W., Dickerson, F. B., Dixon, L. A., & Goldberg, R. E. A. (2004). The Schitzophrenia Patient Outcomes Research Team (PORT). Updated treatment recommendations 2003. *Schizophrenia Bulletin, 30,* 193–217.

Leigh, J., & Johnson, A. (2004). *Giving presentations the EVL way.* Retrieved from www.evl.uic.edu/aej/PresentinginEVL

Lembke, E. S., & Strichter, J. P. (2006). Utilizing a system of screening and progress monitoring within a three-tiered model of instruction: Implications for students with emotional/behavioral disorders. *Beyond Behavior,* 3–9.

LeMoine, N. R. (2001). Language variation and literacy acquisition in African American students. In J. L. Harris, A. G. Kamhi, & K. E. Pollock (Eds.), *Literacy in African American communities* (pp. 169–194). Mahwah, NJ: Erlbaum.

Lenz, B. K. (1983). Promoting active learning through effective instruction: Using advance organizers. *Pointer, 27*(2), 11–13.

Lenz, B. K., & Deshler, D. D. (2004). *Teaching content to all: Evidence-based inclusive practices in middle and secondary schools.* Boston: Allyn & Bacon.

Lenz, B. K., Deshler, D. D., & Kissam, B. R. (2003). *Teaching content to all: Evidence-based inclusive practices in middle and secondary schools.* Boston: Pearson Education.

Lenz, B. K., Schumaker, J. B., Deshler, D. D., & Beals, V. L. (1984). *The word identification strategy* (Learning Strategies Curriculum). Lawrence, KS: University of Kansas.

Lerman, J. (2006). *101 best websites for teacher tools and professional development.* Washington, DC: International Society for Technology in Education.

Lerner, J. (2006). *Learning disabilities and related disorders: Characteristics and teaching strategies* (10th ed.). Boston: Houghton Mifflin.

Lerner, J. W., Lowenthal, B., & Lerner S. R. (1995). *Attention deficit disorders: Assessment and teaching.* Pacific Grove, CA: Brooks/Cole.

Lessow-Hurley, J. (2009). *The foundations of dual language instruction* (5th ed.). Boston: Pearson.

Levendoski, L. S., & Cartledge, G. (2000). Self-monitoring for elementary school children with serious emotional disturbances: Classroom applications for increased academic responding. *Behavioral Disorders, 25,* 211–234.

Lewis, R. B. (1993). *Special education technology: Classroom applications.* Pacific Grove, CA: Brooks/Cole.

Lewis, T. J., Lewis-Palmer, T., Newcomer, L., & Stichter, J. (2004). Applied behavior analysis and the education and treatment of students with emotional and behavioral disorders. In R. B. Rutherford, M. M. Quinn, & S. R. Mathur (Eds.), *Handbook of research in emotional and behavioral disorders* (pp. 523–545). New York: Guilford Press.

Liederman, J., Kantrowitz, L., & Flannery, K. (2005). Male vulnerability to reading disability is not likely to be a myth: A call for new data. *Journal of Learning Disabilities, 38*(2), 109–129.

Linan-Thompson, S. (2007). *Research-based methods of reading instruction for English language learners.* Alexandria, VA: ASCD.

Linan-Thompson, S., & Vaughn, S. (2007). *Research-based methods of reading instruction for English language learners: Grades K–4.* Alexandria, VA: Association for Supervision and Curriculum Development.

Linan-Thompson, S., Vaughn, S., Hickman-Davis, P., & Kouzekanani, K. (2003). Effectiveness of supplemental reading instruction for second-grade English language learners with reading difficulties. *The Elementary School Journal, 103,* 221–238.

Lindamood, P. A., & Lindamood, P. (1998). *The Lindamood phoneme sequencing program for reading, spelling, and speech: The LiPS program.* Austin, TX: PRO-ED.

Loeber, R., Wung, P., Keenan, K., Giroux, B., Stouthamer-Loeber, M., Van Kammen, W., & Maughan, B. (1993). Developmental pathways in disruptive child behavior. *Development and Psychopathology, 51*(1/2), 103–134.

Lovett, M. W., Barron, R. W., & Benson, N. J. (2003). Effective remediation of word identification and decoding difficulties in school-age children with reading disabilities. In H. L. Swanson & K. R. Harris (Eds.), *Handbook of learning disabilities* (pp. 273–292). New York: Guilford Press.

Lucangeli, D., Coi, G., & Bosco, P. (1997). Metacognitive awareness in good and poor math problem solvers. *Learning Disabilities Research and Practice, 12*(4), 209–212.

Lucas, T., Henze, R., & Donato, R. (1990). Promoting the success for Latino language minority students: An exploratory study of six high schools. *Harvard Educational Review, 60,* 315–334.

Luckasson, R., Borthwick-Duffy, S., Buntinx, W. H. E., Coulter, D. L., Craig, E. M., Reeve, A., Schalock, R. L., Snell, M., Spitalnik, D. M., & Spreat, S. (2002). *Mental retardation: Definition, classification, and systems of support* (10th ed.). Washington, DC: American Association for Mental Retardation.

Luckner, J., Bowen, S., & Carter, K. (2001). Visual teaching strategies for students who are deaf or hard of hearing. *Teaching Exceptional Children, 33*(3), 38–44.

Lucyshyn, J. M., Dunlap, G., & Albin, R. W. (2002). Families and positive behavior support: Addressing problem behavior in family contexts. *Adolescence, 37*(148), 863.

Lucyshyn, J. M., Horner, R. H., Dunlap, G., Albin, R. W., & Ben, K. R. (2002). Positive behavior support with families. In J. M. Lucyshyn, G. Dunlap, & R. W. Albin (Eds.), *Families and positive behavior support: Addressing problem behavior in family contexts* (pp. 3–43). Baltimore, MD: Paul H. Brookes.

Lue, M. S. (2001). *A survey of communication disorders for the classroom teacher.* Boston: Allyn & Bacon.

Lusthaus, E., & Forest, M. (1987). The kaleidoscope: A challenge to the cascade. In M. Forest (Ed.), *More education integration* (pp. 1–17). Downsview, Ontario: G. Allan Roeher Institute.

Lynch, E. W., & Hanson, M. J. (1992). *Developing cross-cultural competence: A guide for working with young children and their families.* Baltimore, MD: Paul H. Brookes.

Lynne, B. (2007). *Technology for hearing impaired.* Retrieved from www.teachingtechnology.suite101.com/article.dfm/technology_for_hearing_impaired

Lyon, G. R., Fletcher, J. M., & Barnes, M. C. (2003). Learning disabilities. In E. J. Mash and R. Barkley (Eds.), *Child psychopathology* (2nd ed., pp. 520–588). New York: Guilford Press.

Maag, J. W. (2006). Social skills training for students with emotional and behavioral disorders: A review of reviews. *Behavioral Disorders, 32,* 5–17.

MacGinitie, W. H., MacGinitie, R. K., Maria, K., Dreyer, L. G., & Hughes, K. E. (2006). *Gates-MacGinitie Reading Tests.* Riverside, CA: Riverside.

Mack, K. (2004). Explanations for conduct disorder. *Child & Youth Care Forum, 33*(2), 95–112.

Maheady, L., Harper, G. F., & Sacca, M. K. (1988). Peer mediated instruction: A promising approach to meeting the needs of learning disabled adolescents. *Learning Disability Quarterly, 11,* 108–113.

Mallette, M. H., Henk, W. A., Waggoner, J. E., & Delaney, C. J. (2005). What matters most? A survey of accomplished middle-level educators' beliefs and values about literacy. *Action in Teacher Education, 27,* 33–42.

Mann, V. A. (1984). Longitudinal prediction and prevention of early reading difficulty. *Annals of Dyslexia, 34,* 117–135.

March of Dimes. (2006). *What's inside?* Retrieved from www.marchofdimes.com/14332_1169.asp

Marino, M. T., Marino, E. C., & Shaw, S. F. (2006). Making informed assistive technology decisions for students with high incidence disabilities. *Teaching Exceptional Children, 38,* 18–25.

Marks, S. U. (2008). Self-determination for students with intellectual disabilities and why I want educators to know what it means. *Phi Delta Kappan, 90*(1), 55–58.

Marsh, L. G., & Cooke, N. L. (1996). The effects of using manipulatives in teaching math problem solving to students with learning disabilities. *Learning Disabilities Research and Practice, 11* (1), 58–65.

Marston, D. (1996). A comparison of inclusion only, pull-out only, and combined service models for students with mild disabilities. *The Journal of Special Education, 30*(2), 121–132.

Marston, D., Muyskens, P., Lau, M., & Canter, H. (2003). Problem solving model for decision-making with high-incidence disabilities: The Minneapolis experience. *Learning Disabilities Research and Practice, 18*(3), 187–200.

Marzano, R. J., & Haystead, M. W. (2008). *Making standards useful in the classroom.* Alexandria, VA: Association for Supervision and Curriculum Development.

Marzano, R. J., & Marzano, J. S. (2003). The key to classroom management. *Educational Leadership, 61,* 6–13.

Mason, C., Field, S., & Sawilowsky, S. (2004). Implementation of self-determination activities and student participation in IEPs. *Exceptional Children, 70*(4), 441–451.

Mason, L. H., & Graham, S. (2008). Writing instruction for adolescents with learning disabilities: Programs of intervention research. *Learning Disabilities Research & Practice, 23*(2), 103–112.

Mastropieri, M. A., & Scruggs, T. E. (1997). Best practices in promoting reading comprehension in students with learning disabilities: 1976–1996. *Remedial and Special Education, 18,* 197–213.

Mastropieri, M. A., Leinart, A., & Scruggs, T. E. (1999). Strategies to increase reading fluency. *Intervention in School and Clinic, 34*(5), 278–283.

Mastropieri, M. A., & Scruggs, T. E. (2005). Feasibility and consequences of response to intervention: Examination of the issues and scientific evidence as a model for identification of individuals with learning disabilities. *Journal of Learning Disabilities, 38,* 525–531.

Mastropieri, M. A., Scruggs, T. E., Graetz, J., Norland, J., Gardizi, W., & McDuffie, K. (2005). Case studies in co-teaching in the content areas: Successes, failures, and challenges. *Intervention in School and Clinic, 40*(5), 260–270.

Mathes, P. G., Fuchs, D., Roberts, P. H., & Fuchs, L. S. (1998). Preparing students with special needs for reintegration: Curriculum-based measurement's impact on transenvironmental programming. *Journal of Learning Disabilities 31,* 615–624.

Mattingly, J. C., & Bott, D. A. (1990). Teaching multiplication facts to students with learning problems. *Exceptional Children, 56*(5), 438–449.

Mattison, R. E. (2004). Psychiatric and psychological assessment of emotional and behavioral disorders during school mental health consultation. In R. B. Rutherford, M. M. Quinn, & S. R. Mathur (Eds.), *Handbook of research in emotional and behavioral disorders* (pp. 163–180). New York: Guilford Press.

Matus, R. (2009). *Bright students still get bored.* Retrieved from www.tampabay.com/news/education/k12/article970309.sec

Mayes, S. D., & Calhoun, S. L. (2006). Frequency of reading, math, and writing disabilities in children with clinical disorders. *Learning and Individual Differences, 16,* 145–157.

Mayo Clinic. (2002). How common is attention-deficit/hyperactivity disorder? *Archives of Pediatrics and Adolescent Medicine, 156*(3), 209–210.

McCaleb, J., & White, J. (1980). Critical dimensions in evaluating teacher clarity. *Journal of Classroom Interaction, 15,* 27–30.

McCoy, J. D., & Ketterlin-Geller, L. R. (2004). Rethinking instructional delivery for diverse student populations: Serving all learners with concept-based instruction. *Intervention in School and Clinic, 40,* 88–95.

McDougall, D. (1998). Research on self-management techniques used by students with disabilities in general education settings: A descriptive review. *Remedial and Special Education, 19,* 310–320.

McEvoy, A., & Welker, R. (2000). Antisocial behavior, academic behavior, and school climate: A critical review. *Journal of Emotional and Behavioral Disorders, 8,* 130–140.

McGregor, K. K., & Leonard, L. B. (1995). Intervention for word-finding deficits in children. In M. E. Fey, J. Windsor, & S. F. Warren (Eds.), *Language intervention: Preschool through the elementary years* (pp. 85–105). Baltimore, MD: Paul H. Brookes.

McIntosh, K., & MacKay, L. D. (2008). Enhancing generalization of social skills: Making social skills curricula effective after the lesson. *Beyond Behavior,* 18–25.

McIntosh, R., Vaughn, S., Schumm, J. S., Haager, D., & Lee, O. (1993). Observations of students with learning disabilities in general education classrooms. *Exceptional Children, 60,* 249–261.

McKinley, N., & Larson, V. (1991, November). *Seventh, eighth, and ninth graders' conversations in two experimental conditions.* Paper presented at the annual convention of the American Speech-Language-Hearing Association, Atlanta, GA.

McLaughlin, S. (1998). *Introduction to language development.* San Diego, CA: Singular Publishing Group.

McLoughlin, J. A., & Lewis, R. B. (2005). *Assessing students with special needs* (6th ed.). Upper Saddle River, NJ: Merrill/Prentice Hall.

McMaster, K., Shu-Hsuan, K., Insoon, H., & Cao, M. (2008). Peer-assisted learning strategies: A "Tier 1" approach to promoting English learners' response to intervention. *Exceptional Children, 74*(2), 194–214.

McMillan, J. H., & Hearn, J. (2008). Student self-assessment: The key to stronger student motivation and higher achievement. *Educational Horizons, 87,* 40–49.

McNamara, J. K., & Wong, B. (2003). Memory for everyday information in students with learning disabilities. *Journal of Learning Disabilities, 36* (5), 394–406.

McNeill, D. (1970). *The acquisition of language: The study of developmental psycholinguistics.* New York: Harper & Row.

McTighe, J., & Lyman, F. T., Jr. (1988). Cueing thinking in the classroom: The promise of theory-embedded tools. *Educational Leadership, 45*(7), 18–24.

Mechling, L. C. (2008). Thirty year review of safety skill instruction for persons with intellectual disabilities. *Education and Training in Developmental Disabilities, 43,* 311–323.

Medina, A. L. (2006). The parallel bar: Writing assessment and instruction. In J. S. Schumm (Ed.), *Reading assessment and instruction for all learners: A comprehensive guide for classroom and resource settings.* New York: Guilford Press.

Meichenbaum, D., & Biemiller, A. (1998). *Nurturing independent learners: Helping students take charge of their learning.* Newton, MA: Brookline Books.

Menyuk, P. (1971). *The acquisition and development of language.* Englewood Cliffs, NJ: Prentice Hall.

Menzies, H. M., Lane, K. L., & Lee, J. M. (2009). Self-monitoring strategies for use in the classroom: A promising practice to support productive behavior for students with emotional or behavioral disorders. *Beyond Behavior, 18,* 27–35.

Mercer, C. D., & Miller, S. P. (1992). Teaching students with learning problems in math to acquire, understand, and apply basic math facts. *Remedial and Special Education, 13*(3), 19–35, 61.

Meyer, L. H., Bevan-Brown, J., Harry, B., & Sapon-Shevin, M. (2005). School inclusion and multicultural issues in special education. In J. A. Banks & C. A. M. Banks (Eds.), *Multicultural education: Issues and perspectives* (5th ed., pp. 350–378). Hoboken, NJ: Wiley.

Meyer, M. S., & Felton, R. H. (1999). Repeated reading to enhance fluency: Old approaches and new direction. *Annals of Dyslexia, 49,* 283–306.

Miller, M. C., Cooke, N. L., Test, D. W., & White, R. (2003). Effects of friendship circles on the social interactions of elementary age students with mild disabilities. *Journal of Behavioral Education, 12,* 167–184.

Miyasaka, J. R. (2002, April). *A framework for evaluating the validity of test preparation practices.* Paper presented at the annual meeting of the American Educational Research Association, New Orleans, LA.

Moats, L. C. (2000). *Speech to print: Language essentials for teachers.* Baltimore: Paul H. Brookes.

Moats, L. C. (2009). *The speech sounds of English: Phonetics, phonology, and phoneme awareness.* Longmont, CO: Sopris West Educational Services.

Mobbs, F., Reed, V. A., & McAllister, I. (1993, May). *Rankings of the relative importance of selected communication skills in adolescent peer interactions.* Paper presented at the annual conference of the Australian Association of Speech and Hearing, Darwin, Australia.

Moeller, M. P. (2000). Early intervention and language development in children who are deaf and hard of hearing. *Pediatrics, 106*(2), 43–62.

Moll, L. C., & Greenberg, J. B. (1990). Creating zones of possibilities: Combining social contexts for instruction. In L. C. Moll (Ed.), *Vygotsky and education* (pp. 319–348). Cambridge, England: Cambridge University Press.

Montague, M. (1992). The effects of cognitive and metacognitive strategy instruction on the mathematical problem solving of middle school students with learning disabilities. *Journal of Learning Disabilities, 25,* 230–248.

Montague, M. (2008). Self-regulation strategies to improve mathematical problem solving for students with learning disabilities. *Learning Disability Quarterly, 31,* 37–44.

Montague, M., Enders, C., & Castro, M. (2005). Academic and behavioral outcomes for students with emotional and behavioral disorders. *Behavior Disorders, 31,* 18–32.

Montague, M., & Graves, A. (1993). Improving students' story writing. *Teaching Exceptional Children, 25,* 36–37.

Montague, M., & van Garderen, D. (2003). A cross-sectional study of mathematics achievement, estimation skills, and academic self-perception in students of varying ability. *Journal of Learning Disabilities, 36,* 437–447.

Montgomery, W. (2001). Creating culturally responsive, inclusive classrooms. *Teaching Exceptional Children,* 4–9.

Mora-Harder, M. (2009). *English reading/language arts instruction in first-grade classrooms serving English language learners: A cross-analysis of instructional practices and student engagement* (Unpublished doctoral dissertation). University of Miami, Coral Gables, FL.

Moran, S., Kornhaber, M., & Gardner, H. (2006). Orchestrating multiple intelligences. *Educational Leadership, 64,* 22–27.

Morgan, S. R., & Reinhart, J. A. (1991). *Interventions for students with emotional disorders.* Austin, TX: PRO-ED.

Mueller, T. G. (2009). IEP facilitation. *Teaching Exceptional Children, 41*(3), 60–67.

Mulcahy-Ernt, P. I., & Caverly, D. C. (2009). Strategic study-reading. In R. F. Flippo & D. C. Caverly (Eds.), *Handbook of college reading and study strategy research* (2nd ed., pp. 177–198). New York: Routledge.

Munk, D. D., & Van Laarhoven, T. (2008). Grouping arrangements and delivery of instruction for students with developmental disabilities. In H. P. Parette & G. R. Peterson-Karlan (Eds.), *Research-based practices in developmental disabilities* (2nd ed., pp. 269–290). Austin, TX: PRO-ED.

Murawski, W. W., & Swanson, H. L. (2001). A meta-analysis of co-teaching research. *Remedial and Special Education, 22,* 258–267.

Muscular Dystrophy Association. (2009). *Diseases.* Retrieved from www.mda.org/disease/

Myers, A., & Eisenman, L. (2005). Student-led IEPs: Take the first step. *Teaching Exceptional Children, 37*(4), 52–58.

Nahmias, M. (1995). *Project ADEPT.* Tucson, AZ: University of Arizona, Department of Special Education and Rehabilitation.

National Association for Gifted Children. (2005). *National Association for Gifted Children: Position paper: Differentiation of curriculum and instruction.* Retrieved from www.nagc.org

National Association of School Psychologists. (2006). *New roles in response to intervention: Creating success for schools and children.* Retrieved from http://www.nasponline.org/advocacy/New%20Roles%20in%20RTI.pdf

National Center for Children in Poverty. *Child poverty.* Retrieved from www.nccp.org/topics/childpoverty

National Center for Educational Statistics. (2009). *Fast facts.* Retrieved from http://nces.ed.gov/fastfacts/display.asp?id=59

National Center for Hearing Assessment & Management. (2009). Retrieved from www.infanthearing.org/screening/index.html

National Center on Secondary Education and Transition (NCSET). (2004). *Post secondary supports.* Retrieved from http://ncest.org/topics/preparing

National Council of Teachers of English. (2004). *Beliefs about the teaching of writing.* Retrieved from www.ncte.org/about/positions/category/write/118876.htm

National Council of Teachers of Mathematics. (1989). *Curriculum and evaluation standards for school mathematics* (Report No. SE–050–418). Reston, VA: Author. (ERIC Document Reproduction Service No. ED 304 338).

National Council of Teachers of Mathematics. (2000). Retrieved from www.nctm.org

National Council of Teachers of Mathematics. (2006). *Curriculum focal points for prekindergarten through grade 8 mathematics: A quest for coherence.* Reston, VA: National Council of Teachers of Mathematics.

National Dissemination Center for Children with Disabilities (NICHCY). (2000). *Fact Sheet #11: Info about speech and language disorders.* Retrieved from www.kidsource.com/NICHCY/speech.html

National Dissemination Center for Children with Disabilities. (2006). *Traumatic brain injury.* Retrieved from www.old.nichcy.or/pubs/factshe/fsl8txt.htm

National Down Syndrome Society. (2009). *Myths and truths.* Retrieved from www.ndss.org/index.php?view=article&catid=35%3Aabout-down-syndrome&id

National Federation of the Blind. (2009). *Technology resource list.* Retrieved from www.nfb.org/nfb/Technology_Resource_List1.asp

National Fragile X Foundation. (2009). *What is Fragile X?* Retrieved from www.fragilex.org/html/what.htm

National Health Information Center. (2004). Retrieved from www.health.gov/nhic

National Institute of Mental Health. (2008). *Attention deficit hyperactivity disorder.* Retrieved from www.nimh.nih.gov/health/publications/adhd

National Institute of Mental Health. (2009a). *Anxiety disorders.* Retrieved from www.nimh.nih.gov/health/topics/anxiety-disorders/index/shtml

National Institute of Mental Health. (2009b). *Bipolar disorder in children and teens.* Retrieved from www.imh.nih.gov/health/publications/bipolar-disorder-in-children-and-teens-easy-to-read/

National Institute of Mental Health. (2009c). *Schizophrenia.* Retrieved from www.nimh.nih.gov/health/topics/schizophrenia/index.shtml

National Institutes of Health and Human Development. (2009). *Fragile X syndrome.* Retrieved from www.nichd.nih.gov/health/topics/fragile_x_syndrome.cfm?renderforprint=1

National Institutes of Health. (2001). *Rett syndrome—Autism research at the NICHD* (01-4960). Washington, DC: U.S. Government Printing Office.

National Joint Committee on Learning Disabilities (NJCLD). (2004). State and district-wide assessments and students with learning disabilities: A guide for states and school districts. *Learning Disability Quarterly, 27,* 67–71.

National Middle School Association. (2006). *Highly qualified: A balanced approach.* Retrieved from www.nmsa.org/portals/o/pdf/about/position_statements/EdWeek.pdf

National Organization on Fetal Alcohol Syndrome. (2009). *FAQs.* Retrieved from www.nofas.org/faqs.aspx?id=9

National Reading Panel. (2000). *Teaching children to read: An evidence-based assessment of the scientific research literature on reading and its implications for reading instruction.* Bethesda, MD: National Institutes of Health, National Institute of Child Health and Human Development.

National Research Council. (2001). *Educating children with autism.* Washington, DC: National Academies Press.

Neal, L. V. I., McCray, A. D., & Webb-Johnson, G. (2001). Teachers' reactions to African American students' movement styles. *Intervention in Clinic and Schools, 36,* 168–174.

Neef, N. A., McCord, B. E., & Ferreri, S. J. (2006). Effects of guided notes versus completed notes during lectures on college students' quiz performance. *Journal of Applied Behavior Analysis, 39,* 123–130.

Nelson, J. R., Stage, S., Duppong-Hurley, K., Synhorst, L., & Epstein, M. (2007). Risk factors predictive of the problem behavior of children at risk for emotional and behavioral disorders. *Exceptional Children, 73,* 367–379.

Nelson, N. W. (1998). *Childhood language disorders in context: Infancy through adolescence* (2nd ed.). Boston: Allyn & Bacon.

Ness, M. K. (2008). Supporting secondary readers: When teachers provide the "what," not the "how." *American Secondary Education, 37,* 80–95.

Neubert, D. A. (2003). The role of assessment in the transition to adult life process for students with disabilities. *Exceptionality, 11*(2), 63–76.

Nieto, S. (1992). *Affirming diversity: The sociopolitical context of multicultural education.* New York: Longman.

Nieto, S. (1994). Lessons from students on creating a chance to dream. *Harvard Educational Review, 64,* 392–426.

Nippold, M. A. (1998). *Later language development: The school-age and adolescent years* (2nd ed.). Austin, TX: PRO-ED.

No Child Left Behind Act of 2001. Pub. L. No. 107-110, 115 Stat. 1425. (2001).

Nordness, P. D. (2005). A comparison of school-based and community-based adherence to wraparound during family planning meetings. *Education and Treatment of Children, 28,* 308–320.

Nunley, K. F. (2006). *Differentiating the high school classroom: Solution strategies for 18 common obstacles.* Thousand Oaks, CA: Corwin Press.

O'Connor, R. (2000). Increasing the intensity of intervention in kindergarten and first grade. *Learning Disabilities Research and Practice, 15,* 43–54.

O'Neill, R. E., Horner, R. H., Albin, R. W., Storey, K., & Sprague, J. R. (1997). *Functional assessment and program development for problem behavior: A practical handbook.* Sycamore, IL: Sycamore Publishing.

O'Reilly, M. F., & Glynn, D. (1995). Using a process social skills training approach with adolescents with mild intellectual disabilities in a high school setting. *Education and Training in Mental Retardation and Developmental Disabilities, 30,* 187–198.

O'Reilly, M. F., Lancioni, G., & Kierans, I. (2000). Teaching leisure social skills to adults with moderate mental retardation: An analysis of acquisition, generalization, and maintenance. *Education and Training in Mental Retardation and Developmental Disabilities, 35,* 250–258.

O'Reilly, M. F., Lancioni, G., Sigafoos, J., O'Donoghue, D., Lacey, C., & Edrisinha, S. (2004). Teaching social skills to adults with intellectual disabilities: A comparison of external control and problem-solving interventions. *Research in Developmental Disabilities, 25,* 399–412.

O'Reilly, M., Sigafoos, J., Lancioni, G., Edrishina, C., & Andrews, A. (2005). An examination of the effects of a classroom activity schedule on levels of self-injury and engagement for a child with severe autism. *Journal of Autism and Developmental Disorders, 35,* 305–311.

O'Shea, D. J., & O'Shea, L. J. (2001). Why learn about students' families. In D. J. O'Shea, L. J. O'Shea, R. Algozzine, & D. J. Hammitte (Eds.), *Families and teachers of individuals with disabilities: Collaborative orientations and responsive practices* (pp. 5–24). Boston: Allyn & Bacon.

Oczkus, L. (2009). *Interactive think aloud lessons: 25 surefire ways to engage students and improve comprehension.* Newark, DE: International Reading Association.

Odom, S. L., Horner, M. E., Snell, M. E., & Blacher, J. (2007). The construct of developmental disabilities. In S. L. Odom, R. H. Horner, M. E. Snell, & J. Blacher (Eds.), *Handbook of developmental disabilities* (pp. 3–14). New York: Guilford Press.

Ogbu, J. U. (1978). *Minority education and caste: The American system in cross-cultural perspective.* New York: Academic Press.

Ogbu, J. U. (1990). Minority education in comparative perspective. *Journal of Negro Education, 59,* 45–57.

Ogbu, J. U. (1992). Understanding cultural diversity and learning. *Educational Researcher, 21*(8), 5–14.

Ogle, D. (1986). KWL: A teaching model that develops active reading of expository text. *The Reading Teacher, 39,* 564–570.

Ogle, D. (1989). Implementing strategic teaching. *Educational Leadership, 46*(4), 47–48, 57–60.

Oishi, S., Slavin, R. E., & Madden, N. A. (1983, April). *Effects of student teams and individualized instruction on cross-race and cross-sex friendships.* Paper presented at the annual meeting of the American Educational Research Association, Montreal, Canada.

Orelove, F. P., Sobsey, D., & Silberman, R. K. (2004). *Educating children with multiple disabilities: A collaborative approach* (4th ed.). Baltimore, MD: Paul H. Brookes.

Osborne, A. G., & DiMattia, P. (1994). The IDEA's least restrictive environment mandate: Legal implications. *Exceptional Children, 61,* 6–14.

OSEP Technical Assistance Center on Positive Behavioral Interventions and Supports. (2009). Reducing behavior problems in the elementary school. Retrieved from www.pbis.org/

Ovando, C. J., & Collier, V. P. (1998). *Bilingual and ESL classrooms: Teaching in multicultural contexts* (2nd ed.). Boston: McGraw-Hill.

Ovando, C. J., Collier, V. P., & Combs, M. C. (2003). *Bilingual and ESL classrooms: Teaching in multicultural contexts* (3rd ed.). Boston: McGraw-Hill.

Ovando, C. J., Collier, V. P., & Combs, M. C. (2006). *Bilingual and ESL classrooms: Teaching in multicultural contexts* (4th ed.). Boston: McGraw-Hill.

Owens, G. (2005). *Book review: The dragons of autism: Autism as a source of wisdom.* Germany: Springer.

Owens, R. E., Jr. (2008). *Language development: An introduction.* Boston: Allyn & Bacon.

Padden, C. A., & Humphries, T. L. (2006). *Inside deaf culture.* Cambridge, MA: Harvard University Press.

Palincsar, A. S. (1986). The role of dialogue in providing scaffolded instruction. *Educational Psychologist, 21*(1/2), 73–98.

Palinscsar, A. S., & Brown, A. L. (1984). The reciprocal teaching of comprehension-fostering and comprehension-monitoring activities. *Cognition and Instruction, 1,* 117–175.

Palmer, J. M., & Yantis, P. A. (1990). *Survey of communication disorders.* Baltimore, MD: Williams & Wilkins.

Pardini, P. (2002). The history of special education. *Rethinking Schools Online, 16*(3), 1.

Park, H. S., & Gaylord-Ross, R. (1989). A problem-solving approach to social skills training in employment settings with mentally retarded youth. *Journal of Applied Behavior Analysis, 22* (4), 373–380.

Park, J., Turnbull, P., & Turnbull, H. R. (2002). Impacts of poverty on quality of life in families of children with disabilities. *Exceptional Children, 68,* 151–170.

Parrish, P. R., & Stodden, R. A. (2009). Aligning assessment and instruction with state standards for children with significant disabilities. *Teaching Exceptional Children, 41,* 46–56.

Passenger, T., Stuart, M., & Terrell, C. (2000). Phonological processing and early literacy. *Journal of Research in Reading, 23*(1), 55–66.

Patterson, D. S., Jolivette, K., & Crosby, S. (2006). Social skills training for students who demonstrate poor self-control. *Beyond Behavior, 15,* 23–27.

Pauk, W. (1989). *How to study in college* (4th ed.). Boston: Houghton Mifflin.

Payne, K. T., & Taylor, O. L. (1998). Communication differences and disorders. In G. H. Shames, E. H. Wiig, & W. A. Secord (Eds.), *Human communication disorders: An introduction* (5th ed., pp. 118–154). Boston: Allyn & Bacon.

Peal, E., & Lambert, W. (1962). The relation of bilingualism to intelligence. *Psychological Monographs, 7*(546), 1–12.

Pearson, P. D., Hiebert, E. H., & Kamil, M. L. (2007). Theory and research into practice. Vocabulary assessment: What we know and need to learn. *Reading Research Quarterly, 42*(2), 282–296.

Pearson, P. D., & Johnson, D. D. (1978). *Teaching reading comprehension.* New York: Holt, Rinehart & Winston.

Pecyna-Rhyner, P., Lehr, D., & Pudlas, K. (1990). An analysis of teacher responsiveness to communicative initiations of children with handicaps. *Language, Speech, and Hearing Services in Schools, 21,* 91–97.

Pedulla, J. J., Abrams, L. M., Madaus, G. F., Russell, M. K., Ramos, M. A., & Miao, J. (2003). *Perceived effects of state-mandated testing programs on teaching and learning: Findings from a national survey of teachers.* Boston: National Board on Educational Testing and Public Policy, Boston College.

Pennington, B. F., Groisser, D., & Welsh, M. C. (1993). Contrasting cognitive deficits in attention deficit hyperactivity disorder versus reading disability. *Developmental Psychology, 29,* 511–523.

Peregoy, S. F., & Boyle, O. F. (2005). *Reading, writing, and learning in ESL: A resource book for K–12 teachers* (4th ed.). Boston: Allyn & Bacon.

Peterson, P. E., & Hess, F. M. (2008). Few states set world-class standards. *Education Next, 8,* 70–73.

Peterson, S. K., Mercer, C. D., & O'Shea, L. (1988). Teaching learning disabled students place value using the concrete to abstract sequence. *Learning Disabilities Research, 4,* 52–56.

Pickett, A. L. (2008). Roles and responsibilities of paraeducators working with learners with developmental disabilities: Translating research into practice. In H. P. Parette & G. R. Peterson-Karlan (Eds.), *Research-based practices in developmental disabilities* (2nd ed., pp. 501–520). Austin, TX: PRO-ED.

Pierangelo, R., & Giuliani, G. (2007). *The educator's diagnostic manual of disabilities and disorders.* San Francisco, CA: Wiley.

Pierce, C. D., Reid, R., & Epstein, M. H. (2004). Teacher-mediated interventions for children with EBD and their academic outcomes. *Remedial and Special Education, 25*(3), 175–188.

Pinkus, L. (2006). *Who's counted? Who's counting? Understanding high school graduation rates.* Washington, DC: Alliance for Excellent Education.

Pisecco, S., Baker, D. B., Silva, P. A., & Brooke, M. (2001). Boys with reading disabilities and/or ADHD: Distinctions in early childhood. *Journal of Learning Disabilities, 34,* 98–106.

Plumley, K. (2008). *Assistive listening devices in the classroom.* Retrieved from www.deaf-students.suite101.com/article.cfm/assistive_listening_devices_in_the_classroom

Pocock, A., Lambros, S., Karvonen, M., Test, D. W., Algozzine, B., Wood, W., & Martin, J. E. (2002). Successful strategies for promoting self-advocacy among students with LD: The LEAD group. *Intervention in School and Clinic, 37,* 209–216.

Polsgrove, L., & Smith, S. W. (2004). Informed practice in teaching self-control to children with emotional and behavioral disorders. In R. B. Rutherford, M. M. Quinn, & S. R. Mathur (Eds.), *Handbook of research in emotional and behavioral disorders* (pp. 399–425). New York: Guilford Press.

Portway, S., & Johnson, B. (2005). Do you know I have Asperger's syndrome? Risks of a non-obvious disability. *Health, Risk, and Society, 7,* 73–83.

Prater, M. A., & Dyches, T. T. (2008). Books that portray characters with disabilities: A topic 25 list for children and young adults. *Teaching Exceptional Children, 40,* 32–38.

Presley, I., & D'Andrea, M. (2009). *Assistive technology for students who are blind or visually impaired: A guide to assessment.* New York: American Federation for the Blind Press.

Pressley, M. (in press). Balanced elementary literacy instruction in the United States: A personal perspective. In N. Bascia, A. Cumming, A. Datnow, K. Leithwood, & D. Livingstone (Eds.), *International handbook on educational policy.* Dordrecht: Kluwer.

Pressley, M., & Harris, K. R. (2006). Cognitive strategies instruction: From basic research to classroom instruction. In P. A. Alexander & P. Winne (Eds.), *Handbook of educational psychology* (2nd ed., pp. 265–286). New York: Macmillan.

Pressley, M., Wharton-McDonald, R., Allington, R., Block, C. C., Morrow, L., Tracey, D., Baker, K., Brooks, G., Cronin, J., Nelson, E., & Woo, D. (2001). A study of effective first-grade literacy instruction. *Scientific Studies of Reading, 5,* 35–58.

Pugach, M. C., & Johnson, L. J. (1995). *Collaborative practitioners, collaborative schools.* Denver, CO: Love.

Pugach, M. C., & Johnson, L. J. (2002). *Collaborative practitioners, collaborative schools* (2nd ed.). Denver, CO: Love.

Quay, H. C., & Werry, J. S. (1986). *Psychopathological disorders of childhood.* New York: Wiley.

Quinn, M. M., Rutherford, R. R., Leone, P. E., Osher, D. M., & Poirier, J. M. (2005) Youth with disabilities in juvenile corrections: A national survey. *Exceptional Children, 71*(3), 339–345.

Rafferty, L. A. (2007). "They just won't listen to me": A teacher's guide to positive behavioral interventions. *Childhood Education 84,* 102–105.

Ramirez, J. D., & Merino, B. J. (1990). Classroom talk in English immersion, early-exit & late-exit transition bilingual education programs. In R. Jacobson & C. Faltis (Eds.), *Language distribution issues in bilingual schooling.* Clevedon, England: Multilingual Matters.

Ramirez, M. (1992, Winter/Spring). Executive summary, final report: Longitudinal study of structured English immersion strategy, early-exit and late-exit transitional bilingual education programs for language-minority children. *Bilingual Research Journal, 16*(1/2), 1–62.

Raphael, T. E. (1982). Question-answering strategies for children. *The Reading Teacher, 36,* 188.

Raphael, T. E. (1984). Teaching learners about sources of information for answering comprehension questions. *Journal of Reading, 27,* 303–311.

Raphael, T. E. (1986). Teaching question–answer relationships revisited. *The Reading Teacher, 39*(6), 516–523.

Raskind, M. H., Goldberg, R. J., Higgins, E. L., & Herman, K. L. (1999). Patterns of change and predictors of success in individuals with learning disabilities: Results from a twenty-year longitudinal study. *Learning Disabilities Research and Practice, 14*(1), 35–49.

Rathvon, N. (2004). *Early reading assessment: A practitioner's handbook.* New York: Guilford Press.

Ravitch, D. (1995). *National standards in American education: A citizen's guide.* Washington, DC: Brookings Institution.

Raygor, A. L. (1977). The Raygor readability estimate: A quick and easy way to determine difficulty. In P. D. Pearson (Ed.), *Reading: Theory, research and practice: Twenty-sixth yearbook of the National Reading Conference* (pp. 259–263). Clemson, SC: National Reading Conference.

Rayner, G. (2005). Meeting the educational needs of the student with Asperger syndrome through assessment, advocacy, and accommodations. In K. P. Stoddart (Ed.), *Children, youth and adults with Asperger syndrome: Integrating multiple perspectives* (pp. 184–196). London: Jessica Kingsley.

Reis, S. M., & Renzulli, J. S. (2005). *Curriculum compacting: An easy start to differentiating instruction.* Waco, TX: Prufrock Press.

Resnick, L., & Zurawsky, C. (2005). Standards-based reform and accountability: Getting Back on course. *American Educator,* 1–13.

Reutzel, D. R., & Hollingsworth, P. M. (1993). Effects of fluency training on second graders' reading comprehension. *Journal of Educational Research, 86,* 325–331.

Reyes, E. I., & Bos, C. S. (1998). Interactive semantic mapping and charting: Enhancing content-area learning for language-minority students. In R. M. Gersten & R. T. Jimenez (Eds.), *Promoting learning for culturally and linguistically diverse students* (pp. 133–150). Belmont, CA: Wadsworth.

Reyhner, J. (1992). American Indian bilingual education: The White House conference on Indian education and tribal college movement. *NABE News, 15*(7), 7–18.

Richard-Amato, P. A., & Snow, M. A. (1992). Strategies for content-area teachers. In P. A. Richard-Amato & M. A. Snow (Eds.), *The multicultural classroom: Readings for content-area teachers* (pp. 145–163). White Plains, NY: Longman.

Rinaldi, C., & Samson, J. (2008). English language learners and response to intervention: Referral considerations. *Teaching Exceptional Children, 40,* 6–14.

Rivera, D., & Deutsch-Smith, D. (1988). Using a demonstration strategy to teach midschool students with learning disabilities to compute long division. *Journal of Learning Disabilities, 21,* 71–81.

Robinson, F. P. (1941). *Effective study.* New York: Harper & Row.

Robinson, N., Zigler, E., & Gallagher, J. (2000). Two tails of the normal curve: Similarities and differences in the study of mental retardation and giftedness. *American Psychologist, 55,* 1413–1424.

Rock, M. L. (2005). Use of strategic self-monitoring to enhance academic engagement, productivity, and accuracy of students with and without exceptionalities. *Journal of Positive Behavior Interventions, 7*(1), 3–17.

Roeber, E. (2002). *Setting standards on alternate assessments* (Synthesis Report 42). Minneapolis, MN: University of Minnesota, National Center on Educational Outcomes. Retrieved from http://education.umn.edu/NCEO/OnlinePubs/Synthesis42.html

Roisen, N. J., Blondis, T. A., Irwin, M., & Stein, M. (1994). Adaptive functioning in children with attention-deficit hyperactivity disorder. *Archives of Pediatric and Adolescent Medicine, 148,* 1037–1088.

Rose, D. H., & Meyer, A. (2002). *Teaching every student in the digital age: Universal design for learning.* Alexandria, VA: ASCD Publications.

Rose, M. C. (2005). *Handle with care: The difficult parent–teacher conference.* Retrieved from http://teacher.scholastic.com/products/instructor/handlewithcare.htm

Rosel, J., Caballer, A., Jara, P., & Oliver, J. C. (2005). Verbalism in the narrative language of children who are blind and sighted. *Journal of Visual Impairment and Blindness, 99,* 413–425.

Rosenberg, M. S., Wilson, R., Maheady, L., & Sindelar, P. T. (1997). *Educating students with behavior disorders* (2nd ed.). Boston: Allyn & Bacon.

Rosenshine, B., & Meister, C. (1994). Reciprocal teaching: A review of the research. *Review of Educational Research, 64,* 479–530.

Roth, R. M., & Saykin, A. J. (2004). Executive dysfunction in attention-deficit/hyperactivity disorder: Cognitive and neuroimaging findings. *Psychiatric Clinics of North America, 27*(1): 83-96.

Rourke, B. P. (1993). Arithmetic disabilities, specific and otherwise: A neuropsychological perspective. *Journal of Learning Disabilities, 26*(4), 214–226.

Rubalcava, M. (1991). *Locating transformative teaching in multicultural education.* Unpublished manuscript, Department of Anthropology, Special Project, University of California, Berkeley.

Rubia, K., Oosterlaan, J., Sergeant, J. A., Brandeis, D., & van Leeuwen, T. (1998). Attention deficit/hyperactivity disorder—From brain dysfunctions to behavior. *Behavioral Brain Research, 94,* 1–10.

Rubin, H. (1988). Morphological knowledge and early writing ability. *Language and Speech, 31,* 337–355.

Ruhl, K. L., Hughes, C. A., & Gajar, A. H. (1990). Efficacy of the pause procedure for enhancing learning disabled and nondisabled college students' long- and short-term recall of facts presented through lecture. *Learning Disability Quarterly, 13,* 55–64.

Ruiz, N. T., Garcia, E., & Figueroa, R. A. (1996). *The OLE curriculum guide: Creating optimal learning environments for students from diverse backgrounds in special and general education.* Sacramento, CA: California Department of Education, Specialized Programs Branch.

Rummel, N., Levin, J. R., & Woodward, M. M. (2003). Do pictorial mnemonic text-learning aids give students something worth writing about? *Journal of Educational Psychology, 95,* 327–334.

Rutter, M. (2005). Aetiology of autism: Findings and questions. *Journal of Intellectual Disability Research, 49,* 231–238.

Ryan, A. L., Halsey, H. N., & Matthews, W. J. (2003). Using functional assessment to promote desirable student behavior in schools. *Teaching Exceptional Children, 35*(5), 8–15.

Ryan, J. B., Pierce, C. D., & Mooney, P. (2008). Evidence-based teaching strategies for students with EBD. *Beyond Behavior,* 22–29.

Sacks, G., & Kern, L. (2008). A comparison of quality of life variables for students with emotional and behavioral disorders and students without disabilities. *Journal of Behavioral Education, 17,* 111–127.

Sacks, S. Z., & Wolffe, K. E. (2006). *Teaching social skills to students with visual impairments: From theory to practice.* New York: American Federation for the Blind Press.

Saddler, B. (2004). 20 ways to improve writing ability. *Intervention in School and Clinic, 39,* 310–314.

Salend, S. J. (1994). *Effective mainstreaming: Creative inclusive classrooms* (2nd ed.). New York: Macmillan.

Salend, S. J. (2004). Fostering inclusive values in children: What families can do. *Teaching Exceptional Children, 37,* 64–69.

Salend, S. J. (2008). Determining appropriate testing accommodations. *Teaching Exceptional Children, 40*(4), 4–22.

Salend, S. J., & Duhaney, L. M. (2002). What do families have to say about inclusion?: How to pay attention and get results. *Teaching Exceptional Children, 35*(1), 62–66.

Salend, S. J., & Duhaney, L. M. (2004). Understanding and addressing the disproportionate representation of students of color in special education. *Intervention in School and Clinic, 40,* 213–221.

Salend, S. J., Duhaney, D., Anderson, D. J., & Gottschalk, C. (2004). Using the Internet to improve homework communication and completion. *Teaching Exceptional Children, 36,* 64–73.

Salend, S. J., Duhaney, L. M., & Montgomery, W. (2002). A comprehensive approach to identifying and addressing issues of disproportionate representation. *Remedial and Special Education, 23,* 289–299.

Salend, S. J., Elhoweris, H., & Van Garderen, D. (2003). Educational interventions for students with ADD. *Intervention in School and Clinic, 38*(5), 280–289.

Salend, S. J., & Garrick Duhaney, L. M. (2002). What do families have to say about inclusion? How to pay attention and get results. *Teaching Exceptional Children, 35,* 62–66.

Samuels, C. A. (2007). Minorities in special education studied by U.S. panel. *Education Week, 27,* 18.

Sandomierski, T., Kincaid, D., & Algozzine, B. (2009). Response to intervention and positive behavior support: Brothers from different mothers or different misters? *PBIS Newsletter, 4,* 1–11.

Sands, D. J., Kozleski, E. B., & French, N. K. (2000). *Inclusive education in the 21st century.* Belmont, CA: Wadsworth.

Santa, C. (1988). *Content reading including secondary systems.* Dubuque, IA: Kendall Hunt.

Santa, C. M., Havens, L. T., & Valdes, B. J. (2004). *Project CRISS: Creating independence through student-owned strategies* (3rd ed.). Dubuque, IA: Kendall Hunt.

Sattler, J. M. (1988). *Assessment of children* (3rd ed.). San Diego: Jerome Sattler.

Saxon, J. (2003). *Algebra* (3rd ed.). Norman: OK: Saxon.

Scammacca, N., Roberts, G., Vaughn, S., Edmonds, M., Wexler, J., Reutebuch, C. K., & Torgesen, J. (2007). *Interventions for adolescent struggling readers: A meta-analysis with implications for practice.* Portsmouth, NH: RMC Research Corporation, Center on Instruction.

Schalock, R. L., Luckasson, R. A., & Shogren, K. A. (2007). The renaming of mental retardation: Understanding the change to the term *intellectual disability. Intellectual and Developmental Disabilities, 45,* 116–124.

Schaps, E. (2003). Creating a school community. *Education Leadership 60,* 31–33.

Schatschneider, C., Fletcher, J. M., Francis, D. J., Carlson, C. D., & Foorman, B. R. (2004). Kindergarten predictions of reading skills: A longitudinal comparative analysis. *Journal of Educational Psychology, 96*(2), 265–282.

Schmidt, P. R. (1999). KWLQ: Inquiry and literacy learning in science. *The Reading Teacher, 52*(7), 789–792.

Schmoker, M., & Marzano, R. J. (1999). Realizing the promise of standards-based education. *Educational Leadership, 56,* 17–21.

Schoenfeld, N. A., & Janney, D. M. (2008). Identification and treatment of anxiety in students with emotional or behavioral disorders: A review of the literature. *Education and Treatment of Children, 31,* 583–610.

Schumm, J. S. (2001). *School power: Study skill strategies for succeeding in school.* Minneapolis, MN: Free Spirit.

Schumm, J. S. (2006). Putting it all together in classroom and resource settings: Organizational frameworks for differentiated instruction. In J. S. Schumm (Ed.), *Reading assessment and instruction for all learners* (pp. 460–492). New York: Guilford Press.

Schumm, J. S., & Avalos, M. A. (2009). Responsible differentiated instruction for the adolescent learner: Promises, pitfalls, and possibilities. In K. D. Wood & W. E. Blanton (Eds.), *Literacy instruction for adolescents: Research-based practices* (pp. 144–169). New York: Guilford Press.

Schumm, J. S., Hughes, M. T., & Arguelles, M. E. (2001). Co-teaching: It takes more than ESP. In V. J. Risko & K. Bromley (Eds.), *Collaboration for diverse learners* (pp. 52–69). Newark, DE: International Reading Association.

Schumm, J. S., & Mangrum, C. T. (1991). FLIP: A framework for content area reading. *Journal of Reading, 35*(2), 120–124.

Schumm, J. S., Moody, S. W., & Vaughn, S. R. (2000). Grouping for reading instruction: Does one size fit all? *Journal of Learning Disabilities, 33*(5), 477–488.

Schumm, J. S., & Post, S. A. (1997). *Executive learning: Successful strategies for college reading and studying.* Upper Saddle River, NJ: Prentice Hall.

Schumm, J. S., & Vaughn, S. (1991). Making adaptations for mainstreamed students: General classroom teachers' perspectives. *Remedial and Special Education, 12*(4), 18–27.

Schumm, J. S., & Vaughn, S. (1992). Planning for mainstreamed special education students: Perceptions of general classroom teachers. *Exceptionality, 3,* 81–98.

Schumm, J. S., Vaughn, S., Haager, D., McDowell, D., Rothlein, L., & Saumell, L. (1995a). General education teacher planning: What can students with learning disabilities expect? *Exceptional Children, 61*(4), 335–352.

Schumm, J. S., Vaughn, S., & Harris, J. (1997). Pyramid power for collaborative planning. *Teaching Exceptional Children, 29*(6), 62–66.

Schumm, J. S., Vaughn, S., & Leavell, A. G. (1994). Planning pyramid: A framework for planning for diverse student needs during content area instruction. *The Reading Teacher, 47*(8), 608–615.

Schumm, J. S., Vaughn, S., & Saumell, L. (1992). What teachers do when the textbook is tough: Students speak out. *Journal of Reading Behavior, 24*(4), 481–503.

Schur, L. A. (2003). Barriers or opportunities? The causes of contingent and part-time work among people with disabilities. *Industrial Relations, 42*(4), 589–622.

Schuster, J. W., Stevens, K. B., & Doak, P. K. (1990). Using constant time delay to teach word definitions. *Journal of Special Education, 24,* 306–318.

Schwartz, A. A., Jacobson, J. W., & Holburn, S. C. (2000). Defining person centeredness: Results of two consensus methods. *Journal of Education and Training in Mental Retardation and Developmental Disabilities, 35*(3), 235–249.

Scott, B. J., & Vitale, M. R. (2003) Teaching the writing process to students with LD. *Intervention in School and Clinic, 38,* 220–224.

Scott, T. M., Park, K. L., Swain-Bradway, J., & Landers, E. (2007). Positive behavior support in the classroom: Facilitating behaviorally inclusive learning environments. *International Journal of Behavioral Consultation and Therapy, 3,* 223–235.

Scruggs, T. E., Mastropieri, M. A., & Okolo, C. H. (2008). Science and social studies for students with disabilities. *Focus on Exceptional Children, 41,* 1–24.

Sealey-Ruiz, Y. (2005). Spoken soul: The language of Black imagination and reality. *The Education Forum, 70,* 37–46.

Seals, L. M., Pollard-Durodola, S. D., Foorman, B. R., & Bradley, A. M. (2007). *Vocabulary power.* Baltimore, MD: Paul H. Brookes.

Searfoss, L. W., & Readence, J. E. (1989). *Helping children learn to read* (2nd ed.). Englewood Cliffs, NJ: Prentice Hall.

Seltzer, M. M., Greenburg, J. S., Floyd, F. J., Pettee, Y., & Hong, J. (2001). Life course impacts of parenting a child with disability. *American Journal on Mental Retardation, 106,* 265–286.

Senokossoff, G. W., & Stoddard, K. (2009). Swimming in deep water: Childhood bipolar disorder. *Preventing School Failure, 53,* 89–93.

Seuss, Dr. (1974). *There's a wocket in my pocket.* New York: Random House.

Sexson, S. B., & Madan-Swain, A. (1993). School reentry for the child with chronic illness. *Journal of Learning Disabilities, 26,* 115–125.

Seymour, P. H. K. (2006). Framework for beginning reading in different orthographies. In R. Maltesha Joshi & P. G. Aaron (Eds.), *Handbook of orthography and literacy.* Mahwah, NJ: Erlbaum.

Shaftel, J., Pass, L., & Schnabel, S. (2005, Jan./Feb.). Math games for adolescents. *Teaching Exceptional Children,* 25–28.

Shalaway, L. (2005). *Planning for parent conferences.* Retrieved from http://teacher.scholastic.com/products/instructor/planning_parent_conf.htm

Shaywitz, S. (2003). *Overcoming dyslexia: A new and complete science-based program for reading problems as any level.* New York: Alfred A. Knopf.

Shaywitz, S., & Shaywitz, B. (1988). Attention deficit disorder: Current perspectives. In J. Kavanagh & J. Truss (Eds.), *Learning disabilities: Proceedings of the national conference* (pp. 369–567). Parkton, MD: York Press.

Shippen, M. E., Simpson, R. G., & Crites, S. A. (2003). A practical guide to functional behavioral assessment. *Teaching Exceptional Children, 35*(5), 36–44.

Sigafoos, J., Arthur, M., & O'Reilly, M. F. (2003). *Challenging behavior and developmental disability.* London: Whurr Publishers. (Distributed in the United States by Brookes.)

Sigafoos, J., Green, V., Schlosser, R., O'Reilly, M. F., Lancioni, G. E., Rispoli, M., & Lang, R. (2009). Communication intervention in Rett syndrome. *Research in Autism Spectrum Disorders.* [not yet published]

Simmonds, E. P. (1992). The effects of teacher training and implementation of two methods for improving the comprehension of students with learning disabilities. *Learning Disabilities Research & Practice, 7*(4), 194–198.

Simmons, D., Hairrell, A., Edmonds, M. S., & Vaughn, S. (2008). *Teacher quality research—Reading/writing.* Washington, DC: Institute of Education Sciences.

Simonsen, B., Sugai, G., & Negron, M. (2008). Schoolwide positive behavior supports: Primary systems and practices. *Teaching Exceptional Children, 40,* 32–40.

Simpson, R. L. (1988). Needs of parents and families whose children have learning and behavior problems. *Behavioral Disorders, 14,* 40–47.

Singer, H. (1986). Friendly texts: Description and criteria. In E. K. Dishner, T. W. Bean, J. E. Readence, & D. W. Moore (Eds.), *Reading in the content areas: Improving classroom instruction* (2nd ed., pp. 112–128). Dubuque, IA: Kendall Hunt.

Skiba, R. J., Simmons, A. B., Ritter, S., Gibb, A. C., Rausch, M. K., Cuadrado, J., & Chung, C. (2008). Achieving equity in special education: History, status, and current challenges. *Exceptional Children, 74,* 264–288.

Skoulos, V., & Shicktryon, G. (2007). Social skills of adolescents in special education who display symptoms of oppositional defiant disorder. *American Secondary Education, 35,* 103–115.

Skutnabb-Kangas, T. (1981, February). *Linguistic genocide and bilingual education.* Paper presented at the California Association for Bilingual Education, Anaheim, California.

Slavin, R. E. (1991). Synthesis of research on cooperative learning. *Educational Leadership, 48*(5), 71–82.

Slavin, R. E. (1995). *Cooperative learning: Theory, research and practice* (2nd ed). Boston: Allyn & Bacon.

Slavin, R. E., & Cheung, A. (2005). A synthesis of research on language of reading instruction for English language learners. *Review of Educational Research, 75,* 247–284.

Slavin, R. E., Madden, N. A., & Leavey, M. (1984). Effects of team assisted individualization on the mathematics achievement of academically handicapped and nonhandicapped students. *Journal of Educational Psychology, 76*(5), 813–819.

Smit, A. B. (1993). Phonological error distributions in the Iowa-Nebraska articulation norms project: Word-initial consonant clusters. *Journal of Speech and Hearing Research, 36,* 931–947.

Smith, C. R. (1998). From gibberish to phonemic awareness: Effective decoding instruction. *Teaching Exceptional Children, 30*(6), 20–25.

Smith, J. O., & Lovitt, T. C. (1982). *Computational arithmetic program.* Austin, TX: PRO-ED.

Smith, T. E. C. (2008). Developmental disabilities: Definition, description, and directions. In H. P. Parette & G. R. Peterson-Karlan (Eds.), *Research-based practices in developmental disabilities* (2nd ed., pp. 59–74). Austin, TX: PRO-ED.

Smith, T. W., & Lambie, G. W. (2005, January). Teachers' responsibilities when adolescent abuse and neglect are suspected. *Middle School Journal, 36*(3), 33–40.

Snow, C. E., Burns, M. S., & Griffin, P. (Eds.). (1998). *Preventing reading difficulties in young children.* Washington, DC: National Academies Press.

Snow, C. E., Porche, M. V., Tabors, P. O., & Harris, S. R. (2007). *Is literacy enough?* Baltimore, MD: Paul H. Brookes.

Sobsey, D., & Wolf-Schein, E. G. (1996). Sensory impairments. In F. P. Orelove & D. Sobsey (Eds.), *Educating children with multiple disabilities: A transdisciplinary approach* (3rd ed.). Baltimore, MD: Paul H. Brookes.

Soller, J. (2003). Re-occurring questions about giftedness and the connections to myths and realities. *Gifted and Talented, 7,* 42–48.

Soukup, J. H., Wehmeyer, M. L., Bashinski, S. M., & Bovaird, J. (2007). Classroom variables and access to the general education curriculum of students with intellectual and developmental disabilities. *Exceptional Children, 74,* 101–120.

Sparks, R. L., Javorsky, J., & Philips, L. (2004). College students classified with ADHD and the foreign language requirement. *Journal of Learning Disabilities, 37*(2), 169–180.

Sparks, S. (2008). Culturally and linguistically diverse learners with developmental disabilities. In H. P. Parette & G. R. Peterson-Karlan (Eds.), *Research-based practices in developmental disabilities* (2nd ed., pp. 125–141). Austin, TX: PRO-ED.

Spear-Swerling, L. (2006). *The importance of teaching handwriting.* Retrieved from http://www.ldonline.org/spearswerling/10521

Speckman, N. J., Goldberg, R. J., & Herman, K. L. (1993). An exploration of risk and resilience in the lives of individuals with learning disabilities. *Learning Disabilities Research and Practice, 8,* 11–18.

Speece, D. L. (1994). The role of classification in learning disabilities. In S. Vaughn & C. S. Bos (Eds.), *Research issues in learning disabilities: Theory, methodology, assessment, and ethics* (pp. 69–82). New York: Springer-Verlag.

Speece, D. L., Roth, F. P., & Cooper, D. H. (1999). The relevance of oral language skills to early literacy: A multivariate analysis. *Applied Psycholinguistics, 20*(2), 167–190.

Spina Bifida Foundation. (2009). *FAQ about spina bifida.* Retrieved from www.spinabifidaassociation.org/site/LiKWL7PLLrF/b.2642327/k.5899/FAQ_About_Spina_Bifida.htm

Stach, B. (1998). *Clinical audiology: An introduction.* San Diego, CA: Singular Publications.

Stahl, S. (2004). *The promise of accessible textbooks: Increased achievement for all students.* Wakefield, MA: National Center on Accessing the General Curriculum. Retrieved from www.cast.org/publications/ncac/ncac_accessible.html

Stahl, S. A. (1983). Differential word knowledge and reading comprehension. *Journal of Reading Behavior, 15*(4), 33–50.

Stahl, S. A. (2003). How words are learned incrementally over multiple exposures. *American Educator, 27*(1), 18–19.

Stainback, S., & Stainback, W. (1992). *Curriculum consideration in inclusive classrooms: Facilitating learning for all students.* Baltimore, MD: Paul H. Brookes.

Stanford, P. (2003). Multiple intelligence for every classroom. *Intervention in School and Clinic, 39,* 80–85.

Stanovich, K. E. (1986). Cognitive processes and the reading problems of learning-disabled children: Evaluating the assumption of specificity. In J. K. Torgesen & B. Y. L. Wong (Eds.), *Psychological and educational perspectives on learning disabilities* (pp. 87–131). Orlando, FL: Academic Press.

Stanovich, K. E. (1992). Speculations on the causes and consequences of individual differences in early reading acquisition. In P. B. Gough, L. D. Ehri, & R. Treiman (Eds.), *Reading acquisition* (pp. 307–342). Mahwah, NJ: Erlbaum.

State of Florida. (2009). *Access points for students with significant cognitive disabilities.* Retrieved from www.floridastandards.org/page24.aspx

Stecker, P. M., & Fuchs, L. S. (2000). Effecting superior achievement using curriculum-based measures: The importance of individualized progress monitoring. *Learning Disabilities Research and Practice, 15,* 128–134.

Steinman, B. A., LeJeune, B. J., & Kimbrough, B. T. (2006). Developmental stages of reading processes in children who are blind and sighted. *Journal of Visual Impairment and Blindness, 100,* 36–46.

Stenhoff, D. M., & Lignugaris/Kraft, B. (2007). A review of the effects of peer tutoring on students with mild disabilities in secondary settings. *Exceptional Children, 74,* 8–30.

Stephens, K. R., & Karnes, F. A. (2000, Winter). State definitions for the gifted and talented revisited. *Exceptional Children, 66*(2), 219–238.

Stevens, K. B., & Schuster, J. W. (1987). Effects of a constant time delay procedure on the written spelling performance of a learning disabled student. *Learning Disability Quarterly, 10,* 9–16.

Stevens, K. B., & Schuster, J. W. (1988). Time delay: Systematic instruction for academic tasks. *Remedial and Special Education, 9*(5), 16–21.

Stevens, S. (2001). A teacher looks at the elementary child with ADHD. In B. P. Guyer (Ed.), *ADHD: Achieving success in school and in life* (pp. 67–80). Boston: Allyn & Bacon.

Still, G. F. (1902). Some abnormal psychical conditions in children. *Lancet, 1,* 1008–1012, 1077–1082, 1163–1168.

Stoneman, Z. (2007). Disabilities research methodology: Current issues and future challenges. In S. L. Odom, R. H. Horner, M. E. Snell, & J. Blacher (Eds.), *Handbook of developmental disabilities* (pp. 35–54). New York: Guilford Press.

Strickland, D. S., Galda, L., & Cullinan, B. E. (2004). *Language arts: Learning and teaching.* Belmont, CA: Thomson/Wadsworth.

Stuart, M. (1999). Getting ready for reading: Early phoneme awareness and phonics training improves reading and spelling in inner-city second language learners. *British Journal of Educational Psychology, 69*(4), 587–605.

Stuebing, K. K., Fletcher, J. M., LeDoux, J. M., Lyon, G. R., Shaywitz, S. E., & Shaywitz, B. A. (2002). Validity of IQ-discrepancy classifications of reading disabilities: A meta-analysis. *American Educational Research Journal, 39,* 469–518.

Sugai, G., Horner, R., & Gresham, F. (2002). Interpreting outcomes of social skills training for students with high-incidence disabilities. *Exceptional Children, 67*(3), 331.

Sutton, S. (2009). School solutions for cyberbullying. *Principal Leadership, 9,* 38–40, 42.

Swain, M. (1986). Communicative competence: Some roles of comprehensible input & comprehensible output in its development. In J. Cummins & M. Swain (Eds.), *Bilingualism in education.* New York: Longman.

Swanson, H. L., & Deshler, D. (2003). Instructing adolescents with learning disabilities: Converting a meta-analysis to practice. *Journal of Learning Disabilities, 36*(2), 124–135.

Swanson, H. L., & Hoskyn, M. (1998). Experimental intervention research on students with learning disabilities. A meta-analysis of treatment outcomes. *Review of Educational Research, 68,* 277–321.

Swanson, H. L., & Saez, L. (2003). Memory difficulties in children and adults with learning disabilities. In H. L. Swanson, K. R. Harris, & S. Graham (Eds.), *Handbook of learning disabilities* (pp. 182–198). New York: Guilford Press.

Swanson, H. L., & Siegel, L. (2001). Learning disabilities and working memory deficit. *Educational Psychology, 7,* 1–48.

Swanson, H. L., Hoskyn, M., & Lee, C. (1999). *Interventions for students with learning disabilities: A meta-analysis of treatment outcomes.* New York: Guilford Press.

Swisher, K., & Deyhle, D. (1992). Adapting instruction to culture. In J. Reyhner (Ed.), *Teaching American Indian students* (pp. 81–95). Norman, OK: University of Oklahoma Press.

Sze, S., & Valentin, S. (2007). Self-concept and children with disabilities. *Education, 27,* 552–557.

Tacket, K. (2009). *Response to intervention: Case studies* (Doctoral dissertation). University of Texas, Austin.

TASH. (2000). *TASH resolution on the people for whom TASH advocates.* Retrieved from www.tash.org/resolutions/res02advocate.htm

Taylor, B. (2008). Tier 1: Effective classroom reading instruction in the elementary grades. In D. Fuchs, L. S. Fuchs, & S. Vaughn (Eds.), *Response to intervention: A framework for reading educators* (pp. 5–25). Newark, DE: International Reading Association.

Taylor, B., Harris, L. A., & Pearson, P. D. (1988). *Reading difficulties: Instruction and assessment.* New York: Random House.

Test, D. W., Mason, C., Konrad, M., Neale, M., & Wood, W. M. (2004). Student involvement in individual education program meetings. *Exceptional Children, 70*(4), 391–412.

Tharp, R. G., Estrada, P., Dalton, S. S., & Yamaguchi, L. (1999). *Teaching transformed: Achieving excellence, fairness, inclusion, and harmony.* Boulder, CO: Westview Press.

The Association for Persons with Severe Handicaps (TASH). (2000). *TASH resolution on the people for whom TASH advocates.* Retrieved from www.tash.org/IRR/resolutions/res02advocate.htm

Thomas, C. C., Correa, V. I., & Morsink, C. V. (2001). *Interactive teaming: Consultation and collaboration in special programs* (3rd ed.). Upper Saddle River, NJ: Prentice Hall.

Thomas, W. P., & Collier, V. P. (1997). Two languages are better than one. *Educational Leadership, 55*(4), 23–26.

Thompson, J. R., & Wehmeyer, M. L. (2008). Historical and legal issues in developmental disabilities. In H. P. Parette & G. R. Peterson-Karlan (Eds.), *Research-based practices in developmental disabilities* (2nd ed., pp. 13–42). Austin, TX: PRO-ED.

Thompson, J., Bryant, B. R., Campbell, E. M., Craig, E. M., Hughes, C., Rotholz, D. A., Schalock, R. L., & Whemeyer, M. L. (2004). *Supports intensity scale manual.* Washington, DC: American Association for Mental Retardation.

Thornberry, T. P., Huizinga, D., & Loeber, R. (2004). The causes and correlates studies: Findings and policy implications. *Juvenile Justice, 10*(1), 3–19.

Thousand, J., Rosenberg, R., Bishop, K., & Villa, R. (1997). The evolution of secondary inclusion. *Remedial and Special Education, 18*(5), 270–284.

Thurlow, M. L., Elliott, J. L., & Ysseldyke, J. E. (2002). *Testing students with disabilities: Practical strategies for complying with district and state requirements.* Thousand Oaks, CA: Corwin Press.

Tiedt, P. L., & Tiedt, I. M. (2006). *Multicultural teaching: A handbook of activities, information, and resources* (7th ed.). Boston: Allyn & Bacon.

Tikunoff, W. J. (1983). *Compatibility of the SBIF features with other research instruction of LEP students.* San Francisco: Far West Laboratory.

Tilly, W. D. III, Reschly, D. J., & Grimes, J. (1999). Disability determination in problem solving systems: Conceptual foundations and critical components. In D. J. Reschly, W. D. Tilly, & J. P. Grimes (Eds.), *Special education in transition: Functional assessment and noncategorical programming* (pp. 221–251). Longman, CO: Sopris West.

Todd, A. W., Horner, R. H., & Sugai, G. (2000). Self-monitoring and self-recruited praise: Effects on problem behavior, academic engagement, and work completion in a typical classroom. *Journal of Positive Behavioral Interventions, 1,* 66–76.

Togerson, C. W., Miner, C. A., & Shen, H. (2004). Developing student competence in self-directed IEPs. *Intervention in School & Clinic, 39*(3), 162–167.

Tomlinson, C. A. (2001). *How to differentiate instruction in mixed-ability classrooms* (2nd ed.). Alexandria, VA: Association for Supervision and Curriculum Development.

Tomlinson, C. A. (2003). *Fulfilling the promise of the differentiated classroom: Strategies and tools for responsive teaching.* Alexandria, VA: Association for Supervision and Curriculum Development.

Tomlinson, C. A. (2005). Grading and differentiation: Paradox or good practice? *Theory Into Practice, 44*(2), 262–269.

Tomlinson, C. A., Kaplan, S. N., Renzulli, J. S., Purcell, J. H., Leppien, J. H., & Burns, D. E. (2001). *The parallel curriculum.* Thousand Oaks, CA: Corwin Press.

Torgesen, J. K. (1999). Assessment and instruction for phonemic awareness and word recognition skills. In H. W. Catts & A. G. Kamhi (Eds.), *Language and reading disabilities* (pp. 128–153). Boston: Allyn & Bacon.

Torgesen, J. K., & Burgess, S. R. (1998). Consistency of reading-related phonological processes throughout early childhood: Evidence from longitudinal, correlational and instructional studies. In J. Methsala & L. Ehri (Eds.), *Word recognition in beginning literacy* (pp. 161–188). Mahwah, NJ: Erlbaum.

Torgesen, J. K., Wagner, R. K., & Rashotte, C. A. (1994). Longitudinal studies of phonological processing and reading. *Journal of Learning Disabilities, 27,* 276–286.

Towles-Reeves, E., Kleinert, H., & Muhomba, M. (2009). Alternate assessment: Have we learned anything new? *Exceptional Children, 75,* 233–252.

Townsend, B. L. (2000). The disproportionate discipline of African American learners: Reducing school suspensions and expulsions. *Exceptional Children, 66*(3), 381–391.

Trelease, J. (1995). *The new read-aloud handbook* (4th ed.). New York: Penguin.

Turnbull, A. P., & Turnbull, H. R. (2001). Building reliable alliances. In A. P. Turnbull & H. R. Turnbull (Eds.), *Families, professionals, and exceptionality: Collaborating for empowerment* (4th ed.). Columbus, OH: Merrill/Prentice Hall.

Turnbull, A., & Turnbull, H. R. (2001). *Families, professionals, and exceptionality: Collaborating for empowerment* (4th ed.). Upper Saddle River, NJ: Prentice Hall.

Turnbull, A. P., Turnbull, H. R., Erwin, E. J., & Soodak, L. C. (2007). *Families, professionals, and exceptionality: Positive outcomes through partnership and trust* (5th ed.). Upper Saddle River, NJ: Merrill/Pearson.

Turnbull, A., Turnbull, R., & Wehmeyer, M. L. (2010). Collaborating for exceptional populations. Upper Saddle River, NJ: Merrill/Pearson.

Turnbull, H. R., Stowe, M., & Huerta, N. (2008). *The Individuals With Disabilities Education Act in 2004*. Upper Saddle River, NJ: Prentice Hall.

U.S. Census Bureau. (2008). *An older and more diverse nation by midcentury*. Retrieved from www.census.gov/Press-Release/www/releases/archives/population/012496

U.S. Department of Education. (2002a). *A new era: Revitalizing special education for children and their families.* Jessup, MD: Author.

U.S. Department of Education. (2002b). Retrieved from www.ed.gov

U.S. Department of Education. (2004). *No Child Left Behind: A toolkit for teachers.* Jessup, MD: Author.

U.S. Department of Education. (2005). *To assure the free appropriate public education of all Americans: Twenty-seventh annual report to Congress on the implementation of the Individuals with Disabilities Education Act.* Retrieved from http://www.ed.gov/about/reports/annual/osep/2005/index.html

U.S. Department of Education. (2007a). *27th Annual (2005) report to Congress on the implementation of the Individuals With Disabilities Education Act* (No. ED01CO0082/0008). Washington, DC: Author.

U.S. Department of Education. (2007b). *Individuals With Disabilities Education Act (IDEA) data* (Table 1-3). Washington, DC: Author. [Available online: https://www.ideadata.org/PartBReport.asp]

U.S. Department of Education. (2008). *Foundations for success: The final report of the National Mathematics Advisory Panel.* Jessup, MD: Author.

U.S. Department of Education. (n.d.). *Building the legacy: IDEA 2004.* Retrieved from http://idea.ed.gov

U.S. Department of Health and Human Services. (2009). *Mood disorders.* Retrieved from http://mentalhealth.samhsa.gov/publications/allpubs/KEN98-0049/

Uberti, H. A., Scruggs, T. E., & Mastropieri, M. A. (2003). Keywords make a difference: Mnemonic instruction in inclusive classrooms. *Teaching Exceptional Children, 35,* 56–61.

United Cerebral Palsy. (2009). *Cerebral palsy fact sheet.* Retrieved from www.ucp.org/ucp_general-doc.cfm/1/9/37/37-37/447

Vacca, R. T., & Vacca, J. L. (2005). *Content area reading: Literacy and learning across the curriculum.* Boston: Allyn & Bacon.

Vacca, R. T., & Vacca, J. L. (2008). *Content area reading: Literacy and learning across the curriculum* (9th ed.). Boston: Allyn & Bacon.

van Belle, J., Marks, S., Martin, R., & Chun, M. (2006). Voicing one's dreams: High school

students with developmental disabilities learn about self-advocacy. *Teaching Exceptional Children, 38,* 40–46.

Van der Lee, J. H., Mokkink, L. B., Grootenhuis, M. A., Heymans, H. S., & Offringa, M. (2007). Definitions and measurement of chronic health conditions in childhood. *Journal of the American Medical Association, 297,* 2741–2751.

Van Kleek, A. (1995). Emphasizing form and meaning repeatedly in prereading and early reading instruction. *Topics in Language Disorders, 16,* 27–49.

Van Reusen, A. K., & Bos, C. S. (1990). I PLAN: Helping students communicate in planning conference. *Teaching Exceptional Children, 22*(4), 30–32.

Van Reusen, A. K., & Bos, C. S. (1992). *Use of the goal-regulation strategy to improve the goal attainment of students with learning disabilities* (Final Report). Tucson, AZ: University of Arizona.

Van Reusen, A. K., & Bos, C. S. (1994). Facilitating student participation in individualized education programs through motivation strategy instruction. *Exceptional Children, 60*(5), 466–475.

Van Reusen, A. K., Bos, C. S., Schumaker, J. B., & Deshler, D. D. (1994). *The self-advocacy strategy for education and transition planning.* Lawrence, KS: Edge Enterprises.

Van Tassel-Baska, J., Quek, C., & Feng, A. X. (2007). The development and use of a structured teacher observation scale to assess differentiated best practice. *Roeper Review, 29,* 84–92.

Vanderbilt, A. A. (2005). Designed for teachers: How to implement self-monitoring in the classroom. *Beyond Behavior, 15,* 21–24.

Vandercook, T., York, J., & Forest, M. (1989). The McGill action planning system (MAPS): A strategy for building the vision. *Journal for the Association for Persons With Severe Handicaps, 14,* 205–215.

Vannest, K. J., Temple-Harvey, K. K., & Mason, B. A. (2009). Adequate yearly progress for students with emotional and behavioral disorders through research-based practices. *Preventing School Failure, 53,* 73–83.

Vaughn, B. J., & Horner, R. H. (1997). Identifying instructional tasks that occasion problem behaviors and assessing the effects of student versus teacher choice among these tasks. *Journal of Applied Behavior Analysis, 30,* 299–312.

Vaughn, S., & Bos, C. S. (2009). *Strategies for teaching students with learning and behavior problems* (7th ed.). Boston: Pearson.

Vaughn, S., Elbaum, B., & Boardman, A. G. (2001). The social functioning of students with learning disabilities: Implications for inclusion. *Exceptionality, 9,* 47–65.

Vaughn, S., & Fuchs, L. S. (2003). Redefining learning disabilities as inadequate response to treatment: The promise and potential problems. *Learning Disabilities Research and Practice, 18*(3), 137–146.

Vaughn, S., & Gersten, R. (1998). Productive teaching of English language learners: What we know and still need to know. In R. M. Gersten & R. T. Jimenez (Eds.), *Promoting learning for culturally and linguistically diverse students* (pp. 230–238). Belmont, CA: Wadsworth.

Vaughn, S., Gersten, R., & Chard, D. J. (2000). The underlying message in LD intervention research: Findings from research syntheses. *Exceptional Children, 67*(1), 99–114.

Vaughn, S., & Klingner, J. K. (2007). Response to intervention (RTI): A new era in identifying students with learning disabilities. In D. Haager, J. Klingner, & S. Vaughn (Eds.), *Validated reading practices for three tiers of intervention* (pp. 3–9). Baltimore, MD: Paul H. Brookes.

Vaughn, S., Klingner, J. K., & Bryant, D. P. (2001). Collaborative strategic reading as a means to enhance peer-mediated instruction for reading comprehension and content area learning. *Remedial and Special Education, 22,* 24–38.

Vaughn, S., & Linan-Thompson, S. (2003). What is special about special education for students with learning disabilities? *The Journal of Special Education, 37,* 140–147.

Vaughn, S., Linan-Thompson, S., & Hickman, P. (2003). Response to instruction as a means of identifying students with reading/learning disabilities. *Exceptional Children, 69*(4), 391–409.

Vaughn, S., Linan-Thompson, S., Pollard-Durodola, S. D., Mathes, P. G., & Cardenas-Hagan, E. (2006). Effective interventions for English language learners (Spanish-English) at risk for reading difficulties. In D. K. Dickinson & S. B. Neuman (Eds.), *Handbook of early literacy research* (Vol. 2, pp. 185–197). New York: Guilford Press.

Vaughn, S., Mathes, P. G., Linan-Thompson, S., Cirino, P. T., Carlson, C. D., Pollard-Durodola, S. D., & Francis, D. (2006). Effectiveness of an English intervention for first-grade English language learners at-risk for reading problems. *Elementary School Journal, 107*(2), 153–180.

Vaughn, S., Mathes, P. G., Linan-Thompson, S., & Francis, D. J. (2005). Teaching English language learners at risk for reading disabilities to read: Putting research into practice. *Learning Disabilities Research & Practice, 20*(1), 58–67.

Vaughn, S., & Schumm, J. S. (1994). Middle school teachers' planning for students with learning disabilities. *Remedial and Special Education, 15*(3), 152–161.

Vaughn, S., & Schumm, J. S. (1995). Responsible inclusion for students with learning disabilities. *Journal of Learning Disabilities, 28*(5), 264–270, 290.

Vellutino, F. R., Scanlon, D. M., Sipay, E. R., Small, S. G., Pratt, A., Chen, R., & Denckla, M. B. (1996). Cognitive profiles of difficult-to-remediate and readily remediated poor readers: Early intervention as a vehicle for distinguishing between cognitive and experiential deficits as basic causes of specific reading disability. *Journal of Educational Psychology, 88,* 601–638.

Vellutino, F. R., Scanlon, D. M., Small, S. G., Fanuele, D. P., & Sweeney, J. (2007). Preventing early reading difficulties through kindergarten and first grade intervention: A variant of the three-tier model. In D. Haager, J. Klingner, & S. Vaughn (Eds.), *Validated reading practices for three tiers of intervention.* Baltimore, MD: Paul H. Brookes.

Viadero, D. (2007). Study: Low, high fliers gain less under NCLB. *Education Week, 44,* 7.

Vogel, S. A., Hruby, P. J., & Adelman, P. B. (1993). Educational and psychological factors in successful and unsuccessful college students with learning disabilities. *Learning Disabilities Research and Practice, 8,* 35–43.

Voyager Expanded Learning. (2008). *V-Math: 3–8 Math Intervention.* Dallas, TX: Author.

Vygotsky, L. S. (1978). *Mind in society: The development of higher psychological processes.* Cambridge, MA: MIT Press.

Wagner, E. (2004). Development and implementation of a curriculum to develop social competence for students with visual impairments in Germany. *Journal of Visual Impairment and Blindness, 98,* 703–709.

Wagner, M., Kutash, K., Duchnowski, A. J., Epstein, M. H., & Sumi, W. C. (2005). The children and youth we serve: A national picture of the characteristics of students with emotional disturbances receiving special education. *Journal of Emotional and Behavioral Disorders, 13,* 79–96.

Wagner, R. K., Francis, D. J., & Morris, R. D. (2005). Identifying English language learners with learning disabilities: Key challenges and possible approaches. *Learning Disabilities Research & Practice, 20,* 6–15.

Wagner, R. K., Torgesen, J. K., & Rashotte, C. A. (1999). *Comprehensive test of phonological processing.* Austin, TX: PRO-ED.

Waldron, N. L., & McLeskey, J. (1998). The effects of an inclusive school program on students with mild and severe learning disabilities. *Exceptional Children, 64,* 395–405.

Walker, H. M., Ramsey, E., & Gresham, F. M. (2004). *Antisocial behavior in school: Evidence-based practices* (2nd ed.). Florence, KY: Cengage Learning.

Walker, H. M., & Severson, H. H. (1992). *Systematic screening for behavior disorders* (2nd ed.). Longmont, CO: Sopris West.

Wallach, G. P., & Miller, L. (1988). *Language intervention and academic success.* San Diego, CA: College Hill.

Walsh, J. M., & Jones, B. (2004). New models of cooperative teaching. *Teaching Exceptional Children, 36,* 14–20.

Wanzek, J., & Vaughn, S. (2007). Research-based implications from extensive early reading interventions. *School Psychology Review, 36*(4), 541–561.

Wanzek, J., Vaughn, S., Wexler, J., Swanson, E. A., Edmonds, M., & Kim, A.-H. (2006). A synthesis of spelling and reading interventions and their effects on the spelling outcomes of students with LD. *Journal of Learning Disabilities, 39*(6), 528–543.

Wasburn-Moses, L. (2003). What every special educator should know about high-stakes testing. *Teaching Exceptional Children, 35,* 12–15.

Wehmeyer, M. L. (2007). *Promoting self-determination in students with developmental disabilities.* New York: Guilford Press.

Wehmeyer, M. L., Buntinx, W. H. E., Lachapelle, Y., Luckasson, R. A., Schalock, R., L., & Verdugo, M. A. (2008). The intellectual disability construct and its relation to human functioning. *Intellectual and Developmental Disabilities, 46,* 311–318.

Wehmeyer, M. L., Lattin, D. L., Lapp-Rincker, G., & Agran, M. (2003). Access to the general curriculum of middle school students with mental retardation. *Remedial and Special Education, 24,* 262–272.

Wehmeyer, M. L., Martin, J. E., & Sands, D. J. (2008). Self-determination and students with developmental disabilities. In H. P. Parette & G. R. Peterson-Karlan (Eds.), *Research-based practices in developmental disabilities* (2nd ed., pp. 99–122). Austin, TX: PRO-ED.

Wehmeyer, M. L., Sands, D. J., Knowlton, E., & Kozleski, E. B. (2002). *Teaching students with mental retardation: Providing access to the general curriculum.* Baltimore, MD: Paul H. Brookes.

Wehmeyer, M. L., & Schwartz, M. (1997). Self-determination and positive adult outcomes: A follow-up study of youth with mental retardation and learning disabilities. *Exceptional Children, 63,* 245–255.

Weiner, D. (2005). *One state's story: Access and alignment to the GRADE-LEVEL content for students with significant cognitive disabilities* (Synthesis Report 57). Minneapolis, MN: University of Minnesota, National Center on Educational Outcomes. Retrieved from http://education.umn.edu/NCEO/OnlinePubs/Synthesis57.html

Weintraub, N., & Graham, S. (1998). Writing legibly and quickly: A study of children's ability to adjust their handwriting to meet common classroom demands. *Learning Disabilities Research and Practice, 13,* 146–152.

Weiss, M. P., & Lloyd, J. (2003). Conditions for co-teaching: Lessons from a case study. *Teacher Education and Special Education, 26,* 27–41.

Welch, M. (1992). The P.L.E.A.S.E. strategy: A metacognitive learning strategy for improving the paragraph writing of students with mild learning disabilities. *Learning Disability Quarterly, 15,* 119–128.

Welch, M., & Link, D. P. (1989). *Write, P.L.E.A.S.E.: A strategy for efficient learning and functioning in written expression* (video cassette). Salt Lake City, UT: University of Utah, Department of Special Education, Educational Tele-Communications.

Westling, D. L., & Fox, L. (2009). *Teaching students with severe disabilities* (4th ed.). Englewood, NJ: Prentice-Hall.

Wexler, J., Edmonds, M. S., & Vaughn, S. (2008). Teaching older readers with reading difficulties. In R. J. Morris & N. Mather (Eds.), *Evidence-based interventions for students with learning and behavioral challenges* (pp. 193–214). New York: Routledge.

Wexler, J., Vaughn, S., Edmonds, M., & Reutebuch, C. K. (2008). A synthesis of fluency interventions for secondary struggling readers. *Reading and Writing: An Interdisciplinary Journal, 21*(4), 317–347.

Weyandt, L. L (2001). *An ADHD Primer.* Boston: Allyn & Bacon.

Wheatley, J. P. (2005). *Strategic spelling: Moving beyond word memorization in the middle grades.* Newark, DE: International Reading Association.

White, B. (1975). Critical influences in the origins of competence. *Merrill-Palmer Quarterly, 2,* 243–266.

Whittaker, C. R., Salend, S. J., & Duhaney, D. (2001). Creating instructional rubrics for inclusive classrooms. *Teaching Exceptional Children, 34,* 8–13.

Wiig, E. H., & Semel, E. (1984). *Language assessment and intervention for the learning disabled* (2nd ed.). Columbus, OH: Merrill.

Willcutt, E. G., & Pennington, B. R. (2000). Co-morbidity of reading disability and attention-deficit/hyperactivity disorder: Differences by gender and subtype. *Journal of Learning Disabilities, 33,* 179–191.

Williams, P. (2009). *Exploring teachers' and black male students' perceptions of intelligence* (Unpublished doctoral dissertation). University of Miami, Coral Gables, FL.

Willis, J. (2008). *Teaching the brain to read: Strategies for improving fluency, vocabulary, and comprehension.* Alexandria, VA: ASCD.

Wilson, B. A. (1996). *Wilson Reading System.* Millbury, MA: Wilson Language Training Corporation.

Winebrenner, S., & Espeland, P. (2000). *Teaching gifted kids in the regular classroom.* Minneapolis, MN: Free Spirit Publishing.

Wolery, M. (1989). Transitions in early childhood special education: Issues and procedures. *Focus on Exceptional Children, 22,* 1–16.

Wolery, M., Cybriwsky, C. A., Gast, D. L., & Boyle-Gast, K. (1991). Use of constant time delay and attentional responses with adolescents. *Exceptional Children, 57,* 462–474.

Wolfe, P. S., & Hall, T. E. (2003). Making inclusion a reality for students with severe disabilities. *Teaching Exceptional Children, 35,* 56–61.

Wolfelt, A. D. (2002). Children's grief. In S. E. Brock, P. J. Lazarus, & S. R. Jimerson (Eds.), *Best practices in school crisis prevention and intervention* (pp. 653–671). Bethesda, MD: National Association of School Psychologists.

Wong, B. Y. L., Butler, D. L., Ficzere, S. A., & Kuperis, S. (1997). Teaching adolescents with learning disabilities and low achievers to plan, write, and revise compare-and-contrast essays. *Learning Disabilities Research & Practice, 12*(1), 2–15.

Wong, B. Y. L., Harris, K. R., & Graham, S. (2003). Cognitive strategies instruction research in learning disabilities. In H. L. Swanson & K. R. Harris (Eds.), *Handbook of learning disabilities* (pp. 383–402). New York: Guilford Press.

Wood, J. W., & Wooley, J. A. (1986). Adapting textbooks. *The Clearing House, 59,* 332–335.

Wood, K. D., Lapp, D., Flood, J., & Taylor, D. B. (2008). *Guiding readers through text: Strategy guides for new times* (2nd ed.). Newark, DE: International Reading Association.

Wood, W. M., Karvonen, M., Test, D. W., Browder, D., & Algozzine, B. (2004). Promoting student self-determination skills in IEP planning. *Teaching Exceptional Children, 36*(3), 8–16.

Woodruff, S., Schumaker, J. B., & Deshler, D. D. (2002). *The effects of an intensive reading intervention on the decoding skills of high school students with reading deficits.* Lawrence: University of Kansas Institute for Academic Access.

Worden, J. W. (1996). *Children and grief.* New York: Guilford Press.

Wormeli, R. (2006a). *Fair isn't always equal: Assessing & grading in the differentiated classroom.* Portland, ME: Stenhouse.

Wormeli, R. (2006b). Differentiating for tweens. *Educational Leadership, 63*(7), 14–19.

Wright, C., & Bigge, J. L. (1991). Avenues to physical participation. In J. L. Bigge (Ed.), *Teaching individuals with multiple and physical disabilities* (3rd ed., pp. 132–174). Englewood Cliffs, NJ: Merrill/Prentice Hall.

Wright, C. D., & Wright, J. P. (1980). Handwriting: The effectiveness of copying from moving versus still models. *Journal of Educational Research, 74,* 95–98.

Wylie, R. E., & Durrell, D. D. (1970). Teaching vowels through phonograms. *Elementary English, 47,* 787–791.

Wysocki, K., & Jenkins, J. R. (1987). Deriving word meanings through morphological generalization. *Reading Research Quarterly, 22,* 66–81.

Yavas, M. (1998). *Phonology development and disorders.* San Diego, CA: Singular Publishing Group.

Yell, M. L. (1998). *The law and special education.* Upper Saddle River, NJ: Merrill.

Yopp, H. K. (1995). A test for assessing phonemic awareness in young children. *The Reading Teacher, 49,* 20–29.

Ysseldyke, J., Nelson, R. J., Christenson, S., Johnson, D. R., Dennison, A., Triezenberg, H., & Hawes, M. (2004). What we know and need to know about the consequences of high-stakes testing for students with disabilities. *Exceptional Children, 71*(1), 75–95.

Zaragoza, N. (1987). Process writing for high-risk and learning disabled students. *Reading Research and Instruction, 26*(4), 290–301.

Zaragoza, N., & Vaughn, S. (1992). The effects of process instruction on three second-grade students with different achievement profiles. *Learning Disabilities Research and Practice, 7*(4), 184–193.

Zentall, S. S. (2006). *ADHD and education: Foundations, characteristics, methods, and collaboration.* Upper Saddle River, NJ: Merrill/Prentice Hall.

Zentall, S. S., & Smith, Y. N. (1993). Mathematical performance and behavior of children with hyperactivity, with and without coexisting aggression. *Behavior Research and Therapy, 31*(7), 701–710.

Zhang, Z., & Schumm, J. S. (2000). Exploring effects of the keyword method on limited English proficient students' vocabulary recall and comprehension. *Reading Research and Instruction, 39,* 202–221.

Ziegler, A., & Heller, K. A. (2000). Attribution retraining with gifted girls. *Roeper Review, 23,* 217–248.

Ziegler, J. C., Pech-Georgel, C., George, F., Alario, F. X., & Lorenzi, C. (2005). Deficits in speech perception predict language learning impairment. *Proceedings of the National Academy of Sciences of the United States of America, 102*(39): 14110–14115.

Zigmond, N. (2001). Special education at a crossroads. *Preventing School Failure, 45,* 70–74.

Zigmond, N. (2003). Where should students with disabilities receive special education services? Is one place better than another? *The Journal of Special Education, 37*(3), 193–199.

Zigmond, N., Jenkins, J., Fuchs, L. S., Deno, S., Fuchs, D., Baker, J., & Couthino, M. (1995). Special education in restructured schools: Findings from three multi-year studies. *Phi Delta Kappan, 76,* 531–540.

Zwiers, J. (2008). Academic classroom discussions. In J. Zwiers (Ed.), *Building academic language.* San Francisco/Newark, DE: Jossey-Bass.

Abedi, J., 112, 113
Abikoff, H., 168
Achenbach, T. M., 166, 214
Adams, L., 244
Adams, M. J., 311
Adelman, P. B., 150
Adger, C. T., 110
Adler, L., 165
Adler, S., 178
Afflerbach, P., 440
Agran, M., 260, 266
Ahlberg, A., 310
Ahlberg, J., 310
Al Otaiba, S., 51
Alario, F. X., 188
Alatorre-Parks, L., 442
Albin, R. W., 141
Albrecht, S. F., 218
Algozzine, B., 30, 79, 139, 450, 451
Al-Hassan, S., 94
Al-Hendawi, M., 226
Allen, N., 85
Allington, R., 302
Alper, P., 81
Alper, S., 81
Alsheikh, N., 94
Alsop, L., 265
Alter, P. J., 201, 397
Alvermann, D. E., 423, 424
Amanti, 79
American Academy of Child and Adolescent Psychiatry (AACAP), 206, 207, 208
American Academy of Pediatrics, 289
American Association on Intellectual and Development Disabilities (AAIDD), 254, 258
American Federation of Teachers, 94
American Foundation for Suicide Prevention, 207
American Foundation for the Blind, 276
American Lung Association, 288
American Optometric Association, 274
American Printing House for the Blind, 276
American Psychiatric Association (APA), 161, 205, 232, 253
American Psychological Association, 165
American Speech-Language-Hearing Association (ASHA), 176, 179, 188, 190, 192, 285
Amrein, A. L., 406

Anderson, C. M., 130, 132, 135, 212
Anderson, D. J., 89
Anderson, T. H., 425
Andrade, H., 435
Andrews, A., 239
Andrews-Weckerly, 339
Anthony, J. L., 330
Anxiety Disorders Association of America, 206
Appell, M. W., 268
Archer, A. L., 331
Arguelles, M. E., 72, 75, 77, 78
Armbruster, B., 420, 425, 455
Armstrong, T., 415
Arndt, S. A., 79
Aronson, E., 430
Arter, J., 341
Arthur, M., 245, 247
Arthur-Kelly, M., 255
Association for Persons with Severe Handicaps (TASH), 255
Asthma Allergy Foundation of America, 288
Atkins, M., 139
Atkinson, R. C., 459
Attwood, T., 244
Atwater, J., 29
Atwell, N., 366
August, D., 51, 111, 112, 115
Ault, M., 387
Aultman, L. P., 439
Austin, J., 452
Austin, T. Y., 197
Austin, V. L., 75, 77, 78
Avalos, M. A., 260, 407, 410
Axelrod, S., 137
Ayllon, T., 134

Baca, 112
Bailey, E., 165
Baird, C., 236
Baird, G., 236
Baker, C., 115, 343
Baker, D. B., 164
Baker, S., 114, 115, 149, 159, 323, 339, 343, 350, 371
Baker, S. K., 52, 153
Baldwin, R. S., 428, 440, 441
Ball, E. W., 311
Bandura, A., 224
Banks, J. A., 95, 99, 100, 101, 102
Bankson, N. W., 177
Barker, E. T., 206
Barkley, R. A., 148, 150, 161, 162, 163, 164, 165, 169, 171, 172
Barletta, 95, 112, 113
Barnes, 54

Barnes, M. A., 54, 151, 153, 156, 187
Barnes, M. C., 147
Barone, D. M., 113
Barraga, N. C., 279
Barreras, R. B., 223
Barron, R. W., 149
Bartholome, L. W., 367
Bashinski, S. M., 267
Batsche, G., 47
Baumgart, D., 256
Bauwens, J., 73
Beals, V. L., 320
Bean, T. W., 423, 428, 440, 441, 453
Bear, D. R., 318
Beard, L., 292
Beck, I. L., 314, 324
Becker, M. J., 432
Becker, W., 311
Beegle, 79, 80
Beeler, T., 311
Beers, P. C., 435
Behavioral Research and Reading, 321
Bejoian, L. M., 294
Belanger, S., 387
Belenky, M. F., 96
Bell, J. K., 279
Bello, M., 115, 116
Ben, K. R., 141
Bender, W. N., 43
Bennett, D., 255
Benson, N. J., 149
Bentz, J., 305
Bereiter, C., 345, 380
Berkeley, S., 43
Berliner, D. C., 406
Berner, R., 295
Berninger, V., 364
Bernstein, C., 240
Bernthal, J. E., 177
Berry, R., 343
Bessell, A. G., 294
Best, S. J., 288
Bevan-Brown, J., 114
Biancarosa, G., 318, 331, 440
Biemiller, A., 422
Bigge, J. L., 288, 292
Billings, A. C., 110
Bilton, K. M., 204
Bishop, K., 33
Bivens, 410
Blacher, J., 269
Blachman, B. A., 309, 311
Black, R., 311
Blakesless, 210
Blanchett, W. J., 258
Blanton, W. E., 410, 416, 430

Bley, N. S., 394
Bliss, C., 240
Block, C. C., 421
Blood, G. W., 183
Bloom, L., 179
Blote, A. W., 364
Blue-Banning, 79, 80, 81
Boardman, A., 126, 149, 154, 301, 323, 329
Bode, B. A., 366
Bos, C. S., 18, 79, 109, 116, 192, 194, 195, 197, 302, 310, 313, 314, 316, 317, 330, 348, 363, 384, 397, 399, 419, 432, 446, 447, 449, 450
Bosco, P., 391
Bott, D. A., 387
Bouchard, D., 275
Bovaird, J., 267
Bowen, S., 285
Boyle, E. A., 429
Boyle, J. R., 300, 452, 453, 454, 455
Boyle, O. F., 345
Boyle-Gast, K., 387
Bradley, 23, 41
Bradley, A. M., 324
Bradley, D. H., 351
Bradley, R., 23, 41
Brady, M. P., 260
Brandeis, D., 164
Brazik, E. F., 394
Breen, K., 225
Bremer, C. D., 30, 269
Brengelman, S. U., 76
Brent, D., 207
Brett, A., 324
Brewer, D. M., 450, 451
Brewin, B. J., 234
Briel, L., 290, 291
Brigham, F. J., 203
Brooke, M., 164
Brooke, V., 21
Brophy, J. E., 135, 420, 422, 456
Browder, D., 30, 79, 260, 450, 451
Brown, A. L., 327
Brown, E. T., 397
Brown, J. E., 95
Bruns, E. J., 224
Bryant, B., 292, 375, 458
Bryant, D. P., 292, 329, 371, 375, 458
Bryant, N. D., 362
Buchanan, R. W., 209
Bucholz, J., 260
Buehl, D., 427, 440, 442
Bulgren, J. A., 154, 410
Bulls, J. A., 356

Buntinx, W. H. E., 252, 253
Burgess, S. R., 309
Burish, P., 305
Burks, M., 359
Burniske, R. W., 428
Burns, D. E., 414
Burns, L. D., 427
Burns, M. K., 23, 39, 48, 56, 214, 416
Burns, M. S., 300
Burstein, N., 26, 31
Bursuck, W. D., 70, 434
Butler, D. L., 351

Caballer, A., 275
Cabello, B., 31
Callaway, P., 427
Campbell, A., 212
Campbell, J., 275
Campbell-Whatley, G. D., 450, 451
Cancro, R., 206
Candlelighters Childhood Cancer Foundation, 295
Cangelosi, J. S., 130
Canter, A., 57, 139, 416
Canter, H., 47, 57
Cantrell, S. C., 427
Cao, M., 323
Carlberg, C., 31
Carlisle, J., 323
Carlson, C. D., 309
Carlson, R., 240
Carnine, D., 379, 380, 393
Carnine, L., 311
Carpenter, L. B., 292
Carpenter, S. L., 131
Carr, E. G., 261
Carr, J., 452
Carr, S. C., 324
Carreker, S., 318, 360
Carroll, J., 180
Carter, E. W., 265, 268, 432, 450
Carter, K., 285
Carter, T. P., 107
Cartledge, G., 94, 97, 113, 114, 221
Cash, R. E., 206
Caspi, A., 164
Cassel, P., 132, 138
Cassini, K. K., 295
Castellano, C., 277
Castellano, J. A., 94
Castro, M., 214
Cataldi, E. F., 94
Catts, H., 183
Cauley, K. M., 406
Causton-Theoharis, J., 260, 266
Caverly, D. C., 440
Cawley, J. F., 396
Cea, C. D., 261

Center for Applied Linguistics, 110
Centers for Disease Control and Prevention, 232, 252, 275, 289
Certo, J. L., 406
Cervantes, 112
CHADD (Children and Adults with Attention Deficit Disorder), 161
Chafin, C., 406
Chall, J., 424
Chamberlain, S. P., 94, 96, 113, 128, 129
Chamot, A., 109, 113, 114
Chapman, C., 94, 429
Chappell, G., 195
Chard, D. J., 157, 310, 320, 321, 431
Charles, C., 138
Charman, T., 236
Chatfield, M. L., 107
Checkley, K., 415
Chen, D., 265
Cheung, A., 106
Chiappone, L. L., 417
Children's Defense Fund, 124, 209–210
Children's Educational Services, 306
Christ, T. J., 48
Christenson, S. L., 385
Christian, D., 110
Christodoulou, J. A., 415
Christopherson, K., 452
Chun, M., 451
Chung, J. P-L., 98
Ciancio, D. J., 54
Circle of Inclusion Project, 261
Cirino, 330
Clarizio, H. F., 211
Clark, N. M., 265
Clarke, B., 382
Clausen-Grace, N., 419
Clinchy, B. M., 96
Cloninger, C. J., 261
Coelho, E., 109
Cohen, E. G., 95
Cohen, J. S., 226
Cohen, P., 110
Coi, G., 391
Collier, V. P., 94, 104, 105, 106, 107, 109, 111, 115
Collins, P., 52
Coltrane, B., 112
Combs, M. C., 94, 104, 105, 106, 107, 109, 115
Conderman, G., 434
Conley, M., 405, 406
Conner, C. K., 166
Conner, D. J., 294
Connolly, A. J., 380
Conroy, M. A., 226

Cook, 64, 68, 70
Cook, C. R., 223
Cooke, N. L., 256, 380
Cooper, D. H., 187
Cooper, Harris, 81, 409, 456
Cooper, J. D., 406
Cooper, J. O., 221
Cooper, P., 204
Copeland, S. R., 299
Corn, A. L., 274, 277, 279
Correa, V. I., 86
Cortiella, 53
Cortiella, C., 53
Cosio, 30
Cosio, A., 30
Cotton, K., 367
Council for Exceptional Children (CEC), 53, 269
Courtney, M. E., 168
Cowan, K. C., 206, 416
Cox, P., 276, 277, 279
Cramer, E., 129
Crawford, 112
Crews, S. D., 223, 226
Crites, S. A., 215
Crone, D. A., 216
Cronin, M. E., 221
Crosby, S., 223
Cross, C. T., 23, 42, 79, 94, 96, 128, 129, 166, 204, 210
Crowley, M. J., 207
Cullinan, B. E., 341, 452
Cullinan, D., 139
Cummins, J., 99, 107, 108, 109, 115
Cunningham, P. M., 316, 318
Curran, 79
Curry, C. A., 256
Cushing, L. S., 265
Cybriwsky, C. A., 387

Dale, E., 424
Dalton, S. S., 301
Daly, P. M., 220
D'Andrea, F. M., 279
D'Andrea, M., 279
Danielson, 23, 41
Darling-Hammond, L., 406
Davey, B., 421
Davis, M., 276
Dawson, S., 260
Day, M. H., 247
de Jong, E., 104, 105
De La Paz, S., 351, 357
Dean Qualls, C., 183
Delaney, C. J., 427
Delis, D., 258
Dell, A. G., 292
Demchak, M. A., 267
Demmert, W. G., 113
Deno, S. L., 23, 305
Denton, C., 330
Denton, C. A., 60

DePaepe, P., 289, 290
Deshler, D. D., 18, 153, 154, 318, 320, 331, 410, 418, 440, 450, 456, 459
Dettmer, 64, 67, 71
Dettmer, P., 64, 67, 71, 79
Deutsch-Smith, D., 421
Devine, T. G., 440
Deyhle, D., 95
Diaz, R., 110
Díaz-Rico, L., 97, 106, 110
Dickerson, F. B., 209
Dickson, S. V., 310
Dieker, P., 67, 71, 73, 77
Dieker, L. A., 77
Dietel, R., 113
Dillon, J., 423
DiMattia, A. G., 9
Dion, E., 381
Dirksen, 64
DiVesta, F. J., 193, 452
Dixon, D. R., 258
Dixon, L. A., 209, 258
Doak, P. K., 387
Doan, T., 396
Doelling, J., 289, 290
Doering, 78
Doering, K., 78
Domino, J. A., 311
Donato, R., 107
Donohoe, B., 207
Donovan, M. S., 23, 42, 79, 94, 96, 128, 129, 166, 204, 210
Doolittle, J., 95
Dossey, J. A., 394
Douglas, J., 452
Doukas, G. L., 224
Dowdy, C. A., 197
Downing, J., 257, 268
Downing, J. A., 122, 136, 207, 211, 214, 257
Downing, J. E., 259, 260, 293
Dowrick, P. W., 156
Doyle, P., 387
Drabin, I. R., 362
Dreikurs, R., 132, 138
Drew, A., 236
Driver, J., 186
Duchnowski, A. J., 204
Duff, F., 75, 78
Duhaney, D., 89, 436
Duhaney, L. M., 76, 94, 113
Dunlap, G., 141, 261
Dunsmore, K., 343
DuPaul, G. J., 167
Duppong-Hurley, K., 209
Durand, 216
Durand, V. M., 216, 256
Durando, J., 278
Durkin, D. D., 154
Durrell, D. D., 316
Dweck, 132
Dyches, T. T., 294

Dyck, N. J., 64, 79
Dykes, M., 276, 277, 279

Eber, L., 224, 225, 226
Edmonds, M. S., 322, 359
Edrishina, C., 239
Edrishina, S., 243
Educational Testing
    Services, 12
Edwards, J. K., 51
Edwards, P. A., 68, 114
Edwin, 410
Eggen, P., 423
Egley, A., 208
Ehri, L. C., 149, 309, 312, 314
Eichinger, J., 268
Eisele, J., 311
Eisenman, L., 18
Elbaum, B., 126, 307, 379
Elhoweris, H., 94, 167
Elkonin, D. B., 310
Elliot, 23
Elliot, S. N., 214
Ellis, 410
Ellis, R., 106, 107
Ellison, 161
Emerson, R. S. W., 279
Emery, R. E., 210
Emmer, E., 122, 130, 135
Ender, C., 214
Engelmann, S., 311, 379,
    380, 393
Engleman, M., 276
Englert, C. S., 343
Epilepsy Foundation, 288
Epstein, J. L., 79, 80
Epstein, M., 139, 209
Epstein, M. H., 204, 226,
    227, 434
Erickson, F., 98
Erickson, R. N., 27
Erin, J. N., 279
Ervin-Tripp, S., 109
Erwin, 79
Erwin, E. J., 79, 81
Estrada, P., 301
Everington, C., 261, 263, 264
Everston, C., 122, 135
Ezell, D., 261
Ezzedeen, S. R., 423

Fairbanks, S., 140, 141,
    212, 215
Fanuele, D. P., 51
Farmer, J., 279
Farnan, N., 343
Farrenkopf, C., 279
Fearn, L., 343
Fein, D., 258
Felton, R. H., 322
Feng, A. X., 412
Ferguson, D. L., 150
Ferguson, E. D., 132, 138

Ferguson, P. M., 150
Ferrell, K. A., 275
Ferreri, S. J., 452
Ferretti, 339
Fey, M., 183
Ficzere, S. A., 352
Field, S., 18
Figueroa, R. A., 109
Fink-Chorzempa, B., 344, 349
Fischer, M., 150, 164
Fitzgerald, J., 115
Fitzpatrick, D., 428
Flannery, K. B., 151, 239
Fletcher, J. M., 54, 60, 147, 148,
    151, 153, 156, 187, 309
Flexer, C., 285
Flippo, R. F., 432
Flood, J., 424, 441
Florida Department of
    Education, 356
Florida Sunshine State
    Standards, 406
Floyd, F. J., 81
Flynn, E. M., 341
Flynn, L. A., 341
Foley, T. F., 396
Fontana, J. L., 458, 459
Foorman, B. G., 311
Foorman, B. R., 54, 309, 324
Ford, D. Y., 94, 97, 113, 114
Foreman, P., 255
Forest, M., 256, 261
Forness, S., 223
Forness, S. R., 31, 203,
    206, 223
Foster, S. L., 222
Foulk, D., 289
Fountoukidis, D., 314
Fowler, C. H., 450, 451
Fowler, M., 165
Fowler, S. A., 29
Fox, L., 256
Francis, D. J., 50, 112,
    309, 318
Frankland, 79, 80
Frederickson, N., 256
French, N. K., 167
Friedlander, M. A., 149, 154
Friend, M., 64, 67, 68, 70, 260
Frisbee, K., 266
Frombonne, E., 235
Frose, V., 363
Fry, E. B., 314, 315, 419, 424
Fry, R., 94
Fuchs, 24, 50, 51, 54
Fuchs, D., 31, 34, 44, 46, 48,
    50, 51, 113, 147, 149, 265,
    305, 306, 308, 322, 380, 381,
    384, 385
Fuchs, L. S., 24, 31, 34, 44, 48,
    51, 54, 113, 147, 149, 151,
    153, 156, 187, 305, 306, 308,
    322, 381, 382, 383, 384, 385

Fuchs, Lynn, 265
Fuhler, 64
Furlong, J. J., 204

Gable, R. A., 410
Gajar, A. H., 193, 420
Galambos, N. L., 206
Galambos, S., 111
Galda, L., 341, 452
Gallagher, J., 412
Gallaudet Research Institute, 282
Gambrell, L. B., 366
Garcia, E., 109, 112, 114
Gardner, H., 415
Gardner, R., 94, 97, 113,
    114, 381
Garrick Duhaney, L. M., 90
Garrison-Lane, L., 289, 290
Gaskins, I. W., 311
Gast, D. L., 387
Gay, Geneva, 94, 95, 99
Gaylord-Ross, R., 243
Geary, D. C., 396
Gebauer, 67
Gentry, J. R., 358
George, F., 188
Gerber, A., 195
Gerber, P. J., 150
German, D. J., 195
Germann, G., 322
Gersten, R., 52, 76, 107, 109,
    114, 115, 149, 153, 157, 159,
    323, 339, 343, 350, 371, 431
Gessner, L. J., 289
Gettinger, M., 362
Giangreco, M. F., 260, 261, 292
Gibbs, S. L., 260
Gilberts, G. H., 255
Gilligan, C., 96
Gillon, G. T., 309
Ginsberg, R., 150
Giuliani, G., 209, 253, 254, 287
Glass, T. F., 406, 412
Gleason, Burko, 187
Gleason, M. M., 331, 352
Glennen, S., 241
Glies, D. K., 219
Glomb, 70
Glynn, D., 243
Goetz, L., 77, 78
Gold, M., 207
Goldberg, R. J., 149, 209
Goldberger, N. R., 96
Goldin, L., 445
Goldin-Meadow, S., 111
Gonzalez, 79
Gonzalez, F., 94
Gonzalez, J. E., 226
Gonzalez, N., 96
Good, 306
Good, T. L., 420, 422, 456
Goodwin, M., 458
Gordon, J., 359

Gotheif, C. R., 268
Gottschalk, C., 89
Gouvousis, A., 244
Grabe, M., 452
Graham, S., 149, 154, 156, 159,
    339, 340, 343, 344, 345, 349,
    350, 351, 354, 356, 357,
    362, 364
Grant, C. A., 100
Graves, 114
Graves, A., 339, 354, 355
Graves, D. H., 345, 346, 352
Gray, C., 244
Gray, G. S., 452
Gredler, M. E., 342
Greenberg, J. B., 96
Greenburg, J. S., 81
Gregg, M., 410
Gregg, R. M., 224
Gresham, 203, 204
Gresham, F. M., 140, 202,
    214, 223
Griffin, H., 276
Griffin, P., 300
Griffin-Shirley, N., 279
Griffiths, A., 39, 56, 214
Grimes, J., 49
Groisser, D., 164
Grootenhuis, M. A., 290
Grossman, H., 129
Gulek, 432
Gumpel, T. P., 221
Gunn, B., 330
Gunning, 216, 314
Gunning, T. G., 311, 406, 454
Gunwalk, 132
Guskey, T. R., 76
Guthrie, J. T., 303, 433
Guyer, B. P., 169

Haager, D., 44, 77, 95, 114,
    126, 311
Hacker, D. J., 439
Hagins, R. A., 364
Hakuta, K., 109, 115
Hale-Benson, J. E., 95
Haley, M. H., 197
Hall, L. A., 427
Hall, S. L., 303
Hall, T. E., 264, 408
Hallahan, 23, 31, 41, 79, 80
Hallahan, D. P., 23, 31, 41, 79,
    80, 81, 151, 202, 274, 288,
    361, 365, 412, 444, 446
Hallowell, E. M., 161
Halsey, H. N., 215
Hamill, L., 261, 263, 264
Hamlett, C. L., 305, 306,
    322, 384
Hammill, D., 375
Hamstra-Bletz, L., 364
Hanley, E. L., 219
Hanover, S., 366

Hansen, J., 352
Hanson, M. J., 97
Hardman, M. L., 260
Harper, C., 104, 105
Harper, G. F., 381
Harris, A. A., 260
Harris, J., 72, 410
Harris, K. R., 149, 154, 159,
    340, 343, 344, 349, 354,
    356, 379
Harris, L. A., 302
Harris, S. R., 301
Harry, B., 51, 64, 79, 85, 94, 95,
    96, 114, 128, 129, 166, 204,
    258, 270
Hart, B., 180
Hart, J., 96
Hartman, P., 371, 375
Hasbrouck, J., 330
Hatch, T., 415
Hauge, R., 354
Havens, L. T., 427, 440, 453
Hawken, L. S., 212, 216, 293
Hayes-Jacob, 410
Haystead, M. W., 405, 406
Hazel, J. S., 225
Hear-It Org, 284
Hearn, J., 435
Hebdon, H. M., 260
Hedge, M. N., 177
Heller, K. A., 412
Heller, K. W., 288
Helman, L., 318
Helmstetter, E., 256
Hendley, S. L., 217
Henk, W. A., 427
Henry, B., 164
Henry, M., 316
Henze, R., 107
Herman, K. L., 149
Heron, T. E., 221, 381
Hess, F. M., 406
Hessler, T., 381
Heward, H. L., 79, 80
Heward, W. L., 21, 79, 209, 221,
    255, 275, 287, 288, 289
Heymans, H. S., 290
Hiatt-Michael, D. B., 114
Hickman, P., 47, 321
Hiebert, E. H., 302, 324, 417
Higgins, E. L., 149
Higgins, K., 458
Hill, E. W., 278
Hilton, P., 380
Hirose-Hatae, 78
Hitchcock, C. H., 156, 410
Hofmeister, A. M., 396
Holburn, S. C., 261
Holdnack, J. A., 151
Hollingsworth, P. M., 321
Holloway, P., 94
Holschuh, J. P., 439
Hommersen, P., 207

Honda, H., 232
Hong, J., 81
Hoover, 112, 113
Hoover, J. J., 95, 127, 128
Horner, R., 140, 212, 216
Horner, R. H., 141, 216, 223,
    239, 247, 269
Hoskyn, M., 157
Hosp, J. L., 94
Hourcade, J. J., 73
Howard, M., 177, 186
Howe, K. R., 5
Hruby, P. J., 150
Huai, 23
Hudson, P., 70
Huebner, K. M., 274
Huerta, N., 7
Huges, C., 266
Hughes, C. A., 193, 420, 421,
    432, 456
Hughes, M. T., 77, 78, 307
Huizinga, D., 208
Hulit, L., 177, 187
Humphries, T. L., 282
Hunt, N., 295
Hunt, P., 78, 256, 267
Hurley, M., 324
Hurley, S. R., 112
Hurley-Chamberlain, 67
Hutchinson, N. L., 397
Hutchinson, S. W., 221

IDEA, 252
IDEIA (2004), 39, 40, 42, 146,
    233, 257, 264, 292
Idol, L., 64
Igo, L. B., 452
Insoon, H., 323
International Reading
    Association, 338
Invernizzi, M., 318
Irvine, J. L., 95
Irwin, J. W., 417, 422
Isaacson, S., 352
Israel, S. E., 421
Iverson, V., 261

Jackson, 410
Jackson, C. W., 436
Jacobson, J. W., 261
Jairrels, 64
Janney, D. M., 206
Janney, R., 139
Jansorn, N. R., 80
Jara, P., 275
Javorsky, J., 150
Jayanthi, M., 434
Jenkins, J. R., 316
Jiménez, R. T., 109
Jimerson, S., 204
Jimerson, S. R., 23
Jitendra, A. K., 372
Johnson, A., 420

Johnson, B., 234
Johnson, D., 89, 329
Johnson, D. D., 326
Johnson, D. J., 375
Johnson, D. R., 30
Johnson, D. T., 376, 377
Johnson, G., 311
Johnson, J. M., 256
Johnson, L. J., 68, 70
Johnson, R., 329
Johnson, R. L., 342
Johnson, S., 183, 291
Johnston, C., 207
Johnston, F., 318
Johnston, L., 292
Johnston, P., 302
Johnston, S. S., 293
Jolivette, K., 216, 223
Jones, B., 72, 75, 78
Jones, J., 431
Jordan, L., 459
Jose, R. T., 279
Jung, 76

Kachgal, M., 269
Kagan, 209
Kagan, S., 95
Kalyanpur, M., 270
Kamee'enui, E. J., 157, 384
Kamens, M. W., 77
Kamil, M. L., 417
Kamins, 132
Kaminski, 306
Kania, J. S., 440
Kantrowitz, L., 151
Kaplan, E., 258
Kaplan, S. N., 414
Karasoff, P., 77, 78
Karnes, F. A., 412
Karvonen, M., 30, 79,
    450, 451
Katsiyannis, A., 431
Kauchak, D., 423
Kauffman, J. M., 31, 79, 80, 81,
    202, 203, 204, 205, 224, 274,
    361, 365, 412, 444
Kavale, K. A., 31, 151, 223
Kazdin, A. E., 136, 207
Keating, T., 114
Keefe, E. B., 75, 77, 78, 299
Keenan, S., 224, 225, 226
Keller, C. L., 260
Keller, M., 359
Kelly, J. B., 210
Kelly, M. J., 419
Kelly, S. M., 275
Kennedy, C. H., 265
Keogh, B. K., 148
Kern, 203, 204
Kern, K., 223
Kern, L., 209, 223
Ketterlin-Geller, L. R., 417
KewalRamani, A., 94

Keyes, M. W., 18
Keyser-Marcus, L., 290, 291
Kierans, I., 243
Kiger, N. D., 406
Kim, A., 153, 417
Kim, A-H., 359
Kim, S. A., 371, 375
Kimbrough, B. T., 275
Kincaid, D., 139
King, D. A., 178
King, L. A., 219
King, R., 429
Kirkland, K., 94
Kirstein, I., 240
Kissam, B. R., 154
Kitchel, J. E., 279
Kleinert, H. L., 126, 264
Klein-Ezell, C. E., 261, 263
Klinger, J. K., 51, 166
Klingner, J. K., 31, 40, 41, 44,
    51, 68, 79, 84, 95, 96, 112,
    128, 149, 154, 156, 204, 258,
    270, 301, 323, 329
Klotz, M. B., 139, 416
Knight-McKenna, M., 318
Knitzer, J., 203
Knowlton, E., 261
Koenig, A. J., 274
Koga, N., 408
Konopasek, D., 209
Konrad, M., 79
Koorland, M. A., 289
Koplewicz, H. S., 168
Koppang, A., 410
Korinek, L., 356
Kornhaber, M., 415
Koroghlanian, C., 434
Kovacs, M., 206
Koziol, S., 185
Kozleski, E. B., 167, 261
Kramer, J., 258
Krashen, S., 107
Kress, J. E., 314, 419
Kretlow, A. G., 459
Kreyenbuhl, J., 209
Kübler-Ross, E., 295
Kucan, L., 324
Kuperis, S., 352
Kutash, K., 139, 204

Labbo, L. D., 353
LaBerge, D., 314
Labov, W., 110
Lacey, C., 243
Lachapelle, Y., 252, 253
Lachowicz, J., 219
Ladson-Billings, G., 94, 100,
    103, 114
LaGreca, A. M., 224
Lahey, M., 179
Laird, J., 94
Lambert, M., 258
Lambert, W., 111

Lambie, G. W., 125, 126
Lancelotta, G. X., 208
Lancioni, G., 239, 243
Landers, E., 201, 217
Landrum, T. J., 203, 224
Lane, H. B., 311
Lane, K. L., 220, 224, 269, 450
Lang, R., 237
Langlois, J. A., 287, 291
Lapp, D., 423, 424, 430, 441
Lapp-Rincker, G., 260
Larkin, M. J., 436
Larrivee, B., 132, 219, 220
Larsen, L., 340
Larson, C. N., 388
Larson, N., 380
Larson, V., 185
LaRusso, R., 261
Lash, M. H., 290
Lattin, D. L., 260
Lau, 47
Lau, M., 47
Layton, C. A., 253
Lazar, R. T., 183
Leadbeater, B. J., 206
Leavell, A. G., 260, 410
Leavey, M., 381
Lederer, J. M., 327
Lee, D. L., 137, 371
Lee, J. M., 220
Lee, M., 452
Lee, O., 77
Lee, S-H., 260, 264, 267
Leff, R., 240
Leff, S., 240
Lehman, A. F., 209
Lehr, D., 194
Leigh, J., 420
Leinart, A., 322
LeJeune, B. J., 275
Leland, H., 258
Lembke, E. S., 212, 213
LeMoine, N. R., 110
Lenz, B. K., 154, 155, 320, 410, 418, 459
Leonard, L. B., 195
Leone, P. E., 204
Leppien, J. H., 414
Lerman, J., 83
Lerner, J. W., 167, 366
Lessow-Hurley, J., 99
Levendoski, L. S., 221
Levin, J. R., 458
Lewis, 76, 210, 339
Lewis, J., 110
Lewis, R. B., 76, 240
Lewis, T. J., 136
Lewis-Palmer, T., 136
Liapsun, C. J., 216
Libby, J., 266
Liederman, J., 151
Limber, S. P., 128

Linan-Thompson, S., 47, 52, 58, 115, 118, 318, 329, 330, 332, 333, 334
Lindamood, P. A., 311
Lingnugaris/Kraft, B., 265
Lingo, A. S., 227, 397
Link, D. P., 356
Lipson, 325
Little, T. D., 260, 264, 267
Lloyd, J., 77
Lloyd, J. W., 361, 365
Lo, Y., 459
Lock, R. H., 217, 263
Loeber, R., 207, 208
Loeffler, K. A., 361
London, T. H., 225
Loprete, 77
Loprete, S. J., 77
Lorenzi, C., 188
Lotan, R., 95
Lovett, M. W., 149
Lovitt, T. C., 380
Lucangeli, D., 391
Lucas, T., 107
Luckasson, R. A., 252, 253
Luckner, J., 285
Lucyshyn, J. M., 141
Lue, M. S., 179, 185
Lundberg, I., 311
Lusthaus, E., 256
Lynch, E. W., 97
Lynne, B., 286
Lyon, G. R., 54, 147, 151, 153, 156, 187

MacArthur, C., 344, 349
MacGinitie, W. H., 306
Mack, K., 207
MacKay, L. D., 223
Madan-Swain, A., 294
Madden, N. A., 95, 381
Maddox, M., 186
Magieri, 67, 77
Maheady, L., 204, 381
Mallete, M. H., 427
Malmgren, K., 260, 266
Mangrum, C. T., 425, 426, 444, 448
Mann, D., 207
Mann, V. A., 183
March of Dimes, 254
Marino, E. C., 292
Marino, M. T., 292
Marks, S., 451
Marks, S. U., 19, 114
Marsh, L. G., 380
Marston, D., 32, 47, 48
Martin, J. E., 268
Martin, R., 451
Martinez, E. A., 361, 365
Marzano, J. S., 126, 135
Marzano, R. J., 126, 135, 405, 406

Mason, B. A., 226
Mason, C., 18
Mason, L. H., 149, 154, 343, 345, 351, 354
Mastropieri, M. A., 67, 268, 322, 406, 415, 457, 458
Mathes, P. G., 305, 311, 318, 330
Mathur, S. P., 223
Matthews, W. J., 215
Mattingly, J. C., 387
Mattison, R. E., 210
Matus, R., 406
Mayo Clinic, 165
McAllister, I., 185
McConaughy, S. H., 214
McCord, B. E., 452
McCormack, R. L., 430
McCormick, 302
McCoy, G. F., 211
McCoy, J. D., 417
McCray, A. D., 166
McDonnell, A. P., 293
McDonnell, J., 256, 267
McDonough, J. T., 21
McDougall, D., 221
McDuffie, 67
McEvoy, A., 226
McGee, Cherry A., 102
McGee, R. O., 164
McGregor, K. K., 195
McIntosh, 77
McIntosh, K., 223
McIntosh, R., 131
McKee-Higgins, E., 131
McKeown, M. G., 324
McKinley, N., 185
McKoon, 112
McLaughlin, M., 85
McLaughlin, R., 77
McLaughlin, S., 182
McLeskey, J., 31
McLoughlin, J. A., 76
McMaster, K., 323
McMillan, J. H., 435
McNamara, J. K., 159
McNeill, D., 185
McTighe, J., 341
Mechling, L. C., 265
Medina, A. L., 358
Meichenbaum, D., 422
Meister, C., 327
Mekkelson, 325
Melhem, N., 207
Menyuk, P., 181
Menzies, H. M., 220, 224
Mercer, C. D., 386, 397
Merino, B. J., 106
Merkley, 64
Meyer, A., 157, 410
Meyer, L. H., 114, 311
Meyer, M. S., 322
Miller, L., 187, 362

Miller, M. C., 256
Miller, S. P., 397
Miner, 30
Miner, C. A., 30
Minor, L., 265
Miracle, S. A., 126
Miyasaka, J. R., 432
Moats, L. C., 300, 311, 360
Mobbs, F., 185
Mock, D. R., 50, 203
Moeller, M. P., 283
Moffitt, T. E., 164
Mokkink, L. B., 290
Moll, Luis, 79, 96
Montague, M., 214, 354, 375, 397, 439
Montgomery, W., 94
Moody, S. W., 77, 307
Mooney, P., 226, 227
Moore, V., 75, 78
Moorman, G. B., 416
Mora-Harder, M., 77
Moran, S., 415
Morgan, P. L., 50
Morgan, S. R., 211
Morris, R. D., 112, 258
Morrison, G. M., 204
Morse, S. E., 279
Morsink, C. V., 86
Mosentha, 325
Mostert, M. P., 151, 223
Moxley, K. D., 406
Mueller, T. G., 18
Muhomba, M., 264
Mulcahy-Ernt, P. I., 440
Munk, D. D., 265
Munson, L. J., 295
Munton, S. M., 224
Murawski, W. W., 67, 71, 73, 77
Murdock, J. Y., 221
Murphy, K. R., 150, 164
Murray, 79
Murray, C., 207
Muscular Dystrophy Association, 289
Mutua, K., 94
Muyskens, P., 47
Myers, A., 18
Myklebust, H. R., 375
Myskens, 47

Nahmias, M., 167
Nair, M., 318, 331, 440
National Association for Gifted Children, 414
National Center for Children in Poverty, 94
National Center for Educational Statistics, 202, 257
National Center for Hearing Assessment & Management, 283

National Center on Secondary Education and Transition (NCSET), 30
National Council of Teachers of English, 338, 342
National Council of Teachers of Mathematics (NCTM), 372, 373, 374, 377, 393
National Dissemination Center for Children with Disabilities (NICHCY), 176, 213, 290
National Down Syndrome Society, 253
National Fragile X Foundation, 254
National Health Information Center, 214
National Institute of Mental Health (NIMH), 161, 165, 169, 170, 172, 205, 206, 209
National Institutes of Health, 235
National Institutes of Health and Human Development, 254
National Joint Committee on Learning Disabilities (NJCLD), 27
National Middle School Association, 407
National Organization on Fetal Alcohol Syndrome (NOFAS), 254
National Reading Panel, 300, 312
National Research Council, 232, 236, 237, 374
Neal, L. V. I., 166
Neef, N. A., 452
Neff, 79
Negron, M., 139
Nelson, 79, 80, 410
Nelson, C. M., 216
Nelson, J. R., 209
Nelson, N. W., 185
Ness, M. K., 409
Neubert, D. A., 149
Nevin, 72, 77
Newcomer, L., 136
Newman, R. S., 445
Newton, D., 292
Nicholson, C. B., 183
Nieto, S., 100, 111
Nihira, K., 258
Nippold, M. A., 181, 182, 185
No Child Left Behind, 260, 264, 406
Nobel, M. M., 381
Nordness, P. D., 225
Notari-Syverson, A., 311
Nunley, K. F., 435
Nye, B., 408

O'Brien, R. M., 183
Obrosky, D. S., 206
O'Connor, R., 307, 311
Oczkus, L., 421
Odom, S. L., 269
O'Donnell, C. E., 208
O'Donoghue, D., 243
Offringa, M., 290
O'Flahavan, J. F., 430
Ogbu, J. U., 98, 99, 100, 128
Ogle, D., 324, 325, 441, 442
Ohan, J. L., 207
Oishi, S., 95
Okolo, C. H., 268, 457
Oliver, J. C., 275
Olweus, D., 127
O'Malley, J. M., 109, 113
O'Neill, R. E., 216, 247
Oosterlaan, J., 164
O'Reilly, M. F., 239, 243, 245, 247
Orelove, F. P., 252, 256, 257, 291
Ortiz, Alba, 52
Osborne, P., 9
OSEP Technical Assistance Center on Positive Behavioral Interventions and Supports, 139, 140, 141, 216
O'Shea, D. J., 80
O'Shea, L., 80, 386
Osher, D. M., 204
Ovando, C. J., 94, 104, 105, 106, 107, 109, 111, 115
Owens, G., 176
Owens, Jr., R. E., 176, 177, 180, 182, 184, 185, 195, 197
Owens-Johnson, L., 18

Padden, C. A., 282
Paddock, C., 399
Palinscar, A. S., 318, 327, 331, 440
Palmer, J. M., 178
Paratore, J. R., 430
Pardini, P., 4
Paris, S. G., 440
Park, H. S., 243
Park, J., 210
Park, K. L., 201, 217
Parker, J., 330
Parrish, P. R., 260
Parson, L. B., 39, 56, 214
Pascoe, S., 255
Pass, L., 378
Passenger, T., 183
Patnoe, S., 430
Patterson, D. S., 223
Patton, J. R., 197
Pauk, W., 453
Payne, K. T., 176
Peal, E., 111
Pearson, P. D., 302, 326, 417, 440

Peaster, L. G., 43
Pech-Georgel, C., 188
Peckham-Hardin, K. D., 259, 260
Pecyna-Rhyner, P., 194
Pedulla, J. J., 406
Pennington, B. F., 164
Pennington, B. R., 165
Pepper, 132
Peregoy, S. F., 345
Perez, A., 279
Perrin, D., 339, 354
Person, 132
Peterson, P. E., 406
Peterson, S. K., 386
Petroff, J., 292
Pettee, Y., 81
Philips, L., 150
Phillips, N. B., 305
Pickett, A. L., 260
Pierangelo, R., 209, 253, 254, 287
Pierce, C. D., 226, 227
Pierson, M. R., 269, 450
Pinkus, L., 94
Pisecco, S., 164
Plumley, K., 285
Pocock, A., 451
Poirier, J. M., 204
Pollard-Durodola, S. D., 321, 324
Polloway, E. A., 197
Polsgrove, L., 220
Ponder, P., 278
Pope, G. G., 452
Porche, M. V., 301
Portway, S., 234
Post, S. A., 447
Prater, M. A., 156, 294
Prentice, K., 149
Presley, I., 279
Pressley, M., 156, 379
Pudlas, K., 194
Pugach, M. C., 68, 70
Pullen, 79, 80
Pullen, P. C., 79, 80, 81, 202, 274, 311, 412, 444
Purcell, 414
Purcell, J. H., 414

Quay, H. C., 204
Quek, C., 412
Quinlan, 157
Quinn, M. M., 204

Radencich, Marguerite, 349, 435, 457
Radencich, M. C., 435
Rafferty, L. A., 217
Ramirez, J. D., 106
Ramirez, M., 106
Ramsey, E., 202, 214
Ranalli, P., 220

Raphael, T. E., 326, 327
Rashotte, C. A., 306
Raskind, M. H., 149
Ratey, J. J., 161
Rathvon, N., 54
Ravitch, D., 405
Raygor, A. L., 424
Rayner, G., 234
Rea, 77
Readence, J. E., 422, 428, 440, 441
Reed, V. A., 185
Reid, R., 226, 227
Reiff, H. B., 150
Reinhart, J. A., 211
Reis, S. M., 414
Renwick, R., 234
Renzulli, J. S., 414
Reschly, D. J., 49, 94
Resnick, L., 405, 406
Reutebuch, C. K., 322
Reutzel, D. R., 321
Reyes, E. I., 109
Reyhner, J., 106
Riccoininni, R. H., 452
Rice, M., 323
Richard-Amato, P. A., 117
Rickard, R., 279
Rikhye, C. H., 268
Rinaldi, C., 95
Risley, T. R., 180
Ritchey, W. L., 222
Rivera, D., 421
Roberts, P. H., 305
Robins, C., 110
Robinson, F. P., 440
Robinson, N., 412
Roche, 23
Rock, M. L., 221, 410
Roeber, E., 264
Rogers, J. L., 295
Rogge, Ruth, 74
Roisen, N. J., 166
Rooney, K. J., 169
Rose, D. H., 157, 410
Rose, J., 225
Rose, M. C., 85
Rosel, J., 275
Rosenberg, M. S., 204
Rosenberg, R. L., 33
Rosenshine, B., 327
Roth, F. P., 187
Rothlein, L., 324
Rowe, 422
Rubalcava, M., 99
Rubia, K., 164
Rubin, H., 184
Rubinstein, J., 380
Rueda, R., 270, 339
Ruhl, K. L., 193, 420, 456
Ruiz, N. T., 109
Rummel, N., 458
Rutherford, R. R., 204

Rutland-Brown, W., 287
Rutter, M., 232
Ryan, A. L., 215
Ryan, J. B., 226, 227, 431

Sacca, M. K., 381
Sacks, G., 209
Sacks, S. Z., 275
Saddler, B., 351
Saez, L., 159
Salend, S. J., 27, 76, 89, 90, 94,
    113, 127, 167, 169, 433, 436
Salinas, K. C., 80
Samson, J., 95
Samuels, C. A., 96
Sander, E. K., 177
Sanders, M. G., 79, 80
Sandomierski, T., 139, 141
Sands, D. J., 167, 261, 268
Santa, C. M., 348, 427, 440, 453
Sapon-Shevin, M., 114
Sargeant, J. A., 164
Sattler, J. M., 207
Saumell, L., 425
Saunders, L., 43
Sawilowsky, S., 18
Saxon, J., 380
Scammacca, N., 157, 318
Scanlon, D. M., 51
Scardamalia, M., 345
Scarella, R., 52
Schalock, R. L., 252, 253
Schaps, E., 123
Schatschneider, C., 309
Scheffner Hammer, C., 183
Schloss, C., 81
Schmidt, 64
Schmidt, P. R., 325
Schmoker, M., 406
Schnabel, S., 378
Schoeller, K., 269
Schoenfeld, N. A., 206
Schormans, A. F., 234
Schumaker, J. B., 18, 225, 320,
    410, 450, 456
Schumm, 12, 20, 21, 72, 77, 78
Schumm, J. S., 12, 20, 21, 32,
    72, 76, 77, 78, 84, 116, 260,
    318, 329, 341, 349, 359, 407,
    409, 410, 425, 426, 427, 433,
    447, 450, 451, 452, 453, 454,
    455, 457, 458
Schuster, J. W., 387
Schwartz, A. A., 261
Schwartz, I., 29
Schwartz, M., 17
Schwarzwald, J., 95
Scott, B. J., 349, 351
Scott, T. M., 201, 216, 217
Scruggs, T., 67, 77, 458
Scruggs, T. E., 67, 268, 322,
    415, 457, 458
Sealey-Ruiz, Y., 110

Seals, L. M., 324
Searfoss, L. W., 422
Sears, S., 31
Seltzer, M. M., 81
Semel, E., 185
Senokossoff, G. W., 206
Senter, G., 138
Servilio, K., 201
Seuss, Dr., 310
Severson, H. H., 202
Sexson, S. B., 294
Seymour, P. H. K., 330
Shaftel, J., 378
Shalaway, L., 85
Shanahan, T., 51, 52, 111, 115
Shaw, S. F., 292
Shaywitz, B., 165
Shaywitz, S., 151, 165
Sheehan, A. K., 225
Sheldon-Wildgen, J., 225
Shen, H., 30
Sheppard-Jones, K., 126
Sherman, J. A., 225
Sherrill, J., 206
Sherron-Targett, P., 291
Shicktryon, G., 207
Shinn, M. R., 382
Shipley, K., 186
Shippen, M. E., 215
Shlomit, D., 221
Shogren, K. A., 252, 253
Shu-Hsuan, K., 323
Shumaker, 18
Siegel, L., 159
Sigafoos, J., 239, 245, 247
Silberman, R. K., 252, 291
Silva, P. A., 164
Simizu, Y., 232
Simmonds, E. P., 326
Simmons, D. C., 157, 326
Simon, B. S., 80
Simonsen, B., 139, 140,
    141, 212
Simpson, R. G., 215
Simpson, R. L., 81
Sims, 410
Sindelar, P. T., 204
Singer, H., 425
Skiba, R. J., 204
Skoulos, V., 207
Skutnabb-Kangas, T., 111
Slaughter, H., 388
Slavin, R. E., 95, 106, 381, 409
Slostad, F. A., 77
Small, S. G., 51
Smerdon, B. A., 226
Smit, A. B., 177
Smith, 67
Smith, C. R., 310
Smith, D. A., 193
Smith, J. O., 380
Smith, S. W., 220
Smith, T. E. C., 197

Smith, T. J., 275
Smith, T. W., 125, 126
Smith, Y. N., 375
Snell, M. E., 139, 269
Snidman, 209
Snow, C. E., 300, 301
Snow, M. A., 117
Snyder, A., 226
Sobsey, D., 252, 256, 291
Solano-Flores, G., 51
Soller, J., 412
Soodak, L. C., 79, 81
Soukup, J. H., 260, 264, 267
Spagna, M., 31
Sparks, R. L., 150
Sparks, S., 270
Spaulding, S. A., 130, 132, 135
Spear-Swerling, L., 363
Speckman, N. J., 149
Speece, D. L., 46, 148, 187
Spina Bifida Association, 288
Stage, S., 209
Stahl, S. A., 320, 324, 424
Stainback, S. W., 32, 256
Stanford, P., 415
Stang, K. K., 269, 450
Stanovich, K. E., 301, 302, 309
State of Florida, 260
Stecker, P. M., 113, 383
Steely, D., 393
Stein, C., 430
Steinman, B. A., 275, 278
Stenhjem, P., 127, 128
Stenhoff, D. M., 265
Stephens, K. R., 412
Steubing, K. K., 147
Stevens, K. B., 227, 387
Stevens, S., 167
Stichter, J. P., 136, 212, 213
Stoddard, K., 206
Stodden, R. A., 260
Stoneman, Z., 257
Stoner, G., 167
Stough, L., 130
Stowe, M., 7
Strichart, S. S., 444, 448
Strickland, D. S., 341, 452
Strickler, K., 427
Stuart, M., 183, 330
Sugai, G., 139, 140, 212,
    223, 247
Sumi, W. C., 204
Summers, 79, 80
Suritsky, S. K., 421
Sutherland, K. S., 226
Swain, M., 109
Swain-Bradway, J., 201, 217
Swanson, E. A., 359
Swanson, H. L., 67, 153,
    157, 159
Swanson, P. N., 351
Sweeney, J., 51
Swisher, K., 95

Synhorst, L., 209
Szabo, S., 442
Sze, S., 126
Szeibel, P. J., 168

Tabors, P. O., 301
Tacket, K., 48
Tangel, D. M., 311
Tarule, J. M., 96
Taylor, B., 95, 302
Taylor, D. B., 424, 441
Taylor, J. F., 163
Taylor, O. L., 176
Temple-Harvey, K. K., 226
Templeton, S. R., 318
Terrell, C., 183
Test, D. W., 19, 30, 79, 256,
    450, 451
Tetreault, S., 275
Texas Center for Reading
    and Language Arts, 309
Tharp, R. G., 301
Thomas, C. C., 86
Thomas, K. E., 287
Thomas, W. P., 107
Thompkins, 350
Thompson, B., 324
Thompson, J. R., 252, 253
Thornberry, T. P., 208
Thornton, C. A., 394
Thousand, J., 33, 72, 77
Thurlow, M., 30
Thurlow, M. L., 27, 385
Thurston, L. P., 64, 79
Tiedt, I. M., 99, 101, 111
Tiedt, P. L., 99, 101, 111
Tikunoff, W. J., 114
Tilly, W. D. III, 39, 49, 56
Tinajero, J. V., 112
Todd, A. W., 247
Togerson, C. W., 30
Tomblin, B., 183
Tomlinson, C. A., 351, 408,
    414, 429
Toohey, M. A., 394
Torgesen, J. K., 306, 309,
    310, 311
Towles-Reeves, E., 264
Townsend, B. L., 129
Trela, K., 260
Trelease, J., 321
Trusty, S., 279
Tucker, B. F., 394
Turnbull, A. P., 79, 81, 84,
    270, 287
Turnbull, H. R., 7, 78, 79, 81,
    85, 210, 270
Turnbull, P., 210
Turnbull, R., 287
Turner, J., 256
Tyler, B., 320, 321
Tyrell, G., 95

Uberti, H. A., 458
University of Texas Center for Reading and Language Arts, 24
Unizycki, R. M., 225
U.S. Census Bureau, 94
U.S. Department of Education, 5, 8, 22, 34, 150, 151, 188, 202, 276, 283, 291, 339, 371, 372, 374, 377
U.S. Department of Health and Human Services, 206

Vacca, J. L., 406, 407, 417, 452
Vacca, R. T., 406, 407, 417, 452
Vachon, V., 331
Vadasy, P. F., 311
Valdes, B. J., 427, 440, 453
Valentin, S., 126
Valles, E. C., 339
Valtcheva, A., 435
Van, M. B., 223
van Belle, J., 451
Vanderbilt, A. A., 220
Vandercook, T., 261
VanDerHyden, Amanda, 23, 39, 50, 56, 214
van der Lee, J. H., 290
Van Garderen, D., 167, 375, 410
Van Kleek, A., 183
Van Laarhoven, T., 265
van Leeuwen, T., 164
VanLue, M., 244
Vannest, K. J., 226
Van Ruesen, A. K., 18, 79, 446, 447, 450
Van Tassel-Baska, Joyce, 412, 413
Van Voorhis, F. L., 80
Vaughn, B. J., 247
Vaughn, S., 12, 18, 20, 21, 24, 32, 40, 41, 44, 47, 51, 52, 58, 60, 72, 76, 77, 107, 115, 116, 118, 126, 147, 149, 153, 154, 156, 157, 192, 194, 195, 197, 208, 224, 260, 301, 302, 307, 308, 310, 313, 314, 316, 317, 318, 320, 321, 322, 323, 325, 329, 330, 332, 333, 334, 344, 346, 348, 359, 363, 384, 397, 399, 409, 410, 417, 419, 425, 431, 432, 449, 451
Vaughn Gross Center for Reading and Language Arts, 47
Vellutino, F. R., 51, 54, 309
Verdugo, M. A., 252, 253
Viadero, D., 412
Villa, R., 33, 72, 77
Vitale, M. R., 349, 351
Vo, A., 226
Vogel, S. A., 150
Voltz, 410
Voyager Expanded Learning, 380
Vygotsky, L. S., 301, 345

Waggoner, J. E., 427
Wagner, E., 275
Wagner, M., 204
Wagner, R. K., 112, 306, 309
Wakeman, S., 260
Waldron, C., 244
Waldron, N. L., 31
Walker, H. M., 202, 214
Walker, M., 207
Wall, R. S., 277, 279
Wallach, G. P., 187
Wallerstein, 210
Walrath, C. M., 224
Walsh, J. M., 72, 75, 78
Walther-Thomas, 77
Wanzek, J., 60, 153, 307, 359, 417
Wark, D. M., 432
Warr-Leeper, G. A., 183
Wasburn-Moses, L., 431
Watkins, S., 282
Watson, 306
Weaver, R., 139
Webb-Johnson, G., 166
Weed, K. Z., 106
Wehby, J., 224, 432
Wehman, P., 264, 291

Wehmeyer, M. L., 12, 17, 252, 253, 260, 261, 264, 266, 267, 268, 287
Wehmeyer 2007, 17
Wei, S., 153, 417
Weiner, D., 260
Weintraub, N., 364
Weishaar, M., 455
Weiss, M. P., 77, 361, 365
Welch, M., 356
Welker, R., 226
Welner, K. G., 5
Welsh, M. C., 164
Werry, J. S., 204
Westling, D. L., 256
Wexler, J., 60, 322, 359
Weyandt, L. L., 169
What Works Clearing House, 323
Wheatley, J. P., 359, 360
White, B., 185
White, R. B., 256, 459
Whittaker, C. R., 410, 436
Widaman, K. F., 95
Wigfield, A., 433
Wiig, E. H., 185
Wilcoken, A., 31
Wilcox, K., 279
Willcutt, E. G., 165
Williams, P., 415
Williams, S., 276
Williamson, R. D., 221
Willis, J., 324
Willoughby, S., 380
Wilson, 77
Wilson, B. A., 311
Wilson, R., 204
Windmueller, M. P., 311
Winebrenner, Susan, 413
Wolery, M., 29, 387
Wolf, M. M., 219
Wolfe, P. S., 264
Wolfelt, A. D., 295
Wolffe, K. E., 275
Wolfram, W., 110
Wolf-Schein, E. G., 256
Wolsey, T. H., 430

Wong, B. Y. L., 154, 156, 159, 351
Wood, 30, 79
Wood, J. W., 427
Wood, K. D., 410, 416, 424, 428, 430, 441
Wood, W. M., 30, 79, 450, 451
Woodruff, S., 320
Woodward, M. M., 458
Wooley, J. A., 427
Worden, J. W., 295
Work, R. S., 178
Wormeli, R., 429, 435, 436
Worsham, M. E., 122, 135
Wrick, A., 397
Wright, C. D., 292, 366
Wright, J. P., 366
Wylie, R. E., 316
Wysocki, K., 316

Xu, S. H., 113

Yamaguchi, L., 301
Yantis, P. A., 178
Yasuda, S., 291
Yavas, M., 177
Yawn, C. D, 381
Yell, M. L., 4, 10, 78
Yopp, H. K., 306, 313
York, E. D., 95
York, J., 261
Young, C. L., 50
Ysseldyke, J. E., 27, 48, 385

Zahn, G. L., 95
Zaragoza, N., 344, 346, 353
Zentall, S. S., 148, 375
Zhang, D., 431
Zhang, X., 183
Zhang, Z., 458
Ziegler, A., 412
Ziegler, J. C., 188
Zigler, E., 412
Zigmond, N., 31, 32, 67, 77
Zipprich, M., 355
Zurawksy, C., 405, 406
Zwiers, J., 422, 423

A New Era: Revitalizing Special Education for Children and their Families (2002), 42

AAMR Adaptive Behavior Scale—School, 258

Abilities, focusing on, 123

Absence seizures, 288

Academic language, 109

Academic learning, opportunities for students with emotional and behavioral disorders, 226–227

Acceleration of content for students who are gifted and talented, 414

Acceptance as communication skill, 64

Accommodations
  checklist for, 34
  content versus, 77–78
  determining appropriate accommodations and modifications, 17
  environmental. *See* Environmental accommodations/modifications
  to facilitate student participation, 27
  on high-stakes assessments, 27–28
  instructional. *See* Instructional guidelines and accommodations
  tests, 12, 27

Accountability under NCLB, 5

Acquired immunodeficiency syndrome (AIDS), 289–290

Acronyms, 458
  teaching students to develop, 160

Acrostics, 458

Adaptations, instructional, 25–27. *See also* Instructional guidelines and accommodations
  for differentiated instruction (DI), 408
  for struggling writers, 349–350
  for students with disabilities in general educational classrooms, 21
  for students with emotional and behavioral disorders, 226–227

Adaptations in testing, 434

Adaptive behavior, 252

Additive approach for multicultural education, 101, 102

Advance organizers for students with learning disabilities, 154, 155

Advocacy. *See also* Self-advocacy
  information on, 81
  under IDEA, 7

African American Vernacular English (AAVE), 110

African Americans. *See* Cultural and linguistic diversity

Age of children under IDEA, 7

Aggression. *See also* Violence
  socialized, 207–208
  of students with autism spectrum disorders, 236, 245
  types of, 208

Alliteration, 309

Alphabetic principle, 149
  teaching strategies for, 310–312

Alternative assessment for students with developmental disabilities, 264

American Sign Language (ASL), 282

Americans with Disabilities Act (ADA) of 1990, 6

Amplification for students with hearing loss, 284

Analytic rubrics, 436

Antidepressants, for students with ADHD, 172

Antisocial behavior, 207

Application of learning for students with learning disabilities, 157

Articulation disorders, 177–178

Asian Pacific Islanders. *See* Cultural and linguistic diversity

Asperger syndrome, 232, 233–235
  comparison with other ASDs, 233

Assessment. *See also* Progress monitoring; Test entries
  alternative, 433, 435
  alternative assessment for students with developmental disabilities, 264
  culturally responsive assessment (CRA), 113
  of handwriting, 364
  high-stakes testing. *See* High-stakes tests
  in mathematics, 382–384
  of prior knowledge, 414
  providing feedback to parents about, 86
  in reading instruction, 304–305
  of students with ADHD, 166
  of students with autism spectrum disorders, 237
  of students with communication disorders, 188–190
  of students with cultural and linguistic differences, 112–113
  of students with developmental disabilities, 263–264
  of students with emotional and behavioral disorders, 210–215
  of students with hearing loss, 283–284
  of students with learning disabilities, 151–152
  of students with visual impairments, 276–277
  testing adaptations, 434
  test-taking strategies. *See* Test-taking strategies of writing, 339

Assessment portfolios for content-area assessment, 435

Assistive listening devices (ALDs), 285

Assistive technology for students with physical disabilities and health impairments, 292, 293

Asthma, 288

Atmotrexine for students with ADHD, 172

At-risk students. *See* Students at risk

Attention deficit disorder (ADD), 161

Attention deficit hyperactivity disorder (ADHD), 160–172
  characteristics of students with, 163–165
  definition of, 161
  eligibility for ADHD services and, 166–167
  explaining to others, 164
  identification and assessment of students with, 166
  medication for, 169–172
  prevalence of, 165–166
  types of, 161–163

Audiograms, 281

Auditory brain implants, 284

Augmentative and alternative communication (AAC), 192
  for students with cultural and linguistic differences, 240

Authentic assessment for students with developmental disabilities, 263, 264

Authoring process, 345

Autism, 232–233
  advice for working with students with, 234
  comparison with other ASDs, 233
  definition of, 233–234

Autism spectrum disorders (ASDs), 230–248
  challenging behavior and, 245
  characteristics of students with, 236–237
  curricular and instructional guidelines for students with, 237–244
  definition of, 232
  identification and assessment of students with, 237
  prevalence of, 232
  technology for students with, 242

Autistic leading behavior, 240

Automaticity, 314

Barrier games to promote language, 193

Basic interpersonal communication skills (BICS), 108

Behavioral disorders. *See* Emotional or behavioral disorders

Behavioral improvement plan (BIP), 214

Behavioral inhibition, 164

Behavior management, 120–141
  cultural diversity and, 128–130
  encouraging positive behavior using reinforcers, 132–135
  helping students change inappropriate behavior, 135–137
  PBS for, 139–141
  positive classroom climate and, 122–123
  recognizing students' mistaken goals, 135–137
  rules and consequences for, 135

Belonging, sense of, increasing for students with developmental disabilities in general education classrooms, 265, 266

Big books, 321

Bilingual education, 104–106
historical perspective on, 110–112

Bilingual Education Act of 1968, 111, 112

Bipolar disorder, 206

Black Americans. *See* Cultural and linguistic diversity

Blending, 309

Blindness, 274

Board of Education of Hendrick Hudson Central School District v. Rowley, 4

Boardmaker for students with autism spectrum disorders, 242

Body language, of students with autism spectrum disorders, 236

Bone-anchored implants, 284

Books. *See also* Textbooks
audiobooks, 428–429
big, 321
decodable, 303

Bound morphemes, 183

Braille and braille devices, 277–278

Braillers (braillewriters), 277

Brain injury. *See* Traumatic brain injury

BRIGANCE Diagnostic Comprehensive Inventory of Basic Skills—Revised, 384

Brown v. Board of Education, 4

Bulletins, sending home with students, 87–88

Bullying, preventing, 127–128

Calculators, 396

Calendars for communicating with parents, 88

Cancer, dealing with, 295–296

Cascade of integration options, 264

Cedar Rapids v. Garret F., 4

Cerebral palsy, 288

Challenging behavior
definition of, 245
of students with autism spectrum disorders, 245

Charter schools, 5

Check-in, check-out (CICO) procedure for emotional and behavioral disorders, 212
steps for implementing, 213

Child find, 7

Childhood disintegrative disorder, 232
comparison with other ASDs, 233
definition of, 235

Children and Adults with Attention Deficit Disorders (CHADD), 161

Children with specific learning disabilities, 146

Choosing Outcomes and Accommodations for Children: A Guide to Educational Planning for Students with Disabilities (COACH), 261

Chronic illness, dealing with, 295–296

Circles of Friends activity, 256

Class assignments
completing, 456–457
for differentiated instruction, 409

long-term organizing and planning for, 456–457

Class focus, communication and, 66–67

Class focus, collaboration and, 77

Class meetings, 123–124

Classification in mathematics instruction, 389

Classroom accommodations for students with hearing loss, 284

Classroom climate, establishing, 122–123

Classroom observations in RTI model, 51

Classroom routine, for students with autism spectrum disorders, 238–239

Classroom web page, for communicating with parents, 89

Classwide peer monitoring, 323

Click and clunk in collaborative strategic reading, 328

Closed captioning, 286

Cochlear implants, 284

Cognates, 115–117

Cognitive academic language proficiency (CALP), 108

Collaboration, 67–90
communication skills for, 64–67
family. *See* Collaboration with parents
with professionals. *See* Collaboration with professionals
in RTI model, 56–57

Collaboration with parents, 78–90
from diverse cultural and linguistic backgrounds, 114–115
to extend language concepts, 197
family adjustment and, 80–81
family collaboration, 79–80
forms of school-to-home communication and, 86–90
homework and, 82–84
parent conferences and, 84–86
for students with developmental disabilities, 258, 269–270

Collaboration with professionals, 67–78
collaboration model for, 67, 68, 70–71
consultation model for, 67–69
co-teaching model for, 68, 71–76
issues and dilemmas in, 77–78, 245
resources needed for, 71
support service providers and, 291–292

Collaborative strategic reading (CSR), 327–329

Collective identity, 98

Combined type ADHD, 161–162

Common underlying proficiency, 108

Communication boards for students with autism spectrum disorders, 240, 242

Communication disorders, 174–199
definition of, 176
identification and assessment of students with, 188–190
instructional guidelines and accommodations for students with, 190–197
language content and, 179–182
language disorders as, 179
language form and, 183–185

language use and, 185–186
metalinguistics, 186–187
pervasive developmental disorders, 192
prevalence of, 187
speech disorders as, 176–179
working with parents to extend language concepts and, 197

Communication skills, 64–67
acceptance as, 64
listening as, 64–65
questioning as, 65–66
stayed focused as, 68–69
of students with autism spectrum disorders, 236
of students with developmental disabilities, 255–256
for students with prelinguistic level autism, 240
for students with visual impairments, 275
teaching to students with autism spectrum disorders, 239–241

Communication strategies for students with emotional and behavioral disorders, 220

Community conditions as cause of emotional and behavioral disorders, 210

Co-morbidity, 203

Compensatory skills of students with visual impairments, 277

Composing in writing workshops, 348, 351

Comprehensible input, 107

Comprehensible output, 109

Comprehension
language education affecting, 179
mathematics. *See* Mathematics comprehension
reading. *See* Reading comprehension
teaching, 193

Comprehension monitoring, 301

Comprehension strategies, 323–331

Comprehensive Math Ability Test, 384

Comprehensive Math Assessment, 384

Comprehensive Reading Assessment Battery (CRAB), 306

Comprehensive Test of Phonological Processing (CTOPP), 306

Computation skills, teaching strategic for, 393–398

Computational Arithmetic Program, 380

Computational strategies, 394

Computer assisted instruction (CAI) in spelling, 359

Computers. *See* Technological tools and aids

Concept diagrams for content-area instruction, 418

Concept maps for students with learning disabilities, 154

Concepts
demonstrating connections between, 193–194
development in students with visual impairments, 275
new, presenting, 193, 194
teaching to second language learners, 117

Conceptual density of textbooks, 425
Concerta for students with ADHD, 172
Conduct disorder, 207
Conferencing, 353
Confidentiality of records under IDEA, 7
Conflict resolution, with students with
     emotional and behavioral disorders,
     218–220
Conners Teachers Rating Scale, 166
Consequences for behavior management, 135
Constant time delay procedure, 387
Consultation
     models for, 25, 67–69
     for parents, 81
     in RTI model, 56–57
Content
     accommodation versus, 77–78
     real, in message, 65
     for students who are gifted and talented,
        414
Content integration, 99
Content-area instruction
     activities for, 430
     assessment portfolios for, 435
     demonstrations for, 420–421
     differentiated instruction and, 407
     facilitating student participation for,
        421–424
     graphic organizers for, 417–419
     ideas for demonstrating, 159
     listener-friendly lectures for, 419–420
     prelearning activities for, 416–417
     technology for, 428
     textbooks for, 424–429
Context-embedded communication and
     instruction, 109
Contexts, purposive, teaching language in,
     192–193
Continuum of services, 7, 9
     arguments for, 34–35
Contract, teacher-student (sample), 219
Contributions approach for multicultural
     education, 101, 102
Conversations
     instructional, 301
     for language promotion, 194
     metacognitive, 442–443
Cooperative learning
     for students with developmental disabilities
        in general education classrooms, 267
Cooperative teaching
     concerns about, 77
Co-planning, 72–73, 74, 77
     lesson, 72
     long-range, 72
     planning pyramid and, 72–73, 74
Corrective Mathematics Program, 380
Co-teaching, 68, 71–76
     grading and, 75–76
     lesson, 73
Counseling for parents, 81
Counting by numbers, 388
Crime-oriented gangs, 208

Critical thinking, 424
Cultural and linguistic diversity, 92–118
     assessment of students with, 112–113
     behavior management and, 128–130
     celebrating, 123
     in classrooms, 94–95
     cultural characteristics and, 97–99
     identification of ADHD, 166
     instructional guidelines and
        accommodations for students with,
        114–118
     language and, 197
     macrocultures and microcultures, 95
     multicultural education and, 99–103
     RTI model for, 51–53
     second language acquisition and. See Second
        language acquisition
     technology for, 116
     understanding diverse cultures, 95–97
     working with parents from diverse
        backgrounds, 114–115
Cultural boundaries, 98–99
Cultural characteristics, 97–98
Cultural inversion, 98
Culturally responsive assessment (CRA), 113
Culturally responsive teaching (CRT) style, 95
     characteristics of, 114
Culture, school, empowering, 100
Curricular guidelines, for students with autism
     spectrum disorders, 237–244
Curriculum
     adaptations for students with developmental
        disabilities, 264
     general education, access to, for students
        with developmental disabilities, 257
     integrating math problem solving into, 400
     mathematics. See Mathematics curriculum
     for multicultural education, 101–103
     for writing, current trends in, 337–338
Curriculum-based measurement (CBM),
     305–307
     in mathematics, 383–384
Curriculum compacting, 414
Curriculum enhancement, 408
Curriculum-based assessment (CBA) for
     students with developmental disabilites, 263
Cursive writing, 363, 366
Cybaries (cyber libraries)
     for student research, 428

Deaf, definition of, 281
Death, dealing with, 295–296
Decision-making teams in RTI model, 49
Decodable books, 303
Decodable text, 311
Decoders for closed captioning, 286
Decoding in reading, 300
     teaching strategies for, 315–320
Defiance, 207
Delinquent youth gangs, 208
Demonstrating learning in multiple ways for
     students with learning disabilities, 158–159
Demonstration plus model strategy, 421

Demonstrations for content-area instruction,
     420–421
Department of Public Welfare v. Haas, 4
Depression, 206–207
Developing independence in learning,
     443–459
     active learning in classroom and, 451–455
     difficulties in, 443
     home-school connections and, 455–459
     personal responsibility and, 443–451
Developmental arithmetic disorder, 375
Developmental disabilities, 250–270
     definitions and types of, 250–251
     identification and assessment of students
        with, 257, 263–264
     instructional guidelines and
        accommodations for students with,
        259–270
     prevalence of, 257
     technology for students with, 259
Diagnostic Achievement Battery, 384
Diagnostic Adaptive Behavior Scale (DABS),
     258
Diagnostic and Statistical Manual of Mental
     Disorders, 205
Diagnostic assessments of reading, 305
Dialect, 110
Dialog journal, 366
Dictionary training, 363
Differentiated instruction (DI), 407–416
     assessment, 429, 431
     class assignments and homework for, 409
     components of, 408
     flexible grouping with, 408
     response to intervention (RTI) related,
        415–416
     for secondary learners, 407
     for students who are gifted and talented,
        411–415
Difficulty with zero in mathematics
     instruction, 395
Direct assessments of students with autism
     spectrum disorders, 245–246
Disabilities
     system of federal categories, 22
     use of term, 22
Discrepancy analysis for students with
     developmental disabilities, 262, 263
Discussion web, 423–424
Discussions
     do's and don'ts, 452
     to facilitate student participation, 423–424
     techniques for stimulating, 423
     vibrant, 423–424
Disruptive behaviors of students with autism
     spectrum disorders, 245
DISSECT strategy, 320
Distributed practice, 458
Documentation portfolios, 341
Dopamine for students with ADHD, 172
Down syndrome, 253
Drug gangs, 208
Dual discrepancy of struggling learners, 46

Dual sensory impairments
    definition of, 257
Due process under IDEA, 7
Dynamic Indicators of Basic Early Literacy
    Skills (DIBELS), 306
Dyscalculia, 147
Dysfluency, 179
Dysgraphia, 147, 364
Dyslexia, 147

Early intervening services (EIS), 42
Early intervention
    under IDEIA, 28–29
    for reading difficulties, 308
Early-exit bilingual programs, 105
Echolalia in students with autism spectrum
    disorders, 236
Editing in writing workshops, 348, 351
Education for All Handicapped Children Act
    (EAHCA) of 1975, 5, 6
Education of the Handicapped Act (1970), 4
Education of the Handicapped Act
    Amendments of 1986, 6
Educational Amendments Act of 1974, 6
Educational interventions for students with
    ADHD, 167, 169
Educational placement, 9
Effective listening, 64–65, 66
Elaboration for language promotion, 196
Elementary and Secondary Education Act
    (ESEA) of 1965, 4, 6
Email for communicating with parents,
    88–89
Emotional and behavioral disorders (EBD),
    200–228
    causes of, 209–210
    changing behavior of, 217–218
    check-in, check-out (CICO) procedure for,
        212, 213
    definitions of, 202–203
    identification and assessment of students
        with, 210–215
    prevalence of students with, 203–204
    reasons for underidentification, 203
    recommendations for effective
        interventions, 213
    response to intervention (RTI) for,
        212–214
    teaching guidelines and education for
        students with, 215–227
    technology for students with, 227
    types and characteristics of, 204–209
Emotional disturbance, defining, 202
Empowering school culture, 100
Encoded language in writing process, 342
Encoding function, 452
Encouragement, positive feedback
    versus, 132
English as a second language (ESL)
    instruction. See also English language
        learners (ELLs)
    historical perspective on, 110–112
    situational factors and, 106–107

English language learners (ELLs), 104–105.
    See also English as a second language (ESL)
    instruction; Second language acquisition
    assessment of, 112–113
    best instructional practices for, 114–118
    incidence of, 95
    misconceptions and realities about teaching,
        104, 105
    RTI approaches for, 52–53
    silent or nonverbal period for, 109
    teaching students with reading difficulties,
        329–331
"English only" legislation, 112
Enrichment, 414
Environment
    least restrictive, 7, 9–11
    physical. See Physical environment
    to promote reading, 303–304
    to promote writing, 345–346
    social, promoting writing, 346
    study environment checklist, 448
Environmental accommodations/modifications
    for students with developmental disabilities
        in general education classrooms, 267, 268
    for students with physical disabilities, health
        impairments, and traumatic brain injury,
        292
    for students with visual impairments, 277,
        278
Environmental causes of emotional and
    behavioral disorders, 209–210
Epilepsy, 288–289
Equity pedagogy, 100
Essay writing, teaching strategies, 356
Estimation, in mathematics instruction, 391
ETA/Cuisenaire, 380
Evaluation portfolios, 341
Executive functioning, 164
Executive learners, 440
Expansion for language promotion, 196
Explication in textbooks, 425
Explicit skill instruction, 118
Expository writing, teaching strategies for,
    354, 356
Expressive language, disorders of, 179
Extended practice for students with learning
    disabilities, 157
Externalizing behaviors, 204
External storage function, 452

Failure to shift operations in mathematics
    instruction, 395
Families. See also Collaboration with parents;
    Parent entries
    adjustment of, 80–81
    involvement with RTI model, 53
FAST DRAW strategy, 397
Feedback
    about assessment results, providing to
        parents, 86
    how to provide effective, 58
    in mathematics instruction, 385
    positive, 132

for spelling instruction, 362
    strategies for enhancing student learning,
        385
Fetal alcohol syndrome (FAS), 254
Figurative language, 183
Finger spelling, 282, 283
First drafts, 351
FIRST-letter strategy, 458–459
Flexible groups, for reading
    instruction, 308
FLIP chart strategy, 425, 426
Fluency
    in handwriting, 366
    in reading, 300
    teaching strategies for, 320–323
Fluency disorders, 178–179
Focalin for students with ADHD, 172
Focus, maintaining, as communication skills,
    68–69
Fractions in mathematics instruction, 392–393
Fragile X syndrome, 254
Free and appropriate public education, 166
Free appropriate public education, 7
Free morphemes, 183
Friendliness level of textbooks, 425
Frustration reading level, 307
Full inclusion, 32
    arguments for, 34–35
Functional analysis of students with autism
    spectrum disorders, 246
Functional assessment with developmental
    disabilities, 262, 263
Functional behavioral assessments (FBAs)
    methods, 216
    of students with autism spectrum disorders,
        245–246
    for students with emotional and behavioral
        disorders, 214–215
Functional practice for students developmental
    disabilities in general education classrooms,
    269
Functional vision, definition of, 275
Funding under NCLB, 5
Funds of knowledge, 96

Games
    in mathematics instruction, 388–389
    to promote language, 188, 193
Gangs, 208
Gates-MacGintie Reading Tests, 306
General education classrooms
    adaptations for students with disabilities in,
        21
    mathematics instructional practices for
        gifted students in, 376–377
    promoting language learning in, 118
    support for students with developmental
        disabilities in, 265–269
General education curriculum, access to, for
    students with developmental disabilities,
    259–260
General education teachers, role with students
    with developmental disabilities, 258

Gifted and talented students
  characteristics of students who are gifted
    and talented, 412, 413
  classroom strategies and adaptations for,
    413–414
  learning in the classroom, 411–412
  math instruction for, 376–377
  underidentified high-achieving students,
    412, 414
Gist, getting, in collaborative strategic reading,
  328–329
Goals
  learning, for students with developmental
    disabilities in general education
    classrooms, 266–267
  mathematics, establishing, 380–381
  mistaken, recognizing, 135–137
  personal, helping students establish, 221
  realistic, establishing, 380–381
  setting, 446–447
Grading, 435–436
  co-teaching and, 75–76
  criteria for students with disabilities, 76
Grading rubrics for test taking, 435–436
Grand mal seizures, 288
Graphic organizers for content-area
  instruction, 417–419
Group behavior, 207–208
Group responding, 422
Group work solutions for students with
  emotional and behavioral disorders, 220
Groups for cooperative reading, 329
Grouping (in mathematics), 392
Grouping (instructional)
  flexible, for reading instruction, 308

Hands-on instruction for students with
  developmental disabilities in general
  education classrooms, 267–268
Handwriting instruction, 363–366
  assessment and, 364
  effective, principles of, 364–366
  guidelines for assessing, 365
  Hanover method, 366
  moving model of, 366
  for students with difficulty in handwriting,
    364
  teaching strategies for, 363–366
  traditional, 363–364
Hanover method, 366
Hard of hearing, 281
Head injury. See Traumatic brain injury
Health risks. See Physical disabilities and
  health impairments; Safety
Hearing aids or implants, 284
Hearing loss, 280–286
  definitions and types of, 281
  identification and assessment of students
    with, 283–284
  instructional guidelines and
    accommodations for students with,
    284–286
  mixed, 281

prevalence of, 282–283
technology for students with, 293
Help-seeking behaviors, 440
Help-seeking inventory, 445
Heterogeneous grouping of students, 408
High responders to intervention, 50–51
High schools, RTI model in, 58–60
High-frequency words, 314
Highlighting textbooks, 427
High-stakes tests
  for content areas, 431
  preparing for and taking, 431
Holistic rubrics, 436
Home conditions as cause of emotional and
  behavioral disorders, 209–210
Homebound instruction, 9, 11
Homework (home learning), 82–84
  buddy system for, 82
  completing assignments and, 456–457
  for differentiated instruction, 409
  policy for, 82–83
  special project checklist, 84
  for students with ADHD, 169, 170
Homogeneous grouping of students, 408
Honig v. Doe, 4
Human immunodeficiency virus (HIV),
  289–290
Hyperactive-impulsive ADHD, 163
Hyperactivity, 161

I PLAN strategy, 18, 451
IDEA. *See* Individuals with Disabilities
  Education Act (IDEA) of 1990
IDEIA. *See* Individuals with Disabilities
  Education Improvement Act (IDEIA) of
  2004
Identification
  of students with ADHD, 166
  of students with autism spectrum disorders,
    237
  of students with communication disorders,
    188–190
  of students with developmental disabilities,
    257–258
  of students with disabilities using RTI data,
    57
  of students with emotional and behavioral
    disorders, 210–215
  of students with hearing loss, 283–284
  of students with learning disabilities,
    151–152
  of students with physical disabilities and
    health impairments, 291
  of students with traumatic brain
    injury, 291
  of students with visual impairments,
    276–277
Ignoring, on purpose, 136
Immaturity, 208–209
Impulsivity, 161
Inattentive ADHD, 161, 163
Inclusion, 31–32
  definition of, 31

effectiveness of, 31
full, 32, 34
guidelines for responsible, 32
Independence
  in learning. *See* Developing independence in
    learning
  promoting in students with physical
    disabilities, health impairments, and
    traumatic brain injury, 294
Independent reading level, 307
Indirect assessments of students with autism
  spectrum disorders, 245
Indirect experiences to teach
  reading, 324
Individual interventions under RTI
  model, 51
Individualized education programs
  (IEPs), 7, 11–19
  determining appropriate accommodations
    and modifications, 17
  participants in IEP meetings and, 17
  process for, 19
  sample of, 13–16
  software programs, 12
  student involvement in, 17–18
Individualized family service plans (IFSPs),
  28–29
Individualized-intervention and standardized
  intervention compared, 60
Individualized transition plans, 30
Individuals with Disabilities Education Act
  (IDEA) of 1990, 5, 6
  amendment of (2004), 6
  developmental disabilities under, 257
  hearing loss and, 282
  IEPs and. *See* Individualized education
    programs (IEPs)
  NIMAS under, 277
Individuals with Disabilities Education
  Improvement Act (IDEIA) of 2004, 6
  critical guidelines, 7–8
  discipline problems, 137
  eligibility and identification criteria for, 40
  eligibility of ADHD services under,
    166–167
  expansion of impact of, 28–31
  guidelines, 146
  identifying students with learning
    disabilities prior to, 41
  IEP meeting requirements, 17
  key features of, 8
  RTI promoted in, 42
  teacher responsibilities under, 19–31
Informal reading inventories, 307
Information for parents, 81
Informational writing, teaching strategies for,
  354, 356
Instructional aids for students with visual
  impairments, 279–280
Instructional clarity, 419–420
Instructional conversations, 301
  for students with learning disabilities,
    154–156

Instructional devices in textbooks, 425
Instructional grouping. *See* Grouping (instructional)
Instructional guidelines and accommodations
    for culturally and linguistically diverse students, 114–118
    for students with ADHD, 167–169
    for students with autism spectrum disorders, 237–244
    for students with communication disorders, 190–197
    for students with developmental disabilities, 259–270
    for students with emotional and behavioral disorders, 215–227
    for students with hearing loss, 284–286
    for students with learning disabilities, 152–160
    for students with physical disabilities and health impairments, 291–295
    for students with traumatic brain injury, 291–295
    for students with visual impairments, 277–280
Instructional materials for students with emotional and behavioral disorders, 227
Instructional reading level, 307
Intellectual disabilities, 252
    physical causes of, 253–254
Intellectual functioning, of students with developmental disabilities, 255
Intellectually gifted students. *See* Gifted and talented students
Intelligences, multiple, 415
Intensive interventions, 60
Internalizing behaviors, 204
Internet and websites
    for communicating with parents, 88–89
    for students with traumatic brain injury and visual, hearing, and other physical disabilities, 293
Interpreters for students with hearing loss, 286
Intervention
    multitiered, in RTI model, 42
Intervention, three tiers of, 46–47

Key Math—Revised, 384
Key Math Teach and Practice, 380
Key word method, 459
Keyboarding
    for students with learning disabilities, 158
    teaching strategies for, 366–367
Keyboards for students with traumatic brain injury and visual, hearing, and other physical disabilities, 293
Knowledge construction, 99
K-W-L strategy, 324–325
    introducing, 441
    two variations on, 442

Language. *See* Cultural and linguistic diversity; English as a second language (ESL); English language learners (ELLs); Second language acquisition
Language development
    facilitating, 192–197
Language disorders, 179
Language proficiency
    iceberg analogy of, 108
Language variation, 110
Large print for students with visual impairments, 279
Late bilingual programs, 105
Latino Americans. *See* Cultural and linguistic diversity
Lau v. Nichols, 112
LD. *See* Learning disabilities
Learner characteristics
    second language acquisition and, 107–108
Learning
    application of, for students with learning disabilities, 157
    developing independence in. *See* Development independence in learning
    opportunities for, for students with emotional and behavioral disorders, 224, 225
    transfer of. *See* Transfer of learning, teaching for
Learning and developmental process of second language acquisition, 108–109
Learning communities, creating, 123
Learning contracts, 408
Learning Disabilities Association (LDA), 146
Learning disabilities (LD), 145–160
    adjusting workload and time for, 157–158
    advance organizers and, 154, 155
    characteristics of students with, 147–150
    definition of, 146
    graphic organizers and, 417
    identification and assessment of students with, 151–152
    instructional conversations strategy, 154–156
    instructional techniques and accommodations for students with, 152–160
    keyboarding for students with, 158
    learning tools and aids for, 157
    lifelong outcomes for students with, 149
    memory strategies for, 159–160
    practices associated with academic success, 153
    presenting information and demonstrating in multiple ways for, 158–159
    prevalence of, 150–151
    providing opportunities for extended practice and application and, 157
    reading difficulties and suggestions for instruction, 150
    referral of students with, 152
    signals for, 149

teaching self-regulation and self-monitoring and, 156
    technology for students with, 158
    thinking aloud strategy, 154–155
Learning goals, for students with developmental disabilities in general education classrooms, 266–267
Learning media assessment for students with visual impairments, 277
Learning tools and aids for students with learning disabilities, 157
Least restrictive environment (LRE), 7, 9–11
    checklist, 10
Lectures, listener-friendly, 419–420
    using cues with, 421
Legal blindness, definition of, 274
Legibility of handwriting, 365–366
Lesson co-planning, 72
Lesson co-teaching, 73, 75
Letters, sending home with students, 87–88
Letter strategy mnemonics, 458
Letter-sound correspondence, teaching strategies for, 308–309, 311–312
Lexile levels of textbooks, 424–425
Linguistic diversity. *See* Cultural and linguistic diversity
Linguistic input, second language acquisition and, 107
Listening
    activities for teaching listening skills and, 454
    audiobooks for visually impaired students, 428–429
    in class, 452–455
    as communication skill, 64–66
Literacy developing, promoting, for students with physical disabilities and health impairments, 293
Long-range co-planning, 72
Low vision, definition of, 274

Macroculture, 95
Mainstreaming, definition of, 31
Maintenance bilingual education, 106
Making words, 319
Manipulating, 309
Manuscript writing, 363, 366
Maps for planning narrative writing, 354
MARKER strategy, 446
Massed trials strategy, 239–240
Mastery in mathematics, 388
Math difficulties, students with, 375–376, 377–378
    curricular programs for, 380
Math Exploration and Applications program, 380
Math—Level Indicator: A Quick Group Math Placement Test, 384
Math proficiency standards, 373–375
Mathematics
    ideas for demonstrating, 159
Mathematics ability, influences on, 372–373

Mathematics comprehension
  checking for, 387
  math manipulatives, 386
  teaching for, 386
Mathematics curriculum
  current trends in, 371–372
  evaluating, 377–378
Mathematics instruction, 370–401
  activities for, 398–399
  adapting basal materials for students with
    special needs, 379
  assessment, 382–384
  for basic math skills, 385–389
  for computation skills, 393–398
  cooperative practices for, 381–382
  current trends in, 371–372
  diagnosing student learning needs,
    383–384
  difficulties in learning mathematics and,
    375–376
  effective, 376–377
  fractions and, 392–393
  for gifted students, 376–377
  math proficiency, 373–375
  NCTM standards, 373
  in numeration, 390–392
  place value and, 392
  prenumber skills and, 389–390
  for problem-solving skills, 397–400
  for secondary students with math
    difficulties, 378–379
  standards-based, 405–406
  technology for, 396
McGill Action Planning System (MAPS), 261,
  262
Medically fragile students, 287
Medications for students with ADHD,
  169–172
Memory problems in mathematics instruction,
  395
Memory strategies, 457–459
  for students with learning disabilities,
    159–160
Mental retardation
  classification of, 252–253
  definition of, 252
  problems in classification, 39–40
Metacognition, defined, 439
Metacognitive conversations, 442–443
Metadiscourse in textbooks, 425
Metalinguistics, 111, 186–187
Methadate for students with ADHD, 172
Methylphenidate for students with ADHD,
  169, 172
Microcultures, 95
Middle ear implants, 284
Middle schools, RTI model in, 58–60
Milieu (naturalistic) instruction, 240
Mills v. Board of Education of the District of
  Columbia, 4
Minorities. See Cultural and linguistic
  diversity
Mistaken goals, recognizing, 135–137

Mixed-ability groups
  providing opportunities for students to
    work in, 123
Mnemonic devices, 458
Mobility skills for students with visual
  impairments, 278
Modeling for language promotion, 196
Monitoring of schedules, 449–450
Monoculars, 279
Morphemes, 183–184
Morphology, 183–184
Motivation to spell correctly, 362
Motivator, intrinsic, using language as, 196–197
Motor skills
  instruction in, for students with physical
    disabilities, health impairments, and
    traumatic brain injury, 293
  for students with developmental disabilities,
    255
  of students with visual impairments, 275
Motoric problems in mathematics instruction,
  395
Moving model for handwriting instruction,
  366
MP3 players for students with learning
  disabilities, 158
Multicultural education, 99–103
  curricula for, 101–103
  desired student outcomes and, 101
  dimensions of, 99–100
  guidelines for, 104
Multidisciplinary teams (MDTs), 11
Multiliteracies, 428
Multiple disabilities, definition of, 256–257
Multiple grouping formats, 408
Multiple intelligences, 415
Multiple meanings, 181–182
Multitiered intervention strategy in RTI
  model, 42
Muscular dystrophy, 289

Naming tens in mathematics instruction, 392
Narrative writing, teaching strategies for, 354
Nation at Risk, A, 405
National Instructional Materials Accessibility
  Standard (NIMAS), 277
Native Americans. See Cultural and linguistic
  diversity
NCTM Navigation Series, 380
NCTM standards for mathematics, 373
Negative reinforcement, 132–135
Neuromotor impairment, 287
Newsletters for communicating with parents,
  88
No Child Left Behind Act (NCLB) of 2001,
  5, 6, 27–28
  standards-based instruction related, 406
Noncompliance under IDEA, 7
Nondiscriminatory evaluation under IDEA, 7
Nonoptical aids for students with visual
  impairments, 279–280
Nonresponders to intervention, 50–51
  identifying why, 50

Nonverbal math disabilities, 375–376
Norm-based assessments of reading, 305
Note takers for students with hearing loss, 286
Note taking, 452–455
  activities for teaching note taking, 454
  guidelines for, 453–454
  teaching, 454–455
  two column format, 453
Notes, sending home with students, 87–88
Number sense, 384
Numeration, 390–392

One-to-one correspondence in mathematics
  instruction, 389
Onset-rime, 315–316
Oppositional defiant disorder (ODD), 207
Optical aids for students with visual
  impairments, 279–280
Organization
  personal responsibility and, 448–449
  of textbooks, 425
Orientation skills for students with visual
  impairments, 278
Orthopedic impairment, 287
Other health impairment, definition of, 287
Overcorrection, 136–137
Overlearning, 458

Pace, adjusting, for language promotion,
  195–196
Paragraph writing, teaching strategies for, 356
Parallel curriculum model (PCM), 414
Parallel participation for students with
  developmental disabilities, 264
Parallel talk for language promotion, 196
Paraprofessionals, working with, 69, 245
Parent conferences, 84–86
Parent interviews, 90
Parent participation, under IDEA, 7
Parent surveys, 90
Parental involvement, 258, 269–270. See also
  Collaboration with parents
Parents
  collaboration with. See Collaboration with
    parents
  needs of, 80–81
  providing feedback about assessment results
    to, 86
Partial participation for students with
  developmental disabilities, 264
Partial sight, definition of, 274
Peer assisted learning (PAL), 323
Peer collaboration model, 70–71
Peer editing, 352
Peer support, for students with developmental
  disabilities, 265, 266
Peer tutoring
  in reading, 323
  in spelling, 359
  for students with developmental disabilities,
    265
Peers, educating about physical disabilities and
  health impairments, 294

Pennsylvania Association for Retarded Children v. Commonwealth of Pennsylvania, 4

Personal goals, helping students establish, 221

Personal responsibility, 443–451
  goal setting and self-monitoring and, 446–447
  organization and, 448–449
  self-advocacy and, 450–451
  self-evaluation and, 446
  time management and, 449–450

Personalized knowledge, 95–96

Person-centered planning (PCP), 18
  for students with developmental disabilities, 261–262

Person-first language, 7

Persuasive writing, teaching strategies for, 357–358

Pervasive developmental disorder—not otherwise specified (PDD-NOS), 232
  defined, 235

Pervasive developmental disorders (PDDs)
  communication disorders and, 192
  definition of, 232

Petit mal seizures, 288

Phone calls for communicating with parents, 88

Phonemes, 183

Phonemic awareness, 149

Phonic analysis, 315

Phonological awareness, 183
  teaching strategies for, 309–312, 313

Phonological awareness skills, 300

Phonology, 183

Physical disabilities and health impairments, 286–295. *See also* Hearing loss; Visual impairment
  characteristics of students with, 288–290
  definitions and types of, 286–287
  identification and assessment of students with, 291
  instructional guidelines and accommodations for students with, 291–295
  prevalence of, 290–291
  technology for students with, 293

Physical environment. *See also* Environment
  promoting writing, 345–346
  for students with emotional and behavioral disorders, 217

Physical space, arranging, 122–123

Picture Exchange Communication System (PECS), 242

Place value in mathematics instruction, 392

Planned ignoring, 136

Planning
  in prewriting, 351
  of schedules, 449–450
  story webs for, 354, 355
  teachers' participation in, 22–25

Planning pyramid, 72–73, 74
  for content-area instruction, 411
  for students with developmental disabilities, 260–261

Planning systems for students with developmental disabilities, 260–262

PLEASE strategy, 356

Podcasts for students with learning disabilities, 158

Portfolio assessment
  in content areas, 435
  for students with developmental disabilities, 263–264

Portfolios, writing, 341–342

Positive behavior, focusing on, 131–132

Positive behavioral support (PBS), 139–141
  for managing challenging behavior, 247
  as prevention, 139–140
  response to intervention and, 141
  schoolwide, 140–141

Positive classroom climate, 122–123

Positive feedback, encouragement versus, 132

Positive reinforcement, 132–135

Postschool activities, transition from school to, 29–31

Practice
  in mathematics instruction, 388–389
  for spelling instruction, 360–361, 362

Practice in Effective Guidance Strategies (PEGS), 227

Pragmatics, 185

Preference assessment for students with autism spectrum disorders, 238

Prejudice reduction, 100

Prelearning activities in content-area instruction, 416–417

Prelinguistic level of autism, communication skills for, 240

Prenumber skills, 389–390

Prereferral assistance teams (PATs), 22

Prereferral for special education services, 25

Preschool children, early intervention services under IDEIA for, 28–29

Presenting information in multiple ways for students with learning disabilities, 158–159

Preventing Reading Difficulties in Young Children, 300

Previewing in collaborative strategic reading, 328

Prewriting in writing workshops, 348, 350–351

Prior knowledge, assessment of, 414

Problem-solving
  mathematics, teaching, 397–400

Problem-solving model, 25, 26

Problem-solving model for RTI model, 47–48
  standard protocol model compared, 48–49

Procedural error in mathematics instruction, 395

Process portfolios, 341

Production (of language)
  language disorders affecting, 179
  teaching, 193

Program outlines, 32–33

Progress monitoring
  assessing students' response to intervention with, 54

in handwriting instruction, 365
in mathematics, 382–384
in reading, 305–307
in reading instruction, 305–307
in RTI models, 40, 44–45, 54–55
in spelling, 361–362
steps in conducting, 55
for students with emotional and behavioral disorders, 214
of writing, 339–340

Progress reports, 88

PROJECT strategy, 456

Public Law 91-30. *See* Education of the Handicapped Act (1970)

Public Law 93-380. *See* Educational Amendment Act of 1974; Vocational Rehabilitation Act (VRA) of 1973

Public Law 94-142. *See* Education for All Children Act (EAHCA) of 1975

Public Law 99-457. *See* Education of the Handicapped Act Amendments of 1986

Public Law 101-336. *See* Americans with Disabilities Act (ADA) of 1990

Public Law 101-476. *See* Individuals with Disabilities Education Act (IDEA) of 1990

Publishing in writing workshops, 348, 352

Pull-out services, 32

Punishment, 136–137

Purpose-setting activities in content-area instruction, 416–417

Purposive contexts, teaching language in, 192–193

Question-answer relationships (QAR) strategy, 325–327

Questioning
  as communication skill, 65–66
  to facilitate student participation, 422

Questioning the author (QtA) strategy, 327

Rapid naming, 149

Readability level of textbooks, 424–425

Reading
  learning difficulties in process of, 301
  possible screening measures for, 55
  repeated, 321–322

Reading aloud, 321

Reading comprehension, 301
  strategies for improving, 323–331

Reading instruction, 298–335
  activities for, 313–314
  assessment for, 304–305, 307
  components of, 302–303
  content-area, 424–429
  current trends in, 300
  difficulties and suggestions for instruction, 150
  for first grade, 333
  for fluency, 320–323
  for improving comprehension, 323–331
  intensive, 307
  for kindergarten, 332
  learning difficulties and, 301

for older students, 331
for phonological awareness, letter-sound relationships, and alphabetic principle, 309–313
for second and third grade, 334, 359
for struggling readers, 303–308
for word identification, 314–320
Real content in message, 65
Real world, student's world versus, 78
Receptive language, disorders of, 179
Receptive vocabulary, 180
Reciprocal causation, 301
Recording textbook content, 428–429
Reference software for students with learning disabilities, 158
Referral, teachers' participation in, 22–25
Regard, demonstrating for all students, 123
Register, 185
Regrouping in mathematics instruction, 391
Regular Education Initiative (REI), 34–35
Reinforcement, positive and negative, 132–135
Reinforcement for students with autism spectrum disorders, 239–240
Related services, 11
Reliable alliances, 270
Repeated reading, 321–322
Repetitive motor behaviors of students with autism spectrum disorders, 237
Research paper writing, teaching strategies for, 356–357
Research skills, activities to improve, 457
Research-based writing instruction, 338–339
Residential settings, 9, 10
Residual hearing, 281
Responders to intervention, 50–51
Response cost, behavior management, 137
Response to intervention (RTI), 22, 23–24
    children with specific learning disabilities, 146
    components of, 43–53
    for culturally and linguistically diverse students, 51–53, 95
    decision-making teams, 49
    defined, 39
    differentiated instruction (DI) related, 415–416
    early reading intervention, 308
    for English language learners (ELLs), 52–53
    family involvement with, 53
    four key components of, 44
    identifying students who need help in math, 382
    identifying students with learning disabilities prior to, 41
    implementing interventions, 47–51
    initiatives influencing, 41–43
    in middle and high schools, 58–60
    positive behavioral support and, 141
    previous identification of, 40–41
    progress monitoring, 40, 44–45
    providing interventions, 57–58
    recommended models by state, 43

responders and nonresponders to intervention, 50–51
role of teachers in, 56–58
screening approaches, 53–55
screening struggling readers, 304–305
for students with emotional and behavioral disorders, 212–214
technology for, 45
three tiers of intervention, 46–47
using RTI data to identify students with disabilities, 57
what it can and cannot do, 50
of writing, 340–341
Responsibility. See Personal responsibility
Rett syndrome, 232
    comparison with other ASDs, 233
    definition of, 235
Revising in writing workshops, 348, 351–352
REWARDS program for reading, 331
Rhyming, 309
Ritalin (methylphenidate) for students with ADHD, 169, 172
RTI. See Response to intervention
Rubrics
    grading, for test taking, 435–436
    helping students use, 436
    writing, 341
Rules and consequences
    for behavior management, 135

Safety
    for students with developmental disabilities, 265
Safety, risks to, 124–125
    child abuse and neglect, 125, 126
Saxon Math, 380
Scaffolded questioning, 422
Schedules, planning and monitoring, 449–450
Schizophrenia, 209
School choice under NCLB, 5
School culture, empowering, 100
School support, Circles of Friends activity to provide, 256
School-based wraparound for students with emotional and behavioral disorders, 224–226
Schoolwide positive behavioral support (SWPBS), 140–141
SCORE A method, 356
Screening approaches for RTI model, 53–55
    making educational decisions with, 54
Second language acquisition. See also English as a second language (ESL) instruction; English language learners (ELLs)
    explicit skill instruction and, 118
    focus on meaning and, 117
    framework for, 106–110
    guidelines for making input more comprehensible and, 108
    historical perspective on, 110–112
    iceberg analogy of language proficiency, 108
    language variation and dialect and, 110

learning and developmental process of, 108–109
    programs for promoting, 104–106
    strategic first language use and, 115
Secondary intervention (tier 2) of RTI model, 46
    guidelines, 59
    teacher role, 57–58
    Tier 3 compared, 47
Secondary language output, 109
Section 504. See Vocational Rehabilitation Act (VRA) of 1973
Segmenting, 309
Seizures, 288–289
Self-advocacy, 450–451
    as strategy for IEP meetings, 18
Self-concept, enhancing, 126–127
Self-control, promoting, with students with emotional and behavioral disorders, 218–220
Self-determination, by students, 18–19, 444
Self-determination for students with developmental disabilities, 268–269
Self-evaluation, 446
Self-help by students with visual impairments, 275
Self-injurious behavior of students with developmental disabilities, 256
Self-injury by students with autism spectrum disorders, 236, 245
Self-management
    teaching strategies for, for students with emotional and behavioral disorders, 221–222
Self-monitoring, 444, 446–447
    in mathematics, 381
    for students with learning disabilities, 156
    teaching strategies for, for students with emotional and behavioral disorders, 220–221
    of writing, 343
Self-recording, 446
Self-regulation for students with learning disabilities, 156
Self-talk for language promotion, 196
Semantic feature analysis, 180–181
Semantic maps for content-area instruction, 417–418
Semantics, 179–180, 318
Seriation in mathematics instruction, 390
Service programs, parent-coordinated, 81
Severe disabilities, definition of, 254–255
Sharing in writing workshops, 352–353
Sheltered English, 105
Showcase portfolios, 341
Sight words, 314
Simulations for promoting social acceptance, 129
Situational factors, second language acquisition and, 106–107
SLICK sequence, 429
Sloppy copy, 351

Small groups
 instruction, 58
 for intensive intervention, 60
 mixed-ability, 123
Smart keyboards for students with
 developmental disabilities, 158
Social acceptance
 increasing for students with disabilities and
 exceptional learners, 127–128
 technology for promoting, 129
Social action approach for multicultural
 education, 102, 103
Social environment, promoting writing, 346
Social language, 108
Social learning, providing opportunities for,
 for students with emotional and behavioral
 disorders, 224, 225
Social problem solving for students with
 autism spectrum disorders, 242, 243
Social skills
 of students with autism spectrum disorders,
 236
 of students with developmental disabilities,
 256
 of students with visual impairments, 275
Social skills, teaching strategies for, for
 students with emotional and behavioral
 disorders, 221–222
 asset method, 225
Social skills training
 for students with autism spectrum disorders,
 241–244
Social Story intervention for students with
 autism spectrum disorders, 242, 243–244
Socialized aggression, 206–207
Software. See Technological tools and aids
Spatial organization in mathematics
 instruction, 395
Speaking vocabulary, 180
Special education
 full-time placement in, 9, 10
 part-time placement in, 9
 prereferral for, 25
Special education resource rooms, 10
Special schools, 9, 10
Specific learning disabilities,146. See also
 Learning disabilities
Speech and language pathologists, 174
Speech and language pathologists, working
 with, 190
Speech development, facilitating, 191–192
Speech disorders, 176–179
 articulation disorders as, 177–178
 fluency disorders as, 178–179
 voice disorders as, 179
Spelling instruction
 effective, principles of, 362–363
 flow chart of strategic spelling, 360
 procedure of self-correction and practice,
 362
 spelling rubric, 361
 for students with difficulties in learning to
 spell, 359–362

teaching strategies for, 358–363
 traditional, 358–359
 VCe rule, 359–360
Spelling patterns, 362
Spelling rubrics, 361
Spina bifida, 288
Spiral curriculum, 379
Standard English Language Learners (SELLs),
 110
Standard treatment protocol for RTI model,
 47
 problem-solving model compared, 48–49
Standardized intervention and individualized
 intervention compared, 60
Standards-based instruction, 405–406
 general guidelines, 406
 sample history standards, 406
Standards-based writing instruction, 338–339
Stereotypic behaviors of students with
 developmental disabilities, 256
Stimulant medications
 for students with ADHD, 169–172
Stimulus, 132
STOP and DARE strategy, 357
Story retelling, 325
Story webs, 354, 355
Story writing
 PLEASE strategy, 356
 STOP and DARE strategy, 357
 story check, 355
 TREE method, 356
Story writing, teaching strategies for, 354
Strategies, defined, 439
Strategy guides, 441
 developing, 442
Strategy instruction
 choosing strategies to meet students' needs,
 441
 goals of, 440
 guidelines, 440–443
 teaching-learning connection, 439
Strategy Satisfaction Survey, 443
Structural analysis, 316, 317
Struggling readers, effective reading instruction
 for, 303–308
Struggling writers, adaptations for, 349–350
Student involvement at IEP meetings, 18–19
Student outcomes, desired, for multicultural
 education, 101
Student ownership, 77
Student participation
 in class, 451–452
 facilitating, 421–424
Student-centered model of writing, 345
Student's world, real world versus, 78
Study habits checklist, 444
Study skills, instruction in, 440–443
Study strategies
 stages in learning, 440–441
Stuttering, 179
Success, providing opportunities for, for
 students with emotional and behavioral
 disorders, 227

Suicide, 206–207
Support. See also Positive behavioral support
 (PBS)
 peer, for students with developmental
 disabilities, 265, 266
 for students with developmental disabilities
 in general education classrooms, 265–269
 systems of, 253
Support service providers
 for students with physical disabilities and
 health impairments, 291–292
 working with, 291–292
Supreme Court cases, 4
Syllabification, 316, 318
Syntax, 185, 318
Systems of support, 253

Talented students. See Gifted and talented
 students
Talking word processing programs
 for students with learning disabilities, 158
Task analysis for students with developmental
 disabilities, 262
Teacher responsibilities under IDEIA, 19–31
Teacher role in RTI model, 56–58
Teacher-made tests
 for content-area assessment, 444
 writing effective questions for, 434
*Teaching Children to Read: An Evidence-Based
 Assessment of the Scientific Research Literature
 on Reading and Its Implications for Reading
 Instruction,* 300
Teaching "on purpose," 31
Team-assisted individualization, 381
Teams for RTI decision making, 49
Technological tools and aids
 for content-area instruction, 428
 for culturally and linguistically diverse
 students, 116
 for mathematics instruction, 396
 for promoting social acceptance, 129
 for reading instruction, 322
 for students with autism spectrum disorders,
 242
 for students with developmental disabilities,
 259
 for students with emotional and behavioral
 disorders, 227
 for students with learning disabilities, 158
 for students with traumatic brain injury and
 visual, hearing, and other physical
 disabilities, 293
 for writing instruction, 344
Technologically dependent students, 287
Television Circuitry Decoder Act of
 1993, 286
Test approach skills, 432
Test of Early Mathematics Ability, 384
Test of Mathematical Abilities, 384
Test of Oral Reading Fluency (TORF), 306
Test preparedness skills, 432–433
Testing accommodations for students with
 visual impairments, 280

Testing, standardized tests and culturally diverse populations, 112–113

Tests, adapting math tests, 379–380

Tests, high-stakes. *See* High-stake tests

Test-taking skills, 432

Test-taking strategies, 432–435
grading rubrics and, 435–436
instruction cue words for essay questions and, 432

Textbooks, 424–429
adapting, 425–429
alternative materials (multiliteracies), 428
familiarizing oneself with, 424–425
friendly or considerate text, 425
highlighting, 427
recording content of, 428–429
student interaction with and response to, 425

Therapy for parents, 81

Think alouds, 421

Thinking aloud strategy for students with learning disabilities, 154–155

Think-pair-share method, 82

Tier 3 (tertiary) intervention of RTI model, 46–47
role of teacher, 57–58
Tier 2 compared, 47

Tiers of intervention, 46–47
primary instruction (tier 1), 46
secondary (tier 2), 46, 57–58, 59
tertiary (tier 3), 46–47, 57–58

Time, adjusting for students with learning disabilities, 157–158

Time analysis, 449

Time management, personal responsibility and, 449–450

Time management skills, 449–450

Time out, 136

Timelines for content-area instruction, 418–419

Timers to change behavior, 219

To-Do List (Daily Planning Worksheet), 450

Token system (token economy), 132, 134–135

Tonic-clonic seizures, 288

Total blindness, definition of, 274

Tracking, 408

Transdisciplinary teaming for students with physical disabilities and health impairments, 291–292

Transfer of learning, teaching for in spelling instruction, 362

Transformation approach for multicultural education, 101–102, 103

Transitional bilingual education, 105–106

Traumatic brain injury, 286–295
characteristics of students with, 290
definitions and types of, 287
identification and assessment of students with, 291
instructional guidelines and accommodations for students with, 291–295
prevalence of, 291

TREE method, 356

Turf-based gangs, 208

Tutoring, 85
peer. *See* Peer tutoring
tips for tutors, 85

Two-way bilingual programs, 106

Universal screening, 53–54
for students with emotional and behavioral disorders, 214

Varying exceptionalities, 10

Verbal reprimands, 136

Vibrant discussions, 423–424

Violence. *See also* Aggression
as cause of emotional and behavioral disorders, 210
understanding violent behavior, 208

Violent hate gangs, 208

Visual acuity, 274

Visual detail in mathematics instruction, 395

Visual field, 274

Visual impairment, 274–280
audiobooks for students with, 428–429
causes, 274–275
characteristics of students with, 275–276
definitions and types, 274–275
identification and assessment of students with, 276–277
instructional guidelines and accommodations for students with, 277–280
prevalence of, 276
technology with students with, 293

VMath, 380

Vocabulary, 180, 324
preteaching for content areas, 417

Vocabulary development in English language learning, 114–116

Vocal nodules, 179

Vocational Rehabilitation Act (VRA) of 1973, 6
eligibility for ADHD services under, 166–167
provisions, 8–9

Voice disorders, 179

Wait time, 422
for language promotion, 195

Websites. *See* Internet and websites

Wide Range Achievement Test, 384

Within-child factors, 57

Woodcock Johnson III Tests of Achievement, 384

Word categories, 180–181

Word games, promoting language through, 188

Word identification
in reading, 300
teaching strategies for, 314–320

Word relationships, 180–181

Word walls, 319

Words
high-frequency, 314
making, 319
sight, 314
for spelling instruction, selecting, 359–360, 362

Work, transition from school to, 29–31

Workload, adjusting, for students with learning disabilities, 157–158

Wraparound facilitators, 226

Wraparound system of care, for students with emotional and behavioral disorders, 224–226

Wrap-up in collaborative student reading, 329

Writing
assessment of, 357–358
selecting topics for, 350
self-monitoring of, 343
student-centered model of, 345

Writing instruction, 336–368
activities for, 348–349
current trends in, 337–338
environment to promote writing and, 345–346
for expository writing, 354, 356
features of exemplary, 340
handwriting skills and, 363–366
keyboarding and, 366–367
for narrative writing, 354
for persuasive writing, 357–358
progress monitoring of, 339–340
response to intervention (RTI) approach to, 340–341
for spelling skills, 358–363
writing as process and, 342–345
writing workshops and, 347–354

Writing portfolios, 341–342

Writing process, 336–368
constructing meaning and, 344
interactive nature of, 342–343
as socially mediated language-learning activity, 345
strategic nature of, 343

Writing rubrics, 341

Writing standards
IRA/NCTE standards for the language arts, 338

Writing workshops, 347–348, 350–353
composing stage in, 348, 351
guidelines for conducting, 353
prewriting stage in, 348, 350–351
publishing stage in, 348, 352
revising and editing stage in, 348, 351–352
sharing stage in, 352–353
TAG framework, 353

Written intervention plans, 53

Yopp-Singer Test of Phoneme Segmentation, 306

Zero, in mathematics instruction, 392, 395

Zero reject, 7